ISBN 978-0-332-25801-0
PIBN 11214149

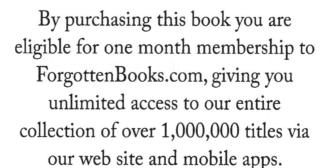

English
Français
Deutsche
Italiano
Español
Português

www.forgottenbooks.com

Mythology Photography **Fiction**
Fishing Christianity **Art** Cooking
Essays Buddhism Freemasonry
Medicine **Biology** Music **Ancient
Egypt** Evolution Carpentry Physics
Dance Geology **Mathematics** Fitness
Shakespeare **Folklore** Yoga Marketing
Confidence Immortality Biographies
Poetry **Psychology** Witchcraft
Electronics Chemistry History **Law**
Accounting **Philosophy** Anthropology
Alchemy Drama Quantum Mechanics
Atheism Sexual Health **Ancient History**
Entrepreneurship Languages Sport
Paleontology Needlework Islam
Metaphysics Investment Archaeology
Parenting Statistics Criminology
Motivational

ARCHER'S
LAW AND PRACTICE
—— IN ——
OIL AND GAS CASES
—— EMBRACING ——

AN ANALYSIS. OF ALL IMPORTANT CASES IN EACH STATE PRODUCING
PETROLEUM OIL AND NATURAL GAS, INCLUDING THE DECISIONS
OF THE FEDERAL COURTS, THE ANALYSIS OF EACH CASE
SHOWING THE LAW OF THE CASE AND THE FACTS
AND PLEADINGS FROM WHICH THE COURTS
DEDUCED ITS CONCLUSIONS.

—— INCLUDING ——

**REMEDIES OF CONFLICTING CLAIMANTS, AND THE
PRACTICE IN OIL AND GAS CASES,**

—— TOGETHER WITH ——

TABLE OF CASES ANALYZED

AND

TABLE OF CASES CITED

WITH

COMPREHENSIVE INDEX

·

BY V. B. ARCHER,
of the Wood County Bar,
PARKERSBURG, WEST VIRGINIA

For Sale By
THE W. H. ANDERSON COMPANY
Cincinnati, Ohio

The Tribune Printing Co.
Charleston, W. Va.
Publishers.

INTRODUCTORY.

Litigation growing out of the production of petroleum oil and natural gas is peculiar to itself. Much of the law and practice applicable to the mining of solid minerals, without modification, owing principally to the migratory character of oil and gas, cannot be applied to cases affecting these minerals. Lessees for oil and gas purposes are held to great diligence and promptness in the performance of the express and implied covenants of the lease. The contract almost universally entered into between the landowner and the prospective producer of oil and gas is commonly called an oil and gas lease. The landowner rarely operates his own premises; and the producer almost universally obtains the oil and gas lease under which to operate rather than title to the surface. The lease confers upon the lessee for a limited time, a license to enter upon the premises for the purpose of exploring for oil and gas. The lessee acquires no vested interest, except his interest and right to enter for explorations, until he discovers oil or gas in paying quantities. Until such discovery the lease remains a license, and when discovery of oil or gas in paying quantities is made the lessee becomes vested with an exclusive right to produce the oil or gas during the term, or to the extent provided for in the lease. Delays and attempted evasions of the duties and obligations devolving upon lessees have been the cause of practically all the litigation growing out of the oil and gas business. The temptation to lessees to obtain leases upon lands for speculative purposes is great, particularly where indications point to a probable development by other lessees, whereby a lessee may be enriched without making explorations himself. The courts have sternly resisted all attempts by the lessee to deprive the landowner of the right to prompt action, either by exploration of the property or surrender of the lease. For failure to exercise these duties the courts have not hesitated to declare the lease forfeited. Excuses for delay in operations must be based upon a substantial consideration, and unreasonable delays for speculative purposes will not be tolerated.

On the other hand, a lessee who for a valuable consideration, however small, obtains in good faith a lease for oil and gas purposes which is not unreasonable, unfair, unjust, or inequitable, is entitled to the benefit of his contract, and the courts have not hesitated to uphold his rights, although the surrounding circumstances may indicate that the landowner might have made a better bargain.

V. B. ARCHER.

Parkersburg, West Virginia, 1911.

EXPLANATORY.

All References are to Pages.

Under the title of each Chapter the substantive law thereof is stated, followed by citations of the cases in support thereof.

Then follows an analyses of the cases, giving the points adjudicated, a statement of the facts, and the pleadings upon which the court predicated the conclusions of law.

Then follows a statement of the practice, and the rights and remedies of the lessor, the lessee, or the claimant to the leasehold, or the oil and gas in place.

Each Chapter is divided into Sections, and the cases analyzed and digested are under separate sections.

CONTENTS BY CHAPTERS.

Introductory ....PAGE.
Table of Cases Analyzed ....
Table of Cases Cited ....
The Lease for Oil and Gas Purposes 1

ERRATA.

In Sec 34, p. 94, next to last line, word "lessor" should be "lessee."
In Sec. 2, p. 323, line 8, "lessee" should be "lessor."
In Sec. 8, p. 330, second line syllabus, "Lessor" should be "Lessee."
In Sec. 17, p. 673, first line, "Sec. 13" should be "Sec. 16."
In Sec. 6, p. 803, first line in syl. 6, "flowing" should be "blowing."

1.. Assignee of Second Lessee with Notice of Prior Lease 385
18. Implied Covenants of the Oil and Gas Lease 393
19. Remedies in Equity for Breaches by Lessee of Implied Covenants 437
20. Remedies at Law for Breaches by Lessee of Implied Covenants .. 453
21. Waiver of Forfeiture of Oil and Gas Lease 467
22. Paying Quantities—Discovery of Oil and Gas in 487
23. Paying Quantities—Remedies 498
24. Forfeiture by Abandonment 501
25. Forfeiture by Abandonment—Lessee's Remedy 546
26. Forfeiture by Abandonment—Lessor's Remedy 550
27. Oil and Gas in Place are Minerals and Part of the Land 558
28. A Void Lease will be cancelled by a court of Equity 601

CONTENTS BY CHAPTERS.

Introductory ....PAGE.

Table of Cases Analyzed ....

Table of Cases Cited ....

1. The Lease for Oil and Gas Purposes   1
2. Construction of Oil and Gas Leases   6
3. Definition—No Estate Vests 20
4. Consideration for the Lease 42
5. Purpose of Grant, Premises Demised and Rights Acquired 67
6. The Term of the Oil and Gas Lease 96
7. Consideration for the Grant of Minerals—Oil 129
8. Reservation for Farming Purposes 144
9. Right to Remove Fixtures Placed upon the Leasehold for Exploration and Development Purposes 150
10. Reservation Around Buildings 170
11. Consideration for the Grant of Minerals—Gas 189
12. Forfeiture and Rental Clause—Lessor's Option 237
13. Forfeiture and Rental Clause—Lessee's Option 290
14. The Surrender Clause of the Oil and Gas Lease 322
15. Assignment of the Lease 350
16. Assignee—Liability of 364
17. Assignee or Second Lessee with Notice of Prior Lease 385
18. Implied Covenants of the Oil and Gas Lease 393
19. Remedies in Equity for Breaches by Lessee of Implied Covenants 437
20. Remedies at Law for Breaches by Lessee of Implied Covenants .. 453
21. Waiver of Forfeiture of Oil and Gas Lease 467
22. Paying Quantities—Discovery of Oil and Gas in 487
23. Paying Quantities—Remedies 498
24. Forfeiture by Abandonment 501
25. Forfeiture by Abandonment—Lessee's Remedy 546
26. Forfeiture by Abandonment—Lessor's Remedy 550
27. Oil and Gas in Place are Minerals and Part of the Land 558
28. A Void Lease will be cancelled by a court of Equity 601

29. Want of Mutuality 608
30. Mining Partnership—Oil and Gas 625
31. Partition of Oil and Gas Rights 650
32. Tenants in Common or Joint Tenants—Right to Execute Oil and Gas Lease, or Develop 660
33. Dry Hole—Effect of Drilling 680
34. Payment of Rental into Bank 696
35. Life Tenants and Remainder Men 709
36. Beginning Operations—What Constitutes 729
37. Shooting Well 737
38. Natural Gas an Article of Commerce When Brought to the Surface 742
39. Waste and Transportation.—Statutory Regulations 745
40. Gas Pump Cannot be used to produce Unnatural Flow 760
41. Nitro-Glycerine to Increase Flow—Right to Use 778
42. Right to Drill Well near Division Line—Drainage 782
43. Right to Operate oil and gas Wells, even where injury results therefrom 788
44. Nuisance 795
45. Waste of Gas Maliciously or Negligently 805
46. Exclusive Right to lay Pipelines Void as against Public Policy ... 814
47. Reservation in Deed of all Minerals Includes Petroleum Oil and Natural Gas 826
48. Reservation in Deed of All Minerals, or Conveyance by Deed of all minerals, does not reserve or convey petroleum oil or natural gas 834
49. Reservation of Oil and Gas 841
50. Several Tracts under one Lease 882
51. Remedies in Equity 895
52. Forfeiture Will not be Enforced by a Court of Equity 923
53. Necessary Parties to Bill in Equity to Settle Controversies between two or more lessees 927
54. Remedy by Ejectment 938
55. Negligence—Injuries to Persons or Property by Corporations or by Persons furnishing Natural Gas for Commercial Purposes .. 944
56. Natural Gas Companies—Duty to Furnish Gas 984
57. Pipeline Companies—Oil 1001

TABLE OF CASES ANALYZED.

With Reference to pages and chapters where analyzed.

A.

Acme Oil etc. Co. r. Williams, 140 Cal. 681; 74 Pac. 296, Chap. 18 .. 428
Acme Oil etc. Co., Perry r. (Ind. App.) 88 N. E. 559, Chap. 9 160
Alexandra etc. Mining Co. r. Irish, 16 Ind. App. 534; 44 N. E. 680;
 Chap. 55 962
Allegheny Heating Co., Benson r., 188 Pa. 614; 41 Atl. 729, Chap. 55 956
Allegheny Oil Co. v. Snyder, 106 Fed. 764; 45 C. C. A. 604, Chap. 4 .. 55
Allegheny Oil Co., Eaton r., 122 N. Y. 416; 25 N. E. 981, Chap. 6 .. 106
Allen and Evans Appeal, 77 Pa. 221, Chap. 10 185
Allred, Murray r., 100 Tenn. 100; 66 Am. St. Rep. 740, Chap. 47.... 827
Anthony, Ind. Nat. & Illum. Gas Co. r., 26 Ind. App. 307, 58 N. E.
 868, Chap. 56 987
American Window Glass Co. r. Williams, 30 Ind. App. 68; 66 N. E.
 912, Chap. 6 113
American Window Glass Co. r. Indiana etc. Gas Co. 37 Ind. App.
 439; 76 N. E. 1006, Chap. 34 702
American Plate Glass Co., Consolidated Gas etc. Co. r., 162 Ind. 392;
 68 N. E. 1020, Chap. 10 181
American Natural Gas Co., Hicks r., 207 Pa. 570; 57 Atl. 55, Chap. 17 389
Ammons r. South Penn Oil Co., 47 W. Va. 610; 35 S. E. 1004, Chap 20 459
Ammons v. Ammons, 50 W. Va. 390; 40 S. E. 490, Chap. 25 712
Ammons v. Toothman, 59 W. Va. 165; 53 S. E. 13, Chap. 49 852
Anderson, Duntley r. 94 C. C. A. 649; 169 Fed. 391, Chap. 21 480
Andrews, Ohio Gas Fuel Co. r., 50 Ohio St. 695; 35 N. E. 1059, Chap. 55 958
Appeal of Allen and Evans, 77 Pa. 221, Chap. 10 188
Appeal of Stoughton, 88 Pa. 198, Chap. 27 580
Apollo Gas Co., Summerville v., 207 Pa. 334; 56 Atl. 876, Chap. 11 .. 210
Armel, Rawlings v., 70 Kan. 779; 79 Pac. 683, Chap. 5 80
Armitage r. Mount Sterling Oil & Gas Co., 25 Ky. Law Rep. 2262;
 80 S. W. 177, Chap. 13 302

Armstrong, Munroe v., 96 Pa. 307, Chap. 5 74
Auer v. Penn, 92 Pa. 444; Chap. 14 349
Aye v. Philadelphia Co., 193 Pa. 451; 44 Atl. 655; 74 Am. St. Rep.
  696, Chap. 2 10

B.

Baden Gas Co., Cleminger v., 159 Pa. 16; 28 Atl. 293, Chap. 36 734
Bailey, Pittsburg etc. Co. v. 70 Kan. 42; 92 Pac. 803, Chap. 27 612
Barnes v. Bee, 138 Fed. 476, Chap. 49 876
Barnes, Bee v. 149 Fed. 727; 79 C. C. A. 433, Chap. 49 878
Barnes, Carney v. 56 W. Va. 581; 49 S. E. 423, Chap. 51 905
Barnard v. Monongahela Gas Co., 216 Pa. 360; 65 Atl. 801, Chap. 42 .. 782
Barnsdall v. Boley, 119 Fed. 191, Chap. 22 494
Barnsdall v. Bradford Gas Co. (Pa.) 74 Atl. 207, Chap. 3 40
Barnsdall, Cortelyou v., 236 Ill. 138; 86 N. E. 200, Chap. 12 260
Barnhart, Murray v., 117 La. 1023; 42 So. 489, Chap. 24 526
Barnhart v. Lockwood, 152 Pa. 82; Ch. 33 691
Barrickman v. Marion Oil Co., 45 W. Va. 634; 32 S. E. 327; 44 L. R.
  A. 92 945
Bartlett and Stancliff v. Boyles, 66 W. Va. 327; 66 S. E. 474, Chap. 30 631
Bartlett, Koen v. 41 W. Va. 559; 23 S. E. 664; 56 Am. St. Rep. 884;
  31 L. R. A. 128, Chap. 35 710
Bartley v. Phillips, 165 Pa. 325; 30 Atl. 842, Chap. 12 264
Bartley v. Phillips, 179 Pa. 175; 36 Atl. 217, Chap. 17 386
Bay State Petroleum Co. v. Penn Lubricating Co., 22 Ky. L. Rep. 1133;
  87 S. W. 1102, Chap. 22 490
Beale, Indiana etc. Nat Gas Co. v., 166 Ind. 684; 76 N. E. 520, Chap. 34 704
Beardsley v. Kansas Nat. Gas Co., 78 Kan. 571; 96 Pac. 589, Chap. 31 653
Becker v. Penn Lubricating Co., 162 Fed. 627 (C. C. A.), Chap. 3 .. 32
Behling v. Southwest Penn. Pipelines, 160 Pa. 359; 28 Atl. 777; 40
  Am. St. Rep. 724, Chap. 57 103
Bell, Bluestone Coal Co. v., 38 W. Va. 297; 27 S. E. 220, Chap. 24 .. 502
Bellevue Oil & Gas Co. v. Pennell, 76 Kan. 785; 92 Pac. 1101, Chap. 11 213
Bennett-Summers v.   W. Va.   ; 69 S. E. 690, Chap. 32 678
Benson v. Allegheny Heating Co., 188 Pa. 614; 41 Atl. 729, Chap. 55 .. 956
Bettman v. Harness, 42 W. Va. 433; 26 S. E. 271, Chap. 6 99
Bettman v. Shadle, 22 Ind. App. 542; 53 N. E. 662, Chap. 14 325
Bettman, Roberts v., 45 W. Va. 143; 30 S. E. 95, Chap. 12 245
Bee, Barnes v., 138 Fed. 476 (C. C.) Chap. 49 876

Bee v. Barnes, 149 Fed. 727; 79 C. C. A. 433, Chap. 49 878

Blackmarr v. Williamson, 57 W. Va. 249; 50 S. E. 254, Chap. 30 627

Blaes, Federal Betterment Co. v., 75 Kan. 69; 88 Pac. 555, Chap. 24 523

Blair, Bradford Oil Co. v., 113 Pa. 33; 4 Atl. 218, Chaps, 16-20 ..367, 454

Blakley v. Marshall, 174 Pa. 425; 34 Atl. 564, Chap. 27 575

Bliven Petroleum Co., Union Petroleum Co. v., 72 Pa. 173, Chap. 54 .. 941

Bluestone Coal Co. v. Bell, 38 W. Va. 297; 27 S. E. 220, Chap. 24 ... 502

Board of Commissioners, Kansas Nat. Gas Co. v., 75 Kan. 325; 89
Pac. 750, Chap. 3 31

Boley, Barnsdall v., 109 Fed. (C. C.) 191, Chap. 22 494

Boyd v. Brown, 47 W. Va. 238; 38 S. E. 668, Chap. 29 620

Boyer, Stage v., 183 Pa. 560; 38 Atl. 1035, Chap. 24 511

Boyles, Bartlett and Stancliff v., 66 S. E. 474; 66 W. Va. 327, Chap. 30 631

Bradford Oil Co. v. Blair, 113 Pa. 83; 4 Atl. 218, Chaps. 16-20 367-454

Bradford Gas Co., Barnsdall v., (Pa.) 74 Atl. 207, Chap. 3 40

Breckenridge v. Parrot, 15 Ind. App. 417; 44 N. E. 66, Chap. 16 ... 376

Brenneman, Ziegler v., 237 Ill. 15; 86 N. E. 597, Chap. 31 657

Brewster v. Lanyon Zinc Co., 140 Fed. 801; 72 C. C. A. 213, Chap. 4 51

Brice, Hodges v., 32 Tex. Civ. App. 358; 74 S. W. 590, Chap. 29 617

Bridgeport Oil Co., Powers v., 238 Ill. 397; 87 N. E. 381, Chap. 18 .. 433

Bridgewater Gas Co., Pope Bros v., 52 W. Va. 252; 43 S. E. 87, Chap. 44 800

Bridgewater Gas Co., Parish Fork Oil & Gas Co. v., 51 W. Va. 583;
42 S. E. 655, Chap. 5 70

Bridgewater Gas Co., McKenna v., 193 Pa. 633; 45 Atl. 52; 47 L.
R. A. 790, Chap. 55 955

Brown v. Vandergrift, 80 Pa. 142, Chap. 12 246

Brown v. Spilman, 155 U. S. 665, Chap. 10 183

Brown v. Fowler,

Brown v. Ohio Oil Co.   65 Ohio St. 507; 63 N. E. 76, Chap. 4 45

Brown, Boyd v., 47 W. Va. 238; 38 S. E. 668, Chap. 29 620

Brown, Pfeiffer v., 165 Pa. 267; 30 Atl. 844, Chap. 43 792

Brown, Tennessee Oil Co. v., 131 Fed. 696; 65 C. C. A. 524, Chap 24 516

Brookshire Oil Co. v. Casmalia Ranch, Oil and Development Co.,
(Cal.) 102 Pac. 927, Chap. 46 814

Buffalo etc. Co. v. Jones, 75 Kan. 18; 88 Pac. 537, Chap. 24 529

Burford, Lynch v., 201 Pa. 52; 50 Atl. 238, Chap. 10 180

Burton v. Forest Oil Co., 204 Pa. 249; 54 Atl. 266, Chap. 16 377

Bush, Silver v., 213 Pa. 195; 62 Atl. 832, Chap. 48 835

Butler Savings Bank v. Osborne, 159 Pa. 10; 28 Atl. 163; 28 Am. St.
Rep. 665, Chap. 30 632

C.

Calhoun v. Neely, 201 Pa. 97; 50 Atl. 967, Chap. 24 515
Calor Oil & Gas Co. v. McGehee, 117 Ky. 71; 77 S. W. 368; 70 L. R.
A. 558, Chap. 39 756
Calor Oil & Gas Co. v. Franzell, and Kentucky Heating Co. v. Calor
Oil & Gas Co., 128 Ky. 715; 109 S. W. 328; 33 Ky. L. Rep. 98,
Chap. 45 ..../...... 808
Camden, McGregor v., 47 W. Va. 193; 34 S. E. 936, Chap. 44 795
Cameron Oil & Gas Co., Marshall Window Glass Co. v., 63 W. Va. 202;
59 S. E. 959, Chap. 55 948
Campbell v. Rock Oil Co., 151 Fed. 191; 80 C. C. A. 467, Chap. 21 .. 478
Campton Fuel & Light Co., Hollon v., 127 Ky. 266; 105 S. W. 426;
32 Ky. L. Rep. 178, Chap. 55 976
Carnegie Nat. Gas Co., Iams v., 194 Pa. 72; 45 Atl. 54, Chap. 11 .. 197
Carnegie Nat. Gas Co. v. South Penn Oil Co., 56 W. Va. 402; 49 S. E.
548, Chap. 15 357
Carnegie Nat. Gas Co. v. Philadelphia Co., 158 Pa. 317; 27 Atl. 95,
Chap. 17 387
Carney v. Barnes, 56 W. Va. 581; 49 S. E. 423, Chap. 51 905
Carpenter, Great Western Oil Co. v., 43 Tex. Civ. App. 229; 95 S. W.
57, Chap. 13 299
Carrell, Manhattan Oil Co. v., 164 Ind. 526; 73 N. E. 1084, Chap. 22   496
Carter, Coffeyville Min. & Gas Co. v., 68 Kan. 565; 70 Pac. 635,
Chap. 55 974
Casmalia Ranch, Oil & Development Co., Brookshire v., (Cal.) 102
Pac. 927, Chap. 14 814
Cassell v. Crothers, 193 Pa. 359; 44 Atl. 446, Chap. 6 109
Central Kentucky Nat. Gas Co., McKinney's Heirs v.; Perry, and
Becraft v.,   Ky.   ; 120 S. W. 314, Chap. 48 836
Central Ohio Natural Gas & Fuel Co. v. Eckert, 70 Ohio St. 127; 71
N. E. 281, Chaps. 4-6 ....53, 114
Chaison Town Site Co., J. M. Guffey Petroleum Co. v., (Tex. Civ.
App.), 107 S. W. 609, Chap. 20 463
Chaney v. Ohio etc. Gas Co., 32 Ind. App. 193; 69 N. E. 477, Chap. 6   104
Charleston Nat. Gas Co., Creel v., 51 W. Va. 129; 41 S. E. 174; 90
Am. St. Rep. 772, Chap. 55 947
Charleston Nat. Gas Co. v. Lowe & Butler, 52 W. Va. 662; 44 S. E.
410, Chap. 56 984
Chartiers Oil Co., Glasgow v., 152 Pa. 48; 25 Atl. 232, Chap. 13 294

Chartiers Valley Gas Co., Collins v., 131 Pa. 143; 18 Atl. 1012, Chap. 43 .790

Chartiers Block Coal Co. v. Mellon, 152 Pa. 286; 25 Atl. 597; 18 L.
R. A. 702; 34 Am. St. Rep. 645, Chap. 49 867

Chautauqua Oil Co., Davis v., 78 Kan. 97; 96 Pac. 47, Chap. 11 214

Childers v. Neely, 47 W. Va. 70; 34 S. E. 827, Chap. 30 626

Christy, Thompson v., 138 Pa. 230; 20 Atl. 934, Chap. 12 ·........ 252

Chrystal Window Glass Co., Consumers Gas Trust Co. v., 163 Ind. 190;
70 N. E. 366, Chap. 11 205

·Citizens Nat. Gas Co., Hartman v., 210 Pa. 19; 59 Atl. 315, Chap. 55 954

Citizens Natural Gas Co., Springer v., 145 Pa. 430; 22 Atl. 986,
Chap. 12 246

Clemenger v. Baden Gas Co., 159 Pa. 16; 28 Atl. 293, Chap. 36 734

Clever, Guffey v., 146 Pa. 548; 23 Atl. 161, Chap. 15 355

Cochran v. Pew, 159 Pa. 184; 28 Atl. 219, Chap. 12 262

Coffeyville, etc. Co., Dickey v., 69 Kan. 106; 76 Pac. 398, Chap. 22 .. 492

Coffeyville Min. & Gas Co. v. Carter, 68 Kan. 565; 70 Pac. 635, Chap. 55 974

Coffeyville Min. & Gas Co., Maxwell v., 68 Kan. 821; 75 Pac. 1047,
Chap. 55 975

Coffinberry v. Sun Oil Co., 68 Ohio 488; 67 N. E. 1069, Chap. 19 .. 451

Colgan v. Forest Oil Co., 194 Pa. 234; 45 Atl. 119; 75 Am. St. Rep.
695, Chap. 18 402

Collier v. Munger, 75 Kan. 550; 89 Pac. 1111, Chap. 2 15

Collins v. Chartiers Valley Gas Co., 131 Pa. 143; 18 Atl. 1012, Chap. 43 790

Collins, Hazelgreen Oil & Gas Co. v., (Ky.), 110 S. W. 343, Chap. 6 .. 121

Compton v. Peoples Gas Co., 75 Kan. 573; 89 Pac. 1039; 10 L. R. A.
(N. S.) 785, Chap. 17 390

Commonwealth v. Trent, 25 Ky. Law Rep. 1180; 77 S. W. 390, Chap. 39 754

Consumers Gas Co., Shirey v., 215 Pa. 399; 64 Atl. 541, Chap. 55 .. 953

Consumers Gas Trust Co. v. American Plate Glass Co., 162 Ind. 392;
68 N. E. 1020, Chap. 10 181

Consumers Gas Trust Co. v. Littler, 162 Ind. 320; 70 N. E. 363,
Chap. 11 201

Consumers Gas Trust Co. v. Chrystal Window Glass Co., 163 Ind. 190;
70 N. E. 366, Chap. 11 205

Consumers Gas Trust Co. v. Corbaley, 14 Ind. App. 549; 43 N. E. 237,
Chap. 55 973

Consumers Gas Trust Co. v. Worth, 163 Ind. 141; 71 N. E. 489,
Chap. 11 206

Consumers Gas Trust Co. v. Perrigo, 144 Ind. 350; 32 L. R. A. 146;
43 N. E. 306, Chap. 55 967

Consumers Gas Trust Co., State ex. rel. Wood v., 157 Ind. 345; 61 N.
    E. 674; 55 L. R. A. 245, Chap. 56   991
Consumers Gas Trust Co. v. Ink, 163 Ind. 174; 71 N. E. 477, Chap. 11   209
Corbaley, Consumers Gas Trust Co. v., 14 Ind. App. 549; 43 N. E. 237,
    Chap. 55   973
Core v. N. Y. Pet. Co., 52 W. Va. 276; 43 S. E. 128, Chap. 20   459
Cortelyou v. Barnsdall, 236 Ill. 138; 86 N. E. 200, Chap. 12   260
Coulehan, Eastern Oil Co. v., 65 W. Va. 531; 64 S. E. 836, Chap. 11   216
Courtney, Toothman v., 62 W. Va. 167; 58 S. E. 915, Chap. 49   854
Coy v. Indianapolis Gas Co., 146 Ind. 655; 46 N. E. 17; 36 L. R. A.
    535, Chap. 56   994
Craig v. Hukill, 37 W. Va. 520; 16 S. E. 363, Chap. 52   923
Craig, Kellar v., 61 C. C. A. 366; 126 Fed. 630, Chap. 18   409
Crawford v. Ritchie, 43 W. Va. 252; 37 S. E. 320, Chap. 5   84
Crawford, Kennedy v., 138 Pa. 561; 21 Atl. 19, Chap. 12   254
Crawford, Woodland Oil Co. v., 55 Ohio St. 161; 44 N. E. 1093,
    Chap. 14   326
Creel v. Charleston Nat. Gas Co., 51 W. Va. 129; 41 S. E. 174; 90 Am.
    St. Rep. 772, Chap. 55   947
Crothers, Cassell v., 193 Pa. 359; 44 Atl. 446, Chap. 6   109

                                    D.

Dailey v. Heller, (Ind. App.) 81 N. E. 219, Chap. 16   381
Dailey v. Heller, 28 Ind. App. 555; 63 N. E. 490, Chap. 16   370
Dailey, Zeigler v., (Ind. App.) 76 N. E. 819, Chap. 33   690
Daley, Huggins v., 99 Fed. 606; 40 C. C. A. 12; 48 L. R. A. 320,
    Chap. 6   103
Dark v. Johnson, 55 Pa. 154, Chaps. 3-15 22,   351
Davenport, Richmond Nat. Gas Co. v., 37 Ind. App. 25; 76 N. E. 526,
    Chap. 35   717
Davidson v. Humes, 188 Pa. 335; 41 Atl. 649, Chap. 37   738
Davis v. Chautauqua Oil Co., 78 Kan. 97; 96 Pac. 47, Chap. 11   214
Davis, Freer v., 52 W. Va. 1; 43 S. E. 164, Chap. 27   588
Davis, Freer v., 52 W. Va. 35; 43 S. E. 172, Chap. 27   590
Delaplain, Fowler v., 79 Ohio St. 279; 87 N. E. 261, Chap. 8   145
Delaware & Hudson Canal Co. v. Hughes, 183 Pa. 66; 63 Am. St. Rep.
    743, Chap. 49   869
Derden, Stanley & Barnsdall v., (Tex. Civ. App.) 121 S. W. 1136,
    Chap. 3   36

Detamore, Ohio Oil Co. v., 165 Ind. 243; 73 N. E. 906, Chap. 24 .. 535

Detlor v. Holland, 57 Ohio St. 492; 49 N. E. 690; 40 L. R. A. 266, Chap. 27 585

DeWitt, Westmoreland Nat. Gas Co. v., 130 Pa. 235; 18 Atl. 724; 5 L. R. A. 731, Chap. 11 222

Diamond Plate Glass Co., Hancock v., 162 Ind. 146; 70 N. E. 149, Chap. 12 280

Dickey v. Coffeyville etc. Co., 69 Kan. 106; 76 Pac. 398, Chap. 22 492

Dill v. Fraze, 169 Ind. 53; 59 N. E. 971, Chap. 24 532

Doddridge Oil & Gas Co. v. Smith, 154 Fed. 970, Chap. 18 416

Doddridge Oil & Gas Co. v. Smith, 173 Fed. 386, Chap. 5 90

Double v. Heat & Light Co., 172 Pa. 388; 33 Atl. 694, Chap. 11 196

Douglass Oil Fields v. Hamilton, 95 Pac. 849 (Wyo.), Chap. 18 432

Douthett v. Fort Pitt Gas Co., 202 Pa. 416; 51 Atl. 981, Chap. 2 12

Duffield v. Hue, 129 Pa. 94; 18 Atl. 566, Chap. 10 177

Duffield v. Hue, 136 Pa. 602; 20 Atl. 526, Chap. 10 172

Duffield v. Rosenzweig, 144 Pa. 520; 23 Atl. 4, Chap. 10 174

Duffield v. Rosenzweig, 150 Pa. 543; 24 Atl. 705, Chap. 10 177

Dulaney, Jackson v., (W. Va.) 67 S. E. 795, Chap. 49 864

Dunham v. Loverock, 158 Pa. 197; 27 Atl. 990, Chap. 30 634

Dunham v. Kirkpatrick, 101 Pa. 36; 47 Am. Rep. 696, Chap. 48 839

Duntley v. Anderson, 94 C. C. A. 647; 169 Fed. 391, Chap. 21 480

E.

Eakin v. Hawkins, 48 W. Va. 364; 37 S. E. 622, Chap. 35 721

Eakin v. Hawkins, 52 W. Va. 124; 43 S. E. 211, Chap. 35 726

Eastern Oil Co. v. Coulehan, 65 W. Va. 531; 64 S. E. 836, Chap. 11 .. 216

Eastern Oil Co., Harness v., 49 W. Va. 232; 38 S. E. 662, Chap. 18 .. 406

Eaton v. Allegheny Gas Co., 122 N. Y. 416; 25 N. E. 981, Chap. 6 .. 106

Eckert, Central Ohio Nat. Gas & Fuel Co. v., 70 Ohio St. 127; 71 N. E. 281, Chaps. 4-6 .... 53, 114

Eclipse Oil Co. v. South Penn Oil Co., 47 W. Va. 84; 34 S. E. 293, Chap. 4 49

Eclipse Oil Co. v. Garner, 53 W. Va. 151; 44 S. E. 131, Chap. 29 609

Eclipse Oil Co., Trees v., 47 W. Va. 107; 34 S. E. 933, Chap. 14 329

Edgell, South Penn Oil Co. v., 48 W. Va. 348; 37 S. E. 596, Chap. 11 220

Edwards v. Hale, 37 W. Va. 193; 16 S. E. 487, Chap. 14 347

Elk Fork Oil & Gas Co. v. Jennings, 84 Fed. 839; 90 Fed. 178; 32 C. C. A. 560, Chap. 4 56

Elk Fork Oil & Gas Co. *v.* Jennings, 99 Fed. 495; 39 C. C. A. 615,
    Chap. 4 56
Elm Grove Coal Co., Wallace *v.*, 58 W. Va., 449; 52 S. E. 485, Chap. 49   850
Emory *v.* League, 31 Tex. Civ. App. 474; 72 S. W. 603, Chap. 31   654
Enterprise Nat. Gas Co., Richmond Nat. Gas Co. *v.*, 31 Ind. App. 222;
    66 N. E. 782, Chap. 40 768
Enterprise Oil & Gas Co. *v.* National Transit Co., 172 Pa. 421; 33 Atl
    687, Chap. 30 646
Eric Crawford Oil Co. *v.* Meek, (Ind. App.) 81 N. E. 518, Chap. 13 ..   317

F.

Farrell, Henderson *v.*, 183 Pa. 547; 38 Atl. 1018, Chap. 24 510
Fayette County Gas Co., Greensboro Nat. Gas Co. *v.*, 200 Pa. 388; 49
    Atl. 768, Chap. 51 915
Federal Oil Co. *v.* Western Oil Co., 121 Fed. 674; 57 C. C. A. 528,
    Chap. 29 610
Federal Oil Co. *v.* Western Oil Co., 112 Fed. 373; Chap. 24 519
Federal Betterment Co. *v.* Blaes, 75 Kan. 69; 88 Pac. 555, Chap. 24 ..   523
Fennel *v.* Guffey, 139 Pa. 341; 20 Atl. 1045, Chap. 16 366
Fisher *v.* Guffey & Queen, 193 Pa. 393; 44 Atl. 452, Chap. 16 380
Fisher Oil Co., Steelsmith *v.*, 47 W. Va. 391; 35 S. E. 15, Chap. 53 ..   928
Flannagan *v.* Marsh, 32 Ky. L. Rep. 184; 105 S. W. 424, Chap. 24 ..   524
Fleming Oil & Gas Co. *v.* South Penn Oil Co., 37 W. Va. 645; 17 S. E.
    202, Chap. 36 730
Florence Oil etc. Refining Co. *v.* Orman, 19 Colo. App. 79; 73 Pac.
    628, Chap. 5 78
Florence Oil Co. *v.* McCumber, 38 Colo. 366; 88 Pac. 265, Chap. 24 ..   528
Florence Oil Co., Harrington Bros. *v.* 178 Pa. 444; 35 Atl. 855,
    Chap. 30 635
Forest Oil Co., Hays *v.*, 213 Pa. 556; 62 Atl. 1072, Chap. 13 319
Forest Oil Co., Burton *v.*, 204 Pa. 249; 54 Atl. 266, Chap. 16 377
Forest Oil Co., Colgan *v.*, 194 Pa. 234; 45 Atl. 119; 75 Am. St. Rep.
    695, Chap. 18 402
Forest Oil Co., Jones *v.*, 194 Pa. 379; 44 Atl. 1074, Chap. 40 775
Forest Oil Co., Marshall *v.*, 198 Pa. 83; 47 Atl. 927, Chap. 24 512
Forest Oil Co., Young *v.*, 194 Pa. 243; 45 Atl. 121, Chap. 18 404
Forney *v.* Ward, 25 Tex. App. 443; 62 S. W. 108, Chap. 36 732
Forst, Hooks *v.*, 165 Pa. 238; 30 Atl. 846, Chap. 24 513
Fort Pitt Gas Co., Douthett *v.*, 202 Pa. 416; 51 Atl. 981, Chap. 2   12

Fort Wayne Gas Co., Roberts v. 40 Ind. App. 528; 82 N. E. 558,
Chap. 11 230
Foster v. Weaver, 118 Pa. 42; 12 Atl. 213, Chap. 30 644
Fowler, Brown v., 65 Ohio St. 507; 63 N. E. 76, Chap. 4 45
Fowler v. Delaplain, 79 Ohio St. 279; 87 N. E. 261, Chap. 8 145
Fowler, Williams v., 201 Pa. 236; 50 Atl. 969, Chap. 54 939
Franzell, Calor Oil & Gas Co. v., 128 Ky. 715; 109 S. W. 328; 33 Ky.
L. Rep. 98, Chap. 45 808
Fraze, Dill v., 169 Ind. 53; 73 N. E. 971, Chap. 24 532
Freeman, Lanyon Zinc Co. v., 68 Kan. 691; 75 Pac. 995, Chap. 27 ... 583
Freer v. Davis, 52 W. Va. 1; 43 S. E. 164, Chap. 27 588
Freer v. Davis, 52 W. Va. 35; 43 S. E. 172, Chap. 27 590
Fretts, Venture Oil Co. v., 152 Pa. 451; 35 Atl. 732, Chap. 5 77
Friend v. Mallory, 52 W. Va. 53; 43 S. E. 114, Chap. 4 47
Fulton Oil & Gas Co., Gillespie v., 236 Ill. 188; 86 N. E. 218, Chap. 13 313
Funk v. Halderman, 53 Pa. 229, Chap. 7 135

G.

Gadberry v. Ohio etc. Gas Co., 162 Ind. 9; 67 N. E. 259, Chap. 11 .. 190
Gaffney Oil Co., New Dominion Oil & Gas Co. v., (Ky.) 121 S. W.
699, Chap. 12 272
Galey v. Kellerman, 123 Pa. 491; 16 Atl. 474, Chap. 12 250
Garrett v. South Penn Oil Co., 66 W. Va. 587; 66 S. E. 741, Chap. 49 860
Garner, Eclipse Oil Co. v., 53 W. Va. 151; 44 S. E. 131, Chap. 29 609
Gartlah v. Hickman, 56 W. Va. 75; 49 S. E. 14, Chap. 9 156
Gartlan, Steelsmith v., 45 W. Va. 27; 29 S. E. 977, Chap. 5 73
George, Western Penna. Nat. Gas Co. v., 161 Pa. 47; 28 Atl. 1004,
Chap. 6 97
Gillespie v. Fulton Oil & Gas Co., 236 Ill. 188; 86 N. E. 219, Chap. 13 313
Glasgow v. Chartiers Oil Co., 152 Pa. 48; 25 Atl. 232, Chap. 13 294
Goldstein, Wilson v., 152 Pa. 524; 25 Atl. 49, Chap. 32 674
Gormley, Wettengel v., 160 Pa. 559; 28 Atl. 934; 40 Am. St. Rep. 733,
Chap. 50 883
Gormley, Wettengel v., 184 Pa. 354; 39 Atl. 57, Chap. 50 884
Great Southern Gas Co., Logan Nat. Gas Co. v., 61 C. C. A. 359; 126
Fed. 623, Chap. 24 517
Great Western Oil Co. v. Carpenter, 43 Tex. Civ. App. 229; 95 S. W.
57, Chap. 13 299
Greenlee v. Steelsmith, 64 W. Va. 353; 62 S. E. 459, Chap. 30 630

Greensboro Nat. Gas Co. v. Fayette County Gas Co., 200 Pa. 388; 49
    Atl. 768, Chap. 51 915
Griest, Ohio Oil Co. v., 65 N. E. 534; 30 Ind. App. 84, Chap. 9 154
Griffin, Moore v., 72 Kan. 164; 83 Pac. 395, Chap. 49 874
Guffey, Fennel v., 139 Pa. 341; 20 Atl. 1045, Chap. 16 366
Guffey & Queen, Fisher v., 193 Pa. 393; 44 Atl. 452, Chap. 16 380
Guffey v. Hukill, 34 W. Va. 49; 11 S. E. 754, Chap. 12 240
Guffey v. Clever, 146, Pa. 548; 23 Atl. 161, Chap. 15 355
Guffey, Hukill v., 37 W. Va. 425; 16 S. E. 544, Chap. 26 553
Guffey, Lowther Oil Co. v., 52 W. Va. 88; 43 S. E. 101, Chaps.
    6-24, ...111, 506
Guffey, Wolf v., 161 Pa. 276; 28 Atl. 1117, Chap. 12 266

H.

Hague v. Wheeler, 157 Pa. 324; 27 Atl. 714; 37 Am. St. Rep. 736;
    22 L. R. A. 141, Chap. 45 805
Halderman, Funk v., 53 Pa. 229, Chap. 7 135
Hale, Edwards v., 37 W. Va. 193; 16 S. E. 487, Chap. 14 347
Hall v. Vernon, 47 W. Va. 295; 34 S. E. 764, Chap. 31 651
Hall, Peterson v. 57 W. Va. 535; 50 S. E. 603, Chap. 49 848
Hamilton, Douglass Oil Fields v., (Wyo.) 95 Pac. 849, Chap. 18 432
Hamilton, Phillips v., (Wyo.) 95 Pac. 846, Chap. 18 430
Hanna, Pheasant v., 63 W. Va. 613; 60 S. E. 618, Chap. 51 911
Hancock v. Diamond Plate Glass Co., 162 Ind. 146; 70 N. E. 149,
    Chap. 12 280
Harrington Bros. v. Florence Oil Co., 178 Pa. 444; 35 Atl. 855, Chap. 30 635
Harris v. Ohio Oil Co., 57 Ohio St. 718; 48 N. E. 502, Chap. 18 411
Harris, Kansas Nat. Gas Co. v., 79 Kan. 167; 100 Pac. 72, Chap. 21 .. 483
Harness, Bettman v., 42 W. Va. 433; 26 S. E. 271, Chap. 6 99
Harness v. Eastern Oil Co., 49 W. Va. 232; 38 S. E. 662, Chap. 18 ... 406
Hartman v. Citizens Nat. Gas Co., 210 Pa. 19; 59 Atl. 315, Chap. 55.. 954
Hartz, Mills v., 77 Kan. 218; 94 Pac. 142, Chap. 24 524
Haskell v. Sutton, 53 W. Va. 206; 44 S E. 533, Chap. 27 594
Haskell, Kansas Nat. Gas Co. v., (C. C.) 172 Fed. 545, Chap. 38...... 742
Hatry, Ogden v., 145 Pa. 640; 23 Atl. 334, Chap. 12 269
Hauck v. Tidewater Pipeline Co., 153 Pa. 366; 26 Atl. 644; 34 Am. St.
    Rep. 710; 20 L. R. A. 642, Chap. 57 1001
Hawkins, Eakin v., 48 W. Va. 364; 37 S. E. 622, Chap. 35 721
Hawkins, Eakin v., 52 W. Va. 124; 43 S. E. 211, Chap. 35 726
Hays v. Forest Oil Co., 213 Pa. 556; 62 Atl. 1072, Chap. 13 319

Hazlegreen Oil & Gas Co. v. Collins, (Ky.) 110 S. W. 343, Chap. 6..... 121
Hazlewood Oil Co., May v., 152 Pa. 518; 25 Atl. 564 Chap. 33 693
Headley v. Hoopengarner, 60 W. Va. 626; 55 S. E. 144, Chap. 18...... 420
Heat & Light Co., Double v., 172 Pa. 388; 33 Atl. 694, Chap. 11....... 196
Heat & Light Co., Moore v., 65 W. Va. 552; 64 S. E. 721, Chap. 55.... 966
Heinhour v. Jones; 159 Pa. 228; 28 Atl. 228, Chap. 32 676
Heintz v. Shortt, 149 Pa. 286; 24 Atl. 316, Chap. 24 540
Heller v. Dailey, 28 Ind. App. 555; 63 N. E. 490, Chap. 16 370
Heller, Dailey v., (Ind. App.) 81 N. E. 219, Chap. 16 381
Henderson v. Farrell, 183 Pa. 547; 38 Atl. 1018, Chap. 24 510
Henderson, Pyle v., 65 W. Va. 39; 63 S. E. 620, Chaps. 6-53......116, 930
Henne v. South Penn Oil Co., 52 W. Va. 192; 43 S. E. 147, Chap. 24... 508
Hickman, Gartlan v., 56 W. Va. 75; 49 S. E. 14, Chap. 9 156
Hicks v. American Nat. Gas Co., 207 Pa. 570; 57 Atl. 55, Chap. 17.... 389
Hicks, United States Nat. Gas. Co. v., 119 S. W. 166, Chap. 55 977
Hillside Coal Co., Plummer v., 160 Pa. 483; 28 Atl. 353, Chap. 5   76
Hinton, Indiana etc. Gas Co. v., 159 Ind. 398; 64 N. E. 224, Chap. 16.. 375
Hochstetter Oil Co., Sult v., 63 W. Va. 317; 61 S. E. 307, Chap. 27... 573
Hodges v. Brice, 32 Tex. Civ. App. 358; 74 S. W. 590, Chap. 29........ 617
Holland, Detlor v., 57 Ohio St. 492; 49 S. E. 690; 40 L. R. A. 266, Chap.
    27 585
Hollon v. Campton Fuel & Light Co., 127 Ky. 266; 105 S. W. 426; 32
    Ky. L. Rep. 178, Chap. 55 976
Hooks v. Forst, 165 Pa. 238; 30 Atl. 846, Chap. 24 513
Hoopengarner, Headley v., 60 W. Va. 626; 55 S. E. 144, Chap. 18..... 420
Houssiere-Lattrielle Oil Co. v. Jennings-Heywood Oil Synd., 115 La.
    107; 38 So. 932, Chap. 13 311
Houssiere-Lattrielle Oil Co., Jennings-Heywood Oil Synd. v., 119 La.
    864; 44 So. 481, Chap. 13 306
Hue, Duffield v., 136 Pa. 602; 20 Atl. 526, Chap. 10 172
Hue, Duffield v., 129 Pa. 94; 18 Atl. 566, Chap. 10 177
Huffman, Starn v., 62 W. Va. 422; 59 S. E. 179, Chaps. 28-51.....603, 909
Huggins v. Daley, 99 Fed. 606; 40 C. C. A. 12; 48 L. R. A. 320, Chap. 6 103
Hughes, Delaware & Hudson Canal Co. v., 183 Pa. 66; 63 Am. St. Rep.
    743, Chap 49 869
Hughes v. United Pipelines, 119 N. Y. 423; 23 N. E. 1042, Chap. 27... 582
Hukill, Craig v., 37 W. Va. 520; 16 S. E. 363, Chap. 52 923
Hukill, Guffey v., 34 W. Va. 49; 11 S. E. 754, Chap. 12 240
Hukill v. Myers, 36 W. Va. 639; 15 S. E. 151, Chap. 12 244
Hukill v. Guffey, 37 W. Va. 425; 16 S. E. 544, Chap. 26 553
Hukill, Schaupp v., 34 W. Va., 375; 12 S. E. 501, Chap. 12 241
Hukill, Thomas v., 34 W. Va. 385; 12 S. E. 522, Chap. 6 118

Humes, Davidson v., 188 Pa. 335; 41 Atl. 649, Chap. 37   738

Humphreys, Plant v., 66 W. Va. 88; 66 S. E. 94, Chap. 49.   858

Huntington Light etc. Co., Ibach v., 23 Ind. App. 281; 55 N. E. 249,
  Chap. 55   964

I.

Iams v. Carnegie Nat. Gas Co., 194 Pa. 72; 45 Atl. 54, Chap. 11   197

Ibach v. Huntington Light etc. Co., 23 Ind. App. 281; 55 N. E. 249,
  Chap. 55 . . . ., ...   964

Indiana, Ohio Oil Co. v., 177 U. S. 190, Chap. 39   747

Ind. Nat. & Illum. Gas Co. v. Anthony, 26 Ind. App. 307; 58 N. E.
  868, Chap. 56   987

Indiana & Ohio Oil, Gas & Min. Co., State, ex rel. Corwin v., 120 Ind.
  575; 22 N. E. 778; 6 L. R. A. 579, Chap. 38.   744

Indiana etc. Gas Co., American Window Glass Co. v., 37 Ind. App. 439;
  76 N. E. 1006, Chap 34   702

Indiana Nat. Gas & Oil Co. v. Leer, 34 Ind. App. 61; 72 N. E. 283,
  Chap. 11   198

Indiana Nat. Gas & Oil Co. v. Hinton, 159 Ind. 398; 64 N. E. 224,
  Chap. 16   375

Indiana Nat. Gas & Oil Co. v. Beale, 166 Ind. 684; 76 N. E. 520, Chap.
  34   704

Indiana Nat. Gas & Oil Co., Jamison v., 128 Ind. 555; 28 N. E. 76,
  Chap. 39   751

Indiana Nat. Gas & Oil Co., Manufacturers Gas & Oil Co., v., 155 Ind.
  461; 57 N. E. 912; 50 L. R. A. 768, Chap. 40   761

Indiana Natural Gas Co. v. McMath, 26 Ind. App. 154; 57 N. E. 593,
  Chap. 55   964

Indiana Nat. Gas & Oil Co., Manufacturers Gas & Oil Co. v., 156 Ind.
  679; 59 N. E. 169; 60 N. E. 1080, Chap. 40   767

Indiana Nat. Gas & Oil Co. v. State ex rel. Armstrong, 162 Ind. 690;
  71 N. E. 133, Chap. 56 . . . .; . . .   995

Indiana Nat. Gas & Oil Co., Manufacturers Gas & Oil Co. v., 155 Ind.
  556; 58 N. E. 851, Chap. 40   765

Indiana Nat. & Illum. Gas. Co. v. State, 158 Ind. 516; 63 N. E. 220;
  57 L. R. A. 761, Chap. 56   996

Indianapolis Nat. Gas. Co. v. Wilhelm, (Ind. App.) 86 N. E. 86, Chap.
  11   228

Indianapolis Gas Co., Coy v., 156 Ind. 655; 46 N. E. 17; 36 L. R. A.
  535, Chap. 56 . . . . ', ...   994

Ink, Consumers Gas Trust Co. v., 163 Ind. 174; 71 N. E. 477, Chap. 11   209

Irish, Alexandra etc. Mining Co. v., 16 Ind. App. 534; 44 N. E. 680,
Chap. 55 962
Isam v. Rex Crude Oil Co., 147 Cal. 659; 82 Pac. 317, Chap. 27 576

J.

Jackson v. Dulaney, (W. Va.) 67 S. E. 795, Chap. 49 864
Jackson v. O'Hara, 183 Pa. 233; 38 Atl. 624, Chap. 16 378
Jamieson v. Indiana Nat. Gas & Oil Co., 128 Ind. 555; 28 N. E. 76,
Chap. 39 751
Jennings, Elk Fork Oil & Gas Co. v., 84 Fed. 839; 90 Fed. 179; 32 C. C.
A. 560, Chap. 4 56
Jennings, Elk Fork Oil & Gas Co. v., 99 Fed. 495; 39 C. C. A. 615,
Chap. 4 56
Jennings-Heywood Oil Synd., Houssierre-Lattrielle Oil Co. v., 115 La.
107; 38 So. 932, Chap. 13 311
Jennings-Heywood Oil Synd. v. Houssierre-Lattrielle Oil Co., 119 La.
864; 44 So. 481, Chap. 13 306
Jennings, Linden Oil Co. v., 207 Pa. 524; 56 Atl. 1074, Chap. 9 156
Jennings-Heywood Oil Synd., Martel v., 114 La. 903; 38 So. 253, Chap.
24 537
Jennings, Moore v., 47 W. Va. 181; 34 S. E. 793, Chap. 27 591
J. M. Guffey Petroleum Co. v. Oliver, (Tex.) 79 S. W. 884, Chap. 18.. 424
J. M. Guffey Petroleum Co. v. Chaison Town Site Co., (Tex. Civ. App.)
107 S. W. 609 463
Johnson v. Price, 172 Pa. 427; 33 Atl. 688, Chap. 30 648
Johnson, Dark v., 55 Pa. 154; Chaps. 3-15 .... 22, 351
Johnson, Washington Nat. Gas Co. v., 123 Pa. 576; 16 Atl. 799, Chap.
16 369
Jones, Buffalo etc. Co. v., 75 Kan. 18; 88 Pac. 537, Chap. 24 529
Jones, Heinhour v., 159 Pa. 228; 28 Atl. 228, Chap. 32 676
Jones v. Western Penna. Nat. Gas Co., 146 Pa. 204; 23 Atl. 386, Chap.
12 265
Jones v., Forest Oil Co., 194 Pa. 379; 44 Atl. 1074; 48 L. R. A. 748,
Chap. 40 775
Jones v. Mount, 166 Ind. 570; 77 N. E. 1089, Chap. 19 448
Jones, Williamson v., 39 W. Va. 231; 19 S. E. 436, Chap. 27 559
Jones, Williamson v., 43 W. Va. 562; 27 S. E. 411, Chap. 27 566

K

Kansas Nat. Gas Co., Beardsley v., 78 Kan. 571; 96 Pac. 589, Chap. 31. 653
Kansas Nat. Gas Co. v. Board of Commissioners, 75 Kan. 335; 89 Pac.
750, Chap. 3 31

Kansas Nat. Gas Co. v. Harris, 79 Kan. 167; 100 Pac. 72, Chap. 21.... 483

Kansas Nat. Gas Co. v. Haskell, (C. C.) 172 Fed. 547, Chap. 38...... 742

Keller v. Craig, 61 C. C. A. 366; 126 Fed. 630, Chap. 18 409

Kellerman, Galey v., 123 Pa. 491; 16 Atl. 474, Chap. 12 250

Kelsey, Lafayette Oil & Gas Co. v., 164 Ind. 563; 74 N. E. 7, Chap. 34. 697

Kelley, Van Etten v., 66 Ohio St. 606; 64 N. E. 560, Chap. 13 291

Kelly v. Keys, 213 Pa. 296; 62 Atl. 811, Chap. 3 140

Kelley v. Ohio Oil Co., 57 Ohio St. 317; 49 N. E. 399; 63 Am. St. Rep.
   721; 39 L. R. A. 765, Chap. 42 784

Keeton, Kimball Oil Co. v., 31 Ky. L. Rep. 146; 101 S. W. 887, Chap. 24 525

Kemper, Newton v., 66 W. Va. 130; 66 S. E. 102, Chap. 52.......:.... 926

Kennedy, McGraw Oil & Gas Co. v., 65 W. Va. 595; 64 S. E. 1027,
   Chap. 18 407

Kennedy v. Crawford, 138 Pa. 561; 21 Atl. 19, Chap. 12 254

Kentucky Heating Co. v. Calor Oil & Gas Co., 128 Ky. 715; 109 S. W.
   328; 33 Ky. L. Rep. 98, Chap. 45 808

Kentucky Heating Co., Louisville Gas Co. v., 117 Ky. 71; 77 S. W. 368;
   70 L. R. A. 558, Chap. 45 756

Kentucky Heating Co., Louisville Gas Co. v., 33 Ky. L. Rep. 912; 111
   S. W. 374, Chap. 45 811

Keys, Kelly v., 213 Pa. 296; 62 Atl. 911, Chap. 3 140

Kilcoyne v. Southern Oil Co., 61 W. Va. 538; 55 S. E. 88, Chap. 18... 435

Kimball Oil Co. v. Keeton, 31 Ky. L. Rep. 146; 101 S. W. 887, Chap. 24 525

Kirchner, Lawson v., 50 W. Va. 344; 40 S. E. 344, Chap. 5 83

Kirkpatrick, Dunham v., 101 Pa. 36; 47 Am. Rep. 696, Chap. 48...... 839

Kiser v. McLean, (W. Va.) 67 S. E. 725, Chap. 49 862

Kleppner v. Lemon, 176 Pa. 502; 25 Atl. 109, Chap. 18 400

Kleppner v. Lemon, 197 Pa. 430; 47 Atl. 353, Chap. 19 441

Kleppner v. Lemon, 198 Pa. 581; 48 Atl. 483, Chap. 19 443

Knotts v. McGregor, 47 W. Va. 566; 37 S. E. 899, Chap. 18 398

Koen v. Bartlett, 41 W. Va. 559; 23 S. E. 664; 56 Am. St. Rep. 884; 31
   L. R. A. 128, Chap. 35 710

Kurt v. Lanyon, 72 Kan. 60; 82 Pac. 459, Chap. 2 13

L

Lackawanna Coal Co., Lillibridge v., 143 Pa. 293; 22 Atl. 1035; 24 Am.
   St. Rep. 544, Chap. 49 871

Lafayette Oil & Gas Co. v. Kelsey, 164 Ind. 563; 74 N. E. 7, Chap. 34.. 697

Lafayette Gas Co., Scott v. 42 Ind. App. 514; 86 N. E. 495, Chap. 12.. 279

Lane, Ohio Oil Co. v., 59 Ohio St. 307; 52 N. E. 791, Chap. 11........ 193

Lanyon Zinc Co., Brewster v., 140 Fed. 801; 72 C. C. A. 213, Chap. 4..   51

Lanyon, Kurt v., 72 Kan. 60; 82 Pac. 459, Chap. 2   13

Lanyon Zinc Co. v. Freeman, 68 Kan. 691; 75 Pac. 995, Chap. 27..... 583

Lanyon Zinc Co., Monfort v., 67 Kan. 310; 72 Pac. 784, Chap. 5......   81

Lawson v. Kirchner, 50 W. Va. 344; 40 S. E. 344, Chap. 5   83

Lebanon Light etc. Co. v. Leak, 139 Ind. 443; 39 N. E. 57; 29 L. R. A.
342, Chap. 55 959

League, Emory v., 31 Tex. Civ. App. 474; 72 S. W. 603, Chap. 31 654

Leak, Lebanon Light Co. v., 139 Ind. 443; 39 N. E. 57; 29 L. R. A.
342, Chap. 55 959

Leer, Indiana etc. Gas Co. v., 34 Ind. App. 61; 72 N. E. 283, Chap. 11.. 198

Lemon, Kleppner v., 176 Pa. 502; 25 Atl. 109, Chap. 18 400

Lemon, Kleppner v., 197 Pa. 430; 47 Atl. 353, Chap. 19 ....:.... 441

Lemon, Kleppner v., 198 Pa. 581; 48 Atl. 483, Chap. 19............. 443

Liggitt v. Shira, 159 Pa. 350; 28 Atl. 218, Chap. 12 263

Lillibridge v. Lackawanna Coal Co., 143 Pa. 293; 22 Atl. 1035; 24 Am.
St. Rep. 544, Chap. 49 871

Linden Oil Co. v. Jennings, 207 Pa. 524; 56 Atl. 1074, Chap. 9 156

Littler, Consumers Gas Trust Co. v. 162 Ind. 320; 70 N. E. 363, Chap.
11 201

Lockwood, Barnhart v., 152 Pa. 82; 25 Atl. 237, Chap. 33 691

Logan, Murdock-West Co. v., 69 Ohio St. 514; 69 N. E. 284, Chap. 6... 101

Logan Nat. Gas Co. v. Great Southern Gas Co., 61 C. C. A. 359; 126
Fed. 523, Chap. 24 517

Logansport etc. Gas Co., v. Seegar, 165 Ind. 1; 74 N. E. 500, Chap. 24.. 531

Logansport & Wabash Valley Gas Co. v. Null, (Ind. App.) 76 N. E. 125,
Chap. 12 277

Louisville Gas Co. v. Kentucky Heating Co., 117 Ky. 71; 77 S. W. 368;
70 L. R. A. 558; 111 Am. St. Rep. 225, Chap. 45 756

Louisville Gas Co. v. Kentucky Heating Co., 33 Ky. L. Rep. 912; 111
S. W. 374, Chap. 45 811

Loverock, Dunham v., 158 Pa. 197; 27 Atl. 990, Chap. 30 634

Low, State v. 46 W. Va. 451; 33 S. E. 271, Chap. 49 843

Lowe & Butler, Charleston Nat. Gas Co. v., 52 W. Va. 662; 44 S. E. 410,
Chap. 56 984

Lowther Oil Co. v. Miller-Sibley Oil Co., 53 W. Va. 501; 44 S. E. 433;
87 Am. St. Rep. 1027, Chap. 5   82

Lowther Oil Co. v. Guffey, 52 W. Va. 88; 43 S. E. 101, Chaps. 6-24.111, 506

Lowther Oil Co., Urpman v., 53 W. Va. 501; 44 S. E. 433, Chap. 5....   82

Lynch v. Versailles Fuel Gas Co., 165 Pa. 518; 20 Atl. 984, Chap. 21.. 470

Lynch v. Burford, 201 Pa. 52; 50 Atl. 238, Chap. 10 180

M

Mack Manufacturing Co., Porter v., 65 W. Va. 636; 64 S. E. 853, Chap.
47 832
Mallory, Wagner v., 169 N. Y. 501; 62 N. E. 584, Chap. 5 87
Mallory, Friend v., 52 W. Va. 53; 43 S. E. 114, Chap. 4 47
Manhattan Oil Co. v. Carrell, 164 Ind. 526; 73 N. E. 1084, Chap. 22.. 496
Manufacturers Nat. Gas. Co., McKnight v., 146 Pa. 185; 23 Atl. 164,
Chap. 11 194
Manufacturers Nat. Gas Co., Wills v., 130 Pa. 222; 18 Atl. 721, Chap. 12 257
Manufacturers Nat. Gas. Co. v. Ind. etc. Gas & Oil Co., 155 Ind. 461;
57 N. E. 912; 50 L. R. A. 768, Chap. 40 761
Manufacturers Nat. Gas & Oil Co. v. Indiana etc. Gas & Oil Co., 156
Ind. 679; 59 N. E. 169; 60 N. E. 1080, Chap. 40 767
Manufacturers Nat. Gas & Oil Co. v. Indiana etc. Gas & Oil Co., 155
Ind. 556; 58 N. E. 851, Chap. 40 765
Mansfield Coal & Coke Co. v. Mellon, 152 Pa. 286; 25 Atl. 596; 18 L. R.
A. 702; 34 Am. St. Rep. 645, Chap. 49 867
Marian Oil Co., Barrickman v., 45 W. Va. 634; 32 S. E. 327; 44 L. R. A.
92 945
Marks, Steiner v., 172 Pa. 400; 33 Atl. 695, Chap. 21 471
Marsh, Flannagan v., 32 Ky. L. Rep. 184; 105 S. W. 424, Chap. 24.... 524
Marshall, Blakley, v., 174 Pa. 425; 34 Atl. 564, Chap. 27 575
Marshall v. Forest Oil Co., 198 Pa. 83; 47 Atl. 927, Chap. 24 512
Marshall v. Mellon, 199 Pa. 371; 36 Atl. 201; 35 L. R. A. 216, 57 Am.
St. Rep. 601, Chap. 27 576
Marshall, Stone v., 188 Pa. 602; 41 Atl. 748-1119, Chap. 51 917
Marshall Window Glass Co. v. Cameron Oil & Gas Co., 63 W. Va. 202;
59 S. E. 959, Chap. 55 948
Martel v. Jennings-Heywood Oil Synd., 114 La. 903; 38 So. 253, Chap.
24 537
Mathes v. Shaw Oil Co., (Kan.) 101 Pac. 998, Chap. 11 212
Matthews v. Peoples Natural Gas Co., 179 Pa. 165; 36 Atl. 216, Chap.
12 271
Maxwell v. Coffeyville Min. & Gas Co. 75 Pac. 1047; 68 Kan. 821,
Chap. 55 975
May v. Hazelwood Oil Co., 152 Pa. 518; 25 Atl. 564, Chap. 33 693
Meek, Erie-Crawford Oil Co. v., (Ind. App.) 81 N. E. 518, Chap. 13.. 317
Mellon, Chartiers Block Coal Co. v., 152 Pa. 286; 25 Atl. 597; 18 L. R.
A. 702; 34 Am. St. Rep. 645, Chap. 49 867
Mellon, Marshall v., 199 Pa. 371; 36 Atl. 201; 35 L. R. A. 216, Chap. 27 576

Mellon, Mansfield Coal & Coke Co. v., 152 Pa. 286; 25 Atl. 597; 18 L. R.
A. 702; 34 Am. St. Rep. 645, Chap. 49 867
Mellon, Riddle v., 147 Pa. 30; 23 Atl. 241, Chap. 6 126
Miller-Sibley Co., Lowther Oil Co. v., 53 W. Va. 501; 44 S. E. 433; 97
Am. St. Rep. 1027 82
Miller v. South Penn Oil Co., 99 C. C. A. 305; 175 Fed. 729, Chap. 53. 931
Mills v. Hartz, 77 Kan. 218; 94 Pac. 142, Chap. 24 524
Monarch Oil, Gas & Coal Co. v. Richardson, 30 Ky. L. Rep. 824; 99 S.
W. 666, Chap. 13 297
Monoghan v. Mount, 36 Ind. App. 188; 74 N. E. 579, Chap. 19....... 446
Monfort v. Lanyon Zinc Co., 67 Kan. 310; 72 Pac. 784, Chap. 5...... 81
Monongahela Gas Co., Barnard v., 216 Pa. 362; 65 Atl. 801, Chap. 42.. 782
Moore v. Heat & Light Co., 65 W. Va. 552; 64 S. E. 721, Chap. 55.... 966
Moore v. Sawyer, 167 Fed. 826, Chap. 16 372
Moore v. Jennings, 47 W. Va. 181; 34 S. E. 793, Chap. 27 591
Moore v. Griffin, 72 Kan. 164; 83 Pac. 395, Chap. 49 874
Mound City Gas & Oil Co., Rhodes v., 80 Kan. 762; 104 Pac. 851,
Chap. 34 700
Mount, Jones v., 166 Ind. 570; 77 N. E. 1089, Chap. 19 448
Mount Sterling Oil & Gas Co., Armitage v., 25 Ky. L. Rep. 2262; 80
S. W. 177, Chap. 13 302
Mount, Monaghan v., 36 Ind. App. 188; 74 N. E. 579, Chap. 19....... 446
Munger, Collier v., 75 Kan. 550; 89 Pac. 1111, Chap. 2 15
Munroe v. Armstrong, 96 Pa. 307; Chap. 5 74
Murray v. Allred, 100 Tenn. 100; 66 Am. St. Rep. 740; 43 S. W. 355,
Chap. 47 827
Murray v. Barnhart, 117 La. 1023; 42 So. 489, Chap. 24 526
Murdock-West Co. v. Logan, 69 Ohio St. 514; 69 N. E. 284, Chap. 6... 101
Myers, Hukill v., 36 W. Va. 639; 15 S. E. 151, Chap. 12 244
Myers, Puritan Oil Co. v., 39 Ind. App. 695; 80 N. E. 851, Chap. 12... 274

Mc.

.

McCalmont Oil Co., Swint v., 184 Pa. 202; 38 Atl. 1020, Chap. 32.... 664
McCoy v. Ohio Valley Gas Co., 213 Pa. 367; 62 Atl. 858; Chap. 55..... 951
McCumber, Florence Oil etc. Co. v., 38 Colo. 366; 88 Pac. 265, Chap. 24 528
McFadden, Roberts & Corley v., 32 Tex. Civ. App. 47; 74 S. W. 105,
Chap. 14 341
McGehee, Calor Oil & Gas Co. v., 117 Ky. 71; 77 S. W. 368; 70 L. R. A.
558; 111 Am. St. Rep. 225, Chap. 39 756

McGraw Oil & Gas Co. v. Kennedy, 65 W. Va. 595; 64 S. E. 1027,
    Chap. 18 407
McGregor, Knotts v., 47 W. Va. 566; 37 S. E. 899, Chap. 18 398
McGregor v. Camden, 47 W. Va. 193; 34 S. E. 936, Chap. 44 795
McIlhenny, Young v., (Ky.) 116 S. W. 728, Chap. 29 614
McIntosh v. Robb, 4 Cal. App. 484; 88 Pac. 517, Chap. 24 522
McIntire, South Penn Oil Co. v., 44 W. Va. 296; 28 S. E. 922, Chap. 27 567
McKenna v. Bridgewater Gas Co., 193 Pa. 633; 45 Atl. 52; 47 L. R. A.
    790, Chap. 55 955
McKinney's Heirs v. Central Ky. Nat. Gas Co., (Ky.) 120 S. W. 314,
    Chap. 48 836
McKnight v. Manufacturers Nat. Gas Co., 146 Pa. 185; 23 Atl. 164,
    Chap. 11 194
McLean, Kiser v., (W. Va.) 67 S. E. 725, Chap. 49 862
McMath, Indiana Natural Gas Co. v., 26 Ind. App. 154; 57 N. E. 593,
    Chap. 55 964
McMillen v. Titus, 222 Pa. 500; 72 Atl. 240, Chap. 24 544
McNeely v. South Penn Oil Co., 58 W. Va. 438; 44 S. E. 508, Chap. 32 665

N.

National Oil etc. Co. v. Teel, 67 S. W. 545, Affirmed 68 S. W. 979; 95
    Tex. 586, Chap. 29 615
National Transit Co., Enterprise Oil & Gas Co. v., 172 Pa. 421; 33 Atl.
    687, Chap. 30 646
Neely, Childers v., 47 W. Va. 70; 34 S. E. 827, Chap. 30 626
Neely, Calhoun v., 201 Pa. 97; 50 Atl. 967, Chap. 24 515
Neill v. Shambourg, 158 Pa. 263; 27 Atl. 992, Chap. 15 353
New American Oil Co. v. Troyer, 166 Ind. 402; 76 N. E. 253; 77 N. E.
    739, Chap. 5   86
New Dominion Oil & Gas Co. v. Gaffney Oil Co., (Ky.) 121 S. W. 699,
    Chap. 12 272
New York Petroleum Co., Core v., 52 W. Va. 276; 43 S. E. 128, Chap.
    20 459
Newton v. Kemper, 66 W. Va. 130; 66 S. E. 102, Chap. 52 926
Northwestern Ohio Nat. Gas Co. v. Tiffin, 59 Ohio St. 420; 54 N. E.
    77, Chap. 6 100
Northwestern Ohio Nat. Gas Co. v. Ullery, 68 Ohio St. 259; 67 N. E.
    494, Chap. 50 887
Null, Logansport & Wabash Valley Gas Co. v., (Ind. App.) 76 N. E.
    125, Chap. 12 277

O.

Oak Harbor Gas Co., State v., 53 Ohio St. 347; 41 N. E. 584, Chap. 39 748
Ogden v. Hatry, 145 Pa. 640; 23 Atl. 334, Chap. 12 269
O'Hara, Jackson v., 183 Pa. 233; 38 Atl. 624, Chap. 16 378
Ohio Oil Co., Brown v., 65 Ohio St. 507; 63 N. E. 76, Chap. 4 45
Ohio Oil Co., Harris v., 57 Ohio St. 718; 48 N. E. 502, Chap. 18...... 411
Ohio Oil Co., Kelly v., 57 Ohio St. 317; 49 N. E. 399; 63 Am. St. Rep.
    721; 39 L. R. A. 765, Chap. 42 784
Ohio Oil Co. v. Griest, 65 N. E. 634; 30 Ind. App. 84, Chap. 9 154
Ohio Oil Co. v. Detmore, 165 Ind. 243; 73 N. E. 906, Chap. 24....... 535
Ohio Oil Co. v. Lane, 59 Ohio St. 307; 52 N. E. 791, Chap. 11........ 193
Ohio Oil Co. v. Indiana, 177 U. S. 190, Chap. 39 747
Ohio Oil Co. v. Westfall (Ind. App.) 88 N. E. 354, Chap. 43 789
Ohio Oil Co., State v., 150 Ind. 694; 40 N. E. 809, Chap. 39 746
Ohio etc. Gas Co., Chaney v., 32 Ind. App. 193; 69 N. E. 477, Chap. 6.. 104
Ohio etc. Gas Co., Gadberry v., 162 Ind. 9; 67 N. E. 259, Chap. 11 190
Ohio River Pipeline Co., West Virginia Transportation Co. v., 22 W. Va.
    600; 46 Am. Rep. 527, Chap. 46 817
Ohio Valley Gas Co., McCoy v., 213 Pa. 367; 62 Atl. 858, Chap. 55.... 951
Ohio Gas-Fuel Co. v. Andrews, 50 Ohio St. 695; 35 N. E. 1059, Chap.
    55 958
Oliver, J. M. Guffey Petroleum Co. v., (Tex.) 79 S. W. 884, Chap. 18.. 420
O'Neill v. Ressinger, 77 Kan. 63; 93 Pac. 340, Chap. 13 303
O'Neill v. Sun Co., (Tex. Civ. App.) 123 S. W. 172, Chap. 3 37
Orman, Florence Oil & Refining Co. v., 19 Colo. App. 79; 73 Pac.
    628, Chap. 5 78
Osborne, Butler Savings Bank v., 159 Pa. 10; 28 Atl. 163; 39 Am. St.
    Rep. 665, Chap. 30 632

P.

Parish Fork Oil & Gas Co. v. Bridgewater Gas Co., 51 W. Va. 583; 42
    S. E. 655, Chap. 5 70
Parrott, Breakenridge v., 15 Ind. App. 417; 44 N. E. 66, Chap. 16 376
Patterson, Windfall Manufacturing Co. v., 148 Ind. 414; 47 N. E. 2;
    62 Am. St. Rep. 532; 37 L. R. A. 38, Chap. 44 797
Penn, Auer v., 92 Pa. 444; Chap. 14 349
Penn Lubricating Co., Bay State Petroleum Co. v., 27 Ky. L. Rep.
    1138; 87 S. E. 1102, Chap. 22 490

Penn Lubricating Co., Becker r., 162 Fed. 627 (C. C. A.) Chap. 3 ...   52

Peunell, Bellevue Oil & Gas Co. r., 76 Kan. 785; 92 Pac. 1101, Chap. 11   213

Pennsylvania Torpedo Co., Zahniser r., 190 Pa. 350; 42 Atl. 707, Chap. 37   739

Peoples Gas Co., Tyner r., 131 Ind. 599; 31 N. E. 61, Chap. 41   781

Peoples Gas Co. v. Tyner, 131 Ind. 279; 31 N. E. 59, Chap. 41   779

Peoples Gas Co., Compton v., 75 Kan. 573; 89 Pac. 1039; 10 L. R. A. (N. S.) 785, Chap. 17   390

Peoples Nat. Gas Co., Matthews r., 179 Pa. 165; 36 Atl. 216, Chap. 12   271

Perrigo, Consumers Gas Trust Co. r., 144 Ind. 350; 32 L. R. A. 146; 43 N. E. 306, Chap. 55   967

Perry v. Acme Oil Co., (Ind. App.) 88 N. E. 559, Chap. 9   160

Peterson r. Hall, 57 W. Va. 535; 50 S. E. 603, Chap. 49   848

Pew, Cochran v., 159 Pa. 184; 28 Atl. 219, Chap. 12   262

Pfeiffer v. Brown, 165 Pa. 267; 30 Atl. 844, Chap. 43   792

Pheasant v. Hanna, 63 W. Va. 613; 60 S. E. 618, Chap. 51   911

Philadelphia Co., Carnegie Nat. Gas Co. r., 158 Pa. 317; 27 Atl. 95, Chap. 17   387

Philadelphia Co., Aye v., 193 Pa. 451; 44 Atl. 655; 74 Am. St. Rep. 696, Chap. 2   10

Philadelphia Co., Snyder v., 54 W. Va. 149; 46 S. E. 366; 102 Am. St. Rep. 941; 63 L. R. A. 896, Chap. 44   802

Phillips, Bartley v., 165 Pa. 325; 30 Atl. 842, Chap. 12   264

Phillips, Bartley v., 179 Pa. 175; 36 Atl. 217, Chap. 17   386

Phillips v. Hamilton, (Wyo.) 95 Pac. 846, Chap. 18   430

Phillips v. Vandergrift, 146 Pa. 357; 23 Atl. 347, Chap. 12   270

Pittsburg etc. Co. v. Bailey, 76 Kan. 42; 90 Pac. 803, Chap. 29   612

Pittsburg Plate Glass Co., Simpson r. 28 Ind. App. 343; 62 N. E. 753   164

Plant v. Humphreys, 66 W. Va. 88; 66 S. E. 94, Chap. 49 ...,......   858

Plummer v. Hillside Coal Co., 160 Pa. 483; 28 Atl. 353, Chap. 5 ...   76

Poe r. Ullery, 233 Ill. 56; 84 N. E. 46, Chap. 14   336

Pope Bros. r. Bridgewater Gas Co., 52 W. Va. 252; 43 S. E. 87, Chap. 44   800

Porter v. Mack Manufacturing Co., 65 W. Va. 636; 64 S. E. 853, Chap. 47   832

Portland Nat. Gas. & Oil Co. r. State, 135 Ind. 54; 34 N. E. 818; 21 L. R. A. 639, Chap. 56   985

Powers v. Bridgeport Oil Co., 238 Ill. 397; 87 N. E. 381, Chap. 18 ..   433

Preston v. White, 57 W. Va. 278; 50 S. E. 236, Chap. 27   578

Price, Johnson v., 172 Pa. 427; 33 Atl. 688, Chap. 30   648

Puritan Oil Co. *v.* Myers, 39 Ind. App. 695; 80 N. E. 851, Chap. 12 .. 274

Pyle *v.* Henderson, 65 W. Va. 39; 63 S. E. 620, Chaps. 6-53 .... 116, 930

Q.

Quigg, Ringle *v.*, 74 Kan. 581; 87 Pac. 724, Chap. 13 304

R.

Rawlings *v.* Armel, 70 Kan. 777; 79 Pac. 683, Chap. 5 80

Ray *v.* Western Pennsylvania Nat. Gas Co., 138 Pa. 576; 20 Atl. 1065,
    Chap. 12 258

Ressinger, O'Neill *v.*, 77 Kan. 63; 93 Pac. 340, Chap. 13 303

Rex Crude Oil Co., Isam *v.*, 147 Cal. 659; 82 Pac. 314, Chap. 27 576

Rhodes *v.* Mound City Gas & Oil Co., 80 Kan. 762; 104 Pac. 851,
    Chap. 34 700

Richardson, Monarch Oil, Gas & Coal Co. *v.*, 30 Ky. L. Rep. 824; 99 S.
    W. 668, Chap. 13 297

Richmond Nat. Gas Co. *v.* Enterprise Nat. Gas Co., 31 Ind. App. 222;
    66 N. E. 782, Chap. 40 768

Richmond Nat. Gas. Co. *v.* Davenport, 37 Ind. App. 25; 76 N. E. 525,
    Chap. 35 717

Riddle *v.* Mellon, 194 Pa. 30; 23 Atl. 241, Chap. 6 126

Ringle *v.* Quigg, 74 Kan. 581; 87 Pac. 724, Chap. 13 304

Ritchie, Crawford *v.*, 43 W. Va. 252; 37 S. E. 220, Chap. 5 84

Robb, McIntosh *v.*, 4 Cal. App. 484; 88 Pac. 517, Chap. 24 522

Roberts *v.* Bettman, 45 W. Va. 143; 30 S. E. 95, Chap. 12 245

Roberts & Corley *v.* McFadden, 32 Tex. Civ. App. 47; 74 S. W. 105,
    Chap. 14 341

Roberts *v.* Fort Wayne Gas Co., 40 Ind. App. 528; 82 N. E. 558,
    Chap. 11 230

Robinson, Vendocia etc. Co. *v.*, 71 Ohio St. 302; 73 N. E. 222, Chap. 21 475

Rock Oil Co., Campbell *v.*, 151 Fed. 191; 80 C. C. A. 467, Chap. 21 .. 478

Rosenzweig, Duffield *v.*, 144 Pa. 520; 23 Atl. 4, Chap. 10 .... 174, 127

Rosenzweig, Duffield *v.*, 150 Pa. 543; 24 Atl. 705, Chap. 10 177

Root, Smith *v.*, 66 W. Va. 633; 66 S. E. 1005, Chap. 51 901

Rymer *v.* South Penn Oil Co., 54 W. Va. 530; 46 S. E. 459, Chap. 50 889

S.

Sawyer, Moore *v.*, 167 Fed. 826, Chap. 16 372

Schaupp *v.* Hukill, 34 W. Va. 375; 12 S. E. 501, Chap. 12 241

Schortt, Heintz v., 149 Pa. 286; 24 Atl. 316, Chap. 24 540
Scott v. Lafayette Gas Co., 42 Ind. App. 614; 86 N. E. 495, Chap. 12 279
Seegar, Logansport etc. Gas Co. v., 165 Ind. 1; 74 N. E. 500, Chap. 24 531
Seep, Turner v., 167 Fed. 646, Chap. 15 361
    Affirmed: Midland Oil Co. v. Turner, 179 Fed. 74; 102 C. C. A. 368 364
Shadle, Bettman v., 22 Ind. App. 542; 53 N. E. 662, Chap. 14 325
Shambourg, Neill v., 158 Pa. 263; 27 Atl. 992, Chap. 15 353
Shaw Oil Co., Mathes v., (Kan.) 101 Pac. 998, Chap. 11 ....·.... 212
Shea, Yoke v., 47 W. Va. 401; 34 S. E. 748, Chap. 34 697
Shellar v. Shivers, 171 Pa. 569; 23 Atl. 95, Chap. 9 151
Shenk v. Stahl, 35 Ind. App. 444; 74 N. E. 538, Chap. 24 541
Shipman, Waterford Oil & Gas Co. v., 233 Ill. 9; 84 N. E. 53, Chap. 14 339
Shira, Liggitt v., 159 Pa. 350; 28 Atl. 218, Chap. 12 263
Shirey v. Consumers Gas Co., 215 Pa. 399; 64 Atl. 541, Chap. 55 ... 953
Shivers, Shellar v., 171 Pa. 569; 23 Atl. 95, Chap. 9 151
Shortt, Heintz v., 149 Pa. 286; 24 Atl. 316, Chap. 24 540
Silver v. Bush, 213 Pa. 195; 62 Atl. 832, Chap. 48 835
Simpson v. Pittsburg Plate Glass Co., 28 Ind. App. 343; 62 N. E. 753 164
Smith, Doddridge Oil & Gas Co. v., 154 Fed. 970, Chap. 18 416
Smith, Doddridge Oil & Gas Co. v., 173 Fed. 386, Chap. 5 90
Smith v. South Penn Oil Co., 59 W. Va. 204; 53 S. E. 152, Chap. 13 .. 296
Smith v. Root, 66 W. Va. 633; 66 S. E. 1005, Chap. 51 901
Snodgrass v. South Penn Oil Co., 47 W. Va. 509; 35 S. E. 820, Chap. 13 292
Snyder, Allegheny Oil Co. v., 106 Fed. 764; 45 C. C. A. 60, Chap. 4 .. 55
Snyder v. Phila. Co., 54 W. Va. 149; 46 S. E. 366; 102 Am. St. Rep.
    941; 63 L. R. A. 896, Chap. 44 802
South Penn Oil Co., Ammons v., 47 W. Va. 610; 35 S. E. 1004, Chap. 20 457
South Penn Oil Co., Carnegie Nat. Gas Co. v., 56 W. Va. 402; 49 S. E.
    548, Chap. 15 357
South Penn Oil Co., Eclipse Oil Co. v., 47 W. Va. 84; 34 S. E. 293,
    Chap. 4 49
South Penn Oil Co., Fleming Oil & Gas Co. v., 37 W. Va. 645; 17 S.
    E. 203, Chap. 36 730
South Penn Oil Co., Garrett v., 66 W. Va. 587; 66 S. E. 741, Chap. 49 860
South Penn. Oil Co., Henne v., 52 W. Va. 192; 43 S. E. 147, Chap. 24 508
South Penn Oil Co., McNeely v., 58 W. Va. 438; 44 S. E. 508, Chap. 32 665
South Penn Oil Co., Rymer v., 54 W. Va. 530; 46 S. E. 459, Chap. 50 889
South Penn Oil Co. v. Edgell. 48 W. Va. 348; 37 S. E. 596, Chap. 11 220
South Penn Oil Co., Smith v., 59 W. Va. 204; 53 S. E. 152, Chap. 13 296
South Penn Oil Co. v. McIntire, 44 W. Va. 296; 28 S. E. 922, Chap. 27 567

South Penn Oil Co., Snodgrass v., 47 W. Va. 509; 35 S. E. 820, Chap. 13   292
South Penn Oil Co. v. Miller, 99 C. C. A. 305; 175 Fed. 729, Chap. 53   931
South Penn Oil Co., Williams v., 52 W. Va. 181; 43 S. E. 214; 60 L.
R. A. 795, Chap. 47   827
South Penn Oil Co., Wade v., 45 W. Va. 380; 32 S. E. 169, Chap. 14 ..   346
Southern Oil Co., Kilcoyne v., 61 W. Va. 538; 55 S. E. 888, Chap. 18   435
Southern Oil Co., Talbott v., 60 W. Va. 423; 55 S. E. 1009, Chap. 45..   807
Southwest Penn Pipelines, Behling v., 160 Pa. 359; 28 Atl. 777; 40
Am. St. Rep. 724, Chap. 57   1003
Spilman, Brown v., 155 U. S. 665, Chap. 10   183
Springer v. Citizens Natural Gas Co., 145 Pa. 430; 22 Atl. 986, Chap. 12   256
Stage v. Boyer, 183 Pa. 560; 38 Atl. 1035, Chap. 24   511
Stahl v. VanVleck, 53 Ohio St. 136; 41 N. E. 35, Chap. 33   680
Stahl, Schenk v., 35 Ind. App. 443; 74 N. E. 538, Chap. 24   541
Staley & Barnsdall v. Derden (Tex. Civ. App.), 121 S. W. 1136, Chap. 3   36
Starn v. Huffman, 62 W. Va. 422; 59 S. E. 179, Chaps. 28-51 ... 603,   905
State ex rel. Armstrong, Ind. N. Gas & Oil Co. v., 162 Ind. 690; 71 N.
E. 133, Chap. 56   995
State ex rel. Ball, Ind. Nat. & Illum. Gas Co. v., 158 Ind. 516; 63 N.
E. 220; 57 L. R. A. 761, Chap. 56   996
State ex rel. Corwin v. Indiana & Ohio etc. Co., 120 Ind. 575; 22 N.
E. 778; 6 L. R. A. 579, Chap. 28   744
State v. Ohio Oil Co., 150 Ind. 694; 49 N. E. 809, Chap. 39   746
State v. Oak Harbor Gas Co., 53 Ohio St. 347; 41 N. E. 584, Chap. 39   748
State v. Low, 46 W. Va. 451; 33 S. E. 271, Chap. 49   843
State, Portland Nat. Gas & Oil Co. v., 135 Ind. 54; 34 N. E. 818; 21
L. R. A. 639, Chap. 56   985
State, Townsend v., 147 Ind. 624; 47 N. E. 19, Chap. 39   749
State ex rel. Wood v. Consumers Gas Trust Co., 157 Ind. 345; 61 N. E.
674; 55 L. R. A. 245, Chap. 56   991
Steelsmith, Greenlee v., 64 W. Va. 353; 62 S. E. 459, Chap. 30   630
Steelsmith v. Gartlan, 45 W. Va. 27; 27 S. E. 978, Chap. 5   73
Steelsmith v. Fisher Oil Co., 47 W. Va. 391; 35 S. E. 15, Chap. 53 ..   928
Steiner v. Marks, 172 Pa. 400; 33 Atl. 695, Chap. 21   471
Stewart v. Tennant, 52 W. Va. 559; 44 S. E. 223, Chap. 32   668
Stone v. Marshall Oil Co., 188 Pa. 602; 41 Atl. 748-1119, Chap. 51 ..   917
Stoughton's Appeal, 88 Pa. 198, Chap. 27   580
Sult v. Hochstetter Oil Co., 63 W. Va. 317; 61 S. E. 307, Chap. 27 ..   573
Summers v. Bennett,   W. Va.   ; 69 S. E. 690, Chap. 32   678
Summerville v. Apollo Gas Co., 207 Pa. 334; 56 Atl. 876, Chap. 11 ..   210

Sun Oil Co., Coffinberry v., 68 Ohio St. 488; 67 N. E. 1069, Chap. 19   451
Sun Oil Co., O'Neill v., (Tex. Civ. App.) 123 S. W. 172, Chap. 3 ...   37
Sutton, Haskell v., 53 W. Va. 206; 44 S. E. 533, Chap. 27   594
Swint v. McCalmont Oil Co., 184 Pa. 202; 38 Atl. 1020, Chap. 32   664

T.

Talbott v. Southern Oil Co., 60 W. Va. 423; 55 S. E. 1009, Chap. 45 ..   807
Taurette, Test Oil Co. v., 19 Okla. 214; 91 Pac. 1025, Chap. 2   14
Teal, National Oil & Petroleum Co. v., 67 S. W. 545; Affirmed 68 S.
    W. 979; 95 Tex. 586, Chap. 29   615
Tennant, Stewart v., 52 W. Va. 559; 44 S. E. 223, Chap. 32   668
Tennessee Oil Co. v. Brown, 131 Fed. 696; 65 C. C. A. 524, Chap. 24   516
Test Oil Co. v. Taurette, 19 Okla. 214; 91 Pac. 1025, Chap. 2   14
Thomas v. Hukill, 34 W. Va. 385; 12 S. E. 522, Chap. 6   118
Thompson v. Christy, 138 Pa. 230; 20 Atl. 934, Chap. 12   252
Tidewater Pipeline Co., Hauck v., 153 Pa. 366; 26 Atl. 644; 34 Am.
    St. Rep. 710; 20 L. R. A. 642, Chap. 57   1001
Tiffin, Northwestern Ohio Nat. Gas Co. v., 59 Ohio St. 420; 54 N. E.
    77, Chap. 6   100
Titus, McMillen v., 222 Pa. 500; 72 Atl. 240, Chap. 24   544
Toothman, Ammons v., 59 W. Va. 165; 53 S. E. 13, Chap. 49   852
Toothman v. Courtney, 62 W. Va. 167; 58 S. E. 915, Chap. 49   854
Townsend v. State, 147 Ind. 624; 47 N. E. 19, Chap. 39   749
Trees v. Eclipse Oil Co., 47 W. Va. 107; 34 S. E. 933, Chap. 14   329
Trent, Commonwealth v., 25 Ky. L. Rep. 1180; 77 S. W. 390, Chap. 39   754
Triple State etc. Co., Ward v., (Ky.) 115 S. W. 819, Chap. 14   325
Troyer, New American Oil Co. v., 166 Ind. 402; 76 N. E. 253; 77 N.
    E. 737, Chap. 5   86
Tupper, Walker v., 152 Pa. 1; 25 Atl. 172, Chap. 30   638
Turner v. Seep, 167 Fed. 646, Chap. 15   361
    Affirmed: Midland Oil Co. v. Turner, 179 F. 74; 102 C. C. A. 368   364
Tyner, Peoples Gas Co. v., 131 Ind. 279; 31 N. E. 59, Chap. 41   779
Tyner v. Peoples Gas Co., 131 Ind. 599; 31 N. E. 61, Chap. 41   781

U.

Ullery, Northwestern Ohio Nat. Gas Co. v., 68 Ohio St. 259; 67 N. E.
    494, Chap. 50   887
Ullery, Poe v., 233 Ill. 56; 84 N. E. 46, Chap. 14   336

Union Petroleum Co. v. Bliven Petroleum Co., 72 Pa. 173, Chap. 54 ..   941
United Pipelines, Hughes v., 119 N. Y. 423; 23 N. E. 1042, Chap. 27   582
United States Nat. Gas Co. v. Hicks, 119 S. W. 166, Chap. 55   977
Urpman v. Lowther Oil Co., 53 W. Va. 501; 44 S. E. 433, Chap. 5 ...   82

V.

Vandergrift, Brown v., 80 Pa. 142, Chap. 12   246
Vandergrift, Phillips v., 146 Pa. 357; 23 Atl. 347, Chap. 12   270
Van Etten v. Kelly, 66 Ohio St. 606; 64 N. E. 560, Chap. 13   291
VanVleck, Stahl v., 53 Ohio St. 136; 41 N. E. 35, Chap. 33   680
Vendocia Oil etc. Co. v. Robinson, 71 Ohio St. 302; 73 N. E. 222,
    Chap. 21   475
Venture Oil Co. v. Fretts, 152 Pa. 451; 35 Atl. 732, Chap. 5   77
Vernon, Hall v., 47 W. Va. 295; 34 S. E. 764, Chap. 31   651
Versailles Fuel Gas Co., Lynch v., 165 Pa. 518; 20 Atl. 984, Chap. 21   470

W.

Wade. v. South Penn Oil Co., 45 W. Va. 380; 32 S. E. 169, Chap. 14 ..   346
Wagner v. Mallory, 169 N. Y. 501; 62 N. E. 584, Chap. 5   87
Walker v. Tupper, 152 Pa. 1; 25 Atl. 172, Chap. 30   638
Wallace v. Elm Grove Coal Co., 58 W. Va. 449; 52 S. E. 485, Chap. 49   850
Ward v. Triple State etc. Co., (Ky.) 115 S. W. 819, Chap. 14   335
Ward, Forney v., 52 Tex. App. 443; 62 S. W. 108, Chap. 36   732
Washington Natural Gas Co. v. Johnson, 123 Pa. 576; 16 Atl. 799,
    Chap. 16   369
Waterford Oil & Gas Co. v. Shipman, 233 Ill. 9; 84 N. E. 53, Chap. 14   339
Weaver, Foster v., 118 Pa. 42; 12 Atl. 213, Chap. 30   644
Western Oil Co., Federal Oil Co. v., 112 Fed. 373, Chap. 24   519
Western Oil Co., Federal Oil Co. v., 121 Fed. 674; 57 C. C. A. 528,
    Chap. 29   610
Western Pennsylvania Nat. Gas Co., Jones v., 146 Pa. 204; 23 Atl. 386,
    Chap. 12   265
Western Pennsylvania Nat. Gas Co., Ray v., 138 Pa. 576; 20 Atl. 1065;
    Chap. 12   258
Western Pennsylvania Nat. Gas Co. v. George, 161 Pa. 47; 28 Atl.
    1004, Chap. 6   97

Westfall, Ohio Oil Co. *v.* (Ind. App.) 88 N. E. 354, Chap. 43 ...... **789**

Westmoreland Nat. Gas Co. *v.* DeWitt, 130 Pa. 235; 18 Atl. 724; 5 L.
R. A. 731, Chap. 11 .... **222**

West Virginia Transportation Co. *v.* Ohio River Pipeline Co., 22 W.
Va. 600; 46 Am. Rep. 527, Chap. 46 .... **817**

Wettengel *v.* Gormley, 160 Pa. 559; 28 Atl. 934; 40 Am. St. Rep. 732,
Chap. 50 .... **883**

Wettengel *v.* Gormley, 184 Pa. 354; 39 Atl. 57, Chap. 50 .... **884**

Wheeler, Hague *v.*, 157 Pa. 324; 27 Atl. 714; 37 Am. St. Rep. 736;
22 L. R. A. 141, Chap. 45 .... **805**

White, Preston *v.*, 57 W. Va. 278; 50 S. E. 236, Chap. 27 .... **578**

Wilhelm, Indianapolis Nat. Gas Co. *v.*, (Ind. App.) 86 N. E. 86,
Chap. 11 .... **228**

Williams, Acme Oil etc. Co. *v.*, 140 Cal. 681; 74 Pac. 296, Chap. 18 .. **428**

Williams, American Window Glass Co. *v.*, 30 Ind. App. 68; 66 N. E.
912, Chap. 6 .... **113**

Williams *v.* South Penn Oil Co., 52 W. Va. 181; 42 S. E. 214; 60 L.
R. A. 795, Chap. 47 .... **829**

Williams *v.* Fowler, 201 Pa. 236; 50 Atl. 969, Chap. 54 .... **939**

Williamson, Blackmarr *v.*, 57 W. Va. 249; 50 S. E. 254, Chap. 30 .... **627**

Williamson *v.* Jones, 39 W. Va. 231; 19 S. E. 436, Chap. 27 .... **559**

Williamson *v.* Jones, 43 W. Va. 562; 27 S. E. 411, Chap. 27 .... **566**

Wills *v.* Manufacturers Nat. Gas Co., 130 Pa. 222; 18 Atl. 721, Chap. 12 **251**

Wilson *v.* Goldstein, 152 Pa. 524; 25 Atl. 493, Chap. 32 .... **674**

Wilson *v.* Youst, 43 W. Va. 826; 28 S. E. 781, Chap. 27 .... **570**

Windfall Manufacturing Co. *v.* Patterson, 148 Ind. 414; 47 N. E. 2;
62 Am. St. Rep. 532; 37 L. R. A. 38, Chap. 44 .... **797**

Wolf *v.* Guffey, 161 Pa. 276; 28 Atl. 1117, Chap. 12 .... **266**

Woodland Oil Co. *v.* Crawford, 55 Ohio St. 161; 44 N. E. 1093, Chap. 14 **326**

Worth, Consumers Gas Trust Co. *v.*, 163 Ind. 141; 71 N. E. 489,
Chap. 11 .... **206**

Y.

Yoke *v.* Shea, 47 W. Va. 401; 34 S. E. 748, Chap. 34 .... **697**

Young *v.* McIlhenny, (Ky.) 116 S. W. 728, Chap. 29 ....**614**

Young *v.* Forest Oil Co., 194 Pa. 243; 45 Atl. 121, Chap. 18 .... **404**

Youst, Wilson *v.*, 43 W. Va. 826; 28 S. E. 781, Chap. 27 .... **570**

Z.

Zahniser et als. *v.* Pennsylvania Torpedo Co., 190 Pa. 354; 42 Atl. 707,
 Chap. 37 739
Zeigler *v.* Brenneman, 237 Ill. 15; 86 N. E. 597, Chap. 31 657
Zeigler *v.* Dailey, (Ind. App.) 76 N. E. 819, Chap. 33 690

CASES CITED.

References are to Pages.

A.

Acme Oil Co. *v.* Williams (140 Cal. 681; 74 Pac. 396) 394, 439

Adams Appeal (113 Pa. 449; 6 Atl. 100) 941

Ahrns *v.* Chartiers Valley Gas Co. (188 Pa. 249; 41 Atl. 473) 283, 289

Alexander *v.* Davis (42 W. Va. 465-467; 26 S. E. 291) 909

Alexandria etc. Co. *v.* Irish (16 Ind. App. 534; 44 N. E. 680) 945, 979, 982

Allegheny Oil Co. *v.* Snyder (106 Fed. 764; 45 C. C. A. 604) 6, 7
                18, 43, 53, 67, 112, 315, 394
                438, 454, 465, 518, 614, 617

Allen *v.* Pullman Palace Car Co. (139 U. S. 658) 938

Allison & Evans Appeal (77 Pa. 221) 170, 174, 188

American Steel & Wire Co. *v.* Tate (33 Ind. App. 504; 71 N. E. 189) 720

American Water Works Co. *v.* State (46 Neb. 194; 64 N. W. 711;
   30 L. R. A. 447; 50 Am. St. Rep. 610) 994

American Window Glass Co. *v.* Indiana etc. Oil Co. (37 Ind.
   App. 439; 76 N. E. 1006-1008) 319, 696, 708

American Window Glass Co. *v.* Williams (30 Ind. App. 685; 66
   N. E. 912) 96, 704

Ammons *v.* Ammons (50 W. Va. 390; 40 S. E. 490) 671, 709
                727, 728, 879

Ammons *v.* South Penn Oil Co. (47 W. Va. 610; 35 S. E. 1004) ..394, 405
                419, 453, 467, 498, 715, 892

Ammons *v.* Toothman (59 W. Va. 165; 53 S. E. 13) 842

Andrews *v.* Andrews (31 Ind. App. 189; 67 N. E. 461) 720

Appeal of Stoughton (88 Pa. 178) 558, 578, 599, 720

Appeal of Thompson (101 Pa. 225) 88

Armentrout's Executors *v.* Gibbons (25 Gratt. 371) 928

Armitage *v.* Mount Sterling Oil & Gas Co. (25 Ky. L. Rep.
   2262; 80 S. W. 177) 290

Armstrong v. Caldwell (53 Pa. 294) 852,   870
Atwater v. R. Co. (48 N. J. L. 55; 2 Atl. 803; 57 Am. Rep. 543)   994
Atwood v. Cobb (15 Pick. 227)   910
Auer v. Penn (92 Pa. 444)   346
Aye v. Philadelphia Co. (193 Pa. 451; 44 Atl. 655; 74 Am. St.
    Rep. 696) 6, 10, 286, 432, 680, 688,   695

B.

Bailey v. State (163 Ind. 165; 71 N. E. 655)   760
Ballard v. Tomlinson (L. R. 29 Ch. Div. 115)   777
Bank v. Stark (106 Cal. 202; 39 Pac. 521)   847
Barnard v. Monongahela Gas Co. (216 Pa. 360; 65 Atl. 801) 782,   788
Barnard v. Sherley (135 Ind. 547; 34 N. E. 600)   799
Barnes v. Bee (138 Fed. 476) 842,   881
Barnhart v. Lockwood (152 Pa. 82; 25 Atl. 237) 64, 680,   695
Barnsdall v. Boley (119 Fed. 191) 125, 488,   498
Barnsdall v. Bradford Gas Co. (225 Pa. 338; 74 Atl. 207) 21,   68
                                            92, 95,   938
Barrickman v. Marion Oil Co. (45 W. Va. 634; 32 S. E. 327;   ·
    44 L. R. A. 92) 945, 979, 980, 981,   983
Bartlett & Stancliff v. Boyles (66 W. Va. 327; 66 S. E. 474) ..625, 640,   641
Bartley v. Phillips (165 Pa. 325; 30 Atl. 842) ... 64, 237, 272, 284,   938
Bartley v. Phillips (179 Pa. 175; 36 Atl. 217) 272, 285,   288
                           385, 393, 680, 687, 696,   938
Barry v. Ranson (12 N. Y. 462)   910
Bay State Petroleum Co. v. Penn Lubricating Co. (27 Ky. L.
    Rep. 1133; 87 S. W. 1102) 488,   498
Beardsley v. Kansas Nat. Gas Co. (78 Kan. 571; 96 Pac. 589)........   651
Bee v. Barnes (149 Fed. 727; 79 C. C. A. 433)   842
Becker v. Penn Lubricating Co. (162 Fed. 629; 89 C. C. A. 419) 21,   32
                                       68, 89,   95
Behling v. Southwest Penn. Pipelines (160 Pa. 359; 28 Atl. 777;
    40 Am. St. Rep. 724)   1001
Bellevue Oil & Gas Co. v. Pennell (76 Kan. 785; 92 Pac. 1101) ...189,   236
Benson v. Allegheny Heating Co. (188 Pa. 614; 41 Atl. 729 945,   983
Benson Min. Co. v. Alta Min. Co. (145 U. S. 428)   90
Bettman v. Harness (42 W. Va. 433; 26 S. E. 271) 6, 7, 64, 96,   219
              222, 287, 558, 587, 598, 603, 704, 896, 898, 899,   910
Bettman v. Shadle (22 Ind. App. 542; 52 N. E. 662) 323, 344,   345

Biddleman v. Brooks (28 Cal. 72) 857
Bitting v. Ten Eyck (85 Ind. 357) 901
Blackmarr v. Williamson (57 W. Va. 249; 41 N. E. 597) 625, 632, 640
Blakley v. Marshall (174 Pa. 425; 34 Atl. 564) ...558, 599, 600, 720, 858
Blodgett v. Lanyon Zinc. Co. (120 Fed. 893; 58 C. C. A. 79) 701, 708
Bluestone Coal Co. v. Bell (38 W. Va. 297; 18 S. E. 493) 64, 192, 438
                                                            501, 502, 550, 603, 910
Boyd v. Brown (47 W. Va. 238; 38 S. E. 668) 608, 624
Braford Oil Co. v. Blair (113 Pa. 83; 4 Atl. 218) 365, 383, 414, 453
Bradley v. Ewart (18 W. Va. 598) 847, 878
Brady v. Insurance Co. (11 Mich. 425) 804
Breckenridge v. Parrott (15 Ind. App. 417; 44 N. E. 66) 365, 384
Brewster v. Lanyon Zinc Co. (140 Fed. 801; 72 C. C. A. 213) ..42, 67, 68
                                        72, 73, 96, 113, 325, 394, 396
                                        439, 445, 553, 555, 608, 612, 625
Breyfogle v. Woods (15 Ky. L. Rep. 782) 36
Brookshire Oil Co. v. Casmalia Ranch etc. Co. (156 Cal. 211; 103
    Pac. 927) 814, 826
Brown v. Beecher (120 Pa. 590-603; 15 Atl. 608) 42
Brown v. Ohio Oil Co. and Brown v. Fowler (65 Ohio St. 507-
    521; 63 N. E. 76) 30, 42, 53, 66, 96, 106, 108
                                        116, 219, 323, 324, 345, 614, 704
Brown v. Spilman (155 U. S. 665) ..6, 11, 170, 188, 585, 762, 782, 787
Brown v. Vandergrift (80 Pa. 142) ... 12, 64, 88, 237, 283, 777, 829
Buffalo Valley Oil etc. Co. v. Jones (75 Kan. 18; 88 Pac. 537)....394, 437
                                        439, 445, 502, 550
Burton v. Forest Oil Co. (204 Pa. 349; 54 Atl. 266) 350, 360, 365, 384
Butler Savings Bank v. Osborne (159 Pa. 10; 28 Atl. 163; 39 Am.
    St. Rep. 665) 625, 643

                                    C

Caldwell v. Copeland (37 Pa. 427) 852, 870, 873
Caldwell v. Fulton (31 Pa. 475; 72 Am. Dec. 760) 829, 873, 910
Calhoun v. Neely (201 Pa. 97; 50 Atl. 967) 502, 551
California v. Southern Pac. R. Co. (157 U. S. 229) 928
Calor Oil & Gas Co. v. Franzell (128 Ky. 715; 109 S. W. 328; 33
    Ky. L. Rep. 98) 745, 805, 813, 814, 826
Campbell v. Rock Oil Co. (80 C. C. A. 467; 151 Fed. 191)........... 468
Carnegie Nat. Gas Co. v. Philadelphia Co. (158 Pa. 317; 27 Atl. 95).. 346
                                        348, 350, 385, 393, 915, 917

Carnegie Nat. Gas. Co. v. South Penn Oil Co. (56 W. Va. 402;
49 S. E. 548) 895, 898
Carney v. Barnes (56 W. Va. 581; 49 S. E. 423) 895, 904
Carter v. Tyler County, (45 W. Va. 806) ......·.................... 850
Cassell v. Crothers (193 Pa. 359; 44 Atl. 446) ... 96, 103, 106, 150, 153
169, 488, 495, 499, 543, 704
Central etc. Tel. Co. v. Fehring (146 Ind. 189; 45 N. E. 64) 995
Central Ohio Gas Co. v. Eckert (70 Ohio St. 127; 71 N. E. 281).. 43, 53
67, 96, 614
Chambers v. Cramer (49 W. Va. 395) 802
Chaney v. Ohio Oil Co. (32 Ind. App. 193; 69 N. E. 477)....365, 376, 384
Charles v. Eshleman (5 Colo. 107) 642
Charleston L. & M. Co. v. Brockmeyer (23 W. Va. 635) 671
Charleston N. Gas Co. v. Lowe & Butler (52 W. Va. 662; 44 S. E. 410). 984
999, 1000
Chartiers Block Coal Co. v. Mellon (152 Pa. 286; 25 Atl. 597;
34 Am. St. Rep. 645; 18 L. R. A. 702) 828, 832, 834, 842, 876, 880
Chicago & N. W. R. Co. v. People (56 Ill. 365; 8 Am. Rep. 699) 994
Childers v. Neely (47 W. Va. 70; 34 S. E. 827) ..130, 143, 625, 632, 640
641, 642
City of Kansas City v. Gilbert (70 Pac. 350) 975
City of Rushville v. Rushville Nat. Gas Co. (132 Ind. 575; 28 N. E.
853; 15 L. R. A. 321 [Note]) ....·.... 995
Clark v. Griest (54 Ohio St. 298; 43 N. E. 962) 414
Clark v. Long (4 Rand. 451) 928
Clayton v. Barr (34 W. Va. 290; 12 S. E. 704) 63
Cleminger v. Baden Gas Co. (159 Pa. 16; 28 Atl. 293) 730, 737
Cleveland v. Gas Light Co. (20 N. J. Eq. 201) 799
Coal Co. v. Kelley (W. Va. 24 S. E. 1020) 852
Cochran v. Pew (159 Pa. 184; 28 Atl. 219) 237, 246, 282, 284
Coffeyville Min. & Gas Co. v. Carter (68 Kan. 565; 70 Pac. 365) 945
980, 982
Coffinberry v. Sun Oil Co. (68 Ohio St. 488; 67 N. E. 1069) 439, 444
Colgan v. Forest Oil Co. (194 Pa. 234; 45 Atl. 119) 83, 394, 407
445, 453, 467 498,501, 784
Collier v. Munger (89 Pac. 1011; 75 Kan. 550) 6
Collins v. Chartiers Valley Gas Co. (131 Pa. 143; 18 Atl. 1012) ..789, 794
Commonwealth v. Trent (117 Ky. 34; 77 S. W. 390) 745, 759
Compton v. Peoples Gas Co. (75 Kan. 572; 89 Pac. 1029; 10 L.
R. A. [N. S.] 758) 385, 393, 661, 664, 673
Congdon v. Olds (18 Mont. 487; 46 Pac. 261) 642

Conger v. National Transportation Co. (165 Pa. 561; 30 Atl. 1038) 246, 283

Connecticut v. Pennsylvania (5 Wheat. 424) 928

Conrad v. Moorehead (89 N. C. 31) 430, 857

Consumers Gas Trust Co. v. American Window Glass Co. (162 Ind. 392; 68 N. E. 1020) 170, 188, 439, 480, 601, 606

Consumers Gas Trust Co. v. Chrystal Window Glass Co. (163 Ind. 190; 70 N. E. 366) 189, 201, 234, 236, 321

Consumers Gas Trust Co. v. Corbaley (14 Ind. App. 549; 43 N. E. 237) 845, 980

Consumers Gas Trust Co. v. Howard (71 N. E. 493) ..201, 468, 474, 707

Consumers Gas Trust Co. v. Ink (163 Ind. 174; 71 N. E. 477) ..189, 201
236, 451, 468, 473, 480, 487, 707

Consumers Gas Trust Co. v. Littler (162 Ind. 320; 70 N. E. 363) 189, 201, 206, 210, 234, 236, 277, 319
321, 451, 468, 472, 480, 487, 704, 707

Consumers Gas Trust Co. v. Perrigo (144 Ind. 350; 43 N. E. 306; 32 L. R. A. 146) 945, 979, 982

Consumers Gas Trust Co. v. Worth (163 Ind. 141; 71 N. E. 489) ..189, 201
234, 236, 277, 319, 321, 439
468, 473, 480, 487, 704, 707

Cook v. Anderson (85 Ala. 99; 4 So. 713) 797

Core v. N. Y. Pet. Co. (52 W. Va. 276; 43 S. E. 128) 289, 303
419, 454, 467

Cortelyou v. Barnsdall (236 Ill. 138; 86 N. E. 200) 237, 287, 289

Couch v. Puryear (1 Rand. 258) 854

Couper v. Shirley (75 Fed. 168; 21 C. C. A. 288) 900

Cowan v. Iron Co. (83 Va. 547; 3 S. E. 120) 603, 657, 910

Coy v. Indianap. Gas Co. (146 Ind. 655; 46 N. E. 17; 36 L. R. A. 535) 984, 991, 994, 999

Craig v. Hukill (37 W. Va. 520; 16 S. E. 363) 914, 923, 925, 927

Crawford v. Bellevue Gas Co. (183 Pa. 233; 38 Atl. 595)............ 289

Crawford v. Oil Co. (55 Ohio St. 161; 44 N. E. 1093) 414

Crawford v. Ritchie (43 W. Va. 252; 27 S. E. 320) 64, 68, 92
130, 131, 219, 501, 503, 550
553, 603, 896, 898, 904, 910

Creel v. Charleston N. Gas Co. (51 W. Va. 129; 41 S. E. 174; 90 Am. St. Rep. 772) 945, 983

Crickard v. Crouch's Admr. (41 W. Va. 503; 23 S. E. 727) 928

Criswell v. Crumbling (107 Pa. 408) 857

Crumley v. Water Co. (99 Tenn. 420; 41 S. W. 1058) 994

Cunningham v. Brown (39 W. Va. 588; 20 S. E. 615) 878

D.

Dailey v. Heller (41 Ind. App. 379; 81 N. E. 219) 365, 383
Dalton v. Railway Co. (144 Ind. 121; 43 N. E. 130) 799
Dark v. Johnson (53 Pa. 164; 93 Am. Dec. 732) 20, 22, 88, 350, 351
Davidson v. Humes (188 Pa. 335; 41 Atl. 649) ....'.......... 737
Dean v. McLain (48 Vt. 412) 808
De Camp v. Carnahan (26 W. Va. 839) ....'...... 909
Decker v. Howell (42 Cal. 636) 642
Deer Lake Co. v. Mich. Land etc. Co. (89 Mich. 180; 50 N. W. 807) .. 839
Delaware & Hudson Canal Co. v.˙Hughes (183 Pa. 66; 63 Am.
   St. Rep. 743) 842, 880, 881
Delaware etc. Co. v. Sanderson (109 Pa. 583) 873
Del Monte Min. & Milling Co. v. Last Chance Min. & Milling Co.
   (171 U. S. 60; 43 L. Ed. 72; 18 Sup. Ct. 395) 762
Denavides v. Hunt (79 Tex. 383; 15 S. W. 396) 37
Detlor v. Holland (57 Ohio St. 492; 49 N. E. 690) 103, 558, 573, 599
                         730, 735, 736, 835, 836, 839, 840, 857
Dickey v. Coffeyville etc. Co. (69 Kan. 106; 76 Pac. 398) ..21, 29, 53, 488
Dill v. Fraze (165 Ind. 53; 75 N. E. 971) 43, 64, 67
                         290, 315, 321, 502, 552
Doddridge County Oil Co. v. Smith (154 Fed. 970) 91, 95, 394
                         453, 454, 466, 467, 899
Doddridge County Oil & Gas Co. v. Smith (173 Fed. 386) 90, 95
Doellner v. Tyrian (38 How. Prac. 176) 799
Donahue v. Fackler (21 W. Va. 125) 928
Double v. Heat & Light Co. (172 Pa. 388; 23 Atl. 694) 189, 204
                         236, 488, 496, 499
Douglass Oil Fields v. Hamilton (95 Pac. 849) 394
Douthett v. Fort Pitt Gas Co. (202 Pa. 416; 51 Atl. 981) 6
Duffield v. Hue (129 Pa. 94; 18 Atl. 566) 64, 78, 88, 467, 469
Duffield v. Hue (136 Pa. 602; 20 Atl. 526) ..170, 177, 188, 558, 598, 601
Duffield v. Rosenzweig (144 Pa. 520; 23 Atl. 4) 170, 188, 454
Duffield v. Rosenzweig (150 Pa. 543; 24 Atl. 705) 170, 188, 462
Duke v. Hague (107 Pa. 57) 42
Duncan v. Hays (22 N. J. Eq. 25) 799
Dunham v. Kirkpatrick (101 Pa. 36; 47 Am. Rep. 696) 829, 835, 836
                         839, 840, 857
Dunham v. Loverock (158 Pa. 179; 27 Atl. 990; 38 Am. St. Rep.
   838) 625, 643
Duntley v. Anderson (94 C. C. A. 647; 169 Fed. 391) 468

Durant Mining Co. v. Percy Con. Min. Co. (93 Fed. 166; 35 C.
  C. A. 252) 90
Duryea v. Burt (28 Cal. 569) 627, 642

E.

Eakin v. Hawkins (48 .W. Va. 364; 37 S. E. 622) 709, 728, 895, 898
Eakin v. Hawkins (52 W. Va. 124; 43 S. E. 211) 671, 709, 728
Eastern Oil Co. v. Coulehan (65 W. Va. 531; 64 S. E. 836) 189, 233
                    235, 236, 438, 548, 549, 895, 898, 904
Eaton v. Allegheny Gas Co. (122 N. Y. 416; 25 N. E. 981) 64, 96
                                                        285, 817
Eclipse Oil Co. v. Garner (53 W. Va. 151; 44 S. E. 131) ...608, 609, 623
Eclipse Oil Co. v. South Penn Oil Co. (47 W. Va. 84; 34 S.
  E. 922) 43, 65, 66, 67, 222, 284, 287, 289, 306, 323
                          328, 343, 344, 350, 608, 617
                          623, 657, 895, 897, 898, 904
Edens v. Miller (147 Ind. 208; 46 N. E. 526) 451
Edgett v. Douglass (144 Pa. 95) 941
Edmonds v. Mounsey (15 Ind. App. 399; 44 N. E. 196) 163, 282
Edwards v. Hale (37 W. Va. 193; 16 S. E. 587) 346
Elk Fork Oil & Gas Co. v. Foster (99 Fed. 495; 39 C. C. A. 615) ..439, 899
Elk Fork Oil & Gas Co. v. Jennings (84 Fed. 839; 90 Fed. 178) ..42, 56
                          66, 285, 553, 603, 896, 910
Emory v. League (31 Tex. App. 474; 72 S. W. 603) 651
Enterprise Oil & Gas Co. v. National Transit Co. (172 Pa. 421;
  33 Atl. 687) 646
Erskine v. Forest Oil Co. (80 Fed. 583) 938
Evans v. Goodwin (132 Pa. 136; 19 Atl. 49) 941

F.

Farmers Co. v. Galesburg (133 U. S. 156) 909
Federal Betterment Co. v. Blaes (75 Kan. 69; 88 Pac. 555) ..32, 502, 551
Federal Oil Co. v. Western Oil Co. (112 Fed. 373) 92, 306, 415
                              438, 502, 608, 610, 623
Federal Oil Co. v. Western Oil Co. (121 Fed. 674; 57 C. C. A. 428) .. 502
                              521, 550, 608, 610, 623, 624
Fennell v. Guffey (139 Pa. 341; 20 Atl. 1048) 364, 383
Ferguson v. Dent (46 Fed. 88) 900
Findlay v. Smith (6 Munf. 134) 671

Fisher v. Guffey & Queen (193 Pa. 393; 44 Atl. 452) 365
Flannagan v. Marsh (32 Ky. L. Rep. 184; 105 S. W. 724) 502, 550
Fleming Oil & Gas Co. v. South Penn Oil Co. (37 W. Va. 645; 17
    S. E. 203) 729, 737
Florence Oil & Refining Co. v. McCumber (38 Col. 366; 88 Pac.
    265) 502, 550
Florence Oil & Refining Co. v. Orman (19 Col. App. 79; 73 Pac.
    628) 20, 26, 68, 92, 130, 141, 680, 689, 695
Fluharty v. Fleming (58 W. Va. 669) 834
Forney v. Ward (25 Tex. App. 413; 62 S. W. 108) 729, 737
Foster v. Elk Fork Oil & Gas Co. (90 Fed. 178; 32 C. C. A.
    560) 64, 415, 419, 502, 551, 680, 688, 695
Foster v. Weaver (118 Pa. 42; 12 Atl. 213) 644
Fowler v. Delaplain (79 Ohio St. 279; 87 N. E. 261)......68, 90, 93, 144
Franklinite Co. v. Condit (19 N. J. Eq. 394) 652
Freeland v. South Penn Oil Co. (189 Pa. 54; 41 Atl. 1000) 289
Freer v. Davis (52 W. Va. 1; 43 S. E. 164) 559, 599, 896, 897
Freer v. Davis (52 W. Va. 35; 43 S. E. 172) 558, 599
Friend v. Mallory (52 W. Va. 53; 43 S. E. 114) .. 42, 67, 287, 323, 333
                               344, 345, 696, 698, 708, 895, 897
Funk v. Halderman (53 Pa. 239) ..20, 22, 88, 130, 135, 172, 350, 351
                               578, 652, 817, 829, 848, 857, 892, 915

G.

Gadberry v. Ohio etc. Nat. Gas Co. (162 Ind. 9; 67 N. E.
    259) 6, 9, 189, 232, 319, 394, 414, 438, 553, 556, 817
Galey v. Kellerman (123 Pa. 491; 16 Atl. 474) 237, 246, 263, 283
Galloway v. Campbell (142 Ind. 324; 41 N. E. 597) ...632, 896, 899, 900
Garrett v. South Penn Oil Co. (66 W. Va. 587; 66 S. E. 741) 502, 541
                                                     547, 842, 882
Gartlan v. Hickman (56 W. Va. 75; 49 S. E. 14; 67 L. R. A.
    694) 150, 163, 169
Gas Light Co. v. Richardson (63 Barb. 437) 987
Geer v. Connecticut (161 U. S. 519-526; 16 Sup. Ct. 600; 40 L.
    Ed. 792) 762
Gerke Brewing Co. v. St. Clair (46 W. Va. 93; 33 S. E. 122) 878
Gerkins v. Kentucky Salt Co. (Ky. 39 S. W. 444; 66 Am. St. Rep. 370) 721
Gibbs v. Gas Co. (130 U. S. 396; 9 Sup. Ct. Rep. 553) 987
Gibson v. Oliver (158 Pa. 277; 27 Atl. 961) 283
Gilbert v. Showerman (23 Mich. 448) 799
Gill v. Weston (110 Pa. 313; 1 Atl. 921) 829, 839, 857

Gillespie v. Fulton Oil Co. (236 Ill. 188; 86 N. E. 219) 290, 322
    385, 392, 696, 699, 708
Glasgow v. Chartiers Oil Co. (152 Pa. 48; 25 Atl. 232) 198, 290
    302, 320, 321, 414
Goldsmith v. Goldsmith (46 W. Va. 426) 848, 909
Goodale v. Tuttle (29 N. Y. 459) 88
Gordon v. Jackson (72 Fed. 86) 938
Great Southern etc. Oil Co. v. Logan Nat. Gas etc. Co. (155 Fed. 114) 36
Great Western Oil Co. v. Carpenter (43 Tex. Civ. App. 229; 95
    S. W. 57 ....290, 321, 608, 620, 624
Greenlee v. Steelsmith (64 W. Va. 353; 62 S. E. 459) 625, 640, 641
Greensboro Nat. Gas Co. v. Fayette County Gas Co. (200 Pa. 388;
    49 Atl. 768) 147, 915, 941
Grubb v. Beard (2 Wall. Jr. 81; Fed. Cases 5849) 652
Grubb v. Grubb (74 Pa. 33) 817
Guffey v. Hukill (34 W. Va. 49; 11 S. E. 754) 64, 104, 160, 192, 237
    284, 288, 333, 438, 862

H.

Haag v. Board (60 W. Va. 511) 800
Hagan v. Warden (3 Gratt. 315) 928
Hague v. Wheeler (157 Pa. 324; 27 Atl. 714; 37 Am. St. Rep.
    736; 22 L. R. A. 141) 805, 813
Hall v. Hall (27 W. Va. 468) 847
Hall v. Vernon (47 W. Va. 295; 34 S. E. 764) 651, 652, 660, 848
Hancock v. Diamond Glass Co. (162 Ind. 146-152; 70 N. E. 149) 163
    238, 277, 284
Hancock v. Diamond Glass Co. (37 Ind. App. 351; 75 N. E. 659) 277
Harding v. Guice (80 Fed. 162; 25 C. C. A. 352) 64
Harner v. Price (17 W. Va. 523) 905
Harness v. Eastern Oil Co. (49 W. Va. 232; 38 S. E. 662) ..394, 419, 453
    457, 467, 622, 624, 883, 886, 894
Harrington v. Florence Oil Co. (178 Pa. 444; 35 Atl. 855) 626, 643
Harris v. Ohio Oil Co. (57 Ohio St. 129; 50 N. E. 1129).....56, 289, 303
    394, 420, 446, 453, 456, 467, 608
Hartman v. Citizens Nat. Gas Co. (210 Pa. 19; 59 Atl. 315) 945, 979
    980, 982
Harvey Coal Co. v. Dillon (59 W. Va. 605; 53 S. E. 928) 857
Haskell v. Sutton(53 W. Va. 206; 44 S. E. 533) 558, 599, 601
    662, 895, 898, 909
Hauck v. Tidewater Pipeline Co. (153 Pa. 366; 26 Atl. 644;
    34 Am. St. Rep. 710; 20 L. R. A. 642) 1001

Haughen v. Water Co. (21 Ore. 411; 28 Pac. 244; 14 L. R. A. 424) .. 994
Haven & Chase Oil Co. v. Jordan (13 Ky. L. Rep. 878) 36
Hays v. Forest Oil Co. (213 Pa. 556; 62 Atl. 1027) 290
Hazelgreen Oil & Gas Co. v. Collins (Ky. ; 110 S. W. 343) 96
Headley v. Hoopengarner (60 W. Va. 26; 55 S. E. 744) 21, 29, 130
　　　　　　　　143, 219, 394, 437, 548, 661, 662
　　　　　　　　673, 867, 895, 898, 923, 925, 927
Heal v. Niagara Oil Co. (150 Ind. 483; 50 N. E. 482) 522, 610
Heinouer v. Jones (159 Pa. 228; 28 Atl. 228) 661, 674
Heintz v. Schortt (149 Pa. 286; 24 Atl. 316) 303, 502, 551
Hellebush v. Blake (119 Ind. 349; 21 N. E. 976) 901
Heller v. Dailey (28 Ind. App. 555; 34 Ind. App. 424; 63 N. E.
　490; 70 N. E. 821) 365, 382
Henderson v. Ferrell (183 Pa. 547; 38 Atl. 1018) 502, 548
　　　　　　　　　　　　730, 735, 737
Hendler v. Lehigh Valley Ry. Co. (209 Pa. 256) 836
Henne v. South Penn Oil Co. (52 W. Va. 192; 43 S. E. 147)..237, 261, 285
　　　　　　　　289, 323, 332, 344, 502, 508
　　　　　　　　547, 680, 686, 696, 895, 897
Hicks v. American Natural Gas Co. (207 Pa. 570; 57 Atl. 55) 385
　　　　　　　　　　　　393, 938
Hiett v. Schull (36 W. Va. 563; 15 S. E. 146) 909
Higgins v. Coal Co. (63 W. Va. 229; 59 S. E. 1064) 867
Hipp v. Babin (19 How. 271) 938
Hitchcox v. Hitchcox (39 W. Va. 607; 20 S. E. 595) 928
Hitchcox v. Morrison (47 W. Va. 206) 852
Hodges v. Brice (32 Tex. Civ. App. 358; 74 S. W. 590) 608, 623
Hollon v. Campton Fuel & Light Co. (127 Ky. 266; 105 S. W. 426; 32
　Ky. L. Rep. 178) 945, 980, 982
Home Co. etc. v. Floding (27 W. Va. 540) 905
Hook v. Garfield Coal Co. (— Ia. —; 83 N. W. 969) 721
Hooks v. Forst (165 Pa. 238; 30 Atl. 846) 502, 553
Hoopes v. Davaugh (43 W. Va. 447; 27 S. E. 251) 64, 909
Hough v. Doyleston (4 Brews. [Pa.] 333) 802
Houssierre-Lattrielle Oil Co. v. Jennings-Heywood Oil Snyd.
　(115 La. 107; 38 So. 932) 290, 323, 342, 345
Huckensteine's App. (70 Pa. 102) 799
Huggins v. Daley (99 Fed. 606; 40 C. C. A. 12; 48 L. R. A.
　320) 6, 9, 19, 21, 28, 35, 68, 92, 96
　　　　　　　　124, 192, 394, 419, 430, 438, 522, 601, 603
　　　　　　　　605, 617, 657, 729, 730, 736, 817, 857, 911

Hughes v. Devlin (23 Cal. 505) .... ·652
Hughes v. United Pipelines (119 N. Y. 423; 23 N. E. 1042) 600
Hukill v. Myers (36 W. Va. 639; 15 S. E. 151) ..112, 204, 237, 285, 286
          288, 468, 474, 548, 549, 553, 896, 897
Hull v. Hull (26 W. Va. 1) 671
Humphrey v. Foster (13 Gratt. 653) 848
Huss v. Jacobs (210 Pa. 145; 59 Am. St. Rep. 991) 852

I.

Iams v. Carnegie Nat. Gas. Co. (194 Pa. 72; 45 Atl. 54) ..189, 232, 233
          235, 500, 501
Ibach v. Huntington etc. Co. (23 Ind. App. 281; 55 N. E. 249) ..945, 983
Indiana etc. Co. v. Anthony (26 Ind. App. 307; 58 N. E. 868) .. 984
          999, 1000
Indiana etc. Co. v. Beale (166 Ind. 684; 76 N. E. 520) 451, 696, 708
Indiana etc. Co. v. Granger (33 Ind. App. 559; 70 N. E. 395) 704
Indiana etc. Co. v. Hinton (159 Ind. 395; 64 N. E. 224) 365, 383
Indiana etc. Co. v. Kibbey (135 Ind. 357; 25 N. E. 392) ...183, 315, 720
Indiana etc. Co. v. Leer (34 Ind. App. 61; 72 N. E. 288) 189, 198
          234, 236, 439
Indiana etc. Co. v. McMath (26 Ind. App. 154; 57 N. E. 593;
   59 N. E. 287) 945, 979, 981
Indiana etc. Co. v. State ex rel. Armstrong (162 Ind. 690; 71
   N. E. 133) 984, 999
Indiana etc. Co. v. State ex rel. Ball (158 Ind. 516; 63 N. E. 220;
   57 L. R. A. 761) 984, 999, 1000
Indianapolis etc. Co. v. Wilhelm (Ind. App. ; 86 N. E. 86) ..189, 233
Insurance Co. v. Boon (95 U. S. 117) 804
Insurance Co. v. Tweed (7 Wall. 44) 804
Iron Co. v. Trout (83 Va. 397; 2 S. E. 713) 64, 104, 911
Isam v. Rex Crude Oil Co. (147 Cal. 659; 82 Pac. 317) 558, 598
Island Coal Co. v. Combs (152 Ind. 579; 53 N. E. 455) 451, 603, 911

J.

Jackson v. Dulaney (W. Va.; 67 S. E. 795) 842, 879, 880
Jackson v. O'Hara (183 Pa. 233; 38 Atl. 624) 238, 268, 280
          282, 284, 350, 360, 365, 384

Jamieson *r.* Ind. Nat. Gas & Oil Co. (128 Ind. 555; 28 N. E.
76) 745, 762,   768
Jennings-Heywood Oil Synd. *r.* Houssierre-Latrielle Oil Co.
(119 La. 864; 44 So. 481) 290,   321
J. M. Guffey Petroleum Co. *r.* Oliver (Tex.   ; 79 S. W. 884 ..   394
439, 445, 454, 608, 611,   623
Johnson *r.* Burns (39 W. Va. 653; 20 S. E. 686)   892
Johnson *r.* Price (172 Pa. 427; 33 Atl. 688)   648
Jones *v.* Clark (42 Cal. 425)   642
Jones *r.* Forest Oil Co. (194 Pa. 379; 44 Atl. 1074) 761,   778
Jones *v.* Mackenzie (122 Fed. 390-393; 58 C. C. A. 96)   938
Jones *r.* Mount (30 Ind. 59; 77 N. E. 1089) 439,   451
Jones *r.* Western Pa. N. Gas Co. (146 Pa. 204; 23 Atl. 386) 237,   263
284,   286
Judge *v.* Brasswell (13 Bush. 67)   642

K.

Kansas Nat. Gas Co. *r.* Board of Comm'rs. (75 Kan. 335;
89 Pac. 750) 21,   653
Kansas Natural Gas Co. *r.* Haskell (172 Fed. 545)   742
Kellar *v.* Craig (126 Fed. 630; 61 C. C. A. 366) 126, 394,   409
453, 454, 466,   467
Kelly *r.* Keys (213 Pa. 295; 62 Atl. 911) 20,   25,   130
Kelly *v.* Ohio Oil Co. (57 Ohio St. 317; 47 N. E. 399; 63 Am. St.
Rep. 721; 39 L. R. A. 765) 782, 788,   889
Kemble *v.* Kemble (44 N. J. Eq. 454; 11 Atl. 733)   652
Kennedy *v.* Crawford (138 Pa. 561; 21 Atl. 19) 237,   283
Kilcoyne *r.* Southern Oil Co. (61 W. Va. 538; 55 S. E. 888) 394,   661
662, 672,   867
Kimball Oil Co. *r.* Keeton (31 Ky. L. Rep. 146; 101 S. W. 887) ..502,   550
Kingsley *r.* Hillside Coal & Iron Co. (140 Pa. 613)   870
Kinney *v.* Koetmaun (Ala. 22 So. 593; 37 L. R. A. 497)   797
Kirchner *v.* Smith (61 W. Va. 434; 58 S. E. 614) 640,   642
Kiser *r.* McLean (W. Va.   ; 67 S. E. 725) 842, 867, 880,   881
Kitchen *r.* Smith (101 Pa. 452)   42
Kleppner *r.* Lemon (176 Pa. 502; 35 Atl. 109).............192, 394,   439
440, 441,   784
Kleppner *r.* Lemon (197 Pa. 430; 47 Atl. 353) 439,   443
Kleppner *r.* Lemon (198 Pa. 581; 48 Atl. 483)   439

Knight v. Coal & Iron Co. (47 Ind. 105; 17 Am. Rep. 692) ..19, 522, 832
Knotts v. McGregor (47 W. Va. 566; 37 S. E. 899) 68, 90
     94, 394, 423, 437, 867
Koch & Balliet's App. (93 Pa. 434) 414
Koelsch v. Phila. Co. (152 Pa. 355; 25 Atl. 522; 18 L. R. A. 759;
    34 Am. St. Rep. 653) ....:................................ 975
Koen v. Bartlett (41 W. Va. 559; 23 S. E. 664; 56 Am. St. Rep.
    884; 31 L. R. A. 128) 709, 728, 842, 876, 879
Kurt v. Lanyon (72 Kan. 60; 82 Pac. 459) 6

L.

Lafayette Gas Co. v. Kelsey (164 Ind. 563; 74 N. E. 7)..451, 480, 696, 708
Lamar's Ex. v. Hale (79 Va. 147) 627
Lanyon Zinc Co. v. Freeman (75 Pac. 995; 68 Kan. 691) ... 53, 558, 598
Lawson v. Kirchner (50 W. Va. 344; 40 S. E. 344) .. 6, 16, 21, 28
    68, 93, 129, 133, 892
Leatherman v. Oliver (151 Pa. 646; 25 Atl. 309) 246, 263, 282
Lebanon Light etc. Co. v. Leep (139 Ind. 443; 39 N. E. 57; 29
    L. R. A. 342) 945, 973, 981, 983
Lenfers v. Henke (73 Ill. 405; 24 Am. Rep. 263) 652, 671
Lewey v. Frick Coal Co. (166 Pa. 536) 870
Lewis v. Cocks (23 Wall. 466) 938
Liggett v. Shira (159 Pa. 350; 28 Atl. 218) 237, 263, 284
Lillibridge v. Lackawanna Coal Co. (143 Pa. 293; 24 Am. St.
    Rep. 544; 22 Atl. 1035) 829, 832, 842, 848, 880
Linden Oil Co. v. Jennings (207 Pa. 524; 56 Atl. 1074) 150, 169
Lindsey v. Eckles (99 Va. 668) 848
List v. Cott (4 W. Va. 543) 848
Logan Nat. Gas Co. v. Great So. Gas Co. (126 Fed. 623; 61
    C. C. A. 359) 18, 36, 315, 502, 550
Logansport etc. Gas Co. v. Seegar (165 Ind. 1; 74 N. E. 5) 502, 550
Logansport & Wabash Valley Gas Co. v. Null (36 Ind. App. 503;
    76 N. E. 125) 238, 285
Lohrs v. Miller's Lessee (12 Gratt. 452) 847
Long's App. (92 Pa. 171) ....:........................... 42, 941
Louisville etc. R. Co. v. Dodenschatz (141 Ind. 251; 39 N. E. 703) .. 415
Louisville Gas Co. v. Kentucky Heating Co. (33 Ky. L. Rep. 912;
    111 S. W. 374) 813

Cases Cited.

Louisville Gas Co. *v.* Kentucky Heating Co. (117 Ky. 71; 77 S.
  W. 368; 70 L. R. A. 558; 111 Am. St. Rep. 225) ...745, 805, 812, 813
Lowman *v.* Crawford (99 Va. 688; 40 S. E. 17) 909
Lowther Oil Co. *v.* Guffey (52 W. Va. 88; 43 S. E. 101) .. 53, 55, 83
                              96, 116, 220, 285, 290, 295, 321, 895, 897
Lowther Oil Co. *v.* Miller-Sibley Oil Co. (53 W. Va. 501; 44 S.
  . E. 435; 97 Am. St. Rep. 1027) 21, 27, 43, 65, 67, 68, 92
                      96, 112, 125, 129, 134, 135, 220, 389, 323, 332
                          344, 418, 419, 487, 489, 498, 500, 502, 506
                              543, 547, 551, 553, 601, 602, 608, 612
                              624, 680, 684, 695, 817, 862, 895, 897
Lyde's App. (106 Pa. 526) 777
Lyford *v.* Putnam (35 N. H. 563) 808
Lynch *v.* Burford (201 Pa. 52; 50 Atl. 228) 170, 188
Lynch *v.* Versailles Fuel etc. Co. (165 Pa. 518; 30 Atl. 984) 468, 487

M.

Manhattan Oil *v.* Carrell (164 Ind. 526; 73 N. E. 1084) 230
                                              480, 488, 501
Manufacturers Gas & Oil Co. *v.* Indiana Nat. Gas & Oil Co. (155
  Ind. 461; 57 N. E. 912; 50 L. R. A. 768) ..522, 610, 759, 761, 775, 778
Manufacturers Gas & Oil Co. *v.* Ind. Nat. Gas & Oil Co. (156
  Ind. 679; 59 N. E. 159; 60 N. E. 1080) 761, 774, 778
Manufacturers Gas & Oil Co. *v.* Ind. Nat. Gas & Oil Co. (155
  Ind. 545; 58 N. E. 706) 774
Manufacturers Gas & Oil Co. *v.* Ind. Nat. Gas & Oil Co. (155
  Ind. 566; 58 N. E. 851) 761, 768, 774, 778
Manufacturers Co. *v.* Patterson (148 Ind. 414; 47 N. E. 2; 37
  L. R. A. 381) 796
Manville *v.* Parks (7 Colo. 128; 2 Pac. 212) 642
Marble Co. *v.* Ripley (10 Wall. 339; 19 L. Ed. 955) 652
Marshall *v.* Forest Oil Co. (198 Pa. 83; 47 Atl. 927) 289, 323, 334
                                              345, 502, 546, 553
Marshall *v.* Mellon (179 Pa. 371; 36 Atl. 201; 57 Am. St. Rep.
  601; 35 L. R. A. 816) 558, 585, 601, 709, 858
Marshall Window Glass Co. *v.* Cameron O. & G. Co. (63 W. Va.
  202; 59 S. E. 959) 945, 980, 983
Martel *v.* Jennings (38 So. 253; 114 La. 903) 306

Martel v. Jennings-Heywood Oil Synd. (114 La. 903; 38 So. 253) 502, 608
Martin v. Crude Oil Co. (77 Kan. 851; 92 Pac. 1119) 653
Martin v. Jones (62 Ohio St. 519; 57 N. E. 238) 219
Marvin v. Brewster (55 N. Y. 533; 14 Am. Rep. 322) 834, 848
Mathes v. Shaw Oil Co. (Kan; 101 Pac. 997) 189
Matthews v. Peoples Nat. Gas Co. (179 Pa. 165; 36 Atl. 216) 238, 284
Mauzey v. Mauzey (79 Va. 537) 848
Maxwell v. Coffeyville Min. etc. Co. (75 Pac. 1047; 68 Kan. 821) 945
                      980, 983
Maxwell v. Todd (112 N. C. 686; 16 S. E. 926) 430, 910
May v. Hazelwood Oil Co. (152 Pa. 518; 25 Atl. 564) 680, 696
Meem v. Rucker (10 Gratt. 506) 905
Messimer's App. (92 Pa. 168) 42
Mills v. Hartz (77 Kan. 218; 94 Pac. 142) 502, 550
Monaghan v. Mount (36 Ind. App. 188; 74 N. E. 579) 439, 451
Monfort v. Lanyon Zinc Co. (67 Kan. 310; 72 Pac. 78) 68, 696, 699
                    708, 720, 729
Montpelier Light & Water Co. v. Stephenson (22 Ind. App. 175;
  53 N. E. 444) 163
Moon v. Pittsburgh Plate Glass Co. (24 Ind. App. 34; 56 N. E.
  108) 232
Moore v. Griffin (72 Kan. 164; 83 Pac. 395) 842, 880
Moore v. Heat & Light Co. (65 W. Va. 552; 64 S. E. 721) ..945, 980, 983
Moore v. Jennings (47 W. Va. 181; 34 S. E. 793) 558, 599, 600, 927
Moore v. McNutt (41 W. Va. 695; 24 S. E. 682) 63
Moore v. Ohio Valley Gas Co. (63 W. Va. 455; 60 S. E. 401) 6, 19
Moore v. Sawyer (167 Fed. 826) 21, 32, 356, 384
Mullen's Ad'mr. v. Carper (37 W. Va. 215; 16 S. E. 527) 64
Mullens v. Shrewsbury (60 W. Va. 694; 55 S. E. 736) 860
Munroe v. Armstrong (96 Pa. 307) 68, 92, 237, 249, 283, 303
                    353, 557, 857
Murdock-West Co. v. Logan (69 Ohio St. 514; 69 N. E. 984) 21, 27
              96, 488, 490, 498, 704
Murdock v. Gilchrist (52 N. Y. 247) 892
Murray v. Allred 100 Tenn. 100; 66 Am. St. Rep. 740; 43 S. W.
  355) 558, 585, 598, 826, 827, 832, 839, 842, 874, 880
Murray v. Barnhart (117 La. 1023; 42 So. 489) 502, 550
Murray v. Graham (117 La. 1023; 42 So. 489) 502, 550

Mc.

McArthur v. Scott (113 U. S. 340) 928
McCaslin v. State (44 Ind. 151) 901
McConihay v. Wright (120 U. S. 201) 64
McConnell v. Denver (35 Cal. 365) 642
McConnel v. Lawrence Gas Co. (30 Pitts. L. Jr. 346) 232
McCoy v. Ohio Valley Gas Co. (213 Pa. 367; 62 Atl. 858) ..945, 979, 982
McCutcheon v. Blanton (59 Miss. 116) 799
McDougle v. Musgrave (46 W. Va. 509) 848
McGahan v. Gas Co. (140 Ind. 335; 37 N. E. 601) 973
McGraw Oil & Gas Co. v. Kennedy (65 W. Va. 595; 64 S. E. 1027) ... 126
                189, 220, 233, 234, 235, 394, 453, 454
                462, 467, 488, 490, 501, 601, 605, 895
McGregor v. Camden (47 W. Va. 193; 34 S. E. 936) 795, 802, 804
McGuire v. Pensacola City Co. (105 Fed. 677; 44 C. C. A. 670) 938
McIntosh v. Robb (4 Cal. App. 484; 88 Pac. 517) 502, 550
McKenna v. Bridgewater' Gas Co. (193 Pa. 633; 45 Atl. 52;
    47 L. R. A. 790) 945, 981
McKinney's Heirs v. Cent. Ky. N. Gas Co. (Ky.   120
    S. W. 314) 835, 840
McKnight v. Kruetz (51 Pa. 232) 414
McKnight v. Manufacturers Nat. Gas Co. (146 Pa. 185; 23
    Atl. 164) 9, 64, 189, 232, 234, 235, 319, 394, 414, 416, 465, 467
McMillen v. Phila. Co. (159 Pa. 142) 112, 246, 283
McMillen v. Titus (222 Pa. 500; 72 Atl. 240) 502, 547
McNeely v. South Penn Oil Co. (58 W. Va. 438; 44 S. E. 508) ..661, 672
McNish v. Stone (152 Pa. 457) 64

N.

National Oil etc. Co. v. Teel (67 S. W. 545; 68 S. W. 779; 95
    Tex. 586) 306, 385, 392, 603, 623, 657
Nease v. Insurance Co. (32 W. Va. 283; 9 S. E. 233) 909
Neb. Tel Co. v. State (55 Neb. 627-634; 76 N. W. 171; 45 L. R. A. 113) 994
Neill v. Shambourg (158 Pa. 263; 27 Atl. 992) 350, 626, 639, 643
New American Oil Co. v. Troyer (166 Ind. 402; 76 N. E. 353;
    77 N. E. 739) 68, 87, 94, 142, 480, 707
New American Oil Min. Co. v. Wolff (166 Ind. 402; 76 N. E. 255) ... 277
New Dominion Oil & Gas Co. v. Gaffney (Ky. 121 S. W. 699) 238, 283

Newman v. Newman (60 W. Va. 371; 55 S. E. 377; 7 L. R. A.
N. S.) 370 860
New Orleans Gas etc. Co. v. Louisiana etc. Co. (115 U. S. 650; 6
Sup. Ct. Rep. 252) 987
New Orleans Water Works Co. v. City of New Orleans (164 U.
S. 471) 928
Newton v. Kemper (66 W. Va. 130; 66 S. E. 102) 923, 927, 931
Northwestern Ohio Nat. Gas Co. v. Tiffin (59 Ohio St. 420; 54
N. E. 77) 96, 103, 704, 889
Northwestern Ohio Nat. Gas Co. v. Ullery (68 Ohio St. 259; 67
N. E. 494) 883, 892, 894
Norton v. Craig (68 W. Va. 275) 808

O.

Ogden v. Hatry (145 Pa. 640; 23 Atl. 334) 238, 263, 284, 286
Ohio Gas Fuel Co. v. Andrews (50 Ohio St. 695; 35 N. E.
1059) 945, 973, 981
Ohio Oil Co. v. Detmore (165 Ind. 243; 73 N. E. 906) 502, 551, 691
Ohio Oil Co. v. Griest (30 Ind. App. 84; 65 N. E. 534) 150, 164, 543
Ohio Oil Co. v. Indiana (177 U. S. 190; 20 Sup. Ct. 576; 44 L.
Ed. 729) 522, 585, 745, 748, 756, 759
Ohio Oil Co. v. Lane (59 Ohio St. 307; 52 N. E. 791) 189, 232, 233
Ohio Oil Co. v. Westfall (Ind. App. 88 N. E. 354) 789, 793, 794
Olmstead v. Proprietors (47 N. J. L. 311) 994
O'Neill v. Ressinger (77 Kan. 63; 93 Pac. 340) 290
O'Neill v. Sun Co. (Tex. Civ. App. 123 S. W. 172) 21
Ore Co. v. Colquitt (28 Tex. Civ. App. 292; 69 S. W. 160) 37
Owens v. Phillips (73 Ind. 284) 799, 800

P.

Parish Fork Oil Co. v. Bridgewater Gas Co. (51 W. Va. 583;
42 S. E. 655) ... 6, 8, 67, 70, 92, 129, 134, 192, 303, 418, 438
502, 505, 519, 551, 680, 685, 695, 857, 895, 897, 904
Peck v. Ayers etc. Tie Co. (116 Fed. 273; 53 C. C. A. 551) 519
Pennsylvania Coal Co. v. Sanderson (113 Pa. 126) 777, 869
People v. Manhattan Gas Light Co. (45 Barb. 136) 987, 994
Peoples Gas Co. v. Tyner (131 Ind. 277; 31 N. E. 59; 16 L. R. A.
443; 31 Am. St. Rep. 433) 522, 779, 610

Perry v. Acme Oil Co. (Ind. App. 88 N. E. 589) 150, 169

Peterson v. Hall (57 W. Va. 535; 50 S. E. 603) 842, 852, 867
　　　　　　　　　　　　　　　　　　　　　　　　882, 895, 897

Petroleum Co. v. Coal & Coke Co. (89 Tenn. 381; 18 S. W. 65) 18, 429, 857

Pfeifer v. Brown (165 Pa. 267; 30 Atl. 844; 44 Am. St. Rep. 660) 789, 794

Pheasant v. Hanna (63 W. Va. 613; 60 S. E. 618)..220, 546, 895, 923, 924

Phillips v. Hamilton (Wyo. 95 Pac. 846) 394

Phillips v. Vandergrift (146 Pa. 357; 23 Atl. 347) 238, 246
　　　　　　　　　　　　　　　　　　　　　　　　263, 284, 286

Pine River Logging Co. v. U. S. (186 U. S. 279-293) 90

Pittsburg Vitrified Paving etc Co. v. Bailey (76 Kan. 42; 90 Pac.
　803) 290, 316, 608, 625

Plant v. Humphreys (66 W. Va. 88; 66 S. E. 725) 842, 864, 880

Plummer v. Hillside etc. Co. (169 Pa. 483; 28 Atl. 853) 35, 68, 93
　　　　　　　　　　　　　　　　　　　　　　　　130, 141, 871

Poe v. Ullery (233 Ill. 56; 84 N. E. 46) 21, 32, 189, 237, 323, 345
　　　　　　　　　　　　　　　　　　　558, 582, 608, 619, 625

Pope Bros. v. Bridgewater Gas Co. (52 W. Va. 252; 43 S. E. 87) ..795, 804

Porter v. Mack Mfg. Co. (65 W. Va. 636; 64 S. E. 853)..........826, 834

Portland Nat. Gas & O. Co. v. State (135 Ind. 54; 34 N. E. 818;
　21 L. R. A. 639) 984, 991, 993, 995, 999, 1000

Powell v. Furniture Co. (34 W. Va. 804; 12 S. E. 1085; 12 L. R.
　A. 53) 796, 802, 804

Powell v. Taylor (11 Leigh 172) 909

Powers v. Bridgeport Oil Co. (238 Ill. 397; 87 N. E. 381) ..:...394, 439
　　　　　　　　　　　　　　　　　　　　　　　　444, 896, 897

Preston v. White (57 W. Va. 278; 50 S. E. 236) ..558, 651, 652, 660, 834
　　　　　　　　　　　　　　842, 847, 850, 852, 864, 867, 879

Priddy v. Griffith (150 Ill. 560; 37 N. E., 997; 41 Am. St. Rep. 397 .. 720

Puritan Oil Co. v. Myers (39 Ind. App. 695; 86 N. E. 495) 238, 283

Pyle v. Henderson (55 W. Va. 122; 41 S. E. 791) 895, 927

Pyle v. Henderson (65 W. Va. 39; 63 S. E. 620) .. 2, 96, 120, 123, 220
　　　　　　286, 288, 322, 323, 330, 385, 390, 393, 394, 424, 468, 475
　　　　　　　548, 601, 606, 608, 611, 625, 661, 662, 672, 673, 897

R.

Railroad Co. v. Madry (57 Ark. 306) 804

Railroad Co. v. Sanderson (109 Pa. 583; 58 Am. Rep. 743) 832

Railroad Co. v. Simon (40 Ind. 278) 800

Randolph v. Frick (57 Mo. App. 400; 53 S. W. 453) 451

Rawlings v. Armel (70 Kan. 778; 79 Pac. 683) 21, 27, 68, 92
130, 142, 653, 680, 689, 695

Ray v. Western Penna. N. Gas Co. (138 Pa. 576; 20 Atl. 1065;
12 L. R. A. 290; 21 Am. St. Rep. 922) 192, 237, 263, 283, 857

Reese v. Zinn (103 Fed. 97) 522

Reichert v. Geers (98 Ind. 73) 800

Resurrection Gold Mining Co. v. Fortune Gold Mining Co. 129
Fed. 668; 64 C. C. A. 180) 90

Rhodes v. Dunbar (57 Pa. 274) 799

Rhodes v. Mound City Gas & Oil Co. (80 Kan. 762; 104
Pac. 851) 696, 708

Rich v. Braxton County (158 U. S. 375) 909

Richmond Nat. Gas Co. v. Davenport (37 Ind. App. 25; 76 N. E. 525) 729

Richmond Nat. Gas Co. v. Enterprise Nat. Gas Co. (31 Ind. App.
222; 66 N. E. 782) 183, 761

Riddle v. Mellon (147 Pa. 30; 23 Atl. 241) 96, 126

Ridgley v. Connewago Iron Co. [C. C.] (53 Fed. 988) 232

Ringle v. Quigg (74 Kan. 581; 87 Pac. 724) 32, 290

Roberts v. Bettman (45 W. Va. 143; 30 S. E. 95) 6, 17, 237, 283
289, 306, 323, 331, 343, 345

Roberts v. Fort Wayne Gas Co. (40 Ind. App. 528; 82 N. E. 558) 189, 237

Roberts & Corley v. McFadden (32 Tex. Civ. App. 47; 74 S.
W. 115) 323, 343, 608, 615, 623

Rorer Iron Co. v. Trout (83 Va. 397; 2 S. E. 713; 5 Am. St.
Rep. 285) 603, 911

Rose v. Lanyon etc. Co. (68 Kan. 126; 74 Pac. 625) 306, 701, 708

Ryan v. Copen (11 Rich. Law, 217; 73 Am. Dec. 106) 799

Ryan v. Hall (13 Metc. [Mass.] 520) 910

Rymer v. South Penn Oil Co. (54 W. Va. 520; 46 S. E. 459) 883, 893

                              S.

Sage v. Railroad Co. (125 U. S. 361) 900

Sanderson v. Scranton (105 Pa. 469) 850, 873

Sayers v. Kent (201 Pa. 38; 50 Atl. 296) 696, 708

Schaupp v. Hukill (34 W. Va. 375; 12 S. E. 501) 112, 237, 285

Scott v. Lafayette Gas Co. (42 Ind. App. 614; 86 N. E. 495) 238, 284

Scranton Gas & Water Co. v. Lackawanna etc. Co. (167 Pa. 136) 871

Scranton v. Phillips (94 Pa. 15) 873
Seegar v. Seegar (16 L. R. A. 247) 671
Selden v. Delaware etc. Co. (29 N. Y. 634) 808
Settembree v. Putnam (42 Cal. 490) 642
Shamburg v. Farmer (18 Ky. L. Rep. 514; 37 S. W. 152) 303
Shellar v. Shivers (171 Pa. 569; 33 Atl. 95) 150, 160, 163, 164
Shenandoah Land Co. v. Hise (92 Va. 238; 23 S. E. 303) 603, 910
Shenk v. Stahl (35 Ind. App. 444; 74 N. E. 538) 547
Shepherd v. Oil Co. (38 Hun. 37) 652
Sheppard's Ex'rs. v. Starke (3 Munf. 29) 928
Shillito v. Shillito (160 Pa. 167) 941
Shirey v. Consumers Gas Co. (215 Pa. 399; 64 Atl. 541) 945, 980
Shriver v. Garrison (30 W. Va. 456; 4 S. E. 660) 905
Siler v. Globe Window Glass Co. (21 Ohio Ct. Ct. Rep. 284) 163
Silver v. Bush (213 Pa. 195; 62 Atl. 832) 835, 840
Simpson v. Edmiston (23 W. Va. 678) 847, 878
Simpson v. Glass Co. (28 Ind. App. 343; 62 N. E. 753) 50, 168, 283
Skillman v. Lachman (83 Am. Dec. 106-107) 627, 642
Smith v. Cooley (65 Cal. 46; 2 Pac. 880) 652
Smith v. Fitzgerald (24 Ind. 316) 800
Smith v. Root (66 W. Va. 633; 66 S. E. 1005) 394, 433, 438, 502, 512
                 540, 550, 552, 696, 699, 707, 895, 899
Smith v. South Penn Oil Co. (59 W. Va. 204; 53 S. E. 152) 6,   19
                                                           295, 321
Snodgrass v. S. Penn Oil Co. (47 W. Va. 509; 35 S. E. 829) 6,   16
                                                      290, 304, 321
Snyder v. Philadelphia Co. (54 W. Va. 149; 46 S. E. 366; 102
    Am. St. Rep. 941; 63 L. R. A. 896) 795, 805, 945, 948, 982
South Penn Oil Co. v. Edgell (48 W. Va. 348; 37 S. E. 596;
    86 Am. St. Rep. 43) 189, 236, 419, 549, 895, 898
South Penn Oil Co. v. Miller (175 Fed. 729; 99 C. C. A. 305) 927
South Penn Oil Co. v. McIntire (44 W. Va. 296; 28 S. E. 922) ..558, 599
Spencer v. Scurr (31 Beavan's Rep. 237) 854
Spies v. R. Co. (60 W. Va. 389; 55 S. E. 446) 914, 925
Springer v. Citizens Nat. Gas Co. (145 Pa. 430; 22 Atl. 986) 237, 238
Stage v. Boyer (183 Pa. 560; 38 Atl. 1035) 502, 547
Stahl v. Van Vleck (53 Ohio St. 136; 41 N. E. 35) 680, 696
Staley & Barnsdall v. Derden (Tex. Civ. App.; 121 S. W. 1135) 21
Starn v. Huffman (62 W. Va. 422; 59 S. E. 179) 601, 220, 895, 904

State r. Butte City Water Co. (18 Mont. 199; 44 Pac. 966; 32 L. R. A. 697; 56 Am. St. Rep. 574) 994
State ex rel. Corwin v. Ind. & Ohio etc. Co. (120 Ind. 575; 22 N. E. 778; 6 L. R. A. 578) 610, 742
State ex rel. Wood v. Consumers Gas Trust Co. (157 Ind. 345; 61 N. E. 674; 55 L. R. A. 245) 984, 999
State r. Columbus Gas Co. (34 Ohio St. 572) 987
State v. Low (46 W. Va. 451; 33 S. E. 271) 842, 843, 850, 852
857, 867, 878, 881
State r. Oak Harbor Gas Co. (53 Ohio St. 347; 41 N. E. 584) 745
State r. Ohio Oil Co. (150 Ind. 694; 49 N. E. 809) 745, 756, 762
State r. South Penn Oil Co. (42 W. Va. 89) 850, 857
Steelsmith v. Fisher Oil Co. (47 W. Va. 391; 35 S. E. 15) 927
Steelsmith r. Gartlan (45 Va. 27; 27 S. E. 978) .. 6, 8, 9, 19, 20
25, 35, 68, 69, 73, 83, 92, 104, 130, 132, 160
219, 220, 286, 289, 303, 394, 399, 418, 438, 501, 504
551, 552, 553, 601, 604, 680, 695, 817, 862, 896, 904
Steiner r. Marks (172 Pa. 400; 33 Atl. 695) 468, 487
Stewart r. Tennant (52 W. Va. 559; 44 S. E. 223) 661, 672, 709
727, 728, 729
Stone r. Marshall Oil Co. (188 Pa. 602; 41 Atl. 748-1119) 285
Storey r. Livingstone (13 Pet. 359) 928
Stoughton's App. (88 Pa. 198) 585, 720, 857, 892
Stuart r. Boulware (133 U. S. 81) 900
Sturm v. Fleming (26 W. Va. 54) 847
Sult r. Hochstetter Oil Co. (63 W. Va. 317; 61 S. E. 307) ..220, 438, 502
507, 551, 558, 600, 607, 826, 842, 857
862, 864, 879, 881, 895, 897, 899, 904
Summers r. Bennett (W. Va. ; 69 S. E. 690) 674
Summerville v. Apollo Gas Co. (207 Pa. 234; 56 Atl. 876) ..126, 189, 232
233, 234, 236, 409, 488, 496
Swearengen v. Watson (35 W. Va. 463; 14 S. E. 249) 347
Swint r. McCalmont Oil Co. (184 Pa. 202; 38 Atl. 1020) ..661, 674, 832

T.

Talbott v. Southern Oil Co. (60 W. Va. 423; 58 S. E. 1009) 805, 814
Taylor v. Castle (42 Cal. 367) 642
Tennessee Oil etc. Co. v. Brown (131 Fed. 696; 65 C. C. A. 524) .. 6, 18
35, 502, 550, 608, 611, 623

Test Oil Co. v. Taurette (19 Okl. 214; 91 Pac. 1025)   6
Thomas v. Hukill (34 W. Va. 385; 12 S. E. 522) 96, 123, 219
                                                    418, 896, 897
Thompson's App. (101 Pa. 232) 850
Thompson v. Christy (138 Pa. 230; 20 Atl. 924) 237, 468, 470, 487
Thompson v. Ketchum (8 John. 189) 910
Thropp v. Field (36 N. J. Eq. 82) 204
Toothman v. Courtney (62 W. Va. 167; 58 S. E. 915) 842, 881, 904
Townsend v. State (147 Ind. 624; 47 N. E. 19) 745, 762
Trees v. Eclipse Oil Co. (47 W. Va. 107; 34 S. E. 933) 42, 64,   66
                                287, 323, 343, 418, 601, 604, 608
                                609, 623, 661, 662, 673, 896, 897
Tuft v. Copen (37 W. Va. 623) 834
Turk v. Skiler (38 W. Va. 404; 18 S. E. 561) 928
Turner v. Seep (167 Fed. 646) 350
Tyner v. Peoples Gas Co. (131 Ind. 599; 31 N. E. 61) 779
                                                    795, 799, 804

                              U.

Uhl v. Ohio River R. Co. (47 W. Va. 59; 34 S. E. 934) 797, 864
Union Petroleum Co. v. Bliven (72 Pa. 173) 88, 814, 939
United States Nat. Gas Co. v. Hicks (Ky.; 119 S. W. 166) 945, 980
University v. Tucker (31 W. Va. 621) 808
Urpman v. Lowther (53 W. Va. 501; 44 S. E. 433) 160, 409, 603
                                                    848, 850, 904, 910

                              V.

Van Etten v. Kelley (66 Ohio St. 605; 54 N. E. 560) 290, 321
Vendocia Oil Co. v. Robinson (71 Ohio St. 302; 73 N. E. 222) ..290, 316
                                                394, 432, 468
Venture Oil Co. v. Fretts (152 Pa. 451; 25 Atl. 732) 21, 30,   35
                        64, 68, 83, 92, 104, 130, 140, 192
                        414, 438, 657, 680, 686, 695, 817, 862
Virginia Coal & Iron Co. v. Kelly (93 Va. 332; 24 S. E. 1020)

                              W.

Wade v. South Penn Oil Co. (45 W. Va. 380; 32 S. E. 169) 345
Wagner v. Mallory (169 N. Y. 501; 62 N. E. 584) 21, 29, 68,   95

Waldron v. Hughes (44 W. Va. 126; 29 S. E. 505) 642
Walker v. Tupper (152 Pa. 1; 25 Atl. 172) ....625, 643 .
Wallace v. Elm Grove Coal Co. (58 W. Va. 448; 52 S. E. 485) 842, 858
860, 867, 881
Ward v. Triple State Gas Co. (Ky. 115 S. W. 819) 323, 344
345, 603, 704
Warren v. Wheeler (8 Metc. [Mass.] 97) 910
Washburn's App. (105 Pa. 480) 941
Washington Nat. Gas Co. v. Johnson (123 Pa. 576; 16 Atl. 799) 365
383, 384
Water Co. v. Wolfe (99 Tenn. 429; 41 S. W. 1060; 63 Am. St.
Rep. 841) 994
Waterford Oil & Gas Co. v. Shipman (233 Ill. 9; 84 N. E. 63) 21, 42
233, 608, 620, 624, 651, 653, 661, 663, 673
Wehrman v. Conklin (155 U. S. 314) 938
West Virginia etc. Co. v. Ohio River Pipeline Co. (22 W. Va.
626; 46 Am. Rep. 527) 810, 814, 826
West Virginia etc. Co. v. Vinal (14 W. Va. 637) 898
Western Union T. Co. v. American Union T. Co. (65 Ga. 160;
35 Am. Rep. 781) 825
Western Union T. Co. v. Chicago etc. R. Co. (86 Ill. 246; 29 Am.
Rep. 28) 825
Western Pennsylvania etc. Co. v. George (161 Pa. 47; 28 Atl.
1004) 96, 99, 103, 106, 287, 910
Westmoreland Coal Co. App. (85 Pa. 344) 720
Westmoreland Gas Co. v. DeWitt (130 Pa. 235-249; 18 Atl.
724; 5 L. R. A. 731) ..12, 68, 88, 94, 144, 147, 170, 171, 174, 183,
188, 189, 219, 235, 468, 469, 558, 597, 601, 777, 782, 784,
729, 842, 879, 881, 915, 917
Wettengel v. Gormley (160 Pa. 559; 28 Atl. 934; 40 Am. St. Rep. 733)
6, 19, 784, 882, 885
Wettengel v. Garmley (184 Pa. 354; 39 Atl. 57) 882, 892
Wheeling etc. Co. v. Town of Triadelphia (58 W. Va. 487; 52 S. E. 499)
914, 927
Whitehead v. Shattuck (133 U. S. 146) 938
Whitham v. Sayers (9 W. Va. 671) 847, 878
Whitlock v. Consumers etc. Co. (127 Ind. 62; 26 N. E. 570) 183
Wilfong v. Johnson (41 W. Va. 283; 23 S. E. 730) 909
Williams v. Fowler (201 Pa. 236; 50 Atl. 969) 42, 938
Williams v. Gas Co. (52 Mich. 499; 18 N. W. 236) 987

Williams v. Guffey (178 Pa. 342; 35 Atl. 875) 232

· Williams v. South Penn Oil So. (52 W. Va. 181; 43 S. E. 214; 60 L.
R. A. 795) 826

Williamson v. Jones (39 W. Va. 231; 19 S. E. 436) ..219, 558, 578,
598, 599, 829, 892, 896, 897

Williamson v. Jones (43 W. Va. 562; 27 S. E. 411) ..133, 558, 585,
598, 599, 600, 661, 672, 709, 711, 720, 727, 729, 808, 896, 898, 904

Williamson v. Yingling (93 Ind. 42) 800

Wills v. Manufacturers N. Gas Co. (130 Pa. 222; 18 Atl. 721) ..163,
237, 246, 263, 283

Wilson v. Goldstein (152 Pa. 524; 25 Atl. 493) 661, 674, 676

Wilson v. Kisel (164 U. S. 248) 928

Wilson v. Pond Mfg. Co. (40 W. Va. 413; 21 S. E. 1035) 797, 804

Wilson v. Youst (43 W. Va. 826; 28 S. E. 781) ..558, 585, 599, 600,
671, 709, 712, 727, 728, 847, 892, 896, 897

Windfall Mfg. Co. v. Patterson (148 Ind. 414; 47 N. E. 2; 62 Am. St.
Rep. 532; 37 L. R. A. 38) 795, 804, 893

Wolf v. Guffey (161 Pa. 276; 28 Atl. 1117) 238, 283, 284

Wood County Petroleum Co. v. W. Va. Transp. Co. (28 W. Va. 210).. 652

Woodenware Co. v. United States (106 U. S. 432) 90

Woodland Oil Co. v. Crawford, 55 Ohio St. (161; 44 N. E. 1093; 34
L. R. A. 62) 30, 55, 116, 163, 282, 303, 323, 365, 371, 384

Y.

Yoke v. Shea (47 W. Va. 40; 34 S. E. 748) 287, 696, 708

Young v. Ellis (91 Va. 297; 21 S. E. 480) 910

Young v. Forest Oil Co. (194 Pa. 243; 45 Atl. 121) ..113, 125, 394,
407, 409, 445, 453, 467, 487, 489, 498, 500, 501, 784

Young v. McIlhenney (116 S. W. 728) 608, 623

Zahniser et als. trading as East End Oil Co. v. Penna. Torpedo Co.
(190 Pa. 350; 42 Atl. 707) 737

Zeigler v. Brenneman (237 Ill. 15; 86 N. E. 597) ..651, 661, 663, 672, 673

Zeigler v. Dailey (37 Ind. App. 240; 76 N. E. 819) 680, 689, 695

Zinc Co. v. Freeman (68 Kan. 691; 75 Pac. 995) 32

Zollman v. Moore (21 Gratt. 213) 905

Archer's Law and Practice

: : IN : :

Oil and Gas Cases

CHAPTER 1.

LEASE FOR OIL AND GAS PURPOSES.

Sec. 1.—Litigation growing out of controversies over oil and gas leases is a subject as distinct and different from the ordinary litigation in which attorneys conducting a general practice engage, as is admiralty practice. No branch of the general practice requires greater skill, quicker action, or more accurate judgment than does the practice in oil and gas litigation. Usually the lawyer must be able to advise his client on the spur of the moment, and upon such advice thousands of dollars depend. The client submits the lease, the subject for the attorney's opinion, with a statement of the facts. An analysis of the lease is the first step necessary to a construction thereof.

Sec. 2.—The form of the oil and gas lease here given contains the usual provisions in grants of this character, which have been the subject of litigation in the oil and gas producing States. These leases are taken by persons, either for the purpose of actual explorations, or for speculative purposes, and generally the lessee uses a printed form prepared by those engaged largely in the production of oil or gas, or by persons furnishing these forms, for sale generally. Modifications are made by the parties—by the landowner usually to obtain what he regards as better terms by the insertion of safe-guards looking to the termination of the lease upon failure within a stipulated time on the part of the lessee to begin explorations. To this end the rental clause is inserted. In taking leases in territories at a distance from production, known as wild cat territory, both the term and the rental period are usually made longer than in leases taken near production.

Sec. 3.—Landowners making leases on wild cat territory usually provide for an income by way of rental or commutation money. In this way the landowner derives an income from his property, regardless of developments. While there is no limi· tation to the modifications found in oil and gas leases, yet these leases are all subject to general rules, both as to the legal effect of the language used, and as to their construction. These leases must necessarily be for a valuable consideration, must have a fixed and determinable term, must be mutual, and as to the rental or commutation money must contain an express promise to pay at fixed periods in lieu of development, or this clause must be an option. Otherwise the lease is void for uncertainty and want of mutuality. The form of oil and gas lease which follows was construed by the Supreme Court of Appeals of the State of West Virginia in 65 West Virginia, 39; 63 S. E. 762. For the purpose of applying the rules laid down by the courts in con· struing oil and gas leases, and in adjudicating the rights of con· flicting claimants, the lease is paragraphed, each essential clause appearing in a separate paragraph, and these paragraphs are considered in separate chapters.

Sec. 4.—*Form of Lease.*—"This agreement made and en· tered into this 3d day of February, A. D. 1897, by and between Thomas Bunfill and Nancy Bunfill, of the county-Tyler and State of West Virginia, parties of the first part, and A. B. Campbell and J. W. Swan, parties of the second part, witnesseth:"

CONSIDERATION FOR THE LEASE OR LICENSE.
(See Chapter 4.)

"That the said parties of the first part, for and in consid· eration of the sum of Fifty-five Dollars, cash in hand paid, the receipt of which is hereby acknowledged, and of the covenants and agreements hereinafter mentioned,

PURPOSE OF GRANT, PREMISES DEMISED AND RIGHTS ACQUIRED.

(See Chapter 5.)

"Do covenant and agree to lease, and by these presents ha— leased and granted the exclusive right unto the party of the second part, his heirs or assigns, for the purpose of operating and drilling for petroleum and gas, to lay pipe-lines, erect necessary buildings, re-lease and sub-divide all that certain tract of land, situate in Ellsworth District, Tyler County, and State of West Virginia, and bounded and described as follows, to-wit: On the north by lands of H. I. Asher and William Prickett; on the east by lands of Roseberry Prickett; on the south by lands of William Ferrell, and John B. Pipes' heirs; on the west by lands of J. A. Maxwell, containing sixty (60) acres, be the same more or less."

TERM.

(See Chapter 6.)

"The parties of the second part to have and to hold the said premises for and during the term of five years from the date hereof, and so long thereafter as oil or gas is produced in paying quantities, or the rental paid thereon."

CONSIDERATION FOR THE GRANT OF MINERALS—OIL.

(See Chapter 7.)

"The parties of the second part agree to give to parties of the first part one-eighth part of the petroleum obtained from said premises, as produced in the crude state, the said one-eighth part of the petroleum to be set apart in the pipe-line running said petroleum to the credit and for the benefit of the said parties of the first part."

RESERVATION FOR FARMING PURPOSES.

(See Chapter 8.)

"The said parties of the first part to fully use and enjoy the said premises for the purpose of tillage, except such parts as shall be necessary for said mining purposes, and a right of way

over and across said premises to the place of mining or operating.''

LESSEE'S RIGHT TO REMOVE FIXTURES.
(See Chapter 9.)

"The said parties of the second part *is* further to have the
privilege of using sufficient gas and water from the premises
herein leased to run the necessary engines, the right to remove
any machinery, fixtures and buildings placed on said premises by
said parties of the second part"

RESERVATION AROUND BUILDINGS.
(See Chapter 10.)

"And is not to put down any well for oil on the lands hereby
leased within ten rods of the buildings now on said premises,
without the consent of both parties."

CONSIDERATION FOR GRANT OF MINERALS—GAS.
(See Chapter 11.)

"It is agreed that if gas is found in paying quantities the
consideration in full to the party of the first part for gas shall
be two hundred dollars per annum for the gas from each well
when utilized off the premises."

FORFEITURE AND RENTAL CLAUSE—LESSEE'S
OPTION.
(See Chapter 12.)

FORFEITURE AND RENTAL CLAUSE—LESSOR'S
OPTION.
(See Chapter 13.)

"Provided, however, that this lease shall become null and
void and all rights hereunder shall cease and determine unless a
well shall be completed on said premises within three months
from the date hereof, or in lieu thereof thereafter the parties of
the second part shall pay to the parties of the first part fifteen
dollars for each three months delay, payable in advance until
such well is completed."

SURRENDER CLAUSE.
(See Chapter 14.)

"And it is further agreed that the second party, his heirs or assigns, shall have the right at any time to surrender up this lease; then and from that time this lease and agreement shall be null and void and no longer binding on either party."

ASSIGNMENT.
(See Chapter 15.)

ASSIGNEE—LIABILITY OF.
(See Chapter 16.)

ASSIGNEE OR SECOND LESSEE WITH NOTICE OF PRIOR LEASE.
(See Chapter 17.)

"And that all conditions between the parties hereto shall extend to their heirs, executors and assigns."

Sec. 5.—Controversies growing out of oil and gas leases must be settled by the construction of some of the express or implied covenants of the ordinary oil and gas lease. In order to arrive at a correct conclusion and give an intelligent opinion on a question arising out of a controversy over an oil and gas lease, it is necessary, first, to consider the rules of construction established by the court in determining such questions. The courts having had before them the construction of these peculiar grants have found it necessary to establish rules applicable to the subject, and have not adhered to the rules governing ordinary leases or contracts. Public policy and necessity for the preservation of private rights, have, together, contributed to the establishment by the courts of certain rules of construction requiring exploration, or surrender of the lease, applicable to no other character of contract.

CHAPTER 2.

CONSTRUCTION OF OIL AND GAS LEASES.

Sec. 1.—In the construction of oil and gas leases different rules obtain from those applied to the construction of ordinary leases, or other mining leases, owing to the peculiar nature of the mineral, and the danger of loss to the owner from drainage by surrounding wells. The general rule is, that oil and gas leases are construed most strongly in favor of the lessor.

Huggins v. *Daley,* 99 Fed. 606; 40 C. C. A. 12; 48 L. R. A. 320.
Allegheny Oil Co. v. *Snyder,* 106 Fed. 764; 45 C. C. A. 60-4-8.
Bettman v. *Harness,* 42 W. Va. 433; 26 S. E. 271.
Steelsmith v. *Gartlan,* 45 W. Va. 27; 29 S. E. 978.
Parish Fork Oil Co. v. *Bridgewater Gas Co.,* 51 W. Va. 583; 42 S. E. 655.
Gadberry v. *Ohio, etc., Gas Co.,* 162 Ind. 9; 67 N. E. 259.
Aye v. *Phila. Co.,* 193 Pa. 451; 44 Atl. 655; 74 Am. St. R. 696.
Brown v. *Spilman,* 155 U. S. 665.
Douthett v. *Ft. Pitt Gas Co.,* 202 Pa. 416; 51 Atl. 981.
Smith v. *South Penn O. Co.,* 59 W. Va. 204; 53 S. E. 152.
Test Oil Co. v. *Taurette,* 19 Okl. 214; 91 Pac. 1025.
Tennessee Oil Co. v. *Brown,* 131 Fed. 696; 65 C. C. A. 524.
Collier v. *Munger,* 89 Pac. 1011; 75 Kan. 550.
Kurt v. *Lanyon,* 72 Kan, 60; 82 Pac. 459.
Lawson v. *Kirchner,* 50 W. Va. 344; 40 S. E. 344, syl. 3.
Snodgrass v. *South Penn Oil Co.,* 47 W. Va. 509; 35 S. E. 820.
Roberts v. *Bettman,* 45 W. Va. 143; 30 S. E. 95.
Wettengel v. *Gormley,* 160 Pa. 559; 28 Atl. 934; 40 Am. St. Rep. 733.
Moore v. *Ohio Valley Gas Co.,* 63 W. Va. 455; 60 S. E. 401.

The Supreme Court of Ohio, in construing oil leases, has held that such grant is more than a mere license. (See Chapter 3.)

Sec. 2.—In *Huggins* v. *Daley,* 99 Fed. 606; 40 C. A. A. 12; 48 L. R. A. 320, analyzed under Chapter 5, the second head note is as follows:

"A different rule of construction obtains as to oil and gas leases from that applied to ordinary leases or to other mining leases, and owing to the peculiar nature of the mineral, and the danger of loss to the owner from drainage, by surrounding wells. such leases are construed most strongly in favor of the lessor."

The court in this case predicated the lessor's right to a forfeiture wholly upon the proviso by which lessee was to commence a well upon the premises within thirty days, and complete the same within ninety days, and held, that the provision as to the payment of Fifty Dollars constituted a mere forfeiture, and that the sole consideration was the drilling of the well. The lessee did nothing as to the drilling of the well, hence, the court concluded that the whole consideration failed and cancelled the lease.

Sec. 3.—In *Allegheny Oil Company* v. *Snyder,* 106 Fed, 764; 45 C. C. A. 504-8, analyzed under Chapter 4, the second paragraph of the head notes is as follows:

"Under the decisions of the Supreme Court of Ohio relating to the construction of oil and gas leases, which have established a rule of property in that State, such leases carry an implied covenant on the part of the lessee that he will drill and operate such number of wells on the premises as would ordinarily be required to develop their production and to afford ordinary protection to their lines; and the lessor may enforce such covenant by action, and is not obliged to permit the lessee to hold the land indefinitely for speculative purposes, notwithstanding the absence of any express limitation in the lease."

Sec. 4.—In *Bettman* v. *Harness,* 42 W. Va. 433; 26 S. E., 271, analyzed under Chapter 6, Judge Brannon, in the opinion, discussing the meaning of the clause in the lease "as much longer, as oil or gas is found in paying quantities, or the rental paid thereon" at page 445 says:

"We want to get at what was the most likely meaning of the words used. Courts may look to language, the subject matter, and surrounding circumstances to get at the meaning, and thus place themselves in the situation the parties were in, to glean their probable purpose * * * . Here are a landowner and

an oil producer negotiating a lease. A term of only two years
is fixed; but plainly that is only the period for completing a
well.   If a good one is obtained, the operator wants longer time,
and he inserts a clause extending the term as long as oil or gas
is produced in paying quantities; but the lessor wants the lease
continued only upon condition that his share of the oil and gas
rent be paid, and he means to have a clause which provides a
continuance of the lease as long as both oil is produced and his
rent paid.''

Sec. 5.—In *Steelsmith* v. *Gartlan*, 45 W. Va. 27; 29 S. E.
978, analyzed under Chapter 3, syl. 3 is as follows:

''Such lease must be construed as a whole, and if there is
no provision therein contained requiring the boring of another
well after the first unsuccessful attempt is completed and abandoned, the lease becomes invalid, and of no binding force as to
any of its provisions.''

Sec. 6.—In *Parish Fork Oil Co.* v. *Bridgewater Gas Co.*, 51
W. Va. 583; 42 S. E. 655, analyzed under Chapter 5, the third
and fourth points of the syllabus are as follows:

''3.   When its terms will permit it, under the rules of law.
an oil lease will be so construed as to promote development and
prevent delay and unproductiveness.
4.   The law recognizes a distinction between the abandonment of operations under an oil lease and an intention to abandon or surrender the lease itself.   Unless bound by the terms of
the lease so to do, it will not permit the lessee to hold the lease
without operating under it, and thereby prevent the lessor from
operating on the land, or leasing it to others.''

In the opinion at pages 592-3, Judge Poffenbarger says:

''A well settled principle of law is, that a contract shall
be construed as a whole and in the light of the purpose and object
for the accomplishment of which it is made.   Oil leases are no
exception to the rule, and, as the subject matter of the lease is
peculiar in its nature, the courts have given this principle great
latitude in their construction.   They are executed by the lessor
in the hope and with an expressed or implied condition that the
land shall be developed and oil produced.   When production takes

place the lease is mutually beneficial. The royalty which it is stipulated in all these leases that the landowner shall receive, is generally the moving cause of the execution of the lease. If there is one principle that is asserted in *Steelsmith* v. *Gartlan,* more vigorously, and with more emphasis than any other, it is that the lessee shall proceed to make the lease profitable to both parties, and that he shall not be permitted to tie up the land. The 'testing' provided for was manifestly a condition upon which the lease depended. If such test showed no minerals then the contract was at an end; if it, on the other hand, showed the presence of valuable mines, then the lessees were bound to operate them in good faith for the joint benefit of themselves and the owners of the fee. Technical words are unnecessary to raise a condition. If a fair and reasonable construction of the instrument shows that a lease shall depend upon the doing or not doing something essential to the purpose of the contract, the law implies the condition."

Sec. 7.—In *Gadberry* v. *Ohio, etc. Gas Co.,* 162 Ind. 9; 67 N. E. 259, analyzed under Chapter 18, Judge Gillette, at page 261 (N. E.) says:

"In determining whether a condition is to be implied, it is important to note that the substantial consideration which moves the grantor to execute such a grant is the hope of profit or royalties, if oil or gas is discovered. Even if the grantee in this case had paid the stated consideration of $1.00—a technical valuable consideration—yet we must construe the instrument with the fact in view that a more substantial reason, or reasons, promoted the making of the grant. *Huggins* v. *Daley,* 40 C. C. A. 12; 99 Fed. 606; 48 L. R. A. 320; *Federal Oil Co.* v. *Western Oil Co.* (C. C.) 112 Fed. 373. In an ordinary agricultural lease, where the rent is payable in kind, it would, of course, be implied, that the tenant would farm the land; and the requirement is implied that lessees in mineral leases, under royalties, will develop the property if exploration warrants it, where the minerals are stable, although the only result of a delay in operating would be to postpone the receipt of profits or royalties. *Island Coal Co.* v. *Combs,* 152 Ind. 379; 53 N. E. 452; *McKnight* v. *Nat. Gas Co.,* 146 Pa. 185; 23 Atl. 164; 28 Am. St. Rep. 790. If a duty to operate is to be implied in such cases, there is much more reason for the implication in the grant of the right to operate for oil and gas upon a royalty, owing to the migratory habit of the fluid. 'Oil leases,' it was declared in *McKnight* v. *Nat. Gas Co.,* supra, must be construed with reference to the known characteristics of the business.''

Sec. 8.—In *Aye* v. *Phila. Co.*, 193 Pa. 451; 44 Atl. 555; 74 Am. St. Rep. 696, (Nov. 6, 1899) the syllabus is as follows:

"Where an oil lease provides for the completion of a test well within a certain time but makes no provision for the contingency of a test well proving dry, there is an implied obligation on the lessee, after having completed a test well which has proved dry, to proceed further with the exploration and development of the land with reasonable diligence according to the usual course of the business, and a failure to do so amounts to an abandonment, which will sustain a re-entry by the lessor. In such a case an unexplained cessation of operations for four years gives rise to a fair presumption of abandonment, and standing alone, and admitted, would justify the court in declaring an abandonment as a matter of law; but it may be capable of explanation, and the question of abandonment is therefore usually a question for the jury on the evidence of the acts and declarations of the parties.

"The rule, that where the parties have expressly agreed on what shall be done there is no room for the implication of anything not so stipulated for, is equally as applicable to oil and gas leases as to any other contracts."

William M. Campbell, on July 11, 1887, executed an oil and gas lease to Fred Aye and others for a tract of 100 acres of land in Armstrong County, Pennsylvania, for the term of twenty years from date, and as much longer as oil or gas could be found in paying quantities. The lessees agreed to drill a test well in the vicinity of the premises demised within six months from the date of the lease, unless prevented by accident, etc., and if oil should be found in paying quantities in said test well the lessees further agreed to complete one test well upon the premises leased within six months from the completion of the well agreed to be drilled within the first six months mentioned, or within one year from the date of the lease, or thereafter to pay the lessor for delay a yearly rental of fifty cents per acre, from the time of completing such well on the leased premises. A failure to complete such well or make such payment should render the lease null and void. On October 2, 1891, Campbell made a second lease to William C. Bailey & Company. This lease contained the following provision:

"It is further agreed, by the parties of the second part, that should lease under date of July 5, 1887, taken by Aye Brothers and R. S. Martin, as the second part thereto, be in full force and effect, then the said parties of the second part hereto agree to release said party of the first part of the demands above described and set forth."

William C. Bailey & Company assigned their lease to the Philadelphia Company. The test well provided for in the original lease was put down on a farm in the vicinity but produced no oil. A second well was drilled on another farm with like results and operations then ceased without any well being drilled on the leased premises. Aye and others instituted their action of ejectment in the Court of Common Pleas of Armstrong County against the Philadelphia Company, the assignee of the second lease, claiming under their lease of July 11, 1887, and obtained a verdict and judgment. The defendant appealed to the Supreme Court of Pennsylvania, and that court reversed the court below.

Sec. 9.—In *Brown* v. *Spilman,* 155 U. S. 665, analyzed under Chapter 10, the syllabus is as follows:

"A grant in a lease of 40 acres of land, described by metes and bounds, for the sole and only purpose of boring, mining, and excavating for petroleum or carbon oil and gas, and piping of oil and gas over all the tract, excepting reserved therefrom ten acres, also described by metes and bounds, upon which no well shall be drilled without the consent of the lessor, is a grant of all the gas and oil under the entire tract, conditioned that the lessee shall not drill wells on the ten-acre plat without the consent of the lessor."

In the opinion delivered by Justice Shiras, 669-670, upon the question of construction it was said:

"Petroleum, gas and oil are substances of peculiar charac- ter and decisions in ordinary cases of mining, for coal and other minerals which have a fixed situs, cannot be applied to contracts concerning them without some qualifications. They belong to the owner of the land, and are part of it, so long as they are on it, or in it, or subject to his control, but when they escape and go into other land, or come under another's control, the title of the former owner is gone. If an adjoining owner drills his own land and taps a deposit of oil or gas, extending under his neighbor's field so that it comes into his well, it becomes his property. *Brown* v. *Vandergrift*, 80 Pa. 142-147; *Westmoreland Nat. Gas Co.'s App.*, 25 Weekly Notes of Cases, (Penn.) 103.''

Sec. 10.—In *Douthett* v. *Fort. Pitt Gas Co.*, 202 Pa. 416; 51 Atl. 981, (April 28, 1902) the first paragraph of the syllabus is as follows:

''Where a contract provided that a well sunk in oil and gas lands should under certain conditions be operated as an oil well. and belong to one of the parties, and if oil should not be found. the other party should drill deeper into another strata, the oral evidence of experts and practical producers of oil and gas in the oil and gas belts is admissable, not to charge, modify or contradict the writing, but to show the surroundings of the parties at the time the contract was made, and thus aid the court in the interpretations of the written agreement.''

On February 25, 1901, Lemuel Douthett, trading as the Thorn Hill Oil Company, entered into a written agreement with the Rochester Tumbler Company wherein, for three thousand dollars and other considerations, he assigned and transferred to the Tumbler Company all the gas rights covered by two leases on two farms including the gas right in a well then drilled on one of said farms. The Tumbler Company agreed to drill a well on one of the farms, commencing within sixty days, and to prosecute the drilling of the same to completion with due diligence. It was agreed that if this well produced no oil it was to be at the cost of the Tumbler Company. If the well produced less than ten barrels per day it was to belong to the Thorn Hill Oil Company, upon payment to the Tumbler Company for the rig and casing at well values, the drilling to be at the cost of the Tumbler Company. If the well produced more than ten barrels per day the Thorn Hill Company should pay the cost of rig and casing at well values, and also pay the cost of drilling, and the well was to belong to the Thorn Hill Oil Company. If neither gas nor oil were found in paying quantities sooner the Tumbler Company was to drill to the fourth sand. The Tumbler Company commenced the drilling of a well on the Douthett farm, one of the farms covered by the leases, under the agreement, about May, 1900, and drilled through what is known as the 100-foot said. The Thorn Hill Company then demanded the right to shoot the well before the Tumbler Company should drill further for the purpose of determining whether oil could be found in this said. This the Tumbler Company refused to allow. Thereupon, Lemuel Douthett, trading as the Thorn Hill Oil Company, filed his bill in equity in the Court of Common Pleas Number 1, Allegheny County, and obtained an injunction against the defendant preventing the further drilling of the well until the plaintiff had been allowed to fairly test the well, or have it tested, for oil in that sand. The defendant claimed that the plaintiff while he had the right to test the well at some time, yet he should not be allowed to do so until the drilling had gone to the fourth sand; and alleged that such test was dangerous to further drilling, and if the well did not produce oil in paying quantities, the shooting would stop its further development by destroying it. The Court of Common Pleas held upon the evidence, which tended to show that while there was danger in shooting the well, that the danger was not so great as to warrant a denial of the right to shoot the well, and granted the relief prayed for. An appeal was taken to the Supreme Court of Pennsylvania, and that court affirmed the Court of Common Pleas.

Sec. 11.—In *Kurt* v. *Lanyon*, 72 Kan. 60; 82 Pac. 459 (October 7, 1905) the syllabus is as follows:

"1. Where two or more written instruments are executed at the same time between the same parties, relating to the same subject matter, and embodied in one transaction, and the execution of one is expressed to be the consideration for the other. the court, in construing one of them, should read them all together, as though all the parts were contained in one writing.

2. Where the owner enters into an agreement to sell certain real estate, excepting the oil and gas therein, and upon the

fulfilment of it a warranty deed is executed to the grantee named in the contract, and at the same time such grantee executes to the grantor a writing purporting to convey to him all oil and gas in the land, and it is expressed in the latter that it is executed for one dollar and the deeding of the premises, the deed and the pretended conveyance of the oil and gas in the land back to the grantor should be read together, and when so read they constitute a deed to the land, excepting the oil and gas therein.''

Sec. 12.—In *Test Oil Co.* v. *Taurette*, 19 Okl. 214; 91 Pac. 1025 (Sept. 5, 1907) the third and fourth points of the syllabus are as follows:

"3. The following covenant in an oil and gas lease, being a restriction of the alienation of the land, and clearly expressing the intention of the parties, will be strictly construed: 'Said first parties hereby further agree that they will, in and by any deed hereafter executed by them, or either of them, for any part of said La Taurette Second Addition to the said Town of Cleveland, prohibit any drilling for oil or gas on any lands so hereafter conveyed in said Second Addition.' *Held*, that the general usage and acceptance of the term 'deed' in the above clause clearly expresses the intention of the parties, not to include 'lease' and thereby prohibit the first parties from leasing the said tract for the purpose of drilling oil and gas wells thereon.
4. The word 'deed' in its common usage and acceptance undoubtedly means the conveyance of real estate, and a deed of conveyance is a sealed writing signed by the parties to be charged which evidences the terms of the contract between the parties whereby the title to real estate is transferred from one to the other, and this is the more usual though somewhat restricted meaning of the word 'deed'.''

On January 27, 1905, Isaac V. La Taurette and wife executed and delivered to John L. Moran an oil and gas lease upon a certain portion of the grantor's property, situated immediately east of the east line of what was known as La Taurette's Second Addition to the Town of Cleveland, Pawnee County, Oklahoma. On March 6, 1905, Moran assigned this lease to the Test Oil Company, and on March 8, 1905, the lease and assignment were filed for record. On March 8, 1905, La Taurette and wife executed and delivered a second oil and gas lease to S. W. Lawrence, covering

a certain tract lying immediately west of the east line of the
Second Addition. Subsequently, Lawrence assigned an undivided one-half interest in the lease to Sornborg and Brother, and
Melrose Oil Company. These assignees of Lawrence drilled wells
for oil and gas on the tract covered by the lease known as the
Second Addition. The Test Oil Company instituted its suit
against Isaac V. La Taurette and the assignees of the lease on
the Second Addition in the District Court of Pawnee County, to
restrain drilling under the second lease. A judgment or decree
was rendered in favor of the defendants, from which the plaintiff
brought error to the Supreme Court of Oklahoma. That court
affirmed the judgment of the District Court.

Sec. 13.—In *Collier* vs *Munger*, 75 Kan. 550; 89 Pac. 1011
(April 6, 1907) syls. 1-2-3 are as follows:

"1. The language of an oil and gas lease will be given its
ordinary and commonly understood meaning where no reason
appears for doing otherwise.
2. A contract to drill an oil and gas well contained the provision which reads: 'The second party agrees to drill one well
for oil or gas * * * and go to the Mississippi limestone
unless a good quantity of oil or gas is struck or otherwise, at the
option of the first party. Second party agrees to do the drilling
in a good workmanlike manner or no pay. First party agrees
to give * * * one dollar per foot for the drilling, provided
it is done in a good, workmanlike manner.' *Held,* that the second party was entitled to the contract price for drilling the well
when he reached the Mississippi limestone if the work was done
in a good, workmanlike manner.
3. To drill a well in a good and workmanlike manner does
not include placing it in a completed condition for permanent
preservation by placing therein a packer and tubing and removing the water therefrom."

Charles P. Collier instituted an action against W. L. Munger
in the District Court of Labette County, to recover the contract
price for drilling the well. The contract contained the conditions stated in the syllabus. Judgment was rendered in favor
of the defendant and plaintiff appealed. The Supreme Court
reversed the District Court.

The defendant claimed that the plaintiff failed to complete the well in that he did not case out the water and put in the packer and tubing, which defendant alleged was necessary to the proper completion of the well.

Sec. 14.—In *Lawson* v. *Kirchner*, 50 W. Va. 344; 40 S. E. 344, analyzed under Chapter 5, syl. 3 and the opinion of Judge Dent, page 348, are as follows:

"3. A person who accepts an oil or gas lease with a stipulation therein contained to pay a monthly rental until a well is completed or until the expiration of a certain fixed term, is bound to pay such rental, although he does not, within such terms, enter upon the land and complete such well, unless he was prevented from doing so by the plaintiffs, and not by mere personal default."

"The last objection is, that the defendant never having signed the lease or conveyance, and never having entered upon or taken actual possession of the property, he cannot be held liable for the rentals reserved. He permitted the court to confirm the sale to him, accepted the conveyance, placed it on record, paid the purchase price, and one month's rental and raised no objection thereto in any manner until the two years' limit had expired."

Sec. 15.—In *Snodgrass* v. *South Penn Oil Co.*, 47 W. Va. 509; 35 S. E. 820, analyzed under Chapter 13, the syllabus is as follows:

"Where a party leases a tract of land for the purpose of mining and operating for oil and gas, the lessee contracting to deliver to the credit of the lessor one-eighth of the oil produced, and saved from the premises, and to pay two hundred dollars per year for the gas from each well drilled, and the lease also contains the following provision: 'Provided, however, that this lease shall become null and void, and all rights thereunder shall cease and determine, unless a well shall be completed on the premises within one year from the date hereof, or unless the lessee shall pay at the rate of three hundred and fifty dollars. quarterly, in advance, for each additional three months such completion is delayed, from the time above mentioned for the completion of such well until a well is completed.' *Held*, that this provision did not bind the lessee to pay any rent for the land, or for delay in commencing to operate for oil and gas, and, in the absence of some other clause binding the lessee to pay for such rent or delay, an action of assumpsit could not be maintained on such lease for failing to pay such rent, or for such delay.''

Sec. 16.—In *Roberts* v. *Bettman*, 45 W. Va. 143; 30 S. E. 95, analyzed under Chapter 12, the first point of the syllabus, and the opinion of Judge Brannon at page 146, are as follows:

"1. A lease for oil and gas contemplates that the lessee have two years in which to bore a well, and provides 'that the party of the second part shall pay to the party of the first part $100 per month in advance, until a well is completed, from the date of this lease, and a failure to complete such well, or to pay said rental when due, or within ten days thereafter, shall render this lease null and void, and can only be renewed by mutual consent, and no right of action shall, after such failure, accrue to either party on account of the breach of any covenant herein contained. * * * It is further agreed that the second party shall have the right at any time to surrender this lease to the party of the first part, and thereafter be fully discharged.' The lessee bored no well, but holds the lease a number of months, and then surrenders it. *Held,* that the forfeiture provisions are for the lessor's benefit, and he can avail himself of them to declare a forfeiture for non-payment of rental or not, as he chooses, and, if he does not, can recover rental until the surrender of the lease. The lessee's mere failure to pay does not release him from obligation to pay. There was tacit consent to renew.''

"The purpose here is plain. If we say that the failure to pay that rental monthly *ipso facto* releases the lessee from its payment, what is the use of the provision for payment? Why provide for payment, if failure to pay alone nullifies the provision for payment? The covenant to pay is brought to birth by the lease only to die at the hands of its mother. This construction renders the instrument self contradictory. The lease cannot mean this nonsense. We must attribute some other meaning to it. If such be the meaning, where is the need of the clause giving the lessee right to surrender the lease at any time and discharge himself? If the other clause was intended to release him from the obligation to pay this second clause, plainly made for the benefit of the lessee, would be useless. The clause stipulating for the payment of rent is the only benefit which the lessor gets until development shall give him what moves him chiefly to make the lease, his share of oil, and he protected himself against the

insolvency of the lessee, or his failure to pay, by the clause forfeiting the lease for failure to complete a well or to pay rental.
That clause of forfeiture was designed for his benefit and not
for the lessee's benefit. It was the lessor's only safety. The
clause giving the lessee a right at any time to surrender the
lease and discharge himself from further liability is his ample
shield. This construction gives all the clauses their full operation.''

Sec. 17.—In *Tennessee, etc. Co.* v. *Brown*, 131 Fed. 696; 65
C. C. A. 524, analyzed under Chapter 24, in the opinion, page 700
Fed. it was held:

''These considerations lead us to the conclusion that the
presence of words of conveyance are not sufficient to require us
to hold that the effect of the instrument was to vest in Colbert
the title to the timber or mineral interest in this land. The
ruling intention, as ascertained from all parts of the agreement,
should be given effect. It is difficult to believe that it was intended that title should pass until these minerals had been removed, and as they were removed. The consideration to be paid
could not be ascertained until the contingency arrived, for no
price in solido is mentioned. Whether any mining should ever
be done or any price ever paid were both dependent upon future
events. The contract was, therefore, for a lease dependent upon
the conditions. That the exploration for minerals should be
made within a reasonable time is of the very essence of the
agreement, and a condition precedent to the accruing of the
right to take the minerals discovered upon the terms of payment
indicated. The failure to make such exploration within a reasonable time, and to make it with such thoroughness and certainty
as to determine the existence of mineral or oil, would be fatal to
the continuance of the agreement. Upon this, we think, this
lease depends as a condition precedent.''

In support of the conclusions reached the court cited the
following authorities: ·

Allegheny Oil Co. v. *Snyder*, 106 Fed. 764; 45 C. C. A. 604.
Logan Gas Co. v. *Great Southern Gas Co.*, 126 Fed. 623;
   61 C. C. A. 359.
Petroleum Company v. *Coal & Coke Co.*, 89 Tenn. 381; 18
   S. W. 65.

Steelsmith v. *Gartlan*, 45 W. Va. 27; 29 S. E. 978.
Conrad v. *Moorehead*, 89 N. C. 31.
Knight v. *Coal & Iron Co.*, 47 Ind. 105; 17 Am. Rep. 692.
Huggins v. *Daley*, 99 Fed. 606; 40 C. C. A. 12.

Sec. 18.—The rule of construction that where there is doubt as to the proper meaning of a contract, the construction the parties have put upon it is entitled to great consideration in its enforcement, applies in the construction of oil and gas leases as in other contracts.

Smith v. *South Penn Oil Co.*, 53 S. E. 150; 59 W. Va. 204. Syl. 3.
Moore v. *Ohio Valley Gas Co.*, 60 S. E. 40; 63 W. Va. 455. Syl. 1.

Sec. 19.—In *Moore* v. *Ohio Valley Gas Co.*, 63 W. Va. 455, 60 S. E. 401, (February 4, 1908) syl. 1 is as follows:

"1.   Where there is doubt as to the proper meaning of a contract, the construction the parties have put upon it is entitled to great consideration in its enforcement."

Sec. 20.—In *Smith* v. *South Penn Oil Co.*, 59 W. Va. 204; 53 S. E. 150, analyzed under Chapter 13, syl. 3 is as follows:

"Such a contract being ambiguous as to what shall constitute a completed well, the conduct of the parties, in treating the completion of an unproductive well as an act sufficient to vest in the lessee a right to make further explorations without additional payments is conclusive upon them, under the principle of practical construction."

Sec. 21.—In *Wettengel* v. *Gormley*, 160 Pa. 559; 28 Atl. 934; 40 Am. St. Rep. 733, analyzed under Chapter 50, the second point of the syllabus is as follows:

"Owing to the vagrant character of oil and gas, a lease of these substances partakes of the character of a lease for general tillage, rather than that of a lease for mining or quarrying the solid minerals."

Sec. 22.—In determining the effect to be given to certain acts of the lessor or lessee of an oil lease, the character of the grant, necessarily, must first be determined. The ordinary oil and gas lease, before developments have been made, or explorations have been commenced by lessee, by whatever name the grant may be called, confers upon the lessee certain rights and privileges which he can lose or preserve, without the execution of any written transfer or releases. The lessor has, by the terms of the grant, enabled the lessee upon the performance of the conditions on his part to be performed, to become vested with the right to produce the oil or gas during the term. It becomes necessary therefore, to define the lease or contract. The courts have not agreed as to the definition of the grant. Some courts hold that it is a mere license, while others, construing the same character of grant, hold it to be a lease, but the courts all hold that the lessee must explore for and develop oil and gas to entitle him to a vested right to produce these minerals.

CHAPTER 3.

DEFINITION—NO ESTATE VESTS.

Sec. 1.—A grant of the exclusive privilege to go on land for the purpose of prospecting for oil and gas is, until oil or gas is discovered in paying quantities, merely a license, and does not vest in the grantee any estate in the surface of the land or the minerals therein; but where by such grant the land is granted with such exclusive privilege, it is a lease conveying an interest in the land and not merely a license to enter and explore for oil or gas.

Funk v. *Halderman*, 53 Pa. 229.
Dark v. *Johnston*, 55 Pa. 164.
Kelly v. *Keys*, 213 Pa. 295; 62 Atl. 911.
Steelsmith v. *Gartlan*, 45 W. Va. 27; 29 S. E. 947; 44 L. R. A. 107.
Florence Oil Co. v. *Orman*, 19 Colo. App. 79; 79 Pac. 628.

Rawlings v. *Armel,* 70 Kan. 778; 79 Pac. 683.

Murdock-West Co. v. *Logan,* 69 Ohio St. 514; 69 N. E. 984.

Lowther Oil Co. v. *Miller-Sibley Oil Co.,* 59 W. Va. 501; 44 S. E. 433; 97 Am. St. 1027.

Huggins v. *Daley,* 99 Fed. 606; 40 C. C. A. 12; 48 L. R. A. 320.

Lawson v. *Kirchner,* 50 W. Va. 344; 40 S. E. 344.

Wagner v. *Mallory,* 169 N. Y. 501; 62 N. E. 584.

Headley v. *Hoopengarner,* 60 W. Va. 626; 55 S. E. 144.

Dickey v. *Coffeyville Vitrified, etc., Co.,* 69 Kan. 106; 76 Pac. 389.

Venture Oil Co. v. *Fretts,* 150 Pa. 451; 35 Atl. 732.

Kan. Nat. Gas Co. v. *Board of Commissioners,* 75 Kan. 335; 89 Pac. 750.

Poe v. *Ulrey,* 233 Ill. 56; 84 N. E. 46.

Staley & Barnsdall v. *Derden,* — Tex. Civ. App. —; 121 S. W. 1135.

O'Neill v. *Sun Co.,* — Tex. Civ. App. —; 123 S. W. 172.

Barnsdall v. *Bradford Gas Co.,* — Pa. —; 74 Atl. 207.

Waterford Oil & Gas Co. v. *Shipman,* 233 Ill. 9; 84 N. E. 53.

Backer v. *Penn Lubricating Co.,* 162 Fed. 627; 89 C. C. A. 419.

Moore v. *Sawyer,* 167 Fed. 826.

Sec. 2.—The contract by which the landowner authorizes the lessee or prospective producer to enter upon the lands for the purpose of prospecting for oil and gas, is commonly called an oil and gas lease. This contract is usually unilateral. By accepting the lease the lessee becomes as much bound by the covenants thereof as though he had signed it. The lease gives to the lessee the right within a fixed term to explore for oil or gas. This term is definitely fixed. If oil or gas is not discovered within the term the lease by its own conditions is void. The term is usually controlled by a rental period, that is, the lessee has a fixed time within which he may enter upon the premises for exploration purposes. For delay in such explorations he is required to pay the rental within a certain time, which is called commutation money for delay.

Sec. 3.—The rental period is subject to modification by oral contract or understanding between the parties. The landowner may waive payment of commutation money at maturity or at the end of the rental period, or he may exact the payment, and if the lease provides for forfeiture in default of payment, the landowner may thereupon declare a forfeiture and put an end to the lease without other notice or legal process. The term of the lease is usually qualified by the expression "or as long thereafter as oil or gas is produced in paying quantities." These qualifying words have no force or application, whatever, unless the lessee discovers oil or gas in paying quantities within the term. If oil or gas is found within the term, then, unless that term is qualified by the provision that the lease shall remain in force as long thereafter as oil or gas is produced in paying quantities, the lease ends at the expiration of the term expressed. But, where the term is qualified by the language above, or similar words, upon the expiration of the fixed term, the lessee may continue operations as long as he produces oil or gas in paying quantities, and pays the royalty or rentals therefor. The lessee or the operator has been usually held to be the sole judge of what constitutes paying quantities.

Sec. 4.—In *Funk* v. *Halderman*, 53 Pa. 229, analyzed under Chapter 7, in a contest between various claimants to the same oil and gas rights, the Supreme Court of Pennsylvania held that the grant did not amount to a lease, nor a sale of the land or the minerals, for the reason that no estate in the oil or minerals was granted; that the right granted to Funk was to experiment for oil, sever it from the soil, and take it on yielding a royalty of one-third to the landlord; that the lessee's right was a license to work the land for minerals; that the lease was a license coupled with an interest, and was not revokable at the pleasure of the licensor.

Sec. 5.—In *Dark* v. *Johnston*, 55 Pa. 154 (March 27, 1867) the syllabus is as follows:

"1. Where a conveyance was to be made of land, if the vendee should find oil upon it, it is to be construed that oil must be found within a reasonable time.
2. Oil, like water, is not the subject of property, except in actual occupancy.

3. A grant of water is not the grant of the soil on which it rests, and it passes nothing for which ejectment will lie.

4. It is essential to an easement that there should be both a dominant and servient tenement.

5. Generally, a parol license is revocable at the will of the licensor; and it is revocable although a consideration has been paid for it.

6. Even a parol license executed, may become an easement on the land, and where acts have been done in reliance upon a license, the licensor will be estopped from revoking it to the injury of the licensee.

7. A license is a personal privilege, and is not assignable; an assignment by a licensee determines his right.

8. McGuire granted to Baird the right to sink one or more wells on his land, and agreed to convey to Baird, if oil was found; also to grant him an exclusive right to sink wells on other land at $100 for every 10 years for every well Baird may continuously pump oil from; if he should fail to find oil, to have the right to remove his machinery, etc.; if oil were found the right to pump to continue as the rent should be paid. *Held, 1.* To be a license to Baird. *2.* That Baird having made improvements McGuire could not revoke the license as to him. *3.* That Baird having assigned the license it was determined.''

Samuel McGuire, on November 26, 1859, was the owner of a farm in Deerfield Township, Warren County, Pennsylvania, of about 250 acres. The landowner made an agreement with Samuel Baird, reciting that petroleum or mineral oil might exist on said lands, and that said McGuire was desirous of having it explored, and in consideration that the said Baird should have the right to sink one or more wells or pits on an island included in the boundaries of said farm, and four trial wells or pits on the farm; and in consideration of $100 to be paid before work was commenced, to said McGuire, and with the provision that should Baird find oil on the island, then McGuire agreed to sell to Baird the island for the sum of $500. The $100 to be paid on commencing work was to be a part of the $500. The remainder of the $500 to be paid upon McGuire delivering a warranty deed for said island to Baird. The agreement provided that McGuire granted to Baird an exclusive right to sink wells and pits for obtaining mineral oil over the rest of said estate, on the following terms and conditions: $100 for each and every period of ten

years, ($10.00 per year) for each and every well or pit that Baird
should continuously pump oil from; the continuous pumping of
said oil to be the evidence that such wells or pits were used. The
rent for each and every well to be paid yearly. The agreement
further provided that Baird should not, in boring or sinking such
wells or pits, or in erecting the necessary buildings and apparatus to obtain, and refine or prepare for market, said oil, injure
any part of said farm valuable as pasture, or tillable; and that
any fences interfered with should be restored to good condition.
It was further agreed that in case Baird should fail to find rock
oil on either the island or the farm, that he should be at full liberty to remove any buildings or machinery that he might have
put up, and the $100 paid to McGuire should be in full for every
demand. It was further agreed that should oil be found, then
the right to pump oil from the wells should continue as the rents
should be paid.

On April 2, 1861, McGuire conveyed the land to C. D. Curtis,
Josiah Hall, and others. Baird took possession of the land and
commenced a well on the main land, gave some twenty leases, and
upon about seventeen of which boring was commenced. Some of
the wells were put down hundreds of feet, and from $20,000 to
$30,000 was expended in boring, building, and other operations.

In 1861, Curtis brought an action of ejectment against Baird,
who received notice from Curtis to quit, and who left in June,
1861. Some of the lessees quit for the war, and at last, all left.
On June 29, 1864, Baird conveyed his interest to William F.
Johnston, Isaac M. Pennock, N. B. Sawyer, and William Bagley.
In December, 1864, a non-suit was taken in the ejectment suit
brought by Curtis against Baird. On September 17, 1864, William F. Johnston, Isaac M. Pennock, N. B. Sawyer, William Bagley and S. A. Baird instituted an action of ejectment in the Court
of Common Pleas of Warren County, against John Dark, Carrolton B. Curtis, and others, for the 250 acres of land, and the
island, claiming under the lease or agreement, made by McGuire
to Baird on November 26, 1859. The jury found for the plaintiffs in the Court of Common Pleas, and a judgment in their
favor was entered, from which judgment the defendants appealed
to the Supreme Court. The real question before the court on

the appeal, was whether or not such title vested in the lessee Baird, and his assignees, as would support an action of ejectment against those claiming under the original lessor or grantor. For the purpose of determining this question it became necessary for the Supreme Court to define the agreement, and to adjudicate the extent of the interests which passed thereby from the grantor to the grantee. The Supreme Court reversed the Court of Common Pleas, and held that the grant passed nothing for which ejectment would lie.

Sec. 6.—In *Kelly* v. *Keys,* 213 Pa. 296; 62 Atl. 911, analyzed under Chapter 7, syl. 1 is as follows:

"The grant of an exclusive privilege to go on land for purpose of prospecting for oil, the grantor to receive part of the oil mined, does not vest in the grantee any estate in the land or oil, but is merely a license or grant of an incorporeal hereditament, and the grantee, if he has never been in possession, cannot maintain an action of ejectment against the grantor or those claiming under him by a subsequent grant, although at the time of the ejectment oil was being produced in paying quantities."

Keys being the owner of a tract of land in Washington County, Pennsylvania, granted the same to Kelly for oil and gas purposes, and Kelly failing to exercise any right under the grant, Keys executed a subsequent lease to C. D. Greenlee and the Southern Oil Company, who proceeded to explore the property, and discovered oil in paying quantities. Thereupon Kelly, the original lessee, instituted an action of ejectment in the Court of Common Pleas of Washington County, against Keys, the landowner, C. D. Greenlee and the Southern Oil Company, lessees under the second lease. The verdict and judgment was rendered in favor of Kelly in the court below, from which judgment the defendants appealed to the Supreme Court. That court reversed the Court of Common Pleas, directed judgment to be rendered in favor of the defendants *non obstante veredicto.*

Sec. 7.—In *Steelsmith* v. *Gartlan,* 45 W. Va. 27; 29 S. E. 945; 44 L. R. A. 107, analyzed under Chapter 5, syl. 1 is as follows:

"A lease for the purpose of operating for oil and gas for the period of five years, and so much longer as oil or gas is found in paying quantities, on no other consideration that prospective oil royalty and gas rental, vests no present title in the lessee, except the mere right of exploration; but the title thereto, both as to the period of five years and the time thereafter, remains inchoate and contingent on the finding, under the explorations provided for in such lease, oil and gas in paying quantities."

Mrs. McGregor executed an oil and gas lease for a tract of land, under which lease Gartlan and others entered and made unsuccessful exploration by drilling one well, and then abandoned the premises. Subsequently Mrs. McGregor made a second lease to Steelsmith, claiming that the original lessee and his assignees had abandoned the search, and forfeited the lease. Steelsmith entered under the second lease and instituted a suit in equity in the Circuit Court of Ritchie County, West Virginia, to cancel the original lease on the grounds of forfeiture by abandonment. The defendants, the original lessee and his assignees, claimed a vested right to hold the lease during the period of five years, the term of the lease, upon the grounds that they had bored a well, and claimed this right without making further explorations. The Circuit Court sustained this position, and upon the cross-bill filed by the original lessees, cancelled the second—the Steelsmith—lease. From this decree Steelsmith appealed to the Court of Appeals, and that court reversed the Circuit Court, and cancelled the original lease.

Sec. 8.—In *Florence Oil & Refining Co.* v. *Orman,* 19 Colo. App. 79; 73 Pac. 628, analyzed under Chapter 5, the contest was between the claimants to two leases made by the State, under the first of which leases some prospecting had been done, but oil in paying quantities not found. The Court of Appeals of Colorado held that under an oil and gas lease until oil or gas was found in paying quantities title of the lessee was for exploration only. In this case the original lessee, not having discovered oil in paying quantities, and having abandoned his search, was held to have forfeited his lease by abandonment.

Sec. 9.—In *Rawlings* v. *Armel,* 70 Kan. 779; 79 Pac. 683, analyzed under Chapter 5, a lease was made by John H. Armel for oil and gas purposes. The lessee entered upon the premises demised and drilled two dry holes, from which the casing was pulled, the wells plugged, and all material, machinery and tools removed from the land and further explorations abandoned. The lessor subsequently brought suit to cancel the lease. The lessees claimed that they had a vested interest by reason of the explorations. The court below cancelled the lease, and the defendants appealed. The Supreme Court of Kansas affirmed the decision of the court below, and held that the lessee had the right to enter and explore, and to operate if oil or gas were discovered; that no estate in the land vested unless minerals should be found and worked; that until that time, the preliminary right was of such a character that it could be lost by abandonment within the lapse of time prescribed by the Statute of Limitations.

Sec. 10.—In *Murdock-West Co.* v. *Logan,* 69 Ohio St. 514; 69 N. E. 984, analyzed under Chapter 6, in a controversy between the holders of two leases the original lessee claiming the right to hold beyond the term, by payment of rental, without having discovered oil in paying quantities, the Supreme Court of Ohio, denying this right, held:

"The stipulation in the lease that the term shall continue 'as much longer thereafter as oil or gas shall be found in paying quantities' requires that oil or gas shall be actually discovered and produced in paying quantities within the term."

Sec. 11.—In *Lowther Oil Co.* v. *Miller-Sibley Oil Co.,* 53 W. Va. 501; 44 S. E. 433; 87 Am. St. Rep. 1027, analyzed under Chapter 5, the first point of the syllabus is as follows:

"Title under a lease only for production of oil and gas is inchoate and contingent, and for purposes of search only, until oil or gas is found. If not found, no estate vests in the lessee, and his right, whatever it is, ends when the unsuccessful search is abandoned. If found, then the right to produce becomes a vested right upon the terms of the lease."

This was a controversy between the claimants to two leases. The claimants to the original lease, having made explorations but not discovering oil in paying quantities, removed practically all the machinery and other property placed on the premises for exploration purposes. The landowner made a second lease, and upon appeal the Court of Appeals held the original lease had been forfeited by abandonment.

Sec. 12.—In *Huggins* v. *Daley,* 99 Fed. 606; 40 C. C. A. 12; 48 L. R. A. 320, analyzed under Chapter 5, in a contest between the claimants to two leases where the claimants to the first lease had made no explorations within the term, within which they were required to put down a well, the Circuit Court of Appeals for the Fourth Circuit held:

"By a course of decisions in West Virginia, which has established a rule of property, it is settled that an oil and gas lease in which the sole compensation to the lessor is a share of the product, is not a grant of property in the oil, or in the land, until oil is actually produced, but merely of a right of possession for the purpose of exploration and development; and there is also an implied if not an express covenant, for diligent search and operation."

This case was in equity, and the original lease was held to be void, and the bill filed by the claimant to the first lease was dismissed.

Sec. 13.—In *Lawson* v. *Kirchner,* 50 W. Va. 344; 40 S. E. 344, analyzed under Chapter 5, syl. 2 is as follows:

"An oil lease for oil and gas purposes is a conveyance or sale of an interest in land, conditional and contingent upon the discovery and reduction to possession of the oil or gas."

Rentals reserved in a lease or sale of infants' interests in the oil and gas in a tract of land made under an order of court, not having been paid by the lessee or purchaser, suit at law was instituted by the infants for the collection of the rentals. The lessee or purchaser denied any liability, claiming that he never entered into possession, and that he did not sign the lease or agreement of sale. Judgment was rendered in favor of the plaintiff by the Circuit Court, which judgment, on writ of error, was affirmed by the Court of Appeals.

Sec. 14.—In *Wagner* v. *Mallory*, 169 N. Y. 501; 62 N. E. 584, analyzed under Chapter 5, the Court of Appeals of New York, in determining the nature of the right of a lessee in an oil and gas lease, and whether it was real estate or personal property, held, syl. 1:

"A lessee acquires no title to oil until it has been taken from the ground under a lease granting him the exclusive right to mine and excavate oil for a specified period; one-eighth of the oil pumped and raised from the premises, to be delivered to the lessor."

In this case the owner of an oil and gas lease died intestate; the executor conveyed certain real estate to purchasers who claimed that the lease was included in this conveyance. The Court of Appeals held that such lease did not constitute real estate, and did not pass with the executor's deed.

Sec. 15.—In *Headley* v. *Hoopengarner*, 60 W. Va. 626; 55 S. E. 144, analyzed under Chapter 18, syl. 2 is as follows:

"The ordinary oil and gas lease, giving the lessee, for a term of years the right to mine and operate for oil and gas, is not a sale of the oil and gas in place, and the lessee has no vested estate therein, until it is discovered; but when found, the right to produce becomes a vested right and when extracted, the title vests in the lessee and the consideration or royalty paid for the privilege of search and production, is rent for the leased premises."

Sec. 16.—In *Dickey* v. *Coffeyville Vitrified Brick & Tile Co.*, 69 Kan. 106; 76 Pac. 398, analyzed under Chapter 22, the fourth point of the syllabus is as follows:

"Gas and oil leases are in a class by themselves. They are not leases in the ordinary sense. They are in the nature of a license with a conditional grant conveying the grantor's interest in the gas or oil conditioned that gas or oil is found in paying quantities. When gas or oil is found the right to produce it becomes a vested right, and the lessee will be protected in exercising agreeably to the terms of the contract.''

Sec. 17.—The Supreme Court of the State of Ohio has held that what is commonly designated an oil and gas lease is more than a mere license, and constitutes a lease.

Brown v. *Fowler*, 65 Ohio St. 507-21; 63 N. E. 76.
Woodland Oil Co. v. *Crawford*, 55 Ohio St. 161; 44 N. E.
   1093; 34 L. R. A. 62.
Martin v. *Jones*, 62 Ohio St. 519-25; 57 N. E. 238.

However, the distinction made by the Ohio Court between what it denominates a ''lease,'' and a writing which other courts have defined to be a ''license'' exercises little or no influence in determining the rights and privileges conferred by the ordinary oil and gas lease, as the conclusions reached by the Ohio Court as to the extent and character of these rights is in harmony with the decisions of the courts of the other oil producing States.

Sec. 18.—In *Venture Oil Co.* v. *Fretts*, 152 Pa. 451; 35 Atl. 732, analyzed under Chapter 5, the syllabus is as follows:

''A vested title cannot ordinarily be lost by abandonment in a less time than that fixed by the Statute of Limitation, unless there is satisfactory proof of an intention to abandon. A lease of a right to mine for oil, etc., stands on different ground. The title is inchoate and for purposes of exploration only until oil is found. If it is not found, no estate vests in the lessee, and his title, whatever it is, ends when the unsuccessful search is abandoned. If oil is found, the right to produce becomes a vested right, and the lessee will be protected in exercising it in accordance with the terms and conditions of his contract.

''An oil lease contained a grant of a right to mine for and remove oil for a fixed period of twenty years, at a royalty of one-eighth of the oil so mined and removed. *Held*, that the right of the lessee was to explore for, and determine the existence of, oil under the land, and if none was found his right ceased when the exploration was finished and the lot abandoned.''

Sec. 19.—In *Kansas Nat. Gas. Co.* v. *Board of Comm'rs of Neosho County,* 75 Kan. 335; 89 Pac. 750 (March 9, 1907), syls. 1, 2, 3 are as follows:

"1. An oil and gas lease conferring on the lessee the right to enter on, operate for, and produce oil and gas upon land described, and containing no provision indicating otherwise, grants a license to enter and explore, and if oil or gas is found, the right to produce and sever it.

2. Until mineral of the kind described is actually produced and severed so that it becomes personalty, the lessee has no title to any specified portion, but the legal title and the possession of the entire mass and volume remains in the owner of the strata in which it is confined.

3. Chapter 244, p. 456, of the Laws of 1897, relating to the taxation of separately owned mineral rights, has no application, except when the right of title to minerals in place has been severed from the right to the title to the remainder of the land, and has become vested in a person other than the one having the right of title to the remainder of the land."

The Kansas Natural Gas Company instituted in the District Court of Neosho County, Kansas, its suit against the Board of Commissioners of Neosho County. The plaintiff was the assignee of an oil and gas lease on the land in Neosho County. The County officials undertook to tax separately from the land itself, whatever mining rights the lease created. Upon non-payment of taxes the Treasurer was about to enforce collection by sale of so much of the "mineral reserve" of the land described in the lease as might be necessary for the payment of the taxes. Plaintiff brought suit to enjoin the sale and annul the tax. The lease in question provided that in consideration of one dollar and the covenants of the parties, the lessor leased to the lessee the exclusive right for ten years to enter upon, operate for, and procure oil and gas upon the lands described. The lessees agreed to deliver to the lessor one-eighth of the oil realized, or at the lessor's option to pay cash for it. Upon the discovery of gas the lessor was to have enough for domestic purposes, free of charge, the lessee to take the remainder, including gas from oil wells, and agreed to pay $50.00 per year if gas should be marketed from wells producing gas only. Provision was made for terminating the lessee's rights, and for continuing them in force. No oil or gas well had been drilled, and the mineral reserves of the land, if any existed, were entirely undeveloped. Judgment was rendered for the defendant, and the plaintiff brought error. The Supreme Court reversed the District Court. Upon the question of the construction of the lease in question the court cited the following cases:

Zinc Co. v. *Freeman,* 68 Kan. 691; 75 Pac. 995.
Federal Betterment Co. v. *Blaes,* — Kan. —; 88 Pac. 555.
Ringer v. *Quigg,* — Kan. —; 87 Pac. 724.

Sec. 20.—In *Poe* v. *Ulrey,* 233 Ill. 56; 84 N. E. 46, analyzed under Chapter 14, syl. 2 is as follows:

"A grant of oil and gas on certain land is a grant of such oil and gas as the grantee may find there, and he is not vested with any title in the oil or gas until it is actually found, since, on account of their wandering nature, and their liability to escape or be withdrawn to other lands, they are not subject to absolute ownership."

Sec. 21.—In *Moore* v. *Sawyer,* 167 Fed. 826, analyzed under Chapter 16, paragraph 3 of the head notes is as follows:

"An instrument in terms, granting all the oil, gas, coal and asphaltum under certain described land, but which was denominated a lease had a definite term of fifteen years, and provided, in addition to a cash payment of $50.00, for the payment of a royalty on all produced, *held,* not a conveyance in fee of the minerals in place, but merely a lease."

Sec. 22.—In *Backer* v. *Penn Lubricating Co.,* 162 Fed. 627; 89 C. C. A. 419 (June 18, 1908) Circuit Court of Appeals, Sixth Circuit, the first, second and fourth points of the head notes are as follows:

"1. An oil lease in ordinary form giving the lessee the exclusive right to explore for, produce and sell oil from the land on payment of a royalty, does not vest in him the title to the oil in place.

2. Such a lessee, however, has a right of action for damages against one who invades his exclusive right by going upon

the land during the term of his lease, without his consent, and drilling wells and removing and selling oil therefrom.

4. In an action by an oil lessee for damages against one who entered upon and took oil from the leased premises, an answer, alleging that defendants' entry was peaceable and made in good faith under a lease which defendant believed to be valid, is not subject to a general demurrer, since such good faith may at least affect the extent of defendant's liability for damages.''

Becker filed his petition under the Kentucky Code of Civil Procedure in the Circuit Court of the United States for the Eastern District of Kentucky, against Penn Lubricating Company, alleging that one Duncan and wife, on November 11, 1902, gave to plaintiff an oil lease upon a tract of land in Wayne County, Kentucky, by an express provision of which the plaintiff was granted the exclusive right to operate or drill thereon for petroleum, gas, or other minerals, for the term of twenty years, and so much longer as such product should be produced in paying quantities, upon payment to Duncan of 10 per cent. of the petroleum extracted, and $25.00 for each gas well; plaintiff agreeing to drill a well within six months, or in lieu thereof pay Duncan $50.00 per year until work should be commenced. The petition alleged that plaintiff, by virtue of the lease, acquired a leasehold estate in the land, by virtue of which he had the sole and exclusive right to enter upon and explore the land for oil and gas, to drill wells for oil and gas; to extract and market the oil and gas therefrom, and to sell and dispose of the oil in and under the tract, excepting the one-tenth, to be paid to Duncan by way of royalty. The petition further alleged that the plaintiff lawfully entered under the lease for the purpose of exploring and developing for oil and gas; and that after such entry, with full knowledge of the plaintiff's lease, and of his rights thereunder, defendant forceably and wrongfully, and against the will and over the protest of both plaintiff and Duncan, entered upon the land, erected derrick and drilled for oil thereon, and extracted therefrom and converted to its own use, upward of 10,000 barrels of petroleum. The petition alleged that the oil so taken by defendant, over and above the one-tenth royalty belonging to Duncan, belonged to and was the property of plaintiff.

The answer alleged that in 1895, Duncan and wife gave to
one Williams an oil lease for twenty years, or as long as oil, gas
or minerals could be obtained in paying quantities upon the land
in question, upon the payment of royalties; that in the year 1896,
and within the time limited therefor by the lease Williams drilled
a well which proved unproductive; that in the year 1902, defendant, who had meanwhile become the owner of the Williams lease,
re-entered and continued the drilling of wells with the knowledge
and consent of Duncan, but failing to find oil in paying quantities,
temporarily left, with the intention, known to Duncan, of return-
ing and continuing the developments; that during defendant's
temporary absence plaintiff obtained his lease with knowledge of
defendant's prior lease and developments under it; and of defendant's intention to continue such development, and for the
purpose of circumventing defendant; that the latter, in pursuance of its original intention re-entered peaceably in 1903, and
from that date until 1905, drilled the wells and produced the oil
referred to in plaintiff's petition, in good faith, and in the belief
that it had an exclusive, prior and superior right as against
plaintiff; that plaintiff made no entry, at least till after defendant's entry in 1903; that to prevent plaintiff from forcibly excluding defendant from the premises, and from himself forceably
drilling wells and producing the oil therefrom, defendant, by suit
in the State Circuit Court, against the plaintiff herein, obtained
judgment, that defendant had a right superior to plaintiff's in
the development and exploration of the premises under the lease,
and perpetually restraining plaintiff herein from entering on
the premises for the purpose of drilling or mining for oil, gas
or other minerals; that the Kentucky Court of Appeals reversed
the judgment of the Circuit Court, holding that defendant herein
had abandoned its right to operate under its lease; that the Circuit Court refused to delay restitution of the premises until an
accounting could be had of profits and improvements made under
defendant's occupancy; that an appeal from said refusal was then
pending in the Kentucky Court of Appeals, and undetermined,
such pendency being urged in abatement of plaintiff's suit; that
when defendant surrendered possession under the judgment of
the Kentucky State Court, it left thereon six producing oil wells,

which had cost defendant, and which enhanced the value of the premises, more than the value of the oil, produced by defendant therefrom; that the plaintiff took possession and had the benefit of all these improvements, thereby escaping the risk and expense of development, and thereby obtaining a profit greater than the value of the oil obtained by defendant, which production cost the latter more than its value; that all defendant's acts complained of were done in good faith and belief in its rightful conduct. The answer denied that the plaintiff was the owner of the oil in question, and denied the latter's right to recovery therefor. Defendant asked judgment on its counter-claim for the value of the improvements made by it in excess of the value of the oil taken.

The plaintiff demurred to the answer, and the court carried the demurrer back to the plaintiff's petition, and held that the latter did not state a cause of action, and on plaintiff's declining to amend, entered judgment dismissing the petition. The sufficiency of the answer and counter-claim was not considered by the Circuit Court. From this judgment the plaintiff obtained a writ of error, and the Circuit Court of Appeals reversed the judgment of the Circuit Court, remanded the cause with directions to over-rule the demurrer, both as affecting the petition and relating to the answer and counter-claim. Upon the question of the defendant's entry and the taking of the oil in good faith, the court held:

"The rule is well established that the ultimate measure of recovery against a trespasser, whether the subject of the taking be timber or minerals, must be determined largely upon the question of good or bad faith of the taking."

Upon the question of the nature of the title of a lessee under an oil and gas lease, and in support of its conclusions thereon, the court cited:

Steelsmith v. *Gartlan*, 45 W. Va. 27; 29 S. E. 978.
Oil Co. v. *Fretts*, 152 Pa. 451; 25 Atl. 732.
Plummer v. *Iron Co.*, 160 Pa. 483; 28 Atl. 853.
Huggins v. *Daley*, 99 Fed. 606; 40 C. C. A. 12.
Tennessee Oil, etc., Co. v. *Brown*, 131 Fed. 696; 65 C. C. A. 524.

Upon the right of a recovery against one who invades the premises claimed by a lessee under an oil and gas lease, the court cited:

Haven & Chase Oil Co. v. *Jordan*, 13 Ky. L. Rep. 878.
Breyfogle v. *Woods*, 15 Ky. L. Rep. 782.
Logan Nat. Gas & Fuel Co. v. *Great Southern Gas & Oil Co.*, 126 Fed. 623; 61 C. C. A. 359.
Great Southern Gas & Oil Co. v. *Logan Nat. Gas & Fuel Co.*, (C. C. A.), 155 Fed. 114.

Sec. 23.—In *Staley & Barnsdale* v. *Derden*, (Tex. Civ. App.) 121 S. W. 1136 (Oct. 16, 1909) syl. 1 is as follows:

"1. Plaintiff conveyed to defendant the oil and other mineral estate in certain land, with the right to drill wells, lay pipe, etc., for the term of 25 years, and as long thereafter as oil, etc., should be found in paying quantities; it being stipulated that the grant was not intended as a franchise merely, but as a conveyance of the property for the purposes stated. As part of the consideration defendant agreed to give plaintiff one-eighth of the oil produced, the same to be delivered to him in the pipelines free of charge. *Held*, that the contract was a conveyance of interest in land, so that the County Court had no jurisdiction to compel defendant by injunction to handle oil to be thereafter severed from the land in a given way, and to deliver one-eighth of it to plaintiff each month."

W. L. Derden instituted an action in the County Court of Navarro County, Texas, against Staley & Barnsdall for an injunction. The judge of the court entered, in chambers, an order restraining Staley & Barnsdall from using and converting the one-eighth part of the product of the oil from the lands of Derden, the same being described in the plaintiff's petition, until the further order of the court, and requiring defendants, pending the litigation, to file monthly statements and requiring them to connect and impound a full one-eighth of the oil produced each month into a single tank located on the premises, free of leaks, and that would hold the oil, and also tanks as was then connected with pipelines of the Navarro Refining Company, which tank the defendants were directed to point out to the plaintiff, W. L. Derden.

After the oil was so delivered the defendants were directed to permit the plaintiff either to remove the one-eighth of the production from the premises in wagons, or by having it run into pipelines of the Navarro Refining Company without interference on the part of defendants.

The defendants filed a plea to the jurisdiction of the court, which was overruled. The plaintiff also asked a recovery from Staley of the sum of $600.00, the value of the oil converted, and for damages done the plaintiff by violation of certain provisions of the oil contract entered into with him, the total amount claimed being $1,000. Barnsdall, after the contract was made, became a partner of Staley and made himself a party defendant to the suit. The terms of the lease are substantially set out in the first point of the syllabus. From the order awarding the injunction the defendants appealed to the Court of Civil Appeals and that court construed the contract of lease to be a sale of an interest in the land, reversed the County Court and dismissed the plaintiff's petition, citing:

Denavides v. *Hunt,* 79 Tex. 383; 15 S. W. 396.
Ore Co. v. *Colquitt,* 28 Tex. Civ. App. 292; 69 S. W. 160.

Sec. 24.—*In O'Neil* v. *Sun Co.,* — Tex. Civ. App. —; 123 S. W. 172 (Nov. 17, 1909) on motion for re-hearing (Dec. 8, 1909) syls. 1, 2, 3, 5 are as follows:

"1. A contract between the owner of land and an oil operator provided that the owner thereby granted, etc., to the operator, all right, title and interest to the oil and gas under the land with a right to enter to drill for oil and gas and operate the wells, and required the operator to drill within a certain time. *Held,* that the contract was not a conveyance of the oil under the ground but merely authorized the operator to exploit the land and acquire title to the oil upon extracting it from the ground, which right was the subject of contract.

2. A contract between the owner of land and the lessee provided that the owner granted all right to the oil and gas thereunder, with the right to enter and drill for oil; the lessee to drill a well within ten days, and when the first well was completed, if it was a paying well, to commence a second well within ten days, and on its completion, if paying, to commence a third well with-

in a certain time. The lease further provided that the lessee
might re-lease all or any part of the tract after completing the
first well, thereby relieving itself of all obligations to the part
released, and on re-leasing any part of the tract, could continue
operations on the part on which it may have drilled any wells,
retaining such part of the tract as might be necessary for operating wells, drilling or then drilled; the amount to be retained to
be based on one-third of the whole tract leased for each well
already drilled or drilling. It was provided that the discharge
of the lessee's obligation to drill the first well should be a sufficient consideration to support the options contained therein. The
lease was to continue in force for one year, and as long thereafter as oil was found in paying quantities, and the lessor was to
receive one-sixth of the oil produced. *Held*, that while the lessee
had the exclusive right to drill any number of additional wells
on unre-leased parts of the tract during the year, if the first well
was non-paying, he was not bound to do so, and need not drill
more than three in any event, either of which could be drilled on
any unre-leased part of the tract without regard to the location
of wells on adjoining tracts, so that where the lessor, to protect
the oil under the tract from exhaustion from a well on adjoining
tracts drilled a well on an unre-leased part without the lessee's
consent, the oil therefrom belonged to the lessee, to be appor-
tioned under the terms of the lease.

3. The lessee could release any part of the tract it desired;
but since it need not drill any wells after drilling the first non-
paying well, its failure to do so, or its abandonment of a well
drilled would not be an abandonment of its exclusive right to drill
on any unre-leased part during the year, nor would the re-lease
of a third of the tract be an abandonment of the whole tract for
drilling purposes; that the provisions of the lease privileged the
lessee to conduct operations on the part of the tract on which it
may have drilled wells upon the release of a part only referring
to the re-leased land.

5. An oil lease gave the lessee the exclusive right to drill
on the land during a certain period and gave the lessor a one-
sixth interest in the oil produced; the lessee to bear the cost of
production. The lessor, without the lessee's consent, drilled a
producing well on the tract and the lessee sued upon the contract to recover the possession of the well and a receiver was
appointed by mutual agreement without prejudice to the contention of either party, to operate the well. The lessee recovered
on the basis of the contract; the lessor being allowed the cost
of drilling the well. *Held*, that since the lessee based its suit on
the contract and the lessor did not occupy the position of a mere

trespasser in the action, the costs of the receivership, being the expenses of production, should be charged against the lessee's share of the proceeds of the oil so as to make the recovery conform to the terms of the contract.''

On February 23, 1907, John O'Neil made an oil and gas lease to the Sun Company for a tract of land in Harris County, Texas, which lease contained in substance the provisions mentioned in the second point of the syllabus. About February 28, 1907, under the lease the Sun Company began a well on the southeast corner of the tract. About March 15, 1907, before the first well, which proves to be dry, was completed lessee began a second well just south of the north line, completing the same about April 25, 1907. The second well produced about 60 or 70 barrels of oil per day, and this was a paying well, though not a large producer. After the lease was made, or about the same time, a well known as the Donohue well was begun on the adjoining tract near the northeast corner of the acre in question, which proved to be a very large producer. Soon after this well came in—early in June— O'Neil, the lessor, began to drill the well in dispute in the northeast corner of the acre, and near the Donohue well and finished it about July 6th or 7th. This well produced 600 or 700 barrels per day and continued to produce until some time in October, when it was abandoned, having produced something over $13,000 worth of oil. The Sun Company brought suit against O'Neil in the District Court of Harris County, Texas claiming the title and right to the well and the production therefrom and seeking a mandatory injunction for possession. The court turned the well over to the receiver by whom it was operated for several months until it quit producing. The proceeds of the sale of the oil, after deducting all expenses amounting to $9,554.35, was invested in certain securities by consent of the litigants.

The case was tried and the trial court eliminated all issues except the reasonable costs incurred by O'Neil in sinking the well and charged the jury that from five-sixths—the share of the Sun Oil Company—of the proceeds, they should deduct the cost of putting down the well, and give plaintiff a verdict for the balance. Judgment was rendered upon this verdict, and the defendant, O'Neil, appealed.

The appellant, lessor, assigned as error the action of the court in charging the receipts of the receivership with the expenses thereof, which contention the appellate court held meant that all the expenses incurred by the receiver should have come out of the Sun Company's share. The appellate court held that inasmuch as the theory upon which the recovery by plaintiff was allowed was, that O'Neil did not occupy the position of a rank trespasser which was entertained by the trial court allowing him the cost of sinking the well, that it would follow that the oil produced from the well should be governed by the terms of the contract and stand for apportionment in accordance with it, O'Neil being interested in the contract and in the subject matter thereof, stood, in equity, in a more favorable light than a mere trespasser, and so the court treated him. The Sun Company founded its suit upon the contract, and, the appellate court held, ought to be willing to abide by it as to all parties thereto; and that when it recovered this oil, or the proceeds thereof, it did so under the contract, and the terms of the contract should determine the respective rights of the parties to the proceeds; and that this being so, the defendants assignment of error should be sustained; and in that regard the judgment was modified and thereupon the expenses of the receivership were charged to the Sun Company's share of the oil.

Sec. 25.—In *Barnsdall* v. *Bradford Gas Co.*, — Pa. —; 74 Atl. 207 (June 22, 1909) the syllabus is as follows:

"1. A contract simply giving the right to take ore from a mine, no estate being granted, confers a mere 'license' and licensee acquires no right to the ore until separated from the freehold; but an instrument demising land for mining purposes for a designated term of years at a fixed rental, and giving the right to erect all necessary buildings is a lease, not merely a mining license.

2. An instrument granting, demising and leasing certain land for the purpose solely of mining and operating for oil, gas, and other minerals, laying pipelines, building tanks and structures to take any of the products is a lease conveying an interest in the land and not merely a license to enter and operate for oil or gas.

3. Ejectment may be maintained by a lessee though he has not entered into possession, where, under his lease he is entitled to the oil and gas and to possession of the premises to remove the same against a third person who claims adversely to lessor.''

William Barnsdall, Jr., instituted in the Court of Common Pleas of Potter County, Pennsylvania, an action of ejectment against the Bradford Gas Company. The plaintiff claimed under an oil and gas lease dated November 8, 1906, in the usual form and for the term of ten years, and as much longer as the premises were operated for oil or gas. The consideration was the delivery in pipelines to the credit of the lessor of one-eighth of the oil produced. The lessee never went into possession of the premises, and brought an action to recover possession from a third party who did not claim under the lessor. The Bradford Gas Company resisted a recovery upon the ground that the lease upon which the plaintiff relied conveyed no interest in the land but was simply a license for the purpose of entering and operating for oil and gas and therefore did not convey a title sufficient to sustain an action of ejectment, the plaintiff never having been in possession. The plaintiff contended that the agreement between him and the lessor conveyed a corporeal interest in the land and was not a mere license to drill and operate for oil; and that being an interest in the land, and he having a right to possession by virtue of his lease, he could recover the possession of the premises in an action of ejectment. The material parts of the lease relied upon by Barnsdall as giving him a right to possession, were as follows:

"The said party of the first part, for and in consideration of one dollar * * * and with the covenants and agreements hereinafter given on the part of the party of the second part * * * has granted, demised, leased and let, and by these presents do grant, demise, lease and let unto the said party of the second part * * * for the sole and only purpose of mining and operating for oil, gas and other minerals, and of laying pipelines and all buildings, tanks, stations and structures thereon, to take any of the said products on the said tract of land * * * containing one hundred acres, more or less * * *"

Upon the trial in the Court of Common Pleas a verdict was

rendered for plaintiff, and the court rendered judgment for defendant *non obstante veredicto*. Plaintiff appealed and the Supreme Court reversed the Court of Common Pleas, citing:

Kitchen v. *Smith,* 101 Pa. 452.
Duke v. *Hague,* 107 Pa. 57.
Brown v. *Beecher,* 120 Pa. 590-603; 15 Atl. 608-9.
Messimer's App., 92 Pa. 168.
Long's App., 92 Pa. 171.
Williams v. *Fowler,* 201 Pa. 336; 50 Atl. 969.

Sec. 26.—In *Waterford Oil & Gas. Co.* v. *Shipman,* 233 Ill. 9; 84 N. E. 53, analyzed under Chapter 14, syl. 2 is as follows:

"2. Oil and gas while in the earth, unlike solid minerals, are not the subject of ownership distinct from the soil, and the grant of the oil and gas, therefore, is a grant not of the oil that is in the ground, but of such a part thereof as the grantee may find, and passes nothing that can be the subject of ejectment or other real action."

CHAPTER 4.

CONSIDERATION FOR THE LEASE.

Sec. 1.—The consideration for an oil and gas lease is the amount the lessee pays to the lessor, if in money, or what he covenants to do, or what is provided he is to do, for the license or privilege of entering upon the premises within a stipulated time to explore for oil or gas.

Brown v. *Fowler.*
Brown v. *Ohio Oil Co.,* 65 Ohio St. 507; 63 N. E. 76.
Friend v. *Mallory,* 52 W. Va. 53; 43 S. E. 114.
Trees v. *Eclipse Oil Co.,* 47 W. Va. 107; Op. 104-5; 34 S. E. 933.
Elk Fork Oil & Gas Co. v. *Jennings,* 84 Fed. 839. Syl. 4.
Brewster v. *Lanyon Zinc Co.,* 140 Fed. 801, syl. 3; 72 C. C. A. 213.

Central Ohio Gas & Fuel Co. v. *Eckert,* 70 Ohio St. 127-135;
   71 N. E. 281.

Allegheny Oil Co. v. *Snyder,* 106 Fed. 764-767, syl. 1; 45
   C. C. A. 604-608.

Dill v. *Fraze,* 169 Ind. 53; 79 N. E. 971.

Eclipse Oil Co. v. *South Penn Oil Co.,* 47 W. Va. 84; 34 S. E.
   293.

Lowther Oil Co. v. *Miller-Sibley Co.,* 53 W. Va. 501; 44 S. E.
   433; 87 Am. St. Rep. 1027.

Sec. 2.—The consideration for the license to enter upon the
premises demised for the purpose of exploration for oil and gas,
may be only nominal, or the consideration may be by way of
stipulation for entry upon premises other than those demised
for the purpose of exploration for oil and gas. Where the consideration is paid, although it may be only nominal, such consideration will be upheld by the courts as a sufficient consideration,
not only for the license granted but for all the other terms and
conditions of the lease, including the right to surrender. The
consideration, if paid, controls as to questions of mutuality, and
in the absence of an express covenant to pay rental or commutation money, at the expiration of the exploration period, the grant
will be held to be an option whereby the lessee has the right to
preserve the grant by the payment within the time stipulated to
the lessor the rental or commutation money. By such payments
the lessee can preserve the option, subject to the right of surrender, where there is a surrender clause, (See Chapter 14) during the term of the lease. Such leases are not void for want of
mutuality, and the lessor has not the right at the expiration of
the exploration period to refuse to accept payment of rental or
commutation money and declare a forfeiture. The lessee, however, has the right to cease further payment, and thereupon the
lease becomes voidable, and in the absence of an express covenant
to pay such commutation money or rental the lessor cannot
recover such rental against the lessee. Where the lease contains
an express covenant to explore or pay the rental or commutation
money, and provides that the lease shall be void for non-payment
thereof, a failure to pay such rental within the stipulated time
gives the lessor the right to terminate the lease by declaring a

forfeiture. In such case the lessor may recover rentals accruing prior to such declaration, the forfeiture clause being for his bene- fit, or, he may waive the forfeiture, and, subject to the right of surrender, collect the installments of rental or commutation mon- ey from the lessee during the term.

Sec. 3.—The consideration which the lessee pays for the lease must not be confounded with the consideration which the lessor is to receive for the oil and gas. The cash consideration, bonus, or whatever it may be called, paid or agreed to be paid by lessee for the lease, is a consideration for the exclusive privilege of entry for exploration. The rental or commutation money is the consideration which the lessor receives for permitting the lessee to further hold his exclusive right of entry for explora- tion. These payments, by whatever name they may be called, do not vest any title in or right to the oil or gas in place. As long as no developments are made resulting in the discovery of oil or gas by lessee, his lease remains a mere privilege to enter and search. When lessee discovers oil or gas in paying quantities, his right to produce them becomes a vested right. He is then, for the first time, authorized and obligated to pay the considera- tion to lessor for the exclusive vested right to produce the oil and gas, the true consideration for such minerals being the royalty of oils and cash rental for gas, as the case may be.

Sec. 4. As long as oil or gas is not found and produced in paying quantities, the lessor has not parted with any right or in- terest in the oil and gas, for which, up to such time, he has re- ceived no consideration whatever. When lessee successfully de- velops the premises, and discovers oil or gas in paying quanti- ties, his right to produce these minerals becomes a vested right. It is no longer a mere privilege. The duty to produce and deliver or pay to the lessor his share or interest in the oil or gas devolves upon the lessee.

Sec. 5.—Where the consideration is not paid, or where no cash consideration is provided for in the lease, and where noth- ing has been done by the lessee, and where there is a provision that lessee may at any time surrender the lease and be relieved of all obligations, such lease is void for want of consideration and mutuality. Even where there is a clause authorizing the lessee to surrender the lease to the lessor and be relieved of all liability, past or future, where such lease is for a good consideration, although nominal, and a provision is made for payment of rental or commutation money for delay in explorations, such lease is not void for want of mutuality, but is an option, and the lessee has the right within the exploration or rental period to pay the commutation money or rental and preserve the lease, which the lessee may continue to do, subject to the right of surrender, during the term.

Sec. 6.—In *Brown* v. *Fowler,* and *Brown* v. *Ohio Oil Co.*, 65 Ohio St. 507; 63 N. E. 76 (February 4, 1902) syl. 1 is as follows:

"1. An oil and gas lease with a granting clause, a habendum clause, a condition subsequent, and a surrender clause, was given in consideration of $1 paid. *Held,* that the $1 so paid was paid for the whole lease, and applied to each clause thereof, so that there was a sufficient consideration, not only for the lease, but for each clause and every part thereof."

Catharine Fowler and husband executed on December 8, 1896, an oil and gas lease to one Snyder for a tract of land in Harrison County, Ohio, in consideration of one dollar, the receipt of which was acknowledged, for the term of two years from the date thereof, and as long thereafter as oil or gas should be found in paying quantities, not exceeding in the whole the term of twenty-five years from the date of the lease. The lease provided that in case no well should be drilled on the premises within twelve months from the date thereof it should become null and void, unless the lessee should pay for further delay at the rate of one dollar per acre at or before the end of each year thereafter until a well should be drilled; that the lessee should have the right at any time to surrender the lease to lessor for cancellation, after which all payments or liabilities to accrue under and by virtue of its terms should cease and determine and the lease become absolutely null and void. Catharine Fowler and husband, on November 26, 1898, claimed that the lease was void and on that day executed another lease of the same premises to one George Gillmor. On December 9, 1898, Gillmor notified the holders of the first lease not to do any work on the premises.

On December 15, 1898, the assignees of Snyder commenced an action against Gillmor and Fowler, the lessors, to enjoin them from drilling on the premises for oil and gas, and these defendants filed a cross-petition to enjoin the plaintiffs from operating on the premises. The facts and conclusions of law in the Circuit Court upon appeal, as far as pertinent, were as follows:

No oil or gas well had been drilled by lessee, Snyder, or his assignee, on the premises within two years from the date of their lease, and no oil or gas had been found thereon, nor had said lessee, or his assignees, taken possession or done any work on said premises until about November 10, 1898, when the Scio Oil & Gas Company, then owning said lease began to place on the lease materials for the erection of a derrick, and continued to work thereon from time to time, and had erected thereon a rig for the purpose of drilling for oil and gas, prior to December 8, 1898, but had not begun to drill. No well had been completed on said leased premises, nor could be drilled and completed by the 8th day of December, 1898, nor had oil or gas been found thereon prior to December 8, 1898. The Scio Oil & Gas Company, after tendering the rental to one of the lessors, deposited it in the Scio Bank, at Scio, Ohio, on December 1, 1898, to the credit of the lessors, to pay for the further delay in drilling for two years after December 8, 1897. The lessors refused to accept said sum of $40.00 so deposited in payment for further delay and the money remained on deposit in said Bank. On November 26, 1898, said Catharine Fowler and husband claimed that said lease was void because no well had been drilled, and because a well could not be drilled within the two years mentioned in the lease. Thereupon the said Fowlers executed another lease for the same premises to one George Gillmor, who had full knowledge of the nature, effect and terms of the Snyder lease. The Circuit Court held the first lease invalid and the second one valid and rendered judgment in favor of the Fowlers and Mr. Gillmor. From this decision the holders of the first lease appealed. The Supreme

Court held that the one dollar was a sufficient consideration for the grant, and that this consideration was paid for the whole lease, and further held that the term of the lease could not be extended by payment of the rentals, and affirmed the judgment of the Circuit Court.

Sec. 7.—In *Friend* v. *Mallory*, 52 W. Va. 53; 43 S. E. 114 (Nov. 29, 1902) syl. 1 is as follows:

"1. An oil and gas lease contained the following provision: 'That this lease shall become null and void, and all rights hereunder shall cease and determine unless a well shall be completed on the said premises within three months from the date hereof, or unless the lessee shall pay at the rate of twenty-two dollars and twenty-five cents quarterly in advance for each additional three months such completion is delayed from the time above mentioned for the completion of such well until a well is completed; and it is agreed that the completion of such well shall be and operate as a full liquidation of all rental under this provision during the remainder of the term of this lease. Such payments may be direct to lessor or deposited to their credit in the Wirt County Bank,' and the further provision that the lessee 'Shall have the privilege at any time to remove all machinery and fixtures placed on said premises, and further shall have the right at any time to surrender this lease to first parties for cancellation, after which all payments and liabilities to accrue under and by virtue of its terms shall cease and determine, and this lease become absolutely null and void.' *Held*, that deposit of a payment by the lessee in such bank to the credit of the lessor on or before the date such payment would fall due, is a sufficient payment to lessor, and it is immaterial whether it is paid in lawful money, or by check, draft, or otherwise; and, *held* further, the lessor cannot avoid such lease or declare a forfeiture thereof within the time for which he has received the stipulated rental, and a lease executed to a third party within such time intended as an act of forfeiture, is void."

Robinsons executed, on March 23, 1900, to Mallory Brothers & Stewart, in consideration of $22.25 cash, an oil and gas lease for a tract of 88 acres of land in Wirt County, West Virginia, for the term of three years, and as long thereafter as oil or gas or either of them should be produced from the premises by the lessees. The lease contained the following provision:

"Provided, however, that this lease shall become null and void, and all rights hereunder shall cease and determine unless a well shall be completed on said premises within three months from the date hereof, or unless the lessee shall pay at the rate of twenty-two dollars and twenty-five cents quarterly in advance, for each additional three months such completion is delayed from the time above mentioned for the completion of such well until a well is completed; and it is agreed that the completion of such well shall be and operate as a full liquidation of all rental under this provision during the remainder of the term of this lease. Such payments may be direct to the lessor or deposited to their credit in the Wirt County Bank."

The lease also contained the following provision:

"It is agreed that the second party shall have the privilege of using sufficient water from the premises to run all necessary machinery, and at any time to remove all machinery and fixtures placed on said premises, and further shall have the right at any time to surrender this lease to first parties for cancellation, after which all payments and liabilities to accrue under and by virtue of its terms shall cease and determine and this lease become absolutely null and void."

Under this lease the lessees deposited in the Wirt County Bank the rentals, on September 20, 1900, on December 20, 1900, March 22, 1901, and June 6, 1901. On June 29, 1901, lessors directed a letter to the agent of Mallory Brothers & Stewart, notifying him to notify Mallory Brothers & Stewart that they, the lessors, had elected and decided to treat the lease held by them on their property forfeited, and that they had re-leased it to other parties; and that they would not receive any further payments under the lease. On July 1, 1901, the Robinsons leased the same property, in consideration of $125.00 to F. J. Friend, for the term of one year, and as long thereafter as oil or gas should be produced in paying quantities. On July 23, 1901, Friend, the second lessee, presented his bill in equity to the judge of the Circuit Court of Wirt County, for an injunction against Mallory Brothers & Stewart to enjoin them from operating the premises for oil and gas under the lease of March 23, 1900, the bill praying that the lease be cancelled as a cloud upon the title of Friend. An injunction was granted as prayed for. On the same day Mallory Brothers & Stewart presented their bill in equity to the same judge, praying for an injunction to restrain and enjoin Friend and Robinson from operating the premises for oil and gas, or from setting up or claiming under any lease or pretended paper executed by Robinson to Friend, and further praying for the cancellation of the Friend lease. An injunction was also awarded to plaintiffs to this bill. Friend in his bill claimed that the lease of March 23, 1900, was at the will of the lessee, and therefore none of its terms and conditions could bind the lessors for the full term, or deprive them of their power to terminate the lease. Upon hearing it was admitted that all rentals had been paid to the Robinsons by the original lessees, up to the 23d day of June, 1901, without the application of the deposit of $22.25 made on June 6, 1901. The Circuit Court decided the injunctions in favor of Mallory Brothers & Stewart against Friend, who appealed to the Court of Appeals. That court affirmed the decree of the Circuit Court.

Sec. 8.—In *Eclipse Oil Co.* v. *South Penn Oil Co.*, 47 W. Va. 84; 34 S. E. 933 (November 28, 1899) the syllabus is as follows:

"1. 'If one party may terminate an estate at his will, so may the other. The right to terminate is mutual.' *Cowan* v. *Iron Co.*, 3 S. E. 120; 83 Va. 347.

2. An executory gas and oil lease, which provides for its surrender at any time, without payment of rent or fulfilment of any of the covenants on the part of the lessee, creates a mere right of entry at will, which may be terminated by the lessor at any time before it is executed by the lessee.

3. The execution of a new lease to other lessees, and possession thereunder, renders such prior executory lease invalid.

4. An executory lease that is unfair, unjust or unreasonable, will not be enforced in equity.

5. If one party to a contract is not bound to do the act which forms the consideration for the promise, undertaking, or agreement of the other, the contract is void for want of mutuality."

On May 11, 1897, Henry Garner made an oil and gas lease
to H. J. and J. C. Stolze. The lease recited that it was made "for
and in consideration of the covenants and agreements hereinafter
mentioned," and also contained the following provision:

"The parties of the second part agree to drill one test well
on the above described premises within six months from the
execution of this lease, or, in lieu thereof, thereafter pay to the
said party of the first part one dollar per acre per annum until
such well is completed; and if said test well is not completed
within six months from the above date, or rental paid thereon,
this lease is null and void, and not further binding on either
party. And it is further agreed that the second parties, their
heirs or assigns, shall have the right at any time to surrender
up this lease, and be released from all moneys due and conditions unfulfilled; then and from that time this lease and agreement shall be null and void and no longer binding on either
party."

There was nothing paid by the lessees, nor did they do anything toward development or exploration. The lessees did not
promise to do anything by way of development or payment of
rental. The lease was assigned by the lessees to the Eclipse Oil
Company. On June 19, 1898, Henry Garner, lessor, again leased
the property to J. A. Phillips, who assigned the lease to the South
Penn Oil Company. This company began explorations, whereupon the Eclipse Oil Company filed its bill in equity in the Circuit
Court of Wetzel County, and obtained an injunction against the
South Penn Company, the bill alleging that the lease held by the
Eclipse Company was still valid, although nothing had been done
thereunder, except the payment of the annual rental provided
for, on November 10, 1898, and alleged acceptance thereof by
lessor. This injunction was dissolved, and the Eclipse Oil Company appealed to the Court of Appeals. That court affirmed the
Circuit Court. In this case, for the reason that there was no consideration paid and no covenant that the lessees should do anything, and in view of the fact that nothing was done by them or
their assignee, the court held that the surrender clause, which
undertook to give the lessee the right either to hold the lease
without paying anything or doing anything, or surrender it at

any time, and relieve himself of any obligations, past or future, invalidated the whole lease. Notwithstanding the provisions of this surrender clause, a valuable consideration although nominal, if paid, would have been sufficient to support the lease, and the consideration would have been sufficient and would have controll-ed the surrender clause.

Sec. 9.—In *Brewster* v. *Lanyon Zinc Company*, 140 Fed. 801; 72 C. C. A. 213 (September 27, 1905) the Circuit Court of Appeals for the Eighth Circuit held:

"The mere inadequacy of consideration or other inequality in the terms of a lease does not in itself constitute a ground to avoid it in equity; that a lease for a definite and permissible term, but which reserves to the lessee an option to terminate it before the expiration of the term, does not create a mere tenancy at will within the operation of the rule that an estate at will of one party is equally at the will of the other; that a lease given upon consideration of one dollar paid at the time is not wanting in mutuality merely because it reserves to one party an option to terminate it which it withholds from the other."

The lease, the subject of the court's construction in this case, was made in consideration of one dollar, the lessee to drill a well upon the premises within two years, or thereafter pay the lessor $78.00 annually, until a well should be drilled or the property re-conveyed to the first party; if no well should be drilled within five years lessee to re-convey the premises to lessor and there-upon the lease should be null and void. It was provided that a failure on the part of the lessee to comply with any of the conditions would render the lease null and void. The lease was made by M. L. Brewster to the Palmer Oil & Gas Company, and was dated October. 28, 1895, for a tract of 312½ acres in Allen County, Kansas, and was assigned in February, 1899, to Thomas L. Hughes, who in March, following, assigned it to the Zinc Company.

Brewster filed a bill in equity on December 31, 1901, in the District Court of Allen County, Kanses, to cancel the lease as a cloud on his title. The suit was removed by the defendant to the United States Circuit Court for the District of Kansas. An

amended bill was filed on February 20, 1904, to which bill defendant demurred, assigning as causes therefor want of equity in the
bill and the existence of an adequate, full and complete remedy
at law. The demurrer was sustained, and as complainant declined
to amend, a decree was entered dismissing the bill, from which
decree plaintiffs appealed to the Circuit Court of Appeals for the
Eighth Circuit. In addition to the facts above stated the amended bill alleged as grounds for cancellation of the lease its want of
mutuality, particularly by reason of the seventh clause of the
lease, which was as follows:

"(7) Second party may at any time remove all his property and re-convey the premises hereby granted, and thereupon
this instrument shall be null and void."   "

In June, 1899, the plaintiff sold and conveyed a part of the
lands so demised to one Holmes, who in July, following, sold and
conveyed it to the Iola Portland Cement Company, which company was not made a party to the suit. The plaintiff continued
to own the residue of the lands demised, and was in the actual
possession thereof, save as defendant may have had occupancy
of a portion of the tract as incident to the operation of the gas
well thereon. No well was drilled during the first four years
after the date of the lease, but the stipulated sum of $78.00 was
paid to complainant during each of the third and fourth years.
In August, 1900, during the fifth year, a well was drilled on the
tract in Section 5 from which gas was obtained in paying quantities. Gas from this well was thereafter used off the premises
by defendant in its business of smelting and refining ores. When
suit was commenced, which was fourteen months after the expiration of the five-year period, and sixteen months after the
drilling of the single well nothing more had been done by defendant in compliance with the terms of the lease, express or implied, save that the required annual payment of $50.00 for the
gas so used off the premises may have been made, as to which
the bill was uncertain. Many oil and gas wells had been drilled
in the territory adjacent to and surrounding the tracts leased,
which produced oil and gas in paying quantities, and new wells
were being drilled and operated in that territory. These wells

were so near to the tracts leased as to drain the same of a good portion of the oil and gas therein, and therefore they rendered the lease of much less value to plaintiff than it would have been had defendant proceeded with reasonable diligence to drill other wells and operate the same for the mutual benefit of the parties. The extent of this drainage was not susceptible of reasonable ascertainment, and therefore the consequent injury to the plaintiff could not be adequately compensated in damages. Defendant had at all times insisted that by drilling the single well it acquired the right to all the oil and gas in the leased tracts, and also the right to hold the lease indefinitely without further development or doing more than paying annually fifty dollars for the gas from that well used off the premises. The court found as a fact, that it had been and was the defendant's purpose to hold the lease either for speculative purposes or to prevent the oil and gas from being used by its rivals in business. Seven days before the institution of the suit the plaintiff notified defendant in writing that she elected to declare the lease terminated, null and void, and demanded surrender and cancellation of the same, but the demand was not complied with. In support of the conclusions reached by the court as to the validity of the lease made upon consideration of one dollar, and that this one dollar was a good consideration for the surrender clause, the court cited:

Lowther Oil Co. v. *Guffy*, 52 W. Va. 88-91; 43 S. E. 101.
Lanyon Zinc Co. v. *Freeman*, (Kan.) 75 Pac. 995.
Dickey v. *Coffeyville, etc. Co.*, (Kan.) 76 Pac. 398.
Brown v. *Fowler*, 65 Ohio St. 507-525; 63 N. E. 76.
Gas Co. v. *Eckert*, 70 Ohio St. 127-135; 71 N. E. 281.
Allegheny Oil Co. v. *Snyder*, 106 Fed. 764-767; 45 C. C. A. 604-608.

The Circuit Court of Appeals reversed the decree of the Circuit Court with instructions to overrule the demurrer to the amended bill.

Sec. 10.—In *Central Ohio Natural Gas & Fuel Co.* v. *Eckert*, 70 Ohio St. 127; 71 N. E. 281 (April 26, 1904) the syllabus is as follows:

"A grant to a corporation, its successors and assigns, without limitation as to time, of 'all the oil' etc., upon the followin terms: 'First. Second party agrees to drill a well upon said premises within six months from this date, or thereafter pay to the first party one hundred and sixty dollars, annually, until said well is drilled, or the property hereby granted is re-conveyed to first party. * * * Seventh. Second party may at any time remove all their property and re-convey the premises hereb granted, which conveyance said first party agrees to accept, and thereupon this instrument be null and void'—after the expiration of six months, and until well is drilled, is a lease, at an annual rental of $160, at the option of the lessee only.''

Henry S. Eckert, Catharine Eckert and Clara Eckert, on January 3, 1894, executed an oil and gas lease to the Central Ohio Natural Gas & Fuel Company, the first and seventh paragraphs of which lease were as stated in the syllabus. The lessee paid the rental stipulated by the first section of the lease in each of the years 1895, 1896, 1897, and 1898, and on the 12th day of July, 1899, tendered the amount for the year thereafter ending in that month. This the lessor refused to accept, and on July 11, 1899, served notice on the gas company that it had no further right under the lease, and that the lessor elected to, and did, terminate the lease. On July 12, 1899, the gas company moved upon the property and undertook to erect a derrick for the purpose of drilling for oil.

The lessor then instituted suit against the lessee and obtained an injunction against the gas company enjoining it from doing anything upon the premises. The petition averred that the lease was a cloud upon the title, and the plaintiff asked that the title be quieted. The Circuit Court found that after the six months stipulated in the written instrument, it was merely a lease from year to year at the rental therein stipulated, and might be terminated by either party at the end of any year. A decree was entered quieting the plaintiff's title, and perpetually enjoining the company from asserting any estate or interest in the premises, or in any way disturbing plaintiff in the possession of the same. Defendant brought error to the Supreme Court, and that court reversed the judgment of the courts below. In support of the conclusions reached the court cited:

Woodland Oil Co. v. *Crawford,* 55 Ohio St. 161; 44 N. E.
    1093.
Lowther Oil Co. v. *Guffey,* 52 W. Va. 88; 43 S. E. 101.

Sec. 11.—In *Allegheny Oil Co.* v. *Snyder,* 106 Fed. 764; 45
C. C. A. 604 (November 7, 1900) the first paragraph of the head
notes is as follows:

"A lease reciting a consideration of one dollar paid by the
lessee gave him the right to drill for oil or gas on the demised
premises, together with such privileges as were incidental to
such operation, and the removal of the oil or gas produced for
the term of two years, and as long thereafter as oil or gas should
be found in paying quantities, not exceeding in the whole the
term of twenty-five years; he to pay a stipulated royalty on the
production. The lease then provides that 'in case no well shall
be drilled on said premises within two years from the date hereof, this lease shall become null and void, unless the lessee shall
pay for the further delay at the rate of one dollar per acre at or
before the end of each year thereafter.' *Held,* that such lease
constituted an entire contract, and that the consideration recited
supported not only the grant of the two years' term, but as well
the privilege of extending the time for drilling by paying the
stipulated price therefor."

On November 12, 1896, William E. Fowler made an oil and
gas lease to one Hiram Snyder upon a tract of land in North
Township, Harrison County, Ohio. The lease contained the following stipulations:

"To have and to hold the same unto the lessee, his heirs and
assigns for the term of two years from the date hereof, and as
long thereafter as oil or gas is found in paying quantities, thereon, not exceeding in the whole the term of twenty-five years from
the date hereof * * * ."
"In case no well shall be drilled on said premises within two
years from the date hereof this lease shall become null and void,
unless the lessee shall pay for the further delay at the rate of
one dollar per acre at or before the end of each year thereafter."
"It is agreed that the lessee shall have the right at any time
to surrender this lease to the lessor for cancellation, after which
all payments or liabilities to accrue under and by virtue of its

terms, shall cease and determine, and this lease become absolutely null and void.''

Nothing was done under this instrument by way of sinking wells, or otherwise taking possession, until after the expiration of the two years named in the lease. On the 10th day of November, 1898, the sum to be paid in the lease for delay at the rate of One Dollar per acre was paid to Fowler. On October 18, 1898, Fowler made another lease to one George Gillmor, which lease was subsequently assigned to the Allegheny Oil Company, and it commenced an action in the United States Circuit Court for the Southern District of Ohio, to remove the cloud of the Snyder lease, and clear its own title, having, in the meantime taken possession of the property. Brown and Myers, the assignees of Snyder, commenced a similar suit in the Court of Common Pleas of Harrison County, which was removed to United States Circuit Court, after an injunction had been obtained in the State Court, restraining the Oil Company from operating under its lease, and under the protection of which Brown and Myers took possession. . A motion having been filed for a temporary injunction in the action commenced originally in the United States Court by the Allegheny Oil Company, and to dissolve the temporary injunction granted in the State Court, the matter came on for hearing on the bill, answer and affidavits. On the hearing the Circuit Court refused the temporary injunction applied for, dismissed the bill of the Allegheny Oil Company, and made perpetual the injunction of the State Court restraining the Oil Company from interfering with the assignees of the Snyder lease. From this decree the Allegheny Oil Company appealed to the Circuit Court of Appeals for the Sixth Circuit, and that court affirmed the decision of the Circuit Court. The court cited in support of its construction of the lease:

Harris v. *Ohio Oil Co.*, 57 Ohio St. 129; 50 N. E. 1129.

Sec. 12.—In *Elk Fork Oil & Gas Co.* v. *Jennings*, 84 Fed. 839 (Jan. 25, 1898) the head notes are as follows:

''1. One in possession of lands under oil and gas leases

may maintain a suit to quiet title against the others claiming possession under other leases.

2. When a court of equity has obtained jurisdiction of a controversy, in order to make effective such jurisdiction, and to give due force to its decree, it will proceed to dispose of all questions properly presented by the pleadings and fairly pertaining to the full and equitable disposition of the cause.

3. A stipulation in a lease of oil and gas lands to the effect that the lessee shall, within a given time, complete one well, 'unavoidable accident' excepted, on pain of forfeiture, or else pay the lessors a certain amount per acre per annum after the time for completing such well shall have passed, will be deemed to have been waived by a recognition by the lessors of the unavoidable character of accidents by which such completion is prevented, coupled with assent to and acquiescence in such delay.

4. By numerous leases, in substantially the same terms, obtained from different parties, a lessee acquired the exclusive right in a large territory 'of drilling and operating for petroleum oil and gas.' He stipulated to give the lessors a certain proportion of the oil obtained and pay them a fixed sum annually for each paying gas well; and he was required on pain of forfeiture to complete one test well within the territory in one year from the date of the leases. *Held*, that he did not, immediately upon the performance of this latter condition become vested with an absolute right for ten years to the oil and gas privileges in the whole territory, but was bound, within a reasonable time thereafter, to search for these minerals on the premises described in each lease, and a failure to do so as to some of the leases was an abandonment thereof.

5. Where, in a subsequent lease of such abandoned property, a clause is inserted to the effect that it is to be held subject to the original lease, such clause is to be construed as meaning that the lessors intended to incorporate into their contract the fact that they had advised their lessee that the land had been theretofore leased, and that he was to take it subject to the old lease, with the understanding that if the latter was valid he should take nothing by the contract, but that if it was invalid the conveyance should then stand as a contract binding upon the parties.''

In December, 1896, and January, 1897, one L. B. Hill leased from certain persons in Tyler County, West Virginia, for oil and gas purposes, certain tracts of land, making the aggregate 1077 acres; soon thereafter under said leases, the Elk Fork Oil &

Gas Company and others under whom they claimed, took possession of said lands, located a well on a 100-acre tract, leased to
Hill by Warren and James Wood, and drilled a well to completion
in pursuance of the terms of the lease. About the 16th of March,
1907, the plaintiffs hearing that defendants, Jennings, Guffey and
Glatzau claimed the right to drill on the land covered by the
lease from Warren and James Wood, and hearing that the said
defendants had contracted for the erection of a derrick thereon,
and were endeavoring to oust the complainants from the possession of the same, filed their bill in equity on March 19, 1897, in
the Circuit Court of Tyler County, West Virginia, against the
said Jennings, Guffey, Glatzau and others, and obtained an injunction restraining the defendants from taking possession of
said 1077 acres situated in said county, for oil and gas purposes,
claiming the right to said land for said purpose under said
leases. This suit was by due proceedings removed to the United
States Circuit Court for the District of West Virginia. On April
2, 1897, the Elk Fork Oil & Gas Company and others filed in the
United States Circuit Court an amended bill against the same
defendants, and also against George E. Foster and others. On
April 14, 1897, the plaintiffs filed an amended and supplemental
bill.

On April 6, 1897, George E. Foster filed his bill against the
Elk Fork Oil & Gas Company and others in the United States
Circuit Court for the District of West Virginia, Foster not having at that time been served with process in the suit, although
named a defendant to the amended bill. Upon his bill he obtained an injunction against the Elk Fork Oil & Gas Company
and the other plaintiffs to the original and amended bills, enjoining and restraining them from operating upon said leasehold premises. It appeared from the record that when Foster
filed his bill he was aware of the fact that the questions raised
by the same concerning what was known as the Hawkins lease
of September 4, 1889, had been presented to the court by the
amended filed on April 2, 1897. When the amended and supplemental bill was filed on April 14, 1897, the Elk Fork Oil &
Gas Company moved for an injunction against Foster as prayed
for in said bill, and also moved to dissolve the restraining order

which had been awarded to Foster on the 6th of April, 1897. The court, upon hearing these motions, directed the causes to be heard together, and ordered that the bill filed by Foster should be treated as a cross bill in the suit brought by the original complainant. The court also at the same time appointed Charles W. Brockunier, receiver, with instructions to drill wells on the 50 acres of land in controversy between Foster and the Elk Fork Oil & Gas Company, at such places and in such manner as he might deem best and proper. All parties in the controversy were enjoined from interfering with the receiver in the exercise of the rights conferred upon him by the order of the court. On April 17, 1897, the defendants, Jennings, Guffey and Glatzau, filed their answer, and at the same time tendered their cross-bill which was filed. On the filing of their answer and cross-bill the court appointed W. A. McCosh receiver so far as the oil and gas rights were concerned in the 100-acre tract of land claimed by the Elk Fork Oil & Gas Company, and known as the Wood lease, and also receiver for the Tuttle lease. On April 30, 1897, the Elk Fork Oil & Gas Company filed their answer to the cross-bill and moved the court to discharge the receiver; the defendant, Foster, at the same time demurring to complainant's bill.

On May 10, 1897, Foster filed an amended bill against the original complainants and certain others, lessors of part of the lands in controversy, and asked for and obtained from the court, an order extending the powers of Receiver Brockunier over the lands of Joshua Hawkins and others. On June 19, 1897, the defendant Foster filed his answer to the complainant's bill. It was alleged in the amended bill of the Elk Fork Oil & Gas Company, filed on April 14, 1897, that defendant served notice on the plaintiff forbidding them to operate for oil on the Wood land, and claiming title to the oil and gas rights thereof, under a lease made to one William Johnson, in September, 1889, by Lyman Wood, the father of Warren and James Wood; that on September 4, 1889, Lyman Wood made an oil and gas lease for 200 acres of land then owned by him, of which the 100 acres leased to complainants by Warren and James Wood was a part, to William Johnson; that on November 14, 1889, said William Johnson assigned to C. G. Dickson, D. C. Gruntz, and Julius McCormick,

thirteen-eighteenths of his holdings in a certain block of leases
(which included the lease of Lyman Wood) and that on March
19, 1897, Johnson, McCormick, Gruntz and Dickson's executors,
assigned the lease to one John Stealey, who on the same day
assigned a one-third interest in the same to one L. E. Smith; and
that on March 20, 1897, Stealey and Smith assigned to George E.
Foster an interest in the said leases, which also included certain
leases made by Eliza and B. F. Hawkins and James Eddy, to
said Johnson, in the year 1889, the lands covered by the same,
being a part of the 1077 acres claimed by the complainants under
the lease executed to L. B. Hill, heretofore mentioned. Complainants also averred that the defendants had no right under
any of the leases so made to William Johnson in 1889, because
the same were void, and therefore all rights that existed under
them had become forfeited; that Johnson and those claiming
under him had made default in the stipulation contained in the
leases to complete a well in one year from the date of the leases,
respectively ·in Ellsworth, Mead, Lincoln, or Union Districts,
unavoidable accidents excepted; that neither Johnson, nor anyone claiming under him had ever drilled a well upon any of the
lands covered by the complainants' leases, and that no developments in fact had been made under any of the leases so given
to Johnson; that certain parties claiming under other and subsequent leases from the owners of the lands had drilled two
wells within Ellsworth District, but finding no oil, had abandoned the territory so tested and leased to Johnson; that neither
Johnson nor anyone else ever paid to Lyman Wood the sum of
ten cents per acre per annum, on account of the payment provided for in the lease made by Wood to Johnson, nor was any
sum paid to any of the lessors of the other leases, nor was any
such amount ever tendered until after oil was produced on the
Wood land by complainants, when the defendant Johnson tendered to Warren Wood, James Wood, and other lessors of Johnson, certain sums of money, alleged to represent the payment
provided for in the leases to him, and that Warren Wood, James
Wood and the other lessors to Johnson had declared forfeiture
of their said leases, and that the leasing of the land by Warren
and James Wood to Hill was a declaration of forfeiture; that

Johnson had abandoned all the leases, including the Lyman Wood lease; that the land owned by Lyman Wood was the property of Warren and James Wood, his sons, and that they leased the land to Hill, at which time, while they regarded the lease made by their father to Johnson as null and void, but still in order to protect themselves from any liability or expense of litigation, they inserted in their lease to Hill the words "this lease is taken subject to the William Johnson lease, September, 1889." In the supplemental bill the plaintiffs alleged that the lease made in September, 1889, by Eliza Hawkins and Benjamin Hawkins to William Johnson, had become forfeited and void; that George E. Foster, claiming under the same, and asserting the right to drill for oil upon the 100 acres of land, leased by said parties to Hill, had undertaken to take possession of the land and had, on April 7, 1897, caused notice to be served upon the plaintiffs requiring them to desist from their operations upon that tract of land; that complainants had taken possession under the Hawkins lease to Hill, had located a well thereon, and were about to drill the same, and that they had a producing well on the Wood tract.

In the cross-bill filed by Foster the execution of the lease by Eliza and Benjamin Hawkins to William Johnson, September, 1889, was alleged, and also that Johnson, at the same time, took a large number of similar leases in the same territory which was then undeveloped for oil or gas; that Johnson procured to be drilled in accordance with the terms of the Hawkins lease, an oil well upon one of the tracts leased to him; that the well was begun in April, 1890, and the work prosecuted continuously until a depth of 1,200 feet was reached, when the tools became fastened, and the work was finally abandoned and the rig moved about twenty feet where another well was started, and drilled to the Big Injun sand, the usual oil bearing sand in Tyler County territory, and no oil being found the well was drilled to the Gordon sand, a depth of 2,700 feet. No oil being then found the well was completed, in December, 1890; that the drilling was attended by numerous accidents; the well caved and caused many delays; that the fastening of the tools and caving of the well were unavoidable accidents whereby at least five months of delay was caused; that the well cost $11,000; that the drilling of said well

complied with the requirements contained in the Hawkins lease
to Johnson, and that but for the delays mentioned it would have
been completed within a year after the date of said lease; that
all the lessors, including Hawkins, were greatly interested in the
well, and were anxious to see it completed and that they conceded
that the failure to complete the same within a year was due to
unavoidable accidents, and therefore none of them demanded
rental or claimed the right to declare a forfeiture; that the well
was drilled in accordance with the terms of the lease to Johnson;
that in all respects the terms of the lease were complied with;
that there was no forfeiture of any of the leases; and that Johnson during the years 1889, and 1890, had either drilled or caused
to be drilled a large number of wells on various leases situated
in the districts of Lincoln, Ellsworth, Union and Mead, at a cost
of over $100,000.

The defendants, Jennings, Guffey and Glatzau, in their
answer admitted the making of the leases by the different lessors
to Hill, as alleged in the bill, but claimed that the same were
void and subordinate to the leases given for the same lands in
1889 to Johnson. They denied that they, or Johnson, ever abandoned any of said leases, and especially any portion of the Lyman
Wood land; they asserted that they had no notice of the lease
made by Warren and James Wood to Hill, or of Hill's assignment of the same, until March 19, 1897, when they notified the
plaintiff that they were the owners of the Lyman Wood lease;
that complainants drilled their well on said land in bad faith,
and with full knowledge of the exclusive right of the defendants
or of Johnson and his assigns to operate upon the same; that they
had been the equitable owners of the lease since August, 1892,
and the legal owners of the same since March 23, 1897. The
material provisions of the lease under which Johnson and his
assignees claimed were as follows:

"The party of the first part for the consideration of the
covenants and agreements hereinafter mentioned, has granted,
demised and let unto the party of the second part, his heirs or
assigns, for the purpose and with the exclusive right of drilling
and operating for petroleum oil and gas, all that certain tract
of land situate * * * to have and to hold the said premises,

* * * for and during the term of ten (10) years from the date hereof, and as much longer as oil or gas is found in paying quantities. * * * One well to be completed within one year in Ellsworth, Meade or Union Districts from the date hereof, unavoidable accidents excepted, and in case of failure to complete operations on a well within such time the party of the second part agrees to pay to party of the first part for such delay the sum of ten cents per acre per annum after the time for completing such well as above specified. * * * And a failure to complete one well, or to make such payments within such time as above mentioned, renders this lease null and void and to remain without effect between the parties hereto."

Upon final hearing the Circuit Court held:

"It follows from what we have said that the Elk Fork Oil & Gas Company, by virtue of the leases executed to Hill, have title to the oil and gas in and under the land as described in said leases, and also that the leases executed to William Johnston in 1889, covering the same land, and now claimed by Jennings, Guffey, Glatzau, Foster and others, are invalid because of abandonment, and that the complainants have a right to have the cloud upon their title caused thereby removed by order of this court. The receivers will be directed to settle their accounts, and report to the court as soon as possible the moneys in their hands to the credit of this consolidated cause so that proper disposition may be made of the same, and said Receivers will be discharged, and the property in their custody will be turned over to the owners thereof. The restraining order granted on the filing of the cross-bill by Foster, as well as the injunction issued when the cross-bill was tendered by Jennings, Guffey and Glatzau, will be dissolved. The injunction granted on the prayer of the Elk Fork Oil & Gas Company restraining the defendants to the original suit from taking possession and operating the leases claimed by that company as set forth in complainant's amended bill, as also the injunction issued against Foster when the amended and supplemental bill of complaints was filed, will be made perpetual."

In support of the court's conclusion as to jurisdiction, the following cases were cited:

Clayton v. *Barr*, 34 W. Va. 290; 12 S. E. 704.
Moore v. *McNutt*, 41 W. Va. 695; 24 S. E. 682.

Hoopes v. *Devaughn* (W. Va.) 27 S. E. 251.
Crawford v. *Ritchie* (W. Va.) 27 S. E. 220.
Harding v. *Guice*, 80 Fed. 162; 25 C. C. A. 352.
McConihay v. *Wright*, 121 U. S. 201.

In support of the conclusions reached as to the construction of the lease the court cited the following cases:

Guffey v. *Hukill*, 34 W. Va. 49; 11 S. E. 754.
Mullen's Administrator v. *Carper*, 37 W. Va. 215; 16 S. E. 527.
Bluestone Coal Co. v. *Bell*, 38 W. Va. 297; 18 S. E. 493.
Bettman v. *Harness*, 42 W. Va. 433; 26 S. E. 271.
Crawford v. *Ritchie*, 27 S. E. 220.
McNish v. *Stone*, 152 Pa. 457.
Brown v. *Vandergrift*, 80 Pa. 142.
Duffield v. *Hue*, 129 Pa. 94; 18 Atl. 566.
McKnight v. *Gas. Co.*, 146 Pa. 185; 23 Atl. 164.
Venture Oil Co. v. *Fretts*, 152 Pa. 451; 25 Atl. 732.
Barnhart v. *Lockwood*, 152 Pa. 82; 25 Atl. 237.
Bartley v. *Phillips*, 165 Pa. 328; 30 Atl. 842.
Cowan v. *Iron Co.*, 83 Va. 547; 3 S. E. 120.
Iron Co. v. *Trout*, 83 Va. 397; 2 S. E. 713.
Eaton v. *Gas Co.*, 122 N. Y. 416; 25 N. E. 981.

The defendants appealed to the Circuit Court of Appeals for the Fourth Circuit, which court affirmed the Circuit Court; *Foster* v. *Elk Fork Oil & Gas Company*, 90 Fed. 178; 32 C. C. A. 560.

Sec. 13.—In *Dill* v. *Fraze*, 169 Ind. 53; 79 N. E. 971, analyzed under Chapter 24, syl. 1 is as follows:

"1. A party to a contract reciting a consideration of one dollar was estopped to deny its consideration as against an assignee of a contract for a valuable consideration who had no knowledge that the original consideration of one dollar was not paid."

Sec. 14.—In *Trees* v. *Eclipse Oil Co.*, 47 W. Va. 107; 34 S. E. 933, analyzed under Chapter 14, syl. 1 is as follows:

"1. An executory oil and gas lease, which does not bind the lessee to carry out its covenants, but reserves to them the right to defeat the same at any time, and relieve themselves from the payment of any consideration therefor, is invalid to create any estate other than the mere optional right of entry which is subject to termination at the will of either party."

Sec. 16.—In *Lowther Oil Co.* v. *Miller-Sibley Co.*, 53 W. Va. 501; 44 S. E. 433; 87 Am. St. Rep. 1027, analyzed under Chapter 5, Judge Brannon at page 505, in the opinion, in discussing *Eclipse Oil Co.* v. *South Penn Oil Co.*, 47 W. Va. 84, said:

"But when once the lessee under even such a lease begins work, whilst he yet has no vested estate, still he has right to go on in search of oil and the lessor cannot then at mere will destroy his right."

It follows therefore that where a lessee has obtained a lease which by reason of insufficient consideration, or want of mutuality, or where the lease is otherwise unconscionable or unreasonable is voidable, such lessee may by entry upon the leased premises obtain a vested right to make explorations by beginning the work of exploration in good faith, and by the discovery of oil or gas in paying quantities by the use of due diligence, become entitled to a vested right to produce oil and gas. And this he may do although his lease may be of such an inequitable character as to preclude specific performance or protection by a court of equity in a proceeding taken by the holder of such lease against the landowner.

LESSOR'S REMEDIES.

Sec. 17.—Where a landowner executes an oil and gas lease voidable for want of consideration, his remedy for relief is by a prompt declaration of forfeiture. And where, after such declaration of forfeiture, lessee attempts to enter and explore for oil or gas, he may enjoin such proceedings and in the same suit cause the lease to be cancelled as a cloud on his title.

Eclipse Oil Co. v. *South Penn Oil Co.,* 47 W. Va. 84; 34 S. E.
    933.
Trees v. *Eclipse Oil Co.,* 47 W. Va. 107; 34 S. E. 933.
Elk Fork Oil & Gas Co. v. *Jennings,* 84 Fed. 839.

Sec. 18.—The distinction between the two classes of leases,
the one which is based upon a nominal consideration to be void
unless future rentals are paid or explorations undertaken, and
the other where there is a substantial consideration paid and an
express covenant and agreement either to explore for oil or gas
or in lieu thereof pay the rental stipulated for, is that in the
first class of leases the lessee has an option either to pay the
commutation money for delay or enter the premises and make
the explorations contemplated by the lease. A failure on the
part of the lessee to do either terminates the lease and no recovery can be had by the lessor against the lessee or his assignee
for rentals or commutation money, or for failure to make the
explorations. In the second class of leases the lessor has the
right, upon the failure of the lessee to pay the commutation
money or explore, to declare a forfeiture or sue for and recover
the rentals from time to time (subject to a surrender clause)
during the term of the lease.

For first class of leases see Chap. 13.
For second class of leases see Chap. 12.

LESSEE'S REMEDIES.

Sec. 19.—Where a lessee has paid a valuable consideration
to the lessor for the lease—the privilege of entering the premises for the purpose of exploring for oil or gas—although nominal, such consideration is sufficient and lessee may hold the
lease during the term upon complying with the other covenants;
such nominal consideration alone will neither authorize lessor
to declare a forfeiture nor constitute grounds for cancellation of
the lease by a court of equity.

Brown v. *Fowler,* and *Brown* v. *Ohio Oil Co.,* 55 Ohio St.
    507; 63 N. E. 76.

Brewster v. *Lanyon Zinc Co.,* 140 Fed. 801; 72 C. C. A. 213.
Central Ohio Nat. Gas & Fuel Co. v. *Eckert,* 70 Ohio St. 127;
    71 N. E. 281.
Allegheny Oil Co. v. *Snyder,* 106 Fed. 764; 45 C. C. A. 604.
Dill v. *Fraze,* 169 Ind. 53; 79 N. E. 971.

Sec. 20.—A lessee holding what purports to be an oil and
gas lease, which is void for want of consideration, may enter
upon the premises demised, before notice of declaration of forfeiture, or before lessor has by the execution of a second lease,
declared a forfeiture, for the purpose of making the explorations provided for in the lease; and where lessor permits lessee
to drill and he discovers oil or gas in paying quantities, lessor
will not be allowed thereafter to declare a forfeiture; nor will a
court of equity either at the suit of the lessor or at the suit of a
second lessee, cancel the original lease on the grounds of want
of consideration.

Friend v. *Mallory,* 52 W. Va. 53; 43 S. E. 114.
Eclipse Oil Co. v. *South Penn Oil Co.,* 47 W. Va. 84; 34 S. E.
    933, syl. 2.
Lowther Oil Co. v. *Miller-Sibley Oil Co.,* 53 W. Va. 501; 44
    S. E. 433; 87 Am. St. Rep. 1027.

CHAPTER 5.

PURPOSE OF GRANT, PREMISES DEMISED, AND RIGHTS AC-QUIRED.

Sec. 1.—The principal purpose and design of the parties to
an oil and gas lease is the production and marketing of the oil
and gas in the land for their mutual benefit. To carry out the
purpose of the grant the lessee acquires the right to enter upon
the premises to make explorations, with the right to lay pipelines, erect necessary buildings, and perform such other acts as
may be necessary to make the grant effective.

Parish Fork Oil Co. v. *Bridgewater Gas Co.,* 51 W. Va. 583;
    42 S. E. 655.

Brewster v. *Lanyon Zinc Co.,* 140 Fed. 901, syl. 8; 72 C. C.
A. 213.
Steelsmith v. *Gartlan,* 45 W. Va. 27.   Op. 34; 29 S. E. 978.
Munroe v. *Armstrong,* 96 Pa. 307.
Plummer v. *Coal & Iron Co.,* 160 Pa. 483; 28 Atl. 353.
Venture Oil Co. v. *Fretts,* 152 Pa. 451; 25 Atl. 732.
Florence Oil Co. v. *Orman,* 19 Colo. App. 79; 73 Pac. 628.
Rawlings v. *Armel,* 70 Kan. 778; 79 Pac. 683.
Monfort v. *Lanyon Zinc Co.,* 67 Kan. 310; 72 Pac. 784.
Lowther Oil Co. v. *Miller-Sibley Co.,* 53 W. Va. 501; 44 S. E.
433; 97 Am. St. Rep. 1027.
Lawson v. *Kirchner,* 50 W. Va. 844; 40 S. E. 344.
Crawford v. *Ritchie,* 43 W. Va. 252; 37 S. E. 220.
Huggins v. *Daley,* 99 Fed. 606; 40 C. C. A. 12; 48 L. R. A.
320.
New American Oil Co. v. *Troyer,* 166 Ind. 402; 76 N. E.
353; 77 N. E. 739.
Wagner v. *Mallory,* 169 N. Y. 501; 62 N. E. 584.
Westmoreland Gas. Co. v. *DeWitt,* 130 Pa. 235; 18 Atl. 724;
5 L. R. A. 731.
Backer v. *Penn Lubricating Co.,* 162 Fed. 627; 89 C. C. A.
419.
Knotts & Garber v. *McGregor,* 47 W. Va. 566; 37 S. E. 899.
Fowler v. *Delcplain,* 79 Ohio State 279; 87 N. E. 261.
Doddridge County Oil & Gas. Co. v. *Smith,* 173 Fed. 386.
Doddridge County Oil & Gas Co. v. *Smith,* 154 Fed. 970.
Barnsdall v. *Bradford Gas Co.,* — Pa. —; 74 Atl. 207.

Sec. 2.—Whether the oil or gas lease be called a mere license
authorizing the lessee to enter upon the premises to explore for
oil or gas, or whether it be called a lease conferring upon the
lessee a present interest, the courts uniformly hold that the general purpose and object of the grant is to authorize the lessee
to enter and make the necessary explorations for oil or gas, and
to confer upon him such incidental rights as laying pipe-lines,
erecting structures, and generally doing that which is necessary
to enable him successfully to explore and produce and market
the oil and gas. Beyond the right to enter and make the explorations the lessee has no vested right in the premises leased until
the search is made and oil or gas discovered in paying quantities.
The real object in view by both parties in making the ordinary
oil and gas lease is the discovery of these minerals. The courts

have universally held this to be the true object of an oil and gas lease, and this being true the lessee must comply strictly with the covenants or he will lose the right that he has acquired by accepting the lease.

Sec. 3.—There is a distinction between a lease for mining coal or other solid minerals or substances and a lease for oil and gas purposes. The distinction is based upon the fugitive character of oil and gas, its liability to drainage and the practical impossibility of proving the loss a landowner sustains by non-development of his premises, and the development and production of oil and gas from the property of adjoining landowners in such close proximity to lessor's lands as to drain the oil and gas therefrom. Where a lessee under a lease for coal fails to develop the premises, the coal remains the property of the owner who simply loses the benefit of his royalties for the time. Where a lessee for oil or gas fails to develop and produce the oil and gas operators on adjoining lands may be securing the oil and gas by drainage. The landowner in this way necessarily suffers irreparable loss. For the purpose of preventing injury thus arising, the oil lease restricts the right of the lessee as to ownership of the oil and gas, to the mere right of production, and usually provides a speedy method for terminating this right by forfeiture.

Sec. 4.—In determining the validity of an oil and gas lease the general object and purpose of the grant must necessarily always be kept in view. Before any right to the oil and gas becomes vested in the lessee, he must discover these minerals; and until such discovery is made his license is subject to forfeiture for breach of express covenants, and will be held the subject of abandonment for breach of implied covenants. It is not sufficient that the lessee enter upon the premises and make explorations; the explorations must be successful. The drilling of a dry hole on a landowner's property is not beneficial to him, nor ordinarily will such result prevent forfeiture for failure to continue explorations. In *Steelsmith* v. *Gartlan, supra,* the lessee having drilled a dry hole, claimed the right to hold the leased premises during the term of five years, without payment of commutation money or further explorations. The landowner made a second lease which lease the Court of Appeals of West Virginia held valid, and on bill in equity filed by the second lessee, cancelled the original lease on the ground of abandonment. In *Parish Fork Oil Company* v. *Bridgewater Gas Company, supra,* a well was drilled and some oil found, but the lessor derived no benefit therefrom. Subsequently the landowner made a second lease, and in a suit involving the validity of the two leases the assignees of the first lease claimed that by drilling one well they could hold the lease, without making further explorations. The court held that the first lease had been abandoned and held the second lease valid.

Sec. 5.—The temptation of a lessee to claim under an oil lease, where he has entered and made fruitless search for oil and gas, or where he has paid rentals for a time and then ceased such payments, and subsequently oil or gas has been discovered near or on the lands so leased, is great, and fruitless efforts have been made by such lessees to secure from the courts a construction of their leases so as to defeat the diligent operator who has, under a second lease made successful operations.

Sec. 6.—In *Parish Fork Oil Co.* v. *Bridgewater Gas Co.*, 51 W. Va. 583; 42 S. E. 655 (March 29, 1902) syl. 2 is as follows:

"2. The principal purpose and design of the parties to such a lease, clearly discernible from its terms, being the production and marketing of the oil and gas in the land for their mutual benefit, 'the right to produce and take the same in accordance with the terms and conditions of the contract vests in him the right to produce and take the same in accordance with the terms and conditions of the contract. In such right the lessee will be protected, but he must proceed to exercise it with reasonable promptness and diligence.' "

On June 4, 1894, J. S. Swisher made an oil and gas lease to E. R. Woodward, which lease Woodward assigned to the Parish Fork Oil & Gas Company, a co-partnership. The Oil Company entered upon the land in August, 1898, and drilled a well about

200 feet deep, which was completed in September, 1898. This well produced oil in small quantities but no oil was marketed. In the Spring of 1899, the drilling machinery with which the well had been drilled was moved away and the well was, to all appearances, abandoned. No further visible work was done upon the land by the lessees until early in June, 1900. The consideration mentioned in the lease was fifty dollars cash, which was stipulated to be the payment of the rental for one year from June 4, 1894, to June 4, 1895. The lease provided that lessee should "complete one well on said premises within one year, or the said E. R. Woodward shall pay to the said Jacob S. Swisher rentals hereinafter provided." The further provision as to rental was as follows: That lessee should pay "fifty cents per acre for each year that the lease may remain in force after the first year." The lease contained the following provision as to the payment of rental: "It is further agreed that when the first well is completed on said premises, then all cash rental shall cease." The term of the lease was stated as follows: "It is agreed that this lease shall remain in force for the term of fifteen years from this date, and as much longer as the premises are operated for oil and gas." The royalty was one-eighth of the oil, and fifty dollars per year for gas from every well on the premises the product of which should be marketed and used off the premises. Rentals were paid in advance each year until June 4, 1899, the last payment having been made on June 2, 1898. Prior to the resumption of work by the lessees, Swisher executed a second lease some time in 1899, to Bell and Hewitt, which was forfeited for non-payment of rental. Then Swisher executed another lease for the same land to Bell who was an employe of the Bridgewater Gas Company, dated February 7, 1900. This lease was assigned to the Bridgewater Gas Company on August 1, 1900.

Early in August, 1900, the claimants to these two conflicting leases each undertook to begin operations on the land, placing materials on the ground and beginning the work of exploration, which resulted in the institution of two suits, the claimants to each lease filing a bill in equity to cancel the other's lease. Injunctions were awarded against each of the parties on their respective bills. The real question at issue was, whether the lessees who drilled the well under the lease of June 4, 1894, had abandoned that lease. At the time the well was drilled the Woodward lease was owned by the parties styling themselves the Parish Fork Oil & Gas Company. One D. C. Mobley was the manager for the company and controlled the operations. After the well had been drilled, shot and cleaned out and a showing of oil found in it, Mobley located another well but nothing was done as to drilling. In the well that was drilled, only two joints of casing were inserted, and these were not of sufficient length to reach down far enough to prevent the well from caving, or to shut off the surface water. The Circuit Court of Wirt County, where the two suits were instituted, held that the claimants to the original lease had abandoned the same, and upon appeal taken by the claimants to the first lease the Court of Appeals affirmed the Circuit Court, and on the question of the completion of one well, held: That after completing one well on the premises and the abandonment of the premises for more than eighteen months, leaving the well unprotected, so that it caved in and partially filled up, the landowner after waiting a year or more from the date of the abandonment, had the right to lease the land to another.

Sec. 7.—In *Brewster* v. *Lanyon Zinc Co.*, 140 Fed. 801; 72 C. C. A. 213, analyzed under Chapter 4, page 51, syl. 8, the court held:

"A lease which grants 'all the oil and gas' under the leased land, together with the right to enter 'at all times' for the purpose of 'drilling and operating' to erect and maintain structures, pipe-lines and machinery necessary for the 'production and transportation' of oil and gas, and to use sufficient water, oil and gas, to run the necessary engines for the 'prosecution of said business,' which reserves to the lessor substantial royalties in kind and in money on the oil produced and saved, and the gas used off the premises, which shows that the promise of these royalties was the controlling inducement to the grant, and which, while expressly requiring the drilling of one well during the first five years, does not expressly define the measure of diligence to be exercised in the work of development, and production, after the expiration of that period, contains a covenant by the lessee arising by necessary implication from the nature of

the lease and other stipulations therein, that if, during the five
years allowed for the original exploration and development oil
and gas, one or both, are found in paying quantities, the
work of development and production shall be continued with
reasonable diligence, that is along such lines as will be reasonably calculated to make the extraction of oil and gas from the
leased land of mutual advantage and profit to the lessor and
lessee.''

Sec. 8.—In *Steelsmith v. Gartlan*, 45 W. Va. 27; 29 S. E.
978 (April 16, 1898) syls. 1-2 are as follows:

"1. A lease for the purpose of operating for oil and gas
for the period of five years, and so much longer as oil or gas is
found in paying quantities, on no other consideration than prospect of oil royalty and gas rental, vests no present title in the
lessee, except the mere right of exploration; but the title thereto both as to the period of five years and the time thereafter,
remains inchoate and contingent on the finding under the explorations provided for in such lease, oil and gas in paying quantities.
2. The completion of a nonproductive well though at great
expense, vests no title in the lessee.''

Mrs. Matilda McGregor, on February 11, 1895, in consideration of one dollar, executed an oil and gas lease to James
Gartlan for a tract of 120 acres of land in Ritchie County. The
granting clause in the lease was as follows:

"Do hereby demise and grant unto the lessee, his heirs or
assigns, all the oil and gas in and under the following described
tract of land, and also the said tract of land, for the purpose and
with the exclusive right of operating thereon for said gas and
oil, together with the right of way, the right to lay pipe over and
use water from, said premises, and also the right to remove at
any time all property placed thereon by the lessee.''

This lease was for the term of five years from date and so
much longer as oil or gas should be found in paying quantities.
It was provided that in case no well should be completed on the
premises within one month from the date of the lease, it should
become null and void and without any further effect whatever,
unless the lessee should pay for further delay at the rate of fifty

dollars per month in advance until a well should be completed. A failure to comply with any of the conditions of the lease should render it null and void and of no effect; the lessor to have the right at any time to surrender the lease for cancellation, after which all payments and liabilities to accrue thereunder should become absolutely null and void. Gartlan, with the assistance of others, drilled a test well about 1800 feet deep by April, 1895, but finding neither gas nor oil in paying quantities, removed the derrick and tools, pulled the casing, plugged the hole and left the premises. During the time the test well was being drilled the lessee paid Mrs. McGregor three months rental on account of delay in completing the well. He then discontinued all payments, and entirely abandoned and ceased all further operations for oil or gas on the premises. Mrs. McGregor, after the abandonment of the premises by the lessee, demanded the surrender of the lease, and notified the parties interested with the original lessee, that she was going to lease the premises to other parties, but no attention whatever was paid to Mrs. McGregor's notice and demand. On October 22, 1896, Mrs. McGregor made a new lease to Amos Steelsmith, who entered upon the premises, drilled a well, and discovered oil in paying quantities. Steelsmith filed a bill in equity in the Circuit Court of Ritchie County against Gartlan and the others interested with him, alleging that the Gartlan lease was forfeited by abandonment, and praying for a cancellation of the lease. Gartlan and the others interested with him claimed in their answer and cross-bill that the drilling of the dry hole was sufficient exploration to hold the lease for the term of five years, without the payment of rental. The Circuit Court decided for the defendants, cancelled the Steelsmith lease, and held the original Gartlan lease to be valid. From this decree Steelsmith appealed to the Court of Appeals, and that court reversed the decree of the Circuit Court, and cancelled the Gartlan lease.

Sec. 9.—In *Munroe* v. *Armstrong*, 96 Pa. 307; (November 26, 1880) syls. 1-2 are as follows: •

"1. A lease of land was made exclusively for the purpose of producing oil. The work of boring for oil was to be commenced in ten days and continued with due diligence until success or abandonment; and if the lessees failed to get oil in paying qualities or ceased to work for thirty days at any time, the lease was to be forfeited and void; *Held,* that if the lessees failed to get oil in one well they had a right to put down another, and as many more as they pleased, so long as they worked with diligence to success or abandonment; *held further,* that a cessation of work for thirty days forfeited the lease.

2. Forfeiture for non-development or delay is essential to private and public interests in relation to the use and alienation of property. In general, equity abhors a forfeiture but not where it works equity and protects a landowner from the laches of a lessee, whose lease is of no value till developed."

On July 31, 1877, Eli Reep, the owner of a large tract of land, executed a lease on ten acres thereof, to A. B. Clark and Ross Lilly for oil purposes, for the term of twenty years, reserving as royalty one-eighth of all the oil produced therefrom. The lease provided that the lessee should commence operations within ten days and continue to prosecute the work with due diligence until success or abandonment, with the following provision:

"The party of the second part, if they fail to get oil in paying quantities, or cease to work for thirty days at any time, this article to be forfeited and to be null and void."

The lessee took possession of the premises and made preparations to drill a well within the ten days required, and completed it during the latter part of October, 1877. The well proved to be dry. The lessees Clark and Lilly, within a few days after the completion of the well, pulled the casing and removed the tools from the lease and sold or used them elsewhere. Conditions remained thus until November 1, 1877, nothing whatever having been done thereon until February, 1878, when Reep called upon Lilly and asked him if he and Clark intended drilling another well upon the lease. Lilly said they did not. Reep told Lilly that he would lease to other parties, as their lease was forfeited: Lilly replied: "If I were in your place I would." Reep called upon Lilly a second time with like result. Reep afterwards, on March 21, 1878, executed and delivered to Monroe, a lease for oil purposes of 17 acres embracing the 10 acres theretofore leased to Clark and Lilly. Munroe, about July 1, 1878, drilled a well on another portion of the Reep farm and found oil in large quantities. Armstrong purchased from Clark and Lilly whatever interest they had in the original lease, and under an assignment thereof, in July, 1878, went upon the 10 acres and commenced operating for oil. Munroe then brought suit for possession. The well was completed by Armstrong in December, 1878, which well produced oil in large quantities. The Court of Common Pleas of Butler County held that there was no forfeiture of the lease made by Reep to Clark and Lilly, and instructed the jury to return a verdict for the defendants which was done. From the judgment in favor of Armstrong rendered upon this verdict, Munroe the plaintiff, appealed, and the Supreme Court of Pennsylvania reversed the Court of Common Pleas.

Sec. 10.—In *Plummer* v. *Coal & Iron Co.*, 160 Pa. 483; 28 Atl. 353 (March 26, 1894) a controversy is presented growing out of conflicting claims to leases for coal. In this case an attempt was made by the claimants to apply the principles governing the construction of oil and gas leases to the construction of coal leases or contracts. In distinguishing the rights of lessors and lessees under oil leases from the rights of lessors and lessees under coal leases, Justice Williams in the opinion says:

"The difference in the nature of the two minerals, and the manner of their production, has, however, resulted in considerable differences in the forms of the contracts or leases made use of. When oil is discovered in any given region, the development of the region becomes immediately necessary. The fugitive character of oil and gas and the fact that a single well may drain a considerable territory and bring to the surface oil that when in place in the sand rock was under the lands of adjoining owners, makes it important for such landowner to test his own land as speedily as possible. Such leases generally require, for this reason, that operations should begin within a fixed number of days or months, and be prosecuted to a successful end or abandonment. Coal, on the other hand, is fixed in location. The owner may mine when he pleases, regardless of operations around him. Its amount and probable value can be calculated with a fair degree of business certainty. There is no necessity for haste, nor moving *pari passu* with adjoining owners. The consequence is that coal leases are for a certain fixed term, or for all the coal upon the land leased, as the case may be.''

Sec. 11.—In *Venture Oil Co.* v. *Fretts*, 152 Pa. 451; 25 Atl. 732 (January 16, 1893) the syllabus is as follows:

"A vested title cannot ordinarily be lost by abandonment in a less time than that fixed by the Statute of Limitations, unless there is satisfactory proof of an intention to abandon. A lease for a right to mine for oil, etc., stands on different ground. The title is inchoate and for purposes of exploration only until oil is found. If it is not found, no estate vests in the lessee, and his title, whatever it is, ends when the unsuccessful search is abandoned. If oil is found, then the right to produce becomes a vested right, and the lessee will be protected in exercising it in accordance with the terms and conditions of his contract.

An oil lease contained a grant of a right to mine for and remove oil for a fixed period of twenty years, at a royalty of one-eighth of the oil so mined and removed. *Held*, that the right of the lessee was to explore for, and determine the existence of oil under the land, and if none was found, his right ceased when the explorations were finished and the lot abandoned.''

Joseph M. Gamble, on December 26, 1883, executed an oil and gas lease to C. D. Robbins, in consideration of the stipulations, grants and covenants contained in the lease, for a tract of land in Washington County, Pennsylvania, for the sole and only purpose of mining and excavating for petroleum or carbon oil, gas or other volatile substances, for the purpose of laying pipe, either under or on top of the surface, for transporting oil or gas for a term of twenty years next ensuing the date of the lease, the lessee to commence operations within six months of the date of the execution of the lease, on some one of the farms leased by him in Cecil Township, and when oil should be found in paying quantities the lessee to commence operations within sixty days upon the next adjoining farm leased by him, and so on until all the lands leased in the township should be tested to success or abandonment. The territory covered by the leases obtained by Robbins was at that time wholly undeveloped. Within six months Robbins began operations on the farm of J. L. Scott and drilled a well on it to the depth of 2247 feet. Neither oil nor gas was found. Robbins drew the casing soon after the well was finished, and plugged and abandoned it. He made no further effort to test any other part of the lands covered by his leases, but removed his machinery and drilling tools to other localities in the fall of 1884. Some six or seven years later, nothing having been done by Robbins on any one of the farms covered by his leases of 1883, Gamble made a new lease of his farm to other parties under whom Fretts claimed title, and operations were at once begun on the land. Robbins and the Venture Oil Company holding under him, then brought an action of ejectment to the February Term of the Court of Common Pleas of Washington County, asserting a right of entry under the lease of 1883. Verdict and judgment were rendered by the court in favor of defendant, from which judgment plaintiffs appealed. Upon this appeal the Supreme Court of Pennsylvania reversed the Court of Common Pleas.

In support of the conclusions reached the court cited:

Duffield v. *Hue,* 129 Pa. 94; 18 Atl. 566.

Sec. 12.—In *Florence Oil & Refining Co.* v. *Orman,* 19 Colo. App. 79; 73 Pac. 628 (September 14, 1903) the syllabus is as follows:

"An oil lease gave the exclusive right to mine lands for oil for twenty years in consideration of a per cent. of the oil produced, the lessee covenanting to sink two wells within 18 months, and the lease providing that if the two wells were so sunk, and were not productive, the lessee should pay $50 a year till the drilling of new wells should commence, and failure to pay it would render the lease void. *Held,* that, till oil was found the title of the lessee was for exploration only, and that having done nothing for four years after putting down the two wells without finding oil in paying quantities, he lost his rights through failure to make diligent search."

The State of Colorado made a lease to one Davis for the exclusive right to mine certain lands for oil and gas for a term of twenty years from date in consideration that the lessee agreed to give the State five per cent. of the oils and gases produced and saved from the premises, the lessee to commence operations within two months, and sink two wells to a depth of from 1,500 to 1,800 feet, unless oil in paying quantities should be sooner found. A failure on the part of the lessee to comply with the terms of the lease should render it void. The lease was dated March 20, 1894. Davis assigned the lease to the Florence Oil & Refining Company, which company, within one month began sinking a well and during the year 1894, sunk three wells, each deeper than the required depth. In 1895, the company began a fourth well, which was completed in the summer of 1896. The company did some further work on two of the wells drilled in 1894. This was all that was done by the company in the search for oil, except that in April, 1901, after the lease had been cancelled, and the company knew of this fact, it began the erection of a derrick on the premises. As a result of the search oil was found in a small quantity in one of the wells, but all of the wells proved non-paying and practically dry. Casings were drawn and the wells abandoned in the early part of the summer, 1896. Since that time the company made no further effort to discover oil. On March 8, 1898, the general manager of the company wrote to the representative of the State Board of Land Commissioners, that the company had heard that the lease had been cancelled, and inquired if this was true. The representative replied by letter, dated March 12, 1898, stating that the lease had not been forfeited, and was not subject by its conditions to cancellation. On July 23, 1900, the Board of Land Commissioners, without notice to the Company, cancelled the lease. In March, 1901, Howe applied to lease the land, and in April following, an order was made granting the lease. The Florence Oil Company first heard in April, 1901, of the cancellation, and made immediate application to have it set aside, which was denied.

In July, 1901, the company instituted suit against the State Board of Land Commissioners and the appellee for the purpose of setting aside the order of the Board cancelling the lease, and to obtain an injunction restraining the issuance of the lease ordered to the appellee Howe. Judgment was entered dismissing the action, from which the Oil Company appealed. The Supreme Court of Colorado affirmed the decree of the court below.

Sec. 13.—In *Rawlings* v. *Armel*, 70 Kan. 778; 79 Pac. 683 (Feb. 11, 1905) syls. 1-3 are as follows:

"1. Under the provisions of the oil and gas lease involved in this suit, the lessee had the right to enter upon the leased premises for the purpose of exploration, and to operate if oil or gas were discovered, but no estate vested in the lessee until such minerals were found and produced."

3. The preliminary right of exploration for gas and oil under the lease in question was of such a character that it might be lost by abandonment without the lapse of time prescribed by the Statute of Limitations."

A lease was executed by John A. Armel and wife to the Kansas and Texas Oil, etc. Company for certain lands granting to the lessee the exclusive right for two years from the date of the lease to enter upon and operate for, and procure oil and gas from, the leased premises. If no oil or gas well should be drilled within thirty days from May 21, 1902, on the premises, all rights and obligations under the lease should cease, at the option of the lessor, unless the lessee should pay to the lessor the sum of fifty dollars on or before twelve o'clock on June 20, 1902, such payment to entitle the lessee to an extension of thirty days within which to begin drilling. Several extensions were made by the lessor, the last one for fifteen days—from September 19th to October 4th—it being understood that unless a well was actually commenced by noon on October 4, 1902, the lease should be subject to forfeiture, at the option of lessor. Before noon, on October 12th the lessee commenced drilling and proceeded to sink two dry wells. About November 26th the company pulled the casing from the wells, plugged them, ceased all further explorations, removed all material, machinery and tools from the land, and left the premises. On January 3d following, the lessor notified the lessee that the lease was forfeited for failure to comply with its conditions. Later he demanded the return of the lease, and a release of the premises to him. Subsequent to February 19, 1903, the lessee assigned the lease to Rawlings and others. On February 28, 1903, the lessor notified the assignees of the lease that it was null and void.

No rental was paid or tendered prior to March 17, 1903, and on that day the lessor commenced an action against the lessee and its assignees to cancel the lease on the grounds of abandonment and non-payment of rental. The District Court entered judgment cancelling the lease, from which judgment the defendants appealed, and the Supreme Court affirmed the judgment of the District Court.

Sec. 14.—In *Monfort* v. *Lanyon Zinc Co.*, 67 Kan. 310; 72 Pac. 784 (June 6, 1903) the court held:

"We are of the opinion that the performance of these conditions had the effect of continuing the lease for the period of ten years from the date of its execution, or so long as the lessees or their assignees continued to make this annual deposit. The language used in setting forth the conditions to be performed by the lessees in order to preserve this right is so plain that nothing is left for inference or speculation."

Monfort leased to Bowles and Company, in consideration of one dollar, and in further consideration of the drilling of test wells in Allen County, Kansas, for oil and gas, a tract of 160 acres of land, situated in said county. The lessees were to have the exclusive right for ten years from the date of the lease to enter upon the premises and explore for oil and gas, with a condition that if no oil or gas well should be sunk on the premises within five years from the date of the lease the same should become absolutely null and void unless the lessee should elect from year to year to continue the lease by paying or depositing to the credit of the lessor, each year in advance, $40.00 which deposit was to be made in the Bank of Allen County, Kansas, until a well should be completed on the premises. More than five years after the execution of the lease the lessor brought suit to set aside the lease on the ground that no well had been sunk or undertaken by the lessees or their assignees on the lessor's property. The defendants claimed, and it was not denied, that the one dollar cash consideration was paid, and that wells were sunk and operated in Allen County, and that after the expiration of the five years the lessees each year, in advance, deposited $40.00 in the Bank of Allen County, to the credit of lessors. The District Court rendered judgment for the defendant, from which judgment the plaintiff appealed. The Supreme Court affirmed the District Court, and held the lease valid.

Sec. 15.—In *Lowther Oil Co.* v. *Miller-Sibley Oil Co.*, 53 W. Va. 501; 44 S. E. 433; 97 Am. St. Rep. 1027 (May 2, 1903) syl. 1 is as follows:

"Title under a lease only for production of oil and gas is inchoate and contingent and for purposes of search only until oil or gas is found. If not found, no estate vests in the lessee, and his right, whatever it is, ends when the unsuccessful search is abandoned. If found, then the right to produce becomes a vested right upon the terms of the lease. Point 2 of syllabus in *Oil Co.* v. *Gas Co.*, 51 W. Va. 583 explained."

On May 24, 1907, James Metz made a lease for oil and gas purposes to Miles for a tract of 250 acres of land in Calhoun County, West Virginia. The lease was for a term of three years from date, and "as much longer as oil and gas can be found in paying quantities." There was no provision for rental or forfeiture. The lease provided for payment to Metz of a royalty of one-eighth of the oil produced, and $200 yearly for each gas well. The lessee had the right to remove machinery and "at any time surrender this lease and be relieved from all liability thereunder." Miles assigned the lease to Miller-Sibley Oil Company, which company drilled a well and found some oil, but by reason of its tools becoming fastened in the well, or from an invasion of salt water, this well was abandoned and another well was drilled, and in it a small quantity of oil was found, the quantity being a matter of controversy. This well was pumped for oil and two tanks were partially filled, one of 250 and another of 60 barrels. The first well was pumped some and a little oil obtained from it. The second well was pumped several months. Operations were suspended. The last pumping was in January, 1899. Some of the casing was pulled from the first well, and nearly all was pulled from the second well and taken away. No tools were left. The rigs were left to decay. An engine and boiler were left at the first well but parts of the engine taken away. Then an order was given to Warden, by an agent of the Miller-Sibley Company, authorizing him "to remove the engine, boiler and tanks, casing, tubing, sucker rods; etc.'' Warden at once moved the engine only. This order was dated December 11, 1900. The two rigs were left, and the boiler and some other articles used in the business. The company owned leases on other lands in the vicinity, amounting in all to 800 or 1,000 acres. This tract was stated in the lease to be a part of a block of 800 acres of land leased by Miles. The company drilled two wells on these other lands in developing the territory. These wells were not far from the tract of 250 acres. One of the wells produced gas, not oil. No royalty was ever paid to Metz by the Miller-Sibley Company.

On January 9, 1900, Metz executed to Lowther a lease on the same tract for oil and gas purposes, and Lowther assigned this lease to the Lowther Oil Company. In June, 1900, the Lowther Oil Company went upon the land and endeavored to utilize the first well which had been drilled by Miller-Sibley Company, but failed, and then went to the second well drilled by that company and cleaned and pumped it but did not succeed in producing oil in paying quantities, only producing one barrel a day, and then drilled it to greater depth and found oil in paying quantities. The Lowther Oil Company then brought suit in equity in the Circuit Court of Calhoun County against the Miller-Sibley Company to restrain the latter from entering upon the land or interfering with the possession of the land by the Lowther Oil Company, and to have the first lease made by Metz to Miles cancelled. A decree was entered by the Circuit Court cancelling the first lease, from which decree the Miller-Sibley Company appealed, and the Supreme Court affirmed the decision and held the first lease void for abandonment. The court cited in support of its decision:

Steelsmith v. *Gartlan,* 45 W. Va. 27; 29 S. E. 978.
Lowther Oil Co. v. *Guffey,* 52 W. Va. 88; 43 S. E. 101.
Venture Oil Co. v. *Fretts,* 152 Pa. 451; 25 Atl. 732.
Colgan v. *Oil Co.* 194 Pa. 234; 45 Atl. 119.

Sec. 16.—In *Lawson* v. *Kirchner,* 50 W. Va. 433; 40 S. E. 344 (Nov. 30, 1901) syls. 2-3 are as follows:

''An oil lease for oil and gas purposes is a conveyance or sale of an interest in land conditional and contingent on the discovery and reduction to possession of the oil or gas.

"A person who accepts an oil or gas lease with a stipulation therein contained to pay a monthly rental until a well is completed, or until the expiration of a certain fixed term, is bound to pay such rental although he does not within such term enter upon the land and complete such well, unless he was prevented from doing so by the plaintiffs and not by mere personal default."

In a proceeding instituted under the Statute of West Virginia which provides for the lease or sale of infant's real estate in the Circuit Court of Tyler County, on behalf of some minor heirs for the purpose of obtaining authority from the court to lease or sell the interest of said minors in a tract of land in Tyler County, West Virginia, anthority was given, and a sale or lease was made under the decree of the court, and W. E. Kirchner became the purchaser, or lessee. Kirchner was to have two years within which to drill for oil or gas, and was to pay a monthly rental of one dollar per acre, the first rental maturing September 13, 1895, and thereafter the monthly rental was to be paid on the 13th of each succeeding month until a well should be completed on the premises, or until the expiration of the term of two years. The rental was payable to the infants.

In a suit by the infants against the purchaser or lessee for the recovery of the unpaid rental judgment was rendered by the Circuit Court of Tyler County against Kirchner for the sum of $4,873.89, from which judgment a writ of error was prosecuted in the Court of Appeals, and that court affirmed the judgment of the Circuit Court.

Sec. 17.—In *Crawford* v. *Ritchie,* 43 W. Va. 252; 27 S. E. 220 (April 3, 1897) syl. 1 is as follows:

"Where a lease is made on the 12th day of April, 1889, 'for the sole and only purpose of drilling and operating for petroleum oil and gas, for the term of twenty years, or as long thereafter as oil or gas is found in paying quantities' and providing that the lessee shall commence one well on or before the tenth day of May, 1889, and prosecute the same to completion, unavoidable accidents excepted, and on the 26th day of October, 1889, the time is extended for such commencement of work by written endorsement on the lease, to the 28th day of November, 1889, and nothing is done under said lease for the period of seven years from said last named date, the lessee is presumed to have abandoned the said lease, and a court of equity may entertain a suit to cancel the lease and quiet title.''

On April 12, 1889, Robert Crawford executed an oil and gas lease to J. B. Ritchie, for a tract of 264 acres of land in Marshall County, West Virginia. The consideration was stated as follows: ''In consideration of the stipulations, rents and covenants on the part of the said party of the second part, his executors, administrators and assigns, to be kept and performed.'' The lessee agreed to commence one well in Cameron or Liberty Township, Marshall County, West Virginia, on or before the 10th day of May, 1889, and prosecute the same to completion, unavoidable accidents excepted. The time for the commencement of the test well was on October 26, 1889, by agreement extended to November 25, 1889.

The lessee failed to commence the test well and at April Rules, 1896, the lessor filed his bill in the Circuit Court of Marshall County against the lessee praying to have said lease cancelled as a cloud on his title. An amended bill was filed in the cause by the plaintiff, to which the defendant demurred, and the demurrer was sustained and the plaintiff's bill dismissed. The plaintiff appealed to the Court of Appeals, and that court reversed the Circuit Court.

Sec. 18.—In *Huggins* v. *Daley,* 99 Fed. 606; 40 C. C. A. 12; 48 L. R. A. 320 (February 9, 1900) analyzed under Chapter 6, the court held:

''We are of opinion upon the whole case that the exploration for, and development of, oil and gas was the sole consideration for the lease; that the proviso requiring the boring of a well within ninety days was a consideration precedent to the vesting of any interest in the lessee, and that the forfeiture of $50 was intended merely as a penalty to secure the drilling of a well, and if paid, would have been merely compensation to the landowner for the right of the lessee to possession during the ninety days, and such payment would not be so far a compliance with the conditions of the lease as to vest in the lessee a title in the leased premises for the period of five years; that after the expiration of ninety days from the date of the lease, there being no provision therein for any work to be done by the lessee in the development of the property,

which was the sole consideration therefor, the lessor had the
option to avoid it; that the inaction of the lessee during a period
of eight months, while operations were being commenced on adjoining lands, calculated to drain the land of the lessor and irreparably injure him, fully justified his avoidance of the lease; that
the lease to Huggins and his associates was an unequivocal declaration of his intention to avoid it, and terminated any inchoate
right which Hodges could claim thereunder."

Sec. 19.—In *New American Oil Co.* v. *Troyer,* 166 Ind. 402;
76 N. E. 253, (Dec. 14, 1905) syl. 4 is as follows:

"Where a gas lease required a lessee to pay a quarterly rental
in advance for delay beyond a stated period in drilling a well and
the lessor accepts five quarterly payments of rental without pro-
testing at the delay in drilling the well, his action in commencing
suit for the forfeiture of the contract for failure to sooner drill
the well, only ten days after the expiration of the last quarter,
for which rent was paid, without previously giving notice to the
lessee, and a reasonable time to drill the well, was inequitable and
would not be sustained."

Lucy Troyer made an oil and gas lease to one Thomas Mc-
Donald in consideration of one dollar and the conditions and
agreements in the lease set forth, granting and conveying to the
lessee all the oil and gas in and under the demised premises; together with the exclusive right to enter thereon for the purpose
of drilling and operating for oil or gas, the lessee to drill a well
on the premises within two months from the date of the lease or
thereafter pay in advance for further delay a quarterly rental
of twenty dollars until a well should be drilled. No well having
been drilled, the lessor instituted an action to quiet the title.
The Circuit Court rendered judgment for the plaintiff, from
which defendant appealed to the Supreme Court. That court
reversed the Circuit Court, and in the opinion Judge Hadley
says:

"Prior to the commencement of this suit no well had been
drilled and no possession of the premises had been taken for the
purpose of drilling. In this, as in other contracts of its class, the
purpose of the parties is exploration for oil and gas. The landowners intention to part with, and the operator's intention to
acquire no other right than the exclusive privilege of entering

upon, and with as little injury as possible to the possession of the freehold and for mutual profit in the discovery, put down wells and mine and market the product.''

This case was again taken to the Supreme Court of Indiana, 77 N. E. 739, and on April 26, 1906, that court held:

"An oil and gas lease conveying to the lessee the oil and gas under the lessor's land bound the lessee to drill a well within two months or thereafter to pay $20 quarterly in advance, and stipulated that the failure to make the quarterly payments should terminate the lease, and that the lessee might at any time re-convey the grant, and thereupon the lease should be void. *Held*, that as oil and gas are not the subject of conveyance until placed under control by being diverted into artificial channels, and as such leases are customarily made in advance of the demand for the product, oil and gas leases are not ordinary leases, and the stipulation that the lessee might re-convey the grant did not give the lessor an option to terminate the lease at pleasure.''

Sec. 20.—In *Wagner* v. *Mallory*, 169 N. Y. 501; 62 N. E. 584 (Jan. 28, 1902) the syllabus is as follows:

"1. A lessee acquires no title to oil until it has been taken from the ground under a lease granting him the exclusive right to mine and excavate oil for a specified period; one-eighth of the oil pumped and raised from the premises to be delivered to the lessor.
2. Under laws 1883, c. 372, providing that oil wells and fixtures and rights held by virtue of any lease should be deemed personal property for all purposes except taxation, the right to oil is personalty, and does not pass under a deed from the executors and devisees of the lessee conveying all the land owned by them, or in which they have an interest.''

Job Moses, on October 2, 1877, executed an oil and gas lease upon a tract of land, and died in 1887, testate. At this time one John S. Robinson was the owner of the land, subject however, to the rights reserved in said lease. Mallory and others succeeded to Robinson's rights. The executors of Job Moses, by deed dated October 2, 1888, conveyed twenty parcels of land in Carrollton, Cataraugus County, New York, and five parcels in the town of Red House, in that county, none of which included the lands owned by Robinson or Mallory, Rathbone and Tait, who

succeeded to his title. The executor's deed was made to Wagner
and others, and concluded as follows:

"It is the intent hereof to convey to the parties of the second
part all the lands and premises owned by the parties of the first
part, or in which they had an interest, lying or being in said town
of Carrollton, and the said Town of Red House, whether the same
are hereinbefore particularly described or not."

The lands of Robinson upon which the lease was outstanding were located in the town of Carrolton, and therefore it was
contended on behalf of plaintiff, Wagner, who brought suit
against Mallory and others to enjoin them from appropriating
the oil produced from the premises described in said lease, that
the leasehold interest owned by the testator at the time of his
death passed to them under the provisions of the deed. Mallory, Rathbone and Tait drilled a well on the premises, which
was a producer, and they appropriated the oil to their own use.
The Appellate division of the Supreme Court rendered judgment
for the defendants, and plaintiffs appealed to the Court of Appeals, and the judgment appealed from was affirmed. The Court
of appeals in support of its conclusions, cited the following cases:

Duffield v. Hue, 136 Pa. 502-607; 20 Atl. 526.
Westmoreland Gas Co. v. DeWitt, 130 Pa. 235-249; 18 Atl. 724.
Brown v. Vandergrift, 80 Pa. 142.
Union Petroleum Co. v. Bliven, 72 Pa. 173.
Funk v. Halderman, 53 Pa. 229.
Dark v. Johnson, 55 Pa. 164-168; 93 Am. Dec. 732.
App. of Thompson, 101 Pa. 225-232.
Goodale v. Tuttle, 29 N. Y. 459-460.

Sec. 21.—In Westmoreland, etc. Gas Co. v. Ira DeWitt, 130
Pa. 235; 18 Atl. 725; 5 L. R. A. 731, analyzed under Chapter 11,
the lessee entered upon the leased premises, which was gas territory, drilled a well, and discovered gas in large quantities.
The Gas Company connected the well with a pipe-line but did
not regularly use the gas from said well, which was shut in practically all the time. The company paid rentals but not strictly
in accordance with the provisions of the lease. DeWitt, who

held a second lease upon the premises, undertook to drill on the reserved portion of the farm, claiming that the Gas Company's lease was forfeited, when the Gas Company filed a bill, and obtained an injunction which the Court of Common Pleas of Westmoreland County on final hearing dissolved. The Gas Company appealed to the Supreme Court and that court reversed the Court of Common Pleas, re-instated the injunction, and made the same perpetual and held:

"1. Under a lease of land for the sole purpose of drilling and operating for oil and gas, the lessee's right in the surface of the land is in the nature of an easement of entry and examination with a right of possession arising where the particular place of operation is selected, and the easement of ingress, egress, storage, transportation, etc., during the continuance of operations."

The court held the lease of the Gas Company was not forfeited, because by connecting the well with the pipe-line although the gas was shut in, such connection gave to the lessee possession of the gas and the right to produce the gas vested by means thereof, in the lessee.

Sec. 22.—In *Backer* v. *Penn Lubricating Co.*, 162 Fed. 627; 89 C. C. A. 419, analyzed under Chapter 3, paragraphs 1-3-4 of the head notes are as follows:

"1. An oil lease in ordinary form, giving the lessee the exclusive right to explore for, produce and sell oil from the land on payment of a royalty, does not vest him with title to the oil in place.
2. Such a lessee however, has a right of action for damages against one who invades his exclusive right by going upon the land during the term of his lease without his consent, and drilling wells and removing and selling oil therefrom.
4. In an action by an oil lessee for damages against one who entered upon and took oil from the leased premises, an answer, alleging that defendant's entry was peaceable and made in good faith under a lease which defendant believed to be valid, is not subject to general demurrer since such good faith may at least effect the extent of defendant's liability for damages."

Upon the proposition that the ultimate measure of recovery

against a trespasser depends largely upon the question of good
or bad faith of the taking of the property, the court cited:

> *Durant Mining Co.* v. *Percy Con. Min. Co.*, 93 Fed. 166; 35
>   C. C. A. 252.
> *Woodenware Co.* v. *United States*, 106 U. S. 432.
> *Pine River Logging Co.* v. *United States*, 186 U. S. 279-293.
> *Resurrection Gold Min. Co.*, v. *Fortune Gold Mining Co.*,
>   129 Fed. 668; 64 C. C. A. 180.
> *Benson Min. Co.* v *Alta Min. Co.*, 145 U. S. 428.

Sec. 23.—In *Knotts & Garber* v. *McGregor*, 47 W. Va. 566;
37 S. E. 899, analyzed under Chapter 18, the first, second, third
and fourth points of the syllabus are as follows:

"1.   An action can be maintained against an executor for
breaches of covenant of a lease committed by his testator.
2.   In a lease for oil and gas there is an implied covenant of
right of entry and quiet enjoyment for the purposes of the lease.
3.   The covenant of quiet enjoyment in a lease for oil or gas,
or other purposes, is not broken by the mere fact, alone, that the
lessor makes another lease during the term, of the same premises,
whether the first lessee be in actual possession or not; the second
lessee not entering.
4.   The covenant for quiet enjoyment implied in a lease for
oil is broken by the exclusion by the lessor of the lessee from
taking possession for the purposes of the lease, or his withholding from him the possession of the land for the purposes of the
lease."

Sec. 24.—In *Fowler* v. *Delaplain*, 79 Ohio State, 279; 87 N.
E. 261, analyzed under Chapter 8, syl. 4 is as follows:

"An oil lease which grants to the lessee the exclusive right
to mine for and produce petroleum and natural gas on a certain
tract of land, and the possession of so much of said land as may be
necessary therefor, does not give to the lessee the right to occupy
and use any portion of the land for the purpose of cultivation
or for residences and conveniences for employes, but confines the
occupancy and use of the surface to so much as is strictly necessary for mining and producing purposes."

Sec. 25.—In *Doddridge County Oil & Gas Co.* v. *Smith*, 173
Fed. 386, first reported in 154 Fed. 970, analyzed under Chapter 18, the court held:

"It is insisted by the company that the Master has erred in charging it with the costs and expenses of drilling well Number 3, named in his report, or named Number 6 in the former opinion. This well, it will be remembered, was drilled by Smith after he had unlawfully ousted the company from the lease, as heretofore held by me, and it had been charged in his cross bill as 'a very fair well.' The company now insists, that, notwithstanding the decree herein ascertaining it to be liable to pay the actual expenses for the drilling of this well, this decree was entered under the assumption that the company would and did elect to take over this well under its lease, notwithstanding it had been drilled by Smith de son tort. On the other hand, it is insisted by Smith that the terms of this decree are absolutely final and binding upon the company, requiring it to take this well over and pay the expenses to Smith of its drilling. The master has felt himself bound to adopt this latter view, and has reported something over $2,700.00 in favor of Smith for the drilling of this well. It clearly appears from the evidence that the well was practically worthless, yielding substantially only a half a barrel of oil a day.

In view of the fact disclosed by this record that Smith had unlawfully taken charge and ousted the company from this lease, and in his cross bill represented this well to be a fair one, I do not believe it to be in accord with the dictates of equity and good conscience to require this company to pay for drilling this worthless well against their protests. * * * * * * * * I have therefore determined that, if the company so elect, I will not hold it responsible for the expense of drilling third well, and, of course, will allow it no share or part in the oil that has been received therefrom."

Sec. 26.—In *Doddridge County Oil & Gas Company* v. *Smith*, 154 Fed. 970, analyzed under Chapter 18, the concluding paragraph of the opinion is as follows:

"In conclusion, it seems clear to me that plaintiff company must be restored to its rights under the lease; that this cause must be referred to a commissioner to settle the accounts of the receiver, and ascertain the compensation due him for his services; that all costs of this receivership, other than the actual sums invested by him in preservation of the wells drilled since the lease, must be paid by Smith, as also all direct damages and costs incurred by Smith by reason of its exclusion from the lease; that an account should be stated between the plaintiff company and Smith, charging the former with the fair value of all material and machinery not returned or tendered to be returned to Smith, and with a fair compensation for the use of that returned. On the other hand, charging Smith with all the gas, if any, sold by him from the gas well, with all the oil received by him, less the

⅛ royalty from the two oil wells drilled since the lease; and allowing him, as having finished one and drilled the other de son tort, only the actual value of the work so done by him, without any personal compensation for such. And a decree may be so entered accordingly.''

Sec. 27.—In *Barnsdall* v. *Bradford Gas Co.*, — Pa. —; 74 Atl. 207, analyzed under Chapter 3, syl. 3 is as follows:

"3. Ejectment may be maintained by a lessee though he has not entered into possession where, under his lease he is entitled to the oil and gas and to possession of the premises to remove the same against a third person who claims adversely to lessor.''

LESSOR'S REMEDIES.

Sec. 28.—Where lessee under an oil and gas lease has not within a reasonable time entered upon the demised premises for the purpose of exploring for oil and gas, the law presumes an abandonment; and lessor may by suit in equity cancel the lease as a cloud on his title.

Crawford v. *Ritchie*, 43 W. Va. 252; 37 S. E. 220.
Huggins v. *Daley*, 99 Fed. 606; 40 C. C. A. 12; 48 L. R. A. 320.

Sec. 29.—Where a lessee enters upon the premises demised and drills one or more unproductive wells and then abandons the lease, lessor may declare a forfeiture, retake possession of the premises, and procure a cancellation of the lease as a cloud on his title, upon the grounds of abandonment.

Parish Fork Oil Co. v. *Bridgewater Gas Co.*, 51 W. Va. 583; 42 S. E. 655.
Steelsmith v. *Gartlan*, 45 W. Va. 27; 29 S. E. 978.
Munroe v. *Armstrong*, 96 Pa. 307.
Venture Oil Co. v. *Fretts*, 152 Pa. 451; 25 Atl. 732.
Florence Oil Co. v. *Orman*, 19 Colo. App. 79; 73 Pac. 628.
Rawlings v. *Armel*, 70 Kan. 778; 79 Pac. 683.
Lowther Oil Co. v. *Miller-Sibley Co.*, 53 W. Va. 501; 44 S. E. 433.

Sec. 30.—Where a lessee enters into possession of the premises demised and occupies and uses portions of the land for cultivation or for residences and conveniences for his employes, the landowner may, by proceedings in a court of law, recover possession of all the premises not actually necessary for producing and marketing oil and gas.

Fowler v. *Delaplain,* 79 Ohio St. 279; 87 N. E. 261.

Sec. 31.—Where during the term allowed for the original exploration and development lessee enters the premises and discovers oil or gas in paying quantities, there is an implied covenant in the lease that the work of development and production shall be continued with reasonable diligence so as to make the extraction of oil and gas from the land of mutual advantage and benefit to the lessor and lessee. A failure on the part of the lessee to prosecute the work of development will entitle lessor to recover damages at law for such breaches of the implied covenants of the lease, or cancel the lease as to the undeveloped portions of the land. The remedy depends upon whether the courts of the State prescribe a suit at law for damages, or allow the cancellation of the lease as to such undeveloped portions.

Brewster v. *Lanyon Zinc Co.,* 140 Fed. 901; 72 C. C. A. 212.
For Remedy at Law see Chapter 20.
For Remedy in equity, cancellation of lease, see Chapter 19.
For Distinction between Coal and Oil Leases See:
Plummer v. *Coal & Iron Co.,* 160 Pa. 483; 28 Atl. 353.
For Liability of Lessee to pay rentals see:
Lawson v. *Kirchner,* 50 W. Va. 433; 40 S. E. 344, and see:
Chapter 12, Forfeiture and Rental Clause—Lessor's Option.
Chapter 13, Forfeiture and Rental Clause—Lessee's Option.

LESSEE'S REMEDIES.

Sec. 32.—Where a lessee for a valuable consideration by an oil and gas lease, acquires the right to enter upon the premises demised within a fixed term for exploration purposes he is entitled to the benefit of the term fixed within which to make explorations, upon payment or tender of the rental, according to the stipulations of the lease.

See Chapter 13—Forfeiture and Rental Clause, Lessee's Option.

Sec. 33.—Where an oil and gas lease contains a rental clause which authorizes the lessee to delay explorations from time to time within the term by payment of a fixed rental, and the lessor acquiesces in delays either in beginning operations or in payment of commutation money, as provided by the lease, he waives the right to forfeit the lease therefor, and lessee may hold the lease, notwithstanding such technical forfeiture.

New American Oil Co. v. *Troyer,* 166 Ind. 402; 76 N. E. 353;
     77 N. E. 739.
See Chapter 21, Waiver of Forfeiture.

Sec. 34.—There is an implied covenant in an oil and gas lease of right of entry and quiet enjoyment for the purposes of the lease. The implied covenant for quiet enjoyment is broken by the exclusion of the lessee by lessor from taking possession of the premises for the purposes of the lease, or his withholding from lessee the possession of the land for the purposes of the lease; and lessor may recover damages in an action at law against lessor for such breaches of the implied covenants of the lease.

Knotts & Garber v. *McGregor,* 47 W. Va. 566; 37 S. E. 899.

Sec. 35.—Where lessee has entered the demised premises and discovered oil or gas in paying quantities, he may by bill in equity enjoin lessor from drilling other wells upon the leasehold or from interfering with lessee in his right to the possession of the premises for the purposes of the lease.

Westmoreland Gas Co. v. *DeWitt,* 130 Pa. 235; 18 Atl. 724;
     5 L. R. A. 731.

Sec. 36.—A lessee under an oil and gas lease has a right of action for damages against one who enters upon the demised premises during the term without his consent and drills wells and removes and converts to his own use oil and gas therefrom. The measure of lessee's damages is the value of the oil or gas so taken. Where the person so entering is a trespasser, lessee may recover the value of all the oil taken; but where such per-

son enters under color of title or in good faith believing he has a
right to the oil and gas, the actual expenses of production will
in such case be deducted and lessee is only entitled to recover
the value of the oil or gas taken, less the actual cost of production.   No deduction will be made for drilling dry holes.

Backer v. *Penn Lubricating Co.*, 162 Fed. 627; 89 C. C. A. 419.
Doddridge County Oil & Gas Co. v. *Smith*, 173 Fed. 386.
Doddridge County Oil & Gas Co. v. *Smith*, 154 Fed. 970.
See Chapter 27—Oil and Gas in Place are Minerals and part
   of the land.

Sec. 37.—A lessee entitled under an oil and gas lease to
enter upon the demised premises and extract the oil and gas
therefrom, may maintain an action of ejectment for possession
of the premises against a third person who enters thereon, claiming adversely to him.

Barnsdall v. *Bradford Gas Co.* —— Pa. ——; 74 Atl. 207.

Sec. 38.—Whether an oil and gas lease is real estate or personal property depends upon the statute law of the State wherein the leasehold is situated.

Wagner v. *Mallory*, 169 N. Y. 501; 62 N. E. 584.

Sec. 39.—A lessee may, by bill in equity, or petition in a court
exercising equity jurisdiction and powers, settle and adjust all
questions as to the validity and priority of oil and gas leases
between claimants, where such leases have been made by a common landowner; and the court having taken jurisdiction for one
purpose will adjudicate the rights of all parties and enter such
decrees as may be just and proper.

See Chapter 51, Remedies in Equity.

CHAPTER 6.

TERM OF THE OIL AND GAS LEASE.

Sec. 1.—Where the lease provides that the lessee shall have a specified period of time within which to explore, although the lease may provide that the term shall be as long as rentals are paid or oil or gas produced in paying quantities, yet unless oil or gas is found in paying quantities within the specified period of time, the payment or tender of such rental after the expiration of the definite term will not extend the time, and after the expiration of this specified period of time, the lease becomes a tenancy at will.

Western Pennsylvania Gas Co. v. *George,* 161 Pa. 47; 28 Atl. 1004.
Bettman v. *Harness,* 42 W. Va. 433; 26 S. E. 271.
Northwestern Ohio Nat. Gas Co. v. *City of Tiffin,* 59 Ohio St. 420; 54 N. E. 77.
Murdock-West Co. v. *Logan,* 69 Ohio St. 514; 69 N. E. 984.
Huggins v. *Daley,* 99 Fed. 606; 40 C. C. A. 12; 48 L. R. A. 320.
Chaney v. *Ohio etc Gas Co.* 32 Ind. App. 193; 69 N. E. 477.
Eaton v. *Allegheny Gas Co.* 122 N. Y. 416; 25 N. E. 981.
Brown v. *Fowler,* 65 Ohio St. 507; 63 N. E. 76.
Cassell v. *Crothers,* 193 Pa. 359; 44 Atl. 446.
Lowther Oil Co. v. *Guffey,* 52 W. Va. 88; 43 S. E. 101.
Lowther Oil Co. v. *Miller-Sibley Oil Co.* 53 W. Va. 501; 44 S. E. 433; 97 Am. St. 1027.
Brewster v. *Lanyon Zinc Co.* 140 Fed. 801; 72 C. C. A. 213.
Am. Window Glass Co. v. *Williams,* 66 N. E. 912.
Central Ohio Fuel Co. v. *Eckert,* 70 Ohio St. 127; 71 N. E. 281.
Pyle v. *Henderson,* 65 W. Va. 39; 63 S. E. 620.
Thomas v. *Hukill,* 34 W. Va. 385; 12 S. E. 522.
Hazelgreen Oil & Gas Co. v. *Collins,* —— Ky. ——; 110 S. W. 343.
Riddle v. *Mellon,* 147 Pa. 30; 23 Atl. 241.

Sec. 2.—While a lease may be terminated before the expiration of the term by failure to pay the stipulated rentals or commutation money in the manner provided for, and while the lessor and lessee may agree orally upon extensions of the time for the payment of the rental or commutation money, yet unless the explorations are made and prove successful and oil or gas found in paying quantities within the term, payment of the rental or commutation money will not extend the term beyond that specified in the lease. The term of the lease fixes its life beyond which the only means of preserving it is the discovery by lessee within the term of oil or gas in paying quantities. Where such discovery is made the right to produce vests in lessee to the extent provided for in the lease, and the language of the ordinary lease, which provides that it shall extend as much longer after the term as oil or gas is found in paying quantities, preserves the lease until the oil and gas are exhausted, or the lease abandoned.

Sec. 3.—The term of the lease measures the time during which the lessee is authorized to explore for oil or gas, or for delay in such explorations to pay the commutation money, commonly called rental. Where the lands demised or granted embrace a considerable area it may be that one well constitutes a very imperfect test of the territory. The object of an oil and gas lease being exploration and production of oil and gas the lessee must either prosecute his work of exploration, pay commutation money for delay, or surrender the lease. The law will not tolerate unreasonably tying up property, either for speculative purposes or merely to suit the convenience of the lessee. He must always be diligent. While the lessee may not lose his right to continue explorations by drilling one or more wells which prove unproductive, yet such drilling is not the measure of his diligence unless he desires to abandon the search after such effort. A cessation of explorations for an unreasonable period of time, unless commutation money is paid for delay will be construed to constitute abandonment, which gives the lessor the right to declare a forfeiture and resort to a court for the cancellation of the lease.

Sec. 4.—In *Western Pennsylvania Gas Co.* v. *George*, 161 Pa. 47; 28 Atl. 1004 (April 9, 1894) the syllabus is as follows:

"An oil lease 'for the purpose of drilling and operating for oil and gas' provided that the lessee should hold the leased premises during the term of two years from the date thereof, and as much longer as oil and gas were found in paying quantities or the rental paid thereon. The lessor was to receive one-eighth of the oil produced, and $500.00 per annum for each well from which gas should be obtained in paying quantities, and so long as it should be sold therefrom. The lease further provided that the lessee should commence a well within thirty days and complete it within ninety days 'or in default thereof pay to the party of the first part for further delay an annual rental of Sixty Dollars, payable quarterly in advance on the premises from the time above specified for completing a well, until such well shall be completed. A failure to complete such well or pay said rental within the time specified or within ten days thereafter shall render this lease null and void.' *Held*, that the failure of the lessee to complete a well within the term of two years enabled the lessor to terminate the lease on the expiration of it, and that the lessee could not indefinitely continue the lease by payment of Sixty Dollars per annum after the expiration of the two years.''

Robert S. George made an oil and gas lease whereby he demised to D. J. Sterling a tract of land, and Sterling assigned the lease to the Western Pennsylvania Gas Company. The lease was for a term of two years with a provision as follows:

"And as much longer as oil or gas is found in paying quantities or the rental paid thereon."

The lessee was to commence a well on the premises within thirty days and complete it within ninety days from the date of the lease, and in case of his failure to do so he was to pay to the lessor $60.00 per annum quarterly in advance. Neither the lessee nor his assignee entered upon the leased premises for the purpose of drilling for oil or gas during the term of two years which ended on July 16, 1892. The Gas Company the assignee, claimed the right to hold the lease after the expiration of the two-year term without making explorations, by tendering the quarterly rental provided for. The lessor refused to accept this rental, and the Gas Company brought suit for possession of the premises in the Court of Common Pleas of Washington County, which court without a jury, rendered judgment for the defendant George, from which judgment the Gas Company appealed to the Pennsylvania Supreme Court. That court affirmed the judgment of the Court of Common Pleas.

Sec. 5.—In *Bettman v. Harness,* 42 W. Va. 433; 26 S. E. 271 (Nov. 25, 1896) syl. 4 is as follows:

"A lease for oil and gas contains the clause, 'to have and to hold the said premises unto said party of the second part during and until the full term of two years, and as much longer as oil or gas is found in paying quantities thereon, or the rental paid thereon' and provided for a rent of one-eighth of the oil, and Two Hundred and Fifty Dollars per year for gas, and has a clause reading: 'Operations shall be commenced and one well completed within one month, and, in case of failure to complete one well within such time, the party of the second part agrees to pay the parties of the first part, for such delay, fifteen dollars per month in advance after said time for completing such well, as above specified, and the parties of the first part agree to accept such sum as a full consideration and payment for such delay until one well shall be completed; and a failure to complete one well or to make such payment for such delay is to render this lease null and void at the option of the lessor.' The lessee, having failed to begin operations within the two years, has no right to continue the lease by payment of Fifteen Dollars per month, but the lease is ended."

Harness and wife made two oil and gas leases to Watson, granting the exclusive privilege to drill and operate for petroleum oil and gas on two tracts of land in Pleasants County, which leases Watson assigned to Bettman. No possession was taken under these leases, and later Harness and wife, claiming that the leases had expired, made a lease for oil and gas purposes to Finnegan, under which last lease possession was taken and drilling for oil was commenced, when Bettman instituted a suit in equity in the Circuit Court of Pleasants County against Harness, Finnegan and others, and obtained an injunction enjoining operations under the second lease. The Judge of the Circuit Court over-ruled a motion to dissolve this injunction and the defendants appealed. The Court of Appeals of West Virginia reversed the order of the Circuit Court over-ruling the motion to dissolve the injunction, dissolved the injunction and as the bill was considered purely an injunction bill, dismissed it. Upon the construction of the lease the court cited:

Western Pennsylvania Gas Co. v. *George,* 161 Pa. 47; 28 Atl. 1004.

Sec. 6.—In *Northwestern Ohio Nat. Gas. Co.* v. *City of Tiffin*, 59 Ohio St. 420; 54 N. E. 77 (Jan. 17, 1899) syl. 2 is as follows:

"2. Such a lease or license, granted for a specified term of years, and as much longer as oil or gas is produced or found in paying quantities on the land, expires at the end of the specified term, unless within that time oil or gas is obtained from the land in the designated quantities."

On June 10, 1886, John A. Taylor executed an oil and gas lease in favor of William Duke, Jr., on a tract of one hundred acres of land in Hancock County, Ohio, for the term of five years from the date thereof, and as much longer as oil or gas should be produced in paying quantities the lessee to complete a well on the premises within nine months from the date of the lease or to pay the lessor for delay a yearly rental of fifty cents per acre from the time given to complete such well until the same should be completed, and a failure to complete such well or to make such payment should render the lease null and void. The rentals were to be paid by the first day of March in each year. Payments and extensions of the lease were made, and the lease was assigned by the original lessee to the Northwestern Ohio Natural Gas Company. In March, 1894, Alvin Shoupe purchased one of the tracts of land granted by the lease. The Gas Company had never entered upon the tract for the purpose of making explorations. When Shoupe purchased, the adjoining lands were being operated for gas, and large quantities were being taken therefrom.

In April, 1895, after the expiration of the lease, Shoupe executed to the City of Tiffin an oil and gas lease, granting to the said City the exclusive right to enter upon the land and explore for oil and gas. The City of Tiffin did, in fact, enter upon said land and commenced the construction of the necessary derricks and machinery, and commenced to drill upon the land, when the Northwestern Ohio Natural Gas Company filed a petition against the city and others to enjoin the city and its officers from entering upon and removing the gas from the demised premises. The Circuit Court dismissed the plaintiff's petition and rendered judgment in favor of the defendant for costs. To reverse this judgment error was prosecuted to the Supreme Court of Ohio, which court affirmed the judgment of the Circuit Court.

Sec. 7.—In *Murdock-West Co.* v. *Logan,* 69 Ohio St. 514; 69 N. E. 984 (Feb. 2, 1904) syls. 2-3 are as follows:

"2. The stipulation in the lease that the term shall continue 'as much longer thereafter as oil or gas shall be found in paying quantities' requires that oil or gas shall be actually discovered and produced in paying quantities within the term.

3. Upon the hypothesis that the payment of $50 per month under the stipulations of the lease, was payment of rent, the failure of the lessee to pay $50 for the month from April 22, 1900, to May 22, 1900, rendered their lease null and void from and after April 22, 1900."

On May 23, 1900, John Lightner and wife made an oil and gas lease to Murdock-West Company, a co-partnership. On December 22, 1899, Lightner and wife executed an oil and gas lease to Logan. This lease being prior in time, provided that the lessee should hold the premises for the term of sixty days from date, and as much longer thereafter as oil or gas should be found in paying quantities. The lessee under the first lease did not commence to drill a well on the leased land within sixty days from the date of the lease. The claimants to this first lease claimed that the term thereof was extended to April 22, 1900, and further claimed that within that time oil in paying quantities was found upon the land, which they claimed entitled them to a continuance of the lease thereafter so long as oil or gas should be produced in paying quantities.

The lessees of the first lease founded their pretentions to a continuance of their term upon the principle that where a lessee holds over after the expiration of the term of the lease, the lessor has the option to treat him as a trespasser, or as a tenant under the terms of the original lease. The lessor, John Lightner, in this case, accepted payment from the original lessee of fifty dollars, on March 1, 1900, and fifty dollars on March 22, 1900, and the original lessee claimed that this extended the term of the lease to April 22, 1900, 'and as much longer as oil or gas should be found in paying quantities."

Murdock-West Company instituted suit in the Court of Common Pleas of Washington County, to enjoin the original lessee under the lease dated December 22, 1899, and that court granted a perpetual injunction against the defendant. The defendants appealed to the Circuit Court and that court made special findings of fact: That on April 8, 1900, defendants completed an oil well under their lease, which was drilled through the oil bearing sand, which underlaid said tract of land, and from which oil was then being produced in paying quantities on premises adjoining said tract of land; that after completing said well the defendants pumped the same with the drilling machine which had drilled said well, commencing ·on the morning of April 9, 1900, and continuing until noon on April 12, 1900, when they ceased pumping; that said well was not pumped again until June 1, 1900, when it was pumped by means of a power; that such pumping continued until June 3, 1900, at which time the plaintiff, the lessee under the second lease, obtained the injunction. The Circuit Court further found that the defendants upon the test made, ascertained that the well would probably produce oil in paying quantities, and having decided as a result of such test that such well would produce oil in paying quantities, defendants determined to pump said well by means of a power. The Supreme Court of Ohio, in the opinion rendered by Judge Davis, found that there was no testimony establishing the fact that oil was actually produced on the day the well was completed. The Supreme Court further found, in the opinion, that the pumping found by the Circuit Court to have been done in June, 1900, was done after the lessor had declared the lease void, and after the plaintiffs had acquired their title. Upon the question of discovery of oil by the defendant, Judge Davis, in the opinion, said:

"All this demonstrates that, while the parties interested may have entertained a well founded opinion as to the outcome of the well, oil in paying quantities had not yet been found, obtained or produced. In order to continue their lease beyond the stipulated time it was necessary for the lessees to find oil in paying quantities. For this purpose it was not sufficient to complete a well having some indications of oil, or·a well which might be developed into a well producing oil in paying quantities, but the

lessee must actually find oil in paying quantities, and this is the
same as obtaining and producing it in paying quantities.''

The Supreme Court reversed the Circuit Court and entered
judgment for plaintiffs, and cited in support of its conclusions:

Gas Co. v. *George,* 161 Pa. 47; 28 Atl. 1004.
Cassell v. *Crothers,* 193, Pa. 359; 44 Atl. 446.
Detlor v. *Holland,* 57 Ohio St. 492; 49 N. E. 690.
Gas Co. v. *Tiffin,* 59 Ohio St. 420; 54 N. E. 77.

Sec. 8.—In *Huggins* v. *Daley,* 99 Fed. 606; 40 C. C. A. 12;
48 L. R. A. 320, (Feb. 6, 1900) the third paragraph of the headnotes is as follows:

"3.   Where an oil and gas lease by which the lessor is to be
compensated solely by a share of the product, contains a proviso
requiring the lessee to commence and complete a well on the
property within a specified time, such proviso and the time of
its performance are of the essence of the contract, and it constitutes a condition precedent to the vesting of any estate in the
lessee, without regard to the grammatical construction of the
instrument.   When the lessee makes no attempt to comply with
such provision, and evidences no intention to do so, at the expiration of the time stipulated the lease becomes forfeitable, at the
option of the lessor, although by its terms it is for a definite term
of years; and being in possession, the exercise of such option is
sufficiently evidenced by the lessor's execution of a new lease to
another party.''

F. P. Marshall executed an oil and gas lease upon a fifty-
acre tract of land in Ritchie County, West Virginia, to A. P.
Hodges, who subsequently assigned his lease to Daley.   The
lease bore date March 12, 1887, and recited a consideration of
One Dollar, and demised, granted and let to the lessee, all the
oil and gas in and under said tract of land, and also the tract of
land for the purpose of operating thereon for oil and gas.   The
term of the lease was five years from date and as much longer
as oil or gas should be found in paying quantities, not exceeding
the term of thirty-five years.   The lease contained the following
proviso:

"Provided, however, that a well shall be commenced upon the
above described premises within 30 and completed within 90 days

from the date hereof and in case of failure to commence and complete said well as aforesaid the lessee shall pay to the lessor a forfeit of $50.00.''

Neither the lessee, Hodges, nor his assignee, Daley, entered upon the premises for the purpose of making explorations, either within the thirty days, or the ninety days, mentioned in the proviso of the lease. On November 6, 1897, Marshall executed a second lease to J. J. and J. B. Huggins for the same tract of land. These lessees entered upon the premises and commenced to put down a well, when Daley filed his bill in equity in the Circuit Court of the United States for the District of West Virginia, for an injunction and receiver, and for the cancellation of the Huggins lease, alleging that the second lease was a cloud on the title and claiming that the fifty dollar forfeiture in the proviso was in lieu of rental, and such forfeiture so expressed gave to the assignee of the original lessee the right of exploration for the full term of five years. This position was sustained by the Circuit Court, and a decree entered cancelling the Huggins lease. These second lessees appealed to the Circuit Court of Appeals for the Fourth Circuit, and that court reversed the decree of the Circuit Court, remanded the cause for settlement of the receivership accounts and a restoration of the property to the claimants under the second lease, and directed the dismissal of the bill. In support of the conclusions reached the court cited:

Steelsmith v. *Gartlan*, 45 W. Va. 27; 29 S. E. 978.
Oil Co. v. *Fretts*, 152 Pa. 451; 25 Atl. 732.
Guffey v. *Hukill*, 34 W. Va. 49; 11 S. E. 754.
Iron Co. v. *Trout*, 83 Va. 397; 2 S. E. 713.

Sec. 9.—In *Chaney* v. *Ohio etc. Oil Co.*, 32 Ind. App. 193; 69 N. E. 477 (Jan. 12, 1904) syl. 1 is as follows:

''Where a gas and oil lease provides that the lessee shall hold the premises for one year, and so long thereafter as oil and gas shall be found in paying quantities, the lease expires at the expiration of one year unless gas has been found in paying quantities.''

On April 8, 1896, David Chaney executed an oil and gas lease to J. A. Graves for a tract of 80 acres of land in Jay County, Indiana. The lease was for a term of one year from the date thereof and as long thereafter as oil or gas could be produced in paying quantities, and provided that if there was no well drilled on the south-west corner of the A. J. Bone farm within sixty days the lease should be null and void between both parties; and that after the A. J. Bone well should be completed the lessee should complete a well within thirty days on the demised premises. Otherwise the lease should be null and void unless the lessee should pay the lessor two dollars per day in advance until such well should be completed, and that there should be one well completed every sixty days until eight wells were completed, or the lessee should pay one dollar per day for each undrilled well until such well should be drilled, or forfeit the lease, except the land drilled on at the rate of ten acres to the well. The lessee drilled the well on the A. J. Bone tract, prior to June 15, 1896, and on or about that date the said Graves took actual possession of the demised premises and before the last day of June, 1896, completed a well thereon, which well was completed within the thirty days provided for the A. J. Bone well. No other well was ever completed on said real estate by Graves or by his assignee, and no rental or penalty was paid to the lessor by the lessee or his assignee. The well drilled on the demised premises never produced oil or gas after September 14, 1896. Between September 14th and the first day of December, 1896, Graves removed all his property of every kind out of and from said well, and off the premises, and wholly abandoned the same, and never had actual possession of the real estate for any purpose whatever, after the first of December, 1896. On June 26, 1897, Graves attempted to assign to the Ohio and Indiana Oil Company the lease of April 8, 1896, and made a written transfer of the lease by which he purported to grant, bargain, sell and transfer all his right, title and interest in said lease to the said Oil and Gas Company. Chaney instituted suit in the Circuit Court of Wells County, against the Ohio and Indiana Oil Company to recover from it the penalties for failure to put down the wells mentioned in his lease to Graves. The Circuit Court rendered judgment for the defendant, from which judgment Chaney appealed to the Appellate Court, and that court affirmed the judgment of the Circuit Court, and held, as to the forfeiture as stated in syllabus 2, and as to the recovery of the penalties as against the assignee, the court held, that as the assignment of the lease occurred after the forfeiture thereof, there was no privity of contract or title between the lessor and the assignee of Graves, and therefore that there could be no recovery. Upon the question of the forfeiture of the lease the court cited:

Western Pennsylvania Gas Co. v. *George,* 161 Pa. 47; 28 Atl. 1004·
Brown v. *Fowler,* 65 Ohio St. 507; 63 N. E. 76.
Cassell v. *Crothers,* 193 Pa. 359; 44 Atl. 446.

Sec. 10.—In *Eaton* v. *Allegheny Gas Co.,* 122 N. Y. 416; 25 N. E. 981 (Dec. 2, 1890) the syllabus is as follows:

"1. The owner of land granted it to others by a so-called 'lease' for the purpose of boring for oil and gas thereon, with the right to the grantees to appropriate the oil or gas found therein on payment of a certain royalty to the grantor. The term was expressly stated as being 'twelve years from this date or as long as oil is found in paying quantities.' *Held,* that the length of time during which oil is found in paying quantities fixes the duration of the term.
2. Where the grantees have sought for oil for two years, and, failing to find it, have abandoned the use of the premises for that purpose, the grantor may terminate the lease."

On April 27, 1881, Harvey C. Foster executed an oil and gas lease to W. A. Wilson, A. B. Wheeler and W. T. Eaton for a tract of fifteen acres of land for the term of twelve years from date, or as long as oil should be found in paying quantities, the lease to be null and void and at an end unless the lessees should within six months from date commence and prosecute with due diligence, unavoidable accidents excepted, the drilling of one well on or in the vicinity of the lease to a depth of 1,200 feet, unless oil in paying quantities should be sooner found. The lease further provided that if the lessees failed to keep and perform the covenants and agreements by them to be kept and perform-

ed, then the lease should be null and void and surrendered to
the lessor. The lessees entered upon the leased premises in
June, 1881, erected an engine house, placed therein an engine,
and boiler, with tools and machinery, erected a derrick and began drilling a well, and before the end of July had drilled to a
depth of 1093 feet, and about the middle of August had reached
a depth of 1500 feet. Drilling was then suspended until the
winter and early spring of 1882, when it was resumed and the
well sunk to the depth of 1800 feet. At the depth of 1045 feet
natural gas was found in large quantities. At 1093 feet some oil
was found but not in paying quantities. The well was cased
down to rock, a depth of 285 feet, but was never tubed for the
purpose of obtaining the oil. The gas was conducted about 150
feet away from the well, as a precaution against the destruction
of the buildings and derrick by fire, the pipe turned up at the
end, the gas lighted and allowed to burn. The gas was only
utilized in drilling by the lessees. In the spring of 1883, the lessees ceased to prosecute operations for mining purposes on the
premises, and afterwards did not in any manner attempt to obtain oil therefrom, which they never found in paying quantities.
In the autumn of 1882, the lessees removed from the premises
their engine, boiler and machinery, but left thereon their engine
house, derrick, the casing in the well down to the rock, and the
tubing which conducted the gas from the well. On February 8,
1884, Harvey C. Foster, the lessor entered into a written contract, under seal, with Charles P. Thurston, whereby he leased
to said Thurston 100 acres of land, including the fifteen acres
mentioned in the first lease, for the purpose of mining, drilling
and excavating for petroleum, carbon and gas. The second
lease contained this covenant:

"And it is further agreed that this instrument is subject to
a lease on a part of said lands made to Wilcox, Wheeler and
Eaton, in case the same is not now, or does not become, forfeited
or cancelled."

On the day of the date of the last mentioned lease it was
assigned by the lessee to the Allegheny Gas Company, which
company immediately entered into possession of the premises,

cleaned out and tubed the well, after which it produced gas and
became of great value. Shortly after the Gas Company began
its operations the plaintiffs gave it notice of their claims and
insisted that they were entitled to ten-twelfths of the gas produced, and demanded that they be permitted to enjoy their rights,
which was refused, and thereupon the original lessees brought
suit to restrain the Gas Company from appropriating to itself,
to the exclusion of the plaintiffs, the gas well and its product,
and to recover their respective interests in the property, with
damages for their exclusion. The Court dismissed the complaint, the plaintiffs appealed to the Supreme Court, and that
court reversed the court below and thereupon the case was appealed to the Court of Appeals, and that court reversed the Supreme Court.   .

Sec. 11.—In *Brown* v. *Fowler*, 65 Ohio St. 507; 63 N. E. 76,
analyzed under Chap. 4, syl. 5 is as follows:

"Another lease in every respect like the above except as to
the clause as to drilling a well within twelve months, had the
following clause as to that matter: 'In case no well shall be
drilled on said premises within two years from the date hereof,
this lease shall become null and void unless the lessee shall pay
for further delay at the rate of One Dollar per acre at or before
the end of each year thereafter until a well shall be drilled.' No
well having been drilled and no oil or gas found, within the two
years mentioned in said clause, the payment of $1.00 per acre
could in no event have the effect to extend the lease, or the right
to drill, beyond the term of two years mentioned in the habendum
clause, unless the parties should by a further contract, extend the
time."

Catharine Fowler and husband on December 8, 1896, made
an oil and gas lease for a tract of land to H. A. Snyder. The
lease was for a specified term of two years from date, and as
long thereafter as oil or gas should be found in paying quantities, not exceeding the term of twenty-five years from the date.
The lease provided that in case no well was drilled on the premises within twelve months from the date thereof, it should be
null and void unless the lessee should pay for further delay at
the rate of one dollar per acre at or before the end of each year

thereafter until a well should be drilled. The lease was assigned and finally became the property of Brown and others, the plaintiffs. Catharine Fowler and her husband, on November 26, 1898, claimed that the lease was void, and on that day executed another lease of the same premises to George Gillmor, who on December 9, 1898, notified the holders of the first lease not to do any work on the premises. On December 15, 1898, Brown and others assignees of the first lease, commenced an action against Gillmor and Fowlers to enjoin them from drilling on said premises for oil and gas under the second lease, and the defendants filed a cross-petition to enjoin the plaintiffs from operating on the premises. The case went to the Circuit Court on Appeal, and upon the trial in that court judgment was rendered in favor of defendants Snyder and Fowler, from which judgment Brown and others, the assignees of the original lease, appealed to the Supreme Court of Ohio. The Supreme Court predicated its findings upon the following facts: No oil or gas well was drilled by the original lessee, H. A. Snyder, or his assignees, on the premises within two years from the date of the lease; no oil or gas has been found thereon; neither the lessee nor his assignees had taken possession or done any work on the premises until about November 10, 1898, when the Scio Oil & Gas Company, then owning the said lease, began to place thereon material for the erection of a derrick, and erected thereon a rig for the purpose of drilling for oil and gas, prior to December 8, 1898, but had not begun to drill; no well had been completed on the premises, nor could a well be drilled and completed by December 8, 1898; neither oil nor gas had been found on the premises prior to December 8, 1898; the Scio Oil and Gas Company, after tendering the rental to one of the lessors, on December 1, 1898, deposited it in the Scio Bank, at Scio, Ohio, to the credit of the lessors, to pay for further delay in drilling for two years after December 8, 1897; the amount so credited was $40.00; the lessors refused to accept the deposit. Upon these facts found by the Circuit Court, the Supreme Court affirmed its decision.

Sec. 12.—In *Cassell* v. *Crothers*, 193 Pa. 359; 44 Atl. 446 (Oct. 30, 1899) syl. 1 is as follows:

"1. In an oil lease for a fixed period, and 'as long thereafter as oil is found in paying quantities' where the lessor's compensation is one-eighth of the oil produced, the tenancy as to the surface of the land, after the expiration of the fixed period, and after the fact that oil is not being found and produced in paying quantities, becomes susceptible of proof, is a tenancy in the nature of a tenancy at will, and if not actually terminated by mutual consent, or continued by mutual consent, in order that further explorations be made, may be terminated by either party."

On April 22, 1887, W. B. Crothers leased his farm in Buffalo Township, Washington County, Pennsylvania, containing 96 acres, to the Marshall Oil Company for oil and gas purposes, for the term of ten years, and as long thereafter as oil and gas should be found in paying quantities. The Marshall Oil Company assigned the lease, and it became vested in Cecelia Cassell, on March 18, 1891. A number of wells were drilled on this farm under the lease shortly after its execution, and oil, but not gas, was found in paying quantities. The term of the lease—ten years—expired April 22, 1897, and at that time there were five wells that had been, or were being, pumped for oil. On July 1, 1897, four wells were producing oil, and on November 14, 1897, only three. On the last named day all the oil in the tanks was run into the pipelines, all the wells were shut down, the loose tools were locked up, and the employes in charge of the lease left it, and none of them returned except as hereinafter stated. At the time the wells were thus shut down they were making in all one or two barrels of oil per day, and were not at that time producing oil in paying quantities, a production of eight or ten barrels per day being necessary in order to make the lease produce oil in paying quantities. The wells were shut down and left as indicated by the field manager, in pursuance to directions received from attorney's in fact of Cecelia Cassell, which directions were in a letter in substance stating to the field manager that the attorney in fact had recently written Mr. Mallick to instruct the manager to shut down the Blaney well on the W. B. Crothers farm for the winter; that it was not their intention to clean out any wells in that section before the next spring. This letter was dated November 9, 1897. Some time in April, 1898, W. B. Crothers, the lessor, entered and took possession of all the wells and property theretofore in the possession and operated by Cecelia Cassell, including boilers, engines, steampipe, sucker-rods, tools, etc., under the claim that the term of the lease was ended, and that the leased premises, and everything thereon belonged to him. Crothers shot and cleaned out some of the wells, re-built some of the rigs, repaired some of the machinery, and by July 1, 1889, was producing oil in paying quantities, to-wit, eight or ten barrels per day. On May 15th or 16th, 1898, Cecelia Cassell, knowing what Crothers had done, sent an employe to take charge of her wells on this farm, who was ordered off and threatened with arrest by Crothers, who claimed that the plaintiff no longer had any right under the lease of April 22, 1897. Between November 14, 1897, when the wells were shut down, and May 15th or 16th, 1898, when the employe of Cecelia Cassell made his appearance, no one on her behalf had done anything upon the leased premises. On August 24, 1898, Cecelia Cassell instituted her action of ejectment against Crothers to recover possession of this tract of land for oil and gas purposes. The Court of Common Pleas decided in favor of the defendant, from which decision the plaintiff appealed, and the Court of Appeals affirmed the court below.

Sec. 13.—In *Lowther Oil Co.* v. *Guffey*, 52 W. Va. 88; 43 S. E. 101 (November 29, 1902) the syllabus is as follows:

"Where a grant of oil and gas, and oil and gas privileges, in consideration of One Dollar, without limitation as to time, contains a forfeiture clause in these words: 'In case no well is completed within two years from this date, then this grant shall immediately become null and void as to both parties, provided, that second party may prevent such forfeiture from year to year by paying to the first annually in advance eighteen and seventy-five one-hundredths dollars at her residence until such well is completed,' such lease is thereby converted into a lease from year to year at the option of the lessee until a well is completed. It would then continue so long as oil or gas is produced in paying quantities."

On April 13, 1895, Ella Yoak and Agnes Yoak, in consideration of one dollar, executed to J. M. Guffey and oil and gas lease for a tract of seventy-five acres of land in Calhoun County,

West Virginia, the lessee to have and to hold said premises upon the following conditions: That in case no well should be completed within two years from date the lease should immediately become null and void unless the lessee should prevent such forfeiture from year to year by paying the lessor annually in advance, $18.75. On October 3, 1900, the lessors made a second lease to the Lowther Oil Company. The original lessee Guffey, did not drill a well on the land but kept up the commutation money till April 13, 1901. In March, 1901, Guffey took possession and began drilling and tendered to lessors the commutation money of $18.75, and a further sum increasing the aggregate to $75.00, if they would permit him to continue operations without molestation. The lessors refused to accept the tender, having executed a second lease to the Lowther Oil Company on October 3, 1900, subject to the Guffey lease. The Lowther Oil Company filed their bill in equity in the Circuit Court of Calhoun County for the purpose of cancelling the Guffey lease as a cloud on the title to the premises, and to obtain an injunction perpetually enjoining all operations under the Guffey lease. The Circuit Court rendered a decree in favor of the Lowther Oil Company, which decree cancelled the Guffey lease, from which decree Guffey appealed to the West Virginia Court of Appeals, and that court reversed the decree of the Circuit Court. Upon the construction of the lease the court cited:

Allegheny Oil Co. v. *Snyder,* 106 Fed. Rep. 764; 45 C. C. A. 60.
McMillan v. *Phila. Co.* 159 Pa. 142.

Upon the question of the recital in the Lowther Oil Company lease, and subject thereto, the court in the opinion, said:

"The plaintiff's lease was taken with full knowledge of the subject of, and subject to, the appellant's lease, and hence it has no rights thereunder until appellant's lease is forfeited."

Schaupp v. *Hukill,* 34 W. Va. 375; 12 S. E. 501.
Hukill v. *Myers,* 36 W. Va. 639; 15 S. E. 151.
Elk Fork Oil & Gas Co. v. *Jennings,* 84 Fed. 839.

Sec. 14.—In *Lowther Oil Co.* v. *Miller-Sibley Oil Co.,* 53 W.

Va. 501; 44 S. E. 433; 47 Am. St. Rep. 1027, analyzed under Chapter 5, syl. 4 is as follows:

"Where an oil and gas lease is for a given term, 'and as much longer as oil and gas can be produced in paying quantities' to the lessee, if a well pays a profit, even a small one, over operating expenses, it produces 'in paying quantity', though it never repay its cost, and the operation as a whole may result in loss. The phrase 'paying quantity' is to be construed with reference to the judgment of the operator when exercised in good faith."

In support of the conclusion the court cited:

Young v. *Oil Co.*, 194 Pa. 243; 45 Atl. 121.

Sec. 15.—In *Brewster* v. *Lanyon Zinc Co.*, 140 Fed. 801; 72 C. C. A. 213, analyzed under Chapter 5, the Court as to the term of the lease, held:

"A lease for a definite and permissible term, but which reserves to the lessee an option to terminate it before the expiration of the term, does not create a mere tenancy at will, within the operation of the rule that an estate at the will of one party is equally at the will of the other."

Sec. 16.—In *American Window Glass Co.* v. *Williams,* (Ind. App.) 66 N. E. 912, (April 3, 1903) syl. 1 is as follows:

"A landowner leased his premises to a gas company for ten years, and as much longer as gas was found in paying quantities, or the 'rental' paid as provided. If gas was found in quantities sufficient for manufacturing purposes, the lessor was to receive $100 per annum for each well from the time gas was used therefrom for such purposes. Until the lessee drilled a well and began to use gas therefrom for such purposes, it was to pay $50 a year 'rent.' *Held,* that the lease was not continued in force beyond the 10 years by the lessees completing a paying well, but closing and anchoring it and continuing to pay only $50.00 rent."

Alonzo M. Williams, on February 8, 1890, leased a tract of land for oil and gas purposes, which lease was assigned to the American Window Glass Company. The lease was for the term of ten years from date, and provided that it should continue as much longer as oil or gas should be found in paying quantities or the rental paid. The lease provided that until such time as the lessee should drill an oil or gas well on the premises and should begin to use the gas therefrom for manufacturing purposes, or to save oil therefrom, the lessee should pay an annual rental during the term of $50.00 payable semi-annually upon the first days of January and July. In case gas should be discovered and used by the lessee or his assigns for manufacturing purposes the consideration in full to the lessor should be $100.00 per annum for each and every gas well the gas from which should be used for manufacturing purposes. On February 4, 1900, the Glass Company drilled a well on the premises which resulted in finding gas in paying quantities, which well the company closed and anchored to prevent the escape of the gas. Thereafter the Glass Company did not, nor did anyone for it under the lease, produce any gas or oil from the premises, and did not transport any gas from the premises for manufacturing purposes, or for any other purpose, nor was any oil saved from the premises. No other well was drilled. The $50.00 gas rental mentioned in the lease, was paid from the date of the lease on the first of January and July of each year up to July 1, 1899, which last payment was for the ensuing six months. On February 17, 1900, Williams declared a forfeiture, took possession of the well, laid a service pipe therefrom to his dwelling house on the premises, and thereafter used the gas for domestic purposes. On April 7, 1900, the Glass Company tendered Williams, and offered to pay him $100.00 in gold for the gas from the well and offered to connect the well with a pipeline and to begin then to use gas from the well under the terms of the lease, all of which Williams refused to accept, claiming that the term of the lease had expired. For the purpose of cancelling the lease the lessor instituted suit in the Circuit Court of Wells County, and obtained judgment quieting his title. From this judgment the Glass Company appealed to the Appellate Court of Indiana, and that court affirmed the Circuit Court.

Sec. 17.—In *Central Ohio Nat. Gas & Fuel Co. v. Eckert*, 70 Ohio St. 127; 71 N. E. 281 (April 26, 1904) the syllabus is as follows:

"A grant to a corporation, its successors and assigns, without limitation as to time, of 'all the oil' etc. upon the following terms: 'First. Second party agrees to drill a well upon said premises within six months from this date, or thereafter pay to the first party One Hundred and Sixty Dollars, annually, until said well is drilled, or the property hereby granted is re-conveyed to the first party. * * * * * * * Seventh. Second party may at any time remove all their property and re-convey the premises hereby granted, which conveyance said first party agrees to accept, and thereupon this instrument shall be null and void'—after the expiration of six months, and until, a well is drilled, is a lease, at an annual rental of one hundred and sixty dollars, at the option of the lessee only.''

Henry C. Eckert and others, in consideration of one dollar and of the covenants and agreements contained in the lease, on January 3, 1894, made an oil and gas lease for a tract of land in Fairfield County, Ohio, to the Central Ohio Natural Gas & Fuel Company. The lessee agreed to drill a well on the premises within six months from date, or thereafter pay to the lessor $160.00 annually until a well should be drilled. The lessee was given the right at any time to remove all its property and re-convey the premises, which conveyance the lessors agreed to accept, and thereupon the instrument should be null and void. There was also in controversy a similar lease construed by the court in a suit by the *Gas & Fuel Co.* v. *Kull.* In each case the company paid the rental stipulated by the first clause of the lease in the years 1895, 1896, 1897 and 1898, and on July 12, 1899, tendered the amount for the year thereafter ending in that month. The lessors refused to accept this rental, and on July 11, 1899, served notice on the company that it had no further right under the lease, and that the lessors had elected to and did terminate the same. On July 12, 1899, the company moved upon the property and undertook to erect a derrick for the purpose of drilling for oil. The lessors brought suit and obtained an injunction against the company enjoining it from doing anything upon the premises. The petition in each case alleged that the lease was a cloud upon the title, and the plaintiff asked that the title be quieted. The Circuit Court found in each case that after the six months stipulated in the lease, it was merely a lease from year to year, at the rental therein stipulated, and might be ter-

minated by either party at the end of any year. A decree was
entered quieting plaintiff's title, and perpetually enjoining the
company from asserting any estate or interest in the premises,
or in any way disturbing plaintiff in the possession of the same.
From this decree the Gas Company appealed to the Supreme
Court of Ohio, and that court reversed the decree of the Circuit
Court and remanded the cause.   In support of the conclusions
reached the Court cited:

Woodland Oil Co. v. *Crawford,* 55 Ohio St. 161; 44 N. E. 1093.
Brown v. *Fowler,* 65 Ohio St. 507; 63 N. E. 76.
Lowther Oil Co. v. *Guffey,* 52 W. Va. 88; 43 S. E. 101.

Sec. 18.—In *Pyle* v. *Henderson,* 65 W. Va. 39; 63 S. E. 762
(Jan. 26, 1909) the court, speaking by Judge Brannon, as to the
term of the original lease, said:

"When this second lease was taken, the term of the first lease,
five years, had not expired. If it had, there would be some force
in saying that it could be extended only by a new lease; but such
was not the case. It was then competent for Bunfill to waive the
mere forfeiture; the first lease being still in life."

Thomas Bunfill, on February 3, 1897, made an oil and gas
lease of 60 acres of land to A. B. Campbell and J. W. Swan. The
lessees paid Bunfill a cash bonus or consideration for the lease
of $55.00. The lease was for a term of five years and so long
thereafter as oil and gas should be found in paying quantities,
or the rental paid thereon. The lease contained a clause on
which the litigation turned:

"Provided, however, that this lease shall become null and
void and all rights hereunder shall cease and determine unless a
well shall be completed on said premises within three months from
the date hereof, or in lieu thereof thereafter the parties of the
second part shall pay to parties of the first part fifteen dollars
for each three months delay, payable in advance, until such well
is completed.' "

No well was put down under this lease, nor was the $15.00
commutation money paid. On May 5, 1897, Bunfill made an oil
and gas lease of the same tract to C. E. Pyle. When the first

lease was made Bunfill owned only seven-undivided-ninths of the tract. His brother John owned one-ninth, and the Sindledecker heirs, children of a sister, the other nine. Thomas Bunfill secured a conveyance from John Bunfill of his ninth on March 15, 1897, before the three months limitation in the clause quoted above had expired. He never got in the ninth interest of the Sindledeckers. Some of them were infants, and under a judicial proceeding, Miller, Trustee, acquired that share of the oil and gas. Pyle, the second lessee, assigned an interest in his lease to Hardman, and Pyle and Hardman assigned the second lease to Miller, Trustee, and thus Miller obtained the whole, except reserved royalties to Pyle and Hardman. Campbell and Swan assigned interests to Stealey and Henderson. No possession was taken under the first lease, but under the second wells were drilled and oil produced. Pyle, Hardman, and Miller, Trustee, claiming under the second lease, brought a chancery suit against Henderson and others, claiming in their original and amended bills, under the second lease as superior to the right of those claiming under the first lease; claiming that all right under it had ceased before the second lease was made, because of failure to drill a well or pay the $15.00 commutation money as demanded by the clause of the first lease quoted above; alleging that they were in possession, operating for oil under the second lease; and seeking to enjoin the claimants under the first lease from entering and boring for oil, and to cancel said first lease as a cloud upon their title. The defendants, Campbell, Swan, Stealey and Henderson's executor, filed a cross-bill-answer, setting up their title under the first lease, alleging that the original lessees, Campbell and Swan, before the expiration of the ninety-day limitation, discovered the defect in Bunfill's title, and Bunfill extended the time, or waived the payment of the rental. That Campbell and Swan furnished Bunfill money from time to time, by means of which he was enabled to secure the outstanding interest of his brother John Bunfill; and that jointly, Bunfill and said lessees undertook to obtain the outstanding interest of the Sindledecker heirs, but failed to do so within the period of three months mentioned in the lease; and without any notice to the original lessees, and while the negotiations

were pending or attempted negotiations, for obtaining the Sindledecker interests, the second lease was executed. The defendants in their cross-bill-answer claimed that Thomas Bunfill had
waived forfeiture by his conduct and by his agreement with the
original lessees, by reason whereof, as well as by reason of the
defect in the title to the leased premises, he was not in position
to declare a forfeiture of the first lease. The Circuit Court held
that the first lease was valid, recognized the interest obtained by
Miller from the Sindledecker heirs to be valid, and cancelled the
second lease. The claimants to the second lease appealed to
the West Virginia Court of appeals, and that court affirmed the
Circuit Court. One of the points made by counsel for the claimants to the second lease was, that as the first lessees failed to enter and drill on the premises within the time—three months—
mentioned in the lease, the time could not be extended by Bunfill
without a new lease. Upon this question the court held as quoted
above.

Sec. 19.—In *Thomas* v. *Hukill*, 34 W. Va. 385; 12 S. E. 522
(Dec. 6, 1890) the syllabus is as follows:

"C. of Monongalia County, W. Va., executed to K. & L. an
'oil lease' of one hundred and thirty-one acres, dated 11th August
1885, for the term of twenty years; C. the lessor, retaining full use
and enjoyment of the premises for the purpose of tillage, except
such as may be necessary for oil development purposes, right of
way, etc.; K. & L. to commence operations within one year, or
thereafter pay Five and a half dollars per month until the work
is commenced; a failure to comply with either one or the other
of these conditions to work an absolute forfeiture of the lease.
The lessees assigned to defendant Hukill 29th September, 1885;
and lease and assignment were recorded 29th June, 1886. Hukill
had not commenced to bore for oil up to 7th March, 1888. By lease
of that date C. the owner in fee still in actual possession, demised
said one hundred and thirty one acres, excluding ten acres
around the buildings to R. for the sole and only purpose of drilling, etc., for oil and gas, for the term of two years
or as long thereafter as gas or oil is found in paying quantities;
R. not to disturb unnecessarily growing crops or fences. R. was
to complete one well within six months, or pay forty dollars in
advance for the right to drill during the two years by paying one
hundred and thirty dollars in quarterly payments, and then the
lease was to become null and void unless a well was drilled in on

the premises. This lease was assigned by R. to Thomas and others, plaintiffs, on the 10th day of March, 1888, and on the 30th day of March, 1888, lease and assignments were recorded. No one under this lease ever entered or attempted to enter or operate for oil. On the last day of March, 1889, defendant, Hukill, with C's, the lessor's consent, entered, put down five producing wells at a cost of $30,000 and was producing oil in paying quantities when this action of unlawful entry and detainer was brought against him by plaintiffs for possession on 14th January, 1890. The case was heard, verdict found, and judgment rendered 19th June, 1890, after the two years had expired. *Held;* Plaintiffs were then not entitled to recover possession of the premises from defendant, Hukill. The oil thus produced by Hukill in paying quantities did not then give plaintiffs the right to recover the possession of the premises from defendant, Hukill, in this action.''

William P. Core was the owner of a tract of one hundred and thirty-one acres of land in Monongalia County, West Virginia, and on August 11, 1895, executed a lease of this land to Long and Kennedy for oil and gas purposes for the term of twenty years, operations to commence thereunder within one year, or thereafter lessee to pay a monthly rental of $5.50 for delay. The lease contained the following forfeiture clause:

"The parties of the second part covenant to commence operations for said purposes within one year from and after the execution of this lease, or thereafter pay to the party of the first part $5.50 per month until work is commenced. A deposit in the hands of John Kennedy shall be good and sufficient payment for each and every month till work is commenced, and a failure on the part of said second parties to comply with either one or the other of the foregoing conditions shall work an absolute forfeiture of this lease.''

The lease was subsequently assigned to Hukill, who neither paid rental nor entered upon the premises for exploration, until September 18, 1888, when he paid Core $137.50 in full of rental to that date. On March 7, 1888, Core made a second lease of the same property to O. B. Ryall, for the term of two years with the following forfeiture clause:

"It is further agreed between the parties to this agreement that this lease will be extended by first party for six (6) months from the date of the completion of well, as recited below by second party paying forty ($40) dollars in advance, and it is further

agreed at the end of one year from the date of this lease, the
second party can have this lease extended one year longer by
paying one hundred and thirty ($130) dollars in quarterly pay-
ments; and that this lease becomes null and void, unless a well is
drilled in on the premises described. The party of the second part
agrees to complete one well within six months from the date hereof,
and, in case of failure to complete one well within such time, the
party of the second part hereby agrees to pay thereafter to party
of the first part, for any future delay the sum of $ * * * * * *
A failure to complete one well or make any such payment within
such time * * * renders this lease null and void and to remain
without effect between the two parties.''

On February 16, 1889, Core, in writing acknowledged tender
of payment of all installments of rental past due under the Ryall
lease. Hukill took possession with Core's consent, about the
last of March or first of April, 1889, bored five wells, and discovered oil in July, 1889. On January 14, 1890, Thomas and
others instituted suit in the Circuit Court of Monongalia County, West Virginia, in unlawful entry and detainer against Hukill
to recover possession of the William P. Core tract of land. A
trial was had and at the conclusion of the evidence there was a
demurrer to the evidence and a conditional verdict rendered by
the jury on which verdict the court gave judgment for the plaintiff, to which judgment Hukill obtained a writ of error. The
Court of Appeals reversed the Circuit Court upon the grounds
that when the verdict was rendered the plaintiff's right to the
possession should then have been a subsisting right; that the
plaintiff's lease began on March 7, 1888, and ran for a term of
two years, expiring by its own limitation on the last moment of
March 7, 1890, unless oil or gas had been within that period found
in paying quantities by the lessee, or by some one working under
that lease. Ryall and his assignees had from March 7, 1888, to
March 7, 1889, to begin work without objection from anybody;
and as late as the last of January, 1890, they did not ask for the
privilege of boring, but for an extension of time, alleging as a reason that they had not time enough to comply with the conditions
of their lease. This request Core refused. The discovery of
oil by Hukill did not extend the term of the Ryall lease so as to
vest title in Thomas, as assignee of Ryall, and as the case was
tried after the expiration of the term of the Ryall lease, and as

neither Ryall nor his assignees had, under their lease, discovered oil, Thomas, assignee, was not entitled to possession. This was a suit at law, and what conclusions the court of equity might have reached had Thomas, assignee of Ryall, interposed by bill in equity within the term of the Ryall lease, the court did not indicate. But the duty to develop within the term as a condition to the vesting of any title or right in the oil and gas is clearly affirmed in this case.

Sec. 20.—In *Hazelgreen Oil & Gas Co.* v. *Collins,* — Ky. —; 110 S. W. 343 (May 15, 1908) the syllabus is as follows:

"A lease of land was for the term of three years and as much longer as oil and gas were found on the land, provided wells were completed during the term of the lease which also stipulated that if gas was found in sufficient quantities to market the same the consideration should be $100.00 per year for each well as long as gas from such well was marketed, and that the lessee should sink a test well on the land within one year. *Held,* that the expression 'provided wells were completed during said term' meant that other wells were to be completed during the term, besides the test well, and that the mere sinking of a test well during the term without marketing the gas found in it did not entitle the lessee to an extension of the term beyond the three years, and an agreement by the lessee to furnish the lessor with gas from the test well in consideration of the release from the payment of any royalty while he was using the gas did not excuse it from its obligation to put down other wells."

On February 23, 1903, Holly Wilson made a lease to the Hazelgreen Oil & Gas Company. It put down no wells on the property during the first year of the lease, but paid Wilson royalty as provided therein. In the second year of the lease it put down a well and discovered gas therein, about July 1, 1904. The well flowed about 200,000 cubic feet of gas per day. Lessee did not market the gas or make any use of it but simply capped the well in. Lessee had struck, before that, gas on a neighboring farm in a well that flowed over 700,000 cubic feet of gas per day. This well it had delivered into its mains and supplied all its customers. Wilson learned that the lessee was not using his gas and it was agreed between him and the directors of the company that the lessee would furnish lessor the cost of the pipe and some other articles, and that he could run the gas to his house and use it for heating and lighting purposes if he would release the company from paying any royalties while he was thus using the gas. Lessor agreed to this and did run the gas to his house and used it from that time on. Before this was done the company had torn down its derrick, and moved it to another farm, and was doing no further work on this property. Nothing further was done till the summer of 1906, when Wilson made another lease to S. R. Collins. The lessor entered on the land and was preparing to drill for gas when the Hazelgreen Company entered and hauled off his lumber and other things, preventing him from going to work. Wilson instituted suit in the Circuit Court of Morgan County against the Hazelgreen Oil & Gas Company to recover for trespass, and recovered judgment for $100.00 damages, and the defendant gas company appealed. The Court of Appeals, upon considering the appeal deemed it necessary only to consider whether the lease to the Hazelgreen Oil & Gas Company was in force at the time the lease to Collins was made; that if this lease had terminated the lease to Collins was valid and the gas company had no right to interfere with Collins in his work on the land. The material paragraphs of the lease under consideration are stated in the syllabus. The Court of Appeals affirmed the judgment of the Circuit Court.

REMEDIES.

Sec. 21.—What is called the "rental period" must not be confounded with the "term" of the lease. The term is fixed. The *rental period* while definitely stated, is the subject of modification or waiver during the term by the lessor and lessee at their pleasure, and such modification or waiver need not be in writing, while if oil or gas is not found in paying quantities, to extend the *term* a new lease or writing to that effect is necessary.

Pyle v. *Henderson,* 65 W. Va. 39; 63 S. E. 620.

Sec. 22.—It must not be understood, however, that while the lessee is given a fixed term within which he must prosecute explorations to success, in case the lessee is prevented from taking possession of the property for the purpose of making developments under his lease, by the lessor directly, or by second lessee, the lessee loses the benefit of his license. Where the lessee acts in good faith, but is prevented by the lessor from making the explorations provided for by the lease within the term, and during which a successful exploration is made by the lessor, or by lessees under a junior lease, such junior lease will be cancelled by a court of equity as a cloud upon the title of the original lessee, and the rights of such original lessee will be fully protected and preserved. And this is true although the term of the original lease may have expired before the termination of a successful suit prosecuted by the original lessees. This rule is peculiarly applicable to suits brought in courts of equity to cancel the junior or second lease as a cloud upon the senior lessee's title.

Pyle v. *Henderson,* 65 W. Va. 39; 63 S. E. 620.

Sec. 23.—In some jurisdictions the lessee may maintain an action at law for the possession of the demised premises, but by instituting such suit the lessee runs the risk of losing the benefit of his lease where the statute of the State restricts the right of recovery in possessory actions to cases where the plaintiff at the time of trial is entitled to possession. In a court at law a possessory action tried after the plaintiff's title has expired, the fact that the plaintiff's term had then expired, defeats his right to recovery notwithstanding in equity he might have the right to cancel the junior lease.

Thomas v. *Hukill,* 34 W. Va. 385; 12 S. E. 522.

Sec. 24.—The holder of a second or junior lease, where the right to cancel the senior lease exists, and where such senior lessee enters and holds possession pending the settlement of the question of the rights of the claimants until after the term of the junior lease has expired, has the same rights as to cancellation of the senior lease, as the holders of the junior lease, as stated in Section 21 of this Chapter.

Huggins v. *Daley,* 99 Fed. 606; 40 C. C. A. 12; 48 L. R. A. 20.

Sec. 25.—Where, however, the lessee by his own fault or neglect, fails to exercise his right of exploration within the term specified under the ordinary oil and gas lease, all rights under such lease cease and determine at the end of such term, and the lessee will not be permitted, without the consent of the lessor, to make explorations after the expiration of the term.

(See cases cited under Section 1 of this Chapter).

LESSOR'S REMEDY.

Sec. 26.—Where, notwithstanding the expiration of the term within which by the conditions of the lease the lessee is given the exclusive privilege of entering and making explorations for oil or gas, the lessee does not enter within the term for the purpose of testing the territory, and after the expiration of the term then undertakes to make explorations, the remedy of the lessor is by bill in equity, or by petition or complaint in the nature of a bill in equity against the lessee to cancel the lease as a cloud upon the lessor's title.

(See cases cited under Section 1 of this Chapter.)

Sec. 27.—Where a lessee, under an oil and gas lease which provides for a specific term qualified by the words "and as much longer as oil or gas is produced in paying quantities" enters during the term and discovers oil in paying quantities, the question of whether or not at the expiration of the stipulated term oil or gas is by the lessee being produced from the leased premises in paying quantities, is a question of fact.

(See Sec. 1 Chapter 22 and cases there cited and digested.)

Sec. 28.—While the courts have almost universally held in cases where the question as to the proper construction to be

given leases containing the provision after the specified term:
"And as much longer as oil or gas is produced in paying quantities" that the lessee is the judge of what constitutes paying quantities, yet such judgment must be exercised in good faith and be predicated upon the actual results of the operation of the lease. If there is a fair profit to the lessee in the production, over the actual expenses incident thereto, then so long as these conditions continue oil is being produced in paying quantities. Where, however, these conditions do not exist, the lessor has the right to show, by proper proceeding for the purpose of cancelling the lease, that oil or gas is not being produced in paying quantities; and by establishing the fact that there is not a fair profit to the lessee in the production, then the lessor may have the lease cancelled as a cloud on his title.

Barnsdall v. *Boley,* 119 Fed. 191.
Lowther Oil Co. v. *Miller-Sibley Oil Co.,* 53 W. Va. 501 Syl. 4; 44 S. E. 435; 97 Am. St. Rep. 1027.
Young v. *Oil Co.* 194 Pa. 243; 45 Atl. 121.

LESSEE'S REMEDY.

Sec. 29.—Where under an oil and gas lease providing a fixed term within which lessee is given the exclusive right of exploration, and providing that should oil be found in paying quantities within the term the lease should continue as long thereafter as oil or gas should be produced in paying quantities, and the lessee has within the term discovered oil or gas in paying quantities, he is entitled to continue operations as long after the expiration of the fixed term as he produces oil or gas in paying quantities. Where the landowner seeks a cancellation of the lease, or institutes a possessory action at law, the lessee may defeat either action by proving that he is producing oil in paying quantities; and by establishing the fact that the well or wells are paying a profit to the lessee, even a small one, over the operating expenses, he has established the fact that the lease is producing oil or gas in paying quantities.

Young v. *Oil Co.,* 194 Pa. 243; 45 Atl. 121.

McGraw Oil & Gas. Co. v. *Kennedy* 65 W. Va. 595; 64 S. E.
  1027.
Summerville v. *Apollo Gas Co.* 207 Pa. 234; 56 Atl. 876.
Kellar v. *Craig,* 126 Fed. 630; 61 C. C. A. 366.
(See Paying Quantities, Chapter 22).

Sec. 30.—Where a lessee enters the demised premises and
drills an unproductive well within the term, and after the expiration of the term, re-enters for the purpose of making further
developments under the lease under inducements and encouragement by the lessor so to do, proof of such encouragement and
inducement by lessor will defeat an action of trespass brought
against lessee for such subsequent entry and explorations.

Riddle v. *Mellon,* 147 Pa. 30; 23 Atl. 241.

Sec. 31.—In *Riddle* v. *Mellon,* 147 Pa. 30; 23 Atl. 241 (Jan.
4, 1892) the syllabus is as follows:

"An oil and gas lease was made for the term of 'One year
and as long as oil or gas is found in paying quantities.' The lessee
drilled a well during the year, but failed to develop oil or gas in
paying quantities. The lessor brought trespass against the lessee,
for entering to prosecute further drilling, several months after
the year expired; *held:*
Under the testimony as presented at the trial, that the jury
were properly instructed that, if the lessor after the expiration
of the year, and before the alleged trespass, encouraged and allowed the expenditure of money and labor in operations on the
lease, on the basis of its continuance, he would be estopped from
asserting that it was then at an end."

James W. Riddle instituted an action of trespass in a court
of Common Pleas of Allegheny County, Pennsylvania, against
W. L. Mellon and others to recover damages for an entry made
by defendants upon the plaintiff's farm, for the purpose of
drilling for oil. The defendant's plea was not guilty. At the
trial the following facts were shown: On February 21, 1889,
James W. Riddle executed an oil and gas lease for his farm of
about 50 acres to Samuel Galey, which lease was "for, during
and until the full term of one year next ensuing the day and year
above written, and long as gas or oil is found in paying quantities or rental paid." The lease contained no other provisions

upon the subject of payment of rental. It provided that operations upon the demised promises should be commenced within 30 days from the date of the lease and prosecuted with reasonable diligence to completion or the lease should be null and void, and that all conditions between the parties should extend to their heirs, executors, and assigns. Galey commenced the drilling of the well within thirty days after the date of the lease. The well was not completed to an oil producing sand till February 20, 1890.

The defendants alleged that the delay in its completion was due to various hindrances and difficulties encountered in the course of drilling it. The plaintiff did not concede the truth of this, but he made no objection to the delay in completing the well, and did not seek to take advantage thereof. The well developed some oil, but after working with it, torpedoing it, and cleaning it out, it failed to produce oil in paying quantities. Prior to the completion of the well Galey assigned the lease to W. L. Mellon. In the latter part of April, 1890, the plaintiff called on Mellon and requested him to drill the well deeper to a later discovered sand, known as the Fifth sand. After some conversation, Mellon got out the lease, and sent for a notary public, and the plaintiff acknowledged the lease, so that it might be put on record, and Mellon had it recorded soon afterwards. Testimony for the defendants tended to show that the acknowledgment of the lease was made in accordance with an understanding and agreement between the plaintiff and Mellon to the effect that the lease should continue in force, and that Mellon should drill the well deeper, or drill another well on plaintiff's farm, and that subsequently, at different times the plaintiff recognized Mellon's rights under the lease as still in force. The plaintiff denied that there was any extension or renewal of the lease, unless the mere acknowledgment of it before the notary public operated, *ipso facto* in that way. In May or June, 1890, Mellon had a packer put in the well, but it had no effect in improving its production. In July, 1890, he had a part of the casing pulled, plugged the well in the manner prescribed by law in cases of abandoned wells, and moved the rig over to an adjoining farm for the purpose of making a test there, intending afterwards to return and drill a well upon another part of plaintiff's farm. Testimony for the defendants tended to show that all this was done in accordance with an understanding between Mellon and the plaintiff that this course should be taken. Some of Mellon's machinery, etc., had been left on the farm. On August 1, 1890, the plaintiff made another lease to A. Learn, which contained the following provision:

"The lessee is to indemnify lessor against all damages, costs, and expenses, whatever, which may be incurred by reason of this lease, owing to a lease heretofore made by said Riddle to Samuel Galey, which lessor claims has expired by its terms."

Some time later, in August, 1890, the defendants, against plaintiff's protest, placed on the premises lumber and materials for the erection of a rig, with which to drill a new well. This suit was then brought. About August 29, 1890, Learn, the second lessee, hauled a load of lumber on the premises, and the defendants at once hauled it off again. The defendants kept possession of the premises and erected a rig, which they subsequently moved to the old well. In November, 1890, they commenced to drill that well deeper, and in March, 1891, developed oil in paying quantities therein.

The Judge of the Court of Common Pleas, when the testimony was closed, instructed the jury that the term of the lease was one year, and that when the year expired, if gas or oil had not been found by that time, although the operations might be in progress, yet the right of the defendants to that oil or gas was gone, because it was not found within the time fixed in the contract; that assuming it to be true that Riddle, the lessor, at the end of the year had a right to forfeit the lease, the next question was, did he waive his right? That if he saw fit to forfeit the lease, then the jury were instructed that the law is, that he could immediately turn the defendants out of possession or order them off, or could make a good lease to somebody else; but, if the lessee acknowledged defendant's right or encouraged or allowed them to go on by his conduct, intimating to them that he would still maintain the lease, and allow them to continue boring for oil until they got it, then the lessor would be estopped from claiming the right to forfeit the lease. The court then left the question of whether or not the lessor did waive his right to a forfeiture to the jury for their determination, and instructed them that if he did, that it was too late at any time after that to undertake to forfeit the lease by reason of the expiration of the time fixed. The court further instructed the jury that if they were not satisfied that there was a recognition of the lease, or a waiver by which lessor was estopped, they might stop there and give a verdict for the plaintiff, because his case would be then made out. But if there was a waiver, and if there were such acts done by lessor as the jury would think fairly encouraged the lessee to continue operations there, then the question would be: Whether the lessee or parties or their contractors proceeded with reasonable diligence to operate, or continue their operations for the discovery and production of oil. If they did not, even if up to that time the plaintiff had waived his right to take advantage of the forfeiture, arising from the expiration of the year, he then had a right, without he did some other act during or after that time, to encourage them still further to go on, to repudiate their right to remain in possession, to take possession of the premises himself, or make a new lease.

Verdict and judgment were rendered for defendants and plaintiff appealed. The Supreme Court affirmed the judgment.

CHAPTER 7.

CONSIDERATION FOR THE GRANT OF MINERALS—OIL

Sec. 1.—The consideration for the grant to the lessee by the lessor of the oil interests is the receipt of and the delivery to the lessor of the royalties provided for by the lease.

Lowther Oil Co. v. *Miller-Sibley Oil Co.,* 53 W. Va. 501; 44
    S. E. 433.
Parish Fork Oil Co. v. *Bridgewater Gas Co.,* 51 W. Va. 583;
    42 S. E. 655; 59 L. R. A. 566.
Lawson v. *Kirchner,* 50 W. Va. 344; 40 S. E. 344.

Steelsmith v. *Gartlan,* 45 W. Va. 27; 29 S. E. 978; 44 L. R. A. 107.
Crawford v. *Ritchie,* 43 W. Va. 252; 27 S. E. 220.
Funk v. *Halderman,* 53 Pa. 229.
Florence Oil Co. v. *Orman,* 19 Colo. App. 79; 73 Pac. 628.
Rawlings v. *Armel,* 70 Kan. 778; 79 Pac. 683.
Plummer v. *Hillside Coal, etc. Co.,* 160 Pa. 483; 28 Atl. 853.
Venture Oil Co. v. *Fretts,* 152 Pa. 451; 25 Atl. 732.
Kelley v. *Keys,* 213 Pa. 295; 62 Atl. 911.
Headley v. *Hoopengarner,* 60 W. Va. 626; 55 S. E. 144.
Childers v. *Neely,* 47 W. Va. 70; 34 S. E. 825.

Sec. 2.—Until the discovery of oil in paying quantities by the lessee he has no vested interest in or to the minerals. While he has the right to explore for oil, yet such right is subject to forfeiture for failure to perform the express covenants of the lease, and is subject to forfeiture by abandonment. The only consideration that the lessor can receive for the oil under the ordinary oil and gas lease, is the royalty provided for. Until the discovery of oil the lessee's right is strictly one of exploration. For the protection of the lessor the lease provides for forfeiture, which may be prevented by the lessee by payment of commutation money for delay in drilling. Fixed periods are agreed upon as rental periods within which the lessee may explore, and for the purpose of securing prompt developments the forfeiture clause is inserted, with the right to lessee to prevent such forfeiture by promptly paying the commutation money or proceeding with the explorations—the object in view by both parties to the lease. Upon the discovery of oil in paying quantities the lessee becomes vested with the right of production. He takes no title to the oil in place. He is vested only with the right to produce the oil, which when produced and raised to the surface, becomes personal property and his interest is then for the first time reduced to such possession as vests in him the absolute title thereto.

Sec. 3.—After the discovery of oil in paying quantities lessee's right to produce becomes a vested right, and he can only lose such right by breaches of the express covenants of the lease, by intentional abandonment or breaches of the implied covenants of the lease, constituting fraud upon the rights of the lessor.

The real object of the lease, and that which both parties have in contemplation—the discovery of oil in paying quantities—brings to life the effective terms and conditions of the lease. Prior to this the right is experimental. Nothing tangible exists. Upon discovery of oil in paying quantities title to something vests; not title to the oil and gas in place—the title thereto remains vested in the landowner; he has parted only with the exclusive right to produce the oil, and has transferred that right, or rather by his license has clothed lessee with the right to become vested with the exclusive privilege of producing the oil. No title to the oil in place has vested in lessee, notwithstanding his discovery thereof. He must produce the oil—raise it to the surface— then he becomes vested with the absolute title to his proportion thereof. When he fails to produce the oil, either by intentional abandonment or by exhaustion, he has no further rights in or upon the premises except the right to remove the machinery and fixtures placed thereon for exploration and production; and this right he must exercise according to the terms and conditions of the lease.

Sec. 4.—In *Crawford* v. *Ritchie,* 43 W. Va. 252; 27 S. E. 220, analyzed under Chapter 5, the consideration for the grant of the oil and gas is stated as follows:

"The second party hereby agrees in consideration of the lease of the above described premises, to give said first party one-eighth ($\frac{1}{8}$) of all the oil or mineral produced and saved from said premises, and further agrees to give $300.00 per annum for the gas from each and every well drilled on the above described premises, in case the gas is conducted and used off the above described premises."

The lessee abandoned the premises, and after finding the facts as stated in the analysis of the case, Chapter 5, Judge Brannon, in the opinion, says:

"It was the duty of defendant to begin his work at the time specified, and to complete it in a reasonable time. The defendant has no vested title, and has abandoned the lease, never having done anything under the lease after the lapse of about eight years. * * * * * * * A vested title cannot ordinarily be lost by abandonment in a less time than that fixed by the statute of limitations, unless there is satisfactory proof of an intention to abandon. A lease of a right to mine for oil, etc., stands on different ground. The title is inchoate, and for purposes of explorations only until oil is found. If it is not found, no estate vests in the lessee, and his title, whatever it is, ends when the unsuccessful search is abandoned. If oil is found then the right to produce becomes a vested right and the lessee will be protected in exercising it in accordance with the terms and conditions of his contract. * * * * * *

If defendant (the lessee) had possession under the terms of his contract, and developed gas and oil, or either, he would have vested rights, of which he could not have been ousted, or divested; but the lease being 'for the sole and only purpose of drilling and operating for petroleum oil and gas for the term of twenty years, or as long thereafter as oil or gas is found in paying quantities,' and providing that he shall commence within a month in the first instance, and afterwards a few months when it is by consent renewed and extended from October 26 to November 28, 1889, to begin work, he must be presumed to have abandoned it.''

Sec. 5.—In *Steelsmith* v. *Gartlan*, 45 W. Va. 27; 29 S. E. 978, analyzed under Chapter 5, the consideration in the lease is as follows:

"Yielding and paying to the lessor the one-eighth (⅛) part of all the oil, produced and saved from the premises, delivered free of expense into tanks or pipelines to the lessor's credit; and should any well produce gas in sufficient quantities to justify marketing, the lessor shall be paid at the rate of $200 per year for such well, so long as the gas therefrom is sold. Lessor to have gas for domestic use on the premises, free, she making her own connections.''

After a non-productive well had been drilled the lessee, claiming the right to hold the premises for five years—the term of the lease—by virtue of having drilled the unproductive well, refused to surrender the lease or make further explorations. In a suit instituted by the holder of the second lease against the lessee in the first lease, and his assignee, Judge Dent, delivering the opinion of the court, said:

"The lessee's title being inchoate and contingent both as to the five years limit and the time thereafter, on the finding of oil and gas in paying quantities, did not become vested by reason of his putting down a non-productive well. This gave him no new or more extensive rights than he enjoyed before, but in fact destroyed all his rights under the lease. As said in *Williamson* v. *Jones*, 43 W. Va. 562; 27 S. E. 411, 'as an abortive well neither enhances the value nor yields anything to the true owner he ought not to be charged with the costs thereof.' The lessee would charge the expense of this abortive well as though it were a part of the consideration for this lease, when it was plainly evident that no such thing was ever had in contemplation by parties, but this is a mere desperate after-thought to furnish a non-existant money consideration for the continuance of the lease. A dry hole, plugged up and abandoned, while expensive to the lessee, is no advantage, but an incumbrance, to the lessor. Then why should she pay for it by a non-operating and indefinite extension of the lease, to await the will and pleasure of the lessee, who claims the option to operate, abandon, surrender, or forfeit it at his pleasure, while numerous others are clamoring for the privilege of diligent operation and offering a large bonus therefor? Such a holding would be unconscienable and contrary to both right and justice.''

The Supreme Court cancelled the first lease.

Sec. 6.—In *Lawson* v. *Kirchner*, 50 W. Va. 344; 40 S. E. 344, analyzed under Chapter 5, a recovery was sought against the lessee who obtained a lease under an order of the court in a suit for unpaid rentals. It was held in syllabus 2:

"An oil lease for oil and gas purposes is a conveyance or sale of an interest in land, conditional and contingent on the discovery and reduction to possession of the oil and gas."

In this case the land, or an interest therein, belonged to infants, and a proceeding was instituted under the Statutes of West Virginia for the leasing for oil and gas purposes of this interest. A grant which the court construed to be for oil purposes was directed to be, and in fact was made, and confirmed by the court. The lessee accepted the grant. The consideration therein stated was as follows:

"Seven-eighths of all the oil and gas in and underlying the premises for the term of two years, and as much longer as oil or gas is found in paying quantities, for the sum of Two Thousand Four Hundred and Seventy-One Dollars and Forty-two cents, cash in hand paid by said purchaser, reserving to said infants the usual royalty of one-eighth of five-sevenths of all the oil obtained from said premises, produced in the crude state, the same to be set apart in the pipelines running said petroleum, to credit and for benefit of said infants.''

The court sustained the infants claim for the unpaid rentals, no developments having been made, and gave judgment therefor, and upon writ of error the Court of Appeals affirmed this judgment.

Sec. 7.—In *Parish Fork Oil Co.* v. *Bridgewater Gas Co.*, 51 W. Va. 583; 42 S. E. 655; 59 L. R. A. 566, analyzed under Chapter 5, the consideration for the grant of the oil and gas was that the lessor should receive one-eighth of all the oil produced and saved from the premises, and fifty dollars per year for every gas well, the product of which should be marketed and used off the premises. After the assignees of the original lessee had made an unsuccessful search, and abandoned the lease, the landowner made a second lease, and in a controversy between the claimants to the two conflicting leases, the Court of Appeals of West Virginia, sustained the second lease, and held, in syllabus 2:

''The principal purpose and design of the parties to such a lease clearly discernible from its terms, being the production and marketing of the oil and gas in the land, for their mutual benefit, mere discovery of oil, by explorations under it, vests no title to it in the lessee, but does vest in him the right to produce and take the same in accordance with the terms and conditions of the contract. In such right the lessee will be protected, but he must proceed to exercise it with reasonable promptness and diligence.''

Sec. 8.—In *Lowther Oil Co.* v. *Miller-Sibley Oil Co.*, 53 W. Va. 501; 44 S. E. 433, analyzed under Chapter 5, Judge Brannon, in the opinion, at page 505 (W. Va.) explains the inadvertant use of the language: ''Mere discovery of oil by exploration under it vests no title to it in the lessee'' used in syl. 2 of the case cited, digested in Section 7 above:

''In point 2 of syllabus, is language that ''mere discovery of oil by exploration under it, vests no title to it in the lessee. This language is inadvertent and does not express the meaning intended, as on page 591 it is stated that discovery of oil does vest title. As above stated, when Miller-Sibley Company discovered oil an estate vested in it according to the lease which it could lose only by terms of the lease or by abandonment.''

Sec. 9.—In *Lowther Oil Co.* v. *Miller-Sibley Co.*, 53 W. Va. 501; 44 S. E. 433, analyzed under Chapter 5, the consideration for the grant was a royalty of one-eighth of the oil produced, and $200 yearly for each gas well. After the unsuccessful search had been abandoned by the claimants to the original lease, and after the claimants to the second lease had discovered oil in paying quantities, an equity suit was instituted and in the controversy therein between the two adverse claimants the Court of Appeals of West Virginia, as to title, in syl. 1, sustaining the second lease, held:

"Title under a lease only for production of oil and gas is inchoate and contingent and for the purpose of search only until oil or gas is found. If not found, no estate vests in the lessee and his right, whatever it is, ends when the unsuccessful search is abandoned. If found, then the right to produce becomes a vested right upon the terms of the lease. Point 2 of the syllabus in *Oil Co.* v. *Gas Co.* 51 W. Va. 583 explained."

Sec. 10.—In *Funk* v. *Halderman*, 53 Pa. 229, (Jan. 7, 1867) syls 9-10-11 are as follows:

"9. The right granted to Funk was to experiment for oil sever it from the soil, and take it on yielding one-third to the landlord.

10. The $200 paid was the consideration for the entry to experiment; the consideration for the right to the oil was to be measured by the oil taken.

11. Funk's right was a license to work the lands for minerals; it was a license coupled with an interest not revokable at the pleasure of the licensor."

David McElhany, on October 8, 1859, was the owner of a farm originally consisting of two pieces; one situated in Cornplanter Township, the other in Cherrytree Township, Venango County, Pennsylvania, the two pieces constituting the farm of the said McElhany on each side of Oil Creek. On that day McElhany and wife made an agreement with A. B. Funk, bargaining and selling in consideration "of $200 to Funk, his heirs and assigns, the free and uninterrupted use, privilege, etc., to go on any part of their 200 acres for the purpose of prospecting, digging, etc., to find any ore, oil, salt, coal or other minerals, and of taking the same out of the earth,'' and the exclusive use of one acre of land at each well, with free ingress, etc., over said land by Funk, his hands, teams, tenants, and undertenants, occupiers or possessors of said land. Funk bound himself to commence operations the next Spring—to put a steam engine in operation—to use energetically all reasonable efforts to obtain the oil; to give one-third of all that should be taken out to McElhany; that if the experiments failed the ''premises should revert back'' to McElhany, McElhany to have the privilege of tilling the land subject to the rights of Funk.

On December 2, 1859, McElhany and wife entered into another agreement with John H. Dalzell and Thomas Donnelly, which agreement fully recited the prior agreement of October 8th with Funk, and then proceeded in the form of an indenture to grant, bargain and sell to Dalzell and Donnelly the ''one-half of the oil, coal, salt or other minerals which may be taken from said lands, in accordance with the agreement of McElhany and Funk, aforesaid''; in case Funk should abandon his rights Dalzell and Donnelly were to succeed him, and for the rights so conveyed to them they were to pay McElhany $800.00. A subsequent clause defined that McElhany was to convey only one-half of the portion of the oil, salt or coal which he should receive from Funk. By these conveyances one-sixth of what is called the royalty that Funk was to pay was left in McElhany, and the other one-sixth was conveyed to Dalzell and Donnelly.

On January 28, 1860, McElhany sold and conveyed to William H. Ewing, in consideration of $595.00 one-twelfth of the royalty he was to receive from Funk, together with the right of succession to all Funk's rights in case he abandoned the enterprise and Dalzell and Donnelly elected not to take his place. After the contract of January 28, 1860, made with Ewing, McElhany retained to himself whatever interest in the freehold he had not conveyed to Funk, together with a right to one-twelfth of all the oil, salt or ore that Funk should take out of the earth. On March 22, 1860, Funk and wife in consideration of $20,000. conveyed by indenture to Joseph G. Hussey, William D. McBride and Levi Halderman, both of the tracts of land before mentioned, particularly describing them by metes and bounds, the one in Cornplanter, and the other in Cherrytree Township, and subject only to the three last mentioned agreements, the first with Funk, the second with Dalzell and Donnelly and the third with Ewing.

On March 27, 1860, four days after the last mentioned conveyance, Hussey, Halderman and McBride entered into an agreement with Funk which agreement recited the conveyance by McElhany to Funk and themselves, followed by the following recitation: "And whereas, it is mutually desired by the parties hereto that the boundaries of the land conveyed by the aforesaid grant to A. B. Funk should be more definitely described, and that the part reserved and excepted from said grant should be more clearly ascertained and designated than is done in said recited instrument of writing, by reference to perishable buildings." Then follows the covenant: "The grant of rights and privileges unto the said A. B. Funk shall be deemed, considered and construed, to cover, extend over and include all that certain tract of land situate in Cornplanter Township, bounded and described" by courses and distances, "excepting and reserving from said grant all that part of said tract included in a strip 43 rods wide, and extending along the south side thereof from the east to the west line across the whole breadth of said tract, said strip being of the length of 137 perches and of the depth of 43 perches; and it is further agreed that within said limits and boundaries aforesaid, all and singular the grants, privileges, provisions and stipulations in said recited instrument of writing contained, are hereby ratified, confirmed and renewed; and within the reserved strip aforesaid, said parties of the first part retain to themselves, their heirs and assigns, all the rights of ownership as though none of the grants and agreements aforesaid had ever been made or entered into. It being understood also, and hereby expressly agreed that the said A. B. Funk, his heirs and assigns, at his and their discretion, are to have the right of assigning and transferring the rights and privileges herein granted in whole to any one or more parties, or to sub-divide said lands into suitable lots and assign and transfer his rights and privileges aforesaid, to be exercised and enjoyed by his as-

signees or transferees, severally, within the limits of such lot or
sub-division."

The reservation mentioned in the supplemental covenant to
the original agreement between McElhany and Funk is as follows:

"And in no case shall the said Funk be permitted to occupy
any land within one hundred yards of his (McElhany's) buildings."

The next paper, dated March 29th was said to have been
executed and delivered on May 5, 1860, and was an indenture between Hussey, McBride and Halderman of the first part, and
A. B. Funk of the second part, wherein the parties of the first
part, in consideration of Funk's covenants, and of One Dollar,
granted to him the same right on the tract in Cherrytree Township, which McElhaney had granted to him on the tract in
Cornplanter Township, and in substantially the same terms, reserving, however, from this grant, so much of said tract as was
contained in Lots marked five and six on a plot of a survey made
by S. M. Irwin, dividing said tract into ten parcels, said reserved
lots, five and six being about the center of said tract, and running from the creek to the northern boundary line, and being
the width of about 36 rods, and containing 23 acres, and 145
perches, within which said lots five and six, said parties of the
first part retained to themselves all rights of ownership as
though none of the grants and agreements therein had ever been
made or entered into. But as to the other lots numbered 1, 2, 3,
4, 7, 8, 9 and 10 on the plot aforesaid, the said A. B. Funk, his
heirs and assigns were to have and enjoy all the rights and privileges granted, and the liberty of assigning and transferring said
rights and privileges at his or their option and discretion. Hussey, McBride and Halderman made leases to various parties of
oil rights within their reservations, and Funk sub-divided his
territory (all the unreserved portions of both parts of the Mc-
Elhany farm) into suitable lots and let them to various parties,
individuals and oil companies for oil purposes, all his lessees
being bound to yield the appointed royalty to the landlords.

Hussey, McBride and Halderman claimed a right in common with Funk to mine within his lines upon any land, not actually occupied by him, for mining purposes; and claimed, moreover, that Funk, by sub-dividing his rights had forfeited them so that neither he nor his lessees could lawfully take oil from any part of the premises.

Upon these claims so made by Halderman and others Funk filed his bill in equity against them, praying for an injunction to restrain them from interfering with his rights, and set up the various transactions by conveyances hereinbefore specified. The bill averred a performance by Funk of all his covenants, alleged that Hussey, McBride and Halderman pretended to doubt his right to sub-divide and sublet the land, and that for the purpose of removing said pretended doubts, Funk surrendered a strip of land to them, and they expressly gave him the right to assign and transfer the privileges granted to him, and to sub-let the lands. The bill further charged that complainant had the exclusive right to dig for oil and other minerals, and the right to sub-let, but that the defendants pretended that they had the right in common with the plaintiff to work any portion of the land not actually operated by complainant, and that in pursuance of this pretended right the defendants had entered on the premises and commenced digging for oil. The bill prayed for an injunction to restrain defendants from operating for oil and from using any portion of the premises, except for agricultural purposes.

The defendants, Hussey, McBride and Halderman, filed answers to Funk's bill, and also filed a crossbill, in which they alleged that the right to sub-divide and underlet was given by them in the agreement of March 26, 1860, gratuitously, and without advice of counsel, and that they had entered upon the land to search for oil; that they had laid out lots and had given parol leases to build; they denied that plaintiff's agreements gave him the exclusive right to dig for oil, and averred that the instruments were mere licenses to search in common with the defendants. The defendants further denied complainant's right to subdivide or under-let, and insisted that the plaintiff had surcharged the tenancy of certain lots and forfeited all right to the same. The Court of Common Pleas of Venango County dismissed the plaintiff's bill, from which decree the plaintiff Funk appealed to the Supreme Court of Pennsylvania, which court reversed the Court of Common Pleas, and dismissed the cross-bill.

Sec. 11.—In *Venture Oil Co. v. Fretts*, 152 Pa. 151; 25 Atl. 732, analyzed under Chapter 5, the original lessee assigned, and plaintiff Venture Oil Company, claimed under the original lease. Operations under the original lease were abandoned and the landowner made a second lease. An ejectment suit was brought by the claimants of the original lease. The Court below decided for the defendants; plaintiffs appealed to the Supreme Court of Pennsylvania, and that court affirmed the decision of the court below, and held, in syl. 2:

"An oil lease contained a grant of a right to mine for and remove oil for a fixed period of twenty years, at a royalty of one-eighth of the oil so mined and removed. *Held*, that the right of the lessee was to explore for and determine the existence of oil under the land, and if none was found his rights ceased when the explorations were finished and the lot abandoned."

Sec. 12.—In *Kelly v. Keys*, 213 Pa. 295; 62 Atl. 911, (Jan. 2, 1906) syl. 2 is as follows:

"The grant of an exclusive right to mine for and produce oil, though it be a mineral, is not a sale of the oil that may afterwards be discovered. When, after such a grant, oil has been discovered, it is the grantee's right to produce it and sever it from the soil; so much as is thus severed, belongs to the parties entitled under the terms of the grant, not as any part of the real estate, however, but as a chattel, and only so much as is produced and severed passes under the grant; as to all not produced there is no change of property."

Keys was the owner of a certain tract of land in Washington County, Pennsylvania, and granted to Kelly the exclusive right to mine and produce therefrom petroleum and natural gas, with possession of so much of the land as might be necessary for such purposes, for the term of two years. Kelly never exercised any rights under the grant, and never entered into possession of any part of the premises. Subsequently Keys, claiming that by reason of a default Kelly had forfeited his rights under the

grant, executed a like conveyance to C. D. Greenlee and the
Southern Oil Company, who proceeded to explore the property
and succeeded in producing oil therefrom in paying quantities.
Kelly, averring compliance on his part with all the conditions
and stipulations of the grant under which he claimed, and deny·
ing forfeiture, brought an action of ejectment against the defendants to compel surrender to himself. The action resulted in
a verdict for the plaintiff, subject to the decision of the court on
a question reserved, viz., whether ejectment in such case would
lie. Upon consideration judgment was rendered on the reserved
point in favor of the plaintiff. From this judgment the defendants appealed. The Supreme Court of Pennsylvania reversed the judgment, and directed judgment rendered on the
point reserved in favor of defendant, notwithstanding the verdict.

Sec. 13.—In *Plummer* v. *Hillside Coal, etc. Co.*, 160 Pa. 483;
28 Atl. 853, analyzed under Chapter 5, the last point of the syllabus is as follows:

"The rights of lessors and lessees under oil leases are distinguished from the rights of lessors and lessees under coal leases
by reason of the difference in the nature of the two minerals and
the manner of their production."

This suit related to leases for coal, and upon the question
of the application of the law, applicable to the construction of
oil and gas leases, the Supreme Court of Pennsylvania, in distinguishing the coal lease from the oil and gas lease, held as
stated in the syllabus quoted.

Sec. 14.—In *Florence Oil, etc. Co.* v. *Orman*, 19 Colo. App.
79; 73 Pa. 628, analyzed under Chapter 5, the Court of Appeals
of Colorado held:

"That till oil was found the title of the lessee was for exploration only, and that, having done nothing for four years, after
putting down the two wells without finding oil in paying quantities,
he lost his right through failure to make diligent search."

The State of Colorado caused a lease of certain lands to be made, for oil and gas purposes, for a term of twenty years from date, lessee to begin operations within two months. After an unsuccessful search for oil by lessee and abandonment of the search the State made a second lease, and in a controversy wherein the original lessee claimed that by reason of its operations it had a vested interest, the Court of Appeals, denying the right claimed by the original lessee held, that until oil was found in paying quantities the title of the lessee was for exploration only; and that having done nothing for four years, after drilling the two wells provided for in the lease, without finding oil in paying quantities, the lessee lost his right through failure to make diligent search.

Sec. 15.—In *Rawlings* v. *Armel,* 70 Kan. 778; 79 Pac. 683, analyzed under Chapter 5, syls. 1-3 are as follows:

"1. Under the provisions of the oil and gas lease involved in this suit, the lessee had the right to enter upon the leased premises for the purpose of exploration, and to operate if oil or gas were discovered, but no estate vested in the lessee until such minerals were found and produced.
3. The preliminary right of exploration for gas and oil under the lease in question was of such a character that it might be lost by abandonment without the lapse of time prescribed by the statute of limitations."

A landowner executed a lease for oil and gas purposes. The lessee made explorations but failed to discover oil in paying quantities. Subsequently the landowner executed a second lease, and then instituted suit to cancel the first lease. The original lessee defended, claiming that he had made explorations, and was entitled thereby to the benefit of his term. The Supreme Court of Kansas denied to the claimant of the first lease the rights claimed.

Sec. 16.—In *New American Oil Co.* v. *Troyer,* 166 Ind. 402; 76 N. E. 253, analyzed under Chapter 5, the court held:

"In the oil and gas lease the purpose of the parties was the exploration for oil and gas. The landowners intention to part

with and the operator's intention to acquire no other right than
the exclusive privilege of entering upon, and with as little injury
as possible to the possession of the freehold, and for the mutual
profit in the discovery, put down wells and mine and market the
product.''

Sec. 17.—In *Headley* v. *Hoopengarner,* 60 W. Va. 626; 55
S. E. 144, analyzed under Chapter 18, the last clause of the second point of the syllabus is as follows:

"But when found, (oil or gas) the right to produce becomes
a vested right, and when extracted the title vests in the lessee, and
the consideration or royalty paid for the privilege of search and
production is rent for the leased premises."

REMEDIES.

Sec. 18.—By the express provisions of the oil and gas lease
the parties conclusively settle all questions as to right and title
to the oil produced. Under the modern system of transportation of oil by pipeline companies, the oil must be divided by
division orders, approved by the pipeline company. The lessors
interest—the royalty—is set apart to him as his share of the
production. The lessee's share—the working interest—is likewise set apart to him. From the time the division orders are
approved by the pipeline company the division is complete and
neither party has any title to or interest in the oil of the other.
Practically no controversy arises as to this division. If the lessor is the owner in fee of the leased premises, and the lessee who
has produced the oil is the rightful owner of the lease, there can
be no dispute between these parties as to the consideration for
the oil.

Sec. 19.—In *Childers* v. *Neely,* 47 W. Va. 70; 34 S. E. 825,
analyzed under Chapter 30, syl. 5 is as follows:

"Partners have a lien on personal property for advances or
balance due them, after debts; but if they have divided the property or product of the business giving each his share in severalty,
and separating it from the balance, no such lien exists on the property or product actually divided. Such is the case with 'division
orders' in oil mining."

Judge Brannon in the opinion discussing the effect of ''division orders'' at page 77 of 47 W. Va. says:

"Now, these partners agreed to have division orders when they began business (that is, the pipelines to give each certificate of his share of the oil committed to them, which was a product of the wells); and this effected a separation of that product making each ones share his several property, and severing it from the social property, if it was such at any moment. There being no lien, there was no justification for the injunction. It perhaps disabled Neely from paying as the bill demanded of him.''

Sec. 20.—The landowner by the ordinary oil and gas lease, even after discovery by the lessee of oil in paying quantities, parts with no title to the oil in place. The lease provides for the division of the oil, the royalty to be delivered to the landowner. The lessee never has any title or interest in the royalty. Before the pipeline companies will credit the oil to the parties the execution and delivery to them of a division order, signed by the parties interested, is universally demanded; and before the oil is allowed to be delivered to the owners the pipeline company must have approved the division order.

CHAPTER 8.

RESERVATION FOR FARMING PURPOSES.

Sec. 1.—The landowner in the ordinary oil and gas lease reserves the right to use all the property demised not necessary for use and occupancy by lessee for exploration purposes, and for producing and marketing the oil and gas.

Westmoreland etc. Gas Co. v. *DeWitt*, 130 Pa. 235; 18 Atl.
    724; 5 L. R. A. 731.
Fowler v. *Delaplain*, 79 Ohio St. 279; 87 N. E. 261.

Sec. 2.—The ordinary oil and gas lease is executed for a specific purposes, that is, the exploration for and production and marketing of the oil and gas. As a rule the landowner reserves the right to use the premises not actually necessary for use and occupation by the lessee in exploring for oil and gas, and the production and marketing thereof.

LESSOR'S REMEDIES.

Sec. 3.—Where under an oil and gas lease the lessee has entered into possession of the premises and discovered oil or gas in paying quantities, he is entitled to the use and occupancy of so much of the surface as is actually necessary for mining and producing purposes. Should lessee occupy and use any portion of the land for purposes of cultivation, or for residences and conveniences for his employes, the landowner may by proper proceedings in a court of law recover possession of such portions of the premises as are not actually necessary for mining and producing purposes.

In *Fowler* v. *Delaplain*, 79 Ohio St. 279; 87 N. E. 261, (January 26, 1909) syls. 2, 3, 4 are as follows:

"2. Where a landowner orally gives permission to another to occupy and use certain lands but does not grant or attempt to grant any interest in the land, and the lessor assumes no obligation on his part with regard to such occupancy or use, the possession and use of the land is under a bare license, which is revokable at the option of the lessor; and this will be so although the lessor has silently acquiesced in the making of valuable improvements and the erection of structures on the land by the licensee.

3. Such a license is terminated by the death of either of the parties.

4. An oil lease which grants to the lessee the exclusive right to mine for and produce petroleum and natural gas on a certain tract of land, and the possession of so much of said land as may be necessary therefor, does not give to the lessee the right to occupy and use any portion of the land for the purposes of cultivation or for residences and conveniences for employes, but confines the occupancy and use of the surface to so much as is strictly necessary for mining and producing purposes."

William A. Delaplain and wife executed to F. L. Mooney an oil and gas lease on a farm in Monroe County, Ohio, which lease contained the following provision:

"The lessor does hereby grant unto the lessee for the term of five years (and so long thereafter as oil or gas is produced from the land leased, and the royalty or rentals paid by the lessee therefor) the exclusive right to mine for and produce petroleum oil and natural gas from, and the possession of so much of 430 acres of land in Washington Township, Monroe County, Ohio, as may be necessary therefor. Lessee to have all the rights and privileges necessary for the proper use and enjoyment of the lease."

Delaplain instituted an action in the Court of Common Pleas of Monroe County, against Fowler to recover possession of certain real estate in that County and for damages for unlawful detention of the same. The defendant entered a general denial. He alleged that he was placed in possession of the premises by William A. Delaplain, under whom Fowler claimed title; and was in possession at the time Fowler became seized of the legal title; that he went into such possession under a contract with Delaplain, the plaintiff in error, by which contract he alleged that he should have and retain possession of said premises and quiet enjoyment of the same as long as he was engaged as an employe of the parties who owned the leasehold on the Delaplain farm, and was operating the same for oil and gas; the defendant further alleged that under such contract he erected buildings upon the premises, and occupied them, and that he was still in the employ of the parties owning the leasehold, and that the claimants of the lease were then operating the farm for oil and gas. The defendant's third defense set up a lease for oil and gas purposes given by Delaplain and wife to F. L. Mooney, a portion of which the premises claimed in the action constituted a part. The provisions of the lease relied on in the third defense were as above quoted. The defendant further alleged in his third defense, that he was placed in possession of the premises claimed by the defendant in error, the plaintiff to the action, by the parties owning the lease and operating the farm, and that he was an employe of the lessee; and that such occupancy and possession was reasonably necessary for the proper, economic and safe operation of the premises for the oil and gas under such lease. The plaintiff demurred to the second and third defenses of the answer, and the Court of Common Pleas overruled the demurrer. The defendant in error, the plaintiff in action, then filed a reply admitting the possession of the plaintiff in error at the time of the death of Delaplain, the lessor, admitting that the plaintiff in error, the defendant in the action, was an employe of the parties operating the lease; admitting that the plaintiff in error took possession of the premises during the lifetime of Delaplain; admitting that the title of the defendant in error to said premises came to her by a devise from Delaplain; admitting the execution of a lease for oil and gas, and denying all the other allegations of the second and third defenses of the answer. On the trial a verdict was rendered in favor of the plaintiff in error, the defendant to the original action, and judgment was rendered on the verdict. A petition in error was filed, and the case heard by the Circuit Court. That Court reversed the judgment of the Court of Common Pleas upon the grounds that the Court of Common Pleas erred in admitting testimony adduced by defendant below over the objections of the plaintiff below. The case was appealed to the Supreme Court of Ohio, and that court affirmed the judgment rendered by the Circuit Court, which judgment reversed the judgment of the Court of Common Pleas of Monroe County.

LESSEE'S REMEDY.

Sec. 4.—Where the lessee enters upon the demised premises and is in possession engaged in the development or production of oil or gas, he may maintain a bill in equity for an injunction against lessor who attempts to drill upon the premises and interfere with lessee's exclusive right to the premises for mining purposes.

> *Westmoreland, etc. Gas Co.* v. *DeWitt,* 130 Pa. 235; 18 Atl.
> 724; 5 L. R. A. 731.
> *Greensboro Nat. Gas Co.* v. *Fayette County Gas Co.,* 200 Pa.
> 388; 49 Atl. 768.

Sec. 5.—In *Westmoreland, etc. Gas. Co.* v. *DeWitt,* 130 Pa. 235; 18 Atl. 724; 5 L. R. A. 731, analyzed under Chapter 11, syls. 1, 2, 3, 4. 5 are as follows:

"1. Under a lease of land for the sole purpose of drilling and operating for oil and gas, the lessee's right in the surface of the land is in the nature of an easement of entry and examination with a right of possession arising where the particular place of operation is selected, and the easement of ingress, egress, storage, transportation, etc., during the continuance of operations.

2. The real subject of possession to which the lessee is entitled, is the oil or gas contained in or obtainable through the land; these are minerals feræ naturæ, and are a part of the land and belong to its owner only so long as they are in it and under his control; the lessee, when he has drilled a gas well and controls the gas produced thereby, is in possession of all the gas within the land.

3. The fact that the gas from such well is not kept flowing into the pipeline of the lessee, but is shut in the well as a reserve for use in emergencies, does not affect the possession of it by the lessee when he is in control thereof by means of a connection between the well and his pipeline, so arranged that he can have the gas flow into his line at any time.

4. That the lessor, claiming a forfeiture of the lease, ordered the lessee's agent, who was measuring the pressure of the well, off the premises, and the agent withdrew, or, that in consequence of a like order, agents of the lessee who were on the land to locate a second well, withdrew without doing so, is no evidence of an ouster of the lessee from his possession.

5. Where the lessee is thus in possession of the gas underlying the premises equity has jurisdiction to restrain the lessor from drilling on the leasehold, the rights granted to the lessee being necessarily exclusive, and the damage to arise from the threatened waste, being entirely incapable of measurement at law, even if not irreparable."

On May 31, 1887, the Westmoreland and Cambria Natural Gas Company filed a bill in equity against Ira DeWitt, John H. Brown and others, averring that John H. Brown was the owner of a certain tract of land, and made an oil and gas lease for the same to J. M. Guffey & Company, on December 7, 1885; that the lease was afterwards assigned to the plaintiff, and that plaintiff entered upon the premises, drilled a gas well thereon, and relying upon the supply of gas to be obtained from said well and others in the vicinity, had expended large sums in laying pipelines for its transportation; that Brown, claiming that the lease had been forfeited for the non-payment of a small sum of money, had made a second lease of the lands to the defendant, DeWitt, who, with the assistance of others was about to drill a gas well on the premises; that such well could be drilled and gas obtained in about forty days, and that defendants thereby could commit great waste upon the estate of the plaintiff and do irreparable damage to its property. The bill prayed for an injunction to restrain the defendants from drilling such well, or in any way committing waste upon the plaintiff's estate and for general relief. The lease, a copy of which was filed with the bill, contained the following provision:

"To have and to hold the said premises for the said purpose only, unto the party of the second part, his executors, administrators and assigns for, during and until the full term of twenty years, next ensuing the day and year above written; . . . . . . It is further agreed, that if gas is obtained in sufficient quantities and utilized, the consideration in full to the party of the first part shall be Five Hundred Dollars, for each and every well drilled on the premises herein described, per annum, payable quarterly in advance from completion of each and every well drilled and utilized * * * * The said party of the first part to fully use and enjoy the said premises for the purpose of tillage, except such parts as shall be necessary for said operating purposes."

A preliminary injunction was granted. The defendants answered the bill, denying that plaintiff had expended large sums in laying pipelines for the transportation of gas; denying that the gas from said premises was necessary to the plaintiff, or that its loss would result in irreparable injury; and averring that said lease was forfeited by reason of the plaintiff's default in making the payments therein mentioned, averring that the plaintiff had no claim or title to or rights in the land within a radius of 300 yards from the buildings of the lessor; and that the well proposed to be drilled by the defendants was located within the limits of said radius, and praying that the injunction be dissolved. Issue having been joined upon the bill and answer the case was referred to an examiner and master who filed a report, and held that the plaintiff, the Westmoreland etc. Gas Company was not in possession of the leased premises, and therefore could not maintain a bill in equity. The Court of Common Pleas sustained this report and the Gas Company appealed. The Supreme Court of Pennsylvania reversed the Court of Common Pleas, re-instated the bill, and perpetuated the injunction.

CHAPTER 9.

RIGHT TO REMOVE FIXTURES PLACED UPON THE LEASEHOLD FOR EXPLORATION AND DEVELOPMENT PURPOSES.

Sec. 1.—The lessee in the oil and gas lease usually reserves the right to remove any machinery, fixtures and buildings placed on the premises, for the purpose of making the explorations and for producing oil and gas. The casing in the well, the derrick, and other appliances used in drilling and operating the wells, are trade fixtures and may be removed by the owner or lessee during the term of the lease; but they become the property of the land-owner if not removed by the lessee during the term, or at least within a reasonable time after its expiration.

> *Shellar* v. *Shivers*, 171 Pa. 569; 33 Atl. 95.
> *Cassell* v. *Crothers*, 193 Pa. 359; 44 Atl. 446.
> *Ohio Oil Co.* v. *Griest*, 65 N. E. 534; 30 Ind. App. 84.
> *Linden Oil Co.* v. *Jennings*, 207 Pa. 524; 56 Atl. 1074.
> *Perry* v. *Acme Oil Co.*, (Ind. App.) —; 88 N. E. 589.
> *Gartlan* v. *Hickman*, 56 W. Va. 75; 49 S. E. 14.
> *Simpson* v. *Pittsburg Plate Glass Co.*, 62 N. E. 753; 28 Ind.
>   App. 343.

Sec. 2.—The right to the lessee, when his search has ceased, or when oil or gas, if found, has been exhausted, to remove all machinery, fixtures, and buildings placed on the premises, is usually reserved in the lease. The term "fixtures" used in the oil and gas lease refers to those structures and appliances placed upon the premises for the purpose of exploration and production, and in general, would be of no benefit in place to the lessor; in fact, in cases where the premises are used for farming purposes, if not removed they would prove an injury. The lessor would not be benefitted by the retention of the fixtures in place. Where, however, there is a gas well, which in the judgment of the lessee is not producing in paying quantities, but there is yet a suffi-cient quantity of gas for domestic use, and there is a provision in the lease to the effect that the lessor shall have gas for domes-tic use, and the lessee has agreed that if he abandons the well it shall be left in a condition to be used by the lessor, he will not be permitted to remove pipe, thereby cutting off the supply of gas to lessor's residence.

Sec. 3.—Where a lessee enters the premises under a lease giving him the right to remove all machinery and fixtures placed thereon for exploration and production purposes, and begins explorations and subsequently the lease is cancelled by a court of competent jurisdiction, a prior lessee cannot appropriate to his own use the machinery and fixtures placed on the premises by the second lessee, without being liable to him for the value of the machinery and fixtures so appropriated.

Sec. 4.—In *Shellar* v. *Shivers,* 171 Pa. 569; 33 Atl. 95 (Oct. 24, 1895) the syllabus is as follows:

"The casing in an oil or gas well, the derrick and other appliances used in drilling and operating the well are trade fixtures, and may be removed by the owner or lessee during the term of the lease; but they become the property of the landowner if not removed by the lessee during the term, or at least within a reasonable time after its expiration.

The term of an oil and gas lease was for 'three years, or as much longer thereafter as oil or gas might be found in paying quantities, with the right in the said lessee to enter upon said premises at any time for the purpose of mining,' etc. The lease also provided that the lessee had 'the right to remove at any time all machinery, oil well supplies or appurtenances of any kind belonging to said lessee.' The well never produced oil or gas in paying quantities. *Held,* that after the expiration of four years from the date of the termination of the lease, and five years and six months after the well had been completed and found to be of no use, the lessee could not enter to remove the casing from the well."

On October 27, 1892, Samuel M. Shellar was the owner in fee, and was in possession of, a tract of land situated in Buffalo Township, Washington County, Pennsylvania, containing 255 acres, more or less. On that day Shivers and others, without the consent and against the will of Shellar, entered upon said tract of land for the purpose of taking casing out of a hole that had been drilled for oil and gas in the Spring of 1887, and removing other fixtures which had been used in drilling this well—which produced neither oil nor gas in paying quantities. The casing and fixtures, at the time the well was drilled belonged to Shivers and others. Samuel M. Shellar claiming that this entry upon his land for the purpose indicated was unlawful brought an action of trespass against the defendants. Shellar died before the action was tried, and his heirs and the defendants agreed upon the facts, and submitted them in the nature of a special verdict for the opinion of the court. These facts were: On November 11, 1885, Samuel M. Shellar executed and delivered to J. B. Akin a lease of this 255 acres for oil and gas purposes; the term was for "three years and as much longer thereafter as oil or gas might be found in paying quantities, with the right in said lessee to enter upon said premises for the purpose of mining," etc; the lease also provided that the lessee had "the right to remove at any time any and all machinery, oil well supplies or appurtenances of any kind belonging to the said lessee"; the lessee and those who claimed under him entered under said lease upon this tract of land and drilled a well, completing it in April, 1887; the well produced neither oil nor gas in paying quantities, and the lessee and his assigns ceased operations on the premises. The engine and boiler used in drilling the well was taken away but the casing in the well, and other fixtures, were left, and remained on the premises and were there on the said 27th of October, 1892, and the defendants entered to remove them.

The questions for the consideration of the court were: Were the defendants trespassers? Had they a right to remove the fixtures connected with and used in drilling this well, which was completed and abandoned as worthless, in April, 1887? The Court of Common Pleas upon the facts stated, rendered judgment in favor of the plaintiffs for nominal damages and costs, from which judgment defendants appealed. The lower court held that the defendants claiming under the lease could not, after four years were allowed to expire, remove the fixtures. The Supreme Court affirmed the decision of the lower court.

Sec. 5.—The court in *Shellar* v. *Shivers* draws a distinction between the lessee's right to remove the machinery, fixtures and other property placed upon the leased premises for the purpose of development within the term of the lease, and his right to remove such property after the term has expired. Subject to the rights of lessors who have as a consideration for the grant reserved rights as to use of gas for domestic purposes from wells producing gas at the time lessee attempts to remove the fixtures, the lessee has the absolute right at any time within the term specified in the lease within which he may make explorations, to remove any property placed on the lease for the purpose of exploration or production. After the expiration of the exploration period, or after the expiration of the specified term, the lessee has the right within a reasonable time to remove such fixtures.

Sec. 6.—In *Cassell* v. *Crothers,* 193 Pa. 359; 44 Atl. 446, analyzed under Chapter 6, syl. 2 is as follows:

"Where the lessor terminates an oil and gas lease, and takes possession of the premises and of certain personal property claimed by the lessee the latter cannot maintain an action of ejectment to obtain possession of the premises in order to remove the personal property, but the court will direct judgment in the ejectment in favor of the lessor without prejudice to the lessee's rights to maintain an action against the lessor for taking and appropriating the personal property of the lessee."

On April 22, 1887, W. B. Crothers leased his farm of ninety-six acres to the Marshall Oil Company for oil and gas purposes. The lease provided that the lessee should have the right "to remove at any time any and all machinery, oil well supplies or appurtenances and property of any kind," placed by lessee upon the premises for the purpose of exploration or development. The Marshall Oil Company assigned the lease and Cecelia Cassell became vested with the same and all rights thereunder on March 18, 1891. A number of wells were drilled on the farm under this lease shortly after its execution and oil but not gas was found in paying quantities. The term of the lease was ten years, which expired April 22, 1897, at which time there were five wells that were being pumped for oil. On July 1, 1897, four wells were producing oil, and on November 14, 1897, only three. On the last date all the oil in the tanks was run into the pipeline, the wells shut down, the loose tools locked up, and the employes in charge

of the lease left it and none of them returned, except as hereafter stated.   At the time the wells were thus shut down they
were making in all about one or two barrels of oil per day, eight
or ten barrels being necessary to constitute production in paying quantities.   In April, 1898, W. B. Crothers took possession
of all the wells and property of the plaintiff, Cecelia Cassell, including boilers, engines, steam pipes, sucker rods, tools, etc.,
claiming that the term of the lease had expired, and that the leased
premises and everything found thereon belonged to him.   About
May 15, 1898, the plaintiff, with knowledge of what the defendant
had done, sent an employe to take charge of her wells on the
farm, who was ordered off and threatened with arrest by Crothers who claimed that the plaintiff Cassell had no longer any
rights under the lease of April 22, 1887.   On August 24, 1898,
Cecelia Cassell instituted an action of ejectment against W. B.
Crothers, to recover possession of this tract of land for oil and
gas purposes.   The Court of Common Pleas of Washington
County rendered judgment for defendant,- from which judgment
the plaintiff appealed.   The Supreme Court affirmed the judgment.

Sec. 7.—In *Ohio Oil Co.* v. *Griest*, 65 N. E. 534; 30 Ind. App.
84, (Nov. 25, 1902) syls. 2-3 are as follows:

"2. A complaint alleging that the plaintiff was the owner of
certain land on which was a gas well, and that the well furnished
gas for plaintiff's dwelling house, and that defendant wrongfully
removed the drivepipe, casing, and tubing from the well, cutting
off the flow of gas, thereby damaging the real estate, stated a
cause of action, irrespective of whether or not the gas, when
brought to the surface, was personal property.
3. Where a lease for the privilege of drilling for gas gave
the lessee right to remove machinery or fixtures, but provided
that, if he abandoned the lease while there was a well furnishing
gas sufficient for the lessor's residence on the premises, such well
should be left in a condition to be used by the lessor, the lessee
could not remove pipe, thereby cutting off the supply of gas to
the residence, whether or not such pipe was personal property."

In April, 1893, Jasper N. Hiatt was the owner of and in possession of a tract of land.   On May 3, 1893, the Sheriff of Jay
County, Indiana, by virtue of a decree issued to him by the Clerk

of the Circuit Court of Jay County, sold the real estate at sheriff sale to Reuben Griest, who took a certificate of purchase therefor. On August 18, 1893, while the certificate of sale was held by Griest, Hiatt leased the land to one Huffman, trustee, for oil and gas purposes. In September, 1893, Huffman drilled and completed a gas well thereon. On February 24, 1894, Huffman sold and assigned said lease, well and fixtures to the Ohio Oil Company. On March 3, 1894, Griest leased the same land to Huffman for oil and gas purposes; and Huffman, on March 28, 1894, sold and assigned the lease made to him by Griest to the Ohio Oil Company. Jasper N. Hiatt failed to redeem the real estate from sheriff's sale, and on May 8, 1894, Griest received a sheriff's deed for the land. The well on the land produced gas in marketable quantities for three or four years, and the Ohio Oil Company paid the rental, as stipulated in the lease, and furnished Griest gas for his dwelling on the land. After a few years the flow of gas from the well was so reduced in quantity that it became unprofitable to convey it from the premises, whereupon the Ohio Oil Company entered upon the premises and removed the drivepipe, casing, tubing and other fixtures connected with the operation of the well. The lease from Hiatt and the lease from Griest to Huffman, both contained the following provision:

"The lessee to have the right to remove any buildings, machinery or fixtures placed on said premises by them at any time, either before or after the limitation of this lease."

The lease also contained the following provision: "If the lessee at its option abandons well on said premises, furnishing gas sufficient for said residence, said well shall be left in such condition as to be used by said first party at his (said first party's) expense." Reuben Griest instituted his suit against the Ohio Oil Company for $1500 damages, alleging that the Ohio Oil Company wrongfully removed the drivepipe, casing and tubing from said well, thereby destroying it, and cutting off the flow of gas, by reason whereof the real estate was damaged in the sum of $1500. The Oil Company answered, claiming that a proper construction of the lease gave the right to it to remove all the pipe and fixtures from the well. The plaintiff recovered judgment for $700 against the defendant, from which it appealed, and the Appellate Court of Indiana affirmed the judgment.

Sec. 8.—In *Linden Oil Co. v. Jennings*, 207 Pa. 254; 56 Atl. 1074; (Jan. 4, 1904) the syllabus is as follows:

"Where a lessee under an oil lease entered upon the leased premises with notice of a claim of a prior lessee, and the prior lease is subsequently adjudged valid, the owner of the prior lease has no right to take possession of personal property placed on the premises by the owner of the subsequent lease, nor even of property attached to the land, where the subsequent lessee has the right to remove such property under his agreement with the land-owner."

The land owner made an oil and gas lease, which lease he subsequently claimed to be forfeited, and thereafter executed a second lease under which last lease the lessee's assignee entered for exploration purposes and commenced to drill a well. In a suit between the conflicting claimants, the first lease was held valid, and thereupon the lessee under the first lease took possession of the well commenced by the second lessee and converted the rig, boiler, engine, etc., to his own use. The second lessee instituted suit in trespass for conversion of personal property in the Court of Common Pleas Number 2, Allegheny County, and recovered verdict and judgment, from which judgment the defendants, the first lessees, appealed to the Supreme Court of Pennsylvania, and that court affirmed the judgment.

Sec. 9.—In *Gartlan v. Hickman*, 56 W. Va. 75; 49 S .E. 14 (Oct. 25, 1904) the syllabus is as follows:

"1. The owner of land executes a lease thereon for oil and gas purposes, by which it is agreed that the lessee shall have the privilege, at any time, to remove therefrom all machinery and fixtures placed on said premises. Under this lease the lessees, and their assignees, for the purpose of exploring for oil and gas, placed on the land an engine, wooden oil well rig, wooden oil tanks, casing, pipes, rubber belt, and other appliances of like character, necessary for the prosecution of that work. Afterwards the lease was forfeited and terminated for the non-payment of rental. *Held*, that said machinery and fixtures did not become parts of the freehold, and that said lessees, or the owners of the machinery and fixtures, had a reasonable time after the termination of said lease, in which to remove said property from the land.

2. What is a reasonable time for the removal is to be determined from all the facts and circumstances of the case.''

Miranda A. Hickman and Willie Hickman, her husband, executed to John F. Phillips and J. Perry Thompson an oil and gas lease dated May 29, 1901, on a tract of 112½ acres of land in Harrison County, West Virginia. By successive assignments W. S. Mowris, Thomas Gartlan and the Southern Oil Company acquired an interest in the lease. The lease contained the following stipulations:

"The parties of the first part 'do grant, demise, lease and let unto the parties of the second part, their heirs, executors, administrators or assigns, for the sole and only purpose of mining and operating for oil and gas, and of laying pipelines etc., and of building tanks, stations and structures thereon to take care of said product, all that certain tract of land * * * It is agreed that this lease shall remain in force for the term of five years from this date, and so long thereafter as oil or gas, or either of them, is produced therefrom, by said parties of the second part, their successors and assigns. * * * * * * * * Provided, however, that this lease shall become null and void, and all rights herein shall cease and determine unless a well shall be completed on the said premises within ninety days, from the date hereof, or unless the lessees pay at the rate of $125.00 quarterly in advance for each additional three months such completion is delayed, from the time above mentioned for the completion of such well, until a well is completed; and it is agreed that the completion of such well shall, be and operate as a full liquidation of all rentals under this provision during the remainder of the term of this lease. * * * * * * It is agreed that the second party shall have the privilege * * * * * * at any time to remove all machinery and fixtures placed on the premises.' ''

On December 31, 1901, Willie Hickman commenced a suit in Chancery in the Circuit Court of Harrison County, against Mowris, Gartlan, the Southern Oil Company, Phillips and Thompson. On January 7, 1902, Hickman presented his bill to the Judge of said Court in which he set up said lease and the several assignments thereof and filed therewith copies of the same, and in substance alleged therein that Mowris and the Oil Company, claiming to be equal owners of the lease, had drilled one well on the land, marked on the plat filed, as Number 1, which was completed in January, 1901; that it was afterwards shot and declared by them to be a dry hole, and not worth cleaning out; that said lease had been abandoned by the defendants, and active operations thereon for oil and gas continuously discontinued since the middle of January, 1901, until the 31st day of December, 1901; that the defendant had paid no rental on the land since August 29, 1901; that on December 31, 1901, defendants again entered upon the land with screw, circle, water barrels, bailer, stem and cable, and hauled the same to the well, and proceeded to lay pipe for the purpose of furnishing fuel to said well from another well on a neighboring farm; that the lease and the assignments thereof were null and void, and constituted a cloud on plaintiff's title to the land, the bill praying that the lease and the several assignments thereof be declared forfeited and cancelled as such cloud; and that defendants and each of them, be restrained and enjoined from entering upon the land, and from doing any and all things under said lease or any of the assignments thereof. The injunction was granted as prayed for; the bill was filed at rules, and the cause regularly matured for hearing, and on May 22, 1902, the Circuit Court entered a decree upon the bill taken for confessed, and the cause set for hearing, cancelling the lease bearing date May 29, 1901, and all assignments thereof, and contracts thereunder, and a subsequent lease of the three acres around the buildings in said Phillips and Thompson lease reserved, ordering the defendants to surrender to the plaintiff the lease and all assignments thereof. Hickman, on July 14, 1902, sent by registered mail to Thomas Gartlan, the Southern Oil Company, and others, a notice as follows:

"You are hereby notified that the oil well rig at well number 1, casing, and all fixtures and machinery of every kind or character, and all property now on my farm, in Indian Run, in Harrison County, West Virginia, belong to me and are my property; and you are further notified not to remove the same or any part thereof; and you are still further notified not to trespass upon my said farm or any part thereof, for any purpose whatever."

These copies were received by the parties, from the 14th to the 28th days of July, 1902. It was proven upon the trial that this notice was the first claim of ownership that Hickman had made to the property in controversy, and was the first knowledge that the defendants or any of them had of the determination of the chancery cause, or of such claim. On August 1, 1902, an action of detinue was commenced in the Circuit Court of Harrison County by the said Gartlan, Mowris, the Southern Oil Company, Phillips and Thompson, against Hickman for the recovery of sundry goods and chattels, of the total value of $1,846.53, and $1,000 damages for the detention of the same, being the machinery and fixtures placed by the plaintiffs on the leased premises, and used in the drilling of well Number 1. A trial of the action was had to a jury, and a verdict was rendered in favor of the plaintiff for the property sued for, upon which verdict judgment was rendered that the plaintiffs should retain possession of the property, they having filed the affidavit and bond for the purpose of obtaining possession under the statute, and from this judgment Hickman obtained a writ of error to the Court of Appeals. Upon the trial it was admitted that the plaintiffs placed the property in controversy upon the land of the defendant embraced in the lease of May 29, 1900, for the purpose of drilling and operating for oil and gas under the lease; that one well was drilled and completed about the middle of January, and shot about the thirteenth of February, 1901; plaintiffs paid the rental under the lease on August 29, 1901, for the quarter ending November 28, 1901; the well in question was drilled to a depth of 2,200 feet; casing was inserted at the proper depth—about 2,100 feet; a derrick was built over the well, and the engine sued for was set or placed in an engine house, connected with the drilling tools in the usual way, and the tanks were set or placed about 75 feet from the derrick; all the property sued for was connected in the usual way for drilling and operating the well, and was necessary and used for that purpose; that shortly after November 28, 1901, defendant posted notices in writing upon the outer gates of the land embraced in the lease, notifying plaintiffs, or anyone acting under them, to keep off the property; that plaintiff claimed the lease had been

forfeited for failure to pay rent, neither plaintiffs nor any agent
for them, at that time being on the property; that the same notice and claim were given verbally by defendant to agents of the
plaintiff at the same time; that no rental was paid after August
28, 1901; that on December 31, 1901, employes of plaintiffs, by
their authority, after the notice had been given, went upon the
property and upon warrant sued out on January 1, 1902, were
arrested as trespassers, taken before a Justice of the Peace, and
the cause was continued at the instance of the defendants; that
before trial an injunction was granted in the chancery suit; that
Thomas Gartlan and others were then not further prosecuted
under the warrants and the same were dismissed; that on February 13, 1901, employes of plaintiffs, by their authority, went
upon the land and shot the well a second time; that the property in controversy was taken by the plaintiffs at the time of
the institution of this suit by giving bond and the same was
replevied by the defendant; that a demand was made upon defendant for the property in controversy on July 26, 1902, which
demand was in writing; that all the property in controversy remained in place as it was at the time the well was drilled and
operated, until delivered to plaintiff in the suit by the sheriff.
Verdict and judgment were rendered for plaintiffs and defendant brought error to the Court of Appeals, and that court
affirmed the judgment.

Upon the proposition that the lessees, who were defendants
in the chancery suit and plaintiffs in the detinue suit, only forfeited their right to make further exploration, the court cited:

Guffey v. *Hukill,* 34 W. Va. 49; 11 S. E. 754.
Steelsmith v. *Gartlan,* 45 W. Va. 27; 29 S. E. 978.
Urpman v. *Lowther Oil Co.,* 53 W. Va. 501-505; 44 S. E. 433.

Upon the right to remove property placed on the lease the
court cited:

Shellar v. *Shivers,* 171 Pa. 569-572.

Sec. 10.—In *Perry* v. *Acme Oil Co.,* — Ind. App. —; 88 N.
E. 859, (June 25, 1909) syls. 2, 3, 4, 5, 6 are as follows:

"2. In action for conversion of certain oil or fixtures and machinery against plaintiff's landlord, a special defense that the lease provided that plaintiff might remove all property at any time, and, if it failed to operate any one well for 60 days, or pay defendants one dollar a day for the time it was not operated, the ten acres on which it was located should be returned to defendants; that plaintiff on December 12, 1902, ceased to operate the wells, abandoned the premises and removed therefrom all its machinery and remained away thereafter until the 15th day of April, 1903, when defendants took possession of the wells, casing and drive pipe, and proceeded to operate the same; and that defendants did not appropriate any machinery belonging to plaintiff, but only properly attached to and forming a part of the real estate which could not be removed therefrom without damage—was practicable under the general denial pleaded, and hence the sustaining of a demurrer thereto was not error.

3. Where an oil and gas lease contained a covenant by the lessee to surrender the ten acre tract on which any well was located on the lessee's failure for 60 days to operate the well, or pay one dollar a day for the time of such failure to operate, the lessor was estopped to claim that such provision was enforceable because of uncertainty in the description of the property to be surrendered; it being to select the particular tract to be reconveyed on its failure to operate a well or pay royalty.

4. Machinery and fixtures placed on realty leased for oil and gas purposes did not become permanent fixtures nor parts of the freehold by reason of such annexation as was necessary to develop the premises according to the terms of the lease and the title to such machinery and fixtures did not vest in the lessor on forfeiture of the lease.

5. Where an oil and gas lease authorized the lessee to remove its fixtures 'at any time' such right was not unlimited as to time, but the lessee was only authorized to remove within a reasonable time after the expiration of the lease.

6. Where an oil and gas lease provided for drilling or operating oil or gas wells, and, on failure to do so, to pay an agreed sum per day to the lessor for such failure or delay, and that, upon failure to drill, operate, or to pay the agreed sum, the lease should be void, such provision was for the benefit of the lessor, so that, on a breach of the lease, he might declare a forfeiture by proper notice or waive the forfeiture and proceed against the lessee for failure to perform the covenants of the lease, and hence, title did not re-vest in the lessor immediately on the lessee's default.''

This was an action brought in the Circuit Court of Wells County, Indiana, by the Acme Oil Company against William M. Perry and the King Oil Company for the recovery of the value of certain oil or fixtures, and machinery alleged to have been converted by the said Perry and King Oil Company to their own use. The complaint was in one paragraph and alleged that on the 26th of September, 1899, William M. Perry and wife executed and delivered to the plaintiff Acme Oil Company an oil and gas lease whereby Perry granted to the plaintiff 100 acres of land in Wells County, for the purpose of drilling and operating for gas and oil, with the right to enter thereon and erect and maintain necessary buildings; that lessee entered upon the land in pursuance of said lease, took possession thereof and drilled and completed two wells thereon, and equipped the wells with casing and drive pipe, to the value of $928.30; that defendants took possession of said wells, casing, drive pipe and other materials and machinery and unlawfully converted them to their own use. To this complaint the defendants filed separate demurrers, and before the court decided the demurrers the King Oil Company filed its separate answer in general denial, and Perry filed his separate answer, in two paragraphs, first, general denial; second, admitting that he executed the contract as set out in the complaint, and averring that the lessee submitted a blank printed form of contract for him to execute, which contained among other things, the following:

"The second party shall have the right, free of charge, to use sufficient gas, oil, and water to run all machinery for operating said well, also the right to remove all property at any time."

That there was inserted therein in writing a provision as follows:

"It is further agreed by second party that when they fail to operate any one well for a period of sixty days, or pay to first party one dollar per day from the time they fail to operate said well, the ten acres on which said well is located shall be cancelled and returned to first party. Second party shall have the right to remove their machinery from said ten acres."

The answer further averred that on December 12, 1902, lessee, the plaintiff, ceased to operate the said two wells, and wholly abandoned the premises, removed therefrom all its machinery, and so remained therefrom thereafter; that on April 15, 1903, he took possession of said wells, casing and drive pipe, and employed his co-defendant to operate the wells; that he did not appropriate to his own use any machinery belonging to the lessee, the plaintiff, but only property which was attached to and formed part of the real estate, and which could not be removed therefrom without damage. To the second paragraph of the answer the plaintiff demurred, which demurrer was sustained by the trial court, and proper exceptions reserved as to the ruling thereon. Upon the trial judgment was rendered for plaintiff Acme Oil Company from which judgment the defendants Perry and the King Oil Company appealed. The case was decided February 22, 1907, and was first reported in 80 N. E. 174, where the case was reversed and remanded and upon re-hearing the judgment of the Circuit Court was affirmed.

Upon the right of a lessee who has placed machinery and fixtures on a leasehold property for drilling for oil and gas to remove the same, the court cited:

Montpelier Light & Water Co., v. *Stephenson*, 22 Ind. App. 175; 53 N. E. 444.
Gartlan v. *Hickman*, 56 W. Va 75; 49 S. E. 14; 67 L. R. A. 694.
Siler v. *Globe Window Glass Co.*, 21 Ohio St. Ct. R. 284.
Shellar v. *Shivers*, 171 Pa. 569; 33 Atl. 95.

Upon the question of the right of the lessor upon failure of the lessee to perform the covenants of the lease to declare a forfeiture, or to waive the forfeiture and proceed against lessee for failure to perform the covenants of the lease, the court cited:

Hancock v. *Diamond Glass Co.*, 162 Ind. 146-152; 70 N. E. 149.
Edmonds v. *Mounsey*, 15 Ind. App. 399; 44 N. E. 196.
Woodland Oil Co. v. *Crawford*, 55 Ohio St. 161; 44 N. E. 1093; 34 L. R. A. 62.
Wills v. *Manufacturers Gas Co.*, 130 Pa. 222; 18 Atl. 721; 5 L. R. A. 603.

LESSOR'S REMEDY.

Sec. 11.—Where a lessee under an oil and gas lease has the right to remove the machinery, fixtures and buildings, placed on the lease for exploration and producing purposes, he must remove them during the term or at least within a reasonable time after its expiration. When lessee fails to remove the property within such time he loses his right of removal, and such property becomes the property of the landowner. A lessee who enters the premises for the purpose of removal, after he has lost his right so to do, is a trespasser, and the landowner may recover damages against him for such entry. While lessee reserves the right to remove the property he placed on the premises, yet such property is placed there for the sole purpose of exploration and production, and as lessee's right to possession is limited to exploration and production, when the premises are abandoned for these purposes, he must remove the fixtures placed upon the premises for exploration and development purposes; otherwise the property becomes the property of the landowner.

Shellar v. *Shivers,* 171 Pa. 569; 33 Atl. 95.

Sec. 12.—Where an oil and gas lease provides for the removal of the machinery and fixtures by the lessee, but further provides, that if there is a gas well producing gas upon the premises at the time of abandonment, such well should be left in a condition so as to be used by the lessor such lessee will be liable in damages where, in removing his fixtures and machinery, he cuts off the supply of gas from the residence of the lessor.

Ohio Oil Co. v. *Griest,* 65 N. E., 534; 30 Ind. App. 84.

Sec. 13.—In *Simpson* v. *Pittsburg Plate Glass Co.,* 28 Ind. App. 343; 62 N. E. 753 (February, 1902) syls. 1-5 are as follows:

"1. A natural gas lease granted the lessees three tracts of land out of a 100-acre tract for drilling gas wells, gave them the use of adjoining highways for laying mains, and bound the lessors not to drill or permit others to drill on the entire 100 acres. The lessees agreed to furnish gas for a dwelling house on the premises during the lease; to pay $100 annual rental for each well, and $100 a year until a well was drilled; and to drill one well by a certain date, or to pay for the same *whether drilled* or not. The lease was to terminate whenever gas ceased to be used generally for manufacturing purposes in that county. *Held,* that as, during the continuance of the lease, the lessors and their assigns were forbidden from drilling or permitting others to drill on the 100 acres, the lessees were during such time bound by their stipulation to drill at least one well, and, failing to do so, must pay $100 yearly and supply gas for the dwelling house.

5. Injunction will lie to restrain a lessee under a natural gas lease from cutting off the supply of natural gas which he has agreed to furnish the lessor and his assigns where great injury will result from the cutting off of the gas and there is no adequate remedy at law.''

Lawrence Simpson instituted a suit against the Pittsburg Plate Glass Company in the Circuit Court of Howard County, for the recovery of an installment of rent claimed to be due under a gas lease, and for an injunction to restrain the Glass Company from cutting off plaintiff's supply of gas. The defendant demurred to the petition, which demurrer the Circuit Court sustained, and the plaintiff appealed to the Appellate Court. That court reversed the Circuit Court.

The complaint alleged in substance that Amos T. Parker was the owner and in possession of a tract of 100 acres of land, and on June 1, 1889, executed a gas lease to Levi Barrett and Sylvanus Barrett; that this lease granted to Barretts three tracts of twenty feet square in a certain 100-acre tract, with the exclusive right of drilling a gas well on each side of the three tracts, with the right to erect and remove the necessary machinery or fixtures; that lessor was not to drill or permit others to drill any other gas well on any part of the entire hundred acres during the continuance of the lease; that if any gas well were drilled on the premises the Barretts, their heirs and assigns should thereafter be released from payment of the rental provided for in the contract; but that otherwise the rights of the Barretts should not be affected; that Barretts agreed that they would deliver to Parker during the continuance of the lease gas free of charge necessary for domestic use for the dwelling house on the premises, or that might be erected thereon, not exceeding two dwellings, this gas to be delivered in a main or pipe in a public highway nearest the principal dwelling house then on

the premises, where it was to be received by Parker, who was
to make the necessary attachments; that the Barretts agreed
to furnish gas on or before November 1, 1889; and further agreed
to give or pay to Parker one-sixth of all oil produced; and also
agreed to pay as an additional consideration an annual rental
of $100 each year for each gas well so drilled which should pro-
duce gas in paying quantities sufficient for manufacturing purposes, which payments were to commence and become due and
payable on January 1, as to each gas well after the completion
thereof, and to continue thereafter annually during the continuance of the lease; that until drilling of a gas well on the
premises by the Barretts it was agreed that they should pay
Parker an annual rental of $100, to be paid on the first of Janu-
ary in each year; and that there should be a well drilled by
November 1, 1889, or be paid for whether drilled or not; that
the lease was to be in force from June 1, 1889, and deemed to
have terminated whenever natural gas ceased to be used generally for manufacturing purposes in Howard County, Indiana,
or whenever the Barretts should fail to pay or tender the rental
agreed upon, within sixty days of the date of its becoming due.

The complaint further alleged that the Barretts on July
16, 1889, assigned the lease to the Diamond Plate Glass Company, and the lease, on April 1, 1895, was assigned to the Pittsburg Plate Glass Company; that this last assignee in consideration of the assignment, agreed to perform all the conditions of
the lease and pay all the rentals; that the assignors of the last
named assignee entered upon the land under the lease and laid
in the highway thereof pipes and mains for the transportation
of gas, and maintained the same from November 1, 1889, to
April 1, 1895. The complaint in this behalf alleged that the lease
stipulated that the Barretts, their heirs or assigns, should have
the right to use the highways adjoining any part of the 100
acres for laying mains and pipes for the transportation of gas;
that when the Pittsburg Company became the owner of the
lease on April 1, 1895, it entered upon the land under the lease
for the purpose of maintaining thereon in the highways thereof, pipes for the transportation of natural gas, and had maintained on and across the land, in the highways thereof, from

April 1, 1895, to the commencement of the suit under the lease,
120 rods of 1-inch natural gas pipe, which the company had
continually used for the transportation of natural gas produced
elsewhere; that from April 1, 1895, to October 15, 1898, the Pittsburg Company had maintained on and across the land, in the
highways thereof, 120 rods of 6-inch gas pipe, which it used all
that time for the transportation of natural gas produced elsewhere; that at the date of the execution of the lease and continuously since that time there had been a highway 40 feet wide
along the west side of the 100 acres of land, one-half of the
width of which was on the land owned by the plaintiff; and that
there had been a highway 30 feet wide along the north side of
the land, one-half of the width of which highway was on that
land; that no gas or oil well had been at any time drilled on the
100-acre tract; that the rental maturing on January 1, 1890, including January 1, 1898, had been paid; but the rental of $100
due January 1, 1899, was due and unpaid; that Parker, on March
10, 1890, sold the land to Walter F. Temlin who, on February
27, 1897, sold the land to the plaintiff Simpson; that natural
gas had been at all times since the execution of the lease, and
still was used generally for manufacturing purposes in Howard
County; that the lessor and his grantee, including the plaintiff,
had at all times performed the conditions of the lease on their
part; that the assignors of the Pittsburg Plate Glass Company
duly furnished to the plaintiff's grantors natural gas, free of
charge necessary for domestic use at the dwelling house on the
premises, from November 1, 1889, to April 1, 1895, since which
date the Pittsburg Company had furnished to the plaintiff's
grantor, and to the plaintiff, natural gas free of charge necessary for domestic use at said dwelling house, and was so doing
at the date of the suit; that the Pittsburg Company asserted
that it had the right to remove the pipes for the transportation
of the gas from the plaintiff's said land, and to cease to furnish him gas for domestic use at the house on the land; and
that unless restrained by the court it would in the immediate
future remove the pipes and cut off the supply of gas at the
plaintiff's house, which supply was necessary for domestic use
at said house; that, if the company should so cut off the supply,

it would greatly damage the plaintiff; that natural gas had a great and peculiar value as fuel, and for light and domestic use, there being no known substitute therefor; that the plaintiff would be wholly unable to obtain from any other source natural gas for domestic purposes in said dwelling, and he would be compelled to use wood for fuel and coal oil for light; that the house was fitted up with necessary pipes and fixtures for using natural gas, which would be rendered worthless by cutting off the supply of gas; that the company had an ample and abundant supply of natural gas, and could readily maintain said gas pipelines in the highways and furnish natural gas to the plaintiff necessary for domestic use at said house, in compliance with the terms of the lease. The petition prayed for judgment for $100.00, and that the Glass Company be enjoined and restrained from removing the pipelines and cutting off the supply of gas.

Sec. 14.—Where in an oil and gas lease, as a part of the consideration therefor, lessee covenants to furnish gas free of charge to lessor for domestic use for a fixed term, or until the happening of a certain event, and lessee does furnish such gas for such purpose and lays pipelines for this purpose, upon the demised premises, and subsequently, before the end of the term of the lease or before the happening of the event provided for, lessee undertakes to remove the gas lines, and thereby disable itself from furnishing gas for domestic purposes, lessor may maintain an injunction and restrain lessee from removing the gas line and cutting off the supply of natural gas where the plaintiff proves under proper allegations that great injury will result from the cutting off of the gas, and that he has no adequate remedy at law.

Simpson v. *Pittsburg Plate Glass Co.*, 28 Ind. App. 343; 62 N. E. 753.

LESSEE'S REMEDY.

Sec. 15.—Where, under an oil and gas lease lessee has entered the premises and discovered oil in paying quantities and subsequently abandons the premises, and the lessor declares a forfeiture and takes possession of the wells, derricks, machinery, casing and other property, which lessee had the right to remove at the time of such conversion, the lessor will be liable to the lessee in damages for the value of the property so converted; which damages the lessee may recover in an action at law instituted for the purpose.

Cassell v. *Crothers*, 193 Pa. 359; 44 Atl. 446.

Sec. 16.—Where a lessee under an oil and gas lease containing a provision authorizing him to remove the machinery, fixtures and buildings placed on the premises for exploration and production, enters upon the premises under such lease, commences explorations, and places thereon machinery and fixtures for the purpose, and subsequently the claimants of a prior lease in a controversy between the claimants to the first and second leases cause the second lease to be cancelled by a decree or order of court, and the claimants to such prior lease take possession of the well, derrick and other fixtures placed upon the premises by the second lessee and convert them to their own use, such second lessee may recover against the claimants of the prior lease who have so converted the property of the second lessee, the value of the property in a proceeding at law taken for the purpose.

Linden Oil Co. v. *Jennings*, 207 Pa. 524; 56 Atl. 1074.
Perry v. *Acme Oil Co.*, (Ind App.) —; 88 N. E. 859.

Sec. 17.—Where under an oil and gas lease lessee has the right to remove within a reasonable time after ceasing operations on the lease, the machinery, fixtures and buildings placed thereon for the purpose of development and exploration, and lessor refuses permission to lessee to remove his property within such time, and himself, takes possession of the property, lessee may, in a suit against lessor brought for the purpose, recover possession of his property, if possession thereof can be had, if not, then the value of the property, and in either case, damages for the detention thereof.

Gartlan v. *Hickman*, 56 W. Va. 75; 49 S. E. 14.

CHAPTER 10.

RESERVATION AROUND BUILDINGS.

Sec. 1.—Where a landowner grants the exclusive privilege
to a lessee, by the ordinary oil and gas lease, to explore for and
produce oil and gas upon a tract of land, with a reservation
around buildings upon which no well shall be drilled, such reservation will be construed as a mere limitation whereby the lessee
will not be allowed to drill within the reserved area. The lessor,
however will not be allowed to drill upon the reserved portions,
himself; nor will he be allowed to grant the right to another to
drill thereon. Such reservation is not a reservation of the oil
and gas underlying the reserved portions of the land. The right to
exhaust the oil and gas underlying the reserved portions passes to
the lessee, who is authorized to exhaust such oil and gas by wells
drilled upon other portions of the tract.

> *Westmoreland etc. Nat. Gas Co.* v. *DeWitt*, 130 Pa. 235; 18
>   Atl. 724.
> *Duffield* v. *Hue*, 136 Pa. 602; 20 Atl. 526.
> *Duffield* v. *Rosenzweig*, 144 Pa. 520; 23 Atl. 4.
> *Duffield* v. *Rosenzweig*, 150 Pa. 543; 24 Atl. 705.
> *Lynch* v. *Burford*, 201 Pa. 52; 50 Atl. 228.
> *Consumers Gas Trust Co.* v. *American Plate Glass Co.*, 162
>   Ind. 392; 68 N. E. 1020.
> *Brown* v. *Spilman*, 155 U. S. 665.
> Allison and Evans Appeal, 77 Pa. 221.

Sec. 2.—A provision in an oil and gas lease prescribing a certain acreage or distance around the buildings on the premises
demised upon which the lessee is to drill no wells for oil or gas, is
almost universally inserted in leases for oil and gas made by land
owners in the thickly populated States, and particularly where
the lands are occupied by the owner or his tenants. The object of
this restriction is the protection to the landowner from fire, noise
of drilling, and other objectionable features incident to the drilling for and production of oil and gas. Both the lessor and
lessee have attempted to nullify the effect of this restrictive provision of the lease; The landowner, conceiving that he has not
parted with the oil and gas underlying these reserved portions,

either has attempted himself to drill the reserved premises, or
by other contracts or leases has endeavored to clothe third parties
with the authority so to drill. In all cases where the oil and gas
rights under the whole tract are granted by the lease, such reservations have been held to be mere restrictions as to where the lessee might drill—that is, he could not drill on the reserved portion.
Neither can the lessor drill thereon, nor can he grant to another
the right and privilege so to do.

Sec. 3.—In *Westmoreland etc. Nat. Gas Co.* v. *Dewitt,* 130 Pa.
335; 18 Atl. 724, analyzed under Chapter 11, syl. 6 is as follows:

"When the premises embraced in an oil and gas lease are
described as 'all that certain tract of land' etc., a clause therein
providing that no wells shall be drilled within a limited area is
neither an exception nor a reservation, but simply a limitation
upon the privilege of drilling granted to the lessee confining his
drilling without the area specified."

J. H. Brown, on December 7, 1885, made an oil and gas lease
to J. M. Guffey & Company, containing the following provision:
"No well to be drilled within 300 yards of the brick or stone building belonging to J. H. Brown." J. M. Guffey & Company afterwards assigned the lease to the Westmoreland Natural Gas Company. This company entered upon the leased premises and completed a gas well on April 23, 1886. A pipeline was laid from the
gas well but the gas was never regularly used, it being shut in
nearly all the time. On May 10, 1887, Brown, the landowner,
claiming the lease forfeited made a second lease of the land for
gas purposes to Ira DeWitt, who entered upon the land and began
the erection of a derrick for the purpose of drilling a gas well
within 300 yards of the stone building belonging to Brown. The
Gas Company filed a bill in equity against DeWitt, Brown and
others, praying for an injunction restraining them from drilling
the well, or in any way committing waste upon the plaintiff's
estate and for general relief. The defendants answered the bill,
therein claiming, among other things, that the plaintiff under the
original lease had no claim or title to, or rights in the land within
a radius of 300 yards from the buildings of the lessor, Brown;
and claiming that the well proposed to be drilled by the defend-

ants was located within the limits of said radius. A decree was entered by the Court of Common Pleas of Westmoreland County, dismissing the plaintiff's bill, from which it appealed to the Supreme Court of Pennsylvania. That court reversed the decree of the court below.

Justice Mitchell, delivering the opinion of the court, in reference to drilling on the excepted area, said:

"The well which respondents proposed to bore is within this prohibited distance; and the respondents claim that Brown, and they as his lessees, have the right to drill wells within that part of the territory. But the clause in question is neither a reservation nor an exception as to the land, but a limitation as to the privilege granted. It does not in any way diminish the area of the land leased; that is still the whole tract; but it restricts the operations of the lessee in putting down the wells to the portions outside of the prohibited distance. For right of way and other purposes of the lease, excepting the location of the wells, the space inside of the stipulated line is as much leased to the lessee as any other part of the tract. The terms of the grant would imply the reservation to the lessor of the possession of the soil for purposes other than those granted to the lessee, and the parties have expressed what otherwise would have been implied by the provision that the lessor is 'to fully use and enjoy the said premises for the purpose of tillage, except such parts as shall be necessary for said operating purposes.' From the nature of gas and gas operations, already discussed, the grant of well rights is necessarily exclusive. It was so held even as to oil wells in *Funk* v. *Halderman*, 53 Pa. 229, 247-248, although in that case the plaintiff had a mere license to enter, etc., and not as complainants here, a lease of the land; and it is exclusive, in the present case, over the whole tract. As already said, the clause relative to the 300 yards distance was a restriction on the privilege granted, not a reservation of any land, or any boring rights to the lessor; and a well upon the prohibited portion was just as damaging to the lessees as upon any other portion of the tract. The drilling of the well threatened by respondents is therefore in violation of the lease and should be enjoined if the lease is still in force."

Sec. 4.—In Duffield v. Hue, 136 Pa. 602; 20 Atl. 526 (October 6, 1890) syls. 1-2-3 are as follows:

"1. Under a lease which grants to the lessee for oil producing purposes a certain described tract of land, with the exclusive right of boring for oil thereon but restricts the operations of the lessee to certain specified sites, the lessee has no right of possession, such as will support ejectment as to any land outside the designated sites: *Duffield* v. *Hue,* 129 Pa. 94.

2. The lessee, however, has the protection of the entire premises, and equity has jurisdiction to restrain the lessor or others acting under him, from drilling wells thereon outside of such designated sites, and thereby lessening the production of wells drilled by lessee, such injury being destructive of his rights and incapable of adequate remedy at law.

3. A court of equity may entertain a bill for an injunction against such an intereference with the lessee's right, notwithstanding that the boundaries of the demised premises are disputed, the defendant, who also is in possession under the lessor, denying that the land upon which he is drilling was included by the lessor in the leasehold granted to the plaintiff.''

On January 20, 1882, Thomas and H. W. Brown leased to one F. M. Pratt for oil producing purposes a part of Tract number 497 in Mead Township, Warren County, Pennsylvania, which tract, however, was designated in the lease, as Tract Number 498. This tract was described as containing an area of —————— according to a division of said tract into numbered sites, made by the parties, each site situated on lots numbered respectively on Map: 151 Mill Street; 183 Center Street; 160 and 134 on Elston Street and also sites for three wells situated as per plat Number 1, south side of Philadelphia & Erie Railroad, to be designated and mutually agreed on by both parties. The lease was for a term of fifteen years from date with the sole and exclusive privilege and right during that period, of boring for oil and minerals on said lot, together with the right to put up and keep tanks thereon, together with such other buildings as might be necessary for the production, storage and transportation of oil and gas. The lease contained the following provision: ''It is understood that this lease includes no land south of Robert Thompson's line, and further, said party of the second part to have the privilege of drilling on the premises hereinafter mentioned, other wells, if said first party determines to have more wells drilled, at the same terms and conditions mentioned in this lease.'' On December 16, 1883, C. C. Duffield by divers conveyances became the owner of the leasehold, and entered into possession thereof and drilled six producing wells, and was engaged in drilling a seventh upon a location mutually agreed upon between Duffield and the agent of the lessors when the suit was brought. A portion of the lands leased by Browns to Pratt were subsequently sold at Sheriff sale and purchased by L. Rosenzweig. These sales were made under writs of execution issued upon judgments against Thomas Brown and others, and the title of the Browns subject to the Elston lease was transferred by such sale to said Rosenzweig, who leased, on January 16, 1886, to Hue and Gerould the lot so sold at Sheriff sale. These second lessees entered upon the tract by them leased from Rosenzweig, and located two wells and erected derricks and other structures thereon, and commenced to drill. By the terms of the lease the rights of Pratt, as lessee, for oil mining purposes, were restricted to these sites. It was provided that he should have the privilege of drilling other wells on the same premises, only in the event that Browns might determine to have more wells drilled, and in that case the operations were to be conducted on hte same terms. On March 6, 1886, C. C. Duffield filed his bill in equity in the Court of Common Pleas of Warren County, Pennsylvania, against the said lessees of Hue and Gerould. In his bill Duffield claimed the exclusive right to drill, notwithstanding the original lease restricted the lessee as to the sites upon which wells could be located. The Court of Common Pleas dismissed the plaintiff's bill, from which decree Duffield appealed. The Supreme Court reversed the court below.

In support of the jurisdiction of a court of equity Justice Clark, who delivered the opinion, cited:

Alison & Evans Appeal, 77 Pa. 221.
Westmoreland etc. Nat. Gas Co. v. *DeWitt,* 130 Pa. 235; 18 A. 724; 5 L. R. A. 731.

Sec. 5.—In Duffield v. Rosenzweig, 144 Pa. 520; 23 Atl. 4 (Oct. 26, 1891) syls. 1-2-3-4 are as follows:

"1. Where a lease for oil purposes granted to the lessee a certain tract of land, with the exclusive right of boring for oil thereon, but restricted the operations of the lessee to certain specified sites, the lessee had no such possession as would support ejectment as to land outside the sites designated; *Duffield* v. *Hue,* 129 Pa. 94.

2. The lessee, however, had the protection of the entire lease-hold; and equity had jurisdiction to restrain the lessor, or others acting under him, from drilling wells thereon outside the designated sites, and thereby lessening the production of the lessee's wells, such injury being without adequate remedy at law; *Duffield* v. *Hue*, 136 Pa. 602.

3. But, when wells have been drilled on the leasehold outside the sites designated, either by the lessor, or by those acting under him, under a subsequent lease, the jurisdiction in equity does not oust the jurisdiction at law, and the first lessee may have a remedy at law against the lessor to recover damages actually sustained by him from such drilling.

4. In such case, the damages are not to be measured by the amount of oil taken out of the defendant's well so drilled, nor by the speculative opinions of operators as to how much of it might have been obtained through the plaintiff's wells, but they may be measured by the difference in value of the plaintiff's leasehold before and after the injury was committed."

Prior to January 23, 1880, C. R. Elston had executed to Thomas and Henry W. Brown a lease for general purposes of the surface of certain land, including the lands upon which the oil wells here-inafter mentioned were drilled.   On   January 23, 1880, W. R. Elston and others, heirs at law to C. R. Elston, executed and de-livered a lease to Brown for the purpose of mining and operating for petroleum, of the same land included in the lease of the surface given by their ancestor, C. R. Elston.   The oil lease was for the term of twenty years.   On January 20, 1882, the Browns made a lease to F. M. Pratt for the "exclusive right and privilege of digging and boring for oil and other minerals" for the term of fifteen years.   The description of the property so leased is as follows:

"All that certain lot or piece of land situated in the Township of Mead, County of Warren, and State of Pennsylvania, bounded and described as follows, viz.   Being a part of tract Number Four Hundred and Ninety-Eight according to George O. Cornelius' survey, and containing an area of ———————— according to a division of said tract into numbered sites, made by said first party, each site situated on lots numbered respectively on map 151 Mill Street; 193 Center Street; 160-164 on Elston Street, and also sites for three wells situated per plot Number 1 south side of Philadelphia & Erie R. R., to be designated and mutually agreed upon by both parties . . . . . . It is understood that this lease includes no land south of Robert Thompson's line, and further said party of the second part to have the privilege of drilling on said premises hereinbefore mentioned, other wells if said parties determine to have more wells drilled, at the same terms and conditions mentioned in this lease.''

Henry W. Brown assigned his interest in the lease of W. R. Elston and others, made to Thomas and himself, to Thomas Brown. Afterwards, on judgments against Thomas Brown, and upon executions thereon, said lease was levied upon and on June 8, 1885, was sold by the Sheriff to Louis Rosenzweig. On January 16, 1886, Rosenzweig executed a lease to F. P. Hue and D. L. Gerould, for oil and mineral purposes, which lease was for about two acres of land leased by the Elstons to Brown, and known in the controversy as the "Mill-yard". Upon this Millyard lot Hue and Gerould, under their lease from Rosenzweig entered and put down the wells, which Duffield attempted to enjoin in his suit against Hue, 136 Pa. 602. Hue and Gerould, between the date of their lease of January 16, 1886, and January, 1890, and by virtue of said lease produced oil amounting to 8253 barrels. Neither F. M. Pratt nor C. C. Duffield, his assignee, were ever in possession of the Millyard property, nor was the Millyard property ever divided by the Cornelius Survey, or mapped or plotted into numbered sites, and there were no sites or locations fixed thereon for the drilling of oil wells, as authorized or designated under the lease from the Browns to Pratt. The lease was made by Rosenzweig after Duffield told him that he, Duffield, would not put down any more wells under the Brown-Pratt lease, on the terms thereof. Rosenzweig afterwards told the plaintiff, Duffield, that he might put down the seventh well, Duffield having drilled the six designated sites prior to the drilling of the well consented to by Rosenzweig. Rosenzweig's possession of the Millyard property was by virtue of the Sheriff's sale of the interests of Thomas and Henry W. Brown, on June 8, 1885. On November 21, 1889, Charles C. Duffield instituted an action of trespass against Louis Rosenzweig in the Court of Common Pleas of Warren County, stating damages to the extent of $8,000, claiming that to be the value of the 8253 barrels of oil produced by Rosenzweig's lessees, from the wells on the Millyard. The Court of Common Pleas, upon the facts held that the plaintiff was not entitled to recover. From this decision Duffield appealed to the Supreme Court, and that court reversed the court below, and remanded the cause for further proceedings.

Sec. 6.—In Duffield v. Rosenzweig, 150 Pa. 543; 24 Atl. 705 (July 13, 1892) the syllabus is as follows:

"Where a lease of land for oil mining purposes, with the exclusive right of boring for oil thereon, restricts the operations to certain sites and the lessor or his subsequent grantee drills wells on the leasehold outside of the sites designated, the lessees measure of damages is the difference in value of the leasehold before and after the injury was committed; *Duffield* v. *Rosenzweig*, 144 Pa. 520.

The damages cannot be estimated by the amount of oil which the new wells might drain from the old wells, the proof of damages upon this basis being impracticable in the nature of the case."

This is an appeal taken to the Supreme Court of Pennsylvania from a judgment rendered by the Court of Common Pleas of Warren County after the case has been remanded by the Supreme Court, 144 Pa. 520.

The case was tried in the Court of Common Pleas, and judgment rendered in favor of the plaintiff for $1140.00. The facts upon which the Court of Common Pleas rendered its opinion are:

"1. In the Spring of 1886, the value of the plaintiff's leasehold, freed from the obstructions put upon it by the defendant's lessees for the balance of the term, with the situation, surroundings, production, royalty, and general condition of the oil market and business, was $4500.00.

2. The value of the same for the same term as aforesaid by the obstructions put upon it by the defendant's lessees, was $3375.00.

3. Therefore, the damages to the plaintiff's leasehold, in the defendant's lessees, amounted to $1125.00."

Duffield appealed from this judgement, claiming the damages were insufficient. The Supreme Court affirmed the judgment.

Sec. 7.—In *Duffield* v. *Hue*, 129 Pa. 94; 18 Atl. 566, (Nov. 4, 1889) syl. 1 is as follows:

"1. A grant of 'the exclusive right and privilege of digging and boring for oil and other minerals' for the term of fifteen years from the date thereof, must be treated as a lease for the production of oil and not as a sale of the oil or of an interest in the land."

On July 18, 1888, C. C. Duffield brought ejectment against F. B. Hue and D. L. Gerould for a lot of ground in Clarendon Borough, containing about two acres, with three oil wells thereon, part of tract 497, Mead Township, formerly occupied by a sawmill and used as a sawmill yard, and part of leasehold granted to F. M. Pratt by Thomas and H. W. Brown, on January 20, 1882. Upon the findings of fact as hereinafter stated the court in lieu of a jury rendered judgment for defendant. Plaintiff took a writ of error to the Supreme Court, where the judgment was affirmed. Before January 23, 1880, C. R. Elston had given to Browns a lease for general purposes of the surface of certain land, including that in dispute. On January 23, 1880, William R. Elston and others, heirs at law of C. R. Elston, executed to Browns a lease for oil and gas purposes. The surface of the land was leased by the ancestor of Elstons to the Browns. The oil and gas lease was for the term of twenty years, with the right of renewal thereafter, so long as oil should continue to be found in paying quantities. The outline of the two leases—one of the surface, and the other for mining purposes—were represented upon a map made by E. Gibbs, the boundaries being a diagonal line at the left hand of the map, the creek at the bottom, main street at the top, and the line of R. Thompson and Lapham at the right hand. Some time before January 20, 1882, the Browns procured a survey to be made, dividing a portion of the territory into village lots. The lots thus surveyed were numbered and a map of the same made, called the Cornelius survey. On January 20, 1882, the Browns made a lease to F. M. Pratt of the "exclusive right and privilege of digging and boring for oil and other minerals," on the lands mentioned therein for the term of fifteen years. The number of the tract in the lease was 498, but should have been 497. The rights of F. M. Pratt under this lease by sundry conveyances and assignments, became vested in the plaintiff, C. C. Duffield on December 14, 1883. At the time of the execution of the lease from the Browns to Pratt, the Browns had a sawmill, connected with which was a yard for the storage of logs and lumber, the mill and yard occupying about two acres of land, the same being bound on one side by the railroad, on one side by the plank road and Brown's Avenue, and on one side by Exchange Street. The ejectment suit was brought for the land formerly occupied by the sawmill and sawmill yard. The plaintiff, Duffield, claimed that the land described in his writ was included in the lease made by the Browns to Pratt, and that he was entitled to the possession for the purpose of operating and procuring petroleum and other minerals under the term of the Pratt lease. The defendants, F. P. Hue and D. L. Gerould asserted their right of possession under the following facts: Henry W. Brown assigned his interest in the lease of William R. Elston and others, to Thomas and himself, to Thomas Brown. Afterwards, on judgments against Thomas Brown, executions were issued. On these executions the lease was levied upon and on June 8, 1885, was sold at Sheriff sale, and L. Rosenzweig became the purchaser. On January 16, 1886, L. Rosenzweig executed a lease for oil and gas purposes to the defendants Hue and Gerould, which lease was for the two acres, the land mentioned in the plaintiff's writ, and under which lease the defendants Hue and Gerould were in possession. The defendants further claimed that if the land in dispute included the lease from the Browns to Pratt, Pratt and the plaintiff Duffield had forfeited all their rights in the lease. The lease under which the plaintiff claimed included the tract of two acres, the Millyard, but this lease specifically provided for drilling wells at certain designated points, the millyard not being one of the designated points. The court held that the lease included the exclusive right to produce oil from all the lands, but, that the Millyard was not one of the designated points where the lessee was authorized and directed to drill. Justice Clark, in the opinion, at pages 108-9 said:

"Whatever oil might be produced from the premises leased at these points, the lessees had a right to produce; but they had no right of possession, for any purpose, at any other place, within the bounds of the territory described. If the lessors, or others acting under them, by boring other wells, lessened this production, or otherwise disturbed or interfered with the rights of the lessees, they may have had their remedy, but not in this form; for by no

construction of the contract in question can Pratt be supposed to
have had any right of possession, for any purpose, in any part of
the premises in dispute; and Duffield in his right, has therefore
no standing to recover in ejectment."

Sec. 8.—In *Lynch* v. *Burford,* 201 Pa. 52; 50 Atl. 228 (Nov. 8,
1901) the syllabus is as follows:

"A lessor in an oil and gas lease of five acres carved out of
a large farm 'subject to a reservation of land surrounding farm
buildings and marked by stakes, and as a protection against fire,'
has no right to drill a well on the reservation."

On January 25, 1899, J. R. Burford agreed to lease to George
W. Lynch a tract of land in Armstrong County, Pennsylvania, for
oil and gas purposes, for a period of fifteen years from date, or as
long as oil should be obtained in paying quantities, the tract containing five acres, more or less, subject to a reservation of lands
surrounding the farm buildings and marked by stakes, as a protection against fire; the lessee to drill one well on the lease within
ninety days from the date of the lease, and if oil should be obtained
in paying quantities the lessee to pay one-eighth royalty of all the
oil or gas obtained; the lessor reserving all rights and privileges
to the property, except what were necessary to drill, test, and save
oil or gas from the lease. On April 20, 1899, Lynch commenced
to drill a well, known as "Lynch Well No. 1," on the five acre
tract, and completed it on May 19, 1899, at a cost of $2,000. The
well was pumped and was a paying producing well at the time this
suit was brought. This well was about 800 feet from the reservation in the lease. In the Fall of 1900, Lynch, with the knowledge and consent of Burford, located another well known as
"Lynch No. 2" on the five acre tract. Prior to its location Burford had staked off the reservation mentioned in the lease, making
a circle from 195 to 200 feet around his farm buildings. This well
Number 2 was located one foot one inch without the reservation,
and within 195 feet and 4 inches of the Burford barn, and about
800 feet from the Lynch well Number 1. Lynch finished the rig to
put down this well early in the Fall of 1900, laid his water line, but
never commenced to drill, alleging as an excuse, that he had so
much trouble with Number 1 that he had not time to do so. On

March 27, 1901, Burford prepared two notices which he had served upon Lynch, notifying him to remove his tools and rig, and not to put down any more wells on the lease. In the early part of June, 1901, J. R. Burford erected a derrick on the five acre tract, about twenty-three feet within the reservation staked off by him under the provisions of the lease, and twenty-four feet nearer his buildings than the Lynch Well Number 2, said well being located 195 feet 4 inches from Burford's barn. The Burford well was about 824 feet from the Lynch Well Number 1, which was producing a small amount of oil. About June 13, 1901, Lynch learned that Burford was about to drill his well within the reservation as described. Burford had graded the ground and put in part of the mud-sills. On June 17, 1901, Lynch served a notice on Burford not to drill this well; otherwise he would be met by an injunction. Notwithstanding this notice Burford proceeded to put down the well to a depth of from 1400 to 1600 feet and to within about 100 feet of the oil producing rock. On July 29, 1901 Lynch filed a bill in equity in the Court of Common Pleas of Armstrong County, and obtained a preliminary injunction against Burford which preliminary injunction, on September 23, 1901, was by the court made perpetual. From this decree Burford appealed, and the Supreme Court of Pennsylvania affirmed the Court below.

Sec. 9.—In *Consumers Gas Trust Co.* v. *American Plate Glass Co.*, 162 Ind. 392; 68 N. E. 1020, (Nov. 24, 1903) the syllabus is as follows:

"1. One accepting a lease granting the exclusive right to sink gas wells on certain property is charged with notice of the rights of a railroad occupying the property as a right of way, and in case of conflict, the rights of the railroad are paramount to those of the lessee.

2. A railroad which enters on property without color of title, and occupies it as a right of way, acquires merely an easement in the property for purposes of a right of way.

3. A lessee under a lease giving it the exclusive right to draw gas from the demised tract cannot enjoin a railroad having merely an easement over the land, and no right to draw gas, from sinking a well on its right of way, unless the lessee has a proprietary right in the land, over which the right of way extends.

4. A lessee, under a lease giving it the exclusive right to

draw gas from the demised tract, has a proprietary interest in
the tract, including a part thereof, over which a railroad had
acquired an easement for its right of way; and though it cannot
enter on the railroad's land so as to sink gas wells thereon, so
long as the railroad is in possession, yet it may enjoin the sinking
of a gas well on such land, thereby diminishing the flow of gas
from its own wells.''

On October 26, 1896, Consumers Gas Trust Company obtained a grant for an indefinite time for the exclusive right to
drill gas wells and lay pipe lines for the transportation of gas on
a 400-acre tract of land in Section 6, Township 21, Range 8 in Madison County, Indiana. At the date of this grant the Cleveland,
Cincinnati, Chicago & St. Louis Railway Company was operating
a line of railroad built by the Cincinnati, Wabash and Michigan
Railway Company, about 1871, on a right of way through said
tract of land which was fenced by said company about the year
1877, which fences were afterwards maintained. The entry of the
railroad company was made without color of title, and over the
protest of the holders of the record title. The landowners had not
sought to have their damages assessed. The Railroad Company
occupied the land with a single track railroad, and a line of telegraph poles since its entry. Its possession had been continued
without interruption, and its possession seemed to have been hostile. The Cleveland, Cincinnati, Chicago & St. Louis Railway
Comapny had been using the railroad for a number of years under
an operating agreement with the Cincinnati, Wabash & Michigan
Railway Company. At the date of the institution of the suit the
American Plate Glass Company was engaged in drilling a gas
well on, and laying a line of gas main along the right of way
through said section under and by virtue of a lease made by said
operating company. It appeared from the evidence in the case
that such was the character of the particular gas field that the
sinking of a well into the gas reservoir within two miles of a producing well would appreciably reduce the flow of such well, and
that the injury to it would be still greater if the new well were in
close proximity. The lease of the Gas Company was sufficiently
broad to vest in it the exclusive right to sink gas wells in the
said 400-acre tract; but the Cincinnati, Wabash & Michigan Railway company was in possession of and using the right of way for

railroad purposes at the time of the execution of the lease, and it was evident therefrom that the gas company was charged with notice of whatever rights the railway company had. The Consumers Gas Trust Company instituted its action in the Superior Court of Madison County, against the American Plate Glass Company, and the Cleveland, Cincinnati, Chicago & St. Louis Railway Company, for an injunction to restrain the defendants from drilling a natural gas well on, and laying a gas main along, that part of the railroad right of way which extended through said section 6, Township 21, Range 8. The cause was put at issue, and after a trial the court rendered a finding and decree in favor of said gas company, restraining the defendants from drilling such well; but the court denied the relief prayed for relative to laying the gas main. Each of the parties to the action filed a motion for a new trial, and assigned error on appeal. Both parties appealed. The Supreme Court of Indiana affirmed the finding and decree of the court below, and cited the following cases:

Indianapolis etc. Co. v. *Kibbey*, 135 Ind. 357; 25 N. E. 392.
Westmoreland etc. Co. v. *DeWitt*, 130 Pa. 235; 18 Atl. 724.
Richmond etc. Co. v. *Enterprise etc. Co.*, 31 Ind. App. 222.
    66 N. E. 782.

Whitlock v. *Consumers etc. Co.*, 127 Ind. 62; 26 N. E. 570.

Sec. 10.—In *Brown v. Spilman*, 155 U. S. 665; (Jan. 7, 1895) the syllabus is as follows:

"A grant in a lease of forty acres of land, described by metes and bounds, for the sole and only purpose of boring, mining, and excavating for petroleum or carbon oil and gas, and piping of oil and gas over all the tract, excepting reserved therefrom ten acres, also described by metes and bounds, upon which no well shall be drilled without the consent of the lessor, is a grant of all the gas and oil under the entire tract, conditioned that the lessee shall not drill wells on the ten-acre plat without the consent of the lessor."

John F. Taylor, on July 29, 1889, leased a tract of forty acres of land in Pleasants County, West Virginia, to Joseph S. Brown

for oil and gas purposes, which lease contained the following provision:

"Excepting reserved therefrom ten acres, beginning at the
railroad and running thence to the County road, thence south
with said County road to A. Smith's line, thence with said Smith's
line to a line to be drawn from the railroad to meet it, upon which
no wells shall be drilled without the consent of the party of the
first part."

Brown took possession under this lease and proceeded to exer-
cise his rights by drilling oil wells thereon. On June 30, 1890,
John F. Taylor sold and conveyed said tract of land to B. D.
Spilman and W. N. Chancellor, subject to the lease to Brown,
which lease in this deed is described as a lease of thirty acres of
land for oil and gas purposes.   On July 9, 1890, Spilman and
Chancellor filed in the Circuit Court of the United States for the
District of West Virginia, a bill in equity against Joseph S.
Brown wherein they set up their ownership of said tract of land,
containing forty acres, conveyed to them by Taylor, and complained that Brown, without right, was asserting a claim and title
to the oil and gas in a certain acreage of the land, and was threatening to interfere with the right and possession of the plaintiffs
in drilling oil wells and operating on the said ten acres; and
charged that the claim of Brown constituted a cloud on their title
to the ten acres, and prayed for an injunction and equitable relief.
Brown, on July 18, 1890, filed an answer to the bill, asserting his
right to possession of the entire tract of forty acres for oil and
gas purposes, and denying that the plaintiffs had, under their
deed from Taylor, any right to drill for oil on the ten acres or to
exclude him therefrom. On the same day Brown filed a cross-bill
against Spilman and Chancellor, in which he asked that they be
enjoined from boring or mining for oil and gas on said ten acres,
and from interfering with his right in the same. To this cross-
bill Spilman and Chancellor filed a general demurrer. On February 10, 1891, on final hearing the Circuit Court entered a final
decree, and filed an opinion, reported in 45 Federal Reporter, 291,
sustaining the original bill, and enjoining Brown and all persons
acting under him, from entering upon said ten acres of land, and
from instituting any action or suit against the plaintiffs in re-

spect to said ten acres, and from interfering with, or interrupting the plaintiffs in the use of the ten acres for any purpose. By the decree the demurrer to the cross bill was sustained, and the cross bill dismissed. From this decree Brown appealed to the Supreme Court of the United States, and that Court reversed the Circuit Court wherein the decree sustained the original bill, and also reversed the decree sustaining the demurrer and dismissing the cross-bill.

Sec. 11.—In *Allison and Evans Appeal*, 77 Pa. 221, (Oct. 11, 1875) the syllabus is as follows:

"1. Oil land described by metes and bounds with a 'Protection' of eight rods on the north side and ten rods on the east side, was leased to Evans. *Held*, that the 'protection' extended to the point where the lines on the respective sides of the land would intersect.

2. Oil land on the north-east corner of Evans' lease, was leased to Treat, who sunk a well within the 'protection', injuring Evans' wells on his land. *Held*, that Treat could be restrained from operating on the 'protection' and that in the same proceedings damages could be assessed against him for the injury.

3. As a general principle, when a court of equity has obtained jurisdiction for one purpose it may retain it generally for relief, as well in cases of continuing trespass and waste as in cases of fraud, accident, mistakes and account.

4. To prevent multiplicity of suits, a court of equity will decree an accounting of the damages or waste at the same time with an injunction, and make a decree to settle the entire controversy."

On July 1, 1872, J. W. Allison and A. Evans filed a bill in equity in the Court of Common Pleas of Clarion County against R. W. Porterfield and M. C. Treat. The bill alleged that Joseph Foust, on July 15, 1871, leased for twenty years to Phillip Foust and William Spencer, by metes and bounds, a lot of ground containing three acres and one hundred and twenty-three perches of land, for the sole and only purpose of mining and excavating for petroleum, coal, rock or carbon oil; that the lease provided for a "protection of 10 rods on the east side" of the lot, and "8 rods on the north side"; lessees to deliver to the lessor one-eighth of the petroleum raised on the premises; the lessor to use the premises for tillage, except such parts as should be necessary for mining purposes and right of way; that on March 29, 1872, the lessees transferred their interest in the lease to A. Evans, one of the plaintiffs, and on July 19, 1872, Evans transferred seven-eighths to J. W. Allison, the other plaintiff; that the defendants had entered on "the protection" and after notice from the plaintiffs to desist, had erected machinery on "the protection" and "were boring and drilling thereon for carbon and petroleum, in violation of said notice and rights of the plaintiffs. The bill prayed for an injunction and for an account of all waste, and in the event that oil should be obtained prior to the judicial determination of the case, that the defendants account for all oils so obtained from the premises. The defendants answered alleging that they entered upon the land mentioned in bill under a lease from Joseph Foust, the plaintiff's lessor, and denying that they were in "the protection" set out in the bill; they averred that the land leased by them from Joseph Foust lay north-east of the north-east corner of the plaintiff's leasehold; that their lease from Joseph Foust was bounded by lines which was merely an extension of plaintiff's north and east lines beyond their north-east corner; further averring that they believed that the land leased to them was not covered by "the protection" mentioned in the bill, and that they were advised as a matter of law that "the protection" did not extend to any land included in their lease. The Court of Common Pleas sustained the right of the plaintiffs to an injunction restraining the defendants from further operating on the premises in dispute, and decreed an injunction accordingly, and held, that as to the question of damages, the court had not jurisdiction by bill to award damages, and as to that, dismissed the bill without prejudice. Both parties appealed to the Supreme Court, and assigned for error the portions of the decree against them, respectively. The Supreme Court dismissed the defendant's appeal, and affirmed the decree as to the injunction, and reversed so much of the decree as denied to the plaintiff the right to recover damages by bill in equity, and decreed to the plaintiffs $9,388.89, the amount of damages found by the Master to whom the cause had been referred.

LESSOR'S REMEDY.

Sec. 12.—The reservation around the dwelling house, or other buildings, upon which no wells are to be drilled, is for the protection of lessor against fire, the odors of the oil or gas, the noise and confusion necessarily arising from the drilling of wells and their operation. While the oil and gas underlying the reserved portions are not reserved, yet the right of the lessee to drill for these minerals is restricted to that portion of the premises outside of the reservation. The right of the lessee to possession of the leased premises is for the purpose of exploration and development of oil and gas, and the production and marketing of these minerals, exclusively. By the reservation, the landowner has excepted the reserved portions of the surface from this right of possession for exploration and production. The lessee has no right whatever to enter upon the reservation for the purpose of drilling. The lessor has the right to take any proceeding at law or in equity against a lessee for invading for the purpose of drilling the surface excepted that he would have a right to take against any third person or other trespasser.

LESSEE'S REMEDY.

Sec. 13.—The reservation in the ordinary oil and gas lease, either of an acreage described by metes and bounds, or of an area' or reservation around the buildings on the premises demised, upon which no well shall be drilled by lessee, is not a reservation of the oil and gas but is a restriction as to where lessee is authorized to drill. That is, he shall not drill within the reserved surface. Where the landowner, either himself or through others, attempts to drill wells for oil and gas within the reservation, the remedy of the lessee is not by ejectment or possessory action, as lessee has no right to the possession of the surface so reserved.

Duffield v. *Hue,* 129 Pa. 94; 18 Atl. 566.

Sec. 14.—The remedy of the lessee, where his lease contains a reservation of a part of the surface, either of an acreage or of so much surface around the buildings, upon which no wells shall be drilled, where lessor either himself undertakes to drill upon the reserved portions of the premises, or where he leases to another, and such other lessee or a purchaser of the premises from the lessor, undertakes to drill upon the reservation, is by bill in equity for injunction.

> *Westmoreland etc. Nat. Gas Co.* v. *DeWitt,* 130 Pa. 235; 18 Atl. 724.
> *Consumers Gas Trust Co.* v. *American Plate Glass Co.,* 162 Ind. 392; 68 N. E. 1020.
> *Brown* v. *Spilman,* 155 U. S., 665.
> *Duffield* v. *Hue,* 136 Pa. 602; 20 Atl. 526.
> *Lynch* v. *Burford,* 201 Pa. 52; 50 Atl. 228.

Sec. 15.—When wells have been drilled on the leasehold within the reservation, either by the lessor or by those acting under him under a subsequent lease, the jurisdiction in equity does not oust the jurisdiction at law; and the first lessee may recover at law damages against the lessor or those acting under him, either as subsequent lessees or as purchasers, for the injuries actually sustained by the first lessee from such drilling. In such case the damages are not to be measured by the amount of oil taken out of the defendant's wells so drilled, nor by the speculative opinions of operators as to how much of it might have been obtained through the plaintiff's wells, but such damages may be measured by the difference in the value of the plaintiff's leasehold before and after the injury was committed.

> *Duffield* v. *Rosenzweig,* 144 Pa. 520; 23 Atl. 4
> *Duffield* v. *Rosenzweig,* 150 Pa. 543; 24 Atl. 705

Sec. 16.—Where a lessor or those acting under him, under a second lease, or where a purchaser from such lessor, enters upon the reserved portions of the leasehold and drills for, and discovers, oil or gas in paying quantities, the original lessee may in an equity proceeding taken for that purpose enjoin such lessor or other persons acting through or under him, and obtain a decree for the damages sustained by him by reason of the oil or gas being taken from the land.

> *Allison and Evans Appeal,* 77 Pa. 221.

CHAPTER 11.

CONSIDERATION FOR THE GRANT OF MINERALS—GAS.

Sec. 1.—The consideration to the landowner for gas, usually agreed upon in the ordinary oil and gas lease, is a specific sum per annum to be paid by the lessee for each gas well the product of which is utilized off the premises.

Gadberry v. *Ohio etc. Nat. Gas. Co.*, 162 Ind. 9; 57 N. E. 259.
Ohio Oil Co. v. *Lane*, 59 Ohio State, 307; 52 N. E. 791.
McKnight v. *Manufacturers Nat. Gas. Co.*, 146 Pa. 185; 23 Atl. 164.
Double v. *Heat & Light Co.*, 172 Pa. 388; 33 Atl. 694.
Ind. Nat. Gas. & O. Co. v. *Lear*, 34 Ind. App. 61; 72 N. E. 283.
Consumers Gas Trust Co. v. *Littler*, 162 Ind. 320; 70 N. E. 363.
Consumers Gas Trust Co. v. *Chrystal Window Glass Co.*, 163 Ind. 190; 70 N. E. 366.
Consumers Gas Trust Co. v. *Worth*, 163 Ind. 141; 71 N. E. 489.
Consumers Gas Trust Co. v. *Ink*, 163 Ind. 174; 71 N. E. 477.
Eastern Oil Co. v. *Coulehan*, 65 W. Va. 531; 64 S. E. 836.
McGraw Oil & Gas Co. v. *Kennedy*, 65 W. Va. 595; 64 S. E. 1027.
South Penn Oil Co. v. *Edgell*, 48 W. Va. 348; 37 S. E. 596.
Summerville v. *Apollo Gas Co.*, 207 Pa. 334; 56 Atl. 876.
Mathes v. *Shaw Oil Co.*, — (Kan.) —; 101 Pac. 997.
Bellevue Oil & Gas Co. v. *Pennell*, 76 Kan. 785; 92 Pac. 1101.
Westmoreland Nat. Gas Co. v. *DeWitt*, 130 Pa. 235; 18 Atl. 724.
Davis v. *Chautauqua Oil & Gas Co.* — (Kan.) —; 96 Pac. 47.
Iams v. *Gas Co.*, 194 Pa. 72; 45 Atl. 54.
Poe v. *Ulrey*, 233 Ill. 56; 84 N. E. 46.
Indianapolis Nat. Gas Co. v. *Wilhelm*, (Ind. App.) 86 N. E. 86.
Roberts v. *Fort Wayne Gas Co.*, 40 Ind. App. 528; 82 N. E. 558.

Sec. 2.—The courts have construed somewhat differently the obligations imposed upon a lessee where gas only is found in paying quantities, from the obligations imposed upon a lessee where oil only is found in paying quantities. Where oil is found in paying quantities the lessor receives his compensation in kind, while in the gas lease the lessor receives his compensation in money, and has no interest in the gas when produced.   The courts have not held the lessee in a gas lease to the same strict duties as to developing the territory and protecting the lines as they have in cases where oil in paying quantities is discovered. Under the ordinary oil and gas lease the lessee does not obligate himself to market the gas if found in paying quantities; consequently the lessee may hold his lease, under ordinary circumstances, during the term by the payment of the stipulated rental for delay, notwithstanding he may have discovered gas in paying quantities. Some courts, however, have held, that a failure on the part of the lessee to protect the lines of his lease by drilling additional wells, where gas wells are being operated on adjoining territory in such close proximity to the leased premises as to drain the gas therefrom, constitutes abandonment, which anthorizes the cancellation of the lease by a court of equity. Courts have also held, that where the gas can be marketed so as to produce to the lessor a revenue from the gas wells, it is the duty of the lessee to market the gas; and that he is liable for the gas rental to lessor if he fails to do so. The rule to be deduced from the decisions is, that a lessee may pay the stipulated commutation money as rental, agreed to be paid for delay, and hold the lease during the term, even after he has discovered gas in paying quantities. When however the gas can be marketed off the premises at a profit Lessee must market the gas, or he must pay lessor the amount he would be entitled to receive as rental or royalty for the gas rights. A lessee cannot, after discovering gas in paying quantities, shut the gas in, cease to pay any rental to the landowner, and hold the lease. In such case the landowner would be in no better condition than where an unsuccessful search had been made, and explorations abandoned.

Sec. 3.—In *Gadberry* v. *Ohio etc. Gas Co.*, 162 Ind. 9; 67 N. E. 259 (May 14, 1903) syls. 1-2 are as follows:

"1. The owner of land in consideration of $1.00 granted all the oil and gas in it, with the right to operate it, reserving a certain part of all oil produced; the grantee, in case gas only was found, agreeing to pay $100 a year for the product of each well while it was being used off the premises, and the grantor to have gas free for domestic purposes; the lease to become void if no well was completed in 40 days, unless the grantee thereafter pay $1.00 a day till its completion. *Held*, that there was an implied condition subsequent to develop, so that the lease could be forfeited; the grantee, after constructing a well and finding gas in paying quantities, closing it and failing to work it.

2.   Failure for two years of the grantee of the oil and gas in land to develop it, after constructing a well, finding gas, and then closing it, prima facie authorizes the grantor who was to be paid $100.00 a year for each well while gas was being used off the premises, without demand, to treat the grant as abandoned."

R. R. Gadberry and J. A. Gadberry, on December 1, 1897, executed an oil and gas lease to J. S. Andrews, whereby they granted to the lessee all the oil and gas in and under a tract of 80 acres of land in Blackford County, Indiana, upon the following conditions (as to gas) : If gas only should be found lessee to pay $100 each year for the product of each well while the same should be used off the premises, the lessor to have gas free of cost for domestic purposes. The lease further provided that in case no well should be completed within 40 days from date, then the same should become null and void, unless the lessee should pay to the lessor One Dollar per day thereafter such completion should be delayed. On January 6, 1900, Andrews assigned the lease to the Gas Company. The lessee Andrews completed a well on the premises on February 19, 1898, and paid lessors One Dollar per day during the time that the completion of the well was delayed, after forty days from the date of the execution of the lease, down to February 19, 1898. Gas was found in the well in large and paying quantities. Andrews, immediately upon the completion of the well, closed and anchored the same so as to prevent any gas from escaping therefrom, and neither Andrews nor the Gas Company afterwards produced any gas or oil from said premises, and did not use or transport any gas whatever from the premises. Neither Andrews nor the Gas Company paid the lessors anything for the product of the well, or for the privilege of holding the premises after the completion of the well, but still claimed the right to hold the premises without further developing the same, without producing any oil or gas therefrom, and without paying the plaintiff any consideration whatever for the privilege of so doing, after the completion of the well. Neither Andrews nor the Gas Company furnished the plaintiffs or either of them, any gas for domestic use. On December 28, 1899, the lessors declared the lease forfeited and all rights thereunder terminated under the claim of their right so to do, by failure to develop the premises and produce oil or gas therefrom. The plaintiffs then took possession of the well and connected the same with their dwelling house. After the declaration of forfeiture the lessors instituted a suit in the Circuit Court of Blackford County against the said J. S. Andrews and the Gas Company to quiet their title to the real estate, and to remove the cloud therefrom occasioned by the execution and recordation of the lease of December 1, 1897. The Circuit Court rendered judgment in favor of the de: fendant Gas Company, from which judgment the plaintiffs appealed to the Appellate Court of Indiana, and that court on November 20, 1902, affirmed the judgment of the Circuit Court reported in 65 N. E. 289, from which court the case was transmitted to the Supreme Court of Indiana, which court reversed the decisions of the courts below.

The Supreme Court of Indiana held, that the substantial consideration which moved the grantors to execute the lease was the profits or royalties if oil or gas should be discovered, and that even if the lessee had paid the stated consideration of One Dollar —a technically valuable consideration—yet the instrument must be construed with the fact in view that a more substantial reason prompted the making of the grant, that is, the royalties and profits to be obtained of oil or gas should be discovered. In support of this conclusion the court cited:

Huggins v. *Daley,* 99 Fed. 606; 40 C. C. A. 12; 48 L. R. A. 320.
Federal Oil Co. v. *Western Oil Co.,* 112 Fed. 373.

The court further held, that while the courts have manifested a disposition to protect the lessee after he has discovered oil or gas, by treating his interests as no longer postponed to the happening of a condition precedent, yet that it is thoroughly settled that a lessee cannot omit to develop the property, and hold the grant for speculative purposes purely, citing:

Parish Fork Oil Co. v. *Bridgewater Gas Co.,* 51 W. Va. 583; 42
    S. E. 655.
Bluestone Coal Co. v. *Bell,* 38 W. Va. 297; 18 S. E. 493.
Guffey v. *Hukill,* 34 W. Va. 49; 11 S. E. 754; 8 L. R. A. 759;
    26 Am. St. Rep. 901.
Ray v. *Nat. Gas Co.,* 138 Pa. 576; 20 Atl. 1065; 12 L. R. A.
    290; 21 Am. St. Rep. 922.
Venture Oil Co. v. *Fretts,* 152 Pa. 451; 25 Atl. 732.
Kleppner v. *Lemon,* 176 Pa. 502; 35 Atl. 109.

Sec. 4.—In *Ohio Oil Co.*, v. *Lane*, 59 Ohio St. 307; 52 N. E.
791 (Dec. 13, 1898) the syllabus is as follows:

"A contract between the owner of lands and a company operating in oil and gas, whereby such minerals are granted in place
to operating company upon the stipulation that, if gas only is
found, it will pay a fixed sum per year for each well 'while the
same is being used off the premises', and containing no stipulation
inconsistent therewith, should not be so construed as to require
it to pay such sum for a gas well whose product is not used, even
though the jury should be of the opinion that it might have been
so used off the premises without financial loss to the company."

Thomas A. Lane, on May 5, 1890, in consideration of the sum
of $420, granted to the Ohio Oil Company, its successors and
assigns, all the oil and gas in and under a tract of 120 acres of
land in Mercer County, Ohio, together with the right to enter
thereon at all times for the purpose of drilling and operating for
oil, gas or water, to erect and maintain all buildings and structures,
and lay all pipes necessary for the production and transportation of oil, gas or water, from said premises, excepting and reserving the one-sixth of all oil produced and saved from the
premises; if gas only should be found the lessee agreed to pay
$300 each year, in advance, for the product of each well while the
same should be used off the premises; the grantor to have gas
free of cost to heat six stoves in his dwelling house during the
same time. ' Under this agreement the Oil Company drilled one
well on the land in which gas was found in paying quantities.
This well was completed about February 15, 1891. No payments
were made for gas. The lessor claimed that on May 6, 1891, the
lessee was indebted to him in the sum of $300 for gas rental for
the recovery of which amount the lessor instituted suit against
the Oil Company and recovered judgment in the Court of Common Pleas, which judgment was affirmed by the Circuit Court,
and the Oil Company appealed to the Supreme Court. That court
reversed the judgment of the courts below.

The landowner had received a consideration for the oil and
gas in place. The lease provided that if gas only were found in
paying quantities an annual rental of $300.00 should be paid for
each well, the gas from which should be used by the lessee off the
premises. The court construed the contract as containing no
covenants, express or implied, requiring the lessee to market or
use the gas off the premises. The action was one for rent only,

and the question of whether or not, by failing to utilize the gas off the premises, a forfeiture had been incurred was not before the court for consideration.

Sec. 5.—In *McKnight* v. *Manufacturers Nat. Gas Co.*, 146 Pa. 185; 23 Atl. 164, (Jan. 4, 1892) syls. 2-3-5 are as follows:

"2. The duty imposed upon the lessee in a leasehold operated for gas cannot be measured by the same rule applied in the same manner as in the case of a leasehold operated for oil; the peculiar characteristics of the business of producing and transporting natural gas being such as to distinguish it for some purposes from operations for oil.

3. In an action against a lessee who had drilled one paying gas well upon the premises, for not putting down other wells, to protect the territory against the effect of operations on adjoining lands, it was error to charge that a failure to drill such wells was a breach of an implied covenant imposing a liability in damages, in the absence of a reasonable excuse therefor.

5. Whether, when one paying well has been put down, under a lease containing no express covenant to sink other wells, and the well so drilled has been accidentally destroyed while producing gas in paying quantities, the lessee will be obliged to drill another well in its place, or abandon the premises, not decided."

H. O. McKnight, on October 29, 1884, in consideration of the stipulations, rents and covenants contained in the lease, granted, demised and let unto the Cannonsburg Iron Company for the sole and only purpose of mining and excavating for petroleum, carbon oil or gas, and for the further consideration of the sum of One Dollar, a tract of 250 acres of land, situated in Washington County, Pennsylvania, for the term of twenty years; the lessee to deliver to the lessor the one-eighth part of the petroleum or carbon oil pumped from the premises, and to commence operations within eighteen months from the date of the lease. The lessor reserved the right to locate wells: A failure on the part of the lessee to comply with either one or the other of the conditions to work an absolute forfeiture of the lease. If the lessee should fail to get oil in paying quantities in any well drilled, but a sufficient flow of gas should be found to justify the lessee in utilizing it at some other point, not on the premises, then the lessee to pay to the lessor a money royalty of one-eighth of the net proceeds, in cash, for each and every well the gas from which should be so utilized, as long as such wells should be so utilized. The money royalty to be paid semi-annually in installments at the end of each half year. The lease further provided that if gas should be found in considerable quantities in any well, the lessee should pay the lessor the one-eighth of the amount obtained for said well, in the event of a sale thereof. On December 5, 1885, the oil company became the owner of the lease by assignment. In September, 1886, the oil company completed a producing gas well upon the location made by the lessor, and thereafter the gas from this well was utilized until some time in the Spring of 1889. By an agreement between the lessor and the gas company, dated October 13, 1886, the provisions of the lease were so far modified as to provide that "the Gas Company should pay the lessor $1,000 annually, for "each and every gas well having a pressure of 17 pounds over an open 5⅝ inch casing" and utilized at any point not on the leased premises; and that if the pressure of any well or wells should be decreased materially, the amount of annual rental should be reduced in the same proportion. By another agreement dated August 1, 1888, the lessor agreed to accept $750.00 in satisfaction of the rent on the well drilled, from October 19, 1887, to October 19, 1888, with the following stipulation: "And it is further agreed that, since said well has been drilled deeper and the gas increased so that the same can be utilized, and the pressure sufficient to use in the City of Pittsburg, the annual royalty to be paid to H. O. McKnight shall be $500 per annum so long and during such term as the said well is so utilized; payment of the royalty shall be made semiannually." In the Spring of 1899, the packer in the well drilled by the gas company got out of order, and in the course of an effort to remedy the trouble an accident occurred which, in the judgment of the agent of the gas company, made it necessary to abandon the well, and it was accordingly abandoned and plugged. No other well was drilled to take its place, and this was the only well drilled on the lessor's land. On September 22, 1889, the lessor, McKnight, brought assumpsit against the gas company to recover damages for alleged breaches of covenants contained in the lease, the breaches assigned being mismanagement of the gas well drilled upon the land, and failure to drill other wells requisite to the proper development of the land as gas territory. The jury returned a verdict for the plaintiff for $1,000. Upon the judgment thereon rendered the gas company appealed. The Supreme Court of Pennsylvania reversed the judgment of the court of Common Pleas.

Sec. 6.—In *Double* v. *Heat & Light Co.*, 172 Pa. 388; 33 Atl. 694, (Jan. 6, 1896) the syllabus is as follows: ♦

"If a tenant wishes to avail himself of a privilege which he possesses of terminating the lease by his own act, he must do it before he has entered upon another year of his term.

An oil and gas lease was to terminate by its own limitation two years from its date; after that the lease was to continue 'as much longer as oil and gas is found in paying quantities therein * * * * and should any well produce gas in sufficient quantities to justify marketing, the lessor shall be paid at the rate of two hundred dollars per year for such well so long as the gas therefrom is sold.' *Held,* that after the rental clause became operative by the finding of gas in paying quantities, the lessee could not terminate without giving notice to the lessor of his intention to do so.

The mere cessation of the use of gas from the well did not terminate the lease of its own force, and relieve the lessee from any duty to the lessor."

H. P. Double executed an oil and gas lease upon a tract of land in Butler County, Pennsylvania, for the term and period of two years from date, "and as much longer as oil and gas are found in paying quantities thereon," and should any well produce gas in sufficient quantities to justify marketing the lessee was required to pay at the rate of $200 per year for each well so long as the gas therefrom should be sold. A well was drilled on the premises in the summer of 1891, and gas was found in paying quantities. The rental was paid to the lessor up to November 1, 1892. The Light Company became the owner of the lease and well on December 19, 1892. It went into possession and marketed the gas from the well from that date up to June 1, 1893, when it discontinued its lines from the well, but remained in possession of the lease and well up to February 4, 1894. On that day the lessor instituted suit against the Light Company in assumpsit for the rent due for the year. The defendant claimed that the plaintiff was not entitled to recover the full year's rental, but only for the part thereof that it actually used or sold the gas from the well. The plaintiff insisted that he was entitled to the full year's rental as the Light Company had given no notice of intention to quit. The Court of Common Pleas rendered judgment for the plaintiff for $157.57, from which judgment the defendant appealed, and the Supreme Court affirmed the judgment.

Sec. 7.—In *Otho Iams* v. *Carnegie Nat. Gas Co.*, 194 Pa. 72; 45 Atl. 54 (Dec. 30, 1899) the syllabus is as follows:

"Where an oil and gas lease provides that if gas 'be found in sufficient quantities to justify marketing the same; the lessee is bound to market the gas if found in paying quantities or show some good reason for not having done so. He will not, however, be required to market the gas at a loss, but only at a reasonable profit; and in determining whether it could be so marketed, the distance to market, the expense of marketing and every circumstance of a similar kind should be taken into consideration."

Otho Iams and others leased lands belonging to them in Green County, Pennsylvania, to Timothy Ross, "for the purpose and with the exclusive right of drilling and operating for petroleum and gas." The lease was for the term of two years or for such time as oil or gas should be found in paying quantities on the premises. Shortly after the execution of the lease Ross assigned the gas privileges to the Carnegie Natural Gas Company. The lease provided that all its terms and conditions should extend to the heirs, executors and assignees of the parties to it. The lease also contained the following clause:

"In consideration of said grant and demise, the said party of the second part agrees to give or to pay to the said parties of the first part the full equal one-eighth part of all the oil produced or saved from the premises, and to deliver the same free of expense into tanks or pipelines to the credit of the first parties, and should gas be found in sufficient quantities to justify marketing the same, the consideration in full to the parties of the first part shall be five hundred ($500) dollars per annum, payable semi-annually, in advance, for the gas from each well so long as it shall be sold therefrom, and gas free of cost for household use on the premises to be taken from a well on the same."

The Gas Company entered upon the premises, drilled a well and obtained gas, but thereafter neither paid the rental of $500 per annum nor sold the gas from the well. The lessors instituted their action of assumpsit against the Gas Company in the Court of Common Pleas of Alleghany County, to recover the gas rentals and a verdict and judgment were rendered in favor of the plaintiffs for $1162.52 from which judgment the Gas Company appealed. The Gas Company claimed that it was not liable under the terms of the lease because it had not sold or marketed the gas from the wells. The Supreme Court affirmed the judgment of the Court of Common Pleas.

Glasgow v. *Chartiers Oil Co.*, 152 Pa. 48; 25 Atl. 232.

Sec. 8.—In *Indiana Nat. Gas & Oil Co.* v. *Leer*, 72 N. E. 283; 34 Ind. App. 61 (Nov. 17, 1904) syls. 2-3 are as follows:

"2. Where a landowner, in April, 1889, contracted for the sale of gas and the development of gas wells on his farm, and in September, 1895, plaintiff acquired title to a part of the land by a deed from the heirs of the landowner, with knowledge of the development contract and of the construction that had been given to the same by the parties, plaintiff was not an innocent purchaser, and was therefore bound by such construction.

3. Where a contract for the development of gas land required the grantees to develop the land, pay certain rentals, or to furnish gas for the grantor's use in lieu of rentals, the lease did not terminate at the grantor's death, though possession had not been taken by the lessees, and no development work had been undertaken, gas having been furnished to the grantor, as agreed."

Isaac Rybolt, the owner of a tract of land in Delaware County, Indiana, on April 3, 1899, executed an oil and gas lease thereon to Smith and Ziegler, their heirs or assigns, whereby he granted all the oil and gas in and under the tract, the grantees to have the exclusive right to enter on the land and drill for oil or gas, the lessor to use the land for farming purposes. The lessees agreed "to drill a well upon said premises within twelve months from d·te. or thereafter pay to the first party a yearly rental of $20 until said well is drilled." A failure to pay the rental when due should render the grant null and void; The grantor to have one-eighth of the oil produced, $25.00 for the first, and $200.00 for each subsequent gas well so long as gas should be transported off the premises; The grantor to have "free of expense, gas from the well or wells, to use at his own risk, to light and heat the dwellings on the premises." The lease further provided that lessees "may at any time re-convey this grant and thereupon this instrument shall be null and void. * * * * * * * It is understood that second party shall furnish first party gas in lieu of rental by the first of November, 1889, or this lease shall be null and void." Subsequently the lease was assigned to the Indiana Natural Gas & Oil Company. Isaac Rybolt died and his heirs sold and conveyed a portion of the original premises granted on September, 21, 1895, to Charles Leer. The plaintiff, Charles Leer, instituted suit against the Indiana Natural Gas & Oil Company, in the Circuit Court. of Delaware County, to quiet his title, alleging the foregoing facts and further alleging that no well had been drilled, and no payment made on the lease, and that the plaintiff had received nothing in consideration for the Gas Company's holding the same; that the adjoining territory was being operated, and that gas wells had been put down on all sides of the plaintiff's land; and that these wells would take, and were taking, all the oil and gas from beneath the plaintiff's land; that the Gas Company was holding the lease for speculative purposes. The plaintiff alleged that he had notified the Gas Company to develop the land, and that if they did not make developments he demanded a surrender, a re-conveyance and a release of record, alleging that the gas company had failed and refused to drill and operate after such notice. The Gas Company answered, and alleged that on April 3, 1889, Isaac Rybolt owned in fee the land described in the plaintiff's petition, together with 40 acres adjoining; that these tracts composed one body of land, and were held by Rybolt as one farm; that on April 3, 1889, Rybolt made the grant to Smith and Zeigler, who assigned the same to the gas company; that in June, 1891, the real estate was divided and a portion of the land became the property of John Rybolt, and he was, at the beginning of the suit yet the owner thereof; that the only dwelling house on any part of the total acreage, on April 3, 1889, or at any time thereafter, was on the 40 acres owned by John Rybolt; that no dwelling house had been upon that part of the land claimed by the plaintiff; that it was mutually understood and agreed by the parties to the lease that the lessees and their successors should furnish gas free for the dwelling on the premises, at the time of the making of the conveyance, in lieu of all rentals mentioned in the lease; that at all times thereafter the parties so considered it; that the defendant gas company and its predecessors had at all times furnished gas free to the dwelling house, which gas had been accepted by Isaac Rybolt, and his successor, John Rybolt, in lieu of all rentals; that at and prior to the time Charles Leer purchased the real estate, he had notice of the conveyance of April 3, 1889, and notice of the practical construction placed upon the lease by the gas company and its grantors, and Isaac and John Rybolt, and of the furnishing of gas free; that no other

claim had ever been made under the conveyance till the bringing
of the suit; that the original lessees paid Isaac Rybolt Ten Dollars
provided to be paid in the contract, which was accepted by him
as a consideration therefor; that the grant had never been re-
conveyed by the gas company or its predecessors; and that no
rights granted had ever been abandoned. The gas company disclaimed all interest in the land, except as alleged in the answer.
The Circuit Court sustained a demurrer to the answer, and overruled the demurrer to the second paragraph of the complaint
setting forth the facts above stated. From this decision the gas
company appealed. The Appellate Court reversed the Circuit
Court, and as to the contract between Isaac Rybolt and Smith
and Zeigler, held:

"That such contract entitled the grantor to gas for use in
his dwelling house in lieu of rentals, though no wells were drilled
on the premises, and, such gas having been furnished, the grantees
were not in default for failure to furnish gas from wells developed
on the premises, or pay rent."

Upon the question of the right to cancel the lease on the
grounds that the defendant failed to develop the property, the
court speaking by Judge Robinson, said:

"We do not mean to say that the lease or grant may be continued indefinitely without an effort to develop the territory for
oil or gas."

The lease bore date April 3, 1898. The complaint was filed
on February 5, 1902. The lessees were required to drill a well
on the premises within 12 months, or thereafter pay to the lessor
a yearly rental of $20.00 until a well should be drilled. The lessee,
however, was given the right to furnish the lessor gas in lieu of
rental, by November 1, 1889; otherwise the lease should be void.
The lessee elected to furnish gas to lessor from wells located off
the premises. While there was a term of one year mentioned
specifically, that clause of the lease was immediately modified by
the rental clause providing for the payment of $20.00 per year
cash rental until a well should be completed; and this clause was
likewise modified by the provision giving the lessee the right to
furnish gas for domestic purposes in lieu of the cash rental. In
this way, the lessor was deprived of the benefit of the $25.00 cash
provided in the lease as a bonus for the first gas well, and $200.00

for each subsequent gas well. The court in view of these clauses of the lease, held, that at the date the complaint was filed there had been no abandonment; and that the lessor at that time had not the right to cancel the lease. As to the length of time that these conditions could be continued by the lessee, the court did not indicate an opinion. The court cited the following cases:

> Consumers Gas Trust Co. v. Littler, 70 N. E. 363.
> Consumers Gas Trust Co. v. Chrystal Window Glass Co., 70 N. E. 366.
> Consumers Gas Trust Co. v. Ink, 71 N. E. 477.
> Consumers Gas Trust Co. v. Worth, 71 N. E. 489.
> Consumers Gas Trust Co. v. Howard, 71 N. E. 493.

Sec. 9.—In *Consumers Gas Trust Co.* v. *Littler*, 162 Ind., 320; 70 N. E. 363 (March 15, 1904) the syllabus is as follows:

"1. By a written contract the first party agreed to sell all the oil and gas underlying his land to the second party, with the right to mine and transport it, no time being fixed for the beginning of operations, nor for the completion of a well, and no express provisions being made that a well should ever be drilled; but it was agreed that a sum should be paid annually by the second party till oil or gas was found, or till, in the judgment of the second party, they could not be found. If they were found, the first party was to receive a share. *Held*, that there was an implied engagement by the second party to explore for oil and gas, which, if not performed in a reasonable time, entitled the first party to a forfeiture.

2. In construing a contract giving a license to drill wells in land for oil and gas, the court has judicial knowledge, as a matter of common knowledge, that gas or oil does not exist in paying quantities under all the lands within a recognized distance, and that there is no other generally acknowledged way to determine whether it does exist than putting down a well.

3. Where, under a contract the owner of land had the option to require, by claiming a forfeiture, that the other party should drill for gas and oil within a reasonable time, or to accept a certain sum annually, for delay, his acceptance of an annual payment in advance was a waiver of performance for one year.

4. Where, by the acceptance of an agreed annual payment, the owner of land had waived his right to have the other party drill there for oil and gas up to a certain time, and at the expiration of that time he refused to accept another payment, he could not claim a forfeiture of the contract 15 days later, since that did not afford notice for a reasonable time of his intention to do so."

Joseph W. Littler, on October 15, 1896, made an oil and gas contract with one Walley, who subsequently assigned the contract to the Consumers Gas Trust Company. The lease was made in consideration of One Dollar, the receipt whereof being acknowledged as paid, whereby Littler sold to Walley, his heirs and assigns, all the oil and gas under certain lands in Grant County, Indiana "together with the right to enter upon said land at all times for the purpose of drilling and operating for oil, gas or water, with the right to erect and maintain all necessary telephone lines, buildings and structures for that purpose; and together with the right to lay, maintain and remove all lines of pipe over and across said lands for the conveyance and transportation of oil and gas." In consideration whereof, said Walley agreed to pay to Littler the sum of $40.00 annually, beginning on October 15, 1896, until oil or gas should be found in paying quantities, or the grant should be terminated as therein provided for. The lessee was not to drill any well within 300 feet from any building on the premises, and was not to use more than one acre of ground with each well drilled; The grantor, or lessor to have the use of the land for agricultural or other purposes, except what should be actually occupied in operating for oil or gas. One-sixth of the oil produced to be delivered to the lessor, who was to have free gas for domestic purposes from the wells or pipelines on the premises, and should gas be found in greater quantity than was required for use by the lessor the lessee should pay the grantor "$100 each year for each and every well from which gas is used off the premises." If either gas or oil were found on the premises in paying quantities "the part of oil to be delivered, as aforesaid, or the sum per well for gas, shall be in lieu of the annual payments above provided;" Such annual payments to cease immediately upon the discovery of oil or gas in such quantities. It was further provided that whenever, in the judgment of the lessee, his heirs or assigns, oil or gas, or either, could not be found on the premises, or having been found ceased to exist in paying quantities, the lessee should re-convey to the lessor all the oil and gas in and under said premises; and then all payments of every kind from and after said date should cease and determine. In case of a re-conveyance, the lessee was to have the right to lay and maintain pipelines for the transportation of oil and gas over the premises for ten years from the date of such re-conveyance with the right to the lessee at any time to remove all machinery,

fixtures and property placed on the land. The lease provided that
all payments thereunder should be made on October 15th of each
year at a Bank in Muncie, Indiana. It was also provided that
"in default of complete compliance on the part of the second party
of his assigns, renders this lease null and void." All the parties
to the lease signed it. The lease embraced a quarter section of
land. There was a separate lease for each eighty acres in the
same terms.

Littler instituted suit in the Circuit Court of Grant County
against the Gas Company to secure the cancellation of the leases
or contracts, and for the quieting of his title. The complaint was
in three paragraphs, the first being a general count to quiet the
title, and covered the whole of the quarter section. The second
and third paragraphs of- the complaint were addressed to the
respective eighty acres, and set out the contract in full. In addition to the formal matters, the second and third paragraphs of
the complaint each alleged the recording of the contract, the
assignment thereof by Walley to the defendant gas company, the
recording of such assignment, the payment by the defendant on
or about October 15, 1900, of $40.00 as a consideration for the
gas company's option to drill on the premises for one year from
said date to October 15, 1901, which payment was the exact amount
due the plaintiff under the contract at the time it was paid; that
nothing had been paid on the contract to continue it after that
date; that on October 15, 1901, the plaintiff refused to longer
continue the contract in force or receive any further payment
therefor, and declared the contract then terminated and forfeited;
that neither defendant nor its assignor ever drilled a well on the
premises, nor had gas or oil been found thereon, nor had anyone
under the contract laid a pipeline on the premises for oil or gas;
that neither Walley nor the gas company had ever been in possession of the premises.

The Gas Company answered, and in substance alleged: that
Walley took the lease or made the contract as agent of the gas
company, and afterward executed a formal assignment; that payment was made of the annual sum stipulated—$40.00—on or before
the 15th day of October in each year down to the 15th day of
October, 1901; and an offer was made to pay the installment for
the year commencing on that day, which payment lessee refused
to accept; that the contract had never been terminated; denied
that the $40.00 annually was paid as a consideration for the

option or right to drill for any one year; and averred that the
$40.00 was a part of the consideration for all the rights and privi-
leges granted under the contract. To the answer above, which
was filed to the second and third paragraphs of the petition or
complaint the plaintiff demurred and the demurrer was sustained.
The defendant declined to make further answer, and the court
entered a decree annulling the lease and quieting the plaintiff's
title as against the same. From this decree of the Circuit Court
the gas company appealed to the Appellate Court, from which
court the case was transferred to the Supreme Court. That court
reversed the judgment of the Circuit Court, with instructions to
sustain the demurrer to the second and third paragraphs of the
complaint.

In construing the lease or contract the court held, that while
there was an implied covenant on the part of the lessee to test
the territory for oil and gas, this implied covenant must be treated
as a condition which, if not performed within a reasonable time
would entitle the lessor to claim forfeiture under the clause of
the agreement providing that "in default of complete compliance
on the part of the second party or his assigns, renders this lease
null and void"; and that the lessor had waived the right to exercise his option to declare the lease void by accepting the rentals
in advance, and not giving notice to the lessee of his intention
to declare a forfeiture unless explorations were made; that equity
required such notice for a reasonable time, in support of which
conclusion the court cited the following cases:

Hukill v. *Myers,* 36 W. Va. 639; 15 S. E. 151.
Thropp v. *Field,* 26 N. J. Eq. 82.
Double v. *Heat & Light Co.,* 172 Pa. 388; 33 Atl. 694.

A lessor having the option to terminate a lease for oil and
gas purposes, where he has made a contract such as the one in
this case, if he desires to terminate the lease or contract at any
particular time he must give notice of his intention so to do for
a time sufficient to afford lessee an opportunity to develop. Where
a lessor has attempted to terminate a lease without giving such
notice the lessee's remedy is by bill in equity for relief against
such act. The acceptance of rental as a matter of course precludes a forfeiture at any time within the period for which rental
has been accepted.

Sec. 10.—In *Consumers Gas Trust Co.,* v. *Chrystal Window Glass Co.,* 163 Ind. 190; 70 N. E. 366 (March 17, 1904) the syllabus is as follows:

"Where one by a written contract granted the exclusive right to drill in his land for gas and petroleum for a certain rental and a share of the proceeds, where the drilling was delayed, he cannot, by refusal to accept the rental, immediately terminate the contract, and lease the rights to another party, but must give reasonable notice of his intention before doing so."

This was a suit by the Consumers Gas Trust Company against the Chrystal Window Glass Company and Jones and wife, for an injunction to prevent the Chrystal Window Glass Company from entering upon the lands described in the complaint, and drilling wells thereon and conveying the gas therefrom. The complaint stated the facts upon which it was predicated, as follows: On April 30, 1902, Jones and wife made a contract or lease to the Consumers Gas Trust Company, whereby they granted the company the exclusive right to drill wells for gas and oil and lay pipelines for the transportation of the same upon a tract of 40 acres of land; on the same day Jones and wife executed a similar contract on another 40-acre tract of land; On this tract he had a dwelling house which he occupied; At the date of the filing of the complaint lessee had drilled no well on the first tract; that the gas company with the consent of Jones, put down a line of pipe on the highway on the east side of the first mentioned 40-acre tract; On December 21, 1901, the gas company tapped its pipeline and connected a service pipe therewith for the use of Jones, and commenced furnishing gas to him for use in his residence, which gas the company continued to furnish to the date of the filing of the complaint. The gas company paid Jones, who received the rents under the contract, for each year to and including the year ending April 27, 1902, and tendered in advance the rent for the land for the year ending April 27, 1903; Jones refused to receive the money tendered as rent for the year 1903, attempting to repudiate his contract; That Jones had combined with the Chrystal Window Glass Company to deprive the Consumers Gas Trust Company of its rights under the lease; that on April 30, 1902, Jones and wife made a pretended contract with the Chrystal Window Glass Company, whereby they attempted to grant to said company the exclusive right to drill wells for gas and oil, and to lay pipelines for the transportation of the same upon said land; that it had performed all the duties and obligations imposed upon it by the original lease, and that the same was in full force; that it did not know the particulars of the agreement made by Jones and wife with the Chrystal Window Glass Company, but that said Chrystal Window Glass Company had entered upon the real estate and erected a derrick thereon preparatory to drilling a well and operating for petroleum and gas; that they had commenced drilling such well, and threatened to lay pipes thereon for the transportation of gas or oil if any should be found. The complaint prayed for an injunction against the Chrystal Window Glass Company, and said Jones. Issues were formed, and there was a finding and judgment in favor of the defendants. From this judgment the plaintiff appealed to the Appellate court and the case was transferred therefrom to the Supreme Court. It appeared that the contract or lease made by Jones and wife to the Consumers Gas Trust Company was practically the same as the agreement or lease set forth in *Consumers Gas Trust Co.* v. *Little*, 162 Ind. 320; 70 N. E. 363. The Supreme Court reversed the Circuit Court.

Sec. 11.—In *Consumers Gas Trust Co.* v. *Worth*, 163 Ind. 141; 71 N. E. 489 (June 21, 1904) the syllabus is as follows:

"1. Where a gas lease was for such a period as the lessee should pay the lessor a certain sum of money annually, or so much longer as oil or gas should be found in paying quantities, the acceptance by the lessor of an annual payment in advance was a waiver of performance in developing the property for that year.

2. Where a gas lease is for such a time as the lessee shall pay a specified annual sum in advance to the lessor, or until gas shall be found in paying quantities, and the lessor refuses at the beginning of any year to accept the payment, the lessee is then bound to develop the premises within a reasonable time.

3. Where a gas lease is for such period as the lessee shall pay the lessor a specified sum annually in advance, or until gas shall be found in paying quantities, and the lessor refuses to accept the annual payment and declares the lease forfeited, the failure of the lessee to thereafter commence development proceedings, cannot be regarded as a lack of diligence, entitling the lessee to a forfeiture."

Elizabeth Worth, on March 20, 1902, instituted an action in the Superior Court of Madison County, Indiana, against the Consumers Gas Trust Company. The complaint consisted of two paragraphs, the first being the statutory form to quiet title to certain described real estate, containing in all 54 acres situated in said County. The second count sought to have declared null and void a certain lease relating to the same premises. This count alleged that the lease was executed by Elizabeth Worth and husband to the defendant on March 3, 1897, and granted to the defendant the right to enter upon the real estate described for the purpose of drilling for oil and gas thereon. The grant gave the lessee the right to enter upon the premises, with the exclusive right to drill thereon for petroleum and gas, to lay, maintain and operate its main, pipelines and other lines of pipe, with right of way over the premises, with the right to erect, maintain and operate such buildings as should be necessary to the full enjoyment of the grant, with the right at any time to remove any buildings, machinery, fixtures, pipelines, or pipe placed on the premises. The term of the lease was six months from date, and as much longer as oil or gas should be found in sufficient quantities to justify marketing the same in the opinion of the gas company; The lessee to pay to lessor compensation at the rate of fifty cents per acre for each year in advance, for said lands, until the completion by the lessee of a well. After the completion of the first well, if it should, in the opinion of the lessee, produce gas sufficient to justify it in marketing the same, lessee was to pay to lessor $100.00 per annum for each well on said land, so long as it produced a marketable quantity of gas; the amount for each well to be due January first and July first in each year, and payable within ten days of maturity by depositing the same in the Citizens Bank of Summitville, subject to the order of the lessor. Any failure on the part of the lessor to pay as provided shall render the lease null and void, and the rights of both parties should cease and determine, except the lessee should have the right, without paying a further consideration, to operate, repair, replace or remove any pipeline upon the premises. No well was to be drilled within 300 feet of the buildings on the premises; so long as gas wells should be maintained, or pipelines operated on the premises, lessor to have a sufficient supply of gas therefrom without charge therefor, for use in her residence upon the premises; and also gas for two jumbo burners for lawn purposes; In case lessee should abandon a well it should be packed and tubed; The surrender and cancellation of the lease should not cancel the right of the lessee to continue to replace, repair and maintain its pipes and telephone lines through the land. The contract was to inure to the benefit of heirs, executors, administrators and assigns.   ·

The Gas Company demurred to each paragraph of the complaint. These demurrers were overruled, and thereafter the gas company filed answers to each paragraph of the complaint. In each paragraph of the answer the lease was alleged substantially as above stated. Aside from the contract in question, the first paragraph of the answer alleged: That pursuant to said contract, on March 3, 1897, the defendant gas company paid to the plaintiff $27.00, the amount named in the acreage rental, mentioned in the contract; that on each succeeding third day of March until the third day of March, 1902, it paid a like amount for the same purpose; that on March 3, 1902, defendant tendered a like sum to the plaintiff, and she refused to accept the payment, claiming the right to terminate the contract; that upon this refusal defendant deposited the $27.00 with the Citizens Bank at Summitville, to the credit of the lessor; that on March 3, 1902, the plaintiff lessor notified the defendant lessee in writing that she proposed to terminate the contract on that date; defendant denied that the contract had been terminated as provided for therein, and claimed that the paymen of $27.00 was the sole consideration for the option and right of defendant to drill on the premises for any one year; that the several payments were made by defendant and accepted by plaintiff in full satisfaction for delay in drilling wells down to March 3, 1902. Defendant averred that it had never been ascertained that oil or gas in its judgment, could not be found on said premises in a quantity to justify marketing the same, nor that having developed said premises they ceased thereafter to exist in paying quantities. Defendant averred that the contract was still in full force and that the defendant had done and performed, and had been ready to do and perform all the duties and obligations imposed upon it by the contract. The defendant denied that the delay in taking possession of the premises and operating for oil or gas had been unreasonable. The second paragraph of the answer, which was addressed to the second paragraph of the complaint, was substantially the same as the first paragraph. A demurrer was sustained to each paragraph of the answer, and upon the defendant declining to further plead, the court rendered judgment, quieting the plaintiff's title to the real estate, and declaring the lease and contract referred to in the second paragraph of the complaint and set up in defendant's answer, to be null and void. From this decree the gas company appealed to the Appellate Court, from which court the case was transferred to the Supreme Court and that court reversed the Circuit Court.

The judgment and decree of the court below was reversed and the cause remanded, with instructions to the lower court to overrule the demurrer to each paragraph of the answer, and for further proceedings not inconsistent with the opinion.

The effect of this decision is, that where a lessor has accepted the annual payments by way of commutattion money for delay in drilling, the lease cannot be, by such lessor, terminated at the end of any year by refusal to accept rental, without reasonable notice to the lessee of the intention to so terminate the lease, and without affording to the lessee a reasonable time after notice to enter upon the leased premises for the purpose of making explorations. After giving such notice to lessee, and after affording him a reasonable time, a failure on the part of the lessee to enter upon the premises and make explorations gives the lessor the right to declare a forfeiture.

Sec. 12.—In *Consumers Gas Trust Co.* v. *Ink,* 163 Ind. 174; 71 N. E. 477 (June 23, 1904) the syllabus is as follows:

"1. Where, under a lease of oil lands, the owner had an option to require the lessee to drill for gas or oil within a reasonable time by claiming a forfeiture or to accept a certain sum annually for delay, the acceptance of such sum annually in advance for several years precluded the lessor from claiming a forfeiture before the year in which the last payment made for a postponement of operations had expired.

2. Where a lessor of oil lands demanded a forfeiture of the lease for the lessee's failure to drill for oil at a time when she was not entitled to such forfeiture, such demand was ineffectual as a notice to the lessee to start operations, the claim of forfeiture being equivalent to a denial of the lessee's right thereafter to enter the premises for the purpose of conducting such operations."

Sarah F. Ink, on June 3, 1897, made an oil and gas lease to Consumers Gas Trust Company for a tract of land for the term of six months, and as much longer as gas or oil should be found in marketable quantities, or One Dollar per acre in advance per annum until the completion of a well upon the land, was kept paid. The gas company never took possession, and never drilled or attempted to drill a well. Lessor accepted from lessee $80.00 on the day the contract was executed as payment of rent for the year ending June 3, 1898; and on the latter date, and at the end of each subsequent year, to and including 1901, accepted of lessee a like sum for a like purpose. About May 20, 1902, lessee tendered lessor $80.00 as a like payment for the year beginning June 3, 1902, and ending June 3, 1903. Lessor refused to accept the money and declared the contract forfeited on June 12, 1902, and instituted suit in the Circuit Court of Grant County, Indiana, against the lessee to quiet the title and to have the lease cancelled. An answer was filed by the lessee to which a demurrer was sustained. The lessee, refusing to plead further, judgment was rendered annulling the lease and quieting the title. Defendant appealed to the Appellate Court from which court the case was transferred to the Supreme Court, and that court reversed the Circuit Court, the facts being the same as those involved in *Consumers Gas Trust Company* v. *Littler,* 162 Ind. 320; 70 N. E. 363.

Sec. 13.—In *Summerville* v. *Apollo Gas Co.,* 207 Pa., 334; 56 Atl. 876 (Jan. 4, 1904) the syllabus is as follows:

"Where an oil and gas lease was for two years 'and as much longer as oil and gas are found in paying quantities,' the court may say as a matter of law that the lessor has no right to forfeit the lease at the end of two years because during that time no oil or gas had been marketed, where the undisputed evidence is that the production from a well on the land was one million feet per day, worth, when piped and conveyed to a market, from three to five cents per thousand feet.

In an action of ejectment to recover property covered by an oil and gas lease, where the question before the court is, plaintiff's legal right to possession, and this is to be determined by the construction to be placed upon the lease and upon the undisputed evidence as to the facts, it is proper to exclude evidence offered upon the part of the plaintiff to show that possession had been taken under a claim of forfeiture."

E. M. Summerville, on September 2, 1896, made an oil and gas lease to the Star Drilling Company for a tract of land in Clarion

County, Pennsylvania, which lease by assignment became the property of the Apollo Gas Company. The lease stated the term as follows: "For and during the term of two years from the date hereof and as much longer as oil and gas are found in paying quantities or the hereinafter described rental is paid." The well which was to be put down was begun and completed in contract time, and there was no question of rental or undue delay in the case. The well was completed in October, 1897, and up to the time the Apollo Gas Company took possession in July, 1901, the gas produced by the well was not sold or disposed of, but the evidence showed that the production from the well was one million feet per day, worth, when piped and conveyed to market, from three to five cents per thousand feet.

The lessor instituted an action of ejectment in the Court of Common Pleas of Clarion County against the Apollo Gas Company to recover possession of the demised premises. The plaintiff contended that no matter how much gas was produced it could not be said to be a "paying quantity," unless it was sold at a profit. And as the lease by its terms was only to continue after two years, for as long as the gas was found in "paying quantities," it was at an end before the defendant gas company took possession of the premises. The Court of Common Pleas rendered judgment for the defendant, from which the plaintiff appealed. The Court of Appeals found that the only issue raised by the pleadings was the question of forfeiture; and the only ground upon which the plaintiff claimed the right to declare a forfeiture was, that gas was not found in paying quantities. The Supreme Court found that there was no denial that the well produced a million feet of gas per day, and that this gas was worth from three to five cents per thousand feet. Upon the question of marketing the gas Justice Potter, in the opinion, said:

"It may be that for some time the lessee was not able to find a purchaser for the gas, but that was not the affair of the lessors; they were not interested in the proceeds of the sale of the gas. Their rights under the agreement extended only to the receipt of a stipulated annual rental for each well, and the free use of gas for domestic purposes. Beyond this, the question of whether or not the quantity of gas was profitable, was for the decision of the lessee. It may be that the final disposition of the product of the well was such as to amply remunerate it for the delay in finding a market.''

It appeared from the evidence that one of the lessors received gas from one of the wells for domestic purposes. The judgment of the Court of Common Pleas was affirmed.

Sec. 14.—In *Mathes* v. *Shaw Oil Co.,* (Kan.) 101 Pac. 998 (May 8, 1909) the syllabus is as follows:

"A gas and oil lease, in addition to the usual provisions, contained a clause to the effect that if gas is found in any well sufficient to justify saving and casing, lessor may have enough for domestic purposes, and the lessee the remainder. Immediately following this was a clause which reads: 'If, however, second party shall use, market, or sell gas from any well producing gas, it shall pay therefor $50.00 per year for and during the time such gas shall be sold, marketed or used, except for drilling or for domestic use of the parties leasing to second party.' *Held*, that lessee is liable for stipulated rental if gas is used by it for purposes other than drilling."

May Mathes and J. W. Mathes instituted an action for rental in the District Court of Neosho County, Kansas, against the Shaw Oil Company. The lease under which the plaintiffs sought to recover containing the following provision:

"If oil, gas, or other minerals be found on the premises by said second parties, all rights, benefits and obligations, secured hereby shall continue so long as either can be produced in paying quantities by said second party. If gas is found in any well or wells to justify the expense of saving and casing the same, said first party shall have on demand, sufficient gas from such well or wells, or from any well or wells owned by second party, free of cost, at such well or wells, for domestic purposes on said premises, * * * * * the second party to have the remainder thereof. If, however, second party shall use, market or sell gas from any well producing gas, it shall pay said first party, or assigns, therefor Fifty Dollars per year for and during the time such gas shall be sold, marketed or used, except for drilling or domestic use of the parties leasing to second party, or his assigns, said payment to be made on each well within sixty days after commencing to sell or market gas therefrom and annually thereafter while such gas is sold or marketed from such well."

The defendant answered the plaintiff's petition, and after a general denial, alleged:

"Said defendants, for a further answer to said separate and several causes of action, allege that the wells which plaintiffs claim are producing gas, are also producing oil wells, from which plaintiffs under their said lease have at all times received the royalty provided for, and that it is necessary to remove the gas therefrom in order to successfully operate said wells for oil, and therefore no rental is due for the gas under said lease."

The District Court made the following findings of fact:

"That before these defendants or any of them became the owners of said lease a number of oil wells had been drilled on the premises and the prior owners had laid pipelines from several of these wells to their power house, located on said lease, and utilized the gas therefrom as fuel, and that after the defendants became the owners of the lease they continued to use the gas in the same way; that none of said gas wells were paying gas wells, and in order to operate them as oil wells it was necessary to remove the gas therefrom if not burned and permit it to escape in the air; That the use of the gas from any or all of said wells was incidental to the main business of producing oil on said premises, and that the plaintiffs have received their royalties regularly from each of the wells from which gas was burned. That the plaintiffs have been paid nothing from the date of the making of said lease by these defendants or any other as a royalty or rental for the gas used."

The District Court rendered judgment for the defendants from which judgement the plaintiffs appealed. The Supreme Court reversed the judgment of the District Court. The Circuit Court held, that the defense stated in the answer did not constitute a defense to the action.

Sec. 15.—In *Bellevue Oil & Gas. Co.* v. *Pennell*, 76 Kan. 785; 92 Pac. 1101 (Dec. 7, 1907) the syllabus is as follows:

"An ordinary gas lease contains a clause which reads: 'to pipe gas to the house for domestic purposes as soon as well is completed.' *Held*, that by the provisions the parties intended that the gas furnished thereunder should be supplied without charge."

W. S. Pennell, on August 13, 1903, executed and delivered an oil and gas lease to S. Breckenridge, who assigned the lease and it became the property of the Bellevue Gas & Oil Company. By the terms of the lease the lessor granted to the lessee the exclusive right of searching for and producing petroleum and natural gas upon a tract of land in Chatauqua County, Kansas, for the term of two years, and so much longer as oil or gas could be found in paying quantities, or the royalties paid. The lessee agreed: (1) To deliver to lessor in tanks or pipelines one-sixth of all the oil produced and saved. (2) If gas should be found in paying quantities and utilized away from the farm lessee to pay lessor $100 per annum for the gas from each well so used. (3) To continue operations so as to least interfere with farming privileges. (5) To complete one well every sixty days thereafter until ten wells should be completed while oil should be found in paying quantities in each well so drilled. (6) To pipe gas to the house for domestic purposes as soon as well should be completed. A gas well was completed within the time limited by the lease, and gas was piped therefrom to the home of lessor who used gas therefrom for domestic purposes prior to and since August 13, 1904. On August 13, 1904, the assignee of the original lessee paid $100, stipulated in the lease as the annual rental for a gas well. On August 13, 1905, the oil company presented to the lessor an account for gas used by him, amounting to $97.00, and $3.00 cash, payment on which was refused by the lessor, and thereupon the plaintiff instituted suit in the District Court of Chatauqua County against the gas company for the rental claimed by him to be due. Judgment was rendered on an agreed statement of facts in favor of the plaintiff; and the defendant Oil Company brought error. The judgment of the District Court was affirmed.

Sec. 16.—In *Davis* v. *Chatauqua Oil & Gas Co.*, (Kan.) 96 Pac. 47 (May 9, 1908) it was held:

"The right to claim a forfeiture depends entirely upon the proviso inserted in the paragraph limiting the time when the wells were to be drilled. The subject of rentals had been duly treated in other parts of the lease, and no reference had been made to forfeiture as a penalty for failure to pay them. The paragraph in question did not relate to royalties, at all. It covered the

subject of the drilling of the wells and the consequences to attach
in case no wells were drilled * * * * * * * *. If wells should be
sunk on the leased land the provision for royalties should control
and not the provision relating to cash rental and gas piped from
elsewhere. The proviso has no relation to the subject matter of
the paragraph, except to exclude the idea that anything could be
substituted for the agreed royalties if wells were sunk, and has
no more force than if it were the concluding sentence of the paragraph.''

John J. Davis and wife executed, on May 29, 1902, an oil and
gas lease to L. A. Lockwood and George F. Gurnsey, with the following provision:

"It is mutually agreed that the parties of the second part
shall begin drilling within two miles of A. A. Spires' farm within
eight months of the delivery hereof, or in case of failure to do so,
then and in that case this lease shall become null and void. If no
oil or gas well be drilled on said premises within twelve months
from the date thereof it shall be at the option of the party of the
second part to pay twenty-five cents per acre, annually, thereafter, at their office in Independence, Kansas, or lay pipelines
from mains of wells to within fifty feet of the residence occupied
by first party on the above described lands and furnish gas for
two stoves and two lights.''

The lease contained the following stipulation in relation to the
royalties to be paid the landowners:

"The party of the second part agrees to deliver to the party
of the first part one-tenth of the oil realized from these premises
in tanks at the wells, without cost, or to pay the market price
therefor in cash, at the option of the first party. If oil or gas be
found on these premises, all rights, benefits and obligations secured hereby shall continue so long as either can be produced in
paying quantities. If gas is found in any well or wells first party
is to have, on demand, sufficient gas from such well or wells for
domestic purposes on said premises, free, provided there be more
than there is needed by said party of the second part on said
premises. If, however, said second parties shall sell, or market
gas from any well producing gas only it shall pay first party therefor Fifty Dollars per year for and during the time such gas shall
be sold or marketed.''

The lessees assigned the lease to the Chatauqua Oil & Gas
Company. The company drilled a well in due time which produced
both oil and gas. Subsequently the lessors brought suit in the

District Court of Chatauqua County, to forfeit the lease, claiming
a forfeiture on the ground that the defendant did not pay oil royalties; did not furnish gas for domestic uses; and failed to pay
$50.00 per year gas royalties.   The case was tried by the court,
and upon the conclusion of the plaintiff's evidence a demurrer
thereto was sustained and judgments rendered against the plaintiff. From this judgment an appeal was taken to the Supreme
Court of Kansas, and that court affirmed the judgment.

Sec. 17.—In *Eastern Oil Company* v. *Coulehan,* 65 W. Va. 531
64 S. E. 836, (April 27, 1909) syls. 3-4-5-6-7 are as follows:

"3. Where, in a lease for oil and gas, there is a habendum
'to have and to hold the same unto the lessee for the term of five
years from this date, and as much longer as oil or gas is produced
or the rental paid thereon,' and whereby in order to extend the
term of such lease as provided, oil or gas is required to be produced within such five years limitation, the date of the lease
should be excluded in the computation of time, unless it is plainly
manifest therefrom that it should be included.
    4. The discovery of oil or gas under a lease giving right of
exploration and production, unless there is something in the lease
manifesting a contrary intention, is sufficient to create vested
estate in the lessee in the exclusive right to produce oil or gas
provided for therein—a right, however, which may be lost by
abandonment, by failure to produce oil or gas, or pursue the work
of production, or development of the property.
    5. Such right, once vested by discovery of oil or gas in an
upper sand, will not be lost if the lessee continues to drill deeper
in search of oil or gas in a lower sand, although he does not succeed in finding oil in the lower sand within the limitation prescribed by the lease; but, if oil or gas be not found in the lower
strata, production from the upper sand could not long be deferred
without incurring the penalty of abandonment or forfeiture if
forfeiture be prescribed.
    6. Where, before the time has expired for the performance
of a contract, there has been such a substantial compliance therewith by a party thereto that gross injustice would be done him
by denying him relief, equity will grant him relief as from a
forfeiture.
    7. Judicial notice will be taken that gas, unlike oil, cannot be
brought to the surface and stored to await a market for it, but
must remain in the ground, and, unless allowed to waste away,
taken out only as and when producer may be able to find a customer."

John C. Coulehan and wife, on August 3, 1901, executed and delivered to West Union Gas Company a lease which on the same day was assigned to the Eastern Oil Company. The lease recited a consideration of $250.00 paid, and lessors granted and demised to lessee all the oil and gas in and under a tract of 118 acres in Doddridge County, West Virginia, and also said tract of land for the purpose and exclusive right of operating thereon for oil and gas. The term of the lease was stated as follows:

"To have and to hold the same unto the lessee for the term of five years from this date, and as much longer as oil or gas is produced, or the rental paid thereon."

The lease stipulated that the lessor should be paid a royalty of one-eighth part of all oil produced and saved, and $200.00 yearly for each gas well as long as gas therefrom should be sold, payable within 16 days after commencing to use gas therefrom; the lessor to have gas for his dwelling from any gas well, free, by making connections; and it was provided that in case no well should be completed within three months from the date of the lease the same to become absolutely void and of no further effect whatever unless the lessee should pay for further continuance of the privileges therein mentioned the sum of $50.00 quarterly in advance until a well should be completed. The lessee to have the right at any time to re-convey the premises "thereby granted" and thereupon be forever discharged from all liability to the lessor under any and every provision thereof accruing after such re-conveyance, and the instrument should be no longer binding on either party. After the payment of the cash consideration the quarterly annual installments of rent were regularly paid in advance for the full period of five years; but the assignee of the lessee did not begin the work of drilling for oil or gas until June, 1906, after the last quarter begun. It owned other leases adjoining and in the same neighborhood, on some of which it had put down wells, the wells drilled defining defendants land as gas but not oil producing territory. Having invested in bonus and rental money, twelve hundred dollars, the Eastern Oil Company in June, 1906, began a well on the leased land, and about June 20th struck gas in the salt sand at the depth of 1240 feet, which, when gauged and tested showed a capac ity of about 3,000,000 cubic feet per day. After striking the gas the company concluded to go deeper to the lower or Indian sand. The well was begun in ample time to have completed it in the lower sand, but shortage of water due to the drouth caused a delay of several days. Finding the time growing short, and the lessor declining to extend the term, except upon terms deemed oppressive, the drillers were directed by the Company to work on Sunday, The lessor seeing the drillers at work on Sunday, suggested that they were laying themselves liable to arrest and conviction and they were frightened away and refused to work. About thirty minutes after midnight of August 2, 1906, lessor, with witnesses appeared at the well where the drillers were at work on the night tower and inquiring of and being informed by them that the well was not yet completed in the lower sand, notified them that the lease had expired at midnight; that the rights of lessee had ceased; and that all from that time would be treated as trespassers. The drillers, in the absence of the owners, stopped drilling and work was not resumed until noon of August 3d, a loss of about twelve hours. The drilling then begun and was continued until shortly before one o'clock on August 4th, when gas in immense quantities was struck in the Indian sand. The only interruption was the second appearance of the lessor with witnesses shortly after the previous midnight to again notify the drillers that the lease had expired, and ordering them off the premises. The gas company refused to vacate the premises, and the lessor on August 4, 1906, instituted against the Eastern Oil Company in the Circuit Court of Dodd ridge County, a suit in unlawful entry and detainer to recover possession of the property. The Eastern Oil Company filed its bill in the same Court against the lessor, and on December 8, 1906. obtained from said Circuit Court an injunction protecting it in the possession and occupancy of said land, and enjoining the lessor from in any manner interfering with any of its rights, specified in the lease of August 3, 1901; and from in any manner interfering with it in the use, occupancy and operation of the land for oil and gas purposes under the lease; and also from prosecuting the action of unlawful entry and detainer until plaintiff's rights under the lease should be settled and determined, the bill praying · that the court would decree the plaintiff vested with the title to and interest in all the oil and gas according to, and subject to the terms of the lease, and that the lease be held firm and valid. At January rules. 1907, the plaintiff filed an amended bill amplifying the grounds of relief alleged in the original bill, renewing the prayer thereof, and upon hearing upon the original and amended bill and the separate answer of John C. Coulehan thereto, and upon the depositions and proofs taken, the Circuit Court of Doddridge County entered a decree whereby the injunction was wholly dissolved, and the plaintiff's original and amended bill dismissed; but reserving the right to the Gas Company to interpose the discovery of gas as a defense to the action of unlawful entry and detainer. From this decree the Gas Company appealed to the Court of Appeals, and that court reversed the Circuit Court. Upon the construction of the lease as to whether it was a lease or a license, the court cited upon the theory of the grant being a lease:

> Brown v. Fowler, 65 Ohio St. 507-521; 63 N. E. 76.
> Woodland Oil Co. v. Crawford, 55 Ohio St. 161; 44 N. E. 1093; 34 L. R. A. 62.
> Martin v. Jones, 62 Ohio St. 519-525; 57 N. E. 238.

As to the construction of leases of this character by the Court of Appeals of West Virginia, holding that they are mere licenses and vest no estate, the court cited:

> Crawford v. Ritchie, 43 W. Va. 252; 27 S. E. 220.
> Steelsmith v. Gartlan, 45 W. Va. 27; 29 S. E. 978 44 L. R. A. 107.
> Headley v. Hoopengarner, 60 W. Va. 626; 55 S. E. 744.

Upon the question of the jurisdiction in equity to settle all questions as to the validity and priority of leases for oil and gas, where the parties claim under the same title, the court cited:

> Thomas v. Hukill, 34 W. Va. 385; 12 S. E. 522.
> Williamson v. Jones, 39 W. Va. 231; 19 S. E. 436; 25 L. R. A. 222.
> Bettman v. Harness, 42 W. Va. 433; 26 S. E. 271; 36 L. R. A. 566.
> Crawford v. Ritchie, 43 W. Va. 252; 27 S. E. 220.

Steelsmith v. *Gartlan,* 45 W. Va. 27; 29 S. E. 978; 44 L. R. A.
    107.
Lowther Oil Co. v. *Guffey,* 52 W. Va. 88; 43 S. E. 101.
Lowther Oil Co. v. *Miller-Sibley Co.,* 53 W. Va. 501.; 44 S. E.
    433; 97 Am. St. Rep. 1027.
Pyle v. *Henderson,* 55 W. Va. 122; 46 S. E. 791.
Starn v. *Huffman,* 62 W. Va. 422; 59 S. E. 179.
Sult v. *Hochstetter Oil Co.,* 63 W. Va. 317; 61 S. E. 307.
Pheasant v. *Hanna,* 63 W. Va. 613; 60 S. E. 618.

Sec. 18.—In *McGraw Oil & Gas Co.* v. *Kennedy,* 65 W. Va. 595
64 S. E. 1027 analyzed under Chapter 18, the syllabus is as follows:

"1. A lease for oil and gas is for five years 'and as long
thereafter as oil or gas, or either of them, is produced by the party
of the second part. The lessor cannot forfeit it because he thinks
the gas not in paying quantity; the lessee claiming that it is, and
willing to pay the sum stipulated for the well. It is for the lessee
to say whether the gas is in paying quantity, acting in good faith.
    2. When a producing gas well is developed, but its product
not marketed that fact does not authorize the lessor to forfeit the
lease; the lessee being willing to pay the agreed sum for the gas
well.
    3. An oil and gas lease cannot be cancelled in equity alone for
failure to drill additional wells.
    4. Under the lease in this case a well producing gas is drilled,
and the lessee elects to consider it in paying quantity. An estate
ha sthus vested in him.''

Sec. 19.—In *South Penn Oil Co.* v. *Edgell,* 48 W. Va. 348; 37
S. E. 596, (December 1, 1900) the syllabus is as follows:

"The forfeiture clause in a gas and oil lease under which a
valuable estate vested in the lessee in so far as the rentals are concerned, made payable in gas, oil and money, is in the nature of a
penalty to secure such rental, against which a court of equity will
grant relief when compensation for such rental can be fully made,
and great loss wholly disproportionate to the injury occasioned by
the breach of the contract would otherwise result to the lessee
negligently but not fraudulently in default.''

Mary A. Edgell, the owner of a tract of land in Pleasants
County, made an oil and gas lease thereon which lease became
vested in the South Penn Oil Company and the Victor Oil & Gas
Company. The lease was made in consideration of $500.00 paid,

and the lessor to have $300.00 per year in semi-annual payments for the use of the gas from the well already drilled on the lands, and also one-eighth of the oil produced; and upon a compromise of matters in dispute between the lessor and lessees, an agreement was made containing the following stipulations:

"And it is further agreed as a part of the consideration of this agreement and compromise that the said Mary A. Edgell, her heirs or assigns, shall have the right to connect a service line with the gas line of the first parties, near said gas well, and at her own cost and expense lay a service line from said well connecting to the dwelling house occupied by her on said land, and have the use of the gas from said well for domestic purposes in such dwelling house free of charge so long as the first parties, or those holding under them, use or utilize the gas from said well. Such connections and service line, and all fixtures, shall be made, placed and kept in repair at the expense of said Mary A. Edgell, at her risk; it being understood by the second parties that the pressure of gas from said gas well is uneven and variable, and that the use thereof is dangerous, and that the first parties are not to be liable in any wise and on any account to the second parties, or to the said Mary A. Edgell, or those holding under her, for any injury she or they may receive or any damage which she or they may sustain by reason of her so connecting her said service line with the gas line or said well, the said parties, or Mary A. Edgell, taking all risks; and if from any cause the gas from the said gas well be not used or utilized, then said second parties are to have gas for domestic use free of cost as aforesaid, until said well is abandoned, and should said well be abandoned and there be other well or wells thereafter drilled by said first parties or their assigns, then said second parties are to have gas from said well or wells as aforesaid; and if the said first parties fail or refuse to keep and perform any of the covenants or obligations that they have agreed to or undertaken in the original lease or in the compromise, then and in that event the lease and this compromise contract is at an end as fully and completely as if the lease and compromise had never been made and entered into."

The officers and agents of the South Penn Oil Company, losing sight of this part of the lease which was contained in a compromise agreement, endeavored to compel Mrs. Edgel to sign a new contract of release of risk of damage, and to pay for the gas used by her. She refused to do so, and the lessees disconnected her service pipe, and deprived her of the use of the gas, partly, as they claimed, because she was wasting and misusing the gas, but principally because they were not aware of the foregoing stipulation as belonging to their lease. Mrs. Edgell made application to the Companies to be allowed to re-connect the pipe and use the gas. This they refused. Thereupon Mrs. Edgell declared a forfeiture of the whole contract and seized possession of the property, including the gas and oil well, and all the company's machinery and fixtures used in connection with the well. The lessees then filed their bill in the Circuit Court of Pleasants County for an enforcement of their lease, and for relief from the forfeiture thereof. Mrs. Edgell answered the bill, contested the right to the relief prayed for, and moved to dissolve the injunction awarded against her by the Circuit Court. This motion the court overruled, and Mrs. Edgell appealed. The Court of Appeals affirmed the Circuit Court. The Court cited, upon the question of jurisdiction in equity:

Bettman v. *Harness,* 42 W. Va. 433; 26 S. E. 271.
Eclipse Oil Co. v. *South Penn Oil Co.,* 47 W. Va. 84; 34 S. E. 923.

Sec. 20.—In *Westmoreland Natural Gas Co.,* v. *DeWitt,* 130 Pa. 235; 18 Atl. 724; 5 L. R. A. 731, (November 11, 1889.) The syllabus is as follows:

"1. Under a lease of land for the sole purpose of drilling and operating for oil and gas, the lessees right in the surface of the land is in the nature of an easement of entry and examination, with a right of possession arising where the particular place of operation is selected, and the easement of ingress, egress, storage, transportation, etc., during the continuance of operations.

2. The real subject of possession to which the lessee is entitled, is the oil or gas contained in or obtainable through the land; these are minerals feræ naturæ, and are part of the land and belong to its owner only so long as they are in it and under his control; the lessee, when he has drilled a gas well, and controls t e gas produced thereby, is in possession of all the gas within the land.

"3. The fact that the gas from such well is not kept flowing into the pipelines of the lessee, but is shut in the well as a reserve for use in emergencies, does not affect the possssion of it by the lessee when he is in control thereof by means of a connection between the well and his pipeline, so arranged that he can have the gas flow into the line at any time.

4. That the lessor, claiming a forfeiture of the lease, ordered the lessee's agent, who was measuring the pressure of the well off the premises, and the agent withdrew, or, that in consequence of a like order agents of the lessee who were on the land to locate a second well, withdrew without doing so, is no evidence of an ouster of the lessee from his possession.

5. Where the lessee is thus in possession of the gas underlying the premises, equity has jurisdiction to restrain the lessor from drilling on the leasehold, the rights granted to the lessee being necessarily exclusive, and the damage to arise from the threatened waste, being entirely incapable of measurement at law, even if not irreparable.

6. When the premises embraced in an oil and gas lease are described as 'all that certain tract of land,' etc., a clause therein providing that no well shall be drilled within a limited area, is neither an exception nor a reservation, but simply a limitaton upon the privilege of drilling granted to the lessee, confining his drilling without the area specified.

7. A clause in a lease providing for a forfeiture thereof, in the event of a default by the lessee in the performance of his covenants, is not self operating, so as to make the forfeiture take place, ipso facto, upon the occurrence of the default; but being for the benefit of the lessor, it rests with him to enforce or waive it.

8. Forfeitures are to be construed strictly; and when a lease provides that it shall become forfeited, if any of the payments provided for are not made, a whole payment is meant, not a balance on a running account, wherefore, if a part of a payment be accepted before it is due, no forfeiture is incurred by a failure to pay the remainder in the time specified."

On May 31, 1887, the Westmoreland and Cambria Natural Gas Company filed a bill in equity against Ira DeWitt, John H. Brown and others, averring that the defendant, John H. Brown, being the owner of a certain tract of land in the bill described, demised the same to J. M. Guffey & Company, on December 7, 1885, for the sole and only purpose of drilling and operating for petroleum oil and gas; that this lease was afterwards duly assigned to the plaintiff, and plaintiff entered upon possession and enjoyment of its estate in said land, drilled a gas well thereon, and, relying upon the supply of gas to be obtained from said well, and others in the vicinity, had expended large sums in laying pipelines for its transportation, to engage in the business of supplying natural gas to the public; that said Brown, alleging the forfeiture of said lease by reason of the non-payment of a small sum of money, had made a second lease

of said lands to the defendant, DeWitt, who, with the assistance of
other defendants, was about to drill a gas well on the premises;
That such well could be drilled and gas obtained in about forty
days, and that defendants thereby could commit enormous waste
upon the estate of the plaintiff and do irreparable damage to its
property and business, long before final hearing; praying for an
injunction to restrain the defendants from drilling such a well or
in any way committing waste upon the plaintiff's estate, and for
general relief. The lease from Brown to J. M. Guffey & Company
was, as to the material parts thereof, as follows:

"This agreement, made this 7th day of December, 1885,
* * * * * Witnesseth that the party of the first part (J. H. Brown)
in consideration of the stipulations, rents and covenants hereinafter contained on the part of the said party of the second part,
(J. M. Guffey & Co.) his executors, administrators and assigns,
to be paid, kept and performed, hath granted, demised, and let
unto the said party of the second part, his executors, administrators and assigns, for. the sole and only purpose of drilling and
operating wells, and storing, transporting and conveying petroleum oil or gas through, over, and from it, all that certain tract
of land * * * * * * *; No wells to be drilled within three hundred
yards of the brick or stone building belonging to J. H. Brown. To
have and to hold the said premises for the said purpose only, unto
the party of the second part, his executors, administrators, and
assigns, for, during, and until the full term of twenty years, next
ensuing, the day and year above written; * * * * * * It is further
agreed, that if gas is obtained in sufficient quantities and utilized,
the consideration in full to the party of the first part shall be Five
Hundred Dollars, for each and every well drilled on the premises
herein described, per annum, payable quarterly in advance from
completion of each and every well drilled and utilized * * * * * * *
The said party of the first part to fully use and enjoy the said
premises for the purpose of tillage, except such parts as shall be
necessary for said operating purposes * * * * * * Operations
on the above described premises shall be commenced, and one well
completed, within three months from the date hereof; and in case
of failure to complete one well within such time, the party of the
second part hereby agrees to pay to the party of the first part
for such delay the sum of one hundred and twenty-five dollars,
($125.00) every three months from the date of this agreement,
payable to J. H. Brown; and the party of the first part hereby
agrees to accept such sum as full consideration and payment for
such delay until one well shall be completed; and a failure to complete one well, or to make any of such payments within such time,
and at such place as above mentioned, renders this lease null and

void, and to remain without effect between the parties hereto. It is further agreed, that a second well shall be completed within fifteen months after the completion of the first well. It is further agreed, that if any of the within payments remain unpaid thirty days, then this lease to be null and void * * * * * It is understood by and between the parties to this agreement, that all conditions between the parties hereto shall extend to their heirs, executors and assigns.''

Upon the filing of the bill, a preliminary injunction was granted, and by a subsequent order the injunction was continued until final hearing. The defendants answered the bill, denying that the plaintiff had expended large sums in laying lines for the transportation of gas from the premises leased to J. M. Guffey & Company; that the gas from said premises was necessary to the plaintiff's business, or that its loss would result in irreparable injury; and averring that the lease was forfeited by reason of the plaintiff's default in making the payments therein mentioned; that the plaintiffs had no claim or title to, or rights in, the land within a radius of 300 yards from the buildings of the lessor, and the well proposed to be drilled by the defendants was located within the limits of the said radius; praying that the injunction be dissolved, and the defendants dismissed, etc.

The cause was referred to a Master who filed a report of findings of fact, substantially as follows:

1.—On and prior to December 7, 1885, John H. Brown named as defendant, was the owner in fee of a tract of land in Westmoreland County, adjoining lands of Klingensmith's heirs and others, containing 140 acres, more or less.

2.—On December 7, 1885, Brown executed to J. M. Guffey & Company the lease, which was duly recorded.

3.—J. M. Guffey & Company afterwards assigned the lease to the Westmoreland & Cambria Natural Gas Company, the plaintiff, which assignment was recorded.

4.—That complainant entered upon the premises, drilled and completed a gas well, on April 23, 1886. The well was of great capacity, showing a high pressure of gas. Complainants laid a pipeline from said well but had never to the date of the suit regularly used the gas from the well, the gas being shut in nearly all the time.

5.—J. M. Guffey & Company, or their assignee, the complainant, paid to John H. Brown, on account of the lease, on December 8, 1885, $250.00 and on June 22, 1886, $250.00.

6.—During several months prior to the filing of the bill from January 7, 1887, John H. Brown, claiming a forfeiture of the lease, had taken possession of the premises.

7.—On March 17, 1887, John H. Brown filed a bill in equity in the Court of Common Pleas of Westmoreland County, claiming that the lease had been forfeited and praying *inter alia* the court to order and decree the lease to be null and void. On June 23, 1887, Brown discontinued this action.

8.—On May 10, 1887, Brown leased the tract of land for gas purposes to Ira DeWitt, one of the defendants.

9.—DeWitt under his lease entered upon the land, and with the assistance of the other defendants, collected thereon lumber and other necessary material, and began the erection of a derrick for the purpose of drilling a gas well within 300 yards of the stone building belonging to Brown, and so continued until restrained by the injunction.

10—The tract of land described in the lease was situated wholly within the Grapeville Natural Gas belt, and had become very valuable as natural gas territory. The bill and answer and the evidence in the cause disclosed an earnest contest between complainant and respondents as to who had the legal right to the property described in the lease. The foregoing facts were not disputed in the answer, the pleadings, or the evidence.

The Master, upon the facts concluded that the defendants had taken possession exclusively of the leasehold premises, and reported his conclusions of law that the bill of complaint should be dismissed, and the injunction dissolved. Exceptions were taken to the report of the Master, and the Court of Common Pleas sustained the findings, and entered a decree dismissing the bill, and plaintiff appealed. The Supreme Court reversed the decree, directing the bill to be reinstated, and the injunction reinstated and made perpetual, and remanded the cause to execute the decree.

The court held the lessee in possession of the gas by reason of connecting its gas main with the well, notwithstanding the gas was shut in; disproving physical abandonment of the premises. The lease provided that operations on the premises should be commenced and one well completed within three months from the date thereof; and in case of failure to complete one well within such time the lessee to pay lessor for delay $125.00 every three months from the date of the agreement. The court found that the well was completed on April 23, 1886; that a payment was made in June on account of rental amounting to $250.00; and that on October 23, 1886, a quarter's rent in advance was due, but that one-half of this installment had already been paid. The Court found that no forfeiture, by reason of the last payment of rental, could occur until the quarter beginning January 23, 1887, and that a week prior thereto lessee tendered the rent to lessor and it was refused. The lessor executed the lease to DeWitt, under which lease the declaration of forfeiture of the first lease was claimed to have been made, on May 10, 1887. The lease specifically provided that a forfeiture should not be incurred unless default in the payment of a rental should extend for a period of thirty days. The payment tendered for January 23, 1887, was for rent to April 23, 1887, but the thirty-day clause of the lease would extend the time to May 23, 1887. Upon these facts the court concluded that there had been neither a physical abandonment of the premises nor a failure to pay the rental under the terms of the lease; consequently there had been no forfeiture incurred.

Sec. 21.—In *Poe* v. *Ulrey,* 233 Ill. 56; 84 N. E. 46, analyzed under Chapted 14, syl. 8 is as follows:

"8. A lease of the gas and oil on certain lands provided that a test well should be completed on a certain block of leases, which included the land covered by the lease in question and adjoining the lands, by a certain date, and that the lessee should within twelve months from date of the lease drill a well to completion on the land covered thereby, and further, that in case no well was completed within twelve months the lessee to pay a certain annual rental, payable quarterly. Shortly after procuring the lease in question, and before the date specified therein a test well was drilled on adjoining land with the block of leases referred to, on which gas was found, but there being no market therefor, or pipe-line or other means of transportation to market, the well was shot, cased, tubed, packed and equipped with appliances used in gas wells to pipe gas to market, and was left in that condition, awaiting means of transportation. Another well was drilled on other adjoining land within the block, but abandoned on striking a flow of salt water, which destroyed the value of the well. The lessee failed to complete a well on the land covered by the lease within twelve months of the date of the lease, and upon such failure he exercised the option provided for in the lease for the payment, quarterly, of a specified yearly rental, and tendered the amount thereof to the lessor. *Held,* that the lessee did not fail to perform the conditions required by the lease to be performed on his part, so as to entitle the lessor to have the lease cancelled."

Sec. 22.—In *Indianapolis Nat. Gas Co.* v. *Wilhelm,* (Ind. App.) 86 N. E. 86 (Nov. 24, 1908) syls. 2-4-5 are as follows:

"2. An action for rentals under a gas lease providing that, if gas were found in sufficient quantities to market, and to be piped to such market, plaintiffs compensation should be a certain sum per well, allegations in the complaint that gas was found in sufficient quantities to be marketed, and to be piped to market, and that there were good markets within ten miles, and others further away, where the gas could have been delivered and sold at a profit to defendant, setting out facts which if proved, with the other material averments of the complaint, would entitle plaintiff to recover, and hence were not averments of mere opinions.

4. In an action for rentals under a gas lease, providing that if gas were found in sufficient quantities to market and to be piped to market, plaintiff should receive a certain sum per well, a charge that under the lease gas is found in sufficient quantities to market and to be piped to market, whenever gas is found or exists in any wells drilled on the premises in such quantities that, taking into consideration the opportunity to sell it, and the costs and expenses attendant thereon, it could have been reasonably sold at a profit to the lessee, was not objectionable as leaving out of consideration the rental required to be paid if the gas were marketed.

5. In an action for rentals under a gas lease giving the lessor a certain sum per well if gas were produced in sufficient quantities to make it marketable, where the wells were already producing oil in marketable quantities, the original cost of drilling the wells was not to be considered in determining whether the gas produced could be profitably marketed; but the only expense chargeable to the case would be that of operating and marketing it, including the rental therefor."

Jane Wilhelm instituted an action in the Circuit Court of Grant County, Indiana, against the Indianapolis Natural Gas & Oil Company to recover rentals for gas under the terms of a lease between the parties, for a period of six months for one of the wells, and for a period of one year for each of four other wells. The lease contained the following provision:

"That said party of the second part, in consideration of said grant and demise, agree to give to party of the first part the full equal ⅛ of all the petroleum oil obtained or produced on the premises herein leased and to deliver the same in tanks or pipelines to the credit of the party of the first part. It is further agreed that if gas is found in sufficient quantities to market the same to be piped away from the premises to such market, the consideration in full to party of the first part shall be $200.00 per annum for each and every gas well drilled on the above described land."

Issues were joined and trial had before a jury which returned a verdict for plaintiff for $825.00, and judgment was rendered on the verdict. Defendant appealed, assigning three errors, (1) that the complaint did not state facts sufficient to constitute a cause of action; (2) that the court erred in overruling defendant's demurrer to the amended complaint; (3) that the court erred in overruling defendant's motion for a new trial.

The complaint alleged the drilling of each well and that gas was found in sufficient quantities during the year thereafter following to be marketed, and in sufficient quantities to be piped away from the premises to a market for such gas; that during all such time there were good markets for such gas in Upland, Matthews, Gas City, and Hartford, and in other places, all within ten miles of the well, and also at other places further away at which gas could then have been delivered, used and sold at a profit to the defendant. The reasons assigned for a new trial by appellant were, that the sixth instruction given by the court left out of consideration the original cost of the wells; and also the rental required to be paid each year. This instruction was as follows:

"Under the terms of the contract in suit, gas is found 'in sufficient quantities to market the same and to be piped away from the premises to such market' whenever gas is found or exists in any wells drilled on the premises in such quantities that, taking into consideration the opportunity to sell the same, the costs and expenses attendant thereon, and in connection with the operation of such well for oil, if you find the same to have been so operated the gas in such well could or might have been reasonably sold at a profit to the lessee.''

By the fourth instruction the court told the jury that in order to recover the plaintiff must, by her evidence, affirmatively answer the question: ''Did said wells, or either of them, produce gas in sufficient quantities to enable the defendant to pipe the same away to market therefor, and realize therefrom, and thereon a fair, reasonable and just profit, everything considered? The judgment of the Circuit Court was affirmed. The court cited on the question of wells producing oil and gas at the same time:

Manhattan Oil Co. v. *Carrell,* 164 Ind. 526; 73 N. E. 1084.

Sec. 23.—In *Roberts* v. *Fort Wayne Gas Co.,* 40 Ind. App. 528; 82 N. E. 558 (Nov. 20, 1907) the syllabus is as follows:

''Under a lease of land for the purpose only of drilling and operating for gas and oil, providing that the rental shall be 1-6 of the oil, and, 'if gas is found in sufficient quantities to market the same' the consideration to the lessor shall be $100.00 per annum in advance for each gas well drilled, and that operations shall be commenced and four wells completed within four months from the date, or all paid for after that time and that, if the lessee fail to perform such work or to pay the rental, he shall, in lieu thereof, and in full for damages for his default, pay annually during the term $100.00 for each of such wells—where the lessee seasonably drills four wells no rental is payable therefor, except for the time that they produce gas in marketable quantities, though they produce it in such quantities when first drilled, so that a complaint for gas rental must aver that the wells were so producing gas during the period for which rental is claimed.''

Joseph A. Roberts instituted an action against the Fort Wayne Gas Company and others for certain rentals claimed under a lease entered into between the plaintiff and the gas company. The complaint alleged that on June 19, 1902, the plaintiff leased to the gas company a tract of land in Grant County, Indiana for the pur-

pose of drilling and operating for natural gas and petroleum oil
for the term of ten years from date, setting out the lease, which
provided that if gas should be found in sufficient quantities to market, the consideration in full to lessor should be $100.00 per annum
in advance for each and every gas well drilled on the land; that operations on the land should be commenced and four wells completed
within four months from the date of the lease; and that in case
the lessee should fail to do and perform the work or pay the rental,
such failure should not forfeit lessee's right to hold the leased
premises during the term, but in lieu thereof in full payment for
all damages resulting to lessor by such default, lessee should pay
an annual rental for the premises during the term specified of
$100.00 for each well to be drilled; and that rental should become
due semi-annually, and be paid in advance on the first days of January and July and should be paid within ten days of the maturity
thereof; that the lessee, by giving ten days written notice, and
paying the rental due at the expiration of the ten days, and $5.00
additional, in full of all damages, and rentals due, might terminate
the lease. The complaint averred that defendants agreed to pay
lessor $100.00 per annum in advance for each gas well drilled on
the premises; that they agreed to drill at least four wells within
four months, and if not, all were to be paid for after October 1,
1902; and that these rentals were to be paid for the term of ten
years, semi-annually, provided said lease should not be re-conveyed and surrendered to lessor; that the lessee took possession
of the premises, drilled four gas wells before October 1, 1902, in
which gas was found in sufficient quantities to market the same,
and which gas was transported and marketed by lessee; that one
oil well was drilled on the premises; that lessee had never surrendered, cancelled, reconveyed, or released of record said lease,
but still held possession of the premises; that payment of the
rental had been demanded; that it was past due and unpaid; and
that there was due on rentals $450.00. Defendants demurred to
the complaint which demurrer the court sustained and entered
judgment of dismissal. Plaintiff appealed and the Appellate
Court affirmed the judgment. The Appellate court held that the
lease sued on was a lease to take the profit from the land, and when

the profit became exhausted the liability to pay the consideratio
therefor was abrogated, citing:

> Moon v. Pittsburg Plate Glass Co., 24 Ind. App. 34-39; 5
>   N. E. 108.
> Ridgley v. Connewago Iron Co., (C. C.) 53 Fed. 988.
> McConnel v. Lawrence Gas Co., 30 Pitts. L. J. 346.
> McKnight v. Mfrs. Nat. Gas Co., 146 Pa. 185; 23 Atl. 164
>   28 Am. St. Rep. 790.
> Williams v. Guffey, 178 Pa. 342; 35 Atl. 875.
> Ohio Oil Co. v. Lane, 59 Ohio St. 307; 52 N. E. 791.

LESSOR'S REMEDY.

Sec. 24.—By the terms of the ordinary oil and gas lease th
lessor does not reserve a portion of the gas in kind as he does th
oil. When gas is discovered in paying quantities, the lessees righ
to produce the same becomes a vested right.   The lease usuall
provides that in case gas is discovered in paying quantities lesso
shall receive as a consideration therefor a stipulated annual cas
rental for each well; and usually further provides that the lesse
shall pay this rental when the gas is sold or utilized off the prem
ises. Where the lessee discovers gas in paying quantities and doe
utilize the same off the premises, he becomes liable to the lesso
for the stipulated gas rental. The lessor, however, has no interes
in the gas when produced, but must look to the lessee for payment

> Summerville v. Apollo Gas Co., 207 Pa. 334; 56 Atl. 876.

Sec. 25.—In States where the courts hold the ordinary oil an
gas lease, before discovery of gas, to be a mere license, upon dis
covery by lessee of gas in paying quantities, the right to produc
and market it becomes a vested right subject to forfeiture fo
abandonment or failure to pay the rentals. Under leases so con
strued the lessee cannot, upon discovering gas in paying quanti
ties, shut the well in, claiming a vested right, and hold the lease i
this way, neither paying land rental nor gas rental. The remed
of the lessor under such circumstances, is to declare a forfeitur
for abandonment.

> Gadberry v. Ohio etc. N. Gas Co., 162 Ind. 9; 57 N. E. 259.
> Iams v. Gas Co., 194 Pa. 72; 45 Atl. 54.

Summerville v. *Apollo Gas Co.,* 207 Pa. 334; 56 Atl. 876 syl. 4.
Eastern Oil Co. v. *Coulehan,* 65 W. Va. 531; 64 S. E. 836.
McGraw Oil & Gas Co. v. *Kennedy,* 65 W. Va. 595; 64 S. E.
1027.

Sec. 26.—Upon discovery of gas in paying quantities, if the
lessee can market it at a profit and in this way enable lessor to
realize an income from his property he is bound to do so; and a
failure to so market the gas entitles the lessor to a recovery of the
rental that he would receive under the terms of the lease had lessee
marketed the gas; and lessor may recover from lessee the amount
to which he is thus entitled by an action of assumpsit.

Iams v. *Gas Co.,* 194 Pa. 72; 45 Atl. 54.
Indianapolis Nat. Gas. Co. v. *Wilhelm,* (Ind. App.); 86 N. E.
86.

Sec. 27.—Under the construction given to an oil and gas lease
whereby these minerals are granted, in place, to lessee, and under
a stipulation that if gas only is found lessee shall pay a fixed sum
per year for each well while the gas from the same is used off the
premises, although lessee may discover gas in paying quantities,
and although he could have marketed the gas without financial loss
lessor cannot recover in an action against the lessee the stipulated
gas rental covering the period during which lessee might have
marketed the gas.

  Ohio Oil Co. v. *Lane,* 59 Ohio St., 307; 52 N. E. 791.

Sec. 28.—Unless the lease provides that it shall be forfeited
for non-payment of gas rental, the lessor's remedy, where lessee
has discovered gas in paying quantities and marketed or utilized it
in such manner as under the provisions of the lease would entitle
lessor to receive the gas rental, lessor cannot declare a forfeiture
for failure to pay such rental. His remedy is an' action against
lessee for the recovery of the rentals.

Davis v. *Chautauqua Oil & G. Co.,* 78 Kan. 97; 96 Pac. 47.

Sec. 29.—A lessor in an oil and gas lease cannot in an action at
law upon the implied covenants of the lease recover damages

against the lessee who has drilled one paying gas well on the premises, for not putting down other wells to protect the territory against the effect of operating on adjoining lands. The duties imposed upon the lessee in a leasehold operated for gas cannot be measured by the same rule applied in the same manner in the case of a leasehold operated for oil. The drilling of the second or additional wells upon the leasehold premises might reduce the pressure of gas to such an extent as not only to make valueless the additional well or wells, but also destroy the value of the first well.

> *McKnight* v. *Manufacturers N. Gas Co.*, 146 Pa. 185; 23 Atl. 164, Syl. 2 and Opinion.

Sec. 30.—Where a lessee has entered and discovered gas in paying quantities he has a right to hold the lease where there is no market for the gas by paying to the lessor the gas rental beyond the term mentioned in the lease and the lessor cannot, in a suit in equity, cancel the lease either upon the grounds of abandonment or for failure to further develop the leased premises.

> *McGraw Oil & Gas Co.* v. *Kennedy*, 65 W. Va. 595; 64 S. E. 1027.
> *Summerville* v. *Apollo Gas Co.*, 207 Pa. 334; 56 Atl. 876.

Sec. 31.—Where a lessor has executed an oil and gas lease providing that lessee may at his option, by the payment of an annual rental, delay developments from year to year, the lessor, before he can declare a forfeiture of such lease must give notice to lessee of his intention so to do for a reasonable time so as to enable the lessee to develop the premises if he desires; a failure on the part of the lessee to make the explorations within a reasonable time after such notice will authorize the lessor to declare a forfeiture.

> *Ind. Nat. Gas & Oil Co.* v. *Lear*, 34 Ind. App. 61; 72 N. E. 283.
> *Consumers Gas Trust Co.* v. *Littler*, 162 Ind. 320; 70 N. E. 363.
> *Consumers Gas Trust Co.* v. *Chrystal Window Glass Co.*, 163 Ind. 190; 70 N. E. 366.
> *Consumers Gas Trust Co.* v. *Worth*, 163 Ind. 141; 71 N. E. 489.
> *Consumers Gas Trust Co.* v. *Ink*, 163 Ind. 174; 71 N. E. 477.
> See Forfeiture and Rental Clause, Lessor's Option, Chap. 12.

LESSEE'S REMEDY.

Sec. 32.—Where gas has been discovered lessee, acting in good faith, is the judge as to whether or not the gas is in paying quantities, and is entitled to hold the lease as long as the stipulated gas rental is paid.

> *McGraw Oil & Gas Co.* v. *Kennedy,* 65 W. Va. 595; 64 S. E. 1027.
> *Summerville* v. *Apollo Gas Co.,* 207 Pa. 334; 56 Atl. 876.
> *McKnight* v. *Manufacturers N. Gas Co.,* 146 Pa. 185; 23 Atl. 164.
> *Eastern Oil Co.* v. *Coulehan,* 65 W. Va. 531; 64 S. E. 836.

Sec. 33.—When lessee has discovered gas in paying quantities and can market the same at a profit, in order to entitle him to hold the lease he must either market the gas and in this way produce a revenue to the land owner, or he must pay the stipulated gas rental.

> *Iams* v. *Carnegie Gas Co.,* 194 Pa. 72; 45 Atl. 54.
> *Eastern Oil Co.* v. *Coulehan,* 65 W. Va. 531; 64 S. E. 836. Syl. 4.

Sec. 34.—When lessee has discovered gas in paying quantities he may, where there is no market for the gas, shut the well in and by the payment of the stipulated gas rental hold the lease without making further developments.

> *McGraw Oil & G. Co.* v. *Kennedy,* 65 W. Va. 595, 64 S. E. 1027.
> *McKnight* v. *Manufacturers Nat. Gas Co.,* 146 Pa. 185; 23 Atl 164.
> *Westmoreland Gas Co.* v. *DeWitt,* 130 Pa. 235; 18 Atl. 724.

Sec. 35.—When lessee has discovered gas in paying quantities he becomes vested with the right to produce the same, and where lessee pays or tenders the stipulated gas rental and lessor refuses payment and attempts to declare a forfeiture and re-possess him self of the premises, a court of equity will, at the suit of the lessee enjoin all interference by lessor with the lessee's vested rights under the lease.

> *Westmoreland N. Gas Co.* v. *DeWitt,* 130 Pa. 235; 18 Atl. 724.

Eastern Oil Co. v. *Coulehan,* 65 W. Va. 531; 64 S. E. 836.
South Penn Oil Co. v. *Edgell,* 48 W. Va. 348; 37 S. E. 596.
Sec. 36.—Where the lease provides that the lessee may at his

option, by the payment of a stipulated rental, delay developments from year to year, or from time to time, and where lessor has given notice to lessee of his intention to declare a forfeiture at the expiration of any year, or stipulated time, for which rental has been paid for such delay, where such notice has been given for a reasonable time lessee must, in order to hold the lease, enter and make the explorations within the time provided in the notice; otherwise lessor is entitled to declare a forfeiture.

Indiana Nat. Gas. & Oil Co. v. *Leer,* 34 Ind. App. 61; 72 N. E. 283.
Consumers Gas Trust Co. v. *Littler,* 162 Ind. 320; 70 N. E. 363.
Consumers Gas Trust Co. v. *Chrystal Window Glass Co.,* 163 Ind. 190; 70 N. E. 366.
Consumers Gas Trust Co. v. *Worth,* 163 Ind. 141; 71 N. E. 489.
Consumers Gas Trust Co. v. *Ink,* 163 Ind. 174; 71 N. E. 477.
See Forfeiture and Rental Clause, Lessee's Option, Chap. 13.

Sec. 37.—Where the lease provides that the lessor is to have free gas for domestic purposes, either in whole or part payment for the gas rights, lessee may furnish the gas either from wells drilled on the leased premises or from wells on other lands; while so furnishing gas for such purposes the lessee may hold the lease during the term.

Summerville v. *Apollo Gas Co.,* 207 Pa. 334; 56 Atl. 876.
Bellevue Oil & Gas Co. v. *Pennell,* 76 Kan. 785; 92 Pac. 1101.

Sec. 38.—Where lessee has discovered gas in paying quantities and has utilized it, and desires to terminate the lease he must give notice to the lessor before he enters upon another year of his term.

Double v. *Heat & Light Co.,* 172 Pa. 388; 33 Atl. 694.

Sec. 39.—Where suit is brought against lessee by a lessor for recovery of stipulated gas rentals, the lessor must allege in the declaration or complaint that the wells were producing gas in the quantities provided for by the lease during the time for which he seeks a recovery of rentals. The lessee may defeat the action by proof that the wells were not so producing during such time.

Roberts v. *Fort Wayne Gas Co.*, 40 Ind. App. 528; 82 N. E. 558.

CHAPTER 12.

FORFEITURE AND RENTAL CLAUSE—LESSOR'S OPTION.

Sec. 1.—Where an oil and gas lease provides for the payment of rental or commutation money for delay in explorations, and there is an express covenant to pay such rental or commutation, upon lessee's default in such payment the lessor has the option either to treat the lease as forfeited for such non-payment, or in the absence of a surrender clause based upon a sufficient consideration, and a surrender thereunder, he may waive the forfeiture and collect the commutation money during the term.-

Guffey v. *Hukill,* 34 W. Va. 49; 11 S. E. 754.
Schaupp v. *Hukill,* 34 W. Va. 375; 12 S. E. 501.
Hukill v. *Myers,* 36 W. Va. 639; 15 S. E. 151.
Roberts v. *Bettman,* 45 W. Va. 143; 30 S. E. 95.
Brown v. *Vandergrift,* 80 Pa. 142.
Munroe v. *Armstrong,* 96 Pa. 307.
Galey v. *Kellerman,* 123 Pa. 491; 16 Atl. 474.
Wills v. *Manufacturers N. Gas Co.,* 130 Pa. 222; 18 Atl. 721.
Thompson v. *Christy,* 138 Pa. 230; 20 Atl. 934.
Kennedy v. *Crawford,* 138 Pa. 561; 21 Atl. 19.
Springer v. *Citizens N. Gas Co.,* 145 Pa. 430; 22 Atl. 986.
Ray v. *Western Pennsylvania N. Gas Co.,* 138 Pa. 576; 20 Atl. 1065.
Henney v. *South Penn Oil Co.,* 52 W. Va. 192; 43 S. E. 147.
Cochran v. *Pew,* 159 Pa. 184; 28 Atl. 219.
Bartley v. *Phillips,* 165 Pa. 325; 30 Atl. 842.
Cortelyou v. *Barnsdall,* 236 Ill. 138; 86 N. E. 200.
Jones v. *Western Penna N. Gas Co..* 146 Pa. 204; 23 Atl. 386.
Liggitt v. *Shira.* 159 Pa. 350; 28 Atl. 218.
Bartley v. *Phillips,* 165 Pa. 325; 30 Atl. 842.

Wolf v. *Guffey*, 161 Pa. 276; 28 Atl. 1117.
Jackson v. *O'Hara*, 183 Pa. 233; 38 Atl. 624.
Ogden v. *Hatry*, 145 Pa. 640; 23 Atl. 334.
Phillips v. *Vandergrift*, 146 Pa. 357; 23 Atl. 347.
Matthews v. *Peoples N. Gas Co.*, 179 Pa. 165; 36 Atl. ·216.
New Dominion Oil & Gas Co. v. *Gaffney Oil Co.*, — Ky —;
       121 S. W. 699.
Puritan Oil Co. v. *Myers*, 39 Ind. App. 695; 80 N. E. 851.
Logansport and Wabash Valley Gas Co. v. *Null* 36 Ind. App.
       503; 76 N. E. 125.
Scott v. *Lafayette Gas Co.*, 42 Ind. App. 614; 86 N. E. 495.
Hancock v. *Diamond Plate Glass Co.*, 162 Ind. 146; 70 N. E.
       149.

Sec. 2.—The ordinary oil and gas lease is based either upon a nominal consideration or a bonus paid in advance. The lessee usually has a stipulated number of days within which to enter upon the premises and commence operations. The consideration or bonus, if valuable although nominal, is sufficient to sustain the lease and make it a valid contract for the period from its date to the time at which the lessee is required to enter upon the premises for explorations, which time is the rental period, and must not be confounded with the term of the lease. For the purpose of hastening developments, and in the interest of public policy which forbids unreasonably tying the hands of the lessor, a provision is inserted for the payment of rental or commutation at fixed periods as a consideration for delay within the term. Where the lease contains an express covenant or promise to pay to the landowner the stipulated rental or commutation money, in default of which payment the lease shall become void, the landowner has the option either to declare forfeiture or waive it and collect the stipulated rental.

For the purpose of enabling the lessee to surrender the lease to lessor and be relieved of rentals accruing after the date thereof. a surrender clause is usually inserted in the modern oil and gas lease, whereby, where the lease is made for a valuable consideration, lessee may surrender and relieve himself of the obligation to pay rentals or commutation money thereafter accruing.

Sec. 3.—The forfeiture clause is in the interest, not only of the landowner, but of public policy. He can use this clause of his

lease as a means by which he can either compel the lessee to pay
the stipulated commutation money for delay (by which of course he
necessarily waives forfeiture), or if the lessee manifest a disposition to delay developments either for speculative purposes or to
await developments on other territory situated so as to indicate a
probability of the lease being valuable, upon default on the part of
the lessee in the payment of the commutation money he may declare
a forfeiture and thereby be enabled to secure either a bonus, a higher rental for delay in developments, or developments—the real object of all oil and gas leases. The landowner, however, cannot while
accepting rentals for delay, take an undue or unconscienable advantage of the lessee for a mere technical default and for such
default attempt a forfeiture. Such acts will be subject to control
by a court of equity. Where a landowner has accepted payments
of rental or commutation money from time to time for delay and
has not required lessee to strictly conform to the provisions of the
lease in respect to payment of rental, in case he desires to forfeit
for a failure to meet promptly these stipulated payments at their
maturity equity requires that reasonable notice be given to the
lessee of lessor's intention to demand strict payment or forfeiture.
Any course of dealings that leads the lessee to believe that the lessor will not declare a forfeiture for failure promptly to pay the
rental, affords a reasonable excuse to the lessee for not paying
promptly; and if lessor attempts to declare a forfeiture under
such circumstances without reasonable notice to the lessee of his
intention so to do equity will relieve against such forfeiture. In
the absence, however, of dealings between the lessor and lessee
which would lead lessee to the conclusion that prompt payments
would not be required, lessor has a right, upon default, to declare
a forfeiture.

Sec. 4.—The object of all oil and gas leases and the true consideration therefor being prospective explorations, a strict compliance on the part of the lessee with the terms and conditions of
the lease will be required; and the lessor, in the absence of conduct
which may have lulled the lessee into a feeling of security and as a
result induced or led him into the belief that he would not be required to meet the rentals promptly at maturity has the right when-

ever default has been made by the lessee in the payment of the
rental or commutation money to immediately declare a forfeiture
and end the lease. The development of the property must always
be considered as the real object in view in the execution of the oil
and gas lease. The forfeiture clause will always be construed as
a means to' effect the end in view—development. A landowner
may be warranted by surrounding circumstances and conditions
in accepting these payments of rental or commutation money, thus
securing an income from the property without any outlay or expense to himself; but where developments upon other lands indicate a probability of oil or gas being found in paying quantities
the landowners interest can only be protected and preserved by
explorations; and these explorations should be made so as to an-
ticipate probable drainage by wells on adjacent territory, as well
as to obtain a practical test of the lessor's property, while the inducement is present, that is the probability of his land proving
valuable for oil. When surrounding circumstances and conditions
indicate the probability of discovery of oil or gas, the duty to develop at once devolves upon the lessee and the right of the lessor
to declare a forfeiture for failure either to pay the stipulated commutation money for delay or explore is unquestionable. This right
will be upheld in all cases where the lessee is in default, to which default the lessor has not contributed or consented.

Sec. 5.—In *Guffey* v. *Hukill*, 34 W. Va. 49; 11 S. E. 754 (June
10, 1890) syl. 2 is as follows:

"A lease for years for drilling for petroleum oil and gas contained the following provision: 'The parties of the second part
covenant to commence operations for said purpose within nine
months from and after the executions of this lease, or to thereafter pay to the party of the first part one dollar and thirty-three
and a third cents per month, until work is commenced, the money
to be deposited in the hands of John Kennedy for.each and every
month. And a failure on the part of said second parties to comply
with either one or the other of the foregoing conditions shall
work an absolute forfeiture of this lease',—and there is no covenant for re-entry, and there is failure to commence operations
and to pay money in lieu thereof and the lessor leases to. another
person, *Held*, the first lease is thus avoided and the second lease
is good against it, as the execution of the second lease is a sufficient
declaration of forfeiture without demand and re-entry."

Wise made a lease to Hays for oil and gas purposes on June 30, 1886, for a tract of 30 acres of land for the term of twenty years. This lease, on January 10, 1889, was assigned to Hukill. On July 11, 1888, Wise made a second lease of said thirty acres to Rezin Calvert for twenty years, and Calvert assigned to Ida C. and Vinney Calvert on March 16, 1889, and they assigned to Guffey and Murphy on May 8, 1889. Plaintiffs claimed under this lease. The first lease contained the clause quoted in the syl-labus. About May 1, 1889, Hukill began boring for oil under the lease to Hays of June 30, 1886, and continued to work till November, 1889, when he discovered oil in two wells. No rent was paid under the provisions of the lease until about January 4, 1889, when Hays paid to Wise. In October, 1888 Kennedy offered to pay Wise this rent, but he declined to receive it, but did afterwards receive the rent from Hays. All the rent due Wise under the Hays lease was paid to him. Hukill entered into possession of the premises under the Hays lease and began drilling for oil with the knowledge and consent of Wise. No demand was ever made by Wise on Hays for the rent, except that he called once on Kennedy for it. Judge Brannon delivering the opinion, at page 60, said:

"The payment of the rent or commutation money to Wise and his consent to Hukill's taking possession under the Hays lease could have no effect to waive the forfeiture, because such payment and taking possession occurred after the execution by Wise to Calvert of the second lease, which operated as a declaration of forfeiture, and to divest all estate under the Hays lease and invest it in Calvert; and the after act of payment did not destroy Calvert's right."

Hukill, being in possession of the premises under the first lease, Guffey instituted an action of unlawful entry and detainer and obtained judgment for the possession of the property, from which judgment a writ of error was prosecuted to the Court of Appeals, and that court, affimed the judgment of the court below.

Sec. 6.—In *Schaupp* v. *Hukill*, 34 W. Va., 375; 12 S. E. 501 (Dec. 6, 1890), the syllabus is as follows:

"1. F. having given one 'oil lease' to H. afterwards gives another 'oil lease' of the same property to S. on which second lease was endorsed before execution: 'This lease is to be taken subject to the E. M. Hukill lease.' *Held*, the second lease is not an unequivocal declaration of forfeiture of the first lease.

2. The first lease having by mistake been handed back to the lessor to be cancelled, *held*, the above endorsement saves to H. his right, if any, to have such mistake corrected.''

A. M. Fox, on December 6, 1885, was the owner of a tract of 450 acres of land, subject to the life estate of Nancy Fox, widow of Martin Fox, deceased, in 303¾ acres part thereof. On said date A. M. Fox executed an oil lease of said land to E. M. Hukill & Company for the term of 24 years for the sole and only purpose of drilling for, developing or producing petroleum or carbon oil. The lessees were to commence operations within nine months or thereafter pay Fox Eighteen Dollars per month until work should be commenced. A failure to do one or the other was to work an absolute forfeiture. On November 15, 1886, Hukill paid Fox $54.00 which Fox receipted for as in full of rental to November 6, 1886. On March 7, 1888, E. M. Hukill, by mistake, sent this lease back to Fox, who by a writing under seal accepted its return and agreed that the same might be cancelled as of December 6, 1886. This lease thus remained in the hands of Fox from March 7, 1888, until May 20, 1889, when it was returned to Hukill as having been given up by mistake. During this time the lessees did not commence operations and paid no rent. While Fox held the lease thus given up, he was advised that the mere handing back of the lease, without any writing from Hukill, was not sufficient to put an end to it. On May 20, 1889, C. A. Schaupp applied to Fox for an oil lease of the same land on which he (Fox) was then living and had been living during all this time. Fox showed Schaupp the Hukill lease, told him that it had been returned to him through Garrard, Hukill's agent, and that he had signed and receipted for it as above stated. Fox at length agreed to give Schaupp a lease for the term of twenty years, subject to the E. M. Hukill lease. This lease was executed by Fox and wife and by Schaupp, in duplicate, with the following endorsement written by Schaupp before execution and made and intended to be made a part of the instrument; "This lease is to be taken subject to the E. M. Hukill lease." There was but one Hukill lease—the lease made by Fox to E. M. Hukill &

Company, on November 6, 1885. On the next day after the execution of the Schaupp lease, May 3, 1889, Fox met E. M. Hukill for the first time, the matter up to that time having been carried on by the Hukills through Garrard, the agent. E. M. Hukill saw the Schaupp lease, explained to Fox how his (Hukill's) lease had been sent back to be given up by mistake arising from confusion of names, and apparently convinced Fox that it was done by mistake, as Fox then handed back to Hukill his lease. Hukill paid Fox on May 20, 1885, $558.00 for which Fox receipted as in full for rental on lease to June 6, 1889. On September 16, 1889, Fox gave Hukill a receipt for $54.00 in full of rental on lease to September 6, 1889, and agreed to thereafter accept his rental quarterly. On December 3, 1889, Fox gave Hukill a receipt for $54.00 for rent to December 6, 1889. On November 15, 1889, George P. Hukill; the other part owner, assigned to E. M. Hukill all his interest in various leases, including the Fox lease. Fox gave Hukill possession and he commenced operations on the land about October 1, 1889. Schaupp attempted to make the monthly payments as they fell due on his lease up to some time in the early part of November, 1889, when he also attempted to commence operations on the land but was stopped by Hukill who was then in possession. Fox constantly refused to receive any money tendered by Schaupp or to in any manner recognize him as his tenant, or his lease as of any validity after he had returned to Hukill his lease. On May 8, 1890, C. A. Schaupp and others as plaintiffs, instituted a suit in unlawful entry and detainer in the Circuit Court of Monongalia County against Edwin M. Hukill and others, defendants, to recover from Hukill possession, for the purpose of drilling and operating for petroleum, of the tract of land which Andrew M. Fox had conveyed by the two leases aforesaid. On April 15, 1900, Nancy Fox, the widow of Martin Fox, who was the life tenant mentioned above, in the 303¾ acres, granted to Schaupp and others the exclusive right to drill and operate thereon for oil and gas, the royalties to be paid to A. M. Fox. On June 17, 1890, Nancy Fox executed to Hukill an instrument under seal, giving her consent and license to Hukill to enter upon the 303¾ acres to develop the same for oil and pay the royalties to A. M. Fox. A demurrer was interposed by the defendants in the Circuit Court to the plaintiff's evidence disclosing the foregoing facts, and the jury returned a conditional verdict. The Circuit Court sustained the plaintiff's contention and rendered judgment in his favor for possession of the property, from which judgment the defendants below took a writ of error to the Supreme Court of Appeals. That court reversed the Circuit Court. Judge Holt, who delivered the opinion, at page 382, said:

"The clause of forfeiture in Fox's lease to Hukill was put there for the benefit of Fox, the landlord, and it was for him to manifest in some unequivocal way his purpose to avail himself thereof and terminate the tenancy."

Sec. 7.—In *Hukill* v. *Myers,* 36 W. Va. 639; 15 S. E. 151 (April 23, 1892), the syllabus is as follows:

"1.   Where in an oil lease there is a clause of forfeiture for non-payment of rental, but the lessor consents that it need not be paid at the time when due, and indulges the lessee and acquiesces in his failure to pay, there is no forfeiture for non-payment.

2.   In case of such a lease, if the lessor by his conduct clearly indicates that payment will not be demanded when due, and thus lulls the lessee into a feeling of security, and throws him off his guard, and because of this he does not make payments when due, the landlord cannot suddenly, without demand or notice, declare a forfeiture, and there is no forfeiture which equity would recognize, and if there is in such case technically a forfeiture at law, equity would relieve against it.

3.   If, after such rental has accrued, and it is not paid, whereby a forfeiture exists, the lessor with knowledge thereof receives the rentals accruing after forfeiture, he waives and cannot enforce the forfeiture."

On October 30, 1885, David Myers leased to E. M. Hukill and George P. Hukill for the term of twenty years a tract of 300 acres of land in Monongalia County, for oil purposes. The lease contained a covenant as follows:

"To commence operations for said purpose within one year from and after the execution of this lease or to thereafter pay to the said party of the first part twelve dollars per month until the work is commenced; and a failure of the party of the second part to comply with one or the other of the foregoing conditions shall work an absolute forfeiture of this lease."

Hukill did not commence operations within the year. He paid one months rental, as required by the lease, and paid other money for rentals but not within the time required by the lease, but which money was accepted by Myers. On July 27, 1889, on the theory that by reason of non-payment the lease to Hukill was forfeited under its provisions Myers made a second lease of the same land to J. C. Smith and H. S. Akins and they took possession of the lands under their lease. On July 29, 1889, E. M. Hukill, who had become the sole owner of the lease by assignment by George P. Hukill of his interest therein, attempted to begin operations but was driven off the premises and prevented from taking possession by Smith and Akins. Thereupon E. M. Hukill instituted suit in the Circuit Court of Monongalia County against Smith, Akin and Meyers to enjoin Smith and Akin from operating for oil on said premises, to compel specific performance of the lease to him, and to obtain possession of the premises by the award of a writ of possession, which suit was dismissed and from the decree of dismissal Hukill appealed to the Court of Appeals, and that court reversed the Circuit Court. Judge Brannon, who delivered the opinion of the court, at pages 643-4 said:

"After Myers had thus by his conduct clearly manifested a dispensation or waiver of the strict letter of the lease, without any demand on Hukill for the pittance of twelve dollars due under the letter of the lease on the 30th of June, 1889, if we ignore the said agreement to accept rent quarterly, without any notice to Hukill of dissatisfaction or of an intent to insist on the letter of the lease, and if we recognize said agreement more than a month before the rent for the quarter, whether we count from the close of a year from the date of the lease, from the 30th of November, or 30th May, the dates specified in the receipts for the first payment of twelve dollars, and the last payment of $60.00 as dates to which such payment satisfied the rentals, Myers took the inequitable step of making the second lease. At that date no forfeiture existed and Myers had no title to confer by this second lease."

Sec. 8.—In *Roberts* v. *Bettman*, 45 W. Va. 143; 30 S. E. 95 (April 22, 1898), the first point of the syllabus is as follows:

"1. A lease for oil and gas contemplates that the lessee has two years in which to bore a well, and provides 'that the party of the second part shall pay to the party of the first part $100

per month in advance, until a well is completed, from the date of
this lease, and a failure to complete such well, or to pay said rental
when due, or within ten days thereafter, shall render this lease
null and void, and can only be renewed by mutual consent, and no
right of action shall, after such failure, accrue to either party
on account of such breach of any covenant herein contained.
* * * * * It is further agreed that the second party shall have
the right at any time to surrender this lease to party of the first
part, and thereafter be fully discharged.' The lessee bored no
well but holds the lease a number of months, and then surrenders
it. *Held*, that the forfeiture provisions are for the lessors benefit,
and he can avail himself of them to declare a forfeiture for non-
payment of rental or not, as he chooses, and, if he does not, can
recover rental until the surrender of the lease. The lessee's mere
failure to pay does not release him from obligation to pay. There
was tacit consent to renew.''

Roberts made two leases of two tracts of land to Boyle for oil
and gas purposes, which leases contained the rental, forfeiture
and surrender clause quoted in the first point of the syllabus. These
leases were assigned by Boyle to M. A. and D. Bettman as partners. No well was drilled under the leases. For some time the
rental was paid, and then there was a failure to pay for about nine
months. For several months after the first failure to pay the
monthly rentals the Bettmans made no surrender of the lease, but
finally did so. Roberts afterwards brought an action of covenant
upon the leases for the purpose of recovering the unpaid monthly
rentals. A recovery was had for the rentals accruing up to the
date of surrender. From this judgment Bettmans took a writ of
error to the Court of Appeals, which court affirmed the court
below. In the opinion the following cases are cited in support of
the conclusions reached:

Galey v. *Kellerman*, 123 Pa. 491; 16 Atl. 474.
Wills v. *Gas Co.*, 130 Pa. 222; 18 Atl. 721.
Leatherman v. *Oliver*, 151 Pa. 646; 25 Atl. 309.
Phillips v. *Vendergrift*, 146 Pa. 357; 23 Atl. 347.
McMillan v. *Phila. Co.*, 159 Pa. 142; 28 Atl. 220.
Cochran v. *Pew*, 159 Pa. 184; 28 Atl. 219.
Conger v. *Transportation Co.*, 165 Pa. 561; 30 Atl. 1038.

Sec. 9.—In *Brown* v. *Vandergrift*, 80 Pa. 142; (Nov. 20, 1875),
syls. 1-2 are as follows:

"1. Brady leased to Lambing a lot of land, to have the sole right to bore for oil, etc., for twenty years, Lambing to commence operations in 60 days and continue with due diligence; if he should cease operations twenty days at any one time, Brady might resume possession. There were other covenants in the lease, and it was then stipulated that a failure of Lambing to comply with any one of the conditions should work a forfeiture, and Brady might enter and dispose of the premises as if the lease had not been made. It was further agreed that if Lambing did not commence operations at the time specified, he should pay Brady Thirty Dollars per month until he should commence; *Held,* that the covenant of forfeiture was modified, not abrogated by the clause for payment of rent.

2. Lambing did not commence operation; he paid four months rent; he omitted payment for eleven months, and then tendered the amount for that time; *held,* that the lessor might refuse the tender and insist on the forfeiture."

Owen Brady, on April 20, 1872, being the owner of a tract of 70 acres of land in Butler County, Pennsylvania, made an oil and gas lease for thirty acres thereof to James M. Lambing. Brady received as a consideration or bonus $225.00. The lease was for a term of twenty years. The lessee covenanted to commence operations within 60 days, and to continue with due diligence to prosecute the same to success or abandonment. In case Lambing should cease operations for twenty days at any one time then the lease was to be null and void, and Brady had the right to resume possession. The lease contained the following forfeiture clause:

"It is moreover expressly agreed by and between the parties to this instrument that a failure of (Lambing) to comply with any one of the reservations, conditions or agreements contained in the within instrument, which by its terms are to be done, kept or performed by (Lambing), shall work a forfeiture of the rights hereby granted; and that (Brady) may enter upon said ground and dispose of the same as if this lease had not been made. And further agreed, that should (Lambing) not commence operations at the time specified (he) agrees to pay to (Brady) the sum of $30.00 per month, for each and every month until such time as drilling may be commenced."

Lambing did not commence operations in accordance with the terms of the lease. In September, 1872, Brady sued Lambing for three months rent and recovered judgment for $90.00, which

Lambing paid. In January, 1873, Lambing paid Brady $30.00 more. He made no further payments on account of the rent, nor did he commence operations for oil on the premises, and in a few months afterwards the plaintiff Brown and others became vested with whatever interest Lambing had in the lease. On May 6, 1873, Brady entered into an agreement with Vandergrift and others, by which he agreed to convey to them the whole 70 acres, "free and clear of all encumbrances, excepting 30 acres leased to Lambing." On August 30, 1873, one of the assignees of Lambing tendered to one of the purchasers from Brady $330.00 for eleven months rent under the lease of February 20, 1872. The tender was refused. On July 31, 1874, James E. Brown and others instituted in the Court of Common Pleas of Butler County, an action of ejectment against J. J. Vandergrift and others, for the 30 acres of land, being the land leased by Brady to Lambing and claimed by Brown and others, and being the same land purchased by Vandergrift and others on May 6, 1873, from Brady. Judgment was rendered by the Court of Common Pleas in favor of the defendant, from which judgment Brown and others appealed to the Supreme Court of Pennsylvania, and that court affirmed the judgment of the Court of Common Pleas. Judge Agnew, delivering the opinion of the court, at page 148, said:

"These lease were not valuable, except by means of development, unlike the ordinary terms for the cultivation of the soil, or for the removal of fixed minerals. A forfeiture for non-development or delay, therefore cut off no valuable rights of property, while it was essential for the protection of private and public interest in relation to the use and alienation of property. In the present case the lease was modified by adding, immediately after the clause of forfeiture, a stipulation that should the lessee not commence operations at the time specified, he should pay to the landlord Thirty Dollars for each and every month until such time as drilling should be commenced. The lessee having paid for three months delay, suffered eleven months to elapse without payment or tender, then tendered the whole sum, which the landlord declined to accept, and insisted on the forfeiture, he, in the meantime, having made a new lease to a party who went into possession. The learned judge below held, that the lease was forfeited by the omission to pay the monthly sum, the lessee having done nothing in performance of his covenant. We cannot pronounce this to be an error in view of the nature of the lease, the true intention of the clause of forfeiture, and the want of any, valuable interest acquired by the lessee by performance.''

The concluding paragraph of the opinion is as follows:

"It is true as general statement that equity abhors a forfeiture, but this is when it works a loss and is contrary to equity; not when it works equity and protects the landowner against the indifference and laches of the lessee and prevents a great michief, as in the case of such leases. To perpetuate an oil lease forever by the payment of a monthly sum as here, at the will or caprice of the lessee, would work great injustice. The covenant of forfeiture was not abrogated entirely but only modified.

Sec. 10.—In *Munroe* v. *Armstrong*, 96 Pa. 307, (Analyzed under Chapter 5) syl. 2 is as follows:

"Forfeiture for non-development or delay is essential to private and public interest in relation to the use and alienation of property. In general equity abhors a forfeiture, but not where it works equity and protects a landowner from the laches of a lessee, whose lease is of no value till developed."

The lease contained the following forfeiture clause:

"The party of the second part, if they fail to get oil in paying quantities, or if they cease to work for thirty days at any time, this article to be forfeited, and to be null and void."

The lessees entered and drilled a well which was non-productive and then abandoned the premises. From November 1, 1877, until February, 1878, nothing was done. Then lessor called upon lessee and inquired if he intended drilling another well. Lessee said he did not. Reep, the landowner, on March 21, 1878, made a lease to Munroe. The original lessees afterwards assigned their lease to Armstrong who, in July, 1878, entered upon the premises and commenced operating for oil, and completed a well on December 1, 1878, when Munroe instituted an action of ejectment in the Court of Common Pleas against Armstrong and others who claimed an interest with him. The Court of Common Pleas held there had been no forfeiture and rendered judgment for defendants. From this judgment Munroe appealed to the Supreme

Court and that Court reversed the Court of Common Pleas, and held that the original lease had been forfeited.

Sec. 11.—In *Galey* v. *Kellerman*, 123 Pa. 491; 16 Atl. 474 (Jan. 7, 1889), the syllabus is as follows:

"(a)   The lessee in an oil lease covenanted to commence operations within sixty days from the date of the lease, and to complete one well within three months thereafter; and, in case of failure to complete one well in said time, they covenanted to pay the lessor for such delay the sum of $1,000 per annum within three months after the time of completing such well.

(b)   It was also covenanted by the parties that a failure to complete one well or to make such payment within said time, 'renders this lease null and void, and to remain without effect between the parties hereto.' The lessees did nothing towards drilling a well, nor did they make payment within three months after it should have been completed.

1.   In such case, a forfeiture of the lease did not happen until default made by the lessees both in completing the well and in paying for the delay for failure to complete it.

2.   The lessees having neither drilled the first well nor paid the price of delay, according to the terms of the contract, the lessor was entitled to recover at the stipulated rate for the time the lessees held the exclusive right to operate."

On December 28, 1885, Frederick Kellerman made an oil and gas lease to Galey Brothers for a certain tract of land in Bridgewater Borough, Beaver County, Pennsylvania, containing three acres, for the term of ten years, upon the express condition that one well should be completed during each year at lessor's option. Operations were to be commenced within 60 days, and one well completed within three months, and in case of failure to complete one well within such time, lessees were to pay to lessor for delay the sum of ten hundred dollars per annum, within three months after the time for completing such well. A failure to complete one well or to make any of the payments within the time should render the lease null and void. The lessees neither paid the rental or commutation, nor did they drill, and the time for drilling expired on August 28, 1866. The lessor then demanded from lessee the rental, which was not paid. On September 9, 1886, the lessor instituted in the Court of Common Pleas Number 1 of Allegheny

County, an action of covenant for the recovery of the rentals against the lessee. A jury was empaneled and a verdict rendered in favor of the plaintiff for $458.32, from which judgment the de-fendants appealed to the Supreme Court of Pennsylvania, which court affirmed the judgment of the Court of Common Pleas. The last paragraph of the opinion rendered by Justice Williams is as follows:

"The lessees had the right to enter at any time during the eight months and either drill a well or make the stipulated pay-ments. If they did neither, within the time limited, their right of entry was extinguished and the contract itself was at an end. But the acts that forfeited their rights did not also forfeit those of the lessor. Their liabilities growing out of their non-perform-ance are to be distinguished from their rights under the contract. The latter they could forfeit, but the former belonged to the lessor, and could be lost only by his act. The lessees promised to complete one well within a given time. This was for the benefit of the lessor. If this was not done he was to be compensated in money. If the money was not paid he was at liberty to rid himself of his tenant and resume the possession of his land. But the con-struction contended for by the plaintiff in error transfers the punishment for the breach of the contract from him on whose default it arises, to the innocent injured party. Because the lessees have secured the control of the land of the lessor by cove-nants which they have broken, the lessor shall be ·deprived of all redress at law by the very acts of his lessees which gave him a cause of action. Their default takes away his remedy. The acts or omissions of which he complains are an answer to his com-plaint. We should need the constraint of insurmountable neces-sity to induce us to adopt the construction contended for."

Sec. 12.—In *Wills* v. *Manufacturers N. Gas Co.*, 130 Pa. 222; 18 Atl. 731 (Nov. 12, 1889), syl. 2 is as follows:

"A provision in such a lease that a failure by the lessee to perform any of his covenants shall work an absolute forfeiture, and the lease shall thereupon become null and void, being intended for the protection of the lessor he has the option either to declare the forfeiture or to affirm the continuance of the contract, and if he does not choose to avail himself of the forfeiture it cannot be set up by the lessee as a defense to an action upon the lease; *Galey* v. *Kellerman*, 123 Pa. 491, followed."

On January 18, 1887, John A. Wills made an oil and gas lease to the Manufacturers Natural Gas Company for a tract of 228 acres of land in Washington County, Pennsylvania, for a term of twenty years. The lessee agreed to commence operations on one well within 90 days, and to prosecute the work actively, diligently and continuously, and complete the well on or before September 1, 1887; and upon failure to do so lessee to pay lessor $1,000 annually in advance, payable quarterly after September 1, 1887, until the well should be completed. The lease contained a clause that upon failure of the lessee to keep and perform all the covenants therein such failure or breech of covenants should work an absolute forfeiture of the lease, provided that no such forfeiture should in any way interfere with the collection of any and all sums of money due the lessor at or immediately before such forfeiture. On September 1, 1887, when the period of defaults began, the lessee voluntarily paid the first quarterly payment of $250.00, in advance. The installment of rent due December 1, 1887, was not paid. Suit was brought against the lessee, judgment obtained and collected. The third and fourth quarterly installments, payable March 1st and June 1st, 1888, were unpaid. On June 5, 1888, the lessor, John A. Wills brought assumpsit against the lessee in the Court of Common Pleas of Washington County, and obtained judgment, from which judgment the gas company appealed to the Supreme Court, which court affirmed the judgment.

Sec. 13.—In *Thompson* v. *Christy*, 138 Pa. 220; 20 Atl. 934 (Nov. 10, 1890), syls. 4-5 are as follows:

"4. Upon a covenant in an oil lease, that the lessee shall drill a well within a specified time, and on failure so to do shall pay the lessor $40.00 per annum until such well is commenced, the lessor cannot recover in ejectment for such failure to drill the well, the lease containing no clause providing for a forfeiture of the lessee's rights upon such failure.

5. The rule prevailing in equity is, that to entitle a lessor to declare and enforce a forfeiture, the right so to do must be distinctly reserved; the proof of the happening of the event upon which it is to be exercised must be clear; such right must be exercised promptly, and the result of enforcing the forfeiture must not be unconscienable."

On May 16, 1889, Hugh McClellan was the owner of a tract of land in Butler County, Pennsylvania, and on that date executed an oil and gas lease for a term of 15 years to W. C. Thompson. On December 4, 1889, Thompson instituted an action of ejectment in the Court of Common Pleas of Butler County, against C. C. Christy, W. W. Christy and T. C. Christy for the recovery of the possession of 40 acres of land, being the land described in the lease aforesaid. The defendants claimed under a lease for the same tract of land made by Hugh McClellan to C. L. Jones and others, dated March 6, 1888, which lease came by assignment to the defendants Christys. Upon the trial the defendants put in evidence the lease made by McClellan to Jones, which lease contained the following stipulation:

"The party of the second part agrees to drill a test well in the Township of Connoquenessing, or within two miles of the above described premises within one year from the date hereof; and if oil or gas is found in paying quantities in said test well the party of the second part agrees to complete one well on the above described premises within one year from the completion of said test well, or, in lieu thereof, thereafter pay to the said party of the first part $40.00 per annum till work is commenced.

And it is further agreed, that the second party, his heirs or assigns, shall have the right at any time to surrender up this lease and be released from all moneys due and conditions unfulfilled; then and from that time this lease shall be null and void and no longer binding on either party, and the payments which shall have been made shall be held by the party of the first part as the full stipulated damages for the non-fulfillment of the foregoing contract."

On the trial the defendants offered to prove the assignment of the Jones lease to Christys to be followed by proof of possession of the property in litigation by the parties several months before the assignment, and the expenditure by them of large sums of money, to-wit, about $3,000 in developing and improving the property and paying the consideration for the assignment. The defendants also proved that the plaintiff paid nothing for the lease made to him by McClellan, and that it was procured and written by the plaintiff's father, John M. Thompson, who had notice of the Jones lease at the time he procured the lease to W. C. Thompson. Much evidence was offered in behalf of the defendant, and rejected. Judg-

ment was rendered for the plaintiff, from which judgment defendants appealed. The Supreme Court reversed the Court of Common Pleas and directed a new trial. The principal question decided by the Supreme Court applicable to forfeiture is that stated
in the point of the syllabus above quoted, and the paragraph of the
opinion at page 249, as follows:

"The defendants' fourth point drew attention to the position
of the plaintiff, the kind of relief he was seeking, and the rules
prevailing in courts of equity upon the subject of forfeiture. It
was refused without any explanation of the subjects to which it
referred. This was misleading. The rule undoubtedly is that
the right to declare a forfeiture must be distinctly reserved; that
the proof of the happening of the event upon which the right is
to be exercised must be clear; that the party entitled to do so
must exercise his right promptly; and that the result of enforcing
the forfeiture must not be unconscionable. In this case the existence of a right was denied. There had been no attempt to
exercise it except by means of the devise suggested by counsel
of executing a new lease. The lessees were in actual possession
and for several months had been engaged in the work of drilling
a well on the premises. It would hardly be contended that, if
McClellan was in a court of equity with a bill to reform this lease
for the purpose of enabling him to assert a forfeiture upon the
facts of this case, as they were shown, and as the defendants
offered to show them, the conscience of the chancellor would be
moved to aid him to a decree."

Sec. 14.—In *Kennedy* v. *Crawford,* 138 Pa. 561; 21 Atl. 19
(October 20, 1890) the syllabus is as follows:

"(a)   An oil lease, reserving royalty, provided that the
lessee should commence drilling a well within a specified time,
and 'prosecute said drilling with due diligence to success or
abandonment; and should oil or gas not be pumped or excavated
in paying quantities on or before June 27, 1886, then this lease
to be null and void.' A subsequent clause made the violation of
any stipulation in the lease a cause of forfeiture.
1.   The drilling could not be regarded as prosecuted to success so long as no actual product of oil or gas was obtained; and
the lessee, after drilling into the oil bearing rock and finding oil,
for the production of which it was necessary to pump the well,
was bound by his covenant to exercise due diligence in ascertaining whether the oil could be produced in paying quantities, and,
if it could be, in effecting such production.

2. The provision respecting the production of oil or gas on or before June 27, 1886, did not give the lessee a discretion to suspend operations indefinitely after drilling the well, provided he effected such production by the date named; and, if, having completed such drilling in December, 1885, he ceased operations for three months thereafter, making no effort during that period to produce oil, he thereby incurred a forfeiture."

On June 27, 1885, S. A. Kennedy, the owner of a tract of land in Butler County, Pennsylvania, made an oil and gas lease thereof to W. G. Crawford and W. A. Gilleland. The lease provided that the land should be held by the lessees for the purpose therein specified "for and during the time oil or gas may be found in paying quantities, not exceeding the term of fifteen years from the date of the lease." The lease also contained the following stipulations:

"The said parties of the second part hereby agree to commence drilling on said test well, within ninety days from June 27, 1885, and to prosecute said drilling with due diligence to success or abandonment, and should oil or gas not be pumped or excavated in paying quantities on or before June 27, 1886, then this lease to be null and void.

The second parties do further agree that if oil is found in paying quantities, to protect the property hereby leased by drilling thereon an equal number of wells to any wells that may be started on the lands of other parties adjoining this land; * * * * * * and it is understood and mutually agreed that if said second parties, their heirs or assigns, fail to comply with any of the terms or conditions herein contained, then this lease shall become null and void, and not binding on said first parties."

The lessees took possession of the premises and commenced drilling in August 1885. While the well was drilling Gilleland assigned his interest to Crawford. In December, 1885, the well was drilled into the oil bearing rock with a showing of oil. On May 7, 1889, Kennedy instituted an action of ejectment in the Court of Common Pleas of Butler County, against W. G. Crawford for possession of the tract of land. The defendant upon the trial testified that he had found oil and gas both in paying quantities; and that he pulled the casing with the intention of putting in smaller casing and packing off the salt water, but that, as the weather got very cold he concluded that it would be prudent to suspend operations until spring; and having taken the tools out of

the derrick he went away without having utilized any gas from the
well and without having pumped or produced any oil or made any
preparations for pumping or storing oil, but leaving his engine,
boiler and other machinery upon the leasehold; that in April,
1886, he returned to resume operations, but was notified by the
plaintiff not to go on the premises, and about May 21, 1886, and
on subsequent dates he received written notices to that effect from
the plaintiff; that in November, 1886, the plaintiff warned him off
and kept him from the land. The plaintiff in rebuttal denied that
he gave any notice to or interfered with the plaintiff in any way
prior to June 21, 1886; and testified that the notice bearing date
May 21st was really written on June 21st and misdated by mistake; that the witness intended to give that notice on the day specified in the lease, as that on or before which oil or gas must be
pumped or excavated in paying quantities; and, mistaking the figure seven for the figure one he wrote the notice on June 21st, instead of June 27th. Verdict and judgment were rendered in favor
of the plaintiff. From this judgment the defendant appealed to
the Supreme Court, and that court affirmed the judgment of the
Court of Common Pleas.

Sec. 15.—In *Springer* v. *Citizens Natural Gas Company,* 145
Pa. 430; 22 Atl. 986 (Nov. 9, 1891), the first and second points of
the syllabus are as follows:

"(a) An oil and gas lease contained a covenant that the
lessee should complete a well within a certain time, or thereafter
pay to the lessors certain sums semi-annually, until such completion; and stipulated that the failure to complete said well, or
make said payments, as covenanted, should render the lease null
and void and of no effect between the parties;
1. The forfeiture clause being inserted in the interests of
the lessors, they had the option upon a default by the lessee either
to assert a forfeiture, or to affirm the continuance of the contract;
and when they adopted the latter alternative, the lessee could not
set up a forfeiture, to the action in affirmance of the lease; *Ray* v.
N. Gas Co., 138 Pa. 576.
2. An allegation that 'soon' after the lease was executed
it was 'discovered that the territory was worthless for either
oil or gas.' and that the 'leased land did not contain either gas or
oil in paying quantities at the time' of execution, is inefficient as

a defense to a summary judgment in an action in affirmance of the continuance of the lease.''

On December 17, 1886, Hannah Springer and others made an oil and gas lease for a tract of 145 acres of land in Beaver County, Pennsylvania, to E. L. Barton for the term of five years, "and as much longer as gas or oil is produced in paying quantities.'' The lease contained the following provisions:

"Operations on the above described premises shall be commenced, and one well completed within six months from the date hereof; and in case of a failure to complete one well within such time the party of the second part hereby agrees to pay to parties of the first part for such delay the sum of $300 within three days after the time for completing such well as above specified, payable at above mentioned National Bank, and to pay $250 semi-annually thereafter in advance, until one well shall be completed; and the parties of the first part hereby agree to accept such sum as full consideration and payment for such semi-annual delay until one well shall be completed; and a failure to complete one well or to make any of such payments in this lease mentioned, within such time, and at such place, as above mentioned, renders this lease null and void, to remain without effect between the parties hereto.''

On August 1, 1887, E. L. Barton, assigned the lease to the Citizens Natural Gas Company. On November 12, 1890, Hannah Springer and others, the lessors, brought an action of assumpsit against the Citizens Natural Gas Company in the Court of Common Pleas of Beaver County for the recovery of the rentals and the penalty for a failure to complete the well stipulated to be paid in the lease, no explorations having been made by either the original lessee or his assignee, the gas company. The gas company answered and denied all liability, especially claiming that the forfeiture clause relieved the original lessee and his assignee of any liability. A supplemental affidavit of defense was filed whereby the Gas Company undertook to relieve itself of liability on the following grounds:

"That although the said E. L. Barton paid $100 at the time of the delivery of the said lease it was soon thereafter discovered that the territory was worthless for either oil or gas and the drilling of a well or wells was abandoned by said Barton and said defendant company, and said leased lands did not contain either gas or oil in paying quantities at the time of the execution of the lease upon which suit is now instituted.''

The Court of Common Pleas held that the affidavits of defense were not sufficient, and rendered judgment in favor of the plaintiffs for $1373.30, from which judgment the defendant appealed. The Supreme Court affirmed the judgment.

Sec. 16.—In *Ray* v. *Western Pennsylvania N. Gas Co.*, 138 Pa. 576; 20 Atl. 1065 (Jan. 5, 1891), the first, second and fifth points of the syllabus are as follows:

''(a) An oil and gas lease contained a stipulation that the lessee should complete a well within a certain time, or thereafter pay to lessor certain sums, semi-annually, until such completion, and provided that the lessees failure to complete said well or to make such payment as stipulated, should render the lease null and void and of no effect between the parties;
1. The forfeiture clause being inserted in the interests of the lessor, he had the option, upon a default by the lessee either to declare a forfeiture or to affirm the continuance of the contract; and when he adopted the latter alternative the lessee could not set up a forfeiture as a defense to an action in affirmance of the lease. *Galey* v. *Kellerman*, 123 Pa. 492. *Wills* v. *N. Gas Co.*, 130 Pa. 222.
2. When the lessor, being entitled so to do, by the terms of such a lease, remains in possession of the land subject to the rights of the lessee, and the lessee has never taken any possession, a formal re-entry by the lessor, for conditions broken is not requisite to effect a forfeiture; his occupancy, however, at and after the breach will not operate as an assertion of a forfeiture against his will.
5. A gas lease reserved an annual rent of $500 on each well utilized; stipulated for the payment of $250 to the lessor semi-annually until completion of a well, and after specifying when the $500 rent should be paid, provided in the same sentence that 'a failure to complete one well or make any such payments * . * * * as above mentioned' should avoid the lease. The forfeiture clause would seem not to apply to the half yearly payments for delay.''

On July 7, 1888, James Ray made an oil and gas lease for a tract of land in Washington County, Pennsylvania, for the term of two years, or so long thereafter as oil or gas should be found in paying quantities, to the Western Pennsylvania Natural Gas Company. The lease contained the following stipulations:

"The party of the second part agrees to pay within ten days from the execution of this lease, the sum of $53.00; and if a well is not completed within six months from the execution of this lease, the said second party agrees to pay a further sum of $53.00 and so on continually every six months during the continuance of the term herein specified. The said sum of $500 gas rent, shall be paid within one month from the time said well is completed on said premises, and to be paid annually in advance thereafter. It is further agreed by said second party, that if a well is not completed within fifteen months from the date of this lease they are to pay a further sum of $250.00 said sum to be a credit on well when drilled; and in case of failure to complete one well within such time the party of the second part hereby agrees to pay thereafter to party of the first part, for any further delay, the sum of $106.00 per annum within a month after the time for completing such well, as above specified, payable semi-annually at the First National Bank of Washington, Pa., and the party of the first part hereby agrees to accept such sum as full consideration and payment for such yearly delay, until one well shall be completed. And a failure to complete one well or to make such payments within such time and such place, as above mentioned, shall render this lease null and void, and to remain without effect between the two parties."

On March 14, 1890, the lessor brought an action in assumpsit in the Court of Common Pleas of Washington County, against the lessee for the recovery of the rentals and money due under the lease. The defendant filed an affidavit of defense, whereby it sought to defend the action, first, because the defendant never entered into possession of the premises, or any part thereof, the plaintiff being in possession during all the time; that by the terms of the lease a failure to explore or make the payments rendered the lease *ipso facto* null and void, and thereby relieved the defendant of any further liability to pay or perform. Second, because by the laws of Pennsylvania, the non-payment of any installment of money, or the non-performance of any covenant by the party of the second part in an agreement of the kind sued on, containing a condition and forfeiture clause such as in the agreement sued on, *ipso facto* ended and determined the contract both as to the lessor and lessee. The Court of Common Pleas held this affidavit of de-

fense insufficient and rendered judgment for the plaintiff, from
which judgment the gas company appealed, and the Supreme
Court affirmed the judgment.

Sec. 17.—In *Cortelyou* v. *Barnsdall*, 236 Ill. 138; 86 N. E. 200
(Oct. 26, 1908), the syllabus is as follows:

"1. A lease for mining for oil and gas which grants to the
lessee the right to mine for oil or gas so long as the same is prosecuted and the royalties and rentals are paid but does not bind the
lessee to perform any obligations, is a mere option and the lessor
may withdraw before the lessee has done some act by which he
binds himself to exercise the option.
2. Where a lessor in an oil and gas lease which gives to the
lessee a mere option, notifies the lessee of an election to revoke
the option, before the lessee has done any act binding himself to
exercise the option, the revocation is a withdrawal of an offer
which the lessee has not accepted."

Allen Cortelyou and wife, on July 8, 1905, executed an oil and
gas lease to W. W. Seibert, containing the following stipulations:

" * * * The lessor hereby grants unto lessee for the term
of three(3) years (and so long thereafter as oil or gas. is produced
from the land leased or the royalties and rentals paid by lessee
therefor) the exclusive right to mine for and produce petroleum
and natural gas from * * * * 80 acres of land in Crawford County,
State of Illinois * * * * *. This lease is to be void and no longer
binding on either party if a well is not commenced on this block
of 1,000 acres within twelve months from this date, unless the
lessee shall thereafter pay annually to the lessor twenty-five cents
per acre per year for each years delay in completing said well.
Each payment to extend the time for completion one year. * * * *
All conditions and covenants to extend to the heirs and assigns
of the parties hereto. * * * * * * "

The leases constituting the block mentioned, and including the
one made to Seibert, were by him assigned to T. N. Barnsdall and
others. In March, 1906, Cortelyou gave notice in writing to Seibert and his assigns that he elected to exercise his right to revoke,
and did revoke, said lease and notified the lessee and his assignee
not to enter upon the premises for any purpose.   Prior to the
notice neither Seibert nor his assignees had done anything to-

ward developing the premises for oil and gas; had been at no expense in any manner in relation to the lease, nor had any consideration been paid to the lessor. Cortelyou filed a bill in equity in the Circuit Court of Crawford County against Seibert, T. N. Barnsdall and others, praying for the cancellation of the lease on the grounds that it was unfair, particularly in that it did not bind the lessee to drill for oil or pay lessors anything for failure so to do; and that the drilling or development or payment, so far as Seibert was concerned, was a mere option. Upon final hearing upon answer and proofs the Circuit Court found that there had been no consideration paid for the lease; that neither Seibert nor his assigns had entered upon the premises for the purpose of making developments, nor paid any rentals, and entered a decree cancelling the lease. Defendants appealed to the Appellate Court where the decree of the Circuit Court was affirmed, and from this decree defendants appealed to the Supreme Court of Illinois, where the decree was again affirmed.

Sec. 18.—In *Henne* v. *South Penn Oil Co.*, 52 W. Va. 192; 43 S. E. 147, analyzed under chapter 24, syl. 1 is as follows:

"The clause of forfeiture in an ordinary oil lease is for the benefit of the lessor and no act of the lessee can terminate the lease under the forfeiture clause, without the lessor's concurrence."

After drilling a dry hole the lessee removed its machinery and appliances from the premises and set up the same for drilling a well on other property nearby. The dry hole was completed about April 4, 1900. On April 8, 1900, the lessors made a second lease to C. B. Henne which last lease contained the following provision:

"It is further agreed between the parties hereto that this lease is made and this contract entered into subject to a certain other lease and contract made for the same premises by the parties of the first part to William Michæls, bearing date on October 19, 1898, and recorded in Deed Book 108 page 375, in the County Court of Harrison County; and that the existence of said former lease is made known to the party of the first part and who is fully informed and aware of its conditions."

William Michaels had assigned the lease to the South Penn
Oil Company. In a suit brought by Henne against the South Penn
Oil Company to cancel the original lease the court held as stated
in syllabus 1, and in syl. 4 held, that the lease to Henne was not
a declaration by the lessors to unequivocal forfeiture of the first
lease.

Sec. 19.—In *Cochran* v. *Pew,* 159 Pa. 184; 28 Atl. 219 (Dec.
20, 1892) syls. 1-2 are as follows:

"Covenants in an oil lease for the lease to be void, or to cease
and determine on failure by the lessee to comply with the conditions specified, do not make the lease void, except at the option
of the lessor, and the legal effect of such covenants can only be
changed by an express stipulation that the lease shall be voidable
at option of either party, or of the lessee.

Where the parties to an oil lease stipulate that the test well
shall be sunk upon the land demised, it is no defense, to an action
to recover the rent provided in the lease, that the land demised
was shown by exploration of neighboring territory to be dry, and
that the sinking of a well upon the land would have been a useless
expense."

Cephas Cochran brought suit in the Court of Common Pleas
of Allegheny County, Pennsylvania, against J. N. Pew and E. O.
Emerson for the recovery of Two Hundred Dollars rental under
an oil lease which lease contained the following covenant:

"The party of the second part covenants to commence operations on this land for said purpose within three months from the
execution of this lease, or hereafter pay the party of the first part
One Hundred and Sixty Dollars per annum until work is commenced; to be paid $40.00 at the expiration of each three months.
And after work is commenced, it is to be prosecuted with due
diligence until completion.

It is understood and agreed that any moneys that may hereafter become due on this contract shall be paid at the residence of
Cephas Cochran. The failure of the second party to make any
one of the payments when due, or within ten days thereafter, will
render this lease null and void, and not binding on either party."

The defendants filed an affidavit of defense alleging that they
had assigned the lease to the Peoples Natural Gas Company, a

corporation; and that the corporation paid the plaintiff to May first, 1892; and that after making the last payment, and before the 10th day of February, 1892, the corporation, assignee, ascertained by methods practiced and approved by men skilled in the business of mining for oil and natural gas, that neither oil nor gas existed in the land described in the lease; and that thereupon the corporation executed and tendered to the plaintiff a release of said lease and offered to surrender the same; and that after that date neither the defendants nor said corporation ever claimed or exercised any right or privilege under the lease, and did not, and would not, make any further payments on account of the same. The Court of Common Pleas held, that the affidavit of defense was insufficient and rendered judgment for plaintiff, from which judgment defendants appealed to the Supreme Court, and that court affirmed the judgment, citing the following cases:

Galey v. *Kellerman*, 123 Pa. 491; 16 Atl. 474.
Wills v. *Gas Co.*, 130 Pa. 222; 18 Atl. 721.
Ray v. *Gas Co.*, 138 Pa. 576; 20 Atl. 1065; 12 L. R. A. 290;
    21 Am. St. Rep. 922.
Ogden v. *Hatry*, 145 Pa. 640; 23 Atl. 334.
Jones v. *Gas Co.*, 146 Pa. 204; 23 Atl. 386.
Phillips v. *Vandergrift*, 146 Pa. 357; 23 Atl. 347.
Leatherman v. *Oliver*, 151 Pa. 646; 25 Atl. 309.
Liggett v. *Shira*, 159 Pa. 350; 28 Atl. 218.

Sec. 20.—In *Liggitt* v. *Shira*, 159 Pa. 350; 28 Atl. 218 (Dec. 30, 1893) the first point of the syllabus is as follows:

"An oil lease provided that a failure to commence a test well within a specified time should render the lease null and void. 'But if said party of the second part shall pay the party of the first part a monthly rental of one hundred dollars upon the said premises from and after the time above specified for the completion of said well, such payment shall operate to extend the time for completion of said well during the period for which said rental shall be paid.' *Held*, that the lessor was the only person who could assert a forfeiture, as the provision of the lease was for his protection, and not that of the defaulting lessee."

On August 1, 1889, William M. Shira made an oil and gas lease for a tract of 50 acres of land in Butler County, Pennsylvania, to Thomas Liggitt, the rental clause in which lease was as follows:

"It is further agreed that the party of the second part shall commence a well on the above described premises within forty-five days from the date above, or, in default thereof, pay to the party of the first part for further delay, a monthly rental of one hundred dollars on the said premises from the time above specified for commencing a well until such well shall be commenced, the said rental shall be deposited to the credit of the party of the first part at the Butler Savings Bank, or be paid direct to said party. And a failure to commence such well and to prosecute the same to completion with due diligence, or to pay said rental within the time specified therefor, or within ten days thereafter, shall render this lease null and void and the same can then be renewed, extended, or continued in force, only by the mutual consent of the parties of both parts."

No well was commenced as provided for in the lease. The lessee paid one voluntary payment of monthly rental for delay. At the March Term, 1890, of the Court of Common Pleas of Butler County, the lessor recovered judgment for $300 against lessee for unpaid rentals and instituted another suit which was pending at the September Term, 1892, for additional rental amounting to $3,100.00. Thomas Liggitt, the lessee, instituted a suit in equity against William M. Shira, the lessor, in the Court of Common Pleas Number 1 of Allegheny County, to reform the lease. The bill was dismissed by the Court and the plaintiff appealed to the Supreme Court which court affirmed the decree and upon the construction of the lease held the law to be as stated in the syllabus.

Sec. 21.—In *Bartley* v. *Phillips,* 165 Pa. 325; 30 Atl. 842 (Jan. 7, 1895) the syllabus is as follows:

"In an action of ejectment to recover possession of land under an oil lease, where defendants claim that plaintiffs had abandoned their right under their lease, but this is denied by plaintiffs in their abstract of title, the question of abandonment is a mixed question of acts and intention, which must be submitted to the jury.

As against any but the grantor, an abandonment is not complete until the statutory period of limitation, or the end of the

term granted, and possession may be resumed by the grantee at
any time previous.

Where an oil lease provides that the work shall 'be prosecuted
with due diligence until completion or abandonment' the question
of what is due diligence is a question of fact upon which the parties
may agree apart from the writing, and parol proof of the understanding and agreement of the parties upon the subject is proper
evidence.

The clause of forfeiture in an ordinary oil lease is for the benefit
of the lessor, and no acts of the lessee can terminate the lease
under the forfeiture clause, without the lessor's concurrence.

An action of ejectment cannot be maintained against a lessee
in an oil lease by a stranger on the ground that the lessee had
abandoned the premises, where there is no evidence that the lessor
had exercised his right to forfeit the lease.

In an action of ejectment to recover an oil lease, where the
defendant set up an abandonment by the plaintiff, and avers title
in himself under the lessor, the court cannot enter a non-suit on
the ground that defendant's title under the lessor appeared by his
abstract of title, when the abstract of title had not been offered
in evidence by plaintiffs. An entry of non-suit under such circumstances would be a premature determination of the lease.''

J. A. Hartzell, on September 8, 1888, leased a tract of 70 acres of
land for oil purposes for the term of ten years to Bartley and
others. Lessees were to commence operations for mining purposes within thirty days from the execution of the lease, and when
work was commenced to be prosecuted with due diligence until
completion or abandonment. Lessees commenced operations on
the land within fifteen days after the execution of the lease, and
drilled a well, finishing it the latter part of October, 1888. In 1891
Hartzell made a second lease to Phillips. The original lessees,
Bartley and others, brought ejectment in the Court of Common
Pleas of Butler County, against Phillips, the second lessee. The
court entered a nonsuit in favor of defendant. From this decision
plaintiff appealed. The Supreme Court reversed the Court of
Common Pleas, and upon the construction of the lease held the
law to be as stated in the syllabus.

Sec. 22.—In *Jones* v. *Western Pennsylvania Nat. Gas Co.*, 146
Pa. 204; 23 Atl. 386. (Jan. 4, 1892), the syllabus is as follows:

''(a)   A lessee in an oil and gas lease covenanted to complete a well by a date certain, or in default thereof pay for further delay a certain rental yearly from the time specified: 'And a failure. to complete such well, or to pay said rentals * * * * shall render this lease null and void, and can only be renewed by mutual consent;'

1. The legal effect of the covenant is that the forfeiture is for the benefit of the lessor, and is at his option; and such effect can be changed only by an express stipulation that the lease shall be voidable at the option of either party, or of the lessee.

2. If a lease is to become 'null and void', it is not made any more so by provisions that it 'shall be of no effect between the parties', or 'can only be renewed by mutual consent,' or other merely cumulative phrases of the same meaning.

3. In an action to recover on the lessee's default, an offer of the defendant to show 'the uniform construction placed upon such leases by both lessors and lessees,' is inadmissable. It is no more than an offer to reform an instrument on evidence of popular error as to the law.''

Ellis Jones, on April 29, 1889, made an oil and gas lease to the Western Pennsylvania Natural Gas Company for a tract of 220 acres of land in Washington County, for oil and gas. purposes which lease contained the following covenant:

"It is further agreed that the party of the second part shall complete a well on the above described premises by the 5th of August, 1889, from the date above, or in default thereof pay to the party of the first part for further delay, a yearly rental of $300 on said premises, from the time above specified for completing a well until such well shall be completed * * * * * * * and a failure to complete such well, or pay said rental, or within ten days thereof, shall render this lease null and void, and can only be renewed by mutual consent."

The gas company drilled no well on the premises and paid no rent to the lessor who instituted an action of assumpsit against the lessee for the recovery of the rental, returnable to the first Monday in October, 1890. Issue was taken and judgment rendered in favor of the plaintiff. Defendant appealed. The Supreme Court affirmed the judgment.

Sec. 23.—In *Wolf* v. *Guffey*, 161 Pa. 276; 28 Atl. 1117 (April 20, 1894) the syllabus is as follows:

"A lessee in an oil and gas lease agreed to complete a well within six months or pay the lessor for such delay a certain sum per annum, within three months after the time for completing the well. Six days after the expiration of nine months from the date of the lease, the lessor, without demanding payment of any sum on the lessee, leased the premises to another person for a long term of years. *Held,* that this action of the lessor was an election by him to enforce a forfeiture, and that thenceforth the lease was a nullity."

On May 18, 1886, John M. Wolf executed an oil and gas lease to E. B. Beardsley, who assigned to James M. Guffey. The lease contained the following clause: '

"Operations on the above described premises shall be commenced and one well completed within six months from the date hereof, and in case of a failure to complete one well within such time, the party of the second part hereby agrees to pay to the party of the first part for such delay the sum of two hundred and sixty dollars per annum, within three months after the time for completing such well as above specified, payable at the premises, and the party of the first part hereby agrees to accept such sum as full consideration and payment for such yearly delay until one well shall be completed, and a failure to complete one well or to make any such payments within such time and at such place as above mentioned, renders this lease null and void and to remain without effect between the parties hereto."

On February 24, 1887, Wolf, the lessor, without making any demand upon Guffey, leased his premises to the Philadelphia Company for twenty years. Wolf then instituted an action of assumpsit in the Court of Common Pleas Number 2, Allegheny County, against James M. Guffey, the assignee of the lease, for the recovery of the rental. Judgment was rendered for the defendant, from which plaintiff appealed. The Supreme Court affirmed the judgment, and in the opinion delivered by Justice McCollum, stated the reasons for the affirmance of the judgment, as follows:

"If it be conceded that the lessor could have maintained this action in affirmance of the lease, it does not necessarily follow that he may do so after he has elected to forfeit it and rented the property to another party. The cause of the forfeiture arose when the lessee failed to complete a well on the premises within six months, or to pay the sum sued for within three months there-

after. According to the contention of the lessor, a right of action
for this sum accrued on the 18th day of February, 1887, and he is
still entitled to receive it, although he immediately accepted the
non-payment of it as a forfeiture of the lease and an extinguish-
ment of the rights and liabilities of the parties thereunder.   By
the payment of this sum within the time stipulated the lessor
would have been compensated for past delay and the lessee would
have had another year within which to complete the well.   In other
words, such payment would have been, under the most favorable
construction for the lessor, in the interest and for the benefit of
both parties, as it would have extended the time allowed the lessee
to test or develop the property, as well as satisfied the claim of
the lessor.   The covenant of the lessee to pay this sum and the
mutual agreement of the parties that the non-payment of it should
render the lease void and without effect between them were, in a
certain sense, for the benefit of the lessor, because they enabled
him to forfeit the lease on the occurrence of the default.   But
they did not ipso facto forfeit it and extinguish the rights and
liabilities created by it; they merely rendered it optional with the
lessor to terminate the lease or treat it as still in force.   If he
had accepted payment of this sum the day after the right to declare
a forfeiture was completely vested in him, such acceptance would
have operated as a waiver of the right and would have protected
the lessee as effectually as if the payment had been made or tendered the day before it so vested.''

Sec. 24.—In *Jackson* v. *O'Hara,* 183 Pa., 233; 38 Atl. 624 analyzed under Chapter 16, the syllabus is as follows:

"In an oil and gas lease the lessee covenanted 'to commence
operations and complete one well within one month and, in case
of failure to complete one well within such time, to thereafter
pay as rental to the party of the first part for such delay, the
sum of fifty dollars per month.' The lessee agreed 'to accept such
sum as full consideration, liquidation and payment of all damages
for any delays until one well shall be completed, and a failure
to complete such well or to make any such payments within such
time and at such place above mentioned, renders this lease absolutely null and void, and no longer binding on either party, and
will re-vest the estate herein granted in the lessor and release the
lessee from all his covenants herein contained, he having the
option to drill said well or not, or pay said rental or not, as he
may elect.' The lessee assigned a one half interest in the lease.
No well was ever completed or commenced.   The assignee of the
one-half interest in the lease paid the rental for three months,
but then ceased, and no more was paid.   In an action for the rental
against the lessee and the assignee of the one-half interest.   The

defendants filed an affidavit of defense in which they averred that (1) the lessee had an option to sink a well or pay the monthly rental, or to do neither, and by refusing to do either, the lease was at an end; and (2) there was no joint liability of the defendants. *Held,* that the affidavit of defense was insufficient to prevent judgment."

Sec. 25.—In *Ogden* v. *Hatry,* 145 Pa. 640; 23 Atl. 334 (Jan. 4, 1892) the syllabus is as follows:

"(a)   A covenant in an oil lease provided that a failure of the lessee to perform 'by either completing a well within the term aforesaid, or paying said rental, shall render this lease and agreement null and void * * * * and all rights * * * * * of any and all parties hereunder, shall thereafter upon * * * * be extinguished * * * * * * as if this agreement had never been made."
1.   An action for rental was within the rule of *Wills* v. *N. Gas Co.,* 130 Pa. 222; *Ray* v. *N. Gas Co.,* 138 Pa. 576, that such a covenant was for the benefit of the lessor, and the lessee by his own act and default could not relieve himself of a liability already incurred. The clause after the words 'null and void' added mere verbage, but no more force."

J. M. Ogden obtained judgment before a justice which was appealed to the Court of Common Pleas of Venango County in an action against the defendants for the recovery of rentals on an oil lease. The lease contained the following forfeiture clause:

"A failure on the part of the second party to comply with the terms of this covenant, by either completing a well within the term aforesaid or paying said rental, shall render this lease and agreement null and void, and not to remain or be continued in force or be revived without the consent of both parties in writing, and all rights, claims and demands, of any kind or nature, of any and all the parties hereunder, shall thereupon cease, determine, and be extinguished, with like effect as if this agreement had never been made."

The defendants filed an affidavit of defense wherein they alleged that by the terms of the lease a failure on the part of the lessee to complete a well within the time aforesaid or pay the rental rendered the lease and agreement null and void, and not to remain or be continued in force or be revived without the consent of both parties in writing; and all the rights, claims and demands, of any kind or nature, of all the parties thereunder thereupon ceased and were extinguished with like effect as if said agreement had never been made; that said well was not completed within the time aforesaid, nor was rental paid; and that said lease was never continued in force or revived by the consent of both parties in writing or by any of the defendants; that said lease was returned to the plaintiff and the defendant, Hatry, had the plaintiff's receipt thereunder, dated December 11th. The Court of Common Pleas rendered judgment in favor of the plaintiff, holding that the affidavit of defense was not sufficient. The defendant appealed. The Supreme Court affirmed the judgment.

Sec. 26.—In *Phillips* v. *Vandergrift*, 146 Pa. 357; 23 Atl. 347 (Jan. 4, 1892) the syllabus is as follows:

"(a) The lessee in an oil lease covenanted to complete a well in a time certain, or in default thereof to pay the lessor for further delay a certain yearly rental thereafter; 'and a failure to complete such well or pay said rental, shall render this lease null and void, and not to be revived without the consent of both parties hereto;'
1. An action for rental was within the rule of *Wills* v. *N. Gas Co.*, 130 Pa. 222 and *Ray* v. *N. Gas Co.*, 138 Pa. 576, that such covenant was for the benefit of the lessor; and the lessee by his own act and default could not relieve himself from a liability already incurred; See *Jones* v. *N. Gas Co.*, ante, 204; *Ogden* v. *Hatry*, 145 Pa. 640.''

Thomas Phillips brought assumpsit against T. J. Vandergrift in the Court of Common Pleas Number 1 of Allegheny County for the recovery of one years rental due May 23, 1890, under a covenant in an oil and gas lease of the plaintiff's lands which lease was executed by the plaintiff to the defendant November 23, 1888. The covenant referred to provided that the lessee should drill a well within a certain time or in default thereof pay to the lessor for further delay a yearly rental of $500.00 until such well should be completed, and a failure to complete such well or pay said rental should render the lease null and void, and not to be revived without the consent of both parties thereto. The defendant filed an affidavit of defense admitting that no well had been completed on the leased premises, and that the rental sued for had not been paid; but claiming that defendant had not in any manner consented to revive or continue the lease, and by its terms the same, and all estate thereby created became absolutely null and void as to both parties thereto upon the failure to complete such well or pay the rental sued for. Judgment was rendered by the Court of Common Pleas against the defendant, from which judgment an appeal was taken to the Supreme Court, which court affirmed the judgment.

Sec. 27.—In *Matthews* v. *Peoples N. Gas Co.*, 179 Pa., 165; 36 Atl. 216 (Jan. 4, 1897) the syllabus is as follows:

"Plaintiff leased two vacant lots intended for building purposes, to defendant for oil and gas purposes. The lease contained these provisions: 'The party of the second part covenants to commence operations on this land for said purpose within three months from the execution of this lease, or thereafter pay the party of the first part fifty (50) dollars per month until work is commenced; to be paid each month in advance. * * * * * And after work is commenced it is to be prosecuted with due diligence until completion. * * * * * It is mutually understood and agreed by both parties hereto, that in no case shall the commencing of a well on the above described land be delayed beyond a period of six months from date of this lease, and if no well is commenced inside of said six months the penalty to be a forfeiture of this lease, and neither party being held further. It is further understood and agreed that a well drilled on either of above described lots will hold the lease on the other lot for the full term of the lease.' The lease reserved to the lessor the right to use the premises, except such parts as should be necessary for the drilling of the wells. About one year after the date of the lease plaintiff entered on one of the lots and built a house. At this time, however, a stake had been set by the defendant indicating the site of a future well, and it appeared that the building would not have materially interfered with the operation. Three years after the date of the lease plaintiff conveyed by deed one of the lots to another person, without reservation of any right of defendant as lessee to the oil and gas. *Held.* (1) That the clause of forfeiture contained in the lease was for the benefit of the lessor. (2) That the erection of the building on one of the lots was not an assertion of the right of forfeiture; (3) That the absolute conveyance of one of the lots was a constructive eviction of defendant, and ended his liability for rent; (4) that plaintiff was entitled to recover rent until the date of the absolute conveyance of one of the lots."

James E. Mathews made an oil and gas lease to the Peoples Natural Gas Company containing the provisions recited in the syllabus. The lessor instituted an action of assumpsit for the recovery of the rentals claimed to be due, and upon the facts recited in the syllabus the court entered judgment on December 30, 1895, in favor of the plaintiff for the sum of $2394.40, being the aggregate of the monthly payments provided for in the lease from June 6, 1886, to February 6, 1889, on which last date the plaintiff conveyed by deed one of the lots to John D. Porter, without reservation of any right to the defendant, the lessee, to the oil and gas. From this judgment defendant appealed to the Supreme Court, which court affirmed the judgment.

Sec. 28.—In *Bartley* v. *Phillips*, 179 Pa. 175; 36 Atl. 217 analyzed under Chap. 17, syl. 1 is as follows:

"The clause of forfeiture or termination of the estate usually incorporated in oil and gas leases in this State is for the benefit of the lessor, and as against him no act of the lessee can work a forfeiture without his concurrence."

This case is the sequel to *Bartley* v. *Phillips*, 165 Pa., 325; 30 A. 842.

Sec. 29.—In *New Dominion Oil & Gas Co.* v. *Gaffney Oil Company*, 134 Ky., 792; 121 S. W. 699 (Oct. 14, 1909), syls. 10-11 are as follows:

"10. Where a lessee taking an oil lease, had actual knowledge of the fact that a lessor did not own the land, but that a third person owned it, under a parol purchase, followed by adverse possession for more than fifteen years the second party was not estopped to deny the validity of the lease.

11. The right to declare an oil lease forfeited is a personal privilege of the lessor, and when he elects to waive it, no one else may take advantage of it."

William Dobbs was a patentee of a tract of 63 acres of land in Wayne County in 1859. Some fifty years before the litigation he sold 25 acres of land to one Tom Smith, setting it apart by marked boundary. Smith sold the tract to Davenport and Davenport sold it back to Dobbs. Dobbs subsequently resold to Davenport, putting him in possession of it, and Davenport sold to Henderson Foust some thirty years before the litigation, putting Foust in possession. All of these sales were by parol. Davenport was also the owner by peaceable possession of a tract adjoining, of 50 acres, which he had purchased from Irwin Miller. This latter tract was included in the sale to Henderson Foust, who was placed in possession of the whole boundary, which was marked. Foust took up his residence on the 50-acre tract, claiming to the extent of the exterior lines of the whole 75 acres. In 1901, Henderson Foust executed an oil lease on his lands to one W. R. Cress. A written lease described the property embraced, as follows:

"Being the property whereon the said Henderson Foust now resides and also conveyed to him by Irwin Miller, and bounded substantially as follows: * * * * * * * * containing 75 acres more or less. * * * * * "

The parties regarded that the "deed lay in William Dobbs" as they expressed it; yet for more than 25 years Henderson Foust claimed the land as his own exclusive of Dobbs and all others and lived within the common boundary embracing the 25 acres in question. In 1905, Henderson Foust caused William Dobbs to execute a deed to the 25 acre parcel to Bryant Foust and J. W. Foust, sons of Henderson Foust. This was done by Dobbs, not upon any idea or claim that he owned the land, but to comply with his previous parol contract of sale, he admitting all the while that Henderson Foust owned the land, had paid for it, and was in actual possession of it. In April, 1907, Bryant Foust and J. W. Foust executed the mineral lease on the 25 acres to the New Dominion Oil & Gas Company. The Cress lease, which had in the meantime been assigned to the Gaffney Oil Company, contained the stipulation that the lessee and his assigns should within one year from its date, July 30, 1901, begin the drilling of an oil well on the leased premises—the 75 acres—or in default thereof pay to the lessor $7.50 per year; if oil was found in paying quantities he should deliver to the lessor 1-10 thereof. It was further stipulated in the lease that the payment of the annual rentals might be by deposit to the credit of the lessor in the Bank of Monticello. The lessees from Henderson Foust did not begin drilling within a year from July 30, 1901, but they paid the rental of $7.50 each year, after it became due, down to 1907. On July 30, 1907, the manager for the Gaffney Oil Company, who was charged with the duty of paying the rental, was ill. He was on the opposite side of the river from lessor, and from Monticello. The river was swollen with sudden floods so that he could not get across; but he did get across on the following day when he deposited $7.50 in the Bank at Monticello to the credit of the lessor, Henderson Foust. Learning on the following day that the New Dominion Oil & Gas Company was asserting claim to the property the manager sent for Henderson Foust who demanded $2.50 additional because of delay of one day in paying the rental, and this was paid to him. The Gaffney Oil Company did not know that Henderson Foust had caused the deed to be executed to Bryant and J. W. Foust, although the latter knew that their father had, in 1901, leased the land to the assignor of the Gaffney Oil Company, and that that company had been paying him rental therefor, regularly. Afterwards, over the protest of the Gaffney Oil Company, the New Dominion Oil & Gas Company began drilling on the 25 acres, and suit was brought by the Gaffney Oil Company against it and Bryant and J. W. Foust, in the Circuit Court of Wayne County, Kentucky, to restrain them from taking the oil from the well and to restrain them from asserting claim or title to the oil and minerals in the 25 acre tract. Judgment was rendered for the plaintiffs. Defendants appealed to the Supreme Court and that court affirmed the judgment.

Sec. 30.—In *Puritan Oil Co.* v. *Myers*, 39 Ind. App. 695; 80 N. E. 851 (April 3, 1907) syl. 3 is as follows:

"A gas lease made February 4, 1903, provided that the lessee should drill a well on the premises within six months, or should thereafter pay for a further delay a quarterly rental until the well was drilled, provided the lessor accepted such payments. The lessee failed to drill a well within six months, or within two quarterly periods. On May 7, 1904, notice was served on the lessee that the lessor would not accept any renewals and demanded that the work be begun and pushed to completion. On December 6, 1904, the lessor brought suit to quiet title to the land. The lessee offered no excuse for delay. *Held*, that the lessee had reasonable time to comply with the lease by drilling wells in pursuance thereof entitling lessor to its cancellation.''   •

John W. Myers and wife, as parties of the first part, exe-cuted an oil and gas lease to Shadle and Reedy, as parties of the second part, whereby they assigned all the oil and gas in and under the said tract of land, in consideration of one dollar, for the purpose of drilling and operating for oil, gas or water, with the right to erect and maintain all buildings and structures and lay all pipe lines necessary for the production and transportation of oil, gas or water from the premises, reserving the 1-6 part of the oil produced, to be delivered in pipelines as a royalty to lessor. If gas only should be found lessee agreed to pay $100.00 each year for the production of each well while the same should be used off the premises, lessor to have gas free of cost to heat stoves in dwelling house, and for lights. It was provided in the lease:

"In case no well is completed on the above described prem-ises within six months from this date then this grant shall become null and void unless second party shall pay to said first party $30.00 Dollars year thereafter such work is delayed. Paid quar-terly in advance. * * * * * It is expressly stipulated and agreed that the party of the second part may at any time, at its option, in consideration and payment of one dollar to party of the first part, his heirs or assigns, surrender and cancel this lease and terminate all rights and rescind all obligations of either and all of the parties hereto, their successors, heirs or assigns."

John W. Myers, the lessor instituted in the Circuit Court of Henry County, Indiana, a suit against the Puritan Oil Company to quiet his title. The complaint was in two paragraphs, first, in the usual form for quieting title; second, embraced the substance of the first paragraph, and also sought to cancel an oil and gas lease held by the defendant on the tract of land owned by the plaintiff. Demurrers were filed to each of the paragraphs, which demurrers were overruled. Answers in general denial were filed to each paragraph, and special answers filed to certain paragraphs of the complaint. The second paragraph of the answer alleged the pay-ment to the plaintiff of $7.50 on August 1, 1903, which was ac-cepted by the plaintiff; and further alleging the payment of $7.50 to the Merchants Bank for the quarters beginning February 4, 1904,

August 4, 1904, and November 4, 1904, and credited to plaintiff's account with said Bank. The third paragraph alleged that prior to the notice given by plaintiff to defendant, plaintiff knew of the payments made to the Bank for the quarters ending February 4, and May 4, 1904, and before the bringing of the action plaintiff well knew that other payments had been made to the Bank for him. The fourth paragraph alleged substantially the same facts as the second and third, with the additional allegation that said $30.00 was not paid as an option for any one year, but, on the contrary, was a part of the consideration for all the rights under the contract; and that this action was brought before the end of the second year. Demurrers to each of these paragraphs were filed by plaintiff and overruled. The case was put at issue, tried by the court, findings and judgment for the plaintiff. Defendant appealed assigning as error the overruling of the demurrers to the complaint and overruling the motion for new trial. It was proven upon the trial that the lease was assigned to the Puritan Oil Company; and it was admitted by the parties that there had never been any drilling for oil or gas on the premises; that nothing was done by the defendant under the contract, except making two payments, which were sent to the Mechanics Bank in Muncie for plaintiff, and which he refused to accept; that notice was served on the Bank that plaintiff would not, and did not, accept any payments by reason of the provisions of the lease after the quarter beginning November 4, 1903; that notice to the same effect was served on defendant, with the additional notice that:

"The lease will not be extended beyond such period, nor will any consideration be received and accepted for further extension or delay in operations thereon for gas and oil, and further, you are notified that the sum stipulated for rental due February, 1904, and May, 1904, and which has been deposited in the Mechanics National Bank, Muncie, Indiana, so remains so deposited, and will not be received or accepted for delay in operations. And you are hereby notified and required to proceed with all reasonable promptness and dispatch to operate for oil and gas on said premises under penalty of forfeiture of all rights and privileges under said instrument of lease for failure so to do."

The judgment of the Circuit Court was affirmed, the court citing upon the proposition that it was not the understanding or intention of the parties to extend to the lessee indefinitely the right to begin drilling:

> *Hancock* v. *Diamond Plate Glass Co.*, 37 Ind. App. 351; 75 N. E. 659.
> *Consumers Gas Trust Co.* v. *Littler*, 162 ·Ind. 320; 70 N. E. 363.

Upon ·the proposition that before the landowner will be permitted to have the lease cancelled, the lessee must have a reasonable time within which to comply with his contract, the court cited:

> *Hancock* v. *Diamond Plate Glass Co.*, 162 Ind. 146-151; 70 N. E. 149; Id. 37 Ind. App. 351; 75 N. E. 659.
> *Consumers Gas Trust Co.* v. *Worth*, 163 Ind. 141-149; 71 N. E. 489.
> *New American Oil Mining Co.* v. *Wolf*, 166 Ind. 402; 76 N. E. 255.

Sec. 31.—In *Logansport & Wabash Valley Gas Co.*, v. *Null*, (Ind. App.); 76 N. E. 125 (Nov. 14, 1905) the syllabus is as follows:

"1. Where an oil and gas lease which in its beginning purported to be an absolute grant of all the oil and gas in the land, further provided that the grant was made on the terms which thereafter followed, the word 'terms' was broad enough to make the provisions which followed the consideration or conditions of the lease.

2. Where an oil and gas lease provided that a specified sum should be paid annually as rental in case of a delay in developing the land, that a refusal to pay such rental when due should be construed as a surrender of his rights, and that a failure to pay the rental when due should make the lease null and void, and further provided that the grantee might at any time reconvey and thereby render the lease void, and the grantee made no entry on the land, a refusal by the grantor to accept a land rental after the date it became due was a sufficient declaration of his purpose to regard the lease at an end."

On January 5, 1899, John Null executed an oil and gas lease to the Logansport & Wabash Valley Gas Company for a tract of 50 acres of land in consideration of one dollar and the covenants and

agreements therein contained. The second party agreed to drill a
well on the premises within three months from date, or thereafter
pay the lessor for further delay a yearly rental of $75.00 until the
well should be completed, the rentals to be deposited in Marion
Bank, at Marion, Indiana; and should second party refuse to
make such deposit, or pay to the first party on the premises, or at
their present residence, the rental when due, such refusal should be
considered by both parties as an act of the second party for the
purpose of surrendering the rights granted. Default in the payment of the rentals should render null and void the lease without
further notice from lessor. John Null instituted in the Circuit
Court of Grant County, against the Logansport & Wabash Valley
Gas Company, an action to quiet his title. The defendant answered by general demurrer, and the question was whether the
evidence was sufficient to warrant the cancellation of the lease.
No well was drilled, nor was there any attempt to develop the land
for oil and gas by lessee who never entered on the land or took
possession of it. Nothing was paid at the time of the execution of
the contract. The lessor received from the lessee the first payment of money under the contract on or about April 5, 1900, one
year and three months after the date of the lease. The sum then
paid was $75.00, the amount stipulated to be paid for further delay
after the expiration of three months without the drilling of a well,
as yearly rental until a well should be completed.

The last payment was made on or before April 5, 1901. This
payment was made and accepted to pay up to July 1, 1901, the
amount of the payment being $92.50; the rental thereafter to be
paid annually from the first of July. No other money was ever
paid to the lessor or to anyone on his behalf under the contract or
tendered, on or about July 1, 1902; and no such payments were
deposited in the Marion Bank to the credit of lessor on or before
that day. When receiving the payment on or about April 5, 1900,
the lessor made demand of the lessee for the development of the
land, and like demand was made when the payment was made on
or about April 5, 1901. The lessor, who was the only witness on
the trial testified that he was tendered money on the 7th of July,
1902. The amount tendered was $75.00, and was tendered by the
agent of the defendant who tendered it as rental on the lease.

The Circuit Court entered a decree for plaintiff from which defendant appealed, and the Appellate Court affirmed the decree.

Sec. 32.—In *Scott* v. *Lafayette Gas Co.*, 42 Ind. App 614; 86 N. E. 495 (Dec. 15, 1908) syls. 3-6-8 are as follows:

"3. Where a lease of oil and gas lands required the lessee to drill one well within two years from the date of the lease, and to drill two wells thereafter unless the first should become useless, and also provided that in case the wells were not drilled or utilized then, on payment of the stipulated well rental the agreement should continue as though the wells had been drilled, the latter clause, though optional, in form, did not permit the lessee to refuse either to drill the wells or pay the rental, and thus entirely avoid the contract, and on failure to drill the lessee was liable for the well rental.

6. When the language of a contract has a doubtful construction the interpretation thereof between the parties themselves is entitled to great weight, and may control, and such construction will be adopted by the court unless at variance with the correct legal interpretation.

8. Where a gas and oil lease provided that the lessee might cancel the lease by giving notice, and by paying all rental due, together with the sum of $5.00, and releasing the lease of record, the complainant in an action for rental alleging that defendant had returned to plaintiff the five dollars sued for, but failed to give written notice as agreed, and to pay the rental alleged to be accrued and that the five dollars was due and unpaid was sufficient; there being no averment that defendant had cancelled the lease and the fact that it was in arrears on the rental did not obligate it to cancel the lease and become liable for the cancellation fees."

Addison Scott instituted an action against the Lafayette Gas Company in the Circuit Court of Blackford County, Indiana for the recovery of rental under an oil lease. The complaint alleged that the plaintiff leased a tract of 40 acres of land to the defendant in June, 1897, for the term of five years with an option in the lessee to renew or continue the lease for an additional term of five years by giving notice of its desire so to do; that appellee paid all rentals accruing under the lease up to January 1, 1905, and for the period from January 1, 1905, to July 1, 1905, there became due as rental $50.00, and from the period from July 1, 1905, to December 1, 1905, there became due $50.00, making a total of $100.00. The lease provided that in consideration of the premises lessee should pay at the rate of fifty cents per acre per annum for the land until the completion of a well; and that after the completion of a well on the premises which should in lessee's opinion produce gas in sufficient quantities to justify marketing it, lessee should pay $100.00 per annum for each gas well on the land as long as in his opinion the lease produced a marketable quantity of gas. Said payments to become due semi-annually on the first days of January and July in each year. The second party reserved the right to cancel and terminate the lease by giving lessor written notice of his intention three months before the first day of January or the first day of July in any year; and by or on the first day of January or July by paying to lessor all rentals then due and the sum of five dollars and releasing the lease of record, the lease should cease and determine, except that lessee should have the right without paying any further compensation, to maintain, operate and repair any pipelines laid on the premises. The lessee to drill one well within two years from date, and the second well within——————— from the date dessee should use the first well, unless the first well should become useless before the date for drilling the second well. In case the well or wells were not drilled or utilized as provided for, then upon the payment of the well rental the agreement should continue with the same force and effect as though the wells had been drilled. Judgment was rendered for defendant and plaintiff appealed. The Appellate Court reversed the Circuit Court and remanded the cause, citing:

Jackson v. *O'Hara*, 183 Pa. 233; 38 Atl. 624.

Sec. 33.—In *Hancock* v. *Diamond Plate Glass Co.*, 162 Ind. 146; 70 N. E. 149 (Feb. 16, 1904) syls. 2-3 are as follows:

"2. Where a contract between a landowner and a corporation gave the latter the exclusive right of putting down a gas well on certain property, and provided that until this was done it should pay $20.00 per year for the exclusive privilege, and that the contract should be deemed terminated whenever it should fail to pay the rental price within 60 days after it became due, failure to pay did not terminate the contract, but merely gave the landowner the right to do so.

3. A contract between a landowner and a corporation, giving the latter the exclusive right to bore for gas, and providing that the corporation should pay a certain sum annually until it had put down a gas well, but that the contract should be terminated whenever natural gas ceased to be used generally for manufacturing purposes, or whenever the corporation should fail to pay the annual rental within sixty days after it became due, did not create a tenancy at will within Burns' Rev. Stat. 1901 §7089, providing that all general tenancies in which the premises are occupied by the consent, either express or constructive, of the landlord, shall be deemed tenancies at will."

Anna E. Hancock and others instituted an action in the Superior Court of Howard County, Indiana, against the Diamond Plate Glass Company and others to recover a stipulated sum for delay in putting down a well. The plaintiffs and others made an agreement of lease with the Diamond Plate Glass Company whereby it granted to said company and its assigns twenty foot square of a certain tract of 40 acres for the purpose and with the exclusive right of putting down a gas well thereon. As a consideration for the grant the gas company agreed to deliver to appellants in the highway nearest their dwelling on said forty acres, whatever amount of natural gas was necessary for domestic use in their dwelling; and in addition agreed to pay on September 1st of each year $100 for each producing well drilled on the premises; and until the company should put down a gas well it agreed to pay on September 1st of each year, $20.00. Lessors covenanted for themselves, their heirs, executors and assigns not to drill or suffer or permit others to drill any gas well on any part of the entire 40 acres during the continuance of the lease. The lease provided that it should commence at and run from the date of signing and should be deemed to have terminated whenever natural gas ceased to be used generally for manufacturing purposes, or whenever lessee or its assigns should fail to pay or tender the rental price within 60 days of the date of its becoming due; and in the event of the termination thereof for any cause all rights and liabilities thereunder should cease. The Diamond Company assigned the contract to the Pittsburg Plate

Glass Company, which company assigned to the Logansport &
Wabash Valley Gas Company, each assignee agreeing to perform
the covenants of the assignor. No gas well was ever put down or
commenced nor did the lessee demand or request any drilling. No
possession of the premises was ever taken. Natural gas was furnished lessors free of charge under the contract from November 1,
1891, to December 25, 1900, when the supply was cut off by the
Logansport & Wabash Valley Gas Company. The annual sum of
$20.00 was paid according to the contract on each September 1st
from 1891 to 1895, inclusive, and sued for and recovered by the
appellants for 1896. Natural gas had been, all the time since the
execution of the lease, used generally for manufacturing purposes.
There had been no forfeiture, surrender or termination of the
contract, further than could be implied for the failure of lessee
and its assignees to pay the annual sum of $20.00 since September
1, 1896, and the cutting off of the lessor's free gas on December
25, 1900. The complaint was founded on the written contract, and
sought to recover the stipulated annual sum of $20.00 for several
years from September 1, 1897, to September 1, 1902, inclusive, and
damages in the sum of $75.00 for failure to furnish free gas from
December 25, 1900, to the commencement of the suit. The defendants demurred to the complaint for insufficiency. Plaintiffs refused to amend, and judgment was rendered against them for
costs. Plaintiffs appealed to the Appellate Court and the cause
was transferred to the Supreme Court and that Court reversed
the Circuit Court. Upon the question of the effect of a naked
default or non performance, such as was stated in the complaint,
and that the same could not be held to discharge lessee's obligations, the court cited:

Leatherman v. *Oliver*, 151 Pa. 646; 25 Atl. 309.
Cochran v. *Pew*, 159 Pa. 184; 28 Atl. 219.
Woodland Oil Co. v. *Crawford*, 55 Ohio St. 161-176; 44 N. E.
    1093; 34 L. R. A. 62.
Jackson v. *O'Hara*, 183 Pa. 233; 38 Atl. 624.
Ahrns v. *Gas Co.*, 188 Pa. 249; 41 Atl. 739.
Edmonds v. *Mounsey*, 15 Ind. App. 399; 44 N. E. 196.
Simpson v. *Glass Co.*, 28 Ind. App. 343; 62 N. E. 753.

LESSOR'S REMEDY.

Sec. 34.—When a landowner has executed and delivered an oil and gas lease wherein there is a term, a rental period and a forfeiture clause authorizing lessor to terminate the lease for failure to explore or pay the stipulated rental for delay when payable, a failure on the part of the lessee to begin explorations or to pay the commutation money for delay within the period and at the time provided for, authorizes the lessor to declare a forfeiture; and when such declaration of forfeiture is made by the lessor the lease is at an end. The license which lessee held being for entry for exploration purposes only, is ended.

Brown v. *Vandergrift,* 80 Pa. 142. Syl. 2.
Munroe v. *Armstrong,* 96 Pa. 307. Syl. 2.
Galey v. *Kellerman,* 123 Pa. 491; 16 Atl. 474.
Kennedy v. *Crawford,* 138 Pa. 561; 21 Atl. 19.
Wolf v. *Guffey,* 161 Pa. 276; 28 Atl. 1117.
Puritan Oil Co. v. *Myers,* 39 Ind. App. 695; 80 N. E. 851.
Logansport and Wabash Valley Gas. Co. v. *Null,* 36 Ind. App. 5035; 76 N. E. 125.

Sec. 35.—Where an oil and gas lease contains an express covenant to drill a well within a given time or pay a stipulated rental as commutation money for delay, with a forfeiture clause providing that if lessee fails to do either the lease shall be forfeited, such forfeiture clause is for the benefit of lessor and he can avail himself thereof to declare a forfeiture for non-payment of rental, or non-performance of the covenants to drill, or not as he chooses; and if he does not he can recover rental for the time the lessee held the exclusive right to operate.

Conger v. *Nat. Transp. Co.,* 165 Pa. 561;30 Atl. 1038.
Gibson v. *Oliver,* 158 Pa. 277; 27 Atl. 961.
McMillan v. *Phila. Co.,* 159 Pa. 142; 28 Ttl. 220.
New Dominion Oil & Gas Co. v. *Gaffney Oil C.,* — Ky. —; 121 S. W. 699.
Roberts v. *Bettman,* 45 W. Va. 143; 30 S. E. 95.
Galey v. *Kellerman,* 123 Pa. 491; 16 Atl. 474.
Wills v. *Manufacturers N. Gas Co.,* 130 Pa. 222; 18 Atl. 731.
Springer v. *Citizens N. Gas Co.,* 145 Pa. 430; 22 Atl. 986.
Ray v. *West. Penna. Gas Co.,* 138 Pa. 576; 20 Atl. 1065.

Cochran v. *Pew*, 159 Pa. 184; 28 Atl. 219.
Liggitt v. *Shira*, 159 Pa. 350; 28 Atl. 218.
Jones v. *West, Penna. Nat. Gas Co.*, 146 Pa. 204; 23 Atl. 386.
Jackson v. *O'Hara*, 183 Pa. 233; 38 Atl. 624.
Ogden v. *Hatry*, 145 Pa. 640; 23 Atl. 324.
Phillips v. *Vandergrift*, 146 Pa. 357; 23 Atl. 347.
Matthews v. *Peoples N. Gas Co.*, 179 Pa. 165; 36 Atl. 216.
Scott v. *Lafayette Gas Co.*, 42 Ind. App. 614, 86 N. E. 495.
Hancock v. *Diamond Plate Glass Co.*, 162 Ind. 146; 70 N. E.
        149.

Sec. 36.—Where a lease contains a forfeiture clause authorizing lessor to declare a forfeiture and terminate the lease for non-
payment of commutation money or failure to drill within a certain
time, lessor cannot declare a forfeiture, execute a new lease to a
third party, and then recover from the original lessee rental accruing subsequent to such declaration. If lessor declares a forfeiture the lease is terminated and thereafter no recovery can be
had for rentals thereunder; if he claims the rental he affirms the
continuation of the lease for the period for which he claims.

Wolf v. *Guffey*, 161 Pa. 276; 28 Atl. 1117.

Sec. 37.—Where a lease for years for oil and gas purposes
contains a covenant to commence operations within a stipulated
time after the execution of the lease or to thereafter pay to lessor
a rental or commutation money for delay, and the lease provides
that a failure on the part of the lessee to comply with either one
or the other of the foregoing conditions shall work an absolute
forfeiture of the lease, and the lessee fails to commence operations
and fails to pay the rental or commutation money in lieu thereof
and the lessor leases to another party the first lease is thus
avoided and the second lease is good against it. The execution of
the second lease is a sufficient declaration of forfeiture.

Guffey v. *Hukill*, 34 W. Va. 49; 11 S. E. 754.
Eclipse Oil Co. v. *South Penn Oil Co.* 47 W. Va. 84; 34 S. E.
        923.
Wolf v. *Guffey.* 161 Pa. 276; 28 Atl. 1117.

Sec 38.—Where lessor himself does not declare a forfeiture no
one can do so for him. The execution of a second lease, in order to

constitute a declaration of forfeiture, must be a clear and unequivocal declaration by the landowner of the forfeiture, and the right to forfeiture must have existed at the time of the execution of the second lease. The execution of the second lease, if made subject to the first, is not an unequivocal declaration of forfeiture.

> *Schaupp* v. *Hukill,* 34 W. Va. 375; 12 S. E. 501.
> *Hukill* v. *Myers,* 36 W. Va. 639; 15 S. E. 151.
> *Lowther Oil Co.* v. *Guffey,* 52 W. Va. 88. Op. 92; 43 S. E. 101.
> *Henne* v. *South Penn Oil Co.,* 52 W. Va., 192; syl. 3; 43 S. E. 147.
> *Stone* v. *Marshall Oil Co.,* 188 Pa. 602; 41 Atl. 748-1119.
> *Bartley* v. *Phillips,* 165 Pa. 325; 30 Atl. 842.
> *Bartley* v. *Phillips,* 179 Pa. 175; 36 Atl. 217.

Sec. 39.—Where lessee has either incurred a forfeiture by failing to commence operations or by failing to pay commutation money for delay within the time required, or having entered upon the premises subsequently abandons the same, and the lessor having a right to declare a forfeiture at the time, and acting under such authority, executes a second lease and provides therein or in a contemporaneous written agreement, that the lease is made subject to the first, such clause will be construed as meaning that the lessor intended to incorporate into the contract the fact that he had advised the lessee that the land had been theretofore leased, and that lessee was to take his lease subject to the old lease with the understanding that if the latter was valid he should take nothing by the contract, and that if it was invalid the conveyance should then stand as a contract binding on the parties.

> *Elk Fork Oil & Gas Co.* v. *Jennings,* 84 Fed. 839, syl. 5.
> Op. Judge Goff, 849. Affirmed in *Foster* v. *Elk Fork Oil & Gas Co.,* 90 Fed 178; 32 C. C. A. 560.
> *Eaton* v. *Allegheny Gas Co.,* 122 N. Y. 416; 25 N. E. 981.

Sec. 40.—Where an oil and gas lease provides that in case the lessee fails to commence operations within a specified time or pay rental or commutation money for delay the lease shall become "null and void" it is not made any more so by the provision that it "shall be of no effect between the parties" or "can only be renewed by mutual consent" or other merely cumulative phrases of

Sec. 46.—Where under an oil and gas lease there is a provision for forfeiture for failure to explore or pay commutation money for delay and lessee has either paid the commutation money or entered and commenced developments and thereafter has been excluded from possession for development purposes either directly by lessor or by a third person claiming under a subsequent lease, the original lessee may recover possession of the premises by a possessory action for the purpose of performing the covenants of his lease.

Guffey v. *Hukill,* 34 W. Va. 49; 11 S. E. 754.
Bartley v. *Phillips,* 179 Pa. 175; 36 Atl. 217.

Sec. 47.—Where there is a clause of forfeiture for non-payment of rentals or failure to begin explorations in an oil and gas lease if the lessor by his conduct clearly indicates that payment will not be demanded when due and thus lulls the lessee into a feeling of security and throws him off his guard and because of this he does not make payments when due the lessor cannot suddenly without demand or notice declare a forfeiture; if he attempts to declare a forfeiture lessee may file his bill in a court of equity, or his petition in a court exercising equity powers, and obtain relief from such technical forfeiture. In such case there is no forfeiture of the lease.

Hukill v. *Myers,* 36 W. Va. 639; 15 S. E. 151.
Pyle v. *Henderson,* 65 W. Va. 39; 63 S. E. 762.
See further Relief from Forfeiture, Chapter 25.

Sec. 48.—Where an oil and gas lease gives to the lessee the mere option to enter and explore, which is subject to revocation by lessor, in order to hold the lease lessee must do some act toward developing the property or pay commutation money for delay and in this way exercise the option before notice of lessor's election to revoke and cancel the lease. Where lessee enters upon the premises and begins explorations or pays commutation money for delay he is entitled to hold the lease while prosecuting the explorations with due diligence or during the time for which rental has been paid.

Lowther Oil Co. v. *Meller-Sibley Co.* 52 W. Va. 501. Op. 505;
   44 S. E. 433.
Eclipse Oil Co. v. *South Penn Oil Co.*, 47 W. Va. 84; 34 S. E.
   293.
Cortelyou v. *Barnsdall*, 236 Ill. 138; 86 N. E. 200.
See further Want of Mutuality, Chap. 29.

Sec. 49.—Where the lessee enters the leased premises and
drills a dry hole in order to hold the lease longer he is required to
drill additional wells within a reasonable time after the completion of the first well. Otherwise he will be considered as having
abandoned the lease.

Steelsmith v. *Gartlan*, 45 W. Va. 27; 29 S. E. 978.
Henne v. *South Penn Oil Co.* 52 W. Va. 192; 43 S. E. 147.
See further Effect of Drilling Dry Hole, Chap. 33.

Sec. 50.—Where in an oil and gas lease there is a surrender
clause the lessee may exercise his right of surrender and thereby
be relieved of any liability for rental or other liability accruing
subsequent to the date of such surrender.

Roberts v. *Bettman*, 45 W. Va. 143; 30 S. E. 95.
See Surrender Clause, Chap. 14.

Sec. 51.—Where lessor declares a forfeiture of a lease, lessee
may defend a proceeding at law or in equity to enforce such forfeiture by alleging and proving that he has performed all the
express covenants of the lease, breaches of which are therein
specified as grounds of forfeiture. In the States where breaches
of the implied covenants of a lease are held not to constitute a forfeiture, such defense will defeat the action or proceedings taken
by the lessor either to cancel the lease or to recover possession of
the premises from lessor, the law in such cases being that where
causes of forfeiture are specified it is not to be inferred that there
are other causes of forfeiture, not declared in the lease to be such.

Core v. *Petroleum Co.*, 52 W. Va. 276; 43 S. E. 128.
Marshall v. *Oil Co.*, 198 Pa. 83; 47 Atl. 927.
Harris v. *Ohio Oil Co.*, 57 Ohio St. 118; 48 N. E. 502.
Ahrns v. *Gas Co.*, 188 Pa. 249; 41 Atl. 739.
Crawford v. *Co.*, 183 Pa. 233; 38 Atl. 595.
Freeland v. *South Penn Oil Co.*, 189 Pa. 54; 41 Atl. 1000.

CHAPTER 13.

FORFEITURE AND RENTAL CLAUSE—LESSEE'S OPTION.

Sec. 1.—Where an oil and gas lease contains a provision by which the lessee may pay to the lessor a stipulated rental or commutation money for delay in drilling and there is no express promise to do either the lessee has the option either to drill or pay the rental or commutation money within the time specified in the lease and avoid a forfeiture.

Smith v. *South Penn Oil Co.*, 59 W. Va. 204; 53 S. E. 152.
Van Etten v. *Kelly*, 66 Ohio St. 605; 64 N. E. 560.
Snodgrass v. *South Penn Oil Co.*, 47 W. Va. 509; 35 S. E. 820.
Glasgow v. *Chartiers Oil Co.*, 152 Pa. 48; 25 Atl. 232.
Lowther Oil Co. v. *Guffey*, 52 W. Va. 88; 43 S. E. 101.
Monarch Oil, Gas & Coal Co., v. *Richardson*, 30 Ky. L. Rep. 824; 99 S. W. 686.
Great Western Oil Co. v. *Carpenter*, 43 Tex. Civ. App. 229; 95 S. W. 57.
Armitage v. *Mt. Sterling O. & G. Co.*, 25 Ky. L. Rep. 2262; 80 S. W. 177.
O'Neill v. *Resinger*, 77 Kan. 63; 93 Pac. 340.
Ringle v. *Quigg*, 74 Kan. 581; 87 Pac. 724.
Jennings-Heywood Oil Synd. v. *Houssierre-Lattreille Oil Co.* 119 La. 864; 44 Southern, 481.
Houssierre-Lattreille Oil Co. v. *Jennings-Heywood Oil Synd.* 115 La. 107; 38 Southern, 932.
Gillespie v. *Fulton Oil & Gas Co.*, 236 Ill. 188; 86 N. E. 219.
Pittsburg, etc. Co. v. *Bailey*, 76 Kan. 42; 90 Pac. 803.
Dill v. *Fraze*, 165 Ind. 53; 79 N. E. 971.
Vendocia Oil etc. Co. v. *Robinson*, 71 Ohio St. 302; 73 N. E. 222.
Erie Crawford Oil Co. v. *Meek*. 40 Ind. App. 156; 81 N. E. 518.
Hays v. *Forest Oil Co.*, 213 Pa. 556; 62 Atl. 1072.

Sec. 2.—The old form of the oil and gas lease contained an express covenant either to drill or pay commutation money for delay. The courts held, in construing these leases, that the forfeiture clause is inserted for the benefit of the landowner, and that he can either declare a forfeiture or waive it and collect the rental. The forfeiture clause in the modern oil and gas lease is materially different in respect to rental or commutation money for delay. These leases contain the provision that the lease shall be null and void unless the lessee drills within a certain time, or at the expiration thereof pays to the lessor a specified sum as rental or commutation money for delay; there is no express promise either to drill or to pay commutation money for delay; they are not void for uncertainty or want of mutuality, and the lessee has the option either to keep the lease alive by the payment of the stipulated rental or commutation money, or omit payment and terminate the lease, and after such omission lessee is wholly discharged from all liability under the lease, the lease being ended.   There is no obligation upon the lessee to pay the stipulated rental or commutation money, neither can the lessor waive the forfeiture and collect the rental, as he can do under the lease containing an express promise to pay the rental or drill.

Sec. 3.—In *Van Etten* v. *Kelley*, 66 Ohio St. 605; 64 N. E. 560 (June 24, 1902) the syllabus is as follows:

"An oil lease which requires certain wells to be completed within stated times contained the following: 'In case no well is completed within thirty days from this date, then this grant shall become null and void unless second party shall pay to first party thirty dollars each and every month in advance while such completion is delayed.' *Held*, that this did not constitute a promise or obligation to pay rental; and *held*, further, that the lessee had the option to complete wells or pay rental to keep the lease alive, and that upon breach of the agreement to complete wells no action would lie for the recovery of rentals."

On September 15, 1896, Luceba A. Kelly executed an oil and gas lease to S. Blair for a tract of land in Wood County, Ohio, containing 80 acres, for the term of fifteen years.   The lease contained the following condition:

"In case no well is completed within thirty days from this date, then this grant shall become null and void unless second party shall pay to said first party thirty dollars each and every month in advance while such completion is delayed, * * * The east forty acres of said land shall be drilled first.   Second party agrees to complete a well every sixty days, from date hereof on said east forty acres until six wells are completed, including the first well, and all lines must be protected.   Second party further agrees to complete a well every ninety days on the west forty after the completion of the sixth or last well on the east forty acres. It is understood that the monthly rental shall apply to any well or wells not completed as herein specified."

Subsequent to the execution of the lease the original lessee assigned the same and Van Etten and others became vested with title. The lessor instituted an action against Van Etten and others in the Court of Common Pleas of Wood County for the recovery of rentals and recovered judgment. The petition alleged that the defendants did drill the first well on the east forty acres and completed the same within the time provided for in the lease; and that sixty days thereafter the defendants drilled and completed another well on said east forty-acre tract. The petition then alleged that according to the terms of the lease there should have been another well completed on March 15, 1897, which the assignees of the original lease failed to drill; and that by reason of such failure they became liable for the payment of thirty dollars per month as long as they delayed such completion. The defendants denied the averments of the petition, and averred that oil in paying quantities could not be produced on the premises; and that after ascertaining this to be so they had offered to surrender and cancel the lease; and further pleaded that by a fair construction of the lease they were not required to pay any rental whatever to the plaintiff by reason of the failure to drill the wells or for any other cause. From a judgment in favor of the plaintiff, lessor, the defendants, assignees of the lease, appealed to the Supreme Court of Ohio, and that court reversed the judgment and held the law applicable to the lease to be as stated in the syllabus.

Sec. 4.—In *Snodgrass v. South Penn Oil Co.*, 47 W. Va., 509; 35 S. E. 820 (March 24, 1900) the syllabus is as follows:

"Where a party leases a tract of land for the purpose of mining and operating for oil and gas, the lessee contracting to deliver to the credit of the lessor one-eighth of the oil produced and saved from the premises, and to pay two hundred dollars per year, for the gas from each well drilled, and the lease also contains the following provision: 'Provided, however, that this lease shall become null and void, and all rights thereunder shall cease and determine unless a well shall be completed on the premises within

one year from the date hereof, or unless the lessee shall pay at the
rate of three hundred and fifty dollars, quarterly in advance for
each additional three months such completion is delayed from the
time above mentioned for the completion of such well until a well
is completed.' *Held*, that this provision did not bind the lessee
to pay any rent for the land, or for delay in commencing to operate for oil and gas, and, in the absence of some other clause binding the lessee to pay for such rent or delay, an action of assumpsit
could not be maintained on such lease for failing to pay such rent,
or for such delay.''

C. M. Snodgrass made an oil and gas lease to the South Penn
Oil Company for a tract of three thousand five hundred acres of
land in Gilmer and Braxton Counties, West Virginia. The lease
contained the following provision:

"Provided, however, that this lease shall become null and
void and all rights thereunder shall cease and determine unless
a well shall be completed on the premises within one year from
the date hereof or unless the lessee shall pay at the rate of three
hundred and fifty dollars quarterly in advance for each additional
three months such completion is delayed from the time above mentioned for the completion of such well until a well is completed.''

The lease bore date July 18, 1896, and provided that a well
should be completed within one year, followed by the provision
above quoted as to rental. On September 1, 1898, Snodgrass
brought an action of assumpsit upon the agreement against the
South Penn Oil Company for the recovery of rental claimed thereunder. No well had been commenced on the land at the date of the
institution of the suit. The declaration filed in the case set forth
the terms and conditions of the lease and charged that in the lease
defendant agreed and promised the plaintiff to complete a well on
the premises within one year of the date thereof, and in case of
failure, to pay to plaintiff a rental of $350.00 quarterly in ad-
vance for each three months, and to continue to do so until such
well should be completed. The declaration demanded as rental due
the sum of One Thousand Four Hundred Dollars. The defendant
craved oyer of the writing obligatory in the declaration mentioned,
and demurred to the declaration. The Circuit Court of Braxton
County sustained the demurrer to the declaration and from the
judgment sustaining the demurrer the plaintiff obtained a writ of
error. The court of appeals affirmed the judgment.

Sec. 5.—In *Glasgow* v. *Chartiers Oil Co.*, 152 Pa. 48; 25 Atl.
232 (Nov. 11, 1892) the syllabus is as follows:

"An oil lease demised the oil and gas under the grantor's
land with the right to go upon and operate the land for oil and gas
purposes. The lease was to continue for five years and as much
longer as oil or gas should be found in paying quantities. The
consideration was a bonus of one hundred dollars, and a royalty
of one-eighth part of the oil produced. If gas was found the rental
was fixed at three hundred dollars per year for each well. The
lease then proceeded as follows: 'Provided, however, that this
lease shall become null and void and all rights hereunder shall
cease and determine, unless a well shall be completed on the premises within one month from the date hereof or unless the lessee
shall pay at the rate of one hundred dollars monthly in advance,
for each additional month.' *Held*, that the lease contained no
covenant on the part of the lessee to pay rent or develop the land.
The only penalty imposed upon him for failure to operate the land
or pay one hundred dollars per month for delay, was a forfeiture
of his rights under the agreement.

The legal effect of the agreement is to confer on the grantee the
right to explore for oil on the tract described. If he does not exercise this right within one month, it is lost to him unless he
chooses to pay one hundred dollars in advance, as the price of another month's opportunity to explore. If he does exercise it, and
finds nothing, he is under no obligation to continue his explorations. If he explores and finds oil or gas, the relation of landlord and tenant, or vendor and vendee is established, and the tenant would be under an implied obligation to operate for the common good of both parties and pay the rent or royalties reserved."

On June 10, 1890, John Glasgow executed an oil and gas lease
to the Chartiers Oil Company for a tract of land in Butler County,
Pennsylvania, for the term of five years. The lease contained the
provision quoted in the syllabus. No developments were made on
the property but the defendant paid the monthly rentals on the
lease up to and including January 10, 1891. On April 13, 1891, the
lessor instituted suit in the Court of Common Pleas of Butler
County against the lessee for the recovery of $300.00 claimed to
be rentals due for February, March and April, 1891. The defendant filed an affidavit of defense, denying the liability, which affidavit of defense was held sufficient by the Court of Common Pleas
and judgment rendered for defendant. The plaintiff appealed to

the Supreme Court. That court affirmed the judgment of the
Court of Common Pleas.

Sec. 6.—In *Lowther Oil Co.* v. *Guffey,* 52 W. Va. 88; 43 S. E.
101, analyzed under Chapter 6, the syllabus is as follows:

"Where a grant of oil and gas, and oil and gas privileges, in
consideration of one dollar, without limitation as to time, contains a forfeiture clause in these words: 'In case no well is completed within two years from this date, then this grant shall immediately become null and void as to both parties, provided that
second party may prevent such forfeiture from year to year by
paying to the first annually in advance eighteen and seventy-five
one hundredths dollars at her residence until such well is completed,' such lease is thereby converted into a lease from year to
year at the option of the lessee until a well is completed. It would
then continue so long as oil or gas is produced in paying quantities."

Judge Dent, in the opinion, at pages 91-2, says:

"The question of importance in this case is, whether the lessee
had the option to continue the lease from year to year by the payment annually of the non-forfeiture sum. This is the way in
which the lease reads. The manacles were forged by the lessors
themselves with their eyes open, and the court cannot remove them
unless fraud can be shown or the contract is so unfair and uneven
as to render its enforcement equivalent to the perpetuation of
fraud upon the lessors. It is claimed that this is a case of such
character because the lessee by the prompt payment of the non-
forfeiture sum could perpetually prevent the development of the
land for oil and gas. It is not, however, probable that he would
do so, and he is already actively engaged in drilling. If it could
be shown that such was his purpose it would amount to a fraud
which equity might relieve against, for the reason that the primary object of the lease is the development of the land and production of oil royalties and gas rentals, and equity will not tolerate a fraudulent delay in operations. No such delay has occurred
here, but the lessee has only waited until he could ascertain that
there was a strong probability of obtaining oil or gas before ex-
pending the large sums necessary in the proper development of
the land. This seems to have been the object of the provision in
permitting him to postpone the developments from year to year.
The lessors have become impatient at a delay, to which they consented, and which has not been shown to be unreasonable."

The lease bore date April 13, 1895. Lessee elected not to drill, and paid the commutation money to April 13, 1901. In March, 1901, lessee took possession and began drilling and tendered lessor the commutation money, $18.75, which lessor refused to accept. On October 3, 1900, lessor made a second lease to the Lowther Oil Company, which lease was taken subject to the original lease. The Lowther Oil Company filed a bill in equity in the Circuit Court of Calhoun County, praying for a cancellation of the Guffey lease as a cloud on their title. The Circuit Court entered a decree cancelling the Guffey lease, from which decree Guffey appealed to the Court of Appeals, and that court reversed the Circuit Court.

Sec. 7.—In *Smith* v. *South Penn Oil Co.,* 59 W. Va. 204; 53 S. E. 152 (March 6, 1906) the syllabus is as follows:

"1. The following clause in a lease for oil and gas purposes imposes no obligation to pay rent: 'Provided, however, that this lease shall become null and void and all rights hereunder shall cease and determine unless a well shall be completed on the said premises within three (3) months from the date hereof, or unless the lessee shall pay at the rate of Sixty-five and 25/100 ($65.25-100), Dollars quarterly in advance for each additional three months such completion is delayed from the time above mentioned for the completion of such well until a well is completed.'

2. If, after having drilled one unproductive well under such a lease and paid commutation money until the completion thereof, the lessee is permitted to drill another without making further payments; and without notice that any compensation will be demanded or required of him for such further use and occupation of his premises none can be recovered.

3. Such a contract, being ambiguous as to what shall constitute a completed well, the conduct of the parties in treating the completion of an unproductive well as an act sufficient to vest in the lessee a right to make further explorations without additional payment is conclusive upon them under the principles of practical construction."

Albert H. Smith, on January 18, 1896, made an oil and gas lease to the South Penn Oil Company, which lease contained the following provision:

"Provided, however, that this lease shall become null and void and all rights hereunder shall cease and determine unless a well shall be completed on the said premises within three (3) months from the date hereof, or unless the lessee shall pay at the rate of sixty-five and 25/100 ($65.25/100) Dollars, quarterly, in advance for each additional three months such completion is delayed from the time above mentioned for the completion of such well until a well is completed.''

Seven payments of $65.25 each, for delay in drilling, were made, and a well was completed in December, 1897. The lessee then abandoned the premises until the Spring of 1889, when it re-entered and completed another well in May of that year. Both wells were unproductive, and the tools, machinery and appliances were finally removed from the premises in January or February, 1900. The lessor instituted an action of assumpsit in the Circuit Court of Tyler County against the South Penn Oil Company, the lessee, for the recovery of rentals for the premises during the time from the completion of the first well to the abandonment after drilling the second. Judgment was rendered in favor of the plaintiff for $217.50. The defendant prosecuted a writ of error to this judgment, and the Court of Appeals reversed the judgment.

Sec. 8.—In *Monarch Oil, Gas & Coal Co.* v. *Richardson*, 30 Ky. L. Rep. 824; 99 S. W. 668, (Feb. 13, 1907), the syllabus is as follows:

"A coal, oil, gas and mineral lease provided that the lessor was to receive a pro rata share of all the oil and minerals produced, and should gas be found, then a certain rental from each well; and the lease further provided that lessee should commence a well on the premises within a year or pay thereafter an annual rental of $16.00. A well was never commenced, but lessee paid the annual rental, which was accepted by the lessor. *Held*, that notwithstanding the lessor was entitled to forfeit the lease for failure to develop the premises, yet lessor could not do so until he had first declined to accept the rental and demanded of lessee development of the premises."

On October 10, 1898, Nelson & Ramsey entered into a contract with Richardson, whereby in consideration of the mutual covenants and agreements contained in the contract and the sum of One Dollar the said Richardson granted to the second parties the exclusive right for the sole and only purpose of operating for coal, oil and gas, ore and other minerals, a certain tract of land in Wayne County, Kentucky, for the term of twenty years and so long as oil, gas or any of the specified substances were obtained in paying quantities. Second parties covenanted with the first party to give to him the full equal pro rata share, or one-tenth, of all the oil and other minerals produced from the premises; said one-tenth to be set aside in the pipelines when one should be constructed; and should gas be found in paying quantities to justify second parties in marketing the same, the consideration to first party, instead of one-tenth royalty to be $5 per month for the gas from each well so long as it should be sold therefrom. Second parties were to commence a well on the premises within one year from the date, or thereafter pay an annual rental of $16.00 each. It was further agreed that the second party should have the right at any time to surrender the lease to first party and thereafter be fully discharged from any and all damages arising from any neglect or non-fulfillment of the contract. Nelson and Ramsey assigned the contract to the Monarch Oil, Gas & Coal Company. In 1906, Richardson instituted an action in the Circuit Court of Wayne County to have the contract cancelled on the grounds that the lessee and their assignees had failed and refused to commence a well and develop the premises for any of the products mentioned, and upon the further grounds that the leased premises were located in the oil fields of Wayne County and adjacent to lands that had been operated and developed for the production of oil and gas, which had been marketed in large and remunerative quantities, under leases similar to that held by the defendant company. The defendant answered and affirmatively averred that under the contract it had a right to commence a well on the premises within one year from the date of the lease or thereafter pay an annual rental of $16.00; and although it had not commenced a well it had paid the annual rental each year, the last payment being made in October, 1905, the next annual payment not being due till October, 1906; that the lessor had accepted each annual installment of rental; that the defendant was ready, able and willing to drill and develop the land when and as soon as the lessor made his election to require it to do so; that the lessor had not at any time notified it that he would accept the annual rental, or that he would require it

to develop the land. To this answer a demurrer was interposed
and sustained, and the defendant declining to plead further a decree was entered for plaintiff, from which defendant appealed to
the Court of Appeals. That Court reversed the Circuit Court, and
remanded the cause with directions to proceed in conformity with
the opinion.

Sec. 9.—In *Great Western Oil Company* v. *Carpenter*, 43 Tex.
Civ. App. 229; 95 S. W. 57 (May 15, 1906) syls. 1-2 are as follows:

"1. A consideration of one dollar recited as paid in an oil
and gas lease, and in fact paid, was a mere nominal consideration
which was insufficient to support the contract.
2. Where an oil and gas lease recites a consideration of one
dollar and also imposes on the lessee an unconditional obligation
to sink one or more wells on the leased lands within eighteen
months, and to commence work on the first well within six months
from the date of the contract, and in case of his failure authorized
the lessor to elect to declare a forfeiture subject to the lessee's
right to continue the lease in force for another year by paying ten
cents per acre annual rental, such lease was not a mere unilateral
agreement, but was based upon a sufficient consideration."

On January 28, 1901, M. A. Carpenter and wife executed two
certain contracts or agreements substantially identical in their
terms, except as to the land covered thereby, one contract embracing 400 acres of land in Jefferson County, and the other 145 acres in
Harden County. The cash consideration recited was one dollar, with
the further consideration on the part of the lessee, Fritter, to be
performed. The leases were for ten years unless sooner terminated under the terms of the agreements. The lands were leased
"for the purpose of boring, mining and operating for oil, gas,
coal and other minerals on said land." The leases contained the
usual stipulation for the exclusive right of Fritter to mine for oil,
gas, coal and other minerals, with a royalty provision. Each lease
contained the following clause:

"The party of the second part hereby agrees to sink one or
more wells on said land within eighteen months from the date
hereof, work on the first one of which shall be commenced within
six months from the date hereof. In the event of failure to so
commence work on said well within six months from date hereof

the parties of the first part may at their option cancel this lease unless the same be renewed for one year by the party of the second part by the payment of the annual rental of ten cents per acre.''

Fritter assigned the lease to the Great Western Oil Company which company thereby became vested with all the rights, and bound by all the obligations of Fritter. On July 20, 1901, eight days before the expiration of the six months within which lessee was to commence work on the wells, Carpenter and the Great Western Oil Company entered into a new agreement or contract whereby in consideration of one dollar, acknowledged to have been received by the lessor, with the further consideration of the stipulations of the contract, Carpenter granted and sold to the Great Western Oil Company for a continuous period of fifty years, with the privilege of a renewal of an equal term, ''all the oil, gas, coal and other minerals,'' under and upon the 400-acre tract, covered by one of the first leases, and 120 acres of the 145 acres, covered by the other lease. This contract contained the usual provision as to ingress and egress and occupancy for drilling and operating for coal, gas, oil and other minerals. In consideration of the execution of this contract the Great Western Oil Company released all the land conveyed by the two leases executed to Fritter and assigned to it by said lessee and especially released 25 acres embraced in the 145 acres, and not embraced in the last lease. This last contract also contained the following clause:

''In the event work on a well, sinking pipe either for oil or gas, is not begun within nine (9) months from the date hereof and completed within fifteen months thereafter, on each of the said two tracts of land, and not abandoned until pipe is down at least 800 feet, unless oil is found at a less depth, then this grant and lease shall become null and void as to both parties.''

On March 24, 1902, the parties entered into another contract by which Carpenter agreed to pay to the Great Western Oil Company the sum of one thousand dollars out of the first money realized from the sale of fifty acres of land which were released to Carpenter by the said agreement, and further agreed to deed Lot Number 1 to said company or its assigns. Said lot was situated on the north-east corner of the 120 acres, also released to Carpenter

by said agreement. On March 26, 1902, the Oil Company executed
to Carpenter a special release of all its right, title, claim and interest in and to the agreement of July 20, 1901. At the date of the
contract of March 24, 1902, there remained 26 days of the nine
months within which, under the terms of the contract of July 20,
1901, work on a well had to be begun on each of the two tracts of
land embraced therein, in default of which the contract was to become void as to both parties. The Great Western Oil Company instituted in the District Court of Harden County an action against
F. H. Carpenter et al., for the recovery of one thousand dollars in
money, and also for the recovery of a certain tract of 2.82 acres of
land. The Oil Company in its petition prayed, in the alternative,
that if it was held not to be entitled to recover the money and land,
that it be reinstated in its rights under a certain oil lease which
had been cancelled by agreement of the parties in consideration of
the promise of Carpenter to pay the money and convey the tract
of land sued for. Upon trial in the Circuit Court without a jury
there was a judgment for defendant from which judgment
- the plaintiff oil company appealed. The court found that
no part of the fifty acres of land referred to in the
last contract had ever been sold, and that therefore the basis
for the payment of the $1,000 had never been created. No work was
ever in fact done by either Fritter or the oil company toward
boring for coal, oil, gas or other minerals, under any of the contracts. The one dollar in cash, recited to have been a consideration
for each of the two leases of January 28, 1901, and of July 20, 1901,
was in fact paid as recited. The object of the suit was the recovery of the 2.82 acres of land, the lot mentioned in the agreement of
March 24, 1902, and the $1,000 referred to in said contract. The
trial court held, that the plaintiff was not entitled to recover on the
ground that the contracts or leases were unilateral contracts and without consideration and therefore not binding upon the appellees; the Carpenters; and that the release and cancellation thereof furnished consideration for the contract of March 24, 1902, for the conveyance of the land and the payment of the money, the basis of the suit. The trial court further
concluded that as to the $1,000, the conditions upon which it was to
be paid had not been complied with by the sale of the fifty acres of

land. The Appellate court reversed in part the judgment of the trial court, and held the law to be as stated in the syllabus quoted, and rendered judgment in favor of the plaintiff for the 2.82 acres of land described in the contract of March 24, 1902; and as to the claim for $1,000 the judgment was affirmed without prejudice to the right of the oil company to sue for the recovery of the same whenever it should appear that it could be legally demanded under the terms of the contract. The effect of this decision was that the agreement in the leases by which the lessee obligated himself by accepting the lease, to drill the test wells within the time limited was a sufficient consideration, and that the contracts were not void for this reason, but that the mere nominal consideration of One Dollar, in the absence of other considerations would have rendered the leases void.

Sec. 10.—In *Armitage* v. *Mt. Sterling Oil & Gas Co.*, 25 Ky. L. Rep. 2262; 80 S. W. 177 (April 27, 1904) the syllabus is as follows:

"Where the lessee in an oil lease is to commence operations within six months but the only express stipulation for forfeiture is in case a test well is not completed in three years, a suit to cancel the lease, begun several months before the three years have expired, without an averment that the well cannot be completed in time is premature, though failure to commence operations within the six months is alleged.
Where an oil lease stipulated that it is to be void if the test well is not completed in three years unless the lessee pays rental during the time drilling is delayed, the rights of the lessee, after failure to sink the well as required will not be extended by a mere offer to pay the rental if the lessor elects to treat the lease as terminated."

On May 26, 1900, the Mt. Sterling Oil & Gas Company obtained from H. B. Armitage a lease giving it the exclusive right to drill and operate for petroleum oil and gas, coal, and other minerals, upon a tract of 470 acres of land in Manifee County, Kentucky, for a term of ten years, and as much longer as oil, gas, coal, or other minerals were found thereon. The consideration for the lease recited therein, was that the oil and gas company should give to the lessor one-tenth of the petroleum oil and minerals obtained from the premises. It was further agreed that if gas was

found in sufficient quantities to market, and piped from the prem·
ises, the lessor should receive $100.00 per annum for each well so
long as the gas therefrom was marketed. The lessee agreed to drill
a test well on the land within three years, and to commence operations in the county inside of six months. It was stipulated that
the lease was to become void if the well was not completed within
three years, unless the lessee should pay rental for the premises at
the rate of ten cents per acre during the time drilling was delayed.
On February 13, 1903, Armitage instituted suit for the cancellation
of the lease on the ground that the oil company had failed to commence operations in the County of Manifee within six months from
the date of the lease, and had also failed to drill a test well in accordance with the terms of the contract. The Oil Company demurred to the petition, which demurrer was sustained by the trial
court and the plaintiff's petition dismissed. Plaintiff appealed to
the Court of Appeals, and that court affirmed the decree of the
court below, and cited the following cases:

> *Core* v. *New York Pet. Co.*, 52 W. Va. 276; 43 S. E. 128.
> *Harris* v. *Ohio Oil Co.*, 57 Ohio St. 118; 48 N. E. 502.
> *Munroe* v. *Armstrong*, 96 Pa. 307.
> *Heintz* v. *Schortt*, 149 Pa. 286; 24 Atl. 316.
> *Steelsmith* v. *Gartlan*, 45 W. Va. 27; 29 S. E. 978.
> *Woodland Oil Co.* v. *Crawford*, 55 Ohio St. 161; 44 N. E. 1093.
> *Parish Fork Oil Co.* v. *Bridgewater Gas Co.*, 51 W. Va. 583;
>   42 S. E. 655.
> *Schamberg* v. *Farmer*, 18 Ky. L. Rep. 514; 37 S. W. 152.

Sec. 11.—In *O'Neill* v. *Ressinger*, 77 Kan. 63; 93 Pac. 340 (Jan.
11, 1908) the syllabus is as follows:

"An oil and gas lease giving the lessee the exclusive right for a
term of years to enter upon lands and prospect and procure oil
and gas, and providing that in case no well is drilled within six
months all rights and obligations under the lease shall cease and
determine unless the lessee shall elect to continue the lease in force
by payment in advance of an annual rental of one dollar per acre
for all the land, and which contains no covenant, promise or agreement on the part of the lessee to drill a well or pay the rental, or
to do anything, is a mere naked option and the failure of the lessee
to drill a well within six months or to make a payment of rental
forfeits the lease."

On November 2, 1905, Joseph Ressinger and wife made and delivered to James O'Neill an oil and gas lease on certain lands in Wilson County, Kansas. Two of the provisions of the lease were as follows:

"In case no well for oil or gas be drilled on said premises within six months of the date hereof all rights and obligations secured under this contract shall cease and determine, unless the second party shall elect to continue this lease in effect as to all said premises by paying an annual rental of one dollar per acre, payable annually in advance for all of said premises.

Provided, however, that second party shall have the right at any time to terminate this lease by surrendering this lease, released from records, and shall thereupon be released from all obligations and liabilities under the same."

No well was drilled within six months from the date of the lease, nor at any other time, and the lessee paid no rental. In July, 1906, the owners of the land brought their action in the District Court of Wilson County against James O'Neill to recover the sum of $480 for rental on the lands for one year. The petition set out a copy of the lease and alleged that no well for oil or gas was drilled on any of the premises within six months, nor at any time subsequent. The petition alleged that the defendant, O'Neill, "elected to retain said premises under said lease by failing to surrender the said lease to plaintiffs upon the expiration of the six months within which time a well for oil or gas was to be drilled on said premises." The $480.00 was alleged to be due and unpaid. A demurrer to the petition was overruled by the trial court, and the defendant electing to stand upon his demurrer, judgment was entered for the plaintiffs, and defendant brought error to the Supreme Court. That court reversed the judgment of the court below, and remanded the cause with directions to sustain the demurrer, citing the following cases:

Glasgow v. *Chartiers Oil Co.*, 152 Pa. 48; 25 Atl. 232.
Snodgrass v. *South Penn Oil Co.*, 47 W. Va. 509; 35 S. E. 829.

Sec. 12.—In *Ringle* v. *Quigg*, 74 Kan. 581; 87 Pac. 724 (Nov. 10, 1906) the syllabus is as follows:

"1. In an action by the lessor, to cancel·an oil and gas lease on the ground that it is void, the petition alleged the execution of the lease, giving a copy thereof, which is given hereinafter. No facts outside of the lease itself indicating imposition, fraud or mistake, or that the interests of the lessor were being or would be injuriously affected by any of the provisions of such instrument were stated in the petition. *Held*, that a general demurrer to such petition was properly sustained.

2.   A gas lease is not void merely because the lessee stipulated therein that at the end of five years he shall have the option to keep the lease in force by then doing some act which at the date of the lease he is unable to perform.

3.   A lessor in a gas lease has no right to expect the lessee to perform the conditions therein on his part immediately, when, by the provisions of the instrument he is permitted to delay performance for five years.

4.   A written instrument is not void for ambiguity when the contract of the parties can be clearly and certainly ascertained therefrom.

5.   Although obtaining royalties may be the essence of an oil and gas lease, the time when operations under the lease shall commence is the proper subject of the agreement between the parties. and, in the absence of imposition, fraud or mistake, the provisions of the contract should be upheld."

On December 19, 1900, A. D. Riggle and wife executed an oil and gas lease to A. R. Quigg and others, the material provisions whereof were as follows:

"This agreement made and executed in duplicate this 19th day of December, A. D. 1900, between A. D. Riggle and Sarah Riggle, parties of the first part, and A. R. Quigg, O. L. Hayward, S. S. Harmon, and M. L. Stephens, of the second part, witnesseth: That the said parties of the first part in consideration of One Dollar in hand paid * * * * and other valuable considerations hereinafter mentioned, do hereby lease, demise and let unto said parties of the second part, their heirs or assigns, for the term of twenty years and as much longer as gas or oil may be found in paying quantities * * * * the following described real estate situated in the County of Montgomery and State of Kansas, * * * * containing 159 acres, with full and exclusive power and authority * * * * * * taking upon and removing from said land any machinery or appliances necessary to the prosecution of the work: * * * * In consideration of the premises the parties of the second part agree to pay as royalty to the parties of the first part upon each well gas from which any product is taken having any commercial value, the sum of Five Dollars per month for each month while so taken. * * * * In case that oil or other products than

gas are found the royalty shall be one-eighth of such product, delivered at surface near mouth of well or shaft. It is. mutually
agreed that the party of the second part shall begin operations on
this lease within five years (5 yrs.) from the delivery hereof or in
case of failure to do so, then and in that case, it shall be at the
option of the party of the second part to lay pipes from mains to
wells to within fifty feet of the residence occupied by first parties
on the above described land, and furnish gas for stoves and for
lights, and no other or additional expense shall be incurred under
this lease by second party, and this lease shall be binding so long
as gas shall be thus furnished * * * * * otherwise this lease shall
be null and void and no longer binding on either party. * * * * * *''

The lessees assigned their interest in the lease to the Elk City
Gas & Oil Company and this company executed and delivered to the
R. J. Waddell Investment Company a written instrument as some
sort of security. This instrument was recorded in the office of the
registrar of deeds, and the court found that the same constituted
a cloud upon the plaintiff's title to the leased premises. On July
13, 1903, the lessors notified the lessees and their assigns, that unless they cancelled the lease suit would be brought to compel cancellation thereof as void. Upon failure of the lessees to comply
with this demand, lessors commenced an action in the District
Court of Montgomery County, on July 24, 1903, for the purpose of
cancelling the lease and agreement above mentioned. The petition
was amended from time to time, and the second amended petition
was filed on March 15, 1904, to which the Elk City Oil & Gas Company filed a general demurrer, which demurrer was sustained by
the District Court and judgment entered against plaintiffs and an
appeal was taken to the Supreme Court which Court affirmed the
District Court, citing the following cases:

National Oil & Pipeline Co. v. *Teel*, 67 S. W. 545, Affirmed in
      68 S. W. 779; 95 Tex. 586.
Eclipse Oil Co. v. *South Penn Oil Co.* 47 W. Va. 84; 34 S. E.
      293.
Roberts v. *Bettman*, 45 W. Va. 143; 30 S. E. 95.
Federal Oil Co. v. *Western Oil Co.*, 112 Fed. 373.
Martel v. *Jennings*, 38 Southern, 253.
Rose v. *Lanyon, etc.* 68 Kan. 126; 74 Pac. 625.

Sec. 13.—In *Jennings-Heywood Oil Syndicate* v. *Houssierre.*

Lattreille Oil Co., 119 La. 864; 44 So. 481 (March 4, 1907), on re-hearing the syllabus is as follows:

"2. At the height of the excitement created by the discovery of oil at Beaumont, Texas, indications similar to those at the cele-brated Spindletop were observed at Prairie Mamou, about 90 miles from Beaumont, and it caused great excitement. Specu-lators began taking leases of lands of the neighborhood, and a farmer leased to one of these speculators, the part of his land in the immediate proximity of the oil indications. The lease was for ten years and was declared to be for the sole purpose of operating for oil and gas, and its recited consideration was one dollar and the engagement of the lessee to begin operations within six months, or pay $50.00 quarterly in advance for any delay in commencing operations, and to deliver to the lessor one-eighth of whatever oil or gas might be produced. Lessee reserved to himself the right to retire from the contract at any time upon the payment of $100.00 Just before the expiration of the six months the lessee made the first quarterly payment, and thereafter made two others in advance; but when the time came for making the fourth he over-looked it owing to the fact that a fire was raging in the oil field. He tendered the payment four days late and the lessor declined to receive it claiming that the contract had been forfeited for non-performance, and that the tender of the quarterly payment for further delay had not been made in advance, as stipulated. The lessee did not even then offer to develop the land for oil, but in-sisted that he had the right to postpone doing so indefinitely, on making quarterly payments of $50.00, and he continued to tender $50.00 quarterly to the lessor. When accepting those of the quar-terly payments which he did accept the lessor insisted that the next well should be bored on his land, and at the time of the re-fusal of the fourth quarterly payment a number of wells had been bored in the immediate vicinity of the lessor's land, for all that was known were draining the land of its oil. The evidence showed that the cost of boring the well which the lessee obligated himself to bore within six months, was about $10,000, and it was shown that at the signing of the contract the prospect of striking oil appeared to be excellent. Things continued in this state for eight-een months longer when the lessor having begun making prepara-tions for exploiting the land himself the lessee came upon the land and litigation followed, *held:*

(1) That since the sole object and purpose of the contract was to exploit the land for oil and gas, and the contract left the lessee the liberty to do so or not at his option, there was in reality no contract binding on the lessee.

(2) That if, however, there was a contract, it was either in the nature of an option to the lessee to begin operations within the time fixed in the contract, with the right to prolong the term on

making quarterly payments in advance, or else it was a commuta-
tive contract wherein the obligation was to exploit the land for oil
and gas. If it was the former it came to an end by the lessee not
exercising the option timely. If it was the latter, the lessee broke
it by neither beginning operations nor offering to do so within the
term of the contract, or within a reasonable time thereafter.

(3)   That even if the obligation of the lessee was alternative,
namely, either to exploit the land for oil and gas, or else pay $50.00
in advance, quarterly, it became pure and simple when the alternative right to make the payment vanished from the contract as the
result of the failure to exercise that right in time; and from that
time the only useful offer of performance the lessee could have
made would have been to develop the land for oil and gas.

(4) An option must be exercised within the time limit or the
right will be lost. *Vis major* is no excuse for delay.

(5) If a lease is made in consideration of a payment to be
made in advance the obligation of the lessor does not come
into existence unless the payment is made in advance. The
payment in advance is a suspensive condition, all others precedent.

(6)   Where the contract has been violated by not doing what
was covenanted to be done within the time stipulated, a putting in
default is not a prerequisite to a suit in rescission. Such putting
in default is a prerequisite only to recovery of future damages.

(7)   When the contract has been violated by the obligor, the
obligee who no longer desires that it should be performed, is not
bound to put the obligor in default or bring suit for rescission, but
may refuse to allow the contractor to perform, and in case of suit
by the contractor, may plead the breach of the contract by way of
exception.''

Arthur Lattreille and S. A. Spencer, having entered into a
certain contract, Spencer assigned his rights to S. A. Spencer &
Company who assigned to Jennings-Heywood Oil Syndicate. The
contract so entered into was an oil and gas lease whereby the lessor
for the consideration of One Dollar and the covenants and agreements of the lease, granted, leased and let to said Spencer for the
purpose of mining and operating for oil a certain tract of land in
Acadia Parish, Louisiana, for the term of ten years, or so long
thereafter as oil or gas should be produced therefrom. The lessee
agreed to deliver as a royalty to the lessor $\frac{1}{8}$ of the oil produced,
and to pay $\frac{1}{8}$ of the proceeds of the sale of any gas that might be
marketed and used off the premises, the lessee to commence operations on the premises within six months from date, or pay at the
rate of $50.00 quarterly in advance for each three months such op-

erations should be delayed, until a well should be completed. The lessees, upon the payment of $100.00, had the right at any time to surrender the lease for cancellation, after which all payments and liabilities to accrue should cease. The Jennings-Heywood Oil Syndicate instituted a suit against the Housierre-Lattreille Oil Company and others, in the District Court of Acadia Parish, setting up the making of the lease as above stated, and by its original and amended petition alleged that it had complied with the provisions of the lease; that not having commenced operations within six months, on October 19, 1901, it paid Lattreille the sum of $50.00, as the quarterly rental in advance, and made payments on January 19th and April 19th, 1902; and that its tender of $50.00 on or about July 19, 1902, was declined for no sufficient reason. The petition further alleged that on December, 6, 1901, the Cochran Oil & Development Company instituted suit against Lattréille and others praying to be decreed to be the owner of the land in question; that the judgment in favor of the defendants did not become final until November, 1903, and was then taken by writ of error to the Supreme Court of the United States where the suit was then still pending, for which reason in addition to those alleged, the petitioner claimed that it was justified in delaying active operations under its contract, but that shortly after the suit had been decided by the Supreme Court of the State, it erected a derrick on the land with the intention of drilling for oil and gas, and was engaged on this work when, on January 15, 1904, it was enjoined by defendant from further prosecuting the same, and from entering upon the premises; and though the injunction was ordered by the court to be dissolved, it was nevertheless kept in force by the suspensive appeal from the order of dissolution which appeal the petition alleged to be still pending in the Supreme Court of the State. The petition further alleged that the land in question was the western 40 acres of that portion of Section 47 known as the "Lattreille Tract;" that the Housierre-Lattreille Oil Syndicate asserted title thereto under conveyance from Lattreille, executed and recorded long after the making and recording of the contract sued on by the petitioner; and that defendant had taken possession of said land, and was then, with its assigns, aiders and abettors, engaged in drilling wells, and petitioner was informed had obtained at least 2,000,000 barrels of oil, of which, with its aiders, and abettors, it had appropriated 1,000,000 barrels, leaving 1,000,000 barrels on hand; and for the preservation of its rights petitioner prayed for an injunction and sequestration. In accordance with the prayer, a preliminary in junction was issued which was dissolved on bond at the instance of the proper defendant. The defendants filed various pleas and exceptions which were overruled, and the defense that was made was the answer and supplemental answer of the Housierre-Lat- treille Oil Company, wherein it was alleged that this company was the owner of the property in question, having acquired through mesne conveyance directly from Arthur Lattreille, and was in pos- session of the same; that the contract set up by plaintiff, though never legitimate or binding, had lapsed according to its terms by reason of the plaintiff's failure either to drill a well or make the quarterly payments as stipulated; that the contract was obtained from Lattreille, the plaintiff's grantor, through fraud and misrep- resentation, as the parties for whom he signed the same imposed upon him by representing that they were in position to prevent the bringing of the suit by the Cochran heirs; and further representing that whatever proceeding would be taken by the Cochran heirs would be rendered less inimical if the lease were granted; that such representations were entirely untrue but had the effect of coercing Lattreille into signing the lease; that S. A. Spencer ac- quired the lease in question as a speculation, and with no intention of developing the property, and that the plaintiff had no other as- sets than the said lease and other leases of the same character and was incapable of development; that it was only after the plaintiff found that defendant was moving in the direction of developments that plaintiff made any pretence of drilling; that by the terms of the contract the lessee was not bound to drill for oil but might hold the property until developments elsewhere made it practicable for it to do so; that defendant was unwilling to submit its property to the blight of such contract; that when Lattreille accepted the quarterly payment he did so with the understanding that the next well drilled in that field should be on his property; and that the $100.00 payable on the surrender of the contract was relatively nominal and insuf- ficient to support said contract as a consideration; that the con- tract was not only unconscionable because of the insufficiency of the consideration, but also because the duration of the delay that might be involved at the will of the lessee, by which the property might suffer in its value or be entirely lost, time being an essential factor in the operations under the contract; that in the alternative, if said lease was void it was a mere servitude, not exclusive.   Upon the judgment rendered by the District Court, both the plaintiff and defendant appealed.   The Supreme Court reversed the court below, setting aside the judgment by it rendered, rejected the plaintiffs demand, dismissed its suit, and dissolved the injunction with costs in both courts.

Sec. 14.—In *Housierre-Lattreille Oil Co.*, v. *Jennings-Heywood Oil Syndicate*, 115 La. 107; 38 So. 932 (June 22, 1905), the syllabus is as follows:

"1.   The plaintiff company stepped into the shoes of their vendor who was the owner of property held by defendants under a contract of lease.
2.   Lessor reserved no right to rescind the contract under its terms.
3.   The lessees were privileged to drill a well for petroleum or pay rental.
4.   The plaintiffs, as owners, claim possession and treat the contract or lease as void, or as no longer binding upon them;
(a)   That defendant did not drill for petroleum and permitted the time to pass without complying with the contract.
(b)   Rental was paid for a part of the time.
5.   The contract was not void, and the owners were not entitled to possession (if at all) without an action to set aside the lease to which, as assignees, they must be held to have consented.
6.   The rental was not so inconsiderable as to amount as to render it possible to consider it as vile and a mere nothing.   Insufficiency of the amount cannot be sustained in a suit exclusively for possession.
7.   Delays in offering to pay the rental do not render the contract absolutely null.
8.   There was performance for a time as relates to rental and execution of the contract.
9.   A contract of lease may contain a stipulation fixing an amount enabling the lessee to put an end to the lease, and unless this amount is 'vile' and insufficient, the lessor must resort to the courts to have the contract annulled.   Forfeitures are to be strictly construed in an action to resume possession of the property leased, not directed towards setting aside the contract of lease under which the property is held.

10. If the owners have a right of action to set aside the lease they have no right to an action in which the lease is not mentioned, and no allegation is made to have its dissolution decreed.

11. The right to resume possession could not arise until default made by the lessees is shown in not exploring the land for oil, and in not paying for the delay.

12. Even the appearance of a contract has binding effect after execution. There was for a time at least the appearance of a contract by which plaintiffs are held bound.''

Upon re-hearing syl. 14 is as follows:

''14. A contract purporting to be a lease for a term of ten years of mineral rights in a forty-acre tract of land in an unproven part of the country whereby the contractor agrees to commence operations within six months, or pay $50.00 quarterly in advance, for each additional three months such operations are delayed, until an oil well is completed, and whereby he is given the right to remove his machinery at any time and to cancel the contract upon payment of one hundred dollars at any time, and whereby in the event of discovery of oil and gas the gross yield is to be shared in certain proportions by the contracting parties, is not void upon its face for want of mutuality or as containing a potestative condition.''

Arthur Lattreille leased on April 19, 1901, 40 acres of land to C. A. Spencer & Company, who assigned to the Jennings-Heywood Oil Syndicate, for the term of ten years in consideration of one dollar acknowledged to have been paid, with the further consideration of the payment of one-eighth of the oil produced, and one-eighth part of the gas, with the stipulation that the lessee should begin to explore the land for oil within six months, or in the event of a failure to pay rental at the rate of $50.00 quarterly in advance until a well should be completed. Three of the quarterly payments were made and accepted by the lessor without objection. There were some delays thereafter in the payment of rental. The Houssierre-Lattreille Company brought suit in the District Court of the Parish of Acadia for the possession of the tract of land. Judgment was rendered in favor of the defendants from which judgment plaintiff appealed to the Supreme Court, and that court affirmed the decision of the District Court. The suit being at law, the court held that the plaintiff could not treat the lease as absolutely void; that there were rights and equities growing out of such a contract of which no account could be taken if the contract should be treated as an absolute nullity, citing the following cases:

Harris v. *Ohio Oil Co.*, 57 Ohio St. 118; 48 N. E. 502.
Roberts & Corley v. *McFadden*, 32 Tex. Civ. App. 47; 74 S. W. 115.
J. M. Guffey Petroleum Co. v. *Oliver*, (Tex.), 79 S. W. 884.

Sec. 15.—In *Gillespie* v. *Fulton Oil & Gas Company*, 236 Ill. 188; 86 N. E. 219 (Oct. 26, 1908) syls. 9-10-20-21-22-23-25-26 are as follows:

"9. Equity will not receive evidence contradicting the acknowledgment of the receipt of the consideration in a sealed instrument for the purpose of cancelling it, though in actions for the consideration and in bills for specific performance and the like courts will inquire into the actual consideration, and whether the same has been paid.

10. Where the real consideration for the execution of an oil and gas lease was the exploitation of the mineral resources of the farm of the lessor, and not the receipted consideration of one dollar, the receipt of which was acknowledged, the non-payment of one dollar did not invalidate the lease.

20. An oil and gas lease for five years which required the lessee to drill a test well within twelve months and which provided, in case no well was completed within that time he should pay a rental or specified sum per acre to be paid annually counting from the expiration of the said twelve months, did not require the lessee to pay any rental until the expiration of the first year, and in that time if no test well was completed the rental commenced to accrue, and as the lease did not require the payment of the rental in advance the lessee had all the second year in which to pay rental.

21. Where a lessor in an oil and gas lease, when notified that the money called for as rental had been left for him at a bank, refused to accept it on the ground that the lease was void and he indicated his purpose not to receive any rental under the lease, he waived any duty resting on the lessee to make a legal tender of the rental.

22. Where a lessor in an oil and gas lease repudiated the lease by re-leasing the premises to another, and admitting the latter into possession, before the expiration of the year in which the lessee in the first lease had the right to pay rental, and the lessee before the expiration of the year filed a bill to set aside the second lease in which he tendered performance of all the conditions to be performed by him, and as he averred that he was willing to

perform its covenants, there was a sufficient tender in equity of the rental called for in the lease.

23. A lessee in an oil and gas lease executed June 15, for five years, served notice on September 15th of the following year of his intention to carry out a provision in the lease requiring him to make a test well. The lease provided, that if no well was completed within the first year the lessee should pay a rental of $100.00 which he tendered. September 15th, no work having been done under a subsequent lease executed by the lessor to others, on October 14th following, he went on the land to make a location for drilling a well, when he found a well in operation which had been drilled after his notice was served. *Held*, that the rights of the first lessee were not forfeited.

25. An assignee of the lessee in a lease of oil and gas in premises described, with the right to enter thereon to mine for oil and gas, cannot maintain ejectment against the lessee in a subsequent lease.

26. Equity has jurisdiction to prevent waste and irreparable injury at the suit of an assignee in an oil and gas lease against a subsequent adverse lessee.''

S. C. Bowman, on May 17, 1905, executed an oil and gas lease to T. E. Price, the material provisions of which were as follows:

"In consideration of the sum of one dollar, the receipt of which is hereby acknowledged, S. C. Bowman, party of the first part, hereby grants and leases unto T. E. Price parties of the second part, all the oil and gas in and under the following described premises * * * * * in Crawford County, Illinois, containing 50 acres more or less. * * * * * * * * To have and to hold the above described premises for five years from the date hereof, and as much longer as oil or gas is found in paying quantities on said premises on the following conditions: Second party shall, within twelve months from the date hereof, drill a test well upon said premises. * * * * * * * * If oil is found in paying quantities, first party shall have one-eighth part of all oil produced and saved from said premises * * * * * * * with the * * * * * * * * right to remove any machinery and fixtures placed on the premises by them. * * * * * In case no well is completed on said premises within twelve months from this date, the party of the second part shall pay the party of the first part a rental of twenty-five cents per acre per year, to be paid annually, counting from the expiration of said twelve months. It is further agreed that in case no paying well is completed on said premises within five years from the date hereof, this grant shall be null and void without further agreement of the parties hereto * * * * * * * *

The parties of the second part hereby agree to complete a test well in ————County, Illinois, on or before the ———————— 190— or forfeit all rights under this lease. It is understood by the parties to this agreement that all conditions beween the parties hereto shall extend to their heirs, administrators, successors and assigns. * * * * * * * * * * * * * *''

On October 14, 1905, T. E. Price, the lessee, assigned the lease to E. N. Gillespie. On August 20, 1906, Bowman made a second lease of the same premises to T. N. Rodgers who subsequently assigned the lease to the Fulton Oil & Gas Company. On December 19, 1906, after this suit was brought, Bowman made another lease to T. N. Rodgers. This lease Rodgers assigned to Walter Henning. Henning, or the Fulton Oil & Gas Company entered upon the premises claiming under the last two leases, or one of them, and completed a producing oil well. E. N. Gillespie, Trustee, filed a bill in equity in the Circuit Court of Crawford County against the Fulton Oil and Gas Company, S. C. Bowman T. N. Rodgers and Walter Henning, praying for an injunction and an accounting, the appointment of a Receiver, and the cancellation of the oil and gas leases executed by S. C. Bowman and wife to Rogers, and by him assigned to Walter Henning. Answers were filed, proofs taken, and the Circuit Court found the issues for the defendant, and dismissed the plaintiffs bill for want of equity. Upon appeal to the Appellate Court that court affirmed the decree of the Circuit Court, and from this decree plaintiff appealed to the Supreme Court. That court reversed the decrees of the courts below and remanded the cause, citing the following cases:

Indianapolis N. Gas Co. v. *Kibbey,* 135 Ind. 357; 35 N. E. 392.
Allegheny Oil Co. v. *Snyder,* 106 Fed. 764; 45 C. C. A. 604.
Logan N. Gas etc. Co. v. *Great Southern Gas & Oil Co.* 126 Fed. 623; 61 C. C. A. 359.

Sec. 16.—In *Dill* v. *Fraze,* 165 Ind. 53; 75 N. E. 971, analyzed under Chap. 24, syls. 3-5 are as follows:

"3. An oil and gas lease for five years from its date and as long as oil and gas could be found on the land, or the rental was paid thereon as stipulated in the contract, provided that in case no well was completed within sixty day the grant should be null and void, unless the lessee should thereafter pay at the rate of $40.00 for each year such commencement was delayed, and that the lessee might cancel and annul the contract or any portion thereof, at any time upon payment of one dollar to the lessor, and releas, ing him upon record. *Held,* that while upon the receipt of the first years compensation the lessee would have been entitled to postpone the beginning of operations, yet it was within the power of lessor by appropriate action to prevent such lessee from continuing to hold the right granted in the land without exploration or development for the whole of the contract period.''

"5. The owner was entitled to declare a forfeiture at the end of sixty days where there was no well completed in that time, and where the lessee had failed to pay the consideration stipulated for the delay.''

Sec. 17.—In *Pittsburg Vitrified Paving & Building Brick Co.,* v. *Bailey,* 76 Kan. 42; 90 Pac. 802, analyzed under Chapter 29, syl. 1 is as follows:

"1.   B. and wife, owners of certain lands, entered into a written contract with a corporation, which by its terms granted to the corporation, in consideration of $1.00 and the agreements made by the company, the privilege of entering upon the land, for a term of ten years, and boring gas or oil wells, etc., and, in the event of discovery of oil or gas in paying quantities, conveyed the title to such products for a specified royalty. The company agreed to complete a well within two years or to pay a rental of twenty-five.cents per acre until a well should be completed on the premises. The contract also provided that the term might be extended indefinitely by the discovery of oil or gas on the premises, or so long as either should be produced in paying quantities or the rental be paid thereon; also that the company had the right to surrender the contract at any time, and be thereby discharged from all liabilities for the non-fulfillment thereof. *Held,* that the contract is not, strictly speaking, a lease of the premises, but constitutes a sale by R. and wife to the company of an option to exercise or not to exercise the privileges granted, as the company might choose.''

Sec. 18.—In *Vendocia Oil etc. Co.* v. *Robinson,* 71 Ohio St. 302; 73 N. E 222, analyzed under Chapter 21, the syllabus is as follows:

"1.   A grant, in consideration of one dollar, of all the oil and gas under certain premises, with the right to enter thereon for the purpose of drilling and operating for oil and gas, excepting and reserving to the grantor 1-6 of all the oil and gas produced and saved from the said premises, to be delivered in the pipelines with which the grantee may connect his wells, implies an engagement by the lessee to develop the premises for oil and gas.

2.   The time within which the implied engagement must be per_ formed is postponed by acceptance of the sum specified in the condition of such grant that 'in case no well is completed within 90 days from the date hereof, unavoidable delay excepted, then this grant shall become null and void unless second party shall pay to first party twenty-five cents per acre per year, payable by deposit at the ———, or directly to first party after demand having first been made,' and does not commence to run until the end of the year for which payment is accepted, and the lease does not become null and void at the end of such year on the refusal of the grantor to accept payment for another year.''

Sec. 19.—In *Erie Crawford Oil Co.* v. *Meek*, 40 Ind. App. 156; 81 N. E. 518 (May 28, 1907) syls. 4-5 are as follows:

"4.   An oil and gas lease provided that in consideration of one dollar, plaintiff granted all the oil and gas in and under the land described, with the right to drill therefor, reserving to plaintiff 1-6 of all oil saved, for the term of five years from date, and, if gas only was found, then the lessee should pay $50.00 per year and furnish gas to plaintiff, free; that in case no well was completed in ——— years the lease should be void, unless the lessee should pay fifty cents per acre semi-annually in advance, for each year the completion of the work was delayed. *Held,* that the lease should be construed to run for one year only, unless acreage rental was paid semi-annually.

5.   Where an oil and gas lease did not fix a time when the lessee should begin operating but provided that, in case no well was completed within ——— years from the date of the lease, the grant should be void unless the lessee should pay an acreage in advance, the lessee was only entitled to a reasonable time within which to begin operations.''

Jacob Meek instituted an action in the Circuit Court of Jay County, against the Erie Crawford Oil Company, to quiet his title to certain real estate in Randolph County, Indiana. The cause was transferred to Jay Circuit Court where R. H. Clark, upon an intervening petition filed by him, was admitted as a party defendant. The complaint was in one paragraph, answered by separate general denial on the part of the oil company and Clark. A cross complaint by Clark, and answers by separate denial by

plaintiff and defendant oil company formed the issue. A jury trial
was had and a general verdict rendered for plaintiff, and with the
general verdict answers to a number of interrogatories submitted
by both plaintiff and defendant, were returned. The complaint
averred that the plaintiff was the owner in fee simple title to the
tract of land subject to the rights of one R. H. Clark, under and by
virtue of a certain oil lease executed by the plaintiff to him on
February 8, 1904; that the defendant, the Erie Crawford Oil Company, a corporation, claimed an interest adverse to the plaintiff's
rights; that this claim was without right and unfounded, and was a
cloud on plaintiff's title. To this complaint a demurrer for want
of jurisdiction was overruled. Upon the answers returned by the
jury to the interrogatories, the following facts were found: On
August 16, 1901, Jacob Meeks was the owner of a tract of land in
Jay County, Indiana and on that day   executed to the Woodbury
Glass Company an oil and gas lease in consideration of one dollar,
whereby lessor granted all the oil and gas in and under said real
estate to lessee, reserving as royalty a 1-6 of the oil produced; and
if gas only should be found lessee agreed to pay $50.00 per year for
the production of each well while the same should be sold off the
premises, reserving gas free of cost, to heat the stove and light
the jets in the dwelling house then on the land for a like period. In
case no well was completed in —— years from the date of the
lease, then the grant should become null and void unless the Wood·
bury Gas Company should pay to Meeks, in bank, fifty cents per
acre semi-annually in advance $—— for each year thereafter such
completion was delayed.

By various assignments the Erie Crawford Oil Company, on
January 9, 1909, became the owner of the interest of the original
lessee. Rental in the sum of $30.25 was paid to Meeks on Septem-
ber 6, 1901, and on each March 6th and September 6th thereafter,
the last payment on March 6, 1903. On February 8, 1904, Meeks
executed an oil and gas lease on the same land to Ralph H. Clark,
but Clark neither drilled nor attempted to drill on the land, nor did
he pay any rental for failing to drill a well within the year, as pro·
vided in the lease. The rental paid on March 6, 1903, was on the
lease executed August 16, 1901, and for the six months ending September 6, 1903; and was the last payment made. The Erie Craw.
ford Oil Company, on May 24, 1904, left for appellee at the Parker

Bank. $60.50 as an installment of rental, and also a receipt to be signed by lessor in case he accepted said installment of rental. Other answers returned by the jury to interrogatories showed the payment of $30.25 on each September 6th and March 6th, for rental, every six months in advance, for the period terminating September 6, 1903. The foregoing findings were made in answer to special interrogatories by the jury. Verdict and judgment were rendered for plaintiff, and defendant appealed. The judgment of the Circuit Court was reversed with instructions to sustain appellant's motion for new trial. The appellant claimed that under a proper construction of the lease no rental was due until August, 1902, and that the four payments made thereon aggregated $121.00. In construing the lease the court said:

"Considering the instrument in question denominated a lease, as granting for the consideration of one dollar, an option for one year to appellant to enter upon, explore and develop the land for oil and gas, in connection with the nature and migratory character of the substances granted, impels the belief that a consideration more subsistent than that mentioned induced its execution, and justifies the court in construing the instrument 'with the fact in view that a more substantial reason or reasons, prompted the making of the grant.' *Gadberry* v. *Ohio etc. Gas Co.*, 162 Ind. 9; 67 N. E. 259; 62 L. R. A. 895. These reasons appear from the contract to be the benefit and profits from oil or gas to the landowner in the way of royalty from the oil, or well rental from the gas found, and to the grantee 'anticipating profits in vending the products of the wells it should drill.' *Consumers Gas Trust Co.* v. *Littler*, 162 Ind. 320-326; 70 N. E. 363. * * * * * * * * * * * * The lease is one belonging to its own class, embracing indefinite and peculiar provisions and 'must be construed with reference to the known characteristics of the business.' *McKnight* v. *Nat. Gas Co.*, 146 Pa. 185; 23 Atl. 164; 28 Am. St. Rep. 790, *Leiter* v. *Emmons*, 20 Ind. App. 22; 50 N. E. 40."

The court cited the following authorities:

Consumers Gas Trust Co. v. *Worth*, 163 Ind. 141-149; 71 N. E. 489.
American Window Glass Co. v. *Ind. etc. Oil Co.*, 37 Ind. App. 439; 76 N. E. 1006-1008.

Sec. 20.—In *Hays* v. *Forest Oil Co.*, 213 Pa. 556; 62 Atl. 1072 (Jan. 2, 1906) the syllabus is as follows:

"1. An oil and gas lease provided that it should be void if a well was not completed within three months from its date unless the lessee should pay $500.00 monthly for each months delay in completing a well, each payment to extend the time for completion for one month, held, that the monthly payment was only a condition precedent necessary to maintain the vitality of the lease and was not a covenant to pay $500 per month until the well should be completed, or the lease surrendered.

2. Where an oil lease provided for the completion of a well, and the lessor has treated a well as completed and has accepted royalties for two and a half years, he cannot claim that the well was not completed in the first instance.''

L. O. Hays instituted an action in the Court of Common Pleas of Allegheny County, against the Forest Oil Company in assumpsit to recover for monthly rentals alleged to be due under the provisions of the lease for oil and gas purposes upon a tract of land located in Butler County. The lease contained the following provision:

"10. This lease to be null and void and no longer binding on either party if a well is not completed on the premises within three months from this date, unless the lessee shall thereafter pay monthly to the lessor $500.00 per month for each months delay in completing said well; each payment to extend the time for completion for one month, and no longer.''

A well was drilled on the premises as deep as other wells in the 100-foot sand, and the weight of the evidence was that there was but one pay streak in that sand, through which the well was drilled. The Trial Court held that the lessee had a right to determine when the well was completed; and having determined that it was completed after going below the first pay streak, he was not obligated to take any risks for the benefit of somebody else so long as he acted in good faith.

The lessor, before and after the defendant took over the lease, treated the well as completed, and received the royalties due under the terms thereof from the defendant from February, 1900, to September, 1902. The trial court directed the jury to render a verdict in favor of the defendant, and plaintiff appealed. The Supreme Court affirmed the judgment, citing:

Glasgow v. *Chartiers Gas Co.*, 152 Pa. 48; 25 Atl. 232.

LESSOR'S REMEDY.

Sec. 21.—Where an oil and gas lease contains no express cov·enant binding lessee either to explore or pay rental, but contains a provisions that the lease shall become null and void unless lessee shall make explorations within a specified time or pay rental for delay, lessor, in the absence of fraud, cannot refuse payment and declare forfeiture at the expiration of such specified time and terminate the lease. When lessee fails to pay the rental for delay lessor may declare a forfeiture and terminate the lease between the parties.

> *Smith* v. *South Penn Oil Co.*, 59 W. Va. 204; 53 S. E. 152.
> *Van Etten* v. *Kelly*, 66 Ohio St. 605; 64 N. E. 560.
> *Snodgrass* v. *South Penn Oil Co.*, 47 W. Va. 509; 35 S. E. 820.
> *Glasgow* v. *Chartiers Oil Co.*, 152 Pa. 48; 25 Atl. 232.
> *Great Western Oil Co.* v. *Carpenter*, 43 Tex. Civ. App. 229;
> 95 S. W. 57.
> *Jennings-Heywood Oil Syndicate* v. *Housierre-Lattreille Oil Co.*, 119 La. 864; 44 So. 481.

Sec. 22.—Where an oil and gas lease contains a forfeiture clause by the terms of which lessee may pay a stipulated rental for delay in drilling, lessor cannot ordinarily refuse payment and declare a forfeiture; but when lessee unreasonably delays explorations, when such delay may result in irreparable loss to the lessor by drainage or may prevent lessor from obtaining development of his property contemporaneously with developments in the vicinity, he may give notice to lessee for a reasonable time of his desire to have the property explored, and upon failure or refusal of lessee to make such explorations, after such notice, lessor may refuse to accept payment of rentals for further delay, declare a forfeiture and obtain a cancellation of the lease in a court of equity.

> *Lowther Oil Co.* v. *Guffey*, 52 W. Va. 88; Op. 91-2 43 S. E. 101.
> *Dill* v. *Fraze*, 165 Ind. 53; 75 N. E. 971.
> *Consumers Gas Trust Co.* v. *Littler*, 162 Ind. 320; 71 N. E. 363.
> *Consumers Gas Trust Co.* v. *Chrystal Window Glass Co.*, 163
> Ind. 190.
> *Consumers Gas Trust Co.* v. *Worth*, 163 Ind. 141; 71 N. E. 489.

LESSEE'S REMEDY.

Sec. 23.—Where an oil and gas lease is at the option of the lessee who by the provisions thereof has the right to delay developments by payment of a stipulated rental at a specified time, and there is no express covenant either to drill or pay rental for delay, lessee may, ordinarily, delay developments within the term by payment of the stipulated rental during the term.

See cases cited under Section 1, this Chapter.

Sec. 24.—Where the lessee has the option either to drill within a specified time or to delay developments by payment of a specified rental and lessor refuses to accept payment and declares a forfeiture of the lease, and executes a new lease to a third party, lessee having tendered to lessor the stipulated rental, or deposits the same in bank to the credit of the lessor, where such deposit is authorized, may invoke the aid of a court of equity and obtain a cancellation of the second lease and enjoin all interference by lessor with his right to the full enjoyment of the leased premises for the purposes of the lease.

Gillespie v. *Fulton Oil Co.*, 236 Ill. 188; 86 N. E. 219.
Pyle v. *Henderson*, 65 W. Va. 39; 63 S. E. 620.

CHAPTER 14.

THE SURRENDER CLAUSE OF THE OIL AND GAS LEASE.

Sec. 1.—Where an oil and gas lease is made for a valuable consideration and contains a provision that lessee shall have the right at any time to surrender the lease to lessor for cancellation, after which all payments and liabilities to accrue under and by virtue of its terms shall cease and determine, the consideration for the lease is a sufficient consideration to support the surrender clause; the lease is not void for want of mutuality, and lessee may surrender the lease to lessor in the manner provided for and relieve himself of all liability under the lease accruing subsequent to such surrender.

> *Brown* v. *Fowler,* ⎤
> *Brown* v. *Ohio Oil Co.*⎦ 65 Ohio St. 507; 63 N. E. 76.
>
> *Bettman* v. *Shadle*, 22 Ind. App. 542; 53 N. E. 662.
> *Woodland Oil Co.* v. *Crawford*, 55 Ohio St. 161; 44 N. E. 1093; 34 L. R. A. 62.
> *Roberts* v. *Bettman*, 45 W. Va. 143. Op. 146; 30 S. E. 95.
> *Eclipse Oil Co.* v. *South Penn Oil Co.*, 47 W. Va. 84; 34 S. E. 293.
> *Trees* v. *Eclipse Oil Co.*, 47 W. Va. 107; 34 S. E. 933.
> *Henne* v. *South Penn Oil Co.*, 52 W. Va. 192; 43 S. E. 147.
> *Friend* v. *Mallory*, 52 W. Va. 53; 43 S. E. 114.
> *Marshall* v. *Oil Co.*, 198 Pa. 83; 47 Atl. 927.
> *Ward* v. *Triple State etc. Co.*, — Ky. —; 115 S. W. 819.
> *Roberts & Corley* v. *McFadden*, 32 Tex. Civ. App. 47; 74 S. W. 105.
> *Poe* v. *Ulrey*, 233 Ill. 56; 84 N. E. 46.
> *Housierre-Lattreille Oil Co.* v. *Jennings-Heywood Oil Syndicate*, 115 La. 107; 38 So. 932.
> *Waterford Oil & Gas Co.* v. *Shipman*, 233 Ill. 9; 84 N. E. 53.
> *Brewster* v. *Lanyon Zinc Co.* 140 Fed. 801; 72 C. C. A. 213.
> *Lowther Oil Co.* v. *Miller-Sibley Oil Co.*, 53 W. Va. 501; 44 S. E. 433.
> *Pyle* v. *Henderson*, 65 W. Va. 39; 63 S. E. 762.

Sec. 2.—The modern oil and gas lease usually contains a provision whereby the lessor may surrender the lease to the lessor and in this way relieve himself of all obligations under the lease accruing after such surrender although the lease may contain an express covenant either to drill or pay rental. The provision of the lease authorizing lessee to surrender the lease to the lessor and relieve himself of obligations accruing subsequent to such surrender, is called the surrender clause. Where the lessee receives a valuable consideration for the lease such consideration upholds the surrender clause. Where a lease contains a surrender clause and there is an express covenant to pay rental for delay in drilling lessee cannot hold the lease and relieve himself of rentals accruing during such time by subsequently surrendering the lease. When lessee desires to avail himself of the benefit of the surrender clause he must surrender the lease promptly. The surrender clause must be predicated upon a valuable consideration to lessor.

Where lessee pays no consideration for the lease lessor, while the lease remains executory, may revoke it at any time.

Sec. 3.—In *Brown* v. *Fowler* and *Brown* v. *Ohio Oil Co.*, 65 Ohio St. 507; 63 N. E. 75, analyzed under Chapter 4, the fourth point of the syllabus is as follows:

"Said lease also had the following clause: 'It is agreed that the lessee shall have the right at any time to surrender this lease to lessor for cancellation, after which all payments or liabilities to *occur* under and by virtue of its terms shall cease and determine, and the lease become absolutely null and void.'' *Held,* that this clause, when taken in connection with the granting and habendum clause, does not create an estate at will. *Held,* also, that, as the consideration of $1.00 paid for the whole lease was also a payment for this clause, the lease is not void for want of mutuality.''

On December 8, 1896, Catherine Fowler and husband made an oil and gas lease to H. A. Snyder whereby in consideration of One Dollar, the receipt of which was acknowledged, the lessors granted to the lessee all the oil and gas, and also the tract containing 20 acres, more or less, situated in Harrison County, Ohio, for the term of two years, which lease contained the following provision as to surrender:

"It is agreed that the lessee shall have the right at any time to surrender this lease to lessor for cancellation, after which all payments or liabilities to accrue under and by virtue of its terms shall cease and determine, and the lease become absolutely null and void.''

On November 26, 1898, the lessors claimed that the lease was void, and on that day executed another lease of the same premises to George Gillmore. In a controversy between the two claimants of these conflicting leases the Supreme Court construed the surrender clause as stated in syl. 4 above quoted. Judge Burkett, delivering the opinion in the case, said:

"The term of two years certain and this surrender clause are not inconsistent. Full force can be given to both. This surrender clause is an option, intended to enable the lessee to terminate the lease before the end of the term if it shall appear that there is no oil or gas in that territory. Under this clause the lessee can terminate the lease before the end of the term by surrendering the lease, and under the defeasance clause he can do the same by failing to drill a well and failing to pay for further delay. The right to terminate the lease in either of said ways is a valuable right to the lessee and he paid for both by paying the $1.00 mentioned as consideration for the whole lease. Such options in contracts are sustained by courts. *Theyer* v. *Allison,* 109 Ill. 180. *Oil Co.* v. *Crawford,* 55 Ohio St. 161; 44 N. E. 1093; 34 L. R. A. 62. The error of construing a condition subsequent or an option as creating the term of the lease, when that has been created by the granting and habendum clause, has caused many decisions to be rendered whose soundness may well be doubted. This clause gives the lessee his option and for which he has paid, to hold the lease to the end of the term or surrender it sooner. It is always the right of a person holding an option for which he has paid, to surrender it before the expiration of the time, or to hold it for the full time; but the person who gave the option cannot compel a surrender before the expiration of the full time.''

Sec. 4.—In *Bettman* v. *Shadle,* 22 Ind. App. 542; 53 N. E. 662 (April 27, 1889) the fourth point of the syllabus is as follows:

"An oil lease provided that the lessee should begin a well within one month, failing which to pay $2 per day until commenced, or surrender the lease; lessee to have the right 'at any time to surrender the lease, and be released from all moneys due and conditions unfulfilled, then, and from that time the lease to be void, and the payment made to be the full stipulated damages for non-fulfillment.' *Held,* that the lessees did not have the right to cancel back debts by surrendering the lease; that the provisions referred to future obligations.''

On February 20, 1895, Thomas L. Shadle leased to Henry B. Huffman and Andrew Fouse certain lands for oil and gas purposes for a term of five years, and as long as gas and oil could be produced in paying quantities. The lessee assigned the lease, and ultimately it passed to Bettman, Watson & Bernheimer. The lease contained the following surrender clause:

"And it is further agreed that the second party, his heirs or assigns, shall have the right at any time to surrender up this lease and be released from all moneys due and conditions unfulfilled, then and from that time this lease and agreement shall be null and void and no longer binding on either party, and the payment which shall have been made be held by the party of the first part as the full stipulated damages for the non-fulfillment of the foregoing contract.''

The lessor received $30.00 as rent, on August 2, 1895, and re-ceipted for the same as one months rent until September 2, 1895, this being all the rental paid. Suit was instituted by the lessor against Bettman and others for rentals, and judgment recovered. The defendants claimed that they were not liable because, after the institution of the suit, they surrendered the lease. Defendants appealed to the Appellate Court and that Court affirmed the judgment of the Circuit Court.

Sec. 5.—In *Woodland Oil Co.* v. *Crawford*, 55 Ohio State, 161; 44 N. E. 1093 (Oct. 20, 1896) the first point of the syllabus is as follows:

''1. C. granted, demised and let, by written instrument, a certain tract of land and all the oil and gas in and under the same, to U. and his assigns, for the purpose, and with the exclusive right, of drilling and operating the land for gas and oil for five years, and as much longer as oil or gas should be found thereon in paying quantities, upon the consideration of one dollar paid, and a promise to pay certain rentals for further delay if default should be made in drilling a well within one year, and which instrument had the following forfeiture clause: 'And a failure on the part of U. to complete such well or wells as above specified, or instead thereof pay the rental as above provided, shall render this lease and agreement null and void, together with all rights and. claims and not binding on either party, and not to be revived without the consent of both parties hereto in writing.' Default having been made in drilling, in an action to recover the promised rental, *held:* First, that such instrument is a lease of the land, oil and gas, for the limited time and purpose expressed therein. Second, that the forfeiture is for the benefit of the lessor and at his option. Third, that the promise to drill a well or pay rental cannot be discharged by a mere failure to perform the promise. Fourth, upon failure to drill the well, or instead thereof to pay the agreed rental, such rental may be recovered by action as rental, and need not be sued for as unliquidated damages.''

On March 23, 1889, Thomas L. Crawford and wife executed' an oil and gas lease to Cyrus Underwood for a tract of land in Monroe County, Ohio, whereby in consideration of one dollar the lessees granted, demised and let unto the second party all the petroleum and gas in and under a certain tract of land, and also the said tract of land, containing 128 acres, for the term and period of five years and as much longer as oil or gas should be found in paying quantities. The lessee agreed to complete a test well in the Township of Perry, or within two miles of the demised premises within one year from the date of the lease, or in default thereof pay to the lessor for delay a yearly rental of $128.00 until such well should be completed. The lease contained the following clause:

"And a failure on the part of the second party to complete such well or wells as above specified, or instead thereof to pay the rental as above provided, shall render this lease and agreement null and void, together with all rights and claims, and not binding on either party, and not to be revived without the consent of both parties hereto in writing."

On April 10, 1889, Underwood assigned the lease to the Woodland Oil Company. Crawford instituted suit for the recovery of the rentals provided for in the lease and recovered judgment in the Court of Common Pleas. Appeal was taken to the Circuit Court for Monroe County, and judgment affirmed and defendants then appealed to the Supreme Court of Ohio. That court also affirmed the judgment. The Oil Company as grounds of defense alleged the clause in the lease which provided that a failure on the part of the lessee to complete a well, or wells, or pay rental rendered the lease and agreement null and void, and claimed that this clause relieved it of any obligation to pay. To this defense the plaintiff demurred which demurrer was sustained. The Supreme Court, in relation to the demurrer, said:

"We think that the demurrer was properly sustained. It is also urged that the failure to drill the required well, and failure to pay the agreed rental did not entitle the lessor to recover the amount named as rental, but at most would only entitle him to recover unliquidated damages. We regard the case as one of rental. The amount agreed to be paid was for the exclusive right for drilling and operating the premises for oil and gas. Failure to exercise the right would not relieve the company from payment of the amount agreed upon as the price of such exclusive right."

The Supreme Court, in reference to the attempt of the de-

fendant to plead its own default as a defense, and as to the right
of a lessee to insert a surrender clause in a lease, said:

"The lessee cannot plead his own default or wrong in discharge
of his obligation to drill or pay rental. Parties may agree that in
case of failure to drill, or failure to pay, or both, the lessee shall be
relieved of his obligation upon such terms as the parties may agree
upon in the lease whether the terms be of value to the lessor or
loss or inconvenience to the lessee; but a naked default and non-
performance, as in this lease, cannot be held to discharge the obligation of the lessee."

The court in this case draws a clear distinction between
leases which attempt to provide a method of discharge of lessee
upon his failure to do anything under the lease and leases wherein
there is an express covenant inserted which provides that lessee
may surrender the lease for cancellation and be discharged of all
liability thereafter accruing.

Sec. 6.—In *Eclipse Oil Co.* v. *South Penn Oil Co.,* 47 W. Va. 84;
34 S. E. 293, analyzed under chapter 4, syls. 1-2 are as follows:

"1. If one party may terminate an estate at his will, so may
the other. The right to terminate is mutual· *Conwan* v. *Iron Co.*
3 S. E. 120; 83 Va. 347.
2. An executory gas and oil lease which provides for its surrender at any time without payment of rent or fulfillment of any
of its covenants on the part of the lessee, creates a mere right of
entry at will, which may be terminated by the lessor at any time
before it is executed by the lessee."

On May 11, 1897, Henry Garner, of Wetzel County, West Virginia, made an oil and gas lease to H. G. and J. C. Stolze the material provisions whereof were as follows:

"Agreement made and entered into * * * * * Witnesseth:
that the said party of the first part, for and in consideration of the
covenants and agreements hereinafter mentioned does covenant
and agree to lease, and by these presents has leased and granted
the exclusive right unto the parties of the second part, their heirs
or assigns, for the purpose of operating and drilling for petroleum
and gas * * * * * * that certain tract of * * * * * 102 acres
* * * * * * The parties of the second part their heirs or assigns
to have and to hold the said premises for and during the term of

three years from the date hereof and so long thereafter as oil or gas can be produced in paying quantities. The parties of the second part * * * * * to give to first party 1-8 part of all petroleum obtained from said premises * * * * *. If gas is found in paying quantities the consideration in full to the party of the first part for gas shall be $200.00 (two hundred dollars) per annum for gas from each well when utilized off the premises * * * * *. The parties of the second part agree to drill one test well on the above described premises within six months from the execution of this lease, or, in lieu thereof, thereafter pay to the said party of the first part one dollar per acre per annum until such well is completed; and if said test well is not completed within six months from the above date, or rentals paid thereon, this lease is null and void, and not further binding on either party. And it is further agreed that the second party, their heirs or assigns shall have the right at any time to surrender up this lease, and be released from all moneys due and conditions unfulfilled; then and from that time this lease and agreement shall be null and void, and no longer binding on either party, and the payments which have been made held by the party of the first part as the full stipulated damages for nonfulfillment of the foregoing contract; that all conditions between the parties hereto shall extend to their heirs, executors and assigns.''

The lease was assigned to the Eclipse Oil Company. On June 18, 1898, the lessor again leased this property to J. A. Phillips, who assigned to the South Penn Oil Company. The latter company began developments when the Eclipse Oil Company obtained an injunction upon a bill filed by it in the Circuit Court of Wetzel County, claiming that its lease was still valid although nothing was done thereunder except payment by it of the annual rental provided for, on November 10, 1898; and alleging that the lessor accepted this payment. The injunction was dissolved and a decree was entered for defendant, from which decree plaintiff appealed. The Court of Appeals affirmed the Circuit Court.

Sec. 7.—In *Trees* v. *Eclipse Oil Co.*, 47 W. Va. 107; 34 S. E. 933 (Nov. 28, 1899) the syllabus is as follows:

"An executory oil and gas lease, which does not bind the lessees to carry out its covenants but reserves to them the right to defeat the same at any time, and relieve themselves from the payment of any consideration therefor, is invalid to create any estate other than the mere optional right of entry, which is subject to termination at the will of either party.

Such executory lease is terminated by the death of the lessor.

A person holding a valid, executory oil and gas lease, executed by several of the number of co-tenants, has such an inchoate interest in the land subject to such lease as will enable him to maintain an injunction to prevent a wrongdoer from committing waste by extraction of such oil and gas.''

J. C. Trees filed his bill against the Eclipse Oil Company and others in the Circuit Court of Wetzel County, obtained an injunc· tion thereon, which injunction the court sustained, overruling a motion by the oil company for its dissolution, and defendant appealed to the Court of Appeals. The injunction restrained the oil company from entering upon a tract of 200 acres of land known as the John Hafer land, in Wetzel County, and from drilling or boring oil or gas wells thereon. The defendant Oil Company claimed under a lease similar in all respects to the one construed in Eclipse Oil Company against the South Penn Oil Company. John Hafer, in his lifetime executed the lease bearing date August 16, 1898. Nothing was done under the lease, nor were any payments made thereon during the lifetime of the lessor. Some time after the death of John Hafer, and just within eighteen months of the date of the lease the Eclipse Oil Company, assignee of the lessees, claimed to have paid the annual rental provided for in case of failure to complete a well within the six months men· tioned in the lease to the administrator of the estate of John Hafer, claiming that the rental went into, and was distributed as a part of, his estate. Prior to the time of the payment of the rental the widow and heirs of John Hafer, deceased, some of whom were infants, executed an oil and gas lease to the plaintiff Trees, for the same tract of land. After this lease was executed the Eclipse Oil Company entered upon the land and began preparations for sinking a well. The injunction of Trees followed. The Court of Appeals affirmed the Circuit Court.

Sec. 8.—In *Pyle* v. *Henderson*, 65 W. Va. 39; 63 S. E. 762, ana· lyzed under Chapter 24, syl. 1 is as follows:

"Though a lease for oil and gas, for a money bonus as consideration does not bind the lessor to drill or pay money in lieu of doing so, but leaves it optional with him to do so or not, the lessor cannot annul or revoke it merely on the ground of want of mutuality of obligation.''

The court distinguishes the principles announced in *Eclipse Oil Company* v. *South Penn Oil Company* and *Trees* v. *Eclipse Oil Company*, supra, where no consideration was paid for the exclusive right of entry for explorations, from the principles applicable to the lease under consideration where there was paid a valuable consideration for the privilege, in the opinion rendered by Judge Brannon, as follows:

"One argument made for the second lease is, that the first has no covenant binding the lessees to do anything, unless they wish; that it binds the lessee for nothing until they should get oil, either to drill a well or pay money; that the lessor could have no suit for money, or to compel operations of development of oil. It is thence contended that the contract wants the essential of a binding contract, namely, mutuality. Under this view the lessor could renounce or revoke the lease at any time, because if not binding the lessee for anything, neither would it bind the lessor and hence the second would be an election by Bunfill not to be bound, and would confer good title. For this contention we are cited the case of *Eclipse Oil Co.* v. *South Penn Co.*, 47 W. Va. 84; 34 S. E. 923, and *Glasgow* v. *Chartiers Oil Co.*, 152 Pa. 48; 25 Atl. 232. We differentiate the present case from the Eclipse case, from the fact that no money was paid as a bonus in that case, whereas one of $55.00 was paid for the lease in this case. We cannot see that when a lessee pays a money consideration for the right or privilege of boring for oil within a fixed time, and, in default of so doing, of paying money as an alternative, he has no vested right of exploration, but his privilege may be revoked at any moment, whether the limited time has expired or not. * * * * * * * * It would seem to me that a lease of this character, the lessor receiving valuable consideration for the privilege of exploration for oil would confer a valid right of exploration for the time, and on the terms spoken of in it.''

Sec. 9.—In *Roberts* v. *Bettman*, 45 W. Va. 143; 30 S. E. 95, analyzed under Chapter 12, at page 146, the court said:

"The clause stipulating for payment of rent is the only benefit which the lessor gets until development shall give him what moved him chiefly to make the lease, his share of oil, and he protected himself against the insolvency of the lessee, or his failure to pay by the clause forfeiting the lease for failure to complete a well or to pay rental. That clause of forfeiture was designed for his benefit, and not for the lessee's benefit. It was the lessor's only safety. The clause giving the lessee a right at any time to surrender the lease and discharge himself from further liabilities is his ample shield.''

The lease in this case contained an express covenant to pay rental for delay. There was also a forfeiture clause authorizing lessee to surrender the lease and be relieved from liability thereafter accruing. Lessee held the lease for a number of months, and then surrendered. The court held that lessee was liable to lessor for the payment of the rental accruing up to the date of the surrender.

Sec. 10.—In *Henne* v. *South Penn Oil Co.*, 52 W. Va. 192; 43 S. E. 147, analyzed under Chapter 24, the surrender clause in the lease in controversy was as follows:

"It is further agreed that the second party shall have the right at any time to surrender this lease to first party for cancellation, after which all payments and liabilities to accrue under and by virtue of its terms shall cease and determine, and this lease shall become absolutely null and void.''

The lease was held valid against the claimants to a second lease, made by the same lessor.

Sec. 11.—In *Lowther Oil Co.* v. *Miller-Sibley Co.*, 53 W. Va. 501; 44 S. E. 433, analyzed under Chapter 5, the lease contained the following surrender clause:

"Lessee shall have the right at any time to surrender this lease and be relieved from all liability thereunder.''

A second lease was made by the landowner, and in a controversy between the holders of the two leases the junior lessee undertook to apply the principles laid down in Eclipse Oil Company cases, 47 W. Va., and in distinguishing the case under consideration from the Eclipse Oil Company cases, Judge Brannon, at page 505, says:

"The lease required no rent, only a share of the oil, and gives absolute right to the lessee to surrender it, and under *Eclipse Oil*

Co. v. *South Penn Oil Co.,* 47 W. Va. 84, gives no present vested estate, and might be ended at any time by either party, and a second lease would end it. That is the character of this lease. But when once the lessee under such a lease begins work, whilst he yet has no vested estate, still he has the right to go on in search of oil and the lessor cannot then at mere will destroy his right."

Sec. 12.—In *Friend* v. *Mallory,* 52 W. Va. 53; 43 S. E. 147, analyzed under chapter 4, the lease in controversy contained the following surrender clause:

"It is agreed that the second party shall have * * * * the right at any time, to surrender this lease to the first parties for cancellation, after which all payments and liabilities to accrue under and by virtue of its terms shall cease and determine and this lease become absolutely null and void."

The lessors made an oil and gas lease to Mallory Brothers & Stewart on March 23, 1900. Lessors gave notice to the agent of the lessees of their intention to declare a forfeiture. On July 1, 1901, lessors made a second lease to F. J. Friend, who filed a bill in the Circuit Court of Wirt County, West Virginia, for the cancellation of the original lease. In the opinion delivered by Judge McWhorter, at pages 57-8, the court said:

"It is insisted by appellants that the lease of March 23, 1900, being at the will of the lessees, none of its terms and provisions could bind the lessors for the full term, depriving them of their power to determine their will; and it is claimed, also, that the consideration of twenty-two dollars and twenty-five cents, paid by the lessees to the lessors was a rental for the first three months from the date of the lease, within which time the first well should be completed. Wherever or however the amount of the consideration paid in hand at the time of the execution of the lease was to be applied, it is admitted that all rental was paid up to the 23rd day of June, 1901, without the application of the deposit of twenty-two dollars and twenty-five cents made by the lessees on the 6th day of June, 1901."

Again it is said at pages 60-61.

"It is insisted by appellants that the lease to Friend terminated the lease to Mallory Brothers & Stewart under the authority of *Guffey* v. *Hukill,* 34 W. Va. 49; *Eclipse Oil Co.* case, 47 W. Va. 84; 34 S. E. 929, and other cases cited. * * * * * * * * * * *

In the Eclipse Oil Co. case it was held that an 'executory gas and oil lease which provides for its surrender at any time without payment of rent or fulfilment of any of its covenants on the part of the lessee, creates a mere right of entry at will, which may be terminated by the lessor at any time before its execution by the lessee.' And it is further held: "The execution of any lease to other lessees and possession thereunder renders such prior executory lease invalid.' That was a case in which nothing was done under a prior lease either in the way of exploring for oil or the payment of rent. In the Eclipse case the lease which was forfeited contained this provision: 'And it is further agreed that the second party, their heirs or assigns, shall have the right at any time to surrender up this lease and be released from all moneys due and conditions unfulfilled; then and from that time this lease and agreement shall be null and void and no longer binding on either party.' It is said in the opinion of the court: 'This clause apparently destroys this lease or renders it invalid, at least till some consideration has passed from the lessee to the lessor.' The case at bar is different from the cases cited, in this, the lessee paid the stipulated rent which was to be paid quarterly in advance for each three months that the completion of a well was delayed. And it is not competent for the lessors to terminate the lease by the execution of another lease during any quarter within which the rental was paid, as provided in the lease proposed to be terminated. * * * * * * * The rental mentioned in the lease, One dollar per acre, per annum, is a substantial consideration, and the affidavits of several parties filed at the hearing of the motion for the dissolution of the injunction not only show that the lease was fully read over to the lessors, but they show that the consideration of the rent to be paid quarterly in advance was as much an inducement to the lessors to lease at the time of execution of the lease as the development of their property, if not really a controlling consideration. At that time no producing well had been drilled near them, and it was problematical as to whether this was oil and gas territory."

The court held as to the effect of the surrender clause:

"The lessor cannot avoid such lease or declare a forfeiture thereof within the time for which he has received the stipulated rental, and a lease executed to a third party within such time, intended as an act of forfeiture, is void."

Sec. 13.—In *Marshall* v. *Oil Co.*, 198 Pa. 83; 47 Atl. 927, analyzed under Chap. 24, the lease contained a surrender clause as follows:

"It is further agreed that the second party, his heirs or assigns, shall have the right at any time to surrender up this lease by paying the rentals, if any then due, and be released from all conditions unfulfilled, then and from that time, this agreement shall be null and void and not binding on either party, and the payments made shall be retained by the first party as the full stip‑ulated damages.''

After the execution of the lease the landowner made a second lease, and in a controversy as to the validity of the first lease, the court held that the mere non-payment of rental did not forfeit the lease.

Sec. 14.—In *Ward* v. *Triple State Natural Gas & Oil Co.,* (Ky.) 115 S. W. 819 (Jan. 29, 1909), syls. 4-5 are as follows:

''4. A surrender of an unrecorded gas lease need not be in writing, signed and acknowledged, any notice being sufficient that definitely informs the adverse party that the lease has been sur‑rendered, but the original lease should be either destroyed or returned to the lessor.
5. A recorded gas lease can only be surrendered by an entry duly made and acknowledged on the margin of the record or by an instrument signed and acknowledged by the lessee.''

On June 6, 1890, Ward and wife as lessors entered into an agreement with the Triple State Natural Gas & Oil Company as lessees, by the terms of which agreement the first parties as les‑sors, in consideration of one dollar, granted and leased to the lessee for mining and operating for gas a certain tract of land in Martin County, Kentucky, for the term of thirty years, and as long thereafter as gas should be produced by the lessee, or rentals paid. The lease contained the following provision:

''Provided, however, that this lease shall become null and void and all rights hereunder shall cease and determine unless a well shall be commenced on said premises within 5 years from the date hereof, or unless the lessee shall pay an anual rent of $225.00 per year, such rental to commence on the date thereof, and to be paid within 60 days from date, and yearly thereafter. It is further agreed that lessee shall have the right at any time after the ex‑piration of five years to surrender this lease and be released from all moneys and obligations unfulfilled provided said second party pays all rentals up to the date of said surrender; then and from that time this lease and agreement shall be null and void and no longer binding on either party. Payments which shall have been

made shall be held by the lessor for the full stipulated damages
for the nonfulfillment of the foregoing contract.''

No wells were drilled by the lessee but the annual rental of
$225.00 for five years, ending June 6, 1905, was paid. The lease
was assigned by the lessee to the United States Natural Gas Company. In January, 1907, lessor brought suit to recover from the
gas company the sum of $356.00 the amount alleged to be due as
rental from June 6, 1905, to the date of the institution of the suit,
this amount being made up of $225.00 as stated to be due for the
year ending June 6, 1906, and $131.00, the amount stated to be due
from June 6, 1906, to January 6, 1907; it being alleged that the lessee had failed to pay the rental, and that they had not surrendered
the lease. The companies answered and denied any indebtedness
and averred that the lease was surrendered according to its terms
June 6' 1905. In a reply which was not denied, the lessor averred
that the companies had run a pipe line through the leased land
which was yet on the land, although it did not in any way interfere with the use and enjoyment of the land. The law and facts
being submitted to the court, it was adjudged that the lease had
been surrendered, but that the company owed the lessor $45.62 as
rental from June 6, 1905, to August, 1905. This amount was allowed on the theory that as the rent due June 6, 1905, to August 19,
1905, had not been paid the company should pay rental for the
period of time between the two dates.   From this judgment the
lessors appealed.   The Court of Appeals of Kentucky found from
the evidence that on or before June 6, 1905, an authorized agent of
the companies notified the lessor that unless he would reduce
the rental they would surrender the premises at the expiration of
the five years. Lessor declined to reduce the rental and was
thereupon notified that the lease would be surrendered by the company although the original lease was not delivered to the lessor.
The judgment of the court below was reversed and the law as to
surrender was held to be as stated in the syllabus.

Sec. 15.—In *Poe* v. *Ulrey*, 233 Ill. 56; 84, N. E. 46 (Feb. 20
1908) syls. 1-2-5-7 are as follows:

"1. Oil and gas are classed as minerals, that term not being
confined to metallic substances.

2. A grant of oil and gas on certain land is a grant of such oil and gas as the grantee may find there, and he is not vested with any title in the oil or gas until it is actually found, since, on account of their wandering nature and their liability to escape or be withdrawn to other lands, they are not subject to absolute ownership.

5. Though the recital of a consideration in an instrument may be contradicted to inquire into the real consideration of a contract where the effect is not to impair the instrument as a conveyance, an acknowledgment in an oil and gas lease of the payment of a specified consideration cannot be contradicted by parol for the purpose of invalidating the instrument or impairing its legal effect as a conveyance.

7. A surrender clause in an oil and gas lease giving the lessee the option to surrender it before the expiration of its term upon the payment of one dollar, but not giving the lessor a right to compel a surrender, did not create a tenancy at will, and hence did not render the lease invalid for lack of mutuality."

On January 27, 1905, J. V. Poe and Mary E. Poe, his wife, executed to Clarence Ulrey an oil and gas lease substantially as follows:

"In consideration of the sum of one dollar, the receipt of which is hereby acknowledged, we, J. V. Poe and wife, parties of the first part, hereby grant and lease unto Clarency Ulrey * * * * all the oil and gas in and under the following described premises * * * * together with the right to enter thereon at all times * * * * * *. To have and to hold the above described premises for the term of five years from the date hereof, and as much longer as oil or gas is found in paying quantities on said premises on the following conditions: Second parties shall within twelve months from the date hereof, drill to completion a test well on said premises. If gas is found in sufficient quantities to transport second parties agree to pay first parties the sum of one hundred dollars per year for the gas produced from each well from which gas is transported * * * * * * *. If oil is found in paying quantities the first parties shall have the one eighth part of all oil produced and saved from such premises * * * * * * * * *. In case no well is completed on said premises within twelve months from this date the parties of the second part shall pay to the parties of the first part as rental at the rate of one dollar per acre per year, to be paid quarterly at the close of the first quarter of each such rental year, counting from the expiration of the said twelve months. It is further agreed that in case no paying well is completed on said premises within five years from the date hereof, this grant shall be null and void without further agreement of the parties hereto * * * * * * *. The parties of the second part hereby agree to complete one test well on this block of leases in Martinsville Township, Park

County, Illinois, on or before the first day of May, 1905, or forfeit all rights under this lease. * * * * * * * If said first well is found productive of either oil or gas second parties further agree to continue with due diligence on this block of leases in Martinsville Township as long as paying wells are found. It is agreed that upon the payment of one dollar at any time by the party of the second part, their successors or assigns, to the parties of the first part their successors or assigns, shall have the right to surrender this lease for cancellation, after which all payments and liabilities thereafter to accrue under and by virtue of its terms shall cease and determine and this lease shall become absolutely null and void.''

Ulrey assigned the lease, except a 1-16 interest, to the Illinois Oil & Gas Company. In the Spring of 1905, a few months after the lease was made a test well was drilled on land belonging to A. B. Keith, in Martinsville Township, adjoining the land of Poe on the south, and about 30 rods from the Poe land. Gas was found and the well was capable of producing 200,000 cubic feet of gas per day, and with 115 pounds rock pressure. There was no market for the gas and no pipeline or other means of transportation to a market, and the well was shot, cased and tubed, packed and equipped with appliances used in gas wells to pipe gas to market, and was left in that condition awaiting means of transportation. Another well was drilled to the depth of about 600 feet on the farm of John McNurland, which cornered with the Poe land, and the well was about 8 rods from his line. The McNurland well showed gas but a flow of salt water was struck which destroyed the value of the well, and it was abandoned. The test well was completed within the time agreed upon but no well was completed on the Poe land within the twelve months from the date of the lease. The lessee and his assignee exercised their option to pay as rental one dollar per acre per year, to be paid quarterly, and they tendered such rental to Poe at the end of each quarter and it was refused. The parties agreed upon an amount to be paid as compensation for the rights granted by the lease in case the well should not be drilled on the Poe land within twelve months. On July 10, 1906, Poe filed a bill in equity against Ulrey and his assignee to have the lease declared null and void. A decree was entered by the Circuit Court of Clarke County, in favor of the plaintiffs. The defendants appealed to the Appellate court and that court reversed the Circuit

Court, and from that decision the plaintiffs below, the lessors, appealed to the Supreme Court, where the decision of the Appellate Court was affirmed.

Sec. 16.—In *Waterford Oil & Gas Co.* v. *Shipman*, 233 Ill. 9; 84 N. E. 53 (Feb. 30, 1908) the syllabus is as follows:

"1.   Where a co-tenant leased the lands held in common to plaintiff for the purpose of drilling and operating for oil and gas, but afterwards, with the other co-tenants, granted the oil and gas right to another person, plaintiff, to secure the interest granted him cannot have compulsory partition either of the oil and gas apart from the land or the land itself, since such a lease being merely a grant of the privilege to enter and prospect, and not giving title to the oil or gas until such products are found, is not a conveyance of the interest of one co-tenant in the common property or any part thereof.

2.   Oil and gas while in the earth, unlike solid minerals, are not the subject of ownership distinct from the soil, and the grant of the oil and gas therefore is a grant, not of the oil that is in the ground, but of such a part thereof as the grantee may find and passes nothing that can be the subject of ejectment or other real action.

3.   The right to go upon land and occupy it for the purpose of prospecting, if of unlimited duration is a 'freehold interest,' but such interest being vested for a specific purpose becomes extinct when the purpose is accomplished or the work is abandoned.

4.   A co-tenant leased the lands held in common to plaintiff for the purpose of drilling and operating for oil and gas.   The lease provided that the lessee upon payment of a dollar might surrender the lease.   Thereafter the co-tenants granted the oil and gas rights to another person.   *Held,* that the option to terminate the lease at any time deprived plaintiff of the right to specific performance, directly or indirectly, until he had performed the contract or placed himself in such position that he might be compelled to perform it on his part, and hence he cannot have a compulsory partition either of the oil and gas apart from the land, or of the land, itself.

5.   A lease of land to another to prospect for oil or gas, which provides that the lessee upon payment of a dollar may surrender the lease, is not void *ab initio* for want of mutuality, but it deprives the party for whose benefit it is made, of relief in the nature of specific performance since if such relief were granted the lessee could nullify the decree by exercising his option and equity will not do a vain thing by settling the rights of parties which one of them may set aside at will.

The Waterford Oil & Gas Company filed a bill in the Circuit Court of Crawford County against Nancy E. Shipman and others, praying for an injunction and petition. The bill averred that a tract of land was owned in common by Nancy E. Shipman, Louis Hicks, Betsy Douglass and William Hicks; that on February 5, 1906, Nancy Shipman and her husband executed an instrument called an oil lease by which the whole of the premises were granted to one D. R. Guncheon, Trustee, for the purpose of drilling and op. erating for oil and gas, laying pipe-lines, etc.; that it was stipulated in the lease that it should remain in force for the term of one year from the date and as long thereafter as the premises should be oper. ated for oil and gas. The consideration for the lease was one dollar and ⅛ part of the oil produced, and a rental of $200 per year for each gas well drilled on the premises, the product from which should be marketed and used. The lease provided that it should be void unless a well was commenced on the premises within 45 days of the date thereof, or unless the lessee should pay at the rate of twenty-five cents per acre, quarterly, for each additional three months such completion should be delayed. The lease also provided that the lessee, or his successor and assigns should have the right upon payment of one dollar to surrender the lease for cancellation, after which all payments and liabilities thereafter to accrue should cease and determine and the lease become absolutely null and void. The lessee did not begin drilling within 45 days, but paid $40.00 to, which was accepted by, Nancy Shipman on the 27th of March, 1906, as rental in advance at twenty-five cents per acre for the three months next ensuing. The bill averred that before the expiration of the quarter for which the rentals were paid the lessee tendered to Nancy Shipman $40.00 for the quarter commencing June 22, 1906, which was refused. The bill further alleged that thereafter the amount of money due under the lease was deposited in a Bank to the credit of Nancy Shipman. The bill also alleged that Nancy Shipman and all the other co-tenants entered into another agreement with Lemuel Neely, trustee, by which they were attempting to defeat and destroy the right of the plaintiff under his lease; and that Lemuel Neely had employed the St. Marys Drilling Company and another who had entered upon and taken possession of a portion of the premises, and were drilling and prospecting for oil and gas on the premises. The prayer of the bill was for an injunction to prevent the acts of alleged waste and also for division and partition of the premises between Nancy Shipman and the other co-tenants and that the interest of Nancy Shipman be designated and set off to her and that the plaintiff be permitted by decree of the court to go upon such portion of said premises as should be set off to Nancy Shipman and develop the land for oil and gas under the terms of the lease. A demurrer was sustained to the bill and the plaintiff elected to stand by the bill. A decree therefore was entered dismissing the bill for want of equity, from which the plaintiff below appealed. The Supreme Court affirmed the decree of the Circuit Court.

Sec. 17.—In *Brewster* v. *Lanyon Zinc Co.*, 140 Fed. 801; 72 C. C. A. 213, analyzed under Chapter 4, the first, second, and third points of the syllabus are as follows:

"1. The mere inadequacy of consideration or other inequality in the terms of the lease does not in itself constitute a ground to avoid it in equity.

2. A lease for a definite and permissible term, but which reserves to the lessee an option to terminate it before the expiration of the term does not create a mere tenancy at will within the operation of the rule that an estate at the will of one party is equally at the will of the other.

3. A lease given upon consideration of one dollar paid at the time is not wanting in mutuality merely because it reserves to one party an option to terminate it which it withholds from the other.

The lease in controversy contained a surrender clause as follows:

"Second party may * * * * * re-convey the premises hereby granted, and thereupon this instrument shall be null and void."

Sec. 18.—In *Roberts & Corley* v. *McFadden*, 32 Tex. Civ. App. 47; 74 S. W. 105 (March 31, 1903) the third, fourth and fifth points of the syllabus are as follows:

"3. Where an oil lease is in consideration of one dollar (not in fact paid) the promise to develop the premises and deliver to the lessor a percentage of the oil produced, and it is stipulated that the lessee may terminate the lease at any time, and that the sum paid shall be the lessor's full compensation, the contract is unilateral and void.

4. A sale of the premises by the lessor in such a lease, prior to the commencement of operations by the lessee terminates the lease.

5. Where a lease of oil lands was void the owners thereof, after making a contract for the sale of the land, were under no obligation to make an effort to remove the lease as a cloud on the title.''

The owners of real estate executed an oil and gas lease under which no explorations having been made, the lessors entered into an agreement for the sale of the real estate, but before the sale was consummated the purchasers discovered of record the lease. In a suit for specific performance and for the cancellation of the lease, the court found that the consideration of one dollar recited in the lease as having been paid, was not in fact paid; and the only consideration upon which the lease rested, so far as lessee was concerned, was the promise to develop the leased premises and to deliver to the lessor ten per cent. of the gross oil product. The lease contained a stipulation that the lessee could terminate it at any time, and that the sum paid the lessor should be his full compensation for any injury sustained. The Circuit Court held, on the authority of *Oil Company* v. *Teel,* 67 S. W. 547, that the lease was void.

Sec. 19.—In *Houssierre-Lattreille Oil Co.,* v. *Jennings-Heywood Oil Syndicate,* 115 La. 107; 38 So. 932, analyzed under chapter 13, syl. 9, and syl. 14 upon re-hearing are as follows:

"9. A contract of lease may contain a stipulation fixing an amount enabling the lessee to put an end to the lease, and unless this amount is 'vile' and insufficient, the lessor must resort to the courts to have the contract annulled. Forfeitures are to be strictly construed in an action to resume possession of the property leased, not directly towards setting aside the contract of lease under which the property is held.''

"14. (Upon Re-hearing.) A contract purporting to be a lease for a term of ten years of mineral rights in a 40-acre tract of land in an unproven part of the country whereby the contractor agrees to commence operations within six months, or pay $50.00 quarterly in advance, for each additional three months such operations are delayed, until an oil well is completed, and whereby he is given the right to remove his machinery at any time and to cancel the contract upon payment of $100.00 at any time, and whereby in the event of discovery of oil and gas the gross yield is to be shared in certain proportions by the contracting parties, is not void upon its face for want of mutuality, or as containing a potestative condition."

The Housierre-Lattreille Oil Company, claiming under a second lease, brought suit in the District Court for the Parish of Acadia, for the possession of the land leased by Arthur Lattreille to S. A. Spencer & Company, assignors of the Jennings-Heywood Oil Syndicate, against the Oil Syndicate in possession, and judgment was rendered for defendant, from which judgment plaintiff appealed to the Supreme Court, which court affirmed the judgment.

LESSOR'S REMEDY.

Sec. 20.—Where a lessor executes an oil and gas lease without receiving a valuable consideration therefor, and the lease provides for its surrender at any time without payment of rental or fulfillment of any of its covenants, on the part of the lessee, such lease creates a mere right of entry at will and lessor may terminate the same at any time before execution by the lessee. The execution of a second lease by the lessor, sale of the property, or the death of the lessor, terminates the lease.

> *Eclipse Oil Co.* v. *South Penn Oil Co.,* 47 W. Va. 84; 34 S. E.
>   293.
> *Trees* v. *Eclipse Oil Co.,* 47 W. Va. 107; 34 S. E. 933.
> *Roberts & Corley* v. *McFadden,* 32 Tex. Civ. App. 47; 74
>   S. W. 105.

Sec. 21.—Where an oil and gas lease contains an express covenant to pay a rental for delay in drilling, and also contains a stipulation authorizing lessee to surrender the lease at any time for cancellation and be relieved of all obligations thereafter accruing, lessor may recover from lessee all rentals accruing up to the time of actual surrender of the lease.

> ∴   *Roberts* v. *Bettman,* 45 W. Va. 143; 30 S. E. 95.

Ward v. *Triple State Nat. Gas & Oil Co.,* —(Ky.)—; 115 S. W.
819.

Bettman v. *Shadle,* 22 Ind. App. 542; 53 N. E. 662.

Sec. 22.—Where a land owner executes an oil and gas lease
containing a surrender clause and the lessee records the lease in
the Land Records provided for by law, lessor is entitled to have
the surrender of the lease properly executed and recorded by the
lessee. Where the lease has not been so recorded lessor is entitled
to actual surrender thereof by the lessee.

Ward v. *Triple State Nat. Gas & Oil Co.,* —(Ky.)—; 115 S. W.
819.

LESSEE'S REMEDY.

Sec. 23.—Where a lessee acquires an oil and gas lease, made
without a valuable consideration, which contains a surrender
clause authorizing him to surrender the lease at any time and be
relieved of all liabilities thereafter to accrue, lessee may execute
the lease by entry upon and exploration of the premises, after
which he has the right to hold the lease subject to the conditions
and stipulations thereof. Lessor cannot, after permitting entry
for explorations, declare a forfeiture or procure a cancellation of
the lease upon the grounds that the lease was without consideration and void for want of mutuality.

Eclipse Oil Co. v. *South Penn Oil Co.,* 47 W. Va. 84; 34 S. E.
293.

Lowther Oil Co. v. *Miller-Sibley Co.,* 52 W. Va. 501; 44 S. E.
433.

Henne v. *South Penn Oil Co.* 52 W. Va. 192; 43 S. E. 147.

Sec. 24.—Where the lessee has the option either to enter and
explore or pay a rental for delay and the lease contains a clause
authorizing him to surrender the lease at any time for cancellation
and be relieved of all obligations accruing thereafter lessee may
pay the stipulated rental for delay, the acceptance of which entitles
him to hold the lease during the time for which rental has been accepted.

Friend v. *Mallory,* 52 W. Va. 53; 43 S. E. 114.

Sec. 25.—Where an oil and gas lease contains a surrender clause authorizing lessee to surrender the lease at any time and be relieved of all liabilities thereafter to accrue and contains a clause authorizing lessee to pay a rental or commutation money for delay in drilling, the lessor having received a valuable though nominal consideration for the lease, such consideration is a sufficient consideration to support the surrender clause and the lessee has the right to surrender the lease, explore or may delay explorations by payment of a rental or commutation money for such delay, during the term.

Brown v. *Ohio Oil Co.*, 65 Ohio St. 507; 63 N. E. 76.
Friend v. *Mallory*, 52 W. Va. 53; 43 S. E. 114.
Marshall v. *Oil Co.*, 198 Pa. 83; 47 Atl. 927.
Poe v. *Ulrey*, 233 Ill. 56; 84 N. E. 46.
Brewster v. *Lanyon Zinc Co.*, 140 Fed. 801; 72 C. C. A. 213.
Housierre-Lattreille Oil Co. v. *Jennings-Heywood Oil Synd.* 115 La. 107; 38 So. 932.

Sec. 26.—Where an oil and gas lease contains a surrender clause authorizing the lessee to surrender the lease at any time and be relieved of all payments and liabilities thereafter to accrue, and contains an express covenant to pay rental or commutation money for delay in drilling, lessee, in order to relieve himself of the obligation to pay rental must surrender the lease in the manner provided for therein, and if recorded must execute and acknowledge such surrender of record.   Such surrender when so made relieves lessee of all payments and obligations thereafter, but does not affect lessor's right to recover rentals accruing prior to the date of such surrender.

Bettman v. *Shadle*, 22 Ind. App. 542; 53 N. E. 662.
Roberts v. *Bettman*, 45 W. Va. 143. Op. 146; 30 S. E. 95.
Ward v. *Triple State Gas Co.* —(Ky.) —; 115 S. W. 819.

Sec. 27.—Effect of taking new lease.—The acceptance by lessee of a new lease for the same tract of land for oil and gas purposes from the landowner or from a reversioner, operates as a surrender of the first lease.

Wade v. *South Penn Oil Co.*, 45 W. Va. 380; 32 S. E. 169.

Edwards v. *Hale*, 37 W. Va. 193; 16 S. E. 587.
Carnegie Nat. Gas Co. v. *Phila. Co.*, 158 Pa. 317; 27 Atl. 95.
Auer v. *Penn*, 92 Pa. 444.

Sec. 28.—In *Wade* v. *South Penn Oil Co.*, 45 W. Va. 380; 32 S.
E. 169 (Nov. 26, 1898) the syllabus is as follows:

"1. If a lessee for life or years take a new lease of the reversioner for a longer or shorter term than before, it is a surrender of
the first lease.
2. A lease yielding rent and an option to purchase the fee
outright are not inconsistent, and the taking of such lease during
the term of the option will not abrogate or surrender it.
3. Where there is a lease for years with rent, and an option
to purchase the fee, an election to purchase under the option, and
tender of the purchase price under it, ends the lease and its rent.
4. A purchase of the reversion in fee by the tenant for years
ends the tenancy, and the tenant is not thereafter estopped from
denying further continuing title, or rent in the landlord."

James Wade on June 9, 1898, made a lease for five years to
McCaslin of a tract of land for oil and gas purposes, Wade to receive ⅛ of the oil and $600.00 per year for each gas well as rent,
which lease was assigned, on July 2, 1890, by McCaslin to South
Penn Oil Company. On April 5, 1894, Wade made a deed which in
its granting clause granted to one Smith all the oil and gas in the
tract, but the deed said that it was agreed that Smith had an option
to buy at the end of five years the oil and gas in the tract, and on
payment they were to be conveyed to him; the deed further stating
that it was on the condition that Smith should, within 30 days after
the completion of a well, either pay Wade $1,252 or release and re-
convey; and further stating that it was on condition to be void if
a well should not be completed in five years, unless Smith should
pay $1252.00 before the expiration of that time; and that if "the
above lease became void" then the oil and gas right should draw
one dollar per acre yearly until "this option is paid in full, then
deed to be made by parties of the first part, or surrendered."
Smith assigned his rights under this instrument to the South
Penn Oil Company on April 16, 1894.   Afterwards, on July 31,
1895, the South Penn Oil Company took from Wade a lease of the
same land for production of oil and gas for the term of ten years,
covenanting to pay Wade as rent ⅛ of the oil, and $550.00 per year

for each gas well. The Company made no developments during
the life of the McCaslin lease, but under the lease to itself it developed oil upon the tract in paying quantity, and tendered Wade
$1252.00 in full satisfaction of his rights to the oil and gas, claim-
ing the right to do so under the option; Wade refused to receive
it, and the money was paid into Bank to his credit. Wade filed a
bill in chancery in the Circuit Court of Wetzel County, West Virginia, against the South Penn Oil Company, wherein he demanded
a discovery of the oil produced from the tract, and for an account
thereof. The Circuit Court dismissed his bill and he appealed to
the Court of Appeals, where the decree of the lower court was
affirmed.

Upon the proposition that the option invested Smith, before
the second lease was executed, with only an election to purchase,
and its acceptance after the lease, made a purchase after it, the
court cited:

Swearingen v. *Watson,* 35 W. Va. 463; 14 S. E. 249.

Sec. 29.—In *Edwards* v. *Hale,* 37 W. Va. 193; 16 S. E. 487
(Dec. 3, 1892) the syllabus is as follows:

"If tenant for life or years take a new lease of the reversioner
of the same premises let in the former lease, it is a surrender in
law of the first lease."

T. A. Edwards brought before a Justice in Lewis County, an
action of unlawful detainer against P. M. Hale to recover a house
and lot in Weston; a judgment having been rendered by the Circuit
Court upon appeal, against Hale he took writ of error to the Court
of Appeals. The defendant relied upon the fact that he was a tenant from year to year and could not be required to give up possession without notice to quit. The certificate of facts showed that
in 1861, P. M. Hale and J. G. Vandervort leased from R. P. Camden the ground in controversy at six dollars annual ground rent,
the lease being in writing but afterwards lost; that the term was
for no definite time, but until Camden should desire to sell or build
on the ground; that Hale and Vandervort were to be allowed to
build thereon, with the privilege of removing any building erected

by them; that they built a small house, standing when the case was tried, and afterwards, when Hale came into possession, he placed another small building in the rear of the first; that Hale and Vandervort occupied it for a time; that then Vandervort occupied it until January, 1886; that ground rent was paid to Camden until in 1862, then to Edwards till 1886; that then Vandervort surrendered possession to Hale, notifying Edwards that he must afterwards look to Hale for rent; that Hale took possession and remained therein up to the time of the suit. Upon the trial the plaintiff gave in evidence the following instrument, against the defendant's objection:

"On or before the first day of January, 1889, I promise to pay to Thomas A. Edwards, the sum of twenty-five dollars, for rent on Beef shop on Main Street from January 1, 1888, to January 1, 1889. Given under my hand this 17th day of May, 1888. (Signed) P. M. Hale."

The Court of Appeals affirmed the decree of the Circuit Court upon the grounds that the defendant Hale, as shown by the note for $25.00, and the evidence in support thereof, had taken a new lease.

Sec. 30.—In *Carnegie Nat. Gas Co.* v. *Phila. Co.*, 158 Pa. 317; 27 Atl. 95, analyzed under Chapter 17, the master to whom the cause was referred, in his finding stated:

"The master, therefore, concludes upon this branch of the case, that the rights of the Carnegie Natural Gas Company in the premises do not rise any higher than that of their assignor, John A. Snee, and they are bound by his surrender of the old lease, and acceptance of the new, for the reason that possession of Lytle of the tract described in the lease of December 18, 1891, was notice to the assignees of any rights or equity he might have outstanding against said lease, and that the plaintiff company, obtaining possession under the terms of the lease of August 8, 1892, are concluded by its terms."

The finding of the master was confirmed by the Judge of the Court of Common Pleas, and upon an appeal from the decree confirming the finding to the Supreme Court, that court affirmed the decree.

Sec. 31.—In *Auer* v. *Penn,* 92 Pa. 444, (March 22, 1880) the syllabus is as follows:

"1. The fact that a lease is for a longer term than three years does not prevent a rescission thereof by a parol agreement of the parties when accompanied by a surrender of the lease and possession by the tenant to the landlord, and the acceptance thereof by the latter. It is not like a sale and transfer to a stranger of an interest in land greater than a term of three years, and is not, therefore, within the Statute of Frauds.

2. By such acceptance and surrender, the relation of landlord and tenant is ended; and the landlord, having taken possession of the premises, either personally or by another tenant, is estopped from collecting rent."

Joseph Penn, landlord, instituted an action of covenant upon a lease in Court of Common Pleas, Number 1, of Philadelphia County, Pennsylvania, against John Auer, a surety for the payment of rent upon a lease made by Jacob Brown, tenant. The lease bore date October 15, 1875, and was for a term of five years from date, the rent payable monthly. The plaintiff filed a copy of the lease, and a statement of claim in which latter was an item for "difference between rent agreed to be paid and rent obtained." The defendant, who was surety for the tenant, filed an affidavit of defense, in which he averred that Brown occupied the premises for about the space of one year; and that he then went to plaintiff and delivered to him the possession of the premises, which plaintiff agreed to take, and did take, and released Brown and defendant as security. A supplemental affidavit was filed in which the defendant averred that Brown, "on or about the 15th day of October, 1876, and previous to the falling due of the amount claimed in this case, did surrender to the plaintiff the term of years of him, the said Jacob Brown, then to come and unexpired, of and in the demised premises, under said lease, which surrender the said plaintiff there and then accepted, and the said plaintiff thereby released the defendant from all further liability under said lease, and that the surrender and release stated in the previous affidavit filed, were made before the claim for rent in this case fell due, and before the commencement of the time for which said rent is claimed." Judgment was rendered for plaintiff, and defendant took writ of error to the Supreme Court, where the judgment was reversed.

CHAPTER 15.

ASSIGNMENT OF THE LEASE.

Sec. 1.—A lessee may, unless inhibited by statute or restricted by an express provision in the lease, assign the same without the consent of the lessor.

> *Funk* v. *Halderman,* 53 Pa. 229 Op. 244.
> *Dark* v. *Johnston,* 55 Pa. 164.
> *Neill* v. *Shamburg,* 158 Pa. 263; 27 Atl. 992.
> *Guffey* v. *Clever,* 146 Pa. 548; 23 Atl. 161.
> *Carnegie Nat. Gas Co.* v. *South Penn Oil Co.,* 56 W. Va. 402;
>   49 S. E. 548.
> *Jackson* v. *O'Hara,* 183 Pa. 233; 38 Atl. 624.
> *Burton* v. *Forest Oil Co.,* 204 Pa. 349; 54 Atl. 266.
> *Turner* v. *Seep,* 167 Fed. 646.
> *Eclipse Oil Co.* v. *South Penn Oil Co.,* 47 W. Va. 84; 34 S. E.
>   293.

Sec. 2.—Where an oil and gas lease is executed for a valuable consideration to lessee, his heirs or assigns, while such lease confers upon lessee until oil or gas is found in paying quantities only a license to enter and make explorations, it may be assigned to a third party and such assignment will confer upon and vest in assignee all the rights and privileges conferred by the original lease upon the lessee.

> *Funk* v. *Halderman,* 53 Pa. 229.

Sec. 3.—On January 17, 1867, the Supreme Court of Pennsylvania in *Dark* v. *Johnston,* 55 Pa. 164, held, that where an oil and gas contract (now universally called an oil and gas lease) was given by the lessor to the lessee, and not to his assigns, such contract conferred personal privileges to be enjoyed on the land exclusively by the lessee; and that such contract was not for the benefit of any other tenement and was not appurtenant to any other lands but belonged exclusively to the person of the grantee; and that the assignment by lessee of such contract determined the license.

Sec. 4.—In many if not all the states where oil and gas are found in commercial quantities the ordinary oil and gas lease is by Statute made personal property and, after discovery of oil or gas, chattels real. Consequently having the quality of property they are subject to assignment or grant. At this time the Pennsylvania decision in *Dark* v. *Johnston* has little practical effect for the reason that oil and gas leases are almost universally made to lessee, his heirs or assigns, or contain a clause expressly authorizing assignment of the lease.

Sec. 5.—In *Funk* v. *Halderman,* 53 Pa. 129, analyzed under Chapter 7, the lease was made in consideration of $200.00, and was made to "Funk, his heirs and assigns." In the opinion at page 244, the court said:

"But though we hold the papers in this instance to constitute a license and not a lease, it is a license coupled with an interest; not a mere permission conferred, revokable at the pleasure of the licensor, but a grant of an incorporeal hereditament, which is an estate in the grantee, and may be assigned to a third party."

Sec. 6.—In *Dark* v. *Johnston,* 55 Pa. 164 (Jan. 17, 1867) the syllabus is as follows:

"1.   Where a conveyance was to be made of land, if the vendee should find oil upon it, it is to be construed that oil must be found within a reasonable time.

2.   Oil, like water, is not the subject of property, except in actual occupancy.

3.   A grant of water is not the grant of the soil on which it rests, and it passes nothing for which ejectment will lie.

4.   It is essential to an easement that there should be both a dominant and servient tenement.

5.   Generally a parol license is revokable at the will of the licensor; and it is revokable although a consideration has been paid for it.

6.   Even a parol license executed, may become an easement on the land, and where acts have been done in reliance upon a license, the licensor will be estopped from revoking it to the injury of the licensee.

7.   A license is a personal privilege and is not assignable; an assignment by a licensee determines his right.

8.   McGuire granted to Baird a right to sink one or more wells on his land; and agreed to convey to Baird, if oil was found; also

to grant him an exclusive right to sink wells on other lands at $100
for every 10 years for every well Baird may continuously pump
oil from; if he should fail to find oil, to have the right to remove
his machinery, &c; if oil were found the right to pump to continue
as the rent should be paid. *Held,.* 1. To be a license to Baird.
2. That Baird having made improvements, McGuire could not
revoke the license as to him. 3. That Baird having assigned the
license, it was determined.''

On November 26, 1859, Samuel McGuire being the owner in
fee of a farm in Deerfield Township, Warren County, Pennsylvania, of about 250 acres, and also an island in the Allegheny
River containing about 9 acres, made an agreement with Samuel
Baird reciting:

"That the said McGuire is the owner of a farm * * * * * * *
On this land petroleum or mineral oil may exist, and said McGuire
is desirous of having it explored, and agreed to and with said Baird
as follows, viz:
First. Said Baird, as full consideration for the right to sink
one or more wells or pits on the island, and four trial wells or pits
on the farm, pays to said McGuire One Hundred Dollars before
commencing work; and should said Baird find oil on said island,
then said McGuire agrees to sell to said Baird the above described
island for the sum of Five Hundred Dollars. The one hundred
paid on commencing work to be part of said sum; the remaining
four hundred to be paid on McGuire's giving him a warranty deed
for said island in fee.
Second. Said McGuire covenants and agrees with said Baird
to grant him an *exclusive right* to sink wells and pits for obtaining
mineral oil over the rest of said estate, on the following terms and
conditions, viz: one hundred dollars for each and every period of
ten years (ten dollars per year), for each and every well or pit that
said Baird may continuously pump oil from, the continuous pumping of said oil to be the evidence that such wells or pits are used.
The rent for each and every well shall be paid yearly.
It is understood and agreed on the part of said Baird, that he
will not, in boring or sinking such wells or pits, or in erecting the
necessary buildings and apparatus to obtain, and refine or prepare
for market said oil, injure any part of said farm valuable as
pasture or tillable; and that any fences interfered with shall be restored into good condition.
It is further understood and agreed between the parties to
this instrument, that in case the said Baird shall fail to find rock
oil on either the island or the farm aforesaid, then he shall be at
full liberty to remove any buildings or machinery he may have put

up, and the one hundred dollars paid to McGuire shall be in full of every demand.

And further, should oil be found, then the right to pump oil from the wells shall continue as the said rent is paid, as before mentioned. For and in consideration of the above premises we hereby bind ourselves and our legal representatives for and to the full performance of the above agreement and every part.''

On April 2, 1861, McGuire conveyed the land to C. B. Curtis, Josiah Hall and others. Baird went into possession of the land and commenced a well on the main land, gave some twenty leases at about seventeen of which boring was commenced; some of the wells were drilled hundreds of feet and between twenty and thirty thousand dollars had been expended in boring, building, etc. Curtis, in 1861, brought an action of ejectment against Baird who received notice from Curtis to quit and left in June, 1861. Some of the lessees quit for the war and at last all left. On June 29, 1864, Baird conveyed his interests to William F. Johnston, Isaac M. Pennock, N. P. Sawyer, William Bagley and S. A. Baird, who as plaintiffs brought suit in ejectment against John Dark, Carrolton B. Curtis and others, grantees of McGuire. Verdict and judgment were rendered by the Court of Common Pleas of Warren County in favor of the plaintiffs, the assignees of Baird, the original lessee. From this judgment the defendants, who were the grantees of McGuire, appealed to the Supreme Court of Pennsylvania, and that court reversed the judgment.

Sec. 7.—In *Neill* v. *Shamburg,* 158 Pa. 263; 27 Atl. 992, (Nov. 6, 1893), the second point of the syllabus is as follows:

"A person about to purchase an oil lease is not bound to disclose to his vendor facts in regard to the production of oil upon a neighboring leasehold which he owns, and the failure to disclose such facts is not fraud. Unless exceptional circumstances create a duty to speak, it is the right of every man to keep his business to himself.''

On June 11, 1877, John Wilson and Jane Neill, owners of the fee, made an oil and gas lease to G. Shamburg in consideration of reserved royalties for a tract of fifty acres of land, in Forest County, Pennsylvania, for the term of 20 years. The tract consisted of the western part of lots 10-11-12 of the Manross farm. Shamburg drilled wells numbered 5-6-7. Number 7 was a good producing well. On March 25, 1878, John Wilson and Jane Neill made another oil and gas lease to Shamburg for a like term and consideration for the remaining part of Lots 10-11-12, and the whole of Lot 9, and also lot 8 which was situated immediately east of and contiguous to said Lots 9-10. On April 18, 1878, Shamburg assigned and conveyed to Elizabeth P. Neill the undivided one half of the leasehold covered by the lease last mentioned. On July 29, 1879, Elizabeth P. Neill sold and conveyed back to Shamburg the undivided half of the leasehold which she had purchased of him, in consideration of $550.00 paid to her by said Shamburg, and $100.00 additional when a well should be obtained on the leasehold producing six barrels per day for any thirty days during the first six months after it should be finished. Between the time of the purchase by Elizabeth P. Neill of the half interest in said leasehold and the time that she reconveyed the half interest to Shamburg, he, Shamburg, instructed his employes, or some of them, not to let anybody know anything about his business, so that it was impossible for J. A. Neill, husband of Elizabeth P. Neill, who was acting for her, to obtain accurate information as to the production of the well on the 50-acre lease made by John Wilson and Jane Neill on July 11, 1877, and situated adjoining the leasehold of March 25, 1878. The lessee, Shamburg, died and Elizabeth P. Neill filed her bill in equity in the Court of Common Pleas of Forest County against B. F. and H. W. Shamburg, administrators of G. Shamburg, deceased, the object of which bill was to obtain a re-conveyance of the interest in the oil lease sold back by Elizabeth P. Neill to G. Shamburg on July 29, 1879.

The plaintiff in her bill claimed as ground for her suit for re-conveyance, that during the time she and the lessee Shamburg owned together the 50-acre leasehold, Shamburg was operating the wells on the adjoining tract, and that he had information of the value of these adjoining lands, but caused the production and all facts in relation thereto to be concealed from her. The plaintiff claimed that the relationship of joint owners made it the duty of Shamburg to communicate to her what he knew of the production on the adjoining lands; and that a failure to make such communication constituted a fraud and breach of trust. The question of partnership was also raised, the plaintiff claiming that that relation existed between her and Shamburg. The Court of Common Pleas dismissed the plaintiff's bill, and she appealed to the Supreme Court, where the decree was affirmed,

Sec. 8.—In *Guffey* v. *Clever,* 146 Pa. 548; 23 Atl. 161, (Jan. 4, 1892), the syllabus is as follows:

"(a) A lease of land for oil and gas production, with no clause authorizing an assignment thereof, provided that if oil or gas were found, the lessee should have the refusal for three months of a lease of an adjoining tract of the lessor, on terms 'that may be equal to the best terms offered by any other person or persons therefor.'

(b) The lease having been subsequently assigned, the lessor entered into a written contract with the assignee providing for certain extensions of the time of performance and for the payment of increased royalties, and that the original lease 'shall remain in full force in all particulars in which the same is not hereby modified.'

(c.) The assignee, finding oil, notified the lessor of his election to take the lease of the adjoining tract, and was fraudulently informed by the lessor that he had been offered $20,000 for the lease. Relying upon such representation, the assignee paid said sum and accepted said lease, although the best offer that had been made to the lessor was $10,000;

1. The position that the assignment of the first lease did not carry with it the option for the second lease, was untenable, in view of the new agreement between the lessor and the assignee, especially providing for the continuance of the unmodified covenant of the first lease; and the assignee was entitled to the new lease on the best bona fide offer made.

2. In trespass for the fraud a proper measure of the damages recoverable, was the difference between the amount paid by the assignee for the second lease, and the best offer actually received by the lessor; and offers of evidence on the part of the lessor showing the actual value of the second lease, were irrelevant and inadmissible.

3. Where the vendor of property makes fraudulent representations or is otherwise guilty of fraud in the contract, the purchaser may stand to the bargain and recover damages, or may rescind the contract and recover back the money paid; *Hastings* v. *McGee,* 66 Pa. 384; so that damages were recoverable without tendering a reconveyance of the lease."

On August 10, 1888, A. P. Clever made an oil and gas lease for a tract of about 50 acres of land in Allegheny County, adjoining another tract of the lessor, to G. C. Garnier and S. S. Smith. The lease provided that:

"In case oil or gas is found on said premises, as aforesaid, then the said parties of the second part shall have the refusal, for the term of three months, of the other lands of the said parties of the first part, lying in the same locality, on terms for the lease thereof that may be equal to the best terms offered by any other person or persons therefor."

On December 4, 1888, Garnier and Smith assigned the lease, and the leasehold created thereby, to J. M. Guffey, and on February 12, 1889, A. P. Clever and J. M. Guffey executed an instrument under seal extending the time for completing a well then drilling on the premises in consideration of which Guffey agreed to pay to Clever an increased and graded royalty, "to be paid in addition to all royalty or other payments provided for in said lease, and said lease shall remain in full force in all particulars in which the same is not hereby notified." The well when completed proved to be a good producer, and on April 23, 1889, Guffey sent a letter to Clever notifying him that he would take a lease on the adjoining tract of 179 acres on the terms provided for in the supplemental agreement of February 12, 1889. Thereupon Clever sent to Guffy the following letter:

"J. M. Guffey, Esquire. Dear Sir: In answer to yours of April 23rd, 1889, I beg leave to say that I have an offer to lease the other lands owned by me in the same locality as your fifty acre lease from me, to-wit, a farm in Stowe Township, containing one hundred and seventy-nine and one-half acres, for one-eighth of the oil and a bonus of twenty thousand ($20,000) dollars, and one thousand ($1,000) dollars per annum for each gas well from which gas may be utilized. * * * * * * If you desire the property under the terms of your lease of August 10, 1888, you are hereby required to notify me of such intention within ten (10) days, and comply with the above terms on or before the end of three months after the date upon which you struck oil on your lease with me of August 10, 1888."

Thereupon on May 10, 1889, a lease was executed and delivered by A. P. Clever to J. M. Guffey in consideration of $20,000 paid in cash by the latter for the tract of land mentioned in the letter, upon substantially the same terms as there set out. In the letter from Clever to Guffey he stated that the offer of $20,000 had been made to him by Mr. Peter Goettman, of Atwood street, Oakland, Pittsburg. Guffey made no inquiry of Goettman as to whether the representations of the letter were true or not, but accepted the lease for the adjoining tract on the faith of the representations. J. M. Guffey brought an action of trespass against A. P. Clever and Charles Scarborough in the Court of Common Pleas Number 1, Allegheny County, to first Monday in April, 1890, on the theory that the statement of Clever in his letter to Guffey as to the price which he had been offered for the lease was a mere pretence, and that the only genuine offer which Clever received was one made by a Mr. Aiken of $10,000 for the lease. Upon the trial the plaintiff Guffey offered to prove that the letter of Clever was a pretence, and that the highest offer he had received was $10,000; that Goettman was a man of means; that Scarborough, a son-in-law of Clever, without means, induced Goettman to permit his name to be used as having made the offer on the terms stated in Clever's letter. The jury found a verdict in favor of the plaintiff for $10,000, and defendants appealed. The Supreme Court affirmed the judgment. It was contended in the Supreme Court that the lease to Garnier and Smith was personal, unassignable, and did not run with the land. The court held as to this point that the assignment of the lease was ratified by the new agreement between Clever and Guffey.

Sec. 9.—In *Carnegie Natural Gas Co.* v. *South Penn Oil Co.*, 56 W. Va., 402; 49 S. E. 548 (Dec. 6, 1904), syls. 4-5-6 are as follows:

"4. Carnahan being the owner of a number of oil and gas leases covering a large tract of land, assigned all the gas and gas rights, to which he was entitled, by virtue of them, to another party by a written contract, retaining all the oil and oil rights, and, at the same time, entered into another contract with the assignee, containing this clause: 'The parties hereto shall have the right to operate said territory under their respective interests, and should Carnahan in his operations for oil develop a gas well or wells, the gas company shall have the right or privilege of having any such well or wells transferred to it upon payment of the actual cost of drilling the same, together with the cost of the rig and casing, and should the gas company in its operations for gas develop an oil well or wells, Carnahan shall have the right or privilege of having any such well or wells transferred to him upon payment of the actual cost of drilling the same, together with the costs of the rig and casing. Each party shall have thirty (30) days from the completion of any such well or wells in which to exercise its option to so purchase a well from the other and make payment therefor, and during which time they shall have the opportunity of testing and inspecting any such well drilled by the other. Any gas well drilled by Carnahan, and any oil well drilled by the gas company which shall not be so purchased by the other party within the time above designated, shall, together with the product thereof, be and become the absolute property of the party drilling the same. Either shall give immediate notice to the other of the completion of any well in which the other would have an interest or right to purchase under this paragraph.' *Held;* That upon the development of gas in paying quantities, in drilling for oil, and the election of the gas company within the time limited to pay the cost of drilling the well and of the rig and casing, the party drilling it must deliver possession of the well to the gas company, and cannot continue operations therein in an effort to find oil in a lower stratum.

5. Such election on the part of the gas company, converts the option into an executory contract, specific performance of which will be enforced in equity.

6. Pending the suit for such enforcement, further operations in violation of the contract will be enjoined, to maintain the status quo, and obedience to the final decree may be compelled by prohibitory or mandatory injunction, or both, according to the exigencies of the case.''

The contract mentioned in the fourth point of the syllabus was made with the *Carnegie Natural Gas Company* on October 23, 1899. On February 14, 1902, Carnahan and others, who had obtained interests in the leases with him, conveyed all the interest and estate remaining in them by virtue of the leases to the South Penn Oil Company. Both companies then proceeded with the work of development under the contract, each turning over to the other productive wells pursuant to the agreement until the South Penn Company drilled a large gas producing well known as ''Genuine-Robison No. 19.'' Upon striking gas in this well the workmen withdrew the tools and notified the gas company, but, soon after the agents of that company appeared upon the ground, the gas company was informed by the agents of the South Penn Company

that the latter intended to drill the well on down into the oil bearing stratum and would not then surrender it. Another large gas
producing well, known as "Die-No. 1," was drilled by the South
Penn Oil Company, and this, it decided to drill deeper and refused
to surrender to the gas company. Thereupon the Carnegie Gas
Company instituted two suits in chancery in the Circuit Court of
Wetzel County against the South Penn Oil Company, setting out in
the bills in detail the facts before stated, and praying injunctions.
As to the Genuine-Robison well, the prayer was that the South
Penn Oil Company, its agents, and employes be restrained and
inhibited from, in any manner, interfering with the plaintiff in
its work and effort to pack said well for the purpose of saving the
gas, and that the plaintiff might be protected in its peaceable
possession thereof. As to the Die well, the prayer was that the
defendant be restrained from drilling the well any deeper, and that
it be required and compelled either to close and case in the gas
or allow the plaintiff to do so, to the end that the gas might be
preserved until the matters in dispute between the parties should
be settled by the court. The bill alleged that the Carnegie Company had no immediate use for the gas, in consequence of which,
it desired to have the wells shut in for the time being in order to
prevent loss by its escape. The South Penn Oil Company demurred to the bills, which demurrers were overruled. It then
answered admitting all or substantially all the facts, but claiming the right under the contract to drill the wells into the oil bearing sands, below the "Gordon stray" sand in which the gas was
found; denied that it was permitting the gas to escape, and alleged
that it was possible to operate the wells for both oil and gas and
save both by proper casing and piping and the use of certain appliances made for that purpose. Depositions were taken and filed
by both parties, and upon the hearing the Court decided that the
South Penn Company had the right to continue its operations,
but in doing so was bound to prevent the escape of gas as far as
the same could be avoided by the use of the best methods, means,
devices and appliances known to operators in the oil business.
Accordingly a bond in the penalty of $20,000 with conditions to
take the precautions aforesaid for preventing the escape of gas
was required in each case, and the decrees provided that upon

execution of the bonds the injunction should stand dissolved without further order of the court. From these decrees the Carnegie
Company appealed to the Court of Appeals, and that court reversed the Circuit Court.

Sec. 10.—In *Jackson* v. *O'Hara*, 183 Pa. 233; 38 Atl. 624, analyzed under Chapter 16, the syllabus is as follows:

"In an oil and gas lease the lessee covenanted 'to commence
operations and complete one well within one month and, in case
of failure to complete one well within such time, to thereafter pay
as rental to the party of the first part for such delay the sum of
fifty dollars per month.' The lessor agreed 'to accept such sum
as full consideration, liquidation and payment of all damages for
any delays until one well should be completed, and a failure to
complete such well or to make any such payments, within such time,
and at such place above mentioned, renders this lease absolutely
null and void, and no longer binding on either party, and will re-
vest the estate therein granted in the lessor, and release the lessee
from all his covenants herein contained, he having the option to
drill said well or not, or pay said rental or not, as he may elect.'
The lessee assigned a one-half interest in the lease. No well was
ever completed or commenced. The assignee of the one-half interest in the lease paid the rental for three months, but then ceased,
and no more was paid. In an action for the rental against the lessee
and the assignee of the one-half interest, the defendants filed an
affidavit of defense in which they averred that (1) the lessee had an
option to sink a well or pay a monthly rental, or to do neither, and
by refusing to do either, the lease was at an end; and (2) there was
no joint liability of the defendants. *Held,* that the affidavit of
defense was insufficient to prevent judgment."

Sec. 11.—In *Burton* v. *Forest Oil Co.*, 204 Pa. 349; 54 Atl. 266,
analyzed under Chapter 16, the first point of the syllabus is as
follows:

"Where a lessee of a gas lease assigns an undivided one-half
interest therein to a corporation 'to have and to hold the said interest subject to all royalties of the lessee therein contained,' and subsequently the other undivided one-half interest is assigned to a second company, the first company enters into possession, and operates the land under an agreement by which it is to account to the
second company for one-half of the proceeds of the gas produced,
the latter to be liable for one-half of the expense, the first company
is liable to the lessor for the whole of the royalties stipulated for
in the lease."

Sec. 12.—In *Eclipse Oil Co.* v. *South Penn Oil Co.*, 47 W. Va. 84; 34 S. E. 293, analyzed under Chapter 4, Henry Garner, on May 11, 1897, executed an oil and gas lease for a tract of land in Wetzel County, West Virginia, to H. J. and J. C. Stolz. This lease was assigned by lessees to the Eclipse Oil Company. On June 18, 1898, Garner, the land owner, made a second lease for the same property to J. A. Phillips, who assigned his lease to the South Penn Oil Company. This company entered the premises and commenced development when the Eclipse Oil Company obtained an injunction upon a bill in equity filed by it in the Circuit Court of Wetzel County against the South Penn Oil Company, claiming that its lease was valid, and, in a controversy between these two assignees of the original lessees a decree was entered by the Circuit Court validating the second lease in the hands of the assignee, from which decree the plaintiff, Eclipse Oil Company, the assignee of the first lease, appealed to the Supreme Court of Appeals, which court affirmed the Circuit Court.

Sec. 13.—In *Turner* v. *Seep*, 167 Feb. 646, (Feb. 10, 1909.) syl. 2 is as follows:

"Where an oil and gas lease executed by an Indian in the Indian Territory on a form prescribed by the Interior Department expressly provided that no sublease or assignment of any interest therein could be made without the written consent of the lessor and the Secretary of the Interior, and any attempted assignment or transfer without such consent should be void, a subsequent regulation of the department which contained no requirement of the lessor's consent in such cases could not validate an assignment of such lease made without the lessor's consent."

Susan Turner, a fullblooded Cherokee Indian, at the time of executing the lease hereinafter mentioned, was a minor. On November 16, 1905, J. T. Parks, who prior to that date had been regularly appointed as the legal guardian of Susan Turner, executed to the Midland Oil Company an oil and gas lease for a tract of land in the Cherokee Nation, in Indian Territory, which land was a portion of the allotment to said Susan Turner. The lease was executed upon the form prescribed at the time by the Secretary of the Interior, and was made for a term extending to December

4, 1908. In the execution of the lease the guardian acted under an order of the United States Court for the Northern District of Indian Territory, which court had at that time jurisdiction of such guardianship matters under the law as then in force. Thereafter, on December 9, 1905, the lease was filed with the United States Indian Agent at Muskogee, to be forwarded to the Secretary of the Interior for his approval. In addition to filing the lease with the United States Indian Agent, it was necessary under the rules and regulations of the Secretary of the Interior then in force that the lessee in such case also file an application to accompany the lease upon the form prepared and prescribed by the Secretary of the Interior. The application to accompany the lease was not filed by the lessee, the Midland Oil Company, until September 5, 1906. One of the provisions of the lease was as follows:

"And it is mutually understood and agreed that no sub-lease, assignment, or transfer of this lease, or of any interest therein, or thereunder, can be directly, or indirectly, made without the written consent thereto of the lessor and the Secretary of the Interior first obtained, and that any such assignment or transfer made or attempted, without such consent shall be void."

On April 29, 1907, the Midland Oil Company executed to William J. Seep, of Coffeyville, Kansas, and Theodore N. Barns- dall, of Pittsburg, Pennsylvania, a written instrument purporting to be an assignment of this lease made to Barnsdall and Seep. On the same date Barnsdall and Seep executed a written instrument styled an "acceptance of such assignment." At the time of the execution of these instruments, the lease had not been approved by the Secretary of the Interior, nor had Susan Turner or her guardian consented, either verbally or in writing, to the assignment. But on June 18th following, both the lease and the assignment were approved by the Assistant Secretary of the Interior, as appears from an endorsement reading as follows:

"Department of the Interior, Washington, D. C., June 18, 1907. Lease and assignment approved as recommended. Jesse L. Wilson, Asst. Secretary of the Interior."

The Midland Oil Company never took possession of the property leased. Early in the year 1906, and within a few months af-

ter the date of the execution of the lease, W. J. Seep, appearing
to act for Barnsdall and himself, went upon the property which
consisted of about 50 acres of land, and proceeded to drill wells
thereon until it had developed twelve producing oil wells. Pumps
were put in and the oil was drawn and delivered to the Prairie
Oil and Gas Company a corporation engaged in the business of
buying and piping oil from that field. Early in January, 1907, the
guardian having been advised that developments were being made
upon the land, visited the property and found Seep in possession,
and oil and gas wells drilled on the land, and all equipment set
for drawing oil from the land—tanks erected, pipes laid, and engine and engine house, and a man in charge of the land. Upon inquiry at the office of the Pipeline Company the guardian learned
that they were taking the oil from the land and crediting it to
Barnsdall and Seep. On March 7, 1907, the guardian filed an action
in the United States Court for the Northern District of Indian Territory, styled a "complaint in equity" setting up the majority of
the plaintiff, his guardianship, the execution of the lease, and the
fact that it had never been approved by the Secretary of the Interi-
or; that Barnsdall and Seep were unlawfully in possession of the
land withholding the same from the plaintiff, destroying the timber thereon and withdrawing the oil therefrom, to the irreparable
injury of the plaintiff, and praying that a Receiver be appointed
pending the action; that the defendants be restrained from interfering with the plaintiff's possession and peaceful enjoyment of
the premises, and from removing the oil therefrom, and for an
accounting to the plaintiff for the timber cut from the land, and
the oil and gas or other minerals taken or extracted therefrom, and
for judgment therefor. A Receiver was appointed by the Court
pending the litigation. The Prairie Oil & Gas Company was made
a defendant and filed its separate answer disclaiming interest in
the property, denying any collusion with the other defendants, and
praying that the complaint be dismissed in so far as it was concerned; and the action was dismissed as to the company. On November 5, 1907, the defendants, Seep and Barnsdall, and the Midland Oil Company filed their separate answers admitting the execution of the lease to the Midland Oil Company, and alleging its
approval by the Secretary of the Interior on June 18, 1907; alleg-

ing also the execution and approval of the assignment from the
Midland Oil Company to Barnsdall and Seep; and denying the allegations of the complaint with reference to the conversion of the
oil and timber by them from the land and praying that the Receiver be discharged, and that the complaint be dismissed as
against them. By replication thereafter filed the plaintiff denied
the approval of the lease by the Secretary of the Interior, and also
denied the assignment of the same. The court held that the lease
and assignment had been properly approved by the Secretary of
the Interior, as required by law. As to the provision of the lease
which required the lessor's consent to the assignment, the court
held:

"The requirement that the assignment be with the consent of
the lessor is clear and unequivocal. The lessor did not consent to
the attempted assignment under which Seep and Barnsdall claim,
and therefore, by the plain terms of the lease, the assignment is
void, and gives Seep and Barnsdall no legal right to operate upon
the land."

Upon appeal to the Circuit Court of Appeals for the Eighth
Circuit, the decree of the Circuit Court was affirmed, except as to
charging defendants below with part of the compensation of the
Receiver for operating the wells. The Court held that plaintiffs below should have a fair compensation for the use of their tools and
machinery by the Receiver. *Midland Oil Co.* v. *Turner*, 179 Fed.
74; 102 C. C. A. 368.

CHAPTER 16.

ASSIGNEE—LIABILITY OF.

Sec. 1.—An assignee by accepting an assignment of an oil and
gas lease becomes liable upon covenants which are broken while
the title is held by him, but he is not liable upon covenants broken
before he obtained title or maturing after he parts with it.

Fennell v. *Guffey*, 139 Pa. 341; 20 Atl. 1048.

Bradford Oil Co. v. *Blair*, 113 Pa. 83; 4 Atl. 218.
Washington Nat. Gas Co. v. *Johnston*, 123 Pa. 576; 16 Atl. 799.
Heller v. *Dailey*, 28 Ind. App. 555; 63 N. E. 490.
Woodland Oil Co. v. *Crawford*, 55 Ohio St., 161; 44 N. E. 1093.
Moore v. *Sawyer*, 167 Fed. 826.
Indiana Nat. Gas Co. v. *Hinton*, 159 Ind. 398; 64 N. E. 224.
Chaney v. *Ohio Oil & Gas Co.*, 32 Ind. App. 193; 69 N. E. 477.
Breckenridge v. *Parrott*, 15 Ind. App. 417; 44 N. E. 66.
Burton v. *Forest Oil Co.*, 204 Pa. 249; 54 Atl. 266.
Jackson v. *O'Hara*, 183 Pa. 233; 38 Atl. 624.
Fisher v. *Guffey & Queen*, 193 Pa. 393; 44 Atl. 452.
Dailey v. *Heller*, 41 Ind. App. 379; 81 N. E. 219.

Sec. 2.—An assignee of an oil and gas lease, by accepting the assignment of the lease becomes liable to the lessor for the performance of the covenants of the lease breaches of which occur during the time he holds title. An assignee is liable for the payment of the rentals where there is an express covenant to pay rentals accruing subsequent to the assignment and during the time he holds title; and this liability may be enforced by the lessor against the assignee upon proof of the assignment and the retention of the lease subsequent thereto.

Sec. 3.—Covenants for development of the property demised by an oil and gas lease run with the land and are binding on an assignee, and such covenants may be enforced without any special contract being entered into between the lessor and the assignee.

Sec. 4.—The original lessee, by an assignment of the lease, does not relieve himself of liability to the lessor, but remains liable owing to the privity of contract between him and the lessor. The assignee of a lease being also in privity of contract with the lessor, is liable only upon covenants broken while his privity of estate exists.

Sec. 5.—Each successive assignee is liable upon the covenants broken while the title is held by him; but the assignee is not liable upon covenants broken before he obtained title, nor is the assignee liable on covenants where the liability matures after the assignee has parted with his title. An assignee is not liable to the lessor upon covenants to drill a well on the premises when the time for the performance of such covenant elapsed before the lessee acquired title under the assignment.

Sec. 6.—Where a lessor sues the assignee of his lessee on the covenants of the lease the burden is on the lessor to prove the assignment.

Sec. 7.—Where a lessee assigns the lease and in such assignment stipulates that the assignee shall have and hold the lease under the terms thereof and under and subject to the rents and covenants therein reserved and contained on the part of the lessee to be paid, kept, done and performed, and such assignee accepts the assignment and receives the lease thereunder, thereby the assignee steps into the shoes of the lessee and assumes his obligations and becomes liable not only for the rentals due and unpaid at the time of such assignment, but also for all breaches of covenants which accrue during the time such assignee holds the lease.

Sec. 8.—In *Fennell* v. *Guffey,* 139 Pa. 341; 20 Atl. 1048 (Jan. 5, 1891), the syllabus is as follows:

"1. Covenants to pay rent or royalty run with the land; and the assignee of a lease of land for oil and gas production is liable to the lessor for the payment of all rents or royalties which accrue while he holds an assignment of the lease.
(a) A lease of oil lands required the lessee to complete a well within six months from its date, and, on a failure so to do, to pay to the lessor 'for such delay, the sum of $231 per annum, within three months after the time for completing such well.'
(b) No well was completed; and, about eight months from its date, the lease was assigned to a third person, who continued to hold it but never began operations under it. Subsequently the lessor brought assumpsit for four annual payments of $231.00 each;
2. In such case, the first annual payment had not accrued, nor was there a breach of the covenant to pay it, until after the assignment; and, inasmuch as the installments sued for all accrued while the defendant held the assignment, all were recoverable."

On May 12, 1886, William Fennell made an oil and gas lease to E. C. Beardsley for a tract of land in Allegheny County, Penn-

sylvania for the term of twenty years, which lease contained the
following provisions:

"Operations on the above described premises shall be commenced and one well completed within six months from the date
hereof; and, in case of a failure to complete one well within such
time, the party of the second part hereby agrees to pay to the
party of the first part, for such delay, the sum of $231.00 per
annum, within three months after the time for completing such
well as above described, payable at bank aforesaid; and the party
of the first part hereby agrees to accept such sum as full consideration and payment for such yearly delay, until the well shall be
completed; and a failure to complete one well, or to make any such
payments, within such time and at such place as above mentioned,
renders this lease null and void, and to remain without effect between the parties hereto."

On January 24, 1887, the lessee E. C. Beardsley, assigned the
lease to J. M. Guffey, and no well having been drilled, and no
rentals paid, on August 7, 1890, the lessor instituted suit in the
Court of Common Pleas of Allegheny County, against J. M. Guffey,
the assignee, for the recovery of payments of $231,00 each, coming
due February 12, 1887, 1888, 1889, and 1890, with interest. The
defendant filed an affidavit of defense substantially as follows: (1)
That the defendant never took possession of the premises, and that
the covenant to drill the well was broken before the assignment,
and that as assignee he could not be held for *damages* for such
breach. (2) That the plaintiff's right of action was against the
lessee, Beardsley, and was limited to the damages accrued at the
time of the breach. (3) That by its own terms the parties to the
lease agreed it should be void and of no effect as to either party upon the lessee's failure to drill a well or pay the damages for such
failure; and that plaintiff could only recover $231.00 the amount of
damages accrued at the time of forfeiture. The Court of Common
Pleas held the affidavit of defense insufficient and entered judgment for $1,039.16. The defendant, Guffey, appealed to the Su-
preme Court of Pennsylvania and that court affirmed the judgment
of the Court of Common Pleas.

Sec. 9.—In *Bradford Oil Co.* v. *Blair*, 113 Pa. 83; 4 Atl. 218
(May 15, 1886), the first point of the syllabus is as follows:

"1.   A. leased his farm to B. to explore for and produce oil, at
a royalty of one-eighth of the production.   The lease contained the
following covenant: 'To continue, with due diligence, and without delay, to prosecute the business to success or abandonment;
and if successful, to prosecute the same without interruption for
the common benefit of the parties.'   B. assigned an interest in said
lease to C. and D. and they with B. assigned it to E.   Two wells
were bored on the farm, both of which were producing wells.   E.
refused to bore any other wells.   In an action of covenant brought
by A. against E. for breech of the covenant above quoted, *held*,
that said covenant was not the personal covenant of B. but a covenant that ran with the land, and therefore bound E."

On July 17, 1875, James E. Blair leased to L. B. Peck his farm
in McKean County for oil purposes for one-eighth royalty.   On
July 27, 1876, Peck assigned to W. C. Chambers the one-half and to
J. T. Jones the undivided one-fourth interest in said lease.   On
April 20, 1876, the Bradford Oil Company was organized, and on
the 25th of the same month, Peck, Chambers and Jones assigned
the lease to said company.   The lease contained a covenant on the
part of Peck that he would "continue with due diligence and without delay to prosecute the business to success or abandonment, and
if successful, prosecute the same without interruption for the common benefit of the parties aforesaid."   Peck, Jones and Chambers
went upon the farm in the summer of 1875 and drilled one well
thereon, which was completed about December first of the same
year.   The Bradford Oil Company went into possession of the
farm immediately after its organization in the Spring of 1876, and
drilled one well thereon which was completed about August 1, 1876.
These two wells were fair producers.   The Bradford Oil Company
became the owner of the land, or the oil rights therein upon all but
one side of the Blair farm, and drilled wells on the surrounding
lands all of which produced oil.   The company did not drill any
other wells on the Blair farm until in October, 1878.   Blair repeatedly notified them to go on and prosecute the business as required by the lease.   James F. Blair instituted an action of covenant in the Court of Common Pleas of McKean County against the
Bradford Oil Company to recover damages for a breach of the
covenant above quoted.   The defendant company plead *non est
factum* and covenant performed *absque hoc*.   Judgment was rendered by the court of Common Pleas in favor of the plaintiff, from

which judgment the oil company appealed to the Supreme Court, which court affirmed the judgment.

Sec. 10.—In *Washington Natural Gas Co.* v. *Johnson*, 123 Pa. 576; 16 Atl. 799 (Feb. 18, 1889) the first, second and third points of the syllabus are as follows:

"1. Owing to his privity of contract with the lessor, a lessee's liability upon his covenant in an oil and gas lease, continues after his assignment of the lease; but an assignee of a lease, being in privity of estate only with the lessor, is liable only upon covenants which are broken while his privity of estate exists.

2. Each successive assignee would be liable upon covenants which are broken while the title is held by him, but because of the absence of any contract relations with the lessor, he would not be liable upon covenants broken before he obtained title or maturing after he had parted with it.

3. An assignee of an oil and gas lease is not liable to the lessor upon a covenant of the lease to drill a well upon the demised premises, when the time for the performance had elapsed before the assignee acquired title under the assignment. *Bradford Oil Co.*, v. *Blair*, 113 Pa. 83, distinguished."

On August 5, 1885, M. J. Johnson and others demised to W. S. Guffey & Company a tract of land in Washington County, Pennsylvania, for oil and gas purposes for the term of twenty years. The lease contained, among other provisions, the following:

"It is further agreed that the second well shall be commenced four months after May, 1886, the time stated for the completion of well number 1."

The lease also provided that if gas should be obtained in sufficient quantities and utilized, the consideration in full to the lessors should be $800.00 for each and every well drilled on the premises. On March 18, 1886, W. S. Guffey and Company assigned the lease to C. D. Robbins, who drilled the first well and completed the same in the summer of 1886. Robbins paid the $800.00 royalty for this well. A location for a second well was made and a derrick erected about October, 1886. On January 20, 1887, Robbins assigned the leasehold to the Washington Natural Gas Company. This company went into possession and utilized the gas from well

Number 1. The second well was never drilled. On August 2, 1887, the lessors instituted an action of assumpsit in the Court of Common Pleas of Washington County against the Washington Natural Gas Company for the recovery of $800.00 damages for the failure to commence the second well upon the premises within the time mentioned in the lease. The defendant pleaded non-assumpsit and payment. The plaintiffs offered to prove that a second well could have been drilled and completed if due diligence had been used, by January 1, 1887. Judgment was rendered by the Court of Common Pleas for the plaintiffs. The Gas Company appealed to the Supreme Court of Pennsylvania, which court reversed the judgment. Justice Williams, in the opinion, at page 592, said:

"It is clear, therefore, that when Robbins made his assignment to the Washington Natural Gas Company, the time fixed in the lease for the sinking of the second well had gone by, and the covenant was broken. Guffey & Co. were liable upon their covenant, because, although their assignment had divested them of the lease, it could not relieve them from their contracts. Robbins, who was the owner when the covenant matured, was liable because of the privity of estate; but the gas company had no relations with the lessor or the leasehold until after the covenant was broken. The covenant ran with the land until the breach. It then ceased to run, because it was turned into a cause of action."

Sec. 11.—In *Heller* v. *Dailey*, 28 Ind. App. 555; 63 N. E. 490, (April 2, 1902) the second and third points of the syllabus are as follows:

"2. An assignor of a lease continues after his assignment to be liable on the express covenants therein.
3. Where the lessor of an oil lease sues an assignee of his lessee on a covenant of lease, the burden is on the lessor to prove the assignment."

On April 22, 1896, Lemuel Heller made an oil and gas lease to Dailey and Eddington, for a tract of 80 acres of land in Wells County, Indiana, which lease was upon the following conditions:

"If gas only is found, second party agrees to pay two hundred dollars each, for the product of each well while the same is being used off the premises, and the first party to have gas free

of cost to heat all stoves in dwelling houses and for domestic purposes during the same time. * * * * In case no well is completed within sixty days from this date, then this grant shall be
null and void, unless second party shall pay the first party one
dollar per day in advance for each day thereafter such completion
is delayed. * * * * * And it is further agreed by the party of
the second part that they shall drill a well at the rate of one every
sixty days after date until five wells are completed. In case any
well is not completed in said sixty days as above provided for,
parties of the second part shall pay one dollar per day in advance
until said well is completed. It is understood between the parties
to this agreement that all the conditions between the parties here-
unto shall extend to their heirs, executors and assigns.''

On April 22, 1895, Eddington assigned in writing all his interest in the lease to Dailey, who, on the 28th of the same month,
assigned in writing an undivided one-half interest in the lease to
Waring. Dailey & Waring assigned the lease to the Capital Oil
Company, which company afterwards went into the hands of a receiver and became defunct. The receiver sold the lease to Britton &
Britton. Two wells were drilled on the premises within one hundred
and twenty days from the date of the lease. No other wells were
thereafter drilled, nor were any rentals paid for delay. In March,
1889, the lessor sued Dailey, Eddington and the Brittons, with
Frank L. Waring, who died before the trial, the lessor claiming the
"daily rental," specified in the lease. The Brittons answered making general denial. Judgment was rendered by the Circuit Court
of Wells County in favor of the plaintiffs. From this judgment the
defendants appealed to the Appellate Court of Indiana, which
court affirmed the judgment so far as it related to the liability of
the Brittons, but reversed it as to Dailey and Eddington. The reversal as to the defendants, Dailey and Eddington, was upon the
pleadings, they having pleaded surrender.

Sec. 12.—In *Woodland Oil Co,.* v. *Crawford*, 55 Ohio St., 161;
44 N. E. 1093, analyzed under Chapter 14, the second point of the
syllabus is as follows:

"2. U. assigned the lease to the oil company, and in such assignment stipulated that the oil company should have and hold
the lease under the terms thereof, and under and subject to the
rents and covenants therein reserved and contained on part of the

lessee to be paid, kept, done and performed, and the oil company accepted the assignment and received the lease thereunder. *Held,* that thereby the oil company stepped into the shoes of U. and assumed his obligations, and became liable for the rentals due under the lease."

Sec. 13.—In *Moore* v. *Sawyer,* 167 Feb. 826 (C. C. E. D. Okla. Jan. 5, 1909.) syls 3-5-9 are as follows:

"3.   An instrument in terms granting all the oil, gas, coal, and asphaltum, under certain described land, but which was denominated a lease, had a definite term of 15 years, and provided, in addition to the cash payment of $50.00, for the payment of a royalty on oil produced, *held,* not a conveyance in fee of the minerals in place, but merely a lease.

5.   Any equities in favor of a lessor in an oil lease arising out of suppression of facts, when the lease was made, or failure to pay a bonus provided for therein, and the receipt of which was acknowledged, does not affect the validity of the lease in the hands of assignees, who took it for value in good faith, and without any knowledge of such facts.

9.   An assignee of a second oil lease on Indian land, who took the assignment of the lease with knowledge that a prior lease was outstanding, in reliance on the records of the office of the Indian agent, which showed that the prior lease had been forwarded to the land department for cancellation at the request of the parties, *held,* not a bona fide purchaser, entitled to preference over the prior lease where such prior lease was not in fact cancelled, but was approved by the Secretary of the Interior, the request for cancellation having been through a mistake, which fact would have been disclosed to the assignee of the second lease if he had made inquiry of the parties."

Zeke Moore was a member of the Creek Tribe or Nation of Indians.   He was a negro having no Indian blood, but by virtue of his enrollment as a citizen of said Nation was entitled to, and had allotted to him prior to the transactions involved in this controversy, 160 acres of land in the Creek Nation.   At the time of the allotment, and at the time of the various deeds and leases mentioned in the suit, Moore was confined in the United States penitentiary, at Leavenworth, Kansas, serving a sentence for the crime of larceny, imposed pursuant to a conviction in the United States District Court for the Western District of Indian Territory.   The land in question was located in what is known as the "Glenn Pool District" which first attracted attention as an oil field in 1905, or

1906. On April 12, 1906, Moore executed to Royal S. Litchfield an oil and gas mining lease covering the homestead and that portion of his surplus allotment described as the West half of the northwest quarter of Section 8, designated as West 80, and in all, 120 . acres. This lease was executed upon the form provided for use at that time, pursuant to rules and regulations promulgated by the Secretary of the Interior, and was for the term of fifteen years. In consideration of the royalties, and other stipulations contained in the lease, it purported to demise, grant and let to said Litchfield for said term all the oil deposits and natural gas in and under the said lands with the right to prospect therefor. The lease was approved by the assistant Secretary of the Interior on January 9, 1907. Immediately upon the approval of the lease Litchfield began to sink wells on the portion of the land comprising the homestead, and before the institution of the suit had expended a large sum of money upon the land and had developed a number of producing wells thereon. After the approval of the lease the lessee paid to the lessor Moore, $120.00, the bonus agreed upon, and thereafter paid the stipulated royalties. On June 1, 1906, Moore executed to the United States Loan & Trust Company an instrument, styled "a lease" covering the 120 acres theretofore leased to Litchfield. This lease provided that in consideration of $50,00 cash the lessor granted unto the lessee all the oil and gas in and under the tract of land, describing it, for the production and transportation of oil and gas, excepting and reserving one-tenth part of all oil produced, which lease was for a term of fifteen years, and as much longer as oil or gas should be produced, or the rentals paid. On November 19, 1906, the lessee, the said Loan & Trust Company, assigned to Usher Carson all its interest in said lease. On November 20, 1906, Carson assigned seven-eighths of his interest in the lease to J. R. Sharp; and on January 12, 1907, Carson assigned his remaining one-eighth interest to J. W. Sloan. On January 26, 1906, Moore executed to one Sawyer a general warranty deed to the West 80-acre tract of land in consideration of $1,150.00. On December 17, 1906, the deed was reacknowledged by Moore before W. H. Bond, a Notary Public for Leavenworth County, Kansas. On July 20, 1906, Fred L. Sawyer and wife conveyed by warranty deed to Royal S. Litchfield their undivided one-half interest in the land described in the last mentioned deed. Shortly after acquiring the interest of Carson in the Loan & Trust Company lease Sharp and Sloan commenced to erect a rig and drill for oil on the West 80 acres. Thereupon, in January, 1907, Sawyer instituted suit against Sharp and Sloan in the United States Court for the Indian Territory, at Sapulpa, to enjoin them from interfering with his possession of said land under his deed from Moore. Subsequently by amendment filed February 4, 1907, other parties claiming interests in the land were made parties defendant, so that it became a suit by Sawyer against J. R. Sharp, J. W. Sloan, Usher Carson, Zeke Moore, United States Loan & Trust Company, G. R. McCullough, O. M. Lancaster, and Royal S. Litchfield, the object of which was to establish Sawyer's title to the land, and set aside and annul the instrument under which the various defendants were claiming interests adverse to his, and remove such as clouds on his title. Subsequently, on April 22, 1907, Moore commenced his action against the defendants and other parties as to whom the action was subsequently dismissed, to recover possession of the land, to enjoin defendants from interfering with his possession, for the appointment of a receiver *pendente lite*, and an accounting for oil extracted from the land. The basis for this suit, as originally filed, was the alleged fraud and misrepresentation practiced upon the plaintiff by the defendants in the procurement of the various deeds and leases referred to. By an amendment filed later, Moore also alleged that at the time of the procurement of the Litchfield lease, the Loan & Trust Company lease, and the Sawyer deed, he was a minor; and that he had not ratified the contract after he became of age. Subsequently the two suits were consolidated. As to the validity of the original lease the court held:

"As it does not appear that at the time this lease was executed its terms were inequitable, or the consideration inadequate, in view of the conditions as they then existed, and in view of its approval by the Secretary of the Interior, I find that complainants prayer that it should be cancelled and set aside, should be denied."

As to the lease to United States Loan & Trust Company, the court held that as to the forty acres comprising the homestead, the lease never having been approved by the Secretary of the Interior, was invalid, and should be cancelled, to that extent. As to the contention by Sharp and Sloan that the lease held by them was a conveyance in fee of the oil in place, and therefore an alienation, the court held as stated in syl. 3. As to the rights of an assignee, the court held as stated in syl. 9; and as between the relative rights of Litchfield and the rights of Sharp and Sloan, the assignees of the second lease, the court held that the right of Litchfield was prior and sustained his lease. The concluding paragraph of the opinion is as follows:

"It therefore follows that Sharp and Sloan took the Trust Company lease with notice of and subject to the prior rights of the Litchfield lease, and while, as between themselves and the complainant Moore, the lease is held to be valid as to the West 80, they cannot exercise any rights under it, so far as oil and gas are concerned, during the term of the Litchfield lease, or until such time as it should cease to be a valid and subsisting instrument. As to the forty acres comprising the homestead, the lease is invalid, and should be cancelled, so far as it affects that property."

Sec. 14.—In *Indiana Natural Gas and Oil Company v. Hinton,* 159 Ind. 398; 64 N. E. 224 (May 27, 1902), syl. 2 is as follows:

"2. Covenants in a lease of oil and gas lands for the payment of rent, and the furnishing of gas to heat and light the dwellings on demised premises, are covenants running with the land; and in an action against an assignee of the lessee for a breach thereof, it is not necessary to allege that the assignee agreed to perform such covenants."

On July 25, 1889, Joseph McGraw leased to J. S. Smith and H. C. Ziegler a tract of land in Grant County, Indiana, for oil and gas purposes, which lease contained the following provisions:

"Fourth. First party shall have, free of expense, gas from the well or wells, to use, at his own risk, to light and heat the dwellings now on the premises, with pipe to conduct the same to said dwellings, free of cost. * * * Ninth. Second party agrees to furnish gas to first party for use at his premises on or before the fifteenth day of November."

Shortly after the lease was executed and delivered, Smith and Ziegler sold, assigned and transferred their rights as lessees to the

Indiana Natural Gas & Oil Company. After making the lease the lessor, McGraw sold and conveyed the lands together with his interest in the lease to William S. Beeson. On March 2, 1896, Beeson sold and conveyed said land and his rights under said lease to Albert H. Hinton. The Oil Company paid the $56.00 money rent stipulated for in the lease to the several owners. Albert H. Hinton brought an action against the Gas Company in the Circuit Court of Grant County for damages for breach of the covenant to furnish gas for the purpose of heating and lighting the dwellings on the premises demised. General denial was entered by the Gas Company. A trial by jury was had, judgment for plaintiff, motion for new trial over-ruled, and the case was appealed to the Supreme Court by the Gas Company. That court affirmed the judgment of the Circuit Court. Chief Justice Dowling, who delivered the opinion of the court, said:

"The appellee, who occupied and used the land, was the only person injured by the breach of the covenant to furnish gas. The appellee, therefore, had the right to maintain this action for the damages sustained by him, which were occasioned by the failure of the assignees of the lease to furnish gas to heat and light the buildings on the land."

Sec. 15.—In *Chaney* v. *Ohio Oil Co.,* 69 N. E. 477; 32 Ind. App. 193, analyzed under Chapter 6, syl. 2 is as follows:

"An oil and gas lease was for one year, and so long thereafter as oil and gas could be produced in paying quantities; and it was provided that the lessee should drill a well within a certain time, and additional wells within a specified time, or be liable for a certain penalty. One well was drilled, but gas was not found in paying quantity, and after the expiration of the year the lessee assigned the lease. *Held,* that the assignee of the lessee was not liable to the lessor for the penalties, there being no privity of estate."

Sec 16.—In *Breckenridge* v. *Parrott,* 15 Ind. App. 417; 44 N. E. 66 (May 26, 1896), the syllabus is as follows:

"1. Where a lease of oil and gas privileges requires the lessee to complete an oil well within one year from the date of the lease, or on default, to pay 'for further delay a yearly rental' until the well is completed, and provides that the conditions of the lease shall bind assignees, one who soon after the lease is executed becomes the owner of a half interest therein, and, shortly after the expiration of the first year, becomes, by assignment from the original lessee of his remaining interest, the sole owner of the lease, is liable for rental for the second year if the well is not completed.

  2.   The fact that during the second year he released the lease of record, and sent the original lease to the lessor who kept it, will not change his liability; the release having been executed without the knowledge or consent of the lessor, and the lessor never having released such rental.''

On June 11, 1890, Peter Parrott executed to E. T. Anderson & Company an oil and gas lease on 160 acres of land in Adams County, Indiana, for the term of five years. By the terms of the lease Anderson & Company agreed to complete a well on the premises demised within one year from the date of the lease, or, in default thereof pay to the lessor for further delay a yearly rental of $160.00 until the well was completed. It was expressly agreed in the lease that all the conditions between the parties thereto should extend to their assignees. Soon after the lease was executed, Anderson acquired the sole interest, and afterwards, on June 15, 1891, assigned the lease to Sylvester Breckenridge. On April 8, 1892, Breckenridge without knowledge or consent of Parrott, released the lease of record and sent the original lease by mail to Parrott, who retained possession of the lease. No well was ever completed on the land, and no rental was ever paid to the lessor. Parrott instituted an action for the rental against Breckenridge in the Circuit Court of Wells County and obtained judgment, from which judgment Breckenridge appealed to the Appellate Court, where the judgment was affirmed.

Sec. 17.—In *Burton* v. *Forest Oil Co.*, 204 Pa. 349; 54 Atl. 266 (Jan. 5, 1902) the first point of the syllabus is as follows:

  ''Where a lessee of a gas lease assigns an undivided one-half interest therein to a corporation 'to have and to hold said interest subject to all royalties of the lessee therein contained,' and subsequently the other undivided one-half interest is assigned to a second company, and the first company enters into possession, and operates the land under an agreement by which it is to account to the second company for one-half of the proceeds of the gas produced, the latter to be liable for one-half of the expenses, the first company is liable to the lessor for the whole of the royalty stipulated for in the lease."

On April 3, 1889, B. P. Burton leased a tract of 36 acres of land in Butler County, Pennsylvania, for oil and gas purposes to W. S. Guffey and Emmett Queen for the term of ten years. The gas rental clause in the lease was as follows:

"It is further agreed that if gas is obtained in sufficient quantities to utilize, the consideration in full to the party of the first part shall be five hundred dollars ($500) per annum for each and every well drilled on the premises herein described, as long as the same is utilized."

In August, 1889, Guffey & Queen assigned the lease to J. M. Guffey, who by an assignment dated November 15, 1890, assigned to the Forest Oil Company a one-half interest therein. This assignment contained the following provision:

"To have and to hold the said interest in the above described lease, leasehold and premises, subject to all royalty, rents, and covenants of the lessee therein contained, to be rendered, paid and performed, on and after November 8, 1890."

By another assignment dated February 1, 1890, another undivided one-half interest in the lease was vested in the Chartiers Oil Company. A well was drilled on the premises in the Fall of 1889, producing large quantities of oil and gas. The Chartiers Oil Company had the management and control of the lease until January, 1893, when the Forest Oil Company took possession of the premises, and operated the well for oil and gas until 1898. Burton, the lessor, instituted suit in the Court of Common Pleas of Butler County, against the Forest Oil Company for the recovery of the gas rental of $500.00 per annum, claimed to be due from the Forest Oil Company during the time it had the management and control of the leased premises. Judgment was rendered in favor of the plaintiff, from which judgment the oil company appealed to the Supreme Court; and that court affirmed the judgment.

Sec. 18.—In *Jackson* v. *O'Hara,* 183 Pa. 233; 38 Atl. 624 (Nov. 8, 1897), the syllabus is as follows:

"In an oil and gas lease the lessee covenanted 'to commence operations and complete one well within one month, and, in case of failure to complete one well within such time, to thereafter pay as rental to the party of the first part for such delay the sum of fifty dollars per month.' The lessor agreed 'to accept such sum as full consideration, liquidation and payment of all damages for any delays until one well shall be completed, and a failure to complete such well or to make any such payments within such time, and at such place above mentioned, renders this lease absolutely null and void, and no longer binding on either party, and will revest the estate therein granted in the lessor and release the lessee from all his covenants therein contained, he having the option to drill said well or not, or pay said rental or not, as he may elect.' The lessee assigned the one-half interest in the lease. No well was ever completed or commenced. The assignee of the one-half interest in the lease paid the rental for three months, but then ceased, and no more was paid. In an action for the rental against the lessee and the assignee of the one-half interest, the defendants filed an affidavit of defense in which they averred that (1) the lessee had an option to sink a well or pay the monthly rental, or to do neither, and by refusing to do either the lease was at an end; and (2) there was no joint liability of the defendant. *Held*, that the affidavit of defense was insufficient to prevent judgment." ˙

On January 29, 1891, Jane M. Jackson leased to C. K. O'Hara for oil and gas purposes a tract of land in Allegheny County, Pennsylvania, which lease contained the following rental clause:

"The party of the second part agrees to commence operations and complete one well on the premises within one month from the date hereof, unavoidable accidents excepted, and in case of failure to complete one well within such time the party of the second part agrees to thereafter pay as rental to the party of the first part for such delay the sum of fifty (50) dollars per month payable monthly in advance at the Burgettstown National Bank, at Burgettstown, Pa., and the party of the first part hereby agrees to accept such sum as full consideration, liquidation and payment of all damages for any delays until one well shall be completed, and a failure to complete such well or to make any such payment within such time, and at such place as above mentioned renders this lease absolutely null and void, and no longer binding on either party, and will revest the estate herein granted in the lessor and release the lessee from all his covenants herein contained, he having the option to drill said well or not, or pay said rental or not, as he may elect."

On May 1, 1891, the lessee assigned the lease to the Ohio Valley Gas Company. No well was ever drilled. The $50.00 rental was

paid for three months, to-wit, for March, April and May, 1891.
Fifty Dollars was also paid for February, 1891. The three months
rental was paid by the Ohio Valley Gas Company. Payments
then ceased. The lessor instituted an action for the recovery of
the unpaid rentals in the Court of Common Pleas Number 2 of
Allegheny County, and obtained judgment. The suit was brought
against the original lessee, O'Hara, and the Gas Company, his
assignee, jointly. The defendants appealed from the judgment to
the Supreme Court of Pennsylvania, which court affirmed the
judgment.

Sec. 19.—In *Fisher* v. *Guffey & Queen*, 193 Pa. 393; 44 Atl. 452
(Oct. 30, 1899) the syllabus is as follows:

"An assignment of an oil and gas lease in consideration of a
certain sum paid at the time of the assignment, 'and the further
consideration of the sum of $1,000 if oil is found in any well drilled
on any of the territory herein described, and said well or territory
be further operated by the said assignee,' creates no covenant running with the land, and the assignor is not entitled to recover from
an assignee of the assignee the $1,000 mentioned in the assign-
ment."

J. L. Fisher sold and assigned a number of leases covering
about 4,000 acres of land to B. F. Tomb. The assignment was as
follows:

"For and in consideration of the sum of five hundred dollars
($500) to me in hand paid by F. B. Tomb, receipt whereof is
hereby acknowledged, and the further consideration of the sum of
one thousand dollars ($1,000) if oil is found in any well drilled on
any of the territory herein described, and said well or territory
be further operated by said F. B. Tomb (or assigns) I, J. L.
Fisher, hereby sell, assign and transfer unto F. B. Tomb, of Wil-
kinsburg, Pennsylvania. his heirs and assigns, all the following
described leasehold interests in and leases, of property in Jackson,
Aleppo and Spring Hill Townships, Green County, Pennsylvania,
and Clay District, Wetzel County, West Virginia, aggregating
about four thousand (4,000) acres; together with all my rights,
licenses, and privileges in, to or concerning the premises described
in said leases or intended so to be. To have and to hold the said
interests unto the said F. B. Tomb, his heirs and assigns, subject
to the rents, royalties and conditions in said leases contained."

F. B. Tomb assigned the leases mentioned in the foregoing assignment to W. S. Guffey and Emmett Queen; and James L. Fisher instituted an action of assumpsit for the use of Rachel J. Fisher, against W. S. Guffey and Emmett Queen, trading as Guffey & Queen, and the South Penn Oil Company, for money alleged to be due under said original assignment. Guffey & Queen had assigned the leases to the South Penn Oil Company, which company drilled a well and found oil in paying quantities, and was operating the well at the time the suit was brought. The contention of the plaintiff was, that the obligation of Tomb to pay the $1,000 additional if oil should be found, was a covenant running with the land, and that by reason of the assignments mentioned, the South Penn Oil Company became liable for the payment of this amount to him. The Court of Common Pleas of Green County sustained a demurrer to the statement of plaintiff's claim, and dismissed the plaintiff's suit. From the judgment of dismissal the plaintiff appealed to the Supreme Court. That court affirmed the judgment.

Sec. 20.—In *Dailey* v. *Heller,* 41 Ind. App. 379; 81 N. E. 219, (May 16, 1907), the third point of the syllabus is as follows:

"3. Where a lease of oil lands provided that in case no well was completed within 60 days from date the grant should be null and void, unless the lessee should pay to lessor one dollar per day in advance for each day thereafter such completion was delayed, and that the lessee should drill a well at the rate of one well every sixty days after date, until five wells were completed, and in case any well was not completed in 60 days, the lessee should pay one dollar per day in advance until the said well was completed, and only two wells were completed, the first provision applied only to the first well, and under the last provision the lessee was liable for one dollar per day on each well not drilled within the respective 60 day periods from the date of the contract."

Lemuel Heller instituted in the Circuit Court of Wells County, Indiana, against Michael Dailey, and others, an action for the recovery of alleged rentals, claimed to be due by virtue of an oil and gas lease. From a judgment in favor of plaintiffs defendants appealed, and assigned as error, first, that the complaint did not state facts sufficient to constitute a cause of action, and second, that the court erred in sustaining the plaintiff's demurrer to the amend third paragraph of the defendant's answer; third, that the court erred in overruling the motion for a new trial, and fourth, overruling the appellant's motion to modify the judgment.

This was the third appeal in this action. (See *Heller* v. *Dailey*, 28 Ind. App. 555; 63 N. E. 490; *Heller* v. *Dailey*, 34 Ind. App. 424; 70 N. E. 821.) The court overruled the first assignment of error, upon the ground that the complaint showed an assignment of the lease, and that it was held on first appeal that the assignment did not release the defendant from liability on the express covenants to pay rentals. The court overruled the second assignment of error upon the grounds that a comparison of the answer with the answers considered by the Appellate Court upon the second appeal disclosed that the second answers were substantially the same. The court overruled the third assignment of error, and held that from the direct evidence given, and upon inference properly drawn therefrom, it could not be said that the evidence failed to show a breach of the contract. Upon the fourth assignment of error the court held, that the motion to modify the judgment was based on the theory that the plaintiff in no event was entitled to more than one dollar per day for the delay in sinking wells, instead of three dollars, as found by the court; but that it was not error to overrule the motion, based upon the clause in the lease, providing:

"In case no well is completed within 60 days from this date then this grant shall be null and void unless second party shall pay to the first party one dollar per day in advance, for each day thereafter such completion is delayed * * * * * * * and it is further agreed that the party of the second part shall drill a well at the rate of one well every sixty days after date until five wells are completed. In case any well is not completed in sixty days as above provided for, party of the second part shall pay one dollar per day in advance until said well is completed."

The Court found that two wells were drilled, and that the lease meant that one well should be drilled within 60 days from the date of the lease, and another within 120 days, and another within 60 days from the completion of the first; The time for drilling each well was definitely fixed in the lease and did not depend upon any contingency; that it appeared that within 120 days from the date of the lease the two wells were completed; that the parties were carrying out the provision, "one well every sixty days after date" and they were required to continue so doing until "five wells were completed; that the provision "in case any well is not completed in 60 days, as above provided for, party of the second part shall pay one dollar per day in advance until said well is completed" provided for a payment in addition to the payment provided for by the first provision of the lease as a penalty for failing to drill a well within 60 days; and was not to be considered as determining the liability for a failure to drill the last three wells, for the reason that the first provision became ineffective after the first well was drilled within the time, and the liability for failure to drill the wells, for which the suit was brought, was to be determined by the concluding clause that "in case any well is not · · completed in said 60 days" etc., the second party should pay one dollar per day in advance until said well was completed.

LESSOR'S REMEDY.

Sec. 21.—A lessor in an oil and gas lease may recover damages from an assignee of the lessee for breaches of covenants which occur during the time such assignee holds title to the leased premises under the assignment.

> *Fennel* v. *Guffey*, 139 Pa. 341; 20 Atl. 1048.
> *Bradford Oil Co.* v. *Blair*, 113 Pa. 83; 4 Atl. 218.
> *Washington Natural Gas Co.* v. *Johnson*, 123 Pa. 576; 16 Atl. 799.
> *Indiana Natural Gas & Oil Co.* v. *Hinton*, 159 Ind. App. 398; 64 N. E. 224.
> *Dailey* v. *Heller*, 41 Ind. App. 379; 81 N. E. 219.

Sec. 22.—A lessor may recover for breaches of the covenants from each successive assignee, but an assignee is only liable to lessor for breaches which occur while he holds title to the lease.

> *Washington Natural Gas Co.* v. *Johnson*, 123 Pa. 576; 16 Atl. 799.

Sec. 23.—Where the lessor in an oil and gas lease sues an assignee of his lessee on a covenant of the lease, the burden is on the lessor to prove the assignment.

> *Heller* v. *Dailey*, 28 Ind App. 555; 63 N. E. 490.

Sec. 24.—A lessor in an oil and gas lease may recover from an assignee of such lease rentals and royalties which accrue during the time the assignee holds title to the lease.

Washington Natural Gas Co. v. *Johnson,* 123 Pa. 576; 16 Atl. 799.
Woodland Oil Co. v. *Crawford,* 55 Ohio St. 161; 44 N. E. 1093.
Breckenridge v. *Parrott,* 15 Ind. App. 417; 44 N. E. 66.
Burton v. *Forest Oil Co.,* 204 Pa. 349; 54 Atl. 266.
Jackson v. *O'Hara,* 183 Pa. 233; 38 Atl. 624.

ASSIGNEE—DEFENSES.

Sec. 25.—An assignee of an oil and gas lease in a suit brought by the lessor against him for breaches of the covenants of the lease, may defeat the action by proving, (1) that the breaches occurred prior to the time he acquired title to the lease, or (2), by proving that the breaches of the covenants occurred subsequent to the time he parted with title to the lease.

Washington Natural Gas Co. v. *Johnson,* 123 Pa. 576; 16 Atl. 799. Syl. 3.
Chaney v. *Ohio Oil Co.,* 32 Ind. App. 193; 69 N. E. 477.

Sec. 26.—An assignee of an oil and gas lease against whom the lessor seeks to enforce equities or claims arising out of suppression of facts when the lease was made; or where lessor seeks to recover from assignee a bonus provided for in the lease, the receipt of which was by the lease acknowledged to have been paid, may defeat all such equities or the enforcement of such demands or recovery of such claim for bonus by proof that the assignee took the lease for value, in good faith, and without any knowledge of the facts upon which such equities or claims were based.

Moore v. *Sawyer,* 167 Fed. 826.

CHAPTER 17.

ASSIGNEE OR SECOND LESSEE WITH NOTICE OF PRIOR LEASE.

Sec. 1.—An assignee of an oil and gas lease with notice of an outstanding prior lease takes no better title than that of his assignor, and it is the duty of the assignee to make inquiry as to whether the prior lease has been terminated. And one who takes a second lease subject to a prior lease stands in the same position.

> *Bartley* v. *Phillips,* 179 Pa. 175; 36 Atl. 217.
> *Carnegie Nat. Gas Co.* v. *Phila. Co.,* 158 Pa. 317; 27 Atl. 95.
> *Hicks* v. *Gas Co.,* 207 Pa. 570; 57 Atl. 55.
> *Pyle* v. *Henderson,* 65 W. Va. 39; 63 S. E. 762.
> *Compton* v. *Peoples Gas Co.,* 75 Kan. 572; 89 Pac. 1029; 10 L. R. A. (N. S.) 758.
> *National Oil & Pipeline Co.* v. *Teel,* 95 Tex. 586; 67 S. W. 545. Affirmed 68 S. W. 797.
> *Gillespie* v. *Fulton Oil & Gas Co.,* 236 Ill. 188; 86 N. E. 219. Syls. 25-26.

Sec. 2.—An assignee of an oil and gas lease, where there is an outstanding prior lease upon the same property, takes no better title than was held by the assignor.

Sec. 3.—Where a landowner has already executed and delivered a lease for oil and gas purposes, and thereafter makes a second lease without declaring a forfeiture of the first lease, the second lessee does not possess the power of declaring a forfeiture, and he will take the second lease subject to all the rights and equities existing in favor of the first lessee against the lessor.

Sec. 4.—Where a lessee is in possession of real estate exercising his rights as such lessee for oil and gas purposes, although his lease may not be of record, a second lessee with knowledge of such occupancy will be held to have had notice of the prior lease.

Sec. 5.—It is the duty of a second lessee, or the assignee of a prior lease, with notice of an outstanding lease to make diligent inquiry as to whether or not the prior lease has been forfeited or abandoned.

Sec. 6.—Where a lease provides for forfeiture in certain cases, it is the duty of the assignee of such lease to make inquiry as to whether or not the lease has been forfeited upon any of the grounds of forfeiture provided for in the lease.

Sec. 7.—In *Bartley* v. *Phillips,* 179 Pa. 175; 36 Atl. 217, (Jan. 4, 1897,) the second and third points of the syllabus are as follows:

"Parties who lease or buy oil or gas lands, with a term apparently outstanding, without inquiry of the lessees, and without the exercise of the lessor's powers to forfeit, take the risk of the fact of abandonment of the first lease as the facts may be found by the jury.
Defendant leased oil and gas lands from the owner. He had notice of the fact that there was an outstanding lease of ten years to plaintiff, only three years of which had expired. The grantor of the lessor of defendant refused in his deed to assert a forfeiture of the first lease. Defendant made no inquiry of the plaintiffs as to whether their lease had been terminated. *Held,* (1) that the defendant had sufficient notice to put upon him the duty of inquiry, (2) that it was a question for the jury to determine whether there had been an abandonment of the first lease."

On September 8, 1888, J. A. Hartzell leased to W. E. Bartley and others a tract of seventy acres of land for oil purposes, in Butler County, Pennsylvania. The lease was for the term of ten years. Lessees, by the terms of the lease, were to commence operations for mining purposes within thirty days from the execution of the lease and when work was commenced it was to be prosecuted with due diligence until completion or abandonment. Lessees commenced operations on the land within fifteen days after the execution of the lease, and drilled a well, and finished it in the latter part of October, 1888. After the date of the lease Hartzell conveyed the land by deed to one Zeigler, and in the deed expressly excepted the lease to Bartley and others from the covenant of warranty. Zeigler executed an oil and gas lease to Samuel Walker, who assigned it to Thomas W. Phillips. Phillips, having entered into possession of the premises, an action of ejectment was instituted by Bartley and others in the Court of Common Pleas of

Butler County, against Phillips, and verdict and judgment were rendered in favor of plaintiff. From this judgment Phillips appealed, and the Supreme Court of Pennsylvania affirmed the judgment.

Sec. 8.—In *Carnegie Natural Gas Co.* v. *Philadelphia Co.*, 158 Pa. 317; 27 Atl. 95 (Nov. 6, 1893), the fourth and fifth points of the syllabus are as follows:

"Where a lease provides for forfeiture in certain cases, the assignee of the lease is bound at his peril to ascertain whether or not it has been forfeited.
A lessor is not affected by a mere general rumor that the lease has been assigned by the lessee to another person. The information as to such assignment must come from some person interested in the property, and must be directly communicated to the lessor."

Joseph Lytle, on December 18, 1891, made an oil and gas lease of a tract of about 400 acres of land in Allegheny County, Pennsylvania, to John A. Snee. On August 5, 1892, Snee assigned the lease to the Carnegie Natural Gas Company, which company, on August 11, 1892, entered upon the premises and on October 6, 1892, completed a producing gas well thereon. The lease contained the following words: "The test to be drilled on above described lease or forfeit this lease." On January 26, 1892, Lytle agreed with Jesse L. Wall to convey five acres of the demised premises, and this agreement contained the following provision:

"The party of the second part hereby covenants and agrees to take said five acres, more or less, subject to the lease of the Philadelphia Gas Company, now existing and in full force."

The words "Philadelphia Gas Company," having been written by mistake of the Justice of the Peace, they were erased, and the words "John A. Snee" written over them before the delivery of the article to Wall. About the middle of May, 1892, Snee, who was also lessee of the Wright farm situated between the Lytle farm and the river, began drilling a well thereon. This well which turned out to be a large gas well, was completed on August 2, 1892. On July 26, 1892, Lytle met Mr. Owings, the agent of Snee, and a conversation took place which Lytle stated to be as follows:

"I asked him, or told him, I would like him to send me up the lease. He asked me why, and I told him the lease was dead, and it was forfeited. Q. Did you tell him why the lease was dead? A. I don't mind whether I told him why or not. I made some remark about not getting the well, and his answer then was, if I would re-lease, he would give me the next well. *By the Master:* What was that? A. He said: 'I suppose you would not hesitate to re-lease if we would give you the next well.'"

On August 3, 1892, Owings again met Lytle, and it was arranged that Mr. Snee should come personally and arrange for a new lease. Accordingly, on August 8th, Mr. Lytle met Snee and a new lease bearing that date exclusive of the five acres sold to Wall, was executed, Snee paying Lytle a bonus of $1,000 for the new lease. In the meantime, on August 5, 1892, John A. Snee had, by deed bearing that date, acknowledged on August 6th, assigned to the Carnegie Natural Gas Company his right, title and interest in 32 oil leases, including the Lytle lease of December 18, 1891. On August 11, 1892, Snee, as contractor for the Carnegie Natural Gas Company, proceeded to erect a derrick and drill a well on the Lytle farm, which was completed October 6, 1892. On October 6, 1892, Jesse S. Wall leased the five-acre tract above mentioned, to the Philadelphia Company, and that company, shortly thereafter entered upon the five acre tract for the purpose of drilling a well, put up a derrick and commenced drilling, but was stopped by the injunction granted in the case. The Carnegie Natural Gas Company filed its bill in Equity in the Court of Common Pleas, Number 2, Allegheny County, against the Philadelphia Company for an injunction to restrain the Philadelphia Company from drilling on the Lytle farm. The Philadelphia Company answered, averring that the lease of December 18, 1891, was never accepted by Snee, he not having signed it till after August 5, 1892, further alleging that if said lease operated to vest any title in Snee it was forfeited and determined prior to August 5, 1892, of which fact the Carnegie Company had notice. The answer further alleged that on August 8, 1892, Snee, recognizing the forfeiture, obtained from Lytle a new lease in lieu of the lease of December 18, 1891; and that this lease excepted the five acres which Lytle had, in the meantime, sold to Jesse Wall. The answer further alleged that Snee, or his assignee, entered on the lands of Lytle under the terms of his second lease and not that of December 18, 1891. Defendant claimed no rights to any other portion of the farm, except the five acres. The Court of Common Pleas dismissed the bill in equity. The plaintiff appealed to the Supreme Court, and that Court affirmed the decree of dismissal.

Sec. 9.—In *Hicks* v. *American Natural Gas Company*, 207 Pa. 570; 57 Atl. 55 (Jan. 4. 1904.) the second point of the syllabus is as follows:

"Where a vendee of land takes title without actual personal notice of an unrecorded oil and gas lease, but it appears that his agent who made the contract was on the land, saw the plant of the lessees in operation, and was informed by the vendor of the lease, and it also appears that the lease provided for an accurate system of measuring the gas, and that the lessees were operating one well and were about to drive another, the vendee is not entitled to a preliminary injunction against the lessee because (1) his right was not clear, as he was bound by the knowledge of his agent; (2) he showed no irreparable damage;(3) the preliminary injunction would not maintain the status quo, and (4) the exclusive remedy was at law by an action of ejectment."

On May 14, 1892, Peter and Margaret Stewart granted to the American Natural Gas Company all the oil and gas under their farm consisting of 189 acres, in Westmoreland County, Penn. The grant was in writing, duly executed and acknowledged by the parties to it. It stipulated that the gas company should have the right at all times to drill and operate for oil and gas upon the farm. In August, 1902, the gas company went upon the premises and commenced drilling a gas well. It erected a derrick, an engine house, and connected by belt the engine with the derrick. A well was then drilled 2700 feet deep, and gas was struck on November 18, 1902. The gas company connected the well by pipes with its mains, and in the following year removed its machinery and derrick a short distance from the first well, and in July, 1903, commenced drilling another well. On May 12, 1903, Alfred Hicks sent his agent, John Taylor, to the Stewarts and solicited an option for the purchase outright of the farm from which the oil and gas had been granted to the gas company. Taylor obtained a 60-day option for $75,000. Before the expiration of the option Hicks elected to purchase, and obtained an absolute deed for the farm on July 3, 1903, which deed he recorded four days afterwards.

The gas company did not leave its contract for record until August 3, 1903, thirty days after the date of the deed to Hicks. There was no reservation of the oil and gas in the deed from the Stewarts to Hicks. Alfred Hicks filed his bill in equity against the American Natural Gas Company for an injunction in the Court of Common Pleas of Westmoreland County, and obtained a preliminary injunction. Taylor, the agent of Hicks, who took the option in his own name, admitted at the hearing that he examined the farm, and knew its boundaries before taking the option. He saw the derrick and Stewart called his attention to it, but Taylor made no further inquiry about it. The gas company appealed from the order awarding the preliminary injunction to the Supreme Court, and that court reversed the Court of Common Pleas and dismissed the bill.

Sec. 10.—In *Pyle* v. *Henderson*, 65 W. Va. 39; 63 S. E. 762, analyzed under Chapter 25, Judge Brannon, delivering the opinion, at page 47 says:

"When Pyle took the second lease he had full knowledge of the first lease, and solicited Bunfill to lease to him. A court of equity cannot look with much favor on his suit to enforce a forfeiture to his benefit. When this second lease was taken the term of the first lease, five years, had not expired. If it had there would be some force in saying that it could be extended only by a new lease; but such was not the case. It was then competent for Bunfill to waive the mere forfeiture, the first lease being still in life, from want of title and waiver of payment by Bunfill, it was the binding duty of Pyle to learn, by inquiry, from the first lessees, as to the right they claimed and how they claimed, and we may say that he would have learned that Bunfill had agreed to procure good title for the benefit of the first lessees and had waived the forfeiture. Knowledge of the first lease put Pyle on inquiry and he is affected with notice of the right of the first lessees and the waiver of the forfeiture. Authorities for this proposition are given in *Reed* v. *Bachman*, 61 W. Va. at page 464. Pyle was thus, under the law, guilty of gross negligence, to say the least."

Sec. 11.—In *Compton* v. *Peoples Gas Company*, 75 Kan. 572; 89 Pac. 1029; 10 L. R. A. 758 (April 6, 1907,) syls. 2-3-4 are as follows:

"2. An oil and gas lease upon lands of which a widow owns an undivided one-half, and the other half belongs to the children, and a part thereof is occupied by the family as a homestead, is not void because executed by the widow alone. It conveys her undivided interest in the oil and gas privileges, subject to the right of those occupying the premises as a homestead.

3. A subsequent oil and gas lease of the same lands to a third party, executed by the children after the youngest child has reached majority, conveys the undivided interest of the children in the oil and gas privileges. Each lessee is entitled to the premises for the purpose of mining for oil and gas but neither is entitled to exclusive possession.

4. Where an oil and gas lease has been accepted by the lessee and valuable improvements made thereunder, and the lessor has accepted the benefits and consideration, one who takes a subsequent lease with notice of the fact and of the terms and conditions of the former lease, takes subject thereto, and will not be permitted to question the validity of the former on the ground that it lacks mutuality or that it has been revoked by the giving of the subsequent lease.''

Elizabeth Phillips was the owner of a one-half interest in 201 acres of land in Montgomery County, Kansas, the other one-half belonging to her children. In May, 1900, Mrs. Phillips executed an oil and gas lease to the Pennsylvania Oil Company, which company subsequently assigned the lease to the Peoples Gas Company. The husband of Mrs. Phillips, who originally held the title to the land, died in 1883, and at the time the lease was executed some of the children were minors, and a portion of the premises was occupied by the family as a homestead. None of the children joined in the execution of the lease. On November 4, 1904, Mrs. Phillips executed a lease in which the children, all of whom were then of age, joined. This lease was made to O. W. Compton, who instituted in the District Court of Montgomery County his action against the Peoples Gas Company to enjoin that company from operating on the lands under the gas lease executed on May, 1900, and to have the lease decreed void. The gas company filed a cross-petition, setting up its lease, and praying that it be decreed valid, and for an injunction against the plaintiff's lease. The lease under which the Peoples Gas Company claimed was recorded soon after its execution, and contained the following provision:

"If no oil or gas well is sunk on the premises within twelve months from this date, this lease shall become absolutely null and void unless the second party shall pipe gas to within 100 feet of the residence of the parties of the first part, and give the parties of the first part the right to use gas for three stoves and four lights.''

No well was completed within twelve months, but within that time the owners of the lease laid pipelines and piped gas to within 100 feet of the residence of Mrs. Phillips, and supplied the family with fuel from that time. The gas company had fully complied with, and performed the conditions and requirements of the lease, and at a cost of $1,250.00 drilled a producing well on the premises. The trial court, however, found that the material for the drilling of this well was placed on the land on October 25, 1904, and that the drilling was commenced on November 15th and the well completed on December 1, 1904. The court also found that the plaintiff, on November 8, 1904, notified the Peoples Gas Company in writing of his lease, and warned them not to drill any wells on the premises. The District Court rendered judgment that plaintiff and defendant each owned an undivided one-half interest in the oil and gas, subject to the rights reserved by the owners of the land; and that each was as much entitled to the possession of the premises as the other, but that neither was entitled to the exclusive possession.

The temporary injunction granted to Compton at the beginning of the suit, was dissolved and the costs were divided between the parties. From this decree the plaintiff Compton appealed to the Supreme Court, and that court affirmed the decree, and as to a lease on lands owned by tenants in common, and occupied as a homestead, cited with approval *Zinc Co.* v. *Freeman,* 68 Kan. 691; 75 Pac. 995.

Sec. 12.— In *National Oil & Pipeline Co.* v. *Teel,* 95 Tex. 586; 67 S. W. 545, affirmed 68 S. W. 979, analyzed under Chapter 29, syl. 1 is as follows:

''1. The assignee of an oil option is not bound by the fraud of an assignor in procuring the contracts, though the grantors are in possession, and the rights claimed under the option are consistent with such possession.''

Sec. 13.—In *Gillespie* v. *Fulton Oil & Gas Co.,* 236 Ill. 188; 86 N. E. 219, analyzed under Chapter 13, syls. 25-26 are as follows:

"25. An assignee of the lessee in a lease of oil and gas in premises described, with the right to enter thereon to mine for oil and gas, cannot maintain ejectment against the lessee in a subsequent lease.

26. Equity has jurisdiction to prevent waste and irreparable injury at the suit of an assignee in an oil and gas lease against a subsequent adverse lessee."

DUTY AND REMEDIES OF ASSIGNEE OR SECOND LESSEE.

Sec. 14.—It is the duty of an assignee of an oil and gas lease where he has notice that there is an outstanding prior lease upon the same premises, to make diligent inquiry not only as to the terms and conditions of such outstanding lease but likewise to diligently inquire as to whether or not the conditions of such lease have been performed; And if there are grounds of forfeiture in the lease it is the duty of such assignee or second lessee to inquire whether or not the original lessor has elected to declare a forfeiture; and where such assignee or second lessee fails to make such inquiry he takes the risk of all equities existing in favor of the landowner, or of the holder of such prior lease, which a diligent inquiry would have disclosed.

Bartley v. *Phillips,* 179 Pa. 175; 36 Atl. 217.
Carnegie Nat. Gas Co. v. *Phila. Co.,* 158 Pa. 317; 27 Atl. 95.
Hicks v. *Gas Co.,* 207 Pa. 570; 57 Atl. 55.
Pyle v. *Henderson,* 65 W. Va. 39; 63 S. E. 762.
Compton v. *Peoples Gas Co.,* 75 Kan. 572; 89 Pac. 1029; 10 L. R. A. (N. S.) 758.

CHAPTER 18.

IMPLIED COVENANTS OF THE OIL AND GAS LEASE.

Sec. 1.—Leases for oil and gas are subject to the implied covenant that the lessee will do all that is necessary to carry into effect the purposes and objects of the lease. In the absence of a covenant to begin work within a certain time, there is an implied covenant to begin within a reasonable time. When the lessee commences explorations there is an implied covenant that he will diligently prosecute the search, and if oil or gas is found in paying quantities that he will protect the lines and well develop the territory. There is also an implied covenant of right of entry and quiet enjoyment for the purposes of the lease.

Brewster v. *Lanyon Zinc Co.,* 140 Fed. 801; 72 C. C. A. 213.
Knotts v. *McGregor,* 47 W. Va. 566; 37 S. E. 899.
Steelsmith v. *Gartlan,* 45 W. Va. 27. Op. 34-35; 29 S. E. 978.
Kleppner v. *Lemon,* 176 Pa. 502; 35 Atl. 109.
McKnight v. *Manufacturers Nat. Gas Co.,* 146 Pa. 185; 23 Atl. 164; 28 Am. St. Rep. 790.
Harris v. *Ohio Oil Co.,* 57 Ohio St. 118; 48 N. E. 502.
Colgan v. *Forest Oil Co.,* 194 Pa. 234; 45 Atl. 119; 75 Am. St. Rep. 695.
Kellar v. *Craig,* 126 Fed. 630; 61 C. C. A. 366.
Doddridge Oil Co. v. *Smith,* 154 Fed. 970 (C. C. N. D. W. Va.)
Allegheny Oil Co. v. *Snyder,* 160 Fed. 764; 45 C. C. A. 60.
Young v. *Forest Oil Co.,* 194 Pa. 243; 45 Atl. 121.
Harness v. *Eastern Oil Co.,* 49 W. Va. 232; 38 S. E. 662.
McGraw Oil Co. v. *Kennedy,* 65 W. Va. 599; 64 S. E. 1027.
Gadberry v. *Ohio etc. Co.,* 162 Ind. 9; 67 N. E. 257.
Headley v. *Hoopengarner,* 60 W. Va. 626; 55 S. E. 144.
Pyle v. *Henderson,* 65 W. Va. 39; 63 S. E. 762.
Acme Oil etc Co. v. *Williams,* 140 Cal. 681; 74 Pac. 296.
Venedocia Oil etc. Co., v. *Robinson,* 71 Ohio St. 302; 73 N. E. 222.
Aye v. *Phila. Co.,* 193 Pa. 451; 44 Atl. 555; 74 Am. St. 696.
J. M. Guffey Petroleum Co. v. *Oliver* —(Tex.) —; 79 S. W. 884.
Huggins v. *Dailey,* 99 Fed. 606; 40 C. C. A. 12; 48 L. R. A. 320.
Phillips v. *Hamilton,* —Wyo.—; 95 Pac. 846.
Douglass Oil Field v. *Hamilton,* —Wyo—; 95 Pac. 849.
Ammons v. *South Penn Oil Co.,* 47 W. Va. 610; 35 S. E. 1004.
Smith v. *Root,* 66 W. Va. 633; 66 S. E. 1005.
Powers v. *Bridgeport Oil Co.,* 238 Ill. 397; 87 N. E. 381.
Kilcoyne v. *Southern Oil Co.,* 61 W. Va. 538; 55 S. E. 888.
Buffalo Valley etc. Co. v. *Jones,* 75 Kan. 18; 88 Pac. 537.

Sec. 2.—Where lessor has title to the demised premises and executes an oil and gas lease therefor, reserving the right to forfeit the same for non-developments or non-payment of rentals, he has the right upon lessee's failure to either explore or pay commutation money, to promptly declare a forfeiture; and when such declaration is made the lease and all rights and privileges thereunder, so far as conferred conditionally upon lessee, absolutely cease and determine and no legal proceeding or other act is necessary to be taken or performed by lessor.

Sec. 3.—Where the lessor accepts payment of the rental or commutation money within the term of the lease, he is bound thereby, and cannot declare a forfeiture of the lease during the period covered by such payment.

Sec. 4.—When the lease does not provide in express terms for a forfeiture for non-development or non-payment of rental lessor cannot declare a forfeiture for such failure alone. Such failure must continue for such time as to warrant the presumption that the lessee has abandoned the lease. In every lease, in the absence of an express covenant, there is an implied covenant for development. A majority of the courts hold, that a breach of an implied covenant will not, of itself, work a forfeiture of the lease. The remedy of the lessor, who has not provided for forfeiture by express covenant for non-payment of rental or non-development, is not so clear and effective as where he has made such express provision.

Sec. 5.—Where an oil and gas lease contains an express covenant for the payment by lessee of rentals or commutation money as indemnity for non-development and contains no clause providing for a forfeiture of the lease for failure to pay or develop, such failure alone will not constitute grounds to authorize lessor to declare a forfeiture.

Sec. 6.—Where there is no express covenant providing for forfeiture of the lease for non-payment of rentals, before the lessor can declare forfeiture or procure a cancellation of the lease, there must be abandonment. Non-payment of rental, alone, is not sufficient. Non-payment of rental, however, continued beyond a reasonable time will not only authorize lessor to declare forfeiture, but will constitute grounds for cancellation of the lease, as a cloud upon lessor's title.

Sec. 7.—A lessor, under some circumstances, may compel development or procure cancellation of the lease. Where wells on

adjacent territory are producing oil or gas in such close proximity
to lessor's lands as to drain the oil or gas therefrom, lessee will
not be permitted to evade the implied covenants of his lease which
require protection of lines by refusing to protect lessor by drilling a sufficient number of wells on the leased premises to protect
the lines from such drainage. Lessee cannot refuse to develop the
property and hold the grant for purely speculative purposes.

Sec. 8.—In *Brewster* v. *Lanyon Zinc Co.*, 140 Fed. 801; 72 C.
C. A. 213, analyzed under Chapter 4, syls. 8-16, inclusive, are as follows:

"8.   A lease which grants 'all the oil and gas' under the leased
land, together with the right to enter 'at all times' for the purpose of 'drilling and operating' to erect and maintain structures,
pipelines and machinery necessary for the 'production and transportation' of oil and gas, and to use sufficient water, oil, and gas
to run the necessary engines for the 'prosecution of said business', which reserves to the lessor substantial royalties in kind and
in money on the oil produced and saved and the gas used off the
premises, which shows that the promise of these royalties was the
controlling inducement to the grant, and which, while expressly requiring the drilling of one well during the first five years, does
not expressly define the measure of diligence to be exercised in
the work of development and production after the expiration of
that period, contains a covenant by the lessee, arising by necessary
implication from the nature of the lease and the other stipulations
therein, that if, during the five years allowed for original exploration and development oil and gas, one or both are found in paying quantities, the work of development and production shall be
continued with reasonable diligence; that is along such lines as
will be reasonably calculated to make the extraction of oil and gas
from the leased land of mutual advantage and profit to the lessor
and lessee.
9.   Whether a covenant is also a condition is essentially a
question of intention, and where in an oil and gas lease the covenants of the lessee are introduced with the statement that the
grant is made 'on the following terms', and are followed by a
stipulation that the lessee's failure to comply with 'any of the
above conditions,' shall render the lease null and void, this stipulation has reference to the spirit and legal effect, and not the mere
letter, of what precedes, and if that by necessary implication contains a covenant by the lessee to exercise reasonable diligence in
prosecuting the work of development and production, such covenant is also a condition, a plain and substantial breach of which,
in view of the actual circumstances at the time, as distinguished

from mere expectations on the part of the lessor and conjecture on the part of mining enthusiasts will entitle the lessor to avoid the lease.

10.   Where the object of the operations contemplated by an oil and gas lease is to obtain a benefit or profit for both lessor and lessee, neither is, in the absence of a stipulation to that effect, the arbiter of the extent to which, or the diligence with which the operations shall proceed; But both are bound by the standard of what, in the circumstances, would be reasonably expected of operators of ordinary prudence, having regard to the interests of both.

11.   An oil and gas lease contained a covenant, which was also made a condition, that the lessee would continue with reasonable diligence the work of development and production after the expiration of the period allowed for original exploration and development, if during that period oil and gas, one or both, were found in paying quantities. The lease covered two tracts owned by the lessor, which were widely separated and embraced 232.50 acres. Both were in a recognized oil and gas field. These minerals were being produced in paying quantities from the lands surrounding each tract. Near the expiration of the period allowed for original exploration and development the lessee drilled a single well on one of the tracts, in which gas was found in paying quantity, and thereafter took and maintained the position that by drilling that well and paying the stipulated price for gas used therefrom it acquired the right to hold the lease indefinitely without further development. This situation continued for fourteen months, when the lessor elected to terminate the lease for breach of the covenant and condition for the exercise of reasonable diligence. *Held*, that in these circumstances, the prolonged failure of the lessee to continue the work of development and production though due to a mistaken view of the obligations imposed by the lease, was a plain and substantial breach of the covenant, and condition, and entitled the lessor to terminate the lease.

12.   A remedy at law is not adequate, in the sense that it will deprive a court of equity of jurisdiction unless it is as certain, prompt, and efficient to the ends of justice as the remedy in equity.

13.   Equity will not relieve against a breach of condition in respect of a leasehold where the elements of fraud, accident, and mistake are wanting and the measure of compensation is uncertain, but will allow the forfeiture to be enforced if such is the remedy provided by the contract.

14.   Because forfeitures are usually harsh and oppressive, and because they can ordinarily be enforced at law, courts of equity generally refuse to aid in their enforcement; but the rule is not absolute or inflexible. Its influence and operation do not extend beyond the reasons which underlie it, and in cases otherwise cognizable in equity, there is no insuperable objection to the enforcement of a forfeiture in a court of equity when that is more consonant

with the principles of right, justice and morality, than to withhold equitable relief.

15.   A suit, the primary and only purpose of which is to establish a forfeiture as matter of record and to cancel the thing forfeited—in this instance a lease—is a suit to give effect to, and therefore to aid in, the enforcement of a forfeiture, and the equity which it presents must be strong enough to overcome the general indisposition of courts of chancery towards granting such relief.

16.   A forfeiture of an oil and gas lease was incurred under circumstances which do not entitle the lessee to relief in equity. Although actually terminated by the default of the lessee and the assertion of a forfeiture by the lessor, the lease appears, as spread upon the public records, and is claimed by the lessee, to be still effective as a disposal of all the oil and gas in the lessor's land. It embarrasses, if it does not prevent, the exercise of the right to make other disposition of these minerals, and this at a time when they are being exhausted by the lawful multiplication and operation of wells on surrounding lands. The lessor is in possession, save of a small portion of the land, occupied by the lessee, in the operation of a single gas well which it has drilled. The State statute permits the defeated party in ejectment to demand and obtain a second trial as matter of right. *Held*, that a bill disclosing these facts states a case which calls for a measure of relief not attainable at law, and which entitles the lessor to a decree giving effect to the forfeiture by its establishment as matter of record, and by the cancellation of the lease as a cloud upon the title.''

Sec. 9.—In *Knotts* v. *McGregor*, 47 W. Va. 566; 37 S. E. 899 (March 24, 1900), syls. 1-2-3-4 are as follows:

''1.   An action can be maintained against an executor for breach of a covenant of a lease committed by his testator.

2.   In a lease for oil and gas there is an implied covenant of right of entry and quiet enjoyment for the purpose of the lease.

3.   The covenant of quiet enjoyment in a lease for oil or gas, or other purposes, is not broken by the mere fact, alone, that the lessor makes another lease during the term, of the same premises, whether the first lessee be in actual possession or not; the second lessee not entering.

4.   The covenant for quiet enjoyment implied in a lease for oil is broken by the exclusion by the lessor of the lessee from taking possession for the purposes of the lease, or his withholding from him the possession of the land for the purposes of the lease.''

Knotts & Garber obtained a lease on August 30, 1899, from David McGregor of certain lands for oil and gas purposes for the term of five years, which land was situated in Ritchie County,

West Virginia. The lease provided, that the lessees should complete a well within one year from the date of the lease; and a failure to do so should render the lease null and void, unless the lessees should pay the lessor a rental of twenty-five cents per acre per year for delay. On February 13, 1890, McGregor executed a second lease to A. L. Gracey for the same land for oil and gas purposes. The lessor died within the term of the first lease, and Matilda McGregor was appointed by his will its executrix and qualified as such. The original lessees did not drill within the year specified in their lease, but claimed to have tendered to David McGregor before his death the rental within the rental period, which he refused to accept, and which rental the original lessees claimed to have then deposited in the Second National Bank at Parkersburg, the depository provided for in the lease. After the death of David McGregor, Matilda McGregor, the executrix, on February 10, 1895, executed to James Gartlan another lease for oil and gas purposes for the same property, originally leased to Knotts & Garber. Knotts & Garber instituted in the Circuit Court of Ritchie County an action of covenant against Matilda McGregor, executrix of the last will and testament of David McGregor, deceased. In their declaration filed in the cause they claimed, in the first count thereof, damages for the breach of covenant of David McGregor in his lifetime, committed by the execution of the lease to Gracey; and in the second count, the plaintiffs claimed damages against the executrix by reason of the lease by her as such executrix made to Gartlan. A demurrer was, by the Circuit Court, sustained to the declaration and the suit dismissed. A writ of error was taken to this judgment, and the Supreme Court of Appeals of West Virginia affirmed the judgment on the grounds of misjoinder of action, that is, that the cause of action against the defendant's estate could not be joined in the same action with a cause of action against the personal representative, individually.

Sec. 10.—In *Steelsmith* v. *Gartlan,* 45 W. Va. 27; 29 S. E. 978, analyzed under Chapter 5, in the opinion at pages 34-5 the law is stated as follows:

"Contracts unperformed, optional as to one of the parties, are optional as to both, nor can there be a different conclusion if it is held that the lease, being for the purpose of operating for oil and gas, is subject to the implied precedent condition according to the decisions of some of the states, notably North Carolina, that the lessee shall diligently prosecute the search and operation, for in such case the forfeiture would follow in a much less time than eighteen months under the general clause, to-wit: 'A failure to comply with any of the conditions of this lease shall render the same null and void and of no effect,' which necessarily applies to implied as well as express conditions.''

In this case the plaintiff, Steelsmith, took a second lease, entered into possession of the premises, and then brought suit in equity to cancel the first lease under the claim that it constituted a cloud on his title, and that the lease was forfeited by abandonment. Upon the question of forfeiture for breach of covenant, Judge Dent quotes the clause in the lease sought to be cancelled: "A failure to comply with any of the conditions of this lease shall render the same null and void and of no effect," in support of the conclusion that the lease had been forfeited, not only by abandonment, but by breach of this express covenant, which covenant Judge Dent held would render the lease the subject of cancellation by a court of equity for the breach of implied covenant for diligent explorations.

Sec. 11.—In *Kleppner* v. *Lemon*, 176 Pa. 502; 35 Atl. 109, (July 15, 1896), the syllabus is as follows:

"It is an implied condition of every lease of land for the production of oil therefrom, that when the existence of oil in paying quantities is made apparent the lessee shall put down as many wells as may be reasonably necessary to secure the oil for the common advantage of both lessor and lessee. In determining when and where such wells shall be located, regard must be had to the operations on adjoining lands, and to the well known fact that a well will drain a territory of much larger extent when the sand rock in which the oil or gas is found is of coarse and loose texture than when it is of fine grain and compact character. Whatever ordinary knowledge and care would dictate as the proper thing to be done for the interests of both lessor and lessee under any given circumstances is that which the law requires to be done as an implied stipulation of the contract.

A lease conferred on the lessee 'the exclusive right of drilling and operating for petroleum and gas on the plaintiff's land.' If oil and gas were found certain royalties were to be paid. There was no distinct covenant for putting down wells on the land, except that which related to the first or experimental well, which was to determine the value of the land for oil purposes. The right to divide the leasehold and sublet the parts into which it was divided, for oil purposes was distinctly reserved by the lessee. The defendant had oil and gas leases on adjoining properties. He put down one well on plaintiff's land, and other wells on adjoining land near the boundaries of plaintiff's land with the express purpose of securing the oil under plaintiff's land through these wells. · *Held,* (1) that the lease contemplated the production of oil underlying the plaintiff's lot by means of operations conducted on its surface; (2) that the number and location of the wells necessary to carry out the purposes of the contract, was a subject belonging primarily to the lessee; (3) That in disposing of this question the lessee was bound to take into consideration the fact that his lessor was the owner of the oil, and to arrange and conduct his efforts to bring it to the surface in such manner as should best protect the interests of both parties to the contract; (4) that he was not bound to put down more wells than were reasonably necessary to obtain the oil of his lessor, nor to put down wells that would not be able to produce oil sufficient to justify the expenditure; (5) that the fact that the oil might be obtained in time through other wells on the lands of other owners, was not enough to excuse the lessee from his implied undertaking to operate the land for the best interests of both owner and operator.

In such a case the court may decree on bill in equity filed that unless the defendant shall drill another well within a certain time specified, his leasehold estate in said land shall be deemed to be abandoned, except as to the well actually drilled on plaintiff's land, and a certain specified space around it.''

John Kleppner, on June 15, 1894, made a lease for oil and gas purposes to D. P. Lemon for a tract of about eight acres of land in Allegheny County, Pennsylvania for a term of two years, the lessor to receive one-eighth of the oil, and if gas were produced in sufficient quantities to justify marketing it, he was to receive $500.00 for each well so producing, the lessee to commence a well within thirty days, or in default thereof, pay the lessor $35.00 monthly in advance until a well should be commenced or the lease abandoned. The lessee formed a partnership with the other parties in this lease, and also in leases of several other properties in the neighborhood embracing lands adjoining the property of said lessor. No well was begun on the lessor's property until in February, 1895, when a well was commenced and completed in the spring of 1895, which well produced about five barrels of oil per day. This well was within fifteen or twenty feet of the line on the southern side of lessor's property. In March, 1895, the lessee and his partners began a well on the farm of Stotler, adjoining the lessor's property, and within 157 feet of the line of lessor's property, which well was completed in May, 1895, and at first produced about 120 barrels per day; and at the time the suit was brought was producing about 40 barrels per day. The lessee and his partners also put down several wells on adjoining property, some of which were good producing wells, and at the date of the suit they were putting down a well on an adjoining tract, within 250 feet of the lessor's line. The well on lessor's land was on high ground, and was drilled through hard or compact rock. The Stotler well was through loose rock and on lower ground near the creek, and a large portion of lessor's land adjoining this land was of the same character. The lessee and his partners declared their intention not to put down more wells on lessor's property, alleging that the probabilities of getting a good well would not justify the expenditure. Under these circumstances the lessor, Kleppner, filed a bill in equity in the court of Common Pleas of Allegheny County, against his lessee to compel him to put down additional wells. The Court of Common Pleas entered a decree giving the lessee well Number 1, and 300 feet around the same, and enjoined him from any operations on the residue of the tract, unless he should, within ten days from notice of the decree, file in the case a declaration to the effect that he would proceed to put down another well on said land in the lower part thereof at such place as might be designated by the plaintiff and should also within thirty days from the date of the decree begin to put down such well and should thereafter with due and reasonable diligence proceed with the drilling of the same to the depth required for obtaining the oil in the 100-foot sand where the oil was shown to be located and found by the producing well already sunk on the plaintiff's land. From this decree the defendants appealed and the Supreme Court of Pennsylvania affirmed the decree.

Sec. 12.—In *Colgan* v. *Forest Oil Co.* 194 Pa. 234; 45 Atl. 119; 75 Am. St. Rep. 695 (Dec. 30, 1899), the second and fourth points of the syllabus are as follows:

"A court of equity will not assume jurisdiction to enforce specifically covenants in an oil and gas lease which are merely implied and to whose extent depends altogether on oral evidence of opinions, unless it appears that the lessee is fraudulently evading his obligations to the lessor.

Where a lessee in an oil lease has bound himself by covenants to develop a tract, and has entered and produced oil, he has a vested estate in the land which cannot be taken away on any mere difference of judgment; and a court of equity, in the absence of any allegation of fraud, has no jurisdiction to compel the lessee to sink additional wells, nor to forfeit the lease and oust him from possession, in order to allow the lessor to experiment.''

William Colgan leased a farm in Allegheny County, Pennsylvania, for oil and gas purposes to Thomas Liggett. The lessor received $65.00 in cash, and by the terms of the lease was to receive one-eighth of the oil produced, and an annual rental of $500 for each gas well so long as the gas from the same should be utilized off the premises. One well was to be completed within one year from December 3, 1890, or in default a rental of $130.00 per annum was to be paid. The lease was subsequently assigned to the Forest Oil Company. Five wells were drilled on the farm, Numbers 1 and 2 producing gas for a time, but were subsequently abandoned. Numbers 3-4-5 produced oil. The oil company held oil and gas leases on the lands adjoining Colgan's land on the north, south and west, upon which the defendant had drilled. The company refused to drill additional wells on Colgan's land, claiming that the probabilities were, they would not get a paying well, while they would be compelled to pay $4,500.00 for drilling the well. The lessor filed a bill in equity for a forfeiture of the lease, or in the alternative, for specific performance of the covenants in the lease by requiring the sinking of additional wells. The Court of Common Pleas sustained the plaintiff's bill, and decreed that the defendant should put down a well on the western portion of plaintiff's farm and begin the same within thirty days after the decree and prosecute the drilling thereof with all reasonable diligence and in good faith. In default of such drilling the defendant should be deemed to have abandoned its lease, except as to wells 3-4-5, and a space 500 feet around said wells on all sides, together with the rights of way and other rights incident thereto under the terms of the lease necessary to the operation of said wells. The defendant appealed to the Supreme Court of Pennsylvania which court reversed the decree and dismissed the bill.

Sec. 13.—In *Young* v. *Forest Oil Co.*, 194 Pa. 243; 45 Atl. 121 (Dec. 30, 1899), the second and third points of the syllabus are as follows:

"Where a lessee under an oil and gas lease has entered upon land and sunk wells he is entitled, in determining whether he shall sink additional wells, to follow his own judgment. If that is exercised in good faith, a different opinion by the lessor or the expert, or the court, or all combined, is of no consequence and will not authorize a decree interfering with him.

A bill in equity will not lie by the lessor of an oil and gas lease against the lessee or his assigns to compel the latter to test part of the leased lands not yet drilled, or upon his failure to do so, to surrender the land to the lessor, unless it is shown that the failure of the lessee to drill amounts to a fraud upon the rights of the lessor."

Andrew B. Young, on October 21, 1889, leased a tract of land in Allegheny County, Pennsylvania, for oil and gas purposes, to T. J. Vandergrift. The lease was subsequently assigned, and on January 26, 1898, became the property of the Forest Oil Company. Five wells were drilled on the premises. The plaintiff filed a bill in equity in the Court of Common Pleas of Allegheny County to forfeit the lease, or, in the alternative, for the specific performance of the covenants therein for the sinking of additional wells. A decree was rendered in favor of the plaintiff. The Oil Company appealed to the Supreme Court of Pennsylvania, and that court reversed the decree, and directed the bill to be dismissed. The facts found by the Judge of the Court of Common Pleas upon which the decree of that court was predicated were substantially as follows: On October 21, 1889, the plaintiff was the owner of 53 acres of land in Allegheny County, subject to the dower interest of his mother, until her death which occurred on January 7, 1892. On October 21, 1889, plaintiff and his mother executed the lease to T. J. Vandergrift. Under the lease five wells were drilled on the premises, which were known and designated as Numbers 1-2-3-4-5. Number 1 was located on the north-west corner of the farm, 224 feet from Frank Schuler's line. This well was completed in 1890, and produced oil at an average of 150 barrels an hour for the first thirty days, its output gradually decreasing until January, 1891, when its production was 25 barrels per day, and which production continued to decrease until, at the date of the institution of the suit, or at the hearing, it was only producing one-half barrel per day. Immediately after the completion of Well Number 1 wells Numbers 2-3-4 were drilled, and each produced oil for a time, and were abandoned in the latter part of 1892, on account of their small output, their production at the time of abandonment being as follows: Wells two and three, each one-fourth barrel daily, and well Number 4 one-half barrel per day; well Number 5, located 252 feet west of plaintiff's east line and nearly midway between his north and south line, was drilled in 1896 through both the 100-foot and fourth sands without obtaining either oil or gas. The district in which plaintiff's farm was situated was known as the Forest Grove Oil Field, and in all wells drilled in that field oil was obtained from what was known as the 100-foot sand, except in one well known as the Sarah J. Phillips, Number 3, in which the oil was obtained in what was known as the fourth sand, found below the 100-foot; The Phillips Number 3, was about 1000 feet south of the south-west corner of plaintiff's farm, and about 2,000 feet south-west of his well Number 5. Wells had been drilled on all farms adjoining plaintiff's farm, and in every instance oil had been obtained except in the well known as Parsonage Oil Company, Number 1, which was a gas well, and plaintiff's Number 5, which produced neither oil nor gas; The defendant company had refused to drill additional wells on plaintiff's land, contending that this land had been sufficiently developed, and that the probabilities of getting a well with a production sufficient to pay drilling and operating expenses, and a reasonable profit, were not sufficient to warrant the expense. The nature of the sand from which oil was produced determines the extent of the area which a well will drain. A well producing from a coarse and pebbly sand will drain from a greater distance than one producing from a hard and compact sand. The sand from which oil was obtained in the Forest Grove Oil Fields was of a loose, coarse nature and wells producing from that sand would draw from a distance of 500 feet. The plaintiff could, were it not for the lease held by defendants, have leased his farm in its then condition for oil and gas purposes, and could have had the east portion thereof tested by having drilled thereon one or more wells.

Sec. 14.—In *Ammons* v. *South Penn. Oil Co.*, 47 W. Va., 610; 35 S. E. 1004, analyzed under Chapter 20, syl. 2 is as follows:

"2. S. purchased of A. seven-eighths of the undivided one-
half interest of A. in the oil in and under two hundred and forty-
three acres of land, and paid three hundred dollars cash therefor;
and, as part of the terms and conditions of sale, S. was to begin
to operate, mine, and bore for oil and gas within and under said
tract of land, free of cost to A. within sixty days, and complete
one well thereon in one year, unavoidable delay and accidents excepted; and, if oil be found thereon in paying quantities, then, after the said first well was completed thereon, S. should immediately commence and drill another well thereon as should seem necessary to protect the oil and gas in and under the said tract of land,
and should also deliver as royalty to the credit of A. free of cost
to him, the one-half of the one-eighth of all the oil produced and
saved from the said land, in pipelines or tanks, and pay to him
the one-half of three hundred dollars per year for the gas from
each and every well drilled thereon producing gas, the product
from which should be marketed. *Held,* that the remedy for violation of said conditions of the sale is not by way of forfeiture of
the rights of S. to bore or drill for oil on the land or any part of it,
but by action or proceeding for damages caused by such breach."

Sec. 15.—In *Harness* v. *Eastern Oil Co.,* 49 W. Va. ¯232; 38 S.
E. 662 (March 16, 1901) the third point of the syllabus is as follows:

"Lessor's remedy for failure on the part of lessee to further
develop the leased premises, or to properly protect the lines thereof from drainage through wells on adjacent property, is ordinarily
by action at law for damages."

On January 25, 1896, Thomas B. Harness and Anna K. Harness executed an oil and gas lease to M. Finnegan for two tracts
of land in Pleasants County, West Virginia. One tract of 152
acres belonged to T. B. Harness, and the other tract of 35 1-2 acres
belonged to Anna K. Harness, the wife of T. B. Harness. The two
tracts adjoined. The lease was for both tracts. No developments
were made on the 35-acre tract, and the lessors claimed that sufficient developments had not been made on the 152-acre tract. At
June Rules, 1899, the lessors filed in the Circuit Court of Pleasants
County their bill in chancery against the Eastern Oil Company
and M. Finnegan, alleging a fraudulent assignment of the lease
by Finnegan to the Eastern Oil Company, and further alleging
that the company was operating extensively on a tract of land adjacent to the leased premises, and was using the gas from well
Number 1, on the 152-acre tract in the pumping and production of

oil on the adjacent farm. The first well drilled on the leased premises was a gas well, which the plaintiffs claimed would have been
an oil well if it had been properly tested. A second well was
drilled which was abandoned. The lessors claimed that their
property was being drained by development on adjoining property
upon which defendants held leases; that no attempt had been made
to develop the 35-acre tract, the lessors claiming an absolute forfeiture of the lease as to that tract. The lessors further claimed
that the defendants had failed to protect the lines of the leased
premises, and in their bill prayed for a cancellation of the lease
as to both tracts. Defendants answered, denying the allegations
of the bill as to forfeiture. The company claimed the right to hold
both tracts because it had paid the gas rental on Well Number 1.
A decree was entered by the Circuit Court granting the plaintiffs
the relief in part by assigning a certain acreage around wells, a
number of wells having been drilled pending the litigation, and
cancelled the lease as to the territory not tested. From this decree
the defendants appealed to the Court of Appeals and that court
reversed the decree, and cited in support of its conclusion:

Colgan v. *Forest Oil Co.*, 194 Pa. 234; 45 Atl. 119.
Young v. *Forest Oil Co.*, 194 Pa. 243; 45 Atl. 121.

Sec. 16.—In *McGraw Oil & Gas Co.* v. *Kennedy*, 65 W. Va. 599;
64 S. E. 1027 (June 12, 1909) the syllabus is as follows:

"1.   A lease for oil and gas is for five years, 'and as long
thereafter as oil or gas, or either of them, is produced by the party
of the second part.' The lessor cannot forfeit it because he thinks
the gas not in paying quantity; the lessee claiming that it is, and
willing to pay the sum stipulated for the well. It is for the lessee
to say whether the gas is in paying quantity, acting in good faith.
    2.   When a producing gas well is developed, but its product
is not marketed, that fact does not authorize the lessor to forfeit
the ease; the lessee being willing to pay the agreed sum for a gas
welll
    3.   An oil and gas lease cannot be cancelled in equity only
for failure to drill additional wells.
    4.   Under the lease in this case, a well producing gas is drilled,
and the lessee elects to consider it in paying quantity. An estate
has thus vested in him."

conditions, or pay the cash consideration in the lease mentioned, at the time and in the manner agreed, then the lease is to be null and void, and not binding on either party, and oil being produced in paying quantities through wells drilled on the land by the lessee under the lease, *Held,* that the lessee has a vested interest in the land; that, to work a forfeiture of the lease, there must be a breach of a condition or covenant which is mentioned in the lease; that a breach of an implied covenant does not work a forfeiture of the lease; and that certain causes of forfeiture being specified in the lease others cannot be implied.

3. Under such lease, the remedy for a breach of an implied covenant is not by way of forfeiture of the lease, in whole or in part, but by an action for damages caused by such breach.''

William Snyder and Cordelia Snyder, on December 16, 1887, made an oil and gas lease for a tract of land in Wood County, Ohio, to Carey C. Harris. The lessee covenanted and agreed to commence and complete one well within six months. A failure so to do should render the lease null and void, unless the lessee should pay $100.00 to lessor for each three months the drilling should be delayed. It was also agreed that a failure on the part of the lessee to comply with the conditions, or to pay the cash consideration mentioned in the lease at the time and in the manner agreed, that then and in that event the lease should be null and void and not binding on either party. The lessee, Harris, took possession of the premises and drilled and operated nine oil wells thereon, and then assigned all his interest in the lease to the Ohio Oil Company, on February 22, 1889, and delivered possession to said Company. The oil company drilled and operated three additional wells, which produced oil in paying quantities. On January 5, 1892, Carey C. Harris purchased the land from the lessors, William Snyder and wife and then claimed that at least ten additional oil wells should be drilled upon the lands in order to reasonably and properly develop the same, protect lines and prevent the wells on surrounding lands from draining the oil from under the lands to his injury. Harris notified the company to drill more wells; and further notified the company that unless such additional wells were drilled within a reasonable time he would regard the lease as forfeited as to the undrilled parts of the land, and would proceed to drill the wells on said part of the lands, himself. The company refused to comply with this request, claiming that it had the exclusive right to drill wells on the land by virtue of its lease. After repeated notices

by Harris, and refusals by the company, Harris made preparations
to drill a well on the undrilled part of the land, and thereupon the
company filed its petition in the Court of Common Pleas of Wood
County, against Harris and obtained a temporary injunction restraining him from producing oil on the demised premises. Harris
filed his answer, averring that at the time the lease was made there
existed a well known custom throughout the County of Wood to
the effect following: That a lessee should protect the lines of
lands leased for oil and gas purposes from wells producing oil on
adjoining lands; that upon the completion of the first paying well
other wells should be completed and operated so as to develop
the leased lands; that one well, at least, should be drilled and
operated on each five acres of the demised premises. The defendant also averred that the plaintiff operated lands adjoining his
property on every side, and had operated the same since the 22d
of February, 1889; that on the 160 acres of land west of defendant's land the plaintiff owned and operated twenty oil wells; that
on the 80-acre tract on the east it owned and operated ten oil wells;
that on the quarter sections on the north, north-west and south-
west the plaintiff owned and operated nineteen oil wells, and within a distance of about one-half mile from defendant's land plaintiff owned and operated over one hundred and twenty oil wells;
that many of said wells were near the lines of defendant's land, and
drew the oil from under and in said land, and was doing him irreparable injury. The case was tried in the Circuit Court upon
appeal, and that court entered a decree that the plaintiff be quieted
in its exclusive rights to drill for and produce oil and gas in and
upon the leased premises, and perpetually enjoined the defendant
from drilling for and producing oil or gas upon the lands or any
part thereof during the continuance of the lease, and from in any
manner interrupting or interfering with the plaintiff oil company
in the exercise of its exclusive right to drill for and produce oil or
gas upon said land. A motion for a new trial was filed, and overruled by the Circuit Court. Exceptions were taken and petition in
error was filed in the Supreme Court by Mr. Harris, seeking to
reverse the judgment or decree of the Circuit Court. The Supreme
Court affirmed the Judgment.

Judge Burkett delivering the opinion of the court, said:

"This lease is, in its terms, an entire contract, without any words of severance; and there is no implication of severance as is sometimes the case when all wells are to be drilled within a shorter time than the period of the lease. In such cases, even though the lease is in terms a sale of all the oil contained in the land, whatever oil remains in the undeveloped parts of the land at the expiration of the time in which drilling can be done by the terms of the lease inherent in the land, and lapses into the fee, and remains the property of the landowner, the same as standing trees which are sold to be removed within a given time remains the property of the owner of the land after the expiration of such time.

In support of its conclusion the court cited:

Glasgow v. *Oil Co.*, 152 Pa. 48; 25 Atl. 232.
Koch's and Balliet's Appeal, 93 Pa. 434.
McKnight v. *Gas Co.*, 146 Pa. 188; 23 Atl. 164.
Clark v. *Guest*, 54 Ohio State 298; 43 N. E. 962.
Crawford v. *Oil Co.*, 55 Ohio St. 161; 44 N. E. 1093.
Venture Oil Co. v. *Fretts*, 152 Pa. 451; 25 Atl. 732.
McKnight v. *Kreutz*, 51 Pa. 232.
Bradford Oil Co. v. *Blair*, 113 Pa. 83; 4 Atl. 218.

Sec. 19.—In *Gadberry* v. *Ohio etc. Co.* 162 Ind. 9; 67 N. E. 259, analyzed under Chapter 11, the syllabus is as follows:

"The owner of land, in consideration of $1.00 granted all the oil and gas in it, with the right to operate, reserving a certain part of all the oil produced; the grantee, in case gas only was found, agreeing to pay $100.00 a year for the product of each well while it was being used off the premises, and the grantor to have gas free for domestic purposes; the lease to become void if no well was completed in 40 days, unless the grantee thereafter paid $1.00 a day till its completion. *Held* that there was an implied condition subsequent to develop so that the lease could be forfeited; the grantee after constructing a well and finding gas in paying quantities, closing it and failing to work it.

Failure for two years of the grantee of the oil and gas in land to develop it, after constructing a well, finding gas, and then closing it, prima facie authorizes the grantor, who was to be paid $100 per year for each well while gas was being used off the premises, without demand, to treat the grant as abandoned.

E. R. Gadberry and J. A. Gadberry granted all the oil and gas in and under a tract of land to J. S. Andrews, his successors and assigns. The lease provided that if gas only should be found the lessee should pay $100.00 each year for the product of each well while the same should be used off the premises, the lessor to have gas free of cost for domestic purposes. In case no well should be completed within forty days from the date of the lease it was to become null and void unless lessee should pay lessor One Dollar per day thereafter during the time the completion of a well was delayed. Andrews completed a well on the premises on February 19, 1898, and paid the lessor one dollar per day during the time completion of the well was delayed, after the forty days stipulated in the lease. Gas was found in the well in large and paying quantities. Andrews, upon completion of the well, closed and anchored it so as to prevent any gas from escaping therefrom. On January 6, 1900, Andrews assigned the lease to the Ohio etc., Gas Company. The gas was not utilized by Andrews or the gas company nor did either of them pay the lessors anything for the product of the well or for the privilege of holding the premises after completion of the well. The gas company claimed the right to hold the premises without further development, and without paying lessor anything for the privilege. The lessors on December 28, 1899, declared the lease forfeited for failure to develop and produce oil or gas under the lease, and then connected the gas with their dwelling house on the premises. The lessors instituted suit in the Circuit Court of Blackford County, Indiana, against the gas company for cancellation of the lease. The Circuit Court decided for the defendants and the plaintiff appealed to the Appellate Court of Indiana and that court affirmed the judgment of the Circuit Court. The case was then taken by the plaintiffs to the Supreme Court of Indiana, which court reversed the judgments of the courts below. In the opinion, Judge Gillett said:

"In the case in hand specific performance could not be enforced (*Louisville etc. R. Co.* v. *Dodenschatz,* 141 Ind. 251; 39 N. E. 703); and the completion of the first well having cut off the liquidated damages of $1.00 per day for con-completion, and as no gas has been disposed of off the premises, there remains no measure of damages for, while the damages would be substantial, they would be speculative. *Foster* v. *Elk Fork etc. Co.,* 32 C. C. A. 560; 90 Fed. 178: *Federal Oil Co.* v. *Western Oil Co.* (C. C.) 112 Fed. 373. The lack of any other remedy, and the danger that the gas might be withdrawn through wells on other lands, makes a case of this kind appeal to the conscience of the chancellor and calls upon him to enforce the incurred forfeiture by removing the cloud from the title."

Sec. 20.—In *McKnight* v. *Manufacturers Nat. Gas. Co.*, 146 Pa. 185; 23 Atl. 164; 28 Am. St. Rep. 790, analyzed under Chapter 11, the syllabus is as follows:

"1. A leasehold, operated for oil production imposes upon the lessee, after ascertaining the existence of oil, the duty of sinking so many wells as may be reasonably necessary, in view of operations on adjoining lands, to secure so much of the oil from the lands demised as may be obtained with profit; per Mr. Justice Williams.

2. The duty imposed upon the lessee in a leasehold operated for gas, cannot be measured by the same rule applied in the same manner as in the case of a leasehold operated for oil; the peculiar characteristics of the business of producing and transporting natural gas being such as to distinguish it for some purposes from operation for oil.

3. In an action against the lessee who had drilled one paying gas well upon the premises, for not putting down other wells, to protect the territory against the effect of operations on adjoining lands, it was error to charge that a failure to drill such wells was a breach of an implied covenant imposing a liability in damages in the absence of a reasonable excuse therefor.

4. Moreover, when a lease provides that all wells shall be located by the lessor, he may not maintain an action against the lessee for not drilling additional wells if he never fixed upon a location for any additional well, or called upon the lessee to locate one for him; the lessee having no right to drill except at points indicated by the lessor.

5. Whether, when one paying well has been put down, under a lease containing no express covenant to sink other wells, and the well so drilled has been accidentally destroyed while producing gas in paying quantities, the lessee will be obliged to drill another well in its place, or must abandon the premises, not decided."

Sec. 21.—In *Doddridge Oil and Gas Co.* v. *Smith*, 154 Fed. 970 (C. C. N. D. W. Va.) (July 24, 1907) the third and fifth paragraphs of the headnotes are as follows:

"3. While courts of equity, contrary to their rules, will enforce forfeitures of oil and gas leases where necessary to protect the rights and equities of the landowner, owing to their exceptional character, their powers cannot be invoked as against a lessee who has carried on the work in good faith and expended large sums in developing the leased property to enforce a forfeiture created by the lessor by an act of bad faith, which caused a default on the part of lessees.

5.   Where an owner leases land for oil and gas purposes, his remedy for failure on the part of the lessee to further develop the leased premises or to properly protect the lines from drainage, through wells on adjoining property, is ordinarily by action at law for damages, and not by way of forfeiture of the lease.''

On October 19, 1904, Frank Smith and wife executed an oil and gas lease to Anson H. Russell, Junior, upon a tract of 800 acres of land owned by them in Doddridge County, West Virginia, which lease on January 31, 1905, Russell assigned to the Doddridge County Oil and Gas Company. The lease was for a term of five years, or as long as oil or gas should be found in paying quantities, the lessors to receive one-eighth of the oil as royalty and $300.00 annually for each gas well. The drilling of the first well was to commence within forty days after the date of the lease, a second well within forty days from the completion of the first, and in like manner the whole property was to be developed. Two wells were drilled by the company, when, on April 21, 1905, the lessors claimed a forfeiture of the lease and entered thereon, took possession of the wells and all the property and machinery of the company, drove its agents and servants from the premises, and threatened to drill other wells. On January 17, 1906, the Doddridge Oil and Gas Company filed in the United States Circuit Court for the Northern District of West Virginia, its bill against the landowners setting up the foregoing facts, and alleging that the defendants fraudulently conceived the plan of seizing and taking possession of the premises under a pretended and fraudulent claim of forfeiture of the company's rights. The defendant landowners answered the bill and filed a cross-bill. The company filed an amended bill, to which also the landowners filed their answer. In the cross-bill and answer the landowners claimed that Martha J. Smith was the wife of Frank Smith, and had no interest in the land leased, except her inchoate right of dower. The landowners further alleged that prior to the execution of the lease to Russell, and his assignment thereof to the Company, three wells had already been drilled on the property; and that the defendant had upon the property certain machinery and material, such as engines, boilers, derricks, tanks, casing and pipe; and that Smith gave to Russell a written option running six months to purchase at an agreed price the output less one-eighth royalty of these three wells, and all the machinery and material; that when the Doddridge Oil & Gas Company drilled its first well, which was a gas well, it used Smith's boiler and engine, and consumed a portion of his pipe; also erected a derrick of his material; and when it started its second well it used Smith's boiler and engine, and after the work progressed the option to buy the machinery, material and output, having expired without compliance, Smith served notice upon the company to drill no longer with, but to surrender to him, his engine and boiler or pay him therefor, upon the reception of which notice the company ceased drilling and after a lapse of time, Smith further served notice of the forfeiture of the lease and took possession of the premises (including the company's property) and employed W. H. Carr to finish the well, agreeing to give him a fourth interest therein, which interest Carr sold and conveyed afterwards to Thomas B. Smith, who, in turn sold and conveyed it back to Frank Smith. The cross bill and answer therefore claimed that by reason of the cessation of drilling by the company upon the notice aforesaid, it had failed to keep and perform the terms of the original lease, and by reason thereof said lease had become forfeited. The cross bill contained a prayer for an injunction against the company to inhibit it from disposing of or removing from the premises any property or from disposing of its rights or interests, it being alleged that the company was insolvent; and also prayed for a cancellation of the lease and an accounting for Smith's damages. Upon hearing Judge Dayton held, that the oil company must be restored to its rights under the lease.

For the proposition that while courts of equity abhor forfeitures the rule does not apply when instead of working a loss or injury contrary to equity the enforcement of a forfeiture will promote justice and equity and protect the owner of real estate against the indifference, laches and injurious conduct of lessees for oil and gas purposes, Judge Dayton cites the following authorities:

Thomas v. *Hukill*, 34 W. Va. 385; 12 S. E. 522.
Steelsmith v. *Gartlan*, 45 W. Va. 27; 29 S. E. 978; 44 L. R. A. 107.
Trees v. *Eclipse Oil Co.*, 47 W. Va. 107; 34 S. E. 933.
Parish Fork Oil Co. v. *Bridgewater Gas Co.*, 51 W. Va. 583; 42 S. E. 655; 59 L. R. A. 566.
Lowther Oil Co v. *Guffey*, 52 W. Va. 88; 43 S. E. 101.

Lowther Oil Co. v. *Miller-Sibley Oil Co.,* 53 W. Va. 501; 44 S.
E. 433; 97 Am. St. Rep. 1027.
Foster v *Elk Fork Oil and Gas Co.,* 32 C. C. A. 560; 90 Fed.
178.
Huggins v. *Daily,* 40 C. C. A. 12; 99 Fed. 606; 48 L. R. A. 320.

For the proposition that the remedy of the lessor who leases
land for oil and gas purposes for failure on the part of the lessee
to further develop the leased premises or to properly protect the
lines thereof from drainage through wells on adjoining property is
ordinarily by action at law for damages, and not by way of forfeiture of the lessee's right to bore or drill for oil, Judge Dayton
cites the following authorities:

Harness v. *Eastern Oil Co.,* 49 W. Va. 232; 38 S. E. 662.
Ammons v. *South Penn Oil Co.,* 47 W. Va. 610; 35 S. E. 1004.
South Penn Oil Co. v. *Edgell,* 48 W. Va. 348; 37 S. E. 596; 86
Am. St. Rep. 43.
Core v. *New York Petroleum Co.,* 52 W. Va. 276; 43 S. E. 128.
Lowther Oil Co. v. *Miller-Sibley Oil Co.,* 53 W. Va. 501; 44 S.
E. 433; 97 Am. St. Rep. 1027.

Sec. 22.—In *Allegheny Oil Co.* v. *Snyder,* 45 C. C. A. 604; 106
Fed. 764, analyzed under Chapter 4, the second point of the head
notes is as follows:

"Under the decisions of the Supreme Court of Ohio relating
to the construction of oil and gas leases which have established
a rule of property in that State such leases carry an implied covenant on the part of the lessee that he will drill and operate such
number of wells on the premises as would ordinarily be required
to develop their production, and to afford ordinary protection to
their lines; and the lessor may enforce such covenants by action,
and is not obliged to permit the lessee to hold the land indefinitely
for speculative purposes, notwithstanding the absence of any express limitation in the lease."

William E. Fowler, on November 12, 1896, made an oil and gas
lease for a tract of land in Harrison County, Ohio, to Hiram Snyder. The lease was for the term of two years from date and as long
thereafter as oil or gas should be found in paying quantities, not
exceeding ·twenty-five years. In case no well should be drilled
within two years from the date of the lease, the same to be null and
void unless the lessee should pay for further delay at the rate of

One Dollar per acre at or before the end of each year thereafter. Nothing was done under the lease by way of sinking wells or otherwise taking possession until after the expiration of the two years named in the lease. On October 18, 1898, Fowler made another lease to George Gillmor, which lease was recorded on the 16th day of November, 1898. This lease was subsequently assigned to the Allegheny Oil Company. On November 10, 1898, the sum to be paid in the lease of November 12, 1896, at the rate of One Dollar per acre, was paid to Fowler. The Allegheny Oil Company instituted suit in equity in the Circuit Court of the United States for the Southern District of Ohio to cancel the original lease made by Fowler to Snyder. Snyder assigned the lease to Brown and Myers, who instituted a suit in the Court of Common Pleas of Harrison County to cancel the Gillmor lease. This suit was removed to the United States Circuit Court after an injunction had been obtained in the State Court, restraining the Allegheny Oil Company from operating under its lease. On hearing the United States Circuit Court refused the temporary injunction applied for by the Allegheny Oil Company and dismissed its bill and perpetuated the injunction of the State Court. The Allegheny Oil Company appealed to the Circuit Court of Appeals, where the decision of the Circuit Court was affirmed. The Court, in support of its conclusions, cited:

Harris v. *Ohio Oil Co.*, 57 Ohio St. 129; 48 N. E. 502.

Sec. 23.—In *Headley* v. *Hoopengarner*, 60 W. Va. 626; 55 S. E. 144 (Nov. 27, 1906), syl. 1 is as follows:

"The word 'grant' 'Demise' or 'lease' in a lease for years creates a covenant in law for good title and quiet enjoyment of the land demised during the term."

Thomas J. Headley, the father of Mansfield Headley, was the owner in his lifetime of two contiguous tracts of land in Tyler County, West Virginia, containing 24 and 46 acres, respectively. On February 6, 1896, Thomas J. Headley and his wife granted to the South Penn Oil Company one-half of the oil and gas within and underlying the 46-acre tract, and on April 14, 1897, Headley and wife granted to L. R. Loomis one-half of the oil and gas within and underlying the 24-acre tract. Both of these grants were recorded in the office of the Clerk of the County Court of Tyler County, the one to the South Penn Oil Company, on April 1, 1896, and the one to Loomis on April 14, 1897. Soon after the execution of the grant to Loomis, Thomas J. Headley died intestate, leaving surviving him his widow, Mary Jane Headley, and five children, Mansfield, Elisha, Albert, Florence and Susanna, infants. Mansfield became of age on March 17, 1899. Elisha Lemasters was appointed guardian of the infants. On March 17, 1899, as such guardian he united with Mary J. Headley, the widow, and Mansfield Headley, the adult, in a lease to H. L. Hoopengarner, M. W. Wharton and S. A. Carnes & Company, leasing for oil and gas purposes these two tracts of land. Inasmuch as the guardian had no authority to make it, this lease was ineffective to pass the interests of the infants, and on August 8, 1899, the guardian filed his petition in the Circuit Court of Tyler County, reciting the execution of the lease by the widow, the adult Mansfield and the petitioner as guardian of the infants, and filed the lease as an exhibit with his petition. The petition set out the advantage it would be to the infants to sell or lease their interest in and to the "undivided seven-eighths of all the oil and gas within and underlying said tract of land" reserving unto said infants their proportionate share of the one-eighth royalty of oil not sold, and prayed for authority to make such sale. On the same day the court entered a decree authorizing such sale, and the guardian reported that he had sold at private sale the undivided interest of the infants in and to the undivided four-fifths of the seven-eighths of all the oil, and all the gas within and underlying said tract of land, to the original lessees Hoopengarner, Wharton, Carnes & Company; and the court entered a decree confirming the sale. On the same day the guardian made a deed to the purchasers for the oil and gas sold. By various assignments the undivided seven-eighths working interest on April 23, 1900, came into the hands of N. S. Snyder and W. L. Mellon, and they were the owners of such working interest when, in that month, oil was first struck on the 24 acres. The interests which the South Penn Oil Company and Loomis had acquired by their conveyance from the ancestor Headley and his wife had never been discovered by the lessees, and consequently had never been taken into account by them until they came to divide the royalty interest in the oil. Oil being first struck on the 24 acres the question arose as to what interest Loomis owned and a division order was agreed upon signed by Mansfield Headley, Elisha Lemasters, guardian, N. S. Snyder, L. R. Loomis, and W. L. Mellon, giving to Mansfield Headley one-eightieth as royalty, LeMasters four-eightieths, and to Loomis five-eightieths, and to Snyder and Mellon the seven eighths working interest. Later, oil was discovered on the 46 acres, and another division order was agreed upon identical with the first, with the exception that the South Penn Oil Company received the seven-eightieths royalty. On October 21, 1900, Snyder and Mellon assigned the whole of the working interest to Henry Goodkind and Phillip Kleeberg, and on January 2, 1902, Goodkind and Kleeberg, assigned the same to the Colonial Oil Company. The operators of the leasehold divided the royalty as stipulated in the division orders until some time in July, 1903, when Mansfield Headley instituted his suit in chancery against the lessees and their assigns claiming that inasmuch as the original lease reserved one-eighth royalty, and as it was void as to the infants, the entire one-eighth should be accounted for to him, alone. At the same time LeMasters, guardian of the infants, two of whom had, in the meantime, become of age, and the two thus becoming of age instituted their suit in ejectment against the Colonial Oil Company which was then in possession of the property to recover possession of the same. This suit was based upon the theory that the decree in the summary proceedings required the purchaser to pay four-fifths of the royalty oil to the guardian, and provided that a failure to comply with the terms of the lease should operate as a forfeiture; and that inasmuch as the purchasers had paid only two-fifths, the right, title and interest of the infants should revert back to them.

The Colonial Oil Company, Goodkind and Kleeberg filed their answer and cross bill to the bill of Mansfield Headley, in which they set up the lease executed by Mansfield Headley and others, and the summary proceeding case, and insisted that under the lease Mansfield Headley was entitled to one-fifth of the royalty, and the infants to four-fifths, subject to the widow's dower, and they plead the lease and record in the summary proceeding case as an estoppel; They also plead the division orders signed by Mansfield Headley as an estoppel, and asked by way of affirmative

relief that all questions should be settled and that the ejectment
suit be enjoined. Answers were filed by the South Penn Oil Company, the Eureka Pipeline Company, Snyder and Mellon, and
the guardian LeMasters and his former wards, Albert and Florence Headley. Depositions were taken and on final hearing the
Circuit Court decreed that the lessees should account to the heirs
for the full one-eighth royalty. From this decree the lessees appealed to the Supreme Court of West Virginia, where the questions
to be determined were: First, were the Headley heirs entitled to
participate in the full one-eighth royalty; and second, were the
lessees and their assigns liable to account for the additional one-
sixteenth of the oil over and above the one-sixteenth that had
gone to the Headley heirs, and in addition to the one-sixteenth
which had been given to the grantees of the ancestor, Headley. As
to the implied covenant the court held the law to be as stated
in the first point of the syllabus and in the opinion pages 631-2
Judge Sanders said:

"It is contended by plaintiff's counsel that there is no implied covenant of warranty in an oil and gas lease. This is based
upon the theory that the lease from Headley heirs to Hoopengarner, Wharton, Karnes & Company was a sale of the oil in place,
and passed a fee simple estate, and not merely a lease or a rental
contract. If this claim were correct, and it had been a grant of
the oil in place, creating an estate in fee, then the authorities unan-
imously hold that there is no implied covenant of warranty, but
that such covenant must be expressed in the deed. But, also, on
the other hand, if the title passes an estate for years, with a reversion to the lessor, then there need be no express warranty of title
or for peaceable and quiet enjoyment of the demised premises, but
such covenant is implied in law. Where the lease contains such
language as the one we have here, which says: 'Have granted, demised, leased and let, and by these presents does demise, grant,
lease and let unto the parties of the second part, it is universally
held that there is an implied covenant of title for quiet and peaceable enjoyment for the purposes of the lease, when there is no
statute restricting or qualifying the meaning of such words. This
is not an open question in this State. In the case of Knotts, et
al., v. McGregor, 47 W. Va. 566, this is held to be the law, where
it is said: 'In a lease for oil and gas there is an implied covenant
of right of entry and quiet enjoyment for the purposes of the lease.'
'With respect to estates less than freehold, covenants for title were
from the earliest times implied, not only from the words of leasing
such as demisi, concessi, or the like, but even from the relation
of landlord and tenant, such is the law at the present day, unless

where, as in some of the United States, it has been altered by legislation.' Rawle on Covenants (5th Ed.) Section 272. In 18 Am. &
En. Ency. Law (2d Ed.) 612, it is said: 'It is a well settled rule
at the present time that the law will, in the absence of an express
covenant imply a covenant on the part of the lessor for the quiet
enjoyment of the premises by the lessee.''

The court held, that the South Penn Oil Company was entitled
to one-sixteenth of all the oil produced on the 46-acre tract; and
that Loomis was entitled to one-sixteenth of all the oil produced
from the 24-acre tract; and that the infants were entitled to an
accounting for their full share of four-fifths of one-sixteenth of
the royalty oil since the first production in addition to the four-
fifths of one-sixteenth which they had already received, this interest being subject to the widow's dower. The court held that
Mansfield Headley, having signed the division order for his interest, was estopped from claiming any additional amount. The decree of the Circuit Court was reversed and the cause remanded
for the accounting.

Sec. 24.—In *Pyle* v. *Henderson,* 65 W. Va. 39; 63 S. E. 762,
analyzed under Chapter 25, syl. 2 is as follows:

"2. Where, in an oil lease there is a clause that it shall be
void if a well is not completed, or in lieu of it, money paid within
a given time, and before the expiration of the time is found that
the lessor's title is defective and he agrees to perfect it, and agrees
that the money need not be paid when due and gives an extension
for payment until the title can be perfected, he cannot declare a
forfeiture and make a second lease. A second lease, taken with
notice of the first is void as to the first lease.''

Sec. 25.—In *J. M. Guffey Petroleum Co.* v. *Oliver* — Tex. —;
79 S. W. 884 (Feb. 2, 1904), syl. 1 is as follows:

"1. Though a lease of land for oil and gas development which
was executed in consideration of royalties reserved to the lessor
is silent as to the extent of development it implies a condition for
diligence, good faith and reasonable development.''

On March 8, 1901, T. J. Oliver executed an oil and gas lease
for three several tracts of land comprising about 470 acres in
Harden County, Texas, whereby the lessor granted, bargained.

leased and let unto the lessee, its successors and assigns for the sole and only purpose of mining and operating for oil and gas. It was agreed that the lease should remain in force for the term of ten years from the date thereof and as long thereafter as oil or gas should be produced upon the premises by the lessee, its successors or assigns. The lessee covenanted, in consideration of the grant, to deliver to the credit of the lessor, free of cost, in the pipe-lines with which it should connect its wells, the one-eighth part of all the oil produced and saved from the premises, or the lessee might take and pay the market price for his part of the oil; the lessee to pay $200.00 for the gas from each well drilled on the premises, the product of which should be used off the premises. It was also provided that upon payment of $2.00 at any time by the lessee, its successors or assigns, to the lessor, his heirs or assigns, the lessee should have the right to surrender the lease for cancellation after which all payments and liabilities thereafter to accrue under and by virture of the terms of the lease should cease and determine and the lease should become absolutely null and void.

Work was begun under the lease within the time agreed, and the drilling had progressed to a depth of 820 feet when, on June 27, 1901, the parties entered into an agreement omitting the formal parts as follows:

"Whereas, the first parties on or about March 7, 1901, made a lease for oil and gas purposes of his land comprising 885 acres, to J. M. Guffey Company, and has since passed into the possession of J. M. Guffey Petroleum Company, complication has arisen as to the title of said land, and whereas second parties under the terms and conditions of the said lease are drilling a well on same, and whereas in view of such complication it seems expedient and necessary in the mutual interests of the parties hereto that further development of the oil or gas be suspended pending a decision or settlement as to their rights in and to said land, and to this end first party for and in consideration of Ten ($10.00) Dollars in hand paid, the receipt of which is hereby acknowledged, agrees to permit second party to suspend drilling on the above tract of land until such time as either the court of said County or State shall definitely and permanently decide as to the first parties' interest, or until such a time as the question of title or division shall be compromised or settled to the mutual satisfaction of both parties hereto, and said lease, pending such decision or compromise, shall be and remain in full force and virtue as if such delay in completing or suspension had never occurred."

When the lease was executed, the lessee, J. M. Guffey Petroleum Company, was notified of adverse claims to the land by J. A. Bordages and others; and the purpose of Oliver in executing the agreement of June 27, 1901, for the suspension of work was to settle the question of his title before the discovery of oil. Work was accordingly suspended and negotiations for settlement of the title resulted in an agreement between Oliver and the defendant J. M. Guffey Petroleum Company, which company had succeeded to the rights of the J. M. Guffey Company on the one part, and Bordages on the other part. This agreement was reduced to writing and bore date August 1, 1901, and was signed by all the parties named in it, except Ambrose Jackson and the defendant J. M. Guffey Petroleum Company. Jackson never signed it. The Petroleum Company signed it on March 28, 1902. By this agreement the parties divided among themselves the lands included in the original lease. Three tracts aggregating 487 acres were released and conveyed to Oliver. It was provided in the agreement that the partition should be confirmed by a consent decree of the District Court of Jefferson County, to be rendered in a suit to be brought for this purpose by some of the parties.

Another agreement was entered into by all the parties to the original agreement, except Ambrose Jackson, reciting the fact that he had failed to sign, and agreeing that the settlement should be carried out without him, and obligating Bordages, Davis and Gilbert, parties to the agreement, to settle with Jackson or his vendees, and declaring and agreeing that the agreement of August 1, 1901, should otherwise remain in full force. This agreement was not signed by the defendant till March 28, 1902. A suit was brought. A suit was pending in the District Court of Dallas County affecting a portion of the leased land. After all these transactions, Oliver came to the conclusion that he would forfeit the lease, and on April 30, 1902, gave notice of his election to do so in writing to the defendant, and tendered the sum of Ten Dollars and notified the oil company to keep off the premises, and to take no further action under the lease. The sum of Ten Dollars was tendered because it could not be certainly said that the sum mentioned in the contract read "ten" or "two" dollars.

On May 19, 1902, a judgment was entered in the partnership suit partitioning the land among the parties named to the suit, except Ambrose Jackson, and as to him suit was discontinued. At the time the decree was entered Oliver had conveyed a one-fourth interest in the lands owned by him, or such as might be awarded to him under the agreement and judgment to the co-plaintiffs. When Oliver gave the oil company notice of his election to forfeit the lease, it had commenced to drill only one well on the premises. This well was drilled on the 365-acre tract, and did not produce oil in paying quantities. After Oliver had declared the lease forfeited, the oil company prosecuted the work of development and found oil in paying quantities in two wells. In drilling the well, prior to suspension, on June 27, 1901, several oil bearing strata were struck, which were cased off and passed by direction of the oil company's superintendent, without any attempt to develop them. Oliver was present much of the time during the process of drilling and had considerable experience in oil wells, but not enough to determine whether a stratum was oil bearing sufficient to pay without bailing, while the superintendent, on the other hand, from a superior knowledge, could tell and did know when oil was discovered in paying quantities. After the agreement for settlement had been signed by all the parties except the oil company it commenced work again in September, 1901, and drilled the original well to the depth of 1140 feet, when a stratum of oil was struck, but it was cased off by order of the superintendent, and the drillers directed to go deeper and prospect. At the depth of 1,400 feet drilling was stopped and the pipe drawn back to the stratum at 1,140 feet. A third liner was put in here, but the efforts to bail amounted to nothing and the well did not produce much. There was delay in the work and it was finally abandoned in October. Oliver grew impatient and urged the oil company to go ahead with developments, and in February, 1902, men were put at work to fish out the liner, but never succeeded in getting it out and the well was never made a producer. The J. M. Guffey Petroleum Company had been, and were, the lessees of several tracts of land supposed to have underlying them oil and gas, and were producers of oil and gas in large quantities in the Beaumont field. This company was still endeavoring to gain control of oil bearing land when, on September 8, 1902, T. J. Oliver and the others to whom Oliver had conveyed, instituted an action in the District Court of Harden County, Texas, against the J. M. Guffey

Petroleum Company to cancel the lease of March 8, 1901. The facts were submitted to a jury who found in favor of the plaintiffs. A decree was rendered thereon cancelling the lease, from which decree the oil company appealed to the Court of Civil Appeals of Texas, and that court affirmed the decree and as to implied covenants held the law to be as stated in the first point of the syllabus. There were a number of other questions involved in this case, among others, the fraudulent purpose of the Oil Company as to suspension of developments and withholding its signature from the settlement agreement of August first and twenty-fourth, 1901, until March 28, 1902. The court held that the evidence was sufficient to warrant the finding of the jury; that the defendant oil company acted with fraudulent purpose in delaying development of the land.

Sec. 26.—In *Acme Oil, etc. Co.* v. *Williams,* 140 Cal. 681; 74 Pac. 296 (Oct. 17, 1903), the first point of the syllabus is as follows:

"An oil lease in consideration of royalties which are covenanted to be paid at a certain time contains an implied covenant for diligent operations if oil is struck; and a failure to operate for two months followed by an execution sale of the leasehold and all appliances of the lessee justifies a forfeiture and re-entry by the lessor."

H. L. Williams, on June 7, 1897, leased certain lands in Santa Barbara County, California, to Acme Oil & Mining Company for oil and gas purposes. The lessee agreed to begin operations on the premises and to complete the sinking of two wells within ninety days, and complete the sinking of ten wells within a year from the date, and agreed to pay the lessor on the 5th day of each and every month during the existence of the lease for the privileges conferred, and as rental in full for the premises, a royalty of ten cents per barrel for each and every barrel of merchantable oil taken from the premises and sold or disposed of by them. It was further agreed that if default should be made by the lessee in the payment of the royalties for more than ten days or to keep any of the covenants or agreements by it to be kept or performed, the lessor should have the right to re-enter and take possession of the premises, and at his option terminate the lease. The lessor entered upon the premises and sunk two wells within the required time, and on August 11, 1897, commenced pumping oil and paid the lessor the stipulated royalty for August and September. On January 5, 1898 having execution upon a judgment obtained against the oil company, all the oil pumped from said wells and stored in tanks on the premises, all the tanks, buildings, plant and personal property were sold to W. W. Burton, who, on February 2, 1898, purchased the leasehold interest of the oil company which had likewise been sold under execution. On January 15, 1898, Williams entered into possession of the premises claiming forfeiture of the lease, and pumped the wells. On February 2, 1898, the premises were sold and Burton entered into possession of the leased premises and appurtenances, claiming the right of possession by virtue of his purchase of the leasehold at such sale, and pumped said wells, and thereafter bored and pumped additional wells—eight in number. On February 15, 1898 the Acme Company tendered to said Williams as royalty the sum of $11.00 which Williams refused to accept, claiming the lease was forfeited. On March 2, 1898, Williams served upon the oil company written notice that he had taken possession, and declared the lease forfeited for covenants broken, for abandonment of the premises for more than two months, and for having permitted the leasehold and the property and appliances necessary to the operation of the wells to be sold at judicial sale, and for failure and neglect to work the wells or pay royalty for the same.

About the time of the service of this notice Williams executed a lease of the same premises to other parties. On May 26, 1898, the oil company tendered to Burton, the purchaser of the leasehold premises at execution sale, a sum sufficient to redeem, and demanded possession of, the premises from him. Burton refused either to accept the tender or surrender the premises. The Acme Company instituted, in the Superior Court of Santa Barbara County an action in ejectment against H. L. Williams and the second lessee of Williams. The case was decided in favor of the defendants, from which judgment the oil company appealed to the Supreme Court of California, which court affirmed the judgment.

In support of the right of the lessor to re-enter the premises for breach of the conditions of the lease, the court cited:

Petroleum Co. v. *Coal and Coke etc. Co.*, 89 Tenn. 391; 18 S. W. 65.

Conrad v. *Moorehead,* 89 N. C. 35.
Maxwell v. *Todd,* 112 N. C. 686; 16 S. E. 926.

Sec. 27.—In *Huggins* v. *Dailey,* 99 Fed. 606; 40 C. C. A. 12; 48 L. R. A. 320, analyzed under Chapter 6, paragraph 1 of head notes is as follows:

"1. By a course of decisions in West Virginia which has established a rule of property, it is settled, that an oil and gas lease in which the sole compensation to the lessor is a share of the product is not a grant of property in the oil or in the land until oil is actually produced, but merely of the right of possession for the purpose of exploration and development, and there is always an implied, if not an express, covenant for diligent search and operation."

Sec. 28.—In *Phillips* v. *Hamilton,* ——(Wyo.)——; 95 Pac. 846 (May 25, 1908), the syllabus is as follows:

"1. Plaintiff leased land to defendant for the purpose of boring for oil and gas; the lease being for ten years and so long thereafter as the oil or gas was found in paying quantities, the lessor to receive a certain per cent. of any oil or gas found and so much per year for the gas from each well drilled, and the lessee to commence operations within one year therefrom. The lessee drilled the well on the land within a year thereafter to the depth of 460 feet, and no gas being found in commercial quantities the well was cased and he moved the rigging to an adjoining tract where some drilling was done, and some four months after drilling the first well the lessee returned with a portable rig and cleaned out the well and then removed the rig and some seven months thereafter selected another site on plaintiff's land for drilling a well, and had begun to erect a derrick when plaintiff, for the first time, objected to the lessee's performance under the lease, and revoked the lease by written notice on the ground that the lessee had failed to commence operations within a year as required by the lease, and at the trial contended that the lease required the lessee to commence operations within a year and continue without cessation until the land was fully developed or the absence of oil was shown. *Held,* that while the lease contained an implied covenant that the lessee would prosecute the work of development with reasonable diligence he was not obligated to continue it without intermission, and under the circumstances there was no lack of good faith or diligence in developing the land."

2. It is not the duty of courts to make contracts for parties, but to interpret the language they have used and construe the contract they have entered into according to established legal principles.

3. 'Abandonment' is the relinquishment or surrender of the rights of property by one person to another, and includes both the intention to abandon and the external act by which the intention is carried out.

4. In determining whether one has abandoned his property or rights the intention is a paramount subject of inquiry, as there can be no abandonment without an intention to do so, and where plaintiff leased certain lands to defendant for the purpose of boring for oil and gas, operations to be commenced within a year, and operations were begun within that time, and the well drilled, and some seven months after drilling the first well the lessee returned to erect another rig and drill another well when plaintiff revoked the lease, there was no intention by the lessee to abandon the lease.''

On August 4, 1902, Hamilton leased to J. B. Phillips, Trustee, a tract of 360 acres of land in Converse County, Wyoming, for oil and gas purposes. The terms and conditions of this lease are set forth in the syllabus above quoted. About October 6, 1902, the lessee went on the premises with a portable derrick and commenced drilling, and during that month drilled the well to a depth of about 466 feet, when some gas was found but not in commercial quantities. The well was then cased and the drilling machinery removed to adjoining property. A pipe was laid from the well to this adjoining property, and the gas was there used for drilling for some time during the Fall of 1902.

In February or March, 1903, the lessee returned to the premises with a portable rig and cleaned out the well, replaced the casing and then moved the rig off, leaving the casing in the well. About October 15, 1903, the lessee selected a site for another well, and hauled and placed on the land some lumber for a standard derrick. On December 14, 1903, Hamilton mailed to Phillips a notice stating that lessor had rescinded and cancelled the lease. On December 24, 1903, Phillips assigned the lease to Douglass Oil Fields, a corporation, which at the time of the assignment had notice of the attempted cancellation of the lease by the notice of December 14th. On March 26, 1904, Douglass Oil Fields moved a drilling rig on the premises and commenced drilling the second well, and continued drilling till about April 28, 1904, when they had the well sunk to a depth of about 368 feet, and put in 360 feet of 8 inch casing, and were preparing to sink it deeper when they were stopped from further work by a temporary injunction. Hamilton instituted suit in the District Court of Converse County, against the lessee J. B. Phillips and another to enjoin defendants from drilling the well on the land. The claim upon which the plaintiff predicated his right to a cancellation of the lease—the object of the suit—was that under its terms the lessee was obligated to commence operations for oil and gas upon the premises within one year and to continue such operations diligently and in good faith until the oil and gas thereunder had been fully developed, or it had been effectually demonstrated that oil and gas were not to be found thereunder in commercial quantities; and that any cessation of such prospecting would work a forfeiture of the lease and authorize its cancellation. The District Court entered a decree awarding the injunction, from which decree the defendants appealed to the Supreme Court. That court reversed the decree and held the law to be as stated in the syllabus, and remanded the case for a new trial.

Douglass Oil Fields filed a bill in the same court against Hamilton to restrain him from interfering with it in drilling for oil on the leased premises. On this bill a temporary injunction was awarded, and the District Court dissolved this injunction and entered a decree cancelling the lease. From this decree the plaintiff, Douglass Oil Fields, brought error to the Supreme Court, and that court reversed the District Court and remanded the cause for a new trial and held the law to be as stated in the syllabus. *Phillips* v. *Hamilton*, 95 Pac. 846.

Sec. 29.—In *Aye* v. *Philadelphia Co.*, 193 Pa. 451; 44 Atl. 555; 74 Am. St. Rep. 696, analyzed under Chapter 2, the second paragraph of the syllabus is as follows:

"The rule, that where the parties have expressly agreed on what shall be done there is no room for the implication of anything not so stipulated for, is equally as applicable to oil and gas leases as to any other contract."

Sec. 30.—In *Vendocia Oil etc. Co.* v. *Robinson*, 71 Ohio State, 302; 73 N. E. 222, analyzed under Chapter 21, syl. 1 is as follows:

"1. A grant, in consideration of one dollar, of all the oil and gas under certain premises, with the right to enter thereon for the purpose of drilling and operating for oil and gas, excepting and reserving to the grantor 1-6 of all the oil and gas produced and saved from the said premises, to be delivered in the pipelines with which the grantee may connect his wells, implies an engagement by the lessee to develop the premises for oil and gas."

Sec. 31.—In *Smith* v. *Root,* 66 W. Va. 633; 66 S. E. 1005 analyzed under Chapter 51 syls. 2-3 are as follows:

"2. An oil and gas lease giving the lessee the right, for the period of ten years, to explore for oil and gas, and providing that if a well is not completed on the leased premises within three months from the date of the lease the lessee shall pay to the lessor, in advance, a quarterly cash rental for each additional three months the completion of a well is delayed, is an executory contract and vests no title in the lessee to the oil and gas in place.

3. Such a contract contemplates development of the leased premises within a reasonable time, and the lessee may lose his right thereunder before the expiration of the ten years by abandonment of the lease, notwithstanding there is no forfeiture clause in the contract."

Sec. 32.—In *Powers* v. *Bridgeport Oil Co.,* 238 Ill. 397; 87 N. E. 381 (Feb. 19, 1909), syls. 4-5 are as follows:

"4. It is not error for the court, on declaring forfeiture of a lease for failure of the lessee to put down the required number of wells, to refuse to allow the lessee to remove the casing from the wells that were put down where such casing could not be removed without destroying the wells.

5. The lessee in an oil lease may be required promptly to develop the oil in the land, especially where he controls adjoining lands, from which he is taking oil."

On March 14, 1906, W. H. Pemberton executed an oil lease to C. E. Gibson whereby Gibson was to have the right to prospect for oil on the premises, and in case oil was found it was agreed that Pemberton was to have 1-8 part thereof. On January 25, 1907, Pemberton and wife gave to R. F. Powers and H. S. Piper an option to purchase the farm for $3,000. On March 21, 1907, Powers paid the purchase money to Pemberton and received a deed from Pemberton and wife for the land. On March 20, 1907, the day before the option was closed, an oil well which was being drilled by Gibson and others on the land was brought in. On receipt of his deed from Pemberton, Powers notified Gibson that he had purchased the land, and that the lease to him from Pemberton was invalid as the homestead of the Pembertons had been reserved in said land. There was an interview between the parties, and on March 25, 1907, a new contract was entered into between Powers and Gibson and one of his partners, whereby it was agreed that the lease from Pemberton should be confirmed and ratified by the parties in consideration that the firm of Gibson should put down six wells on the land; and if the land covered by the lease would sustain eight wells, that number should be put down. The firm of Gibson put down, within the Spring and Summer, in all five wells. On September 25, 1907, the Gibson firm sold and assigned the lease together with other leases which they held on land in the vicinity of the Pemberton land, to the Bridgeport Oil Company, with which Gibson and his firm were connected. The Bridgeport Company, by this transfer, obtained title to a lease on a fifteen-acre tract of land situated immediately north of the Pemberton land, known as the Willie land, upon which there were three wells. Wells were also put down by the oil company, or by other parties, upon the lands immediately east, south and west of the Pemberton land. In the contract between the firm of Gibson and Powers it was agreed that the outside lines of the Pemberton land should be protected by drilling wells on the Pemberton line to offset any wells which might be put down on the adjoining land, such wells to be so located as to prevent oil under the Pemberton land from being drained into and produced through wells on adjoining lands. R. F. Powers filed a bill in equity in the Circuit Court of Lawrence County against the Bridgeport Oil Company and others to cancel the lease made by Pemberton to Gibson, as a cloud on his title. The oil company answered, replication was filed, and upon a hearing upon the pleadings and proofs a decree was entered in favor of the plaintiff. From this decree the oil company appealed, and the Supreme Court of Illinois affirmed the decree. The Supreme Court found from the evidence that as soon as well number 5 was put down on the Pemberton land, well Number 1 on the same land failed to produce oil; and that no wells were put down on the Pemberton land to offset wells 1 and 2 on the Willie land; and that in consequence of the failure to put down wells to offset the wells on the Willie land some correspondence was had between the parties with Gibson and the Bridgeport Oil Company, and Gibson, or the

Bridgeport Oil Company, failed to take any action in the matter, and Powers notified Gibson and the Oil Company that they had forfeited their right to take oil from the Pemberton land under their lease. Within a short time thereafter Powers filed his bill.

Sec. 33.—In *Kilcoyne* v. *Southern Oil Co.*, 61 W. Va., 538; 55 S. E. 881 (March 12, 1907), the syllabus is as follows:

"1. There is an implied covenant for good title and peaceable and quiet possession in a lease for years for oil and gas.
2. Such implied covenant of warranty is not limited to the right of exploration for oil and gas but when produced the right to the a ount stipulated for in the lease is likewise thereby protected."m

S. B. McDougle, the owner of 16 1-4 acres of land in Wetzel County, West Virginia, on August 24, 1899, conveyed to T. J. Conaway 1-16 of all the oil and gas underlying the same. On January 26, 1903, McDougle leased the same tract to C. L. Johnson for oil and gas purposes for the period of five years and as much longer as oil or gas, or either, should be produced therefrom. The lessee covenanted to deliver, in case of production and operation, to the lessor, his heirs or assigns, in the pipeline, one-eighth part of all the oil produced and saved from the premises, and $300.00 per year for gas for each well drilled thereon. On September 26, 1904, McDougle granted to H. M. Sartelle 1-16 of all the oil underlying the same tract of land, and 1-2 of all the gas royalties that might be paid thereon, or arise therefrom; and on May 16, 1905, McDougle granted to Kilcoyne, with covenants of special warranty, all his right, title and interest in and to the oil and gas in and underlying said tract of land. The lease executed by McDougle to C. L. Johnson was assigned to the Southern Oil Company, and this company on or about November 22, 1904, produced oil in paying quantities on the tract. Kilcoyne, the grantee of McDougle, on the 16th of May, 1905, filed his bill in equity in the Circuit Court of Wetzel County against the Southern Oil Company and others, setting up the various conveyances, and the lease aforesaid, and alleging that by reason of his purchase and deed from McDougle he had acquired an interest in the oil and gas, and claimed to be entitled to the full 1-16 of the oil produced, and one-half of the gas royalties, which he averred had not been conveyed under the previous conveyances. The defendant Southern Oil Company demurred and answered and the cause proceeded to final decree, wherein it was determined that H. M. Sartelle or his assignees were entitled to eight-one hundred and twenty-eighths of the oil, the plaintiff Kilcoyne to seven one hundred and twenty eighths thereof, and the Southern Oil Company to the remainder, subject to the rights of T. J. Conaway, which were not adjudicated; the decree providing further that Kilcoyne was entitled to one hundred and forty dollars and seventy-five cents, part of the three hundred dollars royalty from each and every gas well, the product of which should be used or marketed off the premises. From this decree the Southern Oil Company appealed to the Court of Appeals, which court reversed the decree of the Circuit Court, sustaining the demurrer and dismissing the plaintiff's bill. The plaintiff claimed that Conaway, under and by virtue of his conveyance from McDougle, obtained one-sixteenth of the oil and gas in place, which was before there was any lease whatever upon the land, and that Johnson, the lessee, took his lease with record notice of the conveyance of the 1-16 to Conaway, and having this notice, stipulated and agreed to pay to the lessor his heirs or assigns, the 1-8 of all the oil produced; and that therefore the Southern Oil Company was liable to and must account for 3-16 of the oil produced and saved, taking 3-16 as the working interest, with the possible right to deduct from Conaway's interest the pro rata share of the cost of its production. The court held that the conveyance from McDougle to Conaway passed to him a 1-16 of the oil and gas, whether in place or royalty was immaterial in the determination of the case, and was not affected in any way by any of the subsequent conveyances or lease. McDougle, having parted with the 1-16 interest which vested in Conaway, then leased the entire tract of land to Johnson for oil and gas purposes, reserving the prevailing 1-8 royalty, and by this lease McDougle passed to the lessee, Johnson, the seven-eighths working interest. Subsequent to the Johnson lease McDougle conveyed a 1-16 interest to Sartelle. The court held that Sartelle was entitled to this interest, because at the date of the conveyance to Sartelle, McDougle owned that interest. The court further held, that after the conveyance to Sartelle there remained no interest in the oil and gas in McDougle; and that therefore his deed to the plaintiff Kilcoyne passed nothing. The court predicated its conclusion that under the lease the Southern Oil Company could only be required to pay a 1-8 royalty in all the oil, upon the theory that a lease for years implies a warranty of good title and peaceable and quiet possession of the leased premises, citing in support of this conclusion:

Knotts v. *McGregor*, 47 W. Va. 566; 35 S. E. 899.
Headley v. *Hoopengarner*, 60 W. Va. 26; 55 S. E. 744.

Sec. 34.—In *Buffalo Valley Oil and Gas Co.*, v. *Jones*, 75 Kan. 18; 88 Pac. 537, analyzed under Chapter 24, syl. 1 is as follows:

"Where an oil and gas lease covering lands located in a field which is being actively developed, is given for a term of two years, and contains a provision that in case oil or gas is found on the premises, the lease may be continued in force by lessee so long as he diligently develops the land and markets the product, the failure of the lessee to use reasonable diligence in the respects named will cause said lease to lapse."

For Remedies see Chapter 19.

CHAPTER 19.

REMEDIES IN EQUITY FOR BREACHES BY LESSEE OF IMPLIED COVENANTS.

Sec. 1.—Where an oil and gas lease contains an express covenant for the payment by lessee of rental or commutation money as indemnity for delay in development, and contains no clause providing for a forfeiture of the lease for failure to pay such rental or commutation money, or for failure to develop, the lessee cannot refuse to make the explorations and hold the lease for speculative purposes, but must develop within a reasonable time, or pay the commutation money in lieu thereof; otherwise the lease will be forfeited. The remedy of the landowner is by declaration of forfeiture, and a court of equity, or a court exercising equity powers, will cancel the lease upon the grounds of abandonment, as a cloud upon lessor's title.

Guffey v. *Hukill,* 34 W. Va. 49; 11 S. E. 756.
Bluestone Coal Co. v. *Bell,* 38 W. Va. 297; 18 S. E. 493.
Steelsmith v. *Gartlan,* 45 W. Va. 27; 29 S. E. 978.
Parish Fork Oil Co. v. *Bridgewater Gas Co.,* 51 W. Va. 583;
 42 S. E. 655.
Smith v. *Root,* 66 W. Va. 633; 66 S. E. 1005.
Venture Oil Co. v. *Fretts,* 152 Pa. 451; 25 Atl. 732.
Huggins v. *Daley,* 99 Fed. 606; 40 C. C. A. 12.
Federal Oil Co. v. *Western Oil Co.,* 112 Fed. 373; (C. C. D.
 Ind.)
Allegheny Oil Co. v. *Snyder,* 106 Fed. 764; 45 C. C. A. 604.

Sec. 2.—Where a lessee under an oil and gas lease enters upon the demised premises and discovers gas in paying quantities,
he cannot shut in the well, refuse to pay either a land rental as commutation money for delay, or the gas rental provided for in the
lease, and hold the lease indefinitely. Where a lessee fails to
market the gas within a reasonable time after its discovery, and
also fails to pay the landowner rental or commutation money for
delay, a court of equity, at the suit of the landowner, lessor, will
cancel the lease upon the grounds of abandonment.

Gadberry v. *Ohio etc. Gas Co.,* 162 Ind 9; 67 N. E. 257.
Eastern Oil Co. v. *Coulehan,* 65 W. Va. 531; 64 S. E. 836.

Sec. 3.—Where a lessee under a lease with a rental·clause
which provides for the payment of commutation money for delay
in drilling refuses to make developments, and there are wells on
adjoining territory producing oil or gas in such close proximity to
the leased premises as to produce drainage, lessor should, after demand and notice to lessee of his intention so to do, refuse to accept rental and apply to a court exercising equity powers for relief by specific performance, or cancellation of the lease for failure
to develop the territory. Upon proof that the leasehold premises
are being drained by wells producing oil or gas on adjoining territory, the court will direct specific performance, or in the alterative,
decree a cancellation of the lease. In case of urgency a receiver
will be appointed to protect the premises by making the necessary
developments.

Sult v. *Hochstetter Oil Co.,* 63 W. Va. 317; 61 S. E. 307. Syl.
 9.

Elk Fork Oil and Gas Co. v. *Foster*, 39 C. C. A. 615; 99 Fed. 495. Op. 498-9.

Indiana Nat. Gas and Oil Co. v. *Leer*, 34 Ind. App. 61; 72 N. E. 283.

Consumers Gas Trust Co. v. *Chrystal Window Glass Co.*, 163 Ind. 190; 70 N. E. 366.

Consumers Gas Trust Co. v. *Worth*, 163 Ind. 141; 71 N. E. 489.

Sec. 4.—Where a lessee has entered and discovered oil or gas in paying quantities, and is evading and refusing to perform the obligations to the lessor to further develop the leased premises, or to properly protect the lines from drainage caused by the production of oil from wells on adjoining territory, and the lessor's right to have further developments or protection of his lines does not depend upon mere differences of opinion between lessor and lessee, or upon expert evidence, as to the necessity for the developments or protection, but where the fact of drainage or failure to develop is supported by clear proof a court of equity will assume jurisdiction to enforce specifically the implied covenants of the lease for such developments and protection of lines, and will decree a cancellation of the lease, unless within a given time, lessee further develops or protects the lines, as the case may be.

Kleppner v. *Lemon*, 176 Pa. 502; 35 Atl. 109.
Kleppner v. *Lemon*, 197 Pa. 430; 47 Atl. 353.
Kleppner v. *Lemon*, 198 Pa. 581; 48 Atl. 483.
Acme Oil Co. v. *Williams*, 140 Cal. 681; 74 Pac. 396.
J. M. Guffey Petroleum Co. v. *Oliver*, (Tex.) 79 S. W. 884.
Brewster v. *Lanyon Zinc Co.*, 140 Fed. 801; 72 C. C. A. 213.
Powers v. *Bridgeport Oil Co.*, 238 Ill. 397; 87 N. E. 381.
Buffalo Valley etc. Co. v. *Jones*, 75 Kan. 18; 88 Pac. 537.
Jones v. *Mount*, 166 Ind. 570; 77 N. E. 1089.
Monaghan v. *Mount*, 36 Ind. App. 188; 74 N. E. 579.
Coffinberry v. *Sun Oil Co.*, 68 Ohio State, 488; 67 N. E. 1069.

Sec. 5.—Contra.—After the decision by the Supreme Court of Pennsylvania, in *Kleppner* v. *Lemon*, 176 Pa. 502; 35 Atl. 109, that court in the cases of *Colgan* v. *Forest Oil Co.*, 194 Pa. 234; 45 Atl. 119; 75 Am. St. Rep. 695, and *Young* v. *Forest Oil Co.*, 194 Pa. 243; 45 Atl. 121, has practically overruled the principles laid down in that case. In these later cases the court held that in order to maintain jurisdiction in equity the lessor must allege and prove that lessee was fraudulently evading the implied covenants of his lease.

These later cases have been followed by the Supreme Court of Appeals of West Virginia in *Harness* v. *Eastern Oil Co.*, 49 W. Va. 232; 38 S. E. 662, analyzed under Chapter 18; and while that court has expressed dissatisfaction with the conclusions reached by the Pennsylvania Court and by its own former decisions, in *McGraw Oil & Gas Co.* v. *Kennedy*, 65 W. Va. 595; 64 S. E. 1027, the court adhered to the Pennsylvania rule and refused to modify its own former decisions by decreeing specific performance or cancellation of the lease for failure to develop and protect the lines. While that court under the pleadings and proofs in *McGraw Oil and Gas Co.* v. *Kennedy*, was fully justified in refusing specific performance or cancellation of the lease, nevertheless the courts which have adopted the rules laid down in Section 4, supra, have unquestionably properly solved the problem confronting the lessor where lessee has become vested by the discovery of oil or gas in paying quantities, with the right to take lessor's oil and gas, but has refused to sufficiently develop the property or properly protect the lines.

Sec. 6.—In *Kleppner* v. *Lemon*, 176 Pa. 502; 35 Atl. 109, analyzed under Chapter 18, John Kleppner executed an oil and gas lease to D. P. Lemon, who was the owner of leases on adjoining lands upon which were wells near the boundary of the leasehold in question, upon which only one well was drilled. Kleppner filed a bill in equity in the Court of Common Pleas, Allegheny County, for the specific performance of his lease by causing to be drilled additional wells for the development of the lands and for protection of lines. The court found that the lessee who owned the leases on adjoining lands, drilled the wells thereon with the express purpose of securing the oil from plaintiff's land through these wells. Upon these findings the court held that under the circumstances a court of equity would decree that unless the lessee drilled another well within a certain time specified, upon the leasehold estate of the plaintiff, his estate in the land should be deemed to be abandoned, except as to the well actually drilled on plaintiff's land, and a certain specified space around it. The case was appealed and the Supreme Court affirmed the decree. In the subsequent cases of *Colgan* v. *Forest Oil Co.*, and *Young* v. *Forest Oil Co.*, the principles which the Supreme Court upheld in *Kleppner* v. *Lemon* were for all practical purposes, except in that case, overruled. This case was again appealed to the Supreme Court of Pennsylvania (Section 7.) and re-argued and another opinion delivered. (Section 8.) The two appeals simply announced the law necessarily applicable to the execution of the decree affirmed upon first appeal.

Sec. 7.—In *Kleppner* v. *Lemon*, 197 Pa. 430; 47 Atl. 353 (Oct. 31, 1900), the syllabus is as follows:

"Where a lessee, in order to evade paying royalties under an oil and gas lease, instead of drilling a well and operating the land in accordance with his covenants, drills a well on adjoining property, which he controls, in such a way as to drain the oil and gas from under the leased land, and to render it impossible to determine how much oil was drawn from the lessor's land, the lessee will be liable to pay royalties to the lessor on all the oil produced by the well operated on the adjoining land.

The decree entered in *Kleppner* v. *Lemon*, 176 Pa. 502, slightly modifying the decree of the court below, did not annul or in any manner abridge the appointment of the master and examiner, whose duties were the same, subsequent to the decision as before the appeal on which it was based."

This was the second appeal. The Court of Common Pleas referred the cause to a master, and to the findings of the master exceptions were taken. The master found the facts substantially as follows: (1) The defendant never filed the declaration ordered by the Supreme Court, and never drilled a well at the point indicated by the court, or at any other place on the land, except the one he had drilled in the spring of 1895, and did nothing further to develop the land, except to pump the small well already mentioned. (2) The plaintiff did not himself do anything towards the further development of the land. (3) The well on the Stotler farm, adjoining plaintiff's property, and within 157 feet of plaintiff's line, which was owned by the defendant, and was known as Stotler Number 2, continued to produce oil from the time it was completed, in April or May, 1895, to May, 1897. No evidence was given as to amount of its production from the time it was completed to July 1, 1895. From July 1, 1895, to May, 1897, the total production was 22,182.62 barrels. Production and royalty paid to Stotler who owned the land upon which it was located, constantly diminished from 2358.72 barrels in August, 1895, to 374.16 barrels in April, 1897. The defendant owned and operated other producing wells on other tracts adjoining the land of the plaintiff, but no evidence as to their production was adduced. (4) No oil was brought to the surface on plaintiff's land except that produced from the well on the higher portion thereof, being the same mentioned in the second finding of the court. At the average price, the value of 1-8 of the oil produced by the well known as Stotler Number 2, owned by defendant, from July 1, 1895, to August 31, 1896, being thirty days after defendant could and should have had notice of the decree of the Supreme Court, computed at the average price of oil, was $3,088.33. (5) The plaintiffs land was oil producing land, and the well known as Stotler Number 2, and other wells in the vicinity, owned and operated by defendant, had continuously since April, 1895, to the time of the master's report, drawn oil from plaintiff's land, and thereby greatly diminished the supply of oil on plaintiff's land, to the great benefit of defendant, and to the great damage of plaintiff. (6) It was the duty of the defendant to have developed the plaintiff's land as soon as possible, after the lease to him, in June, 1894, and especially was it his duty to have sunk a well on plaintiff's land indicated by the Supreme Court, immediately after he struck oil at Stotler Number 2, in April, 1895; and that defendant wholly neglected and failed to perform his duty in that respect. (7) It had not been possible at any time since April, 1895, when oil was struck at Stotler Number 2, to ascertain the quantity which might have been produced from plaintiff's land, if defendant had complied with the obligation resting upon him. The failure of defendant to drill a well on the lower portion of plaintiff's tract, near the creek, and his continued operation of other producing wells on tracts near to and adjoining the tract of plaintiff, thereby draining oil from plaintiff's land, rendered it impossible to ascertain the quantity of oil which might have been obtained from plaintiff's land if he had developed it in good faith and according to the obligation resting upon him. The master concluded that there had been such a course of conduct on the part of the defendant, and such an intermixture of the productions of the plaintiff's tract of land with the production of the adjacent tracts of land as to prevent the possibility of ascertaining the production of each and separating them; that as a result John Kleppner, the plaintiff, was entitled to have and receive from D. P. Lemon, defendant, a royalty equal to 1-8 of the production of Stotler Number 2, from July 1, 1895, to August 31, 1896. The production of Stotler Number 2, between these dates was 18,803.66 barrels, and the royalty 1-8 barrels, 2,350.45 barrels, was of the value of $3,088.33, with interest from August 31, 1896. To these findings defendant excepted, which exceptions the Court of Common Pleas dismissed, and entered a decree in accordance with the recommendation of the master, in favor of the plaintiff, from which decree defendant appealed. The Supreme Court affirmed the decree.

Sec. 8.—In *Kleppner* v. *Lemon,* 198 Pa. 581; 48 Atl. 483 (March 25, 1901) upon re-hearing the syllabus is as follows:

"Where a lessee instead of drilling a well and operating the land in accordance with the lease, drills a well on adjoining property which he controls, in such a way as to drain the oil and gas from under the leased land, the measure of the lessor's damages is royalties on a portion of the oil produced through the well, ascertained by comparing it with the total production through the well, in the same proportion as the lessee's land within the circle drained bears to the whole area of drainage, the oil producing capacity of every part of the area being the same.

In such a case the rule as to wrongful confusion of goods should not be applied so as to give to the plaintiff royalties on all the oil produced through the well, it being possible approximately to determine the amount of oil drawn from the lessor's land."

After the decision in *Kleppner* v. *Lemon,* 197 Pa. 430, had been announced, the court ordered a re-argument, and on March 25, 1901, after re-argument, modified the decree of the Court of Common Pleas, the last paragraph of the opinion being as follows:

"The proper measure of damages was the market value of 1-8 of the oil taken from the plaintiff's land and brought to the surface through the Stotler well. The basis of the decree is the reasonable probability because of the nature of the soil, the proximity of the well to the plaintiff's land, and the effect produced on this well by the flow of other wells in the vicinity, that a part of the oil produced came from the plaintiff's land. As it came by drainage from the porous rock with 500 or 600 feet of the well, it is not more difficult to determine approximately the amount taken than it is to determine that any was taken. Presumably the drainage was uniform, and the plaintiff's land contributed a part which bore the some proportion to the whole amount produced, as his land within the circle drained, bore to the whole area of drainage. This proportion is about one to eight, and the defendant should not be held liable for more than 1-8 of the royalty, on the whole. The damages awarded by the decree are reduced to $444.91. With this modification the decree is affirmed at the cost of appellant.''

Sec. 9.—After the announcement of the principles as held by the Supreme Court of Pennsylvania in *Kleppner* v. *Lemon*, the suit of *Ammons* v. *South Penn Oil Company*, 47 W. Va. 610; 35 S. E. 1004, and of *Harness* v. *Eastern Oil Company*, 49 W. Va. 232; 38 S. E. 662, were decided by the Circuit Courts in West Virginia, granting relief to the lessors practically as was decreed lessor in *Kleppner* v. *Lemon*. The cases were each appealed by the lessees to the Supreme Court of West Virginia, which court reversed the Circuit Courts. Both cases were decided after the decision of the Pennsylvania Supreme Court on December 30, 1899, in the cases of *Colgan and Young* v. *Forest Oil Company*. The West Virginia Court of Appeals held, that the effect of the decisions in *Colgan and Young* v. *Forest Oil Company* was to overrule *Kleppner* v. *Lemon*. Syl. 3, *Harness* v. *Eastern Oil Company*, is:

"Lessors remedy for failure on part of lessee to further develop the leased premises, or to properly protect the lines thereof from drainage through wells on adjacent property, is ordinarily by action at law for damages.''

Sec. 10.—In the States of Illinois, Ohio, Texas and Kansas, and in the United States Circuit Court of Appeals for the Eighth Circuit, it has been held, that even after a lessee has discovered oil or gas in paying quantities and is in possession, operating the wells, but fails to either protect the lines from drainage by wells on adjoining territory or to make the developments either provided for by express covenant or that are necessary under the implied covenants of the lease, a court of equity will enforce the express or implied covenants of the lease for such protection and development or will cancel the lease as to the unprotected portions thereof.

Coffinberry v. *Sun Oil Co.*, 68 Ohio State 488; 67 N. E. 1069. *Powers* v. *Bridgeport Oil Co.*, 238 Ill. 397; 87 N. E. 381.

J. M. Guffey Petroleum Co. v. *Oliver,* (Tex.) 79 S. W. 884.
Buffalo Valley Oil etc. Co. v. *Jones,* 75 Kan. 18; 88 Pac. 537.
Brewster v. *Lanyon Zinc Co.,* 140 Fed. 801; 72 C. C. A. 213.

Sec. 11.—In *Colgan* v. *Forest Oil Company,* 194 Pa. 234; 45
Atl. 119, and *Young* v. *Forest Oil Company,* 194 Pa. 243; 45 Atl.
121, the Supreme Court of Pennsylvania again had under consideration the questions determined in *Kleppner* v. *Lemon,* as to the
jurisdiction in equity to specifically enforce the implied covenants of an oil and gas lease, and on December 30, 1899, in each
of these' cases denied relief to lessors who had proceeded by bill
in equity in the courts of Common Pleas of Pennsylvania for relief
upon the ground seemingly afforded them by the Supreme Court
in *Kleppner* v. *Lemon.* In each of these cases the Court of Common Pleas decreed specific performance, or in the alternative forfeiture and cancellation of the lease, except a specified area
around each well drilled. The cases were appealed and in *Colgan*
v. *Forest Oil Company,* the first point of the syllabus is as follows:

"A court of equity will not assume jurisdiction to enforce
specifically covenants in an oil and gas lease which are merely implied, and whose extent depends altogether on oral evidence of
opinion unless it appears that the lessee is fraudulently evading his
obligations to the lessor."

In *Young* v. *Forest Oil Company,* 194 Pa. 243; 45 Atl. 121, analyzed under Chapter 18, the second and third points of the syllabus are as follows:

"Where a lessee under an oil and gas lease has entered upon
land and sinks wells he is entitled, in determining whether he shall
sink additional wells, to follow his own judgment. If that is exercising good faith, a different opinion by the lessor, or the experts,
or the court, or all combined, is of no consequence, and will not
authorize a decree interfering with him.

A bill in equity will not lie by the lessor of an oil and gas
lease against the lessee or his assigns, to compel the latter to test
part of the leased land not yet drilled, or, upon his failure to do
so, to surrender the land to the lessor, unless it is shown that the
failure of the lessee to drill amounts to a fraud upon the rights
of the lessor."

In *Colgan* v. *Forest Oil Company,* 194 Pa. 234; 45 Atl. 119, analyzed under Chapter 18, the Supreme Court of Pennsylvania expressly disclaimed overruling *Kleppner* v. *Lemon,* and held that equity jurisdiction would be sustained where the lessee was fraudulently evading his obligations to the lessor.

Sec. 12.—In *Harris* v. *Ohio Oil Co.,* 57 Ohio St. 118; 48 N. E. 502 (November 23, 1897), William Snyder, on December 16, 1887, made an oil and gas lease to Carey C. Harris for a tract of land in Wood County, Ohio. The lessee entered upon the premises and drilled nine wells, and on February 22, 1889, assigned the lease to the Ohio Oil Company. The oil company drilled three additional wells, all the wells producing oil in paying quantities. On January 5, 1892, Harris purchased the lands from Snyder. Harris claimed that at least ten additional wells should be drilled on the land in order to develop the same, and protect the lines and notified the company to drill more wells or he should regard the lease as forfeited as to the undrilled parts of the land. The company refused to further develop, and Harris made preparations to drill a well on the undrilled parts of the land. Thereupon the company filed its petition and obtained a temporary injunction against the defendant. The defendant answered the petition alleging failure to drill additional wells as demanded by him. The Circuit Court rendered a decree quieting the title of the oil company in its exclusive right to drill for and produce oil and gas in and upon the lands. From this decree the defendant Harris appealed to the Supreme Court of Ohio, which court affirmed the decree and held, syl. 3:

"Under such a lease, the remedy for a breach of an implied covenant is not by way of forfeiture of the lease in whole or in part, but by an action for damages caused by such breach."

Sec. 13.—In *Monaghan* v. *Mount,* 36 Ind. App. 188; 74 N. E. 579 (May 23, 1905), the syllabus is as follows:

"1. Where a grantor of an oil lease conveyed only the right to drill for oil on his land, together with the oil and gas recovered, and the right to go on the land for such purposes only, subject to certain conditions, such right was an incorporeal hereditament incapable of livery of seisin, and therefore not subject to re-entry.

2.   Where a contract granting the right to drill for oil and gas on plaintiff's land required the grantee to complete a well in every period of 90 days from the completion of the first paying well, or to surrender the lease, except ten acres for each paying well, but the contract did not further describe such ten acres to be excepted out of 100 acres, covered by the lease, plaintiff, on a breach of the contract, was not entitled to arbitrarily set off such separate parcels and have his title quieted as to the balance.

3.   Where a grant of a right to mine for oil and gas provided that the grant was subject to certain conditions, one of which was that the grantee should complete an oil well in every period of 90 days from the completion of the first paying well, or surrender the lease, excepting ten acres for each paying well, the grantee's obligation to continue to drill wells on the land was fixed when the first well proved to be a paying well.

4.   Where a grant of a right to mine for oil required the grantees to complete a well in every period of 90 days from the completion of the first well, if it proved to be a paying well, or surrender the lease, excepting ten acres for each paying well, the grantees were bound, after the first well proved to be a paying well, either to continue to drill wells as provided, or themselves select tracts of ten acres each appurtenant to each well drilled.''

Patrick T. Monaghan instituted in the Circuit Court of Wells County an action against Harry Mount and others. In the second paragraph of the complaint it was shown: That plaintiff, on August 21, 1899, was the owner of certain real estate in Wells County, containing 80 acres, and also another tract containing 20 acres; that on that date he entered into a written agreement with one Day, who, on September 29, 1899, assigned the contract to Mount and others. This contract was in consideration of $100.00, and granted to J. C. O. Day all the oil and gas under said lands, the lessor to have 1-8 of the oil produced. The lease was made upon the following conditions: If gas only should be found in sufficient quantities to transport, lessee to pay $100 for the production of each and every well the gas from which was so transported; in case no well was completed within 60 days the grant should become void unless the lessee thereafter paid at the rate of one dollar in advance for each day such completion should be delayed. The lessee agreed to complete a well each ninety days from the completion of the first, if the first well should be a paying one, or surrender the lease, excepting ten acres for each paying well. Defendants, about December 16, 1899, entered upon the premises and drilled well Number 1, this well being 250 feet West and 193 feet South of the north-east

corner thereof. On January 4, 1900, defendants drilled well number 2, being 250 feet east and 93 feet south of the north-west corner
of the land; that on March 5, 1900, defendants drilled well number
3, this well being 250 feet (?) and 825 feet south of said well number 2; that on May 10, 1900, defendants drilled well number 4 being 250 feet east and 423 feet south of well number 3; that on September 10, 1900, defendants drilled well number 5 being 250 feet
west and 683 feet South of well Number 1; that all these wells were
paying wells, and had been operated and pumped ever since; that
no other wells had been drilled on the premises since the completion of well number 5; that it was agreed by the terms of the said
written contract that the lessee and assigns should complete a well
every ninety days from the completion of the first well, if the first
well was a paying well, or surrender the lease and all except ten
acres for each paying well; that the lessee and the defendants failed
to drill any wells on certain parts of the said realestate; (describing
such parts) that at least five wells should have been drilled on said
tracts pursuant to said contract to properly develop the real estate
for oil purposes; that said lease should be surrendered to the plaintiff and declared forfeited as to said undrilled portions. It was
further alleged that all of the tract of 100 acres contained and was
underlaid with valuable quantities of natural gas and oil, which
could be at all times since the execution of the contract easily
obtained in paying quantities; and that paying wells could have
been and still could be drilled and completed and operated on the
portions of the said tract of land described as not having been
developed. The plaintiff prayed that the contract be decreed
null and void as to the portions described as not having been
drilled; that defendants be ordered to surrender and forfeit the
same to the plaintiff and that a commissioner be appointed to cancel of record the contract as to the undrilled portions. Defendants demurred to the complaint, which demurrer the court sustained. Plaintiff appealed, and the Appellate Court affirmed the
judgment

Sec. 14.—In *Jones* v. *Mount*, 166 Ind. 570; 77 N. E. 1089 (May
29, 1906), the syllabus is as follows:

"A gas and oil lease of an eighty-acre tract contemplated that
eight wells might be drilled thereon and stipulated that 'on failure

to drill any of these wells within the specified time the second party (lessee) shall surrender the right to drill on all of these grants, except ten acres for each well drilled.' Only one well was drilled. Held, that the owner of the land could not, in a suit to quiet title, recover either the entire tract or all of it except a specific ten acres in a·square surrounding the well drilled, because of the uncertainty of the provisions compelling a surrender.''

William L. Jones, the owner of a tract of 80 acres of land, entered into a contract in writing with Jennings, under whom Mount and others claimed, for the exploration and development of the land for oil and gas. The contract contemplated that eight wells might be drilled. Only one well was drilled. The lease contained the following provision:

"On failure to drill any of these wells within the specified time the second party shall surrender the right to drill on all of this grant execept ten acres for each well drilled."

The lessor Jones, instituted suit against Mount and others in the Circuit Court of Wells County to quiet his title. The first paragraph of the complaint was the ordinary action to quiet title to the tract. The second paragraph averred that on September 29, 1899, plaintiff owned 80 acres of land, and leased the same to one Jennings for oil and gas purposes; that by this lease plaintiff granted to Jennings the oil and gas in the 80-acre tract, and the lease provided that if no well was completed within 40 days, the grant should be void unless the lessee should pay lessor one dollar per day in advance for the time thereafter such completion should be delayed. A second well to be drilled within 90 days from the completion of the first well, provided said first well was a paying well and so on until eight wells should be drilled, provided the preceding wells should be paying wells. The petition then averred the clause providing for the surrender of the right to drill, above quoted; that the lessee, on November 15, 1899, drilled a well which was being operated at the time of the suit, and was producing gas and oil in paying quantities; that no other well than the first well was drilled; and that if the wells had been drilled each would have been a paying well; that the ten acres belonging to this well, and in which the well was most

clearly located, in the center thereof, was described as follows:
(Here follows description of ten-acre tract.)   It was further
averred that all the eighty acres was underlaid with large and
valuable quantities of gas and oil, which could be, and since the
first well was drilled, could have been, easily obtained in paying
quantities and that paying wells could still be drilled thereon; that
on all sides on adjoining tracts eight wells had been drilled and
operated during the three past years, and that paying gas and
oil wells were still being drilled; that the wells on adjoining lands
were within 290 to 300 feet of the plaintiff's land; that defendants
had purposely and fraudulently failed and neglected to drill other
wells and had wilfully, fraudulently, and negligently permitted
large and valuable quantities of oil to be drained from plaintiff's
land, and to be pumped out of wells on adjoining lands, and were
still so permitting the gas and oil to be so drained to the great
damage of the plaintiff; that plaintiff had no remedy under the
terms of the contract to protect himself and the land from still
greater injury, and had no remedy except cancellation of the
lease, except as to the ten acres around the well drilled, in which
event he could lease the land to operators who would drill wells;
that he could not secure operators on the land as long as defendant's lease constituted a cloud on the undrilled portion; that by
virtue of the terms of the contract and plaintiff's election to terminate the same, except as to the ten acres, defendants had forfeited all rights in and under the contract to all the land except
the ten acres.   The petition then prayed that the lease be declared
forfeited as to the 70 acres, and that a commissioner be appointed
to cancel the contract as to the 70 acres.   The third paragraph of
the complaint averred that the plaintiff owned in fee the land described therein, to-wit, the 70 acres, and that defendants claimed
some right or interest in the same, which was without right and
unfounded, and which was a cloud upon and adverse to plaintiff's
title.   A demurrer to the second and third paragraphs of the
complaint were overruled, and defendants answered in two paragraphs; (1) general denial, and (2) former adjudication.   A demurrer to the second paragraph of the answer being overruled,
plaintiff replied in denial.   A trial was had by the court and
judgment for defendants.   Plaintiff appealed.   The case was decided by the Appellate Court of Indiana on June 22, 1905, where

the judgment of the Circuit Court was affirmed. Judge Robinson, in the opinion, said:

"It is not sought to cancel the entire contract. But the contract does not in itself, furnish any sufficient description of either the drilled or undrilled portion, nor does the evidence disclose any method by which the parties to the contract might determine these facts. The court is asked to quiet title to land, the certainty of the description of which is not shown by any evidence. This it cannot do."

The court cited in support of this conclusion:

Monaghan v. *Mount,* 74 N. E. 579.
Jones v. *Mount,* 30 Ind. App. 59; 63 N. E. 798.
Edens v. *Miller,* 147 Ind. 208; 46 N. E. 526.

The cause was transferred to the Indiana Supreme Court and the decision of the courts below were affirmed: citing,

Consumers Gas Trust Co. v. *Ink,* 163 Ind. 174; 71 N. E. 477.
Lafayette Gas Co. v. *Kelsey,* 164 Ind. 563; 74 N. E. 7.
Indiana, etc. Co. v. *Beales,* (Ind.) 76 N. E. 520.

Upon the question that what is a reasonable time, is a question of fact, and not one of law, and its determination largely depends upon the circumstances surrounding the particular case. and the means and ability of the person by whom the contract is to be performed, the court cited:

Consumers Gas Trust Co. v. *Littler,* 162 Ind. 320; 70 N. E. 363,
    and cases cited in the opinion.
Island Coal Co. v. *Combs,* 152 Ind. 379-387.
Randolph v. *Frick,* 57 Mo. App. 400; 53 N. E. 452.

Sec. 15.—In *Coffinberry* v. *Sun Oil Co.,* 68 Ohio 488; 67 N. E. 1069 (June 16, 1903), the syllabus is as follows:

"1. Where a petition filed by the lessor and owner of land, consisting of about 160 acres against the lessee or his assignee of the lease, on or about January 8, 1901, alleges in substance, that the plaintiff lessor, on or about May 29, 1890, executed said lease for a term of five years, and as much longer as oil or gas should be found in paying quantities, whereby the lessee obtained the exclusive right to produce oil and gas on the leased premises; and that the lease further provides that one well should be completed thereon within one year from the date of the lease, which condition has been complied with, and a paying well completed; and which further alleges that the lessee covenanted that, if the first well should be a paying well, he would drill, as soon thereafter as he could reasonably do so, a sufficient number of wells to fully develop said land, and deliver to the lessor one-sixth of all the oil produced therefrom; and that the lessee, after taking possession and completing the first well, assigned the lease to the defendant, who took possession and drilled two additional wells, the three being in one corner of the premises, and also drilled two wells on one side thereof, and all paying wells, and being completed prior to July, 1898; and, further, that defendant had ever since refused, and still refuses to further drill and develop or test said lands for oil and gas, or permit the plaintiff's lessor, or anyone for him, to do so; and which further alleges that the defendant neglects, to protect the exterior lines of the leased premises from several producing oil wells, already drilled and in operation on lands of others adjoining lands of the plaintiff; and that to properly develop the leased premises at least twenty-six additional wells, should be drilled thereon, which could have been done within three years from the date of the lease; and that owing to the migratory nature of oil, and the impossibility of proving the presence and amount of oil in the land, except by drilling, plaintiff has no adequate remedy at law—such petition states a good cause of action for the cancellation of the lease as to the undrilled portions of the premises, and it is error to sustain a general demurrer thereto, and dismiss the petition of the plaintiff.

2. Upon a cause of action containing such facts, followed by a prayer for specific performance, and a further prayer, in the alternative, 'for such other and further relief in the premises as equity and good conscience require' a court of equity may decree the cancellation of the lease as to the undrilled portions of the premises in lieu of specific performance.''

Henry D. Coffinberry, on January 8, 1901, filed an amended petition against the Sun Oil Company, in the Court of Common Pleas of Wood County, Ohio, containing in substance the allegations mentioned in the first paragraph of the syllabus. The defendant demurred generally to the petition, which demurrer was sustained by the Court of Common Pleas. On appeal to the Circuit Court the demurrer was sustained and the amended petition dismissed. The case was then appealed to the Supreme Court, and that court reversed the lower courts.

LESSEE'S REMEDY AND DEFENSE.

Sec. 16.—Where suit in equity is brought by lessor for specific performance or cancellation of the lease for default in developments or failure to protect lines, lessee may defeat the action by alleging and proving in defense that his management of the premises is founded upon good, honest business judgment; that whether there should be additional wells drilled is a question of opinion; and that it is doubtful whether the drilling of additional wells would be profitable to lessee.   In the absence of fraud, and where lessee's management of the lease is founded upon good honest business judgment, a court of equity will not, after lessee has entered and discovered oil or gas in paying quantities and is operating the wells and delivering the royalties or paying the gas rental, decree specific performance or forfeiture of the lease.

> *Harness* v. *Eastern Oil Co.,* 49 W. Va. 232; 38 S. E. 662.
> *Ammons* v. *South Penn Oil Co.,* 47 W. Va. 610; 35 S. E. 1004.
> *Young* v. *Forest Oil Co.,* 194 Pa. 243; 45 Atl. 121.
> *Colgan* v. *Forest Oil Co.,* 194 Pa. 234; 45 Atl. 119; 75 Am. St.
>   Rep. 695.
> *Kellar* v. *Craig,* 126 Fed. 630; 61 C. C. A. 366.
> *McGraw Oil Co.* v. *Kennedy,* 65 W. Va. 599; 64 S. E. 1027.
> *Doddridge County Oil Co.* v. *Smith,* 154 Fed. 970. (C. C. N.
>   D. W. Va.)

CHAPTER 20.

REMEDIES AT LAW FOR BREACHES BY LESSEE OF IMPLIED COVENANTS OF THE OIL AND GAS LEASE.

Sec. 1.—The remedy of a lessor for a breach of the implied covenants to reasonably operate the premises and protect the lines from drainage is ordinarily by action at law for the recovery of damages for breach of such covenants.

> *Bradford Oil Co.* v. *Blair,* 113 Pa. 83; 4 Atl. 218.
> *Harris* v. *Ohio Oil Co.,* 57 Ohio St. 118; 48 N. E. 502.
> *Harness* v. *Eastern Oil Co.,* 48 W. Va. 232; 38 S. E. 662.
> *Ammons* v. *South Penn Oil Co.,* 47 W. Va. 610; 35 S. E. 1004.

Core v. *New York Petroleum Co.*, 52 W. Va. 276; 43 S. E. 128.
McGraw Oil Co. v. *Kennedy*, 65 W. Va. 595; 64 S. E. Op. 1029.
Duffield v. *Rosenzweig*, 150 Pa. 543; 24 Atl. 705.
Doddridge Oil Co. v. *Smith*, 154 Fed. 970.
Kellar v. *Craig*, 126 Fed. 630; 61 C. C. A. 366.
J. M. Guffey Petroleum Co. v. *Chaison Town Site Co.*, (Tex.
    Civ. App.) 107 S. W. 609.
Allegheny Oil Co v. *Snyder*, 106 Fed. 764; 45 C. C. A. 60.

Sec. 2.—The remedy of a lessor for breaches of the covenants,
either express or implied, for further developments or for the
protection of lines is ordinarily by an action at law for damages
against lessee or his assignee. After oil or gas has been discovered
in paying quantities by a lessee it becomes his duty to reasonably
develop the premises demised, and to protect the lines from drainage through wells on adjoining land whether there is in the lease
an express covenant to do so, or not. After the discovery of oil
or gas in paying quantities the right to produce them vests in the
lessee and ordinarily courts of equity will not cancel the lease or
decree specific performance for failure on the part of the lessee to
reasonably develop the property or protect the lines. Where the
lessee is fraudulently endeavoring to evade the obligations imposed upon him as to development and protection of lines either
by the express covenants of the lease or by implication a court
of equity will, upon proof of such fraud, require additional developments and protection of lines, and in default thereof will
cancel the lease, as to the undeveloped or unprotected portions.

Sec. 3.—In *Bradford Oil Co.* v. *Blair*, 113 Pa. 83; 4 Atl. 218
(May 31, 1886) the syllabus is as follows:

"1. A. leased his farm to B. to explore for and produce oil
at a royalty of one-eighth of the production. The lease contained
the following covenants; 'To continue with due diligence, and without delay, to prosecute the business to success or abandonment,
and if successful, to prosecute the same without interruption for
the common benefit of the parties.' B. assigned an interest in said
lease to C. and D, and they, with B. assigned it to E. Two wells
were bored on the farm, both of which were producing wells. E.
refused to bore any other wells. In an action of covenant brought
by A. against E. for breach of the covenant above quoted, *Held*,
that said covenant was not the personal covenant of B. but a
covenant that ran with the land, and therefore bound E.

2. It was not error for the court to instruct the jury, that the damages for the breach of said covenant would be found as follows: Ascertain how much more oil the plaintiff ought to have received than he actually did receive, and the value of it during the time when it should have been delivered to him; from this deduct the cost of producing what ought to have been produced at the time, under the circumstances, and with the appliances then known; and add to this remainder the interest on it from the time when the oil ought to have been produced to the present time, and this will be the measure of damages sustained by the plaintiff."

On July 17, 1875, James E. Blair leased to L. G. Peck his farm in McKean County, Pennsylvania, containing 150 acres, for oil purposes at a one-eighth royalty. On July 27, 1876, Peck assigned to W. C. Chambers the undivided one-half, and to J. T. Jones the undivided one-fourth interest. On April 20, 1876 the Bradford Oil Company was organized and on April 25, 1876, Peck, Chambers and Jones assigned the lease to the said company. The lease contained, among other things, a covenant on the part of Peck that he would "continue with due diligence and without delay to prosecute the business to success or abandonment, and if successful to prosecute the same without interruption for the common benefit of the parties aforesaid." Peck, Jones and Chambers went upon the farm in the summer of 1875, and drilled one well which was completed about December 1st of that year. The Bradford Oil Company entered into possession in the Spring of 1876 and drilled one well, which was completed about August 1st of that year. The two wells were fair producers. The Bradford Oil Company became the owner of oil rights in lands upon all but one side of the Blair farm, and drilled wells upon said surrounding lands, all of which wells produced oil. The company did not drill any other wells on the Blair farm until in October, 1878. Blair repeatedly notified the company to go on and prosecute the business as required by the lease. Blair instituted in the Court of Common Pleas of McKean County an action of covenant against the Bradford Oil Company to recover damages for breach of the covenant aforesaid, to which suit the defendant company pleaded, among other things, covenants performed. There was evidence adduced upon the trial of the action to show that proper development of the farm required the drilling of a well to every five acres of land, and that within every forty days with only one set of drilling tools a well could be completed. There was also evidence adduced to show that during two years in which the farm was not drilled the defendant drilled several wells on the land surrounding the Blair farm, near enough to the lines to drain oil from it to some extent. The defendant claimed that the covenant to prosecute the business of developing and removing the oil from the farm without interruption for the common benefit of the lessor and the lessee was, under the circumstances, complied with by the drilling of one well in 1875, and another in 1876. A verdict for the plaintiff in the sum of $7,500.00 was returned by the jury, and judgment rendered thereon by the court. From this judgment the defendant appealed to the Supreme Court where the judgment was affirmed, the Court rendering the following opinion:

"Per Curiam. The agreement imposed on the company an obligation to use due diligence in operating on the premises. That was necessary for the common benefit of both parties. We do not think damages for not securing flowing oil are to be ascertained exactly as if it were a stationary mineral.

If oil be not utilized at a proper time it may be lost forever by reason of others operating nearby. Not so the stationary mineral. It remains for future development. While there is some difficulty in the way the damages were ascertained in this case, yet no better or more accurate manner is pointed out.

Looking at the whole case we see no sufficient cause to justify a reversal of the judgment.

Sec. 4.—In *Harris* v. *Ohio Oil Co.*, 57 Ohio St. 118; 48 N. E. 502, analyzed under Chapter 18, the first and third points of the syllabus are as follows:

"1. Where lands are granted, demised and let for the purpose and with the exclusive right of drilling and operating for oil and gas, in consideration that a certain part of the oil produced should be delivered to the lessor, the lease providing that one well should be completed within six months, and in default the lease to be null and void, and the lease being silent as to the drilling of other wells for the protection of lines, *Held*, that in such a lease there is an implied covenant on part of the lessee that he will drill and operate such number of oil wells on the land as would be ordinarily required for the production of oil contained in, such lands, and afford ordinary protection to the lines.

3. Under such lease, the remedy for a breach of an implied covenant is not by way of forfeiture of the lease in whole or in part, but by an action for damages caused by such breach.''

The last paragraph of the opinion is as follows:

"It is strongly urged that it is inequitable for the lessee to hold on to his lease and still fail to so operate the premises as to produce reasonable results, and that he should either reasonably operate the premises or get off and permit his lease to be forfeited. The answer is, that while there is an implied covenant to reasonably operate the premises, there is no implied or express covenant to get off and forfeit his lease for a breach of such covenant. The lease in question provides for a forfeiture for failure to comply with the conditions, or to pay the cash consideration in the lease mentioned, at the time and in the manner agreed; but the implied covenant to reasonably operate the premises, is not mentioned in the lease, and is therefore not included in the causes of forfeiture. Some causes of forfeiture being expressly mentioned none other can be implied. *McKnight* v. *Kreutz*, 51 Pa. St. 232. The remedy for a breach of the implied covenants to reasonably operate the premises is therefore not by way of forfeiture of the lease, in whole or in part, but must be sought in a proper action for breach of such covenant. *Blair* v. *Peck*, 1 Penny, 247. As to the rule of damages in such cases, see *Oil Co.* v. *Blair*, 113 Pa. St. 83; 4 Atl. 218."

Sec. 5.—In *Harness* v. *Eastern Oil Co.*, 49 W. Va. 232; 38 S. E. 662, analyzed under Chapter 18, the third point of the syllabus is as follows:

"3. Lessor's remedy for failure on part of lessee to further develop the leased premises, or to properly protect the lines thereof from drainage through wells on adjacent property is ordinarily by action at law for damages."

Sec. 6.—In *Ammons* v. *South Penn Oil Co.*, 47 W. Va. 610; 35 S. E. 1004 (March 31, 1900) syl. 2 is as follows:

"S. purchased of A. seven-eights of the undivided one-half interest of A. in the oil in and under two hundred and forty-three acres of land and paid three hundred dollars cash therefor; and, as part of the terms and conditions of sale, S. was to begin to operate, mine and bore for oil and gas within and under said tract of land, free of cost to A. within sixty days, and complete one well thereon in one year, unavoidable delays and accidents excepted, and, if oil be found thereon in paying quantities, then, after the said first well was completed thereon, S. should immediately commence and drill other wells thereon as should seem necessary to protect the oil and gas in and under the said tract of land, and should also deliver as royalty to the credit of A. free of cost to him, the one-half of the one-eighth of all the oil produced and saved from the said land, in pipelines or tanks, and pay to him the one-half of three hundred dollars per year for the gas from each and every well drilled thereon producing gas, the product from which should be marketed. *Held,* that the remedy for violation of said conditions of the sale is not by way of forfeiture of the right of S. to bore or drill for oil on the land, or any part of it, but by an action or proceeding for damages caused by such breach.''

On May 27, 1889, Milton A. Ammons and wife leased a tract of 243 acres of land in Monogalia County, West Virginia, together with other lands, making in the aggregate 300 acres, for oil and gas purposes to Charles J. Ford for the term of five years from date, and as much longer as oil or gas should be found in paying quantities. On July 17, 1889, Ford assigned the lease to the South Penn Oil Company. An interest in the land was outstanding in the infant children of Armina Ammons. By proceedings in the Circuit Court, as provided for by statute, these infants interests were sold under a decree for the sum of $300.00 in cash, to the South Penn Oil Company, and a commissioner was appointed to convey and did convey the same to said company, the conveyance containing the conditions set forth in the second point of the syllabus. On August 28, 1895, the infants whose interest was so sold, by their next friend instituted a suit in chancery and filed therein their bill against the South Penn Oil Company, wherein they alleged that the said tract of land was located in what was known as the Doll's Run and Mannington Oil Field; that the oil was found in said land in a porous sand rock strata; that at the time their interests were sold to the defendant the land was practically tested and was very valuable oil territory; That if it had been properly and fairly developed and the oil and gas thereunder properly and fairly protected by the drilling of such wells as seemed to be and were necessary their interests so sold would have been worth several hundred thousand dollars for oil purposes; that the defendant oil company was largely interested and engaged in the oil business in said field and owned leases for oil and gas purposes on many thousands of acres in the belt, and near thereto; that said defendant owned leases for oil and gas purposes on all the lands adjoining said tract, and had developed, or partially developed, said adjoining territory and leases; and that owing to the nature and porous character of the oil producing sand-

rock in that field a well drilled to that rock would drain and produce the oil from a considerable distance around or away from
the place where the well was drilled; that a number of wells
drilled around and close to said tract of land would drain the oil
and gas, or the greater part thereof, from said tract, and leave
t practically valueless for oil purposes unless wells were drilled
and operated on such tract in such proximity to the lines thereof
as would protect the oil and gas under the same. The bill alleged
hat the defendant had drilled wells on the adjoining tracts near
he line and had not drilled wells on the tract opposite thereto to
protect the lines. The bill further alleged that there had not been
a sufficient number of wells drilled within the time to properly develop the lands as provided for by the terms of the sale. The
plaintiffs claimed $25,000 damages for breaches of the covenants
by reason of the facts stated in their bill. The defendants demurred to the plaintiff's bill, and also answered denying the allegations as to failure to protect lines and failure to develop. The
Circuit Court entered a decree upon final hearing whereby the
defendant oil company was enjoined from further operations upon
certain portions of the land which it had not drilled at the date
of the institution of the suit, in case said company failed within
ten days from the entry of the decree to file in the cause a declaration stipulating that it would begin to drill within twenty days a
well upon each of the said undrilled portions of the land, and thereafter prosecute and complete such wells with all reasonable diligence. From this decree the oil company appealed to the Court
of Appeals where the decree of the Circuit Court was reversed.

Sec. 7.—In *Core* v. *New York Petroleum Co.*, 52 W. Va. 276;
3 S. E. 128, (December 13, 1902) the syllabus is as follows:

"1. To work a forfeiture of an oil and gas lease there must
be a breach of a condition or covenant expressed in the lease; ordinarily a breach of an implied covenant will not work a forfeiture
of the lease.
2. Where in such lease causes of forfeiture are specified, it
not to be inferred that there are other causes of forfeiture not
declared in the lease to be such.
3. Under such a lease the remedy for a breach of an implied
covenant is ordinarily not by way of forfeiture of the lease, in
whole or in part, but by an action for damages caused by such
breach."

On July 27, 1889, Bion L. Core leased to Joseph S. Brown a tract of 77 acres of land for oil and gas purposes for a term of two years from the date, and so long thereafter as oil or gas should continue to be found in paying quantities, the lessee, his heirs or assigns to deliver in the pipelines one-eighth of the oil and a yearly rental of $200.00 for each gas well. The lease contained the following provision:

"The party of the second part agrees to, and within one month from this date, commence a test well for gas and oil in the vicinity of this farm, and complete the same within two months thereafter, unavoidable accidents and delays excepted. Said second party to commence and drill a well on the within described land within nine months after the completion of the said test well, and to prosecute said drilling with reasonable diligence to its completion; he is also to pay to first party a monthly rental of ten dollars in advance until said drilling is commenced. Failure of the party of the second part to make said payment will render this lease null and void."

This lease, together with other property, became the property by assignment of the New York Petroleum Company. Under the lease two wells were completed in the early part of 1891, which wells when completed produced considerable quantities of oil but had run down in their production to a very small amount at the time of the bringing of the suit. At September Rules, 1898, the original lessor, B. L. Core, filed his bill in the Circuit Court of Pleasants County against the New York Petroleum Company and others, being the different assignors of the Petroleum Company, claiming damages in the amount of $10,000, based upon the alleged failure and neglect of the said company to develop the property under the lease by drilling other wells, and by not protecting the lines of the same and by careless operations, and holding the lease while the land was being drained through wells on adjoining lands; and praying for the cancellation of the lease in case it should be found that oil was not being produced in paying quantities, and for damages for the negligent and careless manner of operating said wells and for the non-production and drainage of said premises; and in case it should be ascertained that oil was being produced in paying quantities, then for a decree that unless the defendant, New York Petroleum Company should commence

rithin a reasonable time, to be fixed by the court, the drilling of
ther wells thereon for oil and gas in sufficient number to properly
levelop and protect the said land from drainage, then so much of
aid leasehold should be cancelled and annulled as should not be
iecessary to protect the two wells already on the land. The de-
endant oil company demurred to the bill, which demurrer was
verruled, and then answered. Depositions were taken by plaintiff
nd defendant oil company, and on June 20, 1900, the Circuit Court
scertained that the lease had been executed by the plaintiff for
he term of two years, and so long thereafter as oil or gas should
e found in paying quantities; that the lease had been executed
or the purpose of having the land developed for oil and gas; that
he covenants in the lease had not been complied with on the part
f the lessee and those holding under him; and that sufficient
rells had not been drilled on the land to develop the same. The
ecree then gave to the New York Petroleum Company five acres
round each well drilled, and then being operated, and as to the
esidue of the tract provided that unless the said defendant com-
any should commence within thirty days the drilling of other and
urther wells on the remainder of said 77 acre tract of land, and
hould prosecute the drilling of said wells to completion with all
ue diligence, the remainder of the 77 acres should become entire-
: free from the effect of the lease of July 27, 1899, and be can-
elled as to the remaining tract and surrendered to the plaintiff;
nd that he should, upon failure of defendant to comply with the
ecree, hold the same, free from any claim of the defendants, or any
f them. From this decree the petroleum company appealed to
ie Court of Appeals, and that court reversed the decree. The
ist paragraph of the opinion in this case is as follows:

"In the opinion of the court in *Colgan* v. *Oil Co.*, it is said:
The jurisdiction of equity in a similar case was, however, sus-
iined in *Kleppner* v. *Lemon*, 176 Pa. 502, and we do not now pro-
ose to question it. But that decision was on the ground of fraud,
ie majority of the court being of opinion that the defendant was
·audulently evading his obligations to plaintiff while draining
ie oil from plaintiff's land through wells on adjacent terri
iry. The findings show, says Williams, J., that it is the express
urpose of the defendant to secure Kleppner's oil through
is wells on the Garlack and Stotler tracts of land. The basis
ecessary to sustain the bill, therefore, is fraud, and that, of

- course, must be affirmatively and clearly proved:' From which it
will be seen that while the court apparently sustained the decision in the Kleppner case, in order to do so it bases the jurisdiction
of the court wholly on the question of fraud. In effect, the case
of *Kleppner* v. *Lemon,* by these two cases of Colgan and of *Young*
v. *Oil Co.,* in 194 Pa. St. is overruled, especially in so far as it could
affect the case at Bar. 'Courts will not assume to make a contract
for the parties which they did not choose to make themselves.'
Beach on Mod. L. Contracts, S 707; Co. of *Morgan* v. *Allen,* 103
U. S. 498 (515). The decree is reversed and the bill dismissed.''

Sec. 8.—In *McGraw Oil and Gas Co.* v. *Kennedy,* 65 W. Va.
531; 64 S. E. 1027, analyzed under Chapter 18, syl. 1 is as follows:

"1. A lease for oil and gas is for five years, 'and as long
thereafter as oil or gas or either of them is produced by the
party of the second part.' The lessor cannot forfeit it because
he thinks the gas is not in paying quantities; the lessee claiming that it is, and willing to pay the sum stipulated for the well.
It is for the lessee to say whether the gas is in paying quantities,
acting in good faith.''

Judge Brannon, delivering the opinion in this case, speaking
of the inadequate remedy which the lessor has in a proceeding at
law against the lessee for failure to develop the property, says:

"We have frequently held that, where there is no express
condition requiring additional wells, but only an implied one,
this will not forfeit. *Core* v. *Petroleum Co.,* 52 W. Va. 276; 43 S.
E. 128. *Kellar* v. *Craig,* 126 Fed. 630; 61 C. C. A. 366. I have
never been reconciled to the doctrine that for failure to drill
additional wells the lessor must sue at law for damages, and
equity will not cancel, unless for draining from nearby territory
and thus exhaust oil in the leasehold involved. I have asked:
How many actions must the landowner bring? How can damages
be measured? How can we see into the depths of the earth?
But it has been so held. The reason is that equity will not, as a
rule, enforce a forfeiture of an estate. It will not especially insert such a clause when the parties have not inserted it, especially when they did insert forfeiture for failure to drill or pay
commutation, but did not insert forfeiture for failure to drill additional wells.''

Sec. 9.—In *Duffield* v. *Rosenzweig,* 150 Pa. 543; 24 Atl. 705,
anaylzed under Chapter 10, the syllabus is as follows:

"Where a lease of land for oil mining purposes, with the exclusive right of boring for oil thereon, restricts the operations to certain sites, and the lessor or his subsequent grantee drills wells on the leasehold outside of the sites designated, the lessee's measure of damages is the difference in value of the leasehold before and after the injury was committed; *Duffield* v. *Rosenzweig*, 144 Pa. 520.

The damages cannot be estimated by the amount of oil which the new wells might drain from the old wells, the proof of damages u on this basis being impracticable in the nature of the case." P

This case was before in the Supreme Court of Pennsylvania, and is reported in 144 Pa. 520. The facts upon which this appeal was determined were substantially as follows: Duffield, the plaintiff, was the owner of an oil lease known as the Pratt lease, dated June 20, 1882, for the term of fifteen years, covering some 30 acres of land; the sites where the lessee was to bore for oil were to be restricted; a mill-yard connected with a saw-mill near the center of the tract containing some two acres was reserved from mining operations; Duffield the lessee, drilled wells on lands adjoining the mill-yard lot; Rosenzweig acquired the title of the lessor and then conveyed his interest in the mill-yard lot to Hue and others for oil mining purposes, who drilled three wells on the mill lot in the Spring of 1886. On November 21, 1886, Duffield claiming that the mill lot was included in his lease but was excepted as to actual mining operations, instituted an action of trespass against Rosenzweig, the lessor of Hue and others, and obtained judgment. Defendants appealed to the Supreme Court of Pennsylvania, and that court affirmed the judgment in a per curiam opinion and held the law to be as stated in the syllabus.

Sec. 10.—In *J. M. Guffey Petroleum Co.* v. *Chaison Town Site Co.*, (Tex. Civ. App.) 107 S. W. 609, (Jan. 17, 1908), syls. 1-2 are as follows:

"1. The lessee of oil land agreed to properly develop the land and agreed to give the lessor a specified royalty. Subsequently a new agreement was entered into between the lessor and lessee providing for the operation of the only well on the property (naming it) and limiting it to 1-6 of the output of the well's capacity on account of the low basis and inadquate storage facilities. *Held,* that though the instrument referred to the one well it was intended to limit production upon the whole of the leased premises, and the lessor waived her right to require the lessee to produce larger amounts therefrom in the absence of conditions rendering it necessary for the protection of the lease from drainage by wells on adjoining territory.

2.   Though an oil lease does not specify the number of wells that the lessee shall sink and does not absolutely require the sinking of offset wells to protect the land from drainage, yet from the nature of the contract an implied obligation rests on the lessee to use reasonable diligence to protect the property, which binds him to sink as many wells as the exercise of due diligence and care should suggest to an ordinarily prudent person engaged in the same undertaking under the same circumstances.''

The Chaison Town Site Company instituted an action against the J. M. Guffey Petroleum Company in the District Court of Jefferson County, Texas, to recover damages for the alleged failure of the Guffey Company to use due diligence in the development of a tract of 5.27 acres of oil land belonging to the plaintiff and held by defendant under an oil lease, and for failure to use reasonable care to protect said leased property from drainage by wells operated on adjoining tracts of land. Judgment was rendered for plaintiff and defendant appealed. Upon the question of the protection of the property from drainage, Pleasants, Chief Justice, in the opinion, says:

"Of course, if it became necessary, after the execution of this contract, in order to protect the lease from drainage by wells on adjoining tracts, to take more than 20,000 barrels per month from this well, or to sink other wells, said contract did not relieve appellant of his duty; under the evidence before them the jury might have found that if other wells had been sunk and operated upon the property during the year from March 1, 1902, to March 1, 1903, a much larger quantity of oil than that actually produced by appellant would have been produced from said property, and the charges complained of authorized them to find damages for this deficit, or whether or not the increased production during said time was necessary to reasonably protect the property from drainage by outside wells."

It appeared from the evidence that a contract had been entered into between the parties by which the production from one

well was limited to 1-6 of the well's actual capacity on account of
the low basis and inadequate storage facilities. A new trial was
granted, except as to the judgment in favor of the plaintiff for
$860.00, because of the making of the agreement by which the les-
sor limited the output of the production of the well to 1-6; but the
court held that the plaintiff had a right to recover under the evi
dence for the actual damages sustained by failure to drill other
wells for the protection of the property.

Sec. 11.—In *Allegheny Oil Co.* v. *Snyder*, 106 Fed. 764; 45 C.
C. A. 60, analyzed under Chapter 4, the second paragraph of the
headnote is as follows:

"Under the decisions of the Supreme Court of Ohio relating
to the construction of oil and gas leases, which have established
a rule of property in that state such leases carry an implied
covenant on the part of the lessee that he will drill and operate
such number of wells on the premises as would ordinarily be required to develop their production and to afford ordinary protection to the lines; and the lessor may enforce such covenant
by action, and is not obliged to permit the lessee to hold the land
indefinitely for speculative purposes, notwithstanding the absence
of any express limitation in the lease."

The lease provided that in case no well should be drilled on
the premises within two years from the date of the lease it should
become null and void unless the lessee should pay for further delay
at the rate of One Dollar per acre per year. No well having been
drilled within the two years the landowner made a second lease,
and in a controversy between the two lessees the court held, that
the first lease had been forfeited.

Sec. 12.—In *McKnight* v. *Manufacturers' Nat. Gas. Co.*, 146
Pa. 185; 23 Atl. 164; 28 Am. St. Rep. 790, anaylzed under Chapter
11, syl. 3 is as follows:

"In an action against a lessee who had drilled one paying
gas well upon the premises, for not putting down other wells to
protect the territory against the effect of operations on adjoining land, it was error to charge that a failure to drill such well
was a breach of an implied covenant imposing a liability in
damages, in the absence of a reasonable excuse therefor."

The plaintiff asked the Court to give the following instruction to the jury:

"That having commenced operations on this lease, the lessee and the defendant under it were bound to prosecute the business of developing, drilling for gas or oil, and securing the same, without interruption, for the common benefit of the parties."

The court modified this instruction by adding thereto; "Unless the evidence shows that there was a reasonable excuse for such interruption." The Supreme Court of Pennsylvania held this instruction to be error for the reason that the suit was concerning the development of gas territory, and not oil territory; and that the same rule could not be applied in the same manner to a gas lease that might be applied to a lease for the production of oil.

Sec. 13.—In *Kellar* v. *Craig*, 126 Fed. 630; 61 C. C. A. 366, analyzed under Chapter 18, the third and fifth paragraphs of the headnotes are as follows:

"3. In an oil and gas lease a covenant to 'protect the lines and to 'well develop' the land is implied, and the fact that such covenants are expressed in the same general words adds nothing to the lessee's obligation, and the lease cannot be forfeited for a breach of such covenants where he has in good faith done what in his judgment was required to comply therewith.
5. A court will not decree a forfeiture of an oil lease on the ground that the lessee has abandoned development of the land, where up to the time of the filing of the bill he has drilled the full number of wells specifically required by the lease, and is still in possession of and operating the same."

Sec. 14.—In *Doddridge County Oil and Gas Co.* v. *Smith*, 154 Fed. 970, (C. C. N. D. W. Va.) anaylzed under Chapter 18, the fifth paragraph of the headnote is as follows:

"Where an owner leases land for oil and gas purposes, his remedy for failure on the part of the lessee to further develop the leased premises or to properly protect the lines from drainage through wells on adjacent property is ordinarily by action at law for damages, and not by way of forfeiture of the lease."

Sec. 15.—The general rule deducible from the decisions of courts of last resort in the States of Pennsylvania, West Virginia and Ohio, and Federal Courts for these States is that where a lessee under the ordinary oil and gas lease enters and discovers oil or gas in paying quantities and delivers to lessor his royalties in oil, or if gas only is found the gas rental, the lessor's remedy for failure on the part of lessee to further develop the leased premises or to properly protect the lines from drainage through wells on adjoining property is ordinarily by action at law for damages.

> *Colgan* v. *Forest Oil Co.*, 194 Pa. 234; 45 Atl. 119; 75 Am. St. Rep. 695.
> *Young* v. *Forest Oil Co.*, 194 Pa. 243; 45 Atl. 121.
> *Ammons* v. *South Penn Oil Co.*, 47 W. Va. 610; 35 S. E. 1004.
> *Harness* v. *Eastern Oil Co.*, 49 W. Va. 232; 38 S. E. 622.
> *McGraw Oil and Gas Co.* v. *Kennedy*, 65 W. Va. 599; 64 S. E. 1027.
> *Kellar* v. *Craig*, 126 Fed. 630; 61 C. C. A. 366.
> *Harris* v. *Oil Co.*, 57 Ohio State, 118; 48 N. E. 502.
> *Doddridge Oil and Gas Co.* v. *Smith*, 154 Fed. 970.
> *McKnight* v. *Manufacturers Nat. Gas Co.*, 146 Pa. 185; 23 Atl. 164; 28 Am. St. Rep. 790.
> *Core* v. *Petroleum Co.*, 52 W. Va. 275; 43 S. E. 128. syl. 1.

CHAPTER 21.

WAIVER OF FORFEITURE OF OIL AND GAS LEASE.

Sec. 1.—Where in an oil and gas lease there is a clause providing that it shall be void if a well is not commenced or completed within a specified time or in lieu thereof commutation money paid for delay, and the lessor either expressly or by his conduct waives the forfeiture or acquiesces in the lessee's failure to commence or complete the well, or pay the commutation money, he will be precluded from enforcing the forfeiture. The lessor by acquiescence in delays either in beginning explorations or in making payments of commutation money for delay as provided by the lease, waives the right to forfeit the lease therefor.

> *Duffield* v. *Hue*, 129 Pa. 94; 18 Atl. 566.

Westmoreland etc. Gas Co. v. *DeWitt*, 130 Pa. 235; 18 Atl.
724; 5 L. R. A. 731. Syls. 7-8.
Steiner v. *Marks*, 172 Pa. 400; 33 Atl. 695, Syl. 1.
Consumers Gas Trust Co. v. *Ink*, 163 Ind. 174; 71 N. E. 477.
Consumers Gas Trust Co. v. *Howard*, 163 Ind. 170; 71 N. E.
493.
Consumers Gas Trust Co. v. *Worth*, 163 Ind. 141; 71 N. E.
489.
Consumers Gas Trust Co. v. *Littler*, 163 Ind. 320; 70 N. E.
363.
Vendocia Oil etc. Co. v. *Robinson*, 71 Ohio St. 302; 73 N. E.
222.
Pyle v. *Henderson*, 65 W. Va. 39; 63 S. E. 762.
Hukill v. *Myers*, 36 W. Va. 639; 15 S. E. 151.
Thompson v. *Christy*, 138 Pa. 230; 20 Atl. 924.
Lynch v. *Versailles Fuel etc. Co.*, 165 Pa. 518; 30 Atl. 984.
Monarch Oil etc. Co. v. *Richardson*, 30 Ky. L. Rep. 824; 99
S. W. 668.
Kansas Nat. Gas Co. v. *Harris*, 79 Kan. 167; 100 Pac. 72.
Campbell v. *Rock Oil Co.*, 80 C. C. A. 467; 151 Fed. 191.
Duntley v. *Anderson*, 94 C. C. A. 647; 169 Fed. 391.

Sec. 2.—It is usual in oil and gas leases to insert a forfeiture
clause. The courts contrue this clause as inserted for the benefit
of the lessor. Where there is an express promise to either develop or pay commutation money for delay the lessor has the option to declare a forfeiture for failure to develop or pay the rental
or commutation money as it accrues, or he may waive the forfeiture and recover his rentals from time to time, or at the end
of the term recover the whole amount. A failure to develop or
pay the rental—when there is an express covenant in the lease
providing for forfeiture for such failure—forfeits the lease at
the option of the lessor unless he has waived such forfeiture by
some act, dealings or declarations which makes it inequitable to
declare forfeiture. Where lessor intends to declare a forfeiture
for failure on the part of the lessee to perform express covenants
he must not mislead the lessee as to his intentions and must be
prompt in his declaration of forfeiture. Any course of dealings
between the lessor and the lessee which leads the lessee to believe that the lessor will not require strict performance of the covenants will preclude the lessor from declaring a forfeiture when
the lessee has acted in conformity therewith, under the belief
that by conforming thereto a forfeiture will not be incurred.

Where a lessor has indulged the lessee in the matter of strict performance of the covenants either by not insisting upon payment of rental at maturity or by extending the time for drilling, before the lessor will be allowed to declare a forfeiture equity requires that he give reasonable notice to the lessee of his intention to declare such forfeiture. Within this time the lessee may perform the covenants, make the payments, or begin operations, and if in good faith, he will be relieved of any technical forfeiture. Good faith is required of the lessor as well as of the lessee. The remedy of the lessee where a lessor endeavors to declare a forfeiture which is unconscienable or inequitable is by bill in equity for relief against the effects of the acts claimed to constitute forfeiture. In such cases courts of equity hold that there has been no forfeiture and that the acts of the lessor constitute a waiver.

Where there has been a breach of the implied covenants for quiet enjoyment, and the lessee is willing to accept title of the lessor, the lessor will not be allowed by a court of equity to declare a forfeiture of the lease for the non-payment of rental while the lessor and lessee are mutually endeavoring to cure the defect in the title. Where, under such circumstances, lessor has attempted to declare a forfeiture and has executed a second lease a court of equity will cancel the second lease as a cloud upon the title of the first lessee or his assigns.

Sec. 3.—In *Duffield* v. *Hue*, 129 Pa. 94; 18 Atl. 566 analyzed under Chapter 10, the eighth point of the syllabus is as follows:

"The right of the lessor in an oil lease to insist upon a forfeiture by reason of a failure of the lessees to put down a seventh well in a stipulated time, is waived by his acquiescence in the failure to put down two or three of the preceding six wells within the period stipulated in the lease."

Sec. 4.—In *Westmoreland etc. Gas Co.* v. *DeWitt*, 130 Pa. 235; 18 Atl. 724; 5 L. R. A. 721, analyzed under Chapter 11, the seventh and eighth points of the syllabus are as follows:

"7. A clause in a lease providing for a forfeiture thereof, in the event of a default by the lessee in the performance of his covenants is not self operating so as to make the forfeiture take place ipso facto, upon the occurrence of the default, but, being for the benefit of the lessor, it rests with him to enforce or waive it.

8. Forfeitures are to be construed strictly; and where a lease provides that it shall become forfeited, if any of the payments provided for are not made, a whole payment is meant, not a balance on a running account; wherefore, if a part of a payment be accepted before it is due, no forfeiture is incurred by failure to pay the remainder in the time specified."

Sec. 5.—In *Thompson* v. *Christy*, 138 Pa. 230; 20 Atl. 934, analyzed under Chapter 12, the fifth point of the syllabus is as follows:

"The rule prevailing in equity is that, to enable a lessor to declare and enforce a forfeiture, the right so to do must be distinctly reserved; the proof of the happening of the event upon which it is to be exercised must be clear; such right must be exercised promptly, and the result of enforcing the forfeiture must not be unconscienable."

Sec. 6.—In *Lynch* v. *Versailles Fuel Gas Co.*, 165 Pa. 518; 30 Atl. 984 (Jan. 7, 1895) the syllabus is as follows:

"Where time is not stipulated as essential and a forfeiture for non-payment of money or other matter that admits of accurate and full compensation, is provided as a mere penalty whose object is to enforce performance of another and principal obligation, equity will relieve against it, and will not permit it to be used for a different and inequitable purpose.

An oil lease stipulated for rent payable for delay in putting down a well. No time was specified for the payment of this rent and it accordingly fell due by operation of law at the close of each year. The lessee paid the rent for several years without drilling a well. He then began operations and at large expense succeeded in obtaining oil in paying quantities. Lessor lived on the land and saw the work going on. When the rent fell due the lessee, by an oversight, failed to pay it. Six days afterwards the lessor notified the contractor to take away the machinery, and on the following day declared his election to forfeit the lease. The lessee expended a considerable sum of money between the time when the rent was due and the time of the attempted forfeiture. There was some evidence that in previous years the rent had not been paid upon the precise day when due, but the evidence was not strong enough to establish a usage between the parties. *Held*, that under the circumstances of the case the lessor was bound to give notice before declaring forfeiture, and that his action had been neither prompt nor conscienable.''

On August 21, 1886, John Lynch executed an oil lease to J. T. Vandergrift, which lease became by sundry assignments vested in the Versailles Fuel Gas Company. John Lynch died in 1891, having devised the land to the plaintiff, Abraham L. Lynch. The lease contained the following provision:

"That the party of the second part shall complete a well on the above described premises within one year from the date, hereof, and in case of failure to complete such well within such time the party of the second part agrees to pay to the party of the first part for such delay, a yearly rental of one dollar per acre on the premises herein leased, from the time of completing such well, as above specified, until such well shall be completed, the said yearly rental amounting to one hundred and sixty dollars shall be deposited to the credit of the party of the first part, in the Peoples Bank, McKeesport, or be paid direct to the said First party. And a failure to complete such well or make such deposit or payments above mentioned, shall render this lease null and void, and to remain without effect between the parties hereto."

The lessees did not operate the land for several years but paid the annual rental each year. On July 2, 1892, defendant began to drill a well and soon obtained oil in paying quantities. On August 20, 1892, the rent for the year fell due but by an oversight the lessee failed to pay it. On August 26, 1892, lessor notified defendant's contractor to remove his machinery from the premises, and on the following day declared his election to forfeit the lease. The lessor lived upon the land and saw the work as it progressed. Lynch instituted an action of ejectment against the Versailles Fuel Company for possession of the land in the Court of Common Pleas of Allegheny County, and obtained verdict and judgment, and the Gas Company appealed to the Supreme Court, which court reversed the judgment.

Sec. 7.—In *Steiner* v. *Marks,* 172 Pa. 400; 38 Atl. 695 (Jan. 6, 1896) the syllabus is as follows:

"The lessor in an oil and gas lease will not be permitted to enforce a forfeiture of the lease for a delay of one day in the pay-

ment of rental, where by his acts and declarations he has lured
the lessee into the belief that a forfeiture will not be enforced for
so short a delay.

Upon the evening of the last day upon which rent was to be
paid under an oil and gas lease, the lessee went to the lessor's
house in the evening and roused the lessor from his bed to make
payment. The lessee testified: 'I says to him, I came up to pay
this rental. And he says, what brought you here at this time of
night. I said to him, I thought you would kick, or something of
that kind, if I didn't come. And he says, you ought to have known
me better than that. Tomorrow would have done as well, or something like that.' The second quarter was paid a few days before
it was due. On the third day before the third quarter was due
the lessor, being at the lessee's barn, the lessee asked him to wait
until he could go to his house for the money to pay the rental.
When the lessee returned from the house, which was a short distance from the barn, the lessor had gone. The rent was tendered
the day after it was due. The lessor then declared a forfeiture of
the lease. *Held*, that the case was for the jury under proper instructions to determine whether the acts and declarations of the
lessor were calculated to lead, and did lead, the lessee into a day's
default, and whether by such acts and declarations he had not
waived his right to forfeit the lease for the grounds stated."

After the lessor had declared the forfeiture he instituted suit
against the lessee for damages for trespass. The case was tried
in the Court of Common Pleas of Butler County and verdict and
judgment rendered in favor of the plaintiff, from which judgment
the defendants appealed. The Supreme Court of Pennsylvania
reversed the judgment. The Court of Common Pleas instructed
the jury that there had been a forfeiture of the lease; and that
they should find for the plaintiff. The Supreme Court held that
upon the evidence the question of whether or not there had been
such dealings between the parties as would lead the defendants to
believe that the lessor would not insist upon a strict payment of
the rental was a question for the jury.

Sec. 8.—In *Consumers Gas Trust Co.* v. *Littler*, 162 Ind. 320;
72 N. E. 360, analyzed under Chapter 11, the third and fourth
points of the syllabus are as follows:

"3. Where under a contract the owner of land had the option to require, by claiming a forfeiture, that the other party
should drill for gas and oil within a reasonable time, or to accept

a certain sum annually for delay, his acceptance of such annual payment in advance was a waiver of performance for ,one year.

"4. Where, by the acceptance of an agreed annual payment, the owner of land had waived his right to have the other party drill there for oil and gas up to a certain time, and at the expiration of that time he refused to accept another payment, he could not claim a forfeiture of the contract 15 days later, since that did not afford notice for a reasonable time of his intention to do so."

Sec. 9.—In *Consumers Gas Trust Co. v. Ink,* 163 Ind. 174; 71 N. E. 477, analyzed under Chapter 11, the syllabus is as follows:

"1. Where, under a lease of oil lands, the owner had an option to require the lessee to drill for gas or oil within a reasonable time by claiming a forfeiture or to accept a certain sum annually for delay, the acceptance of such sum, annually in advance for several years precluded the lessor from claiming a forfeiture before the year in which the last payment made for a postponement of operations had expired.

2. Where a lessor of oil lands demanded a forfeiture of the lease for the lessee's failure to drill for oil at a time when she was not entitled to such forfeiture, such demand was ineffectual as a notice to the lessee to start operations the claim of forfeiture being equivalent to a denial of the lessee's right thereunder to enter the premises for the purpose of conducting such operations."

Sec. 10.—In *Consumers Gas Trust Co. v. Worth,* 163 Ind. 141; 71 N. E. 489, analyzed under Chapter 11, the syllabus is as follows:

"1. Where a gas lease was for such a period as the lessee should pay the lessor a certain sum of money, annually, or so much longer as oil or gas should be found in paying quantities, the acceptance by the lessor of an annual payment in advance was a waiver of performance in developing the property for that year.

2. Where a gas lease is for such time as the lessee shall pay a specified annual sum in advance to the lessor, or until gas shall be found in paying quantities, and the lessor refuses at the beginning of any year to accept the payment, the lessee is then bound to develop the premises within a reasonable time.

3. Where a gas lease is for such period as the lessee shall pay the lessor a specified sum annually in advance, or until gas shall be found in paying quantities, and the lessor refuses to accept the annual payment, and declares the lease forfeited, the failure of the lessee to thereafter commence development proceedings cannot be regarded as a lack of diligence, entitling the lessor to a forfeiture."

Sec. 11.—In *Consumers Gas Trust Co.* v. *Howard,* 163 Ind. 170; 71 N. E. 493 (June 23, 1904) syl. 3 is as follows:

"3.   Where the lessee of a gas lease agreed to pay to the lessor a specified sum annually, or until oil or gas should be found in paying quantities, the acceptance by the lessor of an annual payment in advance was a waiver of performance in developing the property for that year."

Isaiah Howard and others, on December 15, 1896, executed an oil and gas lease to one Walley, who subsequently assigned his lease to the Consumers Gas Trust Company. By the terms of the lease the lessors granted to the lessee, his heirs and assigns, the right to enter upon the premises at all times for the purpose of operating for oil, gas and water, and to lay and maintain pipelines thereon, etc.   The lease contained the following provision:

"That in consideration of the premises that the party of the second part agrees to pay to the party of the first part the sum of $30.00 annually beginning on the 15th day of December, 1896, and until oil or gas is found in paying quantities, or this is terminated as herein provided."

On December 15, 1896, Walley paid the lessors in advance the stipulated sum of $30.00; and thereafter on each succeeding 15th lay of December lessee paid a like amount to lessor. These payments were made each year until December 15, 1901, on which day appellees for the first time refused to accept the money although it was tendered and offered to them on that date. Lessors refused to accept payment on the ground that they had a right at that time to terminate the contract, and they declared and announced to the appellant that they proposed to terminate the contract on December 15, 1901. The lessors thereupon instituted a suit in the Superior Court of Madison County against the Consumers Gas Trust Company to cancel the lease. Judgment was rendered in favor of the plaintiff and defendants appealed to the Appellate Court and the case was transferred to the Indiana Supreme Court where the judgment was reversed.

Sec. 12.—In *Hukill* v. *Myers,* 36 W. Va. 639; 15 S. E. 151, analyzed under Chapter 12, the syllabus is as follows:

"1.   Where in an oil lease there is a clause of forfeiture for nonpayment of rental, but the lessor consents that it need not be paid at the time when due, and indulges the lessee, and acquiesces in his failure to pay, there is no forfeiture for nonpayment.

2.   In case of such a lease, if the lessor by his conduct clearly indicates, that payment will not be demanded when due and thus lulls the lessee into a feeling of security and throws him off his guard, and because of this he does not make ayments when due, the landlord cannot suddenly, without demand or notice declare a forfeiture, and there is no forfeiture which equity would recognize, and if there is, in such case technically a forfeiture at law equity would relieve against it.

3.   If after such rental has accrued and is not paid, whereby a forfeiture exists, a lessor with knowledge thereof receives the rentals accruing after the forfeiture he waives and cannot enforce the forfeiture."

Sec. 13.—In *Pyle* v. *Henderson*, 65 W. Va. 39; 63 S. E. 762, analyzed under Chapter 25, the second, third and fourth points of the syllabus are as follows:

"2.   Where in an oil lease there is a clause that it shall be void if a well is not completed, or, in lieu of it, money paid, within a given time, and before the expiration of the time it is found that the lessor's title is defective, and he agrees to perfect it, and agrees that the money need not be paid when due, and gives an extension for payment until the title can be perfected, he cannot declare a forfeiture and make a second lease.   A second lease, taken with notice on the first, is void as to the first lease."

3.   In case of such a lease, if the lessor by his conduct clearly indicates that payment will not be demanded when due and thus lulls the lessee into a feeling of security, and throws him off his guard, and because of this, he does not make payments when due, the landlord cannot suddenly, without demand or notice, declare a forfeiture, and there is no forfeiture which equity would recognize; and if there is in such case technically a forfeiture at law, equity would relieve against it.

4.   A forfeiture will be deemed waived by any agreement, declaration, or course of action on the part of him who is benefitted by such forfeiture which leads the other party to believe that by conforming thereto the forfeiture will not be incurred.

Sec. 14.—In *Vendocia Oil etc. Co.* v. *Robinson*, 71 Ohio State 302; 73 N. E. 222 (Jan. 17, 1905) the syllabus is as follows:

"1.   A grant, in consideration of one dollar, of all the oil and gas under certain premises, with the right to enter thereon for the purpose of drilling and operating for oil and gas, excepting and reserving to the grantor 1-6 of all the oil and gas produced and saved from the said premeises, to be delivered in the pipelines with which the grantee may connect his wells, implies an engagement by the lessee to develop the premises for oil and gas.

2. The time within which the implied engagement must be performed is postponed by acceptance of the sum specified in the condition of such grant that 'in case no well is completed within 90 days from the date hereof, unavoidable delay excepted, then this grant shall become null and void, unless second party shall pay to first party twenty-five cents per acre per year, payable by deposit at the ————— or directly to the first party, after demand having first been made' and does not commence to run until the end of the year for which payment is accepted, and the lease does not become null and void at the end of such year on the refusal of the grantor to accept payment for another year.''

H. O. Robinson and S. M. Robinson made a grant to C. S. King & Company of all the oil and gas in and under a tract of land in Van Wert County, Ohio, with the right to enter thereon at all times for the purpose of drilling and operating for oil and gas, to erect and maintain all buildings and structures, and lay all pipes necessary for the production and disposition of oil or gas, excepting and reserving the 1-6 part of all oil produced, to be delivered in the pipelines with which lessee should connect his wells, which lease was upon the following conditions: If gas only should be found lessee should pay $100.00 each year for the production of each well while the same should be used off the premises, lessors to have gas free of cost to heat all stoves in dwelling houses during the same time; in case no well should be completed within 90 days from the date, unavoidable delays excepted, then the grant should be null and void unless lessee should pay to lessor twenty-five cents per acre per year, payable by deposit in the ————— or directly to lessor after demand had been made. On December 18, 1902, King & Company sold, transferred and assigned the lease to the Vendocia etc. Company. On February 2, 1903, Robinsons entered into an agreement in writing with W. G. Speaker in which it was recited that ''in consideration of five dollars and the further consideration of valuable legal advice to said first party by the second party, said advice being in regard to a contract made on December 3, 1901, between Robinsons and C. S. King & Company, said first party agreeing to use said legal advice as may be directed by second party, and agreeing that if said advice should result in the cancellation of the above mentioned contract, or if said second party shall surrender said contract, or fail to pay rental on same, that the first party will then make a contract with the second party as follows.'' Then follows an oil and gas lease. This lease was filed for record and duly recorded in the Recorder's office of said County. Rental under the first lease was paid to March 2, 1903, and on that day the oil company tendered to Robinsons as rental the further sum of $20.00. On March 6, 1903, Speaker moved a load of lumber on the premises for the purpose of erecting a derrick and drilling a well; and on March 7, 1903, the oil company caused the material to be removed, and itself placed a load of lumber on the premises with the intention of erecting a derrick and drilling a well. The oil company was prevented from drilling a well and thereupon commenced an action in the Court of Common Pleas of Van Wert County setting up its lease and the payment of rental, and averring that it had entered into possession of the premises for the purpose of erecting a derrick and drilling a well; and that it was in possession of the premises. It then set out that Robinsons were interfering with its possession, and that the defendants threatened to and would unless restrained by the court, remove the lumber that had been placed upon the premises, and would prevent the plaintiff from drilling. For a second cause of action the oil company set out that a number of landowners, including the Robinsons, desired to have a block of undeveloped territory tested for oil and gas; that King and Company leased a number of pieces of property in the territory; and the plaintiff then alleged what had been done to develop the property; and that at the time of the filing of the petition no well had been drilled on any land in said block adjoining the land of Robinsons, nor had any well been drilled on any land outside of said block and contiguous to the land of the defendant, which produced oil in paying quantities. The purpose of the petition was to set out facts which would show that the oil company had not unreasonably delayed drilling a well upon the lands covered by the lease. In its petition the oil company prayed for an injunction to restrain the defendant from interfering with it, in developing the premises for oil and gas, and that the lease to Speaker might be declared null and void and be cancelled. The defendants admitted the averments of the first cause of action as to the facts therein stated. The Court of Common Pleas granted the relief prayed for. The case was appealed to the Circuit Court, which found for the defendants and dismissed the petition. Thereupon the oil company appealed to the Supreme Court of Ohio and that court reversed the Circuit Court.

Sec. 15.—In *Campbell* v. *Rock Oil Co.*, 80 C. C. A. 467; 151 Fed. 191, (Jan. 2, 1907) the head notes are as follows:

"1. In a suit by a lessor to terminate the lessee's privilege of exploration under an oil and gas lease which under the law of Indiana could be terminated at the end of any year, and prior to the finding of oil or gas in paying quantities only by the giving of notice a reasonable time before the expiration of each year, the burden rests upon the complainant to prove that the time between the giving of notice and the expiration of the year was a reasonable time within which to ascertain whether oil or gas in paying quantities could be found.

2. Where the notice given by a lessor in an oil and gas lease of an intention to terminate the lessee's privilege of exploration thereunder at the end of a year, because of delay in operating, required the lessee to 'proceed with all reasonable speed and promptness,' under penalty of forfeiture of all its rights, and at the end of the year the lessee was so proceeding and had completed a well, but, owing to an inflow of salt water it was necessary to incur large expense for machinery and pumping to render the well productive, which expenditure was made with the knowledge of the lessor, she was estopped to thereafter claim that the lease was terminated by the notice."

On May 20, 1897, Julia E. Campbell and Charles J. Campbell, of Cook County, Illinois, made an oil and gas lease to the Rock Oil Company, whereby in consideration of the agreements contained the lessors granted, demised and let to the lessee for oil and gas purposes, a certain tract of land in Delaware County, Indiana, for the term of five years from date and as much longer as oil or gas should be found in paying quantities or the rental paid. The lease contained the following stipulation:

"It is further agreed, that the party of the second part shall complete a well on the described premises within one year from the date above, or in default thereof pay to the parties of the first part for such delay a yearly rental of $60.00 on the said premises from the time of completing said well, as above specified, until such well shall be completed. The said yearly rental shall be deposited to the credit of the parties of the first part in the Citizens Bank, Muncie, Indiana, or be paid direct to first parties. And a failure to complete such well, or to pay said rental, shall render this lease null and void. The party of the second part agrees to drill an oil or gas well within one year from the above date or forfeit to the parties of the second part Fifty ($50) Dollars. The party of the second part agrees to pay rental on all lands at rate of 50 cents per acre, as above described, excepting forty (40) acres for each well drilled, or abandon the same.''

No well was drilled prior to 1904, but the stipulated rental was paid each year, including a payment before July 1, 1903, for the year ending May 20, 1904. On March 26, 1904, lessor served upon lessee the following notice:

"You are hereby notified that the lease for gas and oil made by the undersigned to the Rock Oil Company, bearing date May 20, 1897, on the following described real estate in Delaware County, State of Indiana, to-wit: * * * * * * * will not be extended beyond the period for which extension has been made and assented to, to-wit: May 20, 1904; or delay in operations on said premises be delayed beyond such period, nor will a money consideration be received and accepted for further extension or delay in operation thereof. You are hereby notified and required to proceed with all reasonable promptness and dispatch to operate for oil and gas on said premises under penalty of forfeiture of all rights and privileges under said instrument of lease."

After the middle of April, 1904, lessee commenced drilling and drilled to a depth of 1240 feet. Oil bearing rock was found at 955 feet. This rock was penetrated 285 feet, which was a proper depth for finding oil in that territory. On May 18th the well was completed and shot. It was cleaned out on the 19th and the pump started. Only water came. On the 20th and for some days thereafter small quantities of oil were obtained when suddenly large volumes of salt water prevented the well from producing oil. The pumps were kept working day and night until June 10th. During this time lessee in good faith tried to produce oil and operated skillfully in an endeavor to ascertain whether or not the

well could be made a paying one. A well in that territory at that
time could be drilled and shot and equipped for pumping in from
15 to 25 days. Before May 20th lessees expended in their operations $1677.00; After that date $3704.00, of which sum, $1551.00
was for machinery which they subsequently removed. Lessor had
full knowledge of lessee's operations both before and after May
20th and made no objection whatever prior to the beginning of
the suit. On June 10, 1904, lessors instituted suit in equity in the
Circuit Court of the United States for the District of Indiana
for the annulment of the lease. The Circuit Court dismissed the
plaintiff's bill for want of equity. From the decree of dismissal
the lessors appealed to the Circuit Court of Appeals for the
Seventh Circuit, and that court affirmed the decree. The bill alleged as a matter of law that prior to the execution of the lease
the Indiana Courts had settled upon a construction of such contracts whereby the lessor at the end of the original or any renewal period could terminate the lessee's interest without notice. In
this contention the Circuit Court of Appeals did not concur, but
held contra, citing *Hancock* v. *Diamond Plate Glass Co.,* 162 Ind.
146; 70 N. E. 149. The court held that under the Indiana law
lessor had the right to terminate lessee's privilege of exploration
by giving him notice for a reasonable time prior to May 29, 1904,
that no further extension would be granted; and that after such
notice lessee could have held over only by finding gas or oil in
paying quantities within such reasonable period, citing:

> *Consumers Gas Trust Co.* v. *Littler,* 162 Ind. 320; 70 N. E. 363.
> *Consumers Gas Trust Co.* v. *Worth,* 163 Ind. 141; 71 N. E.
>   489.
> *Consumers Gas Trust Co.* v. *Ink,* 163 Ind. 174; 71 N. E. 477.
> *Consumers Gas Trust Co.* v. *Chrystal Co.,* 163 Ind. 190; 70
>   N. E. 366.
> *Lafayette Gas Co.* v. *Kelsey,* 164 Ind. 563; 74 N. E. 7.
> *Manhattan Oil Co.* v. *Carroll,* 164 Ind. 526; 73 N. E. 1084.
> *New American Oil Co.* v. *Troyer,* (Ind. Sup.) 76 N. E. 353; 166
>   Ind. 402; 77 N. E. 739.

Sec. 16.—In *Duntley* v. *Anderson,* 169 Fed. 391; 94 C. C. A.
647 (March 26, 1909) the head notes are as follows:

"1. An oil and gas lease declared that, if no well was sunk within 12 months the lease should be void unless the lessee should pipe gas to within 100 feet of the lessor's premises, and give them free gas until the well was drilled. *Held* that where an assignee of the lessee piped the gas as required and the lessors commenced and continued to use the same, 'under the lease' until the trial of a suit to cancel the same, such use constitutes a waiver of his right to cancel the lease because no well was sunk within 12 months.

2. Where an owner of agricultural land executed an oil and gas lease providing that, if it should be detrimental to a sale of the place, the lease should be returned to him, such provision should be construed only to require a rescission if the lease was detrimental to a sale of the land for agricultural or other purposes to which it was then devoted, and did not authorize a rescission to permit the lessor to dispose of his oil rights to greater advantage.

3. An oil and gas lease provided that, in case no oil or gas well was sunk within 12 months, the lease should be void unless the lessee should pipe gas to within 100 feet of the lessor's residence and give him the right to use gas 'till well is drilled,' and that the lease should be returned if detrimental to a sale of the place *Held,* that the lessor while using gas under the lease, which had been piped to within 100 feet of his residence free of charge, was not entitled to a cancellation of the lease in equity as detrimental to a sale of his property."

On June 28, 1900, T. L. Anderson and wife executed to the Pennsylvania Oil Company an oil and gas lease giving to the company the exclusive right for ten years from date to enter upon and operate for oil and gas the land described in the lease. The lease contained the following provision:

"In case no oil or gas well is sunk on the premises within 12 months from this date, this lease shall become absolutely null and void unless the second parties shall·pipe gas to within 100 feet of the residence of the parties of the first part, and give the parties of the first part the right to use gas for three stoves and four lights in consideration of lease, till well is drilled. If this lease shall be detrimental to the sale of this place, this lease shall be returned to first parties."

On May 21, 1904, lessor served a written notice of cancellation on the lessee, reciting that the lease had then become detrimental to the sale of the property, and demanding that the lease be cancelled of record and returned. The notice prohibited the lessee from going on the land for the purpose of sinking wells for gas or oil. Subsequently Anderson brought suit in the State Court to cancel the lease. The suit was removed to the United States Circuit Court for the District of Kansas, and the cause was referred to a master to take testimony and report his findings of fact, and recommendations as to what decree should be entered in the cause. The master found that Anderson was the owner of the land described in the lease, which was executed by him and wife on June 28, 1900; that the Pennsylvania Oil Company, the lessee, was a partnership; that on January 3, 1901, the Pennsylvania Oil Company sold and assigned the lease to the Coffeyville Gas Company, a corporation; that on September 15, 1902, the Coffeyville Gas Company by warranty deed sold and assigned the lease to the Peoples Gas Company, a corporation; that on October 14, 1902, the Peoples Gas Company sold all the oil rights under the lease, except 1-4, to W. P. Brown; that on August 23, 1903, Brown sold and assigned all his rights to the Calumet Oil & Gas Company, a corporation; that on February 17, 1904, the Calumet Company sold and assigned its rights under the lease to the Southern Development Company, a corporation; that on March 24, 1904, the Southern Development Company assigned its oil rights under the lease to J. W. Duntley, J. A. O'Dell and W. O. Duntley. The master further found that neither the original lessee, nor any of its assignees at any time within 12 months from the date of the lease drilled any wells for oil or gas, and that they did not pipe gas to within 100 feet of the lessor's residence as provided in the lease; that in September, 1901, the Coffeyville Gas Company, the then holder of the lease, did pipe gas to within 100 feet of lessor's residence upon the leased premises and gave him the right to use the gas for three stoves and four lights, and that lessor accepted the gas without protest and continuously used the same until the institution of the suit. The testimony showed that 1-2 mile of pipe was laid for the purpose of conducting the gas to within 100 feet of Anderson's house, and that he at once connected and commenced using the gas and continued using it up to the time his testimony was taken in the case. The master

found that these facts constituted a waiver of the forfeiture otherwise incurred for not acting within twelve months; but recommended the cancellation of the lease under the clause which provided that "if this lease shall be detrimental to the sale of this
place this lease shall be returned to the first party. The Circuit
Court accepted this recommendation, adopted the same, and entered a decree cancelling the lease. From this decree the assignees
of the original lessee appealed to the Circuit Court of Appeals
and that Court reversed the decree of the Circuit Court and held
the law to be as stated in the headnotes.

Sec. 17.—In *Kansas Natural Gas Co.* v. *Harris,* 79 Kan. 167;
100 Pac. 7 (Dec. 12, 1908) the syllabus is as follows:

"1. Where the lessee under an oil and gas lease violates the
provisions of the lease so that the lessor might declare the instrument terminated but does not do so, and afterwards the lessor and
lessee agree that for a valuable consideration to be given by the
lessee the lessor will accept the same as a full compliance with the
conditions of the lease, and such consideration is given and accepted as stipulated the transaction will constitute a waiver of the
prior violation of the lease and will return it to its original validity
and vigor.
2. Where the lessor of a contract for the purchase of the oil
and gas in and under certain real estate commenced an action to
cancel an outstanding lease on the land and the owner of the land
is made a party to such action, but no allegation in the pleadings
indicate that he has done, or intended to do anything adverse to
the rights or interests of the plaintiff, and there is no evidence
presented which shows any such action or intent, and it does not
appear when the decree is entered that the plaintiff then has any
substantial interest in the premises, it is error to grant an injunction in favor of the plaintiff and against such landowner restraining him from interfering with the plaintiff in the use of the land
for the purpose of exploring for gas and oil."

Prior to July 5, 1899, Jennie F. Evans and her husband were
the owners of a tract of land, and on that day they executed a
lease to the Independence Gas Company, for the term of ten
years and as much longer as gas or oil should be found in paying
quantities. The lease contained the following stipulation:

"The lessee shall commence operations under the lease within three months, or in case of failure to do so the lease may be kept alive by furnishing gas at the residence of M. Riser in Independence, for two stoves and two lights, in which case the lease shall be binding as long as gas is so furnished."

Gas was furnished as stipulated until about September, 1901, when Riser left the premises and resided with the tenant. After this the company refused to furnish gas free and requested payment therefor from the tenant. Subsequently Evans, the lessor, became the owner of the property and demanded that gas be furnished there for him, which the company refused to do. The lease was duly recorded on September 28, 1899, but was not properly indexed and therefore escaped the attention of those who subsequently dealt with the land. In August, 1903, the Independence Gas Company assigned this lease to the Consolidated Oil & Gas Company, and on March 9, 1904, the Independence Gas Company, and the Consolidated Oil & Gas Company assigned the lease to R. M. Snyder; and on June 14, 1904, the lease was assigned to the Natural Gas Company, which at the date of the suit claimed to be the owner. On December 11, 1902, Jennie Evans and her husband, the lessors in the lease, conveyed the land to G. H. and Dolly Dow. In October, 1903, Dows requested the lessees in writing to furnish gas to them on the leased premises as follows:

"County of Montgomery, State of Kansas, ss: We hereby request of Consolidated Oil, Gas & Mfg. Co., successors to the Independence Gas Co., to furnish gas to us on the premises on which the within lease is granted, instead of Independence, as agreed when written. We agree to accept the same in satisfaction of the said agreement. It is understood we are now the owners of the premises described in this lease. Witness our hands and seals this 19th day of October, C. H. Dow. Dolly Dow."

The lessee complied with this request and thereafter furnished gas as requested. On February 27, 1903, the Dows entered into a contract of sale with C. C. Harris for all the oil and gas in and under the lands described in the lease. Prior to the compliance with the request of the Dows to furnish gas to them on the leased premises the lessees had done nothing in the way of developing the premises and had not in any respect complied with the provisions of the lease; and by reason of their failure in this respect had forfeited their rights thereto. After the Gas Company had commenced furnishing gas to the Dows, and thereby, as they claimed, renewed the life of the lease, it caused a well to be drilled on the premises which proved to be a good gas well. Thereupon C. C. Harris commenced an action to cancel the lease in order to protect his rights under the contract made by him with Dows. At the expiration of six months after the execution of the Harris contract no well having been commenced, the stipulated rental was paid to August 27, 1906. This contract contained provisions as to developing the land for oil and gas. Although an equity cause a jury was called to which several findings of fact were submitted and answered. The District Court adopted these findings and entered a decree thereon in favor of plaintiff. These questions and findings of fact were as follows:

No. 1.   Did the Independence Gas Company lay pipelines to within 50 feet of the residence of M. Riser in Independence, and furnish gas for two stoves and two lights? A.   Yes.

No. 2.   If yes, then did the Independence Gas Company or any of the subsequent owners of the lease cease furnishing gas for two stoves and two lights on lots fourteen, fifteen and sixteen, block forty, the residence of M. Riser, in Independence? A. Yes, according to the terms of the lease.

No. 3.   If you find that the furnishing of gas for two stoves and two lights, within fifty feet of the residence of M. Riser, in Independence, on Lots fourteen, fifteen and sixteen, block 40, was discontinued, then when and why was it discontinued? A. Because Riser's property was occupied by tenants.

No. 4.   If you find that the Independence Gas Company, or any of the subsequent owners of the lease, ceased to furnish gas for two stoves and two lights, on Lots fourteen, fifteen and sixteen block 40, the residence of M. Riser, in Independence, then was it the intention of the Independence Gas Company, or the subsequent owners of the lease, to forfeit and abandon the lease? A. Yes.

No. 5.   Did Dow and wife know of the existence of the Evans lease at the time of their making the lease to C. C. Harris? A. 'Yes.''

The District Court found against the validity of the Evans lease, and in favor of the validity of the Harris contract, and entered a decree cancelling the lease and perpetually enjoining all

the adverse parties, including Dows, from interfering with Harris
in the exercise of his rights under the contract made by him with
the Dows. The Kansas Natural Gas Company filed its petition
in error in the Supreme Court, and the Dows filed a cross petition.
They each complained of the decree of the Trial Court and asked
for a reversal. The Supreme Court reversed the decree and remanded the cause.

Sec. 18.—In *Monarch Oil, Gas & Coal Co.* v. *Richardson*, 30
Ky. L. Rep. 824; 99 S. W. 668, analyzed under Chapter 13, the
syllabus is as follows:

"A coal, oil, gas and mineral lease provided that the lessor
was to receive a pro rata share of all the oil and minerals produced, and should gas be found, then a certain rental from each
well; and the lease further provided that lessee should commence
a well on the premises within a year or pay thereafter an annual
rental of $16.00. A well was never commenced, but lessee paid
the annual rental, which was accepted by the lessor. *Held*, that
notwithstanding the lessor was entitled to forfeit the lease for
failure to develop the premises, yet lessor could not do so until
he had first declined to accept the rental and demanded of lessee
development of the premises."

LESSOR'S REMEDY.

Sec. 19.—The courts have uniformly held that the forfeiture
clause in an oil and gas lease is for the benefit of the lessor. Where
the lease is for a valuable consideration the right to forfeit for
failure to explore or pay rental or commutation money in lieu
thereof must be distinctly reserved, and the happening of the
event upon which the forfeiture depends must be clear. The right
to declare the forfeiture must be exercised promptly. The result
of enforcing the forfeiture must not be unconscienable. The forfeiture clause being inserted in the lease for the benefit of the
lessor he may waive it or acting promptly and in good faith may
terminate the lease by declaring forfeiture where lessee has incurred a forfeiture by failure to perform the covenants of the
lease on his part. Where lessor has by his acts, conduct, or by any
course of dealings with the lessee waived the forfeiture of the

lease, before he will be authorized to declare a forfeiture he must give notice to the lessee of his intention to do so, and this notice must be sufficient as to time to enable lessee if the lease provides that a well is to be completed, to enter and complete such well; or if the lease requires only the beginning of explorations the lessee must be given a sufficient time to enable him to enter and commence explorations.   Where such notice has been given by lessor and time has thus been afforded lessee to do what was originally necessary to be done to prevent forfeiture of the lease and lessee remains in default and fails to perform the covenants of the lease, the lessor at the time fixed in such notice may declare a forfeiture and terminate the lease as though no waiver had occurred.

> *Steiner* v. *Marks,* 172 Pa. 400; 33 Atl. 695. Syl. 1.
> *Consumers Gas Trust Co.* v. *Ink,* 163 Ind. 174; 71 N. E. 477.
> *Consumers Gas Trust Co.* v. *Worth,* 163 Ind. 141; 71 N. E. 489.
> *Consumers Gas Trust Co.* v. *Littler,* 163 Ind. 320; 70 N. E. 363.
> *Thompson* v. *Christy,* 138 Pa. 230; 20 Atl. 924.
> *Lynch* v. *Versailles Fuel etc. Co.,* 165 Pa. 518; 30 Atl. 984.

LESSEE'S REMEDY.
(See Chapter 25)

CHAPTER 22.

PAYING QUANTITIES—DISCOVERY OF OIL AND GAS IN.

Sec. 1.—Where an oil and gas lease provides that it shall be in force for a given time followed by the clause "and as much longer as oil or gas can be produced in paying quantities" or words to that effect, as a general rule the lessee is the judge as to what amount of oil or gas constitutes "paying quantities" provided his judgment is exercised in good faith.

> *Lowther Oil Co.* v. *Miller-Sibley Oil Co.,* 53 W. Va. 501, Syl. 4; 44 S. E. 433; 97 Am. St. 1027.
> *Young* v. *Forest Oil Co.,* 194 Pa. 243; 45 Atl. 1021.

McGraw Oil etc. Co. v. *Kennedy,* 65 W. Va. 595; 64 S. E. 1027.
Murdock-West Co. v. *Logan,* 69 Ohio St. 514; 69 N. E. 984
Bay State Petroleum Co. v. *Penn Lubricating Co.,* 27 Ky. L.
    Rep. 1133; 87 S. W. 1102.
Dickey v. *Coffeyville Vitrified Brick & Tile Co.,* 69 Kan. 106;
    76 Pac. 398.
Barnsdall v. *Boley,* 119 Fed. 191.
Cassell v. *Crothers,* 193 Pa. 359; 44 Atl. 446.
Double v. *Union Heat etc. Co.,* 172 Pa. 388; 33 Atl. 694.
Summerville v. *Apollo Gas Co.,* 207 Pa. 334; 56 Atl. 876.
Manhattan Oil Co. v. *Carrell,* 164 Ind. 526; 73 N. E. 1084.

Sec. 2.—The courts hold that the lessee, acting in good faith,
is the proper judge of whether or not oil or gas is being produced
in paying quantities. If the lessee has performed the implied
covenants of the lease to reasonably develop the demised premises little injury could be suffered by the landowner where the
lessee attempts to hold beyond the time when the lease may be considered as not producing oil or gas in paying quantities. Where
there has not been development of the whole property leased the
lessor may suffer injury by the lessee attempting to hold the premises beyond the time when they in fact produce oil or gas in paying quantities. In such cases it is inequitable to permit a lessee
to stifle developments under a pretence that the premises are producing oil or gas in paying quantities, when in fact they have not
been fully tested. It has been universally held by the courts which
have construed oil and gas leases that it is the implied duty of a
lessee to develop the premises for the mutual benefit of both lessor
and lessee. This being true it would seem unreasonable to allow
the sole judgment of the lessee to control the question as to whether or not the leased premises are producing in paying quantities.
The lessor's judgment, if exercised in good faith, in cases of this
character should have as much weight given to it by the courts as
is given to the judgment of the lessee. The true rule controlling
the determination of the question as to whether or not the leased
premises are producing oil or gas in paying quantities is, that the
judgment of the lessee should be exercised, not only in good faith,
but in a manner so as not to work a hardship on the landowner
by stifling further developments; and the question of whether the
lease is producing oil or gas in paying quantities is one of fact.

In determining this question of fact the condition of the premises as to the extent of developments thereon, the surrounding circumstances, and if gas only has been discovered, the market therefor, if oil, whether the adjacent properties are producing oil from wells located in such proximity to the leased premises as to drain the oil therefrom; the number of acres in the tract, and the number of wells drilled thereon; and such other facts and circumstances as demonstrate the good faith of the lessee in attempting to hold the lease beyond the term when the whole tract has not been tested, or where apparently oil or gas is not being produced in paying quantities. Where the lessee is holding property under a claim that it is producing oil or gas in paying quantities, and in fact the lease is not so producing, a court of equity should and will upon proof of such fact, cancel the lease.

Sec. 3.—In *Lowther Oil Co.* v. *Miller-Sibley Oil Co.*, 53 W. Va. 501; 44 S. E. 433; 97 Am. St. 1027, analyzed under Chapter 5, syl. 4 is as follows:

"Where an oil and gas lease is for a given term 'and as much longer as oil and gas can be produced in paying quantities' to the lessee, if a well pays a profit, even a small one, over operating expenses, it produces 'in paying quantity' though it never repay its cost, and the operation as a whole may result in a loss. The phrase 'paying quantity' is to be construed with reference to the judgment of the operator when exercised in good faith."

Sec. 4.—In *Young* v. *Forest Oil Co.*, 194 Pa. 243; 45 Atl. 1021, analyzed under Chapter 18, the third and fourth points of the syllabus are as follows:

"A bill in equity will not lie by the lessor of an oil and gas lease against the lessee or his assigns, to compel the latter to test part of the leased land, not yet drilled or upon his failure to do so to surrender the land to the lessor, unless it is shown that the failure of the lessee to drill amounts to a fraud upon the rights of the lessor.
Where a lease is to continue as long as oil or gas is found or produced in paying quantities, the phrase 'found or produced in paying quantities' means paying quantities to the lessee or operator. If oil has not been found, and the prospects are not such

that the lessee is willing to incur the expense of a well (or a second or subsequent well as the case may be) the stipulated condition for the termination of the lease has occurred. So, also, if oil has been found, but no longer pays the expense of production. But if a well, being down, pays a profit, even a small one, over the operating expenses, it is producing in 'paying quantities' though it may never repay its cost, and the operation as a whole may result in a loss. The phrase 'paying quantities' therefore, is to be contrued with reference to the operator, and by his judgment, when exercised in good faith.''

Sec. 5.—In *McGraw Oil & Gas Co.* v. *Kennedy*, 65 W. Va. 595; 64 S. E. 1027, analyzed under Chapter 18, syl. 1 is as follows:

"A lease for oil and gas is for five years, 'and as long thereafter as oil or gas, or either of them, is produced by the party of the second part.' The lessor cannot forfeit it because he thinks the gas not in paying quantity; the lessee claiming that it is, and willing to pay the sum stipulated for the well. It is for the lessee to say whether the gas is in paying quantity, acting in good faith.''

Sec. 6.—In *Murdock-West Co.* v. *Logan*, 69 Ohio St. 514; 69 N. E. 984, analyzed under Chapter 6, the last paragraph of the first point, and the second point of the syllabus are as follows:

"A finding of indications of oil, or the existence of conditions which rendered it probable that oil in paying quantities would be found, if the well were operated in a certain way, is not sufficient of itself, to extend the term of the lease.

The stipulation in the lease that the term shall continue 'as much longer thereafter as oil or gas shall be found in paying quantities' requires that oil or gas shall be actually discovered and produced in paying quantities within the term.''

Sec. 7.—In *Bay State Petroleum Co.* v. *Penn Lubricating Co.*, 27 Ky. Law Rep. 1133; 87 S. W. 1102, (June 15, 1905) syl. 1 is as follows:

"Where an oil lease was for a specified time, or as long as oil was obtained in paying quantities, the lessee had the right to determine when he was no longer obtaining oil in paying guantities.''

On January 25, 1895, Harvey Duncan and wife executed an oil and gas lease to A. M. Williams, whereby the lessor granted to the lessee the exclusive right to operate for coal, oil, gas, salt, ores and all minerals in 300 acres of land in Wayne County, Kentucky. The term of the lease was twenty years, or as long as gas, or any of the above substances should be obtained in paying quantities. The lessee had one year and six months within which to begin work. A failure on the part of lessee to complete one well or make any payments should render the lease null and void. Within eighteen months after the making of the lease Williams put down a well upon the tract something like 375 feet deep. At that time the oil field in Wayne County was little developed, and what oil had been found had been found in the Beaver Creek sand. When Williams, the lessee, passed through this sand and found nothing he ceased drilling and nothing more was done under the lease by him. On February 1, 1897, Williams sold a 4-5 interest in the lease to D. W. Wright & Company, who transferred it to Frank Haskell on February 3, 1900, and Haskell transferred it to the Penn Lubricating Company on February 27, 1900. On July 22, 1900, Williams also transferred his remaining 1-5 interest to this company. In the meantime oil had been found in Wayne County in what was called the "Sunnybrook Sand" which is about 500 feet below the Beaver Creek Sand. In June, 1902, the Penn Lubricating Company concluded to drill the well deeper to the Sunnybrook sand. Duncan, the lessor, said he had leased the land, and objected to the Penn Lubricating Company doing anything on the land, claiming that it had done nothing for years, and had abandoned the lease. The Penn Lubricating Company insisted upon going ahead and Duncan made no further objection, the person to whom he proposed to lease the land not closing the trade with him. The Penn Company drilled the well some 500 feet deeper and getting nothing, after six weeks tore down the derrick and took everything off the land. It had leased some 10,000 acres and found oil in other parts of its territory. Its purpose was to follow the line of the oil and come back to Duncan's tract when it had learned where the line of oil laid. In October, 1900, Duncan went to Booth, President of the Penn Company, and asked him if he was going to pay rental or work the lease. Booth claimed that drilling the well deeper would hold the lease. Duncan replied that he was going to lease the land again if the Penn Company didn't work the lease. After this oil was struck on land adjoining Duncan's tract. On November 11, 1902, Duncan leased part of the land to George C. Backer. On December 20th he leased the remainder to C. W. Locklin. They agreed to give him a royalty of 1-10, and paid him $550.00 in money; but they had full notice at the time of the prior lease. Locklin assigned his interest to the Bay State Petroleum Company. In April, 1903, the Penn Company went upon the land and began building a derrick on the part of the tract north of where the old well was, and near the line of the tract on which oil had been struck. The Bay State Company's men, at night tore down the work which had been done on the derrick and threw it in the creek. Thereupon the Penn Company filed suits against Duncan, the Bay State Company and George C. Backer to enjoin them from interfering with its operations on the land. The defendants filed answers and counter claims, insisting that Williams had not complied with the terms of the lease and had abandoned it, and that nothing passed to the Penn Company under the assignment to it; and that that company abandoned the lease after it failed to find oil in 1902. The Circuit Court of Wayne County decided in favor of the Penn Lubricating Company, and the defendant Bay State Company, apealed. The Kentucky Court of Appeals reversed the Circuit Court and held that the original lease had been forfeited by abandonment.

Sec. 8.—In *Dickey* v. *Coffeyville Vitrified Brick & Tile Co.,* 69. Kans. 106; 76 Pac. 398 (April 9, 1904) the second and third points of the syllabus are as follows:

"The stipulation in an oil and gas lease that 'if wells are put in operation and at any time in future the parties of the second part (the lessee) shall become satisfied that it is not paying, he shall surrender this lease and remove all machinery, pipes and fixtures from the premises, and be released from all further obligations' does not put the lessee in the position of a tenant at will. The lease is not terminable at his option if the production of gas or oil on his assertion that a well is unproductive when the contrary is true.

The clause in the lease set out at page 2 construed to mean that if the lessee become satisfied that a particular well is not paying, and such fact exists, the lease is terminable with respect to the unproductive well, only.''

J. W. Cole and wife, on December 23, 1901, executed to C. D. Martin, Manager of the Kansas & Texas Oil Company, an oil and gas lease for a tract of 138 acres of land in Neosho County, Kansas. In April, 1902, Walter S. Dickey purchased this tract of land from Cole, taking a special warranty deed therefor. The conveyance was made subject to the oil and gas lease, made on December 23, 1901. The third stipulation in the lease provided that if gas were found in any well or wells in paying quantities, the lessor should have, on demand, sufficient gas for his tenants' domestic purposes, free, and lessee should have the remainder; and if lessee should market or use gas from any well or wells he should pay lessor therefor at the rate of $80.00 per year for each and every well during the time that such gas should be sold or utilized; and in case lessee should not sell or use gas from said well or wells he should pay lessor 1-2 as much, or $40.00 per year for each well so long as the gas was not used. By the fourth provision it was provided that if oil should be found in paying quantities upon the premises lessee should continue drilling wells as fast as possible until there should be eight wells drilled within one year from the date. The lease further provided that should lessee fail to have the first well in operation within seven months he should pay lessor $100.00 in cash. By the fifth provision of the lease it was provided that in case gas or oil should not be found in paying quantities upon the land the lease should be void and be surrendered, and the lessee should remove all his fixtures from the premises; and if wells were put in operation and at any time in the future lessee should become satisfied that the well or wells were not paying he should surrender the lease and remove all machinery, pipes and·fixtures from the premises and be relieved of all further obligations. It was further provided that in case the lessee should fail to keep and perform his part of the agreement and covenants of the lease he should thereby forfeit all rights and privileges claimed, and should thereupon, peacefully and without damage, surrender the premises to the lessor. Martin, the lessee, commenced drilling on the premises at once, and on or about January 13, 1902, completed a paying gas well. The lease was assigned

thereafter to the Coffeyville Brick & Tile Company. On May 9,
1902, Dickey, the owner of the land, brought an action against the
Brick Company to set aside and cancel the lease. The District
Court of Neosho County decided in favor of the Brick Company,
and Dickey appealed to the Supreme Court of Kansas, where the
decision was affirmed.

Sec. 9.—In *Barnsdall* v. *Boley*, 119 Fed. Rep. 191 (Ct. Ct. D.
W. Va. December 3, 1902), the fourth point of the headnotes is as
follows:

"Defendant executed to complainant's assignor an oil and gas
lease on royalty covering 74 acres of land, which was to run for
the term of five years, and as much longer 'as oil or gas was found
in paying quantities.' It·required the lessee to complete a well
thereon within three months, which he did, but drilled no other
wells, and made no serious effort to do so during the five years, although he was repeatedly requested to do so by the lessor. The
well drilled was a small producer, and was pumped at intervals
only, during the last year or two of the term, not producing enough
to pay the expenses of pumping. *Held,* that the lessee did not
comply with the implied conditions of the lease which required
him to develop the property in good faith; and that a court of
equity would not sustain and enforce the lease in his behalf after
the expiration of the five years, as against the lessor and others
to whom he had leased after that time, and who had rendered
the property productive."

John Boley executed an oil and gas lease to S. T. Mallory on
January 11, 1895. The lease was for 100 acres of land, and was
for the term of five years and as much longer as 'oil or gas was
found in paying quantities,' paying to the lessor 1-8 of the oil as
royalty. The hundred acres consisted of four tracts, one of 45
acres, one of 25 acres, one of 4 acres, all of which belonged to John
Boley, and one tract said to contain 40 acres, but which turned
out to be 68 acres, which belonged to the heirs of Caroline Boley.
Sometime in February, 1895, Mallory commenced drilling a well
on the 4-acre tract and completed it on March 4, 1895. The well
was pumped and after a short time, shut down. This well was
pumped at intervals from time to time during the lifetime of the
lease, but never continuously pumped. Mallory drilled but one

well, although the lessor repeatedly, during the term of the lease, requested his agent to put down other wells. Subsequent to the drilling of the well Mallory assigned the lease to Barnsdall, who had notice of the demand made by lessor for additional developments. On April 14, 1900, John Boley executed a lease for 45 acres, a part of the premises leased to Mallory, to Watt and others. On May 12, 1900, John Boley leased the 25-acre tract to A. H. Higby. On April 7, 1899, Barnsdall served a written notice on C. J. Watt and others that he claimed the property leased by John Boley to S. T. Mallory on January 11, 1895, by the assignment made by Mallory to him. This notice, however, seems to have been served before Boley leased to Watt and others. On September 5, 1900, Barnsdall filed his bill in equity in the Circuit Court of the United States for the Northern District of West Virginia, against Watt and others, and obtained an order restraining the defendants from interfering with his rights under the lease of January 11, 1895, or from drilling or operating upon any part of the leased premises, and from removing the oil therefrom. The defendants answered Barnsdall's bill and denied the validity of the lease claimed by him, and alleged that whatever right the original lessee had under the lease of January 11, 1895, had been terminated, not only by the expiration of the term but by reason of the fact that the lessee had failed and neglected to prosecute in good faith the development for oil upon the leased premises. The learned District Judge who delivered the opinion found from the evidence that there never was but one well drilled upon the property; and that that well was a small producer; and during the term only produced about 800 barrels; that the well was pumped at intervals from time to time during the lifetime of the lease; that there was no continuous pumping for the reason that the production of the well was so small that it did not justify continuous pumping. The Court held that John Boley had waived in the pleadings his right to enforce a forfeiture of the 4-acre tract, but as to the other lands not developed, the lease was forfeited.

Sec. 10.—In *Cassell* v. *Crothers*, 193 Pa. 359; 44 Atl. 446, analyzed under Chapter 6, the first point of the syllabus is as follows:

"In an oil lease for a fixed period, and 'as long thereafter as oil is found in paying quantities' where the lessor's compensation is 1-8 of the oil produced, the tenancy as to the surface
of the land, after the expiration of the fixed period, and after the
fact that oil is not being found and produced in paying quantities,
becomes susceptible of proof, is a tenancy in the nature of a tenancy at will, and if not actually terminated by mutual consent, or
continued by mutual consent in order that further exploration
may be made, may be terminated by either party."

Sec. 11.—In *Double* v. *Union Heat etc. Co.*, 172 Pa. 388; 33
Atl. 694, analyzed under Chapter 11, the second point of the syllabus is as follows:

"An oil and gas lease was to terminate by its own limitation
two years from its date; after that the lease was to continue 'as
much longer as oil and gas was found in paying quantities therein * * * * * * * * * * and should any well produce gas in sufficient
quantities to justify marketing, the lessor shall be paid at the rate
of two hundred dollars per year for such well so long as the gas
therefrom is sold.' *Held*, that after the rental clause became operative by the finding of gas in paying quantities the lessee could
not terminate without giving notice to the lessor of his intention
to do so."

Sec. 12.—In *Summerville* v. *Apollo Gas Co.*, 207 Pa. 334; 56
Atl. 876, analyzed under Chapter 11, the first point of the syllabus is as follows:

"Where an oil and gas lease was for two years 'and as much
longer as oil and gas are found in paying quantities' the court
may say as a matter of law that the lessor has no right to forfeit the lease at the end of two years because during that time no
oil or gas had been marketed, where the undisputed evidence
is that the production from a well on the land was one million
feet per day, worth, when piped and conveyed to market from
three to five cents per thousand feet."

Sec. 13.—In *Manhattan Oil Co.* v. *Carrell*, 164 Ind. 526; 73
N. E. 1084 (April 19, 1905), the syllabus is as follows:

"A provision in an oil lease that after the completion of the
first well the lessee should drill a specified number of wells, in

case oil should be found in paying quantities, did not mean that if oil was found in the test or first well in a sufficient quantity to pay a profit, however small, in excess of the cost of producing it excluding the cost of drilling the well and of equipment, then oil was found in paying quantities within the meaning of the contract, but meant that additional wells were to be drilled only in case oil was found in such quantities as would, taken in connection with other conditions, induce ordinarily prudent persons in a like position to expect a reasonable profit on the whole sum required to be expended; and whether oil was found in paying quantities was to be exclusively determined by the operator, acting in good faith.''

On August 4, 1897, Harry B. Carrell, in consideration of one dollar, granted to the Manhattan Oil Company, all the oil and gas under a certain described 50·acres of land in Blackford County, Indiana, with the right to enter thereon for the purpose of drilling and operating for oil or gas. The lease contained the following provision:

"It is further agreed that after the completion of the first well the said second party to drill and complete one well each ninety (90) days until there shall be completed five (5) wells, if oil is found in paying quantities. In case any of the additional wells should not be completed within ninety (90) days of the preceding well, then the second party shall pay to the first party thirty (30) dollars in advance for each thirty (30) days delay in completing said well.''

The oil company entered upon the premises, and within 90 days from August 4th, to-wit, on October 24, 1897, completed a well which produced both oil and gas. No other well was drilled or attempted to be drilled but possession of the premises was retained, and repeated efforts were made by the oil company to operate the well for oil up to February 25, 1901, when the lessor brought suit to recover of lessee the penalty provided for failure to drill additional wells. The suit was instituted in the Circuit Court of Wells County. Verdict and judgment were rendered in favor of plaintiff for $3,875. The overruling of the defendant's motion for new trial was the error assigned. The case was appealed to the Appellate Court and from that court transferred to the Supreme Court where the judgment was reversed, the court citing:

Young v. *Forest Oil Co.*, 194 Pa. 250; 45 Atl. 121.
Colgan v. *Forest Oil Co.*, 194 Pa. 242; 45 Atl. 119.
Ammons v. *South Penn O. Co.*, 47 W. Va. 610; 35 S. E. 1004.

REMEDIES.
(See Chapter 23)

CHAPTER 23.

PAYING QUANTITIES—REMEDIES.—LESSOR'S REMEDY.

Sec. 1.—Where a lessee is attempting to hold an oil and gas lease after the expiration of its term under the claim that it is producing oil or gas in paying quantities if in fact the production is not sufficient to pay a profit to the lessee upon the expense of production lessor may declare a forfeiture and recover possession of the property either by a possessory action, or by cancellation of the lease, in a court of equity or a court exercising equity powers, as a cloud upon his title.

Lowther Oil Co. v. *Miller-Sibley Oil Co.*, 53 W. Va. 501; 44
    S. E. 433; 97 Am. St. Rep. 1027.
Murdock-West Co. v. *Logan*, 69 Ohio St. 514; 69 N. E. 984.
Bay State Pet. Co. v. *Penn Lubricating Co.*, 27 Ky. L. Rep.
    1133; 87 S. W. 1102.
Barnsdall v. *Boley*, 119 Fed. 191.

Sec. 2.—Where a lessee has entered and discovered oil in paying quantities but refuses to protect the lines from drainage through wells on adjoining properties or fails to properly develop the premises but claims the right to hold the lease upon the grounds that it is producing oil in paying quantities, lessor may maintain a bill in equity to cancel the lease as to the unprotected or undeveloped portions of the land upon satisfactory proof that the failure of the lessee to drill additional wells amounts to a fraud upon the rights of lessor.

Young v. *Forest Oil Co.*, 194 Pa. 243; 45 Atl. 1021.

Sec. 3.—Where the lease provides for a specific term after which the lease is to continue as long as oil or gas is found in paying quantities, and contains a clause that should any well produce gas in sufficient quantities to justify marketing the lessor shall be paid a yearly rental for each well so long as the gas therefrom is sold, or words to that effect, after the gas rental clause becomes operative by the finding of gas in paying quantities and the marketing thereof unless the lease provides that lessee may surrender the same at any time upon the payment of all rentals due he cannot terminate the lease without giving notice to the lessor of his intention to do so; and lessor may recover the gas rental up to the time of such surrender, or until the lessee terminates the same after notice of his intention so to do.

Double v. *Union Heat etc. Co.*, 172 Pa. 388; 33 Atl. 694.

Sec. 4.—Where an oil and gas lease is for a fixed period and as long thereafter as oil or gas is found in paying quantities and the lessor's compensation is a royalty of the oil produced and an annual rental for gas sold or marketed off the premises and the lessee enters and discovers oil or gas in paying quantities after the expiration of the fixed period and after the fact that oil or gas is not being found and produced in paying quantities becomes susceptible of proof, the tenancy as to the surface of the land is in the nature of a tenancy at will and if not actually terminated by mutual consent, or continued by mutual consent, the lessor may terminate the lease at any time, and re-enter or recover possession by possessory action.

Cassell v. *Crothers*, 193 Pa. 359; 44 Atl. 446.

Sec. 5.—Where an oil and gas lease provides that if gas "be found in sufficient quantities to justify marketing the same" the lessee is bound to market the gas if found in paying quantities or show some good reason for not doing so; he will not, however, be required to market the gas at a loss, but only at a reasonable profit, and in determining whether it could be so marketed, the distance to market, the expense of marketing, and every circumstance of a similar kind should be taken into consideration. Where the lessee fails, after the discovery of gas in paying quantities, to market the same he will not be allowed to shut the gas in and hold the lease without the payment of the gas rental; and lessor may recover from lessee or his assigns the annual gas rental where good cause is not shown by lessee for not marketing the gas.

Iams v. Carnegie Nat. Gas Co., 194 Pa. 72; 45 Atl. 54.

LESSEE'S REMEDY.

Sec. 6.—A lessee who enters the demised premises and discovers oil or gas is the judge of whether or not the oil or gas is in fact in paying quantities. However, this judgment must be exercised in good faith. When oil or gas is so found lessee must go on and operate the property so as to make it of mutual benefit to both lessor and lessee. Lessee is not required to show that the oil or gas discovered is in sufficient quantities to repay his expenses incurred in exploration. Producing in paying quantities means paying a profit on the cost of production; that is, the income from the production must exceed the expense of producing the oil or gas. Where lessor undertakes to forfeit the lease lessee may defeat such forfeiture by showing that the wells on the demised premises produce sufficient oil or gas to pay a profit on the cost of operating.

Lowther Oil Co. v. *Miller-Sibley Oil Co.*, 53 W. Va. 501; 44 S. E. 433; 87 Am. St. Rep. 1027. Syl. 4.
Young v. *Forest Oil Co.*, 194 Pa. 243; 45 Atl. 1021. Syl. 4.

Sec. 7.—Where lessee has entered the demised premises and discovered gas he is the judge of whether or not the gas is in paying quantities, acting in good faith; and where he is willing to pay the gas rental he may shut the well in and hold the lease beyond the fixed term; and in a proceeding by the lessor to forfeit or cancel the lease or to compel additional developments the lessee may defeat such action by showing that the gas could not be profitably marketed; and in determining whether the gas could be profitably marketed the distance to market, the expense of marketing and every circumstance of a similar kind may be shown by lessee, and should be taken into consideration.

> *Iams* v. *Carnegie Nat. Gas Co.*, 194 Pa. 72; 45 Atl. 54.
> *McGraw Oil etc. Co.* v. *Kennedy*, 65 W. Va. 595; 64 S. E. 1027.
> *McKnight* v. *Manufacturers Nat. Gas Co.*, 146 Pa. 185; 23 Atl. 164; 28 Am. St. Rep. 790.

Sec. 8.—Where lessor brings suit to cancel the lease basing his suit upon the allegation of abandoment and alleging failure to develop or protect lines and relies upon the contention that the lease is not producing oil or gas in paying quantities, lessee may prevent cancellation of his lease by proof that he acted upon sound business judgment in view of the production, the surrounding conditions, cost and expense of additional wells, and by making it manifest that to drill additional wells would be a mere venture, and that the further development of the territory is the subject of an honest difference of opinion, and that the property is producing an amount of oil or gas sufficient to more than pay the cost of production.

> *Colgan* v. *Forest Oil Co.*, 194 Pa. 234; 45 Atl. 119; 75 Am. St. Rep. 695.
> *Young* v. *Forest Oil Co.*, 194 Pa. 243; 45 Atl. 1021.
> *Manhattan Oil Co.* v. *Carrell*, 164 Ind. 526; 73 N. E. 1084.

CHAPTER 24.

FORFEITURE BY ABANDONMENT.

Sec. 1.—To constitute abandonment by the lessee of a lease for oil and gas purposes there must be both an intention to abandon and an actual relinquishment of the leased premises.

> *Bluestone Coal Co.* v. *Bell*, 38 W. Va. 297; 18 S. E. 493.
> *Crawford* v. *Ritchie*, 43 W. Va. 252; 27 S. E. 220.
> *Steelsmith* v. *Gartlan*, 45 W. Va. 27; 29 S. E. 978.

Parish Fork Oil Co. v. *Bridgewater Gas Co.*, 51 W. Va. 588; 42 S. E. 655; 59 L. R. A. 566.

Lowther Oil Co. v. *Miller-Sibley Oil Co.*, 53 W. Va. 501; 44 S. E. 433.

Sult v. *Hochstetter Oil Co.*, 63 W. Va. 317; 61 S. E. 307.

Henne v. *South Penn Oil Co.*, 52 W. Va. 192; 43 S. E. 147.

Henderson v. *Ferrell*, 183 Pa. 547; 38 Atl. 1018.

Stage v. *Boyer*, 183 Pa. 560; 38 Atl. 1035.

Marshall v. *Oil Co.*, 198 Pa. 83; 47 Atl. 927.

Calhoun v. *Neely*, 201 Pa. 97; 50 Atl. 957.

Tennessee Oil etc. Co. v. *Brown*, 65 C. C. A. 524; 121 Fed. 696.

Logan Nat. Gas etc. Co. v. *Great Southern Gas etc. Co.*, 61 C. C. A. 359; 126 Fed. 623.

Federal Oil Co. v. *Western Oil Co.*, 112 Fed. 373; (C. C. D. Ind.) Affirmed 121 Fed. 674; 57 C. C. A. 428.

Foster v. *Elk Fork Oil etc. Co.*, 90 Fed. 178; 32 C. C. A. 560, affirming 84 Fed. 839.

McIntosh v. *Robb*, 4 Cal. App. 484; 88 Pac. 517.

Federal Betterment Co. v. *Blaes*, 75 Kan. 69; 88 Pac. 555.

Mills v. *Hartz*, 77 Kan. 218; 94 Pac. 142.

Flanagan v. *Marsh*, 32 Ky. Law Rep. 184; 105 S. W. 424.

Kimball Oil Co. v. *Keeton*, 31 Ky. Law Rep. 146; 101 S. W. 887.

Murray v. *Barnhart and Murray* v. *Graham*, 117 La. 1023; 42 Southern 489.

Florence Oil & Refining Co. v. *McCumber*, 38 Colo, 366; 88 Pac. 265.

Buffalo Valley Oil etc. Co. v. *Jones*, 75 Kan. 18; 88 Pac. 537.

Heintz v. *Shortt*, 149 Pa. 286; 24 Atl. 316.

Longansport etc. Co. v. *Seegar*, 165 Ind. 1; 74 N. E. 500.

Dill v. *Fraze*, 169 Ind. 53; 79 N. E. 971.

Ohio Oil Co. v. *Detamore*, 165 Ind. 243; 73 N. E. 906.

Martel v. *Jennings-Heywood Oil Syndicate*, 114 La. 903; 38 Southern 253.

Smith v. *Root*, 66 W. Va. 633; 66 S. E. 1005.

Federal Oil Co. v. *Western Oil Co.*, 121 Fed. 674; 57 C. C. A. 428.

Hooks v. *Frost*, 165 Pa. 238; 30 Atl. 846.

Garrett v. *South Penn Oil Co.*, 66 W. Va. 587; 66 S. E. 741.

Shenk v. *Stahl*, 35 Ind. App. 444; 74 N. E. 538.

McMillan v. *Titus*, 222 Pa. 500; 72 Atl. 240.

Sec. 2.—In *Bluestone Coal Co.* v *Bell*, 38 W. Va., 297; 18 S. E. 493, analyzed under Chapter 28, syl. 2 is as follows:

"If nothing has been done under said contract for the period of seventeen years from the date of the contract, the lessor had a right to presume the contract has been abandoned and said lessee or his assigns cannot, after having been guilty of such laches, restrain said lessor from cutting and using the timber on the said land, and enjoining him from cutting and removing the same."

In this case the lessee, after failing to do anything under his contract for seventeen years, filed a bill in equity against the lessor to restrain him from permitting the timber to be cut upon the premises. The court held, that such original lessee had abandoned the premises and refused to grant the relief prayed for. Judge English delivering the opinion, at page 309, said:

"In making this agreement to lease the coal mentioned therein and to let the lessor have the timber to aid in its safe and economic mining, it is presumed that said David Bell expected to receive some return in the shape of royalty during his natural lifetime; and, although the agreement provides that the lease is to continue for 99 years, the law contemplates that operations shall be commenced in a reasonable time, in order that the lessor may enjoy his royalty and the lessee the coal; otherwise the presumption arises that the lessee has abandoned his right thereunder."

The lease construed by the court in this case was one for coal and timber. The principles announced have been subsequently by this court frequently applied and cited in the construction of oil and gas leases.

Sec. 3.—In *Crawford* v. *Ritchie*, 43 W. Va., 252; 27 S. E. 220, analyzed under Chapter 5, syl. 1 is as follows:

"1. Where a lease is made on the 12th day of April, 1889, 'for the sole and only purpose of drilling and operating for petroleum oil and gas, for the term of 20 years, or as long thereafter as oil or gas is found in paying quantities;' and providing that the lessee shall commence one well on or before the 10th day of May, 1889, and prosecute the same to completion, unavoidable accidents excepted, and on the 26th day of October, 1889, the time is extended for such commencement of work by written endorsement on the lease to the 28th day of November, 1889, and nothing is done under said lease for the period of seven years from said last named date, the lessee is presumed to have abandoned the said lease, and a court of equity may entertain a suit to cancel the lease and quiet title."

After executing an oil and gas lease to J. B. Ritchie, and nothing having been done under the same for a period of seven years, the lessor, Robert Crawford, filed a bill in equity in the Circuit Court of Marshall County, West Virginia, alleging the forfeiture of the lease by abandonment, the bill praying for a cancellation thereof as a cloud on plaintiff's title. The Circuit Court sustained defendant's demurrer and dismissed the plaintiff's bill. The plaintiff appealed, and the Court of Appeals reversed the Circuit Court. Judge McWhorter, delivering the opinion of the court at page 257, said:

"It was the duty of defendant to begin his work at the time specified, and to complete it in a reasonable time. The amended bill alleges that gas and oil have been developed in and upon other lands near to and in the region of the leased premises, and were, at the time of the filing of the amended bill, being so developed; and that, by reason of said contract of lease, he had not only been impeded in, but prevented from, developing his said territory, alleging that he is injured thereby, and that his title is beclouded, and that he has no adequate remedy at law; he cannot have his action of ejectment, he being in possession; and there is no way of ascertaining the measure of damages. The defendant has no vested title and has abandoned the lease, never having done anything under the lease after a lapse of about eight years. This on the theory that the allegations of the amended bill are true, which by his demurrer, the defendant admits."

Sec. 4.—In *Steelsmith* v. *Gartlan*, 45 W. Va., 27; 29 S. E. 978, analyzed under Chapter 5, syl. 2 is as follows:

"Such lease must be construed as a whole, and if there is no provision therein contained requiring the boring of another well, after the first unsuccessful attempt is completed and abandoned, the lease becomes invalid and of no binding force as to any of its provisions."

Judge Dent, delivering the opinion of the court at page 35, said:

"In this case the condition was expressed, but the same rules applied with equal force to implied conditions. However, as before shown, the lessee having abandoned the only obligatory search provided for in his lease, it died on his hands without surrender, forfeiture, or intentional abandonment on his part, for he was without authority to make further explorations without the consent of, and arrangement as to conditions, with the lessor; In other words, without a new lease or extension of the old. Such leases are construed most strictly against the lessee and favorable to the lessor. *Bettman* v. *Harness*, 42 W. Va. 433 (26 S. E. 271.) When a lease provides the mode, manner and character of search to be made, implications in regard thereto are excluded thereby as repugnant. And the demise for the purpose of operating for oil and gas for the period of five years is dependent upon the discovery of oil and gas in the search provided for, and, if such search is unsuccessful the demise fails therewith, as such discovery is a condition precedent to the continuance or vesting of the demise.''

This lease provided that in case no well should be completed on the premises within one month from the date of the lease it should become null and void unless the lessee should pay for further delay at the rate of $50.00 per month until a well should be completed. The lease was for a term of five years, and lessees paid rental until they completed a well, which was dry. They then abandoned the premises and did nothing further for a period of eighteen months. The landowner made requests for surrender of the lease or payment of the rental, which demands lessees refused, and the landowner then made a second lease and the second lessee filed a bill in equity for the cancellation of the original lease on the grounds of abandonment. The Circuit Court dismissed the plaintiff's bill, and he appealed. The Supreme Court reversed the Circuit Court and directed the cancellation of the original lease upon the ground of abandonment.

Sec. 5.—In *Parish Fork Oil Company* v. *Bridge Water Gas Company*, 51 W. Va., 583; 42 S. E. 655; 59 L. R. A. 567, analyzed under Chapter 5, syl. 4 is as follows:

''4. The law recognizes a distinction between the abandonment of operations under an oil lease and an intention to abandon or surrender the lease, itself. Unless bound by the terms of the lease so to do, it will not permit the lessee to hold the lease without operating under it, and thereby prevent the lessor from operating on the land or leasing it to others.''

The landowner made a lease for oil and gas purposes, and the lessee and his assignees entered upon the premises and explored for oil, but produced none, although they found a showing. Subsequently they abandoned the premises. The lessor made a second lease for the same premises to J. W. Bell for the Bridgewater Gas Company. The claimants to the two conflicting leases each attempted to begin operations at the same time, and each filed a bill in equity against the other for injunction and cancellation of the opposing lease. The second lessee obtained an injunction and upon hearing the Circuit Court cancelled the original lease. The original lessee appealed to the Court of Appeals and that court affirmed the Circuit Court.

Sec. 6.—In *Lowther Oil Co.* v. *Miller-Sibley Oil Co.*, 53 W. Va., 501; 44 S. E. 433, analyzed under Chapter 5, syl. 3 is as follows:

"3. To constitute abandonment by lessee of a lease for oil, there must be both an intention to abandon and an actual relinquishment of the leased premises."

Metz made a lease for oil and gas purposes, which by assignment became the property of Miller-Sibley Oil Company. Two wells were drilled under this lease, and while oil was found in one of the wells it was not saved or marketed. The company then moved its tools and appliances off the Metz farm to other undertakings several miles away. Work was abandoned on the Metz farm under the original lease in January, 1899. Metz made a second lease on January 9, 1900. There had been a cessation of work for a year by the Miller-Sibley Company. The second lessee began work in June, 1900, more than fifteen months after the original lessees ceased work. The original lessees, after the second lease was made, entered upon the premises and discovered oil in paying quantities, and claimed that by their operations they were entitled to the vested right to produce the oil. The Lowther Oil Company, the second lessee, brought suit in chancery in the Circuit Court of Calhoun County, against the Miller-Sibley Company, the assignee of the original lessee, to restrain it from interfering with the premises, and for a decree cancelling its lease. The Circuit Court granted the relief prayed for and cancelled the original lease. The Miller-Sibley Company appealed to the Court of Appeals, and that court affirmed the decree of the court below.

Sec. 7.—In *Sult* v. *Hochstetter Oil Co.*, 63 W. Va., 317·, 61 S. E. 307, analyzed under Chapter 27, syl. 6 is as follows:

"6. A lease for oil and gas purposes may be terminated by express surrender or by a surrender in law, effected by abandonment of the premises by the lessee and resumption of possession thereof by lessor; and whether such surrender in law has occurred is a question of intention."

The original lessee entered into possession of the premises, made some explorations and discovered gas. The gas right was afterward sold to the Hochstetter Oil Company. The oil rights came into the hands of the Shawmut Oil Company, a corporation, which company drilled an unproductive and worthless well on the land, and then removed its machinery and appliances from the premises and the stockholders dissolved the corporation. In the opinion, delivered by Judge Poffenbarger, pages 313-314, he said:

"In *Steelsmith* v. *Gartlan*, 45 W. 'Va. 27; 29 S. E. 978; 44 L. R. A. 107, .the lessee, after having drilled an unproductive well plugged it, removed his derrick and tools, including the casing and left the premises. The lessor made repeated demands upon him to do further work on the property, and on his refusal to do so executed a new lease to Steelsmith. The period of absence from the premises was considerable, but the court in the reasoning by which it reached its conclusion, laid stress, not upon the length of that period, but upon the conduct of the parties, which left no room to doubt the lessee's intention not to do anything more, or the lessor's intention to treat the lease as ended. In *Parish Fork Oil Co.* v. *Bridgewater Gas Co.*, 51 W. Va. 583; 42 S. E. 655; 59 L. R. A. 560, the period of cessation of work or absence of the lessee from the premises was not regarded as having so much weight as the misconception on the part of the lessees of their rights under the contract, and of their having allowed the well they had drilled on the premises to fill up and become worthless, and the contractor who had drilled that well, to remove all of his machinery from the premises. Another illustration of the manner in which the court weighs and gives effect to the acts of the parties may be found in the case of *Lowther Oil Co.* v. *Miller-Sibley Oil Co.*, 53 W. Va. 501; 44 S. E. 433; 97 Am. St. Rep. 1027. All these cases, and numerous others, make it plain that the termination of a lease by operation of law on the theory of abandonment and resumption of possession, depends entirely upon the intention of the parties, and that the materiality or signification of the length of the period of abandonment is its tendency to prove intention on the part of the lessee, to retain or give up the lease."

The court found that the original lease, notwithstanding the discovery of gas thereunder, had been by the claimants thereof abandoned. The claimant of the mineral right under a reservation in a former deed filed a bill in equity against the Hochstetter Oil Company, which company undertook to re-enter the land and develop the same, and obtained an injunction against it, and the appointment of a Receiver for the property. From this decree the Hochstetter Oil Company appealed and the Supreme Court affirmed the decree so far as it enjoined the Hochstetter Oil Company from operating on the 15-acre reservation.

Sec. 8.—In *Henne* v. *South Penn Oil Co.*, 52 W. Va., 192; 43 S. E. 147, (Dec. 6, 1902) syl. 2 is as follows:

"2. M. and M. by deed dated October 19, 1898, leased certain premises to M. for oil and gas purposes, which lease contained the following provision: 'This lease shall become null and void and all rights hereunder shall cease and determine unless a well shall be completed on the said premises within six months from the date hereof, or unless the lessee shall pay at the rate of $25.50 quarterly in advance for each additional three months such completion is delayed from the time above mentioned for the completion of such well until a well is completed, and it is agreed that the completion of such well shall be and operate as a full liquidation of all rental under this provision during the remainder of the term of this lease.' M. the lessee, assigned said lease to S. P. Oil Co., which was the lessee for oil and gas purposes of a large area of territory including all tracts contiguous to said premises, the S. P. Oil Co., drilled a well to completion April 4, 1900, paying the stipulated rental until the well was completed, but which well was 'dry.' It then removed all its material and machinery from the premises and proceeded to drill other wells nearer to developments already made on the line towards the premises in question. *Held*, that under the lease and circumstances of the case the S. P. Oil Co., was entitled to a reasonable time in which to return and make further developments under the lease."

Sarah S. Martin and D. P. Martin executed an oil and gas lease to William Michaels on the 20th day of December, 1898, for oil and gas purposes, for a tract of land in Harrison County, West

Virginia, for the term of ten years, upon the usual royalty and $300.00 per year for each gas well drilled on the premises, the product from which should be marketed and used off the premises, the lease to become null and void unless a well should be completed on the premises within six months from date or unless lessee should pay $25.50 quarterly in advance for each additional three months the completion of a well should be delayed. It was expressly covenanted that the completion of such well should be and operate as a full liquidation of all rental under the provisions of the lease during the remainder of the term thereof; and that the lessee should have the right at any time to remove all machinery and fixtures placed on the premises. On December 22, 1898, Michaels assigned the lease to the South Penn Oil Company, which company completed a well on the premises about April 4, 1900, which was a "dry hole." Shortly after the completion of the well the company removed its machinery and appliances from the premises and set the same up for drilling another well on other property nearby. On October 2, 1900, the South Penn Company located another well known as Number 2, on the Martin property, and in a few days begun work on this well. On October 8, 1900, Sarah S. Martin and D. P. Martin executed to C. D. Henne a lease for the same property in consideration of $300.00 cash, which lease contained the following express provision:

"It is however, agreed between the parties hereto that this lease is made and this contract entered into subject to a certain other lease and contract made for the same premises by the parties of the first part made to William Michaels, bearing date on October 19, 1898, and recorded in Deed Book 108, page 375, in the County Court of Harrison County; and that the existence of said former lease is made known to the party of the second part, who is fully informed and aware of its terms and conditions."

Henne caused notice to be served on the South Penn Oil Company of the execution of the lease to him by the Martins. The South Penn Oil Company, disregarding the notice, continued the drilling on Number 2, and completed the same, and also began and completed a third well, both of which wells were producers of oil in paying quantities. At January Rules, 1901, C. B. Henne filed his bill of complaint against the South Penn Oil Company in the Circuit Court of Harrison County, claiming to be entitled to the possession of the premises under his lease, and praying for an injunction against the South Penn Oil Company, and for the appointment of a receiver to take charge of and operate the premises for oil, and for the cancellation of the original lease. The South Penn Oil Company answered, claiming that it had fully complied with its contract of lease; that it had never abandoned nor intended to abandon its lease, and had paid all the rentals required to be paid up to the time of the completion of the first well. Upon final hearing and upon the depositions taken in the cause the Circuit Court, on June 8, 1901, entered a decree denying the relief prayed for by the plaintiff and dismissing his bill. From this decree the plaintiff appealed, and the Court of Appeals affirmed the Circuit Court. Two questions are presented in this case of controlling influence, aside from the question of abandonment. First, the lessor agreed, in consideration of the drilling of a test well, and the payment of rental until its completion, that such payment and such drilling would liquidate all the rentals otherwise accruing after the completion of the test well, and during the term. Second, the lessor did not, unequivocally declare a forfeiture by the making of the lease to the plaintiff Henne, but made the Henne lease subject to the outstanding lease held by the South Penn Oil Company. Aside from these questions, the time which elapsed between the 4th day of April, 1900, when the first well was completed, and the re-entry of the South Penn Company for the purpose of continuing developments on October 2, 1900, taken in connection with the express authority of the lessee to remove the machinery and fixtures, and the additional fact that this machinery and fixtures were removed to another location which tended to develop the demised premises, was not considered of sufficient length to warrant the court in concluding that the South Penn Company had abandoned the lease.

Sec. 9.—In *Henderson* v. *Ferrell*, 183 Pa., 547; 38 Atl. 1018 (January 3, 1898) the syllabus is as follows:

"In an action of ejectment by the lessee in an oil and gas lease to recover possession of the oil and gas, where it appears that the operations were to be begun on the leased premises within 30 days from the date of the lease, the case is for the jury where the evidence for the lessee, although contradicted, tends to show that he drove a stake on the premises upon the afternoon of the 30th day, and began unloading lumber upon the land, with the bona fide intention of sinking a well, and that he was prevented from so doing by the action of the lessor in driving his employes from the premises, and that the delay in beginning operations sooner was caused by inability to secure the materials, machinery and labor necessary for the proper performance of the work. The lessee did not forfeit his rights if he, in good faith, on the last day, commenced operations preparatory to drilling a well.''

On February 4, 1896, Albert Behling made a lease of a lot of ground to Alex Adams for oil and gas purposes. The lease gave to lessee the exclusive right of drilling and operating for petroleum and gas, lessee to commence operations on· the premises within thirty days from the date of the lease, and if he failed to commence operations within that time, then the lease to be null and void. On February 24, 1896, Adams assigned a half interest in the lease to Henderson. Nothing was done on the premises by the lessees or by their direction until March 5th, that being the last day of the period allowed by the lease within which to commence operations. On that day Henderson drove a stake near the center of the lot to indicate the location of the supposed well, and the point at which the lumber required in the performance of the work, called for by the lease, should be deposited. In the afternoon of the same day, and while an employe of the lessee was unloading some lumber upon the lot, in accordance with their instructions, he was met by the lessor who denied that they had any right to put the lumber on the lot, claiming that the time for the commencement of operations had expired in the forenoon of that day. The lessor was accompanied by a number of persons who were in accord with his manifest purpose to prevent the unloading of the lumber on the lot, or the occupancy of it by the lessees or their workmen. The lessor's insistence that the lumber should not be deposited on the lot resulted in the unloading of the balance of it by the roadside, and in lessor's removal from the lot of the lumber unloaded there. Alexander Adams, the lessee, and T. O. Henderson, the assignee of the one-half interest in the lease, brought an action of ejectment for the oil and gas under the demised premises in the Court of Common Pleas of Washington County, against the lessor, and obtained verdict and judgment. Defendant appealed, and the Supreme Court of Pennsylvania affirmed the judgment.

Sec. 10.—In *Stage* v. *Boyer,* 183 Pa., 560; 38 Atl. 1035, (Jan. 3, 1898) the syllabus is as follows:

"An oil and gas lease for ten years provided that a failure to commence operations and complete a well with one year or pay a fixed sum for delay would be ground for a failure of all rights under the lease, the lessee to have the privilege of abandoning the premises at any time, but an abandonment was not to deprive him of the right to convey oil and gas over this land from other lands, upon the payment of an annual rental for the privilege. The lessee drilled one unproductive well within a year, and he then notified the lessor of his intention to abandon the well. He drew the casing, plugged the well, removed his machinery, and thereafter conducted no further operations on the land. He, however, operated on other lands in the vicinity. Four or five years after the lessee abandoned the search, the lessor demanded a surrender of the lease, but the lessee refused the request, and testified on the trial of an ejectment brought by him to enforce his lease, that he had not abandoned his lease and never had intended to do so. *Held,* (1) that the evidence was sufficient to sustain a finding that the lessee had abandoned the right to operate wells under the lease; (2) that the lessee's refusal to surrender the lease was explained by the fact that he had the right under it to convey oil and gas over the lessor's lands from other lands."

The lessor brought ejectment in the Court of Common Pleas of Butler County against lessee for possession of the tract of land. The case was tried by the court without a jury and judgment rendered for defendant, from which judgment plaintiff appealed and the Supreme Court affirmed the judgment on the grounds that the lease gave the lessee two rights: one to search for oil and gas, the other to convey oil and gas in pipes from other lands through and over the farm leased. For the second right the lessee was not required to pay until he exercised it. The court held that holding the lease under the second right was a reserved right independent of the first right, which the lessee had abandoned.

Sec. 11.—In *Marshall* v. *Forest Oil Co.,* 198 Pa. 83; 47 Atl. 927, (Jan. 7, 1901) the second and third points of the syllabus are as follows:

"2. Where a lessee in an oil and gas lease does not absolutely covenant to develop the land, but merely agrees that he will commence operations within a specified period, or thereafter pay a certain fixed sum, monthly as rental, and there is nothing in the lease providing that it shall be forfeited by the non-payment of the rental, the only forfeiture contemplated being that resulting from an abandonment of the lease, and the removal of the lessee's property from the premises, the lessor cannot, by an action of ejectment, enforce a forfeiture merely because the lessee failed to pay the rental. In such case the lessor's remedy is to proceed for the collection of the rent due, and upon failing to recoover it, the lessee's rights will be divested.

3. Where an oil and gas lease does not provide for a forfeiture for the non-payment of rentals, but only by an abandonment by the lessee, it is error for the court to so charge the jury that the latter may be misled into the belief that a mere failure to pay the rental was a ground for the forfeiture, although the subject of abandonment was submitted to them.''

A. H. Knauff, on August 28, 1895, in consideration of $675 cash, executed an oil and gas lease to George M. Marshall for a tract of land in Butler County, Pennsylvania. The lessee agreed to commence operations on the premises within ninety days, or thereafter pay to lessor a rental of $14.00 per month until operations should be commenced. The lease was for a term of ten years from date and as long thereafter as oil or gas could be produced in paying quantities, and provided that the lessee should have the right at any time to surrender the lease by paying the rental due to the time of such surrender, and be relieved of all conditions unfulfilled, and from that time the agreement to be null and void. The lessee did not commence operations at the expiration of 90 days, but paid the rental up to May 28, 1897. On May 26, 1897, the lessee made a location and was about to commence operations when, as he claimed, he was stopped in pursuance to an understanding with lessor that if he kept a man named Burr off the premises the time for beginning work was indefinitely extended and no rental was to be charged for the interval of inactivity. After May 27, 1897, the lessee did nothing, and on May 22, 1899, Knauff leased the premises for oil and gas purposes to S. S. Reesman, who assigned the lease to the Forest Oil Company. On October 20, 1899, Marshall brought ejectment against the Forest Oil Company for recovery of the possession of the property. Verdict and judgment were rendered for the defendant. Marshall appealed, and the Supreme Court of Pennsylvania set aside the verdict, and granted a new trial.

Sec. 12.—In *Hooks* v. *Forst*, 165 Pa., 238; 30 Atl. 846 (Jan. 7, 1895) the syllabus is as follows:

"Where the lessees under an oil and gas lease have an absolute right to rescind the lease at any time, and such lessees never enter into possession of the demised premises, the rights and privileges under the lease may be surrendered by parol.

An oil and gas lease gave the lessor no right to rescind, but provided that the lessees 'shall have the right at any time to surrender up this lease and be released from all moneys due and conditions unfulfilled.' The lessees did not absolutely covenant to develop the land, but only agreed to bore or pay one hundred dollars per month if they did not. The lessees never entered into possession of the land. The evidence tended to show that after two monthly payments had been made, two of the three lessees asked the lessor for time on the third monthly payment, and that it was agreed between them that the time should be extended three weeks, and if the money was not then paid they would surrender the lease. At the end of three weeks the money was not paid, and one of the lessees told the lessor, that he should go on and lease to anyone, and that the lease would be returned. The lease was never formally re-delivered. Sixteen months afterwards the lessor leased the premises to other parties. *Held*, that the evidence was sufficient to establish a rescission of the lease.

In such a case a tender of monthly rental after the rescission had been consummated could not revive the lessee's rights or privileges.

Under the above lease the lessees were not tenants in common but were joint grantees of a right or privilege which had never been exercised, and were bound jointly to perform the covenants of the contract on which the right depended; the obligation was not severable. The declaration and acts of two of the lessees were therefore binding upon the third."

On October 30, 1889, Thomas Anderson made an oil and gas lease to F. M. Campbell, M. Lahey, and W. R. Stoughton, for a tract of land in Butler County, Pennsylvania. The lease was made in consideration of One Dollar and of the covenants and agreements therein mentioned, for the term of fifteen years, and so long thereafter as oil or gas could be produced in paying quantities, and contained the following stipulations:

"The party of the second part hereby agrees to pay the sum of one hundred dollars per month, the receipt of first payment is hereby acknowledged, until one well is completed.

November 30, 1889, received from Lahey, Campbell and Stoughton one hundred dollars for rent on lease in full to December 30, 1889.

It is further agreed that the second party, their heirs or· assigns shall have the right at any time to surrender up this lease and be released from all moneys due and conditions unfulfilled, and then and from that time this lease and agreement shall be null and void and no longer binding on either party, and the payments which shall have been made be held by the party of the first part as the full stipulated damages for the non-fulfillment of the foregoing contract.''

One Hundred Dollars was paid by lessees for the first month's rental, and also a second one hundred dollars was paid on November 30th, following. Lessees made no further payments, nor did they do anything in the way of developments. When the third one hundred dollars came due, January 1, 1890, lessees were unable to pay, and asked Anderson for an extension of time. This was granted, and, as lessor claimed, on condition that if not paid at the end of three weeks the lease should be surrendered or rescinded. The money was not paid, and on June 17, 1891, about sixteen months after the alleged rescission, Anderson leased the same premises to Forst and others, who went into possession for the purpose of drilling for oil, and who made successful developments. Campbell assigned his interest to Hooks, and he and the other original lessees brought an action of ejectment in the Court of Common Pleas of Butler County against Forst for the recovery of possession of the premises. Judgment was rendered for defendant. Plaintiffs appealed and the Supreme Court affirmed the judgment.

Sec. 13.—In *Calhoun* v. *Neely,* 201 Pa., 97; 50 Atl. 967, (January 6, 1902) the second point of the syllabus is as follows:

''Where a lessee under an oil lease for the term of fifteen years goes upon the leased premises and drills and completes a well which is found to be dry, and thereupon removes from the premises all the machinery used in drilling the well, leaving nothing except an oil tank which was allowed to rot on the ground, and does nothing further and asserts no title until after the expiration of nine years, and until after the premises had been leased to other parties who succeeded in drilling paying wells, the court will assume as a matter of law, that the first lease had been abandoned.'''

Frederick Mohr, on July 28, 1890, made an oil and gas lease

to the Pleasant Valley Oil & Gas Company for a tract of land in
Beaver County, Pennsylvania, for a term of fifteen years from
date, and as much longer as oil or gas should be found in paying
quantities, operations to be commenced on the premises thirty
days from the date, and prosecuted with due diligence to completion. The lease was assigned to Calhoun and others who within
sixty days from the date of the lease erected a rig and drilled a test
well on the premises, but obtained no oil. As soon as the well
was completed the assignees removed from the premises all the
machinery used in drilling the well, leaving nothing except an oil
tank which was allowed to rot on the ground. They did nothing
and asserted no title until Mohr, on June 5, 1899, nearly nine
years after the date of the lease, leased 36 acres of the same land
to Neely, and he, with others as assignees, went into possession
of the premises and succeeded in drilling paying wells. The assignees of the original lease then brought a suit in ejectment in
the Court of Common Pleas of Beaver County against the defendant, the second lessee, and his assigns. Verdict and judgment were rendered for defendants. Plaintiffs appealed, and the
Supreme Court affirmed the judgment.

Sec. 14.—In *Tennessee Oil, etc., Co.* v. *Brown,* 131 Fed. 696;
65 C. C. A. 524, (July 15, 1904) paragraphs 2-3 of head note are
as follows:

"2. Where a mining lease required the grantee to make a
search for minerals on the land within reasonable time as a condition precedent to the right to take minerals discovered on the
terms specified, the duty of exploration includes a search for all
the minerals named in the lease which might reasonably be expected to be found on the land, considering known geological conditions, to such an extent as would not only determine the presence or absence of minerals, but their commercial value, considering their abundance and accessibility.
3. Where a mining lease required the grantee to search for
minerals within a reasonable time as a condition precedent to his
right to take minerals from the land under the lease, his failure
to make any search or examination, except a mere superficial
one, of which the grantor had no notice, for a period of fifteen
years, entitled the lessor to treat the lease as abandoned."

Richard Clayton entered into a written contract with George
W. Colbert, whereby Colbert, as party of the first part, in con-

sideration of one dollar paid, and of the further consideration of the agreements mentioned in the contract, bargained, sold and conveyed unto the second party all the mineral, coal, iron ore, potters' clay, and other minerals, and all rock or petroleum oil and salines, and all timber suitable for lumber in, upon, or under a tract of land in the County of Scott, in the State of Tennessee. The agreement recited the granting to second party the exclusive right to enter upon the said land at any time thereafter to search for coal, iron ore and all other minerals, oil and salines, and when found, to remove the same. The agreement specified the royalties to be paid in case he entered and discovered minerals or oil, coal, or iron ore of the quality and quantity sufficient to market the same, payment to be made within five years after the completion of a railroad built in connection with any leading railroad by which said minerals or oils could be taken to any large market. The sum of ten dollars per year was to be paid to first party until mining should be commenced on the premises or during the continuance of the contract; and a failure to make these payments yearly upon request should be deemed an abandonment of the agreement. The second party reserved the right to abandon the lands and mining at any time and to remove all his buildings and fixtures therefrom. The second party paid nothing except the nominal consideration of one dollar. After a period of over twenty-five years had elapsed, Slavin conveyed the property to the Tennessee Oil, Gas & Mineral Company. This company took possession of the premises and instituted suit in equity in the Circuit Court of the United States for the Eastern District of Tennessee, against Colbert and others to cancel the agreement made between the said Slavin and Colbert as a cloud upon their title. The Circuit Court entered a decree cancelling the contract, from which decree defendants appealed to the Circuit Court of Appeals for the Sixth Circuit and that court affirmed the decree.

Sec. 15.—In *Logan Nat. Gas Co.* v. *Great Southern, etc. Co.,* 126 Fed. 623; 61 C. C. A. 359, (December 21, 1903) the head notes are as follows:

"1. Leases were executed by owners of land purporting to grant the same to an oil company for the purpose only of operating thereon for oil and gas, in consideration of a royalty to be paid the lessors, so long as oil and gas should be found thereon in paying quantities. No other time was stated for the termination of the grant nor was any time fixed for the commencement of operations. *Held,* that it was an implied condition of such leases that the lessee should drill wells and commence operations thereunder within a reasonable time, and that its failure to take any steps to that end for four years entitled the lessors to treat the contract as abandoned, and to lease to other parties.

2. The fact that under a provision of such leases the lessee issued to the lessor what were denominated 'first mortgage bonds' for a certain amount per acre, with interest payable from its net profits, reserving the right to cancel the same and abandon the leases, did not affect the right of the lessor to treat the leases as abandoned, although they had not returned the bond, where they had received no payments thereon, such bonds not being negotiable nor of any validity after the leases were terminated by the act of either party.

3. A lessee under an oil and gas lease, although out of possession, may maintain a suit in equity in a Federal Court to protect his rights thereunder by enjoining the removal of oil and gas from the premises by a claimant under another lease, the effect of which would be to destroy his estate, and, having acquired jurisdiction for that purpose, the court may retain it to settle the question of title as between the parties, and to cancel defendant's lease as a cloud on complainant's title.''

On April 12, 1894, Noah Conrad and Anna E. Sheets, respectively, executed two leases to the Fairfield Gas & Oil Company, conferring upon the company the exclusive right to operate on lands described therein for gas and oil. On May 4, 1898, the same lessors made two other leases to Carr, conferring upon him the exclusive right to operate the lands for gas and oil. The Fairfield leases, by assignment, came into the possession of the Great Southern Gas & Oil Company. The Carr leases were assigned to the Logan Natural Gas & Fuel Company. Nothing was done by the original lessee, or its assignee, for a period of over four years. The assignee of Carr filed a bill in equity in the Circuit Court of the United States for the Southern District of Ohio for the cancellation of the leases of April 12, 1894, as a cloud upon its title. The Circuit Court entered a decree cancelling the leases. The claimants to the leases appealed to the Circuit Court of Appeals for the Sixth Circuit, where the decree was affirmed. As authority for the decree cancelling the lease the court cited:

Allegheny Oil Co. v. *Snyder,* 106 Fed. 764; 45 C. C. A. 604.

Upon the question of jurisdiction the court cited:

Allegheny Oil Co. v. *Snyder,* supra.
Peck v. *Ayers & Lord Tie Co.,* 116 Fed. 273; 53 C. C. A. 551.

Sec. 16.—In *Elk Fork Oil & Gas Co.* v. *Jennings,* 84 Fed. 839, affirmed in *Foster* v. *Elk Fork Oil & Gas Co.,* 90 Fed. 178; 32 C. C. A. 560, analyzed under Chapter 4, paragraphs 2-4-5 of the headnotes are as follows:

"2. When a court of equity has obtained jurisdiction of a controversy, in order to make effective such jurisdiction and to give due force to its decrees, it will proceed to dispose of all questions properly presented by the pleadings and fairly pertaining to the full and equitable disposition of a cause.

4. By numerous leases in substantially the same terms, obtained from different parties, a lessee acquired the exclusive right in a large territory 'of drilling and operating for petroleum oil and gas.' He stipulated to give the lessors a certain proportion of the oil obtained, and pay them a fixed sum annually for each paying gas well; and he was required on pain of forfeiture to complete one test well within the territory within one year from the date of the leases. *Held,* that he did not, immediately on the performance of this latter condition become vested with an absolute right for ten years to the oil and gas privileges in the whole territory, but was bound within a reasonable time thereafter, to search for these minerals on the premises described in each lease, and the failure to do so as to some of the leases was an abandonment thereof.

5. Where, in a subsequent lease of such abandoned property a clause is inserted to the effect that it is to be held subject to the original lease, such clause is to be construed as meaning that the lessors intended to incorporate into their contract the fact that they had advised their lessee that the land had been theretofore leased, and that he was to take it subject to the old lease, with the understanding that if the latter was valid, he should take nothing by the contract, but that if it was invalid the conveyance should then stand as a contract binding upon the parties."

Sec. 17.—In *Federal Oil Co.* v. *Western Oil Co.,* 112 Fed. 373; Ct. C. D. Ind., (Jan. 11, 1902), affirmed in 121 Fed. 674; 57 C. C. A. 428, (Oct. 7, 1902), the headnotes are as follows:

"1. In an action to enforce specific performance of a contract, any fact showing that the contract is unfair, unjust and against good conscience, will justify the court in refusing such decree, though the contract may be enforceable at law, and there is no sufficient grounds for its cancellation.

2. A lease for the nominal consideration of $1.00 for the purpose of drilling and operating for oil and gas—the lessor to receive a certain proportion of the oil and gas obtained,—which does not obligate the lessee to commence or prosecute such operations, and which he may terminate at his pleasure, without compensation to the lessor, is unconscienable and should not be enforced.

3. Where under a lease for the purpose of drilling and operating for oil and gas the only consideration to the lessor is the prospective royalties to arise from the exploration and development, and the lessee fails for eight months to commence such development, the agreement is without consideration and may be abandoned by the lessor.

4. Where in a lease of oil lands, the lessee agrees to complete a second well within ninety days, after the completion of the first well, but does not agree to complete or even to commence the first well, such agreement as to the second well is no consideration for the contract.

5. The court will not decree that one party shall specifically perform a contract which the other party at his option may refuse to carry out."

On February 22, 1901, R. W. Bradford, in consideration of one dollar executed an oil and gas lease to the Federal Oil Company whereby he granted all the oil and gas in and under a tract of land, with the right to enter thereon for the purpose of drilling and operating for oil and gas, and producing and transporting the same, the lessor to have an eighth royalty. If gas only should be found in sufficient quantities to transport, lessee agreed to pay lessor $100.00 annually for the product of each and every well the gas from which should be transported to market. In case no well should be commenced within one day from the date of the lease the grant should become null and void unless lessee should thereafter pay at the rate of $8.75 per month, in advance, for each month the commencement of operations was delayed. A second well to be completed ninety days after the completion of the first well; and thereafter a well was to be completed each ninety days until seven were drilled. The rental was then to cease. The lessee reserved the right to cancel and annul the contract, or any part thereof, at any time. The rentals were paid to October 22, 1901.

The lessor then refused to receive a check mailed by lessee on October 19, 1901. The landowners leased the land to the Western Oil Company, and this company entered into possession of the property and commenced drilling thereon for oil and gas. On November 14, 1901, the Federal Oil Company attempted to take possession of the premises and moved material thereon, which material the Western Oil Company removed. Thereupon the Federal Oil Company filed a bill in equity in the Circuit Court of the United States for the District of Indiana against the lessor, Bradford, and the Western Oil Company, for the purpose of cancelling the lease made by Bradford to the Western Oil Company as a cloud on its title. A demurrer was interposed to this bill by the defendant, and was sustained by the Circuit Court.

Sec. 18.—In *Federal Oil Co.* v. *Western Oil Co.*, 121 Fed. 674; 57 C. C. A. 428, analyzed under Chapter 29 upon appeal from the decree sustaining the demurrer in 112 Fed. 373, the headnotes are as follows:

"1. A court of equity will not decree specific performance of a contract which is unfair or unconscienable, or where performance by the complainant is entirely optional, and no offer of performance is made.

2. An oil and gas lease on eighty acres of land provided that, if a well was not commenced at once the lessee should pay the lessor \$8.75 per month during the delay. The lessor was to receive as a royalty one-eighth of the oil produced, and \$100.00 per year for each producing gas well, together with gas for use in his residence. There was no limit as to time, no provision obliging the lessee to make any well, and the contract was terminable at its option. It drilled no well, but made the monthly payments for about eight months, when the lessor refused to accept further payments, and leased to another party. *Held*, that the contract contemplated the exploration of the property at once; that the monthly payments were not a part performance, but merely a stipulated sum for delay in performance; and that the contract would not be specifically enforced because of its want of mutuality and unfairness."

Upon the question of the legal effect of instruments such as the one in question, the Circuit Court of Appeals for the Seventh Circuit, in the opinion rendered by Judge Jenkins, cited:

Indiana:

State v. *Indiana & Ohio etc. Co.*, 120 Ind. 575; 22 N. E. 778;
    6 L. R. A. 579.
Peoples Gas Co. v. *Tyner*, 131 Ind. 277; 31 N. E. 59; 16 L. R.
    A. 443; 31 Am. St. Rep. 433.
Heal v. *Niagara Oil Co.*, 150 Ind. 483; 50 N. E. 482.
Manufacturers Gas Co. v. *Indiana Gas Co.*, 155 Ind. 461; 57
    N. E. 912; 50 L. R. A. 768.

United States Supreme Court:

Ohio Oil Co. v. *Indiana*, 177 U. S. 190; 20 Sup. Ct. 576; 44 L.
    Ed. 729.

Upon the question of the lessee's, Bradford's, right to receive the stipulated sum for delay and terminate the lease, the
court cited:

Knight v. *Indiana Coal & Iron Co.*, 47 Ind. 105; 17 Am. Rep.
    692.
Huggins v. *Daley*, 40 C. C. A. 12; 99 Fed. 606; 48 L. R. A.
    320.
Reese v. *Zinn*, (C. C. D. W. Va.,) 103 Fed. 97.

Sec. 19.—In *McIntosh* v. *Robb*, 4. Cal. App; 484; 88 Pac. 517
(Jan. 24, 1907), syl. 1 is as follows:

"1. Where a mining lease mentioned no specific term but the
lessee covenants to pay the lessor, semi-annually, and that the
payments shall begin on or before six months from the date of the
lease, the lessee's failure for one and a half years to operate
under the lease, and failure to pay any of the installments during
that time, entitled the lessor to cancellation."

B. McIntosh executed a mining lease to H. W. Robb for the
purpose of mining minerals or gems. In consideration of the lease
the lessee covenanted and agreed to pay a royalty of ten per cent.
of the net proceeds, if any, of all mines operated on the premises
from the date of the lease until the gross sum so paid should aggregate $1500.00, at which time the royalty should be fully paid
up, and thereafter the property should be free to the lessee for a
period of fifteen years; provided that the payments should not

exceed six in number and should be semi-annual, and should begin on or before six months from the date of the lease. The lease bore date December 3, 1903. The lessee entered and took possession of the premises and held possession for one month after the date of the lease, and during that month prospected on the land to the extent of making a cut in the hillside, performing no other work of mining or development on the premises. Thereafter the lessee entirely failed and refused to further enter upon or carry on the work of mining and failed and refused to pay to the lessor any royalty or rent for the premises, or to perform any of the covenants or conditions or pay any of the considerations provided for in the contract. On September 6, 1905, the lessor gave notice to the lessee of his rescission of the contract. For about a year and a half following the execution of the lease, there was an entire failure on the part of the lessee to do anything under the contract. The lessor then instituted an action against the lessee in the Superior Court of San Diego County for the rescission and cancellation of the lease. Judgment was rendered in plaintiff's favor, and defendant appealed to the Court of Appeals for the Second District of California, where the decision of the court below was affirmed.

Sec. 20.—In *Federal Betterment Company* v. *Blaes*, 75 Kan. 69; 88 Pac. 555 (Jan. 5, 1907), syl. 2 is as follows:

"An oil lease provided that, if a well was not completed on the leased premises within six months, it could be kept in force by a quarterly payment of $10.00 until one was completed; That is, at any time after a well was drilled six months should elapse without any revenue being received therefrom, and without any further drilling being done the lease should be termed abandoned. An attempt was made to drill a well, and prosecute it until a depth of 1,000 feet was reached. Then the casing was pulled out, and the hole was plugged. No further drilling was done. More than six months thereafter the lessor brought an action to declare the lessee's rights lost by abandonment. *Held*, (a) There being evidence from which it might be inferred that the drilling did not show the existence of oil in sufficient quantities to warrant shooting, which was not attempted, the court was justified in finding that the operations described amounted to the drilling of a well within the meaning of the contract, and that the cessation of operations for six months thereafter constituted an abandonment of the lease. (b) The receipt of a quarterly payment after the operations described, being less than six months thereafter, did not commit the lessor to the proposition that a well had been drilled since it wasthe completion of a well that was to end such payments, and the court was justified in further finding that a well had not been completed within the meaning of the lease."

Sec. 21.—In *Mills* v. *Hartz,* 77 Kan. 218; 94 Pac. 142 (Feb. 8, 1908), the syllabus is as follows:

"Under a lease of land for gas, oil or coal purposes, the lessee was given the exclusive right to dig and bore for gas, oil or coal, for a term of 20 years, and as much longer as any of these could be found in paying quantities. Also the right of way on and over the land to explore and operate including the right to erect buildings and appliances for producing gas, oil or coal on the lands, and the right to remove all improvements and machinery when the lease was abandoned. The only consideration for the lease, aside from the technical one of one dollar was a royalty of eight cents a ton on coal mined, and $50.00 per annum for the gas produced from each well, and sufficient gas to supply two stoves in the lessor's farm house. No clause of forfeiture was specified. *Held,* in an action to cancel the lease, that it contemplated early explorations and operations, and a failure on the part of the lessee to operate for a period of about seven years is equivalent to a surrender by the lessee, and gave the lessor the right to treat the contract as abandoned."

After the lessee failed to operate for seven years the lessor instituted an action for cancellation of the lease in the District Court of Miami County, Kansas. Judgment was rendered for the plaintiff. Defendant appealed to the Supreme Court, where the judgment was affirmed.

Sec. 22.—In *Flannagan* v. *Marsh,* 32 Ky. Law Rep. 184; 105 S. W. 424 (Nov. 22, 1907), syl. 1 is as follows:

"1. Where a lease for oil lands provided that the lessee should commence drilling for oil, gas, etc., within one year or pay $25.00 per annum until drilling was commenced, the real consideration being a royalty on the production, but the lessees held the land for over five years without beginning operations, proper demand having been made on them to do so, the lease could be cancelled, and especially where he had not paid the rent for the lease."

Granville Marsh and wife executed a mineral lease on 250 acres of land in Wayne County, Kentucky, to Landrom Gaulbery, Waters and Flannagan. The lease by assignment finally became the property of Flannagan, Work and Turner, Flannagan owning one-half and Work and Turner the other undivided one-half interest. Marsh died in 1904, and his widow and the heirs instituted an action against Flannagan, Work and Turner to cancel the lease on the ground that it was a cloud on their title. By the terms of the lease the lessees agreed to drill and operate the lands for oil and gas and other minerals, the consideration paid being $25.00; and the lease provided for the payment of royalties and profits to be derived from operations. No operations were commenced for oil, gas or other minerals. The surrounding lands were drilled for these minerals, and oil and gas were found. The petition alleged that by reason of the production of oil and gas from surrounding lands the leased premises were being drained of these substances; and that lessors could, if the outstanding lease was cancelled, have their lands operated for oil and gas and thereby derive great profits. By the terms of the lease the lessees agreed to commence operations within one year, or in lieu thereof pay lessors $25.00 per annum until work should be commenced. The Circuit Court of Wayne County entered a decree cancelling the lease. Lessees appealed. The evidence in the case showed that on the rent due from June 24, 1904, to June 24, 1905, only $22.50 was paid, and that no part of the rental for the year beginning June 25, 1905, to the year ending June 24, 1906, was paid or tendered. Upon these facts, upon appeal, the judgment of the Circuit Court was affirmed.

Sec. 23.—In *Kimball Oil Co.* v. *Keeton*, 31 Ky. Law Rep. 146; 101 S. W. 887 (May 1, 1907), the syl. is as follows:

"A father and son executed on the same day gas leases of their respective lands to the same lessee. Both lessees fixed the term at 20 years, or so long as gas should be obtained in paying quantities, provided for a payment of royalties, and that a failure of the lessee to commence operations or pay rental rendered the lease void. The lease given by the son stipulated that the lessee should commence operations on the son's premises after completing a well on the premises of his father. The lessee failed to do any work on the father's premises, but sunk a well on that of the son. *Held,* that the father, upon the termination of a reasonable time was entitled to the cancellation of the lease."

On April 30, 1903, J. Shelby Keeton made an oil and gas
lease to R. A. Dempsey and C. O. Kimball on 100 acres of land
owned by him in Wayne County, Kentucky. Dempsey and Kimball transferred the lease to the Kimball Oil Company, and on
February 19, 1906, Keeton brought suit against the Oil Company
to cancel the lease on the ground that it had failed to operate the
premises and thereby deprived him of his benefit therefrom. The
defendant by answer pleaded that on the same day the lease from
Shelby Keeton to Kimball and Dampsey was - made, and prior
thereto, John Keeton, the son of Shelby Keeton, had made to the
same lessees a like lease on 400 acrs of land adjoining, and that
it was agreed between all the parties that the two tracts were
to be worked as one tract, and in conjunction; that it had entered
upon the John Keeton lease and put down wells which it operated,
and thus complied with its contract. The Circuit Court sustained
the demurrer to the defendant's answer, and the defendant appealed. The Supreme Court affirmed the Circuit Court.

Sec. 24.—In *Murray* v. *Barnhart,* and
         Murray v. *Graham,* 117 La. 1023; 42 Southern,
489 (Dec. 10, 1906), syls. 1-5-8 are as follows:

"1. Where the obligation of one party to a contract is indivisible, the corresponding obligation of the other party is necessarily so likewise. Thus the obligation of the lessor of a tract of
land is indivisible among his heirs when the consideration of the
lease is the completion of one well for the exploration of the land
for oil and gas.

5. Where in an oil and gas lease it is stipulated that the
lessee shall commence one well within one year 'or pay at the
rate of $4.00 quarterly, in advance, for each additional three
months such completion is delayed,' and it is expressly declared
that the contract is made 'for the sole and exclusive purpose of
mining and operating for oil and gas,' and it is otherwise manifest from the instrument as a whole that the intention of the
parties was, not that the lessee should have the right to simply
hold the land during the term of the lease—not exploring it himself for oil and gas, and not allowing anyone else to do so—but
that he should be bound to complete a well within one year, the obligation to pay $4 quarterly will be held to be a mere penal clause,
and not an alternative obligation, and the making of said payments will be held not to be a fulfillment of the principal contract,

in whole or in part, but merely the payment of liquidated damages.

8. Payments made by way of liquidated damages for delay in the performance of a contract are not required to be tendered in a suit for the rescission of the contract because of non-performance.''

The oil and gas leases, the subject matter of the controversy in this suit, were made in consideration of the sum of one dollar, and of the covenants and agreements in the lease contained on the part of the second party to be kept and performed. The grantor demised, leased and let to the lessee for the sole and only purpose of mining and operating for oil and gas the lands therein described for the term of twenty-five years from date, and as long thereafter as oil or gas should be produced by the parties of the second part; the lessor to receive as a royalty one-tenth of the oil produced and saved from the premises, and $100.00 per year for each gas well drilled on the premises, the product from which should be marketed and used off the premises. The lessee covenanted to complete a well on the premises within one year or pay at the rate of $4.00 quarterly in advance for each additional three months such completion should be delayed from the date above mentioned for the completion of such well until a well should be completed; and it was agreed that the completion of such well should be and operate as a full liquidation of all rent during the remainder of the term of the lease. It was further agreed that upon the payment of $2.00 at any time by the lessee it should have the right to surrender the lease for cancellation, after which all payments and liabilities thereunder to accrue should cease and determine. The lessees suffered four years to elapse without having done anything towards fulfilling the contract. The lessees were notified that the lessors considered the lease as at an end; and that suit would be brought to have the lease declared a nullity. Suit was brought to cancel the lease. The lease was made by E. J. Pitts to the J. M. Guffey Company, and by this company assigned to W. E. Barnhart. The land was partitioned among the heirs of E. J. Pitts. After the first suit was instituted, and before the other three causes were brought, the lessee erected a derrick on that portion of the land which had fallen to Mrs. Graham, but beyond erecting the derrick and making regular quarterly deposits of $4.00, the lessee did nothing toward the fulfillment of its contract. The defendant continued to make deposits in the name

of E. J. Pitts after the latter's death. Pitts died two years before
the institution of the suits, and defendant knew of his death and
also knew who were his heirs before the institution of the suits.
After the institution of the first suit three others were brought by
other heirs, and all four cases were consolidated. The District
Court, where the suits were brought, annulled the lease. The Court
of Appeals affirmed the judgment, and the case was taken to the
Supreme Court of Louisiana, where the judgments of the courts
below were affirmed. The Supreme Court distinguished the case
from Houssierre-Lattreille Oil Company v. Jennings-Heywood Oil
Syndicate, 115 La. 107; 38 Southern, 932, for the reason that in
that case $100.00 agreed to be paid for the right of putting an end
to the contract was deemed by the court for the purpose of the dis-
cussion to have been a sufficient or serious consideration.

Sec. 25.—In *Florence Oil & Refining Co.* v. *McCumber*, 38
Colo. 366; 88 Pac. 265 (Dec. 3, 1906), syl. 1 is as follows:

"1. A complaint alleging the execution of an oil lease running for twenty years stipulating that lessee should sink three wells
within fifteen months and make payment thereof, and pay a fixed
monthly sum until they were sunk and make monthly payments to
prevent a forfeiture, upon failure to sink the wells within the
time specified, and alleging a failure to sink the wells and default
in other provisions of the lease, including that relating to forfeiture, and that lessee refused to cancel the lease, was sufficient
to sustain a decree for cancellation.

Phillip McCumber instituted in the District Court of Fremont
County, Colorado, an action against the Florence Oil & Refining
Company to cancel an oil lease and to recover penalties thereunder.
The petition alleged that in 1892 the plaintiff, McCumber, executed an oil lease on certain lands in Fremont County, Colorado, to
the defendant for the term of twenty years; that the lessee was,
within fifteen months, to sink to a certain depth three wells for
which it agreed to pay a certain sum of money, and a fixed royalty for the product of oil produced from the premises. Until
these wells were drilled lessee was to pay to lessor a stipulated
amount each month. Another clause was, that if the lessee failed
to drill the wells within the time and in the manner provided for in
the lease, then, to prevent a forfeiture of the lease the lessee
was to pay a certain sum per month for each of the three wells not

sunk until the wells were fully completed. The suit was instituted in 1898. From the complaint it appeared that for a short time the company made the early designated monthly payments; that it wholly failed to sink any wells, and entirely disregarded the other provisions of the lease, including that relating to forfeiture, and notwithstanding such default the lessee refused to cancel the lease, and the plaintiff asked for judgment and decree for the amount of money due him under the lease, and for cancellation. The defendant answered, admitting the substantial averments of the complaint, and alleged that it never drilled on the premises any well for oil or paid the penalty for not doing so; that it never entered into possession of the premises under the agreement or otherwise. The testimony of the plaintiff sustained all the material allegations of the complaint. The District Court entered a decree cancelling the lease, but refusing to decree a money recovery in favor of the plaintiff. Upon error to the Supreme Court, the judgment of the District Court was affirmed.

Sec. 26.—In *Buffalo Valley Oil & Gas Co.* v. *Jones*, 75 Kan. 18; 88 Pac. 537, (Jan. 5, 1907) syl. 1 is as follows:

"1. Where an oil and gas lease covering lands located in a field which is being actively developed is given for a term of two years, and contains a provision that in case oil or gas is found on the premises, the lease may be continued in force by lessee so long as he diligently develops the land and markets the product, the failure of the lessee to use reasonable diligence in the respects named will cause said lease to lapse."

B. E. Jones and Kizzie Jones, on February 1, 1902, were the owners of about 200 acres of land near the town of Buffalo, in Wilson County, Kansas, within the oil and gas belt of that county, which was then being actively developed. On February 1, 1902, these landowners executed an oil and gas lease to Neills Esperson, which lease was assigned on March 15, 1904, to Buffalo Valley Oil & Gas Company. The lease was made in consideration of one dollar and of the covenants therein contained on the part of the lessee to be performed, and granted to the lessee the exclusive right for two years, subject to the conditions of the lease, to enter upon and operate and procure oil and gas from the leased premises. The lessee agreed to deliver to the lessors one-eighth of the oil in tanks at the wells, or pay the market price therefor, in cash, at the option of the lessors. If oil or gas should be found on the premises, all rights, privileges and obligations secured by the lease should continue as long as either oil or gas should be produced in paying quantities, the lessee to diligently market and utilize the oil and gas for the joint benefit of the parties. For any and all wells producing gas in sufficient quantities to be utilized and marketed, the lessee covenanted to pay lessors $50.00 per year during the time such well or wells produced gas. In case no oil or gas wells should be drilled on the premises within one year from the date of the lease all rights secured thereunder should cease; provided, however, that the lessee should have the right at any time to terminate the lease by notice in writing or by surrendering the same, and should thereafter be released from all obligations and liabilities. It was distinctly understood that time was the essence of the contract in all its terms and conditions. The lessee drilled one well on the leased premises and found gas in abundance and a small amount of oil. This well was completed about July 9, 1902, and immediately thereafter the derrick and all drilling apparatus were removed from the land and work thereon ceased. The Buffalo Valley Oil & Gas Company also held a lease on about 400 acres of land owned by one White, which was immediately southwest of and adjoining the tract owned by Jones upon which the gas well was drilled. After abandoning the work of development under the Jones lease the lessee began work on the White land, and drilled seven or eight wells thereon, one of which produced gas and one contained considerable oil. While drilling these wells on the White tract the company used gas from the Jones land for drilling purposes. When gas was found in large quantities on the White lands the company attempted to obtain a contract for supplying gas to the cities of Eldorado, Yates Center, and other places, and in February, 1904, completed an arrangement for furnishing gas to Yates Center. The company also took steps to obtain a contract for lighting the town of Buffalo, and to supply the brick plant at that place with gas for fuel. On April 8, 1904, Jones brought suit in the District Court of Wilson County to cancel the lease. There were several gas wells on the lands adjoining the Jones lands on the north-east, which, taken in connection with those on the Jones and White premises, all active wells with good pressure, and located practically in the lines from the north-east to the south-west across the Jones land, indicated to experts in the oil and gas business and to the officers of the company that large quantities of gas underlaid the entire Jones tract. No rental had been paid until just before the commencement of the suit. The petition set forth substantially these facts. A general demurrer to the petition was overruled and the case was tried to the court without a jury. The court found generally for the plaintiff and annulled the lease, except as to one-half acre square in form in the center of which was the gas well. The Gas Company appealed to the Supreme Court where the judgment was affirmed.

Sec. 27.—In *Logansport, etc. Gas Co.* v. *Seegar,* 165 Ind. 1; 74 N. E. 500, (May 23, 1905) the syllabus is as follows:

"1. Where in a suit by a lessor in a gas lease to quiet title against a lessee, defendant relied on tender of rentals made, the burden of proving the same was on him.

2. Where a gas lease provided that development of the property should be commenced within three months, or else a specified yearly rental paid, and the lessor refused to receive a rental tendered to her after it was past due, it was equivalent to notice that she objected to further delay in the beginning of developments, and the lessee was required to proceed within a reasonable time.

3. Where a gas lease provided for development of the premises within three months, or otherwise a specified yearly rental was to be paid, and the lessor refused to receive a certain payment of rental after it was past due, and the lessee prolonged its delay in development until September of the following year, the delay was unreasonable and entitled the lessor to cancellation of the lease."

On January 10, 1899, Lydia Seegar executed an oil and gas lease to Neely, Clover and Howe, who assigned the lease to Logansport Gas Company. The lease contained the following provision:

"Second parties agree to drill a well on said premises within three months from this date, or thereafter pay the first party for further delay a yearly rental of Thirty ($30) dollars until said well is drilled. Such rental when due shall be deposited in Marion Bank, at Marion, Grant County, State of Indiana. Should second parties refuse to make such deposit or pay to first party on these premises, or at present residence of the first party, the said rental when due as aforesaid, such refusal shall be construed by both parties hereto as the act of the second party for the purpose of surrendering the rights hereby granted, and this instrument, in default of the rental payments shall be null and void without further notice from second party.''

Neither the original lessees nor their assignee took possession of the lands in question, and no wells were drilled thereon, and no attempt whatever was made to explore for gas or oil prior to the commencement of the action. On April 10, 1900, the rental then due for the preceding year was paid. The rental for the second year was paid on April 10, 1901, direct to the lessor, by the agent of the assignee of the lessees. At that time lessor asked the agent to cancel the lease for the reason that the lessees assignee was not developing the land, and therefore, under the circumstances she believed she was not receiving enough rent. The agent stated to the lessor that the company would not cancel the lease, but would proceed to develop the land as soon as it could. At the same time the agent verbally promised lessor that in future the rental should be paid in advance on July 1st of each year, the first advance payment to be made on July 1, 1901. In pursuance to this agreement an amount of rental equal to that which would accrue between April 10, 1901, and July 1st of the same year, was paid to lessor, which, together with the amount paid to April 10th liquidated the rental in full for the year immediately preceding July 1, 1901. No rentals accruing after July 1, 1901, were paid in advance by the company. The last rental received and accepted by lessor was that which was paid to July 1, 1901. In 1902, the company did not deposit the rental due for the preceding year in the bank designated in the lease, but some time in that year it offered to pay the rental to the lessor's husband who was acting as her agent in the matter. He, on her behalf, refused to accept any of the rental. After this refusal the company continued until the commencement of this action—September 23, 1903—to remain inactive and wholly failed to drill any well or in any manner explore or develop the premises in question. The lessor instituted suit against the Gas Company in the Circuit Court of Grant County to quiet her title. Judgment was rendered in her favor, and the company appealed to the Appellate Court, from which court the cause was transferred to the Supreme Court, where the judgment was affirmed.

Sec. 28.—In *Dill* v. *Fraze,* 169 Ind. 53; 79 N. E. 971, (Jan. 17, 1907) syls. 1-6, inclusive, are as follows:

. "1. A party to a contract reciting a consideration of one dollar was estopped to deny its consideration as against an assignee of a contract for a valuable consideration who had no knowledge that the original consideration of one dollar was not paid.

2. A contract giving a lease to drill wells in certain land for oil and gas will be construed in the light of the fact that the principal purpose of the owner of the land in giving such lease is to procure the exploration of his land for oil and gas to be followed by the development of it if circumstances warrant.

3. An oil and gas lease for five years from its date and as long as oil and gas could be found on the land or the rental was paid thereon as stipulated in the contract, provided that in case no well was completed within sixty days the grant should be null and void unless the lessee should thereafter pay at the rate of $40.00, for each year such commencement was delayed, and that the lessee might cancel and annul the contract or any portion thereof at any time upon payment of one dollar to the lessor and releasing him upon record. *Held,* that, while upon the receipt of the first year's compensation the lessee would have been entitled to postpone the beginning of operations yet it was within the power of the lessor by appropriate action to prevent such lessee from continuing to hold the right granted in the land without exploration or developments for the whole of the contract period.

4. The payment of $40.00 should be made in advance since there was no express agreement on the part of the lessee that he would explore for gas or oil, but on the contrary, he reserved the right at any time upon payment of one dollar to cancel and annul the contract, and he made no agreement to pay any sum in the nature of rent.

5. The owner was entitled to declare a forfeiture at the end of sixty days, where there was no well completed in that time, and where the lessee had failed to pay the consideration stipulated for the delay.

6. Where an oil and gas lease resting upon a nominal consideration of one dollar, which was entered into for the purpose of procuring the exploration and development of the lessor's property contemplated a forfeiture on the lessee's failure to complete a well within sixty days, equity would not relieve against such forfeiture since such provision was of the essence of the contract and equity would be promoted by the forfeiture stipulated for.''

Charles F. Dill and wife, as parties of the first part, entered into a contract whereby they granted unto Emmet Fraze as second

party all the oil and gas under a certain 40-acre tract of land for
the purpose of drilling and operating for oil and gas for the term of
five years from date, and as long as oil and gas could be found in
paying quantities or the rental paid. The lease contained the following provision:

"In case no well is completed within sixty days and Number
2 well in sixty days thereafter from this date, then this grant shall
become null and void unless second party shall thereafter pay at
the rate of $40.00 for each year such commencement is delayed. A
deposit to the credit of the first party in Merchants Bank, Muncie, Indiana, will be good and sufficient payment for any money
falling due on this grant. * * * * * * The second party shall have
* * * * the right to remove all the property at any time, and may
cancel and annul this contract, or any undrilled portion thereof at
any time, upon payment of one dollar to said first party and re-
leasing the same of record."

The lease was executed on May 26, 1903. On December 31,
1903, C. F. Dill brought suit against Emmet Fraze and others to
cancel the contract. The case was heard in the Henry Circuit
Court. The plaintiff demurred to the defendant's answer, which
demurrer was overruled. An appeal was taken to the Appellate
Court, which court affirmed the judgment of the Circuit Court, and
the case was appealed to the Supreme Court where judgment was
entered reversing the courts below with directions to sustain the
demurrer. The complaint alleged that operations had not been
commenced on the land; that no sum whatever had been paid or
deposited for delay; that the recited consideration for the execution of the agreement was not in fact paid. There were proofs
showing that the defendants had not taken possession and had
abandoned the lease. An answer was filed by an assignee of the
original lessee alleging that it, the oil company, was an assignee
for a valuable consideration and had taken the assignment without knowledge that the original consideration of one dollar for
the execution of the contract had not been paid; that the company
proposed to enter upon the land and drill for oil and gas in the
Spring of 1904. The answer admitted that the sum fixed as the
price for delay had not been paid, but claimed that the company
had construed the contract as not requiring the payment to be made
in advance; and offered to pay the annual rental should the Circuit Court determine that it was due. Upon overruling the de-

murrer a trial was had and judgment rendered for the plaintiff. Upon appeal the Supreme Court affirmed the judgment.

Sec. 29.—In *Ohio Oil Co.* v. *Detmore,* 165 Ind. 243; 73 N. E. 906, (March 28, 1905) syls. 4-5-6-7 are as follows:

"4. Where an oil and gas lease provided that if no well was completed within six months from its date, it should become null and void, unless the lessee should pay $120.00 in advance for each six months thereafter that such completion was delayed the rights of the lessee were terminated by the drilling of an unsuccessful well and the abandonment of the enterprise within which the period for which payment had been made, and failure to renew the lease by paying in advance for another six months.

5. Where an oil and gas lease was terminated by the abandonment of the same, and the failure to renew it, a subsequent parol agreement between the lessor and lessee whereby the latter was permitted to enter and resume work upon complying with certain conditions similar to those imposed by the original lease did not waive the forfeiture of the lessee's interest under the old lease but constituted a new contract.

6. An oil and gas lease required the lessee to pay $120.00 in advance for each six months that the completion of a well was delayed. The lessee abandoned the enterprise and ceased paying the semi-annual rental, and some years after entered into an oral contract with the lessor whereby it was permitted to resume operations on condition of paying the back rental and completing a well within six months or paying another $120.00 in advance for further time. The lessee thereupon built a well, but on finding it unprofitable took it down and stopped operations without having paid any money or completing a successful well. Nothing was then done for more than seven months. *Held,* that the lessee's rights on the premises, under its renewed contract with the lessee were forfeited.

7. Where a lessee in an oil and gas lease forfeits its rights by failing to pay the stipulated rental or completing a successful well within the stipulated time, it could not, after the expiration of that time, renew its rights by entering on the lessor's land over his objections and commence another well."

On August 29, 1895, Levi Detmore and wife entered into a contract with the Huntington Light & Fuel Company whereby in consideration of $120.00 in hand paid, he conveyed to the Light & Fuel Company all the oil and gas in and under 242 acres of real

estate, described, together with the right to enter thereon for the
purpose of drilling and operating for oil, gas and water, and to
erect such structures and pipe lines as would be necessary. Lessor
was to have one-eighth of all the oil, produced and saved, to be
delivered in pipe lines. If gas only was found the lessor was to
have $100.00 a year for each well. The lease contained the follow-
. ing stipulation:

"In case no well is completed within six months from this
date, then this grant shall become null and void unless second
party shall pay the said first party $120.00 in advance for each
six months thereafter that such completion is delayed, and second
party shall have the right to use sufficient gas, oil or water to run
all necessary machinery for operating said well, and also the right
to remove all its property at any time. * * * * * * All conveyances
and agreements herein set forth between the parties shall extend
to their successors, heirs, executors and assigns."

The Huntington Light & Fuel Company assigned its interest
in the contract to the Ohio Oil Company. After the initial payment
of $120.00 the Ohio Oil Company and its assignor advanced a like
sum three times at the end of consecutive six month periods, thus
postponing the time when a well should be completed to August
29, 1897. In March, 1897, a well was sunk on the land by the
company which was a dry hole. The company took down and removed its machinery and other appliances from the premises.
No further periodical payments were paid or tendered, and no
further steps were taken by the lessee or its assignee to assert a
right under the contract until the Spring of 1901—a period of four
years—when the Ohio Oil Company by E. W. Morin, its district
superintendent, entered upon the land to put down a second well.
Lessor objected and forbade the entry, claiming that the rights
of the company under the contract were at an end. After some
parleying lessor proposed that if the oil company would pay the
back rental, $900 or more, being then due and unpaid, upon the
basis of the old contract being still in force, the oil company might come back. Morin said he would refer the matter to
the General Superintendent for decision, and expressed the belief
that the proposition would be accepted. Subsequently he proceeded to tentatively select a place for a second well, and drove a stake
to mark the spot therefor. Morin then negotiated with lessor for
some trees from which to construct a derrick and other appliances,

and then departed. In three or four days Morin communicated to lessor that he had conferred with the General Superintendent, and was directed by the latter to go ahead with the well. The second well was then commenced and completed in May, 1901. The back rental was neither paid nor tendered, in whole or in part. The well was a small producer of oil. The oil company pumped it till January 1, 1902, obtaining in the meantime 250 barrels of oil, and then took down and removed from the premises all the machinery and appliances it had been using. The matter then rested without any further steps being taken by the oil company to operate or develop the land till August 12, 1902, when the lessor instituted her action to quiet her title against any claim of the oil company. On August 18, 1902, pending the suit, over the lessor's objection, the oil company entered upon the premises and drilled Number 3. The Circuit Court rendered judgment in favor of the plaintiff, and defendant appealed to the Appellate Court from which the case was transferred to the Supreme Court, where the decree of the Circuit Court was affirmed.

Sec. 30.—In *Martel* v. *Jennings-Heywood Oil Syndicate*, 114 La. 903; 38 Southern 253, (Feb. 4, 1905) the syllabus is as follows:

"1.   Where A. and B. owning adjoining tracts of land, joined in a lease of the same to C. for the term of 99 years, for the purpose of prospecting, boring, excavating, etc., for oil, gas, petroleum, coal, salt, sulphur and other minerals, during that period for the consideration of one dollar and the royalty of one cent for each barrel of oil sold, and the same proportionate value for all other minerals, A. to have one-third of the royalty accruing from the land of B. and vice-versa; and while C. did not bind or obligate himself to prospect, or to do any work on the premises, *Held*, that such an agreement is not a contract of lease but a mere permit or license, revokable and terminable at will.

2.   Where, within thirty days thereafter, B. leased his tract of land to C. for one year, and on different terms and conditions, the lessee binding himself to develop the property for oil and other minerals, and the royalty fixed at one-eighth of the oil was made payable to B. alone, *Held*, that the first lease was abandoned and terminated and was no longer binding on A.

3.   Where, after subsequent discovery of oil on the B. tract C. entered on the land of A. for the purpose of erecting a derrick thereon, and was enjoined by A. who soon thereafter sold the one-fifth interest in the land to plaintiff, *Held*, that they acquired title

free of the first lease, and were not affected by the subsequent compromise of the suit, and the recognition by A. of the first lease in a modified form.

4. Where, under such compromise lease the tract of land was developed into an oil bearing territory, *Held,* that plaintiffs as owners of an interest in the land are entitled to a like interest in the oil produced, less all expenses of production.''

Laurent Arnadut and Jules Clement each owned tracts of land near Jennings, Louisiana, having a combined area of 472 acres. On April 6, 1901, these landowners entered into an agreement with one Wilkins, by which they leased to him for the term of 99 years a tract of land described as follows:

"The north one-fourth of section 47 known as the Anthony Cochran claim, and the fractional section 46; also sec. 49, Township 9, S. Range 2 West, La. Merd. containing 442 acres, more or less.''

The consideration was the sum of one dollar and the stipulation that lessee, his heirs and assigns should pay lessors one cent for each barrel of oil marketed or sold by the lessees, and for all other minerals or elements obtained from said lands the same proportionate value as that of oil. It was agreed that two-thirds of the profits should accrue to the owners of the lands upon which wells were drilled. On April 24, 1901, Wilkins transferred his interest in the lease to S. A. Spencer & Company, who on May 8, 1901, entered into a contract with Jules Clement whereby it was stipulated that the lease of April 9, 1901, should be null and void in so far as the interests of Clement appeared; and it was declared that the last lease was to supersede the first. Under this contract of May 8, 1901, Clement leased fractional sections 46-49 and part of the south half of fractional section 53, containing about 300 acres, more or less for oil and gas purposes. This lease was to remain in force for one year, and as long thereafter as oil or gas was produced. The lessor was to have one-eighth part of all the oil produced and saved from the premises, and $250.00 for the gas from each and every well drilled on said premises, the lessee to commence operations within one year or pay at the rate of $25.00 quarterly in advance for delay. Spencer & Company took immediate steps to develop the Clement property. Drilling began in June, and an oil well was brought in in September. During the latter part of October, 1901, Spencer & Company entered upon the lands of Arnadut, and commenced the erection of a derrick thereon for the purpose of drilling a well. Thereupon Arnadut filed a suit to annul the lease of April 9, 1901, on the ground that it was obtained by fraud, and enjoined Wilkins and Spencer & Company from trespassing on this property. In December, 1901, the Cochran Oil & Development Company brought suit against Arnadut and others claiming title to that portion of the Cochran grant involved in the Wilkins lease. The suit was decided in the District Court in favor of the defendants, and the judgment was affirmed by the Supreme Court in November, 1903. Plaintiff sued out a writ of error from the Supreme Court of the United States. On December 20, 1901, Arnadut executed to Martel et al., to compensate them for their professional services a *dation en paiement* of the one undivided one-fifth of the right, title and interest in and to the north quarter section 47, being a portion of the lands described in the Wilkins lease of April, 1901. In October, 1902, Arnadut filed a supplemental petition in an injunction suit in which he alleged that the Wilkins lease was null and void for want of consideration and mutuality, and was a mere *nudum pactum,* not binding on the parties, and that said lease was superseded, abrogated and set aside by'the contract of May 8, 1901, between Jules Clement and Spencer & Company, by which the entire royalties on Clement's premises were to be paid to him; and that said pretended contract had been actively violated by the sale by the parties to the Southern Oil Company of the only portion of the Clement property valuable for oil property. The Jennings-Heywood Oil Syndicate, as claimants to the lease of April, 1901, was made a party to the injunction suit. In February, 1903, the injunction suit of Arnadut was dismissed in accordance with his letter of instructions to counsel for defendant therein, wherein he says that the dismissal was by reason of an agreement reached and entered into by and between himself and the Jennings-Heywood Oil Syndicate, whereby the original contract of April 10, 1901, was modified and enlarged so as to cover any and all complaints which he had against the defendants in his suit. This compromise agreement changed the original lease so as to make it a contract between Arnadut and the syndicate, and to eliminate Clement. The consideration was made the same as stated in the lease from Clement to Spencer & Company, executed in May, 1901, but the syndicate bound and obligated itself to begin drilling and boring for oil within thirty days from the date of the agreement. This was done, and as a result several oil wells were brought in on the Arnadut land, prior to the bringing of the present suit on July 13, 1903. Martel and others sued to be recognized as owners of one undivided one-fifth interest in the Arnadut tract of land and to cancel the recorded lease on the same held by the defendants, so far as the lease affected their interest. The District Court rendered judgment in favor of the defendants, and plaintiffs appealed. The Supreme Court reversed the decision of the Circuit Court and decreed that plaintiffs should be recognized as owners of the undivided one-fifth interest in the Arnadut tract of land containing 145 acres, free from all the leases therein set forth, as recorded against said tract of land; and that said leases be cancelled by the clerk and ex officio recorder of the Parish of Acadia in so far as they affected said undivided one-fifth interest. A decree was entered in favor of the plaintiffs that they recover from the Jennings-Heywood Oil Syndicate and its lessees, one-fifth of all the oil produced by the defendants on said tract of land, on plaintiff's reimbursing one-fifth of all expenses ordinary and incidental, incurred in producing, transporting and preserving the oil, and if sold, the additional expenses of sale.

Sec. 31.—In *Smith* v. *Root,* 66 W. Va. 633; 66 S. E. 1005, analyzed under Chapter 32, syl. 4 is as follows:

"4. If the lessee has not actually entered upon the land, the relinquishment of his right to do so, or his abandonment, becomes purely a question of his intention, and may be established by proof of such facts and circumstances as evidence a voluntary waiver of his rights."

Sec. 32.—In *Heintz* v. *Shortt,* 149 Pa. 286; 28 Atl. 228, (May 23, 1893) the syllabus is as follows:

"An oil lease provided that the lessee should complete the first well within six months, 'or thereafter within sixty days remove all machinery and buildings for the business erected and used and this lease be declared null and void unless further prosecuted after the first well drilled.' The first well was completed within the six months, and oil obtained; but thereafter for some four years nothing was done towards the drilling of any other well. *Held,* that the lease had become void."

George M. Heintz et al. brought ejectment in the Court of Common Pleas of Warren County, Pennsylvania, against Alfred Shortt, and others. The lease, the subject matter of the litigation, contained the following clause:

"The party of the second part covenant to commence operations for said mining purposes so as to complete the first well within six months from the execution of this lease, or thereafter within sixty days remove all machinery and buildings for the business erected and used, and this lease be declared null and void, unless further prosecuted after the first well drilled."

Under this lease, which bore date January 30, 1896, the first well was completed within six months from the date, and oil obtained. Nothing was done thereafter toward drilling by lessees under the lease. The plaintiffs claimed under a second lease with notice of the first lease. The Judge of the Court of Common Pleas directed the jury to return a verdict for plaintiff, and rendered judgment thereon. Defendants appealed, and the Supreme Court affirmed the judgment.

Sec. 33.—In *Garrett* v. *South Penn Oil Co.*, 66 W. Va. 587; 66 S. E. 741, analyzed under Chapter 49, syl. 9, is as follows:

"There is a distinction between 'abandonment' and 'forfeiture,' as applied to oil and gas leases; abandonment resting on the intention of the lessee to relinquish the premises, which is a question of fact for the jury, while forfeiture is based on an enforced release."

Sec. 34.—In *Shenk* v. *Stahl*, 35 Ind. App. 444; 74 N. E. 538, (May 23, 1905) the syllabus is as follows:

"1. The words 'granted and leased' used in a contract by which the grantor 'granted and leased' to the lessee, their heirs, or assigns, certain land for the purpose of a gas well, so long as it was used for the same, etc., amounted merely to a covenant for quiet enjoyment on the condition stipulated in the contract.

2. Where a contract 'granted and leased to the grantees their heirs and assigns, certain land for the purpose of a gas well, so long as it is used for the same' etc., the contract was a mere lease terminable on the parties ceasing to use the property as a gas well.

3. Where a contract granted certain land for use as a gas well 'so long as it is used for the same' and on the ceasing of the flow the use of the well was actually terminated, the subsequent discovery of gas in the well in sufficient quantities for use, and the fact that it was thereafter used by the lessor, did not revive the lease.''

Adam Stahl and others instituted suit in the Circuit Court of Howard County, Indiana, against Reuben Shenk and others. The substance of the first paragraph of the complaint was: In September, 1889, Reuben Shenk and wife owned 100 acres of land in Howard County, and on that day leased to the Diamond Plate Glass Company of Indiana, a 20-foot square tract out of a corner of the tract, for the purpose of drilling a gas well thereon, which was done, and the well properly equipped with necessary casing and fixtures. On October 13, 1890, the lease was assigned to the Diamond Plate Glass company of Chicago. This company, on August 15, 1891, assigned the lease to Dan A. Shenk. On August 22, 1891, Reuben Shenk and wife were the owners of the tract of land, and on that day Dan A. Shenk sold the gas well and its fixtures, excepting 1-7 thereof, to Adam Stahl and others, and to George Ingles and Jacob Reel, who were both deceased at the beginning of the suit. On the last date, Reuben Shenk and wife entered into a written contract with Adam Stahl, George Stahl and others, and with Dan A. Shenk, by which Reuben Shenk granted and leased to the second parties a 20-foot square of land in the northwest corner of the said tract, for the purpose of a gas well, so long as it should be used for that purpose. In consideration of the grant the second parties gave to Reuben Shenk the 1-7 interest in the gas well and fixtures, the same being valued at $100.00. The second parties each had an equal share in the gas well and fixtures and agreed to pay their equal share of the expenses to keep the same in repair. It was averred that all the parties under the contract intended to thereby convey to and fix the respective interests of each, and to lease the gas well, fixtures, pipes and privileges; that by the mutual mistake of all the parties the said writing did not properly describe the land on which the well was located, the complaint then giving the true description. The complaint averred that pursuant to the contract the parties thereto entered into possession of the property, attached the necessary gas pipe and appliances to connect the residence to the gas well, and began and continued to use gas therefrom under said contract "until said gas well ceased to provide gas in sufficient quantities to supply them.'' That the supply of gas in said well thereafter greatly increased and in quantities to supply all said parties; that Reuben and Daniel Shenk reconnected the pipe owned by them to said gas well, and were using the gas therefrom to the exclusion of plaintiffs; that Abraham C. Ingles had succeeded to the rights and privileges of George Ingles under the contract; Isaac Keyton had succeeded to the rights of Jacob Reel, and was entitled to the privileges belonging to Reel under the contract; that each plaintiff had demanded of Reuben Shenk the right to enter upon the premises where the well was located and attach pipes thereto and use gas therefrom, which had been denied them by Shenk, who claimed to be the absolute owner of the gas well and fixtures; that natural gas had a peculiar value as fuel, and plaintiffs were unable to obtain it from any other source; that they had suffered damages by reason of having been unlawfully kept out of possession of said well. The complaint prayed that the contract be reformed so as to give the true description of the real estate; and that plaintiffs each be declared the respective owners of the 1-7 of the said well, together with the fixtures; and that Reuben Shenk be enjoined and restrained from disconnecting plaintiff's pipes from the well; and for damages. Reuben Shenk demurred to each paragraph of the complaint, which demurrer was overruled. The complaint was answered in three paragraphs. The case was tried by the court and a decree entered in favor of the plaintiffs. Defendants appealed. The Appellate Court reversed the Circuit Court and remanded the cause with instructions to the trial court to sustain the demurrer to the complaint. Upon the question that a well drilled on land from the surface to the gas bearing rock is a part of the realty, the court cited:

Ohio Oil Co v. Griest, 30 Ind. App. 84-87; 65 N. E. 534.

Upon the question that if the well for lack of gas or for other causes had ceased to be used as a gas well the lease terminated, and having once terminated, the discovery of gas in the well thereafter in paying quantities, and thereafter utilized, would not, alone, revive the lease, the court cited:

Cassell v. Crothers, 193 Pa. 359; 44 Atl. 446.
Lowther Oil Co. v. Miller-Sibley Oil Co., 53 W. Va., 501; 44 S. E. 433.

Heller v. *Dailey*, 28 Ind. App. 555; 63 N. E. 490; 70 N. E. 821.

Sec. 35.—In *McMillan* v. *Titus*, 222 Pa. 500; 72 Atl. 240, (Jan. 4, 1909) syl. 6 is as follows:

"6. A landowner, in consideration of a sum in hand paid and a further sum to be paid him out of the oil obtained, leased the 'right and privilege of prospecting, examining and searching' for coal, oil or other minerals and 'the right and privilege to take. excavate' and bore for them, if found, and to remove them, with the use of as much wood and coal as might be required to operate the machinery in the oil wells. Oil had been discovered in the vicinity and there had been at least two wells put down on the premises, and the existence of coal was well known. Oil was produced in paying quantities from one of the wells dug, and the additional compensation was paid and the operations were continued for several years. Fifteen years thereafter the premises were abandoned. No mines were operated for coal and no use was made of the premises by the parties nor their successors except for the purpose of prospecting and pumping oil, and the premises were subsequently conveyed 'subject to such restrictions and leases as are now held upon said premises.' *Held*, that interpreting the instrument in the light of the then existing conditions, it was a lease for oil, gas and salt purposes, and not a deed conveying in fee simple the minerals under the land."

In the early part of 1864, Solomon Elliott, of Fayette County, procured a patent for a tract of land containing about 108 acres, lying on both sides of Dunkard Creek and about one mile from the mouth of the creek, in Green County, Pennsylvania. Within a year or two after he obtained the patent Elliott removed to the premises, where he resided until 1870. In that year he sold and conveyed the land to Levi Titus "subject to such restrictions and leases as are now held upon said premises by the Seaton & Pioneer Oil & Mineral Co." Titus at once entered into possession. For seven or eight years Benjamin Titus, the son of the owner, resided on the land. L. C. Titus, another son of the owner, then removed to the land and resided on it at the time of the suit. Levi Titus died in 1886, and shortly after about 77 acres of the farm was awarded to L. C. Titus in partition. Of these 77 acres about 33 acres were underlaid with the Pittsburg or River vein of coal. Titus sold this coal in 1902, and went to Waynesburg, Green County, to procure an abstract of title. He learned for the first time that there was on record an instrument in writing purporting to place the title to the coal in other parties. Upon examination there was found the record of a paper dated June 4, 1864, between Solomon Elliott of the first part, and Charles S. Seaton and George W. K. Minor, parties of the second part, of Fayette County. The paper was signed by both parties. By this instrument Elliott, for the consideration of $300.00 paid, and a further consideration of $500.00 to be paid out of oil obtained on the premises, "granted, bargained, demised and leased * * * * to Seaton & Minor, their heirs and assigns, the sole and separate and exclusive right and privilege of prospecting, examining, and searching for coal, ore or other minerals, and for salt, oil, carbon oil or other substances in and upon" said tract of land "and the right and privilege to dig, excavate, and sink pits and wells for any or all of said coal, ore, salt, oil, carbon oil, or other minerals and substances, and to remove and take the same out of the earth, on the premises aforesaid, hereby granting and releasing the said party of the second part * * * * all interest of the said parties of the first part to the coal, ore, carbon oil, or other minerals and substances, in, upon and under the same." It was further provided in said writing that "in case the said parties of the second part succeed in finding oil in sufficient quantities to justify operating any well sunk upon said land, say ten barrels per day, then the said party of the second part agree to pay the said Solomon Elliott the additional sum of $500.00, as soon as enough oil is realized to amount to that sum, and the same been put into market."

Mary McMillan and others instituted proceedings in the Court of Common Pleas of Green County, against L. C. Titus to determine title to coal and other minerals underlying the land of the said Titus. In August, 1902, Titus presented a petition to the Common Pleas Court of Green County, averring the existence of the Elliott paper, and asked that the court frame an issue under the Act of June 10, 1893, between him and the plaintiffs in this action, "to settle and determine their respective rights and title in and to" the coal and other minerals in and underlying the tract of land of which he claimed to be the owner. An issue was framed in which the successors in title to Seaton & Minor, claiming the 2-3 of the coal and other minerals were made plaintiffs and Titus was made defendant. On the trial of the cause in the Court of Common Pleas the plaintiffs relied upon the paper of June 4, 1864, to establish their title. It was contended by the plaintiffs, and so held by the court, that the paper vested in Minor and Seaton, the coal, oil and other minerals in fee; and therefore the plaintiffs, their grantees of the assignees, took a fee simple title to all the minerals including the coal in and under the defendant's tract of land. The court submitted to the jury to find whether the defendant had established a title to the minerals by adverse possession. A verdict was rendered for the plaintiff and from the judgment entered thereon defendant appealed. The Supreme Court reversed the judgment, and entered judgment for defendants.

LESSEE'S REMEDIES
(See Chap. 25.)

LESSOR'S REMEDIES
(See Chap. 26.)

CHAPTER 25.

FORFEITURE BY ABANDONMENT—LESSEE'S REMEDY.

Sec. 1.—Where a lease contains a clause providing for the payment of a stipulated sum as rental or commutation money for delay in explorations but does not contain a clause of forfeiture the mere non-payment of the rental alone does not constitute abandonment or authorize a court of equity to cancel the lease; and where lessor institutes proceedings for the cancellation of such lease upon these grounds lessee may defeat the action by showing a willingness to perform the covenants of the lease and by proof' that explorations have not been unreasonably delayed.

Pheasant v. *Hanna,* 60 S. E. 618; 63 W. Va. 317.
Marshall v. *Oil Co.,* 198 Pa. 83; 47 Atl. 927.

Sec. 2.—Where a lessee has entered the demised premises for the purpose of making the explorations contemplated by the lease and proceeds to explore for oil or gas, which explorations are unsuccessful, and lessor takes proceedings to cancel the lease or makes a new lease to a second party upon the theory that the first lease has been abandoned, and the second lessee either institutes proceedings to cancel the first lease or endeavors to take possession of the premises for the purpose of exploration under his lease, the original lessee may re-enter within a reasonable time after cessation by him of explorations and may defeat proceedings instituted either by the lessor or by the second lessee by proving that he did not intend to abandon the premises.

Henne v. *South Penn Oil Co.*, 52 W. Va. 192; 43 S. E. 147.
Lowther Oil Co. v. *Miller-Sibley Oil Co.*, 53 W. Va. 501; syl. 3; 44 S. E. 433.

Sec. 3.—Where a lessee enters upon the leased premises and discovers oil or gas in paying quantities his right to produce the oil and gas becomes a vested right, and before such right can be divested it must be proven that he intentionally abandoned the premises, and has relinquished possession thereof. The abandonment must be intentional, and the relinquishment actual. These are questions of fact, and it devolves upon the party asserting such abandonment to prove such facts.

Henne v. *South Penn Oil Co.*, 52 W. Va. 192; 43 S. E. 147.
Lowther Oil Co. v. *Miller-Sibley Oil Co.*, 53 W. Va. 501; 44 S. E. 433.
Garrett v. *South Penn Oil Co.*, 66 W. Va. 587; 66 S. E. 741.
Shenk v. *Stahl*, 35 Ind. App. 443; 74 N. E. 538.
McMillan v. *Titus*, 222 Pa. 500; 72 Atl. 240.

Sec. 4.—Where under an oil and gas lease lessee has the right to use the demised premises for the purpose of laying pipe lines across the same for the transportation of oil or gas from other leases within the term, although lessee may enter and make unsuccessful search for oil or gas and thereafter cease further explorations, thereby forfeiting his right to further explore for these minerals, such forfeiture will not affect lessee's right to transport oil or gas from other leases across the demised premises.

Stage v. *Boyer*, 183 Pa. 560; 38 Atl. 1035.

Sec. 5.—Where in an oil and gas lease lessee is required to begin operations within a specified time from the date of the lease and lessor institutes proceedings to cancel the lease or to recover possession of the demised premises upon the grounds that lessee failed to begin operations within the specified period of time, lessee may defeat the action by proving that he was prevented from taking possession by the acts of the lessor; and he will not be held to have forfeited his rights if in good faith he commenced operations preparatory to drilling a well upon the demised premises within the prescribed time.

Henderson v. *Ferrell,* 183 Pa. 547; 38 Atl. 1018.

RELIEF FROM FORFEITURE

Sec. 6.—Where there has been a technical forfeiture of the lease by failure of lessee to pay the stipulated rental or commutation money for delay where such delay is the result of either such dealings between the lessor and lessee as to lead the lessee to believe that the lessor would not demand strict performance of the covenant for the payment of commutation money, or where there has been defects discovered in the lessor's title and notwithstanding such dealings or understandings the lessor undertakes to forfeit the lease, the lessee's remedy in such case is by bill in equity for relief against such forfeiture.

Pyle v. *Henderson,* 65 W. Va. 39; 63 S. E. 762.
Hukill v. *Myers,* 36 W. Va. 639; 15 S. E. 151.
Headley v. *Hoopengarner,* 60 W. Va. 626; 55 S. E. 144.
Eastern Oil So. v. *Coulehan,* 65 W. Va. 531; 64 S. E. 836.
South Penn Oil Co. v. *Edgell,* 48 W. Va. 348; 37 S. E. 596.

Sec. 7.—In *Pyle* v. *Henderson,* 65 W. Va. 39; 63 S. E. 762, analyzed under Chapter 7, syls. 2-3-4-5 are as follows:

"2.   Where in an oil lease there is a clause that it shall be void if a well is not completed, or in lieu of it, money paid, within a given time, and before the expiration of the time it is found that the lessor's title is defective, and he agrees to perfect it, and agrees that the money need not be paid when due, and gives an extension for payment until the title can be perfected, he cannot declare a forfeiture and make a second lease. A second lease taken with notice of the first is void as to the first lease.
3.   In case of such lease, if the lessor by his conduct clearly indicates that payment will not be demanded when due, and thus lulls the lessee into a feeling of security and throws him off his guard, and because of this he does not make payments when due,

the landlord cannot suddenly without demand or notice, declare a forfeiture, and there is no forfeiture which equity would recognize; and if there is, in such case technically a forfeiture at law equity would relieve against it.

4. A forfeiture will be deemed waived by any agreement, declaration, or course of action on the part of him who is benefitted by such forfeiture which leads the other party to believe that by conforming thereto forfeiture will not be incurred.

5. Courts of equity will not enforce a forfeiture of an estate.''

Sec. 8.—In *Hukill* v. *Myers,* 36 W. Va. 639; 15 S. E. 151, analyzed under Chapter 12, the syllabus is as follows:

''1. Where in an oil lease there is a clause of forfeiture for non-payment of rental, but the lessor consents that it need not be paid at the time when due, and indulges the lessee and asquiesces in his failure to pay, there is no forfeiture for non-payment.

2. In case of such a lease, if the lessor by his conduct clearly indicates, that payment will not be demanded when due, and thus lulls the lessee into a feeling of security and throws him off his guard, and because of this he does not make payments when due, the landlord cannot suddenly without demand or notice, declare a forfeiture, and there is no forfeiture which equity would recognize, and if there is in such case technically a forfeiture at law, equity would relieve against it.

3. If, after such rental has accrued and is not paid, whereby a forfeiture exists, the lessor with knowledge thereof receives the rentals accruing after forfeiture, he waives and cannot enforce the forfeiture.''

Sec. 9.—In *Eastern Oil Co.* v. *Coulehan,* 65 W. Va. 531; 64 S. E. 836, analyzed under Chapter 11, syl. 6, is as follows:

''6. Where, before the time has expired for the performance of a contract, there has been such a substantial compliance therewith by a party thereto, that gross injustice would be done him by denying him relief, equity will grant him relief as from a for· feiture.''

Sec. 10.—In *South Penn Oil Co.* v. *Edgell,* 48 W. Va. 348; 37 S. E. 596, analyzed under Chapter 11, the syllabus is as follows:

''The forfeiture clause in a gas and oil lease, under which a valuable estate vests in the lessee in so far as the rentals are concerned, made payable in gas, oil and money, is in the nature of a penalty to secure such rentals against which a court of equity will grant relief when compensation for such rentals can be fully made, and great loss wholly disproportionate to the injury occasioned by the breach of the contract would otherwise result to the lessee negligently, but not fraudently in default."

CHAPTER 26.

FORFEITURE BY ABANDONMENT—LESSOR'S REMEDY.

Sec. 1.—Where an oil and gas lease contains a rental clause but is silent as to the effect upon the lease of the non-payment of rental, the failure of the lessee either to pay rental or enter and explore for oil or gas within a reasonable time will authorize the lessor to declare a forfeiture of the lease upon the grounds of abandonment, and a court of equity will, for such delay, presume that lessee has abandoned the lease and decree cancellation thereof.

Smith v. *Root*, 66 W. Va. 633; 66 S. E. 1005.
Bluestone Coal Co. v. *Bell*, 38 W. Va. 297; 18 S. E. 493.
Crawford v. *Richie*, 43 W. Va. 252; 27 S. E. 220.
Tennessee Oil etc. Co. v. *Brown*, 65 C. C. A. 524; 131 Fed. 696.
Logan Nat. Gas etc. Co. v. *Great Southern Gas Co.*, 61 C. C. A. 359; 126 Fed. 623.
Federal Oil Co. v. *Western Oil Co.*, 57 C. C. A. 428; 121 Fed. 674.
McIntosh v. *Robb*, 4 Cal. App. 484; 88 Pac. 517.
Mills v. *Hartz*, 94 Pac. 142; 77 Kan. 218.
Flannagan v. *Marsh*, 32 Ky. L. Rep. 184; 105 S. W. 724.
Kimball Oil Co. v. *Keeton*, 31 Ky. L. Rep. 146; 101 S. W. 887.
Murray v. *Barnhart*,
Murray v. *Graham*, 117 La. 1023; 42 So. 489.
Florence Oil & Refining Co. v. *McCumber*, 38 Colo. 366; 88 Pac. 265.
Buffalo Valley Oil & Gas Co. v. *Jones*, 75 Kan. 18; 88 Pac 537.
Logansport etc. Gas Co. v. *Seegar*, 165 Ind. 1; 74 N. E. 500.

Sec. 2.—Where a lessee has entered the leased premises and has made explorations for oil or gas which have proved unsuccessful, and thereafter physically abandons the premises, lessor may, after a reasonable time given lessee to re-enter and continue explorations, file his bill in equity for relief alleging the entry and explorations and failure to find gas or oil in paying quantities and the subsequent physical abandonment of the premises by the lessee; and upon proof of these facts, if denied, the court will presume that lessee abandoned the search and will cancel the lease.

> *Steelsmith* v. *Gartlan*, 45 W. Va. 27; 29 S. E. 987.
> *Parish Fork Oil Co.* v. *Bridgewater Gas Co.* 51 W. Va. 583; 42 S. E. 655; 59 L. R. A. 566.
> *Lowther Oil Co.* v. *Miller-Sibley Oil Co.*, 53 W. Va. 501; 44 S. E. 433.
> *Sult* v. *Hochstetter Oil Co.*, 63 W. Va. 317. Syl. 6; 61 S. E. 307.
> *Calhoun* v. *Neely*, 201 Pa. 97. Syl. 2; 50 Atl. 967.
> *Foster* v. *Elk Fork Oil & Gas Co.*, 90 Fed. 178; 32 C. C. A. 560, affirming 84 Fed. 839.
> *Federal Betterment Co.* v. *Blaes*, 75 Kan. 69; 88 Pac. 555.
> *Ohio Oil Co.* v. *Detamore*, 165 Ind. 243; 73 N. E. 906.

Sec. 3.—Where an oil and gas lease specifies the test to be made and provides for no other, and the lessee enters and makes the test provided for which proves unsuccessful and then physically abandons the premises and does not within a reasonable time re-enter and continue or resume explorations, proof of the fact of such actual cessation of search need not be followed by proof of the intention of the lessee to abandon, as the lessee has performed what the express terms of the lease provided for, and his intentions are proven by proof of his acts.

> *Steelsmith* v. *Gartlan*, 45 W. Va. 27; 29 S. E. 987.

Sec. 4.—Where a lessee under an oil and gas lease enters and discovers oil or gas in paying quantities but fails to operate the well or wells, lessor may after giving lessee a reasonable time within which to operate the lease declare a forfeiture and may cancel the lease in a court of equity.

> *Heintz* v. *Shortt*, 149 Pa. 286; 24 Atl. 316.

Sec. 5.—Under the construction given to oil and gas leases by the Supreme Court of Indiana, where a lease provides for a term and contains a clause authorizing the lessee to pay a stipulated sum and thereby continue the lease in force, non-payment of which sum to forfeit the lease, lessor cannot declare a forfeiture during the period for which he has accepted rental; but he may refuse to accept the rental, and, unless within a reasonable time after the date of such refusal lessee enters and commences explorations, lessor may declare the lease forfeited and procure a cancellation thereof by a court exercising equity powers.

Dill v. *Fraze,* 169 Ind. 53; 79 N. E. 971.

Sec. 6.—Where an oil and gas lease contains a rental clause but is silent as to the effect upon the lease of the non-payment thereof at maturity, and where lessee has not actually entered upon the premises for the purposes of development under the terms of the lease, in a suit or proceeding by lessor for the cancellation of the lease upon the grounds of abandonment, the relinquishment of the lessee's right to enter or his abandonment of the lease becomes purely a question of his intention; and this intention may be established by proof of such facts and circumstances as evidence a voluntary waiver of his rights.

Smith v. *Root,* 66 W. Va. 633; 66 S. E. 1005.

Sec. 7.—The distinction as to the proofs required in cases where lessee has entered and then physically abandoned the premises and where he has never entered for the purpose of development is, that in the former case his acts proven show his intentions while in the latter case, never having entered into possession the intention to abandon must be established by such facts and circumstances as show a voluntary waiver or relinquishment of his rights.

Smith v. *Root,* 66 W. Va. 633; 66 S. E. 1005.
Steelsmith v. *Gartlan,* 45 W. Va. 27; 29 S. E. 978.

Sec. 8.—Where a lease is owned by several persons either under an original grant or subsequent assignment lessor may contract with a majority of the owners for surrender of the lease unless explorations are commenced within a specified time; and in default by such owners in commencing explorations within the time agreed upon lessor may declare and enforce a forfeiture of the lease.

Hooks v. *Forst*, 165 Pa. 238; 30 Atl. 846.

Sec. 9.—Where an oil and gas lease contains a rental clause but is silent as to the effect upon the lease of the non-payment of rental, while the non-payment of the rental at the time specified will not of itself forfeit the lease, lessor may proceed for the collection of the rental due and upon failure to recover it may declare the lease forfeited and divest lessee's rights.

Marshall v. *Oil Co.*, 198 Pa. 83; 47 Atl. 927.

Sec. 10.—The remedy of lessor, where lessee fails to pay the stipulated commutation money for delay, and fails to develop the property, but notwithstanding, claims the right to hold the lease, is by bill in equity to cancel the lease as a cloud on his title. Some courts hold, that where a lessee does not drill a sufficient number of wells either to develop the property or protect the lines from drainage, a court of equity will cancel the lease as to the unprotected and undeveloped portions of the land after putting the lessee upon a condition to make the necessary developments or protect the lines.

Hukill v. *Guffey*, 37 W. Va. 425; 16 S. E. 544.
Brewster v. *Lanyon Zinc Co.*, 140 Fed. 801; 72 C. C. A. 213.
Gadberry v. *Ohio & I. Con. Gas Co.*, 162 Ind. 9; 67 N. E. 259; 62 L. R. A. 895.
Munroe v. *Armstrong*, 96 Pa. 307.
Crawford v. *Ritchie*, 43 W. Va. 252; 27 S. E. 220.
Steelsmith v. *Gartlan*, 45 W. Va. 27; 29 S. E. 978; 44 L. R. A. 107.
Lowther Oil Co. v. *Miller-Sibley Co.*, 53 W. Va. 501; 44 S. E. 433; 97 Am. St. Rep. 1027.
Elk Fork Oil & Gas Co. v. *Jennings*, 84 Fed. 839; Affirmed in *Foster* v. *Elk Fork Oil & Gas Co.*, 90 Fed. 178; 32 C. C. A. 560.

Sec. 11.—In *Hukill* v. *Guffey*, 37 W. Va. 425; 16 S. E. 544, (Dec. 22, 1892), syl. 2 is as follows:

"The tract of land of thirty acres in controversy is situated in an oil field at the time of the senior lease partially developed. The senior lessee, and those claiming under him, had for more than nine months failed to commence to bore for oil, and had failed to pay or deposit for the lessor the one dollar and thirty-three and one-third cents per month. *Held,* under the circumstances of the case, the senior lessee and those claiming under him are not entitled to be relieved against the forfeiture by paying such sum. The damages to be looked to are the damages resulting from the breach of the covenants to bore for oil, and not the failure to pay one dollar and thirty-three and one-third cents per month, in lieu thereof; and the damages resulting from the failure to do the specific thing, viz, to bore for oil, not being susceptible of pecuniary measurement, and therefore not compensable, the relief from such forfeiture is denied."

On June 30, 1886, David Wise executed an oil and gas lease for a tract of land in Monongalia County, to William Hays. This lease contained the following covenant:

"The parties of the second part covenant to commence operations for said purposes within nine months from and after the execution of this lease, or to thereafter pay to the party of the first part one and thirty-three and one-third dollars per month, until work is commenced, the money to be deposited in the hands of John Kennedy for each and every month; and a failure on the part of said second parties to comply with either one or the other of the foregoing conditions shall work an absolute forfeiture of this lease."

On January 10, 1889, William Hayes assigned and transferred this lease to E. M. Hukill. On July 11, 1888, David Wise made a second lease of the same property to Rezin Calvert. On March 16, 1889, Rezin Calvert assigned the lease to Ida C. Calvert and Vinnie J. Calvert, who in turn on May 8, 1889, assigned the lease to J. M. Guffey and M. Murphy. No rentals were paid to Wise on the Hays lease until a short time before January 10, 1889, when all the rentals were paid to him. No work was done on the lease until about May 1, 1889, or later in that month, when Hukill commenced boring for oil and worked continuously boring two wells, one spoiled in the drilling, and in the other striking oil in paying quantities on November 25, 1889. On July 15, 1889, Hukill was notified by Guffey and Murphy, in writing of their claim. On

January 23, 1890, Guffey and Murphy brought an action of unlawful entry and detainer against Hukill for recovery of possession of the tract of land, which action was decided in favor of Guffey and Murphy by the Circuit Court of Monongalia County, and affirmed by the Supreme Court of Appeals, and reported as Guffey v. Hukill, 34 W. Va. 49; 11 S. E. 754. A writ of possession was issued in the unlawful entry and detainer case, and Guffey and Murphy by virtue thereof were placed in possession of the property. On June 28, 1890, E. M. Hukill instituted suit in the Circuit Court of Monongalia County in equity against J. M. Guffey, Michael Murphy, Rezin Calvert, David Wise and Joseph Bushnell, praying, among other things, to be relieved from the forfeiture of what is called the "Hays oil lease," that is the first lease made by Hays to Wise; and also for an injunction against the execution of the writ of possession on the judgment rendered by the Court of Appeals in the case of *Guffey & Hukill.* An amended bill was filed, and also a second amended bill, both of which were answered by the defendants, and the Circuit Court dismissed the plaintiff's bill. The case was appealed to the Circuit Court of Appeals where the decision of the Circuit Court was affirmed.

Sec. 12.—In *Brewster* v. *Lanyon Zinc Co.,* 140 Fed. 801; 72 C. C. A. 213, analyzed under Chapter 4, paragraphs 9-15-16 of the head notes are as follows:

"9. Whether a covenant is also a condition is essentially a question of intention, and where in an oil and gas lease the covenants of the lessee are introduced with the statement that the grant is made 'on the following terms' and are followed by a stipulation that the lessee's failure to comply with 'any of the above conditions' shall render the lease null and void, this stipulation has reference to the spirit and legal effect, and not to the mere letter, of what precedes, and if that by necessary implication contains a covenant by the lessee to exercise reasonable diligence in prosecuting the work of development and production, such covenant is also a condition, a plain and substantial breach of which, in view of the actual circumstances at the time, as distinguished from the mere expectations on the part of the lessor and conjecture on the part of the mining enthusiast will entitle the lessor to avoid the lease.

15. A suit, the primary and only purpose of which is to establish a forfeiture, as a matter of record, and to cancel the

thing forfeited—in this instance a lease,—is a suit to give effect
to, and therefore to aid in, the enforcement of a forfeiture, and
the equity which it presents must be strong enough to overcome
the general indisposition of courts of chancery towards granting
such relief.

16.   A forfeiture of an oil and gas lease was incurred under
circumstances which do not entitle the lessee to relief in equity.
Although actually terminated by the default of the lessee and the
assertion of a forfeiture by the lessor the lease appears as spread
upon the public records and is claimed by the lessee to be still
effective as a disposal of all the oil and gas in the lessor's land.
It embarasses, if it does not prevent the exercise of the right to
make other disposition of these minerals, and this at a time when
they are being exhausted by the lawful multiplication and operation of wells on surrounding land. The lessor is in possession,
save of a small portion of the land, occupied by the lessee in the operation of a single gas well which it has drilled. The State statute
permits the defeated party in ejectment to demand and obtain
a second trial as a matter of right. *Held,* that a bill disclosing
these facts makes a case which calls for a measure of relief not
attainable at law, and which entitles the lessor to a decree giving
effect to the forfeiture by its establishment as matter of record,
and by the cancellation of the lease as a cloud upon the title.''

Sec.   13.—In *Gadberry* v. *Ohio & I. Consolidated Gas Co.,* 162
Ind. 9; 67 N. E. 259; 62 L. R. A. 895, analyzed under Chapter 11,
syl. 2 is as follows:

"Failure for two years of the grantee of the oil and gas in
land to develop it, after constructing a well, finding gas, and then
closing it, prima facie authorizes the grantor, who was to be paid
$100.00 a year for each well while gas was being used off the
premises, without demand, to treat the grant as abandoned.''

Judge Gillett, delivering the opinion, said:

"The duty to develop the property upon the discovery of oil
or gas in paying quantities is not to be regarded as a mere implied covenant, but in a case like this, where practically the whole
consideration must depend upon the implied undertakings, is to
be treated as a condition subsequent. Conditions subsequent are
not ordinarily favored 'because' as declared by Professor Kent
'they tend to destroy estates and the rigorous exaction of them is
a species of *summum jus,* and in many cases hardly reconcilable

with conscience. 4 Kent Com. p. *129· Accordingly, it has been declared in unrestricted terms that equity will not lend its aid to enforce a forfeiture. Where there has been a cause of forfeiture, followed by an entry upon the part of the grantor, so that the title has been lost, it is not strictly the enforcing of a forfeiture for a court of equity to decree a cancellation of the instrument. *McClellan* v. *Coffin*, 93 Ind. 456. *Birmingham* v. *Leasan*, 77 Me. 494; 1 Atl. 151. But even in a case of this kind, where the circumstances do not permit of an entry, the forfeiture may be, in effect, enforced by suit in equity. Forfeitures are usually against conscience, and without equity and it is for these reasons that courts of chancery ordinarily refuse relief in such cases, but an exception to the rule must exist where it be against equity to permit the defendant to longer assert his title. * * * * * * And the completion of the first well, having cut off the liquidated damages of one dollar per day for non-completion, and that no gas has been disposed of off the premises, there remains no measure of damages, for while the damages would be substantial, they would be speculative. *Foster* v. *Elk Fork etc. Co.*, 32 C. C. A. 560; 90 Fed. 178. *Fed. Oil Co.* v. *Western Oil Co.*, (C. C.) 112 Fed. 373. The lack of any other remedy, and the danger that the gas might be withdrawn through wells on other lands makes a case of this kind appeal to the conscience of the chancellor and calls upon him to enforce the incurred forfeiture by removing the cloud from the title.''

Sec. 14.—In *Munroe* v. *Armstrong*, 96 Pa. 307, analyzed under Chapter 5, the syllabus is as follows:

"A lease of land was made exclusively for the purpose of producing oil. The work of boring for oil was to be commenced in ten days, and continued with due diligence until success or abandonment; and if the lessee failed to get oil in paying quantities, or ceased work for thirty days at any time, the lease was to be forfeited and void; *Held*, that if the lessees failed to get oil in one well they had a right to put down another and as many more as they pleased so long as they worked with diligence to success or abandonment; *Held further*, that a cessation of work for thirty days forfeited the lease.

Forfeiture for non-development or delay is essential to private and public interest in relation to the use and alienation of property. In general, equity abhors a forfeiture, but not where it works equity and protects a landowner from the laches of a lessee whose lease is of no value till developed.''

CHAPTER 27.

OIL AND GAS IN PLACE ARE MINERALS AND PART OF THE LAND.

Sec.   1.—Petroleum oil and natural gas, in place, are minerals and a part of the land.   Their unlawful extraction by one lawfully in possession is waste, and by one not lawfully in possession is trespass.   The title to these minerals can only pass by deed.

Williamson v. Jones, 39 W. Va. 231; 19 S. E. 436.
Williamson v. Jones, 43 W. Va. 562; 27 S. E. 411.
South Penn Oil Co. v. *McIntire,* 44 W. Va. 296; 28 S. E. 922.
Wilson v. *Yost,* 43 W. Va. 826; 28 S. E. 781.
Sult v. *Hochstetter Oil Co.,* 63 W. Va. 317; 61 S. E. 307.
Blakly v. *Marshall,* 174 Pa. 425; 34 Atl. 564.
Marshall v. *Mellon,* 179 Pa. 371; 36 Atl. 201; 35 L. R. A. 216.
Isam v. *Rex Crude Oil Co.,* 147 Cal. 659; 82 Pac. 317.
Preston v. *White,* 57 W. Va. 278; 50 S. E. 236.
Appeal of Stoughton, 88 Pa. 198.
Hughes v. *United Pipeline,* 119 N. Y. 423; 23 N. E. 1042.
Poe v. *Ulrey,* 233 Ill. 56; 84 N. E. 46.
Lanyon Zinc Co. v. *Freeman,* 68 Kan. 691; 75 Pac. 995.
Detlor v. *Holland,* 57 Ohio St. 492; 49 N. E. 690; 40 L. R. A. 266.
Bettman v. *Harness,* 42 W. Va. 433; 26 S. E. 271.
Freer v. *Davis,* 52 W. Va. 1; 43 S. E. 164.
Freer v. *Davis,* 52 W. Va. 35; 43 S. E. 172.
Moore v. *Jennings,* 47 W. Va. 181; 34 S. E. 792.
Haskell v. *Sutton,* 53 W. Va. 206; 44 S. E. 533.
Westmoreland Nat. Gas Co. v. *DeWitt,* 130 Pa. 325; 18 Atl. 724.
Duffield v. *Hue,* 136 Pa. 602; 20 Atl. 526.
Murray v. *Allred,* 100 Tenn. 100; 66 Am. St. Rep. 740.

Sec.   2.—Petroleum oil and natural gas are minerals and in place are part of the land.   These minerals can be conveyed only by deed.   The title to the oil and gas under the ordinary oil and gas lease remains in the landowner, and can be affected by lessee only by production. When brought to the surface they become personal property.   The royalty of oil which the lessee pays as consideration for the grant to him of the exclusive privilege of producing belongs to the landowner.   The residue, the working interest, when raised to the surface belongs to the lessee and is then personal property.

Sec. 3.—The practical questions arising out of oil and gas leases as to the nature of these minerals usually arise from attempts by a tenant for life, a tenant in common, or co-tenant, or someone under a void or voidable lease, to explore for and market these minerals; or where a life tenant, tenant in common or co-tenant attempts to confer upon lessee the exclusive privilege of producing these minerals from the premises in which such lessor has only a life estate or an interest less than the fee. In such cases the extraction of oil or gas is waste.

Sec. 4.—A tenant in common, co-tenant or joint tenant, although he is entitled to and may be in the actual possession of the premises, cannot by the execution of an oil and gas lease confer upon the lessee a legal right to produce these minerals. Production under such a lease is waste.

Sec. 5.—A guardian of infants owning real estate cannot without authority of a court having jurisdiction over the property of such infants make an oil and gas lease of the premises of his wards which will authorize the mining and marketing of the oil and gas. In the absence of such authority the lease is void.

Sec. 6.—In *Williamson* v. *Jones*, 39 W. Va. 231; 19 S. E. 436 (April 4, 1894,) the syllabus is as follows:

"1. A person who causes his land to be sold for some purpose of his own under a judicial proceeding which turns out to be void. and receives and retains the proceeds of sale, cannot afterwards be heard to question its validity. He has made his election.
2. If such person afterwards stands by and sees the purchaser expend large sums in developing oil on the property, he may not afterwards set up such defect in the purchaser's title; he is estopped.
3. Petroleum or mineral oil in place is as much a part of the realty as timber, coal, iron ore, or salt water.
4. It is a part of the inheritance, and an unlawful removal thereof is a dishersion of him in remainder constituting waste, which a court of equity in a proper case will restrain and enjoin.
5. A case in which the remainder created by the will is *held*

to be vested, not contingent, and those in remainder not to be parties to the suit by representation.''

The facts material upon the consideration of the case as stated in the opinion are as follows:

David Hickman, of Tyler County, West Virginia, the father or grandfather of the principal plaintiffs below, died in the year 1863, leaving his last will and testament which was duly probated and admitted to record in Tyler County. The seventh clause of the will was as follows:

''I give and bequeath to my daughter, Eliza Williamson, the wife of Dr. William S. Williamson, for life, the shares I own in the Thomas Jones land adjoining Sistersville * * * * * with the power to her to dispose of the same by will amongst her sisters or sisters' children, as she may think proper, and in the event of her death without a will, said shares * * * * * shall revert to her sisters in equal proportion.''

By the eighth clause he gave to his daughter, Eliza Williamson, $400.00, and appointed Mrs. Williamson and Christian Engle executors. The latter, alone, qualified. By a codicil he so modified the seventh clause of the will as to constitute Christian Engle trustee to whom he devised said lands (including also 100 acres not in any way involved in this litigation) for the sole use of his said daughter for life, but the devise in all other respects remained as provided for in the seventh clause. The history of the shares in the Thomas Jones land thus owned and devised to his daughter for life, by David Hickman, is as follows: Robert Greer and wife, by deed dated April 21, 1832, conveyed to Thomas Hanes a tract of about 205 acres which was called in the litigation a tract of 165 acres. Between the defendant, Joseph T. Jones, and the family of Thomas Jones, the former owner of the land, no relationship existed or appeared. In the year 1849, Thomas Jones departed this life intestate, seized and possessed of the tracts of 165 acres and of 54 poles, then regarded as of little value. Thomas Jones left surviving him as his heirs at law ten children, six sons, namely, Lewis, John H., Thomas, David, Joel and Milton; and four daughters, namely, Martha, Sarah, Elizabeth and Emmeline. This land was not partitioned amongst the Jones heirs. Lewis Jones had purchased the interest of John H. Jones, Thomas Jones and Emmeline Jones; and also claimed to be the owner of the undivided share of his brother, David Jones. David Hickman was endorser for Lewis Jones on a negotiable note which Hickman had to pay, and Lewis Jones, to secure the payment thereof by trust deed dated December 15, 1853, conveyed to R. Hickman and Thomas I. Stealey, trustees, these five undivided shares. On March 12, 1855, the trustees sold four of these interests to David Hickman, the trust creditor, and conveyed the same to him by deed of that date, which deed was admitted to record in May, 1855. The trustees did not sell the David Jones interest, as it had previously been sold and conveyed to John Wherry. In September, 1854, Milton Jones conveyed his share to Absalom George. Martha Jones had married John Massey. On March 25, 1861, Martha Massey and her husband, Absalom George, and John Wharry, sold and conveyed these three undivided interests to David Hickman. This deed was recorded on April 25, 1861. At the time of his death, in 1863, David Hickman owned seven undivided tenth parts of the Thomas Jones land. These were the shares mentioned in the seventh clause of his will.

On July 1, 1857, the administrators of James Peden, deceased, instituted a suit in equity in the Circuit Court of Tyler County, against Lewis Jones, curator of the estate of Thomas Jones, deceased, and the children and heirs at law of Thomas Jones, deceased, on a claim for $41.09. In February, 1859, Joshua Russell instituted suit in equity against the curator of the estate and the heirs at law of Thomas Jones, to enforce payment of the balance of $32.63 due on a note from decedent to Russell. On September 23, 1862, these two suits were consolidated and a sale was decreed of the tract of 165 acres of land, and of the tract of 54 poles, to pay these debts. On July 23, 1862, the commissioner to whom the cause had been referred, ascertained the amount due Joshua Russell to be $99.61; and to Peden's administrator, $130.21; and to Samuel Davis, $35.70. A. D. Soper was appointed special commissioner to make the sale. None of the claims were liens on any of these interests bought by David Hickman, but he was a pendente lite purchaser of the 1-10 which was sold and conveyed to him by Martha Massey, nee Jones, and husband by deed of March 25, 1861. David Hickman was not a party to the suit. He was a bona fide purchaser for value, or grantee of such purchaser as to six-tenths, with his deeds duly entered of record before the institution of the suit. He was a pendente lite purchaser as to 1-10. Soper, the commissioner to sell, died, and this decree of sale remained unexecuted. On June 10, 1864, Peden's administrators, by James M. Stephenson, their attorney, assigned their claims to the estate of David Hickman. The two other creditors by decree also assigned their decrees.

On October 10, 1868, the Circuit Court entered in the cause a decree as follows:

"And at another day, to-wit, at a Circuit Court held for said County of Tyler on the 10th day of October, in the year 1868, in the above named causes, one in favor of Joshua Russell for $51.94 and interest, and one in favor of the administrators of James Peden for $83.10 and interest, and $35.75 to Samuel Davis has been assigned to and paid by the executors of David Hickman since the date of the decree; and it also appearing by the said decree that two tracts of land owned by Thomas Jones, deceased were decreed to be sold for the payment of said debts, unless otherwise paid, and it also appearing that the said David Hickman at his death, was the owner of seven-undivided tenth parts of said land, and the executor of said Hickman, not desiring the sale of the parts of said land owned by said estate, but only that part of said land not owned by the estate of David Hickman, deceased—it is therefore adjudged, ordered and decreed that the commissioner heretofore appointed to make sale of said lands, sell the outstanding interests in order to the payment of their portion of the debts aforesaid, the said debts being the debts of Thomas Jones, deceased, and a lien on the whole of said land."

From October, 1868, to December 26, 1881, no orders were entered in the two consolidated causes, save orders of continuance. In the meantime, Eliza Williamson purchased the outstanding 1-10, being the share of Joel Jones, from his children, who conveyed the same to her by deed bearing date January 19, 1870; and on December 6, 1872, she bought from the children of Elizabeth Kester, deceased, nee Jones, her 1-10 share, which was conveyed to her by deed of the last named date; and in December, 1887, she bought at tax sale the remaining share in the name of Thomas Jones estate, which the clerk of the County Court conveyed to her by deed dated April 1, 1890.

On the —— day of ————— ——, 1886, Eliza Williamson, who
had become sui juris by the death of her husband, brought
a suit in equity against C. Engle as executor and trustee
under the will of David Hickman, asking that the will be executed
by directing that her legacy of $400.00 be paid to her; and that the
trust be carried out in regard to the Thomas Jones land. On October 12, 1886, defendant Engle filed his answer, and the final decree in the cause was entered as follows:

"This day came the defendant, Christian Engle, trustee for
Eliza Williamson, the executor of David Hickman, deceased, and
tendered in open court his answer to complainant's bill, together
with exhibits A. and B., C., D., E. and F., to the said answer, and
asked that the same be filed, which was accordingly done, whereupon the complainant by her counsel agrees to abide by and perform the arrangement and agreement entered into between herself and Christian Engle, executors, of David Hickman, deceased,
in relation to the liens against the Thomas Jones land, as alleged
and shown by the answers of Christian Engle, and the exhibits
therewith, filed in this cause, and to accept the said liens against
said Jones land, which are mentioned and fully recited in said
answer of said Engle, and the exhibits B. E. and F. therewith
filed, and amounting, on the 25th day of June, 1864, in all, to the
sum of two hundred and sixty-five dollars and fifty-two cents, with
interest thereon from said 25th day of June, 1864, in full of the
balance of two hundred and sixty-five dollars and fifty-two cents
(and the interest thereon accrued and accruing from June 25,
1864) of the bequest of $400.00 to her by·her father, David Hick-
man, deceased, which she alleges in her bill to be due to her on
account of said bequest; and that said Thomas Jones land may be
sold in the chancery suits of Peden's administrators, and Joshua
Russell, pending in the Circuit Court of Tyler County under the
decree of sale made therein, as stated in said answer of said Engle
for the payment of said liens, and the interest thereon accrued
and accruing. And the complainant further agrees that this
cause be dismissed at her cost but no docket fee to be taxed therein, to which proposition and agreement by the complainant the
defendant, C. Engle, by his counsel, accedes and agrees. It is
therefore ordered that the foregoing agreement of complainant
and defendant, C. Engle, executor, etc., be entered up as the decree
of this court in this cause; and said Jones land be sold under the
decree in said two chancery suits in Tyler Circuit Court for the
payment of said lien and interest thereon for the use and benefit
of said Eliza Williamson, as aforesaid, and that this cause, be and

the same is hereby dismissed at the cost of the complainant, Eliza Williamson, less the docket fee as aforesaid.''

On December 26, 1881, in the cause of Peden's administrator v. Lewis Jones, curator, C. Engle, executor of David Hickman, and Eliza Williamson by Ben Engle, her attorney, filed their petition giving the history of the case, the assignments of the sums decreed therein, the history of the Jones land, the disposition of the seven-tenths by David Hickman, testator, Eliza Williamson's purchase of two of the three outstanding tenths; that since the death of her husband the land had been no profit, but a burden to her. They prayed that they might be made parties defendant in the Peden suit; that the Thomas Jones land might be sold for the liens so held by Engle, executor, etc., to pay Eliza Williamson the amount she was entitled to by reason of the interests held by her in said land in her own right; that the decree of September 23, 1863, and of October, 1868, be set aside and a decree entered appointing a new commissioner to make sale of the land on such terms as the court might deem most advantageous to the parties in interest to Eliza Williamson as devisee and as owner in her own right. Thereupon the court, without making any new parties, on December 26, 1881, entered a decree whereby after reciting the ownership of the Jones lands, the appointment of A. D. Soper, Special Commissioner; his death without having executed the decree; the petition of C. Engle, executor of David Hickman, and the amounts represented by the liens in favor of Joshua Russell, Peden and Samuel Davis; the interest of David Hickman in the shares of the Jones estate; the interest of Eliza Williamson in her own right, being the two undivided one-tenths in the Jones land, it was declared that the said lands could not well be partitioned. The decree then made the finding that C. Engle, as trustee, held the interests for the use and benefit for life, of Eliza Williamson, directing a sale of said lands to be made after four weeks publication of a notice and appointed a commissioner to make the sale.

On April 14, 1882, the court modified the decree of December 26, 1881, and authorized the commissioner to sell the seven undivided interests held by C. Engle as trustee under the will of David Hickman, and the undivided two-tenths then held by Eliza Williamson in her own right in said real estate.

On December 12, 1891, C. Engle, the commissioner, filed his report of sale. He reported that on December 19, 1891, at the front door of the Court House of Tyler County, in pursuance to the decree of sale, he sold the two tracts of land aforesaid; and that J. C. Tennant became the purchaser. This sale was confirmed on December 12, 1891. The decree directed the payment to C. Engle, executor of the last will of David Hickman, deceased, of the sum of $265.52, the amount of charges or liens held by him as such executor, and the payment of three-tenths of the residue of the purchase money to Eliza Williamson; and the remaining seventenths to C. Engle, trustee under the will, to be invested at interest for the benefit of Eliza Williamson for life. Mrs. Williamson held the land up to the date of the confirmation of the sale, in her possession. C. Engle, as trustee, was required to execute and file in the papers a bond in the penalty of $2500.00 conditioned according to law. Benjamin Engel, the commissioner, conveyed the land to Tennant, the purchaser, by deed dated February 4, 1892. Tennant was agent for Joseph T. Jones, and conveyed the land to Jones by deed dated February 8, 1892. Joseph T. Jones took possession, bored 23 producing oil wells, at a cost of $6,000 each. He produced from June, 1892, to September 21, 1893, about 403,681 barrels of oil, for which he received about $189,580.90. His drilling and operating expenses were about $225,000. David Hickman left six daughters who were entitled to take under the seventh clause of his will. Eliza Williamson and W. H. Gillespie, assignee of Eliza Williamson, and numerous grandchildren of David Hickman, remaindermen under the said seventh clause of his will, on July 13, 1893, filed a bill in equity in the Circuit Court of Tyler County, West Virginia, against Joseph C. Jones, J. C. Tennant and others, which bill charged that Joseph C. Jones had no valid title to these lands; and that they were the property of Eliza Williamson, and remainder men under the seventh clause of said will; that the defendant Jones, was committing irreparable injury to and waste of the inheritance in taking the petroleum oil from said lands which constituted its chief value. An injunction was granted restraining the pipe line companies from delivering over to J. C. Tennant and J. T. Jones, or either of them, any of the proceeds of the sale of oils on the Jones tract of 165 acres; and two special receivers were appointed on August 25, 1893. On October 17, 1893, the court entered a decree refusing to dissolve the injunction, from which decree Jones appealed to the Supreme Court, and that court, upon final hearing, modified the decree of the court below, and found as to the ownership of the real estate as follows: That the defendant J. T. Jones was the owner in fee of three undivided tenth parts of the land in controversy, and of the freehold of the residue during the life of the plaintiff, Eliza Williamson, with a vested remainder in fee simple to the sisters and their heirs of Eliza Williamson in the remaining seven undivided tenth parts according to and under the will of David Hickman, deceased; and that the defendant Jones was rightfully in possession with the right to extract and sell the oil, provided he did not take more than his share, and after deducting all expenses incident to the working, and after making a proper allowance, if any, for what he, the said Jones, might be entitled to as the owner of the life estate of Eliza Williamson.

Sec. 7.—In *Williamson* v. *Jones*, 43 W. Va. 562; 27 S. E. 411 (June 11, 1897), syls. 1-5 inclusive, and 13-16 inclusive, and 18 are as follows:

"1. Petroleum oil in place is part of the land. Its lawful extraction by one lawfully in possession is waste, and by a stranger is trespass; in both cases irreparable injury which may be enjoined.

2. It is waste in a tenant for life to take petroleum oil from the land, for which he is liable to the reversioner or remaindermen in fee.

3. A tenant for life may work open salt or oil wells or mines even to exhaustion, without account, but cannot open new ones.

4. It is waste in a tenant in common to take petroleum oil from the land for which he is liable to his co-tenants to the extent of their right in the land.

5. Things part of the land, wrongfully severed by a tenant for life becomes personalty, but belong to the owner of the next vested estate of inheritance or reversion or remainder not the life tenant.

13. A tenant for life, or a tenant in common in sole possession claiming exclusive ownership, taking petroleum oil and converting it to his exclusive use, is liable to account on the basis of rents and profits not for annual rental.

14. A remainder man or reversioner has jurisdiction in equity against a tenant for life to enjoin waste, and to have com-

pensation for the damages, the same as if he sued at law, to avoid
multiplicity of suits. The same is the case between tenants in
common where one is guilty of waste.

15. A tenant for life who, by waste, has severed from the
realty things that are part of it, as petroleum oil, has no right to
have the proceeds invested so he may have interest thereon during
the life estate; but their proceeds go at once to the owner of the
next vested estate of inheritance.

16. One making permanent improvements on land as if his
own, at a time when there was reason to believe his title good, is
to be allowed their value, so far as they enhance the value of the
land; but if, when making them he has notice, actual or constructive, of the superior right of another, he cannot be allowed for
them.

18. Under the circumstances, a party taking petroleum oil
unlawfully, is allowed all costs of production, including costs of
boring productive wells, as a set-off against rents and profits.''

This is the second appeal of *Williamson* v. *Jones*, 39 W. Va.
231; 19 S. E. 436. This appeal was taken to a final decree. The
Circuit Court held that Joseph T. Jones was only accountable to
the remainder men under the seventh paragraph of the will of
David Hickman for their proportional interest in the royalty. The
decree required Jones to pay the owners of the seven-tenths of the
lands for one-eighth of seven-tenths of the oil produced, thus
charging Jones only for one-eighth of the oil, that being the usual
rent, commonly called royalty, being the amount usually paid the
landowner in oil and gas leases. Jones appealed, assigning error
in charging him with anything; and the plaintiffs cross assigned
error in charging Jones with only one-eighth of the oil. The Court
of Appeals reversed the decree of the Circuit Court.

Sec. 8.—In *South Penn Oil Co.* v. *McIntire,* 44 W. Va. 296;
28 S. E. 922 (Jan. 26, 1898), the first, second and third points of
the syllabus are as follows:

"1. The appointment of a committee of an insane person by
the county court or its clerk, without the notice required by statute
is void.

2. In a proceeding by a committee of an insane person, under Chapter 83 Code, to sell the undivided interest of such insane
person in the oil and gas underlying the tract of land, the co-

tenants of such person are not necessary or proper parties to such proceeding.

3. Oil and gas, being a part of the realty in and under which they exist, the committee of an insane person having an interest therein can only sell or lease such interest by decree of court as provided by statute."

On April 29, 1895, A. B. McIntire was, by the Clerk of the County Court of Tyler County, without the notice required by law first served, appointed committee of Lucretia J. Thompson, a lunatic. On May 1, 1895, the committee, together with Elihu Thompson and Erufus G. Thompson, brothers of the lunatic, and sole heirs at law of Mary A. Thompson, deceased, leased to the South Penn Oil Company 90½ acres of land in Tyler County for oil and gas purposes, the lease containing the usual covenants and conditions of an oil and gas lease. The lease was recorded in the Clerk's office of the County Court of Tyler County. On November 21, 1896, after notice served on said lunatic of the application, the said A. B. McIntire was appointed her committee by the Clerk of said Court and gave bond and qualified as such. On December 14, 1896, said committee filed his bill against Lucretia J. Thompson, Elihu and Erufus G. Thompson, alleging that his appointment as committee on April 29, 1895, reported to the Court by the Clerk and confirmed on July 9, 1895, was without notice as required by law and void, the bill setting up his second appointment as valid. The bill further alleged the death of Mary A. Thompson in 1893, seized of 90½ acres of land, situated in McElroy District, Tyler County; and that the heirs of said Mary A. Thompson, to-wit, her two brothers, Elihu and Erufus, for themselves and the plaintiff as committee for Lucretia J. Thompson, the lunatic, had agreed upon a partition of said land between themselves, but had excepted from said partition the oil and gas supposed to lie in and under said land, alleging that the best interests of his ward would be subserved by a sale for cash of seven-eighths of her one-third undivided interest in the gas and oil underlying said tract of land, reserving from such sale the one-eighth of one-third, the usual royalty in the product. The bill prayed that a guardian ad litem be appointed for the lunatic to make answer and protect her interests, and for a decree to sell said seven-eighths of one-third undivided interest in the oil and gas. A guardian ad litem was appointed in this suit, and answered for said lunatic. The other defendants, Elihu and Erufus, answered the bill accepting the partition, and joining in the prayer of the plaintiff for the sale of seven-eighths of their sister's interest in said oil and gas. Depositions were taken, and a special commissioner for the purpose of making the sale was appointed, and subsequently he reported that he had sold said interest to D. H. Courtney, A. L. Lowrie and Joseph McDermott for $1100.00 cash, the purchasers paying all the costs, including attorneys' fees. The court confirmed the sale and directed a deed to be made to the purchasers. On December 17, 1896, A. B. McIntire, the committee for Lucretia J. Thompson, and the special commissioner appointed for the purpose, conveyed to the said purchasers, in pursuance to the decree, all the undivided one-third interest of the said Lucretia J. Thompson in and to the undivided seven-eighths of all the oil and gas underlying the land with the privilege to the purchasers of entering upon the land and drilling, mining, boring and operating for oil and gas. The deed also set forth the usual covenants and conditions as to entry, and the conditions contained in the usual oil and gas lease. At January Rules, 1897, the South Penn Oil Company filed its bill in the Circuit Court of Tyler County against the said A. B. McIntire, committee, the said Thompson, the lunatic, and the purchasers, attacking the proceedings in the cause of McIntire against Lucretia J. Thompson and others, in which the interest of the lunatic in the oil was conveyed to Courtney, Lowrie and McDermott, and setting up their lease of May 1, 1895, made by said committee under his first appointment of April 29, 1895, which lease the company claimed authorized it to take the oil and gas from the tract of land; further alleging that the lease had been executed by the other heirs, the brothers of the lunatic, and by the committee. The oil company claimed that the sale made by the committee as special commissioner to Courtney and others, and the deed in pursuance thereto, constituted a cloud on his title. The bill prayed for an injunction against the defendants to restrain them from in any way interfering with it in its possession of the tract of land, and further prayed that the deed made by the commissioner for the interest of the lunatic be set aside. A preliminary injunction was awarded the plaintiff as prayed for. Answers were filed, and at January Rules, 1897, the defendants, purchasers, filed a demurrer. The Circuit Court of Tyler County, on April 2, 1894, sustained the demurrer and dismissed the bill. The oil company appealed from the decree, and the Court of Appeals sustained the Circuit Court as to the status of the oil and held that the County Court was without authority to appoint the committee in the absence of notice, as required by the Statute law of West Virginia.

Sec. 9.—In *Wilson* v. *Youst,* 43 W. Va. 826; 28 S. E. 781 (Nov. 17, 1897), the syllabus is as follows:

"1. Petroleum oil, as is found in the cavities of the rock is part of the realty, and embraced in the comprehensive idea which the law attaches to the word 'land'.

2. The only manner in which a guardian can lease or sell the land of his ward for the purpose of its development, or any other purpose, is in the manner prescribed by statute under decree of the court.

3. The petroleum oil underlying a tract of land which has been devised to a life tenant who is in possession, and which is to go to certain infant children after the decease of the life tenant may be sold, upon the petition of the guardian of said infants under the provisions of Chapter 82 of the code, or leased; and the life tenant will be entitled to the interest on the royalty during the continuance of the life estate, and then the residue or corpus of the royalty will be paid to the remainder man.

4. An oil lease, investing the lessee with the right to remove all the oil in place in the premises, in consideration of his giving the lessors a certain *per cent.* thereof, is in legal effect, a sale of a portion of the land, and the proceeds represent the respective interests of the lessors in the premises."

J. D. Youst, by will bearing date November 29, 1881, devised a tract of land situated in Marion County, West Virginia, to his wife, Susanna Youst, for life, and at her death to Hermenia Wilson, wife of Alpheus Wilson, during her natural life, to be held by her free from the control of her husband as her separate estate, and to descend to her heirs at her death. Against this devise the testator made a charge and limitation that if the said Hermenia C. Wilson should not survive Susanna Youst, the wife of testator, so as to come into possession of the whole tract of land so devised, and should die during the lifetime of Susanna Youst, and should leave surviving her no children, nor the descendants of any children, then, instead of the tract going to the heirs of Hermenia C. Wilson, the testator directed that one-half of the tract, at the death of his wife, Susanna Youst, should go to Alpheus M. Wilson, husband of Hermenia Wilson, if living; and the other half to the heirs of his sister, Eliza Wade, and heirs of his deceased brother, Nicholas B. Youst, by his first wife. Alpheus Wilson died on November 29, 1891, and left surviving him by his wife, Hermenia, three children, Thomas J., Jehu D. and Clarence L. Another child (Stella May Wilson) was born January 11, 1891, and died in April, 1902. After the death of her husband, Alpheus M. Wilson, his widow, Hermenia, was married on June 8, 1893, to James W. Powell, by whom she had one child, Minnie C. Powell. Hermenia Wilson died in November, 1893, leaving surviving her her husband, James W. Powell, and four children, three by the first husband and one by the last. On June 12, 1890, Susanna Youst, Hermenia C. Wilson, and A. M. Wilson, her husband, and Alpheus M. Wilson as guardian of Thomas J. Wilson, Jehu D. Wilson, and Clarence L. Wilson, infant children of Hermenia C. Wilson, leased said tract of land containing 255 acres to C. E. Wells & Company for oil and gas purposes. In November, 1890, Alpheus M. Wilson, as guardian of Thomas J. Wilson, Jehu Wilson and Clarence L. Wilson, infant children of said Hermenia and Alpheus Wilson, filed a petition in the Circuit Court of Marion County, under Section 12, Chapter 83, Code of West Virginia, for the sale of the interests of his wards in the oil and gas underlying said tract of land. A decree was entered directing that A. M. Wilson, as such guardian, sell the oil and gas underlying the said tract. In pursuance to said decree the guardian of the infants executed a lease of said land, or the infants' interests in the oil therein, to C. E. Wells and others, who subsequently assigned to the South Penn Oil Company, which lease was reported to the court and confirmed in December 1890. The South Penn Oil Company proceeded at once to develop the land for oil, and by June 1, 1894, the ⅛ royalty of oil amounted in value to $22,000. Susanna Youst and Hermenia C. Wilson, shortly after the rendition of the decree, assigned two-thirds of the one-eighth royalty to S. B. Hughes, who up to July 1, 1894, had received about $15,000 as the 2-3 of the royalty.

After the lease of said lands was confirmed, another child was born to Hermenia C. and Alpheus Wilson, which was named

Stella May, and she was admitted by a subsequent decree of the court to share in the royalty. This child was born January 11, 1891, and died in April, 1892. Alpheus Wilson died on November 29, 1891. In 1893 his widow intermarried with James W. Powell, by whom she had one child, Minnie C. Powell, and a few days after the birth of Minnie Powell, Hermenia Powell died intestate, leaving her husband, James W. Powell, and four children. In January, 1894, upon petition, the Intermediate Court of Marion County admitted Minnie C. Powell as a co-owner in the ⅛ of the royalty. Susanna Youst was living at the date of the decision of the case. The infant children, Thomas J. Wilson, Jehu D. Wilson, Clarence L. Wilson and Minnie C. Powell, by their next friend, Harrison Manley, filed in the Circuit Court of Marion County their bill in equity attacking said proceedings as being erroneous and void so far as it was decreed that said infants should share equally with Susanna Youst and Hermenia C. Wilson and Alpheus M. Wilson her husband, in the value and production of the oil and gas in said land, giving to said infants one-third of said royalty. It was claimed in this bill that the oil being part of the real estate, the life tenant, during her natural life was entitled to the interest upon the sum realized as royalty; and that the said Hughes, as assignee of the life tenant should be compelled to account for all moneys received by him as royalty in excess of the annual interest upon the ⅛ of the oil paid by the said lessee. The bill prayed for the appointment of a receiver to collect the royalty during the life of Susanna Youst, and that said Receiver be required to pay the interest annually upon the same to said Hughes; and that the entire principal should, at the death of Susanna Youst, be paid to the petitioners, the infants.

The South Penn Oil Company, assignee of the original lessee, answered the bill, stating the manner in which it claimed the right to the lease of said tract of land for oil purposes, and alleging that it delivered the oil to the Pipeline Company, a common carrier, in accordance with the decrees, contracts and proceedings under which said interests were sold and under which its right accrued to bore for and produce the oil; and that all of the ⅛ royalty, except so much thereof as then remained unsold and in the custody of the Pipeline Company, had been delivered to S. B. Hughes, assignee and grantee of Susanna Youst and Hermenia C. Wilson, and to the guardian of the infants, in accordance with the decrees and contracts. The oil company denied the right of the plaintiffs to set aside or annul, or in any manner change or affect the decrees or either of them, under which the sale was made of the infants' interests. The cause was heard on July 18, 1894, and the court dismissed the plaintiffs bill, and the case was appealed to the Court of Appeals where the decision of the Circuit Court was reversed, and the case remanded to the Circuit Court with directions to ascertain the amount of interest that accrued upon the royalties arising from the oil wells drilled on the land during the lifetime of Susanna Youst, which amount when so ascertained to be paid to the assignee of Susanna Youst; and after deducting said interest, the remainder of the royalty to be paid to Thomas J. Wilson, Jehu D. Wilson, Clarence L. Wilson and Minnie C. Powell, plaintiffs in the suit.

Sec. 10.—In *Sult* v. *Hochstetter Oil Co.*, 63, W. Va., 317; 61 S. E. 307, (Jan. 14. 1908) syls. 3-4-5 are as follows:

"3. Equity jurisdiction for injunction and receivership cannot be defeated on the ground of dispute as to title to the land affected when, the record being free from controversy as to facts, the question of title is one of law, only.

4. A clause in a deed, reserving to the grantor 'the right to all the minerals in and under' a certain portion of the land conveyed not limited or qualified as to intention by any other clause of the deed, or by any facts within the knowledge of the parties which may properly be deemed to have influenced them, embraces and saves to the grantor not only solid minerals such as gold, silver, iron and coal, but petroleum oil and natural gas as well."

(*Contra, Detlor* v. *Holland*, 57 Ohio St. 492; 49 N. E. 690; 40
    L. R. A. 266, Sec. 19.)

"5. Forfeiture of title to minerals in a tract of land for nonentry on the land book cannot be predicated upon mere severance in title of the minerals from the surface and lapse of time since presumptively the land was taxed as a whole when the severance occurred, and has since been carried on in the land book in the same manner and the taxes paid."

Eleanor Marshall, owner of a tract of land containing 215 acres of land, conveyed 100 acres thereof to Eliza I. Harrison by deed dated March 9, 1880, out of which she reserved and excepted "the right to all minerals in and under" a certain 15-acre tract aptly described. J. O. Lynch became the owner of 44½ acres of the Eliza I. Harrison land, including the 15 acres, the minerals under which were reserved. J. O. Lynch made an oil and gas lease to T. N. Barnsdall on March 17, 1897. The gas right under this lease afterwards passed by sale to the Mountain State Gas Company, Barnsdall having developed a gas well on the land, and then sold the gas rights to the said company. That company afterwards sold the gas right to the Hochstetter Company. The oil right under the Barnsdall lease passed by a number of transfers into the hands of the Shawmut Gas Company, which company drilled an unproductive and worthless well on the land, and then removed its machinery from the premises, sold all its leases and dissolved. Peter J. Sult purchased the interests of the Shawmut Oil Company from its stockholders. He also acquired by purchase ½ of the royalty in oil and gas reserved to J. O. Lynch by the lease made to Barnsdall. This purchase was made from S. T. Lynch, to whom J. O. Lynch had sold on April 10, 1901. Lynch's conveyance to Sult was dated March 30, 1904. Sult also claimed to have purchased from the heirs of Eleanor Marshall the interest in the reservation of the minerals in the 15-acre tract. J. O. Lynch made an oil and gas lease to David Dunsburg, who assigned the lease to the Hochstetter Company, which company entered the premises when Peter J. Sult filed his bill in the Circuit Court of Ritchie County for an injunction and receiver, claiming title to the property as stated above. A decree was entered appointing a special receiver to take charge of the wells, machinery and appliances on the land, and operate the same for the production of oil and gas; and enjoining and restraining the Hochstetter Company from interfering with the Receiver's custody; and the Eureka Pipeline Company was enjoined from delivering to the Hochstetter Company the oil produced from the land. From this decree the Hochstetter Company and J. O. Lynch, its lessor, appealed. The Court of Appeals upon final hearing held, that the title to the minerals in the 15-acre tract was vested in the plaintiff, Sult; that the lease made by Lynch to Barnsdall had been abandoned, and so far as the decree appointed a receiver for the lands outside of the 15 acres and enjoined the Pipeline Company from delivering the oil therefrom to the Hochstetter Company, it was reversed. But as to the appointment of a receiver for, and awarding the injunction in relation to the fifteen acres the decree was affirmed.

Sec. 11.—In *Blakley* v. *Marshall,* 174 Pa. 425; 34 Atl. 564 (March 23, 1896) the syllabus is as follows:

"An oil lease, investing the lessee with the right to remove all the oil in place in the premises in consideration of his giving the lessors a certain per centum thereof, is in legal effect a sale of a portion of the land, and the proceeds represent the respective interests of the lessors in the premises.

If the lessors in an oil lease are life tenants and remainder men, the life tenants are entitled to the interest on the royalties during life, and at their death, the corpus of the land made up of the aggregate royalties goes to the remainder men."

Isaac E. Blakley and Louisa Blakley were life tenants of a certain tract of land in Butler County, Pennsylvania, and their children, all of whom were minors at the date of the suit, were remainder men of said farm in fee. The Court of Common Pleas of Butler County appointed Thomas M. Marshall trustee for the minor children of the Blakleys to receive all royalties and invest the proceeds, and to pay to Isaac E. Blakley and Louisa Blakley during life and the life of the survivors the interest annually arising from such funds. Some time prior to August 10, 1894, petroleum oil was discovered about and around said farm and the remainder men and the owners of such other lands began developments for oil upon their properties. Isaac Blakley and Louisa Blakley, on August 10, 1894, made a lease of a portion of the farm to N. B. Duncan for oil and gas purposes. The life tenants at the time of making the lease, had born to them seven children, all but one or two of whom were residing with their parents. Under the lease a well was drilled on the premises and the oil was being run into the lines of the Producers Pipeline Company and the National Transit Pipeline Company. The plaintiffs, the parents of the children and life tenants of the farm, claimed the royalty as their individual property, free of any trust whatever, and instituted suit against the said Thomas Marshall, trustee, in the Court of Common Pleas of Butler County to determine the ownership of royalties under said lease; and upon the facts the court held that

the royalties of oils produced from the tract of land belonged to
the remainder men and entered judgment in favor of defendant.
Upon appeal the Supreme Court of Pennsylvania affirmed the
judgment.

Sec. 12.—In *Marshall* v. *Mellon,* 179 Pa. 371; 36 Atl. 201; 35 L.
R. A. 216 (Jan. 4, 1897) the syllabus is as follows:

"Where no oil or gas operations have been commenced on
land, before an estate for life has accrued, the tenant for life
has no right to operate for oil or gas, himself, and cannot give
such right to any person by lease.
   A life tenant of oil and gas land which had never been operated for oil or gas executed a lease for oil and gas purposes, exclusively. The lessees did not operate the land or perform any
of the covenants of the lease, and refused to pay the rent stipulated. *Held,* that the lessor could not enforce the lease."

On February 17, 1885, Mrs. Joseph Marshall, who at the death
of her husband, became vested with a life estate in a tract of land
executed a lease of the same to W. A. Mellon, for oil and gas purposes, the term of the lease being for the life time of the lessor.
This lease was subsequently assigned to A. W. Mellon and John H.
Galey. The lessees never took possession of the premises, nor was
any attempt made to operate the lands, nor was any payment of
rental made. The lessor, Mrs. Marshall, brought suit against A.
W. Mellon and John H. Galey in assumpsit in the Court of Common Pleas of Allegheny County, for the recovery of accrued rental
on the lease. Judgment was entered for defendants upon a verdict for plaintiff subject to the question of law reserved—whether
the plaintiff was entitled to recover under the evidence. From this
judgment Mrs. Marshall appealed to the Supreme Court, where the
judgment was affirmed.

Sec. 13.—In *Isam* v. *Rex Crude Oil Co.,* 82 Pac. 317; 147 Cal.
659 (September 6, 1905) the syllabus is as follows:

"1.   Where the assignor of a lease procured the same from
the plaintiff by fraud and false representations, and then assigned the lease to defendants, the complaint for the cancellation

of the lease for such fraud failing to allege that the assignee took with notice or knowledge of the fraud, was fatally defective.

2. Civ. Code § 1930 providing that when a thing is let for a particular purpose, the hirer must not use it for any other purpose, and if he does the latter may hold him responsible as to use, or treat the contract as rescinded, is applicable to the ownership of real property.

3. Oil is a mineral and as such is a part of the realty.

4. The unauthorized severence and removal of oil by a tenant constitutes waste.

5. Where defendant's assignor leased certain oil lands for three years with privilege of renewal for five, upon the representation that he wished the premises to erect a tenement building thereon, at an annual rental of $100.00, with permission to the lessee to remove, at the termination of the lease such buildings as he might have erected, the lease was a grant of the use merely of the superfices of the soil, and the lessee and his assignees having drawn oil therefrom, plaintiff was entitled to cancel the lease under Civ. Code, § 1930, authorizing such cancellation for an unauthorized use of the leased premises.

6. Where a lease was for the term of three years, with the privilege of renewal for five years, at an annual rental of $100.00, and at the expiration of two years, the lessor cancelled the same, because the lessee and his assignees had used the property for an unauthorized purpose, the contract should be considered as executed with reference to the expired period, so that the lessor was not required to return the rental paid thereon as a condition to the exercise of her right of cancellation.''

S. McG. Isam was the owner of a piece of land in the City of Los Angeles, and filed her petition in the Superior Court of Los Angeles County against the Rex Crude Oil Company and another. In her petition the plaintiff alleged the ownership of the land; that she was in an eastern State and in ignorance of the condition of her property, and the surrounding property, and was in ignorance of the fact that the land lay in an oil belt or district in the City of Los Angeles; that Book, her lessee, by letter represented to her that he wished to lease the premises for the purpose of erecting a tenement building thereon, and concealed from her the fact that oil existed on the premises; that in fact, Book had already entered upon the land, and was at that time by a well extracting oil therefrom; that she executed to Book a lease for the term of three years, with the privilege of renewal for five years, for the annual rental

of $100.00, payable quarterly in advance, with permission to the
lessee to remove at the termination of the lease such buildings as
he might have erected. The petition then alleged that the defendant oil company took an assignment of the lease, from Book,
and entered into possession of the property under the lease, with
knowledge of the terms thereof. The petition alleged the discovery
of the true condition, and of the fraud of Book, after two years had
expired and two years rental had been paid; the service of notice
upon Book and upon the oil company, and of the vacation of the
lease because of its fradulent procurement, and of the continued
pumping of oil after such notice. Trial was had before the court
without a jury. The court found in accordance with the allegations
of the complaint, decreed a cancellation and annulment of the lease,
gave damages to the plaintiff in the sum of $4,070,00, and enjoined
the defendant from operating the oil well, and from removing
therefrom any of the tubing, machinery, or other appliances. From
this decree the defendant appealed to the Supreme Court, where
the decree was affirmed. For the proposition that oil is a mineral,
and as such a part of the realty, and that its severance and removal
except in proper cases is. waste, the court cited:

> *Funk* v. *Halderman*, 53 Pa. 229.
> *Stoughton's Appeal*, 88 Pa. 198.
> *Williamson* v. *Jones*, 39 W. Va. 231; 19 S. E. 436.

Sec. 14.—In *Preston* v. *White*, 57 W. Va., 278; 50 S. E. 236
(Feb. 28, 1905) the syllabus is as follows:

"Petroleum oil and natural gas are minerals, and in their
place are real estate and part of the land.

A deed conveying a tract of land contains the clause: 'But
it is expressly understood and agreed that there is reserved from
and not included in the above sale or conveyance seven-eighths of
all and any oil and gas that may be on, in or under said land,
with full right and privilege to said Bennett his heirs and assigns
to develop and operate the same.' This excepts and does not
pass to the grantee, the oil and gas in place in the land, and the
oil and gas remain vested in the grantor as an actual vested estate
and property, and are not an incorporeal hereditament, nor a
mere license to produce oil and gas, and title in the grantor to the
oil and gas is not in abeyance to vest only when the oil and gas

shall be developed and brought to the surface by the grantor. A subsequent conveyance by such grantor of such oil and gas vests in the grantee like estate and property in the oil and gas as was vested in such grantor.

In a deed conveying land a reservation of the petroleum oil and natural gas in it has the same effect as an exception of the same would have, if such is the plain intent.

Petroleum oil and natural gas may be severed from the owner ship of the surface by grant or exception, and are then a separate corporeal property from the surface.''

In the division of the lands of J. M. Bennett, deceased, among his children, a tract of 296¾ acres in Lewis County was allotted to Lewis Bennett, the decree, however, making the partition provided that all oil and gas in the tract should be for the joint use of Lewis Bennett, Gertrude B. Howell, Mary B. Bowie, and W. G. Bennett, with the right to develop and operate the same. Lewis Bennett conveyed a tract of 151 acres out of the above tract to G. L. White, by deed dated March 11, 1898, the deed containing the following clause:

"But it is expressly understood and agreed that there is re- served from and not included in the above sale or conveyance, seven-eighths of all and any oil and gas that may be on, in or un- der said land, with full right and privilege to said Bennett, his heirs and assigns, to develop and operate the same, and said White, his heirs and assigns, are to pay the taxes on said oil and gas so reserved, developed and operated, which taxes are to be refunded to said White whenever they assume appreciable taxable value.''

On January 11, 1901, Lewis Bennett and his co-owners of the gas and oil conveyed seven-eighths of the gas in said tract of 296¾ acres to H. M. Preston, F. M. Knapp, and W. S. Hoskins, and by deed of March 16, 1901, Lewis Bennett and his co-owners conveyed to said Preston, Knapp and Hoskins, seven-eighths of the oil in said tract.

Preston, Knapp and Hoskins, subsequent to said conveyance filed a bill in chancery in the Circuit Court of Lewis County claim- ing to be the owners of seven-eighths of the oil and gas in the en- tire tract, and conceding that White owned the one undivided eighth in the 151 acres, and alleging that wells on adjoining land

had shown that there was gas under the 151 acres, and might be
oil; that neighboring wells would drain the oil and gas from the
151 acres to the great loss of the plaintiffs, unless steps should be
taken at once to protect or sell the oil and gas. The bill charged
that the plaintiffs had been unable to induce White to join them in
developing, leasing, or selling the oil and gas, or in saving the
same; and that the plaintiffs were unable to operate, lease or sell
their interests therein. The bill further averred that White denied
that he and the plaintiffs were joint owners as tenants in common
of the oil and gas, and alleged that White claimed that by force of
the deed from Lewis Bennett to him, and of the two deeds from
Lewis Bennett and others to the plaintiffs, the plaintiffs had no
property in the gas and oil in the 151 acres until the same should
be taken out of the ground; that the said White claimed that while
in the ground the oil and gas were his property, and that the reservation in the deed from Bennett to him created only an incorporeal
hereditament, a mere license to enter upon the 151 acres to develop
oil and gas; that said White claimed that the plaintiffs must bear,
alone, the burden of development, free of risk and cost to him.
The bill averred that the oil and gas were not susceptible to partition, and that the interests of all parties would be promoted by sale
of all the oil in the 151 acres. The plaintiffs asked the court to declare them to be entitled to seven-eights of the oil and gas in place
in the tract of 151 acres, and White one-eighth; and that the oil
and gas be sold and the proceeds so divided. The Circuit Court
entered a decree holding Preston, Knapp and Hoskins to be the
owners of seven-eighths, and White to be the owner of one-eighth
of the oil and gas in the tract of 151 acres, with the right to develop
such oil and gas; and that the oil and gas were not susceptible to
partition, and directing their public sale. From this decree White
appealed to the Court of Appeals, and that court affirmed the decree.

Sec. 15.—In *Stoughton's Appeal,* 88 Pa. 198 (Jan. 6, 1879) the
syllabus is as follows:

"A guardian has, ordinarily, power to lease any of his ward's
property of such character as makes it the subject of a lease;
but without the approval of the orphan's court he cannot dispose
of any part of the realty. Oil is a mineral, and being a mineral, is
part of the realty and a guardian cannot lease the land of his

ward for the purpose of its development, as it would, in effect, be the grant of a part of the corpus of the estate of his ward.''

At June Term, 1873, David C. Rankin, the guardian of Lewis and Minerva Brown, minor children of Josiah Brown, deceased, presented a petition to the Orphan's Court of Butler County, praying the court to confirm a lease for 20 years of the lands of his said wards, containing about 100 acres, to W. G. Stoughton, for oil purposes. On June 11, 1873, the court granted the prayer of the petition, and a decree was made accordingly. This Stoughton lease was duly recorded, and subsequently Stoughton sub-let a portion of the land to Peter Grace, and Peter Hutchinson, and the balance to H. L. Taylor & Company. At March Term, 1874, James M. Lambing, John A. Lambing, B. B. Campbell, and R. L. Brown, presented a petition to the Orphan's Court, which set forth that David C. Rankin, Guardian, had executed a lease to A. L. Campbell and James M. Lambing, for 40 acres of said tract of land, belonging to the heirs of Josiah Brown, deceased, for a term of 21 years, for oil purposes which lease by assignments was vested in the petitioners; that said lease was duly recorded in said County. That subsequent to the recording of the lease David C. Rankin leased the whole tract aforesaid to W. G. Stoughton without reserving therefrom the 40 acres leased to petitioners; that said Stoughton lease was recorded and that Grace, Hutchinson and Taylor were claiming under said lease, and denying the right of petitioners to hold and enjoy the 40 acres, notwithstanding the parties had notice of petitioner's lease before the taking of their lease; and that the lease of petitioners was much more beneficial to the Brown heirs than was the Stoughton lease. The petition then prayed for a citation to Rankin, Stoughton, Grace, Hutchinson and Taylor & Company, that the order approving the lease to Stoughton might be rescinded so far as it interfered with the lease of petitioners; and that the court should approve the lease of petitioners, *nunc pro tunc* as of the fourth of December, 1871. A citation issued, and answer was made by Stoughton for himself and the others who held under him. Testimony was taken, and after argument the court confirmed and approved the lease to A. L. Campbell and J. M. Lambing, and vacated the part of the order made at June Term, 1873, affecting the 40 acres. From this decree appeals were taken to the Supreme Court. That court referred the case to a master to take testimony and report the facts, together with his opinion thereon; and the master reported, among other things, that the lease to A. L. Campbell and J. M. Lambing was fairly obtained, and had its conditions been carried out, would have been beneficial to the Brown heirs, but that the lease was forfeited by the failure of said lessees to comply with its conditions. The master reported in favor of a decree to reverse and set aside the decree as to the Campbell and Lambing lease, with directions to dismiss their petition; and as to the W. G. Stoughton lease, that the decree of the Orphan's Court taking off the confirmation of the lease by David C. Rankin, Guardian, so far as the same affected the 40 acres of land, be reversed and set aside. The court confirmed these findings and ordered that the decree reported by the Master for the Stoughton Appeal be adopted; and also that the decree reported by the Master for the Rankin appeal be adopted; and entered judgment accordingly.

Sec. 16.—In *Hughes* v. *United Pipelines,* 119 N. Y. 423; 23 N. E. 1042 (Feb. 25, 1890), the second paragraph of the syllabus is as follows:

"Oil in the earth belongs to the owner of the land, and when unlawfully taken therefrom by a wrong doer the title of such owner remains perfect, and he may pursue and reclaim the property wherever he may find it."

The plaintiff, the owner of an oil well, brought suit against the United Pipelines, to whom the oil from the well had been delivered by one unlawfully producing the same, for the wrongful and unlawful conversion of about 5,000 barrels of oil. The defendant denied liability. The Pipelines had notice of the claim of Hughes to the title of the property from which the oil was produced. Judgment was rendered in favor of the plaintiff upon proof of a final judgment having been rendered in favor of Hughes, establishing his title to the oil well in a suit brought by Stephens who had produced the oil, for the conversion of which the Pipelines were sued. Upon appeal the Court of Appeals of New York affirmed the judgment.

Sec. 17.—In *Poe* v. *Ulrey,* 233 Ill. 56; 84 N. E. 46, analyzed under Chapter 14, Syl. 1 is as follows:

"1. Oil and gas are classed as minerals, that term not being confined to metallic substances."

Sec. 18.—In *Lanyon Zinc Co.* v. *Freeman,* 68 Kan. 691; 75 Pac. 995 (March 12, 1904) the syllabus is as follows:

"1. Petroleum and gas are minerals. So long as they remain in the ground they are a part of the realty. They belong to the owner of the land and are a part of it so long as they are on it, or in it, or subject to his control.

2. A resident of Ohio, owning in Kansas a farm that had never been used for other than agricultural purposes, executed a will therein providing that the executor and trustee should`take charge of said premises, and, 'lease and maintain the same in repair and in good condition with a view to obtain the best income therefrom, without permitting the same to deteriorate in value or quality.' *Held,* that the executor and trustee was not, by said will, authorized to execute an oil and gas lease granting to the lessee all the gas and oil under said premises, and binding the legatees thereby.

3. An executor and trustee, without having sufficient authority under the will to bind the legatees thereby, executed an oil and gas lease on a farm that had never been used for other than agricultural purposes. Prior to the execution of the lease he had individually acquired the interests of one of the legatees in the premises. Soon thereafter he acquired the interests of another of the legatees. *Held,* in an action of partition, under the circumstances of the case, he was estopped from denying that the interest acquired by him was not subject to the lease."

In 1895, William A. Koontz, of Ohio, died testate. Reuben R. Freeman was sole executor and trustee under the will. There were named as legatees: the widow, Louisa C. Koontz, a son, Philip D. Koontz and eight grandchildren—Iosa W. King; Enola C. King; Texas R. Koontz; Charles S. Koontz; Earnest S. Koontz; Mabel C. Koontz, and Helyne L. Koontz. The six last named were minors at the commencement of the suit. The testator owned a tract of and in Allen County, Kansas. These lands were demised to the grandchildren, with condition that in the event the testator should die before the period of 18 years from the date of the will—July 10, 1895, the executor and trustee should take charge of the premises and "lease and maintain the same in repair and good condition with a view to obtain the best income therefrom, without permitting the same to deteriorate in value or quality." Until such period of 18 years should have elapsed the widow, Louisa C. Koontz, not having in writing consented to said will, elected to take under the law of descent and distribution. On March 15, 1898, said Iosa W. King and husband conveyed to Reuben R. Freeman (who was the executor and trustee) all their interest in said premises. On December 30, Reuben R. Freeman, as executor and trustee, and the said Louisa Koontz, in consideration of the sum of $802.41, jointly executed to the Lanyon Zinc Company, a lease granting to the company all the oil and gas under the premises. On February 7, 1900, Enola King and husband conveyed to Reuben R. Freeman all their interest in the premises. On July 21, 1901, E. K. Taylor by deed acquired the interest of Louisa C. Koontz in the premises. On December 13, 1901, E. K. Taylor filed in the District Court of Allen County, Kansas, his petition asking a partition of the premises, therein claiming to be the owner of an undivided ½ thereof. In his petition plaintiff averred that Reuben Freeman was the owner of an undivided 2-16 and each of the minors the owner of an undivided 1-16 in said premises. The petition further averred that the Lanyon Zinc Company, a corporation claimed some interest in the premises, and asked that it be required to set up its interest therein. All the parties were brought into court as defendants, the minors appearing by guardian ad litem. The Lanyon Zinc Company, by answer, and upon the trial, admitted the averments of the plaintiff's petition as to the interest of the plaintiff and defendants in the premises, averring and contending however, that the interest of each was subject to the claim of the company under the oil and gas lease. Plaintiff by reply, and defendants, R. R. Freeman, individually and as executor and trustee, and the minors through their guardian ad litem by answer each denied to the Lanyon Zinc Company any right or interest in the premises by virtue of the lease, and averred that the lease was void and without force or effect. The court found plaintiff Taylor to be the owner of an undivided ½ interest in the premises, subject to the right of the Lanyon Zinc Company under the oil and gas lease; and further found that Reuben R. Taylor was owner of an undivided 2-16 in the premises; that as to the interest of Reuben R. Taylor, and the interests of the minors, the lease of the Lanyon Zinc Company was void and without force or effect; that plaintiff and defendants then owning an interest in the premises were tenants in common. Judgment of partition was by the court entered, setting off and allotting the east half of the premises to the plaintiff, decreeing the lease of the Lanyon Zinc Company in full force and effect upon and against the same. It was found by the commissioners who were appointed, that partition of the west half of the premises could not be made among the owners according to their respective interests, and the same was ordered sold if within 20 days parties in interest failed to file their election to take the same at its appraised value. By the judgment and decree of the court the lease of the Lanyon Zinc Company was held to be without force or effect as to the west half of the premises, and as to these premises the lease was cancelled and held for naught. The decree provided however, that nothing therein should affect the rights, if any, of the Lanyon Zinc Company to maintain an action to recover the money it had paid out in operating the lease as to the lands upon which the lease had been held invalid. To the judgment and decree of the court holding the lease invalid and cancelling the same as to the west half of the premises, or any part thereof, the Lanyon Zinc Company excepted and appealed to the Supreme Court, where the judgment was affirmed. As to the nature of the oil and gas in place the Supreme Court cited:

Brown v. *Spilman,* 155 U. S. 665.
Oil Co. v. *Indiana,* 177 U. S. 190.
Murray v. *Allred,* 100 Tenn. 100; 43 S. W. 355.
Kelly v. *Oil Co.,* 57 Ohio State, 317; 47 N. E. 399.
Wilson v. *Youst,* 43 W. Va. 826; 28 S. E. 781.
Stoughton's Appeal, 88 Pa. 198.
Marshall v. *Mellon,* 179 Pa. 371; 36 Atl. 201.
Williamson v. *Jones,* 43 W. Va. 562; 27 S. E. 411.

Sec. 19.—In *Detlor* v. *Holland,* 57 Ohio State, 492; 49 N. E. 690; 40 L. R. A. 266 (Feb. 1, 1898) the syllabus is as follows:

"1. A conveyance of a mining right in land was made as fol-lows: 'Do hereby grant, bargain, sell, and convey to the said Michael Deaver, his heirs and assigns, forever, all the coal of every variety, and all the iron ore, fire clay, and other valuable minerals, in, on, or under the following described premises: * * * * * * * Together with the right in perpetuity to the said Michael L. Deaver or his assigns, of mining and removing such coal, ore or other minerals; and the said Michael L. Deaver or his assigns, shall also have the right to the use of so much of the surface of the land as may be necessary for pits, shafts, platforms, drains, rail-roads, switches, sidetracks, etc., to facilitate the mining and re-moval of such coal, ore, or other minerals, and no more.' *Held,*

that such deed did not convey title to the petroleum oil and natural gas in the lands described in the deed.

2. A person in peaceable possession of real estate under a
defective deed may have his title quieted by action as against a
stranger who makes claim to such real estate, but has no right or
title thereto.

3. A written instrument was duly executed as follows: 'Do
hereby grant unto second party, their heirs and assigns, the sole
right to produce petroleum and natural gas from the following
named tracts of land * * * *: specifically granting to said second
party for and during the term of ninety (90) days from this date,
and as much longer as oil or gas is found, operated, and produced
in paying quantities, with the exclusive right to drill and operate
oil and gas wells.' *Held,* that such written instrument is not a
lease of the lands, but only a grant of the sole right to produce
petroleum and natural gas for the term mentioned; that the grant
expired by its own limitation at the end of ninety days, unless
within that time at least one well was drilled which produced oil
or gas in paying quantities; and that upon failure to drill one
paying well within ninety days there was no right to drill thereafter.

4. The term of the grant in such instrument, having expired,
and the grantee still claiming a right to drill under such grant, the
grantor has a right to have his title quieted as against such claim,
on the ground that the term of the grant has expired, without resorting to the law of forfeitures.

5. Under such an instrument, the sum paid as a consideration for the grant need not be returned in order to maintain an
action to quiet title.

6. Expenses incurred by the grantees in drilling wells on the
lands after the expiration of the grant, and after notice not to
drill such wells, cannot be recovered from the grantor.

7. Such grant being made to four persons jointly, a notice
addressed to all of them, to the effect that the grant has expired,
and to keep off the premises, and served on one of them is sufficient. In such case notice to one is notice to all. *Baker* v. *Kellog,*
29 Ohio State, 663 followed and approved.''

Francis G. Deaver made a conveyance of a mining right in a
tract of 80 acres of land to Michael L. Deaver, in words as stated
in the first point of the syllabus. Afterwards Michael L. Deaver
made and delivered an oil and gas lease of these lands to James
W. Taylor, claiming that he had title to the oil by virtue of the
mining right. Taylor assigned this oil and gas lease to one of the

defendants, which lease had not expired by limitation at the commencement of the action. After granting the mining right Francis G. Deaver died leaving two sons, one of age and the other a minor for whom a guardian was appointed in the State of Wisconsin, where they both resided. After the death of the father the two sons by separate deeds conveyed the lands to Upton Holland, the plaintiff. The deed from the son who was a minor was signed by himself and his guardian, but there was nothing to show any proceedings in a court authorizing the making of the deed. Mr. Holland went into possession and continued in possession of the lands. On May 26, 1893, Upton Holland and wife executed an oil and gas lease upon the premises to William E. Detlor and others. By the terms of this lease lessees were given 90 days from date, unavoidable casualties excepted, to complete one well in addition to the one already on the premises; and were to continue to complete a well each succeeding 90 days thereafter until four wells were drilled, provided that oil should be found in paying quantities in each succeeding well. After the expiration of 90 days, and after Mr. Holland had notified the grantees that the term of the grant had expired they drilled one well on the land, and thereafter drilled another well, but always refused to pay plaintiff any royalty for oil, and denied his right to royalty, and claimed all the oil themselves, under the James W. Taylor lease. All the wells were drilled without the consent of the plaintiff and against his protest, both verbally and in writing. At the time the mining right was granted petroleum oil was produced in small quantities within ten to twenty miles of these lands. Holland filed his petition against William E. Detlor and others to quiet the title to the 80 acres of land. The case was heard and judgment for plaintiff rendered. A new trial was denied and defendants brought error from the Circuit Court of Perry County to the Supreme Court of Ohio, where the judgment was affirmed.

Sec. 20.—In *Bettman* v. *Harness,* 42 W. Va. 433; 26 S. E. 271, analyzed under Chapter 6, syl. 1 is as follows:

"Equity has jurisdiction by injunction to prevent acts of irreparable injury to land, even though there is controversy as to title between the parties, and having jurisdiction on that ground, will go on to give full relief though in so doing it be necessary to decide between two adverse titles."

Sec. 21.—In *Freer* v. *Davis,* 52 W. Va. 1; 43 S. E. 164, (Nov. 22, 1902) the syllabus is as follows:

"1. A court of equity has no jurisdiction to settle the title and boundary of land between adverse claimants when the plaintiff has no equity against the party claiming adversely to him. In so far as point 1 of the syllabus in *Bettman* v. *Harness,* 42 W. Va. 438, conflicts with this proposition, the same is disapproved.

2. Where irreparable mischief is being done or threatened to real estate going to the destruction of the substance of the estate, such as the extraction of oil and gas, and the title to the land is in dispute, the parties claiming under hostile titles, a court of equity will enjoin the trespass and preserve the property and rights of the parties, pending the determination, in a court of law, of the question of title; and this although no action at law has been instituted, if it appears from the bill that the complainant intends immediately to put the question of title into a course of judicial determination and prosecute it diligently.

3. As consent cannot confer jurisdiction, a plaintiff upon whose bill there is a final decree and adjudication against him, upon matter set up in the bill, is not estopped to assert upon appeal, that the court to which he resorted had no jurisdiction of the subject matter.

4. In such case, although the decree will be reversed at the instance of the plaintiff the costs in the appellate court will be awarded against him."

R. H. Freer and others brought suit in equity against Thomas E. Davis and others in the Circuit Court of Ritchie County to recover title and possession of a tract of real estate, containing about 58 acres. As ground of equitable jurisdiction, it was shown that W. J. Shields, one of the plaintiffs under whom all the others claimed, had been in possession of the land claiming under certain deeds; and those under whom he claimed had taken some timber off it, and he had cultivated a small portion of the land in oats one year. Plaintiffs had also sent a man on the land to get out timber for a derrick. While he was so engaged, some of the defendants came upon the land and notified him that they claimed it, threatened to have him arrested for trespassing, and finally told him that if he did not leave the land they would put him off by force, and then he went. Thereafter the defendants and their agents, took possession of the land and began the work of developing it for oil and gas. They erected a derrick on the land very near the line, but, after notice from the plaintiffs they moved it just over the line, but the engine house seems to have been on the land. The bill alleged that the defendants had entered into and upon the premises, and were erecting a derrick and rig thereon preparatory to drilling for oil and gas, and were about to bore for and take from said premises oil and gas. It was shown that other wells had been drilled on adjacent land and so near as to drain the premises in question of the oil. The prayer of the bill was that the defendants and each of them, their agents, etc., might be enjoined and restrained from erecting derricks, or other machinery on the land, and from removing oil and gas therefrom; and that a Receiver be appointed to take charge of the premises and operate the same under the direction of the court.

It was alleged in the bill that in a previous year the land had been reported to the commissioner of school lands as 30 acres of waste and unappropriated land; and upon survey it was found to contain 58 acres. The commissioner brought a suit to sell the land, and under a decree dated October 28, 1885, it was sold on February 15, 1886, to C. H. Gibboney, and the sale was confirmed and a deed made to him on February 24, 1886. Gibboney conveyed a portion of it to Latoriere, and Latoriere conveyed a portion to V. J. Shields; and then conveyed on December 9, 1892, the balance of his interest to C. H. Gibboney. This portion seems to have been 8 acres, and it was sold for non-payment of taxes for the years 1893 and 1894, and Shields purchased it, and the clerk of the County Court conveyed the land to him by deed dated April 6, 1898. Thus Shields became the owner of all of it, and from him the plaintiffs derived their title and interest by conveyances and a lease for oil and gas purposes.

The defendants deduced their title as follows: Isaac Cox and John Ramsey, assignees of Thomas Proctor, were patentees of 0,000 acres of land under a patent from the Commonwealth of Virginia, dated March 20, 1786. This land was forfeited for non-payment of taxes, and under a decree of the Circuit Superior Court of Wood County, made at the April Term, 1841, it was sold. Before sale, however, it was divided into lots, and Lot Number 1, containing 1949½ acres was conveyed to Cyrus Ross by Commissioners P. G. Van Winkle and M. Chapman. Ross died in 1872, and for the purpose of settling his estate the land was conveyed to Edwin Maxwell and John I. Rogers, trustees. They conveyed to certain of the Ross heirs something over 1300 acres, estimated to be worth $10,000 in part satisfaction of $12,000 which it was agreed they should have out of the estate. Whatever land remained after this transaction stood in the name of Rogers and Maxwell, Trustees. Rogers having died, it stood in the name of Edwin Maxwell, surviving trustee. Claiming that the land in controversy belonged to the Ross estate, and denying that the heirs of said estate had ever been out of possession of it, Maxwell, Trustee, leased it to his co-defendants for oil and gas purposes. The defendants insisted that the land was within the 1949½ acre survey, and that the representatives of the Ross estate never had, in any way, relinquished their claim to it, nor admitted that it was waste and unappropriated land. They also claimed to have paid the taxes on the land. On the other hand, the plaintiffs insisted that the defendants had never asserted any claim to the land, nor exercised any dominion over it. The Circuit Court appointed a receiver, and on final hearing adjudicated the title to the lands in favor of the defendants. Upon appeal by plaintiffs to the Court of Appeals, the Circuit Court having dismissed their bill, the decree was reversed and the demurrer to the bill sustained, and leave granted to plaintiffs to amend their bill, and the cause was remanded.

Sec. 22.—In *Freer* v. *Davis,* 52 W. Va. 35; 43 S. E. 172, (Nov. 22, 1902) the syllabus is as follows:

"1. A receiver will not be appointed to take possession from defendant of land, and drill wells for oil, in a suit involving two conflicting titles, merely because that defendant is drilling the same land for oil, or doing other injury, though irreparable, unless special circumstances additional are shown, such as insolvency or other circumstances.

2. In a suit involving two hostile titles to land, a receiver will not be appointed to take charge of it, merely because of the pendency of such suits. It will be done only with great caution and upon special circumstances calling for it to preserve the property from loss.

3. It does not follow that because injunction lies in a suit between hostile titles to land to restrain irreparable damage a reciever for the land will be appointed."

This is an appeal taken by the defendants from a decree appointing a receiver for the lands in controversy in the case of Freer v. Davis, supra.

Sec. 23.—In *Moore* v. *Jennings*, 47 W. Va. 181; 34 S. E. 793 (Nov. 28, 1899) the syllabus is as follows:

"1.   The unlawful extraction of oil or gas from land, they being part of the land, is an act of irreparable injury, and equity will enjoin it.

2.   Where proper parties are not properly before the court the decree will be reversed and the cause remanded for further proceedings.

3.   When the lessors and lessees of one tract of land bring their suit against the lessees of an adjoining tract to enjoin them from trespassing on the plaintiff's premises, and from continuing to drill a well for oil and gas, which defendants had commenced, as plaintiffs claim, on their premises, and praying in their bill that the boundary line between the tracts claimed by the parties respectively be ascertained, fixed and determined; that plaintiffs be decreed to be the owners of the land on which said well had been located by the defendants, and of all the oil and gas which could or might be obtained through said well; that the defendants be decreed to have no estate, right, title, or interest, whatsoever, of, in, or to said land, or said oil or gas, nor any right whatsoever to the possession of said land or said well— *Held*, in such case, all the owners of the fee of both tracts are necessary parties to the suit, to enable the court to settle the rights of all parties interested or affected by the subject matter in controversy."

On April 1, 1897, E. H. Jennings and others filed in the Clerk's office of the Circuit of Tyler County, against Clint Moore, and others, their bill in chancery, with an order of injunction endorsed thereon by a Judge of the First Circuit, which injunction was according to the prayer of the bill. The bill alleged that the plaintiffs, the Tustins and Woodburns, were owners in fee of a tract of 102 acres of land situated in Tyler County; that they were in full, peaceable and lawful, possession thereof; that on March 1, 1896, a legal and valid lease for oil and gas was executed by the plaintiff, Sarah Tustin in her own right; Minerva Tustin; Mary J. Woodburn; Noah Woodburn; Samantha Tustin; and Sarah Tustin, Guardian of Emma, John and Sarah Tustin, to plaintiffs H. W. Richardson and S. C. Wells, who subsequently, by deed conveyed the full equal undivided ½ interest in the lease to D. H. Cox; that Richardson, Cox and Wells entered into an agreement with plaintiffs, E. H; J. G; and R. M. Jennings, whereby it was agreed that

in consideration of one undivided ½ interest in said lease the said
Jennings would drill an oil or gas well upon said tract of land;
that in pursuance of said agreement they located and drilled a well
upon the premises "which produced oil in paying quantities, and
made the premises and adjoining property very valuable for oil
and gas purposes;" that adjoining said tract belonging to the
Tustin tract, was another tract of 2 acres, more or less, known as
the "Arnett Lot" part of a tract or parcel known as the "J. S.
Haught tract" containing 13½ acres; that defendants Clint Moore,
Henry Rauch and L. M. Gorham held what purported to be a lease
for oil and gas upon the Arnett tract of 2 acres; that by virtue
of said lease they entered upon and proceeded to develop the said
2-acre lot for oil and gas purposes, and made the location at which
said well should be bored; that while said location was pretended
to be upon said 2-acre tract, in truth and in fact, it was upon said
Tustin tract; that in making the location defendants were trespassing upon the premises owned and controlled by, and under the
rights and privileges of plaintiffs; that defendants, shortly after
making the location, were notified that they had located the well
upon the land owned and controlled by plaintiffs; and that defendants were trespassing thereon; yet notwithstanding said notice, defendants, contrary to law and in violation of the rights of
plaintiffs, proceeded to erect the necessary wood rig, a large portion of which was situated on the lands of plaintiffs, and to drill at
said location, and upon plaintiffs' land, a well for oil and gas; that
frequently during the progress of the drilling additional notices
were given to defendants that they were drilling the well upon the
Tustin farm, and upon the premises owned and controlled by
plaintiffs; but that notwithstanding such repeated notices defendants continued to prosecute the drilling of said well; that if the
drilling of the well should be completed it would be of great and
irreparable damage to plaintiffs; that defendants had been advised
by their own surveyor, and had admitted, that the well was on the
land of the plaintiffs. The bill further alleged that if the well
should be completed, and prove to be productive of oil or gas,
plaintiffs would be unable to operate it although on their premises,
for the reason that it was located so near the boundary of their
premises that they would be unable to erect the necessary wood
rig with which to further operate the well; and that the loss and
damage would be irreparable; and alleged the insolvency of defendants, and that plaintiffs were without adequate remedy at law;

and prayed that defendants, their agents and employes might be enjoined and restrained from trespassing upon their premises; from drilling the well any deeper, and from completing the same; and from doing and performing any work or labor whatever thereon, or entering thereon for any purpose; and for general relief.

On March 31, 1897, an injunction was granted, as prayed for in the bill, to take effect upon bond being given in the penalty of $2,000.00. On May 8, 1897, defendants, Clint Moore, Henry Rauch, L. M. Gorham, J. F. Hall and C. Hall, filed their demurrer to the plaintiffs bill, alleging for grounds of demurrer, that the bill was not sufficient in law, and that interested and proper persons, as shown by the bill, had not been made parties to the suit, and for other reasons. In May, 1897, plaintiffs filed an amendment to their bill, making Kora Queen a party thereto, and adding prayer to their bill as follows: "And your orators further pray that the said Clint Moore, Henry Rauch, L. M. Gorham, Kora Queen, H. F. Hall, and C. Hall be made parties to this bill of complaint, and for process to issue; and that the boundary line between the said Tustin farm and Arnett lot be ascertained, fixed, and determined; that your orators be decreed to be the owners of the land upon which said well has been located by the defendants, as herein above set forth, and of all the oil and gas which can or may be obtained through said well; that the defendants be decreed to have no estate, right, title, or interest, whatever, of, in or to said land or said oil or gas, nor any right whatsoever to the possession of said land or said well; and that the defendants and their agents and employes be enjoined, inhibited and restrained from trespassing upon said land of your orators, from entering thereon for any purpose whatsoever, from obtaining or taking any oil or gas out of or through said well, and from selling or disposing of any oil heretofore obtained by them out of said well, and from setting up any claim, right, or title of, in, or to said land or said well, or the oil or gas heretofore obtained, or which may hereafter be obtained therefrom; and for such other and further relief as their case may require, and as to a court of equity may seem just and right."

On May 19, 1897, defendant L. M. Gorham filed his demurrer to plaintiffs' bill as being not sufficient in law, and as not entitling plaintiffs to the relief prayed for. On the same day defendants, J. F. and C. Hall filed their demurrer for the same reason, and because sufficient and proper persons interested in the subject matter

the McKeown lease assigned to them as aforesaid, and commenced operations thereon in search of oil and gas. Written notice was served on these assignees by Haskell and Waldon Morrow notifying them that Haskell held a lease on said 135 acres of land made by Emma Morrow and her sons, the owners of said farm, dated August 4, 1900, and forbidding Suttons from carrying on operations on the farm for oil and gas. On October 18, 1901, Haskell Brothers, a firm composed of William A. Haskell and Frank Haskell (the latter being interested in the lease of August 4, 1900) Emma Morrow, Waldron Morrow and George Morrow presented their bill in equity to the Judge of the Circuit Court of Hancock County, alleging substantially the foregoing facts; and also that Sutton Brothers had commenced operations on the land and held possession thereof for that purpose, and were producing oil therefrom to the irreparable loss and damage of plaintiffs, without any right or title so to do; that Sutton Brothers had produced large quantities of oil from the land, which was then in the lines of the Eureka Pipeline Company unsold, or otherwise disposed of. The bill also alleged that the McKeown lease was illegal, null and void, and did not pass to the lessee the interests of the minor children in the tract of land, for any purpose whatever; that the minors were then of full age and in possession of said land; and that the illegal lease was a cloud upon plaintiffs' title. The bill made the Sutton Brothers and Eureka Pipeline Company defendants, with prayer that the McKeown lease be declared illegal, null and void; that Sutton Brothers be inhibited and restrained from producing and selling any oil from the premises; and that they and the Eureka Pipeline Company be required to account for the oil produced; that Sutton Brothers be restrained and enjoined from interfering with plaintiffs in their rightful possession of the land; and from further production of oil therefrom; and that the plaintiffs' title be quieted. The Judge of the Circuit Court granted the injunction restraining Sutton Brothers from further drilling for oil and gas upon the tract of land, and restraining them, and the Eureka Pipeline Company, from selling or otherwise disposing of any oil which had been run into the lines of the Pipeline Company, or any oil that might be produced from the land, until the further order of the court. On December 31, 1901, a motion was made by the defendants in the Circuit Court to dissolve the injunction, which motion was overruled and disallowed. The answer of Sutton Brothers was filed which answer admitted many allegations of the bill, but denied that the lease made by Emma Morrow in her own right, and as guardian, as aforesaid, to John McKeown was illegal and of no binding force. The answer alleged that the lease was valid; further alleging that the defendants paid to Emma Morrow a cash consideration for the lease of $4500.00; that the said Emma Morrow treated the money so received from McKeown as though it belonged to the estate of James W. Morrow, deceased, and to her wards as heirs and distributees of the estate; and further alleged that out of this money Emma Morrow paid and discharged a large number of debts due from James W. Morrow at the time of his death; and that the personal estate left by the said James W. Morrow was wholly insufficient to discharge these debts; that after the payment of the debts of James W. Morrow, out of the consideration for the lease, there remained in the hands of Emma Morrow a considerable portion of the money, which she invested for the benefit of her wards, a portion of which they received after they arrived at legal age; that a portion of the money at that time remained invested, from which the wards, after their majority had been receiving the benefit. These facts, defendants Suttons claimed as an estoppel against Morrows. Depositions and proofs were taken in the cause, and the Circuit Court entered a decree for the plaintiffs, from which decree defendants appealed to the Court of Appeals, where the decree was affirmed.

Sec. 25.—In *Westmoreland Natural Gas Co.* v. *DeWitt,* 130 Pa. 325; 18 Atl. 724, analyzed under Chapter 11, the second and ifth points of the syllabus are as follows:

"2. The real subject of possession to which the lessee is enitled is the oil or gas contained in or obtainable through the land; hese are minerals *ferae naturae* and are part of the land, and beong to its owner only so long as they are in it and under his conrol, the lessee when he has drilled a gas well and controls the gas roduced thereby, is in possession of all the gas within the land.

5. Where the lessee is thus in possession of the gas underying the premises, equity has jurisdiction to restrain the lessor rom drilling on the leasehold, the rights granted to the lessee beng necessarily exclusive, and the damage to arise from the hreatened waste being entirely incapable of measurement at law, ven if not irreparable."

Sec. 26.—In *Duffield* v. *Hue,* 136 Pa. 602; 20 Atl. 526, analyzed under Chapter 21, the second and third points of the syllabus are as follows:

"2. The lessee, however, has the protection of the entire premises, and equity has jurisdiction to restrain the lessor, or others acting under him, from drilling wells thereon, outside of such designated sites, and thereby lessening the production of wells drilled by the lessee, such injury being destructive of his rights and incapable of adequate remedy at law.

3. A court of equity may entertain a bill for an injunction against such an interference with the lessee's rights, notwithstanding that the boundaries of the demised premises are disputed, a defendant, who also is in possession under the lessor, denying that the land upon which he is drilling was included by the lessor in the leasehold granted to the plaintiff."

Section. 27.—In *Murray* v. *Allred,* 100 Tenn., 100; 66 Am. St. Rep. 740, analyzed under Chapter 47, the second and third points of the syllabus are as follows:

"Petroleum, or coal oil, is a mineral, and hence does not pass to the grantee under a deed reserving all mines, metals, and minerals.

Natural gas is a mineral, and, therefore, does not pass by a conveyance of land reserving all mines and metals."

REMEDY OF OWNER OF OIL AND GAS IN PLACE, FOR THE UNLAWFUL EXTRACTION THEREOF.

Sec. 28.—The unlawful extraction of petroleum oil or gas from land, they being a part of the land, is an act of irreparable injury. The owner in fee or the remainder men of the oil and gas in a tract of land may maintain a bill in equity for injunction to enjoin, restrain and inhibit, upon the grounds of irreparable injury, the unlawful extraction of the oil and gas from such land.

Bettman v. *Harness,* 42 W. Va. 423; 26 S. E. 271.
Williamson v. *Jones,* 39 W. Va. 231; 19 S. E. 436.
Williamson v. *Jones,* 43 W. Va. 562; 27 S. E. 411.
Duffield v. *Hue,* 136 Pa. 602; 20 Atl. 526.
Isam v. *Rex Crude Oil Co.,* 147 Cal. 659; 82 Pac. 317.
Lanyon Zinc Co. v. *Freeman,* 68 Kan. 691; 75 Pac. 995.

Detlor v. *Holland,* 57 Ohio St. 492; 49 N. E. 690; 40 L. R. A.
   266.
Moore v. *Jennings,* 47 W. Va. 181; 34 S. E. 279.
Haskell v. *Sutton,* 53 W. Va. 206; 44 S. E. 533.
Murray v. *Allred,* 100 Tenn. 100; 66 Am. St. Rep. 740.

Sec. 29.—One having a life estate in lands cannot make an oil
and gas lease that will authorize the lessee, against the consent of
the remainderman, to extract the oil and gas from the lands; and
the remedy of the remainderman, where such lease has been executed and attempts have been made to operate thereunder, is by bill in
equity for injunction.

Williamson v. *Jones,* 39 W. Va. 231; 19 S. E. 436.
Williamson v. *Jones,* 43 W. Va. 562; 27 S. E. 411.
South Penn Oil Co. v. *McIntire,* 44 W. Va. 296; 28 S. E. 922.
Wilson v. *Youst,* 43 W. Va. 826; 28 S. E. 781.
Blakley v. *Marshall,* 174 Pa. 425; 34 Atl. 564.
Appeal of Stoughton, 88 Pa. 198.
Haskell v. *Sutton,* 53 W. Va. 206; 44 S. E. 533.

Sec. 30.—A court of equity will not entertain jurisdiction by
bill in equity to settle the title and boundaries of real estate as
between either the claimants to the title or claimants of conflicting
oil leases made by the respective claimants, unless the question of
title is a pure question of law. A claimant, however, of an oil and
gas lease, where the title is in dispute, may maintain a bill in
equity for injunction and restrain the production and marketing
of the oil and gas pending proceedings at law to settle the question
of title.

Freer v. *Davis,* 52 W. Va. 1; 43 S. E. 164.
Freer v. *Davis,* 52 W. Va. 35; 43 S. E. 172.

Sec. 31.—Where there is a dispute as to the location of the
boundary line between two tracts of land, a lessee of one of the
claimants may maintain a bill in equity to settle the question of
boundary against the lessee of the other claimant, where the bill
alleges that the defendant lessee is drilling across the line upon
the premises included in the plaintiff's lease; but all claimants to
the title to the leased premises, including the lessors of the

plaintiff, and the lessees under each lease and those interested with them, are indispensably necessary parties to the suit.

Moore v. *Jennings,* 47 W. Va. 181; 34 S. E. 793.

Sec. 32.—A claimant of an oil and gas lease may maintain a bill in equity for injunction and receivership against an adverse claimant to the title and an adverse lessee, where the question of title is one of law, only, and where there is no controversy as to the facts in relation to the title.

Sult v. *Hochstetter Oil Co.,* 63 W. Va. 317; 61 S. E. 307.

Sec. 33.—The owner of a life estate, or an estate for years, in lands which are producing oil or gas is entitled to the interest on the royalties and rentals of the oil and gas sold during the continuance of such estate, for life, or for years, and may enforce such right by bill in equity for an accounting against those operating such lands.

Wilson v. *Youst,* 43 W. Va. 826; 28 S. E. 78.
Blakley v. *Marshall,* 174 Pa. 425; 34 Atl. 564.

Sec. 34.—A tenant for life who by waste has developed the premises and has produced oil and gas, and has converted to his own use the proceeds thereof, has no right to have these proceeds invested so that he may have interest thereon during the life estate, but the proceeds of such oil and gas go at once to the next vested estate of inheritance; and such owner may maintain a bill in equity for an accounting against such life tenant.

Williamson v. *Jones,* 43 W. Va. 562; 27 S. E. 411. Syl. 15.

Sec. 35.—Where a wrongdoer has entered upon lands of another and has unlawfully taken oil therefrom, the owner of the land may pursue and reclaim the oil wherever he may find it.

Hughes v. *United Pipelines,* 119 N. Y. 423; 23 N. E. 1042.

LESSEE'S REMEDY.

Sec. 36.—Where a lessee under an oil and gas lease has by developments become vested with the exclusive right of producing the oil and gas, he may maintain a bill in equity for an injunction against the lessor or those claiming under him where such lessor or those acting under him attempts to drill upon any portion of the leasehold.

> *Westmoreland Nat. Gas Co.* v. *DeWitt*, 130 Pa. 325; 18 Atl. 724.
> *Duffield* v. *Hue*, 136 Pa. 602; 20 Atl. 526.

Sec. 37.—Where the owner of a life estate, or an estate for years, in lands executes an oil and gas lease providing for the payment of stipulated rentals or commutation money for delay, lessee may refuse to pay such rentals upon the grounds that he is not authorized under the lease to produce the oil and gas from the premises.

> *Marshall* v. *Mellon*, 179 Pa. 371; 36 Atl. 201; 35 L. R. A. 216.

CHAPTER 28.

A VOID LEASE WILL BE CANCELLED BY A COURT OF EQUITY.

Sec. 1.—Where a person enters upon land, without authority, under a void lease, and drills thereon and takes petroleum, oil or natural gas, therefrom, a court of equity will, at the suit of the landowner or his lessee, perpetually enjoin such person from operations under such void lease; and will cancel the lease.

> *Haskell* v. *Sutton*, 53 W. Va. 206; 44 S. E. 533.
> *Lowther Oil Co.* v. *Miller-Sibley Oil Co.*, 53 W. Va. 501; 44 S. E. 433.
> *Starn* v. *Huffman*, 62 W. Va. 422; 59 S. E. 176.
> *Steelsmith* v. *Gartlan*, 45 W. Va. 27; 29 S. E. 978.
> *Trees* v. *Eclipse Oil Co.*, 47 W. Va. 107; 34 S. E. 933.
> *McGraw Oil & Gas Co.* v. *Kennedy*, 65 W. Va. 595; 64 S. E. 1027.
> *Huggins* v. *Daley*, 40 C. C. A. 12; 99 Fed. 606.
> *Consumers Gas Trust Co.* v. *American Plate Glass Co.*, 162 Ind. 392; 68 N. E. 1020.
> *Pyle* v. *Henderson*, 65 W. Va. 39; 63 S. E. 762.

Sec. 2.—Where the owner or claimant of an oil and gas lease is excluded from possession of the land by an adverse claimant who enters and drills thereon and takes gas and oil therefrom, the common law remedy of such claimant by possessory action is wholly unavailing and affords the complaining party practically no relief. The rightful claimant might be kept out of possession pending the trial at law, and the property rendered worthless by producing and selling the oil and gas; and where the claimant ultimately succeeds in establishing his right to possession he would necessarily then be compelled to resort to a suit in equity for a discovery and accounting, as otherwise there is no adequate remedy provided for the recovery of the damages sustained by being so excluded from possession.

Sec. 3.—In *Haskell* v. *Sutton,* 53 W. Va. 206; 44 S. E. 533, analyzed under Chapter 27, the syllabus is as follows:

"Where a person enters upon land, without authority, under a void lease, and drills thereon, and takes petroleum oil therefrom, and removes the same from the premises; and threatens to drill other wells and to take the oil produced therefrom, a court of equity will perpetually enjoin him from all operations under said void lease, will cancel said lease and will retain the cause for all purposes, and proceed to a final determination of all the matters at issue therein; although the plaintiffs may have a remedy at law against the wrongdoer for the trespass."

Sec. 4.—In *Lowther Oil Co.* v. *Miller-Sibley Oil Co.,* 53 W. Va. 501; 44 S. E. 433, analyzed under Chapter 5, John Metz made a lease which by assignment became the property of Miller-Sibley Oil Company. The lease was practically the same as that construed in *Eclipse Oil Company* v. *South Penn Oil Co.,* 47 W. Va. 27, analyzed under Chapter 4, and might have been avoided by Metz at any time before actual entry by lessee. The assignee of the lessee entered upon the premises and after making some tests which were never beneficial to the landowner physically abandoned the premises. Metz than made a lease to Lowther who assigned to the Lowther Oil Company, and this company entered upon the premises, took possession of the wells drilled by the Miller-Sibley Company and succeeded in pumping oil from one of them in paying quantities after drilling the well deeper. Lowther Oil Company instituted in the Circuit Court of Calhoun County a suit in equity against the Miller-Sibley Oil Company to restrain that company from interfering with plaintiff in its operations, and for cancellation of the original lease. The Circuit Court cancelled the lease, and the Miller-Sibley Company appealed. The Court of Appeals affirmed the decree.

Sec. 5.—In *Starn* v. *Huffman,* 62 W. Va. 422; 59 S. E. 179 (October 29, 1907) syl. 1 is as follows: ·

"1. A lease of a coal vein for mining for one year, and as long thereafter as the lessee may continue to mine it, the lessee to receive ten cents per ton for all coal mined, payable at the end of each thirty days, the mining to begin the next day. After the lapse of two years and three months, no mining having been done, equity will cancel the lease at the suit of the lessor."

James Starn made a lease to Samuel S. Huffman of the Pittsburg vein of coal in a tract of 12 acres of land for one year, and as much longer as Huffman should continue to operate the mine. The lease provided that the lessee should pay the lessor ten cents per ton for all coal mined; and that the lessee should, "begin mining said coal on or before December 19, 1902, and pay for said coal every thirty days." The lease bore date December 18, 1902. Huffman assigned the lease to James F. Cook and John P. Hart. On March 23, 1905, Starn instituted a suit in chancery in the Circuit Court of Marion County to cancel the lease for failure to mine, as required by the terms of the lease, and to clear and quiet his title. The Circuit Court entered a decree cancelling the lease. The defendants appealed, and the Court of Appeals affirmed the decree, citing in support of its conclusions:

Urpman v. *Lowther Oil Co.,* 53 W. Va. 505.
Crawford v. *Ritchie,* 43 W. Va. 252.
Bluestone Coal Co. v. *Bell,* 38 W. Va. 297.
Bettman v. *Harness,* 42 W. Va. 433.
Western Pa. Gas Co. v. *George,* 161 Pa. 47.
Elk Fork Oil Co. v. *Jennings,* 84 Fed. 839.
Shenandoah Land Co. v. *Hise,* 92 Va. 238.
Cowan v. *Bradford Iron Co.,* 83 Va. 547.
Island Coal Co. v. *Combs,* 152 Ind. 579.
Rorer Iron Co. v. *Trout,* 83 Va. 397.
Huggins v. *Daley,* 99 Fed. 606.

Sec. 6.—In *Steelsmith* v. *Gartlan*, 45 W. Va. 27; 29 S. E. 978, analyzed under Chapter 5, Mrs. McGregor made a lease for oil and gas of a tract of land in Ritchie County, West Virginia, under which lease Gartlan and others entered and put down a well but failed to discover oil in paying quantities. The lease was for a term of five years and as much longer as oil or gas should be produced in paying quantities. The lessees claimed that by drilling the dry hole they were entitled to the full term within which to return and resume developments at their will. After a physical abandonment of the premises for about eighteen months, the lessees declining either to continue operations or pay commutation money for delay, Mrs. McGregor made a second lease to Steelsmith, who entered and found oil in paying quantities. Steelsmith filed a bill in equity in the Circuit Court of Ritchie County against the lessee and the assignees of the lessee under the original lease, for injunction and cancellation of the first lease. Defendants answered, and after proof the Circuit Court held the second lease invalid, and entered a decree cancelling it and validating the first lease. From this decree Steelsmith appealed to the Court of Appeals and the decree of the Circuit Court was reversed, and the original lease was cancelled upon the grounds of abandonment.

Sec. 7.—In *Trees* v. *Eclipse Oil Co.*, 47 W. Va. 107; 34 S. E. 933, analyzed under Chapter 14, syl. 3 is as follows:

"3. A person holding a valid executory oil and gas lease executed by several of the number of co-tenants, has such an inchoate interest in the land, subject to such lease as will enable him to maintain an injunction to prevent a wrongdoer from committing waste by the extraction of such oil and gas."

John Haffer, of Wetzel County, West Virginia, executed an oil and gas lease, on August 16, 1898, which by assignment came into the hands of the Eclipse Oil Company. This lease was without consideration and void for want of mutuality. The lessor died before the Eclipse Oil Company commenced developments. After his death the widow and some of the heirs at law made a second lease to J. C. Trees. Thereafter the Eclipse Oil Company entered the premises for exploration purposes under the original lease. Trees, who held a valid lease from some of the heirs at law of the lessor, filed a bill for, and obtained an injunction against the Eclipse Oil Company restraining it from operating under the original lease. The Circuit Court entered a decree for the plaintiff, and defendant appealed. The Court of Appeals affirmed the decree.

Sec. 8.—In *McGraw Oil & Gas Co.* v. *Kennedy,* 65 W. Va. 595; 64 S. E. 1027, analyzed under Chapter 18, Hugh Evans, the owner of a 528-acre tract of land in Taylor County, West Virginia, made an oil and gas lease to U. S. Ditman and J. C. Gawthrop. A well was drilled by the Southern Oil Company under an agreement with the lessees, and gas was discovered in paying quantities. The well was shut in, there being no accessible pipeline, and the gas rental was paid to the landowner. The Southern Oil Company and the lessees assigned the lease to the South Penn Oil Company. The gas right under the lease ultimately vested in R. W. Kennedy as trustee for the Chrystal Ice Company. Seven annual payments of $200.00 each were made to the lessor, and he was tendered the rental for the year ending December 20, 1907, which he refused to accept. On March 20, 1907, Evans leased the same tract to the McGraw Oil & Gas Company. This Company, with notice of the first lease, entered upon the premises and drilled a well which produced gas. The McGraw Company then brought suit in equity in the Circuit Court of Taylor County against Kennedy and the Chrystal Ice Company to cancel the original lease. Later Kennedy and the Chrystal Ice Company brought a chancery suit against the McGraw Oil & Gas Company, the South Penn Oil Company, and Evans, setting up the first lease, the object of which suit was to have the McGraw lease cancelled as a cloud upon the title. The South Penn Oil Company which retained the oil rights under the original lease, filed in the case of the Chrystal Ice Company a cross-bill against the McGraw Company, praying to have the second lease cancelled. The Circuit Court sustained a demurrer to the cross-bill of the South Penn Company, and entered a decree dismissing the bill filed by Kennedy and the Chrystal Ice Company, and cancelling the original lease. The Chrystal Ice Company, Kennedy, and the South Penn Oil Company, appealed. The Court of Appeals reversed the Circuit Court and entered a decree cancelling the second lease.

Sec. 9.—In *Huggins* v. *Daley,* 99 Fed. 606; 40 C. C. A. 12, analyzed under Chapter 6, F. P. Marshall made an oil and gas lease to A. P. Hodges, who assigned to Daley. The lease provided

that it should be held for the term of five years, provided a well
should be commenced on the premises within 30 and completed
within 90 days from the date. In case of failure to commence or
complete the well lessor should forfeit $50.00. After the expira-
tion of the 90 days, no well having been commenced or completed,
Marshall made a second lease to J. J. and J. B. Huggins, Daley
filed a bill in equity in the United States Circuit Court for the District of West Virginia against Marshall and the lessees J. J. and
J. B. Huggins for the cancellation of the second lease as a cloud
upon the title. J. J. and J. B. Huggins filed a cross-bill praying for
the cancellation of the original lease. The Circuit Court entered a
decree cancelling the second lease, and Huggins appealed. The
Circuit Court of Appeals for the Fourth Circuit reversed the Circuit Court, held that 90 days was the term of the lease, and cancelled the original lease, upon the cross bill.

Sec. 10.—In *Consumers Gas Trust Co.* v. *American Plate
Glass Co.*, 162 Ind. 392; 68 N. E. 1020, analyzed under Chapter 10,
syl. 4 is as follows:

"A lessee, under a lease giving it the exclusive right to draw
gas from the demised tract, has a proprietary interest in the
tract, including a part thereof, over which a railroad had acquired an easement for its right of way; and though it cannot
enter on the railroad's land so as to sink gas wells thereon, so
long as the railroad is in possession, yet it may enjoin the sinking
of a gas well on such land, thereby diminishing the flow of gas
from its own wells."

The landowner permitted the railroad company to enter upon his
land and acquire by user and possession an easement thereon for
the operation of its railroad. Subsequently the landowner made a
lease for gas purposes of the land without excepting the easement
of the railroad company. The railroad company undertook to
cause a well to be drilled on its right of way, and the holder of the
gas lease applied for an injunction against the railroad company
and its agents to restrain it or them from drilling the well, claiming that all the gas in the whole tract was subject to its lease. The
Supreme Court of Indiana upon appeal by both parties to the suit
held that the lessee was entitled to the injunction.

Sec. 11.—In *Pyle* v. *Henderson*, 65 W. Va. 39; 63 S. E. 762,
analyzed under Chapter 6, Thomas Bunfill made an oil and gas

lease to Campbell and Swan for a tract of 60 acres of land for a term of 5 years. The lease provided that unless a well was commenced within three months or a quarterly rental paid for delay, the lease should be null and void. Before the expiration of the three months the lessees discovered that there was an outstanding interest in the land, title to which the lessor did not have, and pending an effort to obtain this outstanding title the three months expired, and within a few days after the expiration of the time, Bunfill made a second lease to Pyle, who had notice of the first lease. Campbell and Swan and their assignees then undertook to enter upon the premises for the purpose of development, but were enjoined by Pyle and his assignees. The second lessee and his assigns held possession and discovered oil in paying quantities. A bill was filed by Pyle and his assignees against the original lessees and their assignees, to cancel the first lease, and the lessees under the first lease and their assignees, filed a cross bill in the suit for the cancellation of the second lease, and for an accounting. The Circuit Court upon final hearing held, that owing to the defective title, there had been no abandonment or forfeiture of the original lease, and entered a decree cancelling the second lease. The second lessees appealed to the Court of Appeals, where the decree of the Circuit Court was affirmed.

REMEDIES.

Sec. 12.—Where a person claiming under a void lease is taking or attempting to take oil and gas from the premises, the remedy of the landowner or his lawful lessee is by bill in equity or petition in the nature thereof. All parties affected should be made parties either as plaintiffs or defendants in a proceeding of this character. The court can quiet the title, protect the true owner, and make such decree as to the determination of the damages sustained as may be necessary to the determination of all matters in controversy and for fixing the liability against the parties who are legally responsible for the injury. Pending this proceeding, injunction will lie, and in cases of extreme necessity a receiver will be appointed to preserve the property pending the ultimate decision by the court.

Sult v. *Hochstetter Oil Co.,* 63 W. Va. 317; 61 S. E. 307.
See cases cited Section 1, Supra.

CHAPTER 29.

WANT OF MUTUALITY.

Sec. 1.—A lease of lands for oil and gas purposes, made without a valuable consideration, wherein lessee neither agrees to make developments nor pay rental or commutation money for delay, is void for want of mutuality, and before entry and developments thereunder by lessee the lease may be terminated at the will of either party.

Eclipse Oil Co. v. *South Penn Oil Co.*, 47 W. Va. 84; 34 S. E. 293.
Trees v. *Eclipse Oil Co.*, 47 W. Va. 107; 34 S. E. 933.
Eclipse Oil Co. v. *Henry Garner*, 53 W. Va. 151; 44 S. E. 131.
Federal Oil Co. v. *Western Oil Co.*, 112 Fed. 373.
Federal Oil Co. v. *Western Oil Co.*, 121 Fed. 674; 57 C. C. A. 428.
Tennessee Oil etc. Co. v. *Brown*, 131 Fed. 696; 65 C. C. A. 524.
Pyle v. *Henderson*, 65 W. Va. 39; 63 S. E. 762.
J. M. Guffey Petroleum Co. v. *Oliver*, 79 S. W. 884 (Tex.)
Lowther Oil Co. v. *Miller-Sibley Oil Co.*, 53 W. Va. 501; Opinion 505; 44 S. E. 433.
Brewster v. *Lanyon Zinc Co.*, 72 C. C. A. 213; 140 Fed. 801.
Pittsburg Vitrified P. & B. B. Co. v. *Bailey*, 76 Kan. 42; 90 Pac. 803.
Young v. *McIllhenney*, 116 S. W. 728. (Ky.)
Roberts & Corley v. *McFadden*, 32 Tex. Civ. App. 49; 74 S. W. 105.
National Oil & Refining Co. v. *Teel*, 67 S. W. 545; Affirmed in 68 S. W. 779; 95 Tex. 586.
Hodges v. *Brice*, 32 Tex. Civ. App. 358; 74 S. W. 590.
Poe v. *Ulrey*, 233 Ill. 56; 84 N. E. 462.
Great Western Oil Co. v. *Carpenter*, 43 Tex. Civ. App. 229; 95 S. W. 57.
Waterford Oil & Gas Co. v. *Shipman*, 233 Ill. 9; 84 N. E. 53.
Martel v. *Jennings-Heywood Oil Syndicate*, 114 La. 903; 38 Southern, 253.
Boyd v. *Brown*, 47 W. Va. 238; 38 S. E. 668.
Harness v. *Eastern Oil Co.*, 49 W. Va. 232; 38 S. E. 662.

Sec. 2.—In *Eclipse Oil Co.* v. *South Penn Oil Co.*, 47 W. Va. 84; 34 S. E. 293, analyzed under Chapter 4, syl. 5 is as follows:

"5. If one party to a contract is not bound to do the act which forms the consideration for the promise, undertaking, or agreement of the other, the contract is void for want of mutuality."

Sec. 3.—In *Trees* v. *Eclipse Oil Co.*, 47 W. V. 107; 34 S. E. 933, analyzed under Chapter 14, syl. 1 is as follows:

"1. An executory oil and gas lease, which does not bind the lessees to carry out its covenants, but reserves to them the right to defeat the same at any time, and relieve themselves from the payment of any consideration therefor, is invalid to create any estate other than the mere optional right of entry, which is subject to termination at the will of either party."

Sec. 4.—In *Eclipse Oil Co.* v. *Henry Garner*, 53 W. Va. 151; 44 S. E. 131 (April 11, 1903) the syllabus is as follows:

"A lessor executed at different times two sets of oil leases to two different lessees, reserving the usual royalty, and, after the first leases have been avoided by the execution of the second the first lessee pays two years rental or commutation money to the lessor with full knowledge of the execution of the second lease; such payment does not entitle such lessee to claim the reserved royalty or any part thereof, either in law or equity."

The Eclipse Oil Company, the assignee of an original lease made by Henry Garner for a tract of land in Wetzel County, West Virginia, which lease was forfeited and avoided by the execution of a second lease by the landowner, upon the ground of want of mutuality, with knowledge of the execution of the first lease paid to the landowner two years commutation money for delay in operations. It afterward brought suit in equity against the landowner and the holder of the second lease in chancery in the Circuit Court of Wetzel County, claiming that the payment of the commutation money entitled it to the royalty reserved in the second lease. The defendants demurred to the bill, which demurrer the Circuit Court sustained and entered a decree dismissing the plaintiffs bill. The laintiff appealed to the Court of Appeals, and that court affirmed he decree. The lease claimed by the Eclipse Oil Company in this ase is construed in *Eclipse Oil Co.* v. *South Penn Oil Co.*, 47 W. ᵀa. 84; 34 S. E. 293, analyzed under Chapter 4.

Sec. 5.—In *Federal Oil Co.* v. *Western Oil Co.*, 112 Fed. 373, analyzed under Chapter 24, the first point of the headnotes is as follows:

"In an action to enforce specific performance of a contract, any fact showing that the contract is unfair, unjust, and against good conscience will justify the court in refusing such decree, though the contract may be enforceable at law, and there is no sufficient ground for its cancellation."

Sec. 6.—In *Federal Oil Co.* v. *Western Oil Co.*, 121 Fed. 674; 57 C. C. A. 528 (October 7, 1902), the head notes are as follows:

"1. A court of equity will not decree specific performance of a contract which is unfair or unconscienable, or where performance by the complainant is entirely optional and no offer of performance is made.

2. An oil and gas lease on eighty acres of land provided that, if a well was not commenced at once, the lessee should pay the lessor $8.75 per month during the delay. The lessor was to receive as a royalty one-eighth of the oil produced, and $100.00 per year for each producing gas well, together with gas for use in his residence. There was no limit as to time, no provision obligating the lessee to make any well, and the contract was terminable at its option. It drilled no well, but made the monthly payments for about eight months, and the lessor refused to accept further payments, and leased to another party. *Held,* that the contract contemplated the exploration of the property at once; that the monthly payments were not a part performance, but merely a stipulated sum for delay in performance; and that the contract would not be specifically enforced because of its want of mutuality and unfairness."

This is an appeal from the decree entered by the Circuit Court in *Federal Oil Co.* v. *Western Oil Co.*, 112 Fed. 373. The Circuit Court of Appeals for the Seventh Circuit affirmed the Circuit Court and in the opinion cited:

State v. *Indiana & Ohio Gas & Mining Co.*, 120 Ind. 575; 22 N. E. 778.
Peoples Gas Co. v. *Tyner,* 131 Ind. 227; 31 N. E. 59.
Heal v. *Niagara Oil Co.*, 150 Ind. 483; 50 N. E. 482.
Manfs. Gas Co. v. *Ind. Gas Co.*, 155 Ind. 461; 57 N. E. 912.

Sec. 7.—In *Tennessee Oil, Gas & Mineral Co.* v. *Brown,* 131 Fed. 696; 65 C. C. A. 524, analyzed under Chapter 24, the fourth point of the head notes is as follows:

"Where a mining lease provides that the grantee might ter-minate the same at his election, the lease was terminable at the will of either party."

Sec. 8.—In *Pyle* v. *Henderson,* 65 W. Va. 39; 63 S. E. 762, analyzed under Chapter 25, syl. 1 is as follows:

"Though a lease for oil and gas for a money bonus as con-sideration, does not bind the lessee to drill or pay money in lieu of doing so, but leaves it optional with him to do so or not, the lessor cannot annul or revoke it merely on the ground of want of mutuality of obligation."

This lease was for a cash consideration of $55,00.

Sec. 9.—In *J. M. Guffey Petroleum Co.* v. *Oliver,* 79 S. W. 884 (Tex.) analyzed under Chapter 18, syl. 9 is as follows:

"A lease of land for oil and gas development, terminable at the will of the lessee upon the payment of two dollars is termin-able also at the will of the lessor on tender or payment of the value of all labor done and services rendered by the lessee."

In explanation of the conclusions reached by the court, after citing the case of *Eclipse Oil Co.* v. *South Penn Oil Co.,* 47 W. Va. 84; 34 S. E. 923, and *Federal Oil Co.* v. *Western Oil Co.* (C. C.) 112 Fed., 374, the Chief Justice in the concluding paragraph of the opinion said:

"The only distinction observable between the case cited and the one under consideration is that the cited case does not require the payment of a consideration for the exercise of the right to ter-minate the lease. But, as above stated, the consideration named in the lease in this case, is only nominal, and cannot be regarded as a valuable consideration. Since, therefore, the lease was ter-minable at the will of either party, Oliver had a right to put an end to it upon doing equity. and it appearing that an accounting has been taken by the parties, and judgment rendered in favor of the defendant for the amount expended by it upon the land, the judgment should be affirmed independently of the question of the right of forfeiture for failure diligently to develop the premises.''

Sec. 10.—In *Lowther Oil Co.* v. *Miller-Sibley Oil Co.,* 53 W. Va. 501; Opinion 505; 44 S. E. 433, analyzed under Chapter 5, the court said:

"The lease required no rent, only a share of oil, and gives absolute right to the lessee to surrender it, and under *Eclipse Oil Co.* v. *South Penn Oil Co.,* 47 W. Va. 84, gives no present vested estate, and might be ended at any time by either party, and a second lease would end it. That is the character of this lease. But when once the lessee under such a lease begins work, whilst he yet has no vested estate, still he has the right to go on in search of oil, and the lessor cannot then at mere will destroy his right.''

Sec. 11.—In *Brewster* v. *Lanyon Zinc Co.* 72 C. C. A. 213; 140 Fed. 801, analyzed under Chapter 4, paragraphs 1-2-3 of the head notes are as follows:

"1.   Mere inadequacy of consideration or other inequality in the terms of a lease does not in itself constitute a ground to avoid it in equity.

2.   A lease for a definite and permissible term, but which reserves to the lessee an option to terminate it before the expiration of the term does not create a mere tenancy at will within the operation of the rule that an estate at the will of one party is equally at the will of the other.

3.   A lease given upon a consideration of one dollar paid at the time is not wanting in mutuality merely because it reserves to one party an option to terminate it which it withholds from the other.''

Sec. 12.—In *Pittsburg Vitrified Paving & Building Brick Co.* v. *Bailey,* 76 Kan. 42; 90 Pac. 803 (June 8, 1907) the syllabus is as follows:

"1. B. and wife, owners of certain lands, entered into a written contract with a corporation, which by its terms, granted to the corporation, in consideration of $1.00 and the agreements made by the company, the privilege of entering upon the land for a term of ten years, and boring gas or oil wells, etc., and, in the event of discovery of oil or gas in paying quantities, conveyed the title to such product for a specified royalty. The company agreed to complete a well within two years or to pay a rental of twenty-five cents per acre until a well should be completed on the premises. The contract also provided that the term might be extended indefinitely by the discovery of oil or gas on the premises, or so long as either should be produced in paying quantities, or the rental be paid thereon; also that the company had the right to surrender the contract at any time, and be thereby discharged from all liabilities for the nonfulfillment thereof. *Held*, that the contract is not, strictly speaking, a lease of the premises, but constitutes a sale by B. and wife to the company of an option to exercise or not to exercise the privileges granted as the company might choose.

2. Such contract is not void for want of mutuality. It is the essence of an option contract that it is not mutual. The purchaser pays his money, or does what he agrees to do for the privilege of choosing whether or not he will perform or claim performance of the contract, and for the consideration received the seller parts with his right of choice.

3. Where certain terms of a contract are ambiguous, but such terms have been construed and acted upon by the parties interested, such construction will be adopted even though the language used may more strongly suggest another construction.

4. The amount paid in the execution of a contract, and the rental thereafter paid is a sufficient consideration to support the contract in its entirety."

Samuel Bailey and wife executed on September 4, 1902, an oil and gas lease to the Pittsburg Vitrified Paving & Building Brick Company, for a tract of 60 acres of land in Montgomery County, Kansas. The lessors, in consideration of one dollar leased and let to the lessee the tract of land together with the right of way over the premises to places of operations; the right to lay pipelines to convey water and gas; and the right to remove any machinery and fixtures placed on the premises. The lease was for the term of ten years, and as much longer as oil or gas should be found in paying quantities or the rental paid. The lessors reserved the right to fully use the premises for farming and all other purposes, except such parts as should be necessary for the purposes of the grant. All oil or gas should belong to the lessee, provided it should deliver in tanks at the wells one-eighth of all the oil produced from the premises, or pay the market price in cash for the same, if the lessor so desired. Sixty Dollars per year was to be paid for each gas well producing five million or less cubic feet per day, and $100.00 per annum for each well exceeding that production, so

long as gas should be sold therefrom. It was further agreed that
the lessor should have the right to case and own any well abandoned by the second party. The second party agreed to complete
a well on the premises within two years from date, reasonably
unavoidable delays or accidents excepted, or in default thereof
pay the lessor a yearly rental of twenty-five cents per acre for further delay, from the date specified for completing a well until such
well should be completed. A failure to complete such well, or make
such payments, should render the lease null and void. It was
further provided that the lessee should have the right at any time
to surrender the lease and be thereby discharged from all damages or claims arising from the non-fulfillment of the contract.
The company paid $1.00 and the rental for two successive years.
On October 24, 1902, fifty days after the execution of the lease,
the company paid the lessors $40.00 as oil and gas rental to Sep-
tember 4, 1903, and the lessors gave a written receipt therefor. On
September 2, 1903, another payment of $40.00 as rental to Sep-
tember 2, 1904, was made and receipted for. On September 4, 1904,
the company tendered to lessors $40.00 in payment of rentals to
September 4, 1905, but lessors refused to accept the same for the
reason, as they alleged, that the pretended lease by the terms
thereof was merely an option which could be revoked at any time,
at the election of either party thereto; and that upon such election
the same should·cease to be of any validity. The lessors instituted
suit in the District Court of Montgomery County, Kansas, against
the lessee to cancel the lease. The case was tried upon the pleadings and the facts above stated, which were agreed upon, and judgment was rendered in favor of plaintiff, and defendant brought error to the Supreme Court, which court reversed the judgment and
remanded the cause with instructions to render judgment for defendant, citing:

> *Allegheny Oil Co.* v. *Snyder,* 106 Fed. 764; 45 C. C. A. 604.
> *Brown* v. *Fowler,* 65 Ohio St. 507; 63 N. E. 76.
> *Central Ohio Nat. Gas & Fuel Co.* v. *Eckert,* 70 Ohio St. 127;
>   71 N. E. 281.

Sec. 13.—In *Young* v. *McIllhenny,* 116 S. W. 728; (Ky.) (Feb.
24, 1909) the second point of the syllabus is as follows:

"Oil and gas leases and a contract between the parties thereto fixed no term or time for the leases to run, and provided no

consideration for the grantor other than an interest in the pro·
duction where oil was found in paying quantities, and so much
per year where gas was found, and nothing in either required the
lessee to drill within any designated time, though each lease pro·
vided that if no well was commenced within a year the grant
should become null and void, unless the lessee paid the lessor a
certain sum for each year thereafter commencement was delayed.
Held, that the leases were simply options for a year with the
right of renewal on payment of the sums stipulated if the lessee
did not begin operations; that there was nothing in either the
leases or the contract binding the lessee to do anything upon which
the lessor could sue for specific performance, and they were void
for want of mutuality.''

This was a suit instituted in the Circuit Court of Cumberland
County, Kentucky, by a lessor for rent claimed under a lease with
conditions as stated in the syllabus. Judgment was rendered for
defendant, and plaintiff appealed. The Court of Appeals dismissed the appeal.

Sec. 14.—In *Roberts & Corley* v. *McFadden,* 32 Tex. Civ. App.
7; 74 S. W. 105, analyzed under Chapter 14, the third, fourth and
fifth points of the syllabus are as follows:

"3. Where an oil lease is in consideration of one dollar (not
a fact paid) the promise to develop the premises and delivery to
the lessor a percentage of the oil produced, and it is stipulated
that the lessee may terminate the lease at any time, and that the
sum paid shall be lessor's full compensation, the contract is unilateral and void.
4. A sale of the premises by the lessor in such a lease, prior
to the commencement of operations by the lessee, terminates the
lease.
5. Where a lease of oil lands was void the owners thereof,
after making a contract for the sale of the land, were under no
obligation to make an effort to remove the lease as a cloud on the
title.''

Sec. 15.—In *National Oil & Pipe-line Co.* v. *Teel,* 67 S. W.
45; affirmed 68 S. W. 979; 95 Tex, 586 (March 12, 1902) the syllabus is as follows:

"1. The assignee of an oil option is not bound by the fraud
of an assignor in procuring the contracts, though the grantors are

in possession and the rights claimed under the option are consistent with such possession.

2. An instrument executed by landowners and others recited that the owners granted the others all oil and gas on the lands, to be paid for by a certain royalty, and that operations should commence within two years or the instrument be void, but that forfeiture might be averted from year to year thereafter by payment of $100.00 in advance. *Held,* that as the contract could not be regarded as a sale to be defeated on condition subsequently be·cause the real consideration was the development of the property, for which no definite time was fixed, and it being requisite to an option that there be some time for performance, the owners might rescind in the absence of any equity owing to any work having been begun by the others.''

The material portions of the lease in controversy in this case were as follows:

''Know all men by these presents: That Richard Teel and ·Nancy Teel, his wife, * * * * in consideration of the sum of one dollar to said first parties paid by Charles A. Nicholson * * * * * the receipt of which is hereby acknowledged, and the further consideration hereinafter mentioned, has granted, bargained, sold and conveyed, and do by these presents grant, bargain, sell and convey unto said party of the second part * * * * reserving however, to first party one-tenth of all oil produced and saved from said premises * * * * If coal is found second party agrees to pay to first party four cents per ton for each ton of same that is mined and ʲmarketed, payable monthly. * * * * * * To have and to hold the above premises unto the party of the second part, their heirs and assigns, upon the following conditions: * * * * * * * In case operations for either drilling a well for oil, or mining for coal or other minerals, is not begun and prosecuted with due diligence within two (2) years from this date, then this grant shall immediately be·come null and void as to both parties, provided that second party may prevent such forfeiture, from year to year, and no longer, by paying in advance $100.00 at his residence until such well is completed, or their shipments from such mines have begun. * * * * * It is understood between the parties to this agreement that all the conditions between the parties hereto shall extend to their heirs, executors, administrators or assigns.''

Nicholson, the lessee, assigned the lease to John Mundy, and on the same day—September 24, 1901—Mundy who claimed to have acquired the lease from Nicholson without notice of any fraud, for value, assigned the lease to the National Oil & Pipeline Company, and the Empire State Oil, Coal & Iron Company. Nothing had been done by Nicholson, Mundy or the companies in pursuance to the lease, and they had never gone into possession. Teel and wife instituted suit in the District Court of Harden County to cancel the lease. The defendants, the corporations, entered a general denial and to the allegation that the lease had been procured by fraud alleged that they were purchasers without notice of any fraud. The court found that Mundy was a purchaser for a valuable consideration without notice of any equities between the lessor and the original lessee. The District Court found for the plaintiffs, and defendants appealed. The Court of Civil Appeals affirmed the District Court, and cited:

> *Eclipse Oil Co.* v. *South Penn Oil Co.*, 47 W. Va. 84; 34 S. E. 293.
> *Huggins* v. *Daley*, 40 C. C. A. 12; 99 Fed. 606.
> *Allegheny Oil Co.* v. *Snyder*, 45 C. C. A. 60; 106 Fed. 764.

The case was appealed by the defendant corporations from the decision rendered by the Court of Civil Appeals to the Supreme Court of Texas, and that court on June 16, 1902, affirmed the court below, and held:

"The assignee of a contract which does not convey an interest in land, but only an option, is not protected against defects which could be asserted against an assignor, as protection to purchaser for valuable consideration extends only to cases where they have purchased the legal title."

Sec. 16.—In *Hodges* v. *Brice*, 32 Tex. Civ. App. 358; 74 S. W. 90 (May 1, 1903) syls. 2-3 are as follows:

"2. Where an oil lease shows on its face that the real consideration is the prospecting and developing of the land with due diligence, and it is to remain in force only so long as the parties comply with their mutual agreements and no prospecting is done for a year, the lease is void.

3. Such an instrument is, at most, a mere option for a lease which is terminated by the foreclosure of a judgment lien against the land."

On April 12, 1901, S. E. Parker and wife executed an oil and gas lease to W. E. Brice for an alleged cash consideration of $4.00, and the further consideration of the covenants and agreements in the lease contained whereby lessor granted, bargained, sold and conveyed to Brice all the oil and gas under the lands demised, with further provisions as follows:

"Together with the right to enter upon said premises for the purpose of drilling and operating for oil, gas and water, and to erect, maintain and remove all buildings, structures, fixtures, pipelines and machinery necessary for the production, or trans-of oil, gas and water; provided that the second party shall have the right to use said premises for farming purposes. * * * * *. The above grant is made on the following terms: (1) In case second party fails to commence a well upon the said premises within six months from this date, or unless he shall thereafter pay to the first party $4.00 per month, from month to month, until said well is commenced then this lease shall become null and void. (2) If oil should be found in paying quantities on the premises second party agrees to deliver to first party in the pipelines with which it may connect the well or wells, the one-eighth of all oil produced and saved from the leased premises. * * * * * * (5) Second party may at any time remove all its property and may re-convey to the party of the first part, his heirs and assigns, the premises and estate hereby granted, and thereafter be relieved from further liability upon this grant and instrument. * * * * * * It is further agreed that the second party, his heirs and assigns, shall have the right at any time to surrender up this lease and be relieved from all moneys due and conditions unfulfilled; then and from that time this lease shall become null and void and no longer binding on either party, and all payments which shall have been made shall be held by the party of the first part as the whole stipulated damages for the non-fulfillment of the foregoing contract."

Brice made similar leases to other parties. A. G. Hodges instituted suit in the District Court of Harden County, against W. E. Brice and others for the recovery of 200 acres of land in Harden County. Hodges' title was deraigned from S. E. Parker through a sheriff's sale at which the plaintiff purchased the land, and the defendants claimed the land under an oil lease. The case was tried to the court without a jury and judgment was rendered in favor of the defendant. The Court held that the plaintiff should take nothing by his suit, which the court held to be one simply for the cancellation of the lease, but decreed that the defendants should pay to the plaintiff the amount of the judgment under which the sale was made, at which he became the purchaser of the land. It was adjudged that the decree was not intended to divest the plaintiff of any title that he might have in the land sued for. The J. S. Brown Hardware Company recovered a judgment on April 6, 1896, in a Justice Court of Galveston County, against S. E. Parker, for $30.98. Execution was issued to Galveston County on this judgment on April 17, 1896, which was returned *nulla bona.* On January 27, 1897, an abstract of the judgment was properly made and certified by the Justice of the Peace, and said abstract was filed and recorded in the Judgment Record of the Office of the County Court of Harden County. S. E. Parker died on May 21, 1901, and his wife, Jane E. Parker, died on February 6, 1902. They left surviving them as their sole heirs three children, to-wit: W. H; W. C. and S. E. Parker. On September 9, 1901, the J. S. Brown Hardware Company for a valuable consideration transferred its judgment against S. E. Brice to E. D. Pope. A suit was brought in the District Court of Harden County on March 20, 1902, by E. D. Pope against the heirs of Parker, and his wife, to establish and foreclose a judgment lien in his favor against the land in controversy; and on April 9, 1902, the said Pope recovered judgment against the said heirs, adjudging that a lien had been created upon the land by the record of the abstract of said judgment, and decreeing that the land should be sold in satisfaction thereof. In pursuance to an order of sale issued upon the judgment the land was sold on July 1, 1902, and was bought by the plaintiff A. G. Hodges, and a deed therefor was executed and delivered to him by the sheriff. None of the defendants were parties to the suit of Pope against the Parker heirs. The plaintiff appealed from the judgment of the District Court to the Court of Civil Appeals, and that court reversed the District Court. The judgment of the Appellate Court held the lease of April 12, 1901, by Parker and wife to Brice to be void, upon the authority of *Emory* v. *League,* 72 S. W. 602; 6 Tex. Ct. Ct. Rep. 719.

Sec. 17.—In *Poe* v. *Ulrey,* 233 Ill. 56; 84 N. E. 46, analyzed under Chapter 14, syl. 7 is as follows:

"7. A surrender clause in an oil and gas lease giving the lessee the option to surrender it before the expiration of its term upon the payment of one dollar, but not giving the lessor the right to compel a surrender, did not create a tenancy at will, and hence did not render the lease invalid for lack of mutuality."

Sec. 18.—In *Great Western Oil Co.* v. *Carpenter,* 43 Tex. Civ. App. 229; 95 S. W. 57, analyzed under Chapter 13, syl. 1 is as follows:

"1. A consideration of one dollar recited as paid in an oil and gas lease, and in fact paid, was a mere nominal consideration which was insufficient to support the contract."

Sec. 19.—In *Waterford Oil & Gas Co.* v. *Shipman,* 233 Ill. 9; 84 N. E. 53, analyzed under Chapter 14, syl. 5 is as follows:

"5. A lease of land to another to prospect for oil and gas, which provides that the lessee upon payment of a dollar may surrender the lease, is not void *ab initio* for want of mutuality, but it deprives the party for whose benefit it is made, of relief in the nature of specific performance since if such relief were granted the lessee could nullify the decree by exercising his option and equity will not do a vain thing by settling the rights of the parties which one of them may set aside at will."

Sec. 20.—In *Martel* v. *Jennings-Heywood Oil Syndicate,* 114 La. 903; 38 So. 253, analyzed under Chapter 24, syl. 1 is as follows:

"1. Where A. and B. owning adjoining tracts of land, joined in a lease of the same to C. for the term of 99 years, for the pur pose of prospecting, boring, excavating, etc., for oil, gas, petro leum, coal, salt, sulphur and other minerals, during that period, for the consideration of one dollar and the royalty of one cent for each barrel of oil sold, and the same proportionate value for all other minerals, A. to have one-third of the royalty accruing from the land of B. and vice versa, and while C. did not bind or obligate himself to prospect, or to do any work on the premises, *held,* that such an agreement is not a contract of lease but a mere permit or license, revocable and terminable at will."

Sec. 21.—In *Boyd* v. *Brown,* 47 W. Va. 238; 38 S. E. 668, (Dec. 2, 1899) the syllabus is as follows:

"1. A promise lacking mutuality at its inception becomes binding upon the promise or after the performance by the promisee.

2. Lack of mutuality is no defense, even in a suit for specific performance, where the party not bound thereby has performed

ill of the conditions of the contract and brought himself clearly
vithin the terms thereof.''

At November Rules, 1897, W. F. Boyd and A. P. Boyd, part-
iers as Boyd Brothers, and A. J. Malarky and G. B. McMillan,
artners as Malarky & McMillan, filed their bill in chancery in the
Jircuit Court of Tyler County, West Virginia, against W. J.
Brown, alleging that in the month of June, 1897, the plaintiffs and
thers were the owners of an undeveloped lease for oil and gas
urposes in Tyler County, made by D. W. Synder and wife to J.
L. Thompson and H. W. Roberts on a tract of about 30 acres of
and; that said owners being desirous of having a test well drilled
n the lease, in June 1897, made an arrangement to have a test well
rilled by Boyd Brothers and Malarky and McMillan, who were
o drill the test well, and were to carry the interest of each of the
wners of the lease, that is, Boyd Brothers, one-fourth, Malarky
: McMillan, one-twelfth, W. J. Brown, one-eighth, U. S. Randolph
ne-twenty-fourth, H. W. Roberts, one-eighth, M. R. Seal one-six-
eenth, C. C. Marsh one-sixteenth, J. L. Thomson five-twenty-
ourths, and O. Hickok one-twenty-fourth. Boyd Brothers and
Malarky & McMillan were to commence operations at once and
rosecute the drilling of a well with due diligence to completion to
he bottom of the Big Injun sand, unless oil and gas should be
ound in paying quantities, at a less depth; and if said well should
e a flowing producing well, to make the necessary connections and
rovide the same with not less than two 250-barrel tanks, and
hould the well be a paying, pumping producing well, to tube the
ime and provide it with the necessary sucker-rods and complete
umping outfit; The well to be drilled and provided with the
ecessary machinery, material and equipment, by the said Boyd
rothers and Malarky & McMillan, without cost or expense of any
ind whatsoever to the plaintiffs; and if said well should not be a
roducing well, the said Boyd Brothers and Malarky & McMillan
hould have the right to keep, take and remove all machinery and
aterial placed by them on said lease. But if the well should be a
aying producing well, then they should each have, hold and en-
jy the same proportionate interest in said well and in the wood
g, and the other property placed on the lease for operating pur-
oses that they would hold and own in the leasehold upon which
ie well should be situated, after they one and all had complied
ith the terms of the agreement, without cost or expense to the

plaintiffs, of any kind. Plaintiffs further alleged that the said W.
J. Brown, U. S. Randolph, H. W. Roberts, M. R. Seal, C. C. Marsh
and J. L. Thompson, agreed to assign and convey unto the plaintiffs the undivided one-half of the interest then held and owned
by each of them in the Snyder lease; that the foregoing was the
proposition made by the owners of the lease to the plaintiffs,
which proposition they accepted, and that they entered upon the
leasehold and drilled the well, and completed the contract in all respects according to the proposition made to them. After the completion of the well W. J. Brown refused to assign to the plaintiffs
the one-half of his interest in the lease, and as a defense alleged
that the plaintiffs were endeavoring to enforce a verbal contract
which was void, and not enforceable for the reason that it was an
attempt to convey real estate, or such interest therein as required
a deed to pass title. The Circuit Court entered a decree in favor
of the plaintiffs requiring the defendant Brown to assign to the
plaintiffs the one-half of his interest in the leasehold. Brown appealed to the Court of Appeals and that court affirmed the decree
of the Circuit Court.

Sec. 22.—In *Harness* v. *Eastern Oil Co.*, 49 W. Va. 232; 38 S.
E. 662, analyzed under Chapter 18, Judge McWhorter in the
opinion, pages 249-50, distinguishes the lease from the one construed in *Eclipse Oil Co.* v. *South Penn Oil Co.*, and the effect of
the entry by lessee under an executory oil and gas lease, and discovery of oil in paying quantities, reaffirming the doctrine that
although an oil and gas lease may be void for want of mutuality,
yet if lessor permits lessee to execute the lease by entry and discovery of oil, he cannot thereafter forfeit the lease on the ground
of want of mutuality.

LESSOR'S REMEDY.

Sec. 23.—Where a valuable consideration is not paid for an
oil and gas lease and the lease does not bind the lessee to carry
out its covenants, but reserves to him the right to defeat the same
at any time and relieve himself from the payment of any consideration therefor, such lease is invalid to create any estate other
than the mere optional right of entry, and the lessor has the right
to terminate the lease at any time without any legal proceedings
or formality whatever.

Eclipse Oil Co. v. *South Penn Oil Co.*, 47 W. Va. 84; 34 S. E. 293.

Eclipse Oil Co. v. *Henry Garner*, 53 W. Va. 151; 44 S. E. 131.

Federal Oil Co. v. *Western Oil Co.*, 112 Fed. 373.

Federal Oil Co. v. *Western Oil Co.*, 121 Fed. 674; 57 C. C. A. 528.

Tennessee Oil, Gas & Mineral Co. v. *Brown*, 131 Fed. 696; 65 C. C. A. 524.

Young v. *McIllhenny*, 116 S. E. 728; (Ky.)

Roberts & Corley v. *McFadden*, 32 Tex. Civ. App. 47; 74 S. W. 105.

Martel v. *Jennings-Heywood Oil Synd.*, 114 La. 903; 38 So. 253.

Sec. 24.—Where a landowner executes an oil and gas lease ut does not receive a valuable consideration therefor, and where y the terms of the lease the lessee is not bound to develop within specified time or pay a fixed rental for delay, such lease consti- ates a mere option and before entry by lessee for the purpose of xecuting the lease the lessor may revoke the license. The execu- ion of a second lease, the sale of the property by the landowner, ne death of the lessor, or foreclosure and sale by judicial pro- eedings of the property leased effectually terminates the lease.

National Oil & Pipeline Co. v. *Teel*, 67 S. W. 545; Affirmed 68 S. W. 979; 95 Tex. 586.

Trees v. *Eclipse Oil Co.*, 47 W. Va. 107; 34 S. E. 933.

Eclipse Oil Co. v. *Henry Garner*, 53 W. Va. 151; 44 S. E. 131.

Hodges v. *Brice*, 32 Tex. Civ. App. 358; 74 S. W. 590.

Roberts & Corley v. *McFadden*, 32 Tex. Civ. App. 47; 74 S. W. 105.

Sec. 25.—Texas Rule.—Where an oil and gas lease provides iat lessee may, by the payment of a stipulated amount, surrender ie lease at any time and be relieved of all obligations the lessor ay terminate the lease at any time before entry by the lessee and ifore any expenditure of moneys by him in explorations. Lessor ay, after such entry and explorations, revoke the license and ter- inate the lease upon tender or payment to the lessee of the value ' all labor done and services rendered by him in such explorations.

J. M. Guffey Petroleum Co. v. *Oliver*, 79 S. W. 884.

Sec. 26.—Where the terms and conditions of an oil and gas lease are unfair, unjust and against good conscience, the lessor may declare a forfeiture and refuse to permit the lessee to enter the demised premises for the purpose of carrying out the terms of the lease on his part, and a court of equity will not at the instance of the lessee enforce specific performance of such a lease.

Federal Oil Co. v. *Western Oil Co.*, 121 Fed. 674; 57 C. C. A. 528.

Great Western Oil Co. v. *Carpenter*, 43 Tex. Civ. App. 229; 95 S. W. 57.

Waterford Oil & Gas Co. v. *Shipman*, 233 Ill. 9; 84 N. E. 53.

Sec. 27.—Where a landowner has executed an oil and gas lease which is void for want of mutality, or where the lease is unfair or unconscienable, the lessor may procure cancellation of the lease as a cloud upon his title by a court exercising equity powers.

(See Chapter 32.)

LESSEE'S REMEDY.

Sec. 28.—Where a lease is voidable for want of mutuality or is incapable of specific performance by reason of its terms being either unconscienable, unfair or unjust, lessee must enter and explore to entitle him to hold the lease against the lessor or his assigns. And where under such a lease a lessor permits the lessee to incur expenses in developments such lessor will not be allowed subsequently to declare a forfeiture, nor will a court of equity cancel the lease at his instance upon the ground of unfairness or want of mutuality.

Lowther Oil Co. v. *Miller-Sibley Oil Co.*, 53 W. Va. 501; Op. 505; 44 S. E. 433.

Harness v. *Eastern Oil Co.*, 49 W. Va. 232; 38 S. E. 662. Op. 249-50 (W. Va.)

Boyd v. *Brown*, 47 W. Va. 238; 38 S. E. 668.

Sec. 29.—Where a lessee pays a valuable consideration or bonus (although nominal) for an oil and gas lease and has a fixed time within which to enter for explorations or pay commutation money for delay, although the other terms of the lease may be un-

'air or unjust lessee may hold the lease against the lessor by enter-
ng and developing or by paying the stipulated rental during the
.erm.

> *Brewster* v. *Lanyon Zinc Co.,* 72 C. C. A. 213; 140 Fed. 801.
> *Pittsburg Vitrified Paving & Build. Brick Co.* v. *Bailey,* 76
>   Kan. 42; 90 Pac. 803.
> *Poe* v. *Ulrey,* 233 Ill. 56; 84 N. E. 46.
> *Pyle* v. *Henderson,* 65 W. Va. 39; 63 S. E. 762.

CHAPTER 30.

MINING PARTNERSHIP—OIL AND GAS.

Sec. 1.—General Rule. Co-owners or joint owners of a min-
ıg lease, before they operate for oil and gas, are tenants in com-
ıon or joint tenants. When they unite and co-operate in working
ıe lease they constitute a mining partnership.

> *Childers* v. *Neely,* 47 W. Va. 70; 34 S. E. 828; 81 Am. St.
>   Rep. 777; 49 L. R. A. 468.
> *Blackmarr* v. *Williamson,* 57 W. Va. 249; 50 S. E. 254.
> *Greenlee* v. *Steelsmith,* 64 W. Va. 353; 62 S. E. 459.
> *Bartlett & Stancliff* v. *Boyles,* 66 W. Va. 327; 66 S. E. 474.

Sec. 2.—Pennsylvania Rule. Co-owners of an oil and gas
ase engaged in the development and operation thereof, will be
·esumed to hold the same relation to each other as they did be-
re beginning developments. As to third persons they may sub-
ct themselves to liability as partners by a course of dealing, or
ʳ their acts and declarations, but as to each other, their relation
pₑnds on their title until by their agreement with each other
eʏ change it.

> *Butler Savings Bank* v. *Osborne,* 159 Pa. 10; 28 Atl. 163; 39
>   Am. St. Rep. 665.
> *Dunham* v. *Loverock,* 158 Pa. 179; 27 Atl. 990; 38 Am. St. Rep.
>   838.
> *Walker* v. *Tupper,* 152 Pa. 1; 25 Atl. 172.

Harrington v. *Florence Oil Co.*, 178 Pa. 444; 35 Atl. 855.
Neill v. *Shamburg*, 158 Pa. 263; 27 Atl. 992.

Sec. 3.—In *Childers* v. *Neely*, 47 W. Va. 70; 34 S. E. 628; 81 Am. St. Rep. 777; 49 L. R. A. 468 (Nov. 28, 1899) the syllabus is as follows:

"1. Where tenants in common or joint tenants of an oil lease or mine unite and co-operate in working it, they constitute a mining partnership.

2. When members of a mining partnership cannot agree in management, those having a majority interest control its management in all things necessary and proper for its operation.

3. A sale of his interest by a member of a mining partnership to another member or a stranger does not dissolve the partnership, as in ordinary partnerships.

4. If loss comes to the firm by the culpable negligence or breach of duty or wrongful conduct or diversion of the social property from the firm's business to other business by one member, he is personally accountable therefor in an accounting between the members.

5. Partners have a lien on a social property for advances or balance due them, after debts; but if they have divided the property or product of the business, giving each his share in severalty, and separating it from the balance, no such lien exists on the property or product, so actually divided. Such is the case with 'diversion orders' in oil mining.

6. If a bill is filed by a member of a co-partnership for dissolution and account, and cause is shown for dissolution, there should be a decree of dissolution and full account, not one allowing the partnership to continue its business, and making only a partial account, and decreeing on its basis in favor of one against another member for a balance on such partial account, leaving assets untouched by the account.

7. When cause is shown for dissolution of a partnership, and the members are discordant and at ill will, and the partnership hopeless of prosperity, it should be dissolved and a receiver and manager appointed instead of leaving its assets and business wholly in the possession and control of one member, excluding the other.

8. Equity, as a general rule, does not entertain a bill for accounting between partners, unless a dissolution and winding up are asked, and cause therefor shown. Then there should be a dissolution and full final account."

Childers owned one-fourth interest, Ramey a three-fourths interest and Neely a three-eighths interest in two leases of town lots for oil and gas purposes These owners agreed to develop the lots for oil but made no written article of partnership, and in fact there was no express oral formation of a partnership. They simply agreed to develop their common property, each giving his skill, paying his share of outlay proportionate to his ownership. getting his share of the product proportioned to such ownership. Childers and Ramey filed their bill in equity in the Circuit Court of Tyler County, West Virginia, against Neely praying that a partnership between them be dissolved and an account taken of all its dealings and transactions, and that a manager be appointed to take charge of the property. The partnership referred to was the development of the leases for the two town lots. Neely admitted the joint enterprise; denied that there was a partnership; joined in a request for an account, and did not resist a dissolution. The Circuit Court entered a decree making a partial account, decreed a balance on this account against Neely, and denied him further participation in the partnership. Neely appealed and the Court of Appeals reversed the decree, citing as to partnership:

Skillman v. *Lachman*, 83 Am. Dec. 106-107.
Lamar's Ex. v. *Hale*, 79 Va., 147.
Duryea v. *Burt*, 28 Cal. 569.

Sec. 4.—In *Blackmarr* v. *Williamson*, 57 W. Va. 249; 50 S. E. 254 (Feb. 21, 1905) the syllabus is as follows:

"1. One of the partners in a mining partnership may convey his interest in the mine and business without dissolving the partnership.

2. When members of a mining partnership cannot agree in management, those having a majority interest control its management in all things necessary and proper for its operation.

3. A member of a mining partnership may sell his interest therein to whomsoever he may, without the knowledge or consent of his co-owners.

4. In order to dissolve a mining partnership by decree in equity to sell the partnership property, the bill must allege clear and good grounds therefor."

J. M. Williamson, Adelia Williamson, Harry Ihrig and F. L. Blackmarr were the joint owners of a working interest in a certain oil and gas lease upon the A. R. Williamson farm of 80 acres in Tyler County, West Virgina, held by them respectively in the following proportions: J. M. Williamson, 4-16; Adelia Williamson 2-16; Harry Ihrig, 3-16 and F. L. Blackmarr, 7-16. The parties were operating the lease for the production of oil and gas and had found and produced oil in paying quantities and were receiving the production therefrom in the proportion named. At March Rules, 1909, Blackmarr filed his bill in chancery in the office of the Clerk of the Circuit Court of Tyler County against the other three owners as defendants, alleging that there were two wells on the lease, drilled for oil and gas; that the oil produced from the lease was run into the lines of the Eureka Pipeline Company as follows: To A. R. Williamson, the lessor, the 1-8 royalty; and the other interests in the proportion as they owned interests in the lease, as above stated; that the owners of the lease agreed to further develop the same and to drill other wells thereon for oil and gas, and had drilled three additional wells Numbers 3-4-5, and had cleaned out and equipped Numbers 1 and 2; that in drilling the new wells and cleaning out and operating the wells on the lease and equipping them, the owners expended between thirteen and fourteen thousand dollars, which was contributed in proportion to their interests; that the production of the wells had declined; that owing to the discovery of large pools or fields of oil in Texas and Indian Territory the market price of oil had declined, and was liable to decline more; that the production of oil was declining upon the lease, and the same was becoming of less market value each month; that plaintiff was not willing to expend any more money upon the lease; that it was for the best interests of plaintiff that the mining partnership operating said lease be dissolved, and the mining partnership property (as it could not be partitioned in kind) be sold and the debts which might exist be paid, and the proceeds be divided amongst the members of the mining partnership in proportion to their interests therein; that when the production of oil on the lease was at its highest, and the market was $1.85 per barrel, the plaintiff repeatedly requested the other partners to join with him in selling the lease as a whole for the highest and best price that could be obtained for it in the market, for the reason that the production would decline; that they refused to join in the sale of the mining partnership property; that there was a lack of harmony between the partners as to the further operation of the lease. The bill prayed the dis-solution of the partnership; that the property be sold, the debts paid, and out of the proceeds of the property the balance be divided among the partners in proportion to their interests.

The defendants demurred to the bill for the want of equity, and answered admitting in their answer that the parties owned the lease in the proportion set out therein, denying the material al-legations of the bill, denying that the plaintiff ever made any re-quest of them to join in a sale of the property, and alleging that all bills against the partnership for developing and operating had been paid in full, and that there existed no indebtedness against the partnership for developing expenses; denied that any grounds whatever existed for the dissolution of the mining partnership; alleged that respondents had no objection to plaintiff selling his interest to whomsoever he would, for all the money he could get therefor, and had no objection to his remaining in the partner-ship; that they had no authority to prevent such sale; that what-ever differences of opinion might have theretofore existed in the practical work of operation of said leasehold had been adjusted upon a comparison of opinion; and that the work of development had gone regularly along and the property had been developed economically and rapidly and had been made to produce all it could be made to produce by anyone; that plaintiff, although not entitled to do so, had taken full charge of the purchasing of ma-terial for developing, placing it upon the premises, and had prac-tically given directions and controlled the same, and his directions had been, in the main, followed; and that defendants were of opinion that a public sale of the property would sacrifice, instead of promote the interests of the respective owners.

Depositions were taken and filed in the cause which was heard on August 17, 1904, when the demurrer was overruled and a de-cree entered, holding that the plaintiff was entitled to the relief prayed for in the bill. A dissolution of the partnership was de-creed, and a sale of the leasehold property ordered. From this decree the defendants appealed to the court of Appeals, and that court reversed the decree.

Sec. 5.—In *Greenlee v. Steelsmith,* 64 W. Va. 353; 62 S. E. 459 (Sept. 11, 1908) syl. 1 is as follows:

"1. Mining partners operating oil leases have a lien on the social property for advances or balances due them after payment of debts; but, having divided the product of the business by division orders giving to each his share of the product in severalty and separating it from the balance, no such lien exists on the product thus divided, but the lien remains valid on the social property used in operating the said leasehold."

C. D. Greenlee and Amos Steelsmith were the joint owners of leases on tracts of land in Pleasants County, West Virginia, and entered upon development thereof, found oil in paying quantities, and signed division orders, thus disposing of the product in proportion to the ownership of the partners. Greenlee, claiming to have made advances in excess of those contributed by Steelsmith on account of the mining operations for the benefit of the concern, filed a bill in chancery in the Circuit Court of Pleasants County to wind up the partnership and for the payment to him of the excess contributed and a division of the proceeds thereafter, according to the interests of the parties. The Oil Well Supply Company was made a party defendant, and filed its answer claiming a large amount of money for supplies furnished by it, and used in developments and operations on the partnership leaseholds. Steelsmith sold his interest in the property to the Pittsburg Refining Company, taking notes for the purchase money a number of which were turned over to the Butler County National Bank as security for Steelsmith's liability to that institution, which Bank was also made a party to the suit. Before a decree was entered adjudicating the claims of Greenlee the parties interested had an opportunity to dispose of the leasehold premises and sold the property, and set apart by a contract and consent decree $5,000 of the proceeds of the sale subject to a final decree as to whether or not the Oil Well Supply Company was entitled to this money. The Circuit Court entered a decree holding that the $5,000 should be applied to the payment of the claim of the Oil

Well Supply Company. The Butler County National Bank claimed the money as assignee of the Pittsburg Refining Company, and denied the right of the plaintiff Greenlee, or the Oil Well Supply Company, to this fund, under the claim that as division orders had been signed by the partners thereafter Greenlee had no lien against the social assets. The Bank appealed from the decree and the Court of Appeals affirmed the Circuit Court.

Sec. 6.—In *Bartlett & Stancliff* v. *Boyles,* 66 W. Va. 327; 66 S. E. 474 (Nov. 23, 1909) syls. 2-4-5 are as follows:

"2. The members of a mining partnership not agreeing, those having the majority interest have the right to control the management in all things necessary and proper for its operation, and are liable in an accounting only for culpable negligence or breach of duty, or wrongful conduct, or diversion of the property from the business of the firm.

4. Where, in a suit for that purpose, a dissolution, accounting and winding up of a mining partnership has been decreed, it is error on a partial settlement for the court to give a personal decree against one partner in favor of another for a balance found due him on such partial settlement. The social property should be first reduced to money and applied to discharge partnership liabilities, including any balance found due on final settlement from one partner to another, and then a decree over on final settlement for any balance that may remain.

5. Where one member of a mining partnership has advanced money or property to pay the share of another in the operating expenses, he is entitled to interest thereon, as against the delinquent partner on dissolution and final settlement and winding up of the partnership."

Bartlett & Stancliff, a partnership, and Bartlett, individually, instituted by bill in equity a suit against Boyles for a dissolution, accounting and winding up of a mining partnership. The case was referred to a commissioner and an account taken between the partners. A report was made by the commissioner and exceptions thereto taken, and the Circuit Court decreed that Boyles should pay Bartlett, assignee of Bartlett & Stancliff, $502.32 with interest from July 15, 1902, until paid, being Boyles' share of the operating expenses from March 9, 1901, to July 15, 1902, the date Bartlett purchased the interest of Stancliff. The court decreed

the further sum of $753.85 against Boyles, with interest from
September 15, 1904, being Boyles' share of the operating expenses
from July 15, 1902, until September 15, 1904; and further decreed
that the mining partnership in which Bartlett owned the undivided 7-8, and Boyles the undivided 1-8, be dissolved the property
sold, the business wound up, and that there be a proper distribution of the proceeds of the sale of the property among the partners, and appointed commissioners to make sale of the property
for that purpose. From this decree the defendant appealed. The
Court of Appeals reversed in part and affirmed in part the decree, citing:

Childers v. *Neely,* 47 W. Va. 70; 34 S. E. 828.
Blackmarr v. *Williamson,* 57 W. Va. 249; 50 S. E. 254.
Galloway v. *Campbell,* 142 Ind. 324; 41 N. E. 597.

Sec. 7.—In *Butler Savings Bank* v. *Osborne,* 159 Pa. 10; 28
Atl. 163; 39 Am. St. Rep. 665 (Dec. 30, 1893) the syllabus is as follows:

"Tenants in common engaged in the improvement or development of the common property will be presumed in the absence of
proof of a contract of partnership, to hold the same relation to
each other during such improvement or development as before it
began. As to third persons they may subject themselves to liability as partners by a course of dealing, or by their acts and declarations, but as to each other, their relation depends on their title
until by their agreement with each other they change it.

When tenants in common of an oil lease agree to carry on
operations upon their land, each contributing towards the expenses in proportion to his respective interest in the land, they
will be considered both with respect to themselves and third persons as the ordinary owners of land, working their respective
shares of the wells, responsible only for their own acts, subject to
no laws of partnership, whatever, and possessing distinct rights
in the property.

Two tenants in common of an oil lease entered into an agreement with each other to drill wells on the leasehold property, each
to pay one-half of the costs of sinking the well and pumping the
oil. The oil produced was to be run into pipelines serving the district, and there credited one-half to each of the tenants in common. *Held,* that no partnership existed between the tenants in
common.''

The firm of D. Osborne & Brothers was engaged in drilling oil wells and producing oil, and the firm of Carothers & Peters, was engaged in the same business in the same manner. Each of the firms bought an undivided one-half of two leases known as the Cookman and Duncan leases. Both leases were obtained from the same vendor who was engaged in drilling a well on one of them at the time of the sale. The sale included the drilling tools and machinery in actual use, and it was agreed that Duncan, the vendor, should proceed to complete the work of drilling the well which he had begun. When the well was finished the two firms proceeded to prepare the well for pumping, each paying one-half the expenses incurred. As soon as the first well was put in order the owners entered into an agreement with each other to drill another well on the same lease, each to pay one-half the cost of it. They divided the expense incurred in pumping and in the care of the lease, each paying one-half. The oil was credited 1-2 to Osborne & Brothers and 1-2 to Carothers & Peters by the Pipeline Company. On June 29, 1892, the Butler Bank caused an execution to be issued and a second writ was issued on June 30, 1892, by Collins & Heasley, to sell the personal property of D. Osborne & Brothers. These two writs were the ordinary writs commanding the sheriff to levy the debts of the goods and chattels, lands and tenements of defendants. On July 2, 1892, the Oil Well Supply Company caused to be issued a special writ of *fiare facias* under a Pennsylvania Statute relating to executions against interests in partnership. This writ commanded the sheriff to levy the sum of the judgment against the interests of defendants of any personal, mixed or real property, rights claims and credits, in a partnership composed of defendants, D. Osborne & Brothers, and John Carothers and M. J. Peters. The sheriff sold the property of D. Osborne & Brothers. Proceedings were taken before the auditor as to the distribution of the proceeds of the sale, the court having directed payment to be made on the report of the auditor on the executions in favor of the Butler Savings Bank, upon the theory that only the interest of D. Osborne & Brothers was sold, and that there was no partnership between the two firms of Osborne & Brothers and Carothers & Peters. The Oil Well Supply Company excepted to the auditor's report and contended that the defendants in the execution were part-

ners of Carothers & Peters in the business of producing oil and gas upon the property sold; that all that was sold
was the interest of the defendants in the partnership, and all that
the purchasers got by the sale was the right to call upon Carothers & Peters for an account, and that the special writs of the Oil
Well Supply Company, having been issued before any levies had
been taken upon the writs of the Bank, and Collins and Heasley,
was entitled to be preferred to the two last mentioned writs, although they had been first issued. The auditor conceded the position taken by the appellants, but held that the writs of the Bank
and Collins & Heasley were entitled to first money for the reason
that the Osbornes and Carothers & Peters, under the facts, were
not partners in the business of producing oil or gas upon the property sold, but held them as joint tenants or tenants in common.
The exceptions of the Oil Well Supply Company to this finding
and distribution were dismissed by the Court of Common Pleas,
and the Oil Well Supply Company appealed. The Supreme Court
of Pennsylvania affirmed the judgment.

Sec. 8.—In *Dunham* v. *Loverock*, 158 Pa. 197; 27 Atl. 990; 38
Am. St. Rep. 838 (Nov. 6, 1893) the syllabus is as follows:

"Tenants in common may become partners, like other persons, where they agree to assume that relation towards each other;
but the law will not create the relation for them as the consequence of a course of conduct and dealing naturally referable to
the relation already existing between them, which makes such a
course of conduct to their common advantage.

An agreement between two tenants in common of an oil lease
to drill an additional well on the leasehold at the common cost of
the co-tenants, will not, as between themselves create partnership.
In the absence of a distinct agreement between them that their
relations to the property and to each other should be changed, the
presumption is that the old relation continues, and that they
treated with each other as owners of separate interests in an undivided lease."

In 1888 Emma F. Coutant made two leases for oil mining purposes for twenty years, for two acres of land to William Loverock,
and eight acres to B. F. Shamburg, the land being stituated in
Venango County, Pennsylvania. Loverock became the owner of

the 1-2 interest in the 8-acre lease, and the whole of the 2-acre lease became vested in W. P. Black and Loverock, each a 1-2 interest. After January 16, 1889, the leaseholds with the oil wells, machinery and material were owned by M. B. Dunham and George H. Dunham, 1-2 and William Loverock 1-2. These parties carried on the operations until October, 1889, by sinking wells for producing oil under the agreement that each should pay his proportion of the expenses and losses, if any, and share in like manner the receipts and profits. George H. Dunham was in active management of the property purchasing supplies and selling the product. M. B. Dunham expended, for carrying on the business a large amount of money in excess of his proportion of the production. On October 18, 1889, Loverock sold his interest in the property to W. H. Pickett, who had notice of Loverock's indebtedness. M. B. Dunham filed a bill in equity against Loverock, Pickett and George Dunham, in the Court of Common Pleas of Venango County, alleging the foregoing facts, which bill prayed for an account of all partnership transactions growing out of the business, carried on by the plaintiff and defendant, and for a decree that Loverock pay the amount found due from him on an accounting; and that the sum be decreed to be a lien on the interest of the property sold to Pickett; and that that interest be sold to satisfy the plaintiff's claim if necessary. The defendants, Loverock and Pickett, answered denying their liability. The Court of Common Pleas dismissed the plaintiff's bill, and he appealed to the Supreme Court, and that court affirmed the decree of dismissal.

Sec. 9.—In *Harrington Bros.* v. *Florence Oil Co.*, 178 Pa. 444; 35 Atl. 855 (Nov. 11, 1896) the second, third and fourth points of the syllabus are as follows:

"Where an action of account render will lie in Pennsylvania between tenants in common a court of equity has concurrent jurisdiction.

Plaintiff and defendant were tenants in common of an oil lease. The defendant kept all the accounts pertaining to the lease, made all purchases, paid bills, and furnished plaintiffs statements from time to time, deducting plaintiff's proportion of the expenses. *Held*, that plaintiffs might maintain a bill in equity for an account against defendants.

Plaintiffs and defendant were tenants in common of an oil lease; plaintiffs owning 1-6 and defendant 5-6 in the lease. Plaintiffs drilled a well under contract with defendant, and by reason of defendant's delay in furnishing casing the well was destroyed by the falling in of the sides. *Held,* that the plaintiffs and the defendant should bear the loss of the well in proportion to their respective interests."

On February 25, 1892, the firm of Friday, Keil & Company, entered into a contract with Harrington by which Harrington Brothers agreed, at their own cost and expense to complete a well in good producing order and condition on a certain tract of land in Allegheny County, Pennsylvania, on which Friday, Keil & Company had an oil and gas lease. The contract provided that in case the well to be drilled should be a producing well, the second parties were to furnish and set up necessary tankage. Upon the completion of the well and putting it in good producing order and condition, Friday, Keil & Company agreed to transfer and assign to the second parties the 1-6 interest in the lease. It was agreed that the tubing and sucker rods necessary to pump the well should be paid for by the parties in interest in proportion to their holdings. It was further agreed that if the well should be a paying one, the derrick, engine, boiler, casing and everything used in and about the operation of the well should belong to the parties to the contract as a part of the leasehold, the first parties to have a 5-6 interest therein and the second parties a 1-6. The contract further provided that after the completion of the first well all expenses incurred in developing or operating the lease should be borne by them in proportion to their respective interests. Under the contract Harrington Brothers drilled wells on the premises, numbered from one to seven, inclusive. Subsequently, on February 25, 1892, Friday, Keil & Company sold and transferred their interest in the leasehold premises to the Florence Oil Company, a corporation, and the plaintiffs continued to drill wells on the leasehold premises for the corporation under the agreement of February 25, 1892, made with Friday, Keil & Company. Between the fourth and fifteenth days of July, 1892, Harrington Brothers commenced to drill well number 6. This well had to be drilled through the coal, which had become vested in other parties. Owing to the fact that there was at this time a pending, undetermined conflict between the owners of the coal and the operators as to the rights of the owners of the surface, and the underlying strata below the coal, and the coal operators, as to their right to drill through the coal, the oil operators in drilling their wells in this district commenced the "spudding" of a well of the diameter of thirteen inches, and drilled it this size below the coal, so that a ten-inch casing could be put in the well to some point sufficiently far enough below the coal so as to protect in so far as they could the coal workings from injury by leakings of oil into the same, or escape of gas into the mine. After drilling through the coal the diameter of the well was reduced to ten inches, and was drilled of this diameter to the depth of about 700 feet to what was known in the Macdonald field as the "Hurry Up" sand. It appeared in this case that between the point where the 13 inch casing stopped and the bottom of the "hurry up" sand, there was neither cave nor water to any extent found, and therefore no necessity for putting in an eighth and a quarter casing. From the top of the "hurry up" sand the diameter of the well was reduced in Number 6, to ten inches, and was drilled this diameter to the distance of 1280 feet from the surface. Having gone this distance it became necessary to put in the 6 1-4 casing for the purpose of casing off the water. Having reached this point Harrington Brothers called upon the defendants to furnish the necessary casing early in August, 1892. The casing was placed by defendant near the well, and plaintiff commenced lowering it into the well and continued to do so until all the casing furnished by defendant had been used when it was, found that there was lacking from 170 to 200 feet of casing. Harrington Brothers swung the casing already lowered, and while waiting for additional casing that portion of the well became fastened, and being unable to either raise or lower it, the well had to be and was abandoned. Harrington Brothers thereupon filed a bill in equity in the Court of Common Pleas of Allegheny County, against the Florence Oil Company to recover for the loss sustained, that is, they claimed an accounting and for a decree against the Florence Oil Company for the 5-6 of the loss incurred by the destruction of the well. The case was referred to a master who found in favor of the plaintiffs, holding the Florence Oil Company liable for 5-6, amounting to $2,456.03. The defendant excepted to the finding of the master. The Court of Common Pleas overruled and dismissed these exceptions and rendered a decree in favor of plaintiff, and defendant appealed. The Supreme Court in a per curiam opinion affirmed the decree and approved the master's finding.

Sec. 10.—In *Walker* v. *Tupper,* 152 Pa. 1; 25 Atl. 172 (Nov. 7, 1892) the first, second, third and fourth points of the syllabus are as follows:

"Participation in profits is the most generally accepted test of the existence of a partnership, and though its presence is not conclusive in favor of, its absence may be regarded as conclusive against partnership.

The owners of an oil lease assigned an undivided 3-4 interest in the lease to two other persons. The assignees agreed to drill two wells at their own expense, without any liability on the part of the assignors to defray any of the expenses of drilling, but the assignors were to pay 1-4 of the operating expenses of the wells, and 1-4 of the bonus due the lessor. The assignees were to drill a third well, the assignors to pay 1-8 of the expenses thereof. It was further agreed that the assignors should 'be the owners of the full equal 1-4 of all the production (after deducting the royalty) machinery, rigs, casing, buildings and appliances of all descriptions, which may be placed upon said leasehold for use in operating the same.' *Held,* that there was no partnership relation between the assignors and the assignees, and that a contract for drilling a well, entered into by the assignees, would not bind the assignor.

While the division of the production is in specie does not necessarily negative the idea of the partnership, it raises a presumption against it, to overcome which an actual intent to become partners should clearly appear.

In an action to hold several persons liable as partners, the declarations of some of the defendants as to the partnership, are not evidence as to the others."

On July 23, 1889, Kuntz leased to George W. Reed a tract of twenty acres of land, more or less, for oil and gas purposes. On August 2, 1889, Reed assigned to A. M. Todd, an undivided 1-4 interest in the lease. On August 3, 1889, Reed and Todd assigned to B. S. Tupper, and A. G. Hatry, an undivided 3-4 interest in the lease. In this assignment Tupper and Hatry as parties of the second part covenanted to drill upon the leasehold at such points as might be agreed upon two oil wells to be drilled exclusively at their expense; but first parties were to pay 1-4 of the operating expenses of the well when drilled and completed, and 1-4 of the bonus of $500.00 per well, required to be paid to the lessor under the lease. The assignees also agreed to erect a third rig and begin drilling a third well when required by Reed and Todd, their assignors. This well was to be drilled upon the following terms: Second parties, assignees, to pay 7-8 of the expenses of location, construction of rig and drilling, and first parties, assignors, to pay the remaining 1-8 and 1-4 of the bonus; and to pay 1-4 of the operating expenses of the well after completion. Other wells were to be drilled at the expense of the parties, the assignors to pay 1-4 and the assignees 3-4. The assignors were to be the owners of an equal 1-4 of all the production, (after deducting the royalty,) machinery, buildings, rigs, casing and appliances of all description, to be placed upon the lease for use and operating purposes. Tupper and Hatry, the assignees of Todd and Reed, employed Walker to drill a well. Walker instituted an action of assumpsit in the Court of Common Pleas of Washington County against the owners of the lease and obtained verdict and judgment, from which judgment Tupper and others appealed. The Supreme Court of Pennsylvania reversed the Court of Common Pleas as to the judgment against Reed & Todd, the assignors of the 3-4 interest, and affirmed the judgment as to Hatry and Tupper the assignees.

Sec. 11.—In *Neill* v. *Shamburg*, 158 Pa. 263; 27 Atl. 992, analyzed under Chapter 15, the third point of the syllabus is as follows:

"No presumption of partnership arises from the operation of an oil well by tenants in common."

Elizabeth P. Neill filed in the Court of Common Pleas of Forest County, Pennsylvania, a bill in equity against B. F. and H. W. Shamburg, administrators of G. Shamburg, deceased, for the reconveyance of an oil lease.

REMEDIES.

Sec. 12.—The owners of an oil and gas lease who hold the majority interest therein have the right to control and manage the property, and their judgment when fairly and honestly exercised will not be made the subject of inquiry by a court at the instance of the minority owners.

Blackmarr v. *Williamson,* 57 W. Va. 249; 50 S. E. 254.
Bartlett & Stancliff v. *Boyles,* 66 W. Va. 327; 66 S. E. 474.

Sec. 13.—One or more members of a mining partnership may file a bill in equity alleging mismanagement by the partners in control, or fraudulent conduct on their part to the injury of plaintiffs, or that the business is being conducted at a loss, or alleging other clear and good grounds for dissolution; and upon proof of these allegations the court will dissolve the partnership, order an accounting and decree a sale of the partnership property.

Childers v. *Neely,* 47 W. Va. 70; 34 S. E. 828; 81 Am. St. Rep.
    777; 49 L. R. A. 468.
Blackmarr v. *Williamson,* 57 W. Va. 249; 50 S. E. 254.

Sec. 14.—Where one or more mining partners have made advances of money or supplies for the benefit of the firm, they have a lien on the social property for such advances and may file a bill in equity against the other members for an accounting, dissolution and sale of the social assets, and the plaintiffs may have a decree over against the other partners for any balance that may remain due them after exhausting the whole of the firm assets.

Bartlett & Stancliff v. *Boyles,* 66 W. Va. 327; 66 S. E. 474.
Greenlee v. *Steelsmith,* 64 W. Va. 353; 62 S. E. 459.
Kirchner v. *Smith,* 61 W. Va. 434; 58 S. E. 614.

Sec. 15.—Where mining partners have divided the property or production of the business giving each his share in severalty, and separating it from the balance, no lien exists on the property or production so actually divided in favor of one or more partners who have made advances of money or supplies for the firm over and above their just proportion; and the execution between the partners of "division orders" whereby the share of the production of the wells is set apart in the pipelines to each partner, such a severance precludes a partner who has made such advances from claiming a lien against the production so divided.

> Childers v. Neely, 47 W. Va. 70; 34 S. E. 628; 81 Am. St. Rep. 777; 49 L. R. A. 468.
> Greenlee v. Steelsmith, 64 W. Va. 353; 62 S. E. 459.
> Bartlett & Stancliff v. Boyles, 66 W. Va. 327; 66 S. E. 474.

Sec. 16.—One member of a mining partnership, where the mining partners are operating the lease and producing oil or gas, may sell and convey his undivided interest, and the purchaser takes such title as was vested in his vendor; such sale and purchase does not dissolve the mining partnership and does not discharge the interest so conveyed from any lien that may exist thereon in favor of the other partners who may have made advances beyond their just proportion; nor does a purchaser take such interest against the rights of a third person who has furnished supplies to the partners and the other partners may maintain a bill in equity for a dissolution and sale of the property regardless of the sale of such partner's interest.

> Greenlee v. Steelsmith, 64 W. Va. 353; 62 S. S. 459.

Sec. 17.—Where a third person has furnished money or supplies to co-owners of an oil and gas lease, after they have united in the development thereof, he may maintain an action against such co-owners as mining partners and may recover without proof of a special contract or express agreement amongst the partners to become partners or to share the profits and losses of mining. The only proof that is necessary to establish the partnership is, that the co-tenants or co-partners have united in the development of the lease or operation of the well thereon. The relation of mining partners arises from the ownership of shares or interest in the lease, and working the same for the purpose of extracting the oil and gas. But an actual working of the lease-hold is essential and necessary to charge the owners as a mining partnership. Otherwise the owners of the lease are simply ten-ants in common or co-owners.

> *Childers* v. *Neely,* 47 W. Va. 70; 34 S. E. 828; 81 Am. St. Rep.
>   777; 49 L. R. A. 468, citing:
> *Duryea* v. *Burt,* 28 Cal. 569.
> *Decker* v. *Howell,* 42 Cal. 636.
> *Settembree* v. *Putman,* 42 Cal. 490.
> *Taylor* v. *Castle,* 42 Cal. 367.
> *Jones* v. *Clark,* 42 Cal. 425.
> *Kirchner* v. *Smith,* 61 W. Va. 436; 58 S. E. 614.

Sec. 18.—One or more members of a mining partnership may defeat a claim or demand made against the partnership if the de-mand is for supplies, by proof that the supplies were not neces-sary and usual in the transaction of the particular business; and if the demand is on account of money, notes or bills of exchange it may be defeated by proof that the general superintendent, manager, partner, or agent who is charged with incurring the ob-ligation, had no authority to borrow money, execute notes, or ac-cept bills of exchange, for the partnership.

> *Childers* v. *Neely,* 47 W. Va. 70; Op. 74; 34 S. E. 828; 81 Am.
>   St. 777; 49 L. R. A. 468, citing:
> *Charles* v. *Eshleman,* 5 Colo. 107.
> *Skillman* v. *Lachman,* 83 Am. Dec. 96, and Note.
> *McConnel* v. *Denver,* 35 Cal. 365.
> *Jones* v. *Clark,* 42 Cal. 181.
> *Manville* v. *Parks,* 7 Colo. 128; 2 Pac. 212.
> *Congdon* v. *Olds,* 18 Mont. 487; 46 Pac. 261.
> *Judge* v. *Braswell,* 13 Bush. 67.
> *Waldron* v. *Hughes,* 44 W. Va. 126; 29 S. E. 505.

Sec. 19.—One or more members of a mining partnership may, when the members are discordant and at ill will, and the part-nership is hopeless of prosperity, procure by bill in equity the ap-pointment of a receiver for the property, cause a dissolution of the partnership, an accounting and a sale of the assets.

> *Childers* v. *Neely,* 47 W. Va. 70; 34 S. E. 828; 81 Am. St. Rep.
>   777; 49 L. R. A. 468.

Sec. 20.—Pennsylvania Rule. Co-owners or joint owners of an oil or gas lease are tenants in common and when engaged in the improvement or development of the common property cannot be charged as partners in the absence of proof of a contract of partnership; As to third persons, they may subject themselves to liability as partners by a course of dealings or by their acts and declarations. But as to each other their relation depends on their title until by their agreement with each other they change it.

Butler Savings Bank v. *Osborne,* 159 Pa. 10; 28 Atl. 163; 39 Am. St. Rep. 665.
Walker v. *Tupper,* 152 Pa. 1; 25 Atl. 172.
Neill v. *Shamburg,* 158 Pa. 263; 27 Atl. 992.

Sec. 21.—A co-owner or tenant in common of an oil and gas lease while engaged in developing or operating the lease, may sell and convey his undivided interest, and the purchaser will take title thereto clear of any claim for advances made by the other co-owners or tenants in common; and neither the partner selling, the purchaser, nor the interest purchased will be held liable for advances made by the other partners, in the absence of a contract of partnership.

Dunham v. *Loverock,* 158 Pa. 197; 27 Atl. 990; 38 Am. St. Rep. 838.

Sec. 22.—One tenant in common of an oil and gas lease may maintain a bill in equity for an accounting against the other tenant in common where the defendant kept the accounts pertaining to the lease, purchased the supplies, paid the bills and furnished plaintiff statements from time to time, deducting plaintiff's proportion of the expenses.

Harrington Bros. v. *Florence Oil Co.,* 178 Pa. 444; 35 Atl. 855.

Sec. 23.—A joint owner who is a tenant in common under the Pennsylvania Rule, who has been wrongfully deprived by the fraud of his co-tenants of his interest in an oil leasehold, is entitled, in a suit brought for his share of the oil produced and converted by the other co-tenants while in possession, to recover as damages the value of the oil in the tanks, without deduction for the expenses of production.

Foster v. Weaver, 118 Pa. 42; 12 Atl. 213.

Sec. 24.—In *Foster* v. *Weaver*, 118 Pa. 42; 12 Atl. 313, (Jan. 3, 1888) the syllabus is as follows:

"A tenant in common, who has been tortiously deprived by the fraud of his co-tenant of his interest in an oil leasehold, is entitled in a suit brought for his share of the oil produced and converted by the co-tenant while in possession, to recover as damages the value of the oil in the tank, without deduction for the expenses of production."

Josiah Weaver instituted an action of trespass in the Court of Common Pleas of Forest County against Jacob Foster and L. Simon. By agreement of parties the cause was referred to a Referee, who made the following findings of fact: The plaintiff and defendant became tenants in common in an oil lease for 50 acres of land in Forest County, dated November 1, 1884, at 1-8 royalty for a term of 20 years, each owning a 1-3 interest. By the lease a well was to be completed within six months, and a second well to be commenced within six months from completion of the first, if productive, and operations to be carried on diligently, and to the best interests of both parties to the lease. In 1885, the lessees began operating for oil under this lease. The plaintiff, Josiah Weaver, lived in New York, and the defendants Jacob Foster and L. Simon were oil operators and had charge of the drilling. About the middle of March, 1885, an oil bearing sandrock was found, and oil in paying quantities was found therein, and the prospects were favorable for a good well. The defendants ordered the well shut down and drilling stopped, and the well was reported to those inquiring to be a failure. About six weeks after this one of the drillers named Nolan, at the suggestion of the defendants, went to New York to purchase plaintiff's 1-3 interest, and reported to him that the well was a failure, and the prospects for oil poor. Nolan succeeded in getting the plaintiff's interest for $500.00 which was less than the plaintiff had paid out, and a conveyance was made to him dated May 11, 1885. In a few days Nolan conveyed the same interest to defendants for $600.00. The purchase by Nolan was in reality for defendants who obtained other lands and other leases adjoining, by purchase and by lease, and in the early part of June began pumping oil from the well already drilled, which proved to be a good well. During this year, and after they acquired plaintiff's interest, the defendants drilled another well on this lease, which also proved to be a good well. .

Early in 1886, the plaintiff hearing of the oil developments, and learning that defendants were the owners of his interest, went to them, and, tendering the $500.00 paid him by Nolan, demanded a re-conveyance of his 1-3 interest, and his share of all the oil produced, which was refused. During the year following defendants drilled other wells, which proved even more productive. Some efforts were made by plaintiff and defendants to come to some agreement. The defendants offered to re-convey to plaintiff and pay his share of oil if he would pay his share of all the expenses of operating, and also 1-3 of the balance due on a leasehold mortgage they had given on this and other leases of defendants, the plaintiff's share of which would amount to about $200.00 which the plaintiff refused to do, and in April, 1887, he had the defendants and Nolan arrested for conspiracy and was about to bring an action of ejectment or suit in equity, when it was finally agreed that the plaintiff should pay defendant what they had paid Nolan, and they should re-convey to him his 1-3 interest; and the right of defendants to deduct 1-3 of the expenses and cost of production from the proceeds of plaintiff's 1-3 of the oil already produced was left unsettled, and to be determined according to the rights and equities of the parties in some form of action, the same as if the plaintiff had recovered possession by adversary proceedings.

This arrangement and re-conveyance to plaintiff of his interest was made on June 4, 1887, and for his share of the oil up to that date this suit was brought. The sales made by defendants to the pipeline company were taken as giving the correct price of the oil. The proceeds of the 1-3 of the oil, up to June 4, 1887, was $4,596.41, and the 1-3 of the costs and expenses of operating, including carpenters, rigs, boilers, engines, casing, tubing, tanks, torpedoes, expenses pumping, superintending, etc., amounted to $4,874.92; the expense exceeding the receipts for oil.

The Referee reported that the plaintiff was entitled to recover the proceeds of his share, to-wit, 1-3 of the oil taken by defendants from the land sold and converted by them to their own use, which amounted to $4,596.41 on June 4, 1887. Judgment was therefore rendered in favor of the plaintiff against the defendants for the amount found by the Referee, from which judgment defendants took a writ of error. The Supreme Court affirmed the judgment.

Sec. 25.—Where several co-tenants of an oil lease assign the lease to an operator who agrees to deliver to them a part of the product, and one of the joint owners does not join in the assignment, to entitle the co-owner who has not joined in such assignment to recover from the assignee, the operator, or from the other co-tenants, his proportion of the royalty, he must first notify the operator, and in such case his remedy is against the lessee as a co-tenant who has not acquired his title. If such co-owner desires to share in the royalty, in a suit against his co-tenants, he must prove that they have received more than their share of the royalty. All proper charges and expenses will be deducted from the royalty before such co-tenant is entitled to anything.

Enterprise Oil & Gas Co. v. *National Transit Co.*, 172 Pa. 421; 33 Atl. 687.

Sec. 26.—In *Enterprise Oil & Gas Co.* v. *National Transit Co.*, 172 Pa. 421; 33 Atl. 687 (Jan. 6, 1896) the second paragraph of the syllabus is as follows:

"Several co-tenants of an oil lease assigned the lease to an operator who was to deliver to them a part of the product. One of the joint owners did not join in the assignment, and notified the assignee not to deliver any oil to his co-tenants. *Held*, (1) that the party not joining in the assignment was not entitled to his share of the oil without proving that his co-tenants had received more than their share; (2) that if he chose to affirm it, he must take his share with the others upon a distribution of the royalty after deducting all proper charges and expenses; (3) that if he did not affirm the lease, he had no claim to any share in the royalty, and could only look to the lessee as a co-tenant who had not acquired his title."

C. J. D. Strohecker and others, partners under a firm name of Enterprise Oil & Gas Company, instituted an action of assumpsit in the Court of Common Pleas of Butler County, Pennsylvania, against the National Transit Company, to recover royalties under an oil lease. At the trial is appeared that in October, 1889, C. J. D. Strohecker was the owner of several oil and gas leases. In that year he assigned the leases to the Enterprise Oil & Gas Company. It appeared that this company was an association of partnership in which there were thirty-two shares, each share being valued at $100.00. The company was not organized as a limited partnership, nor as a corporation. J. T. Johnson denied that he had joined any such partnership and claimed that Strohecker had sold to him for $200.00 an undivided 1-16 in all the leases. The names of the different members of the firm were: C. J. D. Strohecker; J. H. Latshaw; J. D. Stauffer; J. T. Johnson; W. A. Goehring; Householder and Jones; C. M. Root; S. M. Kidd; George Snyder; S. E. Niece, and R. M. Harper. On October 17, 1890, by an instrument in writing the Enterprise Oil & Gas Company assigned to J. M. Latshaw 1-12 of the leases, retaining a royalty of 1-8. Latshaw subsequently formed a company called the Latshaw Armor Company. A well was drilled and oil found in paying quantities. One-eighth of the oil was run into the lines of the National Transit Company and to the credit of the Enterprise Oil & Gas Company. On October 1, 1893, the latter company had 1068 barrels to its credit. About this time J. T. Johnson notified the National Transit Company not to deliver any oil to the Enterprise Oil & Gas Company. Johnson alleged that he had bought 1-16 of the leases from Strohecker, but that he had never entered into any partnership with the other tenants in common. The attorney for the National Transit Company filed an affidavit of defense, setting forth *inter alia*, "the lease under which said well was drilled was made by Keziah Allen to C. J. D. Strohecker. The said C. J. D. Strohecker, by assignment in writing, bearing date the —day of— assigned and conveyed to J. T. Johnson the undivided 1-16 interest in the lease, covering the western half of the Keziah Allen farm. The said J. T. Johnson has never sold or in any wise parted with his 1-16 interest of the lease in suit. The oil in controversy in this suit was produced from said 1-16 interest so owned by said J. T. Johnson, and was delivered by the said defendant company to the said J. T. Johnson in the usual course of its business. The National Transit Company has not in its custody or posession any oil belonging to the said plaintiffs.'' Johnson filed an affidavit to the same effect. Verdict and judgment for defendant were rendered, and plaintiff appealed to the Supreme Court, where the judgment was reversed and a new trial granted.

Sec. 27.—Where lessees of an oil and gas lease are tenants in common thereof, and are also partners in the machinery and appliances for developing the oil and gas, and in the business of mining and selling the same, and engaged in the development of the leasehold premises, and marketing the oil and gas therefrom, and have expended money upon the enterprise, one or more of the co-owners and partners may maintain a bill in equity for a discovery and for a settlement of the accounts of the expenses, receipts and disbursements incident to the business.

Johnson v. *Price,* 172 Pa. 427; 33 Atl. 688.

Sec. 28.—In *Johnson* v. *Price,* 172 Pa. 427; 33 Atl. 688 (Jan. 6, 1896) the fifth paragraph of the syllabus is as follows:

"Where plaintiffs and defendants are the owners as tenants in common of an oil lease, and are also partners in the machinery and appliances for developing the oil, and in the business of mining and selling the oil produced from the well, and both parties have expended money upon the enterprise, but defendants refuse to furnish to plaintiffs any statement of their expenditures, plaintiffs have a standing in equity for a discovery and for a settlement of accounts.''

K. K. Johnson and J. N. Johnson filed a bill in equity in the Court of Common Pleas of Butler County, Pennsylvania, against E. E. Price, A. C. Price, B. D. Tillinghast, D. Stewart, and C. J.

Watt. The bill prayed for discovery and account, and averred that plaintiffs and defendants were tenants in common of a lease for oil and gas purposes for six acres of land; that after the execution and delivery of the lease it was agreed by the plaintiffs and defendants that the same should be tested and developed, and plaintiffs were employed and engaged to drill two wells on the lease, for the purpose of testing and developing the same, at the rate of one dollar per foot for the first well and ninety cents per foot for the second, the cost of which drilling was to be charged, borne and paid by all the owners of the lease in proportion to their respective interests; In furtherance of the purpose of testing and developing the lease it was agreed by plaintiffs and defendants that plaintiff should furnish the necessary machinery, derrick, tools and other property required to be used in the drilling of the wells, the cost of which was to be charged to, borne, and paid by all the owners in proportion to their interests; in compliance with the agreements entered into between the parties plaintiffs proceeded to drill two oil wells and two water wells on the lease, and completed the same at a cost of $3,500.00; and for the machinery, boilers, and other machinery and supplies furnished for the drilling and completing of the wells they expended $2,000 more, which plaintiffs had paid; that the wells when completed began to produce oil in paying quantities, whereupon it was decided by plaintiffs and defendants to equip the wells for pumping and to operate them as pumping wells which was done in the month of March or April, 1891, and had been pumped continuously from that time, and during this time plaintiffs had laid out and expended for labor and expenses upon and about the lease and wells, and for supplies and material furnished, $7,900.00; that plaintiffs having expended the sum of about $14,000 for and about the development and operation of the property, 5-12 of which, only, was properly chargeable to and payable by them; that there remained large sums of money due and owing on this account from them, the defendants, to plaintiff, the amount of which plaintiffs could not state with exactness; that since the months of March, April and September, 1891, when the work of pumping and operating the wells was commenced, defendants had laid out and expended various sums of money in paying for labor and expenses upon and about the same, and for supplies and materials furnished to and for the wells, but how much money was thus expended, and in what proportion by each of the defendants, plaintiffs were ignorant, and could not state, for want of knowledge, except that it would be much less than the sums laid out and expended upon the joint account by plaintiffs as described in the bill; that upon an account taken of the expenditures and outlay by both plaintiffs and defendants upon the common property, the lease and wells aforesaid, defendants would be entitled to a credit for all legitimate and proper expenditures, and· outlay upon and about the common property; nevertheless, that after deducting all possible proper credits, there would remain a large balance or sum of money due from defendants to plaintiffs; that it was necessary that an account be taken between the plaintiffs and defendants; that defendants while not denying that there was a large sum of money due from them to plaintiffs, would not agree upon the amount thus due, and failed, refused and neglected to pay the balance due plaintiffs; that plaintiffs had made repeated efforts to have a settlement, but had failed to obtain it. Plaintiffs prayed for an accounting and for proper decrees for the balance due. Defendants demurred to the bill, upon the ground that plaintiffs had an ample, adequate, and complete remedy at law under the statutes of Pennsylvania. The court sustained the demurrer and dismissed the plaintiff's bill, and plaintiffs appealed to the Supreme Court, where the decree of dismissal was reversed, and the defendants were directed to answer the bill and the cause was remanded.

CHAPTER 31.

PARTITION OF OIL AND GAS RIGHTS.

Sec. 1.—Partition cannot be made of the rights and privileges granted in the ordinary oil and gas lease. Such lease does not convey an interest in real estate, or any title to the oil and gas which may be in the leased premises. It merely creates the privilege of exploring for oil and gas, and the right to sever the same, if found.

Beardsley v. *Kansas Nat. Gas Co.*, 78 Kan. 571; 96 Pac. 589.
Emery v. *League*, 31 Tex. App. 474; 72 S. W. 603.
Ziegler v. *Brenneman*, 237 Ill. 15; 86 N. E. 597.
Waterford Oil & Gas Co. v. *Shipman*, 233 Ill. 9; 84 N.'E. 53.

Sec. 2.—Partition of oil and gas owned by co-owners, separate from the surface, cannot be decreed except by sale and division of the proceeds. A judicial partition thereof by assignment of the oil and gas under sections of the surface is void.

Hall v. *Vernon*, 47 W. Va. 295; 34 S. E. 764.
Preston v. *White*, 57 W. Va. 278; 50 S. E. 236.

Sec. 3.—In *Hall* v. *Vernon*, 47 W. Va. 295; 34 S. E. 764, (Dec. 2, 1899), the syllabus is as follows:

"Partition of oil and gas owned by co-owners, separate from the surface cannot be decreed, except by sale and division of the proceeds. A judicial partition thereof by assignment of the oil and gas under sections of the surface is void."

Hall, Vernon and Donaho were the owners of the oil, gas and mineral rights in a tract of 1100 acres of land in Wirt County, West Virginia. Hall and Vernon instituted a suit in chancery against Donaho for a partition either by allotment of certain sections of the surface, or if that were not legal or practicable, then by sale of the whole mineral interest, and a division of the proceeds. During the pendency of the suit, after a decree authorizing partition by allotment of sections of the surface, if that could be done, or by sale of the entire mineral rights, and appointing commissioners to make report on the question of partition, Hall and Vernon became dissatisfied with the conduct of each other and ceased to co-operate in the management of the litigation; and Vernon, without Hall's consent or knowledge, caused a report to be made by the commissioners, whereby the commissioners reported that partition could be made of the minerals by allotting the surface in strips, and Vernon proceeded to cause a decree to be entered carrying into effect this scheme of partition. When Hall discovered what had been done by Vernon he filed a bill in equity in the Circuit Court of Wirt County against Vernon and Donaho for the cancellation and rescission of the decree of partition, and all proceedings taken by the commissioners, and the cancellation of the deed, if any, made

by the commissioners appointed to carry out the decree confirming
the commissioner's report. An injunction was awarded Hall, enjoining Vernon from operating wells already drilled on some of the
sections which were allotted to Vernon in the partition. The Circuit Court dissolved Hall's injunction and dismissed his bill. From
this decree Hall appealed to the Court of Appeals, and that court
reversed the Circuit Court, citing:

> *Wood Co. Petroleum Co.* v. *West Va. Transportation Co.*, 28
>   W. Va. 210.
> *Shepherd* v. *Oil Co.*, 38 Hun. 37.
> *Funk* v. *Halderman*, 53 Pa. 229.
> *Smith* v. *Cooley*, 65 Cal. 46; 2 Pac. 880.
> *Kemble* v. *Kemble*, 44 N. J. Eq. 454; 11 Atl. 733.
> *Franklinite Co.* v. *Condit*, 19 N. J. Eq. 394.
> *Grubb* v. *Beard*, 2 Wall Jr. 81; Fed. Case, No. 5849.
> *Hughes* v. *Devlin*, 23 Cal. 505.
> *Lenfers* v. *Henke*, 73 Ill. 405.
> *Marble Co.* v. *Ripley*, 10 Wall. 339; 19 L. Ed. 955.

Sec. 4.—In *Preston* v. *White*, 57 W. Va. 278; 50 S. E. 236,
analyzed under Chapter 27, Judge Brannon, delivering the opinion
of the Court at page 284, said:

"As to the assignment of error that a partition in kind was
not made of the oil and gas, it is enough to say that the case of
Hall v. *Vernon*, 47 W. Va. 295, holds, that joint owners of oil
and gas only, not owning the surface, cannot have partition in
kind by lines upon the surface, but only by sale of the oil and
gas, and division of the proceeds."

The oil and gas interests underlying a tract of land in Lewis
County, West Virginia, formerly owned by Louis Bennett and
others, portions of which became by sale the property of Preston,
Knapp and Hoskins, and a portion became vested in one White.
Preston and others instituted a suit in chancery in the Circuit
Court of Lewis County against G. L. White and others, praying for
a partition of the oil and gas rights. The Circuit Court entered
a decree determining the interests of Preston, Knapp and Hoskins
to be seven-eighths, and the interest of White to be one-eighth of
the oil and gas, decreeing that these oil and gas interests were
not susceptible of partition and directing their public sale. White
appealed, and the Court of Appeals affirmed the Circuit Court.

Sec. 5.—In *Beardsley* v. *Kansas Natural Gas Co.*, 78 Kan. 571; 96 Pac. 589 (July 3, 1908), syls. 3-4-5 are as follows:

"3. In an action by the lessees in an oil and gas lease for a partition of their interests thereunder, the lessors are not necessary parties.

4. The provision of the statute relating to partition applies to real estate, only.

5. An ordinary oil and gas lease does not convey an interest in real estate, or any title to the oil and gas which may be in the leased premises. It merely creates the privilege of exploring for oil and gas, and the right to sever the same if found."

B. L. and Josie Frost were the owners of a tract of land in Montgomery County, Kansas, for which they executed an oil and gas lease. The lease was owned by Henry Beardsley, ½; Mr. White, 1-8, and the Kansas Natural Gas Company, 3-8. Beardsley instituted an action in the District Court of Montgomery County, Kansas, against the other owners of the lease for the purpose of obtaining a partition of the rights held under the lease. Frosts, the landowners, were not summoned in the suit. The defendant, the Kansas Natural Gas Company, demurred to the petition and the demurrer was sustained; the plaintiff declining to plead further, the petition was dismissed and plaintiff brought the case for review to the Supreme Court. That Court affirmed the District Court, and as to the nature of an oil and gas lease, and for the proposition that such lease created a mere license to enter and explore for oil and gas and did not create an interest in the land, the court cited:

Rawlings v. *Armel*, 70 Kan, 778; 79 Pac. 683.
Gas Co. v. *Neosho Co.*, 75 Kan. 339; 89 Pac. 750.
Martin v. *Crude Oil Co.*, 77 Kan. 851; 92 Pac. 1119.

Sec. 6.—In *Waterford Oil & Gas Co.* v. *Shipman*, 233 Ill. 9; 84 N. E. 53, analyzed under Chapter 14, syl. 1 is as follows:

"Where a co-tenant leased the lands held in common to plaintiff for the purpose of drilling and operating for oil and gas, but afterwards, with the other co-tenants granted the oil and gas right to another person, plaintiff, to secure the interest granted him, cannot have compulsory partition either of the oil and gas apart from the land or the land itself, since such a lease being merely a grant of the privilege to enter and prospect, and not giving title to the oil or gas until such products are found, in a conveyance of the interest of one co-tenant in the common property or any part thereof.

Sec. 7.—In *Emery* v. *League*, 31 Tex. App. 474; 72 S. W. 603 (Feb. 25, 1903), the syllabus is as follows:

"1. The owners of an undivided interest in land made a contract in consideration of the payment of the lands value before development, whereby they leased their interest for the purpose of prospecting for petroleum, minerals, etc. The contract gave the grantee the exclusive right to prospect and the right of entry for this purpose, and to construct railroads, buildings, etc., necessary for prospecting and developing any mineral resources discovered, which on discovery, were to become his property, the grantors to have a certain per cent. of the gross output. It was stipulated that the grantee should commence operations within six months after partition, and should have six months after 'said period of time aforesaid' in which to prospect the land and complete a well. The contract was to remain in force so long as the parties should faithfully comply with it, and the grantee was empowered to abandon the contract on its becoming unprofitable. By another instrument the grantee agreed to secure a partition. *Held,* that the instrument was not an executed contract conferring on the grantee vested rights but merely gave him an option so that compliance with its provisions was necessary to secure a vested interest.

2. To retain his rights under the instrument it was necessary that the grantee should secure a partition within a reasonable time.

3. The lease was executed March 14, 1901. On July 3, 1901, a third party began partition proceedings, and on October 1, 1901, the grantee was informed of the stipulation which had been made by his agent for partition. He claimed that his agent had not informed him of it, but that he would comply with it. On February 21, 1902, the lessee filed an answer in the suit already begun offering to pay the costs of partitioning the interests covered by the contract. Two terms of the Circuit Court were held without the execution of the lease, and the term at which the partition suit was brought. *Held,* that this was not such diligence to comply with the provisions of the contract as would prevent a forfeiture of the grantee's rights."

J. C. League instituted a partition suit against Hugh Jackson, L. L. Emery and others to partition a tract of land in Galveston County, Texas. The petition alleged that L. L. Emery was asserting some claim or interest in the land sought to be partitioned. The defendant, Jackson, answered the petition, asserting title to an undivided 11.8 involved in the suit, and asked as against plaintiff and all the other defendants that the interest be set aside to him. Defendant, L. L. Emery, answered, setting up a claim to all the mineral rights in and under the land claimed by Jackson, and averred that he had acquired the mineral rights under and by virtue of a contract executed by the owner of an interest in the land— Neville Montaut. Montaut was the vendor of Jackson, and the instrument under which Emery claimed was prior to the conveyance to Jackson. The option or contract under which Emery claimed contained the following provision:

"And further provided the party of the second part shall begin operations in good faith on the lands hereby leased for the purposes above indicated within six months after the final division setting apart of their respective shares; and said party of the second part shall have six months after said period of time aforesaid, in which to prospect said land, and to complete a well. And said party of the second part shall pay all damages if he interferes with the improvements or growing crops on said lands. This deed and contract shall remain in force and effect between the respective parties hereto, their legal representatives, heirs, successors or assigns, so long as the respective parties hereto comply faithfully with the covenants, stipulations and agreement by each respectively undertaken to be done and performed."

The answer of Emery further averred that as a part of the agreement he was to secure a partition of the property; further averring that Jackson was the owner in fee of the land covered by his contract, and asking that said interest in the land be set apart to Jackson, subject to the rights of Emery in and under his contract with the former owner. To this answer defendant, Jackson, replied by supplemental answer in which he admitted the execution of the contract claimed by Emery, admitted that the interest in the land was covered by the contract, and that he, Jackson, purchased the same with notice; but averred that said contract was void, first, for want of mutuality, second, for failure of consideration in that the real consideration for the same was the promise and agreement of Emery to procure without delay, and free of cost

to his vendors, a partition of the land, and to explore, prospect and
develop the land for oil and other minerals; and that in the performance of the agreement and undertaking Emery had wholly
failed; third, because by the terms of the contract it was provided
that the same should be effective only so long as the parties thereto should faithfully comply with the covenants and agreements
therein undertaken to be performed; and that said Emery, having
never performed or offered to perform any of the covenants
or agreements prior to the filing in the suit on October 7,
1901, his cross bill seeking a cancellation of the contract, the defendant, Jackson, by filing said crossbill elected said contract void,
and that the same was no longer of binding force and effect;
fourth, because said Emery by his unreasonable delay in procuring or attempting to procure a partition of said lands, forfeited his
rights, if any he had, under said contract, and could not be heard
to assert the same. Upon these grounds Jackson asked for a cancellation of Emery's contract. The facts disclosed by the record
of the case were: The lands adjudged to Hugh Jackson by the
court were purchased by him on May 9, 1901, from J. C. League,
who had purchased from Neville and Sylvester Montaut, and F.
Harrington, on April 29, 1901. This land was included in the
lease contract executed by and between Neville Montaut and wife,
and F. Harrington, as parties of the first part, and L. L. Emery as
party of the second part, under date March 14, 1901. Jackson purchased the land with notice of the contract. After the execution of
the contract Emery did nothing towards partition of the land, and
testified that he did not know that his agent, Ostrom, who procured the contract for him, had bound him to secure
a partition of the land, until he was so notified by
the purchaser, Jackson, about October 1, 1901, after he,
Emery, had filed his answer in the suit; and that he then
declared to the parties that he would pay his portion of the cost
of partition. In this conversation Jackson informed Emery that
he did not regard the lease contract as binding on him. Emery
was never in possession of any portion of the land; and never made
any explorations thereon for oil or minerals, nor made any preparation for prospecting or developing the same. The suit was instituted July 3, 1901, by J. C. League, who was the owner of an
undivided interest in the tract of land, of which the land in controversy was a part. No demand was made upon Emery by his
lessors that he should begin operations under the contract, or that

he should proceed to secure a partition of the land. The agreement to secure a partition of the land was made by a duly authorized agent of Emery at the time of the execution of the lease, and was a part of the same. At the time the lease contract was made the lands adjoining that covered by the contract were being prospected upon for oil, and wells were being sunk thereon. If the land covered by the contract should prove not to be oil land, the amount paid by Emery for the rights conveyed by the contract, should be equal to the value of the land; but should oil be discovered on the land its value should be increased to as much as \$3,000 per acre. The trial court entered a decree cancelling the Emery lease, and Emery appealed. The Appellate Court affirmed the decree, and cited:

Oil Co. v. *Teal,* 67 S. W. 545.
Venture Oil Co. v. *Fretts,* 152 Pa. 451; 25 Atl. 733.
Huggins v. *Daley,* 40 C. C. A. 12; 99 Fed. 613.
Eclipse Oil Co. v. *South Penn Oil Co.,* 47 W. Va. 84; 37 S. E. 923.
Cowan v. *Iron Co.,* 3 S. E. 120.

Sec. 8.—In *Ziegler* v. *Brenneman,* 86 N. E. 597; 237 Ill. 15 (Dec. 15, 1908), the syllabus is as follows:

"1. No estoppel arises to assert an interest in premises or to object to their being operated for oil because of silence and acquiescence while others expended large sums and demonstrated the great value of the property while during the time of their silence such parties did not know that they had an interest and within a reasonable time after its ascertainment gave notice thereof.

2. An oil and gas lease made by a tenant in common to a stranger is void as against his co-tenant.

3. An oil and gas lease made by a tenant in common to a stranger, though void as against his co-tenants, is valid as between the parties even while the premises remain undivided.

4. Where a tenant in common leased the lands held in common to another, to drill and operate for oil and gas, and thereafter all the co-tenants joined in a like lease to a different person, neither of the lessees could maintain partition to secure the interest granted him.

5. Nor had either of them a right to operate without the others consent."

George Ziegler, Edgar D. Ziegler, Earnest Ziegler and Annie Price were the owners in fee simple as tenants in common of lands in Crawford County, Illinois, of which George Ziegler was the owner of an undivided 1-2, and Edgar Ziegler, Earnest Ziegler, and Annie Price each owned an undivided 1-6. These lands were in oil and gas territory. George Ziegler and Martha V. Ziegler, his wife, each became the owners of an undivided ½ interest in this land, on February 11, 1865. About nine years before the institution of this suit Martha Ziegler died, seized of her interest in the property, leaving no will, and leaving surviving her her husband, George Ziegler, and Edgar D. Ziegler, Earnest Ziegler, and Annie Price, her children and only heirs at law. After her death her husband continued to occupy the premises, and up to the time prior to the beginning of the suit managed and controlled the same as if it were his own property. On June 9, 1905, George Ziegler and Rachael, his wife, executed an oil and gas lease to W. W. Seibert for the term of three years, and so long thereafter as oil or gas should be produced from the land and royalties and rentals paid, giving to Seibert or his assigns, the exclusive right to mine for and produce oil and gas from said tract of land. Seibert assigned and transferred all his right, title and interest in the lease on April, 3, 1906, to I. E. Ackley, trustee, and on January 29, 1907, Ackley as trustee assigned and transferred all his right, title and interest to L. A. Brenneman and A. T. McDonald. These assignments were duly recorded. During the month of February, 1907, Brenneman and McDonald began drilling on the land and about March 11, 1907, completed a paying well. Shortly after the completion of the well Brenneman and McDonald began the drilling of a second well. After the second rig had been erected by them, Edgar D. Ziegler gave notice to their agent, who was operating the land, that he and his brother and sister had an interest in the land, and warned the agent that his principals should not operate further. On June 25, 1907, George Ziegler, Edgar D. Ziegler and Earnest Ziegler, together with their wives, and Annie Price and her husband, executed an oil and gas lease for the premises to C. A. Rapp for the term of ten years and as long thereafter as oil or gas or either of them should be produced from the land. By a mistake of the scrivener who drew this instrument the land was misdescribed, and on February 17, 1908, on learning of the mistake the lease was re-executed and the land property described. Shortly after the execution of the lease in June, 1907, Rapp went on the premises with his employes and began the erection of the derrick for the purpose of drilling a well, but before he had accomplished much, Brenneman and McDonald removed his tools and machinery from the land. Rapp then procured a force of men, replaced his appliances on the land and proceeded to dismantle and destroy the machinery of Brenneman and McDonald. A truce was then arranged between the various parties, and it was agreed that the matter should be submitted to the courts. Rapp then drilled a well. George Ziegler, Edgar Ziegler, Earnest Ziegler, and Annie Price then filed a bill in equity in the Circuit Court of Crawford County, against L. A. Brenneman, A. T. McDonald and others, praying for a cancellation of the lease executed by George Ziegler and wife, and the assignment of the lease of the land, as a cloud upon the title of the plaintiffs. An injunction was awarded restraining the defendants from in any manner interfering with C. A. Rapp or his assigns in drilling or operating for oil or gas on the premises, and from entering thereon for the purpose of prospecting or drilling for oil or gas, or from doing any act tending to the production of oil therefrom. A receiver was appointed who took charge of and operated the property. The Circuit Court entered a decree in favor of some of the plaintiffs. Brenneman and another appealed, and the Supreme Court reversed the Circuit Court and remanded the cause with specific directions to the Circuit Court to enter a decree cancelling the lease made by George Ziegler and wife to Seibert, in so far as the lease and the assignments thereof conveyed any right, privilege or license in and to the interest in the real estate which Martha V. Ziegler's children inherited from her, but leaving this lease and the assignments in full force and effect so far as they purported to convey the interest of George Ziegler in the real estate, the decree to be entered to provide for the division of the oil already produced, or its proceeds, as follows: The oil produced before June 25, 1907, the date of the first lease to Rapp, or its proceeds, to be divided without any charge for its production, in the following manner: 1-16 to George Ziegler; 7-16 to Brenneman and McDonald; and to each of the three children of Martha V. Ziegler the 1-6 part. All the oil produced on and after June 25, 1907, down to the date of the appointment of the receiver, or its proceeds, without any charge for production, to be divided in the manner following: To George Ziegler 3-48; to Brenneman and McDonald 21-48; to each of the three children of Martha V. Ziegler, 1-36, and to Rapp the 20-48 part. The

oil produced since the date of the appointment of the receiver, or
its proceeds, after disbursements and charges, to be divided in the
same manner as the oil above mentioned, which was produced on
and after June 25, 1907, down to the date of the appointment of the
Receiver.

REMEDIES.

Sec. 9.—One or more co-owners of a lease for oil and gas
purposes cannot maintain a suit for partition in kind against the
other co-owners.

(See autherities, Sec. 1, supra.)

Sec. 10.—Where one or more co-owners of a mining partnership desire a partition, the remedy is by bill in equity for an accounting, dissolution of the partnership, and sale of the partnership assets.

(See authorities, Chapter 30.)

Sec. 11.—Where one or more owners of oil or gas rights or
interests in lands desire a division, the remedy of such owner is by
bill in equity for a sale of the whole oil or gas interest, and division
of the proceeds of the sale. A decree cannot be made partitioning
mining rights and interests in kind.

Hall v. *Vernon,* 47 W. Va. 295; 34 S. E. 764.
Preston v. *White,* 57 W. Va. 278; 50 S. E. 236.

CHAPTER 32.

TENANTS IN COMMON OR JOINT TENANTS—RIGHT TO EXECUTE OIL AND GAS LEASE OR DEVELOP.

Sec. 1.—All joint tenants or tenants in common owning lands
must join in an oil or gas lease to make it valid. One joint tenant
or tenant in common cannot make an oil and gas lease binding
the other joint tenant or tenants in common. Where a lessee en-

ters under a lease made by one joint tenant and engages in the production of oil and gas he may be enjoined by the other joint tenants or tenants in common, as such production constitutes waste. Where such lessee produces the oil or gas and markets the same he is liable to the tenants in common or joint tenants, who did not join in the lease, to the extent of their right in the land. Where one tenant in common is in sole possession of the lands, claiming exclusive ownership, and executes an oil and gas lease for the whole property, and the lessee enters and takes petroleum oil and natural gas under such lease and converts it to his own use, he is liable to account to the joint tenants or tenants in common who did not join in the lease, on the basis of rents and profits, not for annual rental. An oil and gas lease executed by one or more joint tenants or tenants in common, while not binding on the other joint tenants or tenants in common, is good between the parties and is binding on their interests.

Williamson v. *Jones*, 43 W. Va. 562; 27 S. E. 411.
Headley v. *Hoopengarner*, 60 W. Va. 626; 55 S. E. 144.
Kilcoyne v. *Southern Oil Co.*, 61 W. Va. 538; 55 S. E. 888.
Pyle v. *Henderson*, 65 W. Va. 39; 63 S. E. 620.
Waterford Oil & Gas Co. v. *Shipman*, 233 Ill. 9; 84 N. E. 53.
Ziegler v. *Brenneman*, 237 Ill. 15; 86 N. E. 597.
Trees v. *Eclipse Oil Co.*, 47 W. Va. 107; 34 S. E. 933.
Compton v. *Peoples Gas Co.*, 75 Kan. 572; 89 Pac. 1029; 10 L. R. A. (N. S.) 758.
Swint v. *Oil Co.*, 184 Pa. 202; 38 Atl. 1020.
McNeely v. *South Penn Oil Co.*, 58 W. Va. 438; 44 S. E. 508.
Wilson v. *Goldstein*, 152 Pa. 524; 25 Atl. 493.
Heinouer v. *Jones*, 159 Pa. 228; 28 Atl. 228.
Summers v. *Bennett,*— W. Va.·—; 69 S. E. 690.
Stewart v. *Tennant*, 52 W. Va. 559; 44 S. E. 223.

Sec. 2.—In *Williamson* v. *Jones*, 43 W. Va. 562; 27 S. E. 411, analyzed under Chapter 27, syls. 4-13 are as follows:

"4. It is waste in a tenant in common to take petroleum oil from the land, for which he is liable to his co-tenants to the extent of their right in the land.

13. A tenant for life, or a tenant in common, in sole possession, claiming exclusive ownership, taking petroleum oil and converting it to his exclusive use, is liable to account on the basis of rents and profits, not for annual rental."

Sec. 3.—In *Trees* v. *Eclipse Oil Co.*, 47 W. Va. 107; 34 S. E. 933, analyzed under Chapter 14, syl. 3 is as follows:

"A person holding a valid executory oil and gas lease, executed by several of the number of co-tenants, has such an inchoate interest in the land subject to such lease as will enable him to maintain an injunction to prevent a wrongdoer from committing waste by the extraction of such oil and gas."

Sec. 4.—In *Headley* v. *Hoopengarner*, 60 W. Va. 626; 55 S. E. 144, analyzed under Chapter 18, syl. 4 is as follows:

"4. Where, in a summary proceeding instituted under Chapter 83, Code, for the purpose of selling the undivided interests of infants to the oil and gas in certain lands inherited by them from their father, one purchases the interests of the infants sold thereunder, and agrees to pay a stipulated royalty therefor, he will not be relieved from the payment of such royalty after the sale is confirmed and deed made, on the ground that the father, in his lifetime, disposed of one-sixteenth of all the oil and gas produced on said lands; nor can such proceedings be re-opened and corrected, but they are final and conclusive upon all the parties thereto, except for after discovered mutual mistake of material facts, or fraud, and, where relied upon, such mistake or fraud must be clearly and distinctly alleged and proved."

Sec. 5.—In *Kilcoyne* v. *Southern Oil Co.*, 61 W. Va. 538; 55 S. E. 888, analyzed under Chapter 18, the syllabus is as follows:

"1. There is an implied covenant for good title and peaceable and quiet possession in a lease for years for oil and gas.
2. Such implied covenant of warranty is not limited to the right of exploration for oil and gas, but when produced the right to the amount stipulated for in the lease is likewise thereby protected."

Sec. 6.—In *Pyle* v. *Henderson*, 65 W. Va. 39; 63 S. E. 620, analyzed under Chapter 6, syls. 2-3 are as follows:

"2. Where in an oil lease there is a clause that it shall be void if a well is not completed or in lien of its money paid, within a given time, and before the expiration of the time it is found that the lessor's title is defective and he agrees to perfect it, and agrees that the money need not be paid when due, and gives an extension for payment until the title can be perfected, he cannot declare a forfeiture and make a second lease. A second lease taken with notice of the first, is void as to the first lease.

3. In case of such lease, if the lessor by his conduct clearly indicates, that payment will not be demanded when due and thus lulls the lessee into a feeling of security and throws him off his guard, and because of this he does not make payments when due, the landlord cannot suddenly without demand. or notice declare a forfeiture, and there is no forfeiture which equity would recognize, and if there is in such case, technically a forfeiture at law, equity would relieve against it.''

Sec. 7.—In *Waterford Oil & Gas Co.* v. *Shipman,* 233 Ill. 9; 84 N. E. 53, analyzed under Chapter 14, syls. 1-4 are as follows:

''1. Where a co-tenant leased the lands held in common to plaintiff for the purpose of drilling and operating for oil and gas but afterwards, with the other co-tenants, granted the oil and gas right to another person, plaintiff, to secure the interest granted him, cannot have compulsory partition either of the oil and gas apart from the land, or the land itself, since such a lease being merely a grant of the privilege to enter and prospect, and not giving title to the oil or gas until such products are found, in a conveyance of the interest of one co-tenant in the common property or any part thereof.''

4. A co-tenant leased the lands held in common to plaintiff for the purpose of drilling and operating for oil and gas. The lease provided that the lessee upon payment of a dollar might surrender the lease. Thereafter the co-tenants granted the oil and gas rights to another person. *Held,* that the option to terminate the lease at any time deprived plaintiff of the right to specific performance, directly or indirectly, until he had performed the contract or placed himself in such a position that he might be compelled to perform it on his part, and hence, he cannot have a compulsory partition either of the oil and gas apart from the land or of the land itself.''

Sec. 8.—In *Ziegler* v. *Brenneman,* 237 Ill. 15; 86 N. E. 597, analyzed under Chapter 31, syls. 2-3-4-5 are as follows:

''2. An oil and gas lease made by a tenant in common to a stranger is void as against his co-tenant.

3. An oil and gas lease made by a tenant in common to a stranger, though void as against his co-tenants, is valid as between the parties, even while the premises remain undivided.

4. Where a tenant in common leased the lands held in common to another, to drill and operate for oil and gas, and thereafter all the co-tenants joined in a like lease to a different person, neither of the lessees could maintain partition to secure the interest granted him.

5. Nor had either of them a right to operate without the others consent.''

Sec. 9.—In *Compton* v. *Peoples Gas Co.*, 75 Kan. 572; 89 Pac. 1029; 10 L. R. A. (N. S.) 758, analyzed under Chapter 17, syls. 2-3-4 are as follows:

''2. An oil and gas lease upon lands of which a widow owns an undivided one-half, and the other half belongs to the children, and a part thereof is occupied by the family as a homestead, is not void because executed by the widow alone. It conveys her undivided interest in the oil and gas privileges subject to the right of those occupying the premises as a homestead.

3. A subsequent oil and gas lease of the same land to a third party, executed by the children after the youngest child has reached majority, conveys the undivided interest of the children in the oil and gas privileges. Each lessee is entitled to the premises for the purpose of mining for oil and gas, but neither is entitled to exclusive possession.

4. Where an oil and gas lease has been accepted by the lessee and valuable improvements made thereunder, and the lessor has accepted the benefits and consideration, one who takes a subsequent lease with notice of the fact and of the terms and conditions of the former lease, takes subject thereto and will not be permitted to question the validity of the former on the ground that it lacks mutuality, or that it has been revoked by the giving of the subsequent lease.''

Sec. 10.—In *Swint* v. *Oil Co.*, 184 Pa. 202; 38 Atl. 1020 (Jan. 3, 1898), syls. 2-3 are as follows:

''2. Where co-tenants join in a lease reserving a common rent payable to the lessors jointly, either of them may receive and give a valid receipt for the entire rent, until notice by one or more of the co-tenants that his share must be paid to himself.

3. Where there is a joint lease by two tenants in common for an entire rental, and neither tenant in common has given notice to the lessee to pay his share of the rent to himself, an assignment by one of the tenants in common to a stranger of all his interest in

the rental does not cause an apportionment of the rent, or affect in the slightest degree the rights or remedies of the other tenant in common.''

Peter Swint was the owner in fee simple of a farm in Allegheny County, containing about 120 acres. J. E. Swint was his son. In 1885 J. E. Swint was of full age and residing with his father on the farm. It was alleged by him that he was associated with his father in the cultivation of the soil, under some sort of verbal agreement, but no distinct contract between them was shown. In 1885, Peter Swint made a lease for oil purposes of part of his farm to Hunter. Two years later he leased the whole farm, subject to the prior lease of Hunter, to H. H. Locke. J. E. Swint, the son, was joined with his father as a co-lessor in both leases. The royalty reserved in the lease was one-eighth part of the oil produced, which was to be delivered to the lessor in the pipelines of the company transporting the oil from the well. It appeared that the lessees delivered the oil in the pipeline for the royalty to the lessor and that the father, the owner of the land, and his vendees after him, had taken possession of the entire 1-8 of the oil so delivered as royalty, and receipted to the lessees therefor. J. E. Swint gave no notice prior to the bringing of his suit of his claim to have half the royalty paid to him, or of any objection on his part to the payment of the whole royalty to his colessor. Peter Swint and J. E. Swint, for the use of J. E. Swint, brought suit in assumpsit in the Court of Common Pleas, Number 1, Allegheny County, against the McCalmont Oil Company for rentals claimed under an oil lease. J. E. Swint, in this action, sought to recover half the royalties, regardless of the fact that they had been paid to the holder of his father's title, and without objection on his part. Verdict and judgment was rendered for defendant, upon binding instructions given by the court. Plaintiff appealed. The Supreme Court affirmed the judgment.

Sec. 11.—In *McNeely* v. *South Penn Oil Company*, 58 W. Va. 438; 44 S. E. 508 (Dec. 5, 1905), the syllabus is as follows:

''1. The basis of accounting, between tenants in common, joint tenants and co-partners, for waste, effected by the extraction of petroleum oil from the common property, under circumstances which make it reasonably certain that the party, so taking oil, acted without fraud and under the belief of good title to himself to the whole of the property, though not without notice of defect of title, is the value of all the oil produced from the land, less the whole cost of its production, including the cost of drilling producing wells.

2. If one co-tenant executes an oil lease, purporting to convey the whole of the common property under which the lessee produces oil, delivering to the lessors part thereof as royalty, it is proper to require the lessor and lessee jointly to make reparation to the injured co-tenant, and to order satisfaction of the decree against them to be made out of proceeds of the oil in the hands of the sepcial receiver in the cause.

3. In such case, rentals received by the co-tenant in possession for delay in drilling, under a provision of the lease, constitute no part of the damages, and should not be included in the decree, nor are they to be accounted for as rents and profits, unless the lease is ratified, or acquiesced in by the other co-tenants.

4. A mere demand for discovery as to, and accounting for such rentals in a bill, expressly denying the title of the lessor and validity of the lease, does not amount to a ratification or adoption of the lease.''

C. B. McNeely and others filed a bill in equity in the Circuit Court of Wetzel County, West Virginia, against the South Penn Oil Company and others. The facts were as follows: By deed April 4, 1873, Edgell conveyed to Nathan Higgins and Mary Higgins, his wife, a tract of 100 acres of land. By written agreement, September 23, 1873, between Nathan Higgins and John W. Starkey, they exchanged lands, Higgins agreeing to convey to Starkey sai d tract of land, and Starkey agreed to convey to Higgins a tract of 50 acres. Mary Higgins was not a party to this agreement. She died on February 12, 1875, and her husband died in April, 1898. The agreement recited that the land was the Allen Edgell farm, and provided that Starkey should pay Higgins $125.00 in cash, payable in future installments. By deed July 26, 1875, Nathan Higgins conveyed to Starkey the 100 acres, reserving a lien for unpaid purchase money. The agreement provided for immediate delivery of possession of the two tracts under the exchange, and a son of Nathan Higgins, living on the 100 acres, moved from it, and another son moved on the 50 acres, and Starkey moved from the 50 acres, and took actual possession of the 100 acres on October 3, 1873. The deed from Higgins to Starkey referred to date and record of the deed from Edgell to Starkey and wife. By certain conveyances the Corning Oil Company and others derivatively from Starkey, became lessees of 26 acres of the 100 acres, under a lease for oil and gas purposes, and the South Penn Oil Company became lessee of the residue, 74 acres; about February 11, 1897, the Corning Oil Company and others jointly owning with it the lease of the 26 acres went into possession and drilled several producing oil wells on the 26 acres. On August 21, 1895, the South Penn Oil Company under its lease of the 74 acres took actual possession, and drilled several producing wells. McNeely and others acquired the interests of certain children and heirs at law of Mary Higgins, and they, together with certain other heirs, filed their bill calling for an accounting of all oils from the land, and payment to the plaintiffs for the same. The Circuit Court decided the case in favor of defendant, and plaintiffs appealed to the Court of Appeals, and that court reversed the decree and remanded the cause. (52 W. Va. 616.)

This was the second appeal. After the case was remanded to the Circuit Court the South Penn Oil Company filed its second amended and supplemental answer, claiming the right to account on the basis of the value of the oil in place, which it claimed was the value of 1-8 of all the oil produced. Upon exception to the answer, so much of it as set up this claim was stricken out by the court. The cause was then recommitted to a commissioner to take further testimony and ascertain and report the amount and value of all the oil obtained from the land occupied by the company with its oil operations, the amount and value of such part thereof, as had been received by John W. Starkey, the lessor, and the amount of money expended by the oil company in operating for and producing the oil so obtained by it. A receiver had been appointed who, together with the Eureka Pipeline Company, were required to report the amount of oil received by them, respectively, and the disposition made thereof, and the prices at which any of it had been sold. The commissioner reported that the South Penn Oil Company had taken from the 74 acres of land occupied by it, oil amounting in value to $47,800.75, of which amount $3,592.11 had been paid by it to J. W. Starkey, the lessor, as royalty, and that the cost of producing the whole amount of oil thus obtained had been $35,698.24, making the sum of $12,102.51 the value of the production from the land, less the cost thereof. To this report both the plaintiffs and the South Penn Oil Company excepted, the former because the commissioner had allowed the cost of production to be taken out of the value of the oil, and the latter because the commissioner had refused to find and report, as the amount due the plaintiffs, the 1-2 of 1-8 of all the oil produced. The court overruled all the exceptions, and decreed to the plaintiffs on account of oil produced the sum of $6,051.25, and in addition thereto $138.67, 1-2 of the cash rentals which had been paid to Starkey, making a total of $6,189.92. The South Penn Company appealed to the Court of Appeals, where the appeal was modified by striking out the item $138.67, 1-2 the rentals paid to Starkey by the South Penn Oil Company, and also by striking out of the decree in favor of the plaintiffs 5-74 of the amount ascertained to be due from Starkey and the South Penn Oil Company on account of three infant children of Louis Higgins, a son of Mary Higgins, who were defendants in the cause and who were entitled to 5-74 of the amount. The corrections being made the Court of Appeals decreed in favor of plaintiff, against the South Penn Oil Company and Starkey, $5,642.38. With the modifications the decree was affirmed.

Sec. 12.—In *Stewart* v. *Tennant*, 52 W. Va. 559; 44 S. E. 223 (March 28, 1903), syls. 11-12-13 are as follows:

"11. Tenants in common, committing waste against a cotenant, are wrongdoers, and may be sued on account thereof jointly or separately, and when sued jointly, it is not error to dismiss the cause as to one of them, on motion of the plaintiff, and over the objection of the other.

12. Where, before assignment of dower, one claiming by purchase from certain heirs and the widow, drills oil wells upon the land, and extracts large quantities of oil therefrom, without having obtained the consent of his co-tenants to such development, and such non-consenting co-tenant brings his suit for an accounting, it is error to decree to him his entire interest in the oil produced, and thereafter to be produced, free from any charge on account of the dower interest.

13. In such case, the holder of the dower interest is entitled to the interest on one-third of the proceeds of the oil going to the non-consenting co-tenant, until the death of the doweress, and until that date the fund upon which such interest is paid remains under the control of the court through its general receiver."

Lewis Stewart filed a bill in equity in the Circuit Court of Tyler County against Jacob S. Tennant and others for relief from certain alleged erroneous decrees pronounced by the same court in a former chancery suit under which Tennant and one Cassie A. Tennant by judicial sale acquired the title, as they claimed, to a certain tract of land, and afterwards leased the tract for oil and gas purposes to the South Penn Oil Company, and for an accounting on the part of the defendants, for 1-12 of the oil taken from the land. The case was substantially as follows:

James Stewart, the owner of a tract of land containing 176 acres, died in 1889, intestate, and left surviving him a widow and twelve children. Afterwards, and prior to July 1, 1890, Jacob S. Tennant and Cassie A. Tennant purchased the undivided interest of six of said children._ They then brought a partition suit praying for an assignment of the dower and division of the land in which suit a decree was rendered adjudicating the right to partition and appointing commissioners to make it and to assign dower. Before this decree was executed at the August term, 1891, Jacob S. Tennant, by leave of the court, filed in the cause deeds executed by the widow and four others of the children, conveying to him the dower interest and an additional 4-12 of the land, making 10-12 of the entire tract owned by him and Cassie A. Tennant. The other two interests were owned by the plaintiff, Lewis Stewart and Emma Stewart, both infants. Then evidence was introduced at the Bar of the court tending to show that the interests of said infants would be promoted by sale of their interest in the land and payment of the proceeds thereof to their guardian; and a decree was entered setting aside so much of the former decree as ordered a partition of the land, decreeing a sale of the undivided interests of the infants, which decree was, on the 8th day of December, 1891, executed, Jacob S. Tennant becoming the purchaser for the sum of $200.00. This sale was confirmed and on August 31, 1895, the commissioner who sold the land under the decree, executed a deed therefor to Tennant. Immediately afterwards the Tennants took possession of the land, and, by two leases dated respectively, June 28, 1894, and May 1, 1897, leased it to the South Penn Oil Company for oil purposes, and on or about April 9, 1897, the oil company entered upon the land and commenced drilling for oil and gas, and since that time had been in the exclusive and uninterrupted possession of the same for oil and gas purposes, and had drilled eleven wells on the land, all of which were producers, and were producing considerable quantities of oil when the suit was brought. On June 29, 1900, the plaintiff, who had been under age when the decree of sale and leases were made, brought this suit by an original bill filed at July Rules, 1900, alleging his infancy, setting up all said proceedings and transactions, alleging that the decrees and proceedings of the former suit whereby the Tennants claimed to have acquired title to his interest in the land, were erroneous, illegal and void, showing that he had attained the age of 21 years, on May 11, 1900, and praying that Tennants, the South Penn Oil Company and the Eureka Pipeline Company be required to answer the bill under oath, and show the quantity of oil taken by them, and each of them, from the land, the amount held by the Pipeline Company and disposed of by it, or any of the defendants; that an injunction should be awarded restraining Tennants and the South Penn Oil Company from taking and removing any timber, oil, or other material from the lands, and from selling or otherwise disposing of the same, or the proceeds thereof; that if the court should permit them to operate on the land it should appoint a receiver to take charge and control of 1-12 of the oil then on hand, or that might be thereafter produced, and for general relief. The defendants demurred, which demurrers were overruled, and they then filed separate answers. Depositions were taken and filed, and on August 29, 1901, a final decree was pronounced. By this decree the decrees made in the former chancery cause at the August and December Terms, 1891, wherein the plaintiff's interest was decreed to be sold, and the sale to Jacob S. Tennant confirmed, and the deed made to Jacob S. Tennant under said decree, and the lease dated May 1, 1897, in so far as the deed and lease related to and purported to convey the interest of the plaintiff in the land, as clouds upon his title, were cancelled, set aside and annulled; and required Jacob S. Tennant to account to the plaintiff, or to him and his assignee, for 1-12 of the royalties, bonuses and rentals received by him from the land, and required the South Penn Oil Company to account to the plaintiff, or to him and his assignee, for 1-12 of 7-8 of the oil and gas taken from the land on the bases of a charge against the company of the whole of 1-12 of the 7-8, to be credited with 1-12 of the actual cost and expense of production, and the difference to be paid over to the plaintiff or to him and his assigns. The Oil Company and Jacob S. Tennant were, by the decree, required to account to the plaintiff for 1-12 of all the timber taken by them from the land within the five years next prior to the commencement of the suit, and the cause was referred to a commissioner to state and report an account in accordance with directions given in the decree. From this decree defendants appealed to the Court of Appeals, and that court reversed the decree, holding that the plaintiff was not entitled to the dower interest in his 1 -12 of the oil, that is, 1-3 of the 1-12 of all the oil produced, less the cost of production; that this amount or the fund arising from the sale of the oil during the life estate having been brought into court, should be left in the custody of the general receiver of the court, citing as to co-tenants:

Wilson v. *Youst*, 43 W. Va. 26.
Ammons v. *Ammons*, 50 W. Va. 390.
Eakin v. *Hawkins*, 52 W. Va. 124.

As to the right of the purchaser of a dower interest to receive the interest on the fund arising from the sale thereof, the court cited:

Findlay v. *Smith*, 6. Munf. 134.
Lenfers v. *Henke*, 73 Ill. 405; 24 Am. Rep. 263.
Seegar v. *Seegar*, 16 L. R. A. 247.

The court further held that the plaintiff in his bill did not tender the purchase money paid by Jacob S. Tennant, nor did the decree require this money to be paid as a condition precedent to setting aside the sale, citing:

Hull v. *Hull*, 26 W. Va. 1.
Charleston L. & M. Co. v. *Brockmeyer*, 23 W. Va. 635.

The demurrer to the bill, on account of this last error, was sustained, and the cause remanded with leave to the plaintiff to amend, the cause to be proceeded in in accordance with the principles announced, and further, according to the rules and principles governing courts of equity.

REMEDY OF CO-OWNER.

Sec. 13.—Where one or more joint tenants or tenants in common, executes an oil and gas lease for the entire tract of land, the remedy of the other co-owners who have not joined in the lease, for the unlawful extraction of oil and gas under such lease, is by

bill in equity for an injunction, wherein may be recovered all damages sustained by the plaintiffs.

(See Chapter 27 for authorities.)

Sec.   14.—Where one or more joint tenants or tenants in common, lawfully in possession and claiming title to the whole property, executes an oil and gas lease for the entire property, and the
lessee enters and produces oil or gas and converts the working
interest to his own use, or where such co-owner develops the premises himself, the other co-owners may enjoin operations and recover their proportion of the production, less the actual cost of
production, and the actual cost of development, but not including
any cost of drilling unproductive wells.   -

Williamson v. *Jones,* 43 W. Va. 562; 27 S. E. 411.
Pyle v. *Henderson,* 65 W. Va. 39; 63 S. E. 620.
McNeely v. *South Penn Oil Co.,* 58 W. Va. 438; 44 S. E. 508.
Stewart v. *Tennant,* 52 W. Va. 559; 44 S. E. 223.

Sec.   15.—Where one or more joint tenants executes an oil
and gas lease for the whole property and the lessee enters and produces oil or gas and converts the working interest to his own use,
the other co-owners who have not joined in such lease may enjoin
operations and recover their proportion of the oil and gas so
produced, without being charged with any cost of development or
production.

Ziegler v. *Brenneman,* 237 Ill. 15; 86 N. E. 597.

LESSEE'S REMEDIES.

Sec.   16.—Where a lessee has, for a valuable consideration
acquired an oil and gas lease and has agreed to pay the usual
royalty, and the landowner prior to such lease has conveyed away
an interest in the oil and gas equal to one-half the agreed royalty,
the lessee cannot be required to pay more than the royalty stipulated in the lease as such lease implies a covenant of general warranty.

Kilcoyne v. *Southern Oil Co.,* 61 W· Va. 538; 55 S. E. 888.

Sec. 17.—The rule stated in Section 13 does not apply, however, where the interests of minors who are co-tenants or tenants in common are sold under a proceeding taken in a court of competent jurisdiction for the purpose, and where the purchaser, as a consideration for the lease agrees to pay a stipulated royalty. In such case the purchaser will be required to pay the royalty agreed upon as a consideration for his purchase.

Headley v. *Hoopengarner,* 60 W. Va. 626; 55 S. E. 144.

Sec. 18.—A lessee acquiring a lease for a tract of land from one or more joint tenants or tenants in common may maintain a bill in equity to enjoin operations on the leased premises by one holding a lease which is either unconscienable or void for want of mutuality, although signed by all the co-owners.

Trees v. *Eclipse Oil Co.,* 47 W. Va. 107; 34 S. E. 933.

Sec. 19.—Where one or more of the joint tenants or tenants in common of a tract of land for a valuable consideration executes an oil and gas lease for the whole premises, such lease implies a covenant of general warranty, and the lessee may maintain a bill in equity to cancel a subsequent lease made by the same lessors to a third party while he and the lessee were endeavoring to acquire the interests of the other co-owners.

Pyle v. *Henderson,* 65 W. Va. 39; 63 S. E. 620.

Sec. 20.—A lessee of a tract of land acquiring a lease from one joint tenant or tenant in common is not entitled to a partition of the lands, but is entitled as against his lessor to possession for the purpose of operating the premises; and while he cannot lawfully extract the oil and gas from the leased premises, if he does do so he will be required to account to the co-owners, who did not join in his lease, for their part of the production.

Waterford Oil & Gas Co. v. *Shipman,* 233 Ill. 9; 84 N. E. 53.
Ziegler v. *Brenneman,* 237 Ill. 15; 86 N. E. 597.
Compton v. *Peoples Gas Co.,* 75 Kan. 572; 89 Pac. 1029; 10 L.
R. A. (N. S.) 758.

Sec. 21.—Where a lessee acquires a lease from two or more co-tenants or tenants in common, jointly, wherein he agrees to pay a common rent or royalty, jointly, to lessors, the lessee may pay such rent or royalty to either of the co-lessors, and his receipt will be binding on the other lessor. Where, however, one or more of several co-lessors notifies lessee of their intention to collect and receive their proportion of such rent or royalty, separately, lessee must, after the receipt of such notice, pay to such lessors as have given such notice, their proportion of the rent or royalties accruing under the lease, subsequent to such notice.

Swint v. *Oil Co.*, 184 Pa. 202; 38 Atl. 1020.

Sec. 22.—Where the lands covered by an oil and gas lease belong to tenants in common, some of whom are minors, the adult co-owners may declare a forfeiture of the lease for non-development of the premises, or non-payment of rental, and if such declaration of forfeiture is not against the interests of the minors, it is sufficient to terminate the lease. Where after such declaration of forfeiture the co-tenants institute suit for the recovery of rentals accruing subsequently, lessee may defeat the action by alleging and proving the declaration of forfeiture; and that he accepted such declaration as a final termination of the lease, and thereafter neither paid rentals, nor attempted to make explorations.

Wilson v. *Goldstein*, 152 Pa. 524; 25 Atl. 493.
Heinouer v. *Jones,* 159 Pa. 228; 28 Atl. 228.

Sec. 23.—Where land is owned by co-tenants or tenants in common, and has been leased for oil and gas purposes by one of the co-tenants or tenants in common, without the consent of the others, the non-consenting owners may ratify such lease and in a suit in equity for an accounting of the rents and profits they are entitled to an accounting of all money received by the lessor of such lease by way of bonus money, commutation money, royalty oils and gas rentals, accruing under such lease.

Summers v. *Bennett,*——W. Va. ——; 69 S. E. 690.

Sec. 24.—In *Wilson* v. *Goldstein,* 152 Pa. 524; 25 Atl. 493 (Jan. 3, 1893), the syllabus is as follows:

"Where a brother of full age acting for himself and as next friend of his minor sisters, asserts a forfeiture of an oil lease covering lands which he and his sisters have inherited as tenants in common, he cannot afterwards recover for himself his share of the monthly damages stipulated in the lease and accruing between the date of the assertion of forfeiture and the institution of the suit.

It seems that in such a case, if the action of the brother as next friend of his minor sisters was judicious and for the best interest of the minors, the forfeiture asserted by him should be sustained against them."   '

James R. Wilson, for himself, and as next friend of Lydia C. Wilson and Mary F. Wilson, minors, brought an action before a Justice of the Peace against Jacob Goldstein to recover the stipulated damages provided for in an oil lease for failure to explore. The case was appealed to the Court of Common Pleas of Venango County, where it was tried and verdict and judgment rendered for plaintiffs, from which judgment defendants appealed. The action was upon two written instruments, oil and gas leases. The lessor, Elisha Wilson, had died and his heirs were the plaintiffs to whom the title to the land covered by the leases had fallen. The lessee had the right to mine and excavate for petroleum, coal rock or carbon oil, or other valuable minerals or valuable substances at a rent or royalty of 1-8 part of oil or other substances produced. It was stipulated in the lease that lessee should commence operations within 90 days after date, or in default thereof pay the sum of $5.00 per month on each lease as stipulated damages due the lessor because of such default, until operations should begin. Elisha Wilson, the lessor, died in December, 1888. James R. Wilson was at that time of full age, and about a month after his father's death, he gave notice to Goldstein that as he had not drilled a well on the leased premises or paid the commutation money for delay, his rights under the leases were forfeited, and he would not be allowed to enter upon the lands thereafter. Goldstein seemed to . have acquiesced in this action, and in answer to Wilson's demand for a surrender of the lease, delivered up the one which was in his possession, and explained that he could not at that time deliver up the other for the reason that he had assigned an interest in it to another person, who had possession of it. He did not deny, however, that Wilson had the right to assert the forfeiture because of his default as to both leases; nor did he offer to commence operations if the default were waived. After the lapse of more than one year from this assertion of the forfeiture and demand for the delivery of the lease, James R. Wilson brought this suit for himself and his minor sisters for the recovery of five dollars per month on each lease from the death of the father to the time when the suit was brought, as stipulated damages for the breach of covenants in failing to commence operations for the production of oil on the leased premises. The judgment of the Court of Common Pleas was, by the Supreme Court reversed, and a new trial awarded.

Sec.   25.—In *Heinouer* v. *Jones*, 159 Pa. 228; 28 Atl. 228 (Dec. 30, 1893), the syllabus is as follows:

"In an action to recover rent on an oil lease, accruing, by reason of the failure to complete a well within the time specified in the lease, if there is evidence that the lessor, after a monthly installment was due and unpaid, declared that the lease was forfeited and subsequently refused to accept the rent, the question of forfeiture must be submitted to the jury.

Where the lessors are tenants in common and some of them minors, whether or not one tenant in common can bind the others who are minors by a forfeiture, depends upon whether he was in a position to speak for them, and whether or not his action was for their best interest. *Wilson* v. *Goldstein*, 152 Pa. 524, followed."

Lorenz Heinouer, Jr., and others, heirs at law of Lorenz Heinouer, Sr., instituted an action of assumpsit on an oil lease in Court of Common Pleas of Allegheny County against Nathan D. Jones. At the trial it appeared that on April 4, 1889, Lorenz Heinouer leased for five years certain property in Allegheny County to defendants, "for the sole and only purpose of drilling or operating for oil or gas." The material portions of the lease were as follows:

"It is further agreed that if gas is obtained in sufficient quantities and utilized off the premises the party of the second part shall pay as annual rental the sum of five hundred dollars upon each well, so long as gas shall be conveyed away therefrom and used off the premises. As a further consideration, the party of the second part agrees to pay to the party of the first part five hundred dollars on the execution hereof; also to pay all damages to growing crops by reason of the privilege herein granted to lay and maintain oil and gas lines * * * * * * * One well shall be completed within six months, and a second well completed ˙ on the above described premises within ten months from the date hereof, ˙ or thereafter pay the party of the first part thirty dollars per month in advance until the work is commenced. * * * * * A failure of the party of the second part to make any one of said payments when due, at such place as above mentioned, renders this lease null and void, and to remain without effect between the parties hereto, and the moneys paid shall be paid in full of all damages.''

The plaintiffs were the heirs at law of Lorenz Heinouer, deceased. They brought the suit upon the lease made by the father. The lessor died in February, 1890, whose eldest son, Lorenz Heinouer, was appointed to administer upon the estate within two days after his death. No well was completed on the land; nor was the work of drilling commenced. The monthly payments were made to the lessor until his death, and to his son, the administrator, thereafter, until April 4, 1890. When the next monthly payment fell due it was not made, and in reply to Heinouer's question, the holder of the lease informed him that it would not be paid. Heinouer then communicated this fact to Jones, the lessee, and, as Jones asserted, then and there declared the lease to be forfeited, and refused to take the rent, saying that he could obtain a bonus of $500.00 for the lease. Heinouer denied the declaration of forfeiture, but admitted he did not take the rent from Jones, and that for two years, and until this suit was brought, he never asked for payment, and the lessee never entered upon the land. The defense rested upon the alleged forfeiture by Heinouer, who was both administrator and heir at law of the lessor. This, it was urged, divested Jones' title under the lease and relieved him from rent accruing thereafter. Defendant insisted that it estopped Heinouer from recovering his share of the rentals falling due after such forfeiture. There was evidence upon which the question whether a forfeiture had been declared or not was a question of fact for the jury. Verdict and judgment were rendered for plaintiffs, and defendants appealed. The Supreme Court reversed the judgment, and for the reason that the brothers and sisters of Heinouer were not separately considered in the case a new trial was awarded.

Sec. 26.—In *Summers v. Bennett,* —— W. Va. ——;
69 S. E. 690 (Nov. 15, 1910), syls. 2-3 are as follows:

"2. In a suit by one co-tenant against another co-tenant of
land acquired and held for sale and profit, for an accounting of the
proceeds of sales made, and rents, issues and profits, the Statute
of Limitations begins to run from the time plaintiff had right to
demand payment.

3. Where land so held has been leased for oil and gas purposes by a co-tenant or trustee, without the consent of the other
tenant or cestui que trust, but such lease is subsequently ratified
in a suit for an accounting for rents and profits, the accounting
should include all money received by the lessor, co-tenant or
trustee, for such lease, by way of bonus money or commutation
money, and from royalty oils and gas rentals, or otherwise accruing under such lease."

Martha M. Summers and others filed their bill in equity in
the Circuit Court of Marion County against William G. Bennett
and others. The plaintiffs claimed as heirs of Gideon D. Camden, deceased, and by their bill sought to establish their right
and title to one-fourth of the residue of four several tracts of
land originally, in 1844, patented to one John Walden, the
legal title to which for several years prior to the death of Camden, had been acquired by Jonathan M. Bennett, and since then
held by his heirs and devisees; and also for an accounting by the
defendants of the rents and profits, and of the proceeds of the
sale of various parts thereof, and for general relief.

It appeared that by contract of August 4, 1843, between
Walden and Camden, Walden had furnished Camden a treasury
warrant calling for 9990 acres; and that it was understood that the
warrant, and any other warrants Walden might thereafter
furnish Camden, should be located upon such lands as Camden
might deem most advisable. The contract also authorized Camden to contract with such persons as he might think proper to
survey and carry the land into grant in such number of tracts
as he might consider most advisable, stipulating, however, that
for the expenses of surveying and patenting such land, such
persons should be entitled to one moiety thereof, Walden
to make quit claim deeds to them therefor. The contract also stipulated that for Camden's services, Walden should

convey to him by quit claim deed, an equal one-half of the other moiety of the lands, with the provision that such moiety should be subject to the costs of the land warrants, which should be paid Walden out of the first sales made. By deed of May 27, 1873, Walden conveyed to Bennett a three-fourths undivided interest in the land, for the money consideration recited therein, and in consideration of a contract of August 10, 1843, being the contract made with Bennett by Camden, pursuant to his contract with Walden, for surveying and patenting said lands, whereby Bennett became invested with the legal title, not only to the moiety provided for in the contract, but also to the one-half of the other moiety which had been held by Walden for himself and Camden. One of the tracts, a tract of 1800 acres in Gilmer County, except 181 acres thereof, which by contract in 1869, had been sold to and by deed of Walden, Bennett and Camden, of June 20, 1873, had been conveyed to one Vann Noy, was for the years 1871 and 1873 returned delinquent in the name of Walden, and was sold in 1875 for the taxes of those years, as a tract of 1619 acres, and purchased by Bennett, and by deed of December 11, 1876, conveyed to him, by the Clerk of the County Court of Gilmer County. This land, however, except a reservation of the oil and gas in 145 acres thereof, conveyed by the executors of J. M. Bennett to Ruth Hinzman, on May 2, 1895, had all been disposed of prior to the institution of this suit, but the facts recited, and other facts in relation thereto, were relied upon by both sides as evidential facts on the subject of the controversy. Of the tracts a tract of 500 acres and one of 1,000 acres on Spring Fork of Yellow Creek, in Calhoun County, after being assessed in the names of Bennett and Walden, were allowed to be returned delinquent for the non-payment of taxes for the year 1874; and in the year 1875 were sold and purchased by the State; and in proceedings taken by the commissioner of School Lands were subsequently acquired by Bennett by deed of April 7, 1880. The title thus acquired to these tracts remained in Bennett, his heirs and devisees, except such portions thereof as were subsequently sold and conveyed by Camden and Bennett, or by Bennett and his heirs and devisees. Bennett died in 1887. Camden died in 1891. Portions of the lands claimed by the plaintiffs or in which they claimed the ¼ interest, had been leased for oil and gas purposes, and the question of the right of the plaintiffs to

have an accounting, not only of the oils received by way of royalties, but also of the bonuses, land rentals, and gas rentals, on
account of such oil and gas leases, was before the court for consideration. The Circuit Court rendered a decree denying to the
plaintiffs the relief prayed for. Plaintiffs appealed to the Court
of Appeals, where the decree was reversed.   :

CHAPTER 33.

DRY HOLE—EFFECT OF DRILLING.

Sec. 1.—The completion of a nonproductive well, though at
great expense, vests no title in the lessee.

Steelsmith v. Gartlan, 45 W. Va. 27; 29 S. E. 978.
Stahl v. Vanvleck, 53 Ohio St. 136; 41 N. E. 35.
Lowther Oil Co. v. Miller-Sibley Oil Co., 53 W. Va. 501; 44
    S. E. 433.
Parish Fork Oil Co. v. Bridgewater Gas Co., 51 W. Va., 583;
    42 S. E. 655.
Henne v. South Penn Oil Co., 52 W. Va., 192; 43 S. E. 147.
Venture Oil Co. v. Fretts, 152 Pa. 451; 35 Atl. 732.
Bartley v. Phillips, 179 Pa. 175; 36 Atl. 217.
Aye v. Philadelphia Co., 193 Pa. 451; 44 Atl. 655.
Foster v. Elk Fork Oil & Gas Co., 32 C. C. A. 560; 90 Fed.
    178.
Florence Oil etc. Co. v. Orman, 19 Col. App. 79; 73 Pac. 628.
Rawlings v. Armel, 70 Kan. 778; 79 Pac. 683.
Ziegler v. Dailey, 37 Ind. App. 240; 76 N. E. 819.
Barnhart v. Lockwood, 152 Pa. 82; 25 Atl. 237.
May v. Hazlewood Oil Co., 152 Pa. 518; 25 Atl. 564.

Sec. 2.—In Steelsmith v. Gartlan, 45 W. Va. 27; 29 S. E.
978, analyzed under Chapter 5, syl. 2 is as follows:

"2. The completion of a nonproductive well, though at great
expense, vests no title in lessee."

Sec. 3.—In Stahl v. Vanvleck, 53 Ohio St. 136; 41 N. E. 35
(June 11, 1895), the syllabus is as follows:

"1. A, party of the first part, being the owner of three adjoining tracts of land, each containing 40 acres, leased one acre thereof, to be designated by himself to a party of the second part; and in the lease it was 'agreed on the part of the party of the first part that if oil or gas be obtained by the second party, or assigns, in or under the provisions of this contract, upon said tract, or on lands adjoining the same premises of which the foregoing one acre described embraces a part, said second party shall have the right to operate 40 acres of the balance of said premises on the same terms as above.' Held, that the 40-acre tract out of which the one acre was thereafter selected by party of the first part is the 40 acres to be operated under the contract. Walsh v. Ringer, 2 Ohio, 328; Cunningham v. Harper, Wright, 366, and Hay v. Storrs, Id. 711, followed and approved.

2. In said contract it was further 'agreed that, if second party or their assigns, do not commence a test oil or gas well at Rising Sun, or vicinity, in ninety days, this lease to be void.' Held, that a test well at that place having been commenced and completed in 90 days, whereby the existence of oil at that point was ascertained, such performance supplied a sufficient consideration for the contract of lease, even though the test well was immediately plugged and casing withdrawn.

3. The party of the first part having selected the one acre upon which such well was to be drilled, and the second party having acted thereon, the first party is bound thereby, and has no right to make a second selection.

4. It being agreed that such lease should 'continue and be in force for five years from the date thereof,' and the second party, having commenced operations in good faith to drill for oil in ample time to complete a well within said term of five years, was wrongfully enjoined by the lessor, and the injunction kept alive until after the expiration of the term of five years, Held, that the second party is entitled at the close of the litigation to such time in which to perform the contract as still remained of his term when he was first enjoined.''

Arie E. Stahl, of Wood County, Ohio, as party of the first part, on December 15, 1886, made an oil and gas lease to C. W. Manahan, Jr., and A. K. Detwiler, whereby said first party granted to the second parties, their successors or assigns, the right to enter upon a tract of land in Wood County, Ohio, to be designated by the first party, of one acre out of a tract of 40 acres, for the purpose and with the exclusive right to lessees to drill for and develop, oil, gas and other valuable substances, in consideration whereof it was agreed that if oil should be found and developed upon the premises in paying quantities, the lessor should receive a royalty of ⅛; and should gas be found and developed, the first party should have the right to use and consume for lighting and heating his dwelling such amount as might be necessary therefor, and the additional sum of $300.00 per annum for each gas well, the gas from which should be marketed and utilized off the premises; that from and after the expiration of 24 months from the date of the lease, and until lessees should enter the premises and exercise the rights and privileges granted by the lease, second parties should pay lessor during the continuance of the contract the sum of fifty cents per acre per year for each acre contracted for, to be paid out of the first moneys realized or received by second party from the development of oil or gas; that the contract should continue and be in force for five years from date, or as long as oil or gas should be found and developed upon the premises in paying quantities; that the lessee should have the right of necessary roads to and from all wells developed upon the premises, and the right to remove all machinery, fixtures and buildings placed by them upon the premises; that if oil or gas should be obtained by the second parties, or their assigns, in or under the provisions of the contract upon said tract, or on lands adjoining the same premises, of which the one acre described embraced a part, second party should have the right to operate the balance of the premises on the same terms as designated in the lease; that in case the second parties, their successors and assigns, should not commence operations on the premises within five years from the date of the lease, the same should be void; and that if the second parties or their assigns did not commence a test well at Rising Sun or vicinity in 90 days, the lease should be void. The second parties, lessees, assigned the contract to George H. Van Vleck. On August 8, 1891, the lessor, as party of the first part, filed his petition in the Court of Common Pleas of Wood County, Ohio, seeking to enjoin the defendant, Van Vleck, from going on the premises, erecting any derrick, placing any timber thereon, or drilling any wells or removing any oil or gas therefrom, and for a reformation of the agreement, its cancellation, and for equitable relief. The injunction and relief was sought upon the alleged ground that the conditions of the instrument had not been performed, no rental paid, no test well commenced at Rising Sun or vicinity, within the time specified, no consideration paid for the contract, that the same was without consideration, that only 40 acres of land were included in the contract, but by mistake the whole 120 acres were included. The defendant answered and averred that the test well at Rising Sun was commenced and drilled to completion within 90 days from the date of the contract; that thereby it was demonstrated at great expense that oil existed in the lands; that he was about to drill a well on plaintiff's lands, and offered to pay any rental due under the contract, when stopped by the suit; and defendant asked to be protected in his rights. After trial in the Court of Common Pleas the case was appealed, and on trial the Circuit Court made a finding of facts: That the tract was described in the lease as a tract of forty acres; and that the recorder, in recording the instrument, overlooked the interlineation, so that the record was made to appear as a tract of 120 acres; that the contract was assigned by the original lessees to George H. Van Vleck; that the original lessees, Manahan and Detwiler, commenced a well in the vicinity of Rising Sun within 90 days after the execution of the contract, in accordance with the terms thereof; that said well was not situated in plaintiff's land, and was about a mile and a half therefrom; that said Manahan and Detwiler in due time drilled said well to the oil bearing rock and for a sufficient distance therein to determine the character of the land; that oil was found in the well; that immediately after the completion of the well Manahan and Detwiler plugged the same, drew the casing and did not further operate the well; that said lease was assigned to and became the property of the defendant, Van Vleck, on March 30, 1887; that no operations were commenced by anyone under the lease upon the lands of plaintiff until about two weeks previous to the commencement of the suit and no rent was paid on the lease; that at the date last aforesaid, the defendant, through one Graham, his agent, requested the plaintiff to designate the acre of land upon which he desired to have a well located; that plaintiff thereupon designated a location for the well; that pursuant to such designation by plaintiff, and prior to the commencement of the suit, defendant in good faith, and with the intent to drill for oil under said lease, commenced placing machinery at the point so designated for the purpose of drilling; that soon afterwards the plaintiff notified the defendant's agent that he had changed his mind, and that if any of said lands were to be operated for gas and oil he desired to have the operations begun and carried on at another point; that soon after receiving the notice the agent of the defendant drew other loads of derrick timber, and deposited it on the 40-acre tract, at the point first designated by the plaintiff, and was about going on the land with another load when the plaintiff informed him that if the defendant insisted that his lease gave him the right to operate the whole farm, which contained 120 acres of land, in case he was successful in finding gas or oil on the premises, that he would not permit him to commence operations upon said land at all, but would enjoin him. To this the agent of the defendant answered, that he did not know how much land the defendant claimed a right to operate, but would write to defendant and let the plaintiff know, and then deposited another load of lumber prepared for the purpose, and intended to be used in the construction of a derrick on the land at the point first designated by the plaintiff. The defendant at that time claimed a right under his lease to operate the whole farm of 120 acres, in case he found gas or oil upon any one acre of land mentioned in the lease and designated by the plaintiff, and supposed that this right was vested in him by the terms of his lease. No other work or operations had been commenced or done on the land at the commencement of the action. Upon the facts so found the court found the equity of the case to be with the defendant, George H. Van Vleck, as to the 40-acre tract described, and decreed that Van Vleck should have and hold the right to enter upon and operate for gas and oil the 40-acre tract described, in all respects as granted and conferred by the lease, free from all interference by plaintiff. Exceptions were taken, and the case was taken on appeal to the Supreme Court of Ohio. That Court affirmed the judgment.

Sec. 4.—In *Lowther Oil Co.* v. *Miller-Sibley Oil Co.*, 53 W. Va., 501; 44 S. E. 433, analyzed under Chapter 5, in a controversy between the claimants to two conflicting leases where the original lessor had drilled a well, and afterwards physically abandoned the premises, Judge Brannon, in the opinion, said ι

"In this instance Miller-Sibley Co. bored a well, pumped it several months, got but little oil, not filling the tanks, abandoned that well. True, it is said that the tools getting fastened caused its abandonment, but it gave poor prospect. Then the company bored a second well, yielding from two and three quarters to five barrels a day, though pumped for months. The company moved its tools and appliances off the Metz farm to other undertakings several miles away. It left nothing at the well very valuable to use in further efforts. The rigs remained; but in that timber country it would not be practicable to transfer them. The casing was mostly pulled out. An engine and boiler were left for awhile, but the engine was partly dismantled and later taken away. The agent gave an order to remove practically all left on the premises. He left the State. Wells bored on other tracts some distance away produced gas only. The search for oil in four wells in that section was unsuccessful. It was a new field, what oil men call, in homely but expressive language, 'wild cat territory.' March 15, 1900, Lowther wrote Miller-Sibley, saying he held various oil leases in that section, and proposed to put them in with those of Miller-Sibley, and on March 19, 1900, Miller-Sibley Oil Co., by its President, wrote in reply, acknowledging receipt by date of this particular letter, saying 'We have decided not to operate in W. Va. for the present, and consequently do not take advantage of your offer.' Miller-Sibley Co. quit work January, 1899, practically in November, 1898, and the Lowther lease was January 9, 1900. There had been a cessation of work for a year. The lease went to record March 19, 1900. The Lowther Oil Co. began work in June, 1900, more than fifteen months after Miller-Sibley Co. ceased work. The oil in the tanks was not marketed but wasted; the derrick and other parts of the rig went to decay. These circumstances, taken together, establish abandonment by Miller-Sibley Co.''

Sec. 5.—In *Parish Fork Oil Co.* v. *Bridgewater Gas Co.*, 51 W. Va. 583; 42 S. E. 655, analyzed under Chapter 5, Judge Poffenbarger, delivering the opinion of the court on the question of a non-productive well, said:

''On the 24th day of August, 1900, Cox made Swisher a tender of rent up to June 4, 1900, with interest thereon, but he coupled it with a protest to the effect that no rent was due him. This position of the lessees is based upon the assumption that by drilling a well and finding oil they acquired a vested interest in the oil and gas in that tract of land. Until oil is discovered in paying quantities the lessee acquires no title under such lease. It simply gives a right of exploration. *Steelsmith* v. *Gartlan*, 45 W. Va. 27; *Oil*

Co. v. *Fretts,* 152 Pa. St. 451; *Plumbers* v. *Iron Co.,* 160 Pa. 483; *Crawford* v. *Ritchie,* 43 W. Va. 252. After the discovery of oil in paying quantities it is held, that title does vest in the lessee, but there is no case which goes so far as to announce that after mere discovery of oil the lessee, upon the assumption of a vested interest or title may cease operation, refuse to develop the property, tie up the oil by his lease, and simply hold it for speculative purposes or to await his own pleasure as to the time of development. * * * * * * * If there is one principle that is asserted in *Steelsmith* v. *Gartlan* more vigorously and with more emphasis than any other, it is, that the lessee shall proceed to make the lease profitable to both parties, and that he shall not be permitted to tie up the land.''

Sec. 6.—In *Henne* v. *South Penn Oil Co.,* 52 W. Va. 192; 43 S. E. 147, analyzed under Chapter 24, syl. 2 is as follows:

"2. M. & M. by deed dated Oct. 19, 1898, leased certain premises to M. for oil and gas purposes which lease contained the following provisions: 'This lease shall become null and void and all rights hereunder shall cease and determine unless a well shall be completed on the said premises within six months from the date hereof, or unless the lessee shall pay at the rate of $25.50 quarterly in advance for each additional three months such completion is delayed from the time above mentioned for the completion of such well, until a well is completed; and it is agreed that the completion of such well shall be and operate as a full liquidation of all rental under this provision during the remainder of the term of this lease.' M. the lessee, assigned the said lease to S. P. Oil Co., which was the lessee for oil and gas purposes of a large area of territory including all tracts contiguous to the said premises, the S. P. Oil Co., drilled a well to completion April 4, 1900, paying the stipulated rental until the well was completed, but which well was 'dry.' It then removed its material and machinery from the premises and proceeded to drill other wells nearer to developments already made on the line towards the premises in question; *Held,* that under the lease and circumstances of the case, the S. P. Oil Co., was entitled to a reasonable time in which to return and make further developments under the said lease.''

Sec. 7.—In *Venture Oil Co.* v. *Fretts,* 152 Pa. 451; 35 Atl. 732, analyzed under Chapter 5, C. D. Robbins procured leases upon a body of farms in Washington County, Pennsylvania, aggregating about 1500 acres. It was provided in the leases that

operations should be begun on some one of the farms held by
Robbins in the township, within six months from the date of the
lease; and in case oil should be found in paying quantities on any
one of the farms, operations were to be begun on the farm next
adjoining within 60 days thereafter, and continued at the same
rate until all the lands held by Robbins should be tested to success or abandonment. Robbins commenced to drill on the farm
of J. L. Scott, and drilled the well to the depth of 2247 feet.
Neither oil nor gas was found. In the opinion, Justice Williams
said:

"This seems to have been regarded by all parties a sufficient
depth to test the farm, and it is evident that Robbins thought it a
test of the whole of the region, and concluded that the territory
covered by his lease was worthless as oil territory. He accordingly drew the casing soon after the well was finished and then
plugged the well and abandoned it. When asked upon the witness
stand why he abandoned the well he replied: 'Because is was
no good.' He made no further effort to test any part of the
land covered by his leases, but removed his machinery and
drilling tools to other localities in which he prosecuted his
business as an explorer for, and a producer of, oil. This was
in the fall of 1884. Some six or seven years later, nothing further having been done by Robbins on any one of the farms covered
by his leases of 1883, Gamble made a new lease of his farm to
other parties under whom the defendants claim title, and operations were at once begun on the land."

The court held that Robbins had abandoned the leases.

Sec. 8.—In *Bartley* v. *Phillips*, 179 Pa. 175; 36 Atl. 217, analyzed under Chapter 17, J. A. Hartzell, on September 8, 1888,
leased a tract of 70 acres of land to Bartley and others for oil
purposes for the term of ten years. By the terms of the lease
lessees were to commence operations for mining purposes within
30 days from the execution of the lease, and when work was commenced it was to be prosecuted with due diligence until completion or abandonment. Lessees commenced operations on the land
within fifteen days after the execution of the lease and drilled a
well, finishing it in the latter part of October, 1888. After the
execution of the first lease Hartzell conveyed the tract of land
by deed to one Ziegler, and in the deed expressly excepted the

lease to Bartley and others, from the covenants of warranty. Ziegler then executed an oil and gas lease to Samual Walker who assigned it to Phillips. Phillips entered the premises and Bartley and others brought ejectment. The court held that the clause of forfeiture in an oil and gas lease is for the benefit of the lessor; and that Phillips took his lease with a term apparently outstanding, and having failed to make inquiry of the lessee as to whether the lease had been abandoned, took the risk of the fact of whether or not there had been an abandonment, and further held that the question of abandonment was one of fact for the jury.

Sec. 9.—In *Aye* v. *Philadelphia Company*, 193 Pa. 451; 44 Atl. 655, analyzed under Chapter 2, syl. 1 is as follows:

"Where an oil lease provides for the completion of a test well within a certain time, but makes no provision for the contingency of the test well proving dry, there is an implied obligation on the lessee after having completed a test well which has proved dry, to proceed further with the exploration and development of the land with reasonable diligence according to the usual course of the business, and a failure to do so amounts to an abandonment which will sustain a re-entry by the lessor. In such a case an unexplained cessation of operations for four years gives rise to a fair presumption of abandonment, and, standing alone, and admitted, would justify the court in declaring an abandonment as a matter of law; but it may be capable of explanation, and the question of abandonment is therefore usually a question for the jury on the evidence of the acts and declarations of the parties."

Sec. 10.—In *Foster* v. *Elk Fork Oil & Gas Co.*, 32 C. C. A. 560; 90 Fed. 178, analyzed under Chapter 4, as Elk Fork Oil & Gas Co., v. Jennings, William Johnson obtained leases covering about 20,000 acres in four districts in Tyler County, West Virginia. Each lease was several; all in the same form, containing the same provisions, covenants and stipulations. Each lease provided for the drilling within a year of one well in the District of Ellsworth, Lincoln, Union or Meade. Within the year Johnson drilled a well within one of these districts, which well was dry. After that time, no well was drilled within either or any of the four districts under any of the Johnson leases. Subsequently one

of the landowners made a second lease and Johnson or his assigns claimed the original lease by reason of the drilling of the
dry hole. Upon appeal from the decision of the Circuit Court,
84 Fed. 839, holding that the drilling of the dry hole vested no title
in Johnson, Judge Simonton, delivering the opinion of the Circuit Court of Appeals, said:

"It is earnestly contended that the lessee was not obliged to
bore a well on every parcel included in the four districts. We do
not say that he was obliged to do this. Perhaps, when he found
by his experiment, that he had gone over 2,000 feet and found
nothing, he was under no obligation to continue his explorations.
Glasgow v. *Chartiers Oil Co.,* 152 Pa. St. 48; 25 Atl. 232. But we
are of the opinion that, when he tried once, and failed, and after
a reasonable time did not try again, he failed to establish his interest in this land, and lost all his rights under the contract."

The decree of the Circuit Court was affirmed.

Sec. 11.—In *Florence Oil etc. Co.* v. *Orman,* 19 Colo. App. 79;
73 Pac. 628, analyzed under Chapter 5, the syllabus is as follows:

"An oil lease gave the exclusive right to mine lands for oil for
twenty years in consideration of a per cent. of the oil produced, the
lessee covenanting to sink two wells within eighteen months, and
the lease providing that if the two wells were so sunk, and were
not productive, the lessee should pay $50.00 a year till the drilling
of new wells should commence, and failure to pay it would render
the lease void. *Held,* that till oil was found the title of the lessee
was for exploration only, and that having done nothing for four
years after putting down the two wells without finding oil in paying quantities he lost his rights through failure to make diligent
search."

Sec. 12.—In *Rawlings* v. *Armel,* 70 Kan. 778; 79 Pac. 683,
analyzed under Chapter 5, John A. Armel and wife executed an
oil and gas lease to the Kansas & Texas Oil Company, for a tract
of land for a term of two years, with a provision that if no oil or
gas well should be drilled within 30 days from May 21, 1902, the
lease should become null and void at the option of the lessor, unless lessee should pay a rental on or before June 20, 1902. Extensions were made by lessor from time to time, and finally lessee

drilled two wells, which were dry, which they completed on October 12, 1902. About November 26, 1902, lessee pulled the casing, plugged the wells, ceased further explorations, removed all
material from the land, and left the premises. After February
19, 1903, the lessee assigned the lease to Rawlings and others. On
March 17, 1903, lessor instituted an action against the lessee and
its assignee, to cancel the lease on the grounds of abandonment
The District Court entered a decree cancelling the lease, which
decree was affirmed by the Supreme Court.

Sec. 13.—In *Ziegler* v. *Dailey,* 37 Ind. App. 240; 76 N. E. 819.
(Jan. 31, 1906), the syllabus is as follows:

"An oil lease provided that, in case no well should be completed within 30 days, the grant should become void unless the
lessee should pay a specified sum annually, for each year completion should be delayed. The lessee failed to complete a well within the required time, but paid for an extension, and within the
period of extension sunk a well, which was worthless. After the
expiration of the extension, and after the demand of the lessor,
the lessee sunk another well which produced oil in paying quantities. *Held,* in a suit between the lessee and the lessor's executors, that the lease had become void and a judgment quieting title
in the executors was proper."

On April 26, 1895, Gideon Wolff owned certain land, and executed to Henry C. Zeigler an oil and gas lease whereby in consideration of one dollar the lessor granted to lessee all the oil and
gas in and under the land, with right of entry for the purpose
of drilling and operating for oil and gas, the lessor to have ⅛
part of the oil produced and saved from the premises. If gas
only should be found in sufficient quantities to transport lessee to
pay lessor $100.00 per year for the production of each well the
gas from which should be transported. In case no well should
be completed within 30 days from the date, the grant should be
null and void, unless lessee should thereafter pay at the rate of
$143.00 annually for each year such completion was delayed.
Ziegler did not complete a well within the 30 days, but paid Wolff
$107.25 for an extension of time for completing the well until
February 26, 1896. In December, 1895, a well was drilled but
neither gas nor oil was found. The casing was withdrawn from

the well and removed from the premises, leaving the derrick and the drive pipe in the well. Wolff, the lessor, died on July 16, 1896, testate. His will was probated on July 21, 1896 in Platt County, Illinois, and letters testamentary were issued to John Wolff and George T. Warren, named as executors in the will, who continued to act as such after October 18, 1899. On September 17, 1896, the will was admitted to probate in Wells County, Indiana. Afterwards the executors acting under the will caused the real estate to be appraised in February, 1899, and advertised the land and sold the same to Michael Dailey and others. Ziegler never paid any sum, whatever, as rental or otherwise, under the lease, except the above sum of $107.25, and never produced any oil or gas or other minerals under the lease, from the well drilled in 1895. The well was wholly worthless and abandoned by Ziegler, who never attempted to put down any other wells on the premises or under the lease, prior to the summer of 1899, and never entered on the premises after the abandonment of the first well, nor attempted to drill or operate thereon prior to the summer of 1899. On October 13, 1899, Ziegler, without any other lease or written contract, or authority so to do, than the lease above mentioned, sunk and completed a well on the land, in which oil was found in paying quantities. Michael Dailey and others, the purchasers, instituted suit in the Circuit Court of Blackford County, against Henry Ziegler to quiet title. Upon the facts the court held that the purchasers, Dailey and others, were the owners in fee of the land, and were entitled to possession, and rendered judgment quieting the title to the land, in them. Ziegler appealed and the Appellate Court affirmed the judgment, citing:

Ohio Oil Co. v. *Detmore*, 165 Ind. 243; 74 N. E. 906.

Sec. 14.—In *Barnhart* v. *Lockwood*, 125 Pa. 82; 25 Atl. 237 (Nov. 11, 1892), the syllabus is as follows:

"Lessees under lease dated March 1, 1876, agreed to go upon demised premises and operate the same for oil within 40 days from the execution of the lease, but did not take possession or carry out their agreement. They afterwards sunk a test well near the demised premises which was a failure and which they abandoned, and nothing was attempted to be done towards the development of the property by lessees until December 18, 1889, when the property increased in value by reason of development of others in the neighborhood. *Held,* that the action of the lessees amounted in law to an abandonment of any right they otherwise might have had under the lease.

The lease in such case is not a grant of property in the oil, but merely a grant of possession for the purpose of searching for and procuring oil.''

E. A. Barnhart and others, trading as Hoch Brothers, instituted an action of ejectment in the Court of Common Pleas of Butler County, Pennsylvania, against M. L. Lockwood, James S Patterson, Charles Young and Edwin Young, for the recovery of the undivided half of a tract of land. Upon the trial the plaintiffs claimed title under an oil lease dated March 1, 1878, from Charles Young, one of the defendants, as party of the first part, which lease was for the term of 18 years and provided that if oil should be found in the vicinity, the second parties should have the refusal of a lease for the balance of the land, granting to lessees, their heirs and assigns, the exclusive possession of the piece of land during the term aforesaid, upon which to explore and produce oil and gas. The lessees covenanted and agreed to go on the land and operate it, and to deliver as royalty to lessor $1/8$ part of the oil obtained, and were to drill a test well at or near Little Connequenessing or Crab Run Creek, commencing inside of 40 days. Lessees never drilled on the premises, but within 40 days they commenced work on a well on the Barnhart farm, belonging to one of the lessees, near the stream mentioned, by hauling upon the ground some timbers for a rig. This was all they did until 1881, when they put up the rig on the Barnhart and drilled a well, which they finished in the Fall of that year. The test well having proved to be a complete failure, they sold the casing and machinery, and permitted the timbers to decay on the ground. No other wells were drilled by them in the neighborhood, nor did they do anything further towards development on the land embraced in the Charles Young lease until December, 1889, nearly twelve years after it was obtained. In the early part of the month a producing oil well was completed by other parties not interested in this controversy, on the Cable farm. This gave market value to the Young farm as oil territory, and on December 11. 1889, Edwin and Charles Young leased the land in controversy, for oil purposes at a bonus of $1500.00 to Lockwood, who afterwards assigned the lease to Patterson, one of the defendants with Youngs in this suit. On December 18, 1889, plaintiffs attempted to take possession of the premisès, but their right to do so was denied, and they were not permitted to enter. They afterwards brought this suit; but before this was done, the premises had been developed by the last mentioned lessee by drilling thereon several wells. Upon the facts, verdict and judgment were rendered for defendants, and plaintiffs appealed. The Supreme Court affirmed the judgment.

Sec. 15.—In *May* v. *Hazlewood Oil Co.*, 152 Pa. 518; 25 Atl. 564 (Jan. 3, 1893), the syllabus is as follows:

"An oil lease provided that the lessee should commence and prosecute to completion a test well for oil or gas on the demised premises, or upon other lands in the vicinity thereof, within 30 days after leases to the amount of five thousand acres shall have been obtained by the lessee, or else forfeit the rights granted by the lease, and should the lessee fail to obtain leases covering five thousand acres by the first day of January, 1887, the lessee should thereupon elect to proceed and drill as before stated in the lease, or, at its option forfeit the lease; and further, it was agreed that the lease should be determined at the option of the lessee, its successors or assigns, should a fair test fail to develop oil or gas in quantities to warrant further operations, notice of such determination to be given to the lessor in writing. The lease further provided for the payment of one dollar per acre for not drilling and prosecuting to completion one well on the premises within one year from the date of the lease.

In an action to recover the rental provided by the said clause, an affidavit of defense is sufficient, which avers that a test well was actually drilled, and that it proved to be a dry hole, yielding neither oil nor gas, and that the test proved that no oil or gas was to be found upon the premises; that defendant openly and publicity removed the drilling machinery from the premises and abandoned all further operations thereon, and that plaintiff, well knowing that the well was a dry hole, and that the premises had been abandoned, made no claim upon the defendant for any sum of money due under the lease for several years and waived the service of any written notice of the forfeiture by defendant; and that subsequently plaintiff granted to another party an option to purchase all the underlying coal from the premises."

John C. May instituted in a court of Common Pleas of Allegheny County, Pennsylvania, an action of assumpsit against the Hazelwood Oil Company for recovery of rental under an oil lease. The plaintiff, on May 4, 1886, executed an oil lease to defendant, containing the following clause:

"And it is further stipulated and agreed by said second party, its successors or assigns, that it will commence and prosecute to completion a test well for oil or gas on said premises, or upon other lands in the vicinity thereof, within 30 days after leases to the amount of 5,000 acres shall have been obtained by the same, or else forfeit the rights hereby granted, and should it fail to obtain leases covering 5,000 acres by the first day of January, A. D. 1887, it shall thereupon elect to proceed and drill as last above stated, or at its option forfeit this lease, and further, covenants to drill no well within 100 yards of any dwelling house, or other building appurtenant thereto, without the consent of first party, first had in writing.

This agreement to be determined at the option of second party, its successors, or assigns, should a fair test fail to develop oil or gas in quantities to warrant further operations, notice of such determination to be given in writing to first party."

The defendant filed an affidavit of defense, alleging the facts stated in the second paragraph of the syllabus, which affidavit of defense the Court of Common Pleas held to be insufficient, and entered judgment for the plaintiff. Defendant prosecuted a writ of error to the Supreme Court, and that court reversed the judgment.

LESSOR'S REMEDY.

Sec. 16.—Where a landowner has executed an oil and gas lease and is to receive as a consideration for the same a percentage of the oil produced, or an annual rental for each gas well, the gas from which is used off the premises, and lessee enters and drills one or more wells which prove unproductive, and thereafter fails, within a reasonable time to continue explorations or pay stipulated rental, where the lease provides for payment of commutation money for delay, lessor may declare a forfeiture upon the grounds of abandonment and recover possession of the property, or cause the lease to be cancelled by a court of equity, or by a court exercising equity powers.

Steelsmith v. *Gartlan*, 45 W. Va. 27; 29 S. E. 978.

Lowther Oil Co. v. *Miller-Sibley Oil Co.*, 53 W. Va. 501; 44 S.
E. 433.

Parish Fork Oil Co. v. *Bridgewater Gas Co.*, 51 W. Va. 583;
42 S. E. 655.

Venture Oil Co. v. *Fretts*, 152 Pa. 451; 35 Atl. 732.

Aye v. *Philadelphia Co.*, 193 Pa. 451; 44 Atl. 655.

Foster v. *Elk Fork Oil & Gas Co.*, 32 C. C. A. 560; 90 Fed.
178.

Florence Oil etc. Co. v. *Orman*, 19 Col. App. 79; 73 Pac. 678.

Rawlings v. *Armel*, 70 Kan. 778; 79 Pac. 683.

Ziegler v. *Dailey*, 37 Ind. App. 240; 76 N. E. 819.

Sec. 17.—Where a lessee drills a dry hole and thereafter fails within a reasonable time to make further explorations or pay commutation money for delay, the landowner may declare a forfeiture and execute a new lease, and the second lessee will be entitled to cancel the outstanding lease and to be quieted in his title and possession, under the terms of his lease.

Steelsmith v. *Gartlan*, 45 W. Va. 27; 29 S. E. 978.

Lowther Oil Co. v. *Miller-Sibley Oil Co.*, 53 W. Va. 501; 44
S. E. 433.

Parish Fork Oil Co. v. *Bridgewater Gas Co.*, 51 W. Va. 583;
42 S. E. 655.

Foster v. *Elk Fork Oil & Gas Co.*, 32 C. C. A. 560; 90 Fed.
178.

Barnhart v. *Lockwood*, 152 Pa. 82; 25 Atl. 237.

LESSEE'S REMEDIES.

Sec. 18.—Where lessee has entered the premises under an oil and gas lease and drilled an unproductive well, to hold the lease he must, within a reasonable time, either make additional explorations or pay commutation money for delay. And where, after drilling a dry hole, the landowner refuses to permit the lessee, within a reasonable time, to continue developments, or refuses to receive commutation money for delay (where the lease provides for commutation money) lessee may, if excluded from the premises, recover possession in a possessory action, or may enjoin the landowner or a second lessee from any interference in making further developments.

Henne v. *South Penn Oil Co.,* 52 W. Va. 192; 43 S. E. 147.
Bartley v. *Phillips,* 179 Pa. 175; 36 Atl. 217.
Stahl v. *VanVleck,* 53 Ohio St. 136; 41 N. E. 35.

Sec. 19.—Where lessees under an oil and gas lease have drilled an unproductive well, and thereafter abandon the same, and neither pay rentals nor make further explorations they may defend an action brought by lessors for non-payment of rentals or commutation money accruing subsequent to such abandonment upon proof that the well drilled was a test well and was unproductive, and that they abandoned the lease with full knowledge and notice to lessor of such abandonment.

May v. *Hazlewood Oil Co.,* 152 Pa. 518; 25 Atl. 564.

CHAPTER 34.

PAYMENT OF RENTAL INTO BANK.

Sec. 1.—Where an oil and gas lease provides for the payment of a stipulated rental or of commutation money for delay in explorations, and further provides that the payments may be made direct to the lessor or deposited in some specified bank to the credit of the lessor, a payment to the bank within the time to the order of the lessor by the lessee, accepted by the bank is a sufficient payment, regardless of whether the deposit is made in legal tender.

Lafayette Gas Co. v. *Kelsey,* 164 Ind. 563; 74 N. E. 7.
Yoke v. *Shea,* 47 W. Va. 40; 34 S. E. 748.
Friend v. *Mallory,* 52 W. Va. 53; 43 S. E. 114.
Monfort v. *Lanyon Zinc Co.,* 67 Kan. 310; 72 Pac. 78.
Gillespie v. *Fulton Oil & Gas Co.,* 236 Ill. 188; 86 N. E. 219.
Smith v. *Root,* 66 W. Va. 633; 66 S. E. 1005.
Rhodes v. *Mound City Gas & Oil Co.,* 80 Kan. 762; 104 Pac. 851.
American Window Glass Co. v. *Indiana etc. Gas. Co.,* 37 Ind. App. 439; 76 N. E. 1006.
Indiana etc. Nat. Gas & Oil Co. v. *Beale,* 166 Ind. 684; 76 N. E. 520.
Sayers v. *Kent,* 201 Pa. 38; 50 Atl. 296.

Sec. 2.—In *Lafayette Gas Co.* v. *Kelsey,* 164 Ind. 563; 74 N. E. 7 (April 28, 1905), syl. 2 is as follows:

"Where a lease provides for the payment of semi-annual rental direct to lessor, or by depositing the same in a specified bank, subject to the lessor's order, a payment to the bank within the time, by deposit in the bank to the order of the lessor, which was accepted by the bank, and the amount thereof credited to the lessor, subject to his order, was sufficient, regardless of whether the deposit was made in legal tender."

In a suit to cancel a lease for non-payment of rental, the lease provided that the rentals might be paid direct to the lessor, or deposited to his credit in bank. The lessee alleged and proved that he had made the payments to the bank agreed upon in the lease as the place of payment, and had made these payments in accordance with the provisions of the lease. The court held that such deposit was sufficient payment of rental and prevented forfeiture as to non-payment.

Sec. 3.—In *Yoke* v. *Shea,* 47 W. Va. 40; 34 S. E. 748 (Nov. 18, 1899), Homer L. Bowser executed an oil and gas lease for a tract of land in Tyler County, West Virginia, to W. J. Steele, and John Matthews, which lease contained the following clause:

"Provided, however, that this lease shall become null and void, and all rights hereunder shall cease and determine, unless a well shall be completed on the said premises within————from the date thereof, or unless the lessee shall pay at the rate of ten dollars ($10.00) per month in advance for each additional month such completion is delayed, from the time above mentioned for the completion of such well until a well is completed. Such payments may be made direct to the lessor or deposited to his credit in Tyler County Bank, at Sistersville. A failure to operate said lease after said well is completed, or pay said rental, for more than thirty days, shall render this lease null and void, and all rights of the second party shall cease."

The lease was acknowledged on March 9, 1897. Under the lease, the lessees began paying their rentals forty-one days after its delivery, by deposit to the credit of the lessor in the Tyler County Bank, in Sistersville, according to the provisions

of the lease. Lessors made a second lease and Yoke, who had
purchased an interest in the original lease, with the other parties
owning the other interests, filed a bill in chancery in the Circuit
Court of Tyler County against Shea and the lessor and others
who claimed under the second lease, to cancel that lease as a
cloud on their title. Decree for plaintiffs. Defendants appealed.
to Court of Appeals; affirmed. The lessor insisted that the
rentals should have been paid sooner, and refused to accept payment when offered, and thereafter the original lessees deposited
the money in the Tyler County Bank according to the terms of
the lease. As to the payment into Bank, the court held:

"The lessor in the lease designated the Bank as the proper
depository, and all the plaintiff was required to do was to make
the deposit and leave the payment to the Bank as it saw fit. The
certificate of deposit was proper as evidence thereof * * * *."

Sec. 4.—In *Friend* v. *Mallory*, 52 W. Va. 53; 43 S. E. 114,
analyzed under Chapter 4, syl. 1 is as follows:

"1. An oil and gas lease contained the provision 'That this
cease and determine unless a well shall be completed on the said
premises within three months from the date hereof, or unless the
lessee shall pay at the rate of Twenty-two Dollars and twenty-five
cents, quarterly in advance for each additional three months such
completion is delayed from the time above mentioned for the completion of such well until a well is completed; and it is agreed that
the completion of such well shall be and operate as a full liquidation of all rentals under this provision during the remainder of
the term of the lease. Such payment may be direct to the lessors
or deposited to their credit in the Wirt Co. bank; and the further
provision that the lessee 'Shall have the privilege at any time to
remove all machinery and fixtures placed on said premises, and
further shall have the right at any time to surrender this lease
to first parties for cancellation, after which all payments and liabilities to accrue under and by virtue of its terms shall cease
and determine and this lease become absolutely null and
void.' *Held*, that deposit of a payment by the lessee in such Bank
to the credit of the lessor on or before the date such payment
would fall due is a sufficient payment to lessor, and it is immaterial whether it is paid in lawful money or by check, draft or otherwise; and *held*, further, the lessor cannot avoid such lease or declare a forfeiture thereof within the time for which he has re-

ceived the stipulated rental, and a lease executed to a third party within such time intended as an act of forfeiture, is void.''

Sec. 5.—In *Monfort* v. *Lanyon Zinc Co.*, 67 Kan. 310; 72 Pac. 78, analyzed under Chapter 5, Monfort leased to Bowles & Company a tract of 160 acres of land for oil and gas purposes, the lease containing a condition that if no oil or gas well should be sunk on the premises within five years from the date of the lease, the same should become absolutely null and void, unless the lessee should elect, from year to year to continue the lease by paying or depositing to the credit of the lessor each year in advance $40.00, which deposit to be made in the Bank of Allen County, Kansas, until a well should be completed. After the expiration of the five years mentioned in the lease, lessor brought suit to cancel the lease upon the grounds that no well had been drilled or undertaken by the lessees or their assignees, within the five years, on the lessor's property. The defendant claimed, and it was not denied, that wells were sunk and operated in Allen County, and that after the expiration of the five years lessees made the deposit in the Bank of Allen County, to the credit of lessors, as provided for by the lease. The court held that the payment by deposit was sufficient, and affirmed the District Court in a decree refusing to cancel the lease.

Sec. 6.—In *Gillespie* v. *Fulton Oil & Gas Co.*, 236 Ill. 188; 86 N. E. 219, analyzed under Chapter 13, syl. 21 is as follows:

"21. Where a lessor in an oil and gas lease, when notified that the money called for as rental had been left for him at a Bank, refused to accept it on the ground that the lease was void, and he indicated his purpose not to receive any rental under the lease, he waived any duty resting on the lessee to make a legal tender of the rental.''

Sec. 7.—In *Smith* v. *Root*, 66 W. Va. 633; 66 S. E. 1005, analyzed under Chapter 51, Hall, executed an oil and gas lease on a tract of land to Goff & Heck, the lease providing that the payment of rentals might be made direct to the lessor or deposited to the credit of the lessor in the Roane County Bank, Spencer, West Virginia. Subsequently two quarterly rentals were paid to Hall, and after the expiration of five quarterly rental

periods without paying any rental, Goff & Heck assigned the
lease to Smith, who deposited the five quarterly rentals to the
credit of lessor in the Roane County Bank. Prior to this payment into Bank, however, the Halls under the belief that the
lease was forfeited, made a second lease. Smith filed a bill in
chancery in the Circuit Court of Roane County, and obtained an
injunction against the second lessee, claiming that the original
lease contained no forfeiture clause, and within the term he had
deposited the rentals in full to date, in the depositary agreed
upon. The defendant, second lessee, filed a cross bill, and the
Circuit Court held that at the date of the execution of the second
lease the first lease was forfeited by abandonment, and cancelled
the same. Smith appealed and the Court of Appeals affirmed
the court below.

Sec. 8.—In *Rhodes* v. *Mound City Gas & Oil Co.*, 80 *Kan.* 762;
104 Pac. 851 (Oct. 9, 1909), the syllabus is as follows:

"1. An assignment of mineral leases conveying real estate
'immediately surrounding,' Mound City, Kansas, was properly in-
terpreted by the District Court to include a lease of land situated
a half mile distant from the town site.

2. In the absence of terms indicating a contrary intention, a
covenant in a gas and oil lease to drill a well on the leased premises within two years, or thereafter pay $80.00 annually until a
well is drilled, does not require the annual payments to be made
in advance, and the covenant is performed by a single payment
of the entire sum at any time before the end of the year for which
it is made."

On June 18, 1902, Henry Carbon made an oil and gas lease
to Robert Fleming, which lease was assigned by Fleming to the
defendant oil company. The lease contained the following provision:

"One. Second party agrees to drill a well upon said premises
within two years from this date, or thereafter pay to first party
$80.00 annually until said well is drilled, or this lease shall be
void.

Eight. A deposit to credit of lessor in Farmers & Mechanics
Bank, Mound City, Kansas, to the account of any of the money
payments herein provided for, shall be a payment under the terms
of this lease."

On April 24, 1905, a tender of $80.00 was made to the lessor according to the terms of the lease, and was refused. On June 16, 1905, less than three years from the date of the lease, the sum of $80.00 was deposited to the credit of the lessor in the Farmers & Mechanics Bank, in Mound City, according to the terms of the eighth condition of the lease. A. B. Rhodes, claiming title to the mineral interests in the Henry Carbon land, instituted in the District Court of Linn County an action against the Mound City company, to enjoin the defendant from interfering with the plaintiff's possession, use and enjoyment of a gas well which had been drilled, and to which plaintiff claimed the paramount right. The defendant claimed the lease by the assignment which described the property assigned as follows:

"All my right, title, claim and interest in and to one certain franchise granted to the undersigned on the 3rd day of March, 1902, by the City of Mound City, Kansas, being ordinances numbers 153 and 154 of said city, and all the gas pipes and gas mains and fixtures not hereinafter reserved, and all my right, title, claim and interest in and to all the oil, gas, coal and other mineral rights of all kinds and description belonging to said undersigned owner, all of which was taken in said undersigned name, and which said lease and franchise cover real estate situated in and immediately surrounding Mound City, Kansas, and this conveyance is intended to cover and convey all the said leases and franchises of the undersigned owner, or which may hereafter be taken in my name."

The Carbon land was a half mile distant from Mound City and the plaintiff claimed that the terms of the assignment excluded it because the word "immediately" forbade existence of intervening space. The plaintiff contended that if no well was drilled the lease became void at the end of two years unless $80.00 was paid in advance to keep it alive, for another year. Judgment was rendered by the District Court in favor of defendant. Plaintiff appealed. The Supreme Court affirmed the judgment, citing as to the construction of the lease, and the payment of the rental:

Rose v. *Lanyon Zinc Co.*. 68 Kan. 126; 74 Pac. 625.
Blodgett v. *Lanyon Zinc Co.*, 120 Fed. 893; 58 C. C. A. 79.

Sec. 9.—In *American Window Glass Co.* v. *Indiana etc. Gas Co.*, 37 Ind. App. 439; 76 N. E. 1006 (March 9, 1906), the syllabus is as follows:

"1. Under an oil and gas lease giving the lessee certain rights 'for a term of 12 years, and so long thereafter as petroleum, gas and mineral substances can be produced in paying quantities or the payments hereinafter provided for are made,' the word 'or' should be read the word 'and' so that the term was limited to 12 years, unless oil or gas was procured.

2. Where an oil and gas lease gave the lessee a right to explore the land for oil and gas for a period of 12 years, and so long thereafter as oil or gas should be produced, and provided for the payment of annual rentals, the acceptance of an annual payment after the expiration of the twelve-year period, and the execution of a receipt stating that the payment continued the lease in form for another term did not extend the lease for an additional term of 12 years, but did constitute a waiver of the right to claim a forfeiture at the end of the twelve-year period, so as to entitle the lessee to notice and a reasonable time thereafter to comply with the terms of the lease before forfeiture.

3. What is a reasonable time within which to perform an act is usually a question of fact, though, if the facts are undisputed or clearly established, it may be a question of law.

4. Where an oil and gas lease provided for a certain annual rental, and stipulated that a deposit in a certain Bank to the credit of the lessor should constitute payment, a deposit of a payment after the expiration of the term limited by the lease which paymen was accepted by the Bank, without notice from the lessor not to do so, was in effect a payment to the lessor."

The American Window Glass Company instituted in the Circuit Court of Wells County an action against the Indiana Natural Gas & Oil Company and others. The plaintiff claimed to be the owner of natural gas, oil and other mineral substances underlying certain real estate in Grant County, Indiana, with the exclusive right to enter upon, prospect for and remove such mineral substances, by virtue of two oil and gas leases executed on April 15th and June 18, 1901, by Frank Wilson, Louie Wilson, his wife, and F. K. Wilson, guardian of Wade H. Wilson, grantees of James S. Wilson. The defendant oil company claimed the said premises by virtue of two leases executed on April 5th and March 12th, 1888, by the then landowner, James S. Wilson, to one Leonard

B. Best. These leases by various assignments, on July 1, 1890, became vested in the oil company. The leases under which both parties claimed stipulated that the leases were for the term of 12 years and so long thereafter as petroleum, gas or mineral substances could be produced in paying quantities, or the payments therein provided for were made according to the terms and conditions of the lease, with the following conditions:

"Lessees to commence operations for said drilling and mining purposes within one year from the execution of this lease, or in lien thereof for delay in commencing such operations, and as a consideration for the agreements herein contained, thereafter to pay * * * * * $36.00 per annum, payable in advance, each year until such operations are commenced, and a well completed. A deposit to the credit of the party of the first part in the Marion Bank of Marion, Indiana, shall be considered a payment under the terms of this lease."

The undisputed facts in the case were: that on February 1, 1893, Frank Wilson and Louie Wilson, his wife, and Wade H. Wilson, by conveyance from James S. Wilson, became the owners of the land leased; that all rentals for the delay in developing the lands until February, March and April, 1901, were duly paid and accepted by the landowners; that the rental for the years 1901, and 1902, ending February, March, and April, 1903, were by appellee deposited in the Marion Bank of Marion; that the landowners had not, nor had anyone for them, on their behalf, notified the bank not to receive the rentals; that the rental for the year ending 1901, was paid in February or March, 1900, by a representative of the appellee to F. K. Wilson; that the landowners, after said last payment, did not receive any payment from appellee or from said Bank; that appellee did not, nor did its assigns, or any other person in its behalf, ever take possession of the real estate for any purpose prior to May 1, 1902; that on said last date, appellee, by its agents and servants, entered upon the real estate over the objection and orders of the lessors and constructed derricks and continued to operate thereon until it had drilled five gas wells, and was about to begin piping the gas therefrom when appellant applied for and obtained a temporary restraining order against appellee restraining it from piping or removing any gas or oil from said wells; that appellant had complied

with all the terms and conditions of the lease under which it was
claiming the right to such oil and gas. Upon final hearing the
restraining order theretofore issued was dissolved and a finding
and judgment entered for defendants. The plaintiff appealed, and
the Appellate Court affirmed the decree.

The court held that had the landowners at the end of the
twelve-year term, notified the oil company that it would not receive any further payments, and refuse to accept the same, and
before payment to the Bank had given it notice not to receive any
payments for their use and benefit, the rights of the oil company
under the lease would have terminated, and cited:

> *American Window Glass Co.* v. *Williams,* 30 Ind. App. 685;
> 66 N. E. 912.
> *Ind. Nat. Gas etc. Co.* v. *Granger,* 33 Ind. App. 559; 70 N. E.
> 395.
> *West Penn Gas Co.* v. *George,* 161 Pa. 47; 28 Atl. 1004.
> *Cassell* v. *Crothers,* 193 Pa. 359; 44 Atl. 446.
> *Murdock-West Co.* v. *Logan,* 69 Ohio St. 514; 69 N. E. 984.
> *Brown* v. *Fowler,* 65 Ohio St. 507; 63 N. E. 76.
> *Northwestern etc. Co.* v. *Tiffin,* 59 Ohio St. 420; 54 N. E. 77.
> *Bettman* v. *Harness,* 42 W. Va. 433; 26 S. E. 271; 36 L. R. A.
> 566.

The court held that under the decision of the Supreme Court
of Indiana, lessors must give the lessee a reasonable time in which
to develop the lands, after notice of intention to declare a forfeiture, citing:

> *Consumers Gas Trust Co.* v. *Littler,* 162 Ind. 320; 70 N. E.
> 363.
> *Consumers Gas Trust Co.* v. *Worth,* 163 Ind. 141; 71 N. E.
> 489.

Sec. 10.—In *Indiana etc. Nat. Gas & Oil Co.* v. *Beale,* 166 Ind.
684; 76 N. E. 520 (Jan. 4, 1906), the syllabus is as follows:

"An oil and gas lease executed on March 29. 1888, provided
that the lessee, or his assigns, should have the right to operate on
the land for petroleum, gas, etc., for 12 years, or so long after the
expiration of such term as petroleum, etc., could be procured in
paying quantities 'or the payments provided for are made ac-

cording to the terms of the lease, which required the commencement of operations within a year', or in lieu thereof, for delay that the lessor pay $21.50 per annum in advance, to a certain specified Bank for the benefit of the lessor. No mining operations were conducted under the lease, but yearly payments in advance were deposited as provided for and until the year ending March 28, 1901. *Held,* that the lessors clearly, without notifying the holder of the leasehold to proceed to develop the premises, was not entitled to have the lease cancelled by merely serving a notice on April 5, 1900, that it had expired."

Idelia Beales instituted in the Superior Court of Madison County, Indiana, an action against the Indiana Natural Gas & Oil Company to quiet title to certain real estate in Grant County, Indiana, and to annul and cancel a certain oil and gas lease which, it was alleged in the complaint, was a cloud on the plaintiff's title. The case was decided by the Superior Court in favor of. the plaintiff, affirmed by the Appellate Court (74 N. E. 551) and the case was transferred from the Appellate Court to the Supreme Court. From the evidence the following facts appeared:

On March 29, 1888, John Roush, the owner in fee of the real estate in question, situated in Grant County, Indiana, executed to Leonard H. Best an oil and gas lease for the tract. The lease became the property of the oil company by assignment on July 1, 1892. On December 16, 1892, Roush and wife conveyed the leased premises to Idelia Beales, and she, from that time, continued to be the owner thereof. The lease stipulated that the lessors leased to Best the real estate therein described for and in consideration of the sum of $10.70 and for the further consideration thereinafter mentioned, and on account of the conditions thereinafter contained for the purpose and with the exclusive right of drilling for petroleum, gas, or any mineral substance for the term of twelve years and so long thereafter as petroleum, gas, or mineral substances could be procured in paying quantities, or the payments thereinafter provided for were made, according to the terms and conditions of the lease; the lease then provided that lessee should have water and wood on the premises for drilling and mining operations, with the right to erect and remove necessary buildings and machinery, tanks, pipes, and other property necessary for the purpose; that the lessor should have 1/8 of all the petroleum or mineral substances aforesaid; that if gas alone should be found in sufficient quantities to make it profitable to pipe the same to other localities, grantor should receive $100.00 per annum for each gas well, and sufficient gas to heat and light his dwelling; no part of the premises leased were to be used for the purpose of mining for minerals, petroleum, or gas, except by the lessee, the lease containing the following provision:

"Party of the second part agrees to commence operations for said drilling or mining purposes within one year from the ex ecution of this lease, or in lien thereof for delay in commencing such operations, and as a consideration for the agreements contained herein, thereafter pay to said party of the firts part (the lessor) $21.50, payable in advance on 29 March in each year, until such operations are commenced and a well completed. A deposit to the credit of the party of the first part (lessor) in the Marion Bank of Marion, Indiana, shall be considered as payment under the terms of this lease. Should party of the second part fail to make such payments or either of them, within thirty days from the time the same is due, then this lease shall be null and void, and of no effect."

The oil company did not take possession of the premises, and no wells were drilled by it, or by any other person under the lease. Plaintiff authorized her husband to act as agent in collecting the rentals. All payments required of the lessee should be paid in lieu of the drilling of wells had been paid to the owners of the real estate, and by them accepted at all times during the entire term of the 12 years, until March, 1900. No money deposited had been received by plaintiff since that time. The rentals had always been paid by deposit in the Marion Bank, in the City of Marion, Indiana, as provided in the contract. On April 5, 1900, the following notice was mailed by the husband and agent of the plaintiff, to the defendant:

"Jonesboro, Ind., April 5, 1900. Indiana Natural Gas & Oil Co., Chicago, Ill: I hereby notify you that your lease expired March 25, 1900, on the land now owned by Idelia Beales in Sections 10 and 15, Township 23 N. Range 8, East, Grant County, Indiana. I kindly ask you to release said lease from the records of Grant County. Respectfully, Idelia Beales."

Receipts for the years 1896-7-8-9 from plaintiff to the oil company for sums due in lieu of drilling under the lease were shown by the evidence. It was agreed by the parties and made a part of the evidence in the trial, that on the 16th day of March, 1900, the oil company deposited to the credit of the plaintiff the sum of $21.50 in the Marion Bank, of Marion, Indiana; that on March 1, 1901, a like sum was deposited in the same bank for the same purpose. On February 25, 1902, a like deposit was made for the same purpose in the same Bank, and on March 13, 1903, a like deposit was made in the same Bank for the same purpose. It appeared that certificates of deposit were made to plaintiff for each of said sums by said Marion Bank. No notice was ever given to the Bank by plaintiff that it should receive no more money or deposits on account of the lease, or that the Bank should no longer act as agent of plaintiff for that purpose; and no notice of the revocation of the agency of the said Bank by plaintiff was at any time given to the oil company. The decree of the courts below was reversed, under authority of the following decisions of the Supreme Court of Indiana:

> *Consumers Gas Trust Co.* v. *Littler,* 162 Ind. 320; 70 N. E. 363.
> *Consumers Gas Trust Co.* v. *Howard,* 163 Ind. 170; 71 N. E. 493.
> *Consumers Gas Trust Co.* v. *Ink,* 163 Ind. 174; 71 N. E. 477.
> *Consumers Gas Trust Co.* v. *Worth,* 163 Ind. 141; 71 N. E. 489.
> *New American Oil Co.* v. *Troyer,* 166 Ind. 402; 76 N. E. 253.

LESSOR'S REMEDY.

Sec. 11.—Where the lessee has abandoned his lease, or incurred a forfeiture by failing to pay the rentals, lessor may declare a forfeiture, and the subsequent deposit by the lessee or his assigns of the unpaid rentals in the depositary agreed upon in the lease will not revive the lease; and notwithstanding such deposit of the rentals lessor or the second lessee may procure the cancellation of the first lease upon the grounds of abandonment, or forfeiture for other causes.

Smith v. *Root,* 66 W. Va. 633; 66 S. E. 1005.

LESSEE'S REMEDIES.

Sec. 12.—Where the lessor refuses to accept the stipulated rentals or commutation money provided for in lieu of explorations, and the lease contains a provision authorizing payment of this rental or commutation money by depositing it in Bank to the credit of the lessor, lessee may pay the stipulated rentals or commutation money to the Bank in the manner provided for by the lease. Where the lessor executes a second lease before the maturity of rentals under the first lease lessee may make such deposit, without making a legal tender to the lessor.

Indiana etc. Nat. Gas & Oil Co. v. *Beale*, 166 Ind. 684; 76 N. E. 520.
Lafayette Gas Co. v. *Kelsey*, 164 Ind. 563; 74 N. E. 7.
Yoke v. *Shea*, 47 W. Va. 401; 34 S. E. 748.
Friend v. *Mallory*, 52 W. Va. 53; 43 S. E. 114.
Monfort v. *Lanyon Zinc Co.*, 67 Kan. 310; 72 Pac. 78.
Gillespie v. *Fulton Oil & Gas Co.*, 236 Ill. 188; 86 N. E. 219.
Rhodes v. *Mound City Gas & Oil Co.*, 80 Kan. 762; 104 Pac. 851.
American Window Glass Co. v. *Indiana etc. Gas Co.*, 37 Ind. App. 439; 76 N. E. 1006.
Sayers v. *Kent*, 201 Pa. 38; 50 Atl. 296.

Sec. 13.—In the absence of terms indicating a contrary intention, a covenant in an oil and gas lease to drill a well on the leased premises within a stipulated time or thereafter pay annually, monthly, or quarterly, a stipulated rental for delay, does not require such stipulated payment of rental to be made in advance, and the lessee by payment or tender of the stipulated sum to the lessor or by payment of said sum into the depositary bank designated by the lease, to the credit of the lessor, in the manner provided for by the lease, at any time before the end of the period designated, sufficiently performs the covenants of the lease, and the lease, upon such tender ,or deposit, is extended to the end of the annual, quarterly, or monthly period provided for by the lease, during which it may be kept alive upon payment of the commutation money.

Rhodes v. *Mound City Gas & Oil Co.*, 80 Kan. 762; 104 Pac. 851.
Rose v. *Lanyon Zinc Co.*, 68 Kan. 126; 74 Pac. 625.
Blodgett v. *Lanyon Zinc Co.*, 120 Fed. 893; 58 C. C. A. 79.

CHAPTER 35.

LIFE TENANTS AND REMAINDERMEN.

Sec. 1.—Where no oil or gas operations have been commenced on land before an estate for life has accrued, the tenant for life has no right to operate for oil or gas himself, and cannot give such a right to any person by lease. Where, however, oil or gas has been discovered in paying quantities before an estate for life has accrued the tenant for life is entitled to the royalty of oil and rental for gas during the continuance of his life estate. Where the petroleum oil underlying a tract of land in possession of a tenant for life is sold or leased by the remainder man, the tenant for life is entitled to the interest on the royalty during the continuance of the life estate, and then the residue or corpus of the royalty will be paid to the remainderman.

> *Marshall* v. *Mellon*, 179 Pa. 371; 36 At. 201; 57 Am. St. Rep. 601; 35 L. R. A. 816.
> *Koen* v. *Bartlett*, 41 W. Va. 559; 23 S. E. 664; 56 Am. St. Rep. 884; 31 L. R. A. 128.
> *Williamson* v. *Jones*, 43 W. Va. 563; 27 S. E. 411.
> *Wilson* v. *Youst*, 43 W. Va. 826; 28 S. E. 781.
> *Ammons* v. *Ammons*, 50 W. Va. 390; 40 S. E. 490.
> *Richmond Nat. Gas Co.* v. *Davenport*, 37 Ind. App. 25; 76 N. E. 525.
> *Eakin* v. *Hawkins*, 48 W. Va. 364; 37 S. E. 622.
> *Eakin* v. *Hawkins*, 52 W. Va. 124; 43 S. E. 211.
> *Stewart* v. *Tennant*, 52 W. Va. 559; 44 S. E. 223.

Sec. 2.—In *Marshall* v. *Mellon*, 179 Pa. 371; 36 Atl. 201; 57 Am. St. Rep. 601; 35 L. R. A. 816, analyzed under Chapter 27, the syllabus is as follows:

"Where no oil or gas operations have been commenced on land before an estate for life has accrued, the tenant for life has no right to operate for oil or gas himself, and cannot give such a right to any person by lease.

A life tenant of oil and gas lands which had never been operated for oil or gas, executed a lease for oil and gas purposes exclusively. The lessees did not operate the land or perform any of the covenants of the lease, and refused to pay the rent stipulated. *Held*, that the lessor could not enforce the lease."

Sec. 3.—In *Koen* v. *Bartlett*, 41 W. Va. 559; 23 S. E. 664; 56 Am. St. Rep. 884; 31 L. R. A. 128 (Dec. 11, 1895), the syllabus is as follows: ·

"1. An owner in fee simple makes an oil and gas lease for a term of five years, and as much longer as the premises are operated for oil and gas, or the rent for failure to commence operating is paid for, among other things, one-eighth part of all the oil produced and saved, to be delivered in the pipelines to the credit of the lessor. The lessor then sells and conveys one undivided moiety of the one-sixteenth part of all the oil produced and saved. Afterwards, but before any oil is bored for or produced, the lessor sells, grants, and conveys the land in fee simple to his six children, to each one a part, by metes and bounds, in consideration of natural love and affection, by deed of general warranty, 'except that the party of the second part takes the same subject to any lease for oil or gas made by the party of the first part or any sale of royalty for oil or gas made by him;' and, by the same deed he retains full control of said land in all respects, and for all purposes, during his lifetime. Soon thereafter oil wells are bored and oil produced, saved, and put in the pipelines in large quantities. *Held,* the one-eighth royalty goes of right to the tenant for life, and his grantees, during the continuance of the estate for life, and not to the owners in fee of the estate expectant thereon.

2. The tenant of an estate for life, unless restrained by covenant or agreement, has a right to the full enjoyment and use of the land and all its profits during his estate therein, including mines of oil or gas open when his life estate begins, or lawfully opened and worked during the existence of such estate."

On September 19, 1892, Elija Kerns, the owner in fee and in possession of a tract of 75 acres of land in Marion County, West Virginia, situated within the productive part of the Mannington oil field, executed to C. S. Nay an oil and gas lease for that part of the tract of land lying north of the county road, for the term of five years, and as much longer as the premises might be operated for oil and gas, at a royalty of one-eighth of the oil delivered in the pipelines. On March 15, 1893, Nay sold, transferred and assigned his lease to O. N. Koen. By deed dated September 28, 1892, Kerns sold and conveyed to O. N. Koen the undivided moiety of the one-sixteenth part of all the oil and gas produced and saved from the lands so leased. On September 30, 1892, O. N.

Koen sold and conveyed one undivided two-thirds of his interests conveyed to him by Kerns to Thornton F. Koen, and J. T. Koen. O. N. Koen by deed dated October 5, 1893, sold and assigned the Nay oil lease to the South Penn Oil Company, and this company drilled the leased premises, and discovered oil in paying quantities, Elija Kerns, by six separate deeds dated December 3, 1892, for natural love and affection, sold and conveyed in severalty by metes and bounds to his six several children in fee simple in expectancy on the grantor's life estate thereby retained and reserved to himself, the said tract of land leased as aforesaid. Whatever interests these expectant owners of the inheritance had, came by various conveyances to O. N. Koen and others. Elija Kerns, by deed dated November 18, 1893, in consideration of $2400.00, sold, granted and conveyed, by deed of general warranty to F. W. Bartlett, H. P. Brand and another, the undivided one-sixteenth part of all the oil and gas in and under the tract of land of 7! acres. Koen filed his bill in the Intermediate Court of Marion County, against Bartlett and others to prohibit the Pipeline Company from delivering the one-sixteenth of the oil conveyed to Bartlett, Brand and another by the deed of November 18, 1893. The plaintiff claimed the sixteenth by virtue and effect of the deeds made by Koen to his children. Bartlett and Brand claimed the sixteenth by virtue of the deed from Kerns, the life tenant by reservation. Koen claimed the sixteenth had passed to the children as owners in fee in expectancy by their deeds. The Intermediate Court of Marion County appointed a receiver to sell and hold the proceeds of the oil; and on final hearing determined that Bartlett and Brand were not entitled to the sixteenth of the oil in the pipelines, but that the plaintiffs, O. N. Koen and others, were entitled thereto, and decreed accordingly. On appeal to the Circuit Court the Intermediate Court was affirmed, and Bartlett and Brand appealed to the Supreme Court. That court reversed the decrees of the Circuit and Intermediate Courts of Marion County, and held in favor of Bartlett and Brand as grantees of the life tenant as to the one-sixteenth of the oil.

Sec. 4.—In *Williamson* v. *Jones* . 43 W. Va. 563: 27 S. E. 411, analyzed under Chapter 27, syls. 2-3-5-6-13-15 are as follows:

"2. It is waste in a tenant for life to take petroleum oil

from the land, for which he is liable to the reversioner or remainder man in fee.

3. A tenant for life may work open salt or oil wells or mines even to exhaustion, without account, but cannot open new ones.

5. Things part of the land, wrongfully severed by a tenant for life, become personalty, but belong to the owner of the next vested estate of inheritance in reversion or the remainder, not the life tenant.

6. Where there is a life tenant, and timber or other thing part of the realty going to loss, and imperative need calls for it, equity may cause it to be cut or otherwise secured for the remainder man or reversioner. Equity has power to do so, if it do no harm to the life tenant, or he be compensated.

13. A tenant for life, or a tenant in common in sole possession claiming exclusive ownership, taking petroleum oil, and converting it to his exclusive use, is liable to account on the basis of rents and profits, not for annual rental.

15. A tenant for life, who, by waste, has severed from the realty things that are part of it, as petroleum oil, has no right to have their proceeds invested so he may have interest thereon during the life estate, but their proceeds go at once to the owner of the next vested estate of inheritance.''

Sec. 5.—In *Wilson* v. *Youst*, 43 W. Va. 826; 28 S. E. 781, analyzed under Chapter 27, syl. 3 is as follows:

''The petroleum oil underlying a tract of land which has been devised to a life tenant who is in possession, and which is to go to certain infant children after the decease of the life tenant, may be sold, upon the petition of the guardian of said infants, under the provisions of Chapter 82 of the Code, or leased; and the life tenant will be entitled to the interest on the royalty during the continuance of the life estate, and then the residue or corpus of the royalty will be paid to the remainder men.''

Sec. 6.—In *Ammons* v. *Ammons*, 50 W. Va. 390; 40 S. E. 490, (Dec. 7, 1901) there was a controversy as to the oil and gas in a tract of 200 acres of land in Monongalia County, West Virginia, formerly owned by Daniel Conaway who died testate several years before the litigation. By his will Conaway devised the tract of land as follows:

"To my daughter, Armina Ammons, to have and to hold during the residue of the term of her natural life, but at her death to go to her heirs, I give and devise the residue of my home farm, being about two hundred acres, subject to an estate for life therein, which I hereby give and devise to my beloved wife, Melinda Conaway."

The Devisee, Armina Ammons, was the wife of Milton A. Ammons. The will was probated on August 29, 1887. On February 17, 1892, Milton A. Ammons, having been appointed guardian for Howard L. Ammons, Clarence L. Ammons, Ashley N. Ammons, Cyrus C. Ammons, Stella M. Ammons, Milliard R. Ammons, Early T. Ammons, and Earnest W. Ammons, all of whom were infants, and being the only children at that time of Armina Ammons, filed his petition in the Circuit Court of Monongalia County under Section 12, and the following Sections of Chapter 83 of the Code, alleging that a lease had been executed by the said Milton A. Ammons and Armina Ammons to C. J. Ford for oil and gas purposes on the tract of land containing about 300 acres, of which about 50 acres was owned by Milton A. Ammons, individually, and the residue was the tract of land devised as aforesaid which by actual measurement was found to contain 243 acres; that said lease had been assigned to the South Penn Oil Company; that Melinda Conaway had conveyed her life estate in the land to Milton A. Ammons and Armina Ammons in consideration of love and affection and their agreement to support, care for and maintain her; that by the terms of the lease the lessees were to deliver to the lessors in the pipelines with which the wells should be connected, ⅛ of all the oil produced and saved, and pay $300.00 annually for every well from which gas should be transported and used off the premises; that until the estate in remainder in the oil and gas in said land should be disposed of no development of oil or gas under the lease could be had; that all the land adjoining said tract so devised had been leased for oil and gas; that said infants had no means to develop the other land; that they had no other estate, real or personal; that it would be greatly to their advantage and interest to have the said estate in remainder in the oil and gas sold; and prayed that sale might be made. A guardian ad litem was appointed for the infants, who filed his answer committing their interests to the protection of the court. Melinda Conaway filed her answer and consented to a sale of the interests of the in-

fant children, and releasing her lien for support to that extent.
Milton A. Ammons and Armina Ammons filed their joint and
separate answer setting up their joint ownership of the interest
of Melinda Conaway under the provisions of the will by reason
of her conveyance to them, and the life estate of Armina Ammons.
as provided by the will, and consented that the said infants might
have an estate *in presenti* of an undivided 1-3 of the oil and gas,
if the court should think the same proper, and that the other 2-3
might be divided equally between Melinda Conaway on the one
side, and themselves on the other side. Upon this petition these
answers, the exhibits therewith filed, and the testimony of the witnesses taken at the hearing, the court decreed a sale of said interests of the infants in the undivided 7/8 of the oil and gas in the
243-acre tract of land upon the following conditions to be performed by the purchaser:

"To begin to operate, mine and bore for the oil and gas within and under said tract of land, free of cost to said infants or
their guardian, within sixty days after the confirmation of the
sale hereunder, and complete one well within one year after said
confirmation, unavoidable delays and accidents excepted, and if
oil be found thereon in paying quantities, then after said first
well is completed thereon, the said purchaser shall immediately
commence and drill other wells thereon as shall seem necessary
and proper to protect the oil and gas in and under the said tract
of land; and shall also deliver as royalty to said infants or their
guardian, free of cost to them or their guardian, the 1-2 of the 1-8
of all oil produced, and saved from the said land, in pipelines or
tanks and pay to said infants or their guardian the one-half of
$300.00 per year for the gas from each and every well drilled
thereon, producing gas, the product from which is marketed or
used off the said premises; and also to pay all damages to growing crops by reason of operations."

Under this decree sale was made, and the South Penn Oil
Company became the purchaser for the sum of $300.00 and costs
of the proceedings. The purchase money was paid and a deed
executed to the purchaser, conforming in all respects to the decree
of sale. Thereafter the South Penn Oil Company entered upon th
land, drilled sixteen or seventeen wells, some of which were dry,
others productive, but not in paying quantities, and still others
which proved to be very valuable, and in pursuance of the terms of

the decree and its deed, it delivered ½ the royalty oil, that is, ½ of the ⅛ of all the oil produced into the pipelines to the credit of Milton A. Ammons, guardian for the infants, and the other ½ to the credit of Armina Ammons, until sometime in the year 1897, when the Oil Company refused to make any further deliveries, and notified the Eureka Pipeline Company, into whose lines and tanks the oil went, to make no more deliveries on account of said royalties. The oil delivered to Armina Ammons amounted when sold to $13,947.19, and the same amount was realized by the sale of the oil delivered to Milton A. Ammons, as guardian. After the cessation of deliveries of oils a further complication arose from the fact that three other children were born to Milton A. Ammons and Armina Ammons after the sale was made in the summary proceedings; and the South Penn Oil Company contended that by the purchase it did not obtain the interests of these children in remainder in the oil and gas in the tract of land.

Howard L. Ammons, and the seven other children, by Milton Ammons, as their next friend, instituted suit in chancery in the Circuit Court of Monongalia County, against the South Penn Oil Company for the purpose of requiring the company to drill and operate the land according to the terms and conditions of the will, in which case a decree was entered in February, 1893, requiring the company to drill certain additional wells on certain parts of the land, or forfeit their right to drill on these portions of the land. An appeal was taken by the Oil Company and the decree was reversed by the Court of Appeals. (See *Ammons* v. *South Penn Oil Co.*, 47 W. Va. 610; 35 S. E. 1004, analyzed under Chapter 20.) The South Penn Oil Company claimed to discover the existence of these three children during the progress of the suit.

Pending the execution of a bond by the guardian, the $300.00 paid as purchase money by the South Penn Oil Company was paid to the general receiver of the court, who some time thereafter died, and the money was never paid by the guardian. Milton A. Ammons and others filed their bill in chancery against Howard L. Ammons and others in the Circuit Court of Monongalia County which resulted in the development of the foregoing facts. The guardian alleged in his bill that he had made a final settlement in which it was ascertained that on the 24th day of October. 1896, there was a balance due from him to Howard L. Ammons amounting to $325.79, all of which he had paid, but that his ward had refused to receipt to him for the money, and had also refused to accept the settlement as final. Three other wards seemed to have gotten beyond the control of their parent and guardian, and their reckless dispositions added to the complication, and the advanced age of the guardian, and some uneasiness on the part of his sureties induced him to bring the suit as guardian of the infants, and as late guardian of Howard L. Ammons, against the South Penn Oil Company and the Eureka Pipeline, all the children of himself and his wife, Armina Ammons, and all the sureties on his bond as guardian. The bill set out all the facts before stated, fully and in detail, and prayed that all matters in difference between the guardian and his wards be adjusted and settled; that all questions of doubt and uncertainty as to how the accounts between him and his wards should be settled, should be adjudicated and determined; that the question as to how the proceeds of the oil should be divided among the infants be settled; that the proper person be designated to receive the money in the hands of the general receiver, when collected; that a proper person be designated to receive and sell the share of the infants in the oil produced from the land thereafter, as well as the oil remaining unsold in the hands of the Eureka Pipeline Company; and for other relief. To this bill, an answer by the South Penn Oil Company was filed, setting forth as the reason for ceasing to make further delivery of the royalty oil the decision of the Court of Appeals in the case of *Wilson* v. *Youst* (43 W. Va. 826, analyzed under Chapter 27), holding that a life tenant is only entitled to the interest upon the money derived from the sale of the royalty oil, and that remainder men are not entitled to the corpus of such fund until after the death of the life tenant, and that such oil should be sold and the proceeds invested for the benefit of the life tenant and those entitled in remainder, and only the interest thereon paid to the life tenant. The Oil Company denied that under the law, as thus settled, Armina Ammons or the plaintiff as guardian, were entitled to demand any of the royalty oil then remaining in the hands of the respondent or that might be obtained thereafter from the land or any gas rental that might result from finding gas on the land. The answer further averred that the decree in the summary proceeding failed to provide for the proper disposition of the royalty and gas rentals as the law then required, and that the Oil Company could not safely deliver the royalty oil then in its possession or which it had delivered to the Eureka Pipeline Company, or which it might thereafter produce, without the direction of the court. By way of affirmative relief the Oil Company prayed that its investment and interest in the oil and gas be protected; that its title thereto be sustained and adjudged valid; that the decrees in the summary proceedings might be so corrected that in future the royalty oil might be sold and the proceeds invested for the use of the life tenant and remainder man in accordance with the law. Milton A. Ammons in his own right and as guardian, and Armina Ammons, filed their separate answers to the cross bill, and their general replication to the answer of the South Penn Oil Company. On February 25, 1901, the Circuit Court entered a decree in which so much of the South Penn Oil Company's answer as sought affirmative relief, and its crossbill were dismissed, the South Penn Oil Company having filed a crossbill in the Clerk's office, at rules in which it set out fully and particularly all the facts and proceedings hereinbefore mentioned, and concluding with a prayer substantially the same as that contained in its answer. A general replication was filed to the remaining portions of the South Penn Oil Company's answer, and it was decreed that Armina Ammons was entitled to ½ of the royalty oil; and that the other half should be divided among all the eleven children. The South Penn Oil Company was required by the decree to deliver only ½ of the future royalty oil into the pipeline to the credit of Armina Ammons. From this decree the South Penn Oil Company appealed to the Supreme Court, and that court reversed the decree, citing *Wilson* v. *Youst.*

Sec. 7.—In *Richmond Natural Gas Co.* v. *Davenport*, 76 N. E. 525; 37 Ind. App. 25 (Dec. 15, 1905), the syllabus is as follows:

"1. Natural gas or petroleum underneath the surface of the ground, and not reduced to actual possession of any person, constitutes a part of the land and belongs to the owner in such sense that he has the exclusive right by operations on his land to reduce the same to possession, though until so reduced to possession such substances is subject to be taken by any other person by proper operations on his own land.
2. One lawfully in possession of land containing natural gas or petroleum, with the right to enjoy the income and profits, but not being the owner of the fee, nor receiving from such owner the

privilege to take minerals from the land is not entitled to extract gas or petroleum therefrom.

3. Where no operations for oil or gas had been carried on by the owner of the fee, his grantee or lessee, and the owner of the fee, had not conveyed such right by lease or grant during the ownership of the fee, a succeeding life tenant was not entitled, as against the remainder men, either to mine for gas or oil on the land himself, or to grant authority to another to do so; and this though unless the land was mined the gas would have been withdrawn therefrom through wells en adjoining property during the continuance of the life estate."

Davenport and others instituted in the Circuit Court of Henry County, Indiana, an action against the Richmond Natural Gas Company. In the complaint it was shown that the gas company was a corporation engaged in drilling natural gas wells and selling the gas for fuel and light to people in the city of Richmond, Indiana, and to other persons; that for such purposes the Gas Company owned, maintained and operated a gas line to convey and transport natural gas from its gas wells in Henry County to the City of Richmond; that it owned and was engaged in drilling gas wells in Henry County, from which was obtained natural gas which it conveyed through its pipelines to consumers and customers; that the plaintiffs on September 19, 1900, and at the date of the suit, were the owners in fee simple of certain land in Henry County; that on that day one Cassandra Davenport, who then held, and still held at the date of the institution of the suit, a life tenancy in and to said real estate, and who had not then, and had not at the date of the institution of the suit, any greater interest therein than as tenant for life; that on that day there was and still remained at the beginning of the suit, under the real estate, a reservoir of natural gas constituting a part of the real estate, and of great value to the same and to the plaintiffs as the owners of the same; that on and prior to that date the natural gas in and under this real estate had never been drilled for nor brought to the surface, or developed in any manner; nor had any experiments or explorations been made thereon for natural gas; that this condition existed at the time Cassandra Davenport acquired the life estate in the land; that on the day last mentioned, she (without the consent of the plaintiffs or either of them, without right) and the defendant entered into a written agreement of lease wherein she, in consideration of the sum of one dollar undertook and assumed to sell to the defendant all the oil and gas in and under the land mentioned. [Here follows a statement of the character of contract entered into, being the ordinary oil and gas lease.] That pursuant to this agreement the defendant entered upon the real estate, erected structures, placed thereon pipe, tools, machinery, and appliances for drilling gas wells, and at the time of the filing of the complaint was engaged in drilling a gas well, and placed therein pipe and appliances for taking and removing the gas under the real estate; and if not restrained and enjoined defendant would permanently occupy the real estate and take and remove therefrom the natural gas lying in and under the same, and would commit great waste and permanent injury to the plaintiff, which could not be compensated in damages. The complaint contained a prayer for injunction. The defendant oil company answered and alleged that at the time Cassandra Davenport acquired the life estate in the real estate described in the complaint, there was, and at the time of the filing of the answer yet was, underlying this real estate, and other real estate adjoining in Henry County, a deposit of natural gas which was utilized for fuel and light by the people of that County and adjoining counties; that this underlying natural gas, at all times mentioned, was contained in and percolated freely through what was known as the Trenton rock, comprising a vast reservoir in which gas was confined, under great pressure and from which it escaped when permitted to do so, with great force. The answer then alleged in substance that it was necessary in order to save the gas from being drained by wells on adjoining property, to drill this land for gas; that Cassandra Davenport was a woman in good health, 68 years of age; her expectancy of life was nine years, and that long before the expiration of that period, to-wit, two years from the filing of the answer, the entire production of natural gas by the process of mining then carried on on other real estate would be drawn out of the reservoir and from beneath all the real estate described in the complaint and would be entirely consumed and lost to Cassandra Davenport, the life tenant, as well as to the remainder men; that under and pursuant to the lease, the defendant had caused a gas well to be drilled on the real estate in question, and had the same properly capped and secured to prevent the escape of gas therefrom; that though it had not operated this well, the pressure of gas and the volume thereof had constantly and steadily decreased since the well was drilled solely because of the operations

for gas being conducted on surrounding real estate and the drawing of gas thereby from the reservoir and from beneath said real
estate; that if the defendant should be permitted to operate the
gas well so drilled it would do so in such manner as not to injure
the real estate, but would only take gas from the well as it would
freely flow therefrom at its natural pressure under the natural law
of flowage of gas. Judgment was entered by the Circuit Court
overruling defendant's demurrer to the complaint and sustaining
plaintiff's demurrer to the defendant's answer, from which
judgment the defendant appealed and the Appellate Court affirmed
the judgment, citing:

Indianapolis Nat. Gas Co. v. *Kibbey*, 135 Ind. 357; 35 N. E.
    392.
American etc. Co. v. *Tate*, 33 Ind. App. 504; 71 N. E. 189.

Upon the proposition that where oil or gas has been taken
from land by means of wells by the owner of the fee or he has by
his contract given the right so to take gas or oil, to another, and
thereafter the possession of the land devolves upon a tenant for
life, such tenant may enjoy the use of such wells or royalty therefrom during such tenancy as profits and income from the land, in
the condition in which it comes to the life tenant, the court cited:

Andrews v. *Andrews*, 31 Ind. App. 189; 67 N. E. 461.
Priddy v. *Griffith*, 150 Ill. 560; 37 N. E. 999; 41 Am. St. Rep.
    397.

Upon the proposition that where no operations for oil or gas
have been carried on by the owner of the fee, or his grantee or
lessee for such use, and he has not developed such right by lease
or grant during his ownership of the fee, a tenant of the land for
life has no right, himself, to operate for oil or gas, or by lease
or grant to give authority to another to do so, the court cited:

Marshall v. *Mellon*, 179 Pa. 371; 36 Atl. 201; 35 L. R. A. 816;
    57 Am. St. Rep. 601.
Blakley v. *Marshall*, 174 Pa. 425; 34 Atl. 564.
Williamson v. *Jones*, 43 W. Va. 562; 27 S. E. 411; 38 L. R. A.
    694; 64 Am. St. Rep. 891.
Westmoreland Coal Co. Appeal, 85 Pa. 344.
Appeal of Stoughton, 88 Pa. 189.

Gerkins v. *Kentucky Salt Co.*, (Ky.) 39 S. W. 444; 66 Am.
St. Rep. 370.
Hook v. *Garfield Coal Co.*, (Ia.) 83 N. E. 963.

Sec. 8.—In *Eakin* v. *Hawkins*, 48 W. Va. 364; 37 S. E. 622,
(Dec. 1, 1900) the syllabus is as follows:

"1. If equity has jurisdiction to grant any part of the relief prayed., and sufficient matter appears on the face of the bill
to authorize such relief, it is error to dismiss the bill.
2.   J. T. A. H. and others by deed of date April 17, 1883,
conveyed to H. and his heirs, to be held by H. during his natural
life, then to his heirs, thirty acres of land.   By deed of lease
dated December 13, 1895, H. sold to an oil company seven-eighths
of the oil underlying the same, reserving to himself the 1-8 of the
oil as royalty.   By deed of June 3, 1896, H. conveyed with general
warranty to F. one-half of the one-eighth of the oil so reserved
to himself.   On July, 1897, proceedings were instituted in the Circuit Court of T. County in which H. was adjudged to be 'not
capable of managing his property and estate,' and H. F. H. was
appointed committee of said H.   H. F. H. was also appointed
guardian of the infant children of H.   On the 20th of August, and
14th of December, 1897, said committee and guardian leased said
thirty acres to B. and C. for oil purposes, reserving to himself, as
such committee and guardian one-eighth of the oil as royalty.
Held, that F. will take under the conveyance of H. dated June 3,
1896, the one-half of the interest in the oil to which H. would be
entitled, when produced, as life tenant, unless it be satisfactorily
established that H. was of unsound mind and incompetent to contract at the time of the excution of said conveyance to F. dated
June 3, 1896."

On January 26, 1852, James Farrel and wife conveyed by deed
to Simon H. Hawkins, two tracts of land in Tyler County, one for
345 and the other for 305 acres.   On September 20, 1875, Simon
conveyed the tract of 305 acres to Joshua T. A. Hawkins, in consideration of $2,000.   Simon died in 188—, leaving surviving him
his children and heirs at law, Isaac N. Hawkns, B. F. Hawkins,
Acena S. Keller, W. C. Hawkins, Delila Pipes, and Joshua T. A.
Hawkins.   On April 17, 1883, Joshua T. A. Hawkins, B. F.
Hawkins, Acena S. Keller, W. C. Hawkins and Delilah E. Pipes
conveyed to Isaac N. Hawkins 30 acres of land.   By deed of lease
dated December 13, 1895, Isaac N. Hawkins and wife granted to the

Fisher Oil Company the tract of 30 acres of land for oil and gas purposes, reserving ⅛ of the oil, the lessors to receive $100.00 for each gas well so long as gas therefrom should be produced and sold. On August 20, 1897, B. F. Hawkins, as committee of Isaac N. Hawkins and as guardian of Isaac N. Hawkins' children, leased the 30 acres to S. P. Boyer and J. H. Caldwell for oil and gas purposes, reserving ⅛ of the oil as royalty, lessor to receive $300.00 for each well producing gas, marketed off the premises, and a cash bonus of $395.00; and on December 14, 1897, the committee and guardian executed a similar lease to the same lessee for the 30 acres of land. On the 30th of August, 1897, the lessees, Boyer and Caldwell, by writing of that date, assigned to the Fisher Oil Company, and its successors or assigns, the undivided half interest in the lease. By deed dated June 3, 1896, Isaac Hawkins and wife, in consideration of $30.00 cash, and other valuable considerations, conveyed to C. S. Fluharty the undivided half of the royalty of ⅛ of the oil reserved to them in the lease of December 13, 1895, and by writing on the back of the deed, Fluharty, on March 4, 1897, assigned to Justus Eakin the ½ of the interest in the royalty so conveyed to him by Isaac N. Hawkins, and by deed of March 12, 1897, Fluharty assigned to W. McG. Hall and J. P. Chaplin, an interest in his remaining one-half interest, and by deed of March 27, 1897, Fluharty conveyed a further interest therein to William McG. Hall, and on the same day W. McG. Hall conveyed to S. B. Hall a part of his interest so conveyed to him by Fluharty and on the some day W. McG. Hall conveyed another interest therein to E. J. Thompson.

Justus Eakin, J. P. Chaplin, E. J. Thompson, W. McG. Hall, S. B. Hall, and C. S. Fluharty filed their bill in chancery in the Circuit Court of Tyler County, on April 14, 1898, and in July, filed their amended bill which named as defendants Isaac N. Hawkins, B. F. Hawkins, committee and guardian, and in his own right, Ora H. Kile, Flora N. Hawkins, John W. Hawkins, Emma J. Hawkins, Rosa N. Hawkins, Bertha F. Hawkins, and Horner F. Hawkins, infants; J. T. A. Hawkins, Acena S. Keller, W. C. Hawkins, Delilah E. Pipes and S. P. Boyer, J. H. Caldwell, Fisher Oil Company, a corporation, and the Eureka Pipeline Company, a corporation, and set out the conveyances and assignments aforesaid, alleging that B. F. Hawkins was, on July 17, 1897, appointed guardian of the infant defendants, who were children of Isaac N. Hawkins, and was, on August 10, 1897, appointed committee of Isaac N. Hawkins; that the deed of September 20, 1875, from Simon to J. T. A. Hawkins, conveying the 305-acre tract of land was without consideration deemed valid in law; that the face of said deed contained and expressed a consideration of $2,000 as passing from Joshua T. A. Hawkins to Simon H. Hawkins, but that Joshua did not pay to Simon, or any other person, the $2,000 or any part of it; that no consideration passed from Joshua for the land; but that the conveyance was for the sole and only purpose, and the land was conveyed to Joshua, for the purpose, use and benefit of the heirs of Simon; that Joshua took the land to divide and convey the same to the heirs of Simon at his death; that Simon died leaving surviving him the children named; that he died seized of the equitable title to the tract of 305 acres; that his children inherited the 305 acres of land as such heirs at law, and immediately on his death, became the owners thereof as co-parceners; that at his death the legal title was in Joshua T. A. Hawkins, and the equitable title was in the heirs at law of Simon; that the legal title was held by Joshua for the use, benefit and in trust of and for the heirs of Simon; that after his death his heirs proceeded to partition the 305 acres of land among themselves and to convey the partitioned parts thereof each to the other by deeds of conveyance; that in the deeds amounts of money for consideration were named, but in fact, no consideration passed between the heirs, or from the other heirs to Joshua, or from them to any other person; that the partition deeds were made as if the deed from Simon to Joshua had not been made, and as if Simon had died intestate and the heirs so regarded and considered the property; that as part and parcel thereof they set off to defendant, Isaac N. Hawkins, the 33 acres partitioned from the 305-acre tract, by paper writing properly describing the same; that the defendants, Joshua T. A. Hawkins, B. F. Hawkins, Acena S. Keller, W. C. Hawkins and Delilah Pipes, by instrument dated April 17, 1883, described and bounded the lands for the purposes of dividing the same as partitioned between the heirs of Simon; and that said instrument failed and was insufficient in law to convey to Isaac N. Hawkins his rightful and true interest in and to the land, and did not contain apt words to describe his interest therein; that Isaac N. Hawkins did not sign the deed, and that the same did not erect a use in Isaac Hawkins, and could be construed only in fee simple in and to him; that Isaac and wife, for a valuable consideration, by deed of December 13, 1895, granted to the Fisher Oil Company all the oil and gas underlying the 30 acres, reserving ⅛ of the oil, lessors to receive $100.00 per year for gas; that B. F. Hawkins as committee and guardian, by the deeds of August 20, and December 14, 1897, pretended to convey the oil and gas under the 30 acres to defendants, Boyer and Caldwell, reserving ⅛ of the oil as royalty, and $—— for the gas reserved as consideration; that under one or more of the leases for oil and gas, but which one being unknown to plaintiff, defendant, Fisher Oil Company, by itself, or with others, took possession of and proceeded to develop and drill for oil and gas, and were actively developing the 30 acres; that defendant, B. F. Hawkins, committee and guardian, set up and made claim to the interest of plaintiffs to the oil and gas under the 30 acres of land, under some pretended claim unknown to plaintiffs, but they believed it to be under the leases made by the committee and guardian of August 20th and December 14, 1897, or one of them; that the oil produced had been run into the pipelines of the Eureka Pipeline Company; that plaintiffs made application to the Pipeline Company for their share of the oil under the grant made to them through the plaintiff Fluharty, and the Pipeline Company refused to deliver them the oil, for the reason that B. F. Hawkins, committee and guardian, claimed the interests of plaintiffs for his insane and wards; that the acts and doings of B. F. Hawkins, committee and guardian, had deprived and kept plaintiffs from their rights in and to the oil; that defendant, Isaac N. Hawkins, was a married man, passed middle life, and had raised a family of children; that he supported and raised the children by his own labor; that he performed and did acts of business continually with his neighbors, and passed title to property without question; that he granted the oil lease of December 13, 1895, to Fisher Oil Company, collected the rent, and accepted the same; that the lease was given long before the Elk Fork Oil field was shown to be productive of oil; that the lease was as fair a lease as was usually given in that neighborhood at that time; that the lease was not questioned at any time, and was a legal and subsisting lease; that the grant of half the royalty by Isaac N. Hawkins to C. S. Fluharty was made for valuable consideration at a time when operations indicated that the land was worthless for oil and gas and nearly a year before the first well in the Elk Fork field was drilled, and long before any leases were taken therein for the purpose, and was made in good faith to Fluharty; that plaintiffs acquired and owned their rights therein before the time Hawkins was appointed committee for Isaac, and guardian for his children; that no inquisition had ever

been had on the insanity of Isaac, until after plaintiffs acquired
their rights in the land; that the acts of defendant, the appointment of Hawkins committee and guardian, the leases of August
20, and December 14, 1897, and all acts thereunder were being
done to cheat and defraud the plaintiffs out of their half interest
in and to the royalty underlying the 30 acres; that Isaac was not
a person of unsound mind at the time of the vesting of the interest
in the royalty in plaintiffs; that Isaac, together with his brother,
B. F. Hawkins, by B. F. Hawkins, guardian and committee, with
others, colluded and conspired to rob, cheat and defraud plaintiffs
out of their right and interest in and to the oil and gas under the
30 acres; that Isaac suffered himself to be declared insane for that
purpose; that said leases of August 20, and December 14, 1897,
were made in furtherance of the purpose; that the infants did not,
nor had they, any legal interest in or title whatever, present or
future, in and to the 30 acres of land; that the leases of August
and December did not vest any legal title in the grantees, or assignees thereof, being insufficient in law for that purpose; that
whatever right defendant, Isaac N. Hawkins, had by virtue of the
deed of April 17, 1883, made by J. T. A. Hawkins and others in the
30 acres, plaintiffs had a like interest under and by the sale to
Fluharty on June 3, 1896. The bill prayed that the plaintiffs be
decreed 1-16 of all the oil and gas mined and produced from and
under the 30 acres of land, or failing in that, the 1-16 of the interest
of the defendant, Isaac N. Hawkins, in and to all the oil and gas
mined and produced therefrom; that B. F. Hawkins, committee
and guardian, be restrained from taking any part of the 1-16 of
the oil and gas belonging to plaintiffs under or by the grants, made
to him as committee and guardian, of August and December; that
the Fisher Oil Company, C. P. Boyer and J. H. Caldwell, any or
all of them, be restrained from delivering to Hawkins, committee
and guardian, or to his credit in the pipelines, the said 1-16 of the
oil theretofore produced under the same, and that the court order
the same to be delivered to plaintiffs; that the Eureka Pipeline
Company be enjoined and restrained from delivering the same to
the guardian and committee; that a receiver be appointed to take
charge of 1-16 part of the oil theretofore produced, or to be thereafter produced; that the court decree that the defendants, the co-
heirs of Isaac N. Hawkins, and especially the defendant, J. T. A.
Hawkins, make a proper and legal deed conveying to said Isaac
his full and rightful title and interest in the 30 acres, and on their

failure to do so, to appoint a commissioner for the purpose of making such deed, and for general relief.

The amended and the original bill contained the same allegations. A demurrer was filed to the amended bill. The demurrer was sustained and the bill dismissed. From the decree of dismissal plaintiffs appealed to the Court of Appeals, and that court reversed the decree.

Sec. 9.—In *Eakin* v. *Hawkins,* 52 W. Va. 124; 43 S. E. 211 (Dec. 6, 1902), the syllabus is as follows:

"1. The sanity of a grantor in a deed, the validity of which is questioned, is presumed by law, and the burden is upon the attacking party to overthrow the presumption.

2. In the absence of fraud, imposition, or undue influence, such presumption will not be overcome by evidence of mere mental weakness, or feebleness of understanding if the grantor has sufficient capacity to understand the nature of the act he does.

3. The interest of a life tenant in the proceeds of royalty oil taken from the premises is the interest on the fund during his natural life.

4. Where petroleum oil is extracted from land, conveyed to a person for life, and remainder in fee to his heirs, under a lease from the life tenant, and a sale of the interest in remainder by order of a court of chancery in a proper proceeding for the purpose, reserving in the lease and order of sale 1-8 of the oil for the owners of the land, it is error to decree, to the life tenant or his grantees, in another suit, the royalty oil or proceeds thereof to hold until the expiration of the life tenancy and take the income thereof, and then pay over the corpus of the fund to those entitled in remainder.

5. It is reversible error to proceed in a suit against an insane person, and enter a decree against him, without the appointment of a guardian ad litem for him, and the filing of an answer by such guardian.

6. When a person has been adjudged to be insane, the presumption of insanity continues until he is discharged, and, in a suit against him, it is necessary to appoint a guardian ad litem for him.

7. The mere formal answer of a guardian ad litem to an infant need not be sworn to unless it be in a proceeding to lease or sell his real estate."

This was the second appeal of the cause, the first reported in
48 W. Va. 364; 37 S. E. 622. After the cause was remanded a
final decree was entered ordering payment by the receiver to the
plaintiffs of the moneys in his hands, arising from the sale of the
½ of the royalty oil, and the delivery to plaintiffs by the Fisher
Oil Company, S. P. Boyer and J. H. Caldwell, of all the oil arising from the royalty not theretofore delivered by them to the receiver, and authorizing the plaintiffs to sell the same. It was
further decreed that the plaintiffs should hold and use said moneys
arising from sales of oil for and during the natural life of the defendant, Isaac N. Hawkins, and upon his death pay the same to
the remainder men entitled thereto. The ½ of the royalty conveyed by Isaac N. Hawkins to C. S. Fluharty was held by Justice
Eakin, William McG. Hall, J. P. Chaplin, S. B. Hall and E. J.
Thompson, by conveyances directly and indirectly from Fluharty,
From this decree the defendants appealed. The first assignment
of error which went to the whole controversy was, that the court
erred in holding that Isaac N. Hawkins was competent to make
the deed by which he conveyed the interest claimed by the plaintiff to C. S. Fluharty. The court overruled this assignment of
error. The Court of Appeals held, that the Circuit Court erred
in decreeing to the plaintiffs payment of the money arising from
the sale by the receiver of the ½ of the royalty oil, and delivery of the unsold half of the royalty oil; that Isaac N. Hawkins
was seized of a life estate only in the land, and his interest in the
proceeds of the royalty oil acquired from the land was limited
to the interest thereon for and during his natural life, and reversed the decree of the Circuit Court and remanded the cause,
citing:

Williamson v. *Jones,* 43 W. Va. 562.
Wilson v. *Youst,* 43 W. Va. 826.
Ammons v. *Ammons,* 50 W. Va. 390.

Sec. 10.—In *Stewart* v. *Tennant,* 52 W. Va. 559; 44 S. E. 223,
analyzed under Chapter 32, the twelfth and thirteenth points of the
syllabus are as follows:

"12. Where, before assignment of dower, one claiming by
purchase from certain heirs and the widow, drills oil wells upon
the land, and extracts large quantities of oil therefrom, without
having obtained the consent of his co-tenants to such develop-

ment, and such non-consenting co-tenant brings his suit for an accounting, it is error to decree to him his entire interest in the oil produced, and thereafter to be produced, free from any charge on account of the dower interest.

13.   In such case, the holder of the dower interest is entitled to the interest on one-third of the proceeds of the oil going to the non-consenting co-tenants, until the death of the doweress, and until that date the fund upon which such interest is paid remains under the control of the court through its general receiver.''

REMEDY OF LIFE TENANT.

Sec. 11.—The life tenant is entitled to the interest on the royalties of oil and the interest on the gas rentals during the continuance of his life estate in lands which are developed and produce oil or gas in paying quantities after such life estate has accrued.   Such life tenant may, by bill in equity, have such rights protected and his right to the receipt of such interest quieted.

Wilson v. *Youst,* 43 W. Va. 826; 28 S. E. 781.
Ammons v. *Ammons,* 50 W. Va. 390; 40 S. E. 490.
Eakin v. *Hawkins,* 52 W. Va. 124; 43 S. E. 211.
Stewart v. *Tennant,* 52 W. Va. 559; 44 S. E. 223.

Sec. 12.—Where there are producing oil and gas wells at the time the estate of the life tenant accrues, he has a right to the royalty of oils and rental for gas during the continuance of his life estate, but may not drill additional wells, and a court of equity will protect the rights of such life tenant.

Koen v. *Bartlett,* 41 W. Va. 559; 23 S. E. 664; 56 Am. St. Rep. 884; 31 L. R. A. 128.

REMEDY OF REMAINDERMEN.

Sec. 13.—Where a life tenant either produces oil or gas and converts the proceeds to his own use, or executes an oil and gas lease to another and the lessee enters and produces oil and gas, the remainder man may enjoin such production and recover from the life tenant or lessee the value of the oil or gas so taken.

Eakin v. *Hawkins,* 48 W. Va. 364; 37 S. E. 622.

Richmond Nat. Gas Co. v. *Davenport,* 37 Ind. App. 25; 76 N.
E. 525.
Williamson v. *Jones,* 43 W. Va. 563; 27 S. E. 411.
Stewart v. *Tennant,* 52 W. Va. 559; 44 S. E. 223.

Sec. 14.—Where there is a life estate in lands in oil producing
territory the remainder man or reversioner may by proceedings
in equity, upon proof that there is danger of drainage and that
there is imperative need, cause the oil or gas to be produced or
otherwise secured for their protection where no harm is done to
the life tenant, or where he is compensated. Such compensation
would be interest on the royalty of oils or rentals for gas during
the continuance of the life estate.

Williamson v. *Jones,* 43 W. Va. 563; 27 S. E. 411, Syl. 6.

Sec. 15.—Where a lessee acquires an oil and gas lease from a
life tenant he may defeat any action brought to enforce the covenants of the lease by allegation and proof that the lessor only has
a life estate in the property, and that the remainder men or reversioners have not joined in the lease.

Marshall v. *Mellon,* 179 Pa. 371; 36 Atl. 201; 57 Am. St. Rep.
601; 35 L. R. A. 816.

CHAPTER 36.

BEGINNING OPERATIONS—WHAT CONSTITUTES.

Sec. 1.—Where an oil and gas lease contains a provision that
unless lessee shall, within a specified time, commence operations
and complete a well on the property within a specified time, and
lessee makes no attempt to comply with such provisions, at the
expiration of the time stipulated the lease becomes voidable at the
option of the lessor.

Huggins v. *Daley,* 99 Fed. 606; 40 C. C. A. 12; 48 L. R. A. 320.
Fleming Oil & G. Co. v. *South Penn Oil Co.,* 37 W. Va. 645;
17 S. E. 203.
Forney v. *Ward,* 25 Tex. App. 443; 62 S. W. 108.

Cleminger v. *Baden Gas Co.,* 159 Pa. 16; 28 Atl. 293.
Henderson v. *Ferrell,* 183 Pa. 547; 38 Atl. 1018.
Detlor v. *Holland,* 57 Ohio State 492; 49 N. E. 690; 40 L. R. A.
    266.

Sec. 2.—In *Huggins* v. *Daley,* 99 Fed. 606; 40 C. C. A. 12; 48
L. R. A. 320, analyzed under Chapter 6, the third point of the
headnotes is as follows:

"Where an oil and gas lease by which the lessor is to be compensated solely by a share of the product contains a proviso requiring the lessee to commence and complete a well on the property within a specified time, such proviso and the time of its performance are of the essence of the contract, and it constitutes a con
dition precedent to the vesting of any estate in the lessee, without
regard to the grammatical construction of the instrument. When
the lessee makes no attempt to comply with such provision and
evidences no intention to do so, at the expiration of the time
stipulated the lease becomes forfeitable, at the option of the lessor,
although by its terms it is for a definite term of years; and, being
in possession the exercise of such option is sufficiently evidenced
by the lessor's execution of a new lease to another party."

Sec. 3.—In *Fleming Oil & Gas Co.* v. *South Penn Oil Co.,* 37
W. Va. 645; 17 S. E. 203 (March 22, 1893), syl. 1 is as follows:

"Where a lease for oil and gas purposes contains a covenant
that the lessee shall commence operations for a test well within
one year from the date thereof at some point in the district, in
which the leased premises are located, and complete said well in
eighteen months after its commencement; and before the expiration of a year from the date of said lease said test well is located
by surveying and levelling; the timbers which are afterwards
used in constructing the derrick at said location are cut down
and hewn; a contract is made with a party for drilling the well;
the machinery is ordered to be hauled to said location but neither
said timber or machinery is hauled to said location within the
year, by reason of the impassable condition of the roads; said
well is, however, completed in less than eighteen months after
the date of said lease—the lease is not liable to forfeiture on the
ground that operations were not commenced within a year from
the date thereof under said circumstances."

On February 22, 1889, David Jones made an oil and gas lease
to T. N. Jackson & Company for a tract of about 140 acres of land

in Marion County, West Virginia. The lease was afterwards assigned and conveyed by T. N. Jackson & Company to the South
Penn Oil Company. The lease contained the following covenant:

"The party of the second part covenants to commence operations for a test well within one year from the date hereof, at some
point in the District of Paw Paw, Marion County, and complete
the same within eighteen months from said commencement provided that unavoidable delays occasioned by mishaps in drilling
shall not cause a forfeiture of this lease; and in case said party
of the second part fails to so commence and complete said test
well, the lease shall be forfeited and void; and, in case said test
well was a success, said party of the second part should commence a well on said property within two years after said test
well is utilized and complete the same in one year from the commencement thereof; and, if said party of the second part failed so
to do, said lease should be forfeited and void, provided that loss
of time spent in the recovery of tools lost in drilling, or unavoidable delays occasioned by any mishaps in connection with drilling,
shall not work a forfeiture of the lease."

Under the provisions of the lease T. N. Jackson & Company
made preliminary surveys in the Fall of 1889, for the purpose of
ascertaining the location of the oil belt with reference to the P.
W. Youst farm, and on January 30, 1890, the point at which the
test well was afterwards drilled was located by him and the spot
pointed out to P. W. Youst. A contract was made with one Ira
DeWitt, in the Fall of 1889, for the drilling of said well, work on
which was to be commenced on January 31, 1899. In pursuance
of this contract Ira DeWitt had the timbers for the derrick which
were afterwards used by him in drilling the test well, cut and hewn
on the Youst farm between January first and sixth; and in the
latter part of January, 1890, DeWitt contracted with J. H. Barry
to haul the machinery, which was afterwards used in drilling the
test well, to the Youst farm, which hauling was delayed for some
time, by reason of the impassable condition of the roads in that
locality. In execution of the contract for drilling DeWitt subsequently got the material and machinery upon the locality selected,
erected a derrick, and completed the well on August 21, 1890. A
second well was commenced on the David Jones farm, on the lands
described in the lease, on September 25, 1890, which was completed on January 5, 1891. On February 28, 1890, David Jones
leased the same tract of land to the Fleming Oil & Gas Company

for oil and gas purposes, but the lease on its face contained a
covenant that "said David Jones was to be held harmless from a
lease made to T. N. Jackson & Co., which expired February 22,
1890." At February Rules, 1891, for the Circuit Court of Marion
County, the Fleming Oil & Gas Company filed its declaration in
ejectment against the South Penn Oil Company and David Jones
for the purpose of recovering the possession of the leased premises. After a demurrer to the declaration had been overruled by
the Circuit Court the defendants pleaded not guilty, and issue was
joined thereon, and the case submitted to a jury. The jury returned a verdict for the plaintiff, which verdict was sustained by
the Circuit Court and judgment rendered thereon. Defendant obtained a writ of error, and the Court of Appeals reversed the Circuit Court.

Sec. 4.—In *Forney* v. *Ward*, 25 Tex. App. 443; 62 S. W. 108
(April 4, 1901), the syllabus is as follows:

"1. Defendant granted plaintiff a part of the oil and minerals in defendant's land, provided that the grant should be void
if no well was begun within four months. The day before the
lease expired plaintiff hauled and placed a load of lumber on the
land, and made defendant an offer for an extension of the lease,
but no agreement was reached, although the offer was not positively declined. The day after the lease had expired plaintiff hauled
lumber to the premises and was refused admittance. *Held*, that
it was not error to refuse to instruct that, if plaintiff expended
money and labor with defendant's consent, on the two days
mentioned defendant was estopped from denying that plaintiff
had complied with the contract, as the issue of estoppel was not
raised by the evidence.

2. Where a contract allowing plaintiff the right to mine for
oil on defendant's premises, provided that the grant should be
void in case no well was begun, and prosecuted with due diligence
within four months, it was not error to refuse to instruct that if the
plaintiff, before the termination of the lease hauled lumber on
defendant's land for the purpose of beginning the well, such act
was the beginning of the well within the contract; as the plaintiff having hauled lumber on the premises the day before the
contract expired, it was not for the court to determine such
question as a matter of law, and it was properly left to the jury
to decide, in connection with testimony as to the general understanding among persons engaged in boring oil wells as to when
a well was begun."

· On November 14, 1898, J. J. Ward and wife made an oil and gas lease to George Forney for a certain tract of land, which lease contained the following provision as to beginning operations:

"In case no well is begun and prosecuted with due diligence within four months from this date, then this grant shall immediately become null and void as to both parties."

Forney made no preparations to begin work under the lease until March 13, 1899, on which day he hauled a load of lumber on the premises, with which he intended to construct a rig to be used in drilling an oil or gas well. The lessor, Ward, was present when the lumber was placed on his land and made no objection and did not claim that the lease was forfeited. The question of the extension of the lease, and the procurement of water with which to drill the well was at the time the lumber was hauled on the premises discussed by Ward and Forney, and Ward proposed to extend the lease for thirty days upon a payment to him by Forney of Thirty Dollars, and Ward also agreed to build a tank and furnish Forney with water for drilling purposes, if he would pay him an additional fifty dollars, which amount Ward was to repay in the water necessary for the drilling of four wells at the rate of $12.50 per well. Forney did not accept Ward's proposition but offered him $15.00 for thirty days extension of the lease. This proposition was not accepted by Ward, though he did not positively decline it, and Forney understood that he would come to town the next day and let him know whether he would accept the offer of Fifteen Dollars for the extension of the lease. Ward did not go to town the next day, and in the evening Forney went to Ward's place to see if he had decided to accept his proposition. They failed to agree upon terms for the extension of the lease, and Forney then told Ward he would go to work on the well under the original agreement, and on the next day, March 15th, sent three wagons with lumber to be used in the prosecution of the work. When the wagons reached the premises the gates were locked, and Ward refused to allow plaintiff to enter the premises, claiming that the lease had been forfeited. When Forney informed Ward on the 14th that he intended to proceed with the work of drilling under the original lease, Ward did not claim that the lease was forfeited, and made no objection to plaintiff's proposal to proceed with the work. Upon Ward's refusal to allow Forney to enter the premises and proceed with the work contem-

plated by the lease, Forney brought suit in the District Court of
Navarro County, Texas, against Ward to enforce his alleged
rights under the lease, and to enjoin the defendant from interfering with the operations contemplated by the lease. The District
Court entered judgment for defendants. Plaintiff appealed and
the Appellate Court affirmed the District Court.

Sec. 5.—In *Cleminger* v. *Baden Gas Co.*, 159 Pa. 16; 28 Atl.
293, (Dec. 30, 1893) the syllabus is as follows:

"Where an oil lease contains a covenant on the part of the
lessee 'to commence operations on the aforementioned premises,
or forfeit this lease within sixty days, and to complete a well on
this lease within five months,' the lessor may forfeit the lease
after the expiration of five months if a well has not been completed within that time.

In the above case there was a delay in starting operations
within sixty days. The lessee desiring to assign the lease had a
conversation with the lessor as to delay. The result of this conversation he stated to be as follows: 'The conclusion was that
Mr. Phillipps (the lessor) acquiesced in the delay and acknowledged the lease on the assurance that there would be a well put
down.' *Held*, that there was no waiver of the right to have a
well completed within five months."

On October 13, 1886, W. J. Phillips and R. A. Phillips executed an oil lease to Ira DeWitt, containing the following clause:

"The party of the second part further covenants and agrees
to commence operations on the aforementioned premises or forfeit this lease within sixty days, and to complete a well on this
lease in five months."

In January, 1887, DeWitt agreed to assign the lease to Frank
J. Cleminger and W. G. Hunter. DeWitt called upon the lessors
in reference to this assignment, and upon the trial testified in
relation thereto that they had a general conversation in regard to
delay, talked about bad roads, difficulty of getting around and
hauling machinery, tools, lumber, etc.; and that the conclusion was
that Mr. Phillips acquiesced in the delay and acknowledged the
lease on the assurance that there would be a well put down. The
well was not completed within five months from the date of the
lease, and the lessors thereupon notified Cleminger and Hunter,

the assignes of DeWitt, that the lease was forfeited; and on April 13, 1887, leased the same land to the Baden Gas Company. Frank J. Cleminger and Hunter, the assignees of DeWitt, instituted in the Court of Common Pleas Number 2, Allegheny County, Pennsylvania, ejectment against the Baden Gas Company, and the lessors, W. J. and R. A. Phillips. Upon the trial there was evidence that in November, 1886, DeWitt hauled lumber on the premises, but apparently there was no actual beginning of operations on the well during the months of November and December, 1896. The court charged the jury that there was no dispute about the fact that the well was not completed within five months, and that under the agreement as a matter of law the defendants had a right to forfeit the lease after the expiration of five months, and they did so; further instructing the jury to find for the defendants. The verdict was so rendered and from the judgment thereon rendered plaintiffs appealed, and the Supreme Court affirmed the judgment.

Sec. 6.—In *Henderson* v. *Ferrell*, 183 Pa. 547; 38 Atl. 1018, analyzed under Chapter 24, the syllabus is as follows:

"In an action of ejectment by the lessee in an oil and gas lease to recover possession of the oil and gas, where it appears that operations were to be begun on the leased premises within 30 days from the date of the lease, the case is for the jury where the evidence for the lessee, although contradicted, tends to show that he drove a stake on the premises upon the afternoon of the thirtieth, and begun unloading lumber on the land with the bona fide intention of sinking a well, and that he was prevented from so doing by the action of the lessor in driving his employes from the premises, and that the delay in beginning operations sooner was caused by inability to secure the materials, machinery and labor necessary for the proper performance of the work. The lessee did not forfeit his rights if he in good faith, on the last day, commenced operations preparatory to drilling a well."

Sec. 7.—In *Detlor* v. *Holland*, 57 Ohio State, 492; 49 N. E. 690; 40 L. R. A. 266, analyzed under Chapter 27, syls. 3-4-5-6 are as follows:

"3. A written instrument was duly executed as follows: 'Do hereby grant unto second party, their heirs and assigns, the

sole right to produce petroleum and natural gas from the following named tract of land; * * * *; Specially granting to said
second party for and during the term of ninety (90) days from
this date, and as much longer as oil or gas is found, operated,
and produced in paying quantities, with the exclusive right to drill
and operate oil and gas wells.' *Held*, that such written instrument is not a lease of the lands, but only a grant of the sole right
to produce petroleum and natural gas for the term mentioned;
that the grant expired by its own limitation at the end of 90 days,
unless within that time at least one well was drilled which produced
oil or gas in paying quantities; and that upon failure to drill
one paying well within 90 days, there was no right to drill thereafter.

4. The term of the grant in such instrument having expired,
and the grantees still claiming a right to drill under such grant,
the grantor has a right to have his title quieted as against such
claim, on the ground that the term of the grant has expired, without resorting to the law of forfeitures.

5. Under such an instrument, the sum paid as a consideration for the grant need not be returned in an action to quiet
title.

6. Expenses incurred by the grantees in drilling wells on
the lands after the expiration of the grant, and after notice not
to drill such wells, cannot be recovered from the grantor.''

LESSOR'S REMEDIES.

Sec. 8.—Where in an oil and gas lease there is a provision
that the lease shall be null and void unless a well shall be commenced within a specified time and completed on or before a certain date, where the lessee fails within the specified time to begin
operations in good faith for the drilling of the well and fails to
complete the same within the stipulated time, lessor may declare
a forfeiture and equity will quiet his title by decree cancelling
the lease as a cloud on his title.

Huggins v. *Daley,* 99 Fed. 606; 40 C. C. A. 12; 48 L. R. A. 320.
Detlor v. *Holland,* 57 Ohio State 492; 49 N. E. 690; 40 L. R.
A. 266.

Sec. 9.—Where an oil and gas lease provides that unless
lessee shall within a specified time commence operations and complete a test well within a certain time, upon the lessee's failure to

comply with these conditions of the lease the lessor may declare a forfeiture; and in a suit brought by lessee either for possession of the premises or in equity for injunction against lessor, he may defeat lessee's action by alleging and proving that lessee failed to commence operations in good faith within the specified time, or complete a well within the time stipulated.

Forney v. *Ward,* 25 Tex. App. 443; 62 S. W. 108.
Cleminger v. *Baden Gas Co.,* 159 Pa. 16; 28 Atl. 293.

LESSEE'S REMEDIES.

Sec. 10.—Where in an oil and gas lease there is a proviso that if operations are not commenced within a specified time, and a well completed on or before a certain date the lease shall become null and void, lessee may defeat an action brought by lessor to cancel his lease, or he may recover possession of the premises in a possessory action against the lessor, upon proof that within the time specified he, in good faith, commenced operations preparatory to drilling a well, even although such preparations were not begun until the last day of the time specified for beginning operations.

Fleming Oil & Gas Co. v. *South Penn Oil Co.,* 37 W. Va. 645; 17 S. E. 203.
Henderson v. *Ferrell,* 183 Pa. 547; 38 Atl. 1018.

CHAPTER 37.

SHOOTING WELL.

Sec. 1.—Where the owner of an oil well employs another to shoot the well, and does not require a guaranty that no damages shall result therefrom, if the well is injured by such shooting, in order to sustain an action for damages it devolves upon the owner to prove negligence in the shooting.

Davidson v. *Humes,* 188 Pa. 335; 41 Atl. 649.
Zahniser, et al., trading as East End Oil Co., et al., v. *Pa. Torpedo Co.,* 190 Pa. 350; 42 Atl. 707.

Sec. 2.—In *Davidson* v. *Humes,* 188 Pa. 335; 41 Atl. 649 (Nov. 7, 1898), the syllabus is as follows:

"In an action of trespass to recover damages for injuries to an oil well by explosion of a torpedo, where it appeared that the defendant contracted with the plaintiff to shoot the well, but without any guaranty that the well should be shot without any resulting injury, the defendant is liable for damages only in case of negligence, the burden of proving which is on the plaintiff."

On July 29, 1897, William Davidson employed the Humes Torpedo Company to shoot an oil well belonging to him. In the performance of the work the torpedo, which was a 15-quart glycerine shot, failed to go off. The torpedo company then dropped a quart glycerine torpedo into the well for the purpose of exploding the first shot. The second shot failed to explode and, as it was being raised, the rope broke and the small shot fell and exploded, injuring the casing of the well. The Torpedo Company had not made any guaranty that the well should be shot without any resulting injury. Davidson instituted suit in trespass against the Torpedo Company for damages in the Court of Common Pleas of Butler County, and there being evidence tending to show that the defendant used reasonable care in the performance of the work of shooting the well a verdict and judgment was rendered for defendant. Plaintiff appealed and the Supreme Court affirmed the judgment. Upon the trial of the cause, among other things, in the Court of Common Pleas, the Judge charged the jury:

"Now, gentlemen, before the plaintiff can recover he must satisfy you by the weight of the evidence that there was negligence in the defendant in putting in this squib. No negligence is claimed as to bringing it there, nor letting it down other than that it was, as I stated, that there was too much slack wire. The plaintiff claims that this squib exploded at least 200 feet from where it was intended to be exploded. His desire was to have it explode at the shell, but it exploded above the shell, and exploded in this casing. That is the plaintiff's theory.

Now, then, gentlemen, if there was negligence on the part of Mr. Humes who put it in, and negligence means the absence of reasonable and ordinary care under the circumstances, and a man who is in a business of this kind handling a dangerous explosive as glycerine is, is required to use a high degree of diligence and care and watchfulness. The law requires the diligence and care

to be increased as the danger of the operation increases. So, it
was the duty of the defendant to use such care and diligence as
was within its power and skill; It was the defendant's duty to
furnish good material and good machinery and good appliances,
and, as I said, take great care and caution. Was that done? The
plaintiff, to prove that the squib exploded in this casing, put on
the stand the witness who cleaned the well out afterwards, Mr.
Johnson, who says that at the request of Mr. Davidson, he
cleaned out this well and took out the casing, and when he took
out the first casing he found no signs of bridging by tin at all
(and it is said by the witnesses who heard the testimony that
where the explosion is successful it does not always carry the tin
out of the hole, the tin that is in the shell); That when he cleaned
out this well he saw no signs of any bridging or of the tin shell,
and the other witnesses with him testify about the same thing.
[Then the proof is that after Mr. Johnson had taken out the casing and fixed the well, he claims he got it down to the depth of
1481 feet, and he claims that he stopped there because Mr. Humes
had cautioned him not to go any deeper on account of the danger.]
Mr. Humes then came back on September 5, and put in another
squib, a part of which was here. The plaintiff alleges that that
squib put off the shot down below and that it was not the big
shot that destroyed the casing, but it was the squib that had fallen
at the top of the well the first time, and that the second squib
brought about the result desired the first time. In support of that,
Johnson and the other men say that after that shot they took a
lot of tin out of the casing; that the casing was bridged with tin
and they took it out, and there was very much more tin there than
would have been, had there been nothing on September 5, but the
squib. You heard this testimony, and the testimony of the other
witnesses as to that. From the testimony in the case, from the
plaintiff's testimony in this case, can you find such proof and
such evidence as will show negligence on the part of the defendant
company? Was this piece of casing shot and destroyed by the
squib? In order to recover you must find that it was. If you
cannot find proof enough to convince you that the squib destroyed
this casing then the verdict must be for the defendant, because
it was the shooting off of the squib, the plaintiff alleges, caused
the accident. How is that?"

Sec. 3.—In *Zahniser et al., trading as East End Oil Co., et
al.,* v. *Pennsylvania Torpedo Co.,* 190 Pa. 350; 42 Atl. 707 (March
20, 1899), the second paragraph of the syllabus is as follows:

"In an action to recover damages for injuries to an oil
well caused by the alleged negligence of the defendant's workmen in shooting the well, plaintiff alleged that the well had been
shot at a point some 200 feet too far above the bottom of the well,
and that this resulted from defendant's workmen failing to run
a measuring line down to the torpedo after it had been lowered
into the well, to make sure of its exact position before firing it.
There was no evidence that it was customary or proper to do so,
or that the workmen did not make the additional test with a
measuring line. No affirmative evidence was given of any negligent act of the defendant, either of omission or commission, but
plaintiff contended that the inference of negligence should be
drawn from the happening of the injury alone. *Held,* (1) that this
was not a case where the circumstances made the happening of
the accident itself sufficient evidence of negligence; (2) that a
non-suit was properly enforced."

The Oil Company brought suit against the Torpedo Company
for damages on account of alleged negligence in shooting an oil
well. The plaintiff alleged that the defendant company whom they
employed to shoot an oil well did it negligently, shot it at the
wrong place, thereby impairing and destroying it, and thereby
seriously injuring plaintiff. The proof showed that immediately
before the agent of the defendant company put in the shot he had
the bailer run to the bottom of the hole, which indicated that it
was clear of obstructions; that he then put in the shell and loaded
it with nitro-glycerine, lowered it in the well and fired it, the plaintiff claiming 200 feet or more above where they had directed it to
be fired. None knew or could testify exactly where it was exploded, but the testimony indicated that it was over 1,000 feet
down, and some 200 feet or more above the point desired. The
plaintiffs claimed that it was the duty of the shooter to run a
measuring line and discover the actual location of the shot when
fired; but they offered no proof to show that the defendant did not
do so. When defendant fired the shot all spectators left the ground
to get out of danger; the shooter was alone and no one knew what
he did. After that he met his death in the business, and did not
testify. The court upon the trial directed a nonsuit and the plaintiff moved to take off this nonsuit. Upon this motion the court
held that if the shooter ran a measuring line, the court might
presume that he fired the shot at the point desired, and fired it
properly; that there was no proof whatever to the contrary; the

hole was clear when the bailer passed down and up; the shooter would have been justified in believing it was still clear for the short time in which he was preparing and lowering the shell. The court held that the duty of the shooter did not require him to take any further precautions; and further held that there was no evidence that the shooter did not take all the precautions known to the business or in his power. The motion was denied, and judgment entered for defendant, and plaintiff appealed. The Supreme Court affirmed the judgment.

REMEDY OF OWNER OF WELL.

Sec. 4.—The owner of an oil well may recover damages against one whom he employs to shoot the well for injuries caused by the negligence of such person, whereby the owner is injured, but in the absence of a contract of guaranty, the defendant can only be held liable upon proof of some act of negligence. The mere injury, alone, is not sufficient to warrant a recovery for plaintiff.

(See Cases cited under Section 1, supra.)

REMEDY OF TORPEDO COMPANY OR PERSON EMPLOYED TO SHOOT WELL.

Sec. 5.—Where the owner of an oil well institutes suit for damages against a person whom he has employed to shoot the well, for injuries claimed to have resulted from the shot, it devolves upon the plaintiff, in the absence of a contract of guaranty, to prove that the defendant was guilty of negligence, and the burden of such proof is on the plaintiff. Where the plaintiff has proven facts from which the jury might be authorized to infer negligence the defendant may defeat a recovery by proof that he used such care and diligence as was within his power and skill; that he furnished good machinery, material and appliances and in and about the shooting exercised a high degree of diligence, care and watchfulness.

(See cases cited under Section 1, supra.)

CHAPTER 38.

NATURAL GAS AN ARTICLE OF COMMERCE WHEN BROUGHT TO THE SURFACE.

Sec. 1.—Natural gas found within the territorial limits of a State, when brought to the surface and placed in pipelines for transportation is an article of commerce, and the owner has the absolute right of property therein with the right to transport and sell and deliver the same as other personal property, of which right he cannot be deprived by the State without just compensation without violating the fourteenth amendment to the Federal Constitution.

Kansas Natural Gas Co. v. *Haskell*, (C. C.) 172 Fed. 545.
State, ex rel Corwin v. *Ind. & Ohio Oil, Gas & Mining Co.*, 120 Ind. 575; 22 N. E. 778; 6 L. R. A. 579.

Sec. 2.—In *Kansas Natural Gas Co.* v. *Haskell*, (C. C.) 172 Fed. 545 (July 3, 1909), the headnotes are as follows:

"1. A suit to enjoin individual defendants from proceeding as officers of a State to enforce an Act of the Legislature of such State which is unconstitutional and void is not a 'suit against the State,' withing the meaning of the eleventh amendment to the Constitution and is within the jurisdiction of a Federal Court.

2. In determining whether a State Statute is within the powers of the State, a court will look beyond the title of the Act, to ascertain its real purpose and effect, from an examination of the body thereof.

3. Natural gas found within the territorial limits of a State is not a product which the State may conserve and preserve by law as a thing in which the people of the State have a common interest, as flowing streams, wild animals, etc; but one who by lawful right reduces it to possession has the absolute right of property therein, with the right to transport and sell and deliver the same as other personal property, of which right he cannot be deprived by the State without just compensation, without violation of the fourteenth amendment to the Federal Constitution, and also, in Oklahoma, of Article 12, § 24 of the State Constitution.

4. Acts, Okl. 1907, p. 586, c. 67, which prohibits, except for private use, the construction of pipelines for the transportation of natural gas within the State, except by corporations organized

thereunder by charters providing that such gas shall not be transported out of the State, nor sold or delivered to anyone else to be taken out of the State, is void as an attempt to interfere with interstate commerce, in violation of the commerce clause of the federal constitution, and, as applied to owners of gas wells in the State, as in violation of Article 12, § 24, of the State Constitution, providing that private property shall not be taken without just compensation.

5. The fee to the land comprising rural highways in the portion of Oklahoma, which was formely Indian Territory is not vested in the State, but in the abutting landowners, subject only to an easement in the public to use the same for highway purposes; and the State has no power to prohibit the laying and maintaining of pipelines over or across such highways by contract with such owners for the transportation of natural gas from within to without the State in interstate commerce, where it does not interfere with the easement in the public property, and subject to such reasonable rules and regulations as the State may impose in the interest of the public health and safety."

At the regular session of the Legislature of the State of Oklahoma, 1907, an Act was passed concerning pipelines, regulating gas and oil pipelines, being Chapter 67 of the laws for the year 1907. This statute provided that no foreign corporation formed for the purpose of, or engaged in the business of transporting or transmitting natural gas by means of pipelines, should ever be licensed or permitted to conduct such business within the State. By Section 2 of the Act, no corporation organized for the purpose of or engaged in the transportation or transmission of natural gas within the State shall be granted a charter or right of eminent domain or right to use the highways of the State, unless it shall be expressly stipulated in its charter that it shall only transport or transmit natural gas through its pipelines to points within the State, and such corporation was forbidden to connect its lines with, transport or deliver natural gas to individuals, companies or corporations engaged in transporting or furnishing natural gas to points, places, or persons outside the State. The object and effect of the Statute was to prohibit the transportation of natural gas outside the State of Oklahoma. The Kansas Natural Gas Company, a corporation created under the laws of the State of Delaware, filed its bill in equity in the Circuit Court of the United States for the Eastern District of Oklahoma to enjoin the enforcement of this Statute. Several other bills were filed for a like purpose by other plaintiffs. All these suits called in question the constitutional validity of the statute. On motion for preliminary injunction, and upon demurrer to the bills, the Circuit Court overruled the demurrers and awarded provisional injunctions.

Sec. 3.—In *State, ex rel, Corwin v. Ind. and Ohio Oil, Gas & Mining Co.,* 120 Ind. 575; 22 N. E. 778; 6 L. R. A. 579, (Nov. 6, 1889, the syllabus is as follows:

"1.   Natural gas, when brought to the surface and placed in pipes for transportation is an article or commerce.
2.   Act, Ind. March 9, 1889, which makes it unlawful for any person, natural or artificial, to conduct natural gas from the State, and imposes a penalty for so doing, is unconstitutional, as it is legislation on interstate commerce, though by other acts it is provided that 'mining' shall include the sinking of gas wells, and natural gas companies are authorized to appropriate and condemn property."

The Acts of the Legislature of Indiana, March 9, 1889, contained the following provision:

"Section 1.   Be it enacted by the general assembly of the State of Indiana, that it shall be unlawful for any person or persons, company, corporation, or voluntary association, to pipe or conduct natural gas from any point within this State to any point or place without this State. Any person or persons, company, corporation, or voluntary organization now or hereafter incorporated, under any law of this or any other State, for the purpose of drilling or mining for petroleum or natural gas, or otherwise acquiring gas or petroleum wells, and the products thereof, and to furnish the same to its patrons, or to convert such product into gas for illuminating purposes or fuel, which shall have entered upon and acquired by deed of conveyance, or appropriated or condemned, any real estate under any law of this State, for the purpose of laying its pipelines, or for any other purpose, which shall permit any gas to be conveyed or carried through its pipelines to any place without this State, or for the purpose of being used without this State, shall forfeit all right, title and interest in and to all real estate so appropriated, conveyed, or condemned, and the pipes laid thereunder, and the same shall revert to and become the property of the persons or corporations, their heirs, successors, or assigns, who owned the same at the time of such appropriation, conveyance, or condemnation; provided, that the provisions of this act shall not be so construed as to prevent towns or cities divided by any of the boundary lines of this State and having a majority of the population of such cities or towns residing within this State, from being supplied with natural gas.''

On February 21, 1889, the Legislature passed an Act declaring that the word "mining" should be deemed to include the sinking of gas wells, and that the incorporation of companies and the subscription of stock under former laws were legalized. On the same day the Legislature passed an Act authorizing gas companies to extend their pipes beyond the corporate limits of cities and towns. On February 20, 1889, the Legislature passed an Act authorizing natural gas companies to appropriate and condemn property. The State of Indiana, at the relation of Cornelius Corwin, instituted an action in the Circuit Court of Jay County, against the Indiana & Ohio, Oil, Gas & Mining Company, to have its franchises forfeited for offenses against said statutes. The Circuit Court rendered judgment for defendant, and plaintiff appealed, and the Supreme Court affirmed the judgment.

<hr>

CHAPTER 39.

WASTE AND TRANSPORTATION OF NATURAL GAS— STATUTORY REGULATION.

Sec. 1.—The State may regulate the pressure at which natural gas may be forced through pipelines, and may also forbid waste of natural gas, and impose reasonable penalties therefor.

State v. *Ohio Oil Co.*, 150 Ind. 694; 49 N. E. 809.
Ohio Oil Co. v. *Indiana*, 177 U. S. 190.
State v. *Oak Harbor Gas Co.*, 53 Ohio St., 347; 41 N. E. 548.
Townsend v. *State*, 147 Ind. 624; 47 N. E. 19.
Jamieson v. *Ind. Nat. Gas & Oil Co.*, 128 Ind. 555; 28 N. E. 76.
Commonwealth v. *Trent*, 25 Ky. L. Rep. 1180; 77 S. W. 390.
Louisville Gas Co. v. *Kentucky Heating Co. and Calor Oil & Gas Co.* v. *McGehee*, 117 Ky. 71; 77 S. W. 368; 70 L. R. A. 558; 111 Am. St. Rep. 225.

Sec. 2.—In *State* v. *Ohio Oil Co.*, 150 Ind. 694; 49 S. E. 809, (March 10, 1898), the syllabus is as follows:

"1. In order to question the capacity of the State to sue in a civil action, a demurrer should embrace the second statutory ground for demurring. (Burns' Rev. Stat. 1894, § 342; Horner's Rev. Stat. 1892, § 339)—"that the plaintiff has not legal capacity to sue."

2. The courts of the State and of the United States are open to the State both in its sovereign capacity and by virtue of its corporate rights.

3. Burns' Rev. Stat. 1894, § 7510 prohibiting any person firm, or corporation, operating any natural gas or oil well, from allowing the escape of gas or oil from such well into open air, is not unconstitutional, as an unwarranted interference with private property, as the title to such gas or oil does not vest in any private owner until it has been reduced to actual possession.

4. Burns' Rev. Stat. 1894, § 7510 which prohibited the permitting of the escape of natural gas into the open air was applicable to the subject of a suit for the preventation of the waste of such gas, though the preamble to such act recited the liability of persons and property to injury as the provocation for such legislation, where it was apparent that the principal object at the passage thereof was to prevent such waste.

5. Under Burns' Rev. Stat. 1894, § 7510, making it unlawful 'to allow or permit the flow of gas or oil, from any such well to escape into the open air', it was unlawful to permit both gas and oil to escape from the same well.

6. Burns' Rev. State, 1894, §§ 290-292 (Horner's Rev. Stat. 1897, §§ 289-291), provide that whatever is injurious to health, or offensive to senses, or an obstruction to the free use of property is a nuisance, and may be enjoined or abated. The complaint, in a suit by the State to enjoin an oil company from wasting natural gas, alleged that a large proportion of the people of the State were dependent upon such gas as an inexpensive fuel; that defendant, in the operation of certain oil wells, producing both oil and gas, has unlawfully permitted the gas produced therein to escape into the open air and become wasted, whereby the supply of such gas has been greatly diminished, and the property of the citizens dependent thereon for fuel greatly damaged; that defendant avows its purpose to permit such gas to escape continuously, and to drill other wells and permit such gas to escape therefrom; that the statutory remedies for such unlawful acts are wholly inadequate, and that such wrongful conduct, if not restrained will result

in the destruction of such supply of gas, and thereby essentially interfere with the property of the State and that of its citizens. *Held,* that such facts constitute a public nuisance which the State has a right to have abated by injunction.''

The State of Indiana, by the attorney general and prosecuting attorney in Madison Circuit Court, brought suit against the Ohio Oil Company for an injunction to restrain it from wasting natural gas. The substance of the complaint is stated in the sixth paragraph of the syllabus. The defendant demurred to the complaint, for want of sufficient facts to constitute a cause of action, and the plaintiff elected to stand on the sufficiency of its complaint, refused to amend or plead further, and the court rendered judgment of dismissal. The State appealed, and the Supreme Court reversed the Circuit Court.

Sec. 3.—In *Ohio Oil Co. v. Indiana,* 177 U. S. 190, (April 9, 1900) the syllabus is as follows:

''The provision in the Act of March 4, 1893, of the State of Indiana 'that it shall be unlawful for any person, firm, or corporation having possession or control of any natural gas or oil well, whether as a contractor, owner, lessee, agent or manager. to allow or permit the flow of gas or oil from any such well to escape into the open air without being confined within such well or proper pipes, or other safe receptacle, for a longer period than two days next after gas or oil shall have been struck in such well; and thereafter all such gas or oil shall be safely and securely confined in such well, pipes, or other safe and proper receptacles,' is not a violation of the constitution of the United States; and its enforcement as to persons whose obedience to its commands were coerced by injunction, is not a taking of private property without adequate compensation, and does not amount to a denial of due process of law, contrary to the provisions of the fourteenth amendment to the constitution of the United States, but is only a regulation by the State of Indiana of a subject which especially comes within its lawful authority.''

This was a controversy between the State of Indiana through the attorney-general, and the Ohio Oil Company, a corporation organized under the laws of the State of Ohio, wherein the State filed a complaint in the Circuit Court of Madison County, Indiana, and presents the same questions as were presented in *State* v.

Ohio Oil Company, 150 Ind. 694; 49 N. E. 809. In this case, however, the Oil Company filed an answer. The case was decided by the Supreme Court of Indiana in favor of the State, and is reported in 50 N. E. 1125. The Oil Company obtained a writ of error to the decree, and the Supreme Court of the United States affirmed the decision.

See also *Ohio Oil Co.* v. *Indiana* (No. 2) 177 U. S. 212, and also *Ohio Oil Co.* v. *Indiana* (No. 3) 213.

Sec. 4.—In *State* v. *Oak Harbor Gas Co.,* 53 Ohio State, 347; 41 N. E. 584, (Oct. 22, 1895) the syllabus is as follows:

"When an oil or gas well is about to be abandoned, or operation thereof ceases, the statute (90 Ohio Laws, 24) requires that, before drawing the casing therefrom it shall be securely filled in such manner as shall prevent the surface or fresh water from penetrating to the oil or gas bearing rock, and also as shall prevent the gas or oil from escaping therefrom. To comply with this statute, it is required that the necessary filling be done while the casing yet remains in the well; and a petition for the violation of this statute need not aver that the casing has been drawn."

The State of Ohio, on complaint of David Gordon, filed a petition against the Oak Harbor Gas Company, alleging that the defendant was a corporation, and for several years had been the operator of a certain well drilled for the production of petroleum oil and natural gas, situated in Ottawa County, Ohio; that the defendant company claimed to own the well, and to be operating the same for the production of oil and natural gas; that said well had ceased to produce either petroleum oil or natural gas, or other profitable mineral substances, and had been wholly unproductive, and of no value or use, and in fact the defendant had ceased to operate the well, and that its condition was such that surface or fresh water penetrated the oil or gas bearing rock through the well; that the defendant ever since the first day of April, 1893, had unlawfully and wilfully neglected and omitted to fill said well with rock sediment or with mortar composed of two parts sand and one part cement, to the depth of 200 feet above the top of the first oil or gas bearing rock, in such manner as to present the surface or fresh water from penetrating to the oil or gas bearing rock, and in such manner as should prevent the gas and oil from escaping from the well, as required by law; that defendant had wholly, wilfully, and unlawfully neglected and omitted to fill the well in any manner whatever, and had omitted to make any attempt to do the same, in any manner, whereby the fresh or surface water penetrated to the oil and gas bearing rock of said well and gas and oil escaped therefrom, contrary to the form of the statute in such case made and provided. The petition prayed that the defendant be found guilty of the facts charged, and required to pay the penalty provided by law; and that a mandatory injunction should issue compelling the defendant to comply with the provisions of the Act of February 9, 1893, entitled "An Act to regulate drilling, operating and abandonment of petroleum oil, natural gas and mineral water wells, and prevent certain abuses connected therewith." To this petition defendants filed a general demurrer to the effect that the petition did not state facts sufficient to constitute a cause of action against the defendant. The Court of Common Pleas overruled the demurrer, exceptions were taken, and the defendant answered and admitted that it was a corporation; that it was the owner of the well described in the petition; that it had not filled up the well; but denied each and every other allegation contained in the petition. Upon the trial of the case to a jury a verdict of guilty was returned and the penalty of $100.00 was assessed against the defendant. A motion for a new trial was filed on the ground that the verdict was against the weight of the evidence, and that the court erred in overruling the demurrer. This motion was overruled, exceptions taken and judgment entered on the verdict. The case was taken to the Circuit Court, where the judgment was reversed on the grounds that the petition did not state facts sufficient to constitute a cause of action; and that the Court of Common Pleas erred in overruling the demurrer to the petition. The defendant filed petition in error in the Supreme Court, and that court in a per curiam opinion reversed the Circuit Court, and affirmed the judgment of the Court of Common Pleas.

Sec. 5.—In *Townsend* v. *State*, 147 Ind. 624; 47 N. E. 19, (May 18, 1897) syls. 1-2-3-4-5-6-9 are as follows:

"1. Rev. Stat. 1894, § 2316, et seq, declaring that the burning of natural gas in flambeau lights is a wasteful use thereof, and forbidding such use under penalty of fine, does not deprive owners of such gas of their property without due process of law (Const. U. S. Amend. 5. 14), nor take property by law without just compen-.sation (Bill of rights, § 21), since the wasteful use of natural gas, which is drawn from a common store in the earth, not reduced to individual possession, is an injury to others.

2.   Nor does such statute violate Bill of Rights, § 1, declaring inalienable their right of liberty and the pursuit of happiness.

3.   Nor does it violate section 23, of the Bill of Rights, pro- viding that no privilege or immunity shall be given to any citizen which shall not on the same terms, belong to all citizens.

4.   The prohibition of wasteful use of natural gas, being within the police power, the legislative determination that the burning thereof in flambeau lights is such wasteful use is final.

5.   Whether such prohibition is unreasonable, or violative of the natural rights of citizens, is a legislative question, the courts having no concern with the justice or policy of enactments violating no provision of the constitution.

6.   The declaration that the burning of natural gas in flam- beau lights is a wasteful use of such gas, in the preamble of Rev. Stat., 1894, Sec. 2316, forbidding such use is not a judicial act so as to be violative of Const. Art. 7, Sec. 1, vesting the judicial power in the courts.

9.   Violation of Rev. Stat. 1894, Sec. 2316, providing that it shall be unlawful to use natural gas in flambeau lights is a con- tinuing offense, and hence, on a prosecution for such violation, the State may show such unlawful use of gas on more than one oc- casion prior to the finding of the indictment.''

Andrew J. Townsend was convicted of wasteful use of natural gas before a Justice of the Peace upon an affidavit charging that on October 9, 1895, and at divers other times at the County of Blackford and State of Indiana, before that, he did then and there knowingly and unlawfully use, light and burn natural gas for illuminating purposes in what was known as a flambeau light. The justice overruled the motion to quash the affidavit, and upon a trial found him guilty and assessed his fine at a dollar, and rendered judgment for the fine and costs. Defendant appealed to the Circuit Court, and there renewed his motion to quash, which that court overruled, and upon his plea of not guilty, a jury upon a trial found him guilty, fixing his fine at One Dollar, upon which the court rendered judgment over defendant's motion for a new trial. Defendant appealed to the Supreme Court, and that court affirmed the judgment. The rulings are stated in the syllabus.

Sec. 6.—In *Jamieson* v. *Indiana Nat. Gas & Oil Co.*, 128 Ind. 555; 28 N. E. 76 (June 20, 1891), the syllabus is as follows:

"1. Act Ind. 1891, prohibiting the transportation of natural gas through pipes at a greater pressure than 300 pounds per square inch, or otherwise than by its natural flow, is a valid exercise of the police power of the State, since natural gas is an intrinsically dangerous substance; and, the legislature having determined what pressure is reasonable and safe, the courts cannot review its action.

2. The court will take judical notice of the fact that natural gas is an inflammable and explosive substance, intrinsically dangerous.

3. The Act, being merely a regulation of the use of property, is not a taking of it, within the meaning of Const. Ind. Art. 1, § 1, prohibiting the taking of property without just compensation, nor does it impair any vested right, nor conflict with Const. U. S. 14th Amend., providing that no State shall deprive any person of property without due process of law.

4. The Act upon its face showing no purpose to usurp federal power over interstate commence, and applying to all persons without discrimination, and being solely for the purpose of regulating the use of a characteristically local and intrinsically dangerous product, and not a prohibition of its transportation, is not a regulation of interstate commerce within the meaning of Const. U. S. Art. 1, § 8, subd. 3, providing that Congress shall have power to regulate commerce among the several States, although its effect may incidentally be to prevent the transportation of gas into another State. Distinguishing *State* v. *Mining Co.*, 120 Ind. 575; 22 N. E. Rep. 778, and *Leisy* v. *Harden*, 135 U. S. 100, 10 Sup. Ct. Rep. 681."

Egbert Jamieson, a stockholder in the Indiana Natural Gas & Oil Company, filed a complaint in the Circuit Court of Porter County, Indiana, for an injunction against said company to prevent it from carrying out a contract alleged to have been in violation of law, which complaint stated the following material facts: The Indiana Natural Gas & Oil Company was a corporation under the laws of Indiana for drilling wells, procuring natural gas, and supplying it to consumers. The plaintiff was a stockholder in that corporation. The Columbus Construction Company was a corporation and the òwner of natural gas wells in many Counties of Indiana. In June, 1890, the gas company entered into a contract with the construction company, wherein it was provided that the latter company should acquire the right of way through Indiana and Illinois, to the City of Chicago; that it should construct for the gas company on the right of way a pipeline for the transportation of natural gas, and furnish necessary machinery and appliances required to obtain and convey gas to consumers. In consideration of the purchase of the right of way, and furnishing and constructing of pipelines, machinery and appliances, the gas company agreed to issue and deliver to the construction company capital stock to the value of $1,500,000, and also issue to the construction company $4,000,000 of its corporate bonds, and secure their payment by a mortgage upon its property and franchises. The construction company proceeded under the contract, acquired a right of way, and purchased and laid a line of pipe for a distance of 20 miles, and distributed pipe along the right of way for a distance of 40 miles. The company had purchased and had in readiness machinery and appliances to be connected with the line of pipes; and it was able, ready and willing to perform its part of the contract; natural gas could only be transported to Chicago by pumping, and under pressure; that it would be impossible to transport it to that point at a pressure which did not exceed 300 pounds to the square inch. The gas company would have no other asset or property than "its plant and system, and no means whatever of paying either the principal or interest" of the corporate bonds which were to be issued to the construction company; that its only means of paying such bonds, or of redeeming its capital stock would be such as were derived from "the plant and system, and the revenues, tolls, income, and profits to be earned thereby in the transportation and sale of natural gas in the city of Chicago; and the sole value of its stock would depend upon the right and ability of the company to engage in and carry on, by means of its natural gas plant and system, the business of transportation of natural gas to Chicago, and there selling the same;" that the plant and system could not be put to any other commercially profitable use than that of transporting natural gas to Chicago, and could only be used to advantage and profit by the use, as aforesaid, of the pumping machines and other artificial devices. The complaint then set forth at length the Act of the Legislature of Indiana of March 4, 1891, and in addition to the averment of the facts above outlined, contained the allegations that the Indiana Natural Gas Company, by reason of the statute aforesaid, was prohibited from transporting the gas through the pipeline at more than the natural flow and pressure or at a pressure in excess of three hundred pounds to the square inch, or from using any artificial device to increase the natural flow of the gas. The natural gas property and plant contracted to be furnished and delivered to the defendant, as aforesaid, would be of no value for the purpose of such plant, and of little or no value for any purpose to the defendant, and the stock and bonds of the defendant would be wasted, and the company deprived of all the means of effecting the object and purposes of its incorporation, and be rendered entirely insolvent; that the statute aforementioned, made it unlawful for the defendant, or any person in the State of Indiana, to transport natural gas through the pipelines at a pressure exceeding 300 pounds to the square inch, or the natural flow and pressure of the gas, or to use in such transportation any artificial device for the purpose, or which should have the effect of increasing or maintaining the natural flow and pressure of the gas. Wherefore, plaintiff averred that it had become and was illegal for either of said defendant companies to further proceed with the execution of the contract, and that the defendant, the Indiana Natural Gas & Oil Company, especially, ought not to be permitted to proceed further in the execution of the contract, the performance of which would result as aforesaid, in a waste and destruction of almost its entire corporate asset, and make it entirely impracticable for it to carry out the objects and purposes of its incorporation, and would also involve it in liability for the payment of heavy penalties for the violation of the statute. Defendant further averred that immediately upon the taking effect of the statute, he demanded of the Board of Directors of the Gas Company, that they and the said company should at once desist from any further proceedings towards executing and carrying out said contract; that they should abandon the enterprise of transporting natural gas by the use of artificial pressure, or pressure in excess of 300 pounds to the square inch, or other than the natural flow and pressure of natural gas; and that they should at once rescind and abandon said contract; that said Board of Directors refused to do so, and declared that notwithstanding the statute, and regardless of the right of the plaintiff, they would proceed to perform fully said contract as to all the obligations of the gas company thereunder, and would not abandon the enterprise of transporting natural gas by artificial pressure in excess of the natural flow and pressure and in excess of 300 pounds to the square inch; and that upon performance by said Columbus Construction Company of its part of the contract the said gas company would issue and deliver to the Construction Company its stock and bonds in all respects according to the terms of the contract. Plaintiff further averred that in execution of the contract the companies had already, and since the taking effect of the statute, connected their pipeline with certain gas wells in the County of Howard, in the State of Indiana, being wells which, under said contract were to be acquired and used by the gas company, and by means of a certain artificial device for pumping known as a "pump" being part of the machinery to be acquired and used by the gas company, did unlawfully transport the natural gas from said wells through a line of pipe in said county, at an artificial pressure, in excess of 300 pounds to the square inch, and in excess of the natural pressure and flow of gas, to-wit, at a pressure of 420 pounds to the square inch; Whereas the natural pressure of gas was but, to-wit, 325 pounds to the square inch; and ever since had continued to, and were then so engaged in violating the provisions of the statute; whereby the gas company had already incurred liability for the penalty prescribed by the statute, and would be subjected to further liability for such penalties, unless defendant companies be enjoined as prayed, which would result in further waste of the corporate assets, and irreparable loss to the plaintiff. Plaintiff averred that the defendant, Indiana Natural Gas & Oil Company, unless enjoined from so doing, would issue to said Columbus Construction Company, its bonds and stock, as provided for by the contract.

An answer was filed by the defendants to which complainant demurred, and the court carried back the demurrer to the complaint, and gave judgment because of the insufficiency of that pleading. An appeal was taken upon the assignments of error to the ruling of the court in holding that the complaint was insufficient. The Supreme Court reversed the Circuit Court, and held the statute of 1891 valid.

Sec. 7.—In *Commonwealth* v. *Trent*, 25 Ky. Law Rep. 1180; 77 S. W. 390 (Dec. 9, 1903), syls. 1-2-5-6 are as follows:

"1. Acts 1891-92, pp. 60-61 (Ky. Stat. 1899 §§ 3910-3914) provide (1) for the confinement of gas in wells until its utilization; (2) for the plugging of abandoned wells; (3) that landowners adjacent to wells the owners of which fail to comply with section 1, may enter on their lands and plug the wells: (4) that owners of land adjacent to abandoned wells may enter and plug them; (5) declare an emergency on account of the number of abandoned wells in the State; *Held*, that since sections 2 and 5 provide expressly and sufficiently for abandoned wells, and section 1 and 4 are not so limited, those latter sections provide for wells not abandoned, although the emergency was declared to exist only as to abandoned wells.

2. Acts of 1891-93, pp. 60-61 (Ky. Stat. 1899 §§ 3910-3914) enacted for the purpose of preventing the waste of gas, provides in Sec. 1 that owners, etc. of gas wells, shall confine the gas until such time as it shall be utilized, and in section 4 that owners of and adjacent to unplugged wells may enter and plug the wells if their owners neglect to do so. Abandoned wells are provided for in Secs. 2 and 5 and Sec. 4, makes no provision for a well that is shut in, the gas escaping from another point than the well itself. *Held*, that section 1, being broader than section 4, imposes a duty on the owners to confine the gas irrespective of the point of its escape, and such owners are liable for permitting gas to escape through pipes at a point other than the well, independently of the liability imposed by Section 4 for permitting the gas to escape at the well.

5. Under Acts 1891-93 pp. 60-61 (Ky. St. 1899, §§ 3910-3914) enacted for the prevention of the waste of gas and adjoining the plugging of wells not in use, it cannot be contended that the owners of wells may do as they please with gas after reduced to possession by them for the gas coming from the gas meter is replaced by other gas coming from the well.

6. Acts 1891-93 pp. 60-61 (Ky St. §§ 3910-3914) enacted for the prevention of the waste of gas and enjoining the plugging of wells not in use was within the legislative power to enact as a protection of the natural resources of the State, to the rights of the public in which the rights of individual owners are subject."

A penal action was instituted by the Commonwealth of Kentucky against J. H. Trent, Jr., et als., in the Circuit Court of Meade County, Kentucky. It was averred in the petition that the defendants conspired and confederated together for the unlawful purpose of obtaining and wasting natural gas from lands embraced in the gas belt of Meade County, Kentucky; that to effectuate and carry out this proposition they drilled six wells in the gas belt, four of them proving to be producing gas wells and yielding about 600,000 feet of gas per day; that these wells were in the possession and under the absolute control of the defendants, either as owners, agents, or managers; and that defendants, under the pretence of manufacturing lampblack, but really with the unlawful purpose to waste the gas and destroy the gas territory in Meade County, willfully and maliciously burned and wasted all the gas from the four wells, after it had been piped into a general tank or gasometer, from the —— day of December, 1901, to the 14th day of June, 1902, in violation of the rights of the owners of the gas land and contrary to the provisions of the statute. It was also alleged that the wells were not utilized by the defendants within three months after they were brought in, nor shut in so as to prevent the gas from wasting by escape; but that the defendants suffered and permitted the gas to waste and escape. The defendants insisted that the facts stated did not make a cause of action under the statute for the reason that it was not charged that the gas was allowed to waste by escape at the well; and that the legislature did not mean to make criminal the use by the citizen of its own property even if that use brought him no pecuniary benefit, or was misuse. It was insisted on behalf of the State that if the defendants willfully and maliciously wasted the gas, the form in which they did so was immaterial under the statute. The court dismissed the complaint, and from the judgment of dismissal the State appealed. The Supreme Court of Kentucky reversed the Circuit Court, citing:

Ohio Oil Co. v. *Indiana,* 177 U. S. 190.
State v. *Ohio Oil Co.,* 150 Ind. 694; 49 N. E. 809.

Sec. 8.—In *Louisville Gas Co.* v. *Kentucky Heating Co., and Calor Oil & Gas Co.* v. *McGehee,* 117 Ky. 71; 77 S. W. 368; 70 L. R. A. 558; 111 Am. St. Rep. 225 (Dec. 11, 1903), the syllabus is as follows:

"1. Though natural gas underlying the soil is not subject to absolute ownership in its natural state, a lessee of natural gas land is limited to a reasonable use of gas obtained from wells sunk on the land, and is not entitled to waste the supply from such wells for the purpose of cutting off the supply and injuring the owners of other wells on adjoining lands.
2. Plaintiff, who was the owner of gas land, leased certain of it to a corporation for the purpose of drawing gas therefrom. Thereafter T. applied to him to lease certain other lands for the same purpose. Plaintiff refused to make a lease if it was intended to do anything to injure the other lessee, but upon being assured that such was not the intention leased the land to T. and there-

after the defendant corporation was organized, and expended
$20,000 putting down gas wells and establishing a lampblack
factory on the ground. Gas in large quantites was obtained from
defendant's wells which was wasted by the defendants, to the injury of the other lessee. *Held,* that such facts did not justify cancellation of defendant's lease on the ground of fraud, plaintiff and
the other lessee being protected by statute against defendants for
the waste of the gas.''

The Kentucky Heating Company and W. C. McGehee brought
actions against the Louisville Gas Company and the Calor Oil &
Gas Company in the Circuit Court of Meade County, Kentucky.
The Louisville Gas Company claimed the exclusive privilege of
selling illuminating gas in the City of Louisville. There was a
long litigation between that company and the Kentucky Heating
Company which resulted in a judgment by the Court of Appeals of
Kentucky that the Heating Company had the right to sell natural gas for heating and illuminating purposes, and also the right
to make and sell artificial gas for fuel, but not the right to sell
artificial gas alone or in mixture with natural gas for purposes of
illuminating without violation of the Gas Company's exclusive
privilege. [Kentucky Heating Co. v. Louisville Gas Co. (Ky.) 63
S. W. 751.] On September 3, 1901, or about three months after
the judgment so rendered the Calor Oil & Gas Company was incorporated. In the winter, before the corporation was formed,
John H. Trent, a lawyer residing in Meade County, who seems to
have been employed by the Gas Company previously, began taking
leases of land for gas in the gas field, and in doing this acted as
the agent, as appeared, of Barrett, Sneed & Speed. After the
organization of the Calor Oil & Gas Company, these leases were
transferred to it. It appeared that for some time before the organization of this company they had been considering the gas field in
Meade County, from which the Kentucky Heating Company obtained its gas, and one of their objects in getting the leases and
organizing the Calor Oil & Gas Company was to interfere with the
supply of that company, and thus cripple it as a rival of the
Louisville Gas Company. They put up between them about $10,000,
which they spent in Meade County in drilling wells and in erecting a lampblack factory. In addition to this, when the depositions were taken they had incurred liabilities for about $10,000
more, which was then unpaid. They succeeded in getting several good gas wells from which the gas was piped to the lamp-

black factory. When they began operations the Kentucky Heating Company had a gas pressure of something over sixty pounds. In five or six months this was run down to less than thirty pounds. Upon these facts, upon the petition of the Kentucky Heating Company, the chancellor enjoined the operation of the lampblack factory on the ground that it was operated only to waste the gas and thus destroy the Kentucky Heating Company. Defendants appealed. A close fence, twelve feet high, was built around the lampblack factory and no one was admitted within the enclosure. It stood on a half acre of ground leased for that purpose, and no one was permitted to come within this enclosure. Fire arms were discharged there to deter the neighbors from coming about. The structure was out in the country where such enclosures were unusual, and, as shown by the evidence, unnecessary. The man in charge of the factory was the lawyer, Trent, who lived at the County seat and knew nothing of the manufacture of lampblack. There were only two other persons employed, one the day man, who was a boy sixteen years old, the other the night man, somewhat older, but both entirely ignorant of the manufacture of lampblack. During the five months the factory was operated they manufactured about three hundred pounds of lampblack, worth four cents per pound. In this time they burned all the gas they could obtain, the total amount being about ninety million feet. No lampblack was shipped away from the factory. The gas was burned night and day, and it was evident from the proof that in a short time more, pressure upon the pipes of the Kentucky Heating Company would have been so low as to destroy its usefulness. The evidence for the defendants showed that it conceived the idea of securing leases on territory connected with the gas reservoir from which the Kentucky Heating Company obtained its supply, and by boring numerous wells to draw off the gas and practically destroy the business of the Kentucky Heating Company. The organization of the Calor Oil & Gas Company and the establishment of the lampblack factory, was a part of the plan to evade the statute against the wasting of natural gas, and to waste the gas. The Circuit Court entered a decree enjoining the Calor Oil & Gas Company from wasting the gas, and the Court of Appeals affirmed this decree, holding, that the Kentucky Heating Company, and also the Calor Oil & Gas Company, had the right to take gas from the common source of supply; but neither had the right by waste to destroy the rights of the other, and as in the case of other like wrongs, the action of redress might be brought in the name of any party in interest, citing:

> Manufacturers Gas Co. v. Indiana Gas Co., 155 Ind. 461; 57 N. E. 912; 50 L. R. A. 768.
> Ohio Oil Co. v. Indiana, 177 U. S. 190.

W. C. McGehee, who leased the land on which the wells referred to, or part of them, were situated, filed an action to cancel the lease on the ground that it was obtained by fraud. McGehee had leased other lands to the Kentucky Heating Company and was getting $700.00 per year from that company. He told Trent this when the lessor applied for the lease, stating that he did not want to do anything that would injure the Kentucky Heating Company. Trent thereupon said to him that the people he represented were lawabiding men, and that they would do a lawful business. The court held that the proofs warranted the conclusion that the wasting of the gas and the consequent injury to the Kentucky Heating Company was a motive inducing the defendants to get the lease, and this purpose was in view when they obtained the lease. McGehee would not have leased them the land if he had understood the facts. The chancellor cancelled the lease upon the ground that it was obtained by fraud, and that fraud vitiates any contract obtained thereby. The defendants had expended something like $20,000 in putting down their wells, perfecting their rights and erecting their buildings and other structures. This was to be a total loss to them if their leases were cancelled. The court held that, as had been held in the case of Commonwealth v. Trent, it was incumbent upon them to confine the gas in the wells until such time as it might be utilized; and if they failed to do this, they became liable to the penalties denounced by the statute. The court further held that it could not be presumed that the defendants would wilfully violate the statute. When McGehee leased the ground for the factory he intended them to have the benefit of the gas if they found any, and intended them to use the gas; yet, notwithstanding the statute, if they should thereafter use the gas unlawfully, he, or any other person aggrieved, might maintain an action for the protection of his rights. The Court of Appeals held that under the circumstances, and in view of all the facts, the rescission of the lease should not be decreed. The judgment in the case of McGehee v. the Calor Oil & Gas Company

was reversed, and the cause remanded with directions to dismiss
the petition.

REMEDIES.

Sec. 9.—Where the State has provided by Statute for the
maximum pressure at which natural gas may be forced through
pipelines, and has also forbidden the waste of natural gas, and
imposed penalties for the violation of the statute, where such
statute is violated punishment may be inflicted by proceedings in
the name of the State; or where the owners of lands or leases
are injuriously affected by such violations such owners may enjoin the further violation of the Statute and may recover damages for injuries resulting therefrom.

(See authorities cited under Section 1, supra.)

Sec. 10.—Upon an indictment for violation of a statute forbidding the waste of gas, and requiring gas wells to be shut in,
where the evidence shows that the lessee or owner of the well discovered gas, and within the time stipulated in the statute confined the same in the well, pipes or other safe receptacle, and
afterwards opened the well for the purpose of repairing or completing the same, and while engaged in such repairs or completion the gas was allowed to escape, such proof entitled the in-
dicted owner or lessee to an acquittal.

Bailey v. *State,* 163 Ind. 165; 71 N. E. 655.

CHAPTER 40.

GAS PUMP CANNOT BE USED TO PRODUCE UNNATURAL FLOW.

Sec. 1.—The owners of lands located in a gas field have the
right to bore or mine for gas on their own lands and to use that portion of it as when left to the natural law of flowage, may rise in the
wells of such owners and into their pipes; but no one of the owners
of such lands has the right, without the consent of all the other
owners, to induce an unnatural flow into or through his own wells

by the use of gas pumps or to do any act with reference to the common reservoir and body of gas therein, injurious to or calculated to destroy it.

> *Manufacturers Gas & Oil Co.* v. *Indiana Nat. Gas Co.*, 155 Ind. 461; 57 N. E. 912; 50 L. R. A. 768.
> *Manufacturers Gas & Oil Co.* v. *Indiana Nat. Gas Co.*, 156 Ind. 679; 59 N. E. 169; 60 N. E. 1080.
> *Manufacturers Gas & Oil Co.* v. *Indiana Nat. Gas Co.*, 155, Ind. 556; 58 N. E. 851.
> *Richmond Nat. Gas Co.* v. *Enterprise Nat. Gas Co.*, 31 Ind. App. 222; 66 N. E. 782.
> *Jones* v. *Forest Oil Co.*, 194 Pa. 379; 44 Atl. 1074.

Sec. 2.—In *Manufacturers Gas & Oil Co.* v. *Indiana Natural Gas & Oil Company*, 155 Ind. 461; 57 N. E. 912; 50 L. R. A. 768, June 28, 1900) the syllabus is as follows:

"1. Since the right to take natural gas exists commonly in the owner of the superincumbent lands, it does not become the property of any of such owners until reduced to actual possession. Hence, objections based on the right of transportation and sale of such gas are not pertinent to a complaint to enjoin the use of artificial means to increase the flow thereof from gas wells.

2. Since the right to mine natural gas, when left to the natural laws of flowage, exists exclusively in the owner of superincumbent lands, and such gas is not subject to public appropriations without their consent, they are entitled to preserve it from destruction, independent of the right of the State to regulate it, and may enjoin any act of one owner to induce an unnatural flow to or through his wells which tends to the injury or destruction of the common supply.

3. Since the right to take natural gas is common to all the surface owners, and the gas does not become the property of any such owners until reduced to actual possession at the surface, Acts 1891, p. 89, prohibiting the use of artificial means to increase the natural flow of gas from a well, is not unconstitutional as a deprivation of property without due compensation, but is a valid regulation for the protection of common property from destruction, recognizing qualified ownership therein."

The Manufacturers Natural Gas & Oil Company and others, instituted suit in the Circuit Court of Grant County, Indiana, against the Indiana Natural Gas & Oil Company, seeking to enjoin the defendant from using devices for pumping and from employing any other artificial process or appliance for the purpose or

having the effect of increasing the natural flow of gas from the
wells of the plaintiffs, or through the pipes conveying and transporting the same. Defendant demurred to the complaint, which
demurrer the Circuit Court sustained, and from which ruling plaintiffs appealed to the Supreme Court, where the decree was reversed, citing: •

State v. Ohio Oil Co., 150 Ind. 21; 49 N. E. 809.
Del Monte Min. & Mill. Co. v. Last Chance Min. & Mill. Co.,
    171 U. S. 60; 18 Sup. Ct. 895; 43 L. Ed. 72.
Brown v. Spilman, 155 U. S. 665; 15 Sup. Ct. 245; 39 L. Ed.
    304.
Jamison v. Oil Co., 128 Ind. 555; 28 N. E. 76; 12 L. R. A. 652.
Townsend v. State, 147 Ind. 624; 47 N. E. 19; 37 L. R. A. 294.
Acts 1891, page 389.
Geer v. Connecticut, 161 U. S. 519-525; 16 Sup. Ct. 600; 40 L.
    Ed. 793.

The complaint alleged: That the Manufacturers Gas & Oil
Company, the Manufacturers Fuel Company, the Ball Brothers
Glass Manufacturing Company; the Swayzee Glass Company; the
Chrystal Window Glass Company, and the Alexandria Window
Glass Company (who were the plaintiffs) were corporations under
the laws of Indiana, as was also the defendant, the Indiana Natural Gas & Oil Company. That the two corporations first named
were engaged, among other things, in supplying natural gas to
manufacturing companies carrying on business at Muncie, Delaware County, Indiana, in which large amounts of capital were invested, and by whom 1600 men were employed and paid, the value
of the annual output of which was $3,500,000.00; that the pipelines
of the said Manufacturers Gas & Oil Company extended to and
some of its wells were situated at a point about nine miles north-
west of the City of Muncie, and fifteen miles from one of the lines
and from some of the wells of the defendant in Grant County; that
the pipelines, and some of the gas wells of the Manufacturers Fuel
Company extended north from the City of Muncie about seven
miles to about eighteen miles from the lines and wells of the de-
dendant; that the Ball Brothers Glass Manufacturing Company
had an annual output of $1,500,000.00; and that it employed 1200
men, with a payroll of $42,000 per month; that the lines through
which it was supplied with gas extended north from the City of

Muncie about 11 miles to within a distance of about 18 miles of the lines and wells of the defendant.

Similar allegation were made as to the Swayzee Glass Company, the Chrystal Window Glass Company, and the Alexandria Window Glass Company; it was further stated that each of the manufacturing establishments required a large amount of fuel to enable it to carry on its operations; that natural gas was more desirable than any other fuel; and that the plants of said plaintiffs were located and built especially with reference to the supply of natural gas in their vicinity, and were entirely dependent upon it; that the defendant was engaged in the business of mining, collecting and transporting natural gas from the natural gas fields in Indiana to the City of Chicago, in the State of Illinois, and that in the conduct of its said business it had established pipelines for the transportation of natural gas through a great part of the Counties of the State from Howard County to the northwest boundary of the State; and that for the purpose of transporting such natural gas, it had established and was maintaining one pumping station in the County of Jasper, and one in the County of Howard, and that it was intending and threatening to and unless restrained by the court it would establish another in the County of Grant, where it had located and drilled wells and laid pipelines connecting with its main pipeline to Chicago; that, underlying the counties in the north-western and central part of Indiana, there was discovered in the year 1886, a great reservoir of natural gas, located in the Trenton Rock at various distances from the surface of the earth, the Counties of Delaware, Madison and Grant being located over the center of the reservoir, and said reservoir extending in every direction from the three counties aforesaid, and underlying the whole of Blackford, and parts of Jay, Wells, Howard, Tipton, Hamilton, Hancock, Henry, and Randolph Counties, the supply of gas being greatest in the Counties of Delaware, Grant and Madison; that said reservoir of natural gas was single, continuous, connected and limited, situated in the Trenton Rock underlying the said several Counties and parts of Counties at a depth of from 900 to 1,000 feet below the surface of the earth; that the said Trenton Rock was a porous substance which permitted the passage of natural gas through it; that said gas was confined in said rock at a great pressure, which had diminished from 325 pounds in 1886, to 165 pounds at the filing of the complaint; that because the said reservoir was continuous,

connected and limited, and diminution, waste, destruction or injury to any part of the reservoir, decreased the entire supply of
natural gas, and diminished the pressure of all natural gas wells
drawing from said reservoir, thereby injuring all other parts of
said reservoir; that beneath and around said reservoir was a vast
body of salt water, which also was confined, and was subject to
great pressure, and which, as the pressure on the reservoir of
natural gas decreased or was diminished, constantly tended to enter the reservoir, and the wells drilled therein, and destroy the
same; that when the pressure within the reservoir should decrease
to about 100 pounds, the effect would be to permit said body of
salt water to enter said entire reservoir and destroy the same, with
all the natural gas wells entering therein, or drawing thereon;
that the gas wells of the plaintiffs would be rendered entirely useless and worthless if the said reservoir should be destroyed; that
for this reason it was of the utmost importance to the plaintiffs and
to all other manufacturing institutions in said gas district that
no excessive unauthorized or unlawful use of said natural gas be
made or permitted; that the defendant had located and drilled,
and drew natural gas from a great number of natural gas wells
in Grant and Howard Counties, and had leased many thousands
of acres of land in said Grant and Delaware Counties, whereon it
had not yet drilled wells, but expected, intended and gave out
that it would drill gas wells on said lands; that much of the land
so leased for the purposes aforesaid lay in the immediate vicinity of the wells owned by the plaintiffs, respectively; that all of the
wells already drilled by the defendant penetrated to and drew from
said reservoir of natural gas, and all wells thereafter drilled upon
said leased land would penetrate and draw upon said reservoir;
that the defendants in violation of the rights of the plaintiffs, and
in violation of Section 2 of an Act, entitled "An Act to regulate
the mode of procuring, transporting, and using natural gas, and
declaring an emergency," which had become a law by lapse of
time, without the governor's approval, March 4, 1891, the defendant had used, was using, and threatened to continue to use
artificial processes or appliances for the purpose, and which had
the effect of increasing the natural flow of the natural gas from its
wells, through tne pipes used for conveying and transporting the
same by maintaining and using at points in the Counties of Jasper,
Howard and Grant, pumping stations, and other devices, to the
plaintiffs unknown, by which the natural gas, while being trans-

orted, was forced into the mains and pipes at a pressure of 400 pounds to the square inch, and largely beyond the natural rock ressure of the natural gas at the wells; that by the use of such evices the back pressure upon the reservoir, which was essential ɔ keep the salt water from entering the wells, and destroying the atural gas, was withdrawn, and the flow of gas from the wells nd in the pipes was greatly increased, and the supply and pres- ure of gas in the reservoir greatly diminished, to the prejudice f the plaintiffs, and of all other manufacturing interests in and roughout the district; and in so forcing the gas through such ipelines by such artificial pressure, the defendant had drawn and as continuing to draw so heavily through its said wells upon the id reservoir as to seriously diminish the supply and pressure of as therein, and draw from the wells owned by the plaintiffs and ther manufacturers in the district the supply of gas upon which ey were dependent for their continued operation; that unless de- ndant was restrained from piping the natural gas by pumping id other artificial appliances for the purpose, and having the fect of increasing the natural flow of gas from any well, and of creasing and maintaining the flow of natural gas through the pes used for conveying and transporting the same, the plaintiffs id all other manufacturing interests located in the said gas dis- ict would suffer irreparable injury, their wells would be wholly stroyed and rendered entirely worthless, the value of their operty would be destroyed in whole or in part, and they would compelled to close down and discharge their employes until ch time as they could re-fit and re-establish their plants for the e of coal; and that even then, the value of their property would greatly diminished, etc. The petition demanded that the de- ndant be perpetually enjoined and restrained from using devices r pumping, or any other artificial process or appliance for the rpose, or that should have the effect, of increasing the natural w of natural gas from any of its wells, and from increasing d maintaining the flow of natural gas through the pipes used for nveying and transporting the same.

Sec. 3.—In *Manufacturers Nat. Gas & Oil Co.*, v. *Indiana Nat. s & Oil Co.*, 155 Ind. 556; 58 N. E. 851 (Dec. 14, 1900), the sylla- s is as follows:

"A complaint for an injunction to restrain defendant from insporting natural gas at a pressure exceeding 300 pounds per

square inch, prohibited by Act March 4, 1891, (Acts 1891, p. 89;
Burns Rev. Stat. 1894 §§ 7507-7509), which failed to allege that the
property or gas wells of complainant were near defendant's pipeline, or that their lives, lives of their servants and employes, and
their property were endangered by the excessive pressure was
demurrable, since it failed to allege injury threatened or apprehended, and did not show that complainants would sustain any
special injury other than which might be inflicted on others simi-
larly situated.''

The Manufacturers Gas & Oil Company instituted suit in the
Circuit Court of Grant County against the Indiana Natural Gas
Company, the object of which was to enjoin the defendants from
transporting natural gas through pipes at a pressure exceeding
300 pounds per square inch, in violation of the provisions of the
Act of March 4, 1891. The principal averments of the complaint,
were: That the plaintiffs (with the exception of the Manufacturers Gas & Oil Company) were manufacturers; that they had invested large sums of money in their factories and business, which
were situated in what was known as the ''Gas Belt of Indiana;''
that they had added largely to the taxable property, wealth and
population of the State; that in making their investments they
relied upon the continuance of the supply of natural gas contained
in the common reservoir described in the complaint; that the defendant was transporting from the gas field natural gas through
pipes at a pressure exceeding 300 pounds to the square inch, in
contravention of the statute, and that such wrongful act was destructive of a common source of supply, and an illegal invasion
of the rights of the plaintiffs. The allegation as to the Manufacturers Gas & Oil Company was that it was the owner of gas
wells in the field in which the defendant was engaged in piping
gas and that it was furnishing gas to certain of the other plaintiffs. It was not averred that the property or gas wells of the
plaintiffs were near the pipelines of the defendant, or that the
lives of the plaintiffs or their servants and employes or their property were exposed to danger by reason of the excessive pressure
of the gas in defendant's pipelines. So much of the Act of 1891,
as related to the controversy was in these words:

''Be it enacted'' etc., ''that any person, or persons, firm, company, or corporation, engaged in drilling for, piping, transporting, using or selling natural gas, may transport or conduct the

same through sound, wrought or cast iron casing and pipes, tested to at least 400 pounds pressure to the square inch, provided such gas shall not be transported through pipes at a pressure exceeding 300 pounds per square inch, nor otherwise than by the natural pressure of the gas flowing from the wells.''

Sec. 2. It is hereby declared to be unlawful for any person, or persons, firm, company, or corporation, to use any device for pumping, or any other artificial process or appliance, for the purpose, or that shall have the effect of, increasing the natural flow of natural gas, from any well, or of increasing or maintaining the flow of natural gas through the pipes used for conveying and transporting the same.

Sec. 3. Any person or persons, firm, company, or corporation violating any of the provisions of this Act, shall be fined in any sum not less than $1,000, or more than $10,000, and may be enjoined from conveying and transporting natural gas through pipes otherwise than in this Act provided.''

The defendant demurred to the complaint, which demurrer the Circuit Court sustained, and plaintiffs appealed. The Supreme Court affirmed the decision of the Circuit Court.

Sec. 4.—In *Manufacturers Gas & Oil Co.* v. *Indiana Nat. Gas & Oil Co.*, 156 Ind. 679; 59 N. E. 169; 60 N. E. 1080 (Jan. 9, 1901) the syllabus is as follows:

''In a suit to prevent the transportation of natural gas through pipes at a pressure in excess of the natural rock pressure, and by means other than the natural pressure of the gas, flowing from the wells, as prohibited by Burns Rev. Stat. 1894 § 7507 (Acts 1891, p. 89) a complaint which does not aver that complainants' property is endangered by the defendants' alleged wrongful acts, nor that they are likely to sustain any special injury peculiar to themselves, is demurrable.''

The Manufacturers Gas & Oil Company and others instituted suit in the Circuit Court of Grant County, against the Indiana Natural Gas & Oil Company for an injunction to prevent defendant from transporting natural gas through pipes at a pressure in excess of the natural rock pressure, and by means other than the natural pressure of the gas flowing from the wells. The ground of the action was the supposed violation of the provisions of the

Act of 1891, which in terms prohibited the transportation of natural gas through pipes at a pressure in excess of the natural rock pressure, or by means other than the natural pressure of the gas flowing from the wells. Defendant demurred to the complaint, which demurrer was by the Circuit Court sustained, and plaintiffs appealed. The Supreme Court affirmed the decision, and upon the proposition that the Act of the Legislature attempted to be invoked was constitutional, cited:

Jamison v. *Oil Co.*, 128 Ind. 555; 28 N. E. 761 12 L. R. A. 652.

Upon the proposition that the statute furnished no basis for relief where the injury alleged was the diminution of the supply of natural gas, the court cited:

Manufacturers Gas & Oil Co. v. *Indiana Nat. Gas & Oil. Co.*, 155 Ind. 556; 58 N. E. 851.

Sec. 5—In *Richmond Nat. Gas Co.* v. *Enterprise Nat Gas. Co.* 31 Ind. App. 222; 66 N. E. 782 (March 19, 1903), the syllabus is as follows:

"1. Burns Rev. Stat. 1901, § 7507, providing that natural gas shall not be transported through pipes at a pressure exceeding 300 pounds per square inch, nor otherwise than by the natural pressure of the gas flowing from the wells, does not prohibit the use of pumps to aid transportation where the pressure is not thereby increased beyond the legal limit, nor does it prohibit the waste of gas; and hence a right in an adoining owner, tapping a common reservoir to injunctive relief, is not made out by merely alleging the use of pumps whereby gas is wasted.

2. Burns Rev. Stat. 1901, §§ 7508-7509, authorizing an injunction to restrain the use of any device for pumping natural gas, or any other artificial pressure or appliance, having the effect to increase the natural flow from any well, or of increasing or maintaining the flow through transportation pipe, are not violated by the use of pumps to a degree not destroying the back pressure, and so not creating a suction in the wells, thereby increasing the natural flow.

3. A finding of an ultimate fact will be disregarded on appeal where primary facts are found negativing it."

The Enterprise Natural Gas Company and others instituted a suit in the Superior Court of Madison County, Indiana, against the Richmond Natural Gas Company, for an injunction to prevent the use by defendant of compressors and appliances to increase the natural flow of gas from wells, and to prevent the transportation of gas through pipelines otherwise than by the natural pressure of such wells. The following facts were by the trial court specially found: All parties to the suit had interests in common in the undeveloped gas within a common reservoir underlying certain described territory, and each owned leases and gas wells in this territory, which were producing gas, which was used in various ways by the respective parties; that the salt water beneath and around this reservoir was held back by the pressure of the gas in the rock, and any reduction of the gas pressure tended to admit the salt water into the rock; whenever the gas pressure was reduced below the pressure of the salt water it at once entered the rock and destroyed the territory to the extent that it was admitted; that the reduction of the gas pressure in the rock tended to the irreparable injury and final destruction of the gas field and common reservoir; that defendant was a corporation engaged in furnishing natural gas to the citizens of Richmond about 38 miles from this gas territory and had a number of pumps and compressors which it was threatening to use for the purpose of forcing gas through its pipelines; that at and prior to the bringing of the suit it had procured leases on a large number of tracts of land within this territory, and had drilled 46 gas wells, and connected them by pipelines with its pumping station, and laid from the station to the City of Richmond an eight inch pipeline. The ninth, tenth, eleventh and twelfth findings were as follows:

"(Nine) That said pumps and compressors are and constitute devices for pumping gas, and gave the effect of stimulating and increasing the general flow of natural gas from the wells, and of increasing and maintaining the flow of natural gas through the pipes used for conveying and transporting the same. That at the bringing of this suit the defendant was threatening and intending to use and operate said pumps and pumping station for the object and purpose aforesaid. That the use of said pumps will give to the defendant an undue proportion of said gas within said reservoir, above what would naturally flow through its pipes and mains by the natural pressure of gas, and will thereby take from all

others, and especially the plaintiffs, having an interest in said field,
a large portion of said gas, which would naturally flow to them if
said reservoir and field was left unaffected by artificial appliances.
That the use of said pumps will unduly reduce the back pressure
of the gas in said field and reservoir, and thereby induce salt water
to enter the same, to the great and irreparable injury of said common reservoir, and of the rights and property of the plaintiffs
therein.

(Ten)   That the defendant could not carry gas from its wells
in Henry County to its patrons in Richmond by the use of its pumps
in greater quantity than would be conveyed by the natural or well
pressure, without increasing the natural flow of gas in its mains.

(Eleven)   That it is the intention of the defendant, and was
when this suit was begun, to use its said pumps and compressors
to transport more gas through its pipelines from its wells in Henry
County to its patrons at the City of Richmond, in Wayne County,
than could or would flow naturally through its lines of pipe by well
pressure, and without the aid or assistance of said pumps or compressors.

(Twelve)   That the use and operation of said pumps and compressors will take more gas from the intake of the said pumps or
the side between said wells and said pumps, than would flow into
and through the said pumps by reason of the natural well pressure,
and would stimulate the flow of gas into said pumps and into defendant's gas mains.''

It was further found that any gas drawn from any lands of
either of the parties to the suit diminished to that extent the common supply contained in the reservoir; that when the suit was
brought the parties had a large number of wells, from which they
were procuring large quantities of natural gas, and that defendant was producing from its wells about 2,000,000 cubic feet of gas
per day to the City of Richmond, which was being transported
through a system of pipes, under the natural pressure of the gas,
without the use of artificial means; that in order to supply its
customers in Richmond it was necessary for defendant to deliver from 2,000,000 to 2,500,000 cubic feet of gas per day; that
the natural gas pressure was sufficient to force through defendant's pipeline a sufficient supply of gas to the City of Richmond
in moderate weather, but was insufficient in extremely cold weather, and the natural pressure was gradually diminishing, and would
continue to diminish as gas should be consumed from the reser-

voir until the gas pressure should not be sufficient to carry an
adequate supply of gas for the use of defendant's customers
without the aid of artificial devices; that the natural gas pressure
would continue to decline because of the consumption of gas until, in the near future, only a small part of the gas required for
defendant's customers could be delivered without the aid of such
artificial devices; that it was the intention of defendant to operate
these pumps and compressors whenever the weather was such
that an adequate supply of gas could not be delivered to its customers by the natural pressure of gas through its pipes, which
would thereafter be a large portion of the year on account of the
diminishing natural pressure.

The seventeenth finding was as follows:

"(Seventeen)   That said natural gas pumps or compressors,
are so constructed and geared as that they may be run either at a
high or low speed, the amount of gas which the same will handle
being regulated by the speed at which the compressors are so operated; that said compressors can be so operated as to take all or any
part of the gas supplied to the same, provided the quantity or
volume of gas so supplied to said pump or compressors does not
exceed the maximum capacity of the same, but that whenever the
quantity of gas supplied to said pumps or compressors exceeds the
maximum capacity of said pumps, or exceeds the volume of gas
being carried forward by said pumps at any given time, the effect
of such excessive supply is to partially damn or back up said gas
in the pipes supplying said compressors so as to retard the flow
thereof in the said pipes, and cause what is known as 'back pressure' in said supply pipes, and in the wells connected therewith."

It was further found that when this case was tried the combined natural flow of gas from defendant's wells was in excess of
29,000,000 cubic feet per day; that all of the wells were connected
with one main line to the intake of the pumps and compressors,
that the wells were so connected that the gas in the pipelines, with
their entire natural flow could be, and was, carried to the pumps
by the natural pressure of the gas, except as the same was retarded by the friction of the pipes, but that this friction was such
that, while more than 29,000,000 cubic feet of gas per day would
naturally flow from the wells to the surface of the ground, between 16,000,000 and 17,000,000 feet of gas, only, would be carried

through the system of pipes to the point where the pumps were
located, by the natural pressure of the gas flowing from the wells;
that the friction of the pipes was so great that, with the entire
output of the wells flowing into the pipes, only about 2,000,000
cubic feet could be delivered at Richmond without the aid of artificial devices; that there would naturally flow from the defendant's
wells through its pipeline to the pumps about 3-5 of the entire natural flow from the wells at the surface of the ground, the flow being
retarded by the friction of the pipes, so that the other 2-5 was held
back in the wells; and that only about 1-15 of the natural flow
could be carried to Richmond without the aid of artificial devices.

The nineteenth finding was as follows:

"(Nineteen)   That the natural pressure of gas, when flowing
from the mouth of defendant's wells, unretarded by any valves or
other artificial devices, does not exceed two or three pounds per
square inch in the largest of said wells, grading downward to less
than one pound to the square inch in the smallest of said welll s; but
that said wells, all being connected with the same line of pipe, leading into said gas compressors, maintain practically an equal
amount of back pressure, so long as the quantity permitted to flow
into said pipes for transportation is less than the quantity carried
to said pumps on the intake side thereof, by said pipeline, leading
to the same; the quantities, character, and expansive power of
natural gas being such as to equalize the pressure at all points in
any given system of wells, pipes, and reservoirs, connected with
each other, except as said pressure may vary on account of the
different degrees of friction at various points in said system, so
that, whenever back pressure is maintained in defendant's said
pipeline, supplying its said pumps or compressors on the intake
side thereof, a slightly greater back pressure will be maintained in
each of the wells connected with said pipes, than in said pipe on the
intake side of the pumping station, varying in each case as the distance is greater or less from each of said wells to said pumping
station; the back pressure increasing with the distance to each of
the said wells, and corresponding with the loss due to friction in
each case."

It was further found that it was the intention of defendant to
maintain at all times a sufficient number of wells to produce naturally a volume of gas largely in excess of the amount required for its

consumers, and take only a portion of the natural flow at any given time, and to maintain in each of the wells and in the lines, a considerable back pressure; that it was defendant's intention to maintain a sufficient number of wells producing naturally a sufficient volume of gas to deliver naturally to the pumps a much larger quantity of gas than was necessary to supply its customers in order that it might at all times, maintain on the intake side of the pumps a considerable back pressure and thereby retard and confine in the wells a portion of the natural flow of each, so as to prevent the entrance of salt water therein; that at no time had it been, or was it defendant's intention to permit the entire natural flow from its wells to be taken by means of pumps or compressors; that it was necessary for the preservation of defendant's own property, that a portion of the natural flow be held back and defendant had intended at all times, to hold back a portion of the natural flow by creating and maintaining back pressure on the intake side of its pumps, and to permit only a portion of the combined natural flow of each well to flow into its pumping station and be transported therefrom. It was further found that the use of pumps would have the effect of increasing the flow from the point where the pumps were located to the City of Richmond, beyond what would naturally flow to that point, by increasing the pressure of gas, and releasing the same on the outflow side of the pumps, at such increased pressure, and, as consequence thereof, increasing the velocity at which the gas would flow from the pumps to the point of consumption; that by the use of the pumps, defendant would get a larger per cent. and proportion of gas from the common reservoir than it could or would get without the use of pumps and by the natural rock pressure.

The first section of the Statute which the plaintiffs sought to enforce, provided, that natural gas "shall not be transported through pipes at a pressure exceeding three hundred pounds per square inch, nor otherwise than by the natural pressure of the gas flowing from the wells." Section 2 provided that it should be unlawful "to use any device for pumping or any other artificial process or appliance for the purpose, or that shall have the effect of increasing the natural flow of natural gas from any well, or of increasing or maintaining the flow of natural gas through the pipes used for conveying and transporting the same."

The third section provides a penalty, and that parties "may

be enjoined from conveying and transporting natural gas through pipes otherwise than in this Act provided.

The Superior Court rendered judgment for plaintiffs, from which judgment defendant appealed. The Appellate Court held, that the complaint was not sufficient as a complaint to enjoin the maintaining of an excessive pressure in the lines, but that giving the complaint the theory that it sought to prevent the use of pumps or other artificial means for the purpose of increasing the natural flow of gas from the wells, it did state a cause of action.

The Appellees, the plaintiffs below, contended that the legislature by statute had conclusively determined that the effect of the use of pumps was necessarily injurious, and had absolutely prohibited their use. The Appellate court held that plaintiff's case was not made out by merely showing the use of pumps for the purpose of transportation; and that the use of pumps or compressors for such purpose was not ipso facto unlawful; and that the Statute was enacted for the purpose of protecting persons and property from the inflammable and explosive character of gas in transit; and fixing the maximum pressure at 300 pounds per square inch, at which it might be transported, whether by natural or artificial pressure, citing:

Manufacturers Gas & Oil Co. v. *Indiana Nat. Gas & Oil Co.*,
156 Ind. 679; 59 N. E. 169; 60 N. E. 1080.

That the plaintiffs presented no such case; that it was not averred that their property was endangered by the alleged wrongful acts of the defendants, nor did it appear that they were likely to sustain any special injury peculiar to themselves in consequence of the violation of the Act by defendant, citing:

Manufacturers Gas & Oil Co. v. *Indiana Nat. Gas & Oil Co.*,
155 Ind. 545; 58 N. E. 706.
Manufacturers Gas & Oil Co. v. *Indiana Nat. Gas & Oil Co.*
155 Ind. 566; 58 N. E. 851.

Upon the proposition that an action will lie for injuries sustained by the use of gas pumps increasing the natural flow, the court cited:

Manufacturers Natural Gas Co· v. *Indiana Nat. Gas & Oil Co.*
156 Ind. 679; 59 N. E. 169; 60 N. E. 1080.

Manufacturers Gas & Oil Co. v. *Indiana Nat. Gas & Oil Co.*
155 Ind. 461; 57 N. E. 912; 50 L. R. A. 768.

Sec. 6.—In *Jones* v. *Forest Oil Co.*, 194 Pa· 379; 44 Atl. 1074
(Jan. 2, 1900) the syllabus is as follows:

"An injunction will not be granted to restrain the use of a gas
pump in an oil well where it appears that gas pumps have been in
constant use in all oil fields except one, to a greater or lesser extent, since the discovery of oil; that they are only used in wells in
territory almost exhausted; that their cost is within the reach of all
operators, and, when used by all, none is injured."

N. D. Jones filed a bill in equity in the Court of Common Pleas,
Number 2, Allegheny County, for an injunction to restrain the
defendant Forest Oil Company from using a gas pump in an oil
well. From the bill, answer, and testimony taken at the trial, the
Judge of the Court of Common Pleas found substantially, the following facts:

1.—Plaintiff was the owner of a tract of land in Allegheny
County, known as the W. H. Kelso farm, bounded by lands of
Tidball, Boyce heirs, Neely, Schaffer, Linton, Noble heirs, and
McCurdy, containing 126 acres. The plaintiff had drilled 6 oil
wells, known as Numbers 2 and 3, located 251 to 204 feet from the
south line of the farm; Number 2 was finished and began producing oil in October, 1901; Number 3 was finished and began producing in November, 1901.

2.—The Forest Oil Company, a corporation, as lessee, had the
exclusive right to drill for oil and gas on the Boyce heirs farm,
adjoining Kelso on the North. On this farm the defendant had
completed and was then operating several oil wells, among them,
Number 1 Boyce, located 162 feet from the line between the Kelso
and Boyce farm, and was 366 feet south from Kelso 3, and 560 feet
south-west of Kelso 2; the well known as Boyce 3, was located 200
feet south from the division line of the Kelso and Boyce farms.

3.—The plaintiff and defendant had each leased numerous
other farms adjoining the Boyce and Kelso for oil and gas purposes, and were then, and had been for some time producing oil
and gas therefrom; the oil was then obtained from all wells in that
field by pumping; the daily production of the wells was small; that

the sand or rock from which oil was obtained in that field was of a loose, coarse, gravelly nature.

4.—The Boyce well Number 1, in the early fall of 1898, was producing from 12 to 15 barrels of oil per day; this production gradually fell off until December 1, 1898, when its output was 7 1-2 barrels, and in January 1899, it was producing less than one barrel per day; In February, 1899, the well was shot and cleaned out, and shortly thereafter there was added to its pumping machinery and apparatus a device known as a gas pump. This device was used by all operators for the purpose of withdrawing gas from the wells by suction, thereby increasing the wells production of oil. The distance from which these pumps will draw oil and gas depends upon the quality and nature of the oil producing sand, its effect being felt to a much greater distance in a coarse and loose sand than in a hard and compact sand. About one week after the use of the gas pump was commenced on the Boyce Number 1, the gas supply in Kelso wells Numbers 2 and 3 of the plaintiff began to fall off, and shortly after the oil production of these wells was decreased. After the use of the gas pump on Boyce well Number 1 was discontinued, Kelso Number 2 went back to its former production, and Number 3, was then producing daily as much as formerly within 55-100 of a barrel, and both wells then had an ample supply of gas.

5.—The production of the three wells claimed to have been affected by the use of the gas pump was as follows: Kelso Number 2, before use of gas pump on Boyce Number 1, 5 barrels in six days; Kelso Number 2, while using gas pump on Boyce Number 1, 4 1-4 barrels in six days; Kelso Number 3 before using gas pump on Boyce Number 1, 3 3-4 barrels in six days; Kelso Number 3, while using gas pump on Boyce Number 1, 2 1-2 barrels in six days; Boyce Number 1, before using pump produced a fraction less than one barrel daily; Boyce Number 2 while using pump produced a fraction more than one barrel daily.

6.—The gas pump had been used in every oil field except that known as the Bradford field, but it was not generally used, except in failing and almost exhausted territory. Its use by one operator necessitated its use by others in the immediate neighborhood, if they desired to prevent the daily production of their wells from being decreased. If pumps were placed in all wells the production of the wells was neither increased nor diminished;

these pumps could be purchased either in Pittsburg, or at various points in the oil fields, and cost from $50.00 upwards according to size; and the pump used on Boyce Number 1 cost $60.00.

7.—Gas pumps were used in the "McCurdy field" the field in which the plaintiffs and defendants wells were located, before being placed in Boyce Number 1, and had been in use in that field for more than one year previous thereto, and were, at the time of the suit, being used on wells in that field.

8.—The farms of plaintiff and defendant, described in findings one and two, lay wholly in what was known as the McCurdy oil field, which field was discovered in 1890, and had been operated since that time; the production of the wells had largely decreased, and at the time of the suit the field was almost exhausted.

From these findings of fact the judge of the Court of Common Pleas concluded that plaintiff was not entitled to the relief prayed for, and that the bill should be dismissed; and dissolved the preliminary injunction and dismissed the bill. Plaintiff appealed and the Supreme Court in a per curiam opinion affirmed the decision of the Court of Common Pleas.

The Court below cited the following authorities:

Lybe's Appeal, 106 Pa. 626.
Pa. Coal Co. v. *Sanderson*, 113 Pa. 145.
Westmoreland Nat. Gas Co. v. *DeWitt*, 130 Pa. 249.
Brown v. *Vandergrift*, 80 Pa. 147.
Ballard v. *Tomlinson*, L. R. 29 Ch. Div. 115.

REMEDIES.

Sec. 7.—When one of the owners of lands or leaseholds having wells producing from a common reservoir or body of gas, attempts to use gas pumps or to do any act to induce an unnatural flow into or through his own wells, with reference to the common reservoir or body of gas injurious to or calculated to destroy it, the other owners may enjoin the use of such pumps or the commission of such acts upon allegation and proof that such use or the performance of such acts, would be a special injury to their property or to their wells located in the gas field and producing from the common reservoir.

Manufacturers Gas & Oil Co. v. *Indiana Nat. Gas & Oil Co.*, 155 Ind. 461; 57 N. E. 912; 50 L. R. A. 768.

Manufacturers Gas & Oil Co. v. *Indiana Nat. Gas & Oil Co.*, 156 Ind. 679; 59 N. E. 169; 60 N. E. 1080.

DEFENCES.

Sec. 8.—Where suit is brought against the owner of an oil or gas well, either in equity for injunction or for damages at law, upon the grounds that such owner is increasing the natural flow through his wells by the use of gas pumps or other devices, the defendant may defeat the action by allegation and proof that the plaintiff has no property rights that are injuriously affected by the acts complained of, or in the absence of a Statute in relation thereto, that such gas pumps or devices have been in constant use in the gas field by other owners and operators and that the cost of such pumps is within the reach of all operators, and when used by all, none is injured.

Manufacturers Gas & Oil Co. v. *Indiana Nat. Gas & Oil Co.*, 155 Ind. 556; 58 N. E. 851.

Manufacturers Gas & Oil Co. v. *Indiana Nat. Gas & Oil Co.*, 156 Ind. 679; 59 N. E. 169; 60 N. E. 1080.

Richmond Nat. Gas Co. v. *Enterprise Nat. Gas Co.*, 31 Ind. App. 222; 66 N. E. 782.

Jones v. *Forest Oil Co.*, 194 Pa. 379; 44 Atl. 1074.

CHAPTER 41.

NITRO-GLYCERINE TO INCREASE FLOW—RIGHT TO USE.

Sec. 1.—The owner of an oil or gas well has the right to explode nitro-glycerine therein for the purpose of increasing the flow of gas or oil, although such explosion may have the effect to draw gas or oil from the lands of another. But such owner cannot accumulate large quantities of nitro-glycerine for that purpose, endangering the lives or property of others.

> *Peoples Gas Co.* v. *Tyner,* 131 Ind. 279; 31 N. E. 59; 31 Am. St.
> Rep. 433; 16 L. R. A. 443.
> *Tyner* v. *Peoples Gas Co.,* 131 Ind. 599; 31 N. E. 61.

Sec. 2.—In *Peoples Gas Co.* v. *Tyner,* 131 Ind. 279; 31 N. E. 59; 31 Am. St. Rep. 433; 16 L. R. A. 443 (April 27, 1892) the syllabus is as follows.

"1.   A person who has a natural gas well on his premises has the right to explode nitro-glycerine therein for the purpose of increasing the flow, although such explosion may have the effect to draw the gas from the land of another.

2.   The fact that the accumulation of nitro-glycerine within the corporate limits of a city is made a crime does not prevent a private citizen from having it enjoined, where, in case of explosion he would suffer an injury in life or property not sustained by the public in general.

3.   The sufficiency of a complaint is not involved where a mere temporary injunction is passed, but the court will grant relief where it appears that the case is a proper one for investigation."

Elbert Tyner brought suit in the Circuit Court of Hancock County, Indiana, against the Peoples Gas Company for an injunction.   The complaint alleged substantially that the plaintiff and his wife were the owners by entireties of real estate, described, which consisted of four city lots in the City of Greenfield; that the lots were enclosed together by a fence; and that his dwelling house and residence, in which he and his family resided, was situated on the lot; that the lots were near the center of the city, and with his residence thereon, were of the value of $4,000; that with full knowledge of all the facts, the defendant, regardless of the rights of the plaintiff, and of the safety, peace, comfort and lives of himself and family, had, without his consent and over his objections, within the last 40 days drilled a natural gas well to the depth of about 1,000 feet, and about 200 feet distant from the plaintiff's residence, with only a street 40 feet in width between the plaintiff's lots and the lot on which the well was drilled; that defendant was about to shoot said well, and would do so unless restrained; that for the purpose of shooting the well the defendant, about midnight of a day in August, 1889, unlawfully procured to be brought and unlawfully permitted a large quantity of nitro-glycerine to be and remain upon Sycamore street, a public street in the city, and within less than 200 feet of plaintiff's residence, for about three hours, in the midst of and surrounded by a large number of people; that defendant by its employes threatened and attempted to shoot said gas well, and still threatened so to do with said nitro-glycerine, or other explosive compound, and would do so unless restrained; that nitro-glycerine is highly explosive and very dangerous to property and life and is liable to explode under any and all circumstances, and at any time or place; and that an explosion of 60 or 100 quarts of the explosive at any given place on the surface of the earth could, and probably would, destroy life and property for a distance of 500 yards in all directions from such explosion; that the handling or storing thereof in or about defendant's gas well would endanger the lives of plaintiff's family, as well as the safety of his property, and that the shooting of the well with nitro-glycerine would greatly injure and damage plaintiff's property, both above and under the surface of the earth, and endanger his life, and the lives of his family. The complaint was verified, and upon it an affidavit filed in support of its allegations, The Circuit Court granted a temporary injunction, and defendant appealed. The affidavits filed by the plaintiff tended to prove that the defendant's gas well was within the corporate limits of the City of Greenfield; that a short time prior to the filing of the complaint the defendant deposited in or about the derrick at the well about 117 quarts of nitro-glycerine, weighing about 340 pounds, with the intention of exploding the same in the well. The affidavits further tended to show that nitro-glycerine is very explosive, and is liable to explode at any time, and that the explosion of that quantity of glycerine on the surface of the earth would be likely to destroy life or property at any point within 500 yards of such explosion. The Supreme Court affirmed the judgment granting the injunction, and upon the question of shooting the well, in the opinion said:

"So far as this suit seeks to enjoin the appellants from exploding nitro-glycerine in their gas well, upon the ground that it would increase the flow of the gas to the injury of the appellee, it cannot, in our opinion, be sustained. The rule that the owner has the

right to do as he pleases with or upon his own property is subject to
many limitations and restrictions, one of which is, that he must
have due regard for the rights of others. It is settled that the
owner of a lot may not erect and maintain a nuisance thereon
whereby his neighbors are injured. If he does so, and the injury
sustained by such neighbor cannot be adequately compensated in
damages, he may be enjoined. *Owens* v. *Phillips,* 73 Ind. 284.

If appellants in this case have been guilty of the folly of sinking a gas well in the center of a thickly populated city, where they
cannot collect the necessary quantity of nitro-glycerine to shoot
it without endangering the property and lives of those who have no
connection with their operations, they should be content with such
flow of gas as can be obtained without such shooting. It certainly
cannot be maintained that the destruction of human life is an injury
which can be compensated in damages. No authority has been
cited, and we know of none, supporting the position of the appellants that the appellee is not entitled to an injunction because the
accumulation of nitro-glycerine within the corporate limits of a
town or city is a crime.''

Sec. 3.—In *Tyner* v. *Peoples Gas Co.,* 131 Ind. 599; 31 N. E.
61 (April 30, 1892) the syllabus is as follows:

"A complaint for an injunction to restrain defendant from
'shooting' a gas well on his land adjoining the land of plaintiff,
and within 200 feet of the residence of himself and family with
nitro-glycerine, which alleges that by shooting the well, and by the
accumulation of a large amount of nitro-glycerine for that purpose,
plaintiff's dwelling and the lives of himself and family will be endangered, if the facts stated are true, shows a private nuisance, and
alleges facts sufficient to warrant the granting of an injunction.''

This was the second appeal. The first is reported as *Peoples
Gas Co.* v. *Tyner,* Supra. After the case was remanded by the
Supreme Court upon an order affirming the award of the injunction, defendant demurred to the complaint. The demurrer was by
the Circuit Court sustained, and from the judgment sustaining
the demurrer the plaintiff appealed, and the Supreme Court reversed the Circuit Court and held the first paragraph of the complaint sufficient.

CHAPTER 42.

RIGHT TO DRILL NEAR DIVISION LINE—DRAINAGE.

Sec. 1.—The owner of lands or his lessee for oil and gas purposes may drill for oil and gas on any portion of the premises although so near the division line as to drain the oil or gas from adjoining lands or from wells thereon.

Barnard v. *Monongahela Gas Co.*, 216 Pa. 362; 65 Atl. 801.
Kelly v. *Ohio Oil Co.*, 57 Ohio State, 317; 49 N. E. 399; 63 Am.
St. Rep. 721; 39 L. R. A. 765.
Brown v. *Spilman*, 155 U. S. 665-669-670.
Westmoreland Nat. Gas Co. v. *DeWitt*, 130 Pa. 235-249-250;
18 Atl. 724.

Sec. 2.—In *Barnard* v. *Monongahela Gas Co.*, 216 Pa. 362; 65
Atl. 801 (Jan. 7, 1907) the syllabus is as follows:

"A landowner may drill an oil well on his farm though he may
draw from an oil well on adjoining land.
Where the owner of land drilled an oil well on his farm, the
only remedy of an adjoining landowner whose oil is drawn upon is
to drill a well on his own land.
Where the same person holds an oil lease on two adjoining
farms, he cannot so collusively drill oil wells as to drain the oil of
one of the farms to the detriment of the other.
Such lessee may, however, drill a well on one farm close to the
line of the other and draw from the latter three-fourths of the gas
therein, if it appears that he also drilled a well on the latter and in
good faith endeavored to develop the land in the performance of
his duty."

Daniel Barnard and Elizabeth Barnard filed a bill in equity
in the Court of Common Pleas of Washington County, against the
Monongahela Natural Gas Company. The plaintiffs were the
owners in fee of a tract of land in Washington County, containing 66 acres. James Barnard owned in fee a tract of land adjoining the plaintiffs, containing 156 acres. The Monongahela Natural
Gas Company, a corporation in the business of producing and
marketing natural gas, held a lease on each of the farms, for the

purpose and with the exclusive right of drilling and operating thereon for petroleum and gas, both of which leases were in full force and effect when the bill was filed. By the terms of these leases the gas company was to pay to the respective lessors a fixed sum per year for the gas from each well drilled, so long as gas should be sold therefrom. The farm of James Barnard adjoined the farm of the plaintiffs in such a way that at one corner of his farm there was an angle of about 12 degrees less than a right angle, and the lines of the adjoining farm that made this angle were respectively 62 and 75 rods long, so that a circle large enough to include ten acres of ground within its center at that corner would enclose less than 2 1-2 acres of the land of James Barnard, and 7 1-2 acres of the land of Daniel and Elizabeth Barnard, the plaintiffs. The gas company had drilled a well on the James Barnard farm in the corner described above, which was 55 feet from the actual corner and about 35 feet from either of the lines dividing the two farms, and upon the completion of this well it was found to be a paying well, such as to entitle the lessor to an annual rental provided for in the lease. This well was drilled on the location chosen after the plaintiffs had protested against it being located so near their lines. Since the well was drilled on the James Barnard farm, the defendant company had drilled a well on the plaintiffs' farm 1350 feet away from the well on the other farm, and not far from the angle. This well failed to produce any gas. A gas well, in time, it was proved, would drain ten acres, more or less, of land, and if the gas producing sand is equally porous the gas would be drawn along all the radii of a circle of which the well is the center. The gas company, the defendant, when it located its well on the corner of the Barnard farm, did not do so with intent to fraudulently deprive the plaintiffs of their rights. The bill sought an injunction and an accounting against the company. The Court of Common Pleas, as conclusions of law found that the drilling of the well on the farm of the Barnards and taking gas therefrom, in no way invaded the plaintiffs property rights; that the defendant company under all the facts of the case was not guilty of either actual or legal fraud in that it drilled the Barnard well where it did, and drained gas from plaintiff's farm. The plaintiffs bill was by the Court of Common Pleas dismissed and the plaintiff appealed. The court below cited in support of its findings:

Wettengel v. *Gormley,* 160 Pa. 559; 28 Atl. 934; 40 Am. St.
Rep. 733.

Kleppner v. *Lemon,* 176 Pa. 502; 35 Atl. 109.

Colgan v. *Forest Oil Co.,* 194 Pa. 234; 45 Atl. 119; 75 Am. St.
Rep. 695.

Young v. *Forest Oil Co.,* 194 Pa. 243; 45 Atl. 121.

The Supreme Court affirmed by per curiam decision the Court
of Common Pleas.

Sec. 3.—In *Kelly* v. *Ohio Oil Co.,* 57 Ohio State, 317; 49 N. E.
399; 63 Am. St. Rep. 721; 39 L. R. A. 765, (Dec. 14, 1897) the syllabus is as follows:

"1.   Petroleum oil is a mineral, and while it is in the earth it
forms a part of the realty, and when it reaches a well, and is produced on the surface, it becomes personal property, and belongs to
the owner of the well.

2.   Whether such oil percolates through the rock or exists in
pools or deposits, it forms a part of that tract of real estate in
which it tarries for the time being and when it leaves one tract,
and enters another, it becomes a part of the realty of the latter, and
thereby the owner of the former loses all right to the oil while it
remains away from his land.

3.   The drilling of wells by each owner of adjoining lands,
along and near the division line, so that each may obtain the
amount of oil contained in his lands, is known as 'protecting lines,'
and such protection affords a certain and ample remedy to prevent
one operator from obtaining more than his share of oil."

Thomas C. Kelly instituted an action in the Court of Common
Pleas of Hancock County, Ohio, against the Ohio Oil Company.
The petition contained the following allegations: That defendant
was a corporation; that John F. Hastings, of said County, was the
owner in fee of 165 acres of oil land; that plaintiff had a contract
and agreement with said Hastings whereby plaintiff had the right
to operate said lands for oil, and take such oil therefrom, paying
as a consideration to Hastings a royalty of the oil produced, the
balance to be retained by plaintiff as his own property; that plaintiff was then at work on the land, had two wells completed, and
a rig up and ready to begin drilling a third well; that the Hastings
land was bounded on the east and west by lands then in posses-

sion and control for oil purposes of defendant, on which land it had producing oil wells; that the Hastings farm was bounded on the south by lands owned in fee by the defendant, on which it had producing oil wells; that underlying the land of Hastings, and the adjoining lands on the south, west and on the east, was a formation of porous sand or Trenton Rock, socalled, which is permeated with mineral oil; that the nature of the mineral oil deposit was such that when in the process of operating, an oil well is drilled from the surface down into and through said oil bearing rock, and the usual pumping appliances attached to and employed on the well to extract the oil; that the oil is drawn to said opening from a long distance through the rock, and all the oil within a radius of from 200 to 250 feet surrounding such well is drawn to and extracted by means of such well, so that, in order to drain and exhaust all the oil in the land it is only necessary to drill the wells from four to five hundred feet apart; that defendants, well knowing the premises, and designing, wilfully and unlawfully to extract the mineral oil from, in and under the Hastings land, by means of surface operations on the lands so owned and controlled by it, in fraud and violation of the plaintiff's right, and from motives of unmixed malice, had located a line of oil wells along the entire east line of said farm, and upon and along the south line which wells were so located just 25 feet from the line of the Hastings land, and just 400 feet apart, all of which wells so located, the defendant threatened and intended to drill at once, with the design and to the unlawful intent and purpose aforesaid; that in view of the well known tendency of said wells to drain a large extent of territory immediately surrounding them, it was the custom and almost universal practice of oil operators when operating adjoining lands to locate their wells at least 200 feet from the line of lands in order that so far as reasonably practicable each operator's well should draw its supply from his own land, and not unnecessarily disturb or detract from the oil mineral wealth of the adjoining lands; that the defendants holdings on the east consisted of about 160 acres in a body, and on the south a very large tract—several hundred acres—and that there was in the defendants operating said land for oil, no necessity or excuse for the location of their said wells so unusually near the Hastings line, as there were no wells at all on the Hastings east or south line, except the wells operated by the defendants, which were more than

200 feet from defendant's line, and by plaintiff's contract with
Hastings, which was of record, well known to the defendant, no
well was to be drilled by the plaintiff within 200 feet of the exterior
line of the farm, unless it became necessary, in order to protect the
line; so that, the only motive of defendant in so locating its said
wells was to injure the plaintiff and to get the oil which would be
available to him in his operations on said farm. The petition alleged that if the defendant was permitted to extract the plaintiff's
oil in the manner aforesaid, the plaintiff would suffer irreparable
injury and would have no adequate legal remedy for the reason that
it would be impossible to determine the exact proportion of the
product belonging to the plaintiff. The petitioner prayed that a
temporary restraining order issue, enjoining the defendant from
drilling and operating any oil well at any point within 200 feet of
the line of said Hastings farm, unless it should become necessary to
approach nearer in order to protect the lines; and that on the final
hearing said injunction be made perpetual. The plaintiff filed a
supplemental petition, containing the following allegation:

"And now comes the plaintiff, by leave of this court, and for
supplemental petition, and in addition to the allegations of the
original petition, alleges that, since the dissolution of the temporary injunction granted in this action, the defendants have proceeded, and located and drilled, and are now operating for oil, or
about to begin operating, twelve oil wells, nine of which are at the
points stated in the petition, and three of which are on the Reimund
farm adjoining the Hastings farm on the west,—all of which wells
are so completed and operating by means of pumping appliances,
and all of which wells are so operating about twenty-five feet from
the lines of said farm. That all of said wells are oil producing
wells of greater or less capacity, and that by means thereof the defendants are daily extracting large and valuable quantities of
mineral oil, a large part of which mineral oil is so drawn and extracted from the deposits thereof in the land of said Hastings, and
which oil the plaintiff has, by his contract with said Hastings, the
right to take and use and enjoy. That said wells draw their supply
so indiscriminately from the mines and lands of said Hastings and
of the defendant that it is impossible to distinguish that of the
defendant from that of the plaintiff, but all of said oil is so being
taken by the said defendant, and converted to its own use. Wherefore, in addition to the prayer of the petition, the plaintiff prays
that the defendant be required to account to the plaintiff for the oil

so taken; that the amount thereof be ascertained, and that the plaintiff may have a decree and judgment against the defendant therefor, and for all proper relief."

The Circuit Court was of opinion that the petition and supplemental petition failed to state a cause of action against the Oil Company, refused to hear any evidence, and upon the pleadings, found for the defendant. Exceptions were taken and the cause appealed to the Supreme Court. That court affirmed the decision of the Circuit Court.

Sec. 4.—In *Brown* v. *Spilman,* 155 U. S. 665, analyzed under Chapter 10, Judge Shiras, delivering the opinion of the court, pages 669-670, said:

."Petroleum, gas and oil are substances of a peculiar character, and decisions in ordinary cases of mining, for coal and other minerals, which have a fixed *situs* cannot be applied to contracts concerning them without some qualifications. They belong to the owner of the land and are part of it, so long as they are on it, or in it, or subject to his control, but when they escape and go into other land, or come under another's control the title of the former owner is gone. If an adjoining owner drills his own land and taps a deposit of oil or gas, extending under his neighbor's field, so that it comes into his well, it becomes his property. *Brown* v. *Vandergrift,* 80 Pa. 142-147; *Westmoreland Nat. Gas Co's. Appeal,* 25 Weekly Notes of Cases, (Penn) 103."

Sec. 5.—In *Westmoreland Nat. Gas Co.* v. *DeWitt,* 130 Pa. 235-249-250; 18 Atl. 724, analyzed under Chapter 11, Justice Mitchell, delivering the opinion, pages 249-250, said:

"If an adjoining, or even a distant owner, drills his own land, and taps your gas, so that it comes into his well, and under his control, it is no longer yours, but his. And equally so as between lessor and lessee in the present case, the one who controls the gas, has it in his grasp, so to speak, is the one who has possession in the legal as well as in the ordinary sense of the word."

REMEDIES.

Sec. 6.—Where two or more owners or lessees of oil and gas lands are operating the lands for oil and gas, and one of such owners drills wells so near the division line as to drain the oil or gas from the lands or wells of adjoining owners, such adjoining owners cannot maintain a suit for injunction, or for damages for such drainage; but the remedy is to drill a sufficient number of off-set wells along the line, and in such proximity as such owner may elect, to protect his property from drainage.

Barnard v. *Monongahela Gas Co.,* 216 Pa. 362; 65 Atl. 801 *Kelly* v. *Ohio Oil Co.,* 57 Ohio State, 317; 49 N. E. 399; 63 Am. St. Rep. 721; 39 L. R. A. 765.

Sec. 7.—Where a lessee holds leases on two or more adjoining tracts of land, he cannot collusively drill wells on one tract so as to drain the oil from the adjoining tracts. If he does so relief in equity will be afforded the injured lessor.

Barnard v. *Monongahela Gas Co.,* 216 Pa. 362; 65 Atl. 801.

Sec. 8.—A lessee holding leases on two or more adjoining tracts of land may drill wells on one farm close to the line of the others and draw oil or gas from the latter, provided he drills wells on the other lands for their protection, or in good faith endeavors to develop them in the performance of his duty as lessor.

Barnard v. *Monongahela Gas Co.,* 216 Pa. 362; 65 Atl. 801.

CHAPTER 43.

RIGHT TO OPERATE OIL AND GAS WELLS, EVEN WHERE INJURY RESULTS THEREFROM.

Sec. 1.—The owner of land or the lessee thereof may drill wells thereon and operate the same for oil or gas although by such operations he may cause damage to real or personal property by the pollution of the waters of a stream by oil or salt water from his wells, where such pollution is necessary to the enjoyment of the wells and the owner is not actuated by malice, and exercises due care to avoid the injury.

Ohio Oil Co. v. *Westfall*, 43 Ind. App. 661; 88 N. E. 354.
Collins v. *Chartiers Valley Gas Co.*, 131 Pa. 143; 18 Atl 1012.
Pfeiffer v. *Brown*, 165 Pa. 267; 30 Atl. 844; 44 Am. St. Rep.
660.

Sec. 2.—In *Ohio Oil Co.* v. *Westfall*, 43 Ind. App. 661; 88 N. E.
354 (May 18, 1909) the syllabus is as follows:

"1. The owner of an oil well is not liable for injuries to real
property caused by the pollution of the water of a stream bordering
the land with oil and salt water, where such pollution is necessary
to the enjoyment of the well, and the owner is not actuated by malice, and has exercised due care to avoid the injury.

2. In an action for injury to land and to crops and cattle thereon caused by the pollution of a stream by oil and salt water from
defendant's oil well, the question whether defendant has made
a reasonable use of the well and has exercised reasonable diligence
to prevent the injury is a question of fact for the jury."

Mary F. Westfall brought an action for damages against the
Ohio Oil Company, in the Circuit Court of Gibson County, Indiana,
the material allegations of the complaint being: That the defendant was engaged in producing and refining petroleum oil; that the
plaintiff was the owner of certain real estate in Gibson County,
used for farming purposes; that it contained a well of water
suitable for domestic purposes; that the defendant owned and operated oil wells and permitted large quantities of oil, salt water and
other water, to flow off the premises where the wells were situated,
down and over the land of the plaintiff; that it gathered great
quantities of crude oil in tanks; that a part of the oil gathered was
unfit for use, and that this oil was emptied from the tanks in great
quantities down over plaintiff's land; that the salt water and oil
polluted the water on the lands of the plaintiff; gathered in pools
on her land and became stagnant, sinking into the land of the plaintiff, and rendering the well on her farm unfit for use; that the salt
water and other mineral waters permitted to flow to plaintiff's
land were injurious to stock and dangerous to hogs, horses and
cattle, and to vegetable life, destroying grass and growing crops,
and emitting unpleasant odors, were nauseous and dangerous to
human beings, injurious to the health of plaintiff and her family
and the occupants of her land; that by reason of the acts and conduct of the defendant in that respect the growing crops upon her

land had been destroyed, and the water for the stock upon her farm had been polluted and her well contaminated and rendered unfit for use and her farm rendered less desirable for residence purposes. Defendant demurred to the complaint, which demurrer was overruled. The defendant answered and the cause was submitted to a jury for trial, and verdict was rendered in favor of the plaintiff. Defendant moved for a new trial, which motion was overruled, and from the judgment for plaintiff and the order denying a new trial the defendant appealed. The Appellate Court affirmed the judgment. The action was not founded upon neglect but upon the maintenance by defendant of a nuisance. The defendant claimed that the things complained of were necessary to the enjoyment by it of its own property, and that, in the maintenance of the offensive oil well it was not actuated by malice; that due care was used to avoid injury to the plaintiff. The court held that whether or not the manner in which the defendant's operations were conducted was a reasonable use, was a question for the jury.

Sec. 3.—In *Collins* v. *Chartiers Valley Gas Co.*, 131 Pa. 143; 18 Atl. 1012 (Jan. 6, 1890) the syllabus is as follows:

"1.   The rule definitely settled in *Penna. Coal Co.* v. *Sanderson*, 113 Pa. 126, that for unavoidable damage to anothers land, in the lawful use of ones own, no action can be maintained, does not exempt a landowner from all obligation to pay regard to the effect of his operations on subterranean waters.

2.   The distinction between rights in surface and in subterranean waters is not founded on the fact of their location above or below ground, but on the fact of knowledge, actual, or reasonably acquirable, of their existence, location and course; in either case, the rule of damnun absque injuria applies only in the absence of negligence; *Wheatly* v. *Baugh*, 25 Pa. 528; *Halderman* v. *Brookhart*, 45 Pa. 514; *Lybe's Appeal*, 106 Pa. 634.

3.   If a person boring for oil or gas have knowledge that neighboring water wells are supplied from a stream of clear water underlying his land, and that there is a deeper stratum of salt water likely to rise and mingle with the fresh when penetrated in such boring, and may prevent this mingling by a reasonable outlay, his failure to use the means available therefor is negligence.

4.   Whether, for an injury to the water well of a neighbor from such commingling, plainly to be anticipated and reasonably preventable, the owner of a gas well, who committed the drilling

of it to an independent contractor, without requiring the use of any means to guard against such injury, is liable, notwithstanding the letting of the drilling out upon such contract, is not decided.''

Nannie R. Collins brought an action of trespass in the Court of Common Pleas of Allegheny County against the Chartiers Valley Gas Company to recover damages for an injury to a water well owned by the plaintiff alleged to have been occasioned by the negligence of the defendant. At the same time Mary L. Osborne brought a similiar suit against the same defendant to recover for a like injury. The two cases were tried together, and the following facts were shown: Each of the plaintiffs was the owner of a small lot with a house thereon in Allegheny County. On each lot was a well used to supply water for domestic use on the premises; on June 7, 1887, the defendant being engaged in the business of producing and supplying natural gas, entered into a written contract with C. J. Hummel, by which Hummel engaged to drill a well for natural gas upon a location about 100 feet from the water well of one of the plaintiffs, and about 125 feet from the other. The contract provided that Hummel should encase said gas well with 8¼ inch casing to the depth of 700 feet, and deep enough to shut off all fresh water, and below that with 6 inch casing, to shut off any water or caving rock found just above the gas rock, and should warrant the well absolutely free from water and do all the work to the satisfaction of the defendants superintendent; all tools, and gas and water connections to be furnished by Hummel, and all casing required for the well to be furnished by defendant. The contract also contained the following clause:

"All springs to be fully protected from damage, and drillings to be carried from the wells to such point as will do least damage to property possible.''

The well was begun some time in June, and finished in August or September, 1887. At the depth of about 70 feet it passed through the vein of fresh water, which supplied the plaintiffs wells and at about 700 feet below the surface it passed through a large quantity of salt water, which rising and mingling with the fresh water ruined the plaintiffs' wells and rendered the water therein utterly unfit for domestic uses. There was evidence tending to establish that the defendant ought to have anticipated that its well would encounter this salt water, and that it would thus affect neighboring water wells, unless precautions were taken to prevent the two kinds of water from co-mingling; that by the use of well known appliances, this co-mingling could have been prevented. which had often been done, though it was not customary, and had been done only in cases where the operator desired to guard against injuring water wells on his own property; and witnesses estimated the cost of one method of effecting this object at about $50.00, and the cost of another method at from $200.00 to $250.00. After the completion of the gas well, the defendant took it off the contractor's hands, and remained in possession of it until the trial. Agents of the defendant were notified of the injurious effects of the salt water upon the plaintiffs' wells, and promised to remedy the injury, but did not do so. The court instructed the jury that plaintiff could not recover and verdicts were returned in favor of the defendant. Judgments were rendered on the verdicts and plaintiffs appealed. The Supreme Court reversed the judgment and awarded a new trial.

Sec. 4.—In *Pfeiffer* v. *Brown,* 165 Pa. 267; 30 Atl. 844; 44 Am. St. Rep. 660 (Jan. 7, 1895) the syllabus is as follows:

"The right of the upper landowner to discharge water on the lower lands of his neighbor is in general a right of flowage only in the natural ways and natural quantities. If he alters the natural conditions so as to change the course of the water, or to concentrate it at a particular point, or by artificial means to increase its volume, he becomes liable for any injury caused thereby.

Where a landowner, by drilling a well and pumping, increases the aggregate quantity of water discharged, concentrates it at an artificial point of flow, and changes its character from fresh to salt, thereby injuring the land of an adjoining owner, he is liable for the injury, if he could have avoided inflicting it by reasonable care and expenditure.

In such a case if the expense of preventing the damage is such as practically to counterbalance the expected profit or benefit, then it is clearly unreasonable, and beyond what the person drilling the well could justly be called upon to assume.

If, on the other hand, however large in actual amount, it is small in proportion to the gain to himself, it is reasonable in regard to his neighbor's right, and he should pay it to prevent damage, or should make compensation for the injury done.

Between these two extremes lies a debatable region, where the cases must stand upon their own facts, under the only general rule that can be laid down in advance, that the expense required would so detract from the purpose and benefit of the contemplated act, as to be a substantial deprivation of the right to the use of ones own property. If damage can be prevented short of this it is an injuria which will sustain an action.

A proper standard of estimating damage in such a case is not given to the jury where the court charges that if the injury could have been avoided 'at slight expense,' or 'at small expense,' it was the duty of defendants to make such expenditures."

The plaintiff Pfeiffer instituted suit in the Court of Common Pleas of Butler County, Pennsylvania, against Brown and others in trespass for injury to land. At the trial the plaintiff claimed damages for the alleged wrongful action of defendants in turning salt water from an oil well on an adjoining farm over and upon her land. The testimony showed that the salt water was pumped up with the oil from the 100-foot sand into the storage tank, and then drawn off, and allowed to flow by a natural depression over plaintiff's land. After it began to flow upon plaintiff's land, she caused a ditch to be plowed along the line of depression and the salt water then flowed in the ditch to a neighboring brook, and thereafter it caused her no damage. In the charge to the jury the trial judge instructed the jury that if the injury could have been avoided at slight expense, or at small expense, it was the duty of defendants to make such expenditure. Verdict and judgment was rendered for defendant, and plaintiff appealed. The Supreme Court reversed the judgment and awarded a new trial.

REMEDIES.

Sec. 5.—Where the owner of an oil or gas well is sued for damages for alleged injuries to property caused by the escape of salt water from his wells, he may defeat a recovery by proof that the use of the well causing the alleged injury was a reasonable use; that he exercised due care to avoid the injury; that he was not actuated by malice; and that the escape of salt water alleged to have caused the injury was necessary to the enjoyment of the well.

Ohio Oil Co. v. *Westfall*, 43 Ind. App. 661; 88 N. E. 354.

Pfeiffer v. *Brown,* 165 Pa. 267; 30 Atl. 844; 44 Am. St. Rep. 660.

Sec. 6.—Where the owner of oil or gas wells, in drilling the same penetrates a stream of clear water underlying the lands, and also penetrates a stream of salt water, which mingles with the fresh water, and thus injures springs or water wells of another, when sued for damages resulting from such injury, he may defeat the action by proof that he had no knowledge that such neighboring water wells were supplied by a stream of clear water underlying his land, and that when he discovered the existence of such stream of clear water and that it supplied such wells, and discovered the existence of the salt water, he made use of the means available to him to prevent the co-mingling of these waters; or by showing that he could not prevent the co-mingling of the waters at a reasonable outlay.

Collins v. *Chartiers Valley Gas Co.,* 131 Pa. 143; 18 Atl. 1012.

Sec. 7.—Where injury is inflicted by pollution of the waters of a stream, or by the co-mingling of salt water with a stream of clear water underlying the land and supplying wells or springs, caused by the drilling or operation of an oil or gas well, the person injured by such pollution may recover damages from the owner of such oil or gas well in an action upon allegation and proof that the act of the owner was malicious; or that such pollution was not necessary to the enjoyment of the well; or that such owner did not exercise due care to avoid the injury; or that the owner had knowledge that neighboring water wells were supplied by a stream of clear water underlying his land, and also had knowledge that there was a deeper stratum of salt water likely to rise and mingle with the fresh water when penetrated, and that such owner, at a reasonable outlay could have prevented the co-mingling of the waters, and failed to use the means available to him therefor; or that the expense of preventing the damage, although large in actual amount, was small in proportion to the gain of the owner of the well.

Ohio Oil Co. v. *Westfall,* 43 Ind. 661; 88 N. E. 354.
Collins v. *Chartiers Valley Gas Co.,* 131 Pa. 143; 18 Atl. 1012.
Pfeiffer v. *Brown,* 165 Pa. 267; 30 Atl. 844; 44 Am. St. Rep. 660.

CHAPTER 44.

NUISANCE.

Sec. 1.—Oil and gas wells are not nuisances *per se*, and the owner thereof may drill and operate the same with regard to public highways, wells on other property, dwelling houses or other buildings and appurtenances, where the effect of the management, location and capacity of the well is not such as to materially diminish the value of the buildings as dwellings, or seriously interfere with the ordinary comfort and enjoyment thereof, and where he exercises care not thereby to inflict injury on other persons or their property.

McGregor v. *Camden*, 47 W. Va. 193; 34 S. E. 936.
Windfall Mfg. Co. v. *Patterson*, 148 Ind. 414; 47 N. E. 2; 62 Am. St. Rep. 532; 37 L. R. A. 38.
Tyner v. *Peoples Gas Co.*, 131 Ind. 599; 31 N. E. 61.
Pope Bros. v. *Bridgewater Gas Co.*, 52 W. Va. 252; 43 S. E. 87.
Snyder v. *Phila. Co.*, 54 W. Va. 149; 46 S. E. 366; 102 Am. St. Rep. 941; 63 L. R. A. 896.

Sec. 2.—In *McGregor* v. *Camden*, 47 W. Va. 193; 34 S. E. 936 (Dec. 2. 1899) the syllabus is as follows:

"1. Oil and gas wells are not nuisances per se. Whether they are nuisances to a dwelling house and its appurtenances depends upon their location, capacity and management.
2. When such a well has such capacity, management, and location, with regard to a dwelling house and its appurtenances as to materially diminish the value thereof as a dwelling, and seriously interfere with its ordinary comfort and enjoyment it is an abatable nuisance.
3. If there is any way that such well can be operated so as not to make it such nuisance, only the unlawful operation thereof will be enjoined."

Matilda McGregor and others instituted a suit in chancery in the Circuit Court of Ritchie County, West Virginia, against Thomas B. Camden and others, for an injunction to prevent the drilling and operation of an oil and gas well. The facts in the case were as follows: The plaintiffs were the owners of a valuable lot and dwelling house and appurtenances, alleged to be worth about $10,000, situated in the town of Cairo, in Ritchie County; the lot was highly improved for the purposes for which it had been used for twenty-five years—a home for the McGregor family; Mrs. McGregor then occupied the same as a life tenant, with remainder in her children, joint plaintiffs, but who had married and lived elsewhere; adjacent to this property was another lot 85 by 115½ feet, on which certain of defendants had commenced drilling a well in 1896, within 70 feet of the dwelling house, and about 50 feet of the line of the lot towards such house, and 15 feet in another direction to the McGregor land. The plaintiffs obtained a temporary injunction to restrain the drilling of the well so close to their property. This injunction was subsequently modified so as to permit defendants to proceed with their well on giving bond in the penalty of $10,000 good for a period of 40 days. The plaintiffs then filed an amended bill, making new parties, and amending the allegations in some respects, and obtained a virtual re-instatement of their injunction, to be effective after the expiration of the 40-day bond limit. Some of the defendants tendered answers, to which plaintiffs excepted. Other of the defendants did not answer, and on January 26, 1897, a vacation order was entered of record as follows:

"It is now, on this 22d day of January, 1897, at New Martinsville, and within the Circuit of which the undersigned is Judge, ordered that the order of injunction entered in this cause upon the amended bill by the Honorable Thomas P. Jacobs, late Judge of said Circuit, be and the same is hereby dissolved and set aside, and the court refuses to reinstate the injunction on the original bill, and overrules the exceptions to the answer of J. H. Kelley and others, and that the defendants be, and are hereby, relieved from all orders of injunction heretofore entered in the cause."

From this decree the plaintiffs appealed. The Court of Appeals reversed the decree, citing:

Mfg. Co. v. *Patterson,* 148 Ind. 414; 47 N. E. 2; 37 L. R. A. 381.
Powell v. *Furniture Co.,* 34 W. Va., 804; 12 S. E. 1085; 12 L. R. A. 53.

Kinney v. *Koetmaun*, (Ala.) 22 South 593; 37 L. R. A. 497.
Wilson v. *Mfg. Co.*, 40 W. Va., 413; 21 S. E. 1035.
Cook v. *Anderson*, 85 Ala. 99; 4 South. 713.
Uhl v. *Ohio River R. Co.*, 47 W. Va. 59; 34 S. E. 934.

Sec 3.—In *Windfall Mfg. Co.* v. *Patterson*, 148 Ind. 414; 47 N.
E. 2; 62 Am. St. Rep. 532; 37 L. R. A. 38 (May 12, 1897) the syllabus is as follows:

"1. Rev. St. 1894, § 5108, providing that lands for gas pipelines shall not be condemned within 75 yards of a dwelling, but
permitting pipes to be laid along a highway, without regard to
nearness of dwellings, has no application to the sinking of a well
and laying pipes on ones own land, between which and dwellings
within that distance is a highway.

2. A plant for manufacture of brick and tiling, even with a
gas well on the property for supplying fuel is not a nuisance
per se.

3. That defendant bought land remote from dwellings for a
brick and tile factory, and there operated the business, with fuel
furnished from a gas well thereon, for three years before plaintiff built a dwelling near the factory, is to be considered on the
question of enjoining the location and use of a gas well near the
dwelling, gas having failed in the original well located in the remote part of the land.

4. Drilling a gas well at a distance of 150 feet from a dwelling will not be enjoined, danger being apprehended only in case
gas, oil or water be found, and it not being certain that either
will be found, and it not being shown that if found, it cannot be
controlled and managed, so as to cause no appreciable injury to
anyone."

Willard E. Patterson and another brought an action in the Circuit Court of Howard County, Indiana, against the Windfall Manufacturing Company, and alleged in their complaint that the defendant was "threatening to and proceeding to drill a gas well," within 152 feet of plaintiff's dwelling, and asked that the defendant
be restrained from drilling said well, and from drilling any well
or laying pipes therefrom, and "at any other point within 300
feet" of plaintiff's property.

The complaint was in two paragraphs, to the first of which
there was a special paragraph of answer, and to this answer a

demurrer was sustained. The cause was submitted to the court
for trial and judgment rendered enjoining the company from drilling the well. Defendant appealed. The main facts were not in
dispute. It appeared that the defendant company was organized
in 1891 for the purpose of buying land and machinery to engage
in the manufacture of brick and drain tile; that in pursuance to
this object the company, during the same year, purchased 22
acres of land near the town of Windfall; the land was believed to
contain an unlimited supply of natural gas, such as was needed
to operate the business in which the defendant was to engage.
During the same year, at a cost of $25,000, the company erected its
plant and machinery, locating the same near the highway on the
west line of the tract, and within 200 feet of the land afterwards
purchased by the plaintiffs; In that year the company drilled a
gas well near the south-east corner of its land, and obtained a
sufficient flow of gas to run its factory until the year 1895, when
the gas failed in that well. It was averred in the answer that the
22-acre tract of land was not large enough to afford more than
two sites for the location of a gas well, such as would probably
furnish gas in sufficient quantities to operate the factory; that on
the failure of the east well it was necessary to suspend the operations of the factory until another well could be located and
drilled; that three years after the location of the plant, the plaintiff, with full knowledge of the facts, purchased the land on which
they erected the dwelling house in question; that in 1895, on the
failure of defendant's first well, and while defendant was prospecting for the location of a second well one of the plaintiffs, Willard Patterson, gave his consent that a well might be sunk on the
west side of defendant's land, not to be nearer than 150 feet to
plaintiff's said dwelling; and that defendant, relying upon
this agreement, proceeded to drill the well in question, and to
lay the gas mains therefrom; that after the company had been
engaged for four days in sinking the well, and when they were
about to begin drilling the rock, the restraining order was issued;
that the point selected for drilling the second well was the greatest
distance possible from the first well, and the best that could be
selected. The reasons given in the complaint to show why the
injunction should be issued, were, that if the proposed well should
be completed there would be a continuous loud noise, depriving
plaintiffs of the enjoyment of their property and greatly depre-

ciating its value; that natural gas is a very explosive and inflammable substance, and when confined under the surface of the earth,
permeates the soil for hundreds of feet, and, as soon as freed in
the air, produces a stench, tarnishes paint, furniture, and silver
ware, and renders the atmosphere unfit to breathe for many feet
around the place of such escape; that the pipeline, if constructed,
to carry gas at rock pressure, as intended, would endanger the
lives and property of plaintiffs and their family, that gas wells
attract electric fluid and are exceedingly liable to be struck by
lightning; that in the digging of the well there was danger of
bringing from the earth other substances, such as water and oil,
and that if the well should overflow with either oil or water, great
damage would result, rendering plaintiff's property unfit for the
purposes for which they held the same. The Supreme Court reversed the Circuit Court. Upon the question of apprehended injury the court cited:

> *Dalton* v. *Ry. Co.*, 144 Ind. 121; 43 N. E. 130.
> *Duncan* v. *Hays*, 22 N. J. Eq. 25.
> *McCutcheon* v. *Blanton*, 59 Miss. 116.
> *Cleveland* v. *Gaslight Co.*, 20 N. J. Eq. 201.
> *Ryan* v. *Copes*, 11 Rich. Law. 217; 73 Am. Dec. 106.
> *Doelner* v. *Tyrian*, 38 How. Prac. 176.
> *Rhodes* v. *Dunbar*, 57 Pa. 274.
> *Huckenstine's Appeal*, 70 Pa. 102.
> *Gilbert* v. *Showerman*, 23 Mich. 448.
> *Owen* v. *Phillips*, 73 Ind. 284.
> *Barnard* v. *Sherley*, 135 Ind. 547; 34 N. E. 600; 35 N. E. 117.

Sec. 4.—In *Tyner* v. *Peoples Gas Co.*, 131 Ind. 599; 31 N. E. 61,
analyzed under Chapter 41, the syllabus is as follows:

"A complaint for an injunction to restrain defendant from
'shooting' a gas well on his land adjoining the land of plaintiff,
and within 200 feet of the residence of himself and family, with
nitroglycerine, which alleges, that by shooting the well, and by
the accumulation of a large amount of nitroglycerine for that
purpose, plaintiff's dwelling and the lives of himself and family
will be endangered, if the facts stated are true, shows a private
nuisance, and alleges facts sufficient to warrant the granting
of an injunction."

The court cited:

Ry. Co. v. *Simon*, 40 Ind. 278.
Haag v. *Board*, 60 Ind. 511.
Owen v. *Phillips*, 73 Ind. 284.
Willimason v. *Yingling*, 93 Ind. 42.
Smith v. *Fitzgerald*, 24 Ind. 316.
Reichert v. *Geers*, 98 Ind. 73.

Sec. 5.—In *Pope Bros.* v. *Bridgewater Gas Co.*, 52 W. Va. 252;
43 S. E. 87 (Dec. 13, 1902) the syllabus is as follows:

"1. To sustain an injunction, inhibiting the drilling of an oil
or gas well or other business, not per se constituting a nuisance,
it must be shown that the danger of injury from it is impend-
ing, and imminent and the effect certain.
2. The drilling of a well on a tract of land adjacent to another on which there is a producing well, and in close proximity
to such producing well, cannot be enjoined on the ground of ignition of gas from the completed well by fires in the furnace and
forges used in drilling the other, when it appears that such danger would arise only in case it should become necessary to open
the producing well for the purpose of repairing the pumping apparatus in case of accident, and that there is no existing cause
for opening it, as mere possible, eventual, or contingent danger
is insufficient."

Pope Brothers & Co., filed a bill in Chancery in the Circuit
Court of Wirt County against the Bridgewater Gas Company for
and obtained, an injunction, restraining the defendant from keeping its fires going in its boiler and forges in drilling an oil well
near a completed well belonging to plaintiff, which was producing
both gas and oil. On the fifteenth day of May, 1901, Pope Bros.
& Co., drilled in their well on a tract of land owned by them and
at a point very near the line between it and a tract of land belonging to one Jacob Swisher on which farm the Bridgewater
Gas Company had a lease for oil and gas purpose. Soon afterwards the Bridgewater Gas Company located a well on its land at
a distance of only about 42 feet from the Pope well, put up its
rig and placed its boiler and other machinery on the grounds.
Before the drilling of the new well was actually commenced, it
became necessary to open the Pope well on account of an accident

to the tubing and pumping apparatus, and in so doing, considerable quantities of both oil and gas escaped from it. So strong was the flow from the well that some of the oil was thrown upon the derrick and rig of the Bridgewater Gas Company, and also upon and beyond said company's boiler, nearly 80 feet away from the flowing well, while the escaping gas enveloped everything around. Seeing this, and realizing the certainty of a conflagration, in case the well should be opened when fires were going in the Bridgewater boiler, the superintendent of the Bridgewater Company was requested to remove his company's boiler to a greater distance from the Pope well. This he refused to do, and later on, after the repairs to the machinery of the Pope well had been completed and the pumping of that well resumed, fire was started in the Bridgewater Company's boiler, and the work of drilling the new well was commenced. On June 1, 1901, the Judge of the Circuit Court of Wirt County granted the injunction upon the bill presented by Pope Brothers. Two days later, on motion of defendants, after notice to dissolve, and after filing a joint and several demurrer and answer, the court so modified the order "as to permit the said defendants to proceed with operations upon their said lease on the Swisher farm so as not to endanger the well and derrick of the said plaintiffs, * * * * * that when it becomes necessary for the plaintiffs to pull the rods in the well and to remove the caps, the said defendant shall, upon request, put out the fires in the boilers and derrick for a reasonable time to enable the work to be done." The motion to dissolve was continued. Affidavits and depositions were taken and filed. The bill alleged that the plaintiffs had taken every precaution and made use of every appliance and method known to close in the well and prevent the escape of gas from it, but that these efforts had been unavailing and gas was constantly escaping and spreading in every direction around the well for a distance of at least 150 feet, so permeating the air that fire, brought within that distance of the well, would ignite it and cause a conflagration that would consume all the structures, stop the production of the well, and necessitate cleaning it out. The bill further showed that the defendant had located its rig within about fifteen feet of the well and its boiler within about 45 feet of it, and intended and was threatening to place fire in the boiler and begin the work of drilling a new well. The facts shown by the evidence negatived the material allegations of the bill. It was admitted by practically all the wit-

nesses for the plaintiffs that the Pope well was thoroughly
packed and closed in at the time the injunction was awarded;
that gas was not escaping therefrom in such quantity as to make
it in the least dangerous to carry on the operations undertaken
by the defendant; that the boiler of the defendant was at a distance of 77 and 8-10 feet from the plaintiff's well, instead of 45
feet. It appeared from the testimony that it would have been
dangerous to have had fire in the boiler and rig of the defendant
at any time when the Pope well might have been open for the purpose of repairing the pump, tubing or other apparatus used in
bringing up the oil; but it was not shown that the defendant ever
refused or expressed an intention to refuse to put out his fire at
any time that it might become necessary to open the Pope well. It
was made clear by the evidence that it was perfectly practicable
for the defendant to drill its well without injury or danger to the
property of the plaintiffs, and without inconvenience other than
a cessation of operations during such times as it might be necessary to have the Pope well open for the purposes of repairs. On
February 14, 1902, the motion to dissolve the injunction was heard
and overruled· From this decree of the Circuit Court the defendant appealed. The Court of Appeals reversed the Circuit Court,
citing:

Powell v. *Bentley & Gerwig,* 34 W. Va. 804.
McGregor v. *Camden,* 47 W. Va. 193.
Chambers v. *Cramer,* 49 W. Va. 395.

Upon the question of mere possible, eventual or contingent
injury, the court cited:

Hough v. *Doyleston,* 4 Brews. (Pa.) 333.
And cases cited above.

Sec. 6.—In *Snyder* v. *Philadelphia Co.,* 54 W. Va. 149; 46 S.
E. 366; 102 Am. St. Rep. 941; 63 L. R. A. 896 (Nov. 21, 1903) the
fourth, fifth and sixth points of the syllabus are as follows:

"4. The owner of a gas well, situated near a public highway,
may lawfully open it for the purpose of allowing the gas to blow
the water out of it, although the noise thereby made is clearly
such as to frighten the horses of persons riding or driving along

the highway; but in doing so, he must exercise care not thereby
to inflict injury upon such persons or their property.

5. Persons using horses on the highway in close proximity
to such well and seeing an agent of the owner at or near it, have
the right to presume that he will not open it without warning,
or first looking for travelers on the road, and are not guilty of
contributory negligence in failing to turn and fly from it, or in
failing to give warning of their presence.

6. When, by the negligent flowing off of such well a teamster's horses became frightened, and, in attempting to control
them a line breaks, causing him to fall from his wagon, whereby
he is injured, the proximate cause of the injury is the blowing off
of the well, although the line is weak and wholly insufficient for
such an emergency.''

Robert Snyder instituted suit in the Circuit Court of Wetzel
County, West Virginia, against the Philadelphia Company, alleging in the declaration filed in the cause that the defendant
owned, controlled and operated a gas well near the public highway, and that it was its duty to use due care in managing and
operating the well, and in blowing the same off so as not to interfere with the lawful use of the highway by persons riding and
driving thereon, but that it neglected to do so; that the plaintiff
on the 28th of April, 1897, was a teamster driving his team upon
and over said highway hauling oil well supplies, merchandise, hay,
etc., in a wagon drawn by two horses driven by him, and when he,
with his team, came to a point on said highway, near to said
gas well, said defendant through its agents, servants and employes, then and there in charge of said gas well not regarding
its duty in the premises, carelessly and negligently managed and
operated said gas well, and so carelessly and negligently caused
and permitted the gas from the well to be discharged and escape
with great force and in large quantities into the air, making a
loud, hissing, unusual and frightful noise, calculated to frighten
horses and cause them to run away, and which did then and there
frighten said horses, and caused them to become unmanageable
and run away, whereby the plaintiff was thrown, etc. Upon trial
verdict and judgment was rendered for plaintiff. Motion to set
aside the verdict was overruled and defendant obtained a writ of
error to the Court of Appeals, and that court affirmed the judgment. Upon the question that the owner of a gas well situated near

a public highway must exercise care in its operation, not to inflict injury upon persons or their property, the court cited:

Powell v. *Furniture Co.*, 34 W. Va. 804.
Wilson v. *Powder Co.*, 40 W. Va. 413.
McGregor v. *Camden*, 47 W. Va. 193.

Upon the question of the proximate cause of an injury or loss, the court cited:

Brady v. *Insurance Co.*, 11 Mich. 425.
Insurance Co. v. *Boon*, 95 U. S. 117.
Insurance Co. v. *Tweed*, 7 Wall. 44.
Ry. Co. v. *Madry*, 57 Ark. 306.

REMEDIES.

Sec. 7.—The drilling and operation of an oil or gas well will not be enjoined by a court or equity unless the bill alleges and the evidence shows that the lives of others will be endangered or their property materially lessened in value. Mere apprehension of injury or damages is not sufficient to warrant an injunction.

McGregor v. *Camden*, 47 W. Va. 193; 34 S. E. 936.
Windfall Mfg. Co. v. *Patterson*, 148 Ind. 414; 47 N. E. 2; 62 Am. St. Rep. 532; 37 L. R. A. 38.
Tyner v *Peoples Gas Co.*, 131 Ind. 599; 31 N. E. 61.
Pope Bros. v. *Bridgewater Gas Co.*, 52 W. Va. 252; 43 S. E. 87.

Sec. 8.—The drilling or operation of an oil or gas well will be enjoined by a court of equity at the instance of other persons whose lives are endangered or whose property is materially diminished in value, or seriously interfered with, where the bill alleges and the proof establishes such danger, diminution in the value of the property, or injury.

McGregor v. *Camden*, 47 W. Va. 193; 34 S. E. 936.
Windfall Mfg. Co. v. *Patterson*, 148 Ind. 414; 47 N. E. 2; 62 Am. St. Rep. 532; 37 L. R. A. 38.
Tyner v. *Peoples Gas Co.*, 131 Ind. 599; 31 N. E. 61.
Pope Bros. v. *Bridgewater Gas Co.*, 52 W. Va. 252; 43 S. E. 87.

Sec. 9.—The owner of an oil or gas well situated near a public highway is liable in damages to a person injured while lawfully using such highway, where such owner fails to exercise due care in the drilling or operation of such well not to inflict injury upon such person or his property.

Snyder v. *Phila. Co.*, 54 W. Va. 149; 46 S. E. 366; 102 Am. St. Rep. 941; 63 L. R. A. 896.

CHAPTER 45.

WASTE OF GAS MALICIOUSLY OR NEGLIGENTLY.

Sec. 1.—A landowner or lessee may, in the absence of malice or negligence and in the absence of a statute forbidding waste, permit gas to escape from his wells and go to waste if no other injury is done to his neighbor than that which would result from the depletion of the gas basin in which his own and his neighbor's wells are situated. But where a lessee abandons a gas well, without having used ordinary care to shut the gas in, he is liable in damages to the owner of the land for injury caused by the escape of gas from the well so abandoned.

Hague v. *Wheeler*, 157 Pa. 324; 27 Atl. 714; 37 Am. St. Rep. 736; 22 L. R. A. 141.
Talbott v. *Southern Oil Co.*, 60 W. Va. 423; 55 S. E. 1009.
Calor Oil & Gas Co. v. *Franzell, and Kentucky Heating Co.* v. *Calor Oil & Gas Co.*, 128 Ky. 715; 109 S. W. 328; 33 Ky. L. Rep. 98.
Louisville Gas Co. v. *Kentucky Heating Co.*, 33 Ky. L. Rep. 912; 111 S. W. 374.

Sec. 2.—In *Hague* v. *Wheeler*, 157 Pa. 324; 27 Atl. 714; 37 Am. St. Rep. 736; 22 L. R. A. 141, (Oct. 2, 1893) the syllabus is as follows:

"In the absence of malice or negligence in draining a well, a landowner may permit gas to escape from it and go to waste, if no other injury is done to his neighbor than that which would result from the depletion of the gas basin, in which his own and his neighbor's lands are situated.

Plaintiffs, an individual and a gas company, were owners of lands in a gas basin, and had opened wells upon their land from which they obtained gas in quantities sufficient for commercial use. Defendants were owners of adjoining lands in the same basin. At the solicitation of the gas company, they opened wells upon their lands, but failed to obtain gas sufficient for commercial use. The object of the gas company in requesting defendants to open the wells was to purchase the land, and the wells were opened in pursuance of a negotiation entered into for that purpose, which afterwards failed. Defendants did not plug the wells, but permitted the gas to escape and go to waste. Plaintiffs entered upon defendants land, and shut in the gas and closed the well. Defendents then threatened to remove the cap and permit the gas to escape. Plaintiffs filed a bill in equity to restrain them from so doing. *Held*, (1) that as there was no evidence that defendants had acted with malice or negligence towards the gas company in opening the well, none could be imputed to them, as to the other plaintiff. (2) That an injunction could not be sustained.''

W. W. Hague and Citizens Gas Company filed a bill in equity in the Court of Common Pleas of Warren County, Pennsylvania, against N. P. Wheeler, L. R. Freeman and others, for an injunction to restrain waste of gas on adjoining premises. The bill averred that plaintiffs were lessees of about 2200 acres of land for oil and gas purposes, and that defendants were neighboring landowners. The bill further averred:

"3. By reason of the geological formation in that locality, the gas bearing sandrock underlying a large part of tracts numbers 5202-5203-5207, and 5208, including those parts of which the plaintiffs and defendants are lessees or owners of the gas and oil respectively, and from which the plaintiffs are producing gas in paying quantities, is subject to rapid drainage by the drilling of wells on any part thereof.

4. The plaintiff, Hague, began drilling wells on his leasehold in the year 1888, and the plaintiff, Citizens Gas Co., in the year 1887. The defendants, lessees, did not drill any wells on the land in which they own the oil and gas, or in the said basin until in the year 1890, when they sunk one well on that part of tract number 5207 situate in Limestone Township, Warren County, about 50 rods from the leasehold of plaintiff, the Citizens Gas Company, and about 80 or 90 rods from the leasehold of the plain-

tiff Hague, in the summer of 1890, and obtained gas in considerable quantities.

5.   The flow of gas from said well of defendants is so great
that it will, if allowed to go to waste, seriously and irreparably
injure the wells of the plaintiff by drainage from the lands adjoining and near to said defendant's wells. The defendants have
not marketed the gas from said well, nor made any use thereof
whatever, but in 1891, said well was opened and the gas permitted
to escape in great quantities, and it having caught fire, the plaintiff Hague and George H. Ahrens caused the same to be extinguished and shut in for the protection of their own land, as well
as to the benefit of the defendants, at the expense of about $200.00.
The defendants at one time offered to shut in said well and give
plaintiffs control thereof for a consideration of $1,650.00 per an-
num, which plaintiffs, being greatly injured by the waste and
drainage of said gas, agreed to pay; but the defendants failed to
perform their agreement, and in September, 1892, sent men to
open said well and allow the gas to escape in great quantities,
and declared their intention to open said well unless plaintiffs
would pay them an extortionate and exorbitant price therefor.
Said defendants are still threatening to open said well, and if
done, the drainage of gas from the territory of plaintiffs will be
such as to cause them great and irreparable damage; and your
orators are informed and believe that on the 25th day of October,
1892, the said defendants again opened said well, and intend to
keep the same open.

6.   The said acts and threats of the defendants, your orators
aver, are contrary to law and equity, and injurious to them and
to the public.''

The bill prayed for an injunction (1) to prevent the opening
of defendant's well, so as to prevent the gas from going to waste,
and (2) for general relief. The court granted a preliminary injunction and subsequently refused to dissolve it. The defendants
appealed, and the Supreme Court reversed the decree of the court
below and dissolved the injunction.

Sec. 3.—In *Talbott* v. *Southern Oil Co.*, 60 W. Va. 423; 55 S.
E. 1009 (Oct. 30, 1906) syl. 3 is as follows:

''3.   For injury to land caused by the escape of natural gas
from a well thereon, drilled and abandoned by a lessee of the
land for oil and gas purposes, the lessor has a right of action for
damages against the lessee.''

E. M. Talbott brought an action in the Circuit Court of Gilmer County against the Southern Oil Company in trespass on the case for damages occasioned by failure on the part of the defendant to plug, as required by statute, an abandoned gas well drilled by the defendant on lands of the plaintiff under a lease authorizing such drilling. Special appearance was made by defendant for the purpose of moving to quash the return of service on the writ. No further appearance having been made, judgment was rendered at the June Term, 1904, in favor of plaintiff. Defendant moved to vacate the judgment, which motion was overruled, and defendant prosecuted error. The Supreme Court affirmed the judgment. Upon the proposition that the licensee is liable for all injury resulting from the negligent exercise of the powers conferred upon him, the court cited:

Lyford v. *Putnam*, 35 N. H. 563.
Norton v. *Craig*, 68 Me. 275.
Dean v. *McLean*, 48 Vt. 412.
Selden v. *Delaware etc. Co.*, 29 N. Y. 634.

Upon the proposition that waste is actionable at common law, whether it results from affirmative wrongful acts, or mere omission to perform duty, the court cited:

University v. *Tucker*, 31 W. Va. 621.
Williamson v. *Jones*, 43 W. Va. 562.

Sec. 4—In *Calor Oil & Gas Co.* v. *Franzell, and Kentucky Heating Co.* v. *Calor Oil & Gas Co.*, 128 Ky. 715; 109 S. W. 328; 33 Ky. Law. Rep. 98 (March 26, 1908) syls. 2-4-5-8 are as follows:

"2. A lease granting to a gas company the exclusive right to construct pipelines across the lessor's land, is void as against public policy in so far as it excludes others from crossing the tract.

4. A lease giving exclusive right to cross lands by pipelines, being against public policy, the owner of the right is not entitled to compensation for the invasion of its exclusive right in condemnation proceedings by another of a similar right of way across the same lands.

5. Nor is the landowner entitled to compensation for loss of

rent because of the abandonment by the owner of the exclusive right of the lease under which such right was claimed.

8. An action will lie by the owner of a gas well against the owner of other wells in the same district for illegal waste or destruction of the gas, but not for exhaustion resulting from legal use or sale of the gas.''

The Calor Oil & Gas Company instituted in the County Court of Meade County, Kentucky, condemnation proceedings against Nicholas Franzell, the Kentucky Heating Company and others. Franzel and wife owned a tract of land in Meade County, between the natural gas field and the City of Louisville. The Kentucky Heating Company was a corporation owning and operating natural gas wells in Meade County, and was engaged in the business of piping the gas from the wells to the City of Louisville and there selling it to its customers under a franchise which it owned and held to lay its pipes through the public streets. The Louisville Gas Company was a corporation engaged in the manufacture of gas in the City of Louisville and selling the same for lighting and heating purposes under a franchise which it owned for the purpose of laying its pipes through the public ways of the city. The latter corporation was not a party to these proceedings, but was a rival to some extent of the Kentucky Heating Company, and it was the theory of the Heating Company that the Calor Oil & Gas Company was but a branch of the Louisville Gas Company, and that the latter was incorporated among other things, to enable the Louisville Gas Company by indirection to pipe natural gas from the gas fields of Meade County, to the City of Louisville, and in this way unlawfully compete wtih the Kentucky Heating Company in its business. The Calor Oil & Gas Company was a corporation having power and authority under its charter to buy and lease oil and gas lands, drill wells, construct pipelines, and do any and all other things connected with such business. The Calor Oil & Gas Company attempted to condemn a strip of land across the farm of Franzell and wife for the purpose of laying thereon a pipeline to convey natural gas from its wells in Meade County, to Louisville. The condemnation proceedings were taken under the Kentucky statutes. The statement required to be filed under these statutes was filed in the clerk's office of the County Court of Meade County, and fully described the strip to be condemned, and the Judge of the Meade County Court appointed three commissioners who, after having qualified, viewed the land, made their report, assessing the damages that would accrue to the owners by reason of the condemnation. Upon the trial of the cause before the County Court on the exceptions of the owners of the land to the report of the commissioners, the court held that the corporation did not have the power of eminent domain and dismissed the proceedings. From this judgment the corporation appealed to the Circuit Court of Meade County where, upon trial de novo, as provided by statute, it was held that the corporation did possess the right of eminent domain and submitted the question of damages to the jury with the result that they returned a verdict for $4,000 in favor of Franzell and wife, and from this judgment all the parties prosecuted an appeal to the Supreme Court. The Kentucky Heating Company was made a defendant to the condemnation proceedings because it claimed under a written contract with Franzell the "the exclusive right and privilege of laying pipe and pipelines for any and all purposes whatsoever on, across, in or upon said land." In addition to this exclusive privilege the Heating Company had under this contract certain mineral rights in the land. On the question of the right to condemn a right of way through the Franzell farm, notwithstanding the Heating Company's claim, to an exclusive right thereon to construct pipelines the court cited:

West Va. Transp. Co., v. Ohio Riv. Pipelines Co., 22 W. Va. 626; 46 Am. Rep. 527.

The judgment on appeal of the Kentucky Heating Company, Nicholas Franzell, and wife, was affirmed and reversed on the appeal of the Calor Oil & Gas Company for a new trial upon the ground that the judgment was excessive.

In the condemnation proceedings the Kentucky Heating Company brought into question the right of the Calor Oil & Gas Company to construct its pipelines for piping gas from the natural gas field of Meade County to the City of Louisville. The Supreme Court held that the trial court should not have permitted any inquiry into the motive of the gas company in this proceeding, and should have excluded all attempts to bring into question whether the venture of the gas company in piping gas from Meade County to Louisville would or would not be profitable, upon the ground that neither the Franzells nor the Kentucky Heating Company

had anything to do with the gas company's rights in this behalf.
The Court further held in the opinion:

"If it be true, as said in the briefs, that the natural gas in
the district of Meade County is contained in a common reservoir
underlying the whole area, of necessity it follows that the gas
company's use of its wells tends to exhaust the wells of the Heating company; and it is equally true that the piping of gas by
the Heating Company from its wells tends to exhaust the gas
company's wells. And undoubtedly the operations of two gas
companies in the same field (assuming that the quantity of gas
is limited) will exhaust it sooner than one of them would. But
each has the legal right, to the legitimate use of the gas underlying its own property and neither can complain of such use by the
other. We have already held, in the case of *Commonwealth* v.
Trent, etc., 117 Ky. 34; 77 S. W. 390, and *Calor Oil & Gas Co.* v.
McGehee, 117 Ky. 71; 77 S. W. 368, that one who illegally wastes
or destroys the gas of a district may be punished under the criminal statutes of the State, and may also be enjoined from committing such wrongful acts. But all parties owning gas wells in
the districts are free to make any legal use of the gas they choose,
and the fact that this legal use tends to exhaust the supply gives
to the other owners of the gas wells in the district no just ground
of complaint."

Sec. 5.—In *Louisville Gas Co.* v. *Kentucky Heating Company,*
33 Ky. L. Rep. 912; 111 S. W. 374 (June 20, 1908) syls. 2-3-4-5-
6-7-8-9 are as follows:

"2. Though an action to enjoin the wasting of natural gas,
and a claim for damages for gas wasted might be joined, and
a court of equity after taking jurisdiction to grant the equitable
relief might retain jurisdiction to assess damages, they are
separate and distinct causes of action, and a suit for injunctive
relief alone will not bar a subsequent action for damages on the
ground that it would be a splitting of the cause of action.

3. In an action for damages for wasting natural gas, defendants are not precluded from showing that they did not waste
gas by judgment against them in a prior action to restrain the
waste of gas, in which, for the purpose of showing that they did
thereafter waste gas, evidence was introduced that they had theretofore wasted it.

4. An allegation in a petition for damages for wasting

natural gas which merely alleges general damages was a sufficient allegation of damages.

5. Under an allegation of general damages, recovery may be had only for such as proximately and naturally flow from the wrongs complained of, and not for any special damages.

6. There is no property in natural gas until taken; before taken it is fugitive in its nature and belongs in common to the surface owners.

7. The right of the surface owners to take natural gas is subject only to the limitation that it must be for a lawful purpose and in a reasonable manner.

8. The measure of damages for injury to the right to take natural gas is the difference at the point where taken between the value of the natural flow and that of the diminished flow directly attributable to the wrong.

9. Punitive damages as well as compensatory may be. had for an injury to the right to take natural gas where malicious and with design to injure one in his business. ''

The Kentucky Heating Company instituted an action in the Circuit Court of Harden County, Kentucky, against the Louisville Gas Company and others for damages for alleged wrongful taking of natural gas from wells in the Meade County gas field. The suit was instituted after the suit of Kentucky Heating Company against the Louisville Gas Company and others, 117 Ky. 71; 77 S. W. 368; 70 L. R. A. 558; 111 Am. St. Rep. 225, had been finally decided. The plaintiff sought to recover damages for the alleged wasting of gas. The suit was prosecuted to judgment in favor of the plaintiff for $60,000 in the Circuit Court of Harden County. Defendant, Louisville Gas Company, appealed. The Court of Appeals of Kentucky reversed the judgment, and in the opinion Judge Lassing said:

"The trial court erred in admitting any evidence of special damages. The error into which the trial court fell in defining appellees measure of damages seems to have been brought about by a misconception of the rights of the appellees. The gas which appellants were wasting was not the property of appellee, and therefore appellee could not recover for this gas as a conversion of his property. Appellants had the same right to take gas in the Meade County field that appellee had as decided by this court in the cases of *Louisville Gas Co.* v. *Kentucky Heating Co.*, 117 Ky. 71; 77 S. W. 368; 70 L. R. A. 558; 111 Am. St. Rep. 225; *Com-*

monwealth v. *Trent,* 117 Ky. 34; 77 S. W. 390, and *Hamby* v. *City of Dawson Springs,* 104 S. W. 259; 31 Ky. Law. Rep. 814; 12 L. R. A. (N. S.) 1164. The right of surface owners to take gas from subjacent fields or reservoirs is a right in common. There is no property in the gas until it is taken. * * * * * The damages sustained is only that which results from an improper interference with the natural flow of the gas in the wells and pipes of another. It is not the value of the gas at the point of distribution, or at any point where it enters artificial conduits, but the value in money for the diminution of the natural flow of the gas at the wells directly and independently of all other causes, attributable to the wrongs complained of.''

REMEDIES.

Sec. 6—The owner of oil or gas wells may enjoin other persons operating in the same field from negligently or maliciously wasting or destroying oil or gas produced from the common reservoir.

> *Hague* v. *Wheeler,* 157 Pa. 324; 27 Atl. 714; 37 Am. St. Rep. 736; 22 L. R. A. 141.
> *Calor Oil & Gas Co.* v. *Franzell, and Kentucky Heating Co.* v. *Calor Oil & Gas Co.,* 128 Ky. 715; 109 S. W. 328; 33 Ky. L. Rep. 98.

(See Chapter 39 and cases analyzed.)

Sec. 7.—Where an owner of oil or gas wells producing from a basin penetrated by gas and oil wells owned and operated by others, maliciously or negligently permits the oil or gas from such common reservoir to go to waste, or destroys the same, whereby the common basin or reservoir is depleted, the person injured by such malicious or negligent waste or destruction may recover damages therefor. The measure of damages for injury to the right to take natural gas or oil from a common basin is the difference at the point where taken between the value of the natural flow and that of the diminished flow directly attributable to the wrong.

> *Louisville Gas Co.* v. *Kentucky Heating Co.,* 33 Ky. L. Rep. 912; 111 S. W. 374.

Sec. 8.—A lessee of lands for oil or gas purposes who has entered, drilled for and discovered gas, and afterwards abandons the well and fails to plug the same or take the necessary means to shut in the gas, and by reason of such failure gas escapes from the well causing injury to the land, is liable in damages to the landowner for the injury.

Talbott v. *Southern Oil Co.,* 60 W. Va. 423; 55 S. E. 1009.

CHAPTER 46.

EXCLUSIVE RIGHT TO LAY PIPE LINES VOID AS AGAINST PUBLIC POLICY.

Sec. 1.—The grant by the lessor in the ordinary oil and gas lease of the exclusive right to lay pipelines upon the demised premises is void as against public policy, being an attempt to impose an unreasonable restriction upon trade.

Calor Oil & Gas Co. v. *Franzell, and Kentucky Heating Co.* v. *Calor Oil & Gas Co.,* 128 Ky. 715; 109 S. W. 328; 33 Ky. L. Rep. 98.
Brookshire Oil Co. v. *Casmalia Ranch Oil & Development Co.,* 156 Cal. 211; 103 Pac. 927.
West Va. Transp. Co. v. *Ohio River Pipeline Co.,* 22 W. Va. 600; 46 Am. Rep. 527.

Sec. 2.—In *Calor Oil & Gas Co.* v. *Franzell, and Kentucky Heating Co.* v. *Calor Oil & Gas Co.,* 128 Ky. 715; 109 S. W. 328; 33 Ky. L. Rep. 98, analyzed under Chapter 45, syl. 4 is as follows:

"4. A lease giving an exclusive right to cross lands by pipelines, being against public policy, the owner of the right is not entitled to compensation for the invasion of its exclusive right in condemnation proceedings by another of a similar right of way across the lands."

Sec. 3.—In *Brookshire Oil Company* v. *Casmalia Ranch Oil & Development Company,* 156 Cal. 211; 103 Pac. 927 (Aug. 25, 1909) the syllabus is as follows:

"1. A lease provided that A. thereby granted to M. the sole right to produce oil and gas from said land, specifically granting to M. for ten years the exclusive right to drill and operate oil and gas wells, to lay and operate pipelines, telegraph and telephone lines, the necessary right of way over the premises, the use of enough land on which to preserve the production, the use of water and wood on the premises till oil is found, that should M. find a paying production of oil or gas on the land during said term, then A. would extend the lease from year to year, so long as such production continued, and that in consideration M. agreed to use and occupy so much of the land as might be necessary for the purposes granted, to commence operations within a year, to pay a royalty on oil and gas produced, also agreeing to use no water necessary for A.'s. stock. *Held,* in view of the general rules of interpretation of contracts, cited by Civ. Code, §§ 1648-1650-1653, and the main object and attendant provisions of the lease, that it gave no general and exclusive right to lay and operate pipelines, but only sufficient rights in that respect to enable the lessee to carry out the main objects of producing and removing the oil and gas, so that he could not interfere with a pipeline subsequently laid by another with the lessor's permission, not affecting his operations.

2. A lease may except right to produce oil and gas from land, and prior rights to lay and operate necessary pipelines. Thereafter with the lessor's permission the third person constructed a pipeline across the land to others, producing from other lands to the market. *Held,* that his use was not adverse to the lessee till the latter began to use the part of the land through which the pipeline ran in a way incompatible with tenancy of such land.

3. That between the times a pipeline for conducting oil to market was torn up and reconstructed the owner was prevented from marketing oil of a certain value, does not show damage from destruction of the line; but if during the interruption the market value of oil depreciated, or if because of the interruption oil was lost or destroyed. or oil which otherwise would have come through the owners wells was, because of their being closed, drawn through the wells of another, and so lost to such owner, and this could be shown, such damages could be recovered.''

Juan B. Arellanes executed in 1899 an oil and gas lease to Casmalia Oil Company, which contained the following provision:

"The first party, (Arellanes) hereby grants unto the second

party * * * * * for and during the term of ten years, from this
date * * * * * the exclusive right to drill and operate oil and gas
wells; to lay and operate pipelines * * * the use of enough land
on which to preserve the production and erect such buildings as
they may desire* * * * to use and occupy only so much of said
land as may be necessary for purposes herein granted.''

Under the lease the Casmalia Oil Company, within three
months after its execution, entered on the land and began drilling for oil, and thereafter continued the work of exploration for
oil, but had not discovered oil or any other substance in marketable quantities at the time of the suit. It had not laid any pipelines over or upon the land, nor had it made any plans for that
purpose. In January, 1905, Arellanes, the lessor, gave a parol
license to the Brookshire Oil Comapny to lay and maintain pipelines over the land. This company entered upon the premises and
laid about 4,000 feet of pipeline over a part of the land leased to
the Casmalia Company, and the Casmalia Company tore up the
line so constructed. The Brookshire company instituted an action in the Superior Court of Santa Barbara County against the
Casmalia Company and others for damages claimed to have been
sustained by the tearing up of its pipeline and for an injunction
to enjoin the defendants from preventing the construction and
maintenance of said pipelines by the plaintiff. The court found
damages in favor of the plaintiff in the sum of $1,232. and further
found that it was not necessary for the defendant to destroy the
pipe in order to preserve its rights under the lease and gave
judgment for said sum against the Casmalia Company. Defendant
appealed. The plaintiff also claimed damages in the sum of
$5,000 for loss incidental to the conduct of oil from the property
of the plaintiff to the railroad. The plaintiff had rebuilt its pipelines after their destruction but was delayed in the use thereof
for a period of 47 days. Upon the issue as to these damages, the
jury found in favor of the defendant. The plaintiff appealed.
An injunction was granted upon the cross complaint of the Casmalia Company against the plaintiff. From this judgment the
plaintiff appealed. The Supreme Court of California affirmed the
judgment for $1,232.00 against defendant, and also affirmed the
lower court in its judgment on the verdict of the jury in finding
no damages on the special issue and reversing the judgment awarding the injunction of the cross-complaint of the Casmalia Oil Com-

pany. The Supreme Court held that the lease did not vest in the lessee any present title in the land; that it granted only the right to do certain things thereon and to take certain mineral substances therefrom, and no title to said substances passed from the original owner until the same should be severed from the realty, and cited:

> *Venture Oil Co.* v. *Fretts*, 152 Pa. 451-460; 25 Atl. 732.
> *Steelsmith* v. *Gartlan*, 45 W. Va. 27-34; 29 S. E. 978; 44 L. R. A. 107.
> *Lowther Oil Co.* v. *Miller-Sibley Co.*, 53 W. Va. 501; 44 S. E. 433; 97 Am. St. 1027.
> *Huggins* v. *Daley*, 99 Fed. 608; 40 C. C. A. 12; 48 L. R. A. 320.
> *Gadberry* v. *Gas Co.*, 162 Ind. 14; 67 N. E. 261; 62 L. R. A. 895.
> *Eaton* v. *Allegheny Gas Co.*, 122 N. Y. 417; 25 N. E. 981.
> *Funk* v. *Halderman*, 53 Pa. 242.
> *Union etc. Co.* v. *Bliven*, 72 Pa. 173.
> *Grubb* v. *Grubb*, 74 Pa. 33.

Sec. 4.—In *West Virginia Transportation Co.* v. *Ohio River Pipeline Co.*, 22 W. Va. 600; 46 Am. Rep. 527 (Nov. 17, 1883) the syllabus is as follows:

"1.　An oil transportation company entered into an agreement with a landowner, whereby the landowner, for a valuable consideration, granted to the company and their assigns, the exclusive right of way and privilege to construct and maintain one or more lines of tubing for the transportation of oil through and under a tract of land containing two thousand acres, which agreement was signed, sealed and delivered by the landowner, *Held*, By the true construction of this instrument it operated, first, as a grant of right of way for such tubing for the transportation of oil through said tract of land, and, secondly, it was intended to operate as a covenant, whereby the landowner agreed, that he would not himself transport oil from or through this tract of land, nor grant rights of way to any other person or company, to lay tubes for the transportation of oil through said tract of land, whether the oil was produced on said tract of land or not.

2.　Such agreement was valid and binding on the landowner and his assigns, so far as it operated as a grant of right of way for such tubing through said tract of land, but so far as it was intended to operate as a covenant, that the landowner would not

himself transport oil from or through said tract of land nor grant
rights of way to any other person or company to lay tubes for the
transportation of oil through said tract of land, whether the oil
was produced upon it or not, this agreement was inoperative, null
and void as contrary to public policy, being an attempt to impose
an unreasonable restraint upon trade.

3. As a general rule any trade or business may legally have
imposed on it by contract a *partial* restraint, as the extent of territory over which it is permitted to extend. Such restraint, when
valid, varies with the character of the trade or business. In some
sorts of trade or business it may be a large extent of country,
hundreds of miles in dimensions, in which a party may contract,
not to carry on his business; but in other sorts of business the
restraint would not be valid, if it were attempted by the contract
to extend it beyond the bounds of a single town; and there are
some sorts of business which the law will not allow to be restrained at all by contract.

4. Whenever the legislature by statute law has authorized
any person or corporation to condemn the lands of others in order
to carry on its business, the courts will regard this as a legislative
declaration, that this character of business is such, as that the
public has so great and direct an interest in, that the courts must
hold it as contrary to public policy to permit any restriction of it
by private contract.

5. A contract, by which an *exclusive* right of way is granted
through any land, however small the parcel, is void, so far as the
right is attempted to be made exclusive, as contrary to public
policy, and as in direct conflict with the State's right of eminent
domain.

6. A landlord may by contract under seal impose on the
lands which he leases, burdens, which will not only be binding on
the tenant, but also on sub-tenants, they being covenants real running with the land. But except between landlord and tenant no
burdens can be imposed on lands by any covenant of the owner
which will run with the land, and bind any grantee of the land;
for such covenants are personal, and are not covenants real running with the land.

7. An agreement by a landowner, that the products of his
land shall be transported to market by a certain common carrier,
is not a covenant real and does not run with the land or bind any
subsequent purchaser of the land.

8. A court of equity would not enforce the performance of
such covenants by subsequent purchaser of the land though he
bought the land with full notice of the existence of such covenant.''

The West Virginia Transportation Company, a corporation under the laws of West Virginia, presented its bill of injunction to the Judge of the Circuit Court of Ritchie County, in which it alleged that it was incorporated as an internal improvement company by several Acts of the Legislature of West Virginia; and that by its charter it was authorized to purchase real estate, erect buildings and improvements thereon, use and hold the same; to have the right to purchase all necessary equipments and append- ages such as tubing, pumps, tanks, telegraph apparatus, and all needed appliances necessary for the transportation of oil through tubing and branch pipes for the convenience, accommodation and purposes of the company; that by Section 5, of its charter, it was authorized to acquire rights of way by condemnation; that Sec- tion 7 regulated its charges for the transportation of oil through such tubing; that the Legislature by Section 12 reserved the right to alter, amend or repeal the Act; that by Chapter 67 of the Acts 1868, its charter was amended, and the company authorized to construct and maintain a line or lines of tubing for the pur- pose of transporting petroleum or other oils through pipes of iron or other material in the Counties of Wirt, Wood, Ritchie and Pleasants, to any railroad or other road or to any navigable stream in or adjoining the counties aforesaid; and to transport from the terminal of said pipe or pipes, petroleum or other oils in tanks, cars, boats, or other receptacles, and to receive and hold said oil on storage, and to buy and sell oils on commission or otherwise; and also power to enter and condemn lands and to ac- quire rights of way in the counties aforesaid for the purposes of said company; and in such cases, when deemed advisable by said company, it should, at its option have the power to acquire a suf- ficient right of way only for the purposes of said improvement over any such lands instead of the fee simple thereof. The bill then stated that pursuant to the authority thus conferred upon it, that is, the right to acquire and hold the right of way, or rights of way over, under or through said lands, or the fee sim- ple as aforesaid, by good and indefeasible title; on September 2, 1868, it obtained the following contract with E. L. Gale and Mary Gale:

"We the undersigned, for and in consideration of the sum of one dollar, receipt of which is hereby acknowledged, do hereby grant unto the West Virginia Transportation Company, a company incorporated under special Act of the Legislature of West Virginia, passed February 26, 1867, and their assigns, the right of way to construct and maintain one or more lines of tubing for the transportation of oil along, through and under lands owned by the undersigned, in Ritchie County, in the State of West Virginia; also the right to construct and maintain a telegraph along said tubing and the privilege to remove said telegraph and tubing at pleasure. Witness our hands and seals this 23d day of September, 1868. E. L. Gale (Seal) Mary Gale (Seal.)''

The bill further alleged that subsequently, on January 31, 1870, and on October 25, 1873, E. L. Gale and Mary Gale granted to it the exclusive right of way for the construction and operation of its lines of tubing through and under lands owned by Gales in the Counties of Ritchie and Wood. These grants were the same, and as follows:

''We, the undersigned, for and in consideration of the sum of one dollar, receipt of which is hereby acknowledged, do hereby grant unto the West Virginia Transportation Company, a company incorporated under special Act of the Legislature of West Virginia, passed February 26, 1867, and their assigns, the exclusive right of way and privilege to construct and maintain one or more lines of tubing for the transportation of oil, water, or other liquids, along, through and under lands owned by the undersigned in Ritchie County, in the State of West Virginia; also the right to construct and maintain a telegraph along said tubing and the privilege to remove said telegraph and tubing at pleasure. Witness our hands and seals this 31st day of January, 1870. E. L. Gale (Seal) Mary Gale (Seal).''

The bill then alleged that the lands mentioned in these three deeds were comprised in a tract of about 2,000 acres, principally in Ritchie County; that acting under these deeds the company laid lines of tubing, erected pumping stations and tanks and necessary appliances on the lands, to all the oil wells thereon, said lines of tubing being several miles in extent, and furnished means of transportation from every well or set of wells upon said tract, the value of the tubing and property amounting to several thousand dollars; that since 1869, the company had furnished complete and efficient transportation for the oil produced from all the wells on said tract; that it had connected its tubing lines with other lines by which transportation for said oil was afforded to Parkersburg, and to the Baltimore & Ohio Railroad at Petroleum and Laurel Junction; that on June 3, 1882, the Secretary of State of West Virginia issued to the Ohio River Pipeline Company a charter whereby its incorporators agreed to become a corporation under that name, for the purpose of transporting petroleum oils by pipe-lines in the Counties of Ritchie, Wood, and Pleasants, for all persons who should deliver to said corporation oil in quantities not less than 50 barrels, at such rates of transportation as may be designated by the corporation, not to exceed the maximum rate for such service as was then prescribed by law; for which purpose said corporation should lay a line, or lines of pipe from at or near Petroleum Station, in Ritchie County, on the railroad along and through what was known as the oil belt in Ritchie and Wood Counties, in a north-westerly course through said counties, to a point in the City of Marietta, in the State of Ohio, and to lay a line of pipe or tubing from any point on its main line on either side thereof, and connecting with the oil wells and points of oil stor-age in said district or belt, in said Counties of Wood and Ritchie, and extending the same to the oil district of Pleasants County; that the Ohio River Pipeline Company thus chartered by Thomp-son Leach, and the Wood County Petroleum Company, by some combination intended as a blind to the acts of the Ohio River Pipe-line Company, had entered upon this 2,000 acre tract called the Gale tract, with the avowed object, and purpose of laying and constructing a line of pipe for the transportation of the oil produced thereon, and in furtherance of their design they had placed upon said tract pipe and tubing in order to lay and construct said line, and had then laid a portion thereof upon the tract of land, and were continuing to lay pipe for the purposes aforesaid; that the said Ohio River Pipeline Company and the persons associated with it were proceeding in this manner without the consent or permission of the West Virginia Transportation Company, and without any proceedings to condemn the land according to law, and without any lawful authority whatever, and in violation of plaintiff's vested rights by their charter and deeds before men-tioned; that the Ohio River Pipeline Company had no property in West Virginia, except a small amount of tubing; that a judg-ment against it would be unavailing. The bill prayed for an in-junction against the Ohio River Pipeline Company and the other defendants to enjoin them from laying and constructing any line of pipe or tubing for the transportation of oil upon and from said tract of land known as the Gale tract, and from removing and transporting through any such line any oil produced, or that might be thereafter produced upon said tract of land, and from interfering in any manner with the sole and exclusive right claimed by the plaintiff. The injunction was awarded as prayed for. The defendants demurred to the bill, and filed their joint and several answers. They admitted the charters of the plaintiff, and the deeds made to it by the Gales. The answer then stated that E. L. Gale and Mary Gale by deed conveyed to the defendants, the natural persons, on June 20, 1875, an undivided one half interest in and to at least 1,000 acres of the said Gale tract being the side of said Gale tract nearest to Volcano; that the grantees in said deed were authorized to grant leases on said 1,000 acres of land, for the purpose of mining for oil or other minerals but no leases were to be granted for a less royalty than 1-4. The answer further stated that on April 4, 1877, said E. L. Gale and wife by deed conveyed to said natural persons, defendants, an additional one undivided 1-8 part of said 1,000 acres, thus vesting in them five undivided eighths in the said thousand acres; that these natural persons used the name "Wood County Petroleum Company" for convenience in the business connected with the interest in said lands; and that Thompson Leach was their agent and manager; that large quantities of valuable oil had been for years, and was then being produced from their 1,000 acres by their tenants under leases which ran for twenty years, and of this 100 acres had been and was leased and worked by the Oil Run Petroleum Company; that the income and profits of the defendants from this 1,000 acres of land would be greatly increased by a speedy, careful, and rightful transportation of their royalty oil to market, upon reasonable and lawful terms, and at reasonable and lawful rates.

The answer denied that the plaintiff had furnished or did then permit transportation from every well or set of wells on said tract of 1,000 acres of land, for the oil produced therefrom; denied that the plaintiff furnished careful, fair and rightful transportation upon reasonable and lawful terms to the defendants at reasonable and lawful rates for the royalty accruing to them from the production of said tract of land; on the contrary, answers affirmed that plaintiff refused to receive royalty oil of the tenants on said tract of land, and to obligate itself to deliver oil of like or equal gravity and value therefor, but it had established an arbitrary system of so-called grades of oil to be delivered by it whereby within the same grade were comprehended oils of different values and gravities, whereby shippers were compelled to suffer loss; and defendants had by these and other specified conduct of plaintiff suffered great loss; and especially when plaintiff as a common carrier of oil had exacted of defendants toll in excess of what was authorized by the statute law, and that plaintiff also deducted more for evaporation than was allowed by statute; that because of these just complaints the defendants determined to forward their own royalty oil to market by some other route, and to this end to provide for its transportation from said tract of 1,000 acres to Petroleum Station, on the B. & O. railroad, a distance of less than three miles, which they could do at much less cost, and without these annoyances and exactions, and that thereupon the said Wood County Petroleum Company, before the granting of the injunction, purchased from the Ohio River Pipeline Company a lot of pipe or tubing sufficient to lay or construct a line from their tanks on the tract of 1,000 acres to the boundary of the tract, and they had about completed laying the same when the injunction was awarded; that it was not their purpose to construct this line beyond the boundaries of the 1,000 acre tract, but to connect it with the line of tubing, extending to said Petroleum Station; but they had no contract with the Ohio River Pipeline Company on the subject, nor did said company take any part in laying said tubing on said 1,000 acres, nor had it any interest therein; that it was not necessary or proper to ask the consent or permission of the plaintiff to lay or construct said line of tubing on the 1,000 acres, because this was the land of defendant, and they, not being a corporation, no condemnation proceedings were necessary or proper; that this tubing laid, and intended to be laid by the defendants did not in any way interrupt or obstruct any tubing lines of the plaintiff, or the operation of the same. The defendants claimed that the plaintiff had not by its charter or deed filed with the bill, any vested right or privilege that was being, or would be interferred with by the laying or construction of the line of pipes or tubing by the defendants; they denied that these deeds to the plaintiff were binding on them, because they were without valuable consideration, because they did not describe any land through which the right of way mentioned was pretended to be granted; and because they were otherwise too vague and uncertain; that these pretended exclusive grants were inconsistent with the retention of the fee simple; they denied that they had any notice of said pretended grants of rights of way; and averred that the recording of the grants was no notice to defendants There was a general replication to this answer. The Ohio River Pipeline Company also filed its anwer, admitting its organization as a corporation, alleged that it sold to the persons composing the Wood County Petroleum Company 2,000 feet of tubing, which the said company laid on their own land, being a part of the Gale tract; but that the Ohio River Pipeline Company had, when this injunction was awarded, no interest in this piping, nor had it any interest when the answer was filed; and that it did not in any way aid in laying the pipe.

Depositions were taken by both parties. The plaintiff proved that the consideration which it gave for the exclusive right of way through the Gale tract, was an undertaking on its part to furnish all necessary and proper facilities for transporting by pipelines, all the oil produced on that tract to Petroleum; and that this it had done. Mr. Gale stated in his deposition that he had been unable to develop the tract because of a want of transportation facilities, and he could get no one to advance money to build pipelines until production of oil on this tract was first assured; that he offered, if the plaintiff would undertake to build pipelines on this tract, to give it an exclusive right of way which would guarantee to it transportation through the pipelines then laid; that the plaintiff on this assurance and guarantee built the pipelines on the Gale tract, connecting it with Petroleum; that without this exclusive grant the plaintiff never would have built the pipelines; that it had occupied and used these lines for 14 years; and that no one else had claimed a right to lay other pipelines during that period. On the back of the receipts given for oil transported in these pipelines were many minute conditions as to terms under which the transportation was made by the plaintiff and which were complained of as unjust. The plaintiffs evidence proved that the Ohio River Pipeline Company had laid some pipelines on the Gale tract. The defendants constituting the Wood County Petroleum Company proved that they had laid down pipelines on their 1,000 acres of land; that it was of advantage to them to have their separate pipelines under their own control, so as to avoid mixing oils of different grades; that this piping on this 1,000 acres was laid by persons constituting the

Wood County Petroleum Company, and not by the Ohio River Pipeline Company; that it did connect with the pipeline of the Ohio River Pipeline Company; that plaintiff's company refused to transport cold test oil through its tubing, with a guaranty by it that it would deliver oil of the same cold test quality to the consignee; that the classification of oil by the plaintiff mixed oils of different degrees of gravity, and of different market value into one so called grade; and this was to the loss of the producers of oil; if for instance the producer ships oil of 31 gravity, he is compelled to accept a shipping receipt of 6 grade oil, which includes all oil between 31 and 33 gravity, and which may be satisfied by the company's delivering 33 gravity which was worth at least one dollar per barrel less than 31 gravity; that the line of tubing of the Wood County Petroleum Company was connected with the line of tubing of the Ohio River Pipeline Company, just on the edge of the 1,000 acre tract, a part of the Gale tract, owned by the Wood County Petroleum Company. On final hearing, November 13, 1882, the Circuit Court of Ritchie County entered a decree dissolving the injunction awarded the plaintiff and dismissing the bill. From this decree the West Virginia Transportation Company appealed to the Supreme Court, and that court affirmed the decree of the Circuit Court.

Upon the question of the construction of the Gale grants to the West Virginia Transportation Company, the court cited:

Western Union Telegraph Co. v. *Chicago & Paducah R. R. Co.*, 86 Ill. 246; 29 Am. Rep. 28.

Western Union Telegraph Co. v. *American Union Telegraph Co.*, 65 Ga. 160; 38 Am. Rep. 781.

REMEDIES.

Sec. 5.—Where a landowner has granted to an individual or corporation the exclusive right to construct and operate pipelines in, upon or across a tract of land, another corporation having the right of eminent domain may condemn a right of way over the same land, notwithstanding the exclusive grant by the landowner; and the grantee claiming such exclusive right is not entitled to compensation in such condemnation proceedings, for the invasion of his exclusive right.

Calor Oil & Gas Co. v. *Franzell; Kentucky Heating Co.* v. *Calor Oil & Gas Co.*, 128 Ky. 715; 109 S. W. 328; 33 Ky. L. Rep. 98.

Brookshire Oil Co. v. *Casmalia Ranch Oil & Development Co.*, 156 Cal. 211; 103 Pac. 927.

Sec. 6.—Where a landowner has made an oil and gas lease or other contract with a lessee or grantee, purporting to grant the exclusive right to construct and operate pipelines for the transportation of oil and gas in, upon and over a tract of land, a subsequent purchaser of such tract may grant rights of way for the construction and operation of pipelines for such purpose to others, or may construct and operate such pipelines for himself; and a court of equity will not, at the instance of the original grantee, enjoin the construction and operation of such lines under such subsequent grant, or by such purchaser.

West Virginia Transportation Co. v. *Ohio River Pipeline Co.*, 22 W. Va. 600; 46 Am. St. 527.   .

CHAPTER 47.

RESERVATION IN DEED OF ALL MINERALS INCLUDES PETRO- LEUM OIL AND NATURAL GAS.

Sec. 1.—A clause in a deed reserving to the grantor all minerals in and under the lands conveyed, not limited or qualified as to intention by any other clause of the deed, embraces and saves to the grantor petroleum oil and natural gas.

Porter v. *Mack Manufacturing Co.*, 65 W. Va. 636; 64 S. E. 853.
Sult v. *Hochstetter Oil Co.*, 63 W. Va. 317; 61 S. E. 307.
Murray v. *Allred,* 100 Tenn 100; 66 Am. St. Rep. 740.
Williams v. *South Penn Oil Co.*, 52 W. Va. 181; 43 S. E. 214; 60 L. R. A. 795.
Contra, See Chapter 48.

Sec. 2.—In *Sult* v. *Hochstetter Oil Co.*, 63 W. Va. 317; 61 S. E. 307, analyzed under Chapter 27, syl. 4 is as follows:

"4. A clause in a deed reserving to the grantor 'the right to all minerals in and under' a certain portion of the land conveyed, not limited or qualified as to intention by any other clause of the deed, or by any facts within the knowledge of the parties which may properly be deemed to have influenced them, embraces and saves to the grantor not only solid minerals such as gold, silver, iron and coal, but petroleum oil and natural gas as well.''

The court cited:

Murray v. *Allred,* 100 Tenn. 100; 66 Am. St. Rep. 740.

Sec. 3.—In *Murray* v. *Allred,* 100 Tenn 100; 66 Am. St. Rep. 740, (September, 1887) the syllabus is as follows:

''A conveyance reserving to the grantor all mines, minerals, and metals in and under the land, does not pass to the grantee any natural gas, or coal, or petroleum oils constituting a part of such land.

Petroleum, or coal oil, is a mineral, and hence does not pass to the grantee under a deed reserving all mines, metals and minerals.

Natural gas is a mineral, and, therefore, does not pass by a conveyance of land reserving all mines and minerals.

The possession of the surface of the soil by the owner for the purpose of tillage, does not give him any possession of gas or other minerals beneath the surface.

Prescriptive title to coal oil and other minerals beneath the surface of the earth is not acquired by the occupation of the land for tillage under a claim of title.''

William T. Murray filed a bill against James A. Allred. The cause was submitted to the chancery court of Jamestown, for a decision, upon the following facts: (1) That John B. Rodgers on October 24, 1853, conveyed to Mathias Wright, a tract of land in Fentress County, Tennessee, in which deed Rodgers reserved to himself all mines, minerals and metals in and under said land. Wright conveyed said land by general warranty deed without any reservation of the mines, minerals and metals, and whatever title said deed communicated under the facts agreed upon, passed to the defendant James A. Allred, to the portion claimed by him, by regular chain of conveyances from Rodgers through Wright and others, which purported to convey an estate in fee ex-

cept the deed from Rodgers to Wright, which reserved the mineral
interests, as above stated; Allred and those through whom he
claimed, had been in actual, open and notorious possession of the
land under color of title for more than seven years, claiming
adversely to the world to the extent of their title papers, which
definitely identified the land intended to be conveyed, but had not
been operating or intending to operate, in any mining business
on said land since the date of the deed from John B. Rodgers to
Wright; neither had any of his vendors attempted to mine on
said land, or drill for petroleum oil or natural gas; there was
no mineral in, under, or on said land, unless petroleum oil or natural gas should be held to be such; that petroleum oil had been
discovered in White County, Tennessee, and in Wayne County,
Kentucky, or Scott County, Tennessee, at which was known as
the Martin Beaty well, prior to the deed from John B. Rodgers
to Mathias Wright, above referred to; And there were petroleum
oil springs in the vicinity of this land which had been discovered
at the date of the deed from Rodgers to Wright.

(2) That John B. Rodgers during his life and his heirs after
his death had claimed said mines, minerals and metals, including
petroleum oil and natural gas, until the same passed out of them,
and passed into William T. Murray, by judicial sale, who then
owned whatever title they owned in the land before the sale.

(3) That William T. Murray by his agent, went upon said
portion of the land last mentioned in said Rodgers deed, claimed
by Allred, and proposed to drill for petroleum oil and natural
gas, and was refused the right to do so by Allred, who conveyed
the same to one Louis Choate, and warranted the title, the said
Allred contending that complainant had no interest in the land; 1,
Because the words "mines, minerals, and metals," did not include
petroleum oil and natural gas; 2.—If they did, the title of said
mines, minerals and metals, had long since been barred by the adverse holding under said deeds.

(4) Complainant Murray contended that petroleum oil and
natural gas were included in the words "mines, minerals, and
metals" and especially so as there was nothing for the reservation to operate upon, and that the possession of Allred and those
through whom he claimed, did not extinguish the title to these
mines, minerals and metals; 1. Because the facts stated and relied upon to effect the bar of the Statute of seven years were not
sufficient to establish the character of adverse holding that would

effect a bar of his rights or perfect the title of defendant; 2. Because their possession was consistent with the complainant's title; 3. The said Murray contended that no cause of action would accrue in such case until the adverse holder invaded mineral rights and, that the cultivation of the soil was not such invasion, and therefore no statute of limitations ran as to said reservation.

Upon this state of facts the chancellor decreed that the words, "mines, minerals and metals," did not include oil and gas; and that there had been seven years adverse holding under the deeds purporting to convey an estate in fee, and this vested the defendant with a perfect title in fee, including the title to oil and gas; and that the adverse holding of James A. Allred and those under whom he claimed, had extinguished the title of John B. Rodgers, claiming under the adverse reservation as to the mines, minerals and metals. He thereupon dismissed complainant's case and rendered judgment against him, and plaintiff appealed to the Court of Chancery Appeals, and the decree of the Chancery Court was reversed; The court of Chancery Appeals held, in an elaborate opinion, that petroleum oil and natural gas were minerals, and were included in the reservation made by John B. Rodgers, and embraced within the terms "mines, minerals and metals", citing:

> *Williamson* v. *Jones*, 39 W. Va. 231.
> *Funk* v. *Halderman*, 53 Pa. 229-249.
> *Westmoreland etc. Gas Co.* v. *DeWitt*, 130 Pa. 235.
> *Brown* v. *Vandergrift*, 80 Pa. 147-8.
> *Dunham* v. *Kirkpatrick*, 101 Pa. 36; 47 Am. Rep. 696.
> *Gill* v. *Weston*, 110 Pa. 313.
> *Caldwell* v. *Fulton*, 31 Pa. 475; 72 Am. Dec. 760.
> *Chartiers Block Coal Co.* v. *Mellon*, 152 Pa. 286; 34 Am. St. Rep. 645.
> *Lillibridge* v. *Lackawanna Coal Co.* 143 Pa. 293; 24 Am. St. Rep. 544.

From the decree of the Court of Chancery Appeals the defendant appealed to the Supreme Court, and that court affirmed the decree of the Court of Chancery Appeals for the complainant, and reversed the decree of the chancellor, rendered in favor of the defendant.

Sec. 4.—In *Williams* v. *South Penn Oil Company*, 52 W. Va.

181; 43 S. E. 214; 60 L. R. A. 795, (Dec. 6, 1902) the syllabus is as follows:

"1. The word 'surface' when specifically used as a subject of conveyance, has a definite and certain meaning, and means only that portion of the land which is or may be used for agricultural purposes.

2. M. and D. jointly owned in fee simple a tract of 180 acres of land. M. conveyed to W. 'all the coal in, on, or underlying the undivided one-half' of the tract, and granted to W. the right to make and maintain on said tract of land such openings as might be necessary for ventilation, for drainage, and for taking out all of the coal without any liability for injury to the surface of said land, or anything thereon, by reason of mining of said coal, and the right to remove same, with right of way etc. D. conveyed to W. his undivided one-half of the tract in fee. W. conveyed to M. 'all the surface of the one hundred and eighty acres undivided, that was so conveyed to him by said D.' retaining the right to make and maintain on said tract of land such openings as might be necessary for ventilation, for drainage, and for the taking out of all the coal without any liability for injury to the surface of the land or anything thereon by reason of the mining of said coal and the right to remove same, and rights of way, etc. *Held;* the said last conveyance from W. to M. was an express grant of the surface only and severed it from all underlying strata.

3. The coal and gas in and under the said tract of 180 acres of land is the joint property of W. and M. or their heirs, assigns or grantees.

4. It is the safest and best mode of construction to give words free from ambiguity their plain and ordinary meaning."

John J. Williams and William T. Williams brought a suit in chancery in the Circuit Court of Harrison County, West Virginia, against the South Penn Oil Company, and others, claiming to be the sole owners of the 1-8 royalty of oil and gas in a tract of 180 acres of land assigned to Deison and Monroe in fee in the partition of a tract of 397 acres of land in Harrison County. On August 20, 1891 the said Monroe conveyed with general warranty to Benjamin Wilson "all the coal in, on, or underlying the undivided one half" of the 180-acre tract and granted also to said Wilson the right to make and maintain on the tract of land such openings as might be necessary in the mining of coal, together with rights of way for that purpose. On September 11, 1891,

Deison, the owner of the other undivided half interest, conveyed to the said Benjamin Wilson his undivided one-half in fee of said tract of land. On September 28, 1891, Benjamin Wilson conveyed to Monroe the surface of the tract, undivided, reserving the right to make and maintain on said tract of land such openings as might be necessary for ventilation, drainage, and for other coal mining purposes. On April 7, 1893, Monroe conveyed the 180 acres of land to John J. Williams an undivided 2-3 interest, and to William T. Williams an undivided 1-3 interest, excepting and reserving the coal in and under the same. On June 12, 1899, Benjamin Wilson and others leased to the South Penn Oil Company, for oil and gas purposes, four several tracts of land, containing in the aggregate about 500 acres, including the tract of about 180 acres, the lease containing the clauses found in the usual oil and gas lease. On June 21, 1899, John J. Williams and W. T. Williams leased for the same purpose to the South Penn Oil Company said tract of 180 acres of land, the lessee to deliver to the credit of the first parties the equal 1-8 part of all the oil produced and saved from the leased premises. In the lease made by Wilson and others the South Penn Oil Company as a royalty was to deliver to the credit of the lessors the 1-8 part of the oil produced; both leases contained a clause for the payment of $200.00 per annum for each gas well, the gas from which should be marketed and used off the premises. The defendant South Penn Oil Company answered denying the allegations of the bill, and denying that it entered upon the said tract of land exclusively under the lease made by the plaintiffs; affirming that it entered under said lease and also under the Wilson lease; denying that it had covenanted in its lease to deliver the 1-8 royalty to the plaintiffs; alleging that it did not pretend to decide and say that plaintiffs might not be entitled to some part of the oil, but if plaintiffs had title to some part thereof, such part was less than the part or amount claimed by them in their bill; asking that plaintiffs be required to show to the court what interest they had in the royalty, as well as their proportionate share of $200.00 per year for gas wells. The defendant, Benjamin Wilson, filed his separate answer to the bill, claiming to be entitled, with his co-lessors, to one-half the royalty, and one-half the price of gas produced from said 180 acres of land, and denied that he had conveyed to Monroe anything more than the surface of the one equal undivided moiety of the tract.

On February 7, 1901, the Circuit Court of Harrison County entered a decree directing the Eureka Pipeline Company to deliver 1-2 of the royalty oil and 1-2 the gas rental to the plaintiffs. The residue of the royalty of oil and gas was directed to remain in the pipelines until the further order of the court. Subsequently Wilson died and the cause was revived in the name of his heirs at law. On October 2, 1901, a final decree was entered, whereby the 1-2 of the royalty oil and gas rental from the 180-acre tract, was divided among the defendants in proportion to which they were entitled; and the court held that the plaintiffs were not entitled to the relief prayed for, and dismissed their bill. Plaintiffs appealed, and the Court of Appeals affirmed the decree, citing:

Knight v. *Coal & Iron Co.*, 47 Ind. 107; 17 Am. Rep. 692.
R. R. Co. v. *Sanderson*, 109 Pa. 583; 58 Am. Rep. 743.
Swint v. *Oil Co.*, 184 Pa. 202; 38 Atl. 1020.
Chartiers, etc. Coal Co. v. *Mellon*, 152 Pa. 286; 34 Am. St. Rep. 645; 25 Atl. 597.
Lillibridge v. *Lackawanna Coal Co.*, 143 Pa. 293; 24 Am. St. Rep. 544.
Murray v. *Allred*, 100 Tenn, 100; 66 Am. St. Rep. 740.

Sec. 5.—In *Porter* v. *Mack Manufacturing Co.*, 65 W. Va. 636; 64 S. E. 853 (May 4, 1909) the syllabus is as follows:

"1. A deed conveying land reserving to the grantor all the clay, fire clay, and other minerals, severs them in ownership from the land, creates two estates therein. The owner of the surface cannot obstruct the mineral owner from a use of the surface for a tramway or other means of transportation fairly useful and necessary.
2. Injunction lies for one owning minerals in land, with right to use the surface for mining and removing them, to prevent the surface owner from unlawfully resisting and obstructing the mineral owner in the legitimate use of the surface for mining and removing the minerals."

Fred G. Porter instituted a suit in chancery in the Circuit Court of Hancock County against the Mack Manufacturing Company. Porter claimed the fire clay, coal and other minerals in a tract of land, and went upon it with his hands to construct a tramroad on the surface for the purpose of conveying fire clay, and other minerals which he owned, in order to use them in the manufacture of fire brick in his plant upon adjoining land. The Manufacturing Company denied his right to construct the road, and in its answer denied the right of Porter to use the surface for taking away the minerals, and absolutely refused, as owners of the surface, to let Porter build the tramroad. It caused a warrant to be sued out from a Justice to arrest the employes of Porter for criminal trespass. In short, the Manufacturing Company admitted in its answer that it opposed and resisted the right of Porter to go upon the land and construct the tramroad or to use the surface. The suit brought by Porter was for the purpose of enjoining the Manufacturing Company from interfering with his use of the surface for the purpose of making a tramroad, and of mining the fire clay, and to have his right to have the tramway for the conveyance of the clay, declared, and to enjoin the Manufacturing Company from intereference with this right, and from obstructing Porter in its exercise. The Circuit Court entered a decree permitting Porter to construct and operate a single tramway over the surface of the tract, by a certain route, of sufficient width, strength and capacity to remove from the mine fire clay and other minerals, and allowing Porter to open one pit or mine in the surface of the land at a certain point designated for the production of fire clay and other minerals, with the provision in the decree that Porter should so operate the mine and so construct and operate the tramway, with due regard to the rights of the Manufacturing Company in the surface.

It appeared that Desselem and Cooper were owners of the whole body, the corpus, of a tract of land, and by deed they conveyed the tract to Evans, the grantors "reserving to themselves all the clay, fire clay, coal, stone and minerals of whatever kind underlying the above tract of land, with the right to mine and remove the same." By conveyance these mineral rights so reserved, became vested in Fred G. Porter, and the right to the surface became vested by conveyance in the Mack Manufacturing Company. From the decree of the Circuit Court the Manufacturing Company appealed to the Court of Appeals, where the decree was affirmed. In the opinion Judge Brannon, speaking for the court, said:

"If the deed of Desselem and Cooper had not reserved the right to mine and remove the minerals, there would have been an implied right to use the surface in such manner, and with such means, as would be fairly necessary for the enjoyment of their estate in the minerals.''

For the conclusions reached the court cited:

Preston v . *White*, 57 W. Va. 278; 50 S. E. 236.
Marvin v. *Brewster Iron Mining Co.*, 55 N. Y. 538; 14 Am. Rep. 322.
Chartiers Block Coal Co. v. *Mellon*, 152 Pa. 286; 25 Atl. 597.
Fluharty v. *Fleming*, 58 W. Va. 669.
Tuft v. *Copen*, 37 W. Va. 623.

REMEDIES.

Sec. 6.—The vendor of lands reserving from the grant all minerals in and under the lands conveyed, retains title to the petroleum oil and natural gas. Such vendor may lease or convey the minerals so reserved, and such lease or conveyance vests in the grantee or lessee the right to enter upon the premises and mine for, produce and market the oil and gas, subject only to the royalty or gas rental agreed upon.

(See cases cited under Section 1, supra.)

Sec. 7.—The owner of the minerals which have been severed from the surface by grant or reservation in a deed, may enjoin the surface owner from interfering with his right to the legitimate use of the surface for mining and removing such minerals.

Porter v. *Mack Manufacturing Co.*, 65 W. Va. 636; 64 S. E. 853.

CHAPTER 48.

RESERVATION IN A DEED OF ALL MINERALS, OR CONVEYANCE BY DEED OF ALL MINERALS IN LANDS, DOES NOT RESERVE OR CONVEY PETROLEUM OIL OR NATURAL GAS.

Sec. 1.—Whether or not petroleum oil or natural gas is conveyed or reserved by a deed wherein all minerals underlying the tract are either reserved or conveyed, is a question of intention.

Such grant or reservation does not convey or reserve petroleum oil or natural gas, unless the deed on its face expressly shows an intention so to do, or unless such intention is proven by competent evidence.

> *Silver* v. *Bush,* 213 Pa. 195; 62 Atl. 832.
> *Detlor* v. *Holland,* 57 Ohio St. 492; 49 N. E. 690; 40 L. R. A. 266.
> *McKinney's Heirs* v. *Central Ky. Nat. Gas Co.,*
>   *Perry* v. *Same, and Becraft* v. *Same,* —— Ky. ——; 120 S. W. 314.
> *Dunham* v. *Kirkpatrick,* 101 Pa. 36; 47 Am. Rep. 696.
> (Contra, Chapter 47).

Sec. 2.—In *Silver* v. *Bush,* 213 Pa. 195; 62 Atl. 832, (Jan. 2, 1906) the syllabus is as follows:

"The cardinal test of the meaning of any word in any particular case is the intent of the parties using it.

Mineral is not per se a term of art or of trade, but of general language, and presumably is intended in the ordinary popular sense which it bears among English speaking people. It may, in any particular case, have a different meaning, more extensive or more restricted, but such different meaning should clearly appear as intended by the parties.

A deed granted certain 'pieces or parcels of land * * * * * * together with all and singular the improvements, ways, waters, water courses, rights, liberties, privileges, hereditaments and appurtenances whatsoever thereunto belonging, or in any wise appertaining, and the reversion and remainders, rents, issues, and profits thereof; and all the estate, right, title, interest, property, claim and demand whatsoever, to the said parties of the first part,' and the habendum in the deed was 'to have and to hold the said piece or parcel of land except the mineral underlying the same and the right of way to and from said mineral which the first parties reserve.' There was no evidence that the parties intended that the word 'mineral' in the deed should include natural gas. *Held,* that the grantee took the natural gas under the deed.''

Mary Silver and others brought suit against U. G. Bush and the Pittsburg Plate Glass Company, in the Court of Common Pleas of Armstrong County, claiming the right as successors in title to Stephen A. Forester, to take the natural gas from under a tract of land in said County, containing 45 acres conveyed to Ulysses G. Bush by Stephen A. Forester, by deed dated May 8, 1891, which deed contained the following reservation:

"Except the mineral underlying the same, and the right of way to and from said mineral, which the said parties reserve."

The defendants were the grantees in said deed, and those claiming under him, and denied that under the above reservation natural gas was excepted. The plaintiff offered to prove that natural gas was being drilled for in the surrounding territory at and prior to the date of the deed. The Court of Common Pleas directed a non-suit which it subsequently refused to take off. Plaintiffs appealed to the Supreme Court, and that court affirmed the Court of Common Pleas, citing:

Hendler v. *Lehigh Valley Ry. Co.*, 209 Pa. 256.
Dunham v. *Kirkpatrick*, 101 Pa. 36.

Sec. 3.—In *Detlor* v. *Holland*, 57 Ohio St. 492; 49 N. E. 690; 40 L. R. A. 266, analyzed under Chapter 27, syl. 1 is as follows:

"1. A conveyance of a mining right in lands was made as follows: 'Do hereby grant, bargain, sell, and convey to the said Michael L. Deaver, his heirs and assigns, forever, all the coal of every variety, and all the iron ore, fireclay and other valuable minerals in, on, or under the following described premises; * * * * * * together with the right in perpetuity to the said Michael L. Deaver, or his assigns, of mining and removing such coal, ore, or other minerals; and the said Michael L. Deaver, or his assigns, shall also have the right to the use of so much of the surface of the land as may be necessary for pits, shafts, platforms, drains, railroads, switches, sidetracks, etc., to facilitate the mining and removal of such coal, ore, or other minerals, and no more.' *Held,* that such deed did not convey title to the petroleum oil and natural gas in the lands described in the deed."

Sec. 4.—In *McKinney's Heirs* v. *Central Kentucky Natural Gas Co; Perry* v. *Same; and Becraft* v. *Same,* (Ky.) 120 S. W. 314, the syllabus is as follows:

"1. In an action to quiet title to lands, in which plaintiff's grantor had previously granted 'all minerals' therein, the deeds granting the mineral rights construed, in connection with other evidence showing the intentions of the parties thereto, held to show that they did not intend to grant the right to the natural gas under the land.

2. Even though deeds purported to convey 'all minerals' underlying the land, if they in connection with the other evidence showed that the parties did not comtemplate a conveyance of the natural gas thereunder the right to the gas did not pass.''

Three separate actions were instituted in the Circuit Court of Manifee County, Kentucky, by the Central Kentucky Natural Gas Company and others against John McKinney's heirs and others, against F. N. Perry and others, and against Cordelia Becraft and others. The object of the suits was to remove the cloud from and quiet the title to the lands described in the three petitions. The defendants answered and controverted the allegations of the petitions. Judgments were rendered for plaintiffs in each case and defendants below appealed. The questions considered upon the appeals were similar and involved the construction of three conveyances. The first was a deed from James Ballard to Gibbs & Dollins, dated March 25, 1871, in the granting clause of which the following language was used:

"Do grant, bargain, sell and convey unto the parties of the second part, his whole entire, right, title and interest in all minerals such as coal, oil, silver, gold, copper, bismuth, antimony, zinc, or any other minerals of any marketable value contained within the following boundary of land, lying and being in the County of Manifee.''

After describing the land the deed contained the following language:

"With the right to explore, prospect, mine and dig upon any of said land for any of the above minerals, or any other of any marketable value, together with the right of timber, stone, or any other material necessary for improvements for mining, to sink, shaft, open drifts, or do anything else on said land necessary to the development of said minerals.''

That part of the deed for construction in the second style of case from James Hodge and wife to Morrison & D. Bard, dated January, 1877, was the language in the granting clause, as follows:

"All the coal and mineral interests and privileges, together with the right of way to and from all the mines or openings, also the right to open mines for and develop the same with a sufficiency of timber for mining purposes, and the construction of cabins for miners."

After the description of the land in the habendum clause, the following language appeared:

"To have and to hold the said minerals of all kinds in and under the said described tract of land, the right of way to and from any mines that may be open or hereafter opened on the same, and all timber necessary for mining the said minerals."

That part of the deed in the last style of case for construction was as follows:

"Party of the first part hereby sells, grants, and conveys to party of the second part * * * * * the following property [describing it] of which E. C. Strong and F. M. Carter (parties of the second part) is hereby entitled to 1-2 of all the minerals or coal on the above described boundary, with all necessary timber and coal, gratis, and rights of way" etc.

This last deed was made by Hulda Ann Coldiron to Strong and Carter, and was dated December 1874. The grantors in the three conveyances, or their grantees or descendants, after the date of the above conveyance, leased or sold to Central Kentucky Natural Gas Company the exclusive right to the natural gas under said land; and this company drilled wells, found gas, and at the time of the institution of the suits was producing gas and furnishing the same to persons in several cities and towns in Kentucky. The grantees of the mining rights which were conveyed in the deeds above mentioned had been setting up claims to this gas by reason of their conveyance. The only question considered by the court was whether the conveyance included natural gas. The court held that gas was not specifically mentioned in either of the deeds, but in all of them the word "minerals" was used, and the question to be determined by the court was: What was the intention of the parties to the deeds at the times they were made? Did the grantors understand at that time that oil and gas were minerals, and would pass with the other minerals named in the conveyance? and did they intend to convey the gas? In other words, did the minds of the parties to the conveyance meet upon the question? Did the one understand that he was conveying, and the other that he was purchasing, the gas thereunder? If not, the gas did not pass with the conveyance. The court affirmed the decision of the Circuit Court and cited:

> Detlor v. Holland, 57 Ohio St. 492; 49 N. E. 690; 40 L. R. A. 266.
> Dunham & Short v. Kirkpatrick, 101 Pa. 36; 47 Am. Rep. 690.
> Deerlake Co. v. Michigan Land & Iron Co., 89 Mich. 180; 50 N. W. 807.

The Court distinguished:

> Murray v. Allred, 100 Tenn. 100; 43 S. W. 355; 39 L. R. A. 249; 66 Am. St. Rep. 740.
> Gill v. Weston, 110 Pa. 313; 1 Atl. 921.

Sec. 5.—In Dunham v. Kirkpatrick, 101 Pa. 36; 47 Am. Rep. 696 (Oct. 2, 1882) the syllabus is as follows:

"A reservation by the grantors in a deed of 'all minerals' does not include petroleum oil. The grantors may not, therefore, by virtue of such reservation, enter and take petroleum oil. If they do they are liable in trespass."

James Kirkpatrick instituted an action of trespass in the Court of Common Pleas of Warren County against C. Dunham and Alfred Shortt, for damages for entering and boring for petroleum oil and cutting timber upon the plaintiff's premises. The defendants entered a plea of not guilty. The case was submitted to the court for an opinion upon certain facts: The plaintiff was the owner of 110 acres of land in Warren County, Pennsylvania, which land he purchased from E. G. Wood and others by article of agreement in pursuance of which he immediately took possession. On November 8, 1881, A. B. Butterfield and E. L.

Butterfield, in whom the legal title of the original vendors had become vested, conveyed the same land to the plaintiff. In the article of agreement, and in the deed to the plaintiff, was inserted the following clause:

"Excepting and reserving all the timber suitable for sawing; also all minerals; also the right of way to take off such timber and minerals."

About February 1, 1881, defendants entered upon the land and erected a derrick and engine house, and drilled an oil well thereon, from which they had continuously taken oil up to March 28, 1882. Defendants claimed by virtue of a lease for oil purposes from said E. L. Butterfield and A. B. Butterfield, dated December 15, 1880. About the time of the first entry by defendants March 7, 1881—written notice was served upon C. Dunham, one of the defendants, by plaintiff. The value of the oil taken was $757.50 including interest to March 27, 1882.

The Court of Common Pleas held that the words "all minerals" used in the exception and reservation in the plaintiff's deed and agreement, did not, in common and ordinary meaning, include petroleum, and entered judgment on the case stated, in favor of plaintiffs against the defendants who claimed under the oil lease. Defendant took a writ of error to the Supreme Court, and that court affirmed the judgment of the court of Common Pleas.

REMEDIES.

Sec. 6.—Where a vendor conveys lands by deed containing a reservation of all minerals, the grantee takes title to the petroleum oil and natural gas underlying the lands so conveyed, notwithstanding such reservation. Such grantee or his vendee or lessee, may, by suit in equity against either the original vendor, or any vendee, or any person claiming under him, quiet the title to his right to take the petroleum and natural gas from the lands conveyed, provided, the adverse claimant does not prove that it was the intention of the vendor to include in the reservation of "all minerals" petroleum oil and natural gas.

Detlor v. *Holland,* 57 Ohio State, 492; 49 N. E. 690; 40 L. R. A. 266.

McKinney's Heirs v. *Central Ky. Nat. Gas Co., Perry* v. *Same, and Becraft* v. *Same,* (Ky.) 120 S. W. 314.

Sec. 7.—Where a landowner conveys lands by deed containing a reservation such as mentioned in Section 6, supra, and the vendor or anyone claiming under him enters upon and takes the petroleum oil or natural gas from the premises conveyed, such person is liable in damages to the vendee or his successors in title for the value of the oil or gas so taken, provided the original vendor or his successors in title do not prove that it was the intention to include in the reservation of "all minerals" petroleum oil and natural gas.

Silver v. *Bush,* 213 Pa. 195; 62 Atl. 832.
Dunham v. *Kirkpatrick,* 101 Pa. 36; 47 Am. Rep. 696.

CHAPTER 49.

RESERVATION OF OIL AND GAS.

Sec. 1.—Petroleum oil and natural gas are minerals. The owner of lands may by deed reserve the oil and gas or convey the same by deed, and possession of the surface by the grantee or his vendee or by the grantor or his vendee will not be considered such possession of the oil and gas as to bar the owners thereof under such reservation or conveyance by the statute of limitations. Where lands subject to such reservation are assessed to the owner of the surface, in the absence of a statute requiring such reservation to be assessed separately, it will be presumed that the land was assessed and taxed as a whole at the time of the severance and has thereafter been carried upon the books in the same manner, and that the taxes have been paid on the land as a whole, when the contrary does not appear. The owner of oil and gas so reserved may operate upon the premises subject to such reservation and produce and market the oil and gas, or may grant the privilege to others so to do; and such owner or his lessee or assigns may, whether the original deed containing the reservation authorizes such entry to be made or not, enter upon, use and occupy suffi-

cient of the surface as may be necessary in the production and
marketing of oil and gas.

> *Koen* v. *Bartlett*, 41 W. Va. 559; 23 S. E. 664; 56 Am. St. Rep.
>   884; 31 L. R. A. 128.
> *State* v *Low*, 46 W. Va. 451; 33 S. E. 271.
> *Preston* v. *White*, 57 W. Va. 278; 50 S. E. 236.
> *Peterson* v. *Hall*, 57 W. Va. 535; 50 S. E. 603.
> *Wallace* v *Elm Grove Coal Co.*, 58 W. Va. 449; 52 S. E. 485.
> *Ammons* v. *Toothman*, 59 W. Va. 165; 53 S. E. 13.
> *Toothman* v. *Courtney*, 62 W. Va. 167; 58 S. E. 915.
> *Sult* v. *Hochstetter Oil Co.*, 63 W. Va. 317; 61 S. E. 307.
> *Plant* v. *Humphreys*, 66 W. Va. 88; 66 S. E. 94.
> *Garrett* v. *South Penn Oil Co.*, 66 W. Va. 587; 66 S. E. 741.
> *Kiser* v. *McLean*, (W. Va.) 67 S. E. 725.
> *Jackson* v. *Dulaney*, (W. Va.) 67 S. E. 795.
> *Chartiers Block Coal Co.* v. *Mellon*, 152 Pa. 286; 25 Atl. 597;
>   18 L. R. A. 702; 34 Am. St. Rep. 645.
> *Delaware & Hudson Canal Co.* v. *Hughes*, 183 Pa. 66; 63 Am.
>   St. Rep. 743.
> *Lillibridge* v. *Lackawanna Coal Co.*, 143 Pa. 293; 22 Atl. 1035;
>   24 Am. St. Rep. 544.
> *Murray* v. *Allred*, 100 Tenn, 100; 66 Am. St. Rep. 740.
> *Moore* v. *Griffin*, 72 Kan. 164; 83 Pac. 395.
> *Westmoreland Nat. Gas Co.* v. *DeWitt*, 130 Pa. 235; 18 Atl.
>   724; 5 L. R. A. 731.
> *Bee* v. *Barnes*, 149 Fed. 727; 79 C. C. A. 433.
> *Barnes* v. *Bee*, 138 Fed. 476.

Sec. 2.—In *Koen* v. *Bartlett*, 41 W. Va. 559; 23 S. E. 664; 56
Am. St. Rep. 884; 31 L. R. A. 128, analyzed under Chapter 35,
syl. 1 is as follows:

"An owner in fee simple makes an oil and gas lease for a term
of five years, and as much longer as the premises are operated
for oil and gas, or the rent for failure to commence operating is
paid, for, among other things, one-eighth part of all oil produced
and saved, to be delivered in the pipelines to the credit of the lessor.
The lessor then sells and conveys one undivided moiety of the 1-16
part of all the oil produced and saved. Afterwards, but before
any oil is bored for or produced, the lessor sells, grants, and conveys the land in fee simple to his six children, to each one a part,
by metes and bounds, in consideration of natural love and affec-

tion, by deed of general warranty 'except that the party of the second part takes the same subject to any lease for oil or gas made by the party of the first part, or any sale of royalty for oil or gas made by him;' and, by the same deed he retains full control of said land, in all respects, and for all purposes, during his lifetime. Soon thereafter oil wells are bored, and oil produced, saved, and put in the pipelines in large quantities. *Held,* the 1-8 royalty goes of right to the tenant for life and his grantees, during the continuance of the estate for life, and not to the owners in fee of the estate expectant thereon.''

Sec. 3.—In *State* v. *Low,* 46 W. Va. 451; 33 S. E. 271, (April 15, 1899) the syllabus is as follows:

''1.   The object of the State is to collect from everyone who claims title to land the taxes thereon at a fair cash valuation.''

2.   Where there is privity of title, one payment of taxes is sufficient and full satisfaction, whether the land is charged as a whole in the name of one, or the various interests separated and charged to the respective owners, dividing the valuation equitably between or among them, as provided in Section 25, Chapter 29, Code.

3.   Where a grantor conveys the gas and oil in a tract of land, and the assessor fails to charge the interest so conveyed on the land book in the name of the grantee for taxation, with its equitable proportion of the valuation of the land of which it is a part, as provided by Section 25, and the land remains charged as a whole to the grantor at the full valuation, and he keeps the taxes paid thereon, there can be no forfeiture of such gas and oil interest for non-entry for five years in the name of the grantee.''

On February 7, 1898, the State of West Virginia filed her bill in the Circuit Court of Doddridge County, for the purpose of selling for the benefit of the school fund various tracts of land, and oil and gas interests in other tracts, alleging that certain of said lands were liable to sale as waste and unappropriated, and others were forfeited for the non-payment of taxes thereon, for the years mentioned, and certain estates or interest in lands in the County of Doddridge had not been charged with taxes thereon upon the land books of the county, for the five consecutive years, of 1892, 1893, 1894, 1895, and 1896, and were therefore forfeited to the State by reason of the owners not having been assessed and charged on the land books of the county with the taxes on the land for the five successive years; and that the State had become the owner thereof, and the lands were liable to sale for the benefit of the school fund, praying that the parties named in the caption be made defendants and required to answer, and that the cause be referred to a commissioner of the court to ascertain and report what of said tracts of land, interests, and estates were liable to sale for the benefit of the school fund, and what were liable to be redeemed, and who might of right, redeem the same. The defendants A. H. Low, S. B. Hughes, L. E. Mallory, C. H. Rathbone, M. C. Trent, John A. Nichol, and others demurred to the bill, and the said six named defendants tendered their joint answer which was filed, and to which plaintiff replied generally. The answer alleged as to their interests in certain oil and gas, conditional grants or options claimed to be forfeited for non-entry for the years alleged; that in the year 1891, respondent, A. H. Low, obtained a number of conditional grants for oil and gas in Doddridge County; that said Low, by assignments, conveyed 3-6 of his interest to and in said grants to respondents, Rathbone, Treat and Mallory, and 2-6 to S. B. Hughes; and that S. B. Hughes assigned his interest to John A. Nichol; that none of said options had been closed or the final amounts paid, except the one tract of 42 acres owned by Dora V. and M. F. Green, November 5, 1892; Peter Ash 111 acres, January 13, 1894; Mildred J. and M. J. Ash, 64 acres, July 12, 1894. That all of said tracts of land on which these conditional grants were given were assessed and valued at the last assessment of real estate in the State as provided by law. That the land was valued, including all the oil and gas and other mineral. That said tracts of land still had the same valuation, and were so charged on the land books of said county in the name of said owners who gave the grant, or their vendees, and were so charged for all of said years, 1892 to 1896, inclusive, for which they were claimed to be forfeited, and the taxes thereon fully paid. That the assessor of Doddridge County never assessed said gas and oil interests on any of their tracts, separately, to respondents, except the three tracts mentioned, on which the options were closed, and that respondents were informed that they had no right or power to have the same done, and could not do so if they desired; and that the apportionment between the owner of the land surface and the owner of the oil and gas could be done only by the assessor. Defendants further alleged that the owners of the said tracts of land who gave the conditional grants thereon, and each of them, and their vendees, had paid all the taxes thereon for the years 1892 to 1896, inclusive, including the whole value of the land, surface, mineral, coal, oil, gas, timber, etc.; that the State had received all her taxes on said land, and each tract thereof for the full value, including oil and gas interests, from the owners of the land, and even if these conditional grants were taxable—which they denied—there was and could have been no forfeiture as long as the taxes had been paid, either by the owners or the owners of the conditional grant; that the conditional grants were not taxable, or the subjects of taxation, and they denied the forfeiture, or that they had been off the land books for said years; that it was true they had not been on the land books in the names of respondents for said years, but they were on the books in the names of the owners of the land, and the taxes paid on each and every parcel and tract of land, and the oil and gas thereon; that said oil and gas conditional grants or options, were not real estate until closed, and could not be the subjects of taxation until closed, and none of those which had been closed were subjects of taxation under the laws; that the interests claimed and owned by respondents on all except those which had been closed were held under agreements, all of which were similar and all identical in form with the one made by James M. and W. F. Squires on 80 acres of land, which was in words and figures as follows:

"In consideration of the sum of eight ($8.00) Dollars, the receipt of which is hereby acknowledged, James M. Squires and William F. Squires, of Doddridge County, West Virginia, grantors, have granted and conveyed, and do hereby convey, subject to the following conditions, unto A. H. Low, of Toledo, Ohio, grantee, all the oil and gas in and underlying the following described premises, to-wit: * * * * * * This grant is subject nevertheless to any rights now existing to the lessee by virtue of the lease heretofore given on said land, for oil and gas; but if said lease has expired or become void, or shall hereafter expire or become void, or if no such lease ever existed, said grantee shall have and is hereby granted all the rights and privileges of drilling and operating of said land to produce, store and remove, the said oil and gas necessary, and usually granted to the lessee in an oil and gas lease. This grant and conveyance is made on condition that said grantee does, within ninety days after a well shall have been drilled on said land, to the usual depth for oil and gas, and been properly completed, tubed, and tested for oil, pay unto the said grantor the sum of ($800.00) Eight Hundred Dollars. If the said grantee shall (as he may do at his option) omit the said sum of Eight Hundred Dollars, within the time aforesaid, then this grant shall become as absolutely null and void as though it had never been made, and the said grantor shall retain the sum first above mentioned as full liquidated damages. Depositing said sum of $800.00 in a bank at Clarksburg, West Virginia, to the credit of said grantor, shall be equivalent to payment of the same to, and its acceptance by said grantor. It is expressly agreed that if said lease is and remains in force, and the said grantee pays the said $800.00 he shall thereafter be entitled to all the royalty and money arising therefrom, but not before said sum is paid. This grant shall expire ten (10) years from this date, if no well shall have been drilled on said land by that time, unless the said sum of $800.00 shall be paid without the well being drilled. This grant, and the conditions, terms, and provisions thereof, shall apply and extend to the said grantor and grantee, their heirs, executors, administrators and assigns. In witness whereof we have hereunto set our hands and seals this 29th day of April, A. D., 1891.'' (Signed and acknowledged.)

An agreement of facts was entered into, which, so far as affected the questions involved, was as follows: The lands on which the grants were given and claimed to be forfeited were valued at the last valuation as the land had always been assessed for taxation, and was placed on the land books of said county, in the year 1892, at that valuation, and continued on the land books for the subsequent years, including 1896, at the same valuation; the taxes thereon as so assessed had all been paid for said years by the persons owning the land and who had executed the grants, or their vendees; that said grants, or the interests therein, except those which had been closed by the payment of the final amount, had never been placed on the land books in the name of J. H. Low, and his assigns for taxable purposes, and they had paid no taxes on the same for said years, that all the grants were similar in form to the one above.

The case was heard and decided by the Circuit Court on July 26, 1898, and the court held, and decreed, that said oil and gas interests and estate were forfeited to the State and liable to sale for the benefit of the school fund, subject to the conditions and

requirements contained in the grant; and the decree directed that
the commissioner of school lands proceed to sell the same at public auction for cash. The defendants appealed, and the Supreme
Court reversed the decree of the court below, citing:

Bank v. *Stark,* 106 Cal. 202; 39 Pac. 531.
Simpson v. *Edmiston,* 23 W. Va. 678.
Whitman v. *Sayers,* 9 W. Va. 671.
Bradley v. *Ewart,* 18 W. Va. 598.
Sturm v. *Fleming,* 26 W. Va. 54.
Hall v. *Hall,* 27 W. Va. 468.
Lohrs v. *Miller's Lessee,* 12 Gratt. 452.

Sec. 4.—In *Preston* v. *White,* 57 W. Va. 278; 50 S. E. 236,
analyzed under Chapter 27, the syllabus is as follows:

"1.   Petroleum oil and natural gas are minerals, and in their
places are real estate and part of the land.
2.   A deed conveying a tract of land contains the clause; 'But
it is expressly understood and agreed that there is reserved from
and not included in the above sale or conveyance, seven-eighths
of all and any oil and gas that may be on, in or under said land,
with full right and privilege to said Bennett, his heirs and assigns,
to develop and operate the same.' This excepts, and does not pass
to the grantee, the oil and gas in place on the land, and the oil and
gas remain vested in the grantor as an actual vested estate and
property, and are not an incorporeal hereditament in him nor a
mere license to produce oil and gas, and title in the grantor to the
oil and gas is not in abeyance to vest only when the oil and gas
shall be developed and brought to the surface for the grantor. A
subsequent conveyance by such grantor of such oil and gas vests in
the grantees like estate and property in the oil and gas as was
vested in the grantor.
3.   In a deed conveying land, a reservation of the petroleum
oil and natural gas in it, has the same effect as an exception of
the same would have, if such is the plain intent.
4.   Petroleum oil and natural gas may be severed from the
ownership of the surface by grant or exception, and are then a
separate corporeal property from the surface."

The Court cited:

Wilson v. *Youst,* 43 W. Va. 826; 28 S. E. 781.

List v. *Cott*, 4 W. Va. 543.
Lillibrídge v. *Lackawanna Coal Co.*, 143 Pa. 293; 24 Am. St.
    Rep. 544.
Marvin v. *Brewster*, 55 N. Y. 533.
Goldsmith v. *Goldsmith*, 46 W. Va. 426.
Humphrey v. *Foster*, 13 Gratt 653.
Mauzey v. *Mauzey*, 79 Va. 537.
Lindsey v. *Eckles*, 99 Va. 668.
McDougle v. *Musgrave*, 46 W. Va. 509.
Urpman v. *Lowther Oil Co.*, 53 W. Va. 501.
Funk v. *Halderman*, 53 Pa. 229.
Hall v. *Vernon*, 47 W. Va. 295.

Sec. 5.—In *Peterson* v. *Hall*, 57 W. Va. 535; 50 S. E. 603,
(March 28, 1905) syls. 2-3-4 are as follows:

"2. There may be separate, distinct estates in different persons in the surface of land and oil and other minerals in it.

3. When the surface of land is owned by one person, the
oil in place by another, a sale for taxes in the name of the owner
of the surface will pass also the oil owned by the other person,
his estate not being charged on the tax books, under Section 25,
Chapter 31, Code 1899.

4. A lessee under an ordinary oil lease for years has no
vested taxable estate in the oil still in the ground either before
or after he has found paying wells. It is taxable in the name of
the surface owner."

B. Walker Peterson filed a bill in chancery in the Circuit
Court of Wetzel County against Camissee Hall and others, alleging substantially, that the plaintiff made a lease on March 5, 1892,
for oil and gas purposes, of a large tract of land in Wetzel
County, to the South Penn Oil Company, the lease reserving to
Peterson 1-8 royalty in oil; the lease was for five years and as
much longer as oil should be produced in paying quantities; Peterson conveyed 64 acres of the land to Camissee Hall by deed
April 15, 1894; this deed stated that the same was subject to the
lease of Peterson to the South Penn Oil Company, and also expressly excepted from the conveyance 1-2 of Peterson's interest
in that lease, that is 1-2 the oil royalty. This 64-acre tract was
sold for the taxes of 1898, in the year 1899, in the name of Hall,
purchased by R. E. L. Snodgrass, who took a tax deed under his
purchase, and subsequently conveyed the 64 acres to C. R. Snod-

grass. Later, on November 19, 1901, C. R. Snodgrass made a lease of the 64 acres to the South Penn Oil Company, for oil purposes, reserving a royalty, and later conveyed half of his royalty of oil to the company. The South Penn Oil Company drilled wells on other parts of the large tract, and afterwards drilled wells on the 64 acres, which produced oil in paying quantities, and the oil was delivered for conveyance to market to the Eureka Pipe Line Company, a common carrier of oil. The 64 acres was not taxed in 1898 to either Peterson or the Oil Company. The Eureka Pipeline Company withheld the royalty because of a conflicting claim between Peterson and Snodgrass to the royalty. It appeared that the South Penn Company drilled on the 64 acres under the Snodgrass lease, and delivered 1-16 to the Eureka Company to his credit. Owing to the conflicting claims of Peterson and C. R. Snodgrass to the rental or royalty oil produced on the 64 acres, Peterson brought a suit in equity in the Circuit Court of Wetzel County against Camissee Hall, the Pipeline Company, the South Penn Company, R. E. L. Snodgrass, C. R. Snodgrass and others, asking that the South Penn Company be enjoined from further developing or taking oil from the 64 acres unless and until it should recognize the continued validity and operation, as to the 64 acre tract, of the lease of Peterson to the South Penn Oil Company, and until that company should deliver to Peterson his 1-16 share of the oil as it should be produced; that C. R. Snodgrass should be enjoined from laying any claim to the sixteenth of oil already produced or still in the land, or from doing anything to interfere with the development of oil on the land under the Peterson lease to the South Penn Company. The bill prayed that the said two companies account for all the oil already produced on the said land, and for decree against them therefor, either by delivery of the oil in kind, or payment of its value in money; that the lease of C. R. Snodgrass to the South Penn Company be set aside and held for naught, as to the plaintiff's right; and that C. R. Snodgrass be held not entitled to any part of Peterson's sixteenth in the oil produced, or to be produced, from the land, and requiring the South Penn Company to develop the land under the lease made to it by Peterson. The bill stated that the plaintiff did not know the amount of oil produced, and asked for discovery. The contest was, whether Peterson or Snodgrass owned the 1-16 oil royalty. The Circuit

Court dismissed the bill and Peterson appealed. The Supreme
Court affirmed the decree, citing:

Preston v. *White*, 57 W. Va. 278; 50 S. E. 236.
Sanderson v. *Scranton*, 105 Pa. 469.
Urpman v. *Lowther Oil Co.*, 52 W. Va. 501.
State v. *South Penn Oil Co.*, 42 W. Va. 80.
Carter v. *Tyler County*, 45 W. Va. 806.
Thompson's Appeal, 101 Pa. 232.
State v. *Low*, 46 W. Va. 451.

Sec. 6.—In *Wallace* v. *Elm Grove Coal Co.*, 58 W. Va. 449;
52 S. E. 485, (Dec. 5, 1905) syls. 1-2 are as follows.

"1. A conveyance of the underlying coal with the privilege
of its removal from under the land of the grantor affects a severance of the right to the surface from the right to the underlying coal, and makes them distinct, corporeal hereditaments. The
presumption that the party having the possession of the surface
has the possession of the sub soil, also does not exist when these
rights are severed.
2. The owner of the surface when the underlying coal has
been so conveyed, can acquire no title to the coal by his exclusive
and continued possession of the surface, nor does the owner of
the coal lose his right or his possession by any length of non-
user. To lose his right he must be disseized, and there can be
no disseizin by an act which does not actually take the coal out of
his possession."

On the first Monday in August, 1903, James Y. Wallace filed
his bill in equity in the Circuit Court of Ohio County against the
Elm Grove Coal Company, alleging that by various deeds of conveyance, he became the owner of a tract of 165 acres of land,
formerly belonging to Blaney, and John McCoy, and that by
various deeds of conveyance of the underlying coal, the Elm
Grove Coal Company, a corporation, claimed the coal underlying
said lands; that the said coal interest had become forfeited to the
State by reason of non-entry on the land books for the purposes
of taxation; that the title of the grantees to said coal had become vested in the State, by reason of such forfeiture; and that
up to the year 1902, no redemption of the property had been made,
nor was there any release or other disposition of the property, or
any part thereof, made by the State of West Virginia; that the con-

veyance made by John McCoy to John Blaney in the year 1864
and by John Blaney to Samuel Roney, in 1870, created in Roney
a title to the coal, which was adverse to that of Connelly, Ford,
Heiskell and Hanlan; that Blaney and McCoy on June 17, 1859,
conveyed to Joseph Connelly, Joseph Ford, Otho W. Heiskell, and
John Hanlan, all the coal underlying two tracts of land, and by
regular conveyance the title to both tracts became vested in John
Blaney, who conveyed the same to Samuel Roney, on October 4,
1870; that Samuel Roney conveyed the land by deed of trust to I.
F. Jones, Trustee, who by deed dated August 22, 1877, conveyed
the same two tracts, amounting in acreage to 165 acres to the
plaintiff; that after the year 1870 no payment by Roney or his
successors in title of any taxes assessed upon said coal, or which
should have been assessed thereon, could inure to the benefit of
Ford, Connelly, Heiskell and Hanlan, as privies in title to the
said Samuel Roney; that the conveyance of the property by Roney
to Jones, Trustee, in 1870, and the conveyance thereof to plaintiff by said Jones, Trustee, in 1877, were also conveyances adverse
to said Connolly and to his co-vendees; that no payment of taxes
made by Jones or the plaintiff could inure to the benefit of Connelly and his co-vendees or privies in title to the said Jones, or
the plaintiff; that the plaintiff had actual, adverse, exclusive, and
constructive possession of the property under claim of title from
1877, to August, 1903, and had paid the taxes thereon from year
to year for each year after 1877, and that those under whom the
plaintiff claimed had like possession and claim, and had paid
taxes for more than 20 years previous to the conveyance to plaintiff; that since April 9, 1873, no person excepting the plaintiff had
actual continuous possession of the coal property under color or
claim of title for ten years, and no person, except plaintiff and
said Jones, under whom plaintiff claimed, had paid the State
taxes on the property, or any part thereof, for any five years
since the last mentioned date; that by operation of law, and in
pursuance of the constitution of the State, the title to said coal
so forfeited to the State, and not having been redeemed, released,
or otherwise disposed of, had been transferred to and vested in
the plaintiff; that the defendant, at the time the conveyance was
made, to it by the heirs at law of the decedent vendees of the coal,
to-wit, the heirs at law of Connelly, Ford, Heiskell and Hanlan,
who by deed dated February 6, 1902, conveyed said coal and mining privileges to the Elm Grove Coal Company, had then full and

actual, as well as constructive knowledge that the title to the said coal privileges vested in its grantors, had been forfeited and become vested in plaintiff; that the deed to defendant coal company constituted a cloud on plaintiff's title; that defendants took by said deed no estate or interest whatever in any of the coal underlying plaintiff's farm; that said deed so far as it undertook to convey any interest in said coal ought to be set aside and annulled. Defendant Coal Company demurred to the bill, which demurrer was sustained by the Circuit Court, and the plaintiff not desiring to amend his bill, the same was dismissed, and plaintiff appealed. The Court of Appeals affirmed the decree, citing:

1. *Cyc.* 194.
Armstrong v. *Caldwell*, 53 Pa. 284.
Caldwell v. *Copeland*, 37 Pa. 427.
1 A & E. E. L. 875 (2d Ed).
Coal Co. v. *Kelly,*   Va.   ; 24 S. E. 1020.
Preston v. *White*, 57 W. Va. 278; 50 S. E. 236.
Peterson v. *Hall*, 57 W. Va. 535; 50 S. E. 603.
Huss v. *Jacobs*, 210 Pa. 145; 59 Am. St. Rep. 991.
State v. *Low*, 46 W. Va. 451.
Hitchcock v. *Morrison*, 47 W. Va. 206.

Sec. 7.—In *Ammons* v. *Toothman*, 59 W. Va. 165; 53 S. E. 13 (Feb. 27, 1906) the syllabus is as follows:

"A deed conveys oil in land, 'except a well now producing oil.' That well ceasing to produce oil is deepened by lessee to a different sandrock, and produces oil from it. The exceptions excepts from the operation of the deed the oil produced from the lower sandrock."

William R. Schumann and wife owned a tract of land and made a lease of it for the production of oil and gas, which lease came by assignment to the South Penn Oil Company. The lease provided for payment to Schumann of 1-8 of the oil as royalty. Schumann sold half of the eighth of the oil, and died owning the other half of the eighth. Under this lease the South Penn Company drilled two wells on the land, one unproductive, the other productive from what is called the Big Injun sand. The producing well was 1900 feet deep; and was called Number 1. On the death of William Schumann said half of the eighth royalty payable to him under the lease went to three heirs, one of them being Charlotte Toothman. The tract was divided between the three heirs, Charlotte Toothman getting for her share a tract of 57 acres; but the oil was not divided but left in common for the three heirs, they owning the half of one-eighth royalty in common. The producing well was on Charlotte Toothman's separate tract, although the oil therefrom belonged to all three heirs. Charlotte Toothman and her husband made a deed, on December 6, 1897, to Corbly Ammons and Isaac Ammons, conveying the said tract of 57 acres in fee, and also conveying one half of the oil and gas owned by Charlotte Toothman in the entire lands which had been owned by her father and mother, William R. and Minerva Schumann "except the well that is now producing oil on said land." The language of the deed containing this exception was as follows:

"The second party is to have one-half of the oil and gas that may hereafter be produced under the land that belonged to Minerva Schumann and William R. Schumann, and the first party reserves the one-half of said oil and gas. This deed means one-half of the first party interest in said oil and gas, except the well that is now producing oil on said land."

At the time the deed was made well Number 1 was producing oil from the Big Injun sand in paying quantities, but later it ceased to produce in paying quantities, and the lessee the South Penn Company drilled the well from 1,000 to 1,100 feet deeper to a different sand, known as the fifth sand rock, and not known to be an oil producing stratum at the date of the deed, as no wells in that section of the country had then been drilled to that stratum. Oil was found there in paying quantities. The South Penn Company recognized Charlotte Toothman as owning her full share in the oil produced from the lower stratum, and delivered it to her credit to the Eureka Pipeline Company for transportation, and did not recognize Ammons as having any interest in the oil from that well. Isaac Ammons sold his interest to Corbly Ammons who brought suit in equity in the Circuit Court of Monongalia County against Charlotte Toothman and the two companies for a discovery and an accounting for the oil produced from the fifth sand through well Number 1, and for a decree against those liable therefor, and to have a decree declaring him entitled to half the share of oil of Charlotte Toothman, produced or to be produced through the well from the fifth sand, the plaintiff claiming that the deed from Toothman to Ammons reserved only the Toothman share produced from the Big Injun sand, and excepted no oil in the lower sand, and that Ammons was entitled to half of that oil. The court sustained a demurrer to the bill as to the claim of Ammons, and dismissed the bill, and Ammons appealed to the Supreme Court where the decree was affirmed, citing:

Spencer v. *Scurr*, 31 Beavan's Rep. 337.
Couch v. *Puryer*, 1 Rand. 258.

Sec. 8.—In *Toothman* v. *Courtney*, 62 W. Va. 167; 58 S. E. 915 (April 12, 1907) syls. 1-6, inclusive, are as follows:

"1. A deed, granting, by the use of appropriate technical terms, all the oil and gas under a tract of land, together with the exclusive right to enter thereon at all times for the purpose of drilling and operating for oil and gas but limiting the estate to a term of seven years, and as much longer as oil or gas may be found thereon in paying quantities, stipulating for the payment of commutation money for delay in drilling, denominating it rental, and providing for the delivery into pipelines for the grantor of one-eighth of all the oil produced and saved from the premises, and also for payment of the yearly rental for every gas well from which gas is transported and used off the premises, does not pass the title to the oil and gas in place. In legal effect it is a mining lease, and the title to the oil and gas in place remains in the grantor.

2. Technical words in a deed, contract or other instrument, will be limited and controlled in their effect by the intention of the parties, gathered from the instrument, considered as a whole, in the light of the nature of its subject matter, and the purpose for which it was executed.

3. An undivided interest in land, or mineral underlying it, can not properly be entered and taxed on the land books, and deed founded upon a sale of such undivided interests, for nonpayment of taxes, is irregular and will be set aside.

4. Such defect in the assessment, sale and deed is not cured by any provision of Section 25, Chapter 31 of the Code.

5. A bill to set aside a tax deed in such case must tender the purchase money and taxes subsequently paid, as a condition precedent to the setting aside of the deed, or aver the willingness and

readiness of the plaintiff to pay the same. A decree which fails to secure to the purchaser such reimbursement is erroneous.

6. On reversing a decree, for insufficiency of the bill in a cause in which a good case is disclosed by the evidence, this court will remand the cause with leave to the plaintiff to amend his bill.''

Daniel L. Toothman, on August 6, 1889, executed to C. J. Ford an instrument in writing purporting to grant to Ford "all the oil and gas in and under" a tract of land, "to have and to hold for the term of seven years, and as much longer as oil or gas is found in paying quantities thereon." The grant was made upon the following terms:

"1st. Second party agrees to drill a well upon said premises within ten months from this date, or thereafter pay to first party a yearly rental of $144. dollars, for further delay until such well is drilled, such rental when due, shall be deposited in First Nat. Bank of Fairmont, State of West Virginia, should second *part* fail to make each deposit or pay to *first part,* on *there* premises, or at present residence of first party, the said rental, then this instrument shall be null and void, and neither party hereto shall be held to any accrued liability or to any damages, or to any stipulations or conditions herein contained.

2nd. Should oil be found in paying quantities upon the premises second *part* agrees to deliver to first *part* in the pipeline with which he may connect the well or wells, the one-eighth part of all the oil produced and saved from the premises.

3rd. Should gas be found, second *part* agrees to pay to first *part* three hundred dollars yearly, payable quarterly on demand for each and every well from which gas is transported or used off the premises so long as the same is so transported or used.

* * * * * * * * * * * * * * * *

7th. Second *part* may at any time remove all his property and reconvey the premises hereby granted, and thereupon this instrument shall be null and void.''

Ford assigned the interest acquired by this paper, along with others, to the South Penn Oil Company, by instrument entitled "Assignment of Leases" dated April 23, 1891 By a paper called "Deed for Oil Royalty" dated May 1, 1894, Toothman conveyed to Joseph McDermott the 1-16 part of all the oil and gas in and under the tract of land, in consideration of $500.00 paid. There were then twelve producing wells on the land, and the following clause of the deed was said to have been intended to apply to additional wells, if any should be drilled: •

"Party of the second part agrees to pay to first party fifty dollars for each and every well drilled on above premises."

By deed dated April 2, 1897, Toothman conveyed to Luther B. Wilson the tract of land, together with a slight interest in the oil and gas. He retained practically 1-16 interest, half the original royalty provided for, by reservation clause, couched in the following terms:

"Party of the first part reserves all the oil rental, there are twelve wells drilled, and if any wells be drilled after the twelve wells is drilled, the second party is to have the sixty-fourth part of the oil."

For the year 1900, an entry was made on the Land Books charging to Toothman an undivided 1-16 of the oil and gas in the tract of land for taxation. The taxes were extended on the same, and being unpaid, that interest was sold by the Sheriff in January, 1903, as delinquent land, to Nicholas C. Vandervort, who assigned his purchase to Courtney by uniting with the Clerk in the deed made to him. Daniel L. Toothman filed a bill in equity in the Circuit Court of Monongalia County, West Virginia, against David H. Courtney and others to set aside the deed made by the Clerk of the County Court conveying to David H. Courtney the undivided 1-16 of the oil and gas in the land conveyed or leased by Toothman to C. J. Ford. No irregularities in the sale or deed were set up in the bill. There was an allegation of fraud, but no evidence to sustain it. It did not appear that the entire tax on the land in which the oil and gas were, was charged to any person or persons, and paid under other entries in the Land Book, so as to make the charge against Toothman in any sense a double assessment on the interest owned by him. The Circuit Court rendered a decree for the plaintiff, from which decree defendant Courtney appealed. The question before the Court of Appeals was, whether Toothman owned any interest in the land, and if so, whether there was a valid assessment, and third, whether the defect in the assessment, if any, invalidated the sale and deed. The Court of Appeals held, that the assessment was invalid, but reversed the decree because the bill did not tender the tax sale purchase money, and the taxes subsequently paid, and did not aver the plaintiff's readiness and willingness to reimburse the purchaser, and for the reason that the decree did not in any way secure to the defendant his right of reimbursement. The decree was reversed, and the cause remanded with leave to the plaintiff to amend his bill, citing:

> State v. South Penn Oil Co., 42 W. Va. 80.
> Harvey Coal Co. v. Dillon, 59 W. Va. 605; 53 S. E. 928.
> Criswell v. Crumbling, 197 Pa. 408.
> Parish Fork Oil Co. v. Bridgewater Gas Co., 51 W. Va. 583.
> Petroleum Co. v. Coal Co., 89 Tenn 381.
> Conrad v. Moorehead, 89 N. C. 31.
> Munroe v. Armstrong, 96 Pa. 307.
> Huggins v. Daly, 99 Fed. 606; 40 C. C. A. 12.
> Ray v. Gas Co., 138 Pa. 576; 20 Atl. 1065.
> State v. Low, 46 W. Va. 451.
> Biddleman v. Brooks, 28 Cal. 72.

Sec. 9.—In *Sult v. Hochstetter Oil Co.*, 63 W. Va. 317; 61 S. E. 307, analyzed under Chapter 27, syls. 4-5 are as follows:

"4. A clause in a deed reserving to the grantor 'the right to all minerals in and under' a certain portion of the land conveyed, not limited or qualified as to intention by any other clause of the deed, or by any facts within the knowledge of the parties which may properly be deemed to have influenced them, embraces and saves to the grantor not only solid minerals such as gold, silver, iron and coal, but petroleum oil and natural gas as well.

5. Forfeiture of the title to minerals in a tract of land for non-entry on the land books can not be predicated on mere severance in title of the minerals from the surface, and lapse of time, since presumptively the land was taxed as a whole when the severance occurred, and has since been carried on the land books in the same manner, and the taxes paid."

The Court cited:

> Dunham v. Kirkpatrick, 101 Pa. 36.
> Detlor v. Holland, 57 Ohio St. 492.
> Stoughton's Appeal, 88 Pa. 198.
> Funk v. Halderman, 53 Pa. 229.
> Gill v. Weston, 110 Pa. 312.

Blakely v. *Marshall*, 174 Pa. 425.
Marshall v. *Mellon*, 179 Pa. 371.
Wallace v. *Elm Grove Coal Co.*, 58 W. Va. 449.

Sec. 10.—In *Plant* v. *Humphreys*, 66 W. Va. 88; 66 S. E. 94 (Nov. 2, 1909) syls. 8-9 are as follows:

"8.   Possession of the surface of land does not carry with it possession of the coal under that surface, where the estate in the coal has been severed as to title.

9.   For the surface owner to aver properly possession of coal severed in title from the land, he must state that he has had actual, physical possession of the coal, apart from his possession of the surface, as by operating mines."

The coal under the land of William G. Plant was sold by his guardian, Dexter G. Fittro, while Plant was an infant. This sale was made under authority of a decree in a suit which the guardian instituted for authority to sell. Plant was sixteen years of age at the institution of the proceedings. A guardian ad litem was appointed for him—John W. Brown, who answered on behalf of the infant, responding that it would be to the infant's interest to sell the coal and invest the proceeds; Plant, the infant also answered in person to the same effect; Depositions tending to establish the propriety of the sale were taken and read in the cause; the guardian, more than two years after the date of the decree authorizing the sale of the coal, reported to the court that he had sold it to Beeson H. Brown, for $19.00 per acre; the court confirmed the sale and directed a deed to be made by the guardian to the purchaser, who was the brother and business partner of John W. Brown, who had been the guardian ad litem. A deed was made by the guardian the day ensuing the entry of the decree confirming the sale. One day before the confirmation of the sale Beeson H. Brown, the purchaser, John W. Brown, the guardian ad litem, and one Smith, styling themselves as Smith, Brown & Company included the Plant coal in a conveyance of a large territory of coal in the same vicinity made to Pennsylvania parties. This conveyance was made for a gross sum by the partners and another person No other conveyance by Beeson H. Brown of the Plant coal to anyone appeared. It appeared therefore, that at the time of the decree confirming the sale to Beeson H. Brown, his brother, John W. Brown, the guardian ad litem, had an interest in the purchase of the infant's coal. Title to the large territory of coal in which Plant's coal was included, conveyed to the Pennsylvania parties, had subsequently passed by several intermediate conveyances, to the Chieftain Coal Company. This company took title in 1902. Plant reached his majority nearly nine years before that time, married soon after becoming of age, settled on the land overlying the coal which he had owned, and continued to own the land and reside upon it, until 1902. Soon after the coal company became interested in the property, the presence of the surveyors on the land caused Plant to make an inspection of the public records, and thereby found that John W. Brown, his guardian, ad litem, in the suit in which divested him of title to his coal, was interested in the purchase of that coal by Brown's brother. The deed to the Pennsylvania parties by Smith, Brown & Company, and another, disclosing this fact, made before the consummation of the sale of the coal, was recorded a few months after its date. For nine years it had been open to the public. Plant, after ascertaining in 1902, the interests of his guardian ad litem in the purchase of his coal, filed his bill in equity in the Circuit Court of Harrison County, against Enoch Humphreys, and others, seeking to annul the decrees of sale and confirmation, in relation to the coal sold on his behalf, and the deed made by his guardian in pursuance thereof, and praying that his title to the coal be quieted, and for general relief. The plaintiff alleged in substance, that his guardian and the guardian ad litem appointed for him colluded in depriving him of his coal property; that John W. Brown and his partners were receiving $30.00 per acre for the coal, when his guardian ad litem, the same Brown, permitted the court to confirm a sale to Brown's brother at $19.00 per acre; that this fact appeared by the deed made to the Pennsylvania parties, of which he knew nothing until a time shortly prior to the institution of his suit; that he knew nothing of the sale of his coal by the court proceedings, and the deed of Fittro, his guardian, or of the interest of his guardian ad litem in the sale and purchase, until his examination of the records, previous to the institution of his suit; and that he had, until that time, been in total ignorance of the fraud and wrongs in the premises. The plaintiff alleged constructive notice to the purchasers subsequent to the date of Beeson H. Brown's deed from the guardian. The Circuit Court, on demurrers, dismissed Plant's original bill and amended bills, except in so far as a reformation of the deed of the guardian to Beeson H. Brown was justified, because of that deed's variance from the decree authorizing its execution. From the decree of dismissal Plant appealed to the Court of Appeals, and that court affirmed the Circuit Court, citing:

> *Wallace* v. *Elm Grove Coal Co.*, 58 W. Va. 449; 52 S. E. 485.
> *Newman* v. *Newman*, 60 W. Va. 371; 55 S. E. 377; 7 L. R. A. (N. S.) 370.
> *Mullins* v. *Shrewsbury*, 60 W. Va. 694; 55 S. E. 736.

Sec. 11.—In *Garrett* v. *South Penn Oil Co.*, 66 W. Va. 587; 66 S. E. 741 (Dec. 21, 1909) syls. 1-5-6-8-9 are as follows:

"1. A deed granting and conveying to grantee one-sixteenth of the oil and gas in and under a tract of land, contains this further provision: 'This grant is subject, nevertheless, to any rights now existing to the lessee, by virtue of the lease heretofore given on said land for oil and gas; but if said lease has expired, or become void, or shall hereafter expire or become void, or if no such lease ever existed; said grantee shall have and is hereby granted, all the rights and privileges of drilling and operating on said land, to produce, store and remove the said oil and gas necessary and usually granted to the lessee in an oil and gas lease.' Construed, in connection with other provisions, to convey not only a one-sixteenth of all the oil and gas, but, subject to the prior lease referred to, to be a lease of said land to grantee for oil and gas purposes with exclusive rights, reserving the usual royalty, and with covenants and agreements usually contained in an ordinary lease for oil and gas purposes.

5. Taking a new lease for oil and gas by one of two lessees in a prior deed or lease, granting to him without reservation or limitation, the right and the exclusive right to enter and bore for oil and gas, is equivalent to a surrender and abandonment by him of all his rights and interests under the former lease; and his assignment of the new lease will invest in his assignee all his right as lessee under either of said leases, and estop and bar him of all right of action as co-lessee in the first lease against his assignee, or any subsequent assignee of such new lease.

6. In an action of ejectment, in which plaintiff, to show right and title, relies on an oil and gas lease, the surrender and abandonment thereof by him, are available as defenses; and whether there has been such surrender or abandonment, is a question of intention to be determined by the jury from all the acts and conduct of

the parties in relation thereto and which may be shown in evidence to the jury under the plea of not guilty.

8.   The Supreme Court will take judicial notice of the fact that mining for oil and gas is a hazardous and dangerous business, involving great risk and requiring large expenditures of money, and that by the usual terms of such a lease the lessor reserves but one-eighth of the oil as a royalty, the other seven-eighths going to the operator.

9.   There is a distinction between 'abandonment' and 'forfeiture' as applied to oil and gas leases; abandonment resting on the intention of the lessee to relinquish the premises, which is a question of fact for the jury, while forfeiture is based on an enforced relief.''

James M. Garrett and others brought an action of ejectment in the Circuit Court of Harrison County, against the South Penn Oil Company. The declaration was in four joint counts. In the first, plaintiff sought recovery of a fee simple estate; in the second of a term of five years, and as much longer thereafter as oil or gas was produced in paying quantities; in the third, of a term of ten years; and in the fourth, of a term of ———— years from the first day of January, 1900, and not yet ended, in and to the fifteen-sixteenths of all oil and gas in and under a tract of 39.38 acres, in the declaration mentioned, with right to go upon said land for the purpose of operating for, producing, storing, and removing the oil and gas. Issue was joined on the plea of not guilty by defendants, and a trial was had thereon before the court and jury, resulting in a verdict and judgment for defendant. After introducing prior deeds, and the stipulation of counsel as to the common source of titles, plaintiffs, to show right and title to operate for oil and gas, and also fee simple title to one-sixteenth of the oil, offered in evidence a contract or deed, from Harrison Nutter, and Cordelia, his wife, dated January 12, 1899, whereby, in consideration of $25.00, acknowledged, the grantors thereby conveyed to the plaintiffs, subject to the conditions therein, one-sixteenth of the oil and gas in and under the premises described in the declaration and containing the provision:

''This grant is subject, nevertheless, to any rights now existing to the lessee, by virtue of the lease heretofore given on said land for oil and gas; but if said lease has expired or become void, or shall hereafter expire or become void, or if no such lease ever existed; said grantee shall have and is hereby granted, all the rights and privileges of drilling and operating on said land, to produce, store and remove the said oil and gas necessary and usually granted to the lessee in an oil and gas lease."

The introduction of the contract for the purpose proposed by plaintiffs was admitted by the court for the time being, but later, when plaintiffs proposed to prove by a witness, R. A. Garrett, that shortly before the deed and lease to plaintiffs, the grantors therein had leased the same property to him, which latter lease he had surrendered, and that at the date of plaintiff's lease the land described was free of lease, defendant again objecting, the court would not permit plaintiffs to prove this fact by the witness, whereupon the Judge of the Circuit Court sustained the objection, and announced that as he construed the contract it was a grant of one-sixteenth of the oil and one-half of the royalty of the gas, if there then existed a valid and subsisting lease on the land for oil and gas; but should such valid and subsisting lease be subsequently relinquished, or expire by limitation, the plaintiffs would then have the right under their contract to go upon the land and take out their one-sixteenth, and if in doing so they should take out sixteen-sixteenths, or the whole, their lease, in his judgment, would not give them fifteen-sixteenths. The case was tried upon this theory of the contract, and the parties limited in all their evidence by the court's construction of the contract. From the judgment for defendant plaintiffs brought error to the Court of Appeals, where the judgment of the Court below was reversed, and a new trial awarded.

Upon the question of the distinction between abandonment and forfeiture, the court cited:

Steelsmith v. *Gartlan,* 45 W. Va. 27; 29 S. E. 978; 44 L. R. A. 107.

Lowther Oil Co. v. *Miller-Sibley Oil Co.,* 53 W. Va. 501; 44 S. E. 433; 97 Am. St. Rep. 1027.

Venture Oil Co. v. *Fretts,* 152 Pa. 451; 25 Atl. 732.

Sult v. *Hochstetter Oil Co.,* 63 W. Va. 317; 61 S. E. 307.

Guffey v. *Hukill,* 34 W. Va. 49; 11 S. E. 759; 26 Am. St. Rep. 901.

Sec. 12.—In *Kiser* v. *McLean,* (W. Va.) 67 S. E. 725 (March 22, 1910) the syllabus is as follows:

"1. In a grant of land, an exception of the oil and gas and
) right to go upon the land for the same, is not defeated by covents for quiet possession of the land and freedom from encum-
ınces thereon. Such covenants relate only to the thing con-
red—the land without oil and gas—the land burdened with the
ht to operate thereon for the oil and gas retained.

2. Covenants in a deed that are plainly intended to defend
:t which has been granted, must be construed to be only co-
ensive with the grant.

3. Mere possession of the surface of land as to which the title
the oil and gas in place thereunder has been severed is not
:session of that oil and gas.

4. Oil and gas, severed in title from that of the land under
:ch they lie, are not in the possession of the owner of the sur-
e, unless he takes actual, physical possession of them, as by
lling wells into the same.

5. On a claim of forfeiture for non-entry of oil and gas
ch have been severed in title from that of the land under
ch they lie, it will be presumed that the land was assessed and
ed as a whole at the time of the severance, that it has since
n carried on the land books in the same manner, and that the
es have been paid on the land as a whole, when the contrary
s not appear."

John P. Kiser filed a bill in equity in the Circuit Court of
kson County against James L. McLean, trustee, and others,
emove a cloud from the title of the plaintiff to lands, and also
ause to be cancelled and annulled an oil and gas lease which
ntiff asserted, others without right had placed upon his land.
endants demurred and answered, and the case was submitted
a an agreed statement of facts. Mary A. D. Bruen, trustee,
·eyed the land to the plaintiff in 1882. The beneficaries in the
t for which the trustee acted, joined in the deed, the granting
se whereof contained the following exception:

"Reserving and excepting, however, from the effects and oper-
1 of this conveyance, all the petroleum and natural gas, togeth-
ith the right of way over and across the above described tract
ınd, and whatever else may be necessary to a full and free
yment of this reservation."

At the time of the conveyance there was an outstanding oil
gas lease on the land. Later leases of this oil and gas were
e by the trustee, or her successor in title. All these prior

leases had expired. Then a lease to John H. Riley was made by McLean, trustee, successor to Bruen. It was this lease to Riley that the bill sought to have cancelled as a cloud on plaintiff's title to the land. The gist of plaintiff's case was that the exception of the oil and gas in the deed was of no avail because it was repugnant to the covenants contained in that deed. The clause containing these covenants was as follows:

"The said parties of the first part hereby covenant that the said John P. Kiser shall have quiet possession of said land free from all encumbrances, and further that they, the said parties of the first part, will warrant generally the property hereby conveyed."

Plaintiff contended that the deed vested in him the title to the oil and gas, and therefore, that McLean, Trustee, had no title thereto which he could lease to Riley. The court dismissed plaintiff's bill, and he appealed. The Court of Appeals affirmed the decree, citing:

Preston v. *White,* 57 W. Va. 279; 50 S. E. 236.
Uhl v. *R. R. Co.,* 51 W. Va. 106; 41 S. E. 340.
Plant v. *Humphreys,* 66 W. Va. 88; 66 S. E. 94.
Sult v. *Hochstetter Oil Co.,* 63 W. Va. 317; 61 S. E. 307.

Sec. 13.—In *Jackson* v. *Dulaney,* (W. Va.) 67 S. E. 795 (March 29, 1910) the syllabus is as follows:

"1. The legal effect of a provision in a deed excepting and reserving out of and from the grant at all times thereafter and forever, unto the grantor, his heirs and assigns one-tenth of all the mineral oil that may be obtained by the grantee, his heirs and assigns, from the land granted, to be delivered on the land to the grantor, his heirs and assigns, his or their agent, free of expense, except the furnishing of barrels or other means of transportation, is to except and reserve in such grantor, his heirs and assigns, to be delivered as stipulated, a royalty of one-tenth of all the oil produced, possessing the same quality of estate as royalty reserved in an ordinary lease for oil and gas purposes.
2. If the owner of the land subject to such an exception and reservation, lease the same for oil and gas, reserving a one-eighth

yalty, without stipulating how the one-tenth of all the oil reserved
such prior grant is to be discharged, his lessee will be entitled
deduct the same from the one-eighth royalty oil reserved in the
ise. Affirming prior decisions involved in the same proposi-
n.''

John S. Morton conveyed a tract of 1125 acres of land in
etzel County to Howard Spencer by deed dated November 25,
34, with covenants of general warranty, but which deed con-
ned the following provision:

"Excepting and reserving however, out of and from the pres-
; grant, at all times hereafter forever unto the said John S.
rton, his heirs and assigns, 1-10 part of all the mineral oil
t may be obtained by the said Howard Spencer, his heirs and
igns, from the said hereby granted tract of land, the said tenth
t of all the mineral oil to be delivered on the said tract of
d to the said John S. Morton, his heirs and assigns, or his, or
ir agent, free of expense to the said John S. Morton, his heirs
issigns, the cost of furnishing barrels or other means for trans-
ting the same from said land shall be at the said expense of
said John S. Morton, his heirs and assigns."

On May 8, 1882, Howard Spencer, disregarding said excep-
1 and reservation, conveyed by deed, with covenants of gen-
l warranty one hundred and one acres of said large tract, in-
ling 65 acres, hereafter mentioned, to "Westley" Dulaney;
aney, by deed dated September 22, 1893, conveyed the said
cres by deed with covenants of general warranty to Catherine
kson, who by deed of the same character, on December 29,
3, conveyed the tract to Stephen W. and Francis M. Jackson,
by deed, June 30, 1903, united in a deed to M. R. Dulaney,
reby they granted and conveyed to him 46 acres out of the 65
tract, reserving "all the oil and gas, coal, and all minerals"
might be underlying the same, with the exception of a one
dredth part of the two-thirds of the one-sixteenth of the royal-
f oil or gas, and also reserving the right to lease and operate
oil and gas, and also mining rights for coal and all minerals,
to take all the rentals that might be paid for oil and gas.
March 22, 1900, Catherine Jackson, F. M. and Stephen W.
son, leased to L. G. Robinson, and W. J. Criswell a tract of
acres, covering the 65 acres, upon the usual terms, reserving

one-eighth of the oil as royalty, and $300.00 per year for each
gas well. Afterwards, on April 13, 1900, Catherine Jackson and
Stephen W. and F. M. Jackson attempted to convey to the Linden
Oil Company 15-16 of all the oil and gas underlying three tracts,
including said 65 acre tract, and together, containing 145 acres,
with the right of entry and to drill for oil and gas, but subject
to the lease then on said land. The Criswell Oil Company ac-
quïred title by assignment to the lease of March 22, 1900, and entered thereunder, and drilled and discovered oil in paying quantities on the 65-acre tract. The South Penn Oil Company, by deed
from Wait H. Conaway, on June 11, 1901, acquired right and
title to the oil and gas reserved in the deed from Morton and wife
to Howard Spencer, Conaway having purchased the same from
Morton, who conveyed to him by deed on March 8, 1901. The
latter deed was recorded on March 12, 1901, the former on January 12, 1903, prior to the discovery of oil on the 65-acre tract by
the Criswell Company. The latter company had actual and constructive notice of the rights claimed by the South Penn Company
under the deed, before drilling. Francis Jackson and others, instituted suit in the Circuit Court of Wetzel County, against Moses
R. Dulaney and others for an accounting for themselves, their
assigns and grantees of the 1-8 of all the oil produced, or that
might be produced, from the 65-acre tract. The Circuit Court
by decree adjudgd that 7-8 of the oil, the working interest, produced, or to be produced from the 65-acre tract, belonged to the
Criswell Oil Company; that the South Penn Oil Company was
entitled to 1-10 of all the oil theretofore or that might thereafter
be produced, being a part of the royalty oil excepted and reserved,
and owned by it under the Morton exception and reservation,
which should be delivered to the pipeline to its credit, free of
cost; and that the Linden Oil Company was entitled to 1-10 of
all the oil, being the balance of the royalty oil, to be likewise delivered to the pipeline, to its credit, free of all cost. The plaintiffs appealed to the Court of Appeals. The Appellants contended
that whereas, at the time of their leases to Robinson and Criswell,
under which the Criswell Company entered and produced oil
from the 65-acre tract, they owned at least 9-10 of all the oil in
and under said tract, with the right to operate, lease or sell the
same, and reserved as the only consideration for the lease, one-
eighth of all oil produced; and that the effect of the decree was to
deprive them of the entire and only consideration therefor, to-

rit, the one-eighth royalty reserved, excepting only the 1-40 de-
reed in favor of their grantee, the Linden Oil Company, which
robably rendered them liable to the latter company for the resi-
lue of the 1-16 conveyed by their deed to that company, on April
3, 1900. The Court of Appeals affirmed the decree.

Upon the question of reservation and exception, the court
ited:

>*Knotts v. McGregor*, 47 W. Va. 566; 35 S. E. 899.
>*Preston v. White*, 57 W. Va. 278; 50 S. E. 236.
>*Headley v. Hoopengarner*, 60 W. Va. 626; 55 S. E. 744.
>*Kilcoyne v. Southern Oil Co.*, 61 W. Va. 528; 66 S. E. 888.

Upon the question presented that Morton and his assignee
ıd lost their rights by adverse possession, non-entry and non-
ıyment of taxes, the court cited:

>*State v. Low*, 46 W. Va. 451; 33 S. E. 271.
>*Peterson v. Hall*, 57 W. Va. 535; 50 S. E. 603.
>*Wallace v. Elm Grove Coal Co.*, 58 W. Va. 449; 52 S. E. 485.
>*Higgins v. Coal Co.*, 63 W. Va. 229; 59 S. E. 1064.
>*Kiser v. McLean,*—(W. Va.); 67 S. E. 725.

Sec. 14.—In *Chartiers Block Coal Co. v. Mellon, and Mans-
ld Coal & Coke Co. v. Mellon*, 152 Pa. 286; 25 Atl. 597; 18 L. R.
702; 34 Am. St. Rep. 645 (January 10, 1893) the syllabus is
follows:

"The owner of the surface of land who has granted to another
rson the coal under his land, has a right, apart from any reser-
tion in the deed, to access through the coal to the strata under-
ng it.

While the surface owner has a legal right to reach in some
y the strata underlying the coal, the regulation of such access
olves too many questions affecting the rights of property, and
injury to the underlying strata, to be settled by a court of
ιity. It is a legislative rather than a judicial question.

An estate in coal is determinable upon the removal of the coal,
l when all the coal is removed, the space it occupied reverts to
grantor by operation of law. The grant of an estate in coal
s not carry with it any interest in the strata underlying the
l.

Where the owner of the coal has not sustained any irreparable injury by the sinking of oil or gas wells through the coal by the owner of the surface, a court of equity will not award an injunction to restrain the sinking of wells, especially where the effect of the injunction would be to destroy the estate of the surface owner in the minerals below the coal.''

The Chartiers Block Coal Company and the Mansfield Coal & Coke Company filed bills in equity in the Court of Common Pleas of Allegheny County Pennsylvania, against Mellon. In the Bill of the Chartiers Company it was averred that plaintiff was a corporation owning all the coal under 187 acres of land conveyed to plaintiff in fee simple by R. L. McCully and wife; that prior to the execution of the deed by R. L. McCully, the absolute title to the land, both surface and mineral, was in Samuel McKown; that McKown vested the fee simple title to the coal with mining privilege in one R. L. McCully, without any reservation to the said McKown, his heirs or assigns, of any right, or easement whatsoever in said coal, and said McCully conveyed the coal and mining privileges to the plaintiff without any such reservation; that defendants, claiming to have permission of some sort from McKown, entered upon the surface over the coal aforesaid, and erected a derrick, and, for the purpose of obtaining natural gas or oil, or both, drilled one well through the coal belonging to plaintiff, to the depth of about 1800 feet, and were threatening, and intended to drill other wells on the property for the same purpose, through said coal belonging to plaintiff; that it was impossible for the wells to be drilled in such a manner as to allow the removal of all the coal in the tract, which was the property of the plaintiff, without exposing the mine to leakage from gas from said wells, and rendering the mining operations then conducted, and thereafter to be conducted upon the property, so hazardous to plaintiff's property, and plaintiff's employes, as to very greatly injure and depreciate the value of the coal property, if not wholly to ruin the value of the same; that it would be impossible to prevent the escape of gas from such wells into such coal mines, if said wells were permitted to be bored, and the presence of such gas in the mine, by reason of the volatile, inflammable and explosive character of such gas, whether natural gas, or the gas emanating from oil wells, would occasion explosion and fires, to the great destruction of plaintiff's property, and to the probable death and serious maiming of plaintiff's employes.

Defendants answered, denying plaintiff's right to an injunction. Numerous affidavits were presented, both by plaintiffs and deendants. On July 18, 1891, the court awarded a writ of injuncion against the defendants to restrain them, their employes, and gents, from interfering with the plaintiff in its rights or to any rells other than the one then completed on the premises described 1 the bill.

In the Mansfield Coal & Coke Company case, the facts were imilar, and the defendants were restrained and enjoined from rilling any well or wells upon or into that certain tract of land escribed in the plaintiff's bill, which would pass into or through 1e Pittsburg vein of coal underlying the tract of land; and the urt upon condition that defendant give bond, further refused 1e preliminary injunction prayed for against any well or wells 1 the tract of land, which at the date of the decree had been illed by defendant through said vein of coal. It was further deeed that the plaintiff file bond with two sureties, to be approved r the court, in the sum of $2,000 conditioned to indemnify the fendant, according to law, for damages arising by reason of the eliminary injunction. On October 3, 1891, upon hearing e injunction was modified as to the two wells which had en commenced, and which had not gone through the Pittsburg in of coal, on defendants giving their bond. From these decrees aintiffs appealed to the Supreme Court, where the decrees were irmed, citing:

Pennsylvania Coal Co. v. *Sanderson,* 113 Pa. 126.

Sec. 15.—In *Delaware & Hudson Canal Co.* v. *Hughes,* 183 . 66; 63 Am. St. Rep. 743; (Oct. 25, 1897) the syllabus is as lows:

"If there is no severance of coal from the surface, an entry in the surface will extend downward and draw to it a title to the lerlying minerals, so that he who disseizes another, and acres title by the Statute of Limitations, will succeed to the estate 1im upon whose possession he has entered; but if a severance is de before his entry, and he has notice of that severance, either the record, or by the state of the possession, acquired both by ervation and by years of service in the employment of the 1er, his entry upon either of the estates will not affect the er."

The Delaware & Hudson Canal Company filed its bill in equity against David Hughes and William Watkins, in the Court of Common Pleas of Lackawanna County, Pennsylvania, praying for an injunction to restrain the defendants from mining coal under certain lands claimed by the plaintiff. The facts disclosed that the plaintiff company was engaged in mining and selling anthracite coal; that as early as 1825, it was the owner of a considerable body of contiguous lands which had been purchased by it because of the underlying coal, a part of which land was a tract known as the Porter tract, containing 200 acres; the coal upon this tract was opened by the company some time before 1830 and 1835, and mining operations begun under it; from that time to the time of the suit the company had been in the possession of its mineral deposits under the Porter tract, by actual mining, and by the use of openings and gangways for purposes connected with the removal of coal from adjoining lands belonging to it. The defendant derived his title from one Alexander McDonald, who was an employe of the plaintiff, and who entered upon the surface of the Porter tract in 1836 or 1837, and began a residence upon and the cultivation of a small portion of it. It appeared that the possession of McDonald and his vendees of the land in controversy had been from 1850 down for a period of more than 21 years, open, notorious, hostile, and exclusive as to the surface; and therefore, the defendant had acquired a title to the surface under the Statute of Limitations. The question raised in the suit was, whether, defendant had also under the circumstances acquired title to the underlying coal. .The bill alleged the exclusive right in plaintiffs to the coal in the lands referred to; and that defendant was taking out and shipping the same by carload by rail in such quantities that he would soon exhaust the mines and leave them without fuel for their steel mills, which was the chief inducement to the purchase. The Court of Common Pleas dismissed the plaintiff's bill, and plaintiff appealed to the Supreme Court, and that court reversed the Court of Common Pleas, citing:

Caldwell v. Copeland, 37 Pa. 427.
Armstrong v. Caldwell, 53 Pa. 284.
Kingsley v. Hillside Coal & Iron Co., 140 Pa. 613.
Lewey v. Frick Coal Co., 166 Pa. 536.

Scranton Gas & Water Co. v. *Lackawanna Iron & Coal Co.,*
    167 Pa. 136.
Plummer v. *Hillside Coal & Iron Co.,* 160 Pa. 483.

Sec. 16.—In *Lillibridge* v. *Lackawanna Coal Co.,* 143 Pa. 293;
? Atl. 1035; 24 Am. St. Rep. 544 (Oct. 5, 1891) the syllabus is
; follows:

"1. The surface of land and the minerals beneath it may be
ssevered in title and become separate tenements. In case of
ıch severance, the mineral becomes a separate corporeal hered-
ıment, and its ownership is attended with all the attributes and
cidents peculiar to the ownership of land.

2. An instrument by which the owners of land 'granted, de-
ised, leased, and to farm-let' all the merchantable coal under
eir land, with the exclusive right to mine and remove the same,
ıbendum, 'until the exhaustion thereof, under the terms of this
denture,' effected a severance of title vesting in the 'lessee' an
tate in fee simple in the coal.

3. Upon a bill filed by the grantors to restrain the grantee
ɔm transporting, through an open space 200 feet below the sur-
ce, made by mining out part of the coal conveyed, other coal
ned by the defendant from an adjoining tract, no actual injury
the plaintiff being averred, a demurrer for want of equity was
operly sustained.

4. As it did not appear from the instrument, or even by
erment, that such use of the open space was contrary to the
:ention of the parties in executing the grant, the defendant,
the owner of the sub stratum of coal, owned also the chamber
space enclosing it, and had the legal right while his ownership
ıtinued, to transport other coal through it.

5. There is no substantial difference between a title by ex-
ɔtion out of a grant, and a title by direct grant of the same sub-
:t. Under an exception from a conveyance of land of all the
ıl therein, the dominion of the grantor over the coal is no
ʒater, and his ownership is no more absolute, than if his title
re acquired by purchase from one owning both coal and surface,

On August 22, 1888, G. L. Lillibridge and John N. Lillibridge,
1 Lucilla, his wife, filed a bill in equity in the Court of Common
ʒas of Lackawanna County, Pennsylvania, against the Lacka-
nna Coal Company, alleging that by a written agreement, dated
.rch 24, 1883, the plaintiffs, with Mrs. Almira Lillibridge, de-
ʒed to defendant, all the merchantable coal underlying a tract

of 45 acres, in Lackawanna County, the lessors then being the owners in fee of the coal; that the plaintiffs had since become the sole owners of the land aforesaid, and of the rights appertaining to the lessors under the agreement; that under said lease the defendant had mined out coal from one of the underlying veins, to such an extent that an open way, of great breadth, about 12 feet in height, and about 200 feet beneath the surface of the land, had been made through said vein from the northerly to the southerly side of said tract; that within two years prior to the filing of the bill defendant had become the lessee or owner of about 350 acres of coal adjoining the plaintiff's land on the northerly side thereof, and was mining the last mentioned coal and carrying it through, under and across plaintiff's land by means of said open way, to its improvements for preparing the coal for market, situated upon other property, and not belonging to the plaintiff, thus unlawfully and wrongfully appropriating plaintiff's property for a road to transport said other coal; praying that for want of an adequate remedy at law, and to avoid a multiplicity of suits, an injunction be granted restraining the defendant from transporting said other coal through plaintiff's land by means of said underground way. By the agreement of March 24, 1883, recited in the bill, the plaintiffs and Mrs. Almira Lillibridge, as parties of the first part, "granted, demised, leased, and to mine—let unto the" defendant, "its successors or assigns, all the merchantable coal, together with the sole and exclusive right to mine and remove the same, under the" tract of land described in the bill; "To have and to hold the coal in and under said land unto the said party of the second part, its successors or assigns, until the exhaustion thereof, under the terms of this indenture." The defendant, by the same instrument, covenanted to prosecute energetically the business of mining coal, and to pay to the parties of the second part certain specified royalties by the ton of mined coal, paying for at least 1500 tons of coal each year, "until such time as the coal under said tract shall become so far exhausted that it is impossible to mine so large an amount in any one year." After stipulating further that the party of the second part, defendant, should pay all taxes and imposts upon the coal mined, but that all taxes upon the surface and unmined coal should be paid by the parties of the first part, that, upon failure of the party of the second part to comply with certain covenants contained in the agreement, the arties of the first part, upon written notice, might "declare this ase forfeited," and retake possession, etc; that the parties of the :st part should have the right to direct that a reasonable amount ! coal be left in pillars as support for the surface; and that the arty of the second part should have the right to take, without iyment therefor, such coal as might be necessary for the makg of steam, for the work of mining, ventilation, etc, the amount ι taken to be "proportioned with the other tracts of land from hich coal is taken by means of" defendant's breaker and other iprovements, the agreement provided as follows:

"All and singular the grants, demises, leases and lettings, venants and agreements hereinbefore contained, shall inure to e benefit of, and be binding upon each and every of the heirs, ecutors, administrators, survivors, successors and assigns of ch and every of the parties to this indenture, the same to all tents and purposes as though they were mentioned and included each of every of said grants, demises, leases, lettings, covents and agreements."

The defendants demurred to the bill, and after argument, the urt held, in substance, that the indenture between Mrs. Almira llibridge and the plaintiffs, of the one part, and the defendant, the other part, was in effect, not a lease or license, but a conyance of the coal; that by the sale and conveyance of the coal ə defendant acquired along with it the right to use the chamber space enclosing it, for any purpose it might see fit until the il was exhausted; that there being no averment that the defendt was interfering with the subjacent or superadjacent soil, the nsportation of foreign coal through the way created in taking ι coal under the indenture, was not an unlawful or wrongful appriation of the property of the plaintiffs, but a legitimate use the defendant of its own property. A decree was entered taining the demurrer and dismissing the bill, and plaintiffs ealed. The Supreme Court affirmed the decree, citing:

Caldwell v. *Fulton,* 31 Pa. 475.
Caldwell v. *Copeland,* 37 Pa. 427.
Scranton v. *Phillips,* 94 Pa. 15.
Sanderson v. *Scranton City,* 105 Pa. 469.
Delaware, Etc., R. Co., v. *Sanderson,* 109 Pa. 583.

Sec. 17.—In *Murray* v. *Allred,* 100 Tenn, 100; 66 Am. St. Rep.
740, analyzed under Chapter 47, the syllabus is as follows:

"A conveyance reserving to the grantors all mines, minerals
and metals in and under the land does not pass to the grantee
any natural gas or coal or petroleum oils constituting a part of
such land.

Petroleum, or coal oil, is a mineral, and hence does not pass
to the grantee under a deed reserving all mines, metals and minerals.

Natural gas is a mineral, and therefore, does not pass by a
conveyance of land reserving all mines and minerals.

The possession of the surface of the soil by the owner for
the purpose of tillage, does not give him any possession of gas or
other minerals beneath the surface.

Prescriptive title to coal, oil, and other minerals, beneath the
surface of the earth, is not acquired by the occupation of the
land for tillage under a claim of title."

Sec. 18.—In *Moore* v. *Griffin,* 72 Kan. 164; 83 Pac. 395 (Nov.
11, 1905) the syllabus is as follows:

"1. A deed to real estate contained the following provision: 'Reserving to said parties of the first part all the rights,
privileges and benefits secured ***** under an oil and gas lease
executed by said parties of the first part, the full power and
right to renew or extend, exchange' or modify said lease *****
as fully and to the same extent as though this conveyance had
not been executed. It is intended hereby to reserve all oil and
gas privileges in and to said premises.' This constitutes an exception, and not a reservation. The title to the oil and gas in said
land remained in the grantors.

2. The owners of the land made a lease of the oil and gas
privileges in the lands. Thereafter they convey the lands by warranty deed excepting and reserving all rights and privileges secured to them by the lease, and all oil and gas priviliges in and to
said premises. Their grantee conveys by general warranty to
another without any reservation or exception. Thereafter the
oil and gas lease is cancelled by the consent of the parties to
the lease. All of the conveyances being of record, a subsequent
purchaser of the lands purchased with constructive notice, and
takes no interest in the oil and gas; and the cancellation of the
lease does not extinguish the rights of the original owner, nor
vest the right to the oil and gas in the owner of the lands at the
time of such cancellation."

M. A. Moore brought a suit against Joel Griffin and another,
the District Court of Wilson County, Kansas, to quiet the title
160 acres of land. On September 24, 1894, the defendants
Ɪꞏned the land in fee. On that day they conveyed by general
ꞏrranty deed to Susan L. Gore, who afterward conveyed to an-
ꞏer, and by regular conveyances, the title passed to plaintiff,
A. Moore, on March 5, 1901. The deed made by defendants to
san J. Gore contained an exception or reservation, out of which
ꞏse the sole contention in the case. The deed recited a consider-
on of $6,000, and in the granting clause, following the descrip-
n of the land, was the provision:

"Reserving to said parties of the first part, their heirs and
ꞏigns, all the rights, privileges and benefits secured to parties
the first part under an oil and gas lease, executed by said
ꞏties of the first part, to Guffey & Galey, dated April 9, 1894,
h full power and right to renew or extend, change or modify
d lease with the said Guffy & Galey, or their heirs and assigns,
fully and to the same extent as though this conveyance had not
n executed. It is intended hereby to reserve all oil and gas
vileges in and to said premises, and to lease and transfer the
ıe."

The warranty clause of the deed closed as follows:

"Except as above set forth, and the right at all times to
ꞏr upon said premises to operate for oil and gas."

The oil and gas lease referred to in the deed had been exe-
ꞏd to Guffey & Galey by defendant several months prior to
conveyance to Susan J. Gore, and contained the usual provis-
ꞏ of an oil and gas lease. It was duly recorded in April, 1896,
prior to the purchase of the lands by the plaintiff. In March
ꞏ, defendant Joel Griffin, made an extension and what pur-
ꞏted to be an assignment of his lease, to the Forest Oil Com-
y, and in August, 1897, with the consent of Guffey & Galey,
the Forest Oil Company, the lease was cancelled. These
ꞏsfers and the release were attached to the original lease and
ꞏ recorded. In none of the conveyances subsequent to the
from the Griffins to Mrs. Gore, was any reference made to this

lease, or to any exception or reservation of the oil and gas, and plaintiff claimed that he purchased without actual or constructive notice of either. The case was tried by the District Court, and judgment was rendered in favor of the defendants, from which judgment plaintiff appealed. The Supreme Court affirmed the judgment, citing:

> *Chartiers Block Coal Co.* v. *Mellon,* 152 Pa. 286; 25 Atl. 597; 18 L. R. A. 702; 34 Am. St. Rep. 645.
> *Koen* v. *Bartlett,* 41 W. Va. 559; 23 S. E. 664; 31 L. R. A. 128; 56 Am. St. Rep. 884.

Sec. 19.—In *Barnes* v. *Bee,* 138 Fed. Rep. 476; (C. C. N. D. W. Va.,) (June 13, 1905) the headnotes are as follows:

"1. Two tracts of land containing 69 1-2 and 2 1-2 acres respectively, as to which the owner had sold an undivided sixteenth interest in all oil, gas, and other mineral substances, in and under the same, were assessed as a whole to such owner, at $6.50 per acre, but the valuation was erroneously set down as $425.00, and $15.00 respectively, instead of $451.75, and $16.25; the levies being properly extended on the true valuation. The same mistakes as to the total valuation of the tracts were made from year to year thereafter, until a re-assessment was made, when the officer neglected to extend the levies on the true valuation, but extended them on the erroneous valuation carried over from the book of the preceding year, prior to which the grantee of the mineral interest had conveyed one-half of such interest to B, who was assessed independently on his undivided interest. *Held,* that the intention was to assess the full taxes on the full valuation of the entire property to the original owner, and, she having paid the amount assessed, the assessment against B. was void.

2. Code, W. Va. 1899, c. 29, § 25, provides that, where a tract or lot of land becomes the property of different owners in several parcels, and one person becomes the owner of the surface, and another of the minerals under the same, or of the timber alone on the land, the assessor shall divide the value at which the whole had before been assessed, among the different owners, having regard to the value of each interest, compared with that of the whole, and Code, 1899, c. 29, § 37, and Acts 1905, p. 303, c. 35, § 49, requires that the 'tract' be assessed in the name of the person who by himself or his tenant has the freehold in possession. *Held,*

at where the owner of certain land conveyed merely an undivided
ie-sixteenth part of all oil, gas or other mineral substances in
id under the same, the grantees of such undivided interest did
it hold by a complete and separate title, and hence their interest
as not subject to a separate assessment for taxes, as an un-
vided interest 'in oil, gas, and other mineral substances.'

3.   Where a tax deed was set aside as absolutely void under
sale unauthorized by law, the owner was not required to pay the
x purchaser his outlay under Code 1899, c. 31, § 25 requiring such
iyment as a condition precedent to the vacation of a tax deed
r irregularities in the proceedings.

4.   Where, in a suit to set aside a tax deed, it was determined
at the deed was absolutely void on the ground that the property
is not subject to the assessment in question, the assessment hav-
g been made by the negligence of the State's officers, costs would
t be allowed to either party.''

• John H. Kelly and Clara V. Kelly, on March 29, 1898, con-
iyed to plaintiff by deed one-sixteenth part of all oil and gas,
id other mineral substances, in and under two parcels of land
tuate in Ritchie County, for the consideration of $2,000 cash.
y deed September, 21, 1898, the plaintiff Barnes conveyed half
this, or one-thirty-second interest to Mallory Brothers, and
ey subsequently, by deed March 29, 1903, re-conveyed this in-
rest to Barnes. The surface and the remaining fifteen-sixteenths
idivided interest of the oil, gas, and other mineral substances,
mained vested in Mrs. Kelly. On the land books of Ritchie
>unty, Mrs. Kelly, for the year 1898, was assessed with these
·o tracts, consisting of 69 1-2 and 2 1-2 acres, separately in fee,
lued each at $6.50 per acre, and a total valuation of $425.00 for
e 69 1-2 acres, instead of $451.75, the true valuation, and for
⁹ 2 1-2 acre tract, $15.00 instead of $16.25, the true valuation.
ese tracts had been acquired by Mrs. Kelly by different deeds
·m different parties. For the year 1899, when Mrs. Kelly was
)wn to be vested with fee simple title in the surface of and in
16 undivided interest in the oil, gas, and other mineral sub-
nces, in and under these two tracts, and when the 1-32 of *the*
ter undivided, was in the plaintiff Barnes, and the remaining
2 was in Mallory Brothers, the said Mallory Brothers were
essed with nothing so far as shown, because of their interest,
; plaintiff Barnes was assessed with 1-16 oil reserved in 72
·es. These taxes were not paid by Barnes, and the· interest

was returned delinquent and sold by the sheriff of Ritchie County, on January 13, 1902, and purchased by the defendant, Bee, who paid a total for taxes and expenses, of $2.35; and on January 19, received from the Clerk of the County Court a deed therefor. On October 20, 1902, Kelly and wife and Barnes made a lease in which Mallory Brothers did not join, to Upham and Ralston, whereby they granted the lessee all the oil and gas in and under these lands, described as 70 acres, for the period of two years for a 1-8 royalty, and upon the usual terms and conditions of an oil and gas lease. This lease was assigned by the lessees to Sarber Brothers & Company, and a valuable 200-barrel a day oil well was drilled in, and the 1-16 undivided interest became of a value estimated at from five to six thousand dollars. Barnes filed his bill in equity in the United States Circuit Court for the Northern District of West Virginia, against Bee, the tax title purchaser, to cancel, set aside and annul the tax deed as a cloud upon his title. The Circuit Court held that there had been a severance of title only as to a fractional undivided interest in the minerals; and that this undivided severance, was not, under the laws of West Virginia, the subject of separate taxation; and rendered a decree cancelling the tax deed.

Upon the proposition that there could not be a separate assessment of the undivided oil and gas interests legally made, and that the payment of the assessment made in the name of Mrs. Kelly, was a payment of the whole tax legally assessable and inured to the benefit of Barnes the other co-tenant, the court cited:

Whithman v. *Sayres,* 9 W. Va. 671.
Simpson v. *Edmiston,* 23 W. Va. 675.
Bradley v. *Ewart,* 18 W. Va. 398.
Gerke Brewing Co. v. *St. Clair,* 46 W. Va. 93; 33 S. E. 122.
State v. *Low,* 46 W. Va. 451; 33 S. E. 371.
Cunningham v. *Brown,* 39 W. Va. 588; 20 S. E. 615.

Sec. 20.—In *Bee* v. *Barnes,* 149 Fed. 727; 79 C. C. A. 433 (Nov. 19, 1906) the head note is as follows:

"Where each of two tracts of land was assessed for taxation at its true value as the property of the owner of the fee, and she paid the full amount of the taxes due thereon, notwithstanding an outstanding one-sixteenth interest in any oil that might be pro-

iced from the land, a sale of such interest for non-payment of
xes assessed thereon, was void."

This was an appeal from the Circuit Court of the United
:ates for the Northern District of West 'Virginia, from the de-
ee rendered in the equity cause of *Barnes* v. *Bee*, 138 Fed. 476,
ction 19, supra, to the Circuit Court of Appeals for the Fourth
rcuit, where the decree of the Circuit Court was affirmed.

Sec. 21.—In *Westmoreland Natural Gas Co.* v. *DeWitt*, 130
ι. 235; 18 Atl. 724; 5 L. R. A. 731, analyzed under Chapter 11,
l. 2 is as follows:

"The real subject of possession to which the lessee is entitled,
'the oil or gas contained in or obtainable through the land:
ase are minerals ferae naturae, and are part of the land and
long to its owner only so long as they are in it and under his
ιtrol; the lessee, when he has drilled a gas well and controls
ε gas produced thereby, is in possession of all the gas within
ε land."

REMEDIES.

Sec. 21.—Where there has been by express grant or reser-
:ion, a severance of the petroleum oil and natural gas or other
ιerals from the surface, such express grant or reservation
sses to the grantee and his vendee or reserves to the grantor
l his vendee, the oil and gas and minerals so reserved or
ιnted, together with the incidental right to open the mines by
king wells or shafts, with the right to use such means as are
essary to produce and market the oil and gas or minerals so re-
ved or granted. The courts have given the same construction
reservations of petroleum oil and natural gas as they have
:oal and other minerals, as to the rights of those entitled to
reservations.

Koen v. *Bartlett,* 41 W. Va. 559; 23 S. E. 664; 56 Am. St. Rep.
884; 31 L. R. A. 128.
Preston v. *White,* 57 W. Va. 278; 50 S. E. 236.
Ammons v. *Toothman,* 59 W. Va. 165; 53 S. E. 13.
Sult v. *Hochstetter Oil Co.* 63 W. Va. 317; 61 S. E. 307.
Jackson v. *Dulaney,* (W. Va.) 67 S. E. 795.

Lillibridge v. *Lackawanna Coal Co.*, 143 Pa. 293; ——Atl.
——; 24 Am. St. Rep. 544.
Murray v. *Allred*, 100 Tenn. 100; 66 Am. St. Rep. 740.

Sec. 22.—Where there has been a severance of petroleum oil
or natural gas from the surface by an express grant thereof, or
where these minerals have been reserved in a deed, the grantor
reserving the minerals under such grant, or the grantor in the
deed, may lease the same to others or operate upon the land
himself and produce and market the oil and gas, and cannot be
prevented by injunction or other proceedings in behalf of the surface owner, from mining and marketing such oil and gas; nor can
he be held liable to the surface owner in damages for so doing.

Kiser v. *McLean*, ——W. Va.,——; 67 S. E. 725.
Jackson v. *Dulaney*, —— W. Va., ——; 67 S. E. 795.
Chartiers Block Coal Co. v. *Mellon, and Mansfield Coal &*
Coke Co. v. *Mellon*, 152 Pa. 286; 25 Atl. 597; 18 L. R. A.
702; 34 Am. St. Rep. 645.
Lillibridge v. *Lackawanna Coal Co.*, 143 Pa. 293; —— Atl. —;
24 Am. St. Rep. 544.
Moore v. *Griffin*, 72 Kan. 164; 83 Pac. 395.
Murray v. *Allred*, 100 Tenn. 100; 66 Am. St. Rep. 740.

Sec. 23.—Where there has been a severance of title of the
petroleum oil or natural gas from the surface, and the surface is
owned by one person and the petroleum oil and natural gas by
another, the owner of the surface is not in possession of the petroleum oil and natural gas unless he has drilled wells and taken
physical possession of such oil and gas. The Statute of Limitations will not begin to run in favor of the owner of the surface
under a claim of possession of the oil and gas thereunder until
such surface owner has taken such physical possession of the oil
and gas.

Murray v. *Allred*, 100 Tenn. 100; 66 Am. St. Rep. 740.
Plant v. *Humyhreys*, 66 W. Va. 88; 66 S. E. 94.
Kiser v. *McLean*, (W. Va.) 67 S. E. 725.
Delaware & Hudson Canal Co. v. *Hughes*, 183 Pa. 66; 63 Am.
St. Rep. 743.

Sec. 24.—When there has been a severance of the title to the
petroleum oil and natural gas from the surface of the land, in the

bsence of a statute requiring separate assessments to be made of
le reservation and the residue of the land, and the land is as-
:ssed at its fair value in the name of the surface owner and the
ixes paid by such surface owner, there can be no forfeiture of
ich oil and gas interests for non-entry on the tax books and non-
ayment of taxes.

State v. *Low,* 46 W. Va. 451; 33 S. E. 271.
Sult v. *Hochstetter Oil Co.,* 63 W. Va. 317; 61 S. E. 307.
Kiser v. *McLean,* (W. Va.) 67 S. E. 725.
Wallace v. *Elm Grove Coal Co.,* 58 W. Va. 449; 52 S. E. 485.

Sec. 25.—Where oil or gas has been severed from the sur-
.ce by deed, either by express grant or by reservation, and has
'en sold for the non-payment or non-assessment of taxes, or
here an undivided interest in such reservation has been so sold,
the absence of a statute requiring such assessment to be made,
e owner may, by bill in equity, upon tender and payment of the
xes and the legal interest and damages lawfully incurred by the
'rson entitled to such reservation or such interest, cause such
·ed to be cancelled, set aside and annuled.

Toothman v. *Courtney,* 62 W. Va. 167; 58 S. E. 915.
Barnes v. *Bee,* 138 Fed. 476, affirmed in *Bee* v. *Barnes,* 149
    Fed. 727; 79 C. C. A. 433.

The Federal Courts held in the last two cases cited, that
1ere mining interests are illegally assessed with taxes, the owner
not required to refund such illegal taxes as a condition prece-
nt to having the tax deed cancelled.

Sec. 26.—The owner of an interest in the oil and gas under-
ng a tract of land, which interest has been severed from the
rface by deed, may, by bill in equity, enjoin the owner of the
rface from producing and marketing the oil and gas.

Westmoreland Nat. Gas Co. v. *DeWitt,* 130 Pa. 235; 18 Atl.
    724; 5 L. R. A. 731.
Delaware & Hudson Canal Co. v. *Hughes,* 183 Pa. 66; 63 Am.
    St. Rep. 743.

Sec. 27.—When the surface of the land is owned by one person, and the petroleum oil and natural gas in place by another, the sale of the lands for non-payment of taxes in the name of the owner of the surface passes title to the oil and gas in place owned by the other person. The purchaser at tax sale takes title to both the surface and the oil and gas, and his deed will not be cancelled upon the sole ground that the assessment was made only against the owner of the surface.

Peterson v. *Hall*, 57 W. Va. 353; 50 S. E. 603.

Sec. 28.—In a suit between conflicting claimants to petroleum oil or natural gas underlying a tract of land either party may prove that the interest of the other was subject to surrender or abandonment, and that such interest has, prior to the trial, been surrendered or abandoned by the adverse claimant; and the question of such surrender or abandonment, becomes a question of fact for the court or jury, as the case may be.

Garrett v. *South Penn Oil Co.*, 66 W. Va. 587; 66 S. E. 741.

CHAPTER 50.

SEVERAL TRACTS UNDER ONE LEASE.

Sec. 1.—Where the owner of two or more tracts of land executes an oil and gas lease covering all the lands, in consideration of one royalty of oil or gas rental, and subsequently, but before oil or gas is discovered on any of the tracts, dies testate having devised the tracts to different divisees in severalty without any devise of the lease or reference thereto in connection with the separate devises, each devisee is entitled to the proportional interest in the royalty or gas rental as his tract in acreage bears to the total acreage covered by the lease.

Wettengel v. *Gormley*, 160 Pa. 559; 28 Atl. 934; 40 Am. St.
    Rep. 733.
Wettengel v. *Gormley*, 184 Pa. 354; 39 Atl. 57.

Sec. 2.—Where two or more persons owning different tracts of land execute a joint lease covering all the lands, in consideration of a joint royalty of oil or gas rental, the question of the right of the owners of the separate tracts to the royalty oils and gas rentals for wells on each separate tract, is a question of fact. A contemporaneous agreement between the lessors that the royalty should be paid and delivered to the owner of the particular tract from which the oil is produced may be proven, in determining to whom royalties or gas rentals are to be paid under such joint lease.

Rymer v. *South Penn Oil Co.*, 54 W. Va. 530; 46 S. E. 459.

Sec. 3.—Where the owners of two or more tracts of land execute a joint lease for oil and gas purposes covering the separate tracts of each owner, for a joint royalty of oil or gas rental, lessee may enter upon one tract and if, within the term, he discovers oil or gas in paying quantities, he is entitled to hold the tracts upon which he does not enter and explore, beyond the term upon payment of the royalties and gas rentals accruing from the wells drilled, to the lessors, as provided for by the lease.

Harness v. *Eastern Oil Co.*, 49 W. Va. 232; 38 S. E. 662.

Sec. 4.—Where the owner of two or more tracts of land executes a lease covering all the lands, and subsequently conveys the separate tracts to different persons, each separate owner is entitled to the royalty of oils or gas rentals from the wells producing upon his tract.

Northwestern Ohio Nat. Gas. Co. v. *Ullery*, 68 Ohio State 259 67 N. E. 494.

Sec. 5.—In *Wettengel* v. *Gormley*, 160 Pa. 559; 28 Atl. 934; 40 Am. St. Rep. 733 (April 2, 1894) the syllabus is as follows:

"Where three tracts of land, all subject to the same oil and gas lease, are devised respectively to the owners three children, the royalties accruing under the lease are divisible among the three divisees, although all of the wells are sunk on one only of the three tracts.

Owing to the vagrant character of oil and gas, a lease of these substances partakes of the character of a lease for general tillage, rather than that of a lease for mining or quarrying the solid minerals."

Annie B. Wettengel brought suit in the Court of Common Pleas, Number 2. Allegheny County, against James P. Gormley, to determine the ownership of oil royalties under an oil lease. The facts were as follows: James Gormley, in his lifetime, owned three contiguous farms, containing, together, about six hundred acres, and in July, 1888, he made an oil lease to Tomlinson, covering all the land. The lease was for fifteen years, reserving a royalty of all the oil produced of 1-8, and giving the lessee the usual privileges on the land, among which was the right to take water from any part of it, and to any extent needed in his operations; a right of way into and over the body of the land; a right to lay pipelines to conduct the oil from the wells, and concluded with the following stipulation:

"It is understood between the parties to this agreement that all conditions between the parties hereto shall extend to their heirs, executors and assigns."

The lessor died in October, 1890. By his will he devised one of the forms to each of his three children, in fee, making no mention of the lease which included the three farms. The devisees entered into possession of their respective farms under the will, and each held in severalty. The holder of the lease put down several wells and was producing oil therefrom; all of the wells happened to be on the farm devised to James P. Gormley, the defendant, who claimed the entire royalty. The question for the court to decide was: Who was entitled to the royalty reserved by the ancestor? The Court of Common Pleas held that the royalty belonged to each of the three heirs, devisees under the will. The Supreme Court affirmed this decision.

Sec. 6.—In *Wettengel* v. *Gormley,* 184 Pa. 354; 39 Atl. 57 (Jan. 3, 1898) the syllabus is as follows:

An owner of three contiguous farms executed an oil and gas lease of the three farms as a single body for a fixed term, reserving a royalty and providing that 'all conditions between the parties hereto shall extend to their heirs, executors, administrators and assigns.' He devised the three farms respectively to his three children. Under this lease a number of wells were sunk upon one of the farms, and no wells were sunk upon the other farms. *Held,* (1) that each child was entitled to receive such share of the total royalty as his or her share of the land bore to the whole tract covered by the lease, no matter on whose farm the wells were located; (2) that the child upon whose land the wells were sunk was entitled to compensation for the decrease in the rental value of his part, caused by the presence of the wells; (3) that the cost of repairing injuries to the realty caused by the sinking of the wells should be postponed until the termination of the lease made it possible intelligently to consider that subject. *Wettengel* v. *Gormley,* 160 Pa. 559, adhered to."

Two suits in equity were instituted in the Court of Common Pleas, Number 2, Allegheny County, one by Albert C. Wettengel, Guardian, etc., against James P. Gormley and others, the other by Anna B. Wettengel against the same defendant. The following facts were shown upon the hearing, the cases being heard together: James Gormley, the father of the plaintiffs, made a lease dated July 14, 1888, to J. A. Tomlinson, which lease became vested in the defendants. The lease was for the exclusive right of drilling and operating for oil and gas upon a tract of 600 acres of land, for a term of 15 years, with a rental of $50.00 a month to be paid until a producing well was obtained, then a 1-8 royalty, and if gas should be obtained a certain gas rental; The lease contained the usual surface privileges, the right to lay pipeline, with right of way for roads, etc; James Gormley died October 1, 1890, leaving a will dated November 13, 1889, devising the land which consisted of three distinct farms to his son, James P. and his daughters Anna B. and Maria J. one farm to each, particularly described; No wells were drilled and nothing done under the lease, except to pay the monthly rental, during the life of James Gormley; One or two wells were drilled after his death on the farm of Mrs. Wettengel, but no oil or gas obtained; Ten wells were put down afterwards on the farm of James P. Gormley, six of which produced, and were still producing at the time the suit was brought; the other four wells produced some oil, but not enough to pay for operating them; James Gormley received the royalty of oil, and sold it; these suits were filed to compel him to account and pay over to the plaintiffs their share of the proceeds, claiming a pro rata share, according to the acreage of the three farms; the three farms touched each other, but were distinct and mainly, wide apart, purchased by James Gormley at different times; in his will they were devised as separate farms, each described by reference to deed of purchase; the will contained no reference to the lease to Tomlinson; There was no clause in the lease which provided that it might be held longer than the term of fifteen years; Seven of the fifteen years had expired when the suit was brought; the monthly rental paid before a producing well was obtained, was divided among the three devisees according to the acreage of their farms; the total amount of money received by the defendant, James P. Gormley, from the sale of the royalty oil from August 19, 1893, to April 18, 1895, was $15,137.83; by common consent of the devisees the widow of James Gormley, who refused to take under the will, was paid 1-3 of the amount, which left $10,091.89, with some oil remaining unsold. After the decision of the Supreme Court in the former case (*Wettengel* v. *Gormley*, 160 Pa. 559) James T. Gormley paid to his two sisters $443.40, which, in proportion to the acreage would be, to Mrs. Lockhart nee Gormley two hundred and forty three dollars and sixty-two and a half cents, and to Mrs. Wettengel, nee Gormley, one hundred and nine ty-nine dollars and seventy-seven and a half cents.

The Court of Common Pleas held, that James T. Gormley should account for royalties, and that the royalty should be paid to the three devisees in proportion as the acreage of each bore to the total acreage, embraced in the lease. Upon appeal the Supreme Court affirmed the decree with some modifications not material here.

Sec. 7.—In *Harness* v. *Eastern Oil Co.*, 49 W. Va. 232; 38 S. E. 662, analyzed under Chapter 18, the first and second points of the syllabus are as follows:

"1. T. B. H. and A. K. H. his wife, leased together in one lease two tracts of land lying contiguous to each other, one hundred and fifty-two acres belonging to T. B. H. and thirty-five and one-half to A. K. H. as one tract of one hundred and eighty-seven and one-half acres, for oil and gas purposes. A well was bored on the one hundred and fifty-two acres; the proceeds cash rental for gas paid to both lessors, and receipted for by them jointly, and the royalty of oil run into the pipelines to their joint credit. *Held,* to be a joint lease of one tract of one hundred and eighty-seven and one-half acres, as between the lessors and lessee.

2. Such lease being 'in consideration of the sum of twelve hundred and fifty dollars, the receipt of which is hereby acknowledged, * * * parties of the first part do hereby grant unto * * *, second party, his heirs and assigns, all the oil and gas in and under the following premises,' describing them, with the right to enter and drill and operate for oil, gas, etc., reserving to themselves one-eighth of the oil produced, to be run into pipeline to their credit. 'Term of lease two years, and as much longer as oil or gas is found in paying quantities. If gas only is found, second party agrees to pay two hundred and fifty dollars each year, quarterly in advance, for the product of each well while the same is being used off the premises, gas free for dwelling house purposes,' the production in paying quantities of either gas or oil, and the payment of gas rental, or the delivery of one-eighth of the oil royalty, in the pipeline, as stipulated, will perpetuate the lease during the time of such production."

The bill alleged that defendant's made no attempt to develop the 35 1-2-acre tract, and that the lease as to that tract was absolutely forfeited, and a cloud on plaintiff's title, and should be removed by decree of the court.

Sec. 8.—In *North-western Ohio Natural Gas Co.* v. *Ullery,* 68 Ohio State 259; 67 N. E. 494, (April 28, 1902) the syllabus is as follows:

"Where an oil and gas lease is made by one party to another covering two or more separate tracts of land, and is made to extend to the heirs and assigns of the parties, and different persons becoming the owners of such different tracts, each owner is entitled to the oil and gas produced on his tract, and to the royalty and rental arising from such tract."

John A. Taylor was the owner of two tracts of land cornering each other, one containing 40 acres, and the other 60 acres. He executed and delivered to William Duke, Junior, an oil and gas lease dated June 10, 1886, whereby in consideration of the covenants and agreements mentioned in the lease, he granted, demised and let to the lessee, his heirs or assigns, for the purpose, and the exclusive right of drilling and operating for petroleum oil and gas, 100 acres of land, being the two tracts above mentioned. The lease gave to the lessee the right to use sufficient water from the lands necessary to the operation of the lease, the right of way over and upon the premises, the right to lay pipelines to convey oil or gas, and the right to remove machinery or fixtures, the lease being for the term of five years from date, and as much longer as oil or gas should be produced or found in paying quantities. The lessee agreed to give to lessor the full equal one-eighth part of all petroleum produced or found on the land, and should gas be found in sufficient quantities to justify marketing, the consideration for each well to be $100.00 per annum. Lessee agreed to complete a well on the premises within nine months, and in case of failure to pay to lessor for delay a yearly rental of fifty cents per acre. Second party agreed to furnish to lessor all the gas necessary for domestic use, free of cost. The lease provided that all its conditions should extend to the heirs, executors and administrators of the parties. On May 15, 1891, the lessee, John A. Taylor, assigned the lease to the Northwestern Ohio Natural Gas Company. On March 31, 1894, John A. Taylor conveyed by warranty deed to John J. Ullery the 40-acre tract, with the following exception as to the warranty:

"Except, against gas lease and pipeline privileges granted to the Northwestern Ohio Natural Gas Co."

On the same day Taylor conveyed by warranty deed to Alvin L. Shoop the 60-acre tract, making the following exception to his warranty: "Except, against gas lease held by the Northwestern Ohio Natural Gas Co., including all pipeline right of way." On May 24, 1894, the gas company paid to Ullery and Shoop the sum of $150.00 rental from June 10, 1894, to June 10, 1895, and took a receipt signed by both; and each year thereafter tendered the rental to both, which was refused, as Mr. Shoop had disposed of his interest in the gas. Tender of 4-10 of the gas rental was also made to Mr. Ullery, and refused by him. On or about June 10, 1895, the gas company drilled a well on the 40-acre tract, which had, ever since, produced gas in sufficient quantities to require the payment of a rental of $150.00 per year for that well, as provided at the end of the extension of date of April 15, 1893, on which date John A. Taylor in consideration of $150.00 paid to him, agreed in writing to extend the terms and conditions of the lease from June 10, 1893, to June 10, 1894, and from year to year so long as the $150.00 should be paid, and when the well should be drilled, he should receive $150.00, yearly for the well. In April, 1895, Mr. Shoop made and delivered a gas lease of the 60-acre tract to the City of Tiffin, and in a contest between that City and the plaintiff in error, the gas company, the city of Tiffin, held the gas right. (*Northwestern O. N. G. Co.,* v. *Tiffin,* 59 Ohio State 420; 54 N. E. 77).

The Gas Company lost that case by reason of its failure to have the extension of the lease recorded. In the year 1899, Mr. Ullery filed in the Court of Common Pleas of Wood County his petition against the North-western Ohio Natural Gas Company, for the recovery of the $150.00 rental on the land, under the lease, from June 10, 1895, to June 10, 1898, with interest. The defendant answered, and upon the facts as above stated, judgment was rendered for plaintiff. Defendant took error to the Circuit Court where judgment was again rendered for plaintiff, and defendant then appealed to the Supreme Court, where the decision of the court below was affirmed. The Supreme Court of Ohio, in this case, refused to follow the Supreme Court of Pennsylvania in *Wettengel* v. *Gormley,* 185 Pa. 354; 39 Atl. 57, and *Wettengel* v. *Gormley,* 160 Pa. 559; 28 Atl. 934, citing:

Kelly v. *Ohio Oil Co.,* 57 Ohio St. 317; 49 N. E. 399; 39 L. R. A. 765; 63 Am. St. Rep. 721.

Sec. 9.—In *Rymer* v. *South Penn Oil Co.,* 54 W. Va. 530; 46 S. E. 459 (Feb. 2, 1904) the syllabus is as follows:

"Where several owners in fee of contiguous tracts of land lease the whole as one tract for oil and gas purposes, and the one-eighth royalty oil is to be paid by the lessee in the usual way, by running the same into the pipelines to the credit of 'the parties of the first part' (the lessors) and the lease is silent as to the division of the royalty between the lessors, and where the development is all on one tract owned in severalty by one of the lessors, who claims to be entitled to all the royalty, upon interpleader of the lessee for determination as to whom to pay the royalty as between the lessors, parol evidence is admissable to prove a contemporaneous agreement between the lessors that the royalty should be paid and delivered to the owner of the particular tract from which the oil is produced."

Henry Rymer and Frank L. Rymer, and Edith, his wife, executed to the South Penn Oil Company a lease, whereby, in consideration of one dollar to lessors, and for the further consideration of the covenants and agreements contained in the lease, on the part of the lessee to be paid, kept and performed, the lessors granted demised and leased, to the lessee for the sole and only purpose of operating for oil and gas, laying pipelines, etc., a certain tract of land (describing it as bounded on the North, East, South and West, by lands of other parties) containing 360 acres. The lessee covenanted to deliver to the credit of the parties, their heirs or assigns, in the pipelines 1-8 of all oil produced, and to pay $300 per year for each gas well drilled on the premises the product from which should be marketed and used off the premises. The lessee, the South Penn Company, sub-leased part of the land to Treat and Crawford, who took possession under their sub-lease and drilled two wells which produced oil in paying quantities. The South Penn Company afterwards took possession of the residue, and drilled several wells; near to those drilled by Treat and Crawford, which produced large quantities of oil. The tract of 360 acres, first leased, consisted of a tract of 90 acres, another of 25 acres, both vested in fee at the time of the execution of the lease, in Frank L. Rymer. The residue, 245 acres, was owned in fee by Henry A. Rymer. The wells drilled by Treat and Crawford, as well as those drilled by the South Penn Oil Company, were all on the 90-acre tract, the property of Frank L. Rymer. Treat and Crawford delivered to Frank L. Rymer the 1-8 of the oil produced from the two wells, and he demanded from the South Penn Oil Company an accounting and delivery to him of the full 1-8 royalty from the wells drilled by it, which the Company refused to do, claiming that the lease of the 360 acres was a joint lease; and that the royalties were payable to the lessors, the said Frank L. Rymer, and the heirs at law of Henry A. Rymer, who had died early in the year 1898, soon after making the lease. Henry A. Rymer executed his will, whereby he devised to his daughter, Susan Smith, during her life, remainder to her children in fee, 100 acres of the leased premises, and to the plaintiff, Frank L. Rymer, 100 acres, and the residue of the leased premises to his daughter, Lizzie Boyers, wife of Doctor F. C. Boyers.

Frank L. Rymer filed his bill in chancery in the Circuit Court of Tyler County against the South Penn Oil Company and the Eureka Pipeline Company, alleging that all the wells drilled by the South Penn Oil Company were located on his tract of 90 acres, which being vested in him in fee simple, entitled him to the whole of the 1-8 royalty therefrom, and the gas rentals, the bill praying that the defendant companies be required to answer and make full account and discovery of dates and any oil run into the pipelines from the wells so drilled by the South Penn Company on the 90 acre tract, the amount so run into the lines of the Eureka Pipeline Company; and that said companies be ordered to pay over to plaintiff all oils and money found due on such accounting, and praying for further relief.

The defendant South Penn Oil Company filed its demurrer to the bill for non joinder of parties, claiming that the heirs and devisees of Henry A. Rymer were necessary parties, the lease being a joint lease, and the royalties and rentals payable to the lessors, jointly. The demurrer was overruled, and the South Penn Company filed its answer in the nature of an interpleader, and cross bill, praying that plaintiff be required by amended bill or otherwise, to make the heirs and devisees of Henry A. Rymer parties defendant. By the cross-bill of the South Penn Oil Company all heirs at law of Henry A. Rymer, the Eureka Pipeline Company and Treat and Crawford, were made parties defendant. The defendant Susan Smith, David M. Smith, her husband; Elizabeth Boyers and C. F. Boyers, her husband, filed their answer denying the right of plaintiff Frank L. Rymer, to recover and receive all the royalty oil produced from the 90-acre tract, or any other particular part of the tract of 360 acres leased jointly by Frank L. Rymer and Henry A. Rymer, to the South Penn Oil Company. Depositions were taken and filed in the cause by the plaintiff Frank L. Rymer, for the purpose of proving an oral contract between the lessors, Frank L. Rymer and Henry A. Rymer, contemporaneous with the lease of August 24, 1897, whereby it was understood and agreed that the several lessors should receive the royalty oil produced from their respective tracts of land owned by them in severalty, and comprising the 360-acre tract leased, and to show how rentals paid before the completion of a well had been distributed under the lease. Other depositions were filed by plaintiff and by defendants Susan Smith, and Elizabeth Boyers, objections and exceptions were made by the said defendants to the depositions of plaintiff taken and filed for the purpose of establishing such oral agreement, because incompetent, being contradictory of the language and provisions of the lease. The Circuit Court over-ruled the objections and exceptions to the depositions as to their competency to prove such parol agreement, and decreed all the royalty oil, and the consideration for gas that might be produced from the 90 acres, and the 25 acres of land, under the said lease, to the plaintiff Frank L. Rymer; and that defendants Susan Smith and Elizabeth Boyer take nothing by their answers and cross-bills, and directing the South Penn Oil Company to run the royalty oil produced and saved from said two tracts to the credit of Frank L. Rymer into the pipelines of the Eureka Pipeline Company, which company was directed to credit the same to Frank L. Rymer. Elizabeth Boyer and Susan Smith appealed to the Court of Appeals, where the decree was affirmed, citing upon the proposition that oil in place is a part of the realty to the same extent as is timber, coal, iron ore or salt water:

Williamson v. *Jones*, 39 W. Va. 231.
Wilson v. *Youst*, 43 W. Va. 826.
Lawson v. *Kirchner*, 50 W. Va. 344.
Ammons v. *Ammons*, 50 W. Va. 399.
Gould on Waters, Sec. 291.
Staughton's App. 88 Pa. 198.
Funk v. *Halderman*, 53 Pa. 229.

Upon the question of the right to introduce parol evidence to establish a contemporaneous agreement, the court cited:

Brown on Parol Evidence, Sec. 50.
Johnson v. *Burns*, 39 W. Va. 658; 20 S. E. 686.
Murdock v. *Gilchrist* 52 N. Y. 247.

For the reason that the wells were not producing oil or gas from the tract originally owned by Henry A. Rymer, the court distinguished the Pennsylvania cases, neither approving nor dis-approving them. The Court seemingly approved:

Nat. Gas Co. v. *Ullery*, 68 Ohio State, 259; 67 N. E. 494.

LESSOR'S REMEDY.

Sec. 10.—Pennsylvania Rule.—A devisee of a tract of land which, together with other tracts, was embraced within one lease executed by a testator who devised the different tracts so embraced to different devisees, may recover from a lessee or other devisees the proportion of the royalties of oil or rentals for gas produced from the other tracts so separately devised, as the acreage of his tract bears to the total acreage covered by the lease, regardless of whether any oil or gas is produced from his separate tract. The decreased rental value of the tract producing oil or gas, by reason of the wells thereon, to be charged against the value of the royalty or gas rental produced from the wells on said tract. Each devisee under such lease is entitled to receive such share of the total royalties or rentals as his share of the land bears to the whole tract covered by the lease, no matter upon which sub-division the wells are located.

Wettengel v. *Gormley,* 160 Pa. 559; 28 Atl. 934; 40 Am. St. Rep. 733.
Wettengel v. *Gormley,* 184 Pa. 354; 39 Atl. 57.

Sec. 11.—West Virginia Rule.—The owner of a separate tract of land which has been embraced within a joint lease executed by the owners of separate tracts for a joint consideration, and providing for a joint royalty for oil, and a joint rental for gas wells, is entitled upon a bill in equity filed against the lessee and the owners of the other interests or tracts embraced within the joint lease, to have decreed to him all the royalty of oils, and all the gas rentals, for wells drilled upon his separate tract of land upon proof that there was a contemporaneous oral agreement and understanding between the lessors that the royalty should be paid and delivered to the owner of the particular tract, from which the oil or gas should be produced.

Rymer v. *South Penn Oil Co.,* 54 W. Va. 530; 46 S. E. 459.

Sec 12.—Ohio Rule.—The owner of a separate tract of land which has been embraced with another separate tract or tracts by the owner or owners in a joint lease for all the lands, or in one lease covering the several tracts, for a joint or single royalty of oil or gas, where the provisions of the lease extend to the heirs and assigns of the parties, may recover from the lessee the royalty of oil or rental for gas, produced on his tract

> *Northwestern Ohio Nat. Gas Co.* v. *Ullery,* 68 Ohio St. 259; 67 N. E. 494.

LESSOR'S REMEDY.

Sec. 13.—Where an oil and gas lease is executed jointly by the owners of two or more tracts of land for a joint rental for gas, and joint royalty of oil, the lessee may enter upon either tract for exploration purposes, and upon discovering oil or gas in paying quantities is entitled to hold all the lands upon payment of the royalties or gas rentals during and beyond the term of the lease, in accordance with its terms and conditions, regardless of the failure of lessee to enter upon, explore for, or produce oil or gas from the other separate tract or tracts. And proof by the lessee that the royalties of oil, and rentals for gas have been paid and delivered to the lessors in the manner provided for by the lease will defeat an action instituted by lessors, or either of them, for the cancellation of the lease as to the particular tracts not developed within the term.

> *Harness* v. *Eastern Oil Co.,* 49 W. Va. 232; 38 S. E. 662.

Sec. 14.—There is an apparent conflict between the courts of Pennsylvania, Ohio, and West Virginia, upon the question of the ownership of the royalties of oil and rentals for gas produced from wells upon a separate tract embraced, with other tracts, in a joint lease made by several owners, or under a lease where several tracts have been embraced in a single lease. The Supreme Court of Ohio has expressly disapproved and refused to follow the Supreme Court of Pennsylvania upon the question as adjudicated in *Wettengel* v. *Gormley,* supra. The Court of Appeals of West Virginia has cited with apparent approval, in *Rymer* v. *South Penn Company,* supra, *Northwestern Ohio Nat. Gas Co.* v. *Ullery,* 68 Ohio St. 259; 67 N. E. 494, and distinguished the Wettengel cases as ajudicating questions arising under a will, that particular point not being before the court for consideration. All the courts hold that petroleum oil and natural gas, in place, are minerals, and belong to the owner of the surface. The rule established by the Supreme Court of Ohio seems to be predicated upon reason and justice, and is supported by the great weight of authority on the question of who is the owner, and entitled to the benefit of the deposits of petroleum oil and natural gas under the surface.

CHAPTER 51.

REMEDIES IN EQUITY.

Sec. 1.—A court of equity will entertain jurisdiction to settle all questions as to the validity and priority of oil and gas leases between claimants, where such leases have been made by a common landowner.

Smith v. Root, 66 W. Va. 633; 66 S. E. 1005.

McGraw Oil & Gas Co. v. Kennedy, 65 W. Va. 595; 64 S. E. 1027.

Eastern Oil Co. v. Coulehan, 65 W. Va. 531; 64 S. E. 836.

Sult v. Hochstetter Oil Co., 63 W Va. 317; 61 S. E. 307.

Headley v. Hoopengarner, 60 W. Va. 626; 55 S. E. 144.

Pheasant v. Hanna, 63 W. Va. 613; 60 S. E. 618.

Starn v. Huffman, 62 W. Va. 422; 59 S. E. 179.

Peterson v. Hall, 57 W. Va. 535; 50 S. E. 63.

Carnegie Nat. Gas Co. v. South Penn Oil Co., 56 W. Va. 402; 49 S. E. 548.

Carney v. Barnes, 56 W. Va. 581; 49 S. E. 423.

Pyle v. Henderson, 55 W. Va. 122; 46 S. E. 791.

Haskell v. Sutton, 53 W. Va. 206; 44 S. E. 533

Lowther Oil Co. v. Miller-Sibley Oil Co., 53 W. Va. 501; 44 S. E. 433.

Henne v. South Penn Oil Co., 52 W. Va. 192; 43 S. E. 147.

Lowther Oil Co. v. Guffey, 52 W. Va. 88; 43 S. E. 101.

Friend v. Mallory, 52 W. Va. 43; 43 S. E. 114.

Parish Fork Oil Co. v. Bridgewater Gas Co., 51 W. Va. 583; 42 S. E. 655.

South Penn Oil Co. v. Edgell, 48 W. Va. 348; 37 S. E. 596.

Eakin v. Hawkins, 48 W. Va. 264; 37 S. E. 622.

Eclipse Oil Co. v. South Penn Oil Co., 47 W. Va. 84; 34 S. E. 928.

Trees v. *Eclipse Oil Co.,* 47 W. Va. 107; 34 S. E. 933.
Steelsmith v. *Gartlan,* 45 W. Va. 27; 29 S. E. 978.
Williamson v. *Jones,* 43 W. Va. 562; 27 S. E. 411.
Wilson v. *Youst,* 43 W. Va. 826; 28 S. E. 781.
Crawford v. *Ritchie,* 43 W. Va. 252; 27 S. E. 320.
Bettman v. *Harness,* 42 W. Va. 433; 26 S. E. 271.
Williamson v. *Jones,* 39 W. Va. 231; 19 S. E. 436.
Hukill v. *Myers,* 36 W. Va. 639; 15 S. E. 151.
Thomas v. *Hukill,* 34 W. Va. 385; 12 S. E. 522.
Powers v. *Bridgeport Oil Co.,* 238 Ill; 397; 87 N. E. 381.
Galloway v. *Campbell,* 142 Ind. 324; 41 N. E. 597.
Freer v. *Davis,* 52 W. Va. 1; 43 S. E. 164.
Elk Fork Oil & Gas Co. v. *Jennings,* 84 Fed. 839; 90 Fed. 178;
     32 C. C. A. 560.

Sec. 2.—Owing to the peculiar character of the grant commonly denominated an oil and gas lease, particularly as to the character of the rights and privileges conferred upon the lessee or
grantee, and in view of the purpose for which such lease or grant
is made, a court of equity alone, has power to give that relief as
between conflicting claimants to which the successful claimant is
entitled. A court of law is remediless to award to the owner of a
conflicting or disputed oil or gas lease the rights which he is entitled to exercise under such grant. The courts have defined an
oil and gas lease and have settled the status of oil and gas in place;
and have, so far as general rules can be laid down, determined
the rights and privileges of a holder of a lease; and it is these
questions so determined, taken together, which vest in a court of
equity the general jurisdiction, which it alone is capable of rendering, to afford complete justice to conflicting claimants to oil and
gas leases.

Sec. 3.—The holder of an oil and gas lease claiming thereunder the exclusive right to enter upon and produce the oil and gas
from a tract of land, may file a bill in equity against a claimant
under an adverse lease, made either before or after the date of
his lease, who has entered upon the premises and is producing and
marketing the oil and gas therefrom, for an injunction and accounting, and a court of equity will settle all questions in dispute
between the conflicting claimants and by decree cancel the invalid
lease as a cloud upon the others title; and where the holder of such
invalid lease has converted the oil and gas to his own use, the

court will render decree against such persons in favor of the lessee holding the valid lease, for the value of the oil and gas so taken.

Thomas v. *Hukill*, 34 W. Va. 385-397-9; 12 S. E. 522.
Hukill v. *Myers*, 36 W. Va. 639; 15 S. E. 151.
Trees v. *Eclipse Oil Co.*, 47 W. Va., 107; 34 S. E. 933.
Eclipse Oil Co. v. *South Penn Oil Co.*, 47 W. Va. 84; 34 S. E. 923.
Parish Fork Oil Co. v. *Bridgewater Gas Co.*, 51 W. Va. 583; 42 S. E. 655.
Friend v. *Mallory*, 52 W. Va. 53; 43 S. E. 114.
Henne v. *South Penn Oil Co.*, 52 W. Va. 192; 43 S. E. 147.
Lowther Oil Co. v. *Guffey*, 52 W. Va. 88; 43 S. E. 101.
Lowther Oil Co. v. *Miller-Sibley Oil Co.*, 53 W. Va. 501; 44 S. E. 433.
Pyle v. *Henderson*, 65 W. Va. 39; 63 S. E. 620.
Sult v. *Hochstetter Oil Co.*, 63 W. Va. 317; 61 S. E. 307.
Peterson v. *Hall*, 57 W. Va. 535; 50 S. E. 603.
Powers v. *Bridgeport Oil Co.*, 238 Ill. 397; 87 N. E. 381.

Sec. 4.—A court of equity will not ordinarily entertain jurisdiction to settle questions between claimants under conflicting leases where the lessors claim the lands demised under conflicting titles. To authorize a court of equity to entertain jurisdiction the leases must be made by a common landowner, or the record must disclose no question of fact at issue between the conflicting titles.

Freer v. *Davis*, 52 W. Va. 1; 43 S. E. 164.
Sult v. *Hochstetter Oil Co.*, 63 W. Va. 317; 61 S. E. 307.

Sec. 5.—One tenant in common or co-tenant who produces oil or gas from the common property, or executes an oil and gas lease thereon to another, may be enjoined by the owners of the other interests from producing and marketing the oil and gas, and the tenant in common or co-tenant who has not consented to such production and marketing is entitled to an injunction and an accounting, and to a decree against the other owners, or their lessees, for the value of his proportion of the oil and gas so taken.

Williamson v. *Jones*, 39 W. Va. 231; 19 S. E. 436.
Wilson v. *Youst*, 43 W. Va. 826; 28 S. E. 781.

Williamson v. *Jones,* 43 W. Va. 562; 27 S. E. 411.
Eakin v. *Hawkins,* 48 W. Va. 264; 37 S. E. 622.
Haskell v. *Sutton,* 53 W. Va. 206; 44 S. E. 533. ·
Headley v. *Hoopengarner,* 60 W. Va. 626-646; 55 S. E. 144.
See Chapter 35.—Life Tenants and Remainder Men.
See Chapter 27.—Oil and gas in Place are Minerals and part
     of the Land.

Sec. 6.—The landowner, or a lessee holding a valid lease under him, may cause to be cancelled by a court of equity an outstanding forfeited or void lease, or a lease made without consideration, or a lease that is inequitable, unconscienable or void for
want of mutuality.

Crawford v. *Ritchie,* 43 W. Va. 252; 27 S. E. 220.
Bettman v. *Harness,* 42 W. Va. 433; 26 S. E. 271.
Steelsmith v. *Gartlan,* 45 W. Va. 27; 29 S. E. 927.
See Chapter 26.—Forfeiture by Abandonment—Lessee's
     Remedy.
See Chapter 28.—A Court of Equity will Cancel a void lease.
See Chapter 29.—Want of Mutuality.

Sec. 7.—Where a lessee has, by the discovery of oil or gas
in paying quantities become vested with the right to produce these
minerals, he will be relieved by a court of equity from a technical
forfeiture for breaches of the covenants of the lease, where such
breaches were not committed by the wilful or wanton act of the
lessee.

South Penn Oil Co. v. *Edgell,* 48 W. Va. 264; 37 S. E. 622.
Eastern Oil Co. v. *Coulehan,* 65 W. Va. 531; 64 S. E. 836-38.
See Chapter 25.—Forfeiture by Adandonment—Lessee's
     Remedy Sec. 6.

Sec. 8.—A lessee may enforce specifically the covenants of an
oil and gas lease against the lessor or anyone claiming in privity
of title with him, where lessee has no adequate remedy at law.

Carnegie Nat. Gas Co. v. *South Penn Oil Co.,* 56 W. Va. 402-
     415; 49 S. E. 548.
West Va. etc. v. *Vinal,* 14 W. Va. 637; syl. 5.
Eclipse Oil Co. v. *South Penn Oil Co.,* 47 W. Va. 84; 34 S.
     E. 923.

Bettman v. *Harness*, 42 W. Va. 433; 26 S. E. 271.
Smith v. *Root*, 66 W. Va. 633; 66 S. E. 1005 syl. 1.

Sec. 9.—A court of equity, in a controversy between conflicting claimants to the oil and gas underlying a tract of land claimed under separate leases, may appoint a receiver pending a final decree, for making necessary developments for the protection of lines, and for the purpose of preserving the status quo.

Sult v. *Hochstetter Oil Co.*, 63 W. Va. 317; 61 S. E. 307.
Galloway v. *Campbell*, 142 Ind. 324; 41 N. E. 597.
Elk Fork Oil & Gas Co. v. *Foster*, 99 Fed. 495; 39 C. C. A. 615.
Doddridge County Oil & Gas Co. v. *Smith*, 154 Fed. 970; 173 Fed. 386.

Sec. 10.—The compensation for the services of the receiver and of his attorney, where the court of its own motion makes the appointment, will be paid out of the funds.

Elk Fork Oil & Gas Co. v. *Foster*, 99 Fed. 495; 39 C. C. A. 615.

Sec. 11.—Where, however, the receiver is appointed on the application of one of the parties against whom a final decree is entered, while the compensation of the receiver and his attorney will be paid out of the funds, a decree over will be rendered against the unsuccessful litigant for the amount of such compensation so paid the receiver and his attorney.

Doddridge Oil & Gas Co. v. *Smith*, 154 Fed. 970; 173 Fed. 386.

Sec. 12.—In *Elk Fork Oil & Gas Co.* v. *Foster*, 99 Fed. 495; 39 C. C. A. 615 (Feb. 6, 1900) [for facts and analysis of pleadings, see *Elk Fork Oil & Gas Co.* v. *Jennings*, Chapter 4, supra,] the headnotes are as follows:

"1. A bill was brought for an injunction to prevent defendants from taking possession of certain land. A defendant filed a bill against complainants, praying an injunction, and obtained the usual restraining order. The court, on argument of the two cases, consolidated them, treating the bill of defendant as a cross bill, and, of his own motion, appointed a receiver of the property in dispute. No order was passed dissolving either

of the injunctions. Afterwards other defendants filed a cross
bill, and another receiver of different property was appointed by
the court of its own motion. The suits all related to rights claimed by the several parties in oil and gas rights under certain leases
held by them. All parties concurred in the necessity of operating
the property, and each side desired permission so to do. *Held,*
that the appointment of receivers on the court's own motion was
proper.

2. The cost of a receivership, where the receiver was appointed by the court of its own motion, will be charged against the
fund in the hands of the receiver, rather than against one of the
parties, in the absence of fraud or improper conduct of any of
the parties.

3. It is proper to order a return to a party of advances
made by him to the receiver appointed in the suit, pending the
receivership, where such advances were made under the permission of the court, and in reliance on its order, requiring a re-
payment if the income accruing to the receiver was sufficient
therefor.

4. An allowance may be made to the counsel for a receiver.''

The Court Cited:

Sage v. *Railroad Co.,* 125 U. S. 361.
Ferguson v. *Dent,* 46 Fed. 88.
Couper v. *Shirley,* 75 Fed. 168; 21 C. C. A. 288.
Stuart v. *Boulware,* 133 U. S. 81.

Sec. 13.—In *Galloway* v. *Campbell,* 142 Ind. 324; 41 N. E. 597,
(Oct. 17, 1895) syl. 1 is as follows:

''1. Where it was alleged, in an action to compel defendants
to assign to plaintiff a certain lease to oil lands in possession
of defendants, that defendants were non-residents, and had only
a small amount of property in the State, and it appeared that
neither parties owned the land, but only claimed a leasehold right
therein, the court was justified in appointing a receiver to take
charge of and superintend the production of the oil.''

Frank Campbell instituted suit in the Circuit Court of Wells
County, Indiana, against John Galloway and others for specific
performance of a contract to assign a certain lease, for oil and
gas, and for the right to operate therefor in and under certain

lands described in the complaint, in pursuance of the terms of an alleged contract. It appeared that the defendants had possession of the land in question, and had drilled one well thereon, and were preparing to drill others; the well drilled produced thirty barrels of oil a day, which was run into a tank for the purpose of being shipped and sold; that the defendants were non-residents of the State, and had no property therein, save the machinery on the land, and that if they were permitted to sell or dispose of the oil taken from the well plaintiff would suffer irreparable injury. The defendants answered the application for the appointment of a receiver, and numerous affidavits were filed for and against the appointment. It was a question of discretion in the judge as to appointment of the receiver upon the showing made for and against such appointment, and from the pleadings. A receiver was appointed, and from the order of appointment defendants appealed. The Supreme Court affirmed the order of appointment, citing:

McCaslin v. *State,* 44 Ind. 151.
Bitting v. *Ten Eyck,* 85 Ind. 357.
Hellesbush v. *Blake,* 119 Ind. 349; 21 N. E. 976.

Sec. 14.—In *Smith* v. *Root,* 66 W. Va. 633; 66 S. E. 1005 (Jan. 25, 1910) the syllabus is as follows:

"1. Equity has jurisdiction of a suit brought by the senior lessee in an oil lease against the lessor and a junior lessee of the same land, from the same lessor, for the purpose of enjoining the removal of the oil from the leased premises, and for specific execution of his lease; and in such a suit, the court can settle the conflicting claims of the lessees, and grant such relief to either claimant as the pleadings and proof may warrant.

2. An oil and gas lease giving the lessee the right, for the period of ten years, to explore for oil and gas, and providing that if a well is not completed on the leased premises within three months from the date of the lease the lessee shall pay to the lessor, in advance, a quarterly cash rental for each additional three months the completion of a well is delayed, is an executory contract, and vests no title in the lessee to the oil and gas in place.

3. Such a contract contemplates development of the leased premises within a reasonable time, and the lessee may lose his rights thereunder before the expiration of the ten years by aban-

donment of the lease, notwithstanding there is no forfeiture clause
in the contract.

4. If the lessee has not actually entered upon the land the
relinquishment of his right to do so, or his abandonment, becomes
purely a question of his intention, and may be established by
proof of such facts and circumstances as evince a voluntary
waiver of his rights.

5. A case in which the evidence proves a voluntary abandonment of the lease by the lessee.''

Mrs. D. M. Hall and C. J. Hall, her husband, on February 29,
1904, executed an oil and gas lease to Lee Goff and A. S. Heck for
a tract of 106 acres of land in Roane County, West Virginia, the
lease to remain in force for ten years, and as much longer as
either oil or gas should be produced, and contained the following
provision:

"Second party covenants and agrees * * * * to complete a
well on said premises within three months from the date hereof,
or pay at the rate of $26.50 quarterly in advance, for each addi-
tional three months such completion is delayed from the time
above mentioned for the completion of such well until a well is
completed; and it is agreed that the drilling of such well, productive or otherwise, shall be and operate as full liquidation of all
rental under this provision during the remainder of this lease.
Such payment may be made direct to lessor or deposited to their
credit in the Roane County Bank, at Spencer, W. Va. It is agreed
that the second party is to have the privilege of using sufficient
water from the premises to run all necessary machinery, and at
any time to remove all machinery and fixtures placed on said
premises, and further, upon the payment of one dollar at any time,
by the party of the second part, their successors or assigns, to the
parties of the first part, their heirs or assigns, said party of
the second part, their successors or assigns, shall have the right
to surrender this lease for cancellation, after which all payments
and liabilities thereunder to accrue under and by virtue of its
terms, shall cease and determine and this lease become absolutely
null and void.''

About the same time Goff and Heck procured oil and gas
leases upon other tracts of land in the same neighborhood, some
of which were contiguous to the Hall tract. Shortly after obtaining these leases Goff and Heck and others procured a charter and

organized the Lucky Oil & Gas Company. Goff and Heck assigned
to this company all the working interest in said leases, except one-
eighth, which they retained for themselves. The contract of assignment provided that the Lucky Oil & Gas Company was to pay
the rentals thereafter to become due, and was to carry Goff and
Heck for the full one-eighth interest, free of cost to them, and bound
the corporation to drill at least one test well on the territory covered by the leases, and gave it the privilege of drilling other wells on
the premises. It further provided "that all surrenders and forfeitures of said leases or any of them, shall be to said first parties"
that is, to Goff and Heck; and that "in no event shall any or either
of said leases be forfeited or surrendered by the said second party
to the original lessors or their assignee, or grantee, or any person
or persons for them." The first two quarterly rentals falling due
on the Hall land were paid by the Lucky Oil & Gas Company.
When the third became due, on November 29, 1904, it was not paid,
but Goff and Heck applied to the Halls for an extension of the
time, without payment of the rent, which extension was refused.
No well was ever drilled on the Hall by anyone claiming under this
lease; but the Lucky Oil & Gas Company did, in the summer and
fall of 1904, drill a well on the Donohue tract of land, adjoining
the Hall tract. It was completed just prior to the time the third
quarterly rental on the Hall tract became due, and proved to be a
dry hole. In the drilling of this well the company had exhausted
its capital. It then ceased to do business and immediately surrendered its charter. The casing was removed from the dry well,
the machinery and casing belonging to the company were sold,
and the proceeds applied to the payment of its debts. Nothing
further was done towards the discovery of oil or gas until in the
early part of the year 1906. On June 27, 1905, the Halls made a
second lease to S. L. Thornily. Under this lease the defendants
completed their first well on the Hall farm on June 28, 1906, and
their second well on September 26, 1906, both of which wells produced oil. Defendant commenced to drill the third well on October 25, 1906. The Goff and Heck lease was assigned to H. L.
Smith, and the Thornily lease to C. M. Root and others. Smith
filed a bill in chancery in the Circuit Court of Roane County, West
Virginia, claiming under the first Hall lease, for an injunction
and receiver, and praying to have the second lease cancelled as a
cloud on his title. A temporary injunction was awarded before

the third well was completed, which injunction was modified so as
to allow the completion of this well, which was a producer. These
wells were all drilled by the defendants under the Hall lease of
June 27, 1905, on the Hall tract. The plaintiff Smith claimed the
exclusive right to the oil and gas in the Hall tract, and in a number of other tracts in the vicinity by assignment from Goff and
Heck made on February 6, 1906. At the time of this assignment
five quarterly rentals were past due on the Hall lease to Goff and
Heck, and on the day after the assignment Goff and Heck deposited
to the credit of the Halls, in the Roane County Bank the depositary
provided for by the lease, $132.50 to pay these back rentals, which
rentals were not accepted by the Halls. The Circuit Court dissolved the injunction and dismissed the bill on final hearing, and
plaintiff appealed. The Court of Appeals affirmed the decree, and
upon the question of the jurisdiction of the court in cases involving
the validity of oil and gas leases, cited:

> *Williamson* v. *Jones,* 43 W. Va. 562; 27 S. E. 411; 38 L. R.
>   A. 694; 64 Am. St. Rep. 891.
> *Crawford* v. *Ritchie,* 43 W. Va. 252; 27 S. E. 220.
> *Eclipse Oil Co.* v. *South Penn Oil Co.,* 47 W. Va. 84; 34 S.
>   E. 923.
> *Urpman* v. *Lowther Oil Co.,* 53 W. Va. 501; 44 S. E. 433; 97
>   Am. St. Rep. 1027.
> *Carney* v. *Barnes,* 56 W. Va. 581; 49 S. E. 423.
> *Starn* v. *Huffman,* 62 W. Va. 422; 59 S. E. 179.
> *Eastern Oil Co.* v. *Coulehan,* 65 W. Va. 531; 64 S. E. 836.

Upon the question that where a lessee has taken possession
or begun operations on the leased premises his abandonment of
his lease may be established by proving that he had abandoned
his intention to enter upon the lease for development, the court
cited:

> *Urpman* v. *Lowther Oil Co.,* 53 W. Va. 501; 44 S. E. 433; 97
>   Am. St. Rep. 1027.
> *Steelsmith* v. *Gartlan,* 45 W. Va. 27; 29 S. E. 978; 44 L. R.
>   A. 107.
> *Parish Fork Oil Co.* v. *Bridgewater Gas Co.,* 51 W. Va. 583;
>   42 S. E. 655; 59 L. R. A. 560.
> *Crawford* v. *Ritchie,* 43 W. Va. 252; 27 S. E. 220.
> *Toothman* v. *Courtney,* 62 W. Va. 167; 58 S. E. 915.
> *Sult* v. *Hochstetter Oil Co.,* 63 W. Va. 317; 61 S. E. 307.

Upon the question that relief will not be afforded one who has committed a mistake of law, the court cited:

Zollman v. *Moore,* 21 Gratt, 213.
Meem v. *Rucker,* 10 Gratt. 506.
Harner v. *Price,* 17 W. Va. 523.
Home Co. etc. v. *Floding,* 27 W. Va. 540.
Shriver v. *Garrison,* 30 W. Va. 456; 4 S. E. 660.

Sec. 15.—In *Carney* v. *Barnes,* 56 W. Va. 581; 49 S. E. 423 (Dec. 20, 1904) the first and fourth points of the syllabus are as follows:

"1. Chancery has jurisdiction to cancel a deed granting petroleum oil for failure to perform its covenants, where the deed has a clause annuling it for such failure.
4. To deny equity jurdisdiction because of a remedy at law, the legal remedy must not be merely partial, but it must be adequate, and as complete and efficacious as that given by equity."

Eli Carney and wife, on February 3, 1898, executed a lease to E. H. Jennings and brothers, for oil purposes, for a tract of land, providing that lessee should give lessors 1-8 of the oil produced, to be set apart in the pipelines to the credit of Carney and wife as royalty or rent. Jennings Brothers drilled two wells on the land, getting oil, which was run into the pipelines of the Eureka Pipeline Company. Before operations for oil production were begun, Carney and wife, on September 6, 1900, made a deed conveying to George W. Barnes all the oil in said land except 1-16, the deed recognizing the existence of the lease to Jennings Brothers, and provided that if that lease should expire or become void under its terms, then Barnes should have all the oil, with the right to produce it on the usual terms of leases for oil and gas purposes; thus the deed to Barnes operated to give him half the eighth, Carney retaining 1-2. For the conveyance Barnes paid Carney a bonus of $3,000 cash, and the deed provided that Barnes should, within thirty days after the first well, and thirty days after the second well, should be completed, tubed, and tested for oil, pay to Carney $2,000 for each well if it produced ten barrels of oil per day for 30 consecutive days, Carney to give notice to Barnes

by writing of the wells being drilled and the amount of their production. The deed from Carney to Barnes contained the clause:

"If said grantee shall, as he may do at his option, omit to pay
the said sum of $2,000 for the first well within the time afore-
said, except as hereinafter mentioned, then this grant shall become as absolutely null and void as though it had never been
made, and said grantors shall retain the sum above mentioned
as full liquidated damages."

Eli Carney and wife filed a bill in chancery in the Circuit
Court of Wetzel County, against George W. Barnes and others,
praying to cancel the deed to Barnes. The Circuit Court entered
a decree for plaintiff, from which decree the defendant Barnes
appealed. The Court of Appeals found the facts: that there was
a conflict of evidence as to the quality of oil produced by the two
wells drilled by Jennings Brothers; There was some evidence to
show less than 20 barrels per day, and some showing 22 barrels
per day; Barnes never was on the ground; The deed to him from
Carney, was taken by Umstead, his agent, who transacted for
Barnes all that he did with Carney in the matter; Carney demanded of Barnes who lived in Ohio, by letters, payment of the
$2,000 for each of the wells, as stipulated in the deed, Carney
claiming that the wells produced over 10 barrels per day, each,
so as to entitle him to the money under the deed; Barnes refused
to pay the money, claiming that he could not afford to do so.
Barnes said that he was under the impression that the deed required the wells to produce thirty barrels per day before he was
called on to pay the money; While the matter was in this condition Umstead went to Carney to make some compromise, and
told Carney that Barnes could not afford to pay $2,000 for each
well, and proposed a compromise, by which Barnes should pay
$2,000 instead of $4,000; and if the third well should be drilled
producing 20 barrels per day for 30 days, then Carney should receive $1,000 more; This compromise was reduced to writing and
was signed by Carney and wife, and sent to Barnes in Ohio, who
refused to accept it, and returned it to Umstead claiming that no
compromise was necessary as the wells did not produce oil in
such quantity as to demand anything from him; Then it was that
Carney and wife brought the suit in equity against Barnes, making as defendants also Jennings Brothers and the Eureka

Pipeline Company, alleging in the bill that the wells had produced more than ten barrels each for 30 days; and that though they had thus become entitled to $2,000 for each, Barnes had refused to pay the same, had broken his contract, and that under the clause of the deed it had become null and void by reason of the refusal of Barnes to pay the money. The bill prayed that Jennings Brothers disclose when each of the wells began to produce oil and what quantity they produced per day for thirty days after their completion, and what amount they had produced since they began to produce oil; what oil from the wells had been received by Barnes; and what oil had been run from the wells into the pipelines of the Eureka Pipeline Company. The bill alleged that a division order certifying the rights of Barnes to 1-16, and of Carney to 1-16 of the oil had been issued by the Pipeline Company, and prayed that that company file a copy of it. The bill also prayed that the Pipeline Company state in what proportion the oil was divided, and who received credit therefor, and state the times when Barnes sold oil produced from the wells, and what he received therefor. The bill prayed that the deed from Carney and wife to Barnes be declared by decree to be null and void, and that the court ascertain through a commissioner the amount of oil received by Barnes, and what oil he had sold from the wells, and what money he received therefor; and that a money decree go against Barnes for the proceeds of his sales of oil. The bill further prayed that the Eureka Pipeline Company be enjoined from accounting for or turning over to Barnes the oil already in its lines, or that might thereafter come into its lines from said well. An injunction was granted. Barnes filed an answer to the effect that the true agreement between Carney and wife and Umstead as agent, was as appeared in the deed, except in one particular, that is, that whereas the deed required him to pay $2,000 for each of two wells producing 10 barrels per day, it should have provided that the wells should produce thirty barrels per day; that the deed should in that place read "thirty barrels" not "ten barrels." His answer stated that he was engaged in the business of buying oil royalties in West Virginia, and elsewhere; that he had blank deeds prepared to facilitate the execution of papers showing the purchase of royalty, and had furnished Umstead with a number of such blanks, and that Umstead had used one of those blanks in the transaction with Carney; that the agreement between Umstead

and Carney and wife, was in that respect for wells producing 30
barrels, not 10, and that the presence of the word ten in the deed
was due to a mistake in the omission to strike out the printed
word "ten." from the blank and insert in its place the word
"thirty;" that the matter was overlooked by Umstead, and also
by Barnes when the deed was sent to him; that in instructions to
Umstead he directed him to require a minimum production, from
30 to 35 barrels per day for thirty days, where the sum of additional money for wells was of the amount specified in the deed;
that the territory in which the wells were drilled was known to
be the Gordon or deep sand territory, wherein the drilling of wells
would cost from $8,000 to $10,000; and that wells producing less
than thirty barrels per day would be unprofitable; and that operators under leases in that territory would refrain from drilling
therein; and that wells producing more than thirty barrels would
induce operators to further develop the territory, and that the
payment of $7,000 for wells of less than thirty barrel capacity
would be unreasonable; denied that Carney had ever given him
notice of the true quantity of oil produced by the wells as stipulated in the contract; averred that the actual production of the
first well on the land was between sixteen and seventeen barrels
per day as shown by the reports of the pipeline company; that
neither the first nor the second well produced at any time as much
as twenty barrels per day, each; denied that the deed from Carney and wife to him had become void; and denied that he owed
anything to Carney and wife by reason of said wells. The answer
prayed that as the deed from Carney and wife to him did not
express the true agreement between them and him, it be reformed
and the word "ten" stricken out and the word "thirty" inserted
in its place. The Circuit Court decreed the deed from Carney
and wife to be null and void, and forfeited on account of the provision contained in it, and the failure of Barnes to comply therewith, and denied to Barnes the reformation of the deed, sought by
his answer, and referred the cause to a commissioner for a report, as to the oil which had been received by Barnes, and perpetuated the provisional injunction restraining the Pipeline Company from turning over to Barnes oil produced from the wells and
required it to account to Carney and wife for all oil in its lines
on that date, when the injunction was served upon it, and directed
such oil and all oil produced in future from the wells to be credited

by the Pipeline Company to Carney and wife, and declared them to be entitled to all oil in the lines at the date of the injunction, or thereafter produced, going to Carney and wife under their lease to Jennings Brothers.   The Court of Appeals reversed the Circuit Court, upholding, however, the jurisdiction of the court; and upon that proposition cited:

Hiett v. *Shull*, 36 W. Va. 563; 15 S. E. 146.
Hoopes v. *Devaughn*, 43 W. Va. 447; 27 S. E. 251.
Haskell v. *Sutton*, 43 W. Va. 206; 44 S E. 533.
Alexander v. *Davis*, 42 W. Va. 465-467; 26 S. E. 291.
Rich v. *Braxton*, 158 U. S. 375.
DeCamp v. *Carnahan*, 26 W. Va. 839.
Nease v. *Ins. Co.*, 32 W. Va. 283; 9 S. E. 233.
Farmers Co. v. *Galesburg*, 133 U. S. 156.
Powell v. *Taylor*, 11 Leigh 172.
Lowman v. *Crawford*, 99 Va. 688; 40 S. E. 17.
Wilfong v. *Johnson*, 41 W. Va. 283; 23 S. E. 730.
Goldsmith v. *Goldsmith*, 46 W. Va. 426; 33 S. E. 266.

Upon the evidence the court of Appeals concluded that the word "ten" had been by mistake left in the blank deed, and should have been stricken out and the word "thirty" inserted; upon this finding the court refused the relief prayed for as to cancellation of the deed.   The Court decreed that the reformation of the deed be made in accordance with the answer of defendant Barnes.

Sec. 16.—In *Starn* v. *Huffman*, 62 W. Va. 422; 59 S. E. 179, (Oct. 29, 1907) the syllabus is as follows:

"1.   A lease of a coal vein for mining for one year, and as long thereafter as the lessee may continue to mine it, the lessor to receive ten cents per ton for all coal mined payable at the end of each thirty days, and mining to begin the next day.   After the lapse of two years and three months, no mining having been done, equity will cancel the lease at the suit of the lessor.
2.   Principles upon which equity will cancel a mining lease for failure to operate.
3.   A mere statement in an answer that other persons are interested in the property involved, without proof of their interest, their rights not being affected by the decree, will not be

ground for reversal. Where one is not interested in the controversy between the immediate litigants, but has an interest in the
subject matter, which may be conveniently settled in the suit and
thereby prevent further litigation, he may be a party or not, at
the option of the complainant.''

James Starn made a lease to Samuel S. Huffman of the Pittsburg vein of coal in a tract of 12 acres of land, for one year and
as much longer as Huffman should continue to operate the mine,
which lease provided that the lessee should pay the lessor ten
cents per ton for all coal mined; and that the lessee should ''begin
mining said coal on or before December 19, 1902, and pay for said
coal every thirty days.'' The lease bore date December 18, 1902.
Huffman assigned the lease to James F. Cook and John P. Hart.
On March 23, 1905, Starn instituted a suit in chancery in the Circuit Court of Marion County, West Virginia, against Samuel S.
Huffman and his assignees, to cancel the lease, for failure to mine
as required by it, and to clear and quiet the title of Starn to the
coal. The defendant answered, but introduced no evidence to support the answer. No mining whatever was done under the lease.
The Circuit Court entered a decree cancelling the lease and defendants appealed, and the Court of Appeals affirmed the decree.

Upon the question of the cancellation of a mining lease by a
court of equity for failure to operate, the court cited:

Urpman v. *Lowther Oil Co.*, 53 W. Va. 505; 44 S. E. 433.
Crawford v. *Ritchie*, 43 W. Va. 252; 27 S. E. 320.
Bluestone Coal Co. v. *Bell*, 38 W. Va. 297; 18 S. E. 493.
Bettman v. *Harness*, 42 W. Va. 433; 26 S. E. 271.
Western Pennsylvania Gas Co. v. *George*, 161 Pa. 47; 28 At.
    1004.
Elk Fork Oil & Gas Co. v. *Jennings*, 84 Fed. 839.
Shenandoah Land Co. v. *Hise*, 92 Va. 238; 23 S. E. 303.
Caldwell v. *Fulton*, 72 Am. Dec. 766.
Cowan v. *Radford Iron Co.*, 93 Va. 547; 3 S. E. 120.
Warren v. *Wheeler*, 8 Metc. (Mass) 97.
Atwood v. *Cobb*, 16 Pick, 227.
Ryan v. *Hall*, 13 Metc. (Mass) 520.
Thompson v. *Ketchum*, 8 John. 189.
Barry v. *Ranson*, 12 N. Y. 462.
Young v. *Ellis*, 91 Va. 297; 21 S. E. 480.
Maxwell v. *Todd*, 112 N. C. 677.

Island Coal Co. v. *Combs,* 152 Ind. 579; 53 N. E. 455.
Rorer Iron Co. v. *Trout,* 83 Va. 397; 2 S. E. 713; 5 Am. St.
    Rep. 285.
Huggins v. *Daley,* 99 Fed. 606; 40 C. C. A. 12; 48 L. R. A. 320.

Sec. 17.—In *Pheasant* v. *Hanna,* 63 W. Va. 613; 60 S. E. 618
(Feb. 18, 1908) syls. 1-4, inclusive, are as follows:

"1.   Equity will not enforce a forfeiture.
2.   A court of equity will not cancel a mining lease before
the expiration of the term, for mere delay in paying rent or commutation money, and failure to commence operations at the time
stipulated, if it appears that the lessees are ready and willing to
pay the rent and perform the covenant to open and operate the
mines.
3.   Equity will relieve a mining lessee from a mere technical
forfeiture on his performance of all covenants and duties imposed upon him by the lease, the rights of no third parties having intervened.
4.   A tender of rent to a landlord who has agreed to sell the
premises, but, by a stipulation in the contract of sale, has the right
to receive rents, issues and profits at the time of the tender, is
sufficient."

E. A. Pheasant and others filed a bill in chancery in the Circuit Court of Morgan County, West Virginia, against Henry
N. Hanna and others.   The facts were substantially as follows:
Marion D. Wise, the owner of a tract of 17 acres of land and an
adjoining tract containing about 20 acres, with her husband, F.
S. Wise, executed a lease to H. H. Hunter, on January 9, 1901, the
purpose of which was to enable the lessee to mine and remove
sand from the 17-acre tract, and gave the right of way to an adjacent tract, to a small railroad—a branch of the Baltimore &
Ohio Railroad.   The consideration for the lease was one dollar,
and the covenants and agreements in the lease to be performed
by the lessee.   These covenants were; to pay for the material at
the price of two cents per ton for first class, and one cent per ton
for second class sand; to begin the mining of sand on the land
within one year from the date of the lease, and diligently prosecute the same.   The rights granted were:
"To dig, mine, or blast and remove the sand from any and all
of the lands owned by the parties of the first part on the east side

of Warm Spring Ridge, between the town of Bath and Hancock Station, on the Baltimore & Ohio R. R. in Morgan County, West Virginia" and the "privilege to mine and remove any and all sand from other lands through and over the premises of the party of the first part."

A right of way at least thirty feet wide through and over the lands of the lessors from said Warm Spring Ridge to the Railroad, to be fenced by a good and substantial fence on both sides by the lessee, together with a sufficient quantity of land for the purpose of erecting necessary buildings and sidings, to be used in the preparation of sand for shipment; and an option to lease the land for a period of ninety-nine years, or purchase the same in fee simple, at the price of $100.00 per acre at any time within two years from the date of the lease. A forfeiture clause in the following terms was inserted:

"Should from any cause the work of mining sand and shipping the same cease for the period of two years at any time, or fail to pay the sum of one hundred dollars annually which is to be deducted from the first royalty due, then this lease to be null and void."

Subsequently Hunter disposed of the lease by assignment and John G. Fouse, I. K. Bechtol, S. F. Shelly, and Nathan L. Chappelle, among whom there existed a sort of co-partnership for speculating or operating on lands of the character above described, became the owners of it. Differences having arisen among them, they failed to commence mining operations on the land but made two annual payments of rental; and in a suit instituted by Fouse for the dissolution of the partnership and settlement of its business, the leasehold was sold on July 19, 1904, to Henry N. Hanna, for the sum of $500.00 and the sale was confirmed on October 7, 1904. In the meantime Wise, on January 17, 1903, had entered into an executory contract for the sale of the land with E. A. Pheasant through her husband and agent, A. M. Pheasant, which was carried into effect on February 12, 1903, by a deed conveying the land with a covenant of general warranty to E. A. Pheasant, of Windbar, Pennsylvania, and J. F. Swope, of Colfax, Pennsylvania. On January 17, 1905, another general warranty deed was executed by Mrs. Wise, conveying the adjacent tract to the same parties. No reference was made in either of these deeds to the lease. In May, 1905, Hanna, J. Frank Fields, and William Beard, whom he had associated with him in respect to this lease, began to cut timber on the premises and make surveys for rights of way, and otherwise indicate their purpose and readiness to begin mining on the property. On May 29, 1905, this suit was instituted by E. A. Pheasant, A. M. Pheasant and J. F. Swope, for the purpose of having the lease cancelled, and for an injunction to restrain the assignees of the lease from entry upon the premises. It was admitted that the commutation money was paid for the years 1901 and 1902. The lease did not specify at what time payment should be made. On January 27, 1903, about ten days after Wise had contracted the sale of the land to Pheasant, A. C. McIntire, a member of a firm of attorneys for Fouse and Bechtol in the suit brought for the dissolution of the co-partnership, received a check of $100 with which to pay the rental for the year 1903, and notified Wise of his possession thereof, and asked him to come and get it. Wise came a day or two later and declined to receive the check, saying the lease had expired and was void. Thereupon McIntire had the check cashed and called upon Marion D. Wise, and tendered her the money. She also refused to accept it, saying sand had not been mined within the year, payments had not been made according to contract, and further, that they had sold to Pheasants, and could not take the money. McIntire then deposited it in Bank at Martinsburg. Some time in September, 1904, A. M. Pheasant pursuant to a request, called at the office of Fouse, in Pittsburg, and accompanied him at his request to the office of his attorney where he spoke of the Wise lease, and suggested payment of money on account thereof to Pheasant, whereupon Pheasant replied that he had no right to receive any money on the lease, saying he had transacted the business for his wife, and Swope, and had turned all the papers over to them; and that any business pertaining thereto would have to be transacted with them, and the attorney then so advised Fouse who said: "All right we will have to do that." Sometime between the 5th and 9th of January, 1905, Hanna caused to be drawn the check of the West Virginia and Pennsylvania Sand Company for $100.00 payable to the order of Mrs. E. A. Pheasant, and certified by the International Trust Company of Maryland, and enclosed it in a registered letter addressed to E. A. Pheasant, at Windbar, Pennsylvania, on which a special delivery stamp was placed, which letter was returned and received by him on January 11, 1905, marked, "Refused." A. M. Pheasant testified that notice thereof had been received by Mrs. Pheasant at Windbar late in the evening of January 9, 1905, and that it was refused because it appeared from the card on the envelope to have been sent by a Pottery Company of Baltimore; being asked why neither he nor his wife opened and read it, he said: "We had no business with those people that we knew of." Being asked if he did not know it contained a money order or draft for the rental, he replied, that he did not know what it contained.

The Circuit Court entered a decree declaring the lease for the tract of 17 acres of land to have been forfeited, and perpetuating an injunction restraining the assignees of the lease from entering upon the premises. From this decree Henry M. Hanna, J. Frank Fields, and William Beard appealed to the Court of Appeals. That court reversed the decree and remanded the cause.

Upon the proposition that equity will relieve against a technical forfeiture, the court cited:

Craig v. *Hukill*, 37 W. Va. 520; 16 S. E. 363.
Wheeling, etc. Railroad Co. v. *Town of Triadelphia*, 54 W. Va. 487; 52 S. E. 499.
Spies v. *R. R. Co.*, 60 W. Va. 389; 55 S. E. 464.

Sec. 18.—Pennsylvania Rule.—Where a lessee is in possession of the premises demised by the lease and engaged in the development thereof, or having discovered gas is in possession thereof by connecting the well with his gas lines, equity has jurisdiction to restrain the lessor or anyone acting for or under him, from drilling on the leasehold, the rights granted to the lessee being necessarily exclusive, and the damages to arise from the threatened waste being entirely incapable of measurement at law, even if not irreparable.

Westmoreland Nat. Gas. Co. v. *DeWitt*, 130 Pa. 235; 18 Atl.
   724.
Greensboro Nat. Gas Co., v. *Fayette County Gas. Co.*, 200
   Pa. 388; 49 Atl. 768.

Sec. 19.—A lessee under an oil and gas lease which grants
only the exclusive privilege of mining for oil and gas upon the
premises, and does not grant the lands for the purpose, may maintain a bill in equity against a conflicting claimant to the premises.

Carnegie Nat. Gas. Co. v. *Philadelphia Co.*, 158 Pa. 317; 27
   Atl. 95.
Funk v. *Halderman,* 53 Pa. 229;

Sec. 20.—In *Greensboro Natural Gas Co.* v. *Fayette County
Gas Co.*, 200 Pa. 388; 49 Atl. 768 (July 17, 1901) the syllabus is
as follows:

"A bill in equity should not be dismissed on answer and replication, where it appears from the bill that the complainant was in
actual possession of the land under an oil and gas lease for a definite term, and this fact is not denied by the answer, and the
prayer of the bill is that the defendant be enjoined from the commission of a continuing trespass and the perpetration of wrongs
alleged to be irreparable. The case, as presented by the pleadings,
is one for a hearing and final decree thereon."

The Greensboro Natural Gas Company, a corporation, filed a
bill in equity in the court of Common Pleas of Fayette County,
against the Fayette County Gas Company, a corporation. The
bill averred that the plaintiff was the owner of an oil and gas
lease dated February 23, 1900, for a tract of land formerly owned
by N. B. Johnson; that the lease was for five years from the date
thereof; that on March 8, 1900, the land was sold by the executors of Johnson to Alva L. Morris; that complainant's lease
was recorded before the deed to Morris; that on or about January
28, 1901, Morris executed an oil and gas lease to the defendant,
the Fayette County Gas Company; that defendant took its lease
with full knowledge that plaintiff's lease was a good and a valid
lease, the defendant fraudulently representing to Morris that he

could safely ignore plaintiff's lease, and could safely lease to defendant; that on January 30, 1901, about 2:30 P. M. plaintiff, learning that defendant proposed to enter upon the property and drill for oil and gas in defiance of plaintiff's lease, gave defendant written notice of plaintiff's rights, and notified defendant not to enter upon the property; and that he would be held responsible in damages for any entry thereon with the intention to drill; that notwithstanding such notice, as plaintiff was informed, defendant on January 31, 1901, entered on the premises for the erection of a derrick, and made preparations to begin drilling for oil and gas; that on January 31, 1901, in the morning, plaintiff entered upon the premises, located a well, and began preparations to drill for oil and gas, and had continued the preparations and purposes, and purposed to complete a well forthwith on the property; that plaintiff had leased other properties in the township where the lease from Johnson was located, and had what was designated as a fairly contiguous territory, and the Johnson tract was situated in the heart of said territory, and in the direct line of the productive wells, and was therefore an essential and very valuable part of the territory; that the damages to plaintiff from being deprived of the exclusive right to drill for oil and gas on the Johnson tract were not capable of being determined in an action at law, and no adequate reparation could be made to the plaintiff for interference with and the loss of the exclusive right to drill on the tract; that the entry on the land for the purpose of drilling by the defendant was a trespass, and continuance thereon for that purpose would be a continuing trespass for which plaintiff had no adequate remedy at law; that plaintiff was a corporation of the State of Pennsylvania, and defendant a corporation of the State of West Virginia. The bill prayed an injunction, preliminary until hearing, and to be made perpetual thereafter, restraining defendant and its agents and employes from erecting on the land any derricks or other structures used in drilling for oil and gas and restraining them from drilling on the land for oil or gas, and from in any way trespassing upon or interfering with plaintiff's exclusive rights on the land.

The defendant filed an answer in which the possession of the plaintiff was not denied. Plaintiff filed a replication and subsequently defendant moved the court to dismiss the bill, and the court granted the motion and dismissed the bill. Plaintiff appealed, and the Supreme Court reversed the decree of dismissal and reinstated the cause.

Sec. 21.—In *Westmoreland Nat. Gas Co.* v. *DeWitt*, 130 Pa. 235; 18 Atl. 724; 5 L. R. A. 731, analyzed under Chapter 7, syl. 5 is as follows:

"5. Where the lessee is thus in possession of the gas underlying the premises, equity has jurisdiction to restrain the lessor from drilling on the leasehold, the rights granted to the lessee being necessarily exclusive, and the damages to arise from the threatened waste, being entirely incapable of measurement at law, even if not irreparable.

Sec. 22.—In *Carnegie Nat. Gas Co.* v. *Philadelphia Co.*, 158 Pa. 317; 27 Atl. 95, analyzed under Chapter 17, the last paragraph of the syllabus is as follows:

"Equity has jurisdiction to award an injunction in a contest over the right to operate land for oil, where the lease under which the right is claimed does not grant a conveyance in fee, but merely an incorporeal hereditament."

Sec. 23.—In *Stone* v. *Marshall Oil Co.*, 188 Pa. 602; 41 Atl. 748-1119 (Nov. 14, 1898) the syllabus is as follows:

"When covenant is for the performance of some duty in connection with the possession of land, and relating thereto, or in the nature of rent or royalty for the use and enjoyment of the premises, it is a covenant running with the land. The rent need not be money; it may be a share in the product, as the share of oil in an oil lease, or the share of the proceeds of the sale of gas in a gas lease.

Where an owner of land executes an oil and gas lease, and, subsequently, after a default in the payment of rental, but without any declaration of forfeiture, executes a second lease to other parties in which it is expressly provided that such parties should stand between him, 'and all who may have claims to this lease.'

the execution of the second lease is not a declaration of forfeiture
of the first lease.

G., the owner of 150 acres of land, exécuted an oil and gas
lease to A. in consideration of one-eighth of the oil and a certain
sum per annum for gas if discovered, with a stipulation that failure to pay rentals would render the lease void. Subsequently A.
and Co., composed of A. and the persons to whom he had assigned
1-2 of the lease, executed two leases of portions of the land to
M., an oil company. In these leases it was provided that M.
should drill an additional well, and that A. and Co., should receive 1-4 of the profits of the gas, if any were discovered. In
1888, M. drilled a well on the land which proved to be a very valuable gas well. About a month after this well was drilled, G.
who had never declared a forfeiture of his lease to A. although
there had been a failure to pay rental, executed an oil and gas
lease on the whole 150 acres to M. which did not require the drilling of the additional well. In this lease M. agreed to stand between G. 'and all who may have claims to this lease.' About one
month after the execution of the latter lease, M. sold and leased
the gas well and fifteen acres surrounding it to W., an oil company.
About a year afterwards W. not being able under its charter to
conduct the gas business, sold the well to a natural gas company
which it had organized, and most of the stock of which it held.
W. knew before it leased from M. that M. had drilled and completed a well on this property under a lease with plaintiffs. The
lease from G. to A. was recorded. In 1893, a bill in equity was
filed by A. & Company against M., W. and the gas company for discovery, to ascertain the facts as to the relations of the different
defendants to the gas leases, the disposal of the gas, and for an
account of the profits of the gas well. *Held*, (1) that equity had
jurisdiction of bill; (2) that plaintiffs were not guilty of laches;
(3) that the statute of limitations did not apply; (4) that the execution of the second lease by G. was not a forfeiture of his first
lease; (5) that M. in procuring the second lease from G. acted
in bad faith, and was guilty of legal fraud upon the plaintiff; (6)
that W. was not an innocent purchaser, or lessee; (7) that W.
was a sub-lessee under the plaintiff's lease; (8) that the sale of
the gas by W. to the gas company was virtually a sale of the
well, and a part of the leasehold realty; (9) that the gas company
was a sub-lessee of the lease from the plaintiff's to M., and as such
subject to all the covenants in said lease; (10) that the covenants in plaintiff's lease to M. ran with the land; (11) that the
plaintiffs were entitled to an account from all three of defendant
companies of the profits realized from the sale of the gas.''

C. W. Stone, R. B. Stone, A. J. Hazeltine, and J. B. Akin
filed a bill in equity in Court of Common Pleas Allegheny County,
Pennsylvania, against the Marshall Oil Company, the Washington
Oil Company, and the Taylorstown Natural Gas Company. The
Judge of the Court of Common Pleas found the following facts:

1.—On November 13, 1885, John Grimes executed an oil and
gas lease to J. B. Akin for 150 acres of land in Washington County
Pennsylvania; Lessor to have ⅛ royalty of oil, and to receive
$700 per annum for the gas from each and every gas well, the gas
from which should be conducted and used off the premises, lessee
to complete one well within a year from date of lease; lessee to
pay lessor $150.00 per annum commencing six months after date,
payable quarterly, which sum lessor agreed to accept as full consideration and payment for each yearly delay until one well should
be completed; a failure to complete one well, or to make any of
said payments within such time rendered the lease null and void.
The lease was acknowledged on December 3, 1885, and recorded in
Washington County, July 22, 1886.

2.—Akin sold and assigned a 1-2 interest in the lease to R.
B. Stone, A. J. Hazeltine and C. W. Stone, on December 2, 1886,
which assignment was acknowledged and recorded the same day,
in Washington County. Akin & Company drilled no well but paid
the quarterly installments of rental. On October 19, 1887, they
executed a lease to the Marshall Oil Company of 50 acres of the
farm, reciting the lease from Grimes to Akin and its provisions.
The lease was "for the sole and only purpose of drilling and operating for petroleum oil or gas for the period of one year, and as
long thereafter, less than the term of the original lease, as oil
or gas may be found in paying quantities, subject, however, to all
the reservations, stipulations, rents and covenants in said original
lease contained, all of which are to be faithfully kept and performed by the said party of the second part (the Marshall Oil
Company) its successors and assigns." The Marshall Oil Company agreed to drill four wells, one to be completed within four
months, one in eight months, one in twelve months, and one in
sixteen months. This lease contained the further provision:

"In further consideration of the lease hereby granted, the said parties of the second part, the Marshall Oil Company, for itself, its successors and assigns, agrees to give to said parties of the first part, their executors, administrators and assigns, 1-4 of all pretroleum produced from said premises;" one-eighth to the credit of John Grimes, the original lessor, and one-eighth to the lessors of this lease. "It is also agreed that in case gas shall be discovered and conducted off the premises for use or sale, the said parties of the first part, in the proportionate interests aforesaid, shall receive 1-4 of the profits thereof above cost and bonus of seven hundred dollars to the original lessor."

This lease was acknowledged on August 19, 1887, and recorded in Washington County, on August 20, 1887.

3.—On December 25, 1887, Akin & Company made a supplemental lease to the Marshall Oil Company of thirty acres more of the Grimes farm on the same terms, stipulations and conditions as the lease of the fifty acres, reciting it, and providing that in place of four wells—none of which had been drilled—two wells should be drilled, one on the 50-acre tract and one on the 30-acre tract, and that one well should be completed within four months, "and as to all wells that may be drilled on either portion of said premises, the royalty of oil and gas shall be as fixed in the lease, of the fifty-acre tract.

4.—The Marshall Oil Company then proceeded to drill a well which was completed on May 8, 1888, the only well ever drilled on the Grimes farm. It was drilled down to the oil rock, but produced no oil. It was a strong gas well. The Marshall Oil Company did not attempt to utilize the gas, but for a month or so, endeavored to sell the well. After some delay in negotiations they sold it to the Washington Oil Company in connection with a lease for fifteen acres, for $4,000.

5—While these negotiations were going on, and while the well was being gauged to ascertain the pressure of the gas, the Marshall Oil Company obtained a lease for the whole farm, dated June 19, 1888, from John Grimes. This lease was nearly identical with the lease from Grimes to Akin, except that $600.00 instead of $700.00 should be paid for every gas well, when the gas should be conducted and used off the premises, and for the gas well then completed, $700 per annum should be paid; and there was no requirement in this lease to put down any additional well. This lease was acknowledged by Grimes on July 4, 1888. Grimes, by a separate agreement, agreed to reduce the annual rental of the gas well to $500.00. The Marshall Oil Company, then, by sale and lease dated July 5, 1888, sold the well and leased 15 acres to the Washington Oil Company, in consideration of $4,000 cash paid, and subject to all the terms and conditions of the lease of June 19, 1888.

6.—The Washington Oil Company tubed the well and conducted the gas off the premises for sale or use from August, 1888, to September 2, 1889, and then sold the gas to the Taylorstown Natural Gas Company, by bill of sale dated September 2, 1889; and that company had been conducting the gas off the premises and selling it to the date of the suit.

7.—The rent due to Grimes on his lease to Akin was paid promptly until February 13, 1888. The rent for the quarter ending May 13, 1888 was not paid.

8.—Grimes never declared a forfeiture of his lease to Akin, of November 13, 1885. When he made the lease to the Marshall Oil Company, of June 15, 1888, he required a statement to be inserted in the lease before he would sign it as follows:

'The party of the second part (the Marshall Oil Company) agrees to stand between the party of the first part (himself) and all who may have claims to this lease.''

After the lease was signed he said to Mr. Akin that he signed it because he wanted to get all the money out of the farm he could; that he didn't know whether his lease was good or not, but the Marshall Oil Company had agreed to stand between him and harm.

9.—The Taylorstown Natural Gas Company was simply a device of the Washington Oil Company to get certain privileges and advantages which it could not get under its charter. It wanted the power to secure the right of way for laying pipes and conducting gas to distant points and selling it, which it could not do under its charter as an oil company. The large majority of the stock of the Taylorstown Natural Gas Company was owned by the Washington Oil Company, the officers of the two companies were nearly the same; the Washington Oil Company had the entire management and control of the business, and received all, or nearly all of the profits. The paper of September 2, 1889, although called a bill of sale, was virtually a lease. No cash was paid. It sold the gas of the well for twenty years, if it should so long pay to pipe it, the Taylorstown Company to pay the annual royalty to Grimes, and $400.00 a year to the Washington Oil Company.

10.—When the drilling ceased, May 8, 1888, the flow of gas indicated a strong gas well. Several tests were made to ascertain the pressure, and each test showed an increased pressure and indicated a very strong gas well. By July 4th, when the Marshall Oil Company sold to the Washington Oil Company it was known to be a remarkably strong gas well. It had produced an immense volume of gas, sufficient to supply the boiler for drilling forty or fifty wells at the same time, and continued at the expiration of nine years to produce gas with little or no diminution of volume.

11.—After the gas well was completed, May 8, 1888, by the Marshall Oil Company, the plaintiffs did nothing under the Grimes lease to Akin, and although they knew of the Grimes lease to the Marshall Oil Company, of June 19, 1888, they took no legal steps to test that lease, and made no demand of any of the defendant companies for a share of the profits of the gas until about the time the bill was filed, July 25, 1893, five years after the Marshall Oil Company had sold to the Washington Oil Company.

The Court of Common Pleas held that these matters brought the case properly within the jurisdiction of a court of equity, and entered a decree, that the plaintiffs were entitled to an account from the defendant companies of the profits realized from the sale of the gas from the well on the Grimes farm; and that to ascertain the profits, all expenses of every kind should be first deducted from the proceeds of the sale of the gas; that if the gas was used by the Washington Oil Company, or the Taylorstown Natural Gas Company, in drilling wells of their own, or the gas was used otherwise, in their own business, they should be charged with said gas at the same rate as though sold to others, or at what said gas was really worth; the expenses to include $700.00 annual rental to Grimes under the original lease, the costs of pipes and other material in keeping up the well, payments for rights of way, payments to all employes engaged in attending to the wells, pipes, etc., and the business, generally, of saving, transporting and selling the gas, and appointed a master to take testimony and state an account against the Washington Oil Company and the Taylorstown Natural Gas Company, and that upon his report coming in, the court would consider the liability of the Marshall Oil Company and any other questions that might properly arise. From this decree the Washington Oil Company and the Taylorstown Gas Company appealed, and the Supreme Court by a per curiam opinion, affirmed the decree.

CHAPTER 52.

FORFEITURE WILL NOT BE ENFORCED BY A COURT OF EQUITY.

Sec. 1.—A court of equity will not enforce a forfeiture. It will not divest a vested estate by enforcing a forfeiture for the breach of a subsequent condition. In such case the party is left to his legal remedy.

Craig v. *Hukill,* 37 W. Va. 520; 16 S. E. 363.
Pheasant v. *Hanna,* 63 W. Va. 613; 60 S. E. 618.
Headley v. *Hoopengarner,* 60 W. Va. 626; 55 S. E. 144.
Newton v. *Kemper,* 66 W. Va. 130; 66 S. E. 102.

Sec. 2.—In *Craig* v. *Hukill,* 37 W. Va. 520; 16 S. E. 363, (Dec. 22, 1892) the syllabus is as follows:

"Equity will not enforce a forfeiture. It will not divest a vested estate by enforcing a forfeiture for the breach of a subsequent condition. In such case the party is left to his legal remedy."

W. M. Davis executed to David Kennedy a lease of a tract of land for a term of years for oil and gas purposes which lease became by assignment the property of E. M. Hukill. The lease contained a covenant on the part of the lessee to begin operations within nine months or pay a sum of money per month as commutation money until commencement of work with a forfeiture clause providing that the lease should be forfeited in case lessee failed to do one or the other. After making the lease Davis executed an instrument by which he agreed to sell to H. P. Griffith all the oil and gas under the tract, and Griffith transferred all his right in the tract to Joseph W. Craig. Davis had a life estate in the tract, with remainder in fee to his children; and by the death of one of them he inherited an undivided 1-5 share therein. Hukill, claiming under the first mentioned lease, as also under a lease from the guardian of the surviving children, drilled for and discovered oil on the premises. Craig brought a suit in equity in the Circuit Court of Monongalia County against Hukill, Davis and others, praying that the tract be partitioned, and 1-5 be assigned as the share of Davis in fee and that all the oil and gas under it be assigned the plaintiff Craig. The theory of Craig for relief was, that by reason of failure to commence operations or to pay money in lieu thereof as provided in the lease to Kennedy, it had become forfeited, and he had, by the agreement between Davis and Griffith become entitled in exclusion of all rights under the Kennedy lease, to all oil which Davis could convey. The Circuit Court decreed to the plaintiff the relief sought, and defendants appealed. The Court of Appeals reversed the Circuit Court upon the grounds that though equity has jurisdiction in partition, yet it will not exercise such jurisdiction when it can be exercised only by enforcing a forfeiture, when the plaintiff's right grows only out of a forfeiture. The Court further held, that the estate under the Kennedy lease had become vested in Hukill, and that plaintiff sought by suit in equity to divest this estate.

Sec. 3.—In *Pheasant v. Hanna*, 63 W. Va. 613; 60 S. E. 618, analyzed under Chapter 51, syl. 1 is as follows:

"Equity will not enforce a forfeiture."

The Court cited:

Craig v. *Hukill*, 37 W. Va. 520; 16 S. E. 363.
Railroad Company v. *Town of Triadelphia*, 58 W. Va. 487;
52 S. E. 499.
Spies v. *R. R. Co.*, 60 W. Va. 389; 55 S. E. 464.

Sec. 4.—In *Headley* v. *Hoppengarner*, 60 W. Va. 626; 55 S. E.
144, analyzed under Chapter 18, the court speaking through Judge
Saunders, at pages 646-7 in 60 W. Va. said:

"The plaintiff assigns as cross error that the court erred in
perpetuating the injunction enjoining the prosecution of the ejectment suit of Elisha LeMasters, guardian, and others, against the
Colonial Oil Company. This is based upon the fact that the
lessees failed to pay the full share of the royalty to the infants
to which they were entitled. While there is a provision in the
deed made by the guardian in the summary proceeding to the effect that a failure to comply in all respects with the terms and
stipulations of the deed would work a forfeiture and that the
property would revert to the heirs, there is no claim that the lessees have failed, in any respect, to comply with the contract, except as to the payment of 4-5 of 1-16 of the oil production, and
this was because of the complications which gave rise to this litigation. They placed a different construction upon the contract
from that given it by the heirs, and have so confided in their construction as to litigate it through this court for decision. This is
not such a voluntary and wilful failure and refusal to comply with
its provisions as should work a forfeiture of the estate acquired
under the deed. It appears from the record that their failure
to pay must have been in good faith, relying upon their construction of the deed. To impose a forfeiture is a harsh penalty
and courts of equity are slow to do so, except where it is plainly
demanded. While the common law courts recognize and will enforce forfeitures in proper cases, yet courts of equity will never
do so, but on the contrary, will relieve against them. It is said in
Craig v. *Hukill*, 37 W. Va. 523, 'Affirmative relief against penalties and forfeitures was one of the springs or fountains of
equity jurisdiction, and the jurisdiction was very early exercised,
and it would be going in the very opposite direction, and acting
contrary to its essential principles to affirmatively enforce a forfeiture. The elementary books on equity jurisprudence state the
rule as almost an axiom that equity never enforces a penalty or
forfeiture.' 2 Story Eq. Jur. Section 1319; 1 Pom. Eq. Jur. Sec-

tion 459; Bisp. Eq. Section 181; Beach Mod. Eq. Jur. Section 1013. And also it is said in *Hukill* v. *Myers*, 36 W. Va. 645; 'Courts of equity were originally founded, among other purposes, to relieve against the hardness of courts of common law, and notably to relieve against forfeiture, even where it clearly exists; and very safely it can be said that equity looks with disfavor upon forfeitures, and will not be quick, active, or alert to see or declare, or enforce them.' The infants have at all times, had their remedy for pecuniary reimbursement. And not only that, but they are now in this suit, asking that the lessees be compelled to pay the back royalties and have their future interests determined. They certainly cannot claim under the deed future royalties, and at the same time claim the benefit of a forfeiture. This would be extremely inconsistent, and not to be countenanced. Therefore, even if a violation of the provisions of the deed would forfeit the estate, yet under the facts of the cause, there is no forfeiture, and the prosecution of the ejectment suit was properly enjoined.''

Sec. 5.—In *Newton* v. *Kemper,* 66 W. Va. 130; 66 S. E. 102 (Nov. 2, 1909) syl. 1 is as follows:

"While a court of equity will, in a proper case, sometimes give relief against, it will never lend its aid in the enforcement of a forfeiture."

Jennie M. Newton filed a bill in chancery in the Circuit Court of Mason County, West Virginia, against Thomas H. Kemper and others. The plaintiff sought cancellation and removal of a lease as a cloud on her title, and an injunction to prevent the drilling for oil and gas by the defendants under a lease from plaintiff, charging the lease to be void for want of consideration, want of mutuality in the covenants, and for uncertainty in the description of the land, and because by its terms the lease if otherwise valid, had become forfeited for failure of the lessee to drill a well on the premises as soon as the well then being drilled on another tract should be completed. The lease recited a consideration of one dollar, acknowledging the payment thereof, and that it was upon a further consideration of the covenants and agreements of the lessee therein. The Circuit Court entered a decree for defendants, from which plaintiff appealed. The Court of Appeals modified and affirmed the decree, citing:

Headley v. *Hoopengarner,* 60 W. Va. 626-646; 55 S. E. 744.
Craig v. *Hukill,* 37 W. Va. 523; 16 S. E. 363.

Sec. 6.—While a court of equity will not entertain jurisdiction of a bill brought for the sole purpose of having a lease declared forfeited, yet where the bill alleges other facts giving to the court jurisdiction, and it is made to appear that the lease has been forfeited by the lessee, a court of equity will entertain jurisdiction and will cancel a forfeited lease as a cloud upon plaintiff's title.

(See Chapter 28.—Equity will cancel a void lease.)

CHAPTER 53.

NECESSARY PARTIES TO BILL IN EQUITY TO SETTLE CONTROVERSIES BETWEEN TWO OR MORE LESSEES.

Sec. 1.—Where a lessee files a bill in equity to settle a controversy between himself and the holder of another lease, or other leases, executed either prior or subsequent to the date of the complainant's lease all parties interested under either one or the other of such leases, including the lessor, are necessary parties.

Moore v. *Jennings,* 47 W. Va. 181; 34 S. E. 793.
Steelsmith v. *Fisher Oil Co.,* 47 W. Va. 391; 35 S. E. 15.
Pyle v. *Henderson,* 55 W. Va. 122; 46 S. E. 791.
Newton v. *Kemper,* 66 W. Va. 130; 66 S. E. 102.
South Penn Oil Co. v. *Miller,* 99 C. C. A. 305; 175 Fed. 729.

Sec. 2.—In *Moore* v. *Jennings,* 47 W. Va. 181; 34 S. E. 793, analyzed under Chapter 27, the second and third paragraphs of the syllabus are as follows:

"2. Where proper parties are not properly before the court, the decree will be reversed and the cause remanded for further proceedings.
3. When the lessors and lessees of one tract of land bring their suit against the lessees of an adjoining tract, to enjoin

them from trespassing upon the plaintiff's premises, and from
continuing to drill a well for oil and gas which defendants had
commenced, as plaintiff's claim, on their premises, and praying
in their bill that the boundary line between the tracts claimed
by the parties respectively, be ascertained, fixed and determined;
that plaintiffs be decreed to be the owners of the land on
which said well had been located by the defendants, and of all the
oil and gas which could or might be obtained through said well;
that the defendants be decreed to have no estate, right, title, or
interest whatsoever of, in, or to said land, or said oil or gas, nor
any right whatsoever to the possession of said land or said well—
held, in such case, all the owners of the fee of both tracts are
necessary parties to the suit, to enable the court to settle the
rights of all parties interested or affected by the subject matter
in controversy."

The Court cited:

Sheppard's Ex'r v. *Starke,* 3 Munf. 29.
Clark v. *Long,* 4 Rand. 451.
Armentrout's Ex'rs v. *Gibbons,* 25 Gratt. 371.
McArthur v. *Scott,* 113 U. S. 340.
Hagan v. *Wardens,* 3 Gratt. 315.
Hitchcox v. *Hitchcox,* 39 W. Va. 607; 20 S. E. 595.
Donahue v. *Fackler,* 21 W. Va. 125.
Crickard v. *Crouch's Ad'mr* 41 W. Va. 503; 23 S. E. 727.
Turk v. *Skiles,* 38 W. Va. 404; 18 S. E. 561.
California v. *Southern Pac. Co.,* 157 U. S. 229.
Wilson v. *Kisel,* 164 U. S. 248.
New Orleans Water Works Co. v. *City of New Orleans,* 164
    U. S. 471.
Storey v. *Livingstone,* 13 Pet. 359.
Conn v. *Penn,* 5 Wheat. 424.

Sec. 3.—In *Steelsmith* v. *Fisher Oil Co.,* 47 W. Va. 391; 35
S. E. 15 (Jan. 24, 1900) the second point of the syllabus is as
follows:

"When the lessees of an oil and gas lease bring their suit
against the lessees of an adjoining tract to enjoin them from trespassing upon the plaintiff's premises, and from proceeding to
drill a well for oil and gas which defendants claim is on their
own lease, but which plaintiffs claim is on their premises, the lessors of both leases and all persons having an interest in the oil or

gas which might be produced from the well, the drilling of which is sought to be enjoined, are necessary parties to the suit, to enable the court to settle the rights of all parties interested or affected by the subject matter in controversy.''

Amos Steelsmith and A. J. Yoke filed their bill in chancery in the Circuit Court of Tyler County, West Virginia, against the Fisher Oil Company, a corporation, alleging that they were the owners of a certain oil and gas lease executed on June 6, 1898, by C. P. Lowry and wife to A. J. Yoke, who afterwards conveyed a part of the lease to Amos Steelsmith, which lease was for a tract of land situated in Ellsworth District, in Tyler County, containing 44 acres, more or less, the bill describing the lands by names of contiguous landowners; that under the terms of their lease they had the exclusive right to drill and operate for oil and gas on the tract of land, and had taken possession and proceeded to drill a well which was a good producer; that the defendant company operated an adjoining lease and had entered upon and erected a derrick on their land and were proceeding and were about to drill the same, and take the oil therefrom, notwithstanding the notices and protests of plaintiffs; that the location and drilling of the well upon their leasehold to take the oil was an act of trespass, and would cause waste and irreparable injury and damage, not susceptible of complete pecuniary compensation, and would lead to vexatious litigation, if permitted to proceed; that the machinery and boiler attached to the derrick and lights used for drilling at night in the derrick erected by the defendant on plaintiff's land, were placed within a dangerous proximity to the tank, rig and well of plaintiffs, which was a large producer and flowing oil and what was called ''lively oil'' (full of gas); that the location of the boiler and rig being within a short distance of plaintiff's 300-barrel tank full of oil and the gas exuding therefrom made it not only liable to destruction from fire from the boiler and lights in the derricks, but a constant menace to the lives of plaintiffs and their employes working and managing their property; that the same was liable to cause irreparable damage in its nature, but the danger to life as aforesaid made the location of the same a dangerous nuisance; that plaintiffs were wholly without remedy, save in a court of equity, and if compelled to submit to the slow, tedious process of a law court they would suffer irreparable loss and injury and have their lives endangered by the acts complained of. The prayer was for an injunction against defendant, its agents and employes, and each of them, and all of those interested with them, restraining defendant from doing the things complained of, and from committing acts of trespass or waste, or in any manner interfering with plaintiffs in the possession of their lease.

Plaintiffs filed with their bill a copy of their lease from C. P. and M. R. Lowry. An injunction was awarded the plaintiffs as prayed for. The defendants, on June 27, 1899, demurred to the plaintiff's bill, and answered. The answer denied that C. P. Lowry and M. R. Lowry leased to Yoke the tract of land described in the bill, and averred that the land belonged to Kate Morrow who held the title in fee, and that Kate Morrow and John Morrow, her husband, made an oil and gas lease for the 44 acres to C. P. Lowry and M. R. Lowry, dated June 27, 1897, which lease was recorded; and that by assignment of June 6, 1898, of record, Lowrys assigned the lease, reserving to themselves a 1-16 interest, to A. J. Yoke, and that Yoke assigned an interest in the lease to Amos Steelsmith, and that Yoke also assigned a 1-4 interest in the lease to M. E. Hagen; that at the time of the institution of the suit there were interested in the lease described in the plaintiff's bill, A. J. Yoke, Amos Steelsmith, C. P. Lowry, M. R. Lowry and M. E. Hagen; and that the plaintiff's bill was defective for want of proper parties as plaintiff's therein. The Circuit Court, upon the hearing of the motion to dissolve the injunction entered a decree of dissolution, from which decree the plaintiffs appealed. The Court of Appeals affirmed the decree, and as to the want of proper parties cited:

Moore v. *Jennings*, supra.

See. 4.—In *Pyle* v. *Henderson*, 55 W. Va. 122; 46 S. E. 791 (Feb. 23, 1904) the second appeal of which is analyzed under Chapter 6, the syllabus is as follows:

"1. Where a trustee brings a suit in equity for the benefit of those he represents, the latter ordinarily are necessary parties to such suit.

2. In a controversy between two sets of lessees under two several leases, co-tenants interested under either one or both such leases should be made parties to a bill in equity filed to settle such controversy.

3. The lessor or landlord is a necessary party to a bill in chancery filed by subsequent lessees to enforce the forfeiture of, set aside and annul a prior lease covering the same subject matter."

Sec. 5.—In *Newton* v. *Kemper,* 66 W. Va. 130; 66 S. E. 102, analyzed under Chapter 52, Judge Miller, speaking for the Court in the opinion said:

"In view of the matters thus disclosed by these answers, the question is presented whether the court below, if requested, should have permitted plaintiff to amend and convert her bill into a bill to settle the conflicting claims of the Frys and of Kemper under his lease from them, and to remove said lease as a cloud, from their title, and if not, whether the court erred in dismissing the plaintiff's bill, without saving to the parties any rights they may have to prosecute or defend any other suit in respect to the matters complained of or asserted in bill or answers. The object of the bill was to stop defendants from drilling under plaintiff's lease and to remove it as a cloud. Failing in that purpose, to have permitted her to amend and convert the bill into one against Kemper and the Frys, to remove the Fry lease to Kemper as a cloud on her title, would have been to wholly change the object of the relief sought by the original bill, a practice not permitted by our decisions and the rules of equity practice."

Sec. 6.—In *South Penn Oil Co.* v. *Miller,* 175 Fed. 729; 99 C. C. A. 305 (Nov. 4, 1909) the third and fourth headnotes are as follows:

"3. A court cannot adjudicate rights under conflicting oil leases of the same property, executed by different lessors, and each providing for the payment of royalties, in a suit between the lessees to which the lessors are not parties.

4. All persons who have such an interest in the subject matter of a suit in a Federal Court as to render their presence necessary in order to make the final decree effectual, are indis-

pensable parties, and must be joined, although their citizenship is
such as will oust the jurisdiction of the court.''

J. T. Miller and others filed a bill in equity in the Circuit
Court of the United States for the Northern District of West
Virginia against the South Penn Oil Company and the Eureka
Pipeline Company. The original bill alleged that the complainants were citizens and residents of the State of West Virginia,
and that the two defendants, the South Penn Oil Company, and
the Eureka Pipeline Company, were corporations organized under
the laws of the State of Pennsylvania, and citizens of that State;
and that the amount in controversy was largely in excess of the
sum of $2,000; that complainants were the owners for develop-
ment of oil and gas, of a tract of land in Wetzel County, West
Virginia, containing about 33 acres; that they held the same by
virtue of two certain instruments of writing known as ''oil leases''
in which the grantors reserved a royalty of 1-8 of the oil produced, and were to receive $300.00 per year for each gas well; that
complainants drilled a productive oil well on the land, as required
by the terms of the leases; that the defendant, the Eureka Pipeline
Company, a corporation which carried on the business of receiving oil, produced at different wells in that locality, and transporting it through pipelines to places where it could be marketed, received the oil from the well, and transported it to Pittsburg to be
there sold to such persons as complainants might direct; that from
June 26, 1902, to October 1, 1902, said company received about
22,100 barrels of oil from that well, and that since last mentioned
date, all the oil produced from the well had passed into the lines
of that company for transportation; that the drilling of an additional well on the lands was commenced by complainants as required by the leases, but not completed, because of the mishaps
incident to such business, and also because of the acts of the
defendants; that the market price of oil at Pittsburg had been,
since the oil was delivered, $1.22 per barrel, and that complain-
ants owning 7-8 thereof, were entiled to receive for the same about
$23,592.00; that the South Penn Oil Company was engaged ex-
tensively in the business of leasing property for the development
of oil and gas; that it had many wells in West Virginia; and that

the Eureka Pipeline Company transported the oil of the South
Penn Oil Company through its lines; that either because the South
Penn Oil Company, or persons interested in it, held large quantities of the stock of the Eureka Pipeline Company, or for other
reasons, it had a great and unreasonable influence over the acts
and conduct of the Eureka Pipeline Company; that until complainants drilled in the first producing well on the property the
South Penn Oil Company made no claim to any such rights to the
same; but that soon after the producing well was finished, the
company set up a claim that it was the owner of the land for oil
and gas purposes; that it claimed to have valid leases for the
property from grantors other than those complainants claimed
under; that the leases under which it so claimed did not entitle
it nor had it any title that did entitle it to the land so claimed by
complainant; that the two companies, defendants, entered into
a conspiracy between themselves, for the purpose of asserting
a claim on behalf of the South Penn Oil Company, to the land so
leased to complainants, and for the purpose of compelling them
to surrender the land, and the oil produced from it, to that company; that in pursuance of such conspiracy, the South Penn Oil
Company served a notice on the Eureka Pipeline Company in
which it was stated that said company was the owner, for oil
and gas purposes, of the land which had been so leased to complainants, and the owner of the oil so produced and run into the
pipeline; and that in pursuance of such conspiracy the Eureka
Company refused to deliver the oil either to complainants or to
the persons to whom they gave orders for it; that the South Penn
Oil Company held oil and gas leases upon other properties in close
proximity to the property so leased to complainants, and upon
both sides of the same, and was drilling wells at places so close
to complainant's leases that they would have the effect of draining the oil which belonged to complainants, and which was under
the land so leased to them, unless they could proceed promptly
and vigorously to drill other and successive wells on the property, so as to extract the oil therefrom; that the market price of oil
remained at $1.22 per barrel from June 26, 1902, to October 1,
1902, and had since increased in price, and that complainants

were entitled to have the Eureka Pipeline Company account to
them for all the oil at the highest price at which oil might have
been sold in the general market at any time between June 26, 1902,
and the time when their oil might be delivered to them under the
order of the court; that complainants were entitled to a decree
against said company so engaged in such conspiracy for the
amount which might represent the difference between the highest
market price and the market price which might be in effect at the
time when such delivery should be made; that by reason of the
circumstances mentioned, complainants had been and were, seriously injured, and had sustained loss because of the interference
with their development of the property, and that if such situation
continued they would suffer irreparable loss and injury of such a
character that the amount of it could not be definitely measured
or ascertained, and could not be compensated for by any damages
which complainants might recover in an action at law against the
companies. The prayer of the bill was that a preliminary injunction issue restraining the South Penn Oil Company from interfering in any manner with the delivery to complainants by the
Eureka Pipeline Company of the oil so held by it; restraining
the last named company from retaining the possession of the oil,
and from preventing complainants from taking and disposing of
the same; directing such company to deliver to complainants,
without delay, the oil in its possession received from the well
mentioned; that the Eureka Pipeline Company be required to
render a specific account of the oil so received by it, and that a
decree be entered in favor of complainants against the companies
for the amount representing any difference between the highest
market price during the period such oil was so retained and the
market price prevailing when the oil should be so delivered to
them; that if it were found necessary, a receiver be appointed to
take charge of and manage the property, develop the same, and
receive and dispose of the oil and gas therefrom; that a decree
be entered finally determining that the South Penn Oil Company had no right or interest of any kind in or to the property;
and also for such other and general relief as to equity might
be proper.

The bill and exhibits were on October 13, 1902, presented in the court below (U. S. Ct. Ct. N. D. W. Va.) when, on consideration thereof an order was entered in which it was stated that the facts presented established "prima facie" the right of complainants to the possession of 7/8 of the oil which had been produced from the well mentioned. The order authorized complainants to enter into bond in the penalty of $30,000 with security conditioned that complainants would comply with any future order of the court relative to the oil referred to, and pay all damages which might be incurred by the defendants should the order thereafter be set aside. It then required that the South Penn Oil Company cease to interfere in any way with the sale by complainants of the 7-8 of the oil produced from the well, and directed the Eureka Pipeline Company to deliver to complainants the 7-8 of such oil. The court designated October 18, 1902, for the hearing of a motion made by complainants for the appointment of a Receiver, and on that day entered a decree appointing the receiver, and directing him to take possession of the property and proceed to complete the wells commenced by complainant, to drill other wells, and to do all other things necessary to be done for the proper development of the land for oil and gas. The receiver was directed to take possession of the oil produced from the wells on the land, and sell the same. The Eureka Pipeline Company was ordered to deliver to the receiver the oil that might be produced in future. A subpoena in chancery was issued summoning defendants to answer the bill, at December Rules, 1902, and was served on the Eureka Pipeline Company on October 15, 1902, and on the South Penn Oil Company on October 17, 1902. At said rules the defendants appeared under protest, for the purpose only of pleading to the jurisdiction of the court, and filed a plea alleging that the Eureka Pipeline Company was not a corporation under the laws of the State of Pennsylvania, nor an inhabitant of that State; but that it was a corporation organized under the laws of the State of West Virginia, and was an inhabitant of that State; that complainants and each of them were citizens and inhabitants of the State of West Virginia, and that therefore, not the Circuit Court of the United States for the Northern District of West Virginia, but in the Circuit Court for the County of Wetzel, in the State of West Virginia, where complainants resided, and where said cause of action arose, was jurisdiction in the premises to be found. The Eureka Pipeline Company, at said rules, also filed a separate and similar plea to the jurisdiction of the court, as did also the South Penn Oil Company, which company also filed a plea to the jurisdiction alleging that prior to the institution of this suit by complainants it had filed its bill in the Circuit Court of Wetzel County, West Virginia, against complainants and others, and that that court had assumed jurisdiction and had issued an injunction against the defendants therein; that the bill and injunction had reference to the same property, rights and controversies, as were set forth in the complainant's bill in this case, and therefore, the South Penn Oil Company claimed that the Circuit Court of Wetzel County, West Virginia, acquired and had jurisdiction in the premises.

These pleas to the jurisdiction were not then formally disposed of, but the decree entered on March 8, 1903, was regarded as in effect determining the questions raised by them. By that decree the motion of the South Penn Oil Company to dismiss the suit on the ground that the court had no jurisdiction, was denied, and the motion of complainants that they be permitted to file an amended and supplemental bill against the South Penn Oil Company as the sole defendant, and that the Eureka Pipeline Company be dismissed from the suit, was granted. Thus, the plea of the Eureka Pipeline Company as to the want of jurisdiction by reason of its being a West Virginia corporation, was sustained, but the defect in jurisdiction caused thereby was supposed to be cured by the dismissal of the suit as to that company. By such decree the court also in effect held, that the Circuit Court of Wetzel County, West Virginia, had not acquired jurisdiction of the controversy. The amended and supplemental bill was in substance the same as the original bill, save only that the allegations relating to the Eureka Pipeline Company were omitted and its prayer was for relief against the South Penn Oil Company asked for in the original bill. The case was matured, depositions taken, exhibits filed, arguments heard, and final decree entered. By the decree the demurrer of the South Penn Oil Company to the amended bill, incorporated in its answer, was considered by the court and overruled and the questions raised by the special pleas to the jurisdiction of the court were formally found against defendant. The decree then proceeded to dispose of the real estate in controversy, giving to the plaintiffs that portion thereof situated west of a certain designated line, and to the defendant the part east thereof. The money in the hands of the receiver was distributed between the parties, each to receive the portions arising from the oil obtained from the land, respectively assigned to them. The South Penn Oil Company applied for and was granted an appeal to the Court of Appeal. That Court reversed the decree of the Circuit Court, and remanded the cause with directions to dismiss the bills.

In the opinion rendered by Circuit Judge Goff, it was said:

"We also think the record discloses the fact that parties absolutely essential to the proper disposition of the questions decided by the court below, were not before it, and that consequently, even had the subject matter of the controversy been properly within its jurisdiction, the court could not have effectively disposed of it. Neither the lessors of the complainants nor of the defendant, were made parties to the suit, and yet the final decree disposed of the funds in which they were interested, and decided the title to the property which they claim to own in fee simple. It takes from one and gives to the other set of claimants portions of the land claimed respectively, by those not made parties. It adjudges that the complainants are the owners by virtue of their leases for oil and gas, of the real property in dispute that is located to the west of a certain line, although such property is claimed in fee simple by the lessors of the South Penn Oil Company, who were not permitted to defend their title."

Upon the proposition that in suits regarding the title to real estate instituted on the equity side of the Federal Courts where objection has not been made by demurrer, plea or answer, nor suggested by counsel, the court, itself, should, in the discharge of a duty imposed on it, dismiss the action, the court cited:

Hipp v. *Babin*, 19 How. 271.
Lewis v. *Cocks*, 23 Wall. 466.
Whitehead v. *Shattuck*, 133 U. S. 146.
Allen v. *Pullman Palace Car Co.*, 139 U. S. 658.
Wehrman v. *Conklin*, 155 U. S. 314.
Gordon v. *Jackson*, (C. C.) 72 Fed. 86.
Erskine v. *Forest Oil Co.*, (C. C.) 80 Fed. 583.
McGuire v. *Pensacola City Co.*, 105 Fed. 677-679; 44 C. C.
    A. 670.
Jones v. *Mackenzie*, 122 Fed. 390-393; 58 C. C. A. 96.

CHAPTER 54.

REMEDY BY EJECTMENT.

Sec. 1.—Pennsylvania Rule.—Where a lease demises, grants and lets a tract of land with the exclusive right of entering thereon for mining and producing oil and gas, such grant is a lease conveying an interest in the land, and lessee may maintain ejectment against one who has entered into possession and claims adversely to him, although lessee, himself, has never entered into possession of the premises.

Barnsdall v. *Bradford Gas Co.*, 225 Pa. 338; 74 Atl. 207.
Hicks v. *American Nat. Gas Co.*, 207 Pa. 570; 57 Atl. 55.
Williams v. *Fowler*, 201 Pa. 336; 50 Atl. 969.

Sec. 2.—A lessee of an oil and gas lease, where he has entered into possession of the premises demised, for the purposes of the grant, may maintain ejectment against one entering into possession and claiming under a second lease from the same grantor, upon proof that he had not abandoned the lease.

Bartley v. *Phillips*, 165 Pa. 325; 30 Atl. 842.
Bartley v. *Phillips*, 179 Pa. 175; 36 At. 217.

Sec. 3.—Where a lessee under the terms of a lease has only the privilege and exclusive right granted to him to enter and explore for oil and gas, and the land, itself, is not granted, his remedy for the disturbance of this right is not by ejectment but by action for damages.

Union Petroleum Co. v. Bliven Pet. Có., 72 Pa. 173.

Sec. 4.—In *Williams v. Fowler*, 201 Pa. 236; 50 Atl. 969 (Jan. 6, 1902) the syllabus is as follows:

"Where a bill in equity for an injunction to restrain opera-tions upon land leased for oil purposes, shows on its face that the plaintiffs were not in posession, and that the defendants were in possession under an alleged lease prior in date to that of the plaintiffs the bill is an ejectment bill and equity has no jurisdic-tion of it.   The fact that an injunction and account are prayed for in the bill, is immaterial, inasmuch as they are incidental to and de-pend upon the determination of the disputed title.

In such a case where the lack of jurisdiction is manifest, the defendant may object at any time, and if he does not do so at the beginning he may do so at the end of the proceeding."

C. M. Williams and others filed a bill in equity in the Court of Common Pleas, Number 2, Allegheny County, against Charles T. Fowler and others, for an injunction and for an accounting. The bill alleged: That Henry A. Allman, on October 30, 1901, leased to plaintiffs for one year, and as long thereafter as oil or gas was found, a tract of 50 acres of land in Marshall Township, Allegheny County, Pennsylvania, with the exclusive right to plain-tiffs to mine for oil and gas, the lease to become null and void unless plaintiffs completed a well on the premises within sixty days of the date of the lease; that plaintiffs were ready to enter upon the premises when they discovered defendants wrongfully on the premises engaged in the work of drilling a well; that on November 14, 1900, plaintiffs notified defendants in writing to re-move from the premises the machinery, tools, and other property placed thereon by them, informing defendants of plaintiff's title to said premises; but that defendants refused to comply with the notice and continued in possession of and operation on the prem-ises; that the plaintiffs, not wishing to commit a breach of the

peace by forceable entry on the premises, being prevented from
peaceably entering thereon by the act of the defendants, were
unable to complete a well within 60 days as their lease required, in
lieu of which they paid the owners, their lessors, the sum of $250,
which secured to them the lease, absolutely; that defendants
wrongfully and illegally, against plaintiffs' ownership and notice,
were continuing the drilling of the well on plaintiffs land to their
irreparable loss, injury and damage; that defendants pretended
to have a right in the land under a prior lease from George Allman, the grantor of Edward H. Allman, dated July 23, 1900, but
that the lease to defendants had become null and void, for failure
on the part of the defendants to comply with the terms thereof,
to-wit: To have either begun a well within three months from
the date thereof, or completed a well within three months thereafter, or pay the sum of $696.00 per annum, payable quarterly in
advance until the well was completed; and that by reason of the
default, the lease to defendants had been declared forfeited, and
they were notified of the forfeiture, after which the lease had been
made to plaintiffs; that plaintiffs had no adequate remedy at
law. The bill prayed for preliminary injunction, to be made perpetual on final hearing, enjoining and restraining the defendants
from further operations on the land; that defendants be required
to remove machinery, rig, tools and other property placed on
plaintiff's land; that defendants be required to account and pay
for all oil or gas, or either, mined on the land, and pay damages
to the plaintiffs. Defendants answered and denied that the plaintiffs were the legal lessees of the land, and averred that the defendants entry was in accordance with their rights under their
lease. After the court had filed its findings of fact and conclusions
of law, and after arguments had been had upon the exceptions to
such findings and conclusion, an exception was filed to the jurisdiction of the court. The court entered a decree dismissing the
bill for want of jurisdiction, and plaintiffs appealed. The Supreme Court affirmed the decree, and upon the question that disputed titles had not been settled at law, and it was too soon for
equity to hear complaints of continuing trespass and irreparable
wrongs, cited:

Long's Appeal, 92 Pa. 171.
Washburn's Appeal, 105 Pa. 480.
Greensboro Nat. Gas Co. v. *Fayette County Gas Co.,* 200 Pa. 388; 49 Atl. 768.

Upon the proposition that defendants could object to the jurisdiction upon final hearing, the court cited:

Adam's Appeal, 113 Pa. 449; 6 Atl. 100.
Evans v. *Goodwin,* 132 Pa. 136; 19 Atl. 49.
Edgett v. *Douglas,* 144 Pa. 95.
Shillito v. *Shillito,* 160 Pa. 167.

Sec. 5.—In *Union Petroleum Co.* v. *Bliven Pet. Co.,* 72 Pa. 173 (Oct. 28, 1872) syls. 1-6 inclusive are as follows:

"1.   An agreement was to lease 'the exclusive right and privilege of boring for oil, etc., upon the farm upon which the first party now resides, with the right of access to and from such place as may be selected by the party of the second part * * * * said boring to be done so as to do the least possible injury to the farm:' the consideration was $150.00 and 1-3 of product, the holes to be sunk to satisfy the parties as to practicability and profit for oil.   This was incorporeal hereditament, only.

2.   The only possession the grantee had was such as was necessary to the exercise of the right.

3.   The remedy for disturbance of the right was case: Ejectment could not be maintained.

4.   An ejectment was brought for the land on which wells had been sunk by persons claiming under the grant, at the suit of persons claiming title to the *land,* under the same grantor, served on persons in possession, a verdict for plaintiffs and they put into possession by an *habere. Held,* not to be conclusive in an action for disturbance against persons claiming under the plaintiffs in the ejectment.

5.   There being but one verdict it was not conclusive of the title; it was persuasive evidence only.

6.   The possession of the land is not necessary to enable the owner of an incorporeal hereditament to maintain an action for its disturbance."

On September 3, 1869, the Bliven Petroleum Company instituted an action on the case against the Union Petroleum Company in the Court of Common Pleas of Venango County. The declaration alleged that the plaintiffs were the owners in fee of "certain incorporeal hereditaments, to-wit, the right and privilege of digging and boring for salt, oil and minerals, upon certain lots, parts of a tract of land known as the John McClintock farm * * * * with the right of ingress and egress * * * * for the pur- pose of digging for said salt, oil and minerals, * * * giving to John McClintock one-third part thereof. Yet the defendants * * * * * entered on said lots * * * * and into the possession of certain oil wells which the plaintiffs had thereon and excluded the plain- tiffs therefrom, and from the enjoyment of their said right and privilege, and obtained and collected large quantities of oil * * * * * which the plaintiffs could have collected for their own use." The defendants pleaded not guilty. The cause was tried on No- vember 8, 1870. By the plaintiffs evidence it appeared that the land on which the wells were located belonged to John McClin- tock, situated in Venango County; On September 26, 1859, an agreement was entered into between John McClintock of the first part, and Bradford R. Alden and Cornelius S. Chase, of the second part, with the clauses mentioned in the first point of the syllabus; That by partition subsequently the title became vested in Alden alone; on January 28, 1865, Alden conveyed to the Bliven Petro- leum Company, the plaintiff; that defendants had occupied by their agents a portion of the land leased to Alden and Chase, had worked the wells put down by Alden, and excluded the plain- tiffs from occupying it; plaintiffs proved the quantity and value of the oil produced and appropriated by defendants; gave evidence as to the lines of the land included in their lease; gave evidence that Allen Wright had a lease from Alden and Chase which af- terwards passed to the "Allen Wright Oil Co.," and drilled wells known as Numbers 81 and 84, on what was claimed to be covered by the lease to Alden and Chase. The defendants claimed the wells to be on their lands; this suit was brought for the disturb- ance of the plaintiffs' rights and privileges in these wells.

The defendants gave in evidence the records of the Circuit Court of the United States for the Western District of Pennsyl- vania, in an action of ejectment in which the Union Petroleum

Company, a citizen and corporation of the State of New York, plaintiff, and George King, S. A. Lyon, and R. Greene, citizens of Pennsylvania, were defendants. The records showed that the marshal returned the writ served on the defendants, and also on D. F. Myer, George Crippen and Samuel Davidson. The premises described in the writ were:

"A strip of land in Cornplanter Township, Venango County, containing six acres; being 160 perches long by 6 perches and 2-10 wide; bounded on the north by the Rynd Farm; on the east by other lands of this plaintiff; on the south by the Buchanan Farm, and on the west by land known as the McClintock farm."

The record also showed that on October 6, 1865, a rule was taken on the defendants to appear in six weeks. The marshal returned that the rule had been duly served on King, Lyon and Green; that an affidavit of defense was made by Allen Wright, a director of the Allen Wright Oil Company "which has the lease management and control of the land and property from which the plaintiffs seek to eject the defendant," and averred that the defendants had "a just and legal defense on the merits." This affidavit was filed on November 29, 1865. On March 5, 1866, the defendants pleaded not guilty. On March 10, 1866, the court appointed William Hilands, "to survey the claims of both parties and to ascertain the quantity and interference of each party, and to note such circumstances as may effect or be deemed material to the title of the parties." The jury found for the plaintiffs, "and fixed the western line of the plaintiff's land as the line run by William Hilands, the artist appointed by the Court, and marked on his plot by the signature of the Clerk of the Court, which plot is now filed of record as part of the verdict in the case." A writ of habere facias was issued on January 25, 1867, to which the marshal returned:—"And now, this 31st day of January, 1867, entered upon the within named premises 'defendants all being absent' and placed E. W. Hinds, agent Union Petroleum Company of New York, in full possession of same. No property of defendants found."

The defendants then gave in evidence the map made by Hilands under direction of the United States Circuit Court; also deed

dated May 19, 1860, from John McClintock to John Nelson Mc-
Comber, granting to McComber for the consideration of $1,500.00,
a piece of land in Cornplanter Township, describing it.   They
then gave evidence tracing this title to the defendants, on June 29,
1864.   They also gave evidence that McClintock had contracted
by articles for the sale of this land to Richard Dempsey who sold
his interest to McComber, and the deed made as above stated
directly from McClintock to McComber.   The evidence was, that
at the time of the contract between McClintock and Dempsey, the
land was unimproved and in wood, and was so when sold by Dempsey to McComber.   Hilands testified that according to the line
run by him well 84 would be within the claim of the defendants, and
that the line ran through well 81.   There was evidence of a line
run by Irvine, which put both wells on the plaintiff's claim; and
also of acquiescence in that line by McClintock, Dempsey and Mc-
Comber, predecessors in title to the defendants; and that the
plaintiffs had been using the wells until defendants were put into
possession by the habere facias from the Circuit Court of the
United States.   After the jury had been charged they returned
a verdict for plaintiffs for $8,190.00.   Defendants prosecuted a
writ of error.   The Supreme Court affirmed the judgment.   The
Supreme Court held that plaintiffs claim was an incorporeal hereditament, issuing out of, annexed to and exerciseable within the
land, and that, unless such incorporeal right was derived by grant
from the party against whom the recovery in ejectment was had,
such recovery would not bar the plaintiffs, the claimants of such
incorporeal hereditament.

CHAPTER 55.

NEGLIGENCE—INJURIES TO PERSONS OR PROPERTY BY COR-
PORATIONS OR BY PERSONS FURNISHING NATURAL GAS
FOR COMMERCIAL PURPOSES.

Sec. 1.—A person or corporation engaged in furnishing natural gas to consumers for purposes of domestic light, heat, and
fuel, is bound to exercise such care, skill and diligence in all oper-

ations as is called for by the delicacy, difficulty and dangers in the nature of the business, that injury to others may not be caused thereby; that is to say, if the delicacy, difficulty and danger are extraordinarily great, extraordinary skill and diligence is required.

> *Barrickman* v. *Marion Oil Co.,* 45 W. Va. 634; 32 S. E. 327; 44 L. R. A. 92.
>
> *Creel* v. *Charleston Nat. Gas Co.,* 51 W. Va 129; 41 S. E. 174; 90 Am. St. Rep. 772.
>
> *Snyder* v. *Phila. Co.,* 54 W. Va. 149; 46 S. E. 366; 63 L. R. A. 890; 102 Am. St. Rep. 941.
>
> *Marshall Window Glass Co.* v. *Cameron Oil & Gas Co.,* 63 W. Va. 202; 59 S. E. 959.
>
> *McCoy* v. *Ohio Valley Gas Co.,* 213 Pa. 367; 62 Atl. 858.
>
> *Shirey* v. *Consumer's Gas Co.,* 215 Pa. 399; 64 Atl. 541.
>
> *Hartman* v. *Citizens Nat. Gas Co.,* 210 Pa. 19; 59 Atl. 315.
>
> *McKenna* v. *Bridgewater Gas Co.,* 193 Pa. 633; 45 Atl. 52; 47 L. R. A. 790.
>
> *Benson* v. *Allegheny Heating Co.,* 188 Pa. 614; 41 Atl. 729.
>
> *Ohio Gas Fuel Co.* v. *Andrews,* 50 Ohio St. 695; 35 N. E. 1059.
>
> *Lebanon Light, etc. Co.* v. *Leap.* 139 Ind. 443; 39 N. E. 57; 29 L. R. A. 342.
>
> *Alexandria etc. Mining Co.* v. *Irish,* 16 Ind. App. 534; 44 N. E. 680.
>
> *Ibach* v. *Huntington Light etc. Co.,* 23 Ind. App. 281; 55 N. E. 249.
>
> *Ind. Nat. etc. Gas Co.* v. *McMath,* 26 Ind. App. 154; 57 N. E. 593; rehearing refused, 59 N. E. 287.
>
> *Moore* v. *Heat & Light Co.,* 65 W. Va. 552; 64 S. E. 721.
>
> *Consumers Gas Trust Co.* v. *Perrigo,* 144 Ind. 350; 43 N. E. 306; 32 L. R. A. 146.
>
> *Consumers Gas Trust Co.* v. *Corbaley,* 14 Ind. App. 549; 43 N. E. 237.
>
> *Coffeyville Mining & Gas Co.* v. *Carter,* 68 Kan. 565; 70 Pac. 365.
>
> *Maxwell* v. *Coffeyville Mining etc. Co.,* 75 Pac. 1047; 68 Kan. 821.
>
> *Hollon* v. *Campton Fuel & Light Co.,* 127 Ky. 266; 105 S. W. 426; 32 Ky. L. Rep. 178.
>
> *United States Nat. Gas Co.* v. *Hicks,* (Ky.) 119 S. W. 166.

Sec. 2.—In *Barrickman* v. *Marion Oil Co.,* 45 W. Va. 634; 32 S. E. 327; 44 L. R. A. 92 (Dec. 14, 1898) the syllabus is as follows:

"1. A person or corporation engaged in furnishing natural gas to stoves, heaters, pipes, etc., for purposes of domestic light, heat and fuel, in a dwelling house, is bound to exercise such care, skill and diligence in all its operations as is called for by the delicacy, difficulty, and dangerousness of the nature of the business, that injury to others may not be caused thereby, that is to say, if the delicacy, difficulty and danger are extraordinarily great, extraordinary skill and diligence is required.

2. If the defendant, so furnishing such gas, negligently and carelessly suffer and permit a greater amount of pressure of said gas to be furnished than is reasonably proper for said purpose, by reason whereof the house or building being so furnished is consumed or injured by fire, resulting from such negligence, the defendant is liable in damages for such loss.

3. If such defendant suffer and permit its regulators or other appliances to be and remain for an unreasonable time in such condition that they do not control the amount and pressure of gas so furnished so that more than a safe and proper amount of gas is so furnished, the defendant is guilty of negligence and liable in damages for injuries proximately caused by such negligence.

4. If such injury is the natural consequence of such negligence and such as might have been foreseen and reasonably anticipated as the result of such negligence, then such negligence must be regarded as the proximate or direct cause of the injury, in the absence of intervening negligence.

5. The mere fact that a building so furnished with gas was set on fire from the gas is not sufficient to justify the inference that an increased pressure of gas caused the fire.

6. In the trial of an action against a corporation so furnishing natural gas to a dwelling house, for damages for causing the destruction of such house by fire by negligently permitting too great a pressure of gas, it is not competent to prove by a witness the bare fact of what pressure the guage of another gas company usually indicated.''

Franklin Barrickman brought an action of trespass on the case in the Circuit Court of Monongalia County, against the Marion Oil Company, claiming damages for the destruction of a dwelling house by fire occasioned by the negligence of the defendant in furnishing natural gas at said house for domestic purposes. The case was tried to a jury, and a verdict was rendered for the plaintiff. A motion to set aside the verdict was overruled by the Circuit Court. Upon judgment for the plaintiff, defendant brought error to the Court of Appeals, where the judgment was reversed.

Sec. 3.—In *Creel* v. *Charleston Nat. Gas Co.*, 51 W. Va. 129; 41 S. E. 174; 90 Am. St. Rep. 772 (Jan. 11, 1902) the syllabus is as follows:

"If a tenant open a service pipe and knowingly permit the same to remain open and the gas escape therefrom into and under the property occupied by him, and then carelessly ignites the same, his landlord cannot recover from the gas company the damages occasioned by the resulting explosion, although such gas company was guilty of negligence in not having cut the gas off from such service pipe."

T. M. Creel instituted an action in the Circuit Court of Kanawha County against the Charleston Natural Gas Company. Upon the trial the following facts were proven: John J. Cavin, a tenant of plaintiff, had natural gas put into plaintiff's building, in the City of Charleston, for heating purposes. Several years before this suit was instituted, Cavin directed the Gas Company to cut off the gas. The company shut off the gas by closing the service pipe, but did not cut the gas off at the street main. Cavin re-rented the building, and directed a plumber in his employ to unscrew the arm of the service pipe which extended through the floor. The plumber discovered that the gas was still in the service pipe and was escaping therefrom, under the floor. Instead of at once restoring the pipe into the condition he found it, he notified the gas company to turn it off at the street main. After some time the gas company managed to find the stopcock and turned off the gas, but in the meantime it had accumulated by escaping from the service pipe under the floor. Cavin threw a lighted match down the hole in the floor. An explosion followed which wrecked the building. The plaintiff brought this suit to recover damages for the destruction of the building. The Circuit Court excluded the plaintiff's evidence and directed a verdict for the defendant. Upon writ of error the Court of Appeals affirmed the judgment.

Sec. 4.—In *Snyder* v. *Phila. Co.*, 54 W. Va. 148; 46 S. E. 366; 63 L. R. A. 890; 102 Am. St. Rep. 941, analyzed under Chapter 44, syls. 4-5-6 are as follows:

"4.   The owner of a gas well, situated near a public highway, may lawfully open it for the purpose of allowing the gas to blow the water out of it, although the noise thereby made is clearly such as to frighten the horses of persons riding or driving along the highway, but in doing so, he must exercise care not thereby to inflict injury upon such persons or their property.

5.   Persons using horses on the highway in close proximity to such well, and seeing an agent of the owner at or near it, have the right to presume that he will not open it without warning, or first looking for travellers on the road, and are not guilty of contributory negligence in failing to turn and fly from it, or in failing to give warning of their presence.

6.   When by the negligent blowing off of such well, a teamsters horses become frightened, and, in attempting to control them, a line breaks, causing him to fall from his wagon, whereby he is injured, the proximate cause of the injury is the blowing off of the well, although the line is weak and wholly insufficient for such emergency."

Sec. 5.—In *Marshall Window Glass Co.* v. *Cameron Oil & Gas Co.*, 63 W. Va. 202; 59 S. E. 959 (Sept. 10, 1907) the syllabus is as follows:

"1.   The duty devolving upon a person or corporation engaged in furnishing to consumers thereof natural gas for fuel and light, is not that of insurer, but to exercise such care, skill and diligence in all its operations as called for by the delicacy, difficulty and dangerousness of the nature of the business, that injury or damage to others may not be caused thereby.

2.   The application of the rules *res ipsa loquitur* depends upon the facts and circumstances of each individual case; but the mere fact of explosion of a gas regulator, which up to the time of the accident had properly performed its functions, is not a circumstances to which the rule may be applied."

The Marshall Window Glass Company instituted an action against the Cameron Oil & Gas Company in the Circuit Court of Marshall County. The plaintiff sought to recover from the defendant damages for the loss by fire of its factory due to the explosion of gas, the alleged result of negligence of defendant. It appeared by the evidence that gas was furnished by defendant under a written contract, by which the defendant agreed, among other things to supply gas to plaintiff for one year from August 1, 1903 at a stipulated price per thousand feet, to maintain pipes or connections to plaintiff's plant, and to place on plaintiff's premises meters and regulators to control the flow of gas: The plaintiff agreed to furnish, put in place and keep in repair all pipes, valves and fittings necessary to distribute and burn the gas. The contract provided that the defendant should at all times have access to said premises, to inspect the pipes, regulators and meters; that the pressure of gas should be determined by it under the supervision of its superintendent; that the ownership of the regulators, and all other fixtures placed by it on said premises should remain in it, and that it might remove or replace the same before or after the termination of the contract; that, "as production of gas wells and conveyance of it over long distance are subject to accidents, interruptions and failures which cannot be foreseen or prevented by any reasonable care or expenditure, the company does not by this contract, undertake to furnish to the consumer a full and uninterrupted supply of gas for the period named herein, but only to furnish such a supply and for such length of time, limited to the term hereof, as its wells and pipelines are reasonably capable of, it being understood that the company may require a block or discontinuance of operations at any time by the consumer temporarily, in whole or in part, without prejudice to its rights to continue its supply to other consumers;" that "it is expressly agreed by the consumer that the company shall not be liable for any loss, damage or injury that may result either directly or indirectly from such shortage or interruption;" that "the company shall not be liable to the consumer or to any other person for any loss, damage or injury resulting from the use of the gas in the said plant, all risks in the said use being assumed by the consumer."

The declaration was in two counts. The only charge of negligence was, that the defendant negligently permitted gas to pass

through the plaintiff's pipes, etc., in such quantities, and at such
pressure that the same were rent asunder, causing escape of
gas, and consequent ignition and destruction of the factory; that
it permitted its regulators and other fixtures to be and remain
out of proper order and repair so that an excessive pressure of
gas passed into the pipes and fittings of plaintiff, causing ignition and destruction of the factory.   The plaintiff did not charge
negligence and inadequate construction by the defendant of its
system of pipes and regulators.   In support of the charge of excessive quantities and excessive pressure the plaintiff relied upon
the evidence of its President and other employes who testified
that shortly before the explosion there was a shortage of gas resulting in complaint on its part to the defendant, followed shortly, as was claimed, by such quantities of gas and pressure as could
not be resisted or controlled by the pipes and fittings of the plaintiff.   There was no evidence that the quantity of gas and pressure
at the time of the explosion were greater than usual.   The plaintiff claimed that, after the complaint of shortage, there was a
sudden on rush of gas, causing flames therefrom in the furnace
and ovens of the plaintiff to ignite and destroy the building and
property therein; that these facts, accompanied by the further
fact, proven, that one of defendant's regulators, about the same
instant exploded in the regulator house, furnished evidential circumstances to make a prima facie case of negligence in the particular charge, as such results could not have followed in the ordinary course of events.   But, in this connection, the plaintiff's witnesses testified that they noticed no unusual pressure at their
places in the factory.   There was other evidence tending to show
no unusual pressure and that on account of the low pressure shortly prior to the explosion, the valves in the factory had all been
thrown wide open, and were left in that condition when the gas
came on again in quantities sufficient to bring about the condition at the time of the explosion.   As to the regulator explosion, the evidence was that the president, with the blacksmith and
another employe, without notice to the gas company, almost at
the instant that the gas came on, and immediately after they had
unsuccessfully attempted to reach the valves at the flattening

oven, to control the gas there, ran to the regulator house, where the blacksmith, by direction of the president, suddenly shut off the gates on the outlet or low pressure side of the regulator, which exploded, and that almost instantly the explosion occurred. There were admissions by the witnessess for the plaintiff of other prior interferences by its employes with at least one of the regulators of the defendant, in piling weights upon it, against which protests were made by the defendant. The blacksmith explained that the reason why he did not shut off the inlet gates, in place of the outlet gates, was because there was no wheel on the inlet gates; that he knew the proper thing to do was to shut the inlet gates, but he then had no wrench with which to do so. There was no affirmative evidence to support the charge in the declaration of want of proper repair of pipes, regulators, etc.

The plaintiff relied in the Court of Appeals, entirely upon the fact that the explosion occurred, and the regulator was blown open, and sought to apply the rule *res ipsa loquitur* to the fact of the explosion in support of both branches of the case.

Upon the trial in the Circuit Court the defendant moved to exclude the plaintiff's evidence, and direct a verdict, which motion the court sustained, and plaintiff took a writ of error to the Court of Appeals, and that Court affirmed the judgment.

Sec. 6.—In *McCoy* v. *Ohio Valley Gas Company,* 213 Pa. 367; 62 Atl. 858; (Jan. 2, 1906) the syllabus is as follows:

"In an action against a natural gas company by one of its employees to recover damages for personal injuries sustained while repairing a pipe, it appeared that at the point where the explosion occurred a landslide had pushed some of the sections of the pipe from their original location; to what extent did not appear, but sufficient to cause a leak where two of the pipes joined. Plaintiff had no control over the work, but simply obeyed orders; and while the work was being done the company did not check or moderate the flow of gas, although this could have been done. The defendant claimed that the accident was the result of a latent defect in the pipe. The evidence showed that at the time of the accident there was a pressure upon the pipe of about 225 pounds to the square inch; that the pipe had been in the ground for four years, subjected continuously to a usual pressure of about

400 pounds. Before it had been placed in the ground it had been subjected to a test of 800 pounds, and after it had been placed in the ground it had been subjected to a test of 450 pounds. *Held,* that the case was properly submitted to the jury, inasmuch as the circumstances connected with the happening of the accident, were sufficient to warrant an inference of negligence in failing to shut off the gas or regulate its flow.''

George McCoy instituted in the Court of Common Pleas of Washington County an action of trespass against the Ohio Valley Gas Company to recover damages for personal injuries. The plaintiff was injured by an explosion which occurred in the pipe-line of the defendant company, at a point where he and others of the company's workmen were engaged in the work of repairing, under the following circumstances: The pipeline was some three feet under ground on the side of a hill; a landslide had pushed some of the sections of pipe from their original location sufficient to cause a leak, where two pipes joined. To relieve the line of the pressure, and to restore it to its place, the earth on the high side was being removed, and the pipe uncovered to admit of its repair. The plaintiff was engaged in this work. It had been ascertained that the leak was about the collar of a joint, but it did not appear that examination had been made to ascertain whether other or further injury had resulted from the slide. At the time the work was being done there was no interruption in the use of the line; the distribution of gas through the line continued at a pressure of about 225 pounds to the square inch, although by the use of safety valves and gates which were placed along the line at intervals of three miles, the gas could have been wholly shut off or its flow regulated at the pleasure of the defendant company, not, however, without serious inconvenience to the consumers who depended on the line for a regular and constant supply. The explosion occurred at the end of the pipe where the leak was discovered to be, breaking out a piece of pipe, varying in width from six to ten inches, and extending back from the mouth, some three feet. From the opening thus made the gas escaped against the earth about the pipe, and with great violence threw such material as was in its way against the plaintiff, inflicting upon him serious bodily injury. Verdict and judgment were rendered for plaintiff for $4,000. Defendant appealed and the Supreme Court affirmed the judgment.

Sec. 7.—In *Shirey* v. *Consumers Gas Co.*, 215 Pa. 399; 64 Atl. 541 (May 24, 1906) the syllabus is as follows:

"In an action against a gas company to recover damages for injuries caused by the explosion of gas, it was admitted that defendant's gas main broke, that gas escaped therefrom, and found its way into the plaintiff's house, where it exploded. A policeman testified that he had smelled gas in the street in the vicinity a night or two before the explosion. Three witnesses testified that the fractured edges of the gas pipe, when examined after the explosion showed in part indications of an old fracture. There was a dispute as to the cause of the break of the gas main. *Held*, that the case was for the jury, and that a verdict and judgment for plaintiff should be sustained.

A company dealing with a substance so dangerous as gas must be held to a high degree of care, and the exercise of every reasonable precaution in guarding against accidental injury."

Myron L. Shirey instituted in the Court of Common Pleas of Berks County an action of trespass to recover damages for personal injuries caused by an explosion of gas, against the Consumers Gas Company. It was admitted on the trial that the defendant's gas main broke, and that gas escaped therefrom and found its way into the house of the plaintiff where it exploded and caused damage. There was some evidence on the part of the plaintiff, given by a policeman, that he had smelled gas in the vicinity a night or two before the explosion. Three witnesses testified that the fractured edge of the gas pipe, when examined after the explosion, showed in part indications of an old fracture. There was a dispute as to the cause of the break in the gas main. The defendant maintained that it was due to the undermining of the supporting earth beneath it by a jet of water issuing from a leak in the water service pipe. The plaintiff, on the other hand, denied the existence of this leak in the water pipe prior to the explosion of the gas, and contended that the leak in the water pipe was the result of the explosion. There was verdict and

judgment for plaintiff for $2,296.80. Defendant appealed and
the Supreme Court affirmed the judgment.

Sec. 8.—In *Hartman* v. *Citizens Nat. Gas Co.*, 210 Pa. 19; 59
Atl. 315 (Nov. 4, 1904) the syllabus is as follows:

"In an action against a natural gas company to recover
damages for injuries to a house and personal property resulting
from an explosion of natural gas, there was evidence that the
odor of escaping gas had been detected in the vicinity of the
house for two years consecutively. There was also evidence that
after the explosion the service pipe leading from the main to
the house was excavated and a leak found therein; that the service pipe when dug up was rusted through in places, that in the
construction of a sewer this pipe had been lowered and thereby
subjected to a strain likely to cause a break; and that several
years before the accident, when the street was excavated on the
opposite side, the earth was discolored and smelt of gas. *Held*,
(1) that the evidence as to the odor of gas was admissible; and,
(2) that the case was for the jury, and that a verdict and judgment for plaintiff should be sustained.
Natural gas companies are held to a degree of care which is
commensurate with the dangerous character of the agency which
is handled. The measure of care is not that of an insurer to
every one who sustains loss by reason of gas escaping and exploding, but it is liable for an explosion where it knew, or by the
exercise of ordinary care should have known, of the defect of its
pipe or mains."

Margaret Hartman instituted suit in trespass in the Court of
Common Pleas of Beaver County, against Citizens Natural Gas
Company to recover damages for injuries to a house and personal property. Judgment was rendered for plaintiff for $2,541.50.
Defendant prosecuted writ of error to the Supreme Court. The
Judge of the Court of Common Pleas, upon a motion for a new
trial, in his opinion thereon, stated the evidence to be in substance
as follows: That the odor of escaping gas had been detected
in the vicinity of the plaintiff's house for two years consecutively
prior to the accident; that after the explosion the service pipe
leading from defendant's main to the house of the plaintiff was
excavated, and a leak found therein; that the ground at the time

of the accident was frozen with a considerable crust; the pipe itself, was taken out of the ditch, and was introduced in evidence; it was shown to be a part of the old service pipe; that the house was blown up as the result of a natural gas explosion. The Court of Common Pleas left to the jury the question of whether or not the defendant company had notice, or ought to have had notice of the existence of the leak in its pipe. The trial court determined that the proximate cause of the explosion was escaping gas from the defendant company's line, but this fact, together with the fact as to whether the defendant company had notice or should have had notice that its gas was escaping, was left to the jury to find. The judgment was affirmed.

Sec. 9.—In *McKenna* v. *Bridgewater Gas Co.*, 193 Pa. 633; 45 Atl. 52; 47 L. R. A. 790 (Dec. 30, 1899) the syllabus is as follows:

"In an action against a natural gas company to recover damages for the death of plaintiff's wife, caused by an explosion of gas in plaintiff's house, it appeared that the defendant and another gas company operated lines in the same borough. The superintendent of the other company, an expert workman, in an effort to supply the urgent need of its customers, searched for one of its old lines, and supposing that he had found it, with expert tools pried open the box of the defendant which enclosed the by-pass. This connected its low and high pressure lines, leaving the gas uncontrolled by the regulator, thus causing the death. Nothing external indicated that the box had been opened and the gas tampered with. *Held*, (1) that the defendant was not bound to maintain a line of sentries the length of its route to keep off trespassers, nor by personal inspection at frequent intervals during the day to ascertain whether some other gas company had mistaken defendant's line for its own, and tampered with its valves; (2) that there was no evidence to convict the defendant of negligence; (3) that the superintendent of the other gas company was the direct, efficient, and dominant cause of the injury for whom the defendant was in no way answerable; (4) that a judgment on a verdict for plaintiff should be reversed without a new venire."

Plaintiff, Patrick Henry McKenna, brought suit in trespass in the Court of Common Pleas of Beaver County, against the

Bridgewater Gas Company for damages claimed for the death of
his wife. From a judgment for the plaintiff the defendant appealed to the Supreme Court. Justice Dean, of that court, stated
the facts as follows: The Bridgewater Gas Company and the
Citizens Natural Gas Company both maintained gas lines in the
borough of New Brighton, Beaver County. On September 27,
1897, an employe of the Citizens Company, one Miller, opened the
gate of what is known as the by-pass of the Bridgewater Company, and thus connected its low and high pressure lines, leaving
the gas uncontrolled by the regulator. This line introduced gas
into the dwelling of Mr. McKenna, the plaintiff. In consequence
of this opening of the gate the pressure rose in the low pressure
line, with which McKenna's house was connected, and an explosion in the house followed, which blew it to pieces, and so severe-
ly burned and otherwise injured plaintiff's wife, that she soon
after died. Plaintiff sued the Bridgewater Company for damages,
alleging that this company was guilty of negligence in leaving the
by-pass in such an exposed condition that anyone had access to
and could so manipulate it as to cause injury to the company's
customers; and further that defendant's system of inspection
was loose and inefficient. The defendant denied any responsibility
for the act of Miller, who was not its servant, and was to them
unknown. Defendant also denied any negligence in any of the
particulars charged. The Court of Common Pleas submitted
the evidence bearing on the question of negligence to the jury,
instructing them that the burden was on defendant to rebut the
inference of negligence fairly derivable from the circumstances.
There was a verdict for plaintiff in the sum of $15,000. Motion
for new trial was made, which was overruled, and judgment entered on the verdict. Defendant appealed, assigning for error the
refusal of the court to peremptorily instruct the jury to render
a verdict for defendant. The Supreme Court reversed the judgment.

Sec. 10.—In *Benson* v. *Allegheny Heating Company*, 188 Pa.
614; 41 Atl. 729 (Nov. 14, 1898) the syllabus is as follows:

"In an action against a natural gas company to recover
damages for a loss by fire, alleged to have been caused by escaping

gas igniting a lamp, binding instructions for defendant will be sustained where the only evidence of an explosion of gas was that two windows near where the lamp stood were found after the fire in the alley outside of the building, but it did not appear whether they were blown out or not. The lamp was lying on the floor, unbroken, and after the fire was extinguished. Two witnesses noticed a strong smell of gas near the service pipe but made no test and could not tell whether the gas was escaping or not. Two witnesses who were within thirty yards of the building when the fire broke out, heard no explosion and one of the plaintiffs who was in the building fifteen minutes before the fire broke out did not notice any smell of gas.''

Elizabeth Benson and Allison B. Benson, Executors of Samuel Benson, instituted an action of trespass in the Court of Common Pleas Number 1 of Allegheny County, against Allegheny Heating Company, to recover damages for the burning of a building. The building injured was used as a pump factory. The portion of the building in which the fire occurred was the engine room. It fronted on Ridge Avenue, and was eighteen feet wide and seventy-five feet deep. The defendant company had a gas main on Ridge Street, and a service pipe entered the building to which a meter had been attached. On December 10, 1890, the meter was detached and the service pipe was left open. There was, however, a stop-off in the street near the main pipe. The fire occurred on the night of December 12th at about 9:00 o'clock. In the engine room was a furnace, at the distance of about 12 1-2 feet from the gas pipe under the boilers which extended back about 22 feet. Back of these, on a table, was an oil lamp, about 13 feet from the end of the boiler. The plaintiff's theory was that the gas escaped from the pipe, and finally reached the lamp which caused an explosion and a fire. The lamp was about 47 1-2 feet from the gas pipe. The testimony was that of Allison Benson, one of the plaintiffs, and L. L. Currier, a foreman in the shop. The only facts upon which the theory of plaintiff was based, were that two windows near where the lamp stood were found in the alley along the side of the shop, the lamp lying on the floor unbroken, and after the fire was extinguished the witnesses noticed a strong smell of gas near the service pipe. No one noticed any escape of gas until after the fire on the 12th; during this time the fires had been used in the furnace and the lamp burned at night. On the night of the fire Mr. Benson testified that he was in the building about fifteen minutes before the fire was discovered, and that when he came out of the stable the shop was all aflame, and the house on the other side of the alley burning so that they could not enter the alley. The uncontradicted testimony on the part of the defendant was that the next morning, on going to the premises, taking out the plug which Mr. Currier had put in the pipe, and testing it with fire, no escaping gas was found. This was testified to by four men, and was not disputed. The court directed verdict and judgment for defendant, from which judgment plaintiff appealed, and the Supreme Court affirmed the judgment in a per curiam opinion.

Sec. 11.—In *Ohio Gas-Fuel Co.* v. *Andrews*, 50 Ohio St. 695; 35 N. E. 1059 (Dec. 19, 1893) the syllabus is as follows:

"The provisions of Section 3561-a Rev. St. imposes on plaintiff in error the duty of keeping under its control natural gas while it is transporting the same, and if damages should result to others, without their fault by its explosion, while being thus transported, the plaintiff in error will be held liable therefor, although not negligent in regard thereto."

Andrews instituted suit against the Ohio Gas-Fuel Company and recovered judgment in the Court of Common Pleas for Mahoning County. On appeal by the defendant the Circuit Court affirmed the judgment. Defendant appealed to the Supreme Court. The Fuel Company, a body corporate, was engaged in transporting in pipes natural gas to the City of Youngstown, and underground along its streets to supply its inhabitants with fuel. The plaintiff Andrews owned valuable improved real estate in said city, the improvements on which were substantially destroyed by an explosion of gas while in course of transportation in said city along a street adjacent to the improvements. Upon the trial of the action in the Court of Common Pleas, the court charged the jury as follows:

"If * * * you find that the defendant was engaged in the transportation of natural gas for the purposes mentioned; that the same escaped from the pipeline of the defendants, at the gate or valve therein, while the same was being so transported, at the time and place and in the manner claimed by the plaintiff in her petition, and that the buildings were in fact destroyed by reason thereof, and that the same was the proximate and direct cause of the destruction of the buildings mentioned, and that the plaintiff's own acts and conduct did not contribute to the injury of which she complained,—then your verdict should be for the plaintiff, in such sum as the evidence shows you she has actually been damaged."

The statute 3561-a contains the following provision:

"But said company shall be liable for any damages that may result from the negligent transportation of the same." [Referring to the transportation of natural gas.]

The Supreme Court affirmed the judgments of the Courts below.

Sec. 12.—In *Lebanon Light etc. Co.* v. *Leap,* 139 Ind. 443; 39 N. E. 57; 29 L. R. A. 342 (Nov. 27, 1894) the syllabus is as follows:

"1. Laying pipe in highway without permission is unlawful, and persons doing so are liable to others injured thereby.

2. A gas company contracted for the construction of a gas plant. The contractor sublet the contract for boring the gas wells. The subcontractor after boring one well, laid pipe which was furnished by the contractor, to get gas from the well to use in boring others. Part of the pipe so laid was taken up by the contractor, and the rest used in conducting gas to a town for the use of the company. *Held,* that, though the plant had not been turned over to the company, it and both contractors were liable for injuries to others caused by the negligent manner in which the pipe was laid.

3. In an action for personal injuries caused by the explosion of natural gas, alleged to have been due to the negligent manner in which the pipe for conducting it was laid, evidence that before the explosion plaintiff had, with other boys, though cautioned against doing so, meddled with the pipe after it was

laid, so as to cause its joints to become loose, should be considered in determining the question of contributory negligence, it being claimed by the defenses that the action was the result of such loosening of the joints."

Amos Leap instituted an action in the Circuit Court of Hamilton County against the Lebanon etc. Company and others, for damages claimed as the result of an accident which occurred on September 20, 1890. It appeared that the Lebanon Company had contracted with Charles T. Doxey to construct a natural gas plant and Doxey entered into a contract with John E. Snow by which Snow was to drill four gas wells to supply gas for the plant. After well Number 3 had been completed Doxey's men took up the pipe on the highway from the "T" at the crossing north to well Number 2. There was then no gas in the pipe at the crossing. Snow was drilling Number 4, and getting his gas from wells Numbers 1 and 2, and had nothing to do further with well Number 3, or with the pipe on the highway. Doxey's assistant testified that he began taking up the pipe north from the crossing by cutting the second joint north of the "T"; they then took two pair of tongs, one to hold the first joint in place, and to keep it from turning in the "T" while the other was used to unscrew the "T" of the second joint which had been cut off. They then plugged up the end of the first joint with a 2-inch wooden plug, and went on and took up the rest of the pipe north to well Number 2. When cutting the second joint and unscrewing the piece from the first joint, and plugging the end of the latter, they did not examine the "T" to see if the joint of pipe was tight in it, but it seemed tight. There was no gas on the line at the time. The "T" was cast iron, of heavier make than the pipe, and would weigh about 25 pounds. The joint of pipe left attached to it was about 19 feet long, and was about 12 feet from the nearest fence. It did not appear how soon after the taking up of the pipe north of the "T" that the gas was again turned on, nor did it appear who turned it on, nor for what purpose or use it was turned on. Snow had not used gas through this line since he completed Number 3, two weeks previous to the accident. It did appear that a line was completed into the City of Lebanon, and gas furnished to the city in the

month of August, 1890. For whatever purpose the gas was turned
into the pipe between wells one and two, after taking up the pipe
north of the "T" it was certain that between that time and the
time of the accident, the leak of gas at the "T" was observed frequently. It also seemed probable that the leak was noticed before
the taking up of the pipe, but it was clear that the leak grew
worse from time to time up to the date of the accident.

The plaintiff was about eighteen years of age, and lived with
his father about 40 rods from the crossing. Several persons
testified that they saw gas on fire at the leak in the "T" on the
day of the accident, and at other times previous. John Griffin,
who lived near the crossing, testified that there had been a leak
at the "T" ever since the pipe had been laid, and that the leak
had been quite bad for some time previous to the accident. Others
who had passed there frequently had never noticed the leak before
that day. Some had smelled gas for a few days previously, but
saw no fire. John Leap, father of the plaintiff had seen the gas
on fire two weeks before, and put out the fire with a bucket of
water. The plaintiff testified that he had noticed the leak on fire
about two months before the accident, and at different times up to
the time of the accident; The last time previous to the time of
the accident was on the preceding Monday night; The accident
happened on Saturday; that on Monday night the gas burned for
about five minutes when he, and others with him, put it out; that he
did not touch the pipe or set the gas afire himself; that he saw two
of the party lift up the end of the link of pipe about four feet
and then let it fall; that he next saw the leak afire on Saturday,
the day of the accident, about 10:00 o'clock in the morning; the
blaze was about four feet high; the pipe at the "T" and across the
traveled part of the road, was covered with about an inch or two
of earth; it was so covered when first laid: that he again saw the
leak between one and two o'clock on Saturday afternoon, while
on his way, on foot, to a town about a mile north of the crossing:
that when he came up to the fire he saw Warren Griffin, a boy of
about 12 years of age, standing there; he noticed the boy with a
small stick scraping along the dirt where the fire was burning;
while they were standing there a neighbor came along and asked
plaintiff to go along, and he replied he was not quite ready; the

two boys were standing without talking during this time, when plaintiff said to Warren, "if that plug was taken out of that pipe it would make a nice fire." Warren asked "What plug?" plaintiff went around and pointed to the plug; Warren walked around to the end of the pipe and raised the end up something about three inches, and that was the last plaintiff knew. The explosion followed, the joint of pipe being thrown out, and the two boys thrown violently back and burned by the gas. There was a judgment for plaintiff, and defendant appealed to the Supreme Court where the judgment was reversed.

Sec. 13.—In *Alexandria etc. Mining Co.* v. *Irish*, 16 Ind. App. 534; 44 N. E. 680 (Sept. 25, 1896) paragraphs 1-2-4-6, and 9 of the syllabus are as follows:

"1. A complaint alleging that defendant natural gas company negligently and knowingly suffered its pipelines to become rotten and incapable of retaining the gas, and continued to use them for conveying gas, knowing of such defective condition, and that, by reason of such carelessness and negligence, one of the pipes sprung a leak in front of the building in which plaintiff's intestate was employed, permitting the gas to escape into the earth, which it permeated, accumulating in said building and exploding when it came in contact with fire, whereby the building was blown down causing intestate to be buried under the debris and to be burned by the fire immediately following the explosion, and to be injured, from the effects of which he died, charges the proximate cause of the death to be the negligence of defendant.

2. A complaint for death caused by an explosion of gas escaping from the pipeline of a natural gas company, need not allege that defendant knew gas was escaping from the broken pipes, and percolating through the ground to the place of explosion, or that it knew the danger of an explosion, it being bound to know that gas would escape, and that there was danger of an explosion, if, as charged, it had knowledge of the imperfect condition of the pipes.

4. Under Rev. Stat. 1894, Sec. 7507, et seq., declaring it the duty of gas companies to conduct natural gas only through sound wrought or cast iron pipes and casing tested to a pressure of at least 400 pounds to the square inch, and that they shall not convey natural gas through such pipes and casings at a pressure exceeding 300 pounds per square inch, failure to apply tests at a pres-

sure of more than 100 pounds is negligence, making the company liable for resulting injury.

6. A special verdict in an action against a natural gas company for negligence in allowing its pipes in the street to remain in an unsafe condition whereby gas escaped, percolated through the ground, and collected in a building on the side of the street, causing an explosion, as a result of which one lawfully occupying a room in the building in the ordinary pursuit of his business, was killed, need not find that deceased had no knowledge of the dangerous and defective condition of the pipes, and that they had burst, and gas was escaping therefrom, if his freedom from fault is fairly inferable from the verdict.

9. In an action against a gas company for death caused by an explosion of gas escaping from its pipes in the street, defendant being charged with negligence in permitting its pipes to remain out of repair at a specified point, evidence of defects at other points in the line is admissible, though some of such defects were not noticed until after the explosion: the evidence warranting a legitimate inference that they existed long before.'*

John Irish, administrator, instituted suit in the Circuit Court of Madison County against the Alexandria Company to recover damages on account of the death of the plaintiff's intestate through the alleged negligence of the defendant. The suit was removed to the Tipton Circuit Court. The special verdict disclosed the following facts: Defendant operated a natural gas plant in the City of Alexandria; the pipes used for conveying gas from the wells to consumers houses were, on March 31, 1894, and for a long time prior thereto, rotten, decayed and rusted, and unsafe to convey gas at high pressure, which the verdict found the defendant well knew; that said pipe was of a weak and inferior quality, unfit and unsafe to convey or control natural gas at a high pressure, which defendant knew; that by reason of the conditions named the pipes leaked at different points along the line for a long period of time before March 31, 1894; that at no time prior to said date did the gas company subject the pipes etc. to an examination or make the same stand a test to exceed 100 pounds to the square inch: that the gas company with knowledge of such conditions allowed the gas to pass through said lines at a pressure beyond the power and capacity of the pipes, during a period of more than one year prior to said date; that on or about the date mentioned the pipes burst,

broke and gave way, and allowed natural gas contained therein
to escape into the earth surrounding such pipes, and permeate
the same and percolate through the ground, and beneath the foundation and building in which the intestate was engaged in the
business of a barber; that on said day the escaping gas at said
point came in contract with fire in said building and there was an
explosion therefrom which wrecked the building and killed said intestate.   Verdict and judgment were rendered in favor of the
plaintiff, and defendant appealed to the Appellate Court where
the judgment was affirmed.

Sec. 14.—In *Ibach* v. *Huntington Light etc. Co.*, 23 Ind. App.
281; 55 N. E. 249 (Nov. 17, 1899) the syllabus is as follows:

"A complaint against a natural gas company for negligently
increasing the pressure, and setting fire to plaintiff's house, showed that plaintiff had control of all the gas appliances within her
house, except the mixer; that the company changed, over plaintiff's protest, a number 5 for a number 7 mixer, but did not show
that it was legally bound to furnish such a mixer as the consumer
wished, or that the fire might not have occurred with either mixer;
that the gas passed through the mixer into a burner, and in front
of the mixer was a valve regulating the flow, and used to turn off
the gas, but that the amount of the flow depended upon the pressure which was regulated by the company.   It averred, further,
that plaintiff had 'carefully adjusted the valve to suit the
pressure before her absence'; indicating that she knew the pressure was not uniform, and that it was controlled by the valve.
Held, not to show negligence of the company."

Mattie W. Ibach brought suit in the Circuit Court of Huntington County against the defendant Fuel Company, her declaration or complaint charging the cause of action as stated in the
syllabus.   Judgment for defendant was rendered, and plaintiff
appealed to the Appellate Court, where the judgment was affirmed, the only question being the sufficiency of the complaint.

Sec. 15.—In *Indiana Natural Gas Co.* v. *McMath*, 26 Ind. App.
154; 57 N. E. 593; 59 N. E. 287 (June 5, 1900) syls. 1-2-4 are as
follows:

"1. A complaint is sufficient which states that defendant negligently maintained a natural gas pipe on the top of the ground on a public highway and allowed it to be covered by grass and weeds, and that plaintiff, in the exercise of due care, without knowing of such pipe, while going from the highway into a field with a traction engine, ran over and broke such pipe, and was injured by an explosion caused by the gas being ignited from the fire in the engine.

2. It is unlawful to lay a natural gas pipe on the surface of a highway, and the person maintaining it is liable for an injury resulting therefrom, even if the particular injury could not have been foreseen.

4. A natural gas pipe on the surface of a highway had been there for years, and was covered by grass and weeds. Plaintiff, who was not a resident of the neighborhood, was injured by an explosion caused by taking a traction engine over the pipe, in order to make a turn to enter a field on the other side of the highway. He sent one of his employes ahead to examine the way before he entered the field. The evidence was in conflict as to plaintiff's knowledge of existence of such gas pipe. *Held,* sufficient to sustain a finding that plaintiff was not guilty of contributory negligence."

John H. McMath brought suit against the Indiana Natural etc. Company, in the Circuit Court of Tipton County for personal injuries. From a judgment in favor of plaintiff, and an order denying a motion for a new trial the defendant appealed to the Appellate Court. In discussing the evidence, that court found that the gas pipe was one-half an inch in diameter, the thickness of the iron being one-eighth of an inch: It lay upon the surface of the highway, along the south side thereof, about three or four feet from the fence on that side, where it had lain for some years, the grass and weeds hiding it: The plaintiff, who did not reside in that neighborhood, was proceeding, with a traction engine driven by steam, to enter a clover field on the north side of the road, which was 24 feet in width, the entrance being through a gap in the north fence. To make the turn he caused the engine to run upon the south side of the traveled track, first sending one of his employes ahead to examine the way for obstructions. Without knowledge of the position or of the existence of the gas pipe, he ran the engine upon it, and thereby crushed it. The escaping gas was ignited by the fire in the fire box of the engine, and the appellee was injured by the explosion and flame. The Appellate Court affirmed the judgment for plaintiff.

Sec. 16.—In *Moore* v. *Heat. & Light Co.*, 65 W. Va. 552; 64 S. E. 721 (April 27, 1909) the syllabus is as follows:

"In an action for tort, the plaintiff bearing the burden of proof, a verdict for him can not be found on evidence which affords mere conjecture that the liability exists, and leaves the minds of jurors in equipoise and reasonable doubt. The evidence must generate an actual rational belief in the existence of the disputed fact.

2. Where a liability is asserted on the ground of tort, the plaintiff bears the burden of proof of the fact on which the liability rests, and the burden to disprove such fact does not shift to the shoulders of the defendant, until plaintiff's evidence shows a state of facts sufficient to establish a rational belief of the existence of such fact."

T. E. Moore instituted suit in the Circuit Court of Ritchie County against the West Virginia Heat & Light Company for damages for the destruction of the house of plaintiff. The company owned a natural gas well about 5580 feet from Moore's house, and a pipe conveying its gas to within 150 yards of Moore's house, and from that pipe a smaller one conveyed gas to the house for Moore's use. He used gas in two stoves. The company shut off the gas to connect with a pipe to convey the gas to Cairo and then, without notice turned on the gas again, and, as Moore claimed, this caused the fire. Upon the trial the defendant company demurred to the evidence, upon which demurrer the Circuit Court gave judgment for Moore for $950.00 from which judgment the company sued out the writ of error. The evidence showed that the house was a board house, one story and a half: one stove was in the kitchen, another in the sitting room. The upstairs, including part of the house, was not used as a room but as a place to store away things; it was over the sitting room. The gas was turned off from the well, and the fire went out in the stoves; then Mrs. Moore left the house and went to a neighbors, to get him to put up a stove for coal, as she had been told some time before by an agent of the company that owing to a sale of the well, the gas would be cut off from the house at some future time, and when cut off, it would not be restored to the house. Shortly after she left, the house was discovered to be on fire; there was then no one in the house, and no one saw the commencement of the fire, or could give any account of its commencement, or how it started. It was first observed at a school house in the vicinity by fire issuing from the roof, and when the teacher and others went to the house, he opened the sitting room door and saw that the fire was in the garret, and was consuming the ceiling over the sitting room. Mrs. Moore had been ironing, and had the stove quite hot. From the stove in the sitting room a pipe ran to the ceiling, and there connected with a flue of iron running from the ceiling up through the tin roof, the flue being an iron casing used in oil wells. When the teacher and others looked into the sitting room they saw no fire in the stove. The plaintiff's theory was that the gas passed into the burner in that stove and went up the pipe and flue. The Court of Appeals reversed the judgment, set aside the verdict and rendered judgment for defendant upon the demurrer to the evidence.

Sec. 17.—In *Consumers Gas Trust Co.* v. *Perrigo*, 144 Ind. 350; 32 L. R. A. 146; 43 N. E. 306, (March 20, 1896) paragraph 2 of the syllabus is as follows:

"2. In an action for personal injuries caused by an explosion of natural gas which, leaking from a sleeve in defendant's pipes percolated through the ground and accumulated in plaintiff's cellar, 90 feet distant, where it appeared that plaintiff's house was supplied by gas by another company, the failure of plaintiff to notify defendant of the leak, even if she knew of its existence, did not constitute contributory negligence."

Frances Perrigo instituted suit in the Superior Court of Marion County against the Consumers Gas Trust Company and others to recover for personal injuries caused by the explosion of natural gas: It was alleged in the complaint that on February 14, 1893, the plaintiff was lawfully an accupant of a dwelling house in the City of Indianapolis, and that defendant gas company was engaged in drilling for natural gas, and conveying the same to said city by mains, service pipes and regulators laid along and in Illinois street, in front of, and adjacent to said dwelling house; that defendant carelessly, negligently and unskillfully maintained its pipes, mains and regulators so that they leaked and permitted gas to escape from control in large quantities in the immediate vicinity of plaintiff's dwelling; that such escaping gas penetrated and percolated through the loose sand and gravel until it reached and accumulated in large quantities within the foundation under said dwelling house, without the knowledge or fault of plaintiff, and that the same became ignited without any fault or negligence of plaintiff, thereby causing a violent explosion within and under said dwelling completely demolishing the same, destroying the personal property of plaintiff and causing her great mental and physical pain and injury. A general denial was filed, and the cause was submitted to a jury for trial. Verdict was rendered for plaintiff for $6,000 on which judgment was rendered. A motion for a new trial was overruled, and defendant appealed.

The testimony disclosed the following material facts: The ground was frozen solid at the time of the explosion; the leak from which the gas escaped into the earth was in the large main at a point where it was covered by a sleeve: In the fall and winter of 1887 the Broad Ripple Natural Gas Company laid its high pressure main line from the City of Indianapolis north-ward along Illinois Street, to the gas wells from which the gas was obtained; the pipe was eight-inch screw joint wrought iron; two forces of men engaged in laying the sections in the City and north to the wells met south of the dwelling under which the explosion occurred; at the point of intersection the pipes could not be screwed together; they were brought up close and connected by a sleeve, which was fitted over the pipes, and calked with lead; the Consumers Gas Trust Company purchased the Broad Ripple line in July, 1889.

The main question for decision was, whether the Consumers Gas Trust Company, Appellants, was careless and negligent in the purchase, inspection and maintainance of the line during the three and a half years from said purchase until the accident in

February, 1893. The evidence submitted to the jury upon this question was voluminous. It appeared that there was no connection by pipes between oppellant's main and plaintiff's house. The latter was supplied with gas by the Indianapolis Natural Gas Company, which company also had its gas main in Illinois Street close to plaintiff's line. The location of the sleeve on appellant's pipe where the gas leaked was across the street, 90 feet distant from plaintiff's dwelling. The sleeve was smooth on the inside, as was the pipe on the outside. The inner diameter of the sleeve was an inch and a half greater than the pipe over which it fitted. This open space was filled with lead. There was evidence that there had been a leak at this point, and that gas escaped through the earth from the first laying of the pipe six years before the explosion. It was the theory of the plaintiff that during all these years the gas permeated the surrounding earth; that it escaped more readily from the surface during the summer, but that when the ground was frozen over the gas was forced to greater distance under the hardened crust. At the time of the purchase of the line by the appellant, a test of the line was made by turning on full gas pressure nearly or quite 300 pounds to the square inch. Appellee argued that there being a leak even at that time under the sleeve the great pressure thus turned on still further opened and displaced the lead between the pipe and the sleeve, and conse- quently that the escape of gas was greater after that test.

It was argued for the appellent that there was no negligence in the purchase, care and maintenance of the pipeline; (1) be- cause appellant employed as superintendent of its pipeline and gas wells a man of large experience in such work; (2) that before the purchase from the Broad Ripple Company the line was care- fully tested and found in good condition; (3) that appellant did not know and had no means of knowing without digging up its entire line of the existence of the sleeve in question; (4) that after the inspection and purchase of the line, the appellant by its line- walkers and other employes, kept up a careful supervision and in- spection of its pipeline, including that on Illinois Street, almost every day up to the time of the explosion; (5) that the line was properly laid, and the sleeve and joint were properly and skill-

fully constructed; (6) that the appellant did not know of the existence of this sleeve, or of a leak at that point, until after the
explosion; its employes, Watson, the foreman of field work, laying
pipe, making repairs, etc., and the line walkers who walked over
the line every few days had never discovered any evidence of a
leak at that point, although it was their special business to look for
leaks.

Mr. Shackelton, General Superintendent of Appellant, who
had full charge of the lines gave as the only test or examination
of the condition of the line made at the time of the purchase
from the Broad Ripple Company, that a full pressure or about
300 pounds was turned on at the wells; that the line stood the
pressure all right, apparently, and that he did not know of any
leak thereby disclosed; he knew that the main pipe was eight
inches in diameter; that he did not learn of the existence of the
leak until after the accident; that at the time of the purchase
he did not make any inquiry as to the location of the sleeve on the
line; they received from the Broad Ripple Company a surveyed
chart of the line, but he did not examine it particularly; that he
had never looked on the chart for sleeves; but he knew that they
were not indicated on the chart; he did not make inquiry of anyone
in regard to sleeves, and did not find out whether or not there were
any on the line; in the city they ordinarily kept memoranda of all
sleeves, so that if there was a break or a leak they could examine
the memoranda and determine where it was located; they had
never examined the place where the leak was at the sleeve in question; no repairs had ever been made by the company at that point
until after the explosion.

Mr. Watson, General foreman of the company and assistant
to the superintendent, in charge of all repairs, testified: After
the explosion he had the earth dug up at the sleeve, and found
a leak on the under side of the sleeve where the lead seemed to
have been drawn out; he had the leak calked by hammering the
lead all back with calking tools; that it had not since leaked; that he
found the earth all around blackened by the gas, and thought
it would take some time to discolor the earth in that way. Mr.
Lyman, the Secretary, testified that there was but little gas turned

on the main line in summer; that there was no regular inspection during that time. Mr. Everett, who lived in the neighborhood, testified that he had smelled gas on the street for a long time, but he thought it came from a regulator below Twenty-sixth street, or from one above that street. Mr. Reichardt, a linewalker of the company whose business it was to examine the line for leaks and to calk them when found, testified that a few months before the explosion he smelled gas a few feet north of Twenty-Sixth Street, but he thought it came from a regulator about 200 feet further north. Mr. Harrison, a linewalker, testified that he was told by a Mr. Watson that he (Watson) smelled gas near Twenty-Sixth Street, but that he (Harrison) could not discover any leak, and did not report the matter to the office; at other times he smelled gas himself, but thought it came from a regulator; this was about two years before the explosion. Mr. Page, who lived on Illinois street, had frequently smelled gas near the locality of the sleeve, but until the explosion had no knowledge as to where it came from.

The plaintiff produced a large number of witnesses, a contractor, and other persons who had aided in digging and covering up the trench when the Broad Ripple line was first laid, plumbers, gas fitters, and others who had occasion to pass along the sidewalk where the sleeve was placed and many neighbors and other persons residing on the street in the immediate vicinity. These witnesses without exception testified that there had been a leak at the sleeve almost from the time the main was first put down, six years prior to the explosion; that it was common talk in the neighborhood; that the odor was sometimes so strong that passers-by crossed the street to avoid it. One witness, going along the sidewalk with a lantern, turned out the lantern at that point, fearing the escaping gas. Several witnesses at different times saw the gas on fire as it came out through the earth. After rains and when water stood in the gutter the gas was often seen to bubble up through the water. In at least two instances appellant's agents the linewalkers, were notified of the escaping gas at the sleeve, and were asked to repair the leak. No repairs, however, were ever made at that point until after the explosion.

The plaintiff testified as to the particulars of the accident: That it occurred in the evening; she had lighted the lamp; there was on one else in the house at the time; she went to the cellar to take down a crock of milk; opened the cellar door, and set the lamp on a bench nearby to show light down the cellarway; as she went down she thought the light grew dimmer; as she returned, when half way up the stairs, she looked up at the lamp standing on the bench, and saw that the light had grown small and burned blue; immediately after, and before she reached the top of the stairway, she saw the lamp blaze up; she remembered no more until she found herself fastened in the ruins of the house which had blown up and was already on fire; her neighbors extricated her from the wreckage; she had not smelled the gas, having been deprived of the sense of smell for many years; she had no thought of there being any gas in the cellar.

As plaintiff's house was supplied with gas by the Indianapolis Company, it was thought at first that the explosion had been caused by an escape from that company's pipes. Accordingly the Indianapolis company spent some time uncovering its service pipe from the house across the street, and also its main pipe for some distance, but found no leak. It was sixteen days after the explosion before appellant company began to uncover its main to discover whether there was a leak there, and on uncovering the pipe at the sleeve, the gas rushed out from the leak with great force. During the whole period of sixteen days from the explosion to the uncovering of the sleeve, the escaping gas continued to burn in jets from two to eight inches high all around the inside of the north, south, and west foundation walls of plaintiff's house. The gas came out between the brick, and from the ground along the bottom of the walls. Within two minutes after the uncovering of the sleeve, as shown by the evidence, the jets of gas in the foundations of the house ceased to burn, and no gas could be discovered there afterward. The earth around the sleeve was found blackened with gas. The ground was frozen above the pipe, and the pipe itself lay in loose gravel and sand.

The Supreme Court affirmed the judgment. Upon the question of the liabilities arising in cases of explosions of natural gas, the court cited:

Ohio Gas Fuel Co. v. *Andrews,* 50 Ohio St. 695; 35 N. E. 1059.
Lebanon etc. Co. v. *Leap,* 139 Ind. 443; 39 N. E. 57.
McGahan v. *Gas Co.,* 140 Ind. 335; 37 N. E. 601.

Sec. 18.—In *Consumers Gas Trust Co.* v. *Corbaley,* 14 Ind. App. 549; 43 N. E. 237, (March 10, 1896) the second point of the syllabus is as follows:

"2. Where, in an action against a natural gas company for damages to plaintiff's house, caused by the explosion of gas, which escaped from its pipeline through the ground into the plaintiff's house, there is evidence that the defendant was aware for several years of the leak, or could have discovered it by the exercise of reasonable care, a finding that defendant was negligent in the maintenance of its pipeline will not be disturbed."

William H. Corbaley brought suit in the Superior Court of Marion County against the Consumers Gas Trust Company to recover damages for the destruction of a house resulting from the explosion of natural gas. A trial by jury resulted in a verdict and judgment in favor of the plaintiff for $1,100.00. Defendant appealed, assigning as error, that the court erred in overruling defendant's motion for a new trial. In the opinion Judge Davis found the evidence substantially as follows: That in the construction of an 8-inch high pressure natural gas line along Illinois street in the City of Indianapolis in 1887 for the Broad Ripple Company, two gangs of men one working from the north and the other from the south met at a point nearly opposite the property in question; in order to connect the two ends of pipe so laid and brought together by the separate gangs, a piece of wrought iron 10-inch gas pipe eighteen inches or two feet in length was used as a sleeve; that the joints at each end of the sleeve were calked with lead; that the line was purchased by appellant in 1889; and thereafter was under its management; that the joints at each end of the sleeve were calked with lead; that a leak at said point occasioned by the lead drawing out between the sleeve and the main pipe caused the explosion which destroyed appellee's house in 1883; that the gas was escaping through said leak for several years before the explosion; that the gas so escaping penetrated through and under the ground to, under, and in appellee's house, and there ignited, causing the explosion; that the appellee never resided on the premises; that the house was occupied by a tenant; that the leak which was evidenced by the escaping gas might have been discovered by the appellant by the exercise of ordinary care in the operation and management of the line before the accident; that an employe of appellent—a linewalker, whose duty it was to inspect the line for leaks—had notice of the fact that there was a leak in the sleeve at this point long prior to the explosion. The Appellate Court affirmed the judgment.

(See Section 17)

Sec. 19.—In *Coffeyville Mining & Gas Co.* v. *Carter*, 68 Kan. 565; 70 Pac. 635 (Nov. 8, 1902) an action was brought by Lulu Carter against the Coffeyville Mining etc. Company, to recover damages for the death of David Carter. A judgment was rendered for plaintiff and defendant brought error to the Supreme Court where the judgment was affirmed. It was proven that defendant put down and was the owner of a natural gas well in the City of Coffeyville. East of this well, about fifty feet, there was erected a two-story brick building. Immediately south of this building stood a small frame building used as a blacksmith shop, where David Carter was employed, on May 21, 1896, at his trade. By reason of defects in the materials used, or the manner of the construction of the gas well, gas escaped through crevices in the earth to a cellar or foundation underneath the brick building. This accumulation of gas from some unknown cause was exploded. The explosion demolished the brick building, threw the south wall on the blacksmith shop, and instantly killed Carter. There was testimony tending to show that at the time the brick building was constructed and thereafter, gas escaped from the well through crevices into the bottom of the cellar; that the water in drinking wells in the neighborhood of the well, free from gas before the drilling of the well, afterwards became contaminated by gas and unfit for use. The cellar or basement under the brick building was rented by one Irwin and had been closed for about ten days prior to the explosion. Matches had been lighted during the day preceding the accident without harm. At the time of the explosion Irwin had gone to the cellar with some help to carry out water therefrom. The explosion followed upon opening the cellar door. The Supreme Court cited in support of its conclusions:

> *Koelsch* v. *Phila. Co.*, 152 Pa. 355; 25 Atl. 522; 18 L. R. A. 759; 34 Am. St. Rep. 653.
> *City of Kansas City* v. *Gilbert*, 70 Pac. 350.

Sec. 20.—In *Maxwell* v. *Coffeyville Mining & Gas Co.*, 75 Pac. 1047; 68 Kan. 821 (March 12, 1904) the syllabus is as follows:

"Evidence merely that defendant maintained a gas well fifty feet from plaintiff's premises, and that gas accumulated in plaintiff's cellar causing an explosion, and that gas was found in water wells within a radius of 200 feet of the gas well is not sufficient to warrant a conclusion that the gas came from defendant's well, or that defendant was negligent."

A. S. Maxwell and others brought an action in the District Court of Montgomery County against Coffeyville Mining etc. Company for the recovery of damages caused to a store of goods by the explosion of natural gas in the cellar of a building, in which the plaintiff was doing business. The evidence showed that the defendant drilled, and was maintaining a gas well within 50 or 60 feet of the premises occupied by the plaintiff; that three wells of water within a radius of 200 feet from the gas well, subsequent to its drilling, became impregnated with gas so as to become unfit for use; that gas had at various times prior and subsequent to the explosion escaped from some source into the cellar of the building occupied by the plaintiff; that gas escaped along the ·curb of the street in front of the plaintiff's place of business. The defendant demurred to the plaintiff's evidence, which demurrer the court sustained, and plaintiff brought error to the Supreme Court, where the judgment was affirmed.

Sec. 21.—In *Hollon* v. *Campton Fuel & Light Co.*, 127 Ky. 266; 105 S. W. 426; 32 Ky. L. Rep. 178 (Nov. 22, 1907) syls. 1-2-3-4-5-7 are as follows:

"1.   Where in an action against a fuel and light company for the destruction of a customers house by fire in that the company negligently permitted an unusal flow of gas to flow through its lines, there was nothing in the complaint to show that the unusual flow was of such force as to destroy the valve in the customer's house by which he was enabled to regulate the flow, it is to be presumed that the flow was not of such a pressure.

2.   Where an unusual flow of gas is permitted by a fuel and light company to pass through its lines, it is not of such pressure as to destroy the valve which the customer has to regulate the volume of gas which is supplied to his light or fire burners, the company is not liable for damages resulting from such flow.

3.   Evidence of the customers neighbors that along about the time the house burned the flow of gas through the pipes in their houses was unusually strong was competent without proof that such houses were located, with reference to the main line practically the same as the house burned, and that the equipment for regulating the flow was practically the same, where the size of the town was such that the pipe and equipment were necessarily practically the same, and the company did most, if not all, of the work of installation.

4.   Evidence that about a year and a half before the fire witness tested the pressure in one of the pipes of the company in another house and found it above the reasonable and proper pressure, was not connected sufficiently close to the time of the fire to entitle it to any weight and should not have been admitted.

5.   Evidence as to the condition in which the 'by-pass' and 'regulator' which were the appliances by means of which the pressure of the gas was regulated, were found the morning following the night of the fire, was improperly admitted.

6.   Where the evidence is equally consistent with either view, the existence or non-existence of negligence, the court should not submit the case to the jury, for the party affirming negligence has failed to prove it.

7.   Evidence, *held*, to show that the fire might have been due to any one or other causes as likely as that of the company's negligence; and hence it was error not to direct a verdict for the company.''

I. R. Hollon brought an action in the Circuit Court of Wayne County against the Campton etc. Company, for damages claimed for the loss of a dwelling house in the town of Campton. The plaintiff claimed that the house was set on fire and burned by reason of the negligence and carelessness of the company, in this, that the company through its agents and employes had turned into the gas pipes which supplied gas to the plaintiff's house an unusual quantity of gas, thereby increasing the flames to such an extent as to cause the destruction of his house. At the close of the plaintiff's testimony, the court, on motion of the defendant, peremptorily instructed the jury to find for the defendant. From the judgment on the verdict plaintiff appealed. The character of evidence and the facts proven were as stated in the syllabus. The Supreme Court affirmed the judgment.

Sec. 22.—In *United States Natural Gas Co.* v. *Hicks,* (Ky.) 119 S. W. 166 (May 19, 1909) the syllabus is as follows:

"1.   Defendant maintained a defective gate valve in his pipeline underneath the street. The box wherein the valve had fallen into disrepair and the valve leaked gas. Plaintiff with other boys were playing in the street when one of the boys four years old threw a match into the box, which caused an explosion by which plaintiff was injured. *Held,* that the defendant's negligence in failing to properly construct and keep its valve box in repair and not negligence of the child was the proximate cuase of the accident.

2.   Where a gas company maintained a pipeline in a highway it was bound to so protect it as to prevent injury from explosion to persons and children lawfully in the highway.

3.   Where a child eight years old was injured while playing in the highway by the explosion of gas from defendant's gas pipeline and he had been previously warned to keep away from the gas valve box where the explosion occurred the presumption was that he was not negligent on account of his age under the rule that a child between seven and fourteen is presumed *non sui juris,* and the question of his negligence was for the jury.''

Talmage Hicks brought suit by his next friend against the United States Natural Gas Company in the Circuit Court of Lawrence County for damages for injuries sustained by a gas explosion. Judgment was rendered in favor of the plaintiff upon verdict of a jury for $250.00. The Gas Company appealed. The gas company owned and operated pipelines for conveying natural gas from its wells in Martin County, Kentucky, to its consumers in West Virginia, Ohio and Kentucky. One of its lines passed through a small town in Lawrence County, Kentucky, called Buchanan. In the construction and operation of gas lines it was necessary for the purpose of cutting off and turning on the gas to place at intervals along the line what is known as gate valves, to be used in case of breaks in the line, so that the people between the break and the well might have the use of gas uninterrupted. Plaintiff introduced testimony tending to show that the gas company negligently failed to place at the place referred to in Buchanan a reasonably safe gate valve and to keep the same in reasonably safe condition and repair. The manner in which the plaintiff received his injuries was as follows: At the time of his injuries appellee was about eight years of age; he, with his brother who was about four years old, and a neighbor boy who was about seven years old, had been in the public road near the box for some time before the explosion, playing marbles; one of the marbles rolled through a crack into the box; It appeared that about this time the neighbor boy went to his home, got some tar paper and some matches and returning with them placed the paper on top of the box and set fire to it. Plaintiff at the time was on the box, as he stated, looking for the marble, and his four-year old brother struck a match and threw it through a crack into the box causing an explosion burning plaintiff's hands, face and arms, and singeing his eye brows and hair. Plaintiff's evidence also tended to show that the leakage of gas at the valve was considerable and had continued for several months before the explosion. One witness stated that he had trouble in getting the animal he was riding to pass by it because of the noise made by escaping gas. The testimony further showed that the box was out of repair; that it had rotted near the upper edge leaving a hole immediately under the lid; that there were holes in the lid the full length thereof caused by decay and shrinkage of the boards. The evidence showed that the place in the road where the box was situated was frequented by the children of the village for the purpose of play; and that this was known to the agents of the gas company who represented it in that section. Plaintiff testified that he had been told by both his father and his mother to keep away from the box, that it was dangerous. The testimony for the Gas Company tended the contradict the alleged fact that the valve was defective or improperly attached to the pipes, or that the gas escaped in any considerable quantity, or that the box was made insecure by reason of the defects referred to; and that it had used care in making inspections of the valve and box and in keeping them in repair. The Court of Appeals affirmed the judgment.

REMEDIES.

Sec. 23.—Where a person or corporation engaged in furnishing natural gas for purposes of domestic light, heat, and fuel, negligently and carelessly suffers and permits a greater amount of pressure of gas to be furnished than is reasonably proper for the purpose, or if such person or corporation suffers and permits its regulators or other appliances to be and remain for an unreasonable time in such condition that they do not control the amount of pressure of gas so furnished, so that more than a safe and proper amount of gas is furnished, such person or corporation is guilty of negligence and is liable in damages for personal injuries, or injuries to the property of others, proximately caused by such negligence.

Barrickman v. Marion Oil Co., 45 W. Va. 634; 32 S. E. 327; 44 L. R. A. 92.
McCoy v. Ohio Valley Gas Co., 213 Pa. 367; 62 Atl. 858.
Hartman v. Citizens Nat. Gas Co., 210 Pa. 19; 59 Atl. 315.
Lebanon Light etc. Co. v. Leap, 139 Ind. 443; 39 N. E. 57; 29 L. R. A. 342.
Alexandria etc. Mining Co. v. Irish, 16 Ind. App. 534; 44 N. E. 690.
Ind. Nat. Gas Co. v. McMath, 26 Ind. App. 154; 57 N. E. 593; rehearing refused, 59 N. E. 287.
Consumers Gas Trust Co. v. Perrigo, 144 Ind. 350; 43 N. E. 306; 32 L. R. A. 146.

Consumers Gas Trust Co. v. *Corbaley,* 14 Ind. App. 549; 43
   N. E. 237.
Coffeyville Min. & Gas. Co. v. *Carter,* 68 Kan. 565; 70 Pac.
   635.
Hollon v. *Campton Fuel & Light Co.,* 127 Ky. 266; 105 S.
   W. 426; 32 Ky. L. Rep. 178.
United State Nat. Gas Co. v. *Hicks* (Ky.) 119 S. W. 166.

Sec. 24.—A person or corporation engaged in furnishing
natural gas for purposes of heat, light and fuel, in dwelling
houses or manufacturing establishments, is bound to exercise such
care, skill and diligence in all its operations as is called for by the
delicacy, difficulty and dangerousness of the nature of the business,
that injury to others may not be caused thereby, that is to say, if
the delicacy, difficulty and danger are extraordinarily great, extraordinary skill and diligence is required. In an action against a
person or corporation for damages claimed as the result of the
failure of such person or corporation to exercise that degree of
skill and diligence required, it devolves upon the plaintiff not only
to prove the injury for which damages are claimed, but he must
go farther and show that the defendant failed to exercise that extraordinary degree of skill and diligence required in furnishing
natural gas for heat, light, or fuel.

   Barrickman v. *Marion Oil Co.,* 45 W. Va. 634; 32 S. E. 327;
     44 L. R. A. 92.
   Marshall Window Glass Co. v. *Cameron Oil & Gas Co.,* 63
     W. Va. 202; 59 S. E. 959.
   Shirey v. *Consumers Gas Co.,* 215 Pa. 399; 64 Atl. 541.
   Hartman v. *Citizens Nat. Gas Co.,* 210 Pa. 19; 59 Atl. 315.
   Moore v. *Heat & Light Co.,* 65 W. Va. 562; 64 S. E. 721.
   Maxwell v. *Coffeyville Min. & Gas. Co.,* 68 Kan. 821; 75 Pac.
     1047.

Sec. 24-a.—Where a person or corporation maintains a pipeline in a highway, such person or corporation is bound to protect
it to prevent injury from explosions to persons and children
lawfully using such highway.

   United States Nat. Gas Co. v. *Hicks,* (Ky.) 119 S. W. 166.

Ind. Nat. Gas Co. v. *McMath,* 26 Ind. App. 154; 57 N. E..593; rehearing denied, 59 N. E. 287.

Sec. 25.—In an action gainst a person or corporation for damages claimed as the result of an explosion of natural gas caused by the negligence of such person or corporation while engaged in furnishing natural gas for heat, light or fuel, it devolves upon the plaintiff to prove that the injury sustained was the natural consequence of the defendant's negligence, and was such as might have been foreseen and reasonably anticipated as the result of such negligence; and when the plaintiff adduces evidence tending to establish these facts, then such negligence must be regarded as the proximate or direct cause of the injury, in the absence of intervening negligence.

> *Barrickman* v. *Marion Oil Co.,* 45 W. Va. 634; 32 S. E. 327; 44 L. R. A. 92.
> *Lebanon Light etc. Co.* v. *Leap,* 139 Ind. 443; 39 N. E. 57; 29 L. R. A. 342.
> *McKenna* v. *Bridgwater Gas Co.,* 193 Pa. 633; 45 Atl. 52; 47 L. R. A. 790.

Sec. 26.—Where the statute imposes upon a person or corporation engaged in furnishing natural gas for light, heat and fuel, the duty of keeping under its control such gas while it is transporting the same, or prescribes the maximum pressure at which such gas shall be transported through the pipelines of the company, and where the statute provides that such person or corporation shall be liable for any damages which may result from the negligent transportation of the gas, the failure of such person or corporation to observe the statutory requirements is negligence per se; and where damages results to another without his fault, by the explosion of gas while being transported or furnished in contravention to the statutory regulations by persons or corporations, such persons or corporations will be held liable therefor although not otherwise negligent in relation thereto.

> *Ohio Gas & Fuel Co.* v. *Andrews,* 50 Ohio St. 695; 35 N. E. 1059.

Alexandria etc. Min. Co. v. *Irish,* 16 Ind. App. 534; 44 N.
E. 680.

Sec. 27.—In an action for personal injuries, or for damage
to property caused by an explosion of natural gas, where the plaintiff proves the injury and adduces evidence tending to show the
defendant's failure to keep the gas pipes, service pipes and other
appliances in a safe condition, which may be established by proof
that the odor of gas was perceptible in the neighborhood of the
explosion, or that gas was seen burning prior to the time of the
explosion near the place where the explosion occurred; or that the
defendant permitted its pipes to remain out of repair at other
points, or that the defendant negligently permitted an unusual
flow of gas to flow through its lines; in such case the question of
defendant's negligence is one of fact, for the determination of the
jury.

> *McCoy* v. *Ohio Valley Gas Co.,* 213 Pa. 367; 62 Atl. 858.
> *Hartman* v. *Citizens Nat. Gas Co.,* 210 Pa. 19; 59 Atl. 315.
> *Alexandria etc. Min. Co.* v. *Irish,* 16 Ind. App. 534; 44 N.
>   E. 680.
> *Consumers Gas Trust Co.* v. *Perrigo,* 144 Ind. 350; 43 N. E.
>   306; 32 L. R. A. 146.
> *Coffeyville Min. & Gas Co.* v. *Carter,* 68 Kan. 565; 70 Pac.
>   635.
> *Hollon* v. *Campton Fuel & Light Co.,* 127 Ky. 266; 105 S. W.
>   426; 32 Ky. L. Rep. 178.

Sec. 28.—The owner of a gas well situated near a public highway, in opening the well for the purpose of allowing the gas to
blow the water out of the well, must use due care while so engaged so as not to cause injury to others. When by the negligent
blowing off of such a well the horses of another become frightened
causing injury to the owner thereof or to other persons lawfully
using the highway, the blowing off of the well is the proximate
cause of the injury, and in an action against the owner of the well
he will be held liable for the damages sustained.

> *Snyder* v. *Philadelphia Co.,* 54 W. Va. 148; 46 S. E. 366; 63
>   L. R. A. 890; 102 Am. St. Rep. 941.

DEFENSES.

Sec. 29.—Where in an action for personal injuries or for damages to property claimed as the result of a gas explosion, proof of the mere fact of the injury, or that the building or property was set on fire by the gas, is not sufficient to justify the inference that the defendant was guilty of negligence; and the court should direct a verdict for the defendant.

> *Barrickman* v. *Marion Oil Co.*, 35 W. Va. 634; 32 S. E. 327; 44 L. R. A. 92.
> *Marshall Window Glass Co.* v. *Cameron Oil & Gas Co.*, 63 W. Va. 202; 59 S. E. 959.
> *Benson* v. *Allegheny Heating Co.*, 188 Pa. 614; 41 Atl. 729.
> *Ibach* v. *Huntington Light etc. Co.*, 23 Ind. App. 281; 55 N. E. 249.
> *Moore* v. *Heat & Light Co.*, 65 W. Va. 552; 64 S. E. 721.
> *Maxwell* v. *Coffeyville Min. & Gas. Co.*, 68 Kan. 821; 75 Pac. 1047.
> *Hollon* v. *Campton Fuel & Light Co.*, 127 Ky. 266; 105 S. W. 426; 32 Ky. L. Rep. 178.

Sec. 30.—In an action against a person or corporation for damages claimed as the result of a gas explosion caused by the negligence of the defendant, proof that the plaintiff was guilty of contributory negligence, and that such contributory negligence was the proximate cause of the injury, will defeat the plaintiff's right to recovery.

> *Creel* v. *Charleston Nat. Gas Co.*, 51 W. Va. 129; 41 S. E. 174; 90 Am. St. Rep. 772.
> *Lebanon Light etc. Co.* v. *Leap*, 139 Ind. 443; 39 N. E. 57; 29 L. R. A. 342.

CHAPTER 56.

NATURAL GAS COMPANY—DUTY TO FURNISH GAS.

Sec. 1.—A natural gas company, occupying the streets of a city or town with its mains, owes to the owners and occupants of houses abutting on such streets the duty of furnishing them with such gas as they may require, where they make the necessary arrangements to receive the gas and comply with the reasonable regulations of the company.

Charleston Nat. Gas Co. v. *Lowe & Butler,* 52 W. Va. 662; 44 S. E. 410.

Portland Nat. Gas & Oil Co. v. *State,* 135 Ind. 54; 34 N. E. 818; 21 L. R. A. 639.

Ind. Nat. & Illum. Gas. Co. v. *Anthony,* 26 Ind. App. 307; 58 N. E. 868.

State ex rel. Wood v. *Consumers Gas Trust Co.,* 157 Ind. 345; 61 N. E. 674; 55 L. R. A. 245.

Coy v. *Indianapolis Gas Co.,* 146 Ind. 655; 46 N. E. 17; 36 L. R. A. 535.

Indiana Nat. Gas & Oil Co. v. *State ex rel. Armstrong,* 162 Ind. 690; 71 N. E. 133.

Indiana Nat. & Illum. Gas Co. v. *State ex rel. Ball,* 158 Ind. 516; 63 N. E. 220; 57 L. R. A. 761.

Sec. 2.—In *Charleston Nat. Gas Co.* v. *Lowe & Butler,* 52 W. Va. 662; 44 S. E. 410, (March 30, 1901) the syllabus is as follows:

"1. Supplying an incorporated city or town, and its inhabitants with natural gas for the purpose of heating and illumination, by a corporation organized under the general laws of the State, and occupying the streets and alleys of such city or town for the purpose by means of the location therein of its pipes, connections, boxes, valves, and other fixtures, under an ordinance of the city or town, is a public use for which such company may take private property in the manner prescribed by Chapter 42 of the Code, upon which to locate its pipeline.

2. Such company is bound to furnish gas to every inhabitant of such city or town who applies therefor, and complies with the regulations prescribed by the ordinance of the town, or fixed by contract between the council and the company."

This was a proceeding by the Charleston Natural Gas Company in the Circuit Court of Kanawha County against Lowe & Butler, Trustees, and others, for the condemnation of real estate for the purpose of acquiring the necessary right of way for the gas main of the company from its gas well to the City of Charleston, where it had obtained an ordinance authorizing it to construct its plant for the purpose of supplying natural gas to the inhabitants of said City for light, heat and fuel. The owners of the land sought to be taken denied the right of the gas company to condemn the property upon the grounds that the purposes for which it proposed to use the property were not public purposes within the meaning of the constitution and statutes of the State. The Circuit Court entered judgment for defendants. The plaintiff took error to the Court of Appeals where the only question considered was whether the use for which the land was sought to be taken was a public use. That court held that the company had the right of eminent domain, and reversed the Circuit Court.

Sec. 3.—In *Portland Nat. Gas & Oil Co.* v. *State,* 135 Ind. 54; 34 N. E. 818; 21 L. R. A. 639, (Sept. 26, 1893) the syllabus is as follows:

"1. A natural gas company occupying the streets of a town or city with its mains, owes to the owners and occupants of houses abutting on said street the duty of furnishing them with such gas as they may require, where they make the necessary arrangements to receive it, and comply with the regulations of the company; and, on its refusal or neglect to perform such duty, it may be compelled to do so by writ of mandamus.

2. To entitle the owner of such a house to the right of being supplied with natural gas, it is not necessary that he should own an interest in the company, different from that held by other citizens.

3. In mandamus to compel a natural gas company to furnish relator's house with gas, an allegation in the answer that relator is already being provided with natural gas by another company is not sufficient to show that it will be necessary for defendant, in order to supply relator's house, to violate Acts 1891, p. 382 §1, which makes it unlawful for anyone to change, alter, or extend any service or other pipe or attachment owned by a gas company without the latter's consent."

This was an action in the Circuit Court of Jay County in mandamus by the State of Indiana, at the relation of William W. Keen, against the Portland Natural Gas & Oil Company, to compel the company to supply the relator's home with natural gas, to be used as light and fuel. The complaint alleged that the defendant was a corporation under the laws of Indiana, organized for the purpose of supplying natural gas to be used for light and fuel; that the common council of the City of Portland had, by an ordinance, permitted the said company to lay its pipes for the purpose of supplying natural gas to the inhabitants, and said company had laid its pipes in the streets and alleys of the city for that purpose; that the relator resided on Walnut Street on the line of one of the company's main pipes; that his house was properly and safely plumbed for the purpose of obtaining natural gas; that in May, 1890, relator demanded of the gas company gas service, and tendered to it the usual and proper charges for such service, but the company refused to so furnish the gas, where upon this proceeding was taken. By the second paragraph of the answer the defendant averred that at the time of the demand for gas relator was being furnished with natural gas by another gas company, which company had ever since continued to furnish gas to him. By the third paragraph the defendant averred that relator had no interest in the gas company, except what he might hold under the laws of the State, in common with all other citizens of the City of Portland. By the fourth paragraph defendant averred that the demand which relator alleged he made on the company to furnish gas was couched in general terms merely, and was not express and distinct, and did not clearly designate the precise thing which relator required. To these paragraphs of the answer relator demurred, which demurrer the Circuit Court sustained. Upon a trial the court awarded a peremptory writ of mandamus against the company, requiring it to furnish the relator with gas, as prayed for in the complaint. The Gas Company appealed to the Supreme Court, where the judgment was affirmed, and the following cases cited:

Beach on Private Corp. Vol. 2, Sec. 835.
Cook on Stockholders and Corp Law, Sec. 674.

State v. *Columbus Gas etc. Co.*, 34 Ohio St. 572.
New Orleans Gas Light Co. v. *Louisiana etc. Co.*, 115 U. S.
   650; 6 Sup. Ct. Rep. 252.
People v. *Manhattan Gas Light Co.*, 45 Barb. 136.
Gibbs v. *Gas Co.*, 130 U. S. 396; 9 Sup. Ct. Rep. 553.
Williams v. *Gas Co.*, 52 Mich. 499; 18 N. W. 236.
Gas Light Co. v. *Richardson*, 63 Barb. 437.
8 Am. & Eng. Ency Law, pp. 1284-1289.

Sec. 4.—In *Indiana Natural and Illuminating Gas Co.* v. *Anthony*, 26 Ind. App. 307; 58 N. E. 868 (Dec. 13, 1900) syls. 1-2-5-6-10-16-18 and 19 are as follows:

"1. A penalty imposed by a city ordinance granting certain privileges to a gas company for failure to comply with its conditions, does not preclude one from maintaining an action for damages sustained by the wrongful act of the company.

2. A complaint in an action against a gas company averring that plaintiff was receiving gas under contract with defendant, when the latter, without right and against the plaintiff's protest, shut off his gas supply, and refused to furnish him with gas, when he had no other adequate means of heating his house, though the charges had been paid in advance, whereby he and his family suffered great pain and distress from the cold weather, states an action in tort, since the contract is but a statement of the reasonable conditions under which the company was required to perform its duty, and hence is not an improper joinder with other causes of action sounding in tort.

5. One receiving gas under a contract with a company is not entitled to remove the mixer placed in his house by the company and burn gas without the use of any mixer, without the company's consent, though the company fails to furnish sufficient gas through the mixer.

6. The fact that one receiving gas under a contract with a company wrongfully removes the mixer and burns gas without the use of any mixer, does not prevent a recovery by him from the company for injuries resulting from failure to furnish gas for which it had received pay in advance.

10. Findings by the jury in an action for damages against a gas company that defendant's pipes were made of the approved kind of material, and such as were in general use, and that defendant maintained a sufficient force of men to keep its lines in repair are not in irreconcilable conflict with a general verdict which finds that defendant had negligently allowed its lines to be-

come rotten, decayed and broken, and that the pipes were not properly inspected and repaired.

16. In an action for damages for wrongfully shutting off the gas supply to plaintiff's house, it is not error to permit a witness to answer a question regarding the supply of gas in other buildings, if an offer is made to show that those buildings were attached to the pipes by means that would furnish as much or more gas than the appliances in plaintiff's house.

18. In an action against a gas company, having, by virtue of certain ordinances, certain privileges and franchises, for damages for wrongfully shutting off plaintiff's gas supply, the ordinance under which the company operates its plant is admissable in evidence to show that defendant had assumed a duty to supply citizens with gas on application, and to show the rates it might lawfully charge.

19. Where plaintiff paid defendant for gas to supply his heating stove in advance, the defendant is legally bound to furnish him with sufficient gas for his stove; and it is no defense in an action for damages for failure to do so, for the company to show that it had furnished all the gas it had, so long as it retained the money it received in payment for gas.''

James R. Anthony instituted suit in the Circuit Court of Boone County against the Indiana Natural & Illuminating Gas Company to recover damages for the wrongful turning off of gas from a heating stove, and for injuries resulting from the alleged negligence of defendant, and to recover alleged excessive charges wrongfully extorted from the plaintiff.

In the first paragraph of the complaint it was averred that the defendant was a corporation having by virtue of ordinances certain privileges and franchises to lay gas mains, and pipes, in the streets of the City of Lebanon, and to furnish and supply the citizens with gas for light and fuel; that plaintiff owned a dwelling house fitted for using gas along the gas line, and on November 24, 1897, he attached an upright stove to the service pipe, made application to defendant for gas, and paid the monthly charge therefor in advance; that appellant thereupon commenced to supply the stove with gas which it continued to February 17, 1899, when defendant's servants, without right, and over the protest of plaintiff's daughter, forcibly entered plaintiff's house, disconnected the stove from the service pipe, and shut off the

gas; that plaintiff was not in arrear of rates, but had paid in advance, all of which defendant knew; that the weather was excessive-
ly cold, and plaintiff had no other means of warming his house, except a cooking stove, which was wholly inadequate; that plaintiff
made immediate demand on defendant to turn on the gas, informing it that on account of the coldness of the weather, himself and
family would suffer from the cold; that defendant refused to turn
on the gas, and for four days and nights deprived plaintiff of gas
for his stove, during which time he and his family suffered greatly
from the cold, and suffered great bodily and mental pain and distress from the cold weather.

The second paragraph of the complaint averred in substance
that the ordinances under which the gas company were authorized
to construct its line and furnish gas to the citizens, prescribed
certain duties and liabilities on defendant's part; that defendant
charged plaintiff a greater rate for gas than it was entitled to
charge; that since November 24, 1897, and to March 10, 1899,
defendant wrongfully, illegally and extortionately compelled plaintiff to pay a monthly rate for gas in excess of the rates fixed by
the ordinance, to-wit, twenty-five per cent. in excess of the rate
fixed; that such excessive rates were collected under threats of
turning off the gas, and plaintiff having no other means to heat
his house, and to prevent the gas from being turned off, paid the
excessive rate under protest.

The third paragraph of the complaint set out the duties of
the defendant under the ordinance granting its franchise, and
averred that the plaintiff had for a long time been a consumer
of gas furnished by defendant for heating his dwelling house;
that he was dependent upon defendant for fuel, having no other
means of heating his house, all of which defendant knew; that
defendant furnished gas brought through its pipes from a point
about twenty miles distant, and had knowingly, purposely, and
negligently permitted the pipes to become rotten, decayed, and
broken, whereby large quantities of gas escaped and were wasted;
and that by reason of such negligence, and neglecting to keep the
pipes in repair, defendant was unable to furnish gas in proper
and sufficient quantities to plaintiff; that defendant for a long

time failed, neglected and refused to furnish plaintiff with gas
in sufficient quantities for the purpose of warming his house;
that by reason of such neglect and refusal during the cold weather
of 1898 and 1899, and without plaintiff's fault, he was, by such
refusal and neglect, almost wholly deprived of gas for heating his
dwelling; that on account of such negligent, failure and refusal
plaintiff's dwelling was destitute of warmth or heat to the extent
that his family suffered greatly in body and health, and from
mental anxiety on account of the extreme cold, all of which was occasioned by defendant's failure and neglect to keep its pipes in
proper and reasonable repair, and failure to supply him with
gas in proper and sufficient quantities.

Defendant demurred to the complaint, alleging that the plaintiff had joined several causes of action, one for breach of contract
in the first paragraph, and the second and third sounding in tort.
The Circuit Court overruled the demurrer. Defendant answered
in five paragraphs. A demurrer was interposed to the fourth and
fifth paragraphs of the answer which demurrer was sustained.
The fourth paragraph of the answer was addressed to the third
paragraph of the complaint, and denied that the defendant had
any contract with plaintiff to furnish gas to him, but alleged
that the contract to furnish gas for the house in question was
with a person other than the plaintiff. The court held that this was
a denial of any obligation to furnish gas because of any agreement with the plaintiff, and that such facts were provable under
the general denial, which the defendant had pleaded. The fifth
paragraph of the answer was addressed specifically to the third
paragraph of the complaint, only. The court held that if the
lines were kept in proper repair, that fact was provable under the
general denial. The first and second paragraphs of the answer
addressed to the first paragraph of the complaint alleged, among
other things, that by the terms of the contract under which defendant was furnishing gas, it had the right to disconnect the
stove from its service pipe for the purpose of repairs or inspection, for non-payment of bills when due, for fraudulent representations in relation to consumption of gas, or for changing, stop-
ping air holes, or enlargement in size of mixer, and for making

changes in the connection without written consent of the company; that at the time the stove was disconnected, plaintiff had removed the mixer, and was conducting gas into the stove by a large pipe, without the use of the mixer, without the company's consent.

The first paragraph of the plaintiff's reply to so much of the first and second paragraphs of the answer, above, admitted that the plaintiff did remove the mixer and did burn gas through a pipe without the use of any mixer, and alleged for the reason for so doing, that defendant did not furnish him sufficient gas through the mixer to heat his house; and that he had no other means of warming his house; that the weather was exceedingly cold, and the gas furnished through the mixer was wholly insufficient to prevent plaintiff and his family from suffering from the severe cold; that the mixer was removed for the sole purpose of obtaining sufficient gas to prevent plaintiff and his family from suffering from the cold, and that the gas obtained through the pipes, after the mixer was removed, was not more than sufficient to warm the room, and was not more than he was entitled to under the contract; that when defendant informed him that the removal of the mixer was a violation of defendant's rules, he offered to replace the mixer and use the same on his stove if defendant would turn on the gas which defendant refused to do until after the space of four or five days, as averred in the complaint. The reply denied all the other allegations of the answer. A demurrer to this reply was overruled, and while the Supreme Court held that part of the reply was bad, yet that there was enough matter well pleaded therein to sustain the Circuit Court's judgment in overruling the demurrer thereto. Judgment was rendered for the plaintiff, and defendant appealed, and the Appellate Court affirmed the judgment, citing:

> *Portland Nat. Gas & Oil Co.* v. *State*, 135 Ind. 54; 34 N. E. 818; 21 L. R. A. 639.
> *Coy* v. *Gas Co.*, 146 Ind. 655; 46 N. E. 17; 36 L. R. A. 535.

Sec. 5.—In *State ex rel Wood* v. *Consumers Gas Trust Co.*, 157 Ind. 345; 61 N. E. 674; 55 L. R. A. 245 (Nov. 1, 1901) the syllabus is as follows:

"A natural gas company, which a city has permitted to lay
its mains in the street to furnish its citizens with gas, cannot
refuse to furnish gas to a citizen in front of whose premises the
pipes were laid, on the ground that there was an unavoidable
deficiency in the amount of gas produced by it, and that if it furnished gas to such citizen, it would inconvenience other patrons."

Ann E. Wood instituted suit in the Superior Court of Marion
County by mandamus to compel the gas company, which was a corporation engaged in supplying natural gas to the inhabitants of
the City of Indianapolis for fuel, to lay a service pipe from its
main, and permit the relatrix to connect therewith, and use the
gas for fuel in her residence. An alternative writ was issued.
Defendant for return to the writ filed an answer in two affirmative paragraphs. A demurrer to the second was overruled and
to the third was sustained. The relatrix elected to stand on her
demurrer to the second paragraph of the answer or return, and declining to plead further judgment was rendered against her for
costs. Relatrix appealed to the Supreme Court. The second
paragraph of the return admitted that the defendant was a corporation engaged in the business of operating a natural gas plant,
and selling and distributing gas to the City of Indianapolis and
its inhabitants for fuel. After setting out at great length the organization of the company, its authorized capital stock, and the
amount of stock actually sold, the construction of its plant, and
the expense incident thereto, it was alleged in the return that the
company had expended all its revenues, funds and resources in
the construction and equipment of its plant, and in acquiring a
large acreage of gas leases, and in the construction and equipment
of a compressing station; that the well pressure on its gas supply had decreased from 325 pounds to the square inch to practically 132 pounds; that in the best gas territory its wells did not exceed 200 pounds pressure to the square inch; that the company
was furnishing natural gas fuel to 13,000 residences in said city,
and to a large number of other houses, and by reason of the
diminution in the quantity of gas and the reduction of pressure,
it had cut off, several years before, during the cold weather,
many of its largest customers including factories, thus discrimi-
nating in favor of residences; that it had been wholly unable during

the last two seasons to furnish a sufficient amount of gas to the consumers already on its lines, when the weather was cold; and that during the winters 1898 and 1899, hundreds of its patrons were left almost entirely without gas; that the colder the weather the greater was the deficiency of gas; that there was a serious menace and danger in the condition that results from an insufficient supply of gas in that the fires in houses insufficiently supplied are liable to go out without notice to the occupants; that in view of the facts and conditions thus set forth it was impossible for the company to remedy these conditions; that because it had become a physical impossibility for it to furnish additional consumers with gas defendant by its Board of Directors, on May 3, 1899, made an order that it could not make any new contracts to furnish consumers with gas; that defendant's refusal to furnish gas to relatrix was by reason of the facts recited; and the said order of the Board of Directors, and not because of a disposition to discriminate against her; that other equally meritorious applications had been refused; that if defendant should comply with the demands of relatrix and others for natural gas fuel, it would have been unable to give them an adequate supply, but by so much as it would give them, it would reduce the supply which it would be able to give to its patrons already connected, and thereby render its service inefficient in a greater degree to all its customers. The Supreme Court held that the second paragraph of the answer or return was insufficient, and that the demurrer thereto should have been sustained, reversing the judgment, and remanding the cause with instructions to sustain the demurrer to the second paragraph of the return to the alternative writ. Upon the proposition that the gas company was under a legal obligation to serve all members of the public contributing to its asserted right, impartially, and to permit all such to use gas who had made the necessary arrangements to receive it, and who applied therefor, and who paid, or offered to pay the price, and offered or agreed to abide the reasonable rules and regulations of the company, the court cited:

Portland Nat. Gas & Oil Co. v. State, 135 Ind. 54; 34 N. E. 818; 21 L. R. A. 639.

Coy v. *Gas Co.*, 146 Ind. 655; 46 N. E. 17; 36 L. R. A. 535.
Haughen v. *Water Co.*, 21 Ore. 411; 28 Pac. 244; 14 L. R.
    A. 424.
People v. *Manhattan Gas Light Co.*, 45 Barb. 136.
Crumley v. *Water Co.*, 99 Tenn. 420; 41 S. W. 1058.
American Water Works Co. v. *State*, 46 Neb. 194; 64 N. W.
    711; 30 L. R. A. 447; 50 Am. St. Rep. 610.
State v. *Butte City Water Co.*, 18 Mont. 199; 44 Pac. 966;
    32 L. R. A. 697; 56 Am. St. Rep. 574.

Upon the proposition that no statute is deemed necessary
to aid the courts in holding that when a person or company has
undertaken to supply a demand which is affected with a public
interest it must supply all alike who are like situated, and not
discriminate in favor of or against any, the court cited:

45 Cent. L. J. p. 278.
Haughen v. *Water Co.*, 21 Ore. 411; 28 Pac. 244; 14 L. R. A.
    424.
Olmstead v. *Proprietors*, 47 N. J. Law, 311.
Chicago & N. W. R. Co. v. *People*, 56 Ill. 365; 8 Am. Rep. 699.
Neb. Tel. Co. v. *State*, 55 Neb. 627-634; 76 N. W. 171; 45 L.
    R. A. 113.
Water Co. v. *Wolfe*, 99 Tenn. 429; 41 S. W. 1060; 63 Am. St.
    Rep. 841.
Atwater v. *R. Co.*, 48 N. J. L. 55; 2 Atl. 803; 57 Am. Rep. 543.

Sec. 6.—In *Coy* v. *Indianapolis Gas Co.*, 146 Ind. 655; 46 N.
E. 17; 36 L. R. A. 535 (Jan. 29, 1897) the syllabus is as follows:

"1. A natural gas company occupying the streets of a city
under a franchise must serve all applications for such service
who comply with its reasonable rules, and make reasonable compensation; and, where the contract between the company and
the consumer is but a statement of the reasonable conditions under which the company was required to perform its duty, the
company's failure to perform the contract is a tort.
    2. In tort, all damages directly traceable to the wrongdoer,
and arising without an intervening agency, and without fault of
the injured party, are recoverable.
    3. A complaint is not demurrable which alleges that defend-
ant natural gas company contracted to furnish fuel gas for plaintiff's house, that relying thereon, plaintiff made no other ar-

rangement for heat; that during severe winter weather, while plaintiff's child was sick, defendant failed to so supply the gas; that defendant was notified of the failure as required by the contract, and also of the child's sickness and plaintiff's vain efforts to get fuel elsewhere; that after plaintiff's failure to get fuel from any source, the house became so cold that the child died by reason of the low temperature, and that its death was proximately caused by defendant's breach of the contract.''

James B. Coy instituted an action in the Superior Court of Marion County against the Indianapolis Gas Company in tort for failure to supply fuel gas to plaintiff's house. The declaration or complaint was in substance as alleged in the third paragraph of the syllabus. The defendant demurred to the complaint which demurrer the Superior Court sustained, and dismissed the action. The plaintiff appealed to the Supreme Court where the judgment was reversed. Upon the proposition that persons or corporations enjoying such public franchises and engaged in such public employment as that charged in the complaint as being exercised by the defendant, are held in return, to owe a duty to the public, as well as to all individuals of that public who in compliance with the established customs or rules, make demand for the beneficial use of the privileges and advantages due to the public by reason of the aid so given by public authority, the court cited:

Central etc. Tel. Co. v. Fehring, 146 Ind. 189; 45 N. E. 64.
Portland Nat. Gas & Oil Co. v. State, 135 Ind. 54; 34 N. E. 818.
City of Rushville v. Rushville Nat. Gas Co., 132 Ind. 575; 28 N. E. 853; 15 L. R. A. 321 (note).

Sec. 7.—In Indiana Nat. Gas & Oil Co. v. State ex rel. Armstrong, 162 Ind. 690; 71 N. E. 133, (May 24, 1904) syl. 2 is as follows:

''2. A corporation engaged in supplying natural gas to the inhabitants of a city may not refuse to supply to one person therewith on the ground that it has not sufficient gas to supply him, and also supply its other customers with their reasonable requirements, or because he may obtain gas from another public service company to which it furnishes a supply.''

Alexander C. Armstrong instituted mandamus proceedings in the Circuit Court of Tipton County against the Indiana Oil & Gas Company, a corporation engaged in the business of supplying natural gas to the inhabitants of the City of Kokomo, to compel the company, which was supplying gas under an ordinance of the City, to connect the residence of relator with defendant's main in the street on which said residence was situated, and to furnish relator with natural gas for use in lighting and heating the residence. Defendant demurred to the alternative writ, which demurrer was overruled. Defendant then filed a special paragraph of return, to which plaintiff demurred, which demurrer was sustained, and defendant refusing to plead further, a peremptory writ of mandamus was issued as prayed. Defendant's return to the alternative writ alleged that it was unable to procure a supply of natural gas beyond what was required to furnish its customers in said city, who were already connected with its lines, with such a supply of natural gas as was reasonably required for their health and comfort, and that another public service corporation, the Kokomo Natural Gas & Oil Company, which had a main in said street, and with which main relator's residence was formerly connected, was able, ready and willing to furnish an adequate supply of natural gas to relator upon his complying with the reasonable rules and regulations of the Company and at the same rate as was charged by defendant. The return showed that the Kokomo Company procured its supply of gas from defendant. The defendant appealed from the order awarding the peremptory writ, and the Supreme Court affirmed the judgment.

Sec. 8.—In *Indiana Nat. & Illum. Gas Co. v. State, ex rel. Ball,* 158 Ind. 516; 63 N. E. 220; 57 L. R. A. 761 (March 11, 1902) the syllabus is as follows:

"1. A natural gas company having laid its mains in town streets, and acquired a monopoly, is impressed with a public character and it must serve the inhabitants without invidious discrimination.

2. Under Const. U. S. Amend. 14, guaranteeing equal protection of the laws, a town ordinance authorizing a natural gas company, doing business of a public character by governmental

authority to charge certain monthly or annual rates, or a certain sum per 1,000 cubic feet to any consumer does not authorize the company to exact the meter rate from one person alone, if the rate is substantially higher than the flat rate charged other consumers; but the mere requirement that one consumer pay for his gas by the meter rate, while others pay by the flat rate, is not forbidden, for an unlawful discrimination must be in some measure unjust and oppressive.''

James A. Ball commenced an action by mandamus in the name of the State in the Circuit Court of Boone County, against the defendant to compel it by mandate to supply the home of the relator with natural gas service on the basis of what was known as a ''flat rate'' as distinguished from a meter rate. Issues were framed, and pursuant to request the Circuit Court, after hearing the evidence, prepared and filed special findings of fact, together with its conclusions of law thereon. The material facts in the case as found by the Circuit Court were: Defendant was a corporation; on November 19, 1901, the Board of Trustees of the Town of Thorntown passed an ordinance prescribing the terms upon which corporations for supplying natural gas might lay and maintain pipes in the streets and alleys of said town for use in supplying said town and its inhabitants with natural gas for heating and illuminating purposes; that it was provided in said ordinance that any corporation accepting such grant should charge certain annual and monthly prices for the service furnished; but that it should have the right if it provided a meter, to require ''any consumer'' to pay for the gas used by him at a rate of not exceeding 20 cents per 1,000 cubic feet of gas supplied; that said ordinance was accepted by the Peoples Natural Gas Company, and that the defendant afterward, on May 15, 1893, became the successor of said gas company, and by virtue of the authority of said ordinance, laid mains in the streets and alleys of said town and entered upon and continued the business of supplying natural gas to said town and its inhabitants for heating and illuminating purposes; that it laid one of its mains in the street in front of the house of relator, and connected the gas pipes in relator's house with said main, and from that time until January 5, 1900, supplied his house with natural gas on the basis of a flat rate, provided for in said ordinance; that on said day defendant's agent requested relator to enter into a new written contract in consideration that defendant would not require him thereafter to pay for the gas he consumed by meter measurement, by which proposed contract, if signed by him, he would have agreed to pay a flat rate, largely in excess of the ordinance requirement, and also have agreed to other conditions not provided for in said ordinance; that relator refused so to do, and tendered payment of the amount which would be due from him for a certain time in the future on the basis of a flat rate which the ordinance provided for; that this tender was refused by the company, and it shut off the flow of gas from relator's premises, and defendant's agent informed relator that he would be required to enter into said proposed new contract before the company would furnish gas to him; that relator afterward, and on the same day, renewed his tender and demanded that the gas be furnished his house; that defendant refused so to do, but the agent immediately informed relator that defendant would supply his house with gas through a meter, and furnish and connect the meter at its own cost, if relator would agree to pay for the gas consumed at the rate of 20 cents per 1,000 cubic feet; that this offer was refused by relator and that gas was not furnished him. The court further found that at that time no other customer in said town was required to pay for gas on a meter basis, but that all others were supplied on the basis of the flat rate provided for in the ordinance. From a judgment in favor of relator the defendant appealed. The Supreme Court reversed the judgment, holding that the gas company had under the ordinance an option to furnish gas on the basis of a flat rate, or on the basis of a meter rate, and that while it was true that the ordinance purported to authorize any natural gas company accepting the ordinance to charge twenty cents per thousand cubic feet for gas to "any consumer" yet that such authorization would not allow the gas company to impose a burdensome discrimination upon relator. The court further held, that under the special findings of fact, it was not shown that under the terms fixed by the ordinance, the use of natural gas upon a meter basis would cost more than on the flat rate, and for these reasons reversed the judgment.

REMEDIES.

Sec. 9.—The owner of property on a street wherein a natural gas company has constructed its mains under an ordinance of a municipality authorizing it to construct and operate a natural gas plant for the purpose of furnishing gas to the inhabitants for heat, light and fuel, may by mandamus compel the company to furnish relator's house with gas, but such relator must conform to the reasonable rules and regulations of the company as to furnishing such gas.

> *Charleston Nat. Gas Co.* v. *Lowe & Butler,* 52 W. Va. 662; 44 S. E. 410.
> *Portland Nat. Gas & Oil Co.* v. *State,* 135 Ind. 54; 34 N. E. 818; 21 L. R. A. 639.
> *State ex rel. Wood* v. *Consumers Gas Trust Co.,* 157 Ind. 344; 61 N. E. 674; 55 L. R. A. 245.
> *Ind. Nat. Gas & Oil Co.* v. *State ex rel. Armstrong,* 162 Ind. 690; 71 N. E. 133.
> *Ind. Nat. & Illum. Gas Co.* v. *State ex rel. Ball,* 158 Ind. 516; 63 N. E. 220; 57 L. R. A. 761.

Sec. 10.—Where a natural gas company has constructed its gas lines and mains in the streets and alleys of a municipality under ordinances conferring upon such company the privileges and franchises for so constructing and operating its gas lines for furnishing natural gas to the inhabitants of such municipality for heat, light or fuel, after connecting its lines with the property of a consumer, it thereafter wrongfully shuts off the gas supply, such consumer may, in an action on contract or in tort, recover from the gas company all damages directly traceable to it, which arise without an intervening agency and without fault of the injured party.

> *Coy* v. *Indianapolis Gas Co.,* 146 Ind. 655; 46 N. E. 17; 36 L. R. A. 535.
> *Indiana Nat. & Illum. Gas Co.* v. *Anthony,* 26 Ind. App. 307; 58 N. E. 868.

RIGHTS AND DEFENSES OF GAS COMPANY.

Sec. 11.—A natural gas company incorporated for the purpose of supplying natural gas to the inhabitants of a municipality, after having constructed its gas lines in such municipality under an ordinance authorizing it to furnish gas to the inhabitants, may prescribe reasonable regulations for furnishing the gas; and where such regulations are not prescribed by ordinance, the gas company may require such regulations to be entered into by contract between it and the consumer, and in a proceeding against the company for damages on contract or in tort for failure or refusal to furnish gas, the company may defeat the action by proof that the plaintiff failed and refused to conform to its reasonable regulations.

> *Portland Nat. Gas & Oil Co.* v. *State,* 135 Ind. 54; 34 N. E. 818; 21 L. R. A. 639.
> *Ind. Nat. & Illum. Gas Co.* v. *Anthony,* 26 Ind. App. 307; 58 N. E. 868.
> *Ind. Nat. & Illum. Gas Co.* v. *State ex rel. Ball,* 158 Ind. 516; 63 N. E. 220; 57 L. R. A. 761.

Sec. 12.—A natural gas company chartered and organized under the general laws of the State for the purpose of supplying natural gas generally to the inhabitants of municipalities for heat, light and power, may take private property where necessary for the purpose of constructing its mains, pipes, connections, boxes, valves, and other necessary appurtenances and fixtures under the general laws prescribing the manner of taking private property for public use.

> *Charleston Nat. Gas Co.* v. *Lowe & Butler,* 52 W. Va. 662; 44 S. E. 410.

CHAPTER 57.

PIPELINE COMPANIES—OIL.

Sec. 1.—A corporation may be chartered and clothed with the right and authority by law to construct its pipelines and works, and operate them; and any injury resulting from such operation, without negligence and without malice is *damnum absque injuria.*

Hauck v. *Tidewater Pipeline Co., Ltd.,* 153 Pa. 366; 26 Atl. 644; 34 Am. St. Rep. 710; 20 L. R. A. 642.
Behling v. *Southwest Penn. Pipelines,* 160 Pa. 359; 28 Atl. 777; 40 Am. St. Rep. 724.

See cases cited under Chapter 46, Section 1.

Sec. 2.—In *Hauck* v. *Tidewater Pipeline Company,* supfa, (Feb. 27, 1893) the syllabus is as follows:

"Where a corporation is clothed with the right ef eminent domain, and is expressly authorized by law to construct its works and operate them, any injury resulting from such operation without negligence, and without malice, is *damnum absque injuria;* but where a corporation has no right of eminent domain, the operation of its works causing consequential injuries to another is a nuisance.

Where an owner of land prosecutes a business which has no necessary relation to the land itself, and is not essential to its development, he is liable for consequential injuries done to the property of another.

Where a pipeline company carries oil from a distance, allows it to escape from the pipes, and to percolate through another's land and destroy his springs, the company is liable in damages for the injury.

Pottstown Gas Co. v. *Murphy,* 39 Pa. 257, and *Robb* v. *Carnegie,* 145 Pa. 324, applied; *Pa. Coal Co.* v. *Sanderson,* 113 Pa. 126, distinguished."

Henry Hauck and wife brought suit in the Court of Common Pleas of Schuylkill County against the Tidewater Pipeline Company, Limited, in case, for injuries to lands, springs, and fish ponds. At the trial it appeared that the defendant, a limited partnership, without the right of eminent domain, constructed a pipeline for the transportation of oil from the oil region, and at the time of the institution of the suit, on March 7, 1897, the terminus of its line was at a point in Schuylkill County. At that point the oil was taken from the pipes and loaded upon tank cars for transportation by railroad. The Company's improvements erected for the purpose of storing and shipping their oil were entirely upon their own land, and separated from plaintiff's land by the railroad tracks and by a public road. Plaintiff introduced evidence which tended to show that oil escaped from defendant's pipes, percolated through the ground, and injured his springs and lands, destroyed the fish in a mill-pond, and rendered a tenement house uninhabitable. There was a verdict and judgment for plaintiffs, and defendants appealed. The Supreme Court affirmed the judgment. In the opinion delivered by Chief Justice Paxton, the court drew the distinction between corporations clothed with authority of eminent domain acting in their corporate capacity as public service corporations, and individuals or limited partnerships not exercising nor authorized to exercise the right of eminent domain, as follows:

"We think the learned judge was right, under the authority above cited [*Pottstown Gas Co.* v. *Murphy*, 39 Pa. 257] in holding that this was not a case of negligence, but of nuisance or of consequential damages. For this reason we think that the case of *The Railroad Company* v. *Lippincott*, 116 Pa. 472, and of *Railroad Company* v. *Marchant*, 119 Pa. 559, have no application. The Railroad companies in those cases were clothed with the right of eminent domain, and were expressly authorized by law to construct their roads and operate them. It was held, therefore, that any injury resulting from such operation, without negligence, and without malice, was damnum absque injuria. In the case in hand the company was clothed with no such power. We think the case closely resembles that of *Robb* v. *Carnegie*, 145 Pa. 324, in which it was held, that the owners of coke ovens, the gases from which injured the growing crops upon the adjoining farm, were liable in damages to the owner of said farm for such injuries. An attempt was made in that case, as it has been made in this, to bring it within the doctrine of *Pennsylvania Coal Co.*

v. *Sanderson,* 113 Pa. 126.   In the latter case the injuries complained of were the natural and necessary result of the development by the owners of the resources of his own land.   In opening a drift for the purpose of mining coal, the mine water, impregnated with the impurities which it had taken up from the earth, coal and other minerals in the mines, either flowed from the mouth of the drift or was pumped from the mines and allowed to take its natural course on its way to the ocean.   It will thus be seen that the flow of the mine water was the natural and necessary result of the development by the owner of his own property.   This was not the case in *Robb* v. *Carnegie,* nor is it the case here.   In *Robb* v. *Carnegie* the refuse coal which was used for making coke, was not mined upon the premises of the company, but was brought from other mines at a distance.   In the case in hand the oil which was the cause of the injury to the plaintiff's property was brought from a distance, allowed to escape from the pipes, and to percolate through plaintiffs land and to destroy his springs.   It was not in any sense a natural and necessary development of the land owned by the company.''

Sec. 3.—In *Behling* v. *Southwest Penn Pipelines,* supra, (March 26, 1894) the syllabus is as follows:

''A proximate cause is one which, in actual sequence, undisturbed by any independent cause, produces the result complained of.

A pipeline company is not liable for the burning of a house where it appears that burning oil from a neighboring property flowed down upon the pipeline causing it to burst and throw a spray of burning oil upon the house.   In such a case the pipeline is not the proximate cause of the injury.   The causa causans, the true proximate cause of the burning of the house, is the descending flood of fire.

In such a case, if the facts are undisputed, it is the duty of the court to determine the question of proximate cause and not to send it to a jury.

It seems that the bursting of a pipeline caused by burning oil flowing over the pipeline from neighboring property is not such an element of danger as the pipeline company is bound to foresee and provide against for the protection of the property of third persons along its line.''

Marie Behling instituted an action of trespass in the Court of Common Pleas of Washington County, against the Southwest

Penn Pipelines for damages claimed for burning a house. The
house of the plaintiff was situated on the Bank of Robbs Run,
in McDonald, and was burned on the night of November 10, 1891.
The defendant company was engaged in transporting oil from
wells in the McDonald oil field to its storage tanks, and to markets in cities. The plaintiff alleged that the burning of her house
was due to the negligence of defendant in laying its lines. There
were several wells above the house, the waste oil from which had
run down Robb's run before the lines reaching there could be
laid. To secure the removal of the product of these wells a four-
inch pipeline was laid up and along the course of the run. This
proved insufficient, and a three-inch line was placed by the side
of the first line. The oil from the wells on the side and top of
the hill was drawn into the lines and conveyed out of the field.
Among the wells served by these lines was the Butler well, which
was about 500 feet from the Behling house, up the hill and near
the run. Another well was known as the Church well, on the opposite side of the run and some distance from it, and connected
with the pipelines along the run by a branch made of two-inch
pipe. The point of junction was about 100 feet from the house,
and lower down the stream. On the night of November 10, 1891,
the Butler well took fire. The derrick, engine house, and machinery were destroyed, and the fire was communicated to the tanks
in which about 150 barrels of oil were standing at the time. The
tanks gave way and the burning oil flowed into Robb's run and
began to descend along its course towards the Behling house, and
the part of the town lower down the stream. The fiery flood
passed the Behling house and reached the dam near where the
branch pipe from the Church well connected with the 4-inch line.
The intense heat caused by the burning oil in and just above the
dam, thrown up by citizens to stop the descent of the oil, caused
the branch pipe to burst and for a few moments, until the oil could
be shut off a spray of oil was thrown towards and upon one corner
of the house, which took fire and was wholly consumed. A verdict
and judgment were rendered for the plaintiff. Defendant appealed and the Supreme Court reversed the judgment.

RIGHTS AND REMEDIES.

Sec. 4.—To exempt a company or persons engaged in the transportation of petroleum oil through pipelines from incidental damages caused to third persons, without negligence and without malice, it is necessary that such company or persons be incorporated under Statutes authorizing the exercise by such corporation of the right of eminent domain.

See cases cited under Section 1.

Sec. 5.—Where, however, incidental damages are inflicted by a pipeline company having the right of eminent domain, where the constitution of the State wherein the damages are inflicted provides that private property shall be neither taken nor *damaged* for public use without just compensation, the person injured is entitled to recover for such incidental damages. Under such Constitutional provisions the rule would be the same as applied to changes in the grade of streets and the operation of steam railroads in public streets as affecting abutting landowners.

INDEX.

ABANDONED WELL,
Statutory Regulation as to plugging or filling, 748.

ABANDONMENT,
Defined, 431.
Distinguished from forfeiture, 541-861.
Forfeiture by—See that title and Chap. 24, 501.
How proven, 902-904.
Lease will be cancelled upon grounds of, 437.
Lessee's rights lost before expiration of term, 433.
Lessee's rights may be lost by—When, 142.
No abandonment where no intention, 431-508.
Question of fact, 541-688.
Remedies—See "FORFEITURE BY ABANDONMENT—LESSEE'S REMEDIES", 546.
　　　　See "FORFEITURE BY ABANDONMENT—LESSOR'S REMEDIES", 550.
Rests on intention, 541-688.
What constitutes, 506.
Where lessee has never entered premises—How proven, 552.

ABANDONMENT OF EXPLORATIONS,
Declared matter of law, 10.
Delay for long period constitutes, 84.
Distinction between—and intention, 8.
Duty to plug gas well after, 805-807.
Effect of, 8-80-92-106.
Law presumes when lessee fails to enter within reasonable time, 92.
Lease will be cancelled for, 92.
Lessee not permitted to hold lease and prevent operations. 8.
Question of fact, 541-688.
Question of intention, 860.
Question of law—when, 688.

ABATABLE NUISANCE, 795.

ACCEPTANCE OF LEASE.
Binds lessee to performance of covenants, 21.
Binds lessee to pay rental, 84.

ACCOUNTING,
Action for by tenants in common or joint tenants, 655.
Bill for—when sustained—*Stone* v. *Marshall O. Co.*, 917.
By life tenants, 600-728.
By non-joining tenant in common or joint tenant—how, 674.
In mining partnership not decreed without dissolution, 626.
What shall be included in, 678.
When statute of limitations begins to run. 678.

ACQUIESCENCE,
Beginning operations—when not waiver of forfeiture, 734.
Delay in payment of rentals, or in beginning operations—when waiver of forfeiture, 94-116-286-467.

ACTION,
By lessor to cancel lease—how lessee may defeat, 125.
Covenant may be maintained against executor, 90.
For cancellation of lease for ambiguity, 305.
For cancellation of lease for failure to drill—premature, 302.
For possession by lessee—cannot be maintained after expiration of term of lease, 119-123.
For possession by lessor—cannot be maintained in absence of proof of failure of lessee to explore and pay rentals, 312.
For possession cannot be maintained on ground of insufficiency of consideration for lease, 311.
For possession may be maintained by lessee, 288.
Lessee may maintain for disturbing right of possession, 32-89.
Lessee may maintain for invasion of his exclusive right, 32-89.
Lessor cannot maintain for damages against lessee for entering after term under inducements by lessor, 126.
Lessor may maintain to recover possession of lands used for farming or for dwellings, 92-93.
Lessor may maintain for damages for lessee's failure to develop or protect lines See Title Remedies at Law, and Chap. 20, 453.
To prevent use of gas pump—See Title Gas Pump, etc., and Ch. 40, 760.

ADDITIONAL WELLS,
Equity will not cancel lease for failure only to drill, 407-462.
Equity will not compel lessee to drill unless his failure constitutes fraud, 404.
Equity will not require—where lessee has drilled number required by lease, 410.
Failure to drill—upon completion of dry hole constitutes abandonment, 688.
Implied obligation to drill, 464.
Lease providing for well on every ten acres, construed, 447-449.
Lessee is judge as to drilling, acting in good faith, 404.
Lessee not required to drill where lease provides for locating wells by lessor until the location is made, 416.
Lessee not required to drill when proven to be mere venture, 501.
Lessor's remedy for failure to drill—action at law for damages, 406.
Lessor's right to have drilled, depends upon lessee's profit and surrounding conditions, 497.

ADJOINING LANDS,
Lessee must protect lines in operating, 433.

ADJOINING OWNER,
May drill, and exhaust oil or gas from neighbor's land, 12-782.

ADVANCES,
Lien for—See title Mining Partnership, and Chap. 30, 625.

AMBIGUITY,
Construction given to lease by parties will be adopted, 613.
Lease not void for when contract of parties can be clearly ascertained, 305.

AMBIGUOUS CONTRACTS,
Construction of by parties conclusive upon them, 19.

ANNUAL RENTAL,
    May be paid at any time during the year, 700.
    May be paid into bank where authorized, 700.

ARTIFICIAL MEANS TO PRODUCE UNNATURAL FLOW,
    See title, "GAS PUMP" etc. and Chap. 40, 760.

ASSIGNEE—LIABILITY OF, Chapter 16, 364.
    Acceptance of lease—assignee liable upon covenants broken while he holds title,
        364-376.
    Assignee of half interest liable for rental, 268-377-378.
    Bound by covenants for development, 365.
    Covenants for development run with the land and bind assignee, 365.
    Covenants to pay rent or royalty run with the land and bind assignee, 366.
    Defenses, 384.
    Each successive assignee liable for covenants broken while title is held by him,
        365-369.
    For failure to supply gas for domestic purposes—when, 375.
    Lessee by assignment does not relieve himself of liability to lessor, 365-381.
    Lessor may recover damages from assignee for breaches of covenants occurring
        while he holds title, 383.
    Lessor may recover from assignee rentals and royalties accruing while he holds
        title to lease, 365-384.
    Lessor suing assignee upon covenants must prove assignment, 366-370-383.
    Liable for payment of rentals while he holds title, 365-366.
    Not affected by equities arising out of suppression of facts when lease was made,
        372-576.
    Not liable for covenants broken after he assigns, 364.
    Not liable for covenants broken before assignment to him, 364-369-376.
    Only liable for breaches occurring while he holds title, 383.
    Upon covenants to drill wells, 368.
    When assignee may defeat lessors suit to enforce equities or recover unpaid
        bonus, 384.

ASSIGNEE OR SECOND LESSEE WITH NOTICE OF PRIOR LEASE, Chapter
    17, 385.
    Assignee cannot maintain ejectment against a lessee in a subsequent lease, 393.
    Assignee of lease not bound by fraud of an assignor in procuring the lease, 392.
    Bound to ascertain whether prior lease has been forfeited, 387.
    Duty to make inquiry as to whether prior lease has been terminated, 385-386-393.
    Effect of failure to make inquiry, 393.
    Lessor not affected by rumor of assignment—notice must come from interested
        party, 387.
    Possession of premises by first lessee notice to second lessee, 385-389.
    Remedies, 393.
    Second lessee affected by notice by first lessee in possession, 385.
    Second lessee cannot declare forfeiture of prior lease, 385.
    Second lessee taking subject to first lease has notice, and stands in position of
        assignee with notice, 393.
    Second lessee with notice of prior lease is bound by its terms, 390-391.
    Takes no better title than that of his assignor, 385.
    Takes subject to rights and equities of first lessee, 385-390-391.
    Where lease provides for forfeiture—duty to inquire, 386-387-393.

ASSIGNMENT,
    of gas rights in lease—oil reserved—effect of subsequent discovery of gas, 357.
        Assignee has right to well upon discovering gas, 357.
        Assignee has right to enjoin assignor from drilling well deeper, 358.
        Assignee after accepting well may enforce his contract in writing, 358.
        Election of assignee to take well converts option into executory con-
            tract, 358.

ASSIGNMENT OF THE LEASE—Chapter 15, 350.
  Assignee assumes existing obligations, 366-371.
  Assignee liable to lessor for gas rentals and royalties, 360.
  Assignee of second lease with notice of first, not innocent purchaser, 372.
  Assignee takes no title where lease prohibits assignment, 361.
  Assignee who is lessee continues liable on express covenants, 370.
  Assignee without notice of fraud in procuring lease takes good title, 372-576
    (Contra 617).   •
  Damages or rescission for fraudulent representation, 355.
  Fraudulent Representations, 355.
  Lessee may assign lease unless inhibited by Stat. or restricted by lease, 350.
  Lessee's liability continues after assignment, 369.
  Lessor may recover rentals from assignee, 360.
  Lessor may waive restrictions forbidding assignment, 355.
  Not vitiated by assignee's failure to disclose facts regarding neighboring lease-
    holds, 353.
  Rescission or Damages for fraudulent representations, 355.

ASSIGNEE WITHOUT NOTICE,
  Rights of not affected by lessee's failure to pay consideration for lease,. 64, 533.

"AS MUCH LONGER AS OIL OR GAS SHALL BE FOUND IN PAYING QUAN-
    TITIES."
  Definition, 27.
  Judgment of lessee must be exercised in good faith, 125.
  Lessee judge as to what constitutes paying quantities, 125.
  Lessee must discover within term to give effect to, 96.
  Requires that oil or gas shall be actually discovered and produced within the
    term, 101.

BANK,
  Payment of rental into sufficient to hold lease, 47-287.
  See title "Payment of Rental into Bank" and Chap. 34, 696.

BEGINNING OPERATIONS—WHAT CONSTITUTES, Chap. 36, 729.
  Acquiescence by lessor—when not waiver of forfeiture, 794.
  Acquiescence in delay—waiver, 94.
  Beginning operations after term—when waiver, 732.
  Beginning operations in good faith within term prevents forfeiture, 737.
  Definition, 729-730.
  Equity will cancel lease for failure, 736.
  Failure to begin within term—lease voidable, 729-730.
  Lessor may declare forfeiture for failure to begin within time, 734-736.
  Operations may be begun on last day of time provided, 737.
  Question of fact—what constitutes, 732-735.
  Remedies, 736-737.
  What constitutes, 729-730.

BILL IN EQUITY.
  Lessee may settle all questions by, 95.
  Necessary Parties—See title "Necessary Parties" etc. and Chap. 53, 927.
  See title "Equity."

BLOCK OF LEASES,
  Lessee developing one tract doesn't acquire vested estate in others, 227-519.

BLOWING OFF WELL near highway, 948.

BONUS,
  Recovery of by tenant in common or joint tenant by ratification of lease, 674.

BOUNDARIES,
  Equity has no jurisdiction to settle, 588.

BURDEN OF PROOF,
  on lessor asserting abandonment, 547.
  on owner of well to establish negligence in shooting well, 728-741.
  on plaintiff in action for injuries, 966-981.

CANCELLATION OF LEASE BY COURT OF EQUITY,
  Abandonment, 84-92-437.
  Breaches of implied covenants, 93.
  Failure to begin operations within specified time, 736.
  Failure to develop and protect lines (Ill.) 433.
  Failure to develop and protect lines (Ohio, Tex., Kan.) 444-445.
  Not cancelled in absence of fraud (Pa. Ind. W. Va.) 453.

CANCELLATION OF LEASE,
  By lessee—provisions of lease as to construed, 279.
  By lessee and subsequent purchaser—does not extinguish rights of lessor, 874.
  By lessor before entry by lessee, 124-616.
  By lessor—consideration or rentals need not be returned, 586.
  Casing in well—lessee not entitled to remove after, 433.
  Remedies in Equity—See title Remedies in Equity, and Chap. 51, 895.

CESSATION OF OPERATIONS,
  After unsuccessful search proof of abandonment, 551, 557.
  Effect of, 10.
  For unreasonable time constitutes abandonment, 512, 515.
  Lessee has reasonable time to resume after, 508. 546, 547.
  Temporary does not constitute abandonment, 508.
  Unexplained construed as abandonment, 10, 688.

CLOUD ON TITLE,
  Owner of land not bound to remove upon sale where created by void lease, 342,
    615.
  See title "Void Lease," etc. and Chap. 28, 601.

COAL,
  Drilling through cannot be enjoined in absence of irreparable injury, 867, 868.
  Estate in determinable upon removal of, 867,
  Grant of does not carry with it underlying strata, 867.

COAL LEASE,
  Abandonment of, 603.
  Analogous to oil and gas lease, 603.

COLLUSIVE DRILLING NEAR DIVISION LINE, 782.

COMMENCING OPERATIONS,
  Test well, 302.
  What constitutes, See title BEGINNING OPERATIONS, and Chap. 36, 729.
  When time is not fixed lessee must begin within reasonable time, 317.

COMMERCE—See title NATURAL GAS AN ARTICLE OF COMMERCE, and Chap. 38, 742.

COMMUTATION MONEY or rental consideration for further delay in explorations,
    44.

COMPLETED WELL,
  Lessor accepting well as such cannot afterwards, dispute, 320.
  Option to purchase, 357.

1012   INDEX.

CONDEMNATION,
    Proceedings to invade exclusive right to lay pipelines, 814.
    See title EMINENT DOMAIN, and 984, 1001, 1005.

CONFLICTING CLAIMANTS,
    Surrender, abandoment or forfeiture may be proven in suits between 882.
    See title REMEDIES IN EQUITY, and Chap. 51, 895.
    See title VOID LEASE WILL BE CANCELLED, etc. and Chap. 28, 601.

CONSIDERATION FOR GRANT OF MINERALS—GAS, Chap. 11, 189.
    Construction, 189, 190.
    Failure to develop after discovering gas—abandonment, 191.
    Is specific sum per annum for product of wells, 189.
    Lease for gas construed differently from lease for oil, 189.
    Lessee after discovering gas cannot shut in well and refuse to pay rental or
        royalty, 190.
    Lessee cannot omit to develop and hold the grant for speculative purposes, 192.
    Lessee does not obligate himself to market gas, 190.
    Lessee may hold lease by payment of rentals, 190.
    Lessee not liable for gas rental when gas not used off premises, 193.
    Remedies, 232-237.
    When gas can be marketed at a profit lessee must market or pay gas rental, 190.
    See title GAS.

CONSIDERATION FOR GRANT OF MINERALS—OIL, Chap. 7, 128.
    Defined, 129.
    Distinguished from consideration for coal, 141.
        Consideration for lease, 135.
    Failure to discover oil constitutes failure of, 131, 132, 133, 134, 135, 140.
        To pay divests lessee of rights, 131.
    Lessee has vested estate upon payment of royalty, 130, 143.
    Receipt and delivery to lessor of royalties constitutes, 129, 135.
    Remedies—143, 144.

CONSIDERATION FOR LEASE, Chap, 4, 42.
    Commutation money or rental—consideration for further delay in explorations,
        44.
    Consideration for lease, 42-135.
    Defined, 42.
    Exploration and development, 85.
    Good, binding on lessor although lessee not obliged to do anything, 611.
    Implies engagement to develop premises, 332, 333.
    Inadequacy of alone not sufficient to cancel lease in equity, 51, 341, 612.
    Lease construed as a whole, 8.
    Lease must be construed with reference to known characteristics of business, 910.
    Lease should be construed to promote developments and prevent delay, 8.
    Lease void for want of, 49-64-65.
    Lease without valuable consideration void, 608.
    Lessee after acceptance bound by covenants of lease, 16.
    Lessee's agreement to explore or pay rental sufficient, 299
    May be only nominal, 43.
    Need not be returned in suit to cancel lease, 586, 736.
    Nominal and substantial distinguished, 66.
    Nominal—Non-payment of will not invalidate lease, 313.
    Not to be confounded with consideration for oil or gas, 44.
    One dollar insufficient to support lease (Tex.) 299, 620.
    One dollar sufficient (Ohio) 45.
    Payment of rental into bank sufficient, 47, 289.
    Recited, cannot be denied against assignee without notice, 64, 533.
        Sufficient to support lease and extension of exploration period, 55.
        Under seal cannot be contradicted for purpose of cancellation, 313.

CONSIDERATION FOR LEASE—*Continued.*
Substantial and nominal distinguished, 66.
Sufficient to support lease in its entirety, 613.
Valuable, though nominal, sufficient, 66.
Vests in lessee right to explore, 331.
Remedies, 65-66-67.
See title PAYMENT OF RENTAL INTO BANK, and Chap. 34, 696.
See title WANT OF MUTUALITY, and Chap. 29, 608.

CONSTRUCTION OF OIL AND GAS LEASES, Chap. 2, 6.
Acceptance of lease binds lessee to pay rental, 16.
   When lessee not bound to pay rental, 16.
Ambiguous construction by parties conclusive upon them, 19, 296.
As a whole, 504.
"As much longer thereafter as oil or gas shall be found in paying quantities"
   defined, 27.
By parties—entitled to great weight, 19, 279, 296.
"Deed" not construed as meaning "lease" 14.
Development and protection of lines required, 7.
Different rules applied to from ordinary leases, 7.
Doubt as to meaning of contract—construction by parties, 19, 279, 296.
Drilling well in good, workmanlike manner, 15.
Duty to develop owing to migatory character of oil and gas, 9.
Express terms excludes implication of others, 10.
Forfeiture clause for benefit of lessor, 17.
General rules, 6.
Implied covenants for development and protection of lines, 7.
Intention of parties cardinal test of meaning of words, 835.
   Should be given effect as ascertained from all parts of lease, 18.
Intention to abandon and abandonment distinguished, 8.
Language must be given ordinary meaning, 15.
Language, subject matter and surrounding circumstances looked to, 7, 12.
Lease construed in favor of lessor and against lessee, 6, 7, 505.
Lease construed with reference to known characteristics of business, 319.
Ordinary mining leases—construction of not applicable, 11, 12.
Partakes of nature of general tillage, 19.
Practical construction, 19.
Reservations construed, 11.
Restriction of alienation, construed strictly, 14.
Rules applicable to, 6.
Rule of property established by, 7.
Second lease made subject to prior lease, 285.
Surrender clause, 17.
Title to oil and gas in place not vested by lease, 18.
Two or more instruments made at same time—same parties, 13.
With reference to vagrant character of oil and gas, 19.
Words free from ambiguity given ordinary meaning, 830.
See title RESERVATION OF OIL AND GAS, and Chap. 49, 841.

CONTROVERSIES—Between Lessees—See NECESSARY PARTIES TO BILL IN EQUITY,
   and Chap. 53, 927.

CONVERSION,
See title RIGHT TO REMOVE FIXTURES etc., and Chap. 9, 150.

CONVEYANCE,
Lease held to be, 36.
of minerals effect a severance, 850.
of oil or gas held to be lease, 854.
of surface does not include oil or gas, 830.
of surface reserving rights under outstanding lease—effect, 874.

COVENANTS RUNNING WITH THE LAND,
to drill wells, 368.
to furnish gas for domestic purposes, 375.
to pay rent or royalty, 366.

COVENANTS NOT RUNNING WITH THE LAND,
By assignee to pay $1,000 if oil is discovered, 380.
Exclusive right to lay pipelines, 818.

COVENANTS,
See title IMPLIED COVENANTS OF OIL AND GAS LEASE, and Chap. 18, p. 393.
See title REMEDIES AT LAW FOR BREACHES. etc., and Chap. 20, p. 453.
See title REMEDIES IN EQUITY FOR BREACHES, etc., and Chap. 19, p. 437.

DAMAGES,
Breach of implied covenants, 93.
Lessee may recover for invasion of his exclusive rights, 33, 35, 38, 39, 89.
From trespasser value of oil taken, 94.
Value of oil taken less cost of production—when, 94-95.
Measure of—depends upon good or bad faith of trespasser, 89.
For oil taken from reservation. 188.
See title RIGHT TO OPERATE OIL AND GAS WELLS, etc., and Chap. 43, p. 788.
See title WASTE OF GAS, etc., and Chap. 45, 809-811-812.

DAMNUM ABSQUE INJURIA—Pipelines, 1005.
Pollution, 790.

DATE OF LEASE excluded in computing time, 216.

DEATH OF LESSOR TERMINATES LEASE void for want of mutuality, 623.

DEED,
Construed to be lease, 544.
Not construed to mean lease, 14.
Reserving oil and gas does not pass title thereto, 578.
Whether reservation of all minerals includes oil and gas—Question of intention. 834.
Whether conveyance of all minerals includes oil and gas—Question of intention, 834.
See title RESERVATION IN DEED, etc., includes oil and gas, and Chap. 47, 826-827.
See title RESERVATION IN DEED, etc., does not reserve oil or gas, and Chap. 48, 834.
See title RESERVATION OF OIL AND GAS, and Chap. 49, 841.

DEFECTIVE PIPES—Admissibility of evidence to prove, 954.
See title NEGLIGENCE, etc., and Chap. 55, 944.

DEFINITION—NO ESTATE VESTS, Chap. 3, p. 20.
Distinction between oil and gas lease and lease for solid minerals, 42.
Grant of minerals held to be lease, 32.
Lease defined, 20.
Expires at expiration of term unless oil or gas is discovered, 22.
Held to convey interest in land, 36.
Is exclusive pdivilege to go upon land to prospect, 20-30-37.
Is mere license until discovery of oil or gas, 20-31-40.
Providing for forfeiture of undrilled portions, 446-447-448.
Providing for re-leasing construed, 38.
Lessee bound upon accepting lease, 21.
Has no vested title until discovery, 27-31-32.
Has right to explore within fixed term, 21.

DEFINITION—NO ESTATE VESTS—*Continued.*
Lessee may hold lease as long as he produces in paying quantities, 22.
    Must find oil within reasonable time, 22.
Lessor may waive payment of commutation money at maturity, 21.
License defined, 23.
No estate in surface vests in lessee, 20-25-26.
Oil and Gas in place—lease vests no title to, 32.
Oil or gas must be discovered within term, 27.
Rental period subject to oral modification, 21.
Term controlled by rental period, 21.
Term—qualification of, 22.
Title of lessee inchoate and contingent, 27-31-32.
Unilateral——lease usually is, 21.
Vested title—how lost, 30.
Where land is granted lease conveys interest, 20.

DEFINITION,
Grant of oil and gas in place passes nothing which can be the subject of eject-
    ment (Ill.) 42.
Lease for oil and gas, 20.
    held to be license, 32.
    held to be license (Pa.) 22-23-25.
    held to be license (Kan.) 31.
    held to be license (Tex.) 37.
    held to be more than license (Ohio) 30.
    mere right of possession for exploration and development (W. Va.) 28.

DELAY,
Caused by lessor not ground of forfeiture, 416-510-547-548.
In beginning operations amounts to abandonment, 184.
Lessee may prove not unreasonable, 546.

DESCRIPTION—Uncertainty, 161-446-447-448.

DEVELOPMENT,
Absence of agreement for—when renders lease void, 608.
Adjoining lands—when lessee required to make, 433.
Express covenant for adds nothing to lessee's obligations, 410.
Implied covenants for, 410.
Lease will not be cancelled for breach of implied covenant for, 410.
Measure of damages for failure to make full—See title REMEDIES AT LAW, and
    Chap. 20, 453.

DILIGENCE—Measure of—is production of oil or gas, 254.

DILIGENT OPERATOR will be protected, 70.

DILIGENT SEARCH—Failure to make forfeits right, 78-141.

DILIGENT SEARCH—Implied covenants for, 424-428.

DISCLOSURE—Person about to purchase oil lease need not make, 353.

DISCOVERY,
of gas does not entitle lessee to hold lease without payment of royalty or rental,
    191-414.
    in abandoned well does not revive lease, 541-542.
of oil not sufficient—Lessee must produce or forfeit, 254-414-540.
of oil or gas after expiration of term does not extend term, 690.

DISCOVERY—*Continued.*
    in one well where lease provides for wells, gas not mentioned, will not extend, 121.
    vests in lessee right to produce, 29-30-82-216-220-227-546-547.

DISCRIMINATION in furnishing gas—See title NATURAL GAS COMPANIES, etc., and Chap. 56, 984.

DISSOLUTION—See title MINING PARTNERSHIP, and Chap. 30, p. 625.

DIVISION LINE—See title RIGHT TO DRILL NEAR, etc., and Chap. 42, p. 782.

DIVISION ORDERS,
    Do not affect property not divided, 630.
    Effect of signing, 143-640-641.
    Lessee's and Lessor's interests set apart by, 143-640-641.
    Partners executing—lose lien on oil for advances, 143.

DOUBT AS TO MEANING OF CONTRACT—Construction by parties entitled to great consideration, 19-279-296.

DOWER,
    Holder of entitled to interest on 1-3 of proceeds of oil and gas, 668-671-727.
    Widow entitled to—is not seized of any part of the land assigned to her, 594.

DRAINAGE—See title RIGHT TO DRILL NEAR DIVISION LINE, etc., and Chap. 42, p. 782.

DRAINING WELL not waste, 805.

DRILLING—When enjoined, 795-797-800-804.

DRILLING THROUGH COAL cannot be enjoined in absence of irreparable injury, 867-868.

DRY HOLE—Effect of Drilling, Chap. 33, p. 680.
    Effect of drilling, 10-78-286-689-690-691.
    Gives lessee no new or more extensive rights, 132.
    Implied covenant to continue operations upon completion of, 688.
    Lessee abandoning after drilling—not liable for rentals, 693.
        drilling must continue developments or forfeit lease, 289.
        entitled to reasonable time to make further developments, 695.
    Lessor may declare forfeiture upon completion of and abandoning explorations, 694-695.
        may execute new lease after completion of and abandonment, 695.
    Remedies, 694-695.
    Vests no title in lessee, 680-685-686-687.

DUE DILIGENCE,
    Defined, 254.
    Imposed on lessee, 456.
    Question of fact, 264.

DUTY TO DEVELOP owing to migratory character of oil and gas, 9.

EASEMENT—Lessee's rights in nature of, 148-222.

EJECTMENT,
    Abandonment in action of—question for jury, 264.
    Action of cannot be maintained for oil and gas in place (Ill.) 42.

EJECTMENT—*Continued.*

Assignee of lessee cannot maintain against a lessee of subsequent lease, 314-393.

Cannot be maintained against a lessee by a stranger on grounds that lessee had abandoned premises—when, 265.

Lessee cannot maintain for possession of reservation, 174.

for purpose of removing fixtures, 153.

may maintain against third person claiming title to premises, (Pa) 40-90-95.

Lessor cannot recover in—under lease which does not contain forfeiture clause, 252.

Plaintiff relying upon lease in—surrender and abandonment may be proven by defendant, 860.

See title REMEDIES BY EJECTMENT, and Chap. 54, p. 938.

EMINENT DOMAIN,

May be exercised by gas company, 984.

May be exercised by pipeline companies, 1001-1005.

ENTRY AND FRUITLESS SEARCH VESTS NO INTEREST IN LESSEE, 70-77-82.

EQUITY,

Abhors a forfeiture but not where it works equity, 249-397-398-533.

Accounting decreed to prevent multiplicity of suits, 185.

When life tenant may have, 600.

Bill in—may be filed for relief from forfeiture, 548.

When lessee may maintain (Pa.) 914-915.

Court of—will relieve against technical forfeiture, 244-911.

Has jurisdiction to prevent acts of irreparable injury, 587.

Unlawful extraction of oil and gas, 598.

Injunction—See title INJUNCTION.

Lease will not be cancelled by court of—for failure to drill additional wells, 220.

Lessee substantially complying with terms of lease—relieved from forfeiture, 216.

Life tenant—when may maintain bill for accounting, 600-728.

Necessary parties to settle controversies between lessees—See that title, and Chapter 53, 927.

Obtaining jurisdiction for one purpose will dispose of all questions, 519-597-595-721.

Relief from forfeiture—See that title and 548, 926, 927.

Specific performance not decreed where lease contains surrender clause, 620.

Title and boundaries—no jurisdiction to settle, 588-599-897.

Will declare forfeiture where lessee not entitled to relief from, 398.

Enjoin operations under void lease—when, 602.

Will not enforce forfeiture of an estate, 549.

Relieve against forfeiture where fraud, accident and mistake are wanting, 497.

Relieve against where forfeiture provision is the essence of the contract, 533.

Will quiet title and decree cancellation for failure to begin operations, 736.

Will relieve against forfeiture when full compensation can be made, 220-470-550.

See title FORFEITURE BY ABANDONMENT—LESSEE'S REMEDY, and Chap. 25, 546.

See title FORFEITURE BY ABANDONMENT—LESSOR'S REMEDY, and Chap. 26, 550.

See title FORFEITURE WILL NOT BE ENFORCED BY COURT OF EQUITY, and Chap. 52, 923.

See title WANT OF MUTUALITY, and Chap. 29, 608.

See title REMEDIES IN EQUITY, and Chap. 51, 895.

See title REMEDIES IN EQUITY FOR BREACHES OF IMPLIED COVENANTS, and Chap. 19, 437.

ESCAPE OF GAS—See title NEGLIGENCE, etc., and Chap. 55, 944.

ESTATE AT WILL,

Execution of new lease terminates, 49.

If one party may terminate so may the other, 49.

ESTATE VESTS IN LESSEE upon discovery of Oil or Gas, 30-220.

ESTOPPEL,
Against assignee without notice, 64.
Does not arise by silence—when, 659.

EXCEPTIONS AND RESERVATIONS, See title RESERVATION OF OIL AND GAS, and
Chap. 49, 841.

EXCEPTION,
Distinguished from reservation, 874.
What constitutes in deed, 874.

EXCLUSION of Lessee from possession—breach of implied covenants, 90.

EXCLUSIVE RIGHT OF ENTRY AND EXPLORATION acquired by lessee, 143.

EXCLUSIVE RIGHT TO DRILL—LEASE AND NOT SALE OF THE OIL AND
GAS, 1-78.

EXCLUSIVE RIGHT TO LAY PIPELINES VOID AS AGAINST PUBLIC POLICY,
Chap. 46, 814.
Agreement for, binding between parties, 817.
Does not bind grantee of land, 818.
Does not prevent landowner from granting right of way, 818.
Not enforced against third person, 818.
Condemnation proceedings to invade, 814.
Covenant running with land—is not, 818.
Exclusive right of way void, 818.
Owners of not entitled to compensation for invasion, 814.
Remedies, 825, 826.

EXECUTOR,
Not authorized to execute oil and gas lease, 583.
Purchasing property after executing lease cannot deny validity thereof, 583.

EXECUTORY LEASE,
Not binding lessee does not create an estate, but is mere option, 65.
Vests no title to oil or gas in place, 433.
Which is unjust will not be enforced in equity, 49-610.
Void for want of consideration—when lessee is entitled to continue de-
velopments, 65.

EXPENSES OF DRILLING,
After expiration of term—when cannot be recovered, 586-736.
And operating—when allowed under void lease, 91-92.

EXPERT EVIDENCE—When admissible, 12.

EXPLORATION PERIOD—Recited consideration in lease sufficient to support extension of, 55.

EXPLORATIONS,
Abandonment of—See title, ABANDONMENT OF EXPLORATIONS, and 8-80-92-106.
Essence of lease, 18-305.
Must be successful to vest interest in lessee, 89.
Object and purpose of lease, 68.
Payment of consideration for lease vests in lessee right of, 331.
Purpose of lease, 142-533.

EXPLORATIONS—*Continued.*
Right of—only until discovery of gas, 68.
Sole consideration, 85.
Time for commencement of—proper subject of agreement, 305.
Unreasonable delay in—entitles lessor to declare forfeiture—when, 321.

EXPLOSION—See title NEGLIGENCE—INJURIES, etc., and Chap. 55, 944.

EXPRESS AGREEMENT,
Excludes implication of anything not expressed, 432-459.

EXTENSION OF EXPLORATION PERIOD—Recited consideration sufficient to support, 55.

FAILURE,
To explore after notice constitutes abandonment, 551-552.
To explore within reasonable time—constitutes forfeiture by abandonment, 551-552.
To pay rental or enter for developments—effect of, 550.
To produce after discovery, 551-556.
To protect lines and fully develop, 553-556.
To resume operations within reasonable time after unsuccessful search, 551.

FIRE—EXPLOSION OF GAS—See title NEGLIGENCE—INJURIES, etc., and Chap. 55, 944.

FIXTURES—See title RIGHT TO REMOVE FIXTURES PLACED UPON THE LEASEHOLD FOR EXPLORATION AND DEVELOPMENT PURPOSES, and Chap. 9, p. 150.

FLAMBEAU LIGHTS,
Statutes forbidding use of, 749.
Use of a continuing offense, 750.
Wasteful use of gas, 749.

FLOWAGE—Rights of landowners, 792.

FORFEITURE,
Acceptance of rental—when precludes lessor from declaring, 86.
Acts and declarations of majority of lessees binding on others, 514.
Based on enforced release, 541.
Beginning operations in good faith within term prevents, 737.
Beginning operations with consent of lessor is waiver of, 732.
By abandonment—See title FORFEITURE BY ABANDONMENT—LESSOR'S REMEDY, and Chap. 26, 550.
Cannot be invoked for insufficiency of consideration without suit to cancel lease, 311.
Causes of—specified in lease—others cannot be inferred, 10-432-459.
Clause in lease—After estate vests is in nature of penalty to secure payment of rentals or royalty, 220.
Construed strictly, 223-311-342.
Declaration of must be clear and unequivocal, 285.
        Must be made promptly, 286-470.
Distinguished from abandonment, 541-861.
Drilling dry hole, abandoning and ceasing operations, amounts to, 286.
Effect of words "null and void" in lease, 266.
Entry and exploration by lessee under voidable lease prevents by lessor, 332-333-334.
Equity abhors except where it works equity. 75-418.
        Will not enforce—See title FORFEITURE WILL NOT BE ENFORCED, etc., and Chap. 52, 923.
        Will relieve against technical, 244-248.
        Will relieve against when compensation can be made, 220.

FORFEITURE—*Continued.*
Erection of buildings on premises by lessor not declaration of, 271.
Essential to public and private interests, 75.
Failure to begin operations within specified time—cause of, 729, 730, 734, 736.
    to develop after notice (Ind.) 274.
    to explore or pay rental grounds of, 514.
    to make diligent search, 78.
    to promptly develop leasehold in oil field, 437.
Forfeiture clause inserted for benefit of lessor, 17-130-161-223-238-244-246-256-258-
    261-265-266-268-269-270-271-272-280-331.
For breaches of subsequent conditions—not enforced, 923.
    Non-payment of rental may be declared by lessor, 237.
    Non-payment of rentals—when prevented by payment of rentals into bank,
    696.
How declared, 283.
Lease conferring option to develop cannot be forfeited without notice, (Ind.) 234.
Lessee's default caused by lessor—not enforced, 416-510-547-548.
    Discovering oil or gas must produce or forfeit lease, 254-414-415-540.
    May prevent by payment of rental into bank where authorized, 47-708.
Lessor after notice may declare—for unreasonable delay in explorations, 321.
    Alone may declare, 223-263-272-284-285.
    Cannot forfeit for failure to pay gas rentals—when, 233.
    Causing delay or default cannot enforce, 416-510-548.
    Entitled to forfeit lease after accepting rentals must give notice (Ky.) 297.
    May declare when lessee ceased developments—when, 92.
    May waive and enforce covenants, 161-223.
No act of lessee can work a forfeiture without lessor's concurrence, 272.
Not incurred by breach of implied covenant, 459.
Notice of intention to forfeit—when must be given, 205.
    of intention to forfeit—when insufficient, 209.
Re-entry by lessor—when not requisite to effect, 258.
Refusal to accept rental—sufficient declaration of, 277.
Relief from—where lessee complies with terms of lease, 216-549.
    See title RELIEF FROM FORFEITURE. and 548-926-927.
Rental—non-payment of in absence of forfeiture clause not alone grounds of, 334.
    Non-payment of or failure to begin operations within time by consent of
    lessor, does not constitute, 288.
Right to claim depends on provisions of lease, 214.
    to declare must be distinctly reserved in lease, 252.
Sale of premises terminates prior voidable lease—when, 342.
    Under execution, of lessee's leasehold and fixtures, constitutes, 428.
Second lease—execution of—sufficient declaration, 49-240-267-284-537.
    Subject to prior—not sufficient declaration, 242-285.
Subsequent conditions—breaches of do not constitute, 923.
Tender of rental may be made in petition or bill for relief from, 313.
Undrilled portions of lease, 446-447-448.
Waiver—See WAIVER OF FORFEITURE, and 244-286.
When failure to pay royalty is not ground of, 214.
When lessee may declare, 22-92.
When lessor must give notice of intention to forfeit, 205.
When not incurred by failure to fully develop, 289.
Where lessor has no other remedy for breach of covenants, equity will decree, 415.
Where lessor indulges lessee in delay he cannot declare—without notice, 288.
Will be declared in equity where lessee is not entitled to relief from, 398.
Will not be enforced by court of equity—See title REMEDIES IN EQUITY, and Chap.
    51, 896, and p. 911.

    See title FORFEITURE WILL NOT BE ENFORCED, etc., and Chap. 52, 923.

Will not be incurred for breaches of implied covenants—See title IMPLIED COVE-
    NANTS, etc., and Chap. 18, 393.

FORFEITURE AND RENTAL CLAUSE—LESSOR'S OPTION, Chap. 12, 237.
  Abandonment question of fact, 264.
  Action for rentals—default of lessee no defense, 258-261-262.
    No defense that premises were shown to be dry, 262.
  Cancellation by lessee, 279.
  Cause of forfeiture specified, none others implied, 289.
  Covenants for forfeiture do not render lease void, 262.
    Option of lessor, 262-283-468.
  Cumulative phrases as to forfeiture, 266-285.
  Declaration of forfeiture by lessor renders lease nullity, 267-284.
  Defined, 237.
  Doubt—construction by parties entitled to great weight, 279.
  Dry hole—when entitles lessor to declare forfeiture, 286.
  Due diligence question of fact, 265.
  Ejectment cannot be maintained against lessee—when, 265.
    When non-suit cannot be directed, 265.
  Enforcement of forfeiture must not be unconscienable, 252.
  Equity abhors forfeiture but not where it works equity, 249.
  Express covenant to drill or pay rental for delay, 283.
  Failure to pay rental for delay, 283.
  Failure to pay rental or develop entitles lessor to declare forfeiture, 240-283.
  Forfeiture essential to public and private interests, 249.
    Not incurred until happening of event upon which it is contingent, 250.
  Grounds of forfeiture—proof of must be clear, 252.
  Inserted for lessor's benefit, 17-130-161-223-238-244-246-256-258-261-265-266-268-269-270-271-272-280-331.
  Lease containing express promise to pay rental or forfeit entitles lessor to waive forfeiture and collect rentals during term, 237-247-250-251-256-258-283-468.
  Lessor alone may declare forfeiture, 263.
    By accepting rental after due, waives forfeiture, 244.
    By accepting rental or commutation money waives forfeiture, 239.
    Concurrence necessary to effect forfeiture, 261-272.
    Conduct may defeat declaration of forfeiture, 244-286.
    Consent to non-payment of rentals is waiver, 244.
    Leading lessee to believe that rental will not be demanded, cannot declare forfeiture without notice, 239-471.
    May dclare forfeiture at any time when lease is mere option, 260.
    May declare forfeiture by executing second lease, 240.
    May waive forfeiture and collect rentals, 245-247.
    Option to forfeit or collect rentals, 237-247-250-256-258-280-468.
    Re-entry not necessary to effect forfeiture—when, 258.
    Has option to declare forfeiture or collect rentals—when, 238.
  Lessee bound to pay rental or drill, 279.
    Drilling dry hole must continue developments, 288.
    Entitled to possession while exploring, 288.
    Excluded from possession may maintain possessory action, 288.
    Failure to pay rental does not forfeit lease or prevent lessor from recovering rental, 245-256-251-258-268-269-270-271.
    May continue lease in force during term by payment of rentals, 287.
    Must comply with covenants strictly to hold lease, 239.
    Must pay rental or explore, 287.
    No act of can work forfeiture without lessor's concurrence, 261-272.
    Relieved from technical forfeiture, 288.
    When not estopped from denying validity of lease, 272.
  Notice of intention to declare forfeiture—effect of, 274-277.
    When required, 244.
  "Null and void"—construction of qualifying words, 266-285.
  Production of oil or gas is measure of diligence, 254.
  Remedies of lessee, 287-289, inc.

FORFEITURE AND RENTAL CLAUSE—LESSORS OPTION.—*Continued.*
  Remedies of lessor, 283-287, inc.
  Rental clause—modification of covenant for forfeiture, 247-249.
  Rental—lessor's refusal to accept is declaration of forfeiture, 277.
  Right to declare forfeiture must be clearly and distinctly reserved, 252.
      Exercised promptly, 252.
      Is personal privilege of lessor, 272.
  Second lease—execution of sufficient declaration of forfeiture, 240-284.
      Subject to prior lease, 242.
      When effective, 284.
  Statute of limitations—abandonment, 264-265.
  Surrender by mistake, 242.
  Surrender clause entitles lessee to terminate lease, 237-238-289.
  Uniform construction, 266.
  Unreasonable delay in developments, 287.
  What language in lease authorizes lessor to declare forfeiture, 283.

FORFEITURE AND RENTAL CLAUSE—LESSEE'S OPTION, Chap. 13, 290.
  Abandonment—Lessee's rights may be lost by, notwithstanding no forfeiture
      clause in the lease, 433.
  Acceptance of well by lessor, 320.
  Action for rental cannot be maintained, 293-294.
  Alternative obligation of lessee, 308.
  Ambiguity—when lease not void for, 305.
  Ambiguous contract—Construction by parties conclusive upon them, 296.
  Annual payments—lease from year to year, 295.
  Assignee cannot maintain ejectment against prior lessee, 314.
  Consideration for lease—payable in advance, lessor not obligated until paid, 308.
  Consideration of one dollar insufficient to support lease, (Tex.) 299.
      When non-payment of will not invalidate lease, 313.
  Covenants to pay rental not contained in, 291.
  Equity will not receive evidence contradicting receipt of acknowledged consid-
      eration, 313.
  Forfeiture Clause in modern lease, 290-291.
  Imposes no obligation on lessee to pay rental, 296.
  Language of lease creating option in lessee to pay rental or develop, 292.
  Lease held to be sale, 316-320.
      Not void for want of mutuality, 305.
      Void for failure to pay rental or explore, 321.
      With no covenants to develop or pay rental is at lessee's option, 291.
  Legal effect, 294.
  Lessee entering after forfeiture incurred, not liable for rental, 296.
      Failing to explore or pay rental, rights terminated, 294.
      Failing to develop upon notice—effect, 321.
      May hold lease during term by payment of rental at maturity, 295.
      May pay rental and hold lease during term, 290-291-292-295-303-305-308-313-
      315-317.
      Not obligated to pay rental or drill, 291-292.
      When may cause cancellation of second lease, 322.
      When may delay developments, 322.
  Lessor cannot annul lease merely on ground of want of mutuality, 330.
      Cannot recover for rentals where lease does not contain express promise
      to pay, 291-292-294-295-303-320-321.
      Cannot waive forfeiture and collect rental, 291.
      Cannot recover for lessee's failure to drill or pay rental, 292.
      May require lessee to drill upon notice—when, 321.
      May terminate lease when lessee fails to pay rental, 308-321.
      Must refuse rental and demand developments before declaring forfeiture,
      (Ky.) 297.
      Not bound to bring suit for rescission, 308.

FORFEITURE AND RENTAL CLAUSE—LESSEE'S OPTION—*Continued.*
    Obligation does not come into existence unless lessee makes payment of
        rental in advance, 308.
  Notice—when lessor may require developments upon, 321.
  Object of Lease—Explorations, 307.
  Option feature does not render lease void, 305.
    Must be exercised within time limit, 308.
  Possession—Lessor not entitled to until default of lessee, 312.
    Suit for not maintainable where lease not void, 311.
  Remedies, 321, 322.
  Rental not recoverable after default in payment, 291-292-294.
    When payable at any time within rental period, 313.
    When sufficient tender of in equity, 313.
    When offer to pay will not extend term, 302.
  Royalties essence of lease, 305.
  Suit to cancel lease on ground of forfeiture—when premature, 302.
  Unconditional obligation to drill, sufficient consideration to support lease, 299.
  Vis Major no excuse for Delay, 308.

FORFEITURE BY ABANDONMENT, Chap. 24, p. 501.
  Abandonment of search constitutes, 504.
  Block of leases, 519.
  Burden of proof on lessee to show payment of rental in suit for rescission, 531.
  Cessation of operations for unreasonable time, constitutes, 512-515-523-544.
    With intention to resume does not constitute, 508.
  Commencing operations on last day of term prevents, 510-511.
  Deed held to be lease, 544.
  Delay caused by lessor does not constitute, 416, 510.
  Depends upon intention, 507, 540.
  Discovery of oil or gas after cessation of production does not revive lease, 542,
    · 543.
  Discovery of oil or gas—lessee must produce or surrender, 540.
  Distinction between abandonment of operations and intention to abandon lease,
    505, 541.
  Does not depend upon length of time lessee absents himself, 507.
  Drilling dry hole and ceasing operations constitutes, 504, 515, 523, 535.
  Entry by lessee without consent of lessor after forfeiture incurred does not revive
    lease, 535.
  Equity will cancel lease on grounds of, 533.
    Will not relieve against forfeiture where it is essence of contract, 533.
    See title REMEDIES IN EQUITY, and Chap. 51, 895.
  Express surrender, 507.
  Failure to begin operations or pay rental constitutes, 514-522-525-528.
    to begin operations within reasonable time constitutes, 517-520-524.
    to continue developments constitutes, 504, 512, 529, 540.
    to drill where lessee has agreed to drill within specified time constitutes,
    526.
    to explore after notice constitutes, 321-531-533
    to operate within reasonable time after discovery, 503-504-519.
    to pay rental alone does not constitute, 512-513.
    to search for all minerals mentioned in lease within reasonable time, con-
    stitutes, 516.
  Holding lease without operating constitutes, 505.
  How enforced, 512-513.
  Intention, 501-540.
    to abandon—how proven, 540.
  Is in law a surrender, 507.
  Lease held to be license revokable at will, 537.
    located in oil field must be diligently developed, 529.

FORFEITURE BY ABANDONMENT—*Continued.*

Lessor estopped to deny consideration recited in lease against assignee, 533.

Lessor's refusal to accept rental is notice to lessee of intention to declare forfeiture, 531.

No time specified—must begin within reasonable time, 522.

Must operate within reasonable time, 524, 525, 526, 528.

Payment of rental after forfeiture incurred does not revive lessee's rights, 523.

Presumption, 503, 504.

Production ceasing, lessee's rights terminate, 541.

Question of intention, 507, 508.

Reasonable time afforded lessee to resume operations, 508.

Relinquishment of premises, 501.

Remedies—See title Forfeiture by Abandonment—Lessee's Remedy, and Chap. 25, 546.

　　See title Forfeiture by Abandonment—Lessor's Remedy, and Chap. 26. 550.

Rentals need not be returned in rescission suit, 527.

Right of way for pipeline prevents—for that purpose, 512.

Second lease terminates prior lease—when, 537.

Subsequent parol agreement does not waive, 535.

Superficial search constitutes, 516.

Surrender by parol, 514.

　　In law, 507.

Tender of rentals after abandonment does not prevent forfeiture, 514.

Unreasonable delay after notice to develop constitutes, 321-531-533.

Unsuccessful search, 504.

What constitutes, 501-503-506.

FORFEITURE BY ABANDONMENT—LESSEE'S REMEDY, Chap. 25, p. 546.

Abandonment must be intentional, 547.

　　of unsuccessful search does not divest lessee of pipeline privileges, 547.

After cessation of explorations lessee has reasonable time to re-enter, 508-546-547.

Covenants—substantial compliance with, 549.

Defective title, 548.

Discovery of oil or gas by lessee vests in him right to produce, 29-30-82-216-220-227-546-547.

Equity will not enforce forfeiture, 549.

Explorations not unreasonably delayed, 546.

Intention to abandon, 547.

Lessee cannot be deprived of right to produce upon discovery of oil or gas, in absence of proof of intention to abandon, 547.

　　May re-enter within reasonable time, 547.

　　May show that lessor prevented possession and performance of covenants, 547-548.

　　Willingness to perform covenants, 546.

Lessor asserting abandonment must prove it, 547.

Pipelines—right to hold lease for right of way, 547.

Question of fact—abandonment, 547.

Relief from forfeiture, 548.

　　When compensation can be made, 549.

Relinquishment of premises must be actual, 547.

Rental—acceptance of after forfeiture, waives, 549.

　　Consent to non-payment of when due, 549.

　　Non-payment of alone does not constitute—when, 546.

　　Non-payment of alone—when cancellation not authorized, 546.

Second lessee with notice of prior lease, 548.

Suit by lessor to cancel lease with no forfeit clause—defenses, 546.

Technical forfeiture—Lessee relieved from, 548.

Waiver of forfeiture, 548.

　　See title Waiver of Forfeiture, and Chap. 21, 467.

FORFEITURE BY ABANDONMENT—LESSOR'S REMEDIES, Chap. 26, p. 550.
Abandonment where lessee has never entered—how proven, 552.
Cessation of explorations constitutes, 557.
 Where unsuccessful, 551-557.
Distinction between proof—entry and Abandonment, and Non-entry, 552.
Equity will cancel lease for, 550-553.
Failure to collect judgment for rentals, 553.
 to explore within reasonable time after notice constitutes (Ind.) 551-552.
 to produce after discovery constitutes, 551-556.
 to protect lines and fully develop, 553-556.
 to pay rental or enter for developments authorizes cancellation, 553.
 to pay rental or enter for developments authorizes lessor to declare forfeiture, 550-553.
 to pay rental or enter for developments within reasonable time constitutes, 550.
 to resume operations within reasonable time after abandoning unsuccessful search, constitutes, 551.
How proven, 552.
Lease containing rental clause but no forfeiture clause is forfeited by failure to pay rental or develop within reasonable time, 550-553.
 With no forfeiture clause—how lessor terminates, 553.
Lessee's entry and physical abandonment is proof of intention, 552.
Lessee making test provided for and ceasing operations, 551.
Lessor may cancel lease for failure to develop and protect lines, 555.
 May cancel lease where lessee is not entitled to relief from forfeiture, 556.
 May execute new lease, 553-554.
 —Remedies where lease contains rental clause but no forfeiture clause, 553.
Physical abandonment of premises after entry constitutes, 551.
Presumption of abandonment where lessee fails to pay rental or explore, 550.
Question of intention, 552.
Relief not afforded lessee where he fails to pay rentals, 554.
Remedies—See title REMEDIES IN EQUITY, and Chap. 51, 895.
Rental—lessor may refuse to accept and demand explorations, 552.
Surrender by one of several lessees, 552.
 By majority of lessees, 552.
Unsuccessful search and physical abandonment constitutes, 550-551-557.

FORFEITURE WILL NOT BE ENFORCED BY A COURT OF EQUITY, Chap. 52, 923.
Enforced in proper case, 925.
For breach of subsequent conditions, 923.
Forfeited lease cancelled, 927.
Not enforced, 923- 924-925-926.
Party left to his legal remedy, 923.
Relief from forfeiture, 926-927.
Vested estate will not be divested, 923.
Void lease cancelled in court of equity—See that title, and Chap. 28, 601.

FOURTEENTH AMENDMENT—Interstate transportation—gas, 742-744-745-747.

FRAUD in purchase of interest in lease, 355.

GAS,
After discovery in paying quantities lessee cannot terminate lease without notice, 496.
After discovery lessee may shut in, pay rentals and hold lease beyond term, 220-222-234-500.
 Lessee cannot shut in, hold lease and refuse to pay rental or royalty, 191-232.
 And marketing lessee becomes tenant from year to year, 196.

GAS—*Continued.*

Article of commerce—See title NATURAL GAS ARTICLE OF COMMERCE, and Chapter 38, 742.

Cessation of use of—does not relieve lessee of duty to pay rental, 196.
  Terminates lessee's rights, 542.
  See title NATURAL GAS COMPANIES, etc., and Chap. 56, 984.

Consideration for grant of—See title CONSIDERATION FOR GRANT OF MINERALS—GAS, and Chap. 11, 189.

Court will decree forfeiture where lessee discovers but fails to pay royalty or rental, 438.

Death of lessor does not terminate lease, 198.

Discovery of—does not entitle lessee to shut in well, and hold lease without payment of rental or royalty, 191-438.
  in abandoned well does not revive lease, 542-543.
  in paying quantities entitles lessee to hold grant as long as he pays gas rental, 235.
  vests in lessee exclusive right to produce, 210-216-220-222-227.

Does not pass by deed reserving all minerals, 598.
  See title RESERVATION IN DEED. etc., and Chap. 47-826.

Duty of gas companies to furnish—See title NATURAL GAS COMPANIES, etc., and Chap. 56, 984.

Escape of—owner liable, 755.

Failure to drill additional wells not breach of implied covenant, 194-465.
  to market does not forfeit lease, 210-220.

Fourteenth Amendment—Statute forbidding waste not contrary to, 747.

Inflammable substance—Court will take judicial notice that gas is, 751.

Injuries to persons or property—See title NEGLIGENCE, INJURIES, etc., and Chap. 55, 944.

Judicial notice taken that gas unlike oil cannot be brought to surface and stored to await market, 216.

Lease for—construed differently from oil lease, 189-194.

Lessee after marketing cannot terminate tenancy without notice, 196.
  Desiring to terminate lease after discovering and utilizing—must give notice before entering upon another year, 236.
  in possession of may maintain bill in equity for protection of his rights, 917.
  is judge as to paying quantities, 210-220-235-407.
  Must give notice of his intention to terminate lease when wells are producing in paying quantities, 499.
  Must market if he can do so at a profit. 197-228-233-235-499.
  Using off premises liable for rental, 232.
  Using—when liable to lessor for rentals, 212.

Lessor cannot recover damages upon implied covenants where lessee has drilled one well, for failure to drill additional wells, 233-234.
  Entitled to rental to date of surrender when lease is producing in paying quantities, 499.
  Interested only in annual rentals, 210, 211.
  May forfeit lease when lessee discovers gas and fails to pay rental or royalty, 232.
  May require developments by giving notice to lessee of intention to declare a forfeiture, 236.
  not interested in proceeds of sale of gas, 210-211.

Market—where none lessee may hold grant by payment of rental, 235.

No property in until brought to surface, 812.

Not reserved in kind, 232.

Pump—See title GAS PUMP, etc., and Chap. 40, 760.

Right to take, 761.

State may enjoin waste of, 746.
  Regulation—See title WASTE AND TRANSPORTATION. and Chap. 39, 745.

GAS—*Continued.*
. Statutes regulating transportation—pressure, 768.
Surface owner must take for lawful purpose, 812.
Waste and Transportation—See that title, and Chap. 39, 745.
Waste of—Maliciously or negligently—See that title, and Chap. 45, 805.
When public nuisance, 746.

GAS FOR COMMERCIAL PURPOSES—See title Negligence, Injuries etc., and
  Chap. 55, 944.
See title Natural Gas Companies, etc., and Chap. 56, 984.

GAS FOR DOMESTIC PURPOSES—Covenant to furnish runs with land, 375.
Injunction to prevent cutting off, 165-168.
Lessee may furnish either from leased premises or from other sources, and hold
  his lease, 236.
Lessor's use of—waiver of forfeiture, 481.
When lessee cannot remove fixtures and cut off supply, 154.
When lessee must furnish free, 213.

GAS PUMP—CANNOT BE USED TO PRODUCE UNNATURAL FLOW, Chap. 40,
  760.
Action will lie for injuries resulting from use of, 774.
Artificial means to produce unnatural flow—may be prohibited by statute, 761.
Defenses, 778.
Gas pump in oil well, 775.
Indiana Statutes, 766-777.
Injunction, 761.
Petition for injunction to prevent use of—what should contain, 765-766-767.
      to enjoin pressure exceeding statutory limit—what should contain, 768.
Pressure, 767.
Property rights must be affected to entitle plaintiff to injunction, 774.
Remedies, 777.
Right to take gas, 761.
Rock pressure, 767.
Special injury necessary, 774.
Statutes regulating pressure not unconstitutional, 745-761-768.
Unnatural flow, 760.
Use of—may be enjoined, 761.
When gas pump may be used, 775.
Who is entitled to injunction to restrain use of, 768-774-777.
Who may enjoin use of—where pressure is beyond statutory limitation, 768.

GATE VALVE—Defective, 977.

GRANT of minerals same as exception, 871.
      of surface does not carry with it minerals—See title Reservation of Oil
      and Gas, and Chap. 49, 841.

GUARDIAN cannot lease ward's estate without authority from court, 580-594.

HIGHWAYS,
Operation of wells near, 802-803.
Pipelines in—Not nuisance, 797.
Pipelines—See title Negligence, etc., and Chap. 55, 944.
Rights of persons using—near wells, 803.

IMPLICATION,
Where parties have agreed upon what shall be done—no room for implication of
  anything not stipulated for, 10.

IMPLIED COVENANTS OF THE OIL AND GAS LEASE, Chap. 18, 393.
 Action at law for failure to drill additional gas wells cannot be maintained, 233-416.
 Breach of—Action at law for damages, 402-410-417-419-453.
  Cancellation of lease for, 93.
  Failure to prosecute development, 93-400-414-433-437.
  Lease will not be cancelled for, alone, 395-402-404-405-406-407-409-411-459.
  Remedies at Law—See title REMEDIES AT LAW, and Chap. 20, 453.
  Remedies in Equity—See REMEDIES IN EQUITY FOR BREACHES, etc., and Chap. 19, 437.
 Broken by exclusion of lessee from taking possession, 90-94-398.
 Cancellation of lease will not be decreed for failure alone to further develop, 443-444-445-446-448.
 Defect in lessor's title constitutes breach, 424.
 Dry Hole—Further Developments, 688.
 Diligent search and operation, 28-394-397-400-428-430.
 Development and production, 93-190-395-397-399-400-411-414-424-433-456.
 Equity will not assume jurisdiction to enforce specifically in absence of fraud, 402.
 Forfeiture for breach of, 399-400.
  Not incurred after discovery of oil or gas for breach of—for full development, 409-412.
 Fraudulent evasion of—grounds of forfeiture, 400.
 Gas Lease—construed differently from oil lease, 416.
 Good title and quiet possession, in lease made by one tenant in common or joint tenant, 662.
 Implication—No room for when express agreement, 432.
 Lease held to contain—for developments, 317.
 Lessor's remedy for breaches of—for development and protection of lines, 410-454.
 New lease—execution of alone not breach of, 90-398.
 Production and protection of lines (Ohio) 7-8-465.
  on adjacent territory, 395-396.
 Protection of lines, 394.
 Quiet enjoyment, 90-394-398-420-423-424-428-435.
 Reasonable diligence, 396.
 Remedy for breaches of—damages or cancellation, 93.
  For full development, 404.
  See title REMEDIES IN EQUITY FOR BREACHES, etc., and Chap. 19, 437.
  See title REMEDIES AT LAW, etc., and Chap. 20, 453
  See title ADDITIONAL WELLS.
 Right of entry and quiet enjoyment, 90-394-398-420-423-424-428-435.
 Title—Defect in lessor's—constitutes breach, 424.
 to begin work within reasonable time, 393.
 to develop within reasonable time, 433-518.
 to drill and operate sufficient number of wells, 411-416-419-464.
 Vested right to produce not divested by court of equity in absence of fraud, 430.
 When covenants will be implied, 9.
 When law presumes, 9.

INFANTS,
 Co-tenants—when bound by declaration of forfeiture by adults, 674-675-676.
 Formal answer of guardian ad litem need not be sworn to, 726.
 Injured by explosion in highway—Right to recover, 977.
 Remainder men entitled to decree or order for sale or lease, 712.

INDIANA—Forfeiture incurred for failure to drill after notice, 274.
  Leases conferring options to drill, 239.
  Statutes regulating transportation and forbidding waste of gas, 745-766-777.

INJUNCTION,
 Lessee kept out of possession by—entitled to extension of term, 681.
  may enjoin lessor or other person from interfering with his rights of

INJUNCTION—*Continued.*
   possession, 94-147-223-597-598-600-601.
  Malicious or negligent waste of gas, 811.
  Remainderman may obtain—When—See title LIFE TENANTS etc., and Chap.
    35; 709.
  Reservation around buildings—See that title, and Chap. 10, 170.
  State may enjoin waste of gas, 746.
  Tenants in common may enjoin operations, 661-672-897.
  Title—Controversies between claimants to, 599-600.
    Question of law, 600.
  to enjoin shooting gas well, 779-799.
    use of gas pump to increase flow, 761-777.
  to prevent drilling, 795-797-800-804.
    See title NUISANCE, and Chap. 44, 795.
    Through, coal, 868.
    Extraction of oil, 591-594-598-599.
    Irreparable injury, 587-588-591-594-598-599.
    Surface owner from producing and marketing, 881.
    Removal of oil and gas, 518.
    Unlawful operation of wells, 795.
    Waste of gas—Who may obtain, 756-758-759-760.
  to protect reservations of mineral, 832.
  Unlawful extraction of oil from leased premises, 598.
  When awarded (Pa.) 917.
  When will be awarded for cutting off gas for domestic purposes, 165.
  Will lie against lessor for protection of lessee—Reservation around buildings,
    173-175.

INJURY,
  Negligence—See title NEGLIGENCE—INJURIES etc., and Chap. 55, 944.
  Resulting from operation of wells—See title RIGHT TO OPERATE OIL AND GAS
    WELLS etc., and Chap. 43, 788.

INNOCENT PURCHASER—Assignee of second lease with notice of first is not, 372.

INSANITY adjudicated continues until discharge, 726.

INTENTION,
  of parties should be given effect as ascertained from all parts of lease, 18.
  to abandon, 501-507.
    Proof of—What constitutes, 552.
  to relinquish essential to abandonment, 541.

INTERSTATE COMMERCE,
  limiting pressure of gas not regulation of, 751.
  Transportation of gas from one State to another is, 742-743-744.

IRREPARABLE INJURY, 587-588-591.
  Unlawful extraction of oil is, 591-594-598.

JOINT LEASE, 836-839.

JUDGMENT FOR RENTALS—Failure to collect considered proof by abandonment, 553.

JUDICIAL NOTICE,
  Gas and oil are not found in paying quantities under all lands, 201.
  Gas is inflammable substance, 751.
  Gas unlike oil cannot be brought to surface and stored to await a market, 216.
  Mining for oil or gas is hazardous and dangerous, 861.

JURISDICTION,
  Consent cannot confer, 588.
  Remedies in equity—See that title, and Chap. 51, 895.
  to quiet title of lessor, 57.

KANSAS RULE—Oil and gas lease mere license, 31.

KENTUCKY RULE AS TO FORFEITURE, 297.

LANDLORD cannot recover for tenant's negligence—When, 947.

LANDOWNER,
  executing lease void for want of mutuality must declare forfeiture promptly, 95.
  May cause void lease to be cancelled—·See title Void Lease Will be Cancelled
      etc., and Chap. 28, 601.
  May enjoin unlawful extraction of oil or gas, 598.

LEAKS—Gas—See title Negligence, Injuries, etc., and Chap. 55, 944.

LEASE FOR OIL AND GAS PURPOSES, Chap. 1, p. 1.
  Ambiguous, 305, 613.
  Analyzed, 2-5.
  Assignee—Liability of, 364.
      With notice, 385.
  Assignment, 350.
  Character of to be. determined to give effect to acts of parties, 20.
  Conditional or contingent sale, 83-133.
  Consideration for, 42.
      For gas, 189.
      For oil, 129.
  Construction, 6.
  Construed most strongly in favor of lessor, 7.
  Containing rental clause but no forfeiture clause, 550.
  Contingent on discovery of oil or gas during term, 27.
  Conveyance held to be, 36.
  Date of lease excluded in computing time, 216.
  Deed construed to be, 544.
  Definition, 20.
      Conveyance or sale conditional and contingent, 28.
      West Virginia rule, 28-430.
  Distinguished from other leases, 9-87.
      From solid mineral lease, 69-76-141-603-884.
  Entire contract without words of severance, 414.
  Exclusive privileges granted vests interest in lessee, 20.
  Execution of new lease terminates prior voidable lease, 49-240.
  Executor without authority under will cannot execute, 583.
  Executory not binding lessee is mere option, 65-609.
      Void for want of consideration, lessee entering under, 65.
      With provision for surrender at any time, 49.
  Fixtures—See title Right to Remove, etc., and Chap. 9, 150.
  Forfeiture—Relief from, 548.
      See title Forfeiture.
      by abandonment—See that title, and Chap. 24, 501.
      See·title Forfeiture and Rental Clause, Lessee's Option, and Chap.
          13, 290.
      See title Forfeiture and Rental Clause, Lessor's Option, and Chap.
          12, 237.
      Clause for lessor's benefit, 17.
  Form of, 2-5.
  Gas lease construed differently from oil ease, 189.
      See title Consideration for Grant of Minerals—Gas, and Chap. 11, 189.

LEASE FOR OIL AND GAS PURPOSES—*Continued.*

Grant of part of corpus of land, 594.

Guardian cannot execute without authority from court, 580.

Held to be lease of land for oil and gas, 326.

Implied covenant by lessee to explore—Forfeiture for breach of, 201.

For development and protection of lines, 393.

See title IMPLIED COVENANTS OF THE OIL AND GAS LEASE, and Chap. 18, 393.

In class by itself, 29.

Judicial knowledge that oil and gas are not found in paying quantities under all lands, 201.

Lessee bound by acceptance of, without signing, 16-21.

Not permitted to hold and prevent operations, 8.

Lessees uniting to operate—When mining partners, 625.

License to go upon premises and explore, 20-31-32-37-135.

Life tenants and remaindermen—See that title, and Chap. 35, 709.

Mining partnership—See that title, and Chap. 30, 625.

Nature of partakes more of general tillage than solid minerals, 19.

Nominal and substantial consideration distinguished, 66.

Ohio Rule, more than mere license, 30.

Oil lease—See CONSIDERATION FOR GRANT OF MINERALS—OIL, and Chap. 7, 129.

One party not bound to performance renders void, 49.

Option—Lease held to be, 54-316-613.

to develop cannot be forfeited without notice (Ind.) 234.

When lease is, 260.

Partition—see title PARTITION OF OIL AND GAS RIGHTS, and Chap. 31, 650.

Paying Quantities—See title, DISCOVERY OF OIL OR GAS IN, and Chap. 22, 487.

Remedies—See title PAYING QUANTITIES—REMEDIES, and Chap. 23, 498.

Pennsylvania Rule—Mere license, 22-23-25.

Purpose and object of, 67.

Real or personal property depends on State Statutes, 95.

Recited consideration sufficient to support lease, and extension of exploration period, 55.

Relief from forfeiture—See title RELIEF FROM FORFEITURE.

Remaindermen—See title LIFE TENANTS AND REMAINDERMEN, and Chap. 35, 709.

Remedies at Law for Breaches of Implied Covenants—See that title, and Chap. 20, 453.

Remedies in Equity for Breaches by lessee of implied covenants—See that title, and Chap. 19, 437.

Rental, See title RENTALS.

Rental for Gas, See that title.

Rental—See FORFEITURE AND RENTAL CLAUSE—LESSOR'S OPTION, and Chap. 12, 237.

Rental—See FORFEITURE AND RENTAL CLAUSE—LESSEE'S OPTION, and Chap. 13, 290.

Reservation around Buildings—See that title, and Chap. 10, 170.

for farming purposes—See that title, and Chap. 8, 144.

of oil and gas—See that title, and Chap. 49, 541.

Sale—Lease held to be, 83.

Second lessee with notice of prior lease, 385.

Several tracts under one lease—See that title, and Chap. 50, 882.

Substantial and Nominal Consideration distinguished, 66.

Surrender—Acceptance of new lease is, 345.

by one of several lessees, 552.

by parol, 514.

Surrender clause of the oil and gas lease—See that title, and Chap. 14, 322.

Tenants in Common or joint tenants—Right to Execute, etc., See that title and Chap. 32, 660.

Term—See title TERM OF OIL AND GAS LEASE, and Chap. 6, 96.

Termination of—If one may terminate at will so may the other, 49.

Title to produce vests in lessee upon discovery, 27.

Unfair or unreasonable not enforced, 521.

Unfair, Unjust and against good conscience, not enforceable, 49-610.

LEASE FOR OIL AND GAS PURPOSES—*Continued.*
Vests no present title in lessee, 73-337-433.
Void for want of consideration, 65.
    Mutality—See title Want of Mutuality, and Chap. 29, 608.
Void lease—Lessee entering under—effect, 67.
    Will be cancelled—See title VOID LEASE WILL BE CANCELLED, etc., and Chap. 28, 601.
Waiver of Forfeiture—See that title, and Chap. 21, 467.

LESSEE,
After beginning operations under void lease may continue, 65.
    declaration of forfeiture may be enjoined from entering, 65.
    discovery of oil must produce or forfeit lease, 245.
Cannot cultivate surface or build residences, 90.
Omit to develop and hold for speculative purposes, 192.
Discovering gas in paying quantities may shut in, pay rental and hold lease beyond term, 220.
Drilling after expiration of term cannot recover expenses of, 736.
    Dry hole—See title DRY HOLE and Chap. 33, 680.
Estate of ends when unsuccessful search abandoned, 132-140.
    vests upon discovery in paying quantities, 132-140-143.
Failure of, after notice, to develop incurs forfeiture (Ind.) 274.
Fixtures—Right to remove—See that title, and Chap. 9, 150.
In possession will be protected by court of equity, 94-147-223.
Judge as to gas in paying quantities, 210-220-225.
Knowledge of ownership and possession in third person, 272.
Life Tenants—and Remaindermen—See that title, and Chap. 35, 709.
Making test provided for and ceasing operations—forfeiture by abandonment, 551.
May continue explorations while making diligent search, When, 75.
    Defeat action to cancel lease or recover possession, 125.
    Maintain action to cancel outstanding lease—See title VOID LEASE, etc., and Chap. 28, 601.
    Ejectment against adverse claimant (Pa.) 40.
    Suit in equity to quiet title, 57.
Must always be diligent, 97.
Option—See title FORFEITURE AND RENTAL CLAUSE—LESSEE'S OPTION, and Chap. 13, 290.
Partition—See title PARTITION OF OIL AND GAS RIGHTS, and Chap. 31, 650.
Prevented by lessor from taking possession, does not lose benefit of lease, 128.
Rentals—cannot refuse to pay and hold lease without development, 279.
    May pay to time sufficient to complete well within term, 302.
Rights cease when explorations finished and lease abandoned, 30-140.
    Easement, 148.
    to explore, 30-77-130.
    to produce, vest upon discovery of oil or gas, 30-140-220.
Tenants in Common or Co-tenants—Lessee of one or more cannot have partition, 339-663-664-673.
Title inchoate and contingent until discovery, 73-82-135.
    not acquired until production, 29.
Void lease—may enter before notice of declaration of forfeiture, 67.

LESSEES,
Acts and declarations of majority binding on others, 514.
Controversies—See title Necessary parties, etc., and Chap. 53, 927.
Mining partnership—See that title, and Chap. 30, 625.
Not tenants in common, 514.

LESSOR,
Abandonment asserted by—must prove, 547.
Cancellation of lease by, 124-616.
    See title VOID LEASE WILL BE CANCELLED, etc., and Chap. 28, 601.

LESSOR—*Continued.*
  Consenting to beginning operations after expiration of term is waiver of forfeiture, 732.
  Has no right to expect lessee to perform covenants immediately when the lease permits delay, 305.
  Forfeiture—can be asserted by, alone, 223-263-274-284-285.
    When may declare, 283.
  Life tenants and Remaindermen—See that title, and Chap. 35, 709.
  Oil and gas in place not parted with, 144.
  Option to declare forfeiture or waive it and collect rentals, 237.
    See title FORFEITURE AND RENTAL CLAUSE—LESSOR'S OPTION, and Chap. 12, 237.
  Permitting lessee to enter under void lease—effect, 67.
  Unauthorized use of premises, 577.
  Remedies at Law for Breaches of Implied Covenants—See that title, and Chap. 20, 453.
  Remedies in Equity for Breaches by Lessee of Implied Covenants—See that title, and Chap. 19, 437.
  Right to recover gas rentals and royalties from assignee of lease—See title Assignment of Lease, and Chap. 15, 350.

LICENSE,
  Lease held to be—22-23-25-26-30-31-32-537.
    (Kansas) 31.
    (La.) 537.
    (Ohio) 30.
    (Penna.) 22-23-25-135.
    (Tex.) 37.
    (W. Va.) 26.
  Lease held to be more than license (Modified Pa. Rule) 40.
    Not binding lessee to do anything is mere license, 620.

LIEN of mining partners—See title MINING PARTNERSHIP, and Chap. 30, 625.

LIFE TENANTS AND REMAINDERMEN, Chap. 35, 709.
  Life tenant—cannot drill new wells, 709-712-717-718-720.
    Cannot recover rental under lease, 601-720.
    Converting oil or gas cannot have proceeds invested, 600-712.
    Entitled to interest on royalty, 600-709-712-726-728-729.
    Entitled to royalty where wells produce before estate vests, 709-710-727.
    Interest of is interest on royalty during lifetime, 726.
    Lease by not binding on remaindermen, 599-718-720-721.
    Liable to account, 712.
    No right to lease, 709.
    No right to operate, 709-712-717-718-720.
    Not entitled to royalty or proceeds, 726.
    Proceeds of production go to owner of next vested estate, 600.
    Remedies, 728.
    Right to accounting, 600-728.
    Right to operate open wells, 712-720.
    Waste to operate, 600-711-712.
  Remaindermen—entitled to corpus of royalty after life estate terminates, 709.
    Infant entitled to decree or order for sale or lease, 712.
    May cause production for his protection, 712-729.
    May enjoin production by life tenant or his lessee, 728.
    May recover from life tenant or his lessee value of oil or gas taken, 728.
    Remedies, 728.

LIMITATION AS TO DRILLING—See title RESERVATION AROUND BUILDINGS, and Chap. 10, 170.

LOCATING WELLS,
Lease providing for—by lessor—effect, 416.
Lessor bound by his selection—when, 681.

LOUISIANA RULE—Lease held to be License, 537.

LOWER STRATA—Regulations for reaching—Legislative question, 867.

MALICIOUS WASTE OF GAS—See title Waste of Gas Maliciously or Negligently, and Chap. 45, 805.

MANDAMUS to compel Gas Company to furnish gas—See title, Natural Gas Companies, etc., and Chap. 56, 984.

MARKET—When none for gas, lessee may hold grant by payment of rental, 235.

MARKETING AND PRODUCTION OBJECT OF LEASE, 67-70-72.
Gas, See title Gas, and p. 189.

MEASURE OF DAMAGES,
Cannot be estimated upon amount of oil taken from premises, 177.
Difference in value of leasehold before and after injury, 177.
For failure to fully develop, 455.
Oil taken by lessor or his grantee or lessee from reservation, 175.
From reservation by lessor or others, 188-463.

MINERALS—OIL AND GAS ARE, See title Oil and Gas in Place are, etc., and Chap. 27, 558.
See title Reservation, etc., Includes, and Chap. 47, 826.
See title Reservation, etc., Does not Include, and Chap. 48, 834.

MINING PARTNERSHIP—OIL AND GAS, Chap. 30, p. 625.
Accounting not decreed without dissolution, 626.
Actual working of lease essential to charge partners, 642.
Advances beyond partner's proportion—Lien for, 641.
Lien for does not attach to property divided, 640-641.
Partners have lien for, 143-626-630-640.
Assignee agreeing to drill well for interest not mining partner, (Pa.) 638.
Assignment—Co-owner not affirming has no interest in royalty, 646.
Co-owner not joining in may affirm and take share of royalty, 647.
Co-owners are tenants in common, not mining partners, (Pa.) 625-632.
Cannot be charged as partners without proof of special contract, (Pa.) 643.
Fraudulently deprived of their interest—Remedy, 644.
Liability for loss of well, (Pa.) 636.
May become partners by special agreement, (Pa.) 634.
of lease not joining in assignment not entitled to recover from other co-owners—when, 646.
Operating leases presumed, 625-641.
Uniting to work lease are, (W. Va.) 625-626.
When liable to accounting, (Pa.) 635-643-648.
Declaration of one co-owner not evidence to establish, 638.
Dissolution—Bill in equity for, 640.
Bill must allege good cause, 627.
Cause for, 626-642.
Decree over against member liable to firm, 631.
Good grounds must be shown for, 640.
Property must be sold and full settlement made, 626-627-631.
Division of production presumption against, 638.
Division Orders—Execution of does not affect property not divided, 630.
Partners executing lose lien for advances on oil divided by, 143-630.

MINING PARTNERSHIP—OIL AND GAS—*Continued.*
General Rule—Co-owners uniting to work are, 625.
Lien for advances does not attach to property divided, 640-641.
    Partners have, 143-626-630-640.
    Partners may enforce, 640.
Majority control management, 626-627-631-640.
    Controlling management—for what accountable, 631.
Member may sell interest without consent of others, 627.
Negligence or wrongful conduct of a member creates personal liability, 626.
Obligations incurred without authority do not bind, 642.
Partial settlement not decreed, 631.
Participation in profits test of, 638.
Partition can only be affected by dissolution and sale of assets, 651-660.
Pennsylvania Rule—Co-owners without special agreement do not constitute, 625-632.
Presumption—None from operating oil well, (Pa.) 639.
Relationship arises from operation of lease, (W. Va.) 641.
Remedies, 640-644.
Sale of member's interest does not discharge lien for advances, 641.
    Discharges lien for advances (Pa.) 643.
    Does not dissolve, 626-627.
Social property applied to discharge liabilities of, 631.
Supplies necessary—Liability for, 642.
Tenants in common—agreeing to drill, not, 632.
    Agreeing to drill additional wells, not, 634.
    Bill in equity for accounting—when, 635-648.
    Damages recoverable, 644.
    Discovery, 648.
    May become partners, 634.
    Not partners, 632.
    Not subject to law of partnership, 632.
    Refusing to furnish statements—Remedy, 648.
    Uniting to operate are, 625-626-627-630-631-641.
    When partners—liability, 648.
    Working lease constitutes, 626.
    Wrongfully deprived of interest—Remedy, 644.
Third persons—Liability to, 625-641.
West Virginia Rule, 625-626-641.

MIXER—Removal of will not preclude recovery, 997.

MULTIPLICITY OF SUITS—Equity will decree accounting to prevent, 185.

MUTUALITY—See title WANT OF MUTUALITY, and Chap. 29, 608.

NATURAL GAS AN ARTICLE OF COMMERCE WHEN BROUGHT TO THE SURFACE, Chap. 38, 742.
Fourteenth Amendment of Federal Constitution applied, 742-744.
Injunction against enforcement of unconstitutional statute, 742.
Just compensation, 742.
Highway—Fee not vested in public, (Okla.) 743.
    State cannot prohibit pipe lines in, 743.
People have not common interest in gas, 742.
Pipelines—Construction and operation of cannot be prohibited, 742-744.
Property—Absolute right of—When title vests, 742.
Sale and delivery, 742.
State cannot deprive owner of gas of right of transportation, without compensation, 742.
Statute prohibiting transportation of gas from State, unconstitutional, 742-744.

NATURAL GAS AN ARTICLE OF COMMERCE, ETC.—*Continued.*
  Transportation of gas from one State to another Interstate Commerce, **742-743-744.**
  When found within territorial limits of State, 742.
  When placed in pipelines for transportation, 742-744.

NATURAL GAS COMPANIES—DUTY TO FURNISH GAS, Chap. 56, 984.
  Abutting owners, 984.
  Arrangements to receive—Owner must make for gas, 984.
  Bound to furnish gas to all, 984-985-992-994.
  Complaint for failure to furnish—Sufficiency of, 994.
  Customers must comply with rules, 984.
  Cutting off gas—Liability for, 987-999.
  Damages recoverable, 994.
  Deficiency no excuse, 992-995.
  Defenses, 1000.
  Defense—None that company furnished all the gas it had, 988.
  Discrimination forbidden, 994-996-997.
  Duty, 985.
  Eminent Domain, 984.
  Evidence of amount of gas furnished other houses, admissible, 988.
  Mandamus—Not necessary that plaintiff be interested in company, 985.
        to compel performance of duty, 985-992-999.
  Mixer—Removal of will not preclude recovery, 987.
        Customer may remove—When, 987.
  Monopoly, 999.
  Negligent maintenance of pipes, 988.
  Occupying streets must furnish gas, 984-992.
        to supply gas is public use, 984.
  Ordinance admissible in evidence, 988.
  Owners of houses must comply with reasonable regulations, 984.
  Payment in advance entitles consumer to gas, 988.
  Penalty imposed by ordinance does not preclude action for damages, 987.
  Refusal to supply, 995.
  Regulations of company, 984.
  Remedies, 999-1000.
  Streets—Use of public, 984.
  Supplying gas public duty, 984.
  Supply in other buildings provable, 988.

NECESSARY PARTIES TO BILL IN EQUITY, Chap. 53, 927.
  All parties interested, landowners and lessees, 591-607-927-928-931.
  All persons interested in subject matter, 928-931.
  Co-tenants, 931.
  Decree reversed for failure to make, 927.
        Where not before the court, 591.
  Landlord, 931.
  Landowner, 927-928.
  Lessees, 928-931.
  Lessor, 927-931.
  Oil and gas—Persons interested in, 928.
  Owners of fee, 928.
  Prior lessees, 927-931.
  Rights of claimants cannot be adjudicated in absence of, 931.
  Subsequent lessees, 927-931.
  Trustees, 931.
  Well—Persons interested, 929.

NEGLIGENCE IN SHOOTING WELL, See title SHOOTING WELL, and Chap. 37, 737.

NEGLIGENCE—INJURIES TO PERSONS OR PROPERTY BY CORPORATIONS OR BY PERSONS FURNISHING NATURAL GAS FOR COMMERCIAL PURPOSES, Chap. 55, 944.
Blowing off well—Negligence—Highways, 948.
Burden of proof on plaintiff in action for injury, 966-981.
Cause—Evidence that accident may have been produced from other causes, 976.
Complaint—Allegations held sufficient, 965.
    Insufficient, 964.
Cellar—Accumulation of gas in, 967.
Conjecture insufficient to warrant verdict, 966.
Contributory Negligence, 959-960.
Defects at different points may be proven, 963.
Defective Gate Valve—Negligence, 977.
Defective pipes—admissibility of evidence, 954.
Defenses, 983.
Degree of care, 953-980.
Diligence and skill required, 946.
Duties defined, 946.
Duty of—furnishing gas, 944-948-954.
Escape of gas from well into cellar—Explosion, 794.
    Into earth—Explosion, 962-967-973.
Evidence insufficient to show escape of gas from well, 975.
    Held insufficient—Negligence, 956-957.
    of condition of by-pass and regulator on day after accident, not admissible, 976.
    of condition of pipes after explosion admissible, 953.
    That other causes were as likely to cause the accident, 976.
    Pressure on other lines—not competent, 946.
    Test of pressure a year before accident—Too remote, 976.
    Unusual flow—When admissible, 976.
Explosion—When liable for, 954-959-962-973.
    of regulator—not negligence, 948.
Facts held insufficient to establish negligence, 964.
Fire caused by gas—fact not sufficient to infer negligence 946.
    Liability for, 946.
Gas well—Maintenance of not negligence, 975.
    Near highway, owner may open, 948.
Gate Valve—Defects—Negligence, 977.
Highway—Infants right to recover for injuries—Explosion, 977.
Highway—See Pipelines, post.
    Persons using—Injuries by explosions—When not guilty of contributory negligence, 965.
    Near well—Persons using not bound to give warning of their presence, 948.
    Persons using not guilty of contributory negligence—when, 948.
Infant—Right to recover for injuries—Explosion in highway, 977.
Injuries natural consequence of negligence—Liability, 946.
Insurers—Persons or corporations not, 948.
Landlord cannot recover for tenants negligence, 947.
Leaks—Duty to repair, 951.
    Failures to notify of not contributory negligence, 967.
  in sleeve—Explosion—Owner liable, 967.
    Known, 973.
Mere fact of fire not sufficient to establish negligence, 946.
Negligence presumed to be proximate cause, 946.
    Question of fact, 952-953.
Negligent use of well, 948.
Odor of gas evidence of negligence, 953-954-957.
Percolating gas, 967.
Pipelines—Interference with by third persons, 955.
    Leaks—Duty to repair, 951.

NEGLIGENCE—INJURIES, ETC.—*Continued.*
    Loose Joints—Liability, 959-960.
    Persons laying—in highways liable for injuries, 965.
    Unlawful to lay—on surface of highway, 965.
    in highway—Liability, 959.
    Owner liable for injuries from explosion, 977-990.
    Persons laying—on surface liable for injury, 965.
  Pressure, 946.
    Negligence, 951-952.
  Prima Facie Case—How made, 932.
  Proximate cause—Negligent use of well, 948.
    Negligence presumed, 946.
  Regulators and appliances insufficient, 946-948-979.
  Remedies, 979-983.
  Res Ipsa Loquitur not applicable, 948.
  Sleeve—Leaks, 957.
  Statutory restrictions—Liability for breach of, 958-962-981.
  Tenant—Negligence of—Landlord not entitled to recover, 947.
  Test of pressure one year before accident—Evidence too remote, 976.
  Trespasser—Not liable for acts of, 955.
  Unusual flow—Evidence held insufficient to establish negligence, 976.
    When not liable for damages, 976.

NEGLIGENT DEFAULT constitutes grounds for relief from forfeiture—See title
    Relief from Forfeiture.

NEGLIGENT OPERATION OF WELLS NEAR HIGHWAY, 802-803.

NEGLIGENT WASTE OF GAS—See title WASTE OF GAS MALICIOUSLY OR NEGLI-
    GENTLY, and Chap. 45, 805.

NEW LEASE—Acceptance of operates as surrender of prior lease, 345-860.
    Execution of, 553-554.
    Not necessary when forfeiture waived within term, 116.

NITROGLYCERINE TO INCREASE FLOW—RIGHT TO USE, Chap. 41, 778.
  Accumulation of may be enjoined, 778-779.
  Complaint to enjoin shooting gas well—what should contain, 781.
  Gas or oil may be drawn from lands of others, 778.
  Injunction to prevent accumulation and explosion, 778-779.
  Owner of well may use, 778-779.
  Shooting well—See that title, and Chap. 37, 737.

NON-PRODUCTIVE WELL vests no title in lessee, 132-133.
    See title DRY HOLE, and Chap. 33. 630.

NOTICE—Lessor's refusal to accept rental is notice of intention to declare for-
    feiture, 531.
    of prior lease—Effect on assignee or second lessee—See title, ASSIGNEE
    OR SECOND LESSEE WITH NOTICE OF PRIOR LEASE, and Chap. 17, 385.
    Possession is notice to subsequent lessee, 181.
    Required to terminate tenancy where gas well is producing in paying
    quantities, 499.
    to one lessee sufficient as to all, 586.

NUISANCE, Chap. 44, 795.
  Abatable—When, 795.
  Depends upon location, capacity and management of wells, 795.
  Drilling enjoined—When, 795-797-800-804.
  Drilling well near residence—when not, 795,797.
    on adjoining tract not enjoined, 800.

NUISANCE—*Continued.*

Dwelling erected after well drilled, 797.

Gas pipe in highway—Not, 797.

Gas well near highway may be opened, 802.

Not, 797.

Injunction—Dangers and injuries must be imminent, 800.

Negligent operation of wells near highway, 802-803.

Oil and gas wells are not—per se, 795.

Owner of well near highway must exercise care in operation, 802-803.

Pipelines in highways not, 797.

Pollution, 788-789.

Remedies, 804-805.

Rights of persons using highways near wells, 803.

Right to operate oil and gas wells even when injury results therefrom. See that title, and Chap. 43, 788.

Shooting well—When enjoined, 799.

Unlawful operations enjoined, 795.

Waste of gas held to be, 746.

Wells—care required of owners, 795.

 Interference necessary to constitute, 795.

 Near buildings and appurtenances, 795.

 Near dwellings, 795.

 Near highways, 795.

NULL AND VOID—Effect of in lease, 266-269.

ODOR of gas evidence of negligence, 954-957.

OHIO RULE—Implied Covenants that lessee will drill sufficient number of wells to fully develop and protect lines, 7-467.

Recovery of gas rental, 233.

Several tracts under one lease—Royalties, 893.

OIL, Consideration for Grant of—See title Consideration for Grant of Minerals—Oil, and Chap. 7, 129.

Owner may pursue and reclaim wherever found, when unlawfully extracted, 600.

Nitroglycerine to increase flow—See that title, and Chap. 41, 778.

Pipelines—See Pipeline Companies—Oil, and Chap. 57, 1001.

OIL AND GAS,

are minerals, 336-559-566-568-570-784.

See title Oil and Gas in Place are Minerals and Part of the Land, and Chap. 27, 558.

Belong to the owner of, and are part of the land, 11-12-582-717.

Grant of held to be lease, 372.

Leases for in class by themselves, 29.

Lessee takes no title to in fee, 89.

Reservation—See title Reservation of Oil and Gas. and Chap. 49, 841.

See title Reservation in Deed of all Minerals Includes Petroleum Oil and Natural Gas, and Chap. 47, 826.

See title Reservation in Deed of all Minerals or Conveyance by Deed of all Minerals in Land does not Reserve or Convey Petroleum Oil or Natural Gas, and Chap. 48, 834.

Title to vests in lessee when raised to the surface, 29.

While in the earth not the subject of ownership distinct from soil, 336-339-351.

OIL AND GAS IN PLACE ARE MINERALS AND PART OF THE LAND, Chap. 27, 558.

Belong to owner of land, 582.

OIL AND GAS IN PLACE, ETC.—*Continued.*
Equity will restrain unlawful extraction, 559.
Jurisdiction in equity to protect—When no controversy as to title, 573.
Lease held to be sale, 575.
    Made by tenant for life cannot be enforced, 576.
Lessee or operator taking oil and gas under belief of good title, entitled to
    expenses of production and operation—nothing for unproductive wells,
    567.
Lessee's Remedy, 600.
Life estate—Termination of, entitles remainderman or reversioner to corpus of
    estate, 575.
Life tenant entitled to interest on proceeds of royalty during estate, 570-575.
May be severed from ownership of surface, 579.
Minerals reserved—Failure to enter on Land Books, Not forfeited, 573.
Remaindermen or reversioners may have sale of, 570.
    May enjoin tenant for life from extracting, 566.
Rental cannot be collected under lease made by tenant for life, 576.
Reservation in deed of all minerals held not to include oil and gas, 585.
    Chap. 49, 841.
    Includes oil and gas, Chap. 47, 826. (See RESERVATION).
    Includes oil and gas, 573.
Reservation or Conveyance does not reserve or convey, Chap. 48, 834.
Tenant for life cannot have proceeds of oil or gas invested for his benefit,
    When, 567.
    Cannot lease for, 576.
    Cannot operate for oil or gas, 576.
    Taking oil or gas commits waste, 566.
Title to passes only by deed, 558-570.
    Does not pass when reserved in deed, 579.
Unlawful extraction by one lawfully in possession is waste, 558-577.
    Not lawfully in possession—trespass, 558.
    Remedy of owner, 598.
When granted, excepted or reserved—separate corporeal property, 579.

OPENING GAS WELL FOR REPAIRS, not waste, 760.

OPERATIONS—See title BEGINNING OPERATIONS. Chap. 36, 729.
    Life tenants and remaindermen—Rights as to, See title LIFE TENANTS
    AND REMAINDERMN, and Chap. 35, 709.
    Under void lease perpetually enjoined, 601.

OPERATION OF OIL AND GAS WELLS—See title RIGHT TO OPERATE OIL AND
    GAS WELLS, EVEN WHERE INJURY RESULTS, and Chap. 43, 788.
    See title NUISANCE, and Chap. 44, 795.

OPTION—Death of lessor revokes, 287.
    Executory lease not binding lessee terminable by either party, 65-537.
    Lease at option of lessee not enforceable in equity, 610.
    Not void for want of mutuality, 305-611.
    Held to be (Ind.) 54.
    Held to be (Kan.) 316.
    is where lessee not bound to pay money or do anything, 260-286-287-307-
    315-329.
Lessee entering under, or paying rental entitled to complete developments or
    hold lease for time rental paid, 288-289.
Lessee's option to terminate before end of term—lease not rendered void for
    want of mutuality, 612-613.
    See title FORFEITURE AND RENTAL CLAUSE, LESSEE'S OPTION, and Chap. 15,
    290.
Lessor's option to declare forfeiture or collect rental, 237.
    See title FORFEITURE AND RENTAL CLAUSE—LESSOR'S OPTION, and Chap. 12,
    237.

OPTION—*Continued*.
Must be exercised within time limit, 308.
New lease revokes, 287.
Notice of revocation terminates lease, 286-287.
Right to terminate at any time deprives holder of specific performance, 339.
When lease is, 66.

PAROL AGREEMENT does not revive forfeited lease, 535.

PAROL EVIDENCE—not received to contradict payment of consideration for lease, 337.

PAROL LICENSE—Revokable at will of licensor, 351.

PARTIES—Necessary to bill in equity—See title NECESSARY PARTIES TO BILL IN EQUITY, etc., and Chap. 53, 927.

PARTITION OF OIL AND GAS RIGHTS, Chap. 31, 650.
Can be affected only by sale and division of proceeds, 651-660.
Cannot be made in kind, 650.
Co-owners cannot have, 651.
Judicial partition cannot be made by assignment of interests, 651.
Lease conditioned upon, 654.
Lessee cannot have partition of land, 653-657.
    of one or more co-tenants cannot have, 339-663-664-673.
Remedies, 660.
Statutes as to partition of land not applicable, 653.

PARTNERSHIP—See title MINING PARTNERSHIP, and Chap. 30, 625.

PAYING QUANTITIES—DISCOVERY OF OIL AND GAS IN, Chap. 22, 487.
Additional drilling contingent on test well producing in, 497.
Cancellation of lease upon proof by lessor that lease is not producing in, 125-494-498-501.
    Not decreed for failure to further develop—when, 501.
Definition, 113-487-489.
Discovery of within term, 96-104.
Gas in, 216.
Indications of oil not, 102-490.
Leasehold not producing in—Tenancy at will, 110-496.
Lessee acting in good faith, judge as to, 487-489-490-497.
    Claiming that lease is producing in—Duties of, 498.
    Discovering gas, may pay rental and hold lease, 500.
    Discovering oil in must operate, 500.
    Entitled to hold lease while lease producing in, 500.
    Judge as to gas, 210-220-235-407.
    May prove that wells are producing in, 501.
    Must market gas if he can do so at profit, 499.

PAYING QUANTITIES—REMEDIES, Chap. 23, 498.
Lessee—Additional developments—when not required, 501.
    Judge as to, 500.
    Required to market gas—when, 500.
Lessor may declare forfeiture, when, 498-499.
Tenancy at will—Lease not producing in, 499.

PAYMENT OF RENTAL INTO BANK, Chap. 34, 696.
Acceptance by bank—effect, 707.
    Sufficient payment—when, 696.
    Past due rental binding on lessor, 702.
After abandonment will not prevent forfeiture, 699-707.

PAYMENT OF RENTAL INTO BANK—*Continued.*
After notice not to accept not binding on lessor, 704.
Annual rentals—when payable, 700.
Authorized by lease—prevents forfeiture 47-708.
Before expiration of rental period, 708.
Legal tender not required, 696.
Prevents forfeiture for time covered, 698.
Sufficient—when, 47-81-696-697-698-699-707.

PENNSYLVANIA RULE—Ejectment, 938.
Lease held to be license, 22-23-25-135.
Modification, 938.
Payment of Royalties—See title Several Tracts Under One Lease, and Chap. 50, 882.

PHYSICAL ABANDONMENT, 551.

PIPELINES—Exclusive right void—See title Exclusive Right to Lay, etc., Void as Against Public Policy, and Chap. 46, 814.
Gas is article of commerce when placed in, 742-744.
In highways, not nuisance, 797.
Negligence—See title Negligence, Injuries, etc., and Chap. 55, 944.
Pipeline Companies—Oil, See that title, and Chap. 57 1001.
Right of way not forfeited by abandoning explorations 547.
State may regulate pressure at which gas may be forced through, See that title, and Chap. 39, 745.

PIPELINE COMPANIES—OIL, Chap. 57, 1001.
Burning house—when not liable, 1003.
Bursting of pipeline—when not liable, 1003.
Consequential injuries—when liable for, 1001.
Corporations chartered to operate, 1001.
Destruction of springs—Liability, 1001.
Eminent Domain, 1001.
Escape of oil—Liability, 1001.
Incidental damages—Liability, 1005.
Injury resulting from operating, 1001.
Liability to owner for oil unlawfully extracted, 582.
Proximate cause, 1003.
Rights and Remedies, 1005.
Third persons injured, liability, 1005.

PLUGGING WELLS—Abandoned gas well, 805-807.
Compliance with Statute—what is, 748.
Statutes construed, 754.
Statutes Regulating—See title Waste and Transportation, etc., Chap. 39, 745.

POLICE POWER—Wasteful use of gas, 750-755.

POLLUTION—Due care required to prevent, 788-789.
See title Nuisance, and Chap. 44, 795.
See title Right to Operate, etc., and Chap. 43, 788.

POSSESSION,
Action by lessor—Proof required, 311.
Cannot be recovered by lessee after expiration of term, 119-123.
Exclusion of lessee—Breach of Implied Covnant, 90.
See title Remedy by Ejectment, and Chap. 54, 938.
Recovery, 288.
Lessee out of may file bill in equity, 518.
Lessee's possession for purpose of lease, 89-145.

POSSESSION—*Continued*.
Nature of easement, 222.
Lessor preventing lessee from taking, 123.
Limited to purpose and object of lease, 90-145.
Not necessary to bind lessee to pay rental, 16.
of gas, how obtained, 148-597.
of gas by lessee, not lost by shutting in well, 148.
 Obtained by connecting with lines 222.
 Protected in equity, 148.
of surface—vests no title in minerals reserved, 850-874-880.
 Not of minerals severed, 858-863-880.
 Not possession of oil and gas, 827.
 Under claim of title—no title to oil or gas, 827.
 Where minerals severed, 869.
Oil and gas in place—remains in landowner till brought to surface, 31.
Remedy—See title Remedy by Ejectment, and Chap. 54, 938.
Vendee or grantee has not of minerals reserved, 841.

POSSESSORY ACTION—Lessee may maintain, 288.

PRESUMPTION OF ABANDONMENT—When arises, 550.

PRESSURE—beyond statutory limitation—Injunction, 768.
 Gas, 946.
 State may regulate, 745-751.

PRIMA FACIE CASE—Negligence—When made, 982.

PRIOR LEASE, 385.

PROOF OF FORFEITURE BY ABANDONMENT, 552.

PRODUCING WELL—Exception of, 852.
 See title PAYING QUANTITIES—DISCOVERY OF OIL OR GAS IN, and Chap. 22, 487.

PRODUCTION—by lessee of one—co-tenant—Waste, 661.
 Right of vests upon discovery, 130.
 Tenant in common—when entitled to expenses, 665-672.

PRODUCTION AND MARKETING OF OIL AND GAS, 67-70-72.

PROTECTION OF LINES—Express covenants for, 410.
 Implied covenants for, 410.
 Lease cancelled for failure, (Ill.) 433.
 Lease cancelled for failure, 438.
 Lease not cancelled for breach of implied covenant for, 410.
 Remedy, See title REMEDIES AT LAW, etc., and Chap. 20, 453.
 Right to drill near division line—See that title, and Chap. 42, 782.

PROVISO—Performance, 103.

PROXIMATE CAUSE—Negligence presumed to be, 946.

PUBLIC POLICY—Exclusive Right to lay pipelines void—See title EXCLUSIVE RIGHT, etc., and Chap. 46, 814.

PUBLIC USE—Occupying streets to furnish gas, 984.

PUMPINGS, 782-792.

PURCHASE OF PREMISES DEMISED, 386.

PURCHASE OF REVERSION BY TENANT FOR YEARS, 346-348-349.

PURCHASER WITH NOTICE of Lessee in possession, 389.

PURPOSE OF GRANT, PREMISES DEMISED AND RIGHTS ACQUIRED, Chap. 5, 6[7].
    Discovery, 68.
    Entry for explorations, 68-86.
    Explorations, 68-142-533.
    Lessee acquires no title to oil or gas until produced, 87-88.
        Entitled to quiet enjoyment, 90-91.
        Restricted to purposes of lease, 90.
    Lessee's Remedy, 93.
    Lessor's Remedies, 92.
    Object of restrictions on lessee, 69.
    Production and marketing oil and gas, 67-70-72-82-142.
    Right of entry, 80.

QUESTION OF FACT—Abandonment, 688.
        Beginning operations, 732-735.
        Due diligence, 265.
        Negligence, 952-953.
        Paying Quantities, 110-124-499.

QUESTION OF LAW—Injunction, when title is, 600.

QUIETING TITLE—Lessee may maintain suit, 56-57.
        Plaintiff in possession of real estate may maintain suit, 586.
        Remedies—See that title and Chap. 51, 895.
        Title Affected by void lease, 607.
    Void lease will be cancelled in court of equity—See that title and Chap. 28, 601.

RATIFICATION—Action for accounting—Lease, 674.
        Demand for discovery and accounting—not, 666.
        of lease entitles non-joining tenant to accounting, 674.

REASONABLE TIME to re-enter for further explorations, 508-546-547.
        Usually question of fact, 702.

RECEIVER—895-899-900.
        Not appointed where title in dispute—when, 590.
        See title REMEDIES IN EQUITY, and Chap. 51, 895.

RECORDED LEASE—How surrendered, 335.
        Landowner—What entitled to, 344.

RE-ENTRY not necessary to effect forfeiture, 258.

REGULATORS AND APPLIANCES, 946-948-979.

RELEASE EXECUTED WITHOUT KNOWLEDGE OF LESSOR, 277.
    of Recorded Lease—Lessor may require, 344.

RELIEF FROM FORFEITURE, 548-926-927.
    Bill in equity may be filed for, 548.
    Conduct of lessor affording, 548.
    Defect in title of lessor affords, 548.
    Fraudulent default does not afford, 550.
    Full compensation affords, 520-470-550.

RELIEF FROM FORFEITURE—*Continued.*
 Lessor's conduct may afford, 416-471-478-483-510-548.
  Consent to non-payment of rentals, 288-549.
 Negligent default—grounds for, 550.
 Substantial compliance affords, 216-549.
 Technical forfeiture, 244-548.
 Waiver of forfeiture affords, 548-549.

REMEDY AT LAW—Equity jurisdiction, notwithstanding, 602.
  When exclusive, 905.
  When not adequate, 397.

REMEDY AT LAW FOR BREACHES BY LESSEE OF IMPLIED COVENANTS,
  Chap. 20, 453.
 Action for damages, 453-454-456-457.
  Failure to further develop, 454.
  Failure to protect lines or develop, 453-456-457-458-459-462-464-465-466.
 Gas wells—failure to drill additional, not actionable, 194-465.
 General Rule, 467.
 Lessor—when may sue, 465.
 Measure of damages—failure to fully develop, 455.
 Ohio rule, 456.
  U. S. Courts, 465.
 Pennsylvania Rule, 463.
 West Virginia Rule, 457-459-462.
  U. S. Courts, 466.

REMEDY BY EJECTMENT, Chap. 54, 938.
 Land not rented—Action for damages, 938-939.
 Lessee excluded after entry, 938.
  Out of possession, 938.
  With exclusive right to produce, 938.
 Pennsylvania Rule, 938.
 When no, 941.

REMEDIES IN EQUITY, Chap. 51, 895.
 Abandonment—How proven, 904.
  May be proven in suit for cancellation, 902.
 Bill for accounting, (*Stone* v. *Marshall*) 917.
 Cancellation of forfeited void lease, 898.
  of lease for failure to perform covenants, 905.
 Co-tenants enjoined from producing, 897.
 Forfeiture not enforced, 911.
 Injunction, 917.
  to prevent removal of oil and gas, 518.
 Jurisdiction, although remedy at law, 905.
  Grounds of, 896.
  to settle all questions, 895-901.
 Lessee in possession of gas, 917.
  Out of possession, 518.
  With exclusive privileges, 915.
 Principles cancellation of lease, 909-910.
 Receiver—Advances to—when refunded, 900.
  Attorneys for—How paid, 899.
  Compensation of—How paid, 899.
  May be appointed, 899-900.
 Relief from technical forfeiture, 911.
 Specific performance, when decreed, 898.
 Title—No jurisdiction to settle, 897.
 Vested rights—protected, 898.

1046 INDEX.

REMEDIES IN EQUITY FOR BREACHES BY LESSEE OF IMPLIED COVE-
    NANTS, Chap. 19, 437.
  Action to cancel lease—Proof necessary, 453.
  California Rule, 439.
  Cancellation of lease, 437-438.
      For failure to develop or protect lines, 439.
      For fraudulent evasion of implied covenants, 439-441.
      What proof necessary, 439.
  Declaration of forfeiture for failure to develop, 437.
      Lessee holding for speculative purposes, 437.
  Illinois Rule, 439-444.
  Indiana Rule, 446-448.
      Kansas Rule, 444.
  Lessee must develop within reasonable time, 437.
      Remedies and Defenses, 453.
  Ohio Rule, 444, 446, 451.
  Pennsylvania Rule, 445.
  Receivership, 438.
  Specific Performance, 438.
  Texas Rule, 439-444.
  West Virginia Rule, 444.

REMAINDERMAN—See title LIFE TENANTS AND REMAINDERMEN, and Chap. 35, 709.
      May maintain bill for accounting, 600.
      May maintain bill in equity to enjoin life tenant, 598-599.

REMOVAL OF FIXTURES—See title FIXTURES.
      See title RIGHT TO REMOVE FIXTURES, etc., and Chap. 9, 150.

RENTAL,
  Acceptance after expiration of term, 702.
      After forfeiture, 244.
      For delay precludes forfeiture, 86.
      In advance waives forfeiture, 201-206.
  Acts conduct and dealings of lessor, 467.
  Acquiescence in delay in payment, 94.
  Assignee—Lessor may recover from, 360.
  Assignment by one joint tenant, 664.
  Cannot be collected under lease by remainderman, 601.
      Recovered by infants—when, 674.
      Recovered by life tenant, 601-729.
  Conveyance of premises ends liability for, 271.
  Failure to pay alone, not forfeiture—when, 205-334.
      Entitles lessor to declare forfeiture, 237-283-514.
  Gas rental—When clause becomes operative, 496.
      When lessee not liable for, 193.
  Lease—express promise entitles lessor to recover during term, 237-247-250-251
    256-258-283.
      Must contain promise to authorize recovery, 16.
  Leasehold proven dry—no defense, 262.
  Lessee bound to pay after accepting lease, 16.
      Although never in possession, 16-84.
      Cannot refuse to pay and hold lease, 279.
      Failure of to pay no defense, 245-247-250-258-269-270-326.
      May surrender lease, and avoid further payment of, 289.
      Non-performance does not discharge, 282.
      Not liable after drilling dry hole, and abandonment, 693-696.
      Where option to pay or develop, 290-292-294.
      See title FORFEITURE AND RENTAL CLAUSE—LESSEE'S OPTION and Chap. 13,
    290.

RENTAL—*Continued.*
   Lessor cannot recover after executing second lease, 284.
      in absence of express promise, 291-292-294-295-303-320-321.
      May refuse to accept after unreasonable delay, 321.
      May terminate lease upon failure to pay—See title FORFEITURE AND RENTAL
        CLAUSE—LESSOR'S OPTION, and Chap. 12, 237.
   Life tenants—See title LIFE TENANTS AND REMAINDERMEN, and Chap. 35, 709.
   Non-payment by consent of lessor—not forfeiture, 288-549.
   Paid after forfeiture need not be tendered in rescission suit, 527.
   Payable annually accrues at end of year, 313-317-476.
   Payable at any time during rental period, 708.
   Payment after expiration of term does not revive lease, 96-108-113.
      Entitles lessee to hold during term, 93.
      Into bank—See title PAYMENT OF RENTAL INTO BANK, and Chap. 34, 696.
      Into Bank—Sufficient when authorized by lease, 287.
      Under void lease—Lessee not entitled to royalties, 609.
   Reasonable notice of intention to forfeit, 201-205.
   Refusal to accept after due is declaration of forfeiture, 277.
      at beginning of rental period, effect, 206.
   Rental or commutation money consideration for delay, 44.
   Return of upon cancellation of lease—Not required, 577.
   Surrender—effect of—See title SURRENDER.
   Tenants in common—one of may receipt for entire, 664-674.
   Tender after abandonment—lease not revived, 514.
      May be made in bill, 313.
      When need not be made, 313.
   Uniform construction cannot be pleaded, 266.
   Void—Lease containing no promise to pay is, 608.
   Waiver of forfeiture, See that title, and Chap. 21, 467.

RENTAL FOR GAS—See title GAS.
      See title CONSIDERATION FOR GRANT OF MINERALS—GAS, and Chap. 11, 189.

RENTAL PERIOD,
   Distinguished from term, 122.
   May be waived or modified during term, 122.
   Subject to modification by oral contract, 21.
   Waiver or modification of, need not be in writing, 122.
   When rental may be paid at any time during, 708.

RESCISSION—Lessor not bound to sue for, when, 308.

RESERVATION—Exception distinguished from, 874.
      of a part of lands leased—construction, 11.
      Same effect as exception, 579.

RESERVATION AROUND BUILDINGS, Chap. 10, 170.
   Accounting for drilling upon, 185.
   Construction, 170-183.
   Damages—How estimated, 177.
   Ejectment does not lie for, 174.
   Injunction for protection of, 173-175-187-188.
   Lessee charged with notice of possession in another, 181.
      Has right of way over, 172.
      Has right to oil from, 170, 183.
      May enjoin lessor from drilling on, 173-175-182.
      May recover from lessor for drilling upon, 188.
      Restricted to certain cites may enjoin others from drilling, 177-182.
   Lessor cannot drill upon, 170-180.
      cannot lease to others, 170.
   Limitation upon privilege of drilling, 171-172-187.

RESERVATION AROUND BUILDINGS—*Continued.*
Measure of damages for oil taken from, 175.
    Difference in value of leasehold before and after injury, 177.
Not reservation of oil and gas, 187.
Object of—protection from fire, 170-180.
Protection for lessee—How construed, 185.
Remedies—Lessees, 187-188.
    Lessors, 187.

RESERVATION IN DEED OF ALL MINERALS INCLUDES PETROLEUM OIL
       AND NATURAL GAS, Chap. 47, 826.
Conveyance of surface does not include oil and gas, 830.
Deed conveying land, reserving mineral is severance, 832.
    Reserving all minerals does not convey oil and gas, 827.
Injunction against surface owner, 832.
Possession of surface not of oil and gas, 827.
Remedies, 834.
Reservation includes oil and gas, 826.
    See title RESERVATION OF OIL AND GAS, and Chap. 49, 841
Title to oil and gas not acquired by possession of surface, 827.

RESERVATION IN DEED OF ALL MINERALS OR CONVEYANCE BY DEED
       OF ALL MINERALS IN LAND DOES NOT RESERVE OR CONVEY
       OIL OR GAS, Chap. 48, 834.
Gas, 835.
Oil, 839.
Oil and gas, 836.
Question of intention, 834-835-836-837.
Remedies, 840.
Reservation—See title RESERVATION OF OIL AND GAS, and Chap. 49, 841.

RESERVATION OF OIL AND GAS, Chap. 49, 841.
Assessment of surface presumed to include, 841-843-857-863.
Cancellation by lessee and subsequent purchaser—effect, 874.
Conflicting claimants—What may be proven, 882.
Construed same as reservation of other minerals, 879.
Conveyance of land reserving outstanding lease, 874.
    of minerals a severance, 850.
    of oil or gas, held to be lease, 854.
Deed reserving all minerals does not pass title to oil and gas, 874.
    Oil or gas does not pass title to these minerals, 578-847.
Drilling through coal cannot be enjoined, 867-868.
    When equity will enjoin, 867-868.
Estate in coal determined upon removal, 867.
Exception distinguished from reservation, 874.
    of producing well, 852.
    Same as grant, 871.
    What constitutes in deed, 874.
Grant of coal does not carry underlying strata, 867.
    of minerals same as exception, 871.
    of surface does not carry minerals, 860.
Included in reservation of all minerals, 857-874.
Legal effect, 864.
Lessee of land subject to reservation may deduct royalty, 864.
    of surface subject to exception, 864.
Lessor—Subsequent conveyance of premises, reserving lease—Effect, 874.
Lower Strata—Regulations for reaching legislative question, 867.
Not subject to forfeiture for non-assessment, 857.
    Taxation in absence of statute, 848-876-881.
Owner entitled to operate and develop, 841-880.
    May enjoin surface owner, 881.

RESERVATION OF OIL AND GAS—*Continued.*
    May convey oil and gas, 841.
    May lease or sell, 841-880.
    May reserve oil and gas, 841-863.
    Not barred by Statute of Limitations—when, 841.
    Possession of surface draws to it possession of minerals—when, 869.
        Title to minerals not vested—when, 850-874-880.
        When not in possession of minerals, 858-863-880.
    Prescriptive title not acquired by possession of surface, 874.
    Remedies, 879.
    Sale of land subject to lease already made—royalty not conveyed, 840.
        For taxes passes reservation—when, 848-882.
    Sale of undivided interest in—voidable, 854-879.
        For taxes, cancelled, 881.
    Separate estate created by, 848.
    Severance in deed—what constitutes, 871.
    Statute of Limitations affecting, 841-869.
    Subsequent purchaser with constructive notice, 874.
    Surface owner—Right to drill through coal, 867.
        Right to reach underlying strata, 867.
        To divest title must have actual possession, 858-863.
    Surface and minerals may be severed, 871.
    Undivided interest in—not subject to separate taxation, 854-877.
    Vendee under deed conveying surface—when not in possession, 841.

RESERVATION FOR FARMING PURPOSES, Chap. 8, 144.
    Landowner—Rights of, 144.
    Lessee's Remedies, 147.
    Lessor's Remedies, 145.

RESIDENCE—Drilling well near, when not nuisance, 795-797.

RES IPSA LOQUITUR, 948.

RIGHT OF WAY—Agreement for exclusive, good between parties for, 817.
    Exclusive to lay pipelines, void—See title EXCLUSIVE RIGHT, etc., and
        Chap. 46, 814.

RIGHT TO DRILL NEAR DIVISION LINE—DRAINAGE, Chap. 42, 782.
    Adjoining owners—Remedies, 784-787-788.
    Collusive drilling near, 782.
    Division line—owner of land may drill near, 782.
    Lessee holding leases on both sides—Duty, 782.
        Must protect lines, 784.
        or owner entitled to produce of well near, 787.
    "Protecting lines" what is, 784.
    Remedies, 787- 788.

RIGHT TO OPERATE OIL AND GAS WELLS EVEN WHERE INJURY RESULTS,
        Chap. 43, 788.
    Cattle— Damage to, 789.
    Course of water, 792.
    Crops—Damage to, 789.
    Damages— Precautions against, 792.
        to property—Lessee not liable, 788, 789.
    Damnum Absque Injuria, 790.
    Due care required to prevent pollution, 789.
    Flowage—Right of landowner, 792.
    Increase of volume of water, 792.
    Knowledge of streams, 790.
    Land—Damage to, 789.

RIGHT TO OPERATE OIL AND GAS WELLS, ETC.—*Continued.*
  Lower landowner—Rights, 792.
  Overflow—care to prevent, 792.
  Pollution of wated by enjoyment of wells, 789.
      by salt water or oil, 788.
  Pumpings, 792.
  Remedies for injuries, 793-794.
  Subterranean and surface water distinguished, 790.
  Subterranean waters—When liable for pollution, 790.
  Upper landowner—Rights, 792.
  Water well—Liability for injury to, 790.

RIGHT TO PRODUCE vests in lessee upon discovery, 27-29.

RIGHT TO REMOVE FIXTURES PLACED UPON THE LEASEHOLD FOR EX-
      PLORATION and development purposes, Chap. 9, 150.
  "At any time" means reasonable time, 161.
  Do not become part of freehold, 157, 161.
  Ejectment cannot be maintained to remove, 153.
  Failure to remove within reasonable time vests title in lessor, 150-151-164.
  Fixtures defined, 151.
  Forfeiture of lease does not forfeit fixtures, 161.
  Injunction to restrain lessee from cutting off gas supply, 165.
  Lessee cannot appropriate when lease under which placed is cancelled, 151-156.
      Cannot remove and cut off gas for domestic purposes, 154.
      Converting fixtures placed by another liable in damages, 169.
      Has reasonable time after termination of lease to remove, 156-164.
      May remove during term or within reasonable time thereafter, 151.
      Must remove within reasonable time after expiration of term, 164.
      Remedies, 168-169.
      Whose lease is cancelled entitled to remove fixtures, 156.
  Lessor liable for conversion—When, 153-169.
      Remedies, 163-168.
      Terminating lease within term not entitled to fixtures, 153.
  Possession of—When may be recovered, 169.
  Reasonable time for removal—Question of fact, 156.
  Right to remove, 150.
  Title to—does not vest in lessor when lessee abandons premises, 161.
  Trade Fixtures—What are, 151.
  When become property of landowner, 150-151-164.

ROYALTIES
  Covenants to pay run with land, 366.
  Division orders to set aside, 143.
  Essence of lease, 305.
  Failure to pay not grounds of forfeiture, 214.
  Joint lease—To whom payable, 886- 889.
  Joint tenant entitled only to proportional, 662-672.
  Lessee of land subject to reservation may deduct royalty reserved, 864.
      Under void lease not entitled to, 609.
  Lessor may recover from assignee—When, 380-384.
  Moving cause for execution of lease, 9.
  Must be divided among all owners, 672.
  Purchaser of infant's interest must pay stipulated, 673.
  Receipt and delivery of, consideration for oil, 129.
  Rights of life tenant and remainder man, See title LIFE TENANTS AND REMAINDER-
      MEN, and Chap. 35, 709.
  Sale of land subject to outstanding lease—does not convey, 842.
  Several tracts under one lease—How Lessee may hold, 886-887.
      See that title and Chap. 50, 882.

RULE OF PROPERTY
Implied covenant for full development and protection of lines (Ohio), 465.
Lease is not a grant of property in oil or gas, 430.
Lessee cannot hold lease for speculative purposes, 7.

SALE
Grantor not bound to remove cloud on title, when, 342-615.
Lease conditional and contingent, 83.
Sale of option to develop, 613.
To be surrendered if detrimental to, 451.
Of leased premises terminates void lease, 615-617-623.

SALT WATER—Pollution by, 788.

SANITY OF GRANTOR presumed, 726.

SECOND LESSEE of tenant in common—When enjoined, 677.
Takes subject to prior lessee in possession, 664.
With notice of prior lease, 385.

SECOND OR JUNIOR LEASE,
Acceptance operates as surrender of prior, 345- 346.
Construction, where made subject to prior, 285-519.
Execution of not forfeiture of prior, 917.
Sufficient declaration of forfeiture, 49-240-267-284-537.
Terminates prior void lease—See title WANT OF MUTUALITY, and Chap. 29-608.
Lessee under may cause prior lease to be cancelled, 123.
Lessor executing cannot recover rentals under first lease, 284.
Prior lease void, lessee under not entitled to royalties under, 609.
Prior lessee may cause to be cancelled, 123.
Subject to prior lease—not declaration of forfeiture, 242- 285.

SEVERAL TRACTS UNDER ONE LEASE, Chap. 50, 882.
Conveyance to separate grantees, 883.
Demise before discovery of oil or gas, 882.
Devisees entitled to proportional royalty, 883-885.
Grantees entitled to royalty from own tracts, 887-888.
Joint lessors for one royalty, 883-886.
Lessor's remedies, 893-894.
Royalties—How paid, Ohio Rule, 887-893.
Penna. Rule, 882-883-884.
West Va. Rule, 886-889-893.

SEVERANCE—Conveyance of surface is of oil and gas, 830.
See title RESERVATION OF OIL AND GAS, and Chap. 49, 841.

SHOOTING WELL, Chap. 37, 737.
Accident not proof of negligence, 740.
Burden of proof on owner to establish negligence, 737-738-741.
Contractor not liable for damages—when, 738.
Proof to escape liability, 741.
Injunction to prevent, 779-799.
Injury alone does not warrant recovery, 741.
To well, 737.
Negligence—Owner must prove, 737.
Owner may recover for, 741.
Nitro-Glycerine to increase flow, See that title, and Chap. 41, 778.
Remedy of owner, 741.
Torpedo company, 741.

SIGNATURE OF LESSEE NOT NECESSARY, 16-21.

SPECULATIVE PURPOSES—Lease cannot be held for, 7-437.
    Lessee holding for—Liable to lessor in damages, 465.

SPECIFIC PERFORMANCE,
    Surrender at any time, defeats, 539-520-521.
    Unfair or unconscienable lease not enforced, 521-610-624.
    Want of mutuality no defense where covenants performed, 620-622.
    When plaintiff has no adequate remedy at law, 898.

SPRINGS— Destruction of—Oil, 1001.
    See title NUISANCE and Chap 44, 795.
    See title RIGHT TO OPERATE, etc., and Chap. 43, 788.

STATE,
    Cannot forbid transportation of gas from, 742.
    Pressure of gas regulated, 745-751.
    Waste of gas enjoined, 746.
        Forbidden, 745, 756.

STATUTE,
    Forbidding waste of gas, 745.
        Not contrary to Fourteenth Amendment, 747.
    Pressure of gas, 767-768.
    Prohibiting transportation of gas from state unconstitutional, 742-744.
        Use of gas pump, 761-766-767.
    Regulating transportation of gas, 745.
    Violation of, as to gas, 958-962-981.
    Waste and transportation—See that title, and Chap. 39, 745.

STATUTE OF LIMITATIONS,
    Applied to reservations, 841.
    When begins to run in action for accounting, 678.
    When runs in favor of one in possession of surface, 869.
    Will not bar owner of reservation, 841-869.

SUBTERRANEAN SPRING, Pollution of, 790.

SURFACE,
    And minerals may be severed, 871.
    Conveyance of does not include oil or gas, 830-860.
    Lessee of subject to exception and reservation, 864.
    Owner has right to reach lower strata, 867.
    Reservation of oil and gas—See that tile and Chap. 49-841.
    Rights of lessee, 89.

SURRENDER,
    Acceptance of new lease for same land—surrender of first, 345.
    By one of several lessees—abandonment, 552.
    By parol, 514.
    In accordance with lease, 345.
    Lessor may recover rentals to date of, 343.
    Lessor's rights—when not affected by, 882.
    Notice to lessor sufficient—of unrecorded lease, 335.
    Of lease if detrimental to sale, 481.
    Of recorded lease must be in writing, 335.
    Of unrecorded lease need not be in writing, 335.

SURRENDER CLAUSE OF THE OIL AND GAS LEASE, Chap. 14, 322.
    Cancellation in equity not authorized, 337.

SURRENDER CLAUSE OF THE OIL AND GAS LEASE—*Continued.*
Consideration for, 322.
    For lease, affecting, 331.
    Sufficient to support, 324-341.
Deprives plaintiff of specific performance, 329.
Held valid, 322.
Is lessee's shield. 332.
Lease with—bars specific performance, 620.
    Does not create tenacy at will, 341.
    Not void, 322-332-333-334.
    Not void for want of mutuality, 322-337-339-341-619.
    Void for want of mutuality, 328-329-341-342.
Lessee may terminate lease before end of term, 325.
    May surrender or pay rentals, 345.
    Must exercise rights promptly, 323.
    Rights under, 322-323.
    Surrender in accordance with lease, 345.
Lessor cannot declare forfeiture, 345.
Modern oil and gas lease contains, 232.
Must be upon valuable consideration. 323-324.
Nominal consideration sufficient to support, 345.
Object, 323.
One dollar sufficient to support, 339.
Option (Ohio) 324.
Recorded lease—How surrendered, 335.
Remedies—Lessees, 344.
    Lessors, 343.
Rental—future discharged, 331.
    Past due not affected, 323-325.
    Tenancy at will not created by, 337.
    Unrecorded lease—How surrendered, 335.

TAKING OF PROPERTY—Statutory Regulations as to gas, not, 751.

TAXATION,
Lease not subject to in absence of Statute, 848.
Of surface includes oil and gas. 841-843-857-863.
Reservation not subject of forfeiture for non-entry, 857.
Not subject to in absence of statute, 848-876-881.
Tax sale of land passes title to. 848-882.
    Undivided interest in, voidable, 854-879.
    When cancelled in equity, 881.

TENANCY AT WILL,
Lease is after expiration of term, not producing in paying quantities, 499.
For definite term, to terminate at lessee's option, not, 113.
Void for want of mutuality is, 608-609.
Leasehold is when not producing in paying quantities, 110-196-499.
Not created by lease, 281.

TENANCY FROM YEAR TO YEAR—Lease held to be, 111-115-317.

TENANT AT WILL—Lessee is after expiration of term, 96, 499.

TENANTS IN COMMON OR JOINT TENANTS—RIGHT TO EXECUTE OIL AND
    GAS LEASE OR DEVELOP, Chap. 32, 660.
Accounting, 661.
    Basis of, 665.
    What should be included in, 678.
    When statute of Limitations begins to run, 678.
All must join in lease, 660.

TENANTS IN COMMON OR JOINT TENANTS—*Continued.*
Bonus recoverable upon ratification, 674.
Committing waste are wrongdoers, 668.
  Liable jointly or severally, 667.
Declaration of forfeiture binding on infants, 674-675-676.
Dower—Right of holder, 668-671-727.
Injunction—Production and marketing, 879.
Joint lessees are not, 514.
Lease by one binding on parties, 657-660-661-663-664.
  Cannot be avoided, lessee willing to accept title, 662.
  Implied covenants in, 662.
  Void as to non-joining, 657-660-661-663.
Lessees before discovery of oil are not, 514.
  Of one cannot have partition, 339-663-664-673.
  Entitled to operate—not to exclusive possession, 664.
  Has no right to operate—when, 657-664.
  Liable to non-joining, 661.
  May be enjoined, 661-672.
  May maintain injunction—when, 662-673.
  Not entitled to cost of unproductive wells, 672.
Non-consenting—Rights of, 668.
Non-joining—May enjoin operations, 661-672.
  Ratification by—Effect, 674.
  Rights of, 665.
One in sole possession—Rights of, 661.
Producing in good faith—Rights of, 665-672.
Production by lessee of one constitutes waste, 661.
Ratification of lease—Action for accounting, 674.
  By non-joining—Effect, 674.
Demand for discovery and accounting not, 666.
Remedy of co-owner, 671-672.
  Lessee, 672-673-674.
  Of non-joining, 671.
  See title OIL AND GAS IN PLACE, etc., and Chap. 27, 558.
Rental—Assignment of by one—effect 664.
  Can be recovered only by ratifying lease, 666-678.
  Cannot be recovered by infants, when, 674.
  May be paid to one of, 664-674.
Royalties proportioned among, 662-672.
  Purchaser of infants interests must pay agreed, 673.
Second lessee—when enjoined, 673.
Statute of Limitations—Accounting, 678.
Waste—Taking by one is, 661-665-668.
  To whom accountable, 661.

TENDER,
Of rental after abandonment—lease not revived, 514.
  In bill or petition, 313.
  When sufficient, 911.

TERM OF THE OIL AND GAS LEASE, Chap. 6, 96.
Acceptance of rental after expiration, effect, 702.
Defined, 96-97.
Discovery of oil or gas within, Lessee's rights, 97-125.
  After expiration does not extend, 690.
Expenses of drilling—when not recovered, 736.
Explorations must be made within, 96-97-118-121-124.
Failure to complete well within terminates lease, 97-98-99-100.
Fixes life of lease, 97.
Indications of oil not sufficient to extend, 490.
In General, 96.

TERM OF OIL AND GAS LEASE—*Continued.*
Lease providing for "wells"—term not extended by one well, 121.
Lessee enjoined entitled to extension—when, 681.
    Excluded—Rights of, 123.
    Holding beyond—Injunction, 96-124-586.
    May hold during by payment of rentals, 93-111-113-115-116.
    Tenant at will after, 96.
Oil or gas must be discovered within, 96-97-104-108.
Paying quantities—Proof of in cancellation suit, 125.
    Time found in fixes term, 106-110-113.
Remedies, 122-123.
    Lessee's, 125-126.
    Lessor's, 124-125.
Rental acceptance does not create new term, 702.
    Failure to pay terminates lease, 96.
    Payment of will not extend, 96-97-100-101-103-104-108-113.
Rental period distinguished from term, 122.

TEST WELL,
Completed within time—effect, 302.
Dry—Effect of, 10-688.
Lessee entitled to time fixed, 302.
Must be drilled within time, 302.

TEXAS RULE—Lease held to be license, 37.
    Nominal consideration for lease, 299.

TIME—Date of lease excluded in computing, 216.

TITLE,
Assignee without notice takes good, 372-576.
Color of—Production under, 945.
Conflicting—not settled in equity, 897.
    When receiver not appointed, 590.
Defect in lessor's—Breach of implied covenants, 424.
    Relief from forfeiture, 548.
Dispute in—when injunction awarded, 599-600.
Drilling dry hole vests none, 680.
Equity has no jurisdiction to settle, 588-599.
Injunction when question of law, 600.
Lessee may sue in equity to quiet, 57.
Lessee's inchoate and contingent, 73-80-142.
Vested—Abandonment—Statute of Limitations, 77.
    Oil and gas stands on different grounds, 77.

TITLE TO OIL AND GAS,
Deed reserving all Minerals does not pass, 874.
    Includes, See that title and Chap. 47, 826.
    Does not include, See that title and Chap. 48, 834.
Inchoate and contingent until discovered 135.
Indications of oil not sufficient, 490.
In place in owner of land, 582.
Lessee has none to oil and gas in place, 89, 140.
Not acquired by possession of surface, 827.
Oil and gas in place—See that title, and Chap. 27, 558.
Prescriptive—not acquired by possession of surface, 874.
Remains in lessor until brought to surface, 31.
Reservation of oil and gas—See that title, and Chap. 49, 841.
Vests in lessee when, 18-29-32-80-87-140-337.

TRANSPORTATION,
Of gas held to be interstate commerce, 742-743-744.
  See title NATURAL GAS ARTICLE OF COMMERCE, etc., and Chap. 38, 742.
Statutes prohibiting—from State held unconstitutional, 742-744.
Statutory Regulation—See title WASTE AND TRANSPORTATION, and Chap. 39, 745.

TRESPASSER,
Charged with total value of oil or gas taken, 94-95.
Liability determined by good or bad faith, 33-35-38-39-89-91.

TWO OR MORE INSTRUMENTS OF SAME DATE, Construction, 13.

UNAUTHORIZED USE OF PREMISES—Effect on rentals, 577.

UNCERTAINTY IN DESCRIPTION, 161-446-447-448.

UNDRILLED Portions of Leasehold—Lease construed, 446-447-448.

UNILATERAL LEASE, 21.
Not binding lessee void for want of mutuality, 615.

UNLAWFUL EXTRACTION of oil does not divest title, 582.
  See title INJUNCTION.
Irreparable Injury, 587-588-591.

UNPRODUCTIVE WELL—See title DRY HOLE—EFFECT OF DRILLING, and Chap.
  33, 680.

UNREASONABLE DELAY in Explorations, 321-531.

UNRECORDED LEASE—How surrendered, 335.

UNSUCCESSFUL SEARCH—Abandonment of— Forfeiture, 504-551-557.
  Abandonment of—Lessee's Rights cease, 140-141.

VAGRANT CHARACTER OF OIL AND GAS, 19.

VALUABLE CONSIDERATION, though nominal, 66.

VESTED ESTATE,
None until discovery, 29-142.
Not divested in equity, 923.
Not ordinarily lost by abandonment, 30-77.
  Oil lease on different basis, 77.
Upon discovery, 30-130-142-143-220-412-546-547.

VESTED RIGHT,
By discovery not lost by drilling deeper, 216.
How may be lost, 216-547.
To produce protected in equity, 989.
  Upon discovery, 29-30-82-216-220-227-546-547-600-601.
  When not divested, 403-404.

VOID LEASE WILL BE CANCELLED IN A COURT OF EQUITY, Chap. 28, 601.
Cancellation, 601- 603-604-605.
Drilling under, 602.
Equity will retain cause for all purposes, 602.
Injunction—Operations, 602-606-607.
Lessee entering without authority—Injunction, 601.
  May cause to be cancelled, 604-606.
Lessor pemitting developments cannot cancel, 602-603.

VOID LEASE, ETC.—*Continued.*
Oil taken under, 602.
Remedies, 607.
Remedy at law not exclusive, 602.
Suit for cancellation—All interested parties should be before court, 607.

WAIVER OF FORFEITURE OF OIL AND GAS LEASE, Chap. 21, 467.   ·
Acceptance of part of rental is, 469-470.
    Rental after forfeiture is, 244-475-476.
    In advance is, 473-475-476.
Acquiescence by lessor in beginning operations—when not, 734.
    In delay is, 94-116-286-467-469.
Acts, conduct and declarations of lessor, 416-468-471-472-475-478-483-501-548.
Beginning operations with consent of lessor, is, 432.
Consent that rental need not be paid when due, is, 286.
Failure to demand development, 486.
    To exercise right promptly is, 470.
Forfeiture clause affecting, 468.
    See RELIEF FROM FORFEITURE, 548.
Indulging lessee, 469-470.
Injunction to protect lessee, 483.
Lessor accepting rental after forfeiture incurred cannot declare without demand
    or notice, 244.
Lessor's conduct may amount to, 244.
    Consent that rental need not be paid when due, 244.
Lessor may waive forfeiture and enforce covenants, 161.
Lessor's Option, 468.
Notice affecting, 478-480.
Remedies—Lessee—See title FORFEITURE BY ABANDONMENT—LESSEE'S REMEDY, and
    Chap. 25, 546.
    See title RELIEF FROM FORFEITURE, 548.
Remedies—Lessor, 486.
Strict performance not required is, 468.
Use of gas for domestic purposes is, 481.
What constitutes, 486-487.
Within term—Execution of new lease not required, 116.

WANT OF MUTUALITY, Chap. 29, 608.
Construction of lease by parties, 613.
Death of lessor terminates lease void for, 343-623.
Execution of second lease terminates lease void for, 343-623.
Executory lease not binding lessee—void for, 609.
Inadequacy of consideration—Lease not void for, 612.
Lease containing surrender clause, not void for, 339.
    For good consideration, not void for, 611-613.
    Held on its face not void for, 342.
    Option from year to year, not void for, 615.
    Terminable at will of lessee—How terminated, 611-623.
    Terminable at will of lessee, void for, 611.
    Void for valid after entry or payment of rental, 333-612-620-664.
    Creates mere tenancy at will, 343.
    May be terminated by lessor at any time before entry, 343-520-521-522-616.
    When one party not bound to performance, 49-342-520-521-537-609-620.
    May be terminated at will of either party, 608-614-615.
    When void for, 608.
    Which is unfair, unjust and against good conscience, 49-610.
    Unfair, unjust and against good conscience—not enforceable in equity, 624.
    Without consideration void for, 343-608-609.
Lessee may enter and hold lease subject to conditions, 344-664
    May enter and make explorations under lease void for, 612-620-624-664.

WANT OF MUTUALITY—*Continued.*
 Lessee's option to terminate before expiration of term—Lease not rendered void
   for, 612.
 Lessor accepting rental cannot declare forfeiture during time covered, 344.
   Cannot declare forfeiture after permitting lessee to enter, 344-624.
   May terminate lease void for before lessee enters, 343-520-521-522-616-622-623.
 No defense where covenants have been performed, 620-622.
 One dollar sufficient consideration, 341-612.
   Not sufficient consideration, 620.
 Remedy of lessee, 624-625.
   Lessor, 622-623.
 Sale of land terminates lease void for, 343-615-623.
 Second lessee cannot question prior lease—When, 664.
 Specific performance not decreed, 610.
 Surrender clause does not render lease void for, 619-620.
 Unilateral lease not binding lessee to do anything, void for, 615.
 When lease is void for, 608-617.

WASTE,
 Accounting—Basis—Tenants in Common or joint tenants, 665.
 Definition, 558.
 Equity will enjoin, 314.
 Gas—See title WASTE AND TRANSPORTATION—STATUORY REGULATION, and Chap.
   39, 745.
   See title WASTE OF, MALICIOUSLY OR NEGLIGENTLY, and Chap. 45, 805.
 Injunction for by injured party, 756-758-759-760.
 Life tenant converting oil or gas, guilty of, 600-711.
 Public nuisance—when waste of gas is, 746.
 Remainderman—accounting for waste, 559-600.
 Statutes forbidding—of gas, constitutional, 747.
 Tenants in Common or joint tenants guilty of, 661-665-668.
   May be sued jointly or severally, 668.
   See TENANTS IN COMMON OR JOINT TENANTS, etc., and Chap. 32-660.

WASTE AND TRANSPORTATION OF NATURAL GAS—STATUTORY REG-
   ULATION, Chap. 39, 745.
 Abandoned well—Plugging, 748.
 Demurrer questioning State's capacity to sue, 746.
 Escape of gas—owners liable for, 755.
 Flambeau lights—Statute forbidding constitutional, 749.
   Use of continuing offense, 750.
   Wasteful use of gas, 749.
 Indana Statutes, 746-747-749-750-751.
 Injunction to prevent waste, 746.
 Injured party may enjoin, 756-758-759-760.
 Judicial notice that gas is inflammable, 751.
 Kentucky Statutes, 754-755.
 Lessee cannot cut off supply, by waste, 756.
 Limiting pressure—Not interstate commerce, 751.
 Ohio Statutes, 748.
 Opening well for repairs not waste, 760.
 Penalties for waste of gas, 745.
 Plugging well—Compliance with Statute—What is, 748.
   Statutes construed, 754.
 Police Power—Forbidding waste of gas within, 750-755.
 Reasonable use, 756.
 Regulation of use of gas, not taking of property, 751.
 Remedies, 760.
 State may enjoin, 746.
   May forbid, 745-756.
   May regulate pressure, 745-751.

WASTE AND TRANSPORTATION, ETC.—*Continued.*
  Statutes forbidding escape of—constitutional, 746-747-750.
    Waste—constitutional, 746-747-750.
    . Waste, not contrary to Fourteenth Amendment, 747.
  Waste of gas—when public nuisance, 746.

WASTE OF GAS MALICIOUSLY OR NEGLIGENTLY, Chap. 45, 805.
  Abandonment of gas well—Duty to plug, 805-807.
  Actionable at common law, 808.
  Damages, 809-811.
    Measure of, 812.
  Punitive may be recovered, 812.
  Draining well not waste, 805.
  Escape of gas—Lessee liable, 807.
  Exhaustion by legal use not, 809.
  Gas—when may be permitted to escape, 805.
  Illegal waste—Liability, 809.
  Injunction, 811.
  Injured party may recover for, 809.
  Liability based upon malice or negligence, 806.
  Plugging abandoned gas well, 805-807.
  Remedies, 813.
  Statutes forbidding—See titleWASTE AND TRANSPORTATION, etc., and Chap. 39, 745.

WATER WELL—When lessee liable for injury, 790.

WELLS,
  Agreement to drill second—no consideration for lease, 520.
  Already opened may be worked by life tenant, 712-720.
  Drilling on another tract sufficient consideration, 681.
  New—cannot be drilled by life tenants, 709-712-717-720.
  Right to operate—See title RIGHT TO OPERATE, etc., and Chap. 43, 788.
  Shooting Well—See that title, and Chap. 37, 737.
  Specified number contingent upon test well producing, 497.
    Lessee required to drill, 447.

WEST VIRGINIA RULE, Several Tracts under One Lease, 893.

WIDOW—not entitled to market oil and gas, 594.

WORDS AND PHRASES,
  "Abandonment," 431-861.
  "All Minerals," 437.
  "As much longer thereafter as oil and gas shall be found in paying quantities,"
    27-101.
  "At any time," 161.
  "Can only be renewed by mutual consent," 285.
  "Deed," 14.
  "Division Orders," 641.
  "Exclusive Right and Privilege of digging and boring for oil and other minerals,"
    178.
  "Forfeiture," 861.
  "Found or produced in paying quantities," 487.
  "Granted and leased," 541.
  "Land," 594.
  "Minerals," 835.
  "Null and Void," 266-269-285.
  "Paying Quantity,"—Oil, 27-101-113.
  "Paying Quantity"—Gas, 210.
  "Paying Quantity," 489-500.

WORDS AND PHRASES—*Continued.*
  "Protection," 185.
  "Protecting Lines," 784.
  "Shall be of no effect between the parties," 285.
  "Surface," 830.
  "Trade Fixtures,"151.
  "While the same is being used off the premises," 193.

WORKING INTEREST—Lessees set apart by division orders, 143.

Lightning Source UK Ltd.
Milton Keynes UK
UKHW012141170119

335727UK00008B/200/P